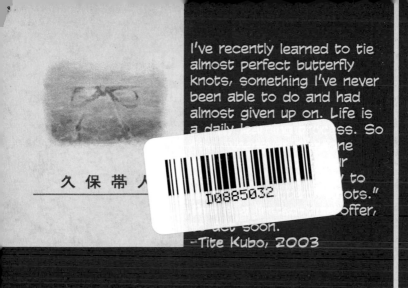

久保帯人

I've recently learned to tie almost perfect butterfly knots, something I've never been able to do and had almost given up on. Life is a daily [...]ss. So [...]ne [...]r [...] to [...]ots." [...] offer, [...]ct soon.

—Tite Kubo, 2003

BLEACH is author Tite Kubo's second title. Kubo made his debut with *ZOMBIE POWDER*, a four-volume series for *WEEKLY SHONEN JUMP*. To date, *BLEACH* has been translated into numerous languages and has also inspired an animated TV series that began airing in Japan in 2004. Beginning its serialization in 2001, *BLEACH* is still a mainstay in the pages of *WEEKLY SHONEN JUMP*. In 2005, *BLEACH* was awarded the prestigious Shogakukan Manga Award in the *shonen* (boys) category.

BLEACH
3-in-1 Edition

SHONEN JUMP Manga Omnibus Edition Volume 4
A compilation of the graphic novel volumes 10–12

STORY AND ART BY
TITE KUBO

English Adaptation/Lance Caselman
Translation/Joe Yamazaki
Touch-up Art & Lettering/Andy Ristaino
Design - Manga Edition/Sean Lee
Design - Omnibus Edition/Fawn Lau
Editor - Manga Edition/Kit Fox
Editor - Omnibus Edition/Pancha Diaz

Printed in the U.S.A.

Published by VIZ Media, LLC
P.O. Box 77010
San Francisco, CA 94107

10 9 8 7 6 5 4 3 2 1
Omnibus edition first printing, February 2013

PARENTAL ADVISORY
BLEACH is rated T for Teen and is
recommended for ages 13 and up. This
volume contains fantasy violence.
ratings.viz.com

www.viz.com

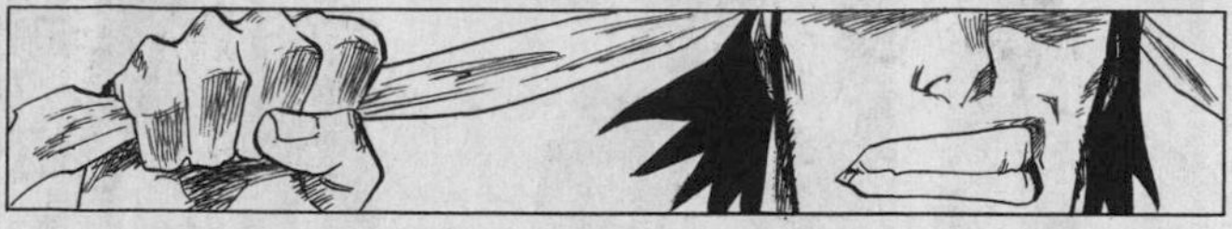

We reach out with our hands
Brush away the clouds and pierce the sky
To grab the moon and Mars
But we still can't reach the truth

BLEACH 10

TATTOO ON THE SKY

Shonen Jump Manga

STARS AND

Kûkaku Shiba

Ganju Shiba

Ichigo Kurosaki

plot

One fateful night, Ichigo Kurosaki encounters Soul Reaper Rukia Kuchiki and ends up helping her do her job—which is cleansing lost souls, called Hollows, and guiding them to the Soul Society. But when Rukia is arrested and taken back to the Soul Society to be executed, Ichigo vows to save her. He and a band of friends make the dangerous journey to the other world. There they attempt to infiltrate the Seireitei, the abode of the Soul Reapers, only to be thwarted by Gin Ichimaru. With time running out, Yoruichi turns for help to Kûkaku Shiba, Rukongai's premier fireworks technician!!

BLEACH ALL

Ikkaku Madarame

藍染惣右介
Sôsuke Aizen

Gin Ichimaru

STORIES

BLEACH 10

TATTOO ON THE SKY

Contents

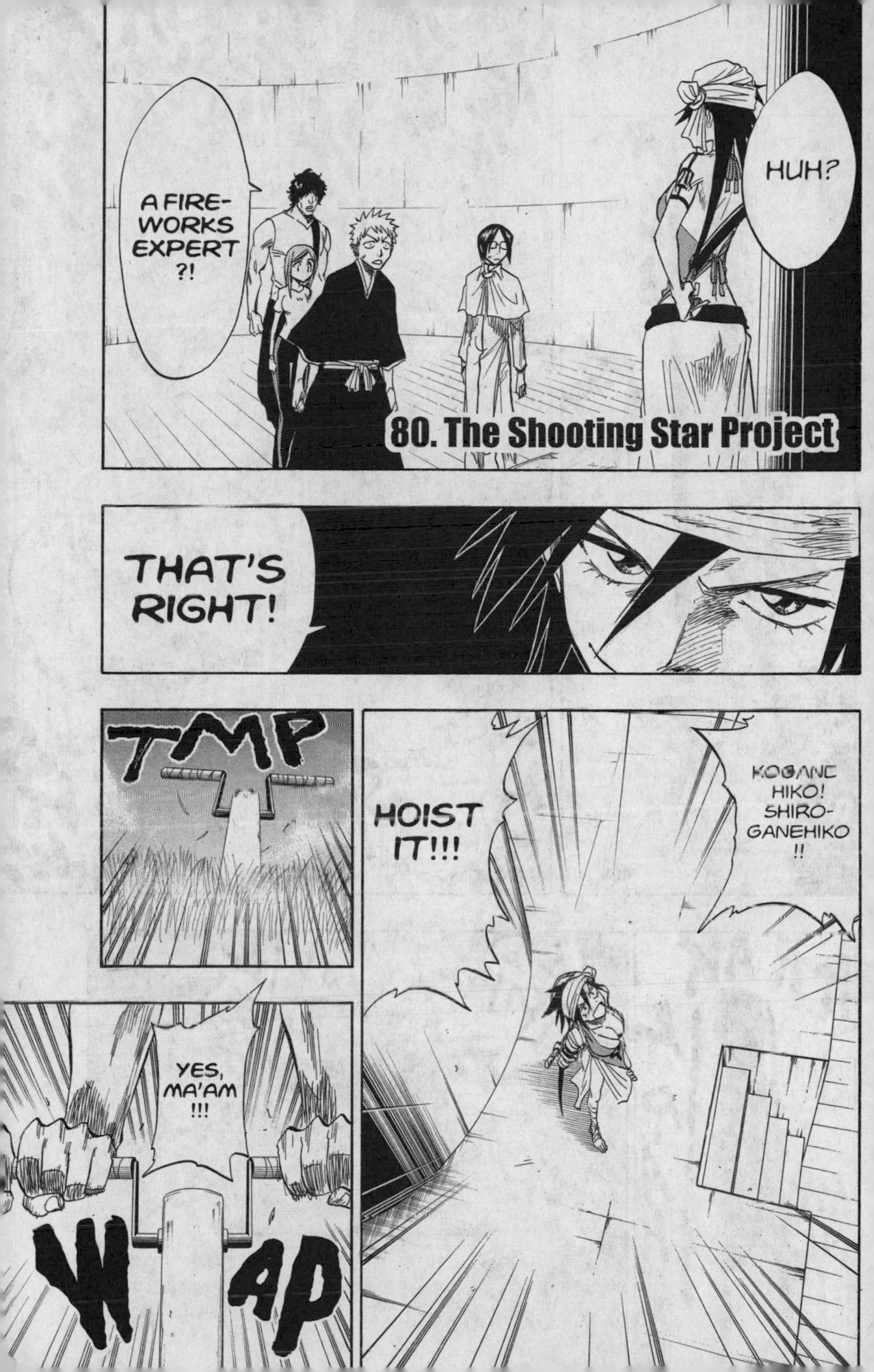
HUH?
A FIRE-WORKS EXPERT?!
80. The Shooting Star Project
THAT'S RIGHT!
KOGANEHIKO! SHIRO-GANEHIKO!!
HOIST IT!!!
TMP
YES, MA'AM!!!
WAP

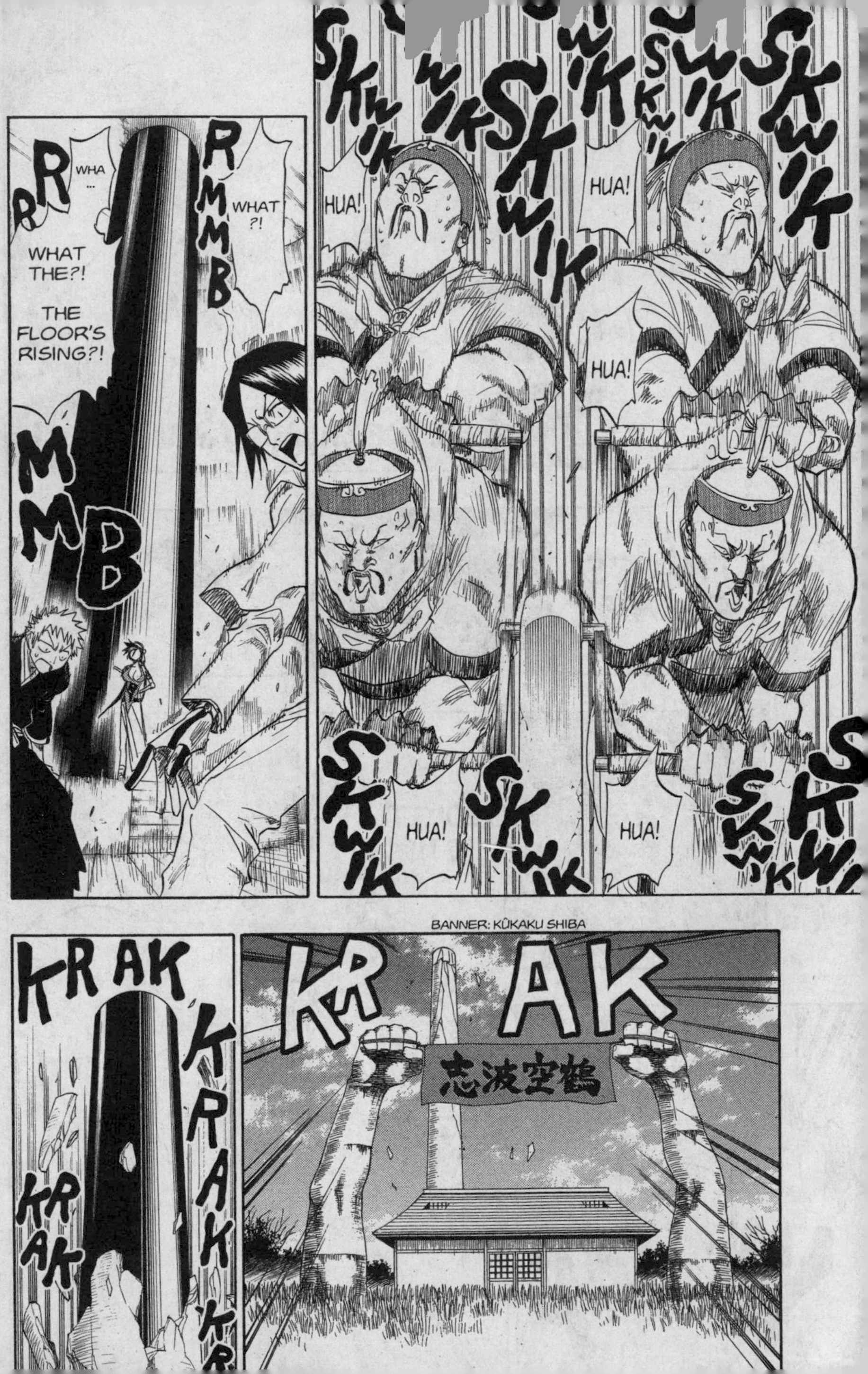

SKWIK
SKWIK
HUA!
HUA!
HUA!
SKWIK
SKWIK
HUA!
HUA!
SKWIK
RRMMB
WHAT?!
WHA...
RR
WHAT THE?!
THE FLOOR'S RISING?!
MMB
BANNER: KÛKAKU SHIBA
KRAK
志波空鶴
KRAK
KRAK
KRAK
KRAK

READ THIS WAY

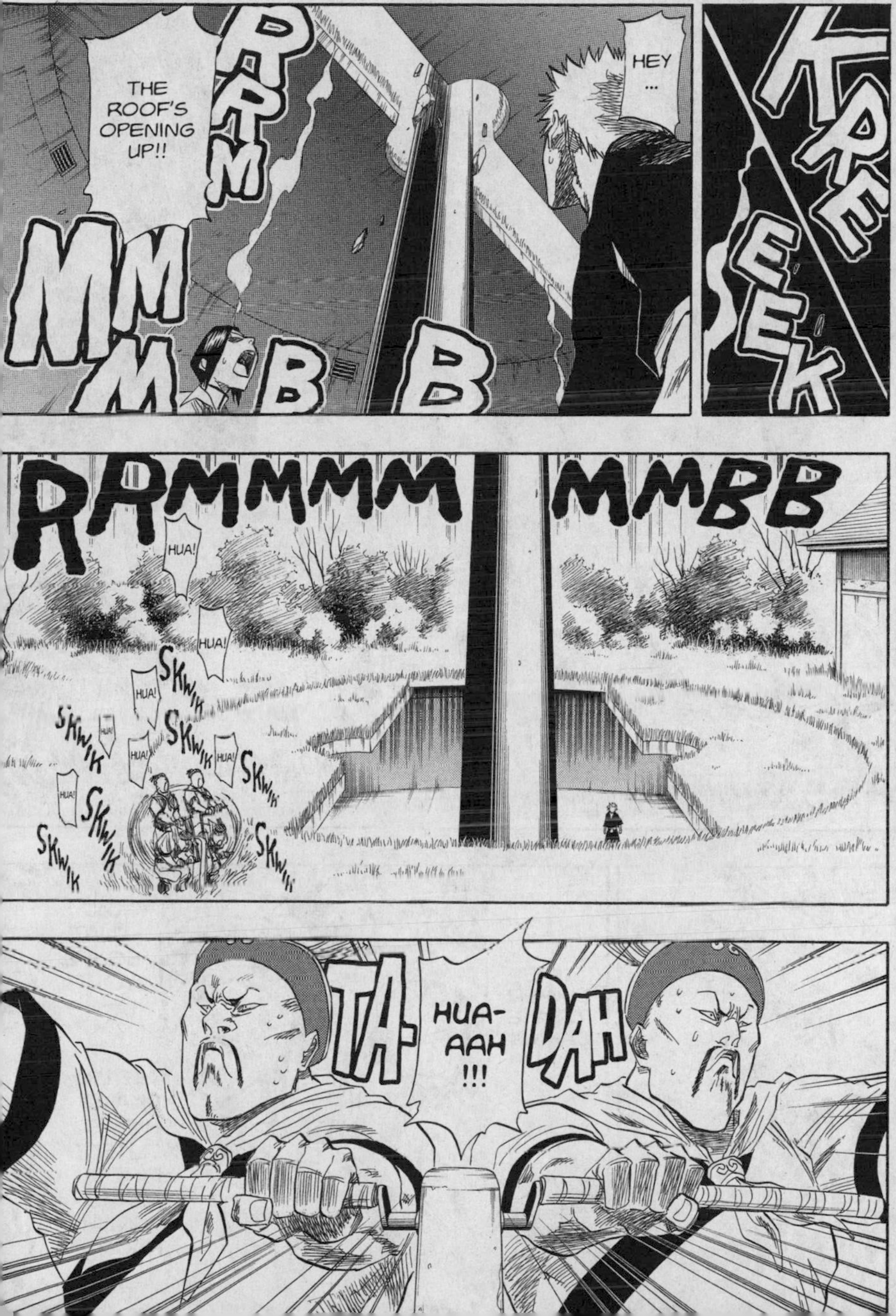
KREEEK
HEY ...
RRM
THE ROOF'S OPENING UP!!
MMMBB
RRMMMMM
MMBB
HUA!
HUA!
HUA!
HUA!
HUA!
HUA!
HUA!
SKWIK
SKWIK
SKWIK
SKWIK
SKWIK
SKWIK
SKWIK
TA-
HUA-AAH!!!
DAH

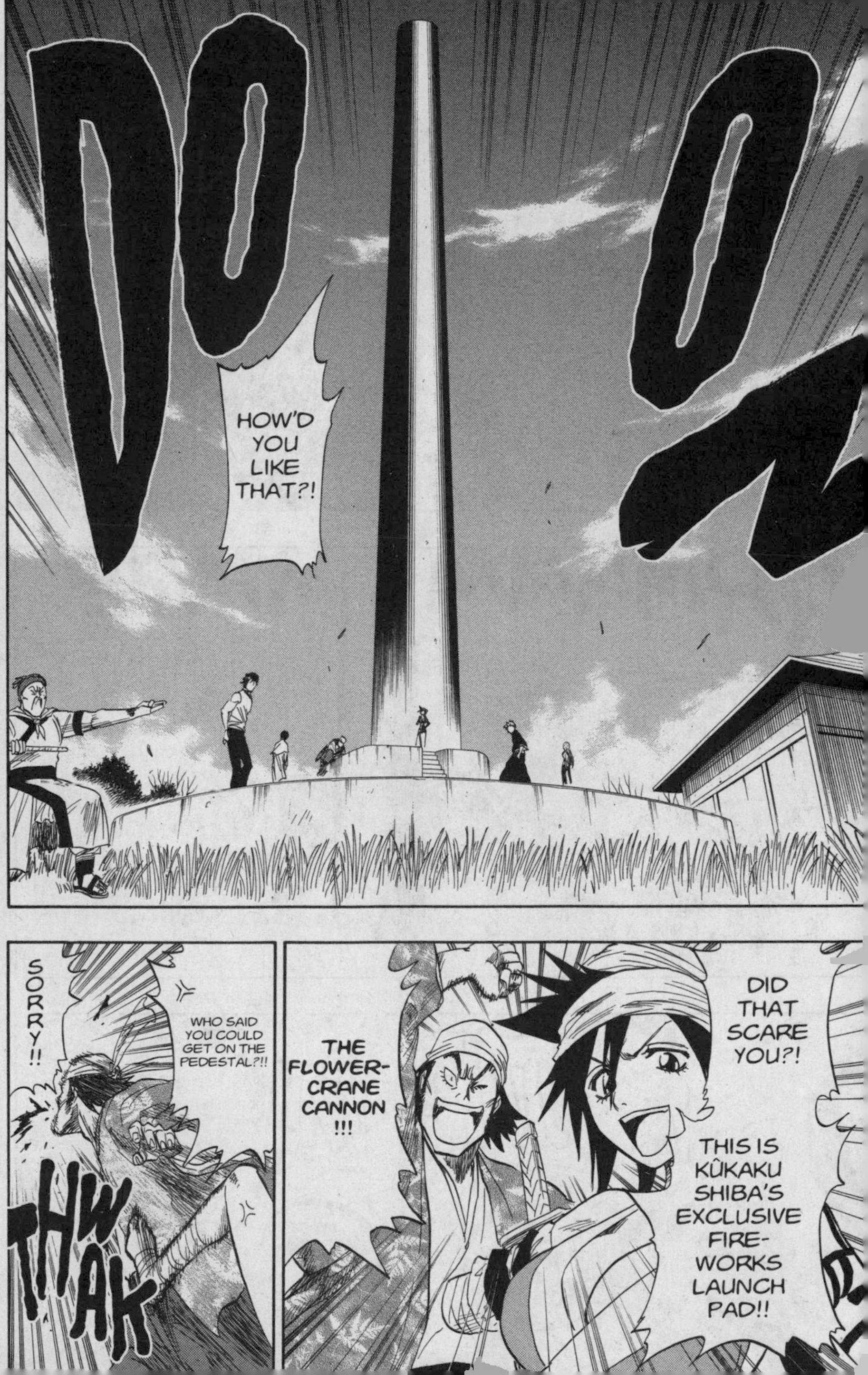
DOO
HOW'D YOU LIKE THAT?!
DID THAT SCARE YOU?!
THIS IS KÛKAKU SHIBA'S EXCLUSIVE FIRE-WORKS LAUNCH PAD!!
THE FLOWER-CRANE CANNON!!!
WHO SAID YOU COULD GET ON THE PEDESTAL?!!
SORRY!!
THWAK

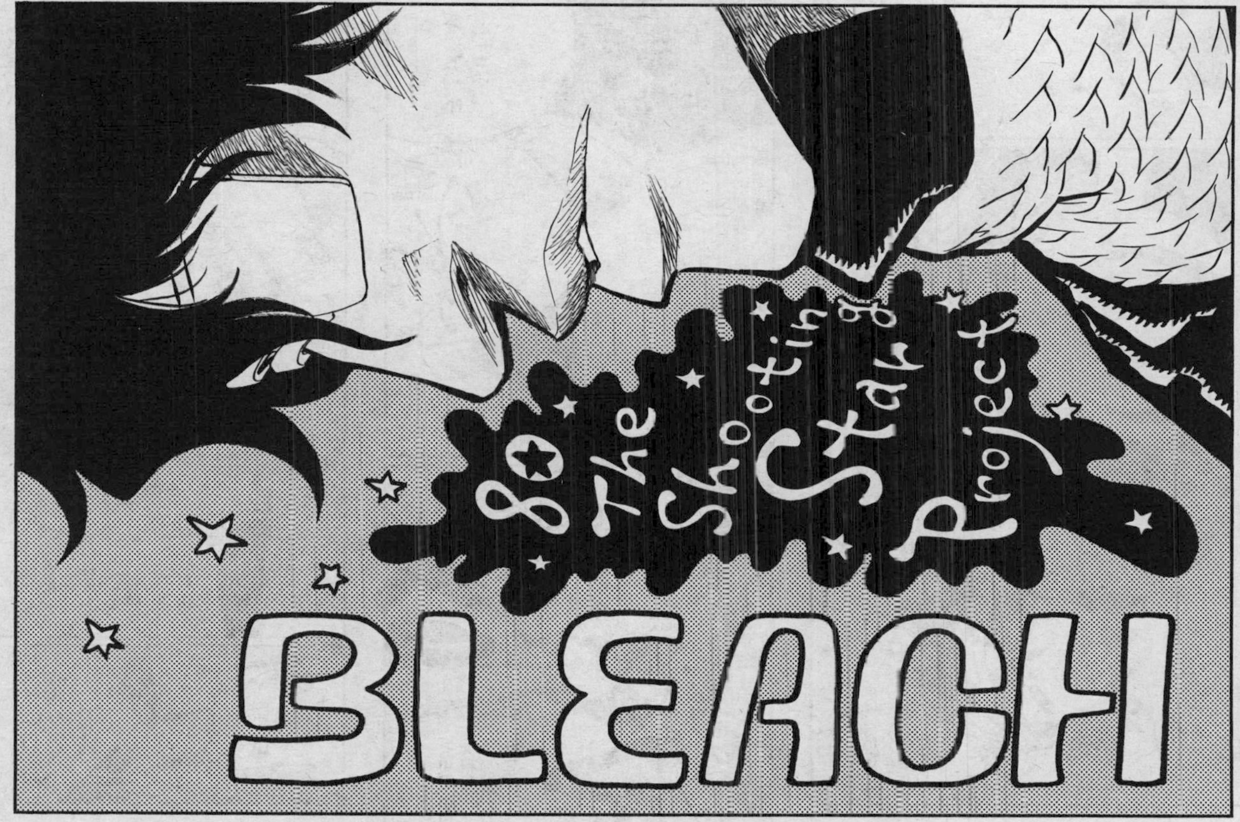
80 The Shooting Star Project
BLEACH

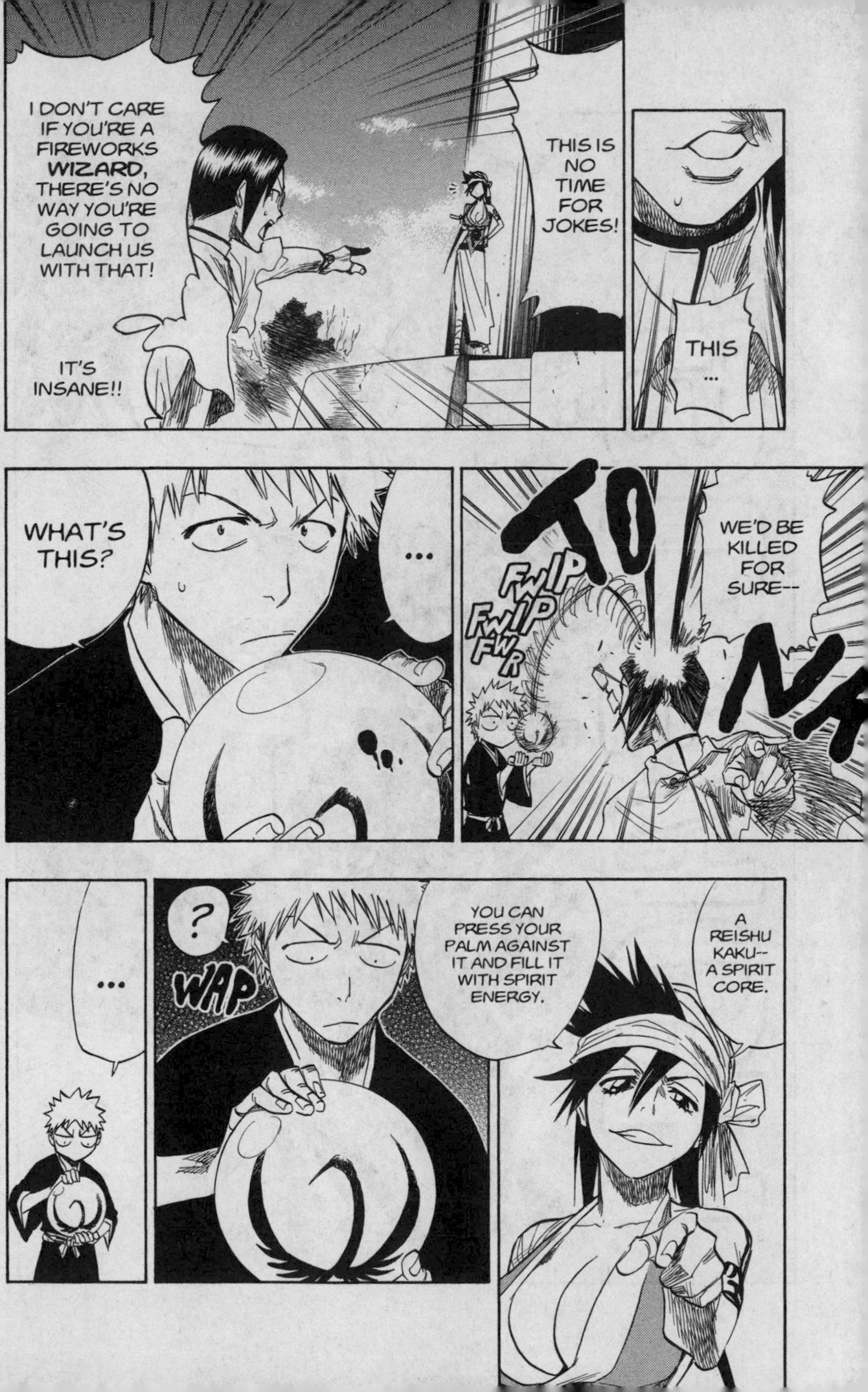
THIS ...
THIS IS NO TIME FOR JOKES!
I DON'T CARE IF YOU'RE A FIREWORKS **WIZARD,** THERE'S NO WAY YOU'RE GOING TO LAUNCH US WITH THAT!
IT'S INSANE!!
TO
WE'D BE KILLED FOR SURE--
NA
FWIP
FWIP
FWR
...
WHAT'S THIS?
A REISHU KAKU-- A SPIRIT CORE.
YOU CAN PRESS YOUR PALM AGAINST IT AND FILL IT WITH SPIRIT ENERGY.
?
WAP
...

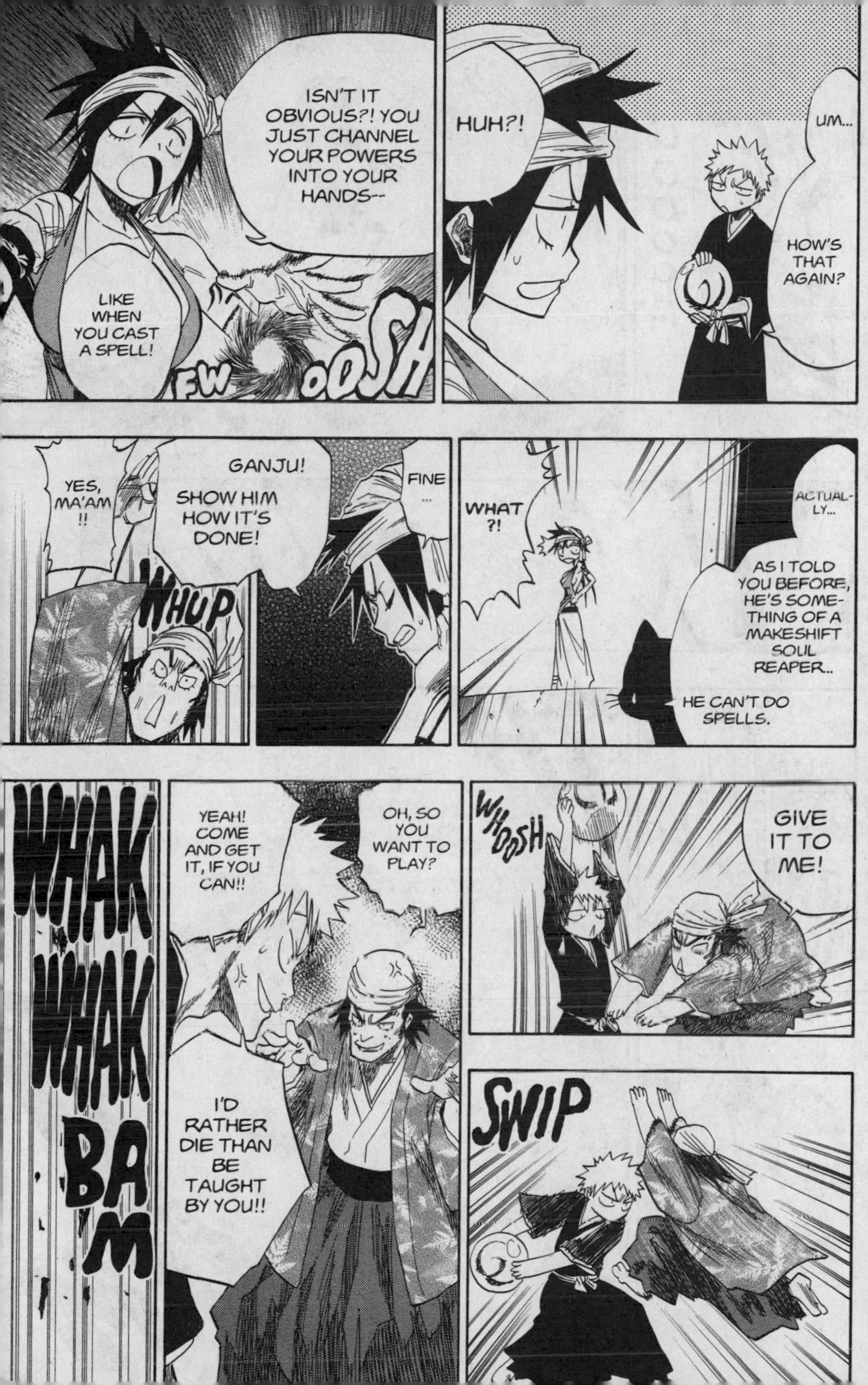
UM...
HOW'S THAT AGAIN?
HUH?!
ISN'T IT OBVIOUS?! YOU JUST CHANNEL YOUR POWERS INTO YOUR HANDS--
LIKE WHEN YOU CAST A SPELL!
FWOOOSH
ACTUAL-LY...
AS I TOLD YOU BEFORE, HE'S SOME-THING OF A MAKESHIFT SOUL REAPER...
HE CAN'T DO SPELLS.
WHAT ?!
FINE ...
GANJU!
SHOW HIM HOW IT'S DONE!
YES, MA'AM !!
WHUP
GIVE IT TO ME!
WHOOSH
SWIP
OH, SO YOU WANT TO PLAY?
YEAH! COME AND GET IT, IF YOU CAN!!
I'D RATHER DIE THAN BE TAUGHT BY YOU!!
WHAK
WHAK
WHAK
BAM

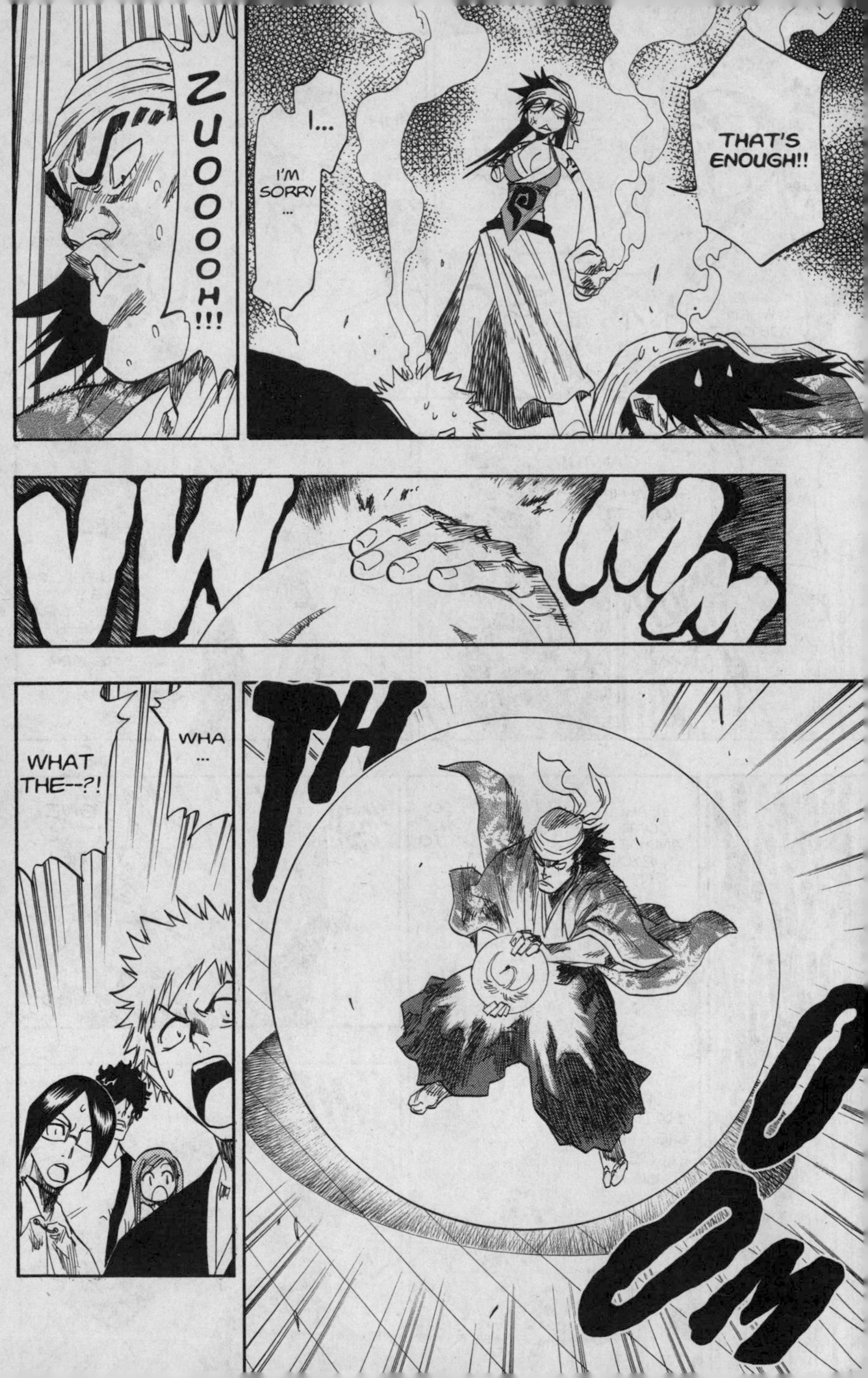
THAT'S ENOUGH!!
I...
I'M SORRY ...
ZUOOOOOH!!!
VWMM
THOOM
WHA ...
WHAT THE--?!

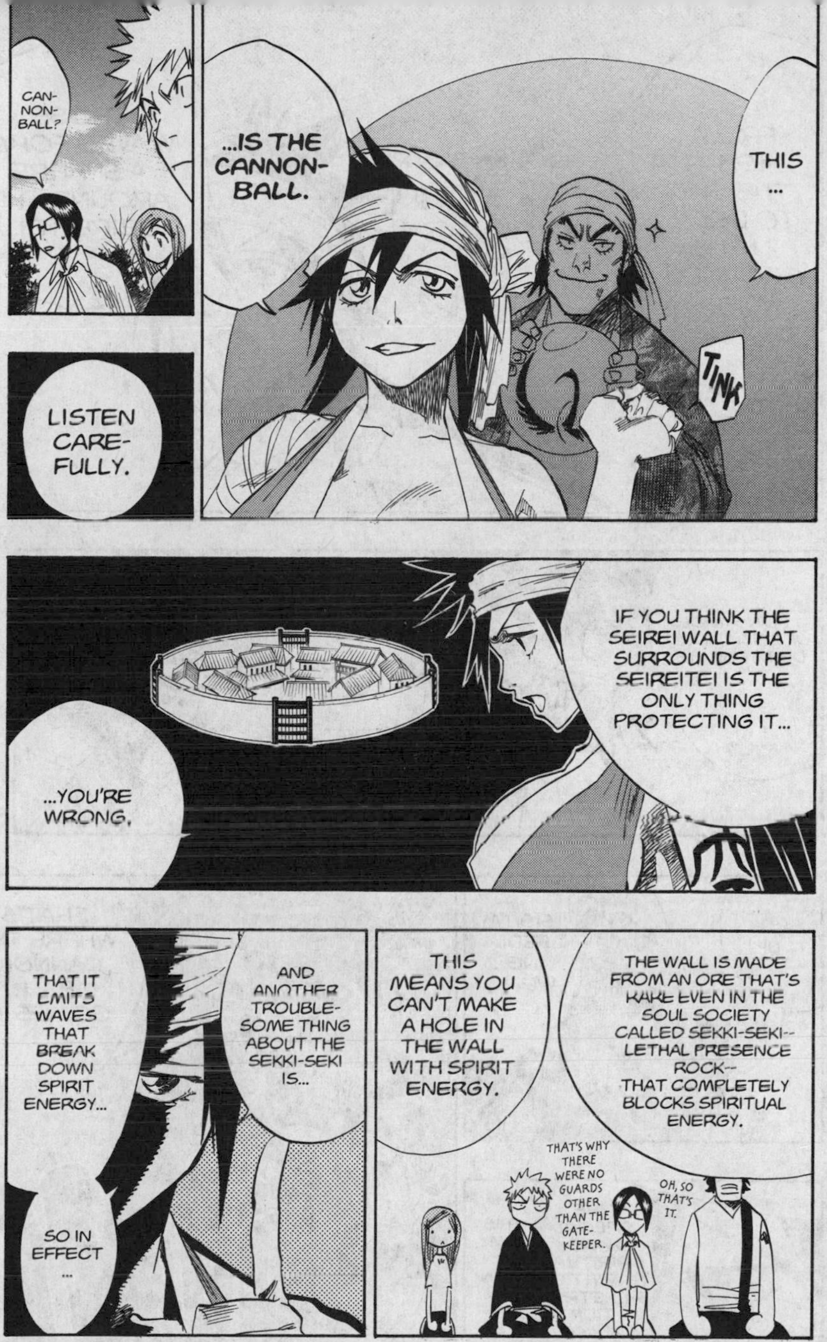
THIS ...
...IS THE CANNON-BALL.
TINK
CAN-NON-BALL?
LISTEN CARE-FULLY.
IF YOU THINK THE SEIREI WALL THAT SURROUNDS THE SEIREITEI IS THE ONLY THING PROTECTING IT...
...YOU'RE WRONG.
THE WALL IS MADE FROM AN ORE THAT'S RARE EVEN IN THE SOUL SOCIETY CALLED SEKKI-SEKI--LETHAL PRESENCE ROCK--THAT COMPLETELY BLOCKS SPIRITUAL ENERGY.
THIS MEANS YOU CAN'T MAKE A HOLE IN THE WALL WITH SPIRIT ENERGY.
OH, SO THAT'S IT.
THAT'S WHY THERE WERE NO GUARDS OTHER THAN THE GATE-KEEPER.
AND ANOTHER TROUBLE-SOME THING ABOUT THE SEKKI-SEKI IS...
THAT IT EMITS WAVES THAT BREAK DOWN SPIRIT ENERGY...
SO IN EFFECT ...

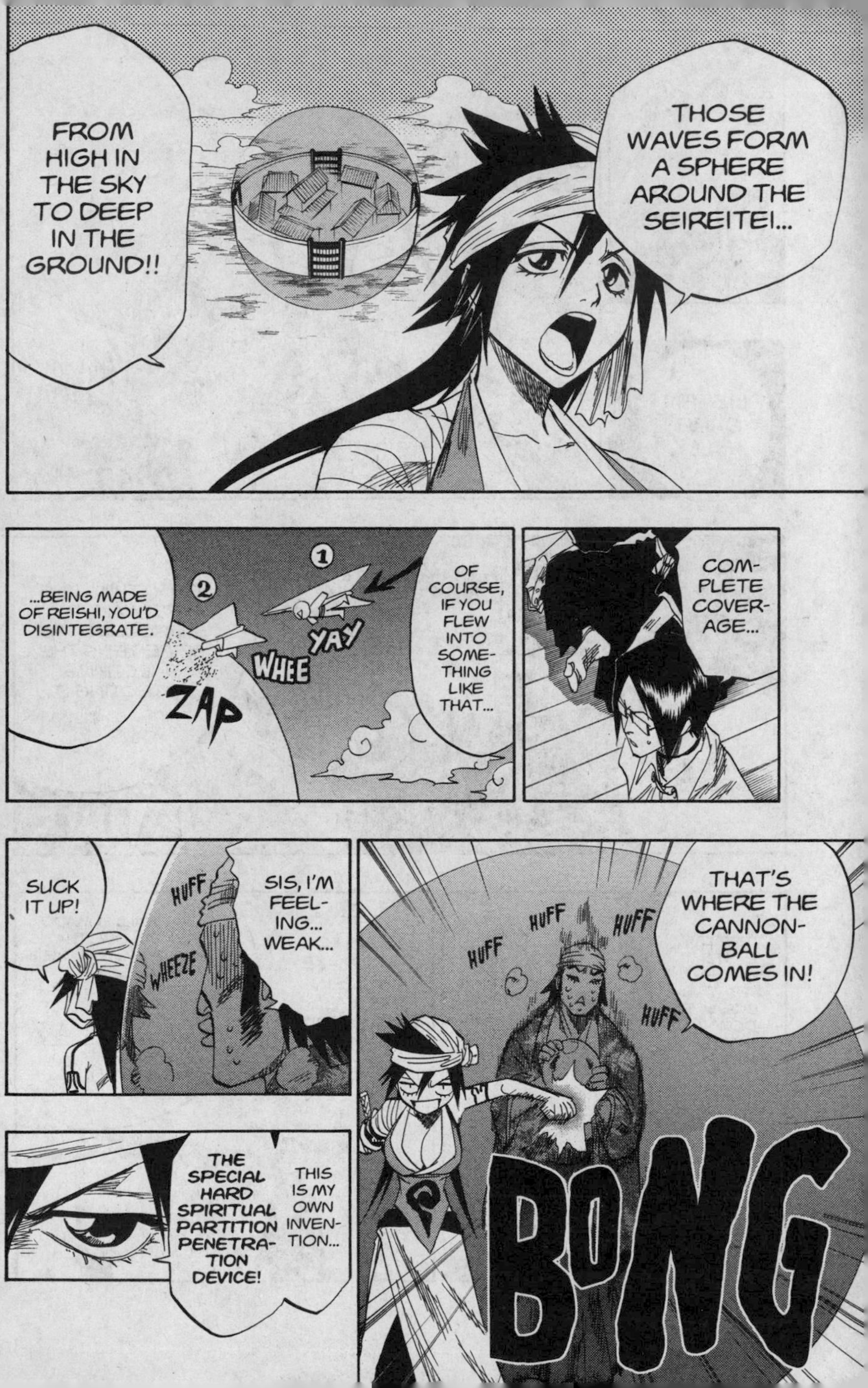
THOSE WAVES FORM A SPHERE AROUND THE SEIREITEI...
FROM HIGH IN THE SKY TO DEEP IN THE GROUND!!
COMPLETE COVERAGE...
OF COURSE, IF YOU FLEW INTO SOMETHING LIKE THAT...
①
②
YAY
WHEE
ZAP
...BEING MADE OF REISHI, YOU'D DISINTEGRATE.
THAT'S WHERE THE CANNONBALL COMES IN!
HUFF
HUFF
HUFF
HUFF
BONG
SIS, I'M FEELING... WEAK...
HUFF
WHEEZE
SUCK IT UP!
THIS IS MY OWN INVENTION...
THE SPECIAL HARD SPIRITUAL PARTITION PENETRATION DEVICE!

READ THIS WAY

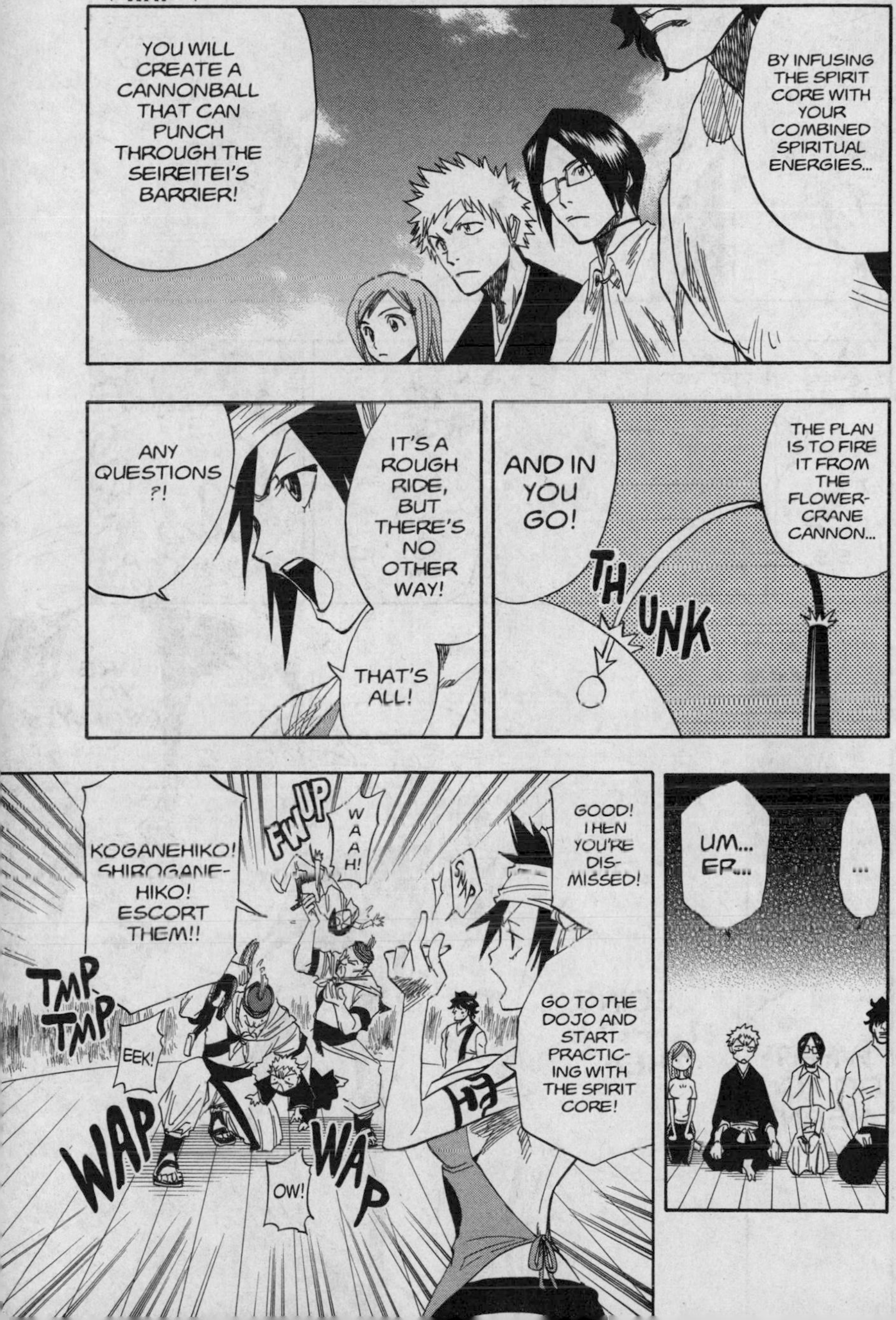

BY INFUSING THE SPIRIT CORE WITH YOUR COMBINED SPIRITUAL ENERGIES...
YOU WILL CREATE A CANNONBALL THAT CAN PUNCH THROUGH THE SEIREITEI'S BARRIER!
THE PLAN IS TO FIRE IT FROM THE FLOWER-CRANE CANNON...
AND IN YOU GO!
THUNK
IT'S A ROUGH RIDE, BUT THERE'S NO OTHER WAY!
ANY QUESTIONS ?!
THAT'S ALL!
...
UM... ER...
GOOD! THEN YOU'RE DIS-MISSED!
GO TO THE DOJO AND START PRACTIC-ING WITH THE SPIRIT CORE!
WAAAH!
FWUP
SNAP
KOGANEHIKO! SHIROGANE-HIKO! ESCORT THEM!!
TMP-TMP
EEK!
WAP
OW!
WAP

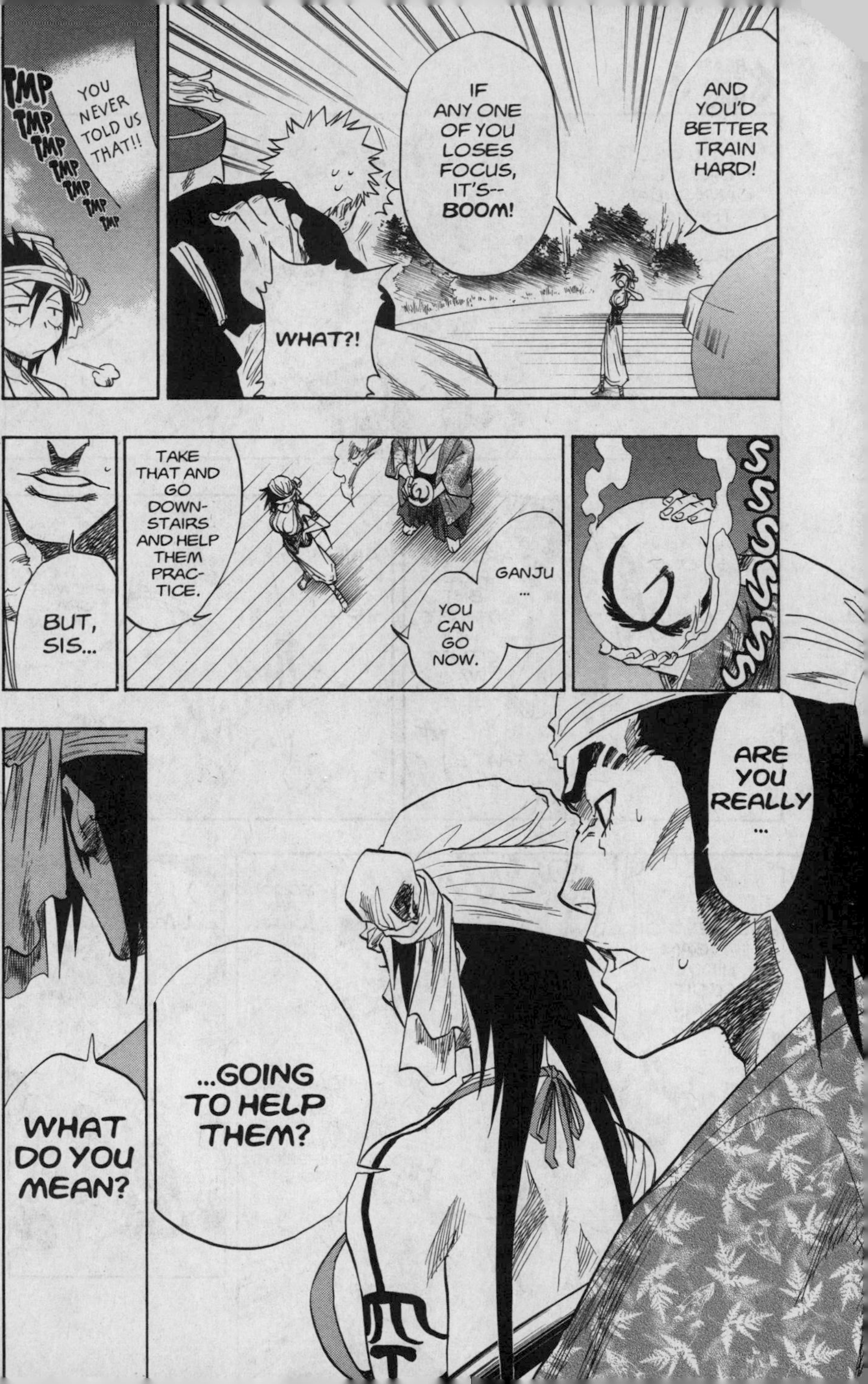
AND YOU'D BETTER TRAIN HARD!
IF ANY ONE OF YOU LOSES FOCUS, IT'S-- BOOM!
WHAT?!
YOU NEVER TOLD US THAT!!
TMP TMP TMP TMP TMP TMP TMP
SSSSSS
GANJU ...
YOU CAN GO NOW.
TAKE THAT AND GO DOWN-STAIRS AND HELP THEM PRAC-TICE.
BUT, SIS...
ARE YOU REALLY ...
...GOING TO HELP THEM?
WHAT DO YOU MEAN?

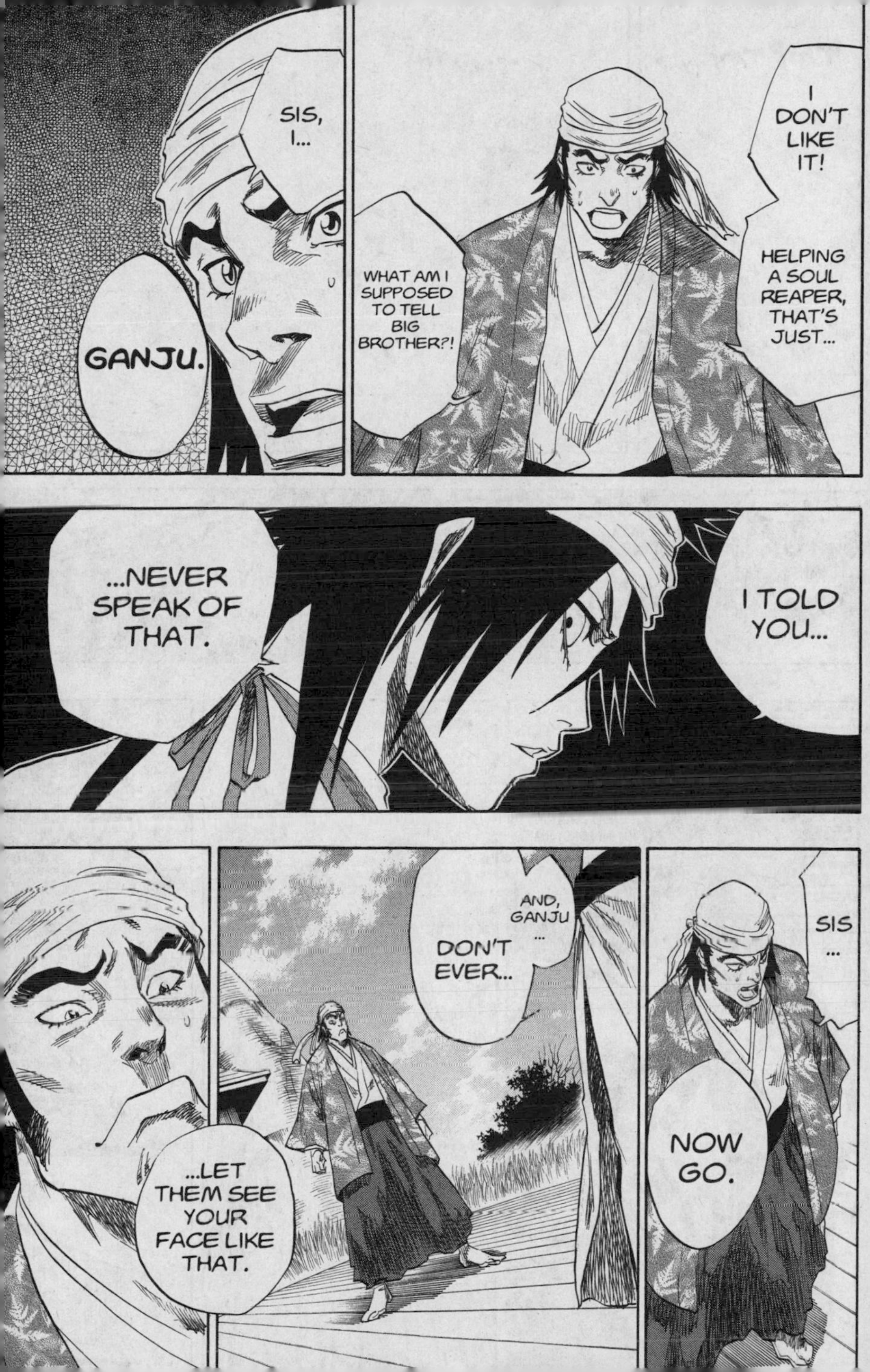
I DON'T LIKE IT!
HELPING A SOUL REAPER, THAT'S JUST...
WHAT AM I SUPPOSED TO TELL BIG BROTHER?!
SIS, I...
GANJU.
I TOLD YOU...
...NEVER SPEAK OF THAT.
SIS...
NOW GO.
AND, GANJU...
DON'T EVER...
...LET THEM SEE YOUR FACE LIKE THAT.

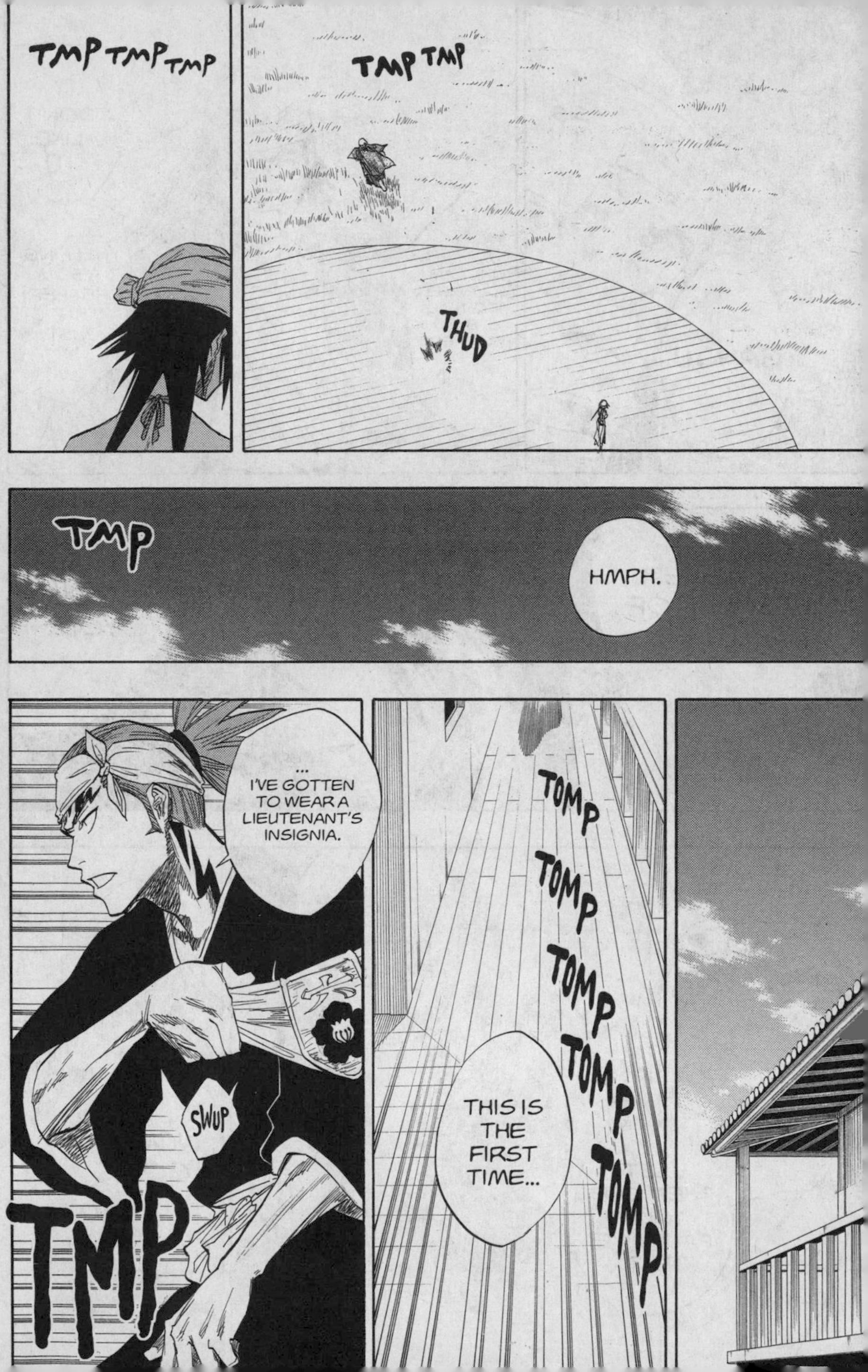
TMP TMP
THUD
TMP TMP TMP
TMP
HMPH.
TOMP TOMP TOMP TOMP TOMP
THIS IS THE FIRST TIME...
... I'VE GOTTEN TO WEAR A LIEUTENANT'S INSIGNIA.
SWUP
TMP

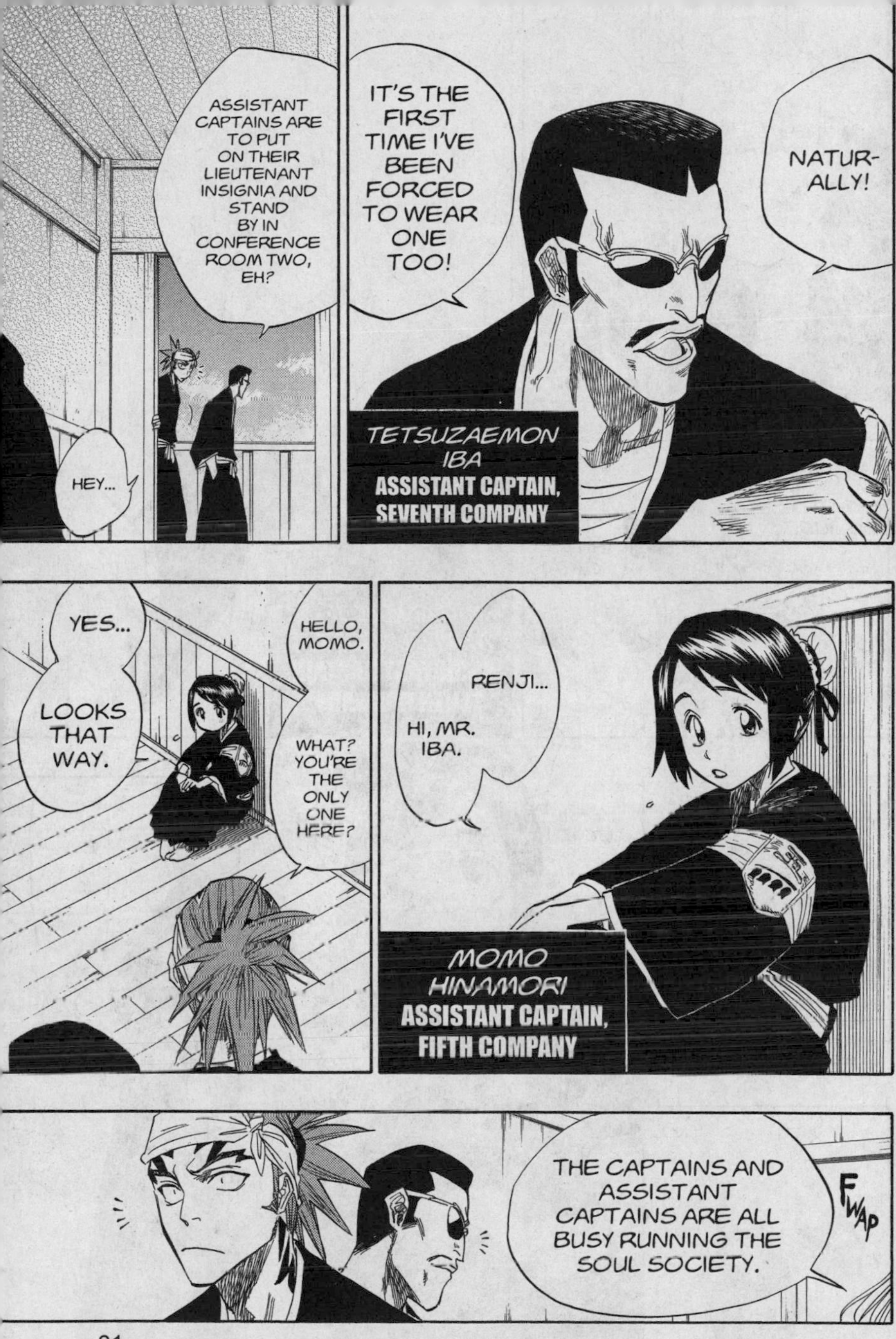

NATURALLY!
IT'S THE FIRST TIME I'VE BEEN FORCED TO WEAR ONE TOO!
TETSUZAEMON IBA
ASSISTANT CAPTAIN, SEVENTH COMPANY
ASSISTANT CAPTAINS ARE TO PUT ON THEIR LIEUTENANT INSIGNIA AND STAND BY IN CONFERENCE ROOM TWO, EH?
HEY...
RENJI...
HI, MR. IBA.
MOMO HINAMORI
ASSISTANT CAPTAIN, FIFTH COMPANY
HELLO, MOMO.
WHAT? YOU'RE THE ONLY ONE HERE?
YES...
LOOKS THAT WAY.
FWAP
THE CAPTAINS AND ASSISTANT CAPTAINS ARE ALL BUSY RUNNING THE SOUL SOCIETY.

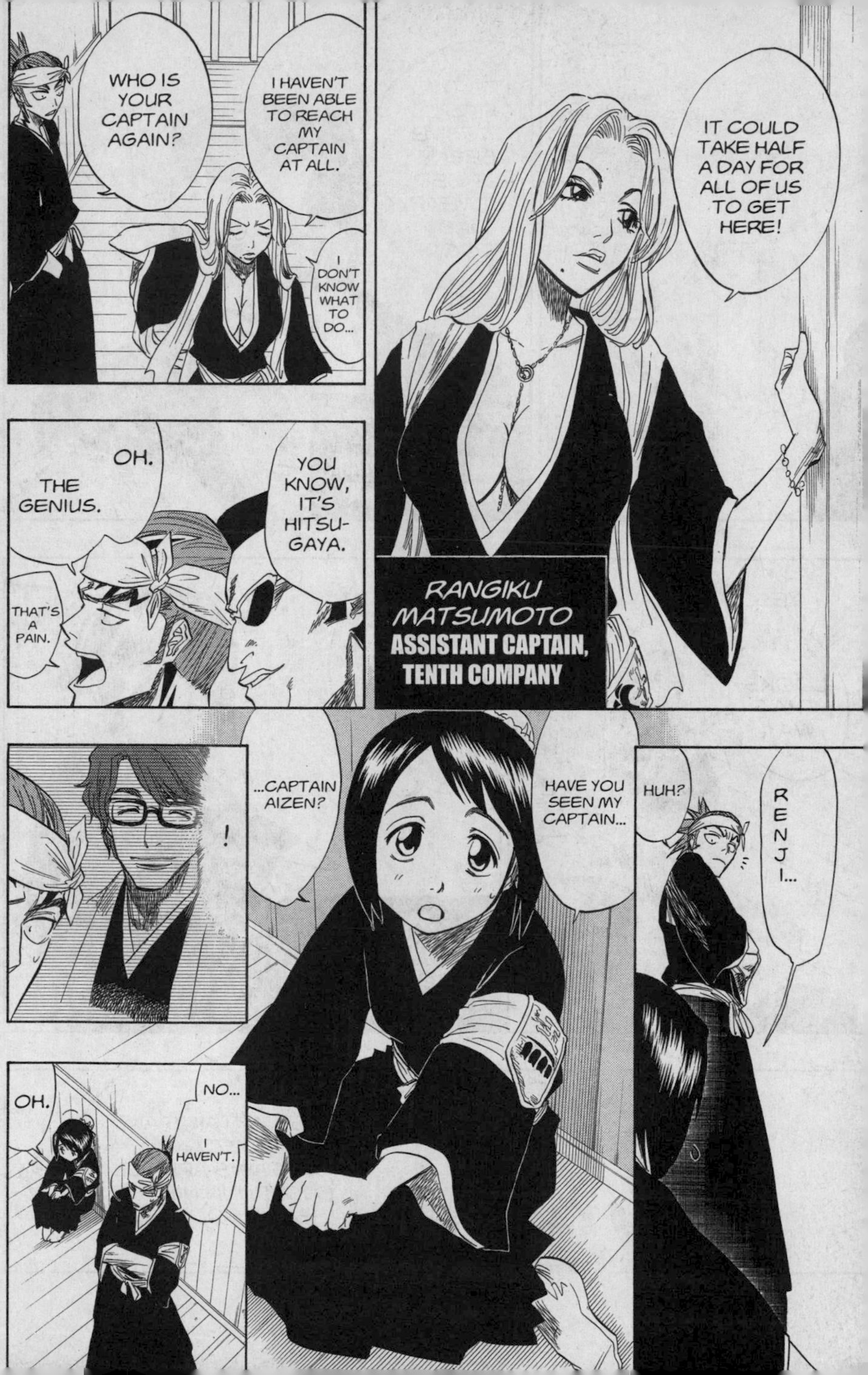
IT COULD TAKE HALF A DAY FOR ALL OF US TO GET HERE!
RANGIKU MATSUMOTO
ASSISTANT CAPTAIN, TENTH COMPANY
I HAVEN'T BEEN ABLE TO REACH MY CAPTAIN AT ALL.
I DON'T KNOW WHAT TO DO...
WHO IS YOUR CAPTAIN AGAIN?
YOU KNOW, IT'S HITSU-GAYA.
OH.
THE GENIUS.
THAT'S A PAIN.
RENJI...
HUH?
HAVE YOU SEEN MY CAPTAIN...
...CAPTAIN AIZEN?
!
NO... I HAVEN'T.
OH.

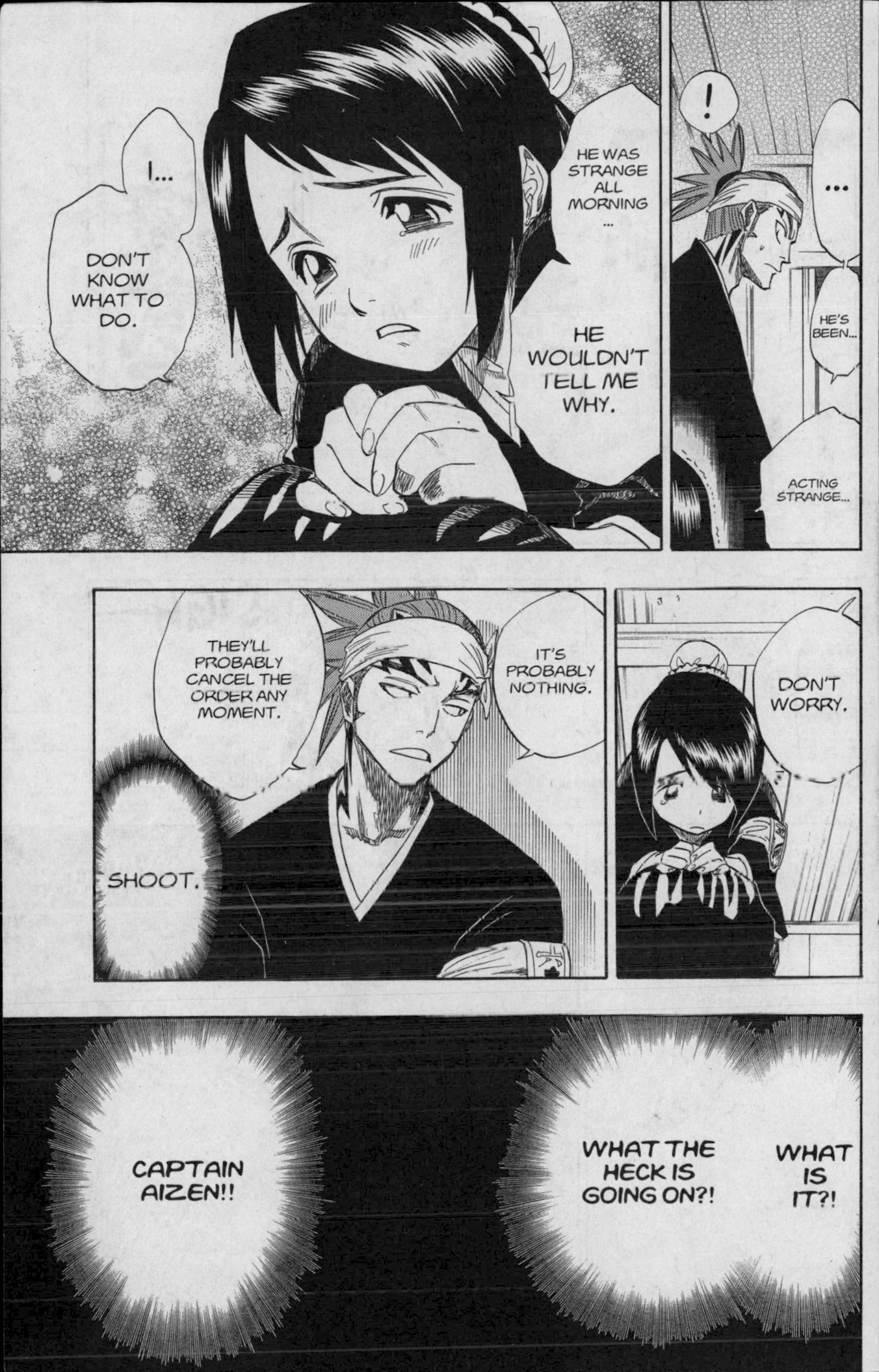
!
...
HE'S BEEN...
ACTING STRANGE...
HE WAS STRANGE ALL MORNING ...
HE WOULDN'T TELL ME WHY.
I...
DON'T KNOW WHAT TO DO.
DON'T WORRY.
IT'S PROBABLY NOTHING.
THEY'LL PROBABLY CANCEL THE ORDER ANY MOMENT.
SHOOT.
WHAT IS IT?!
WHAT THE HECK IS GOING ON?!
CAPTAIN AIZEN!!

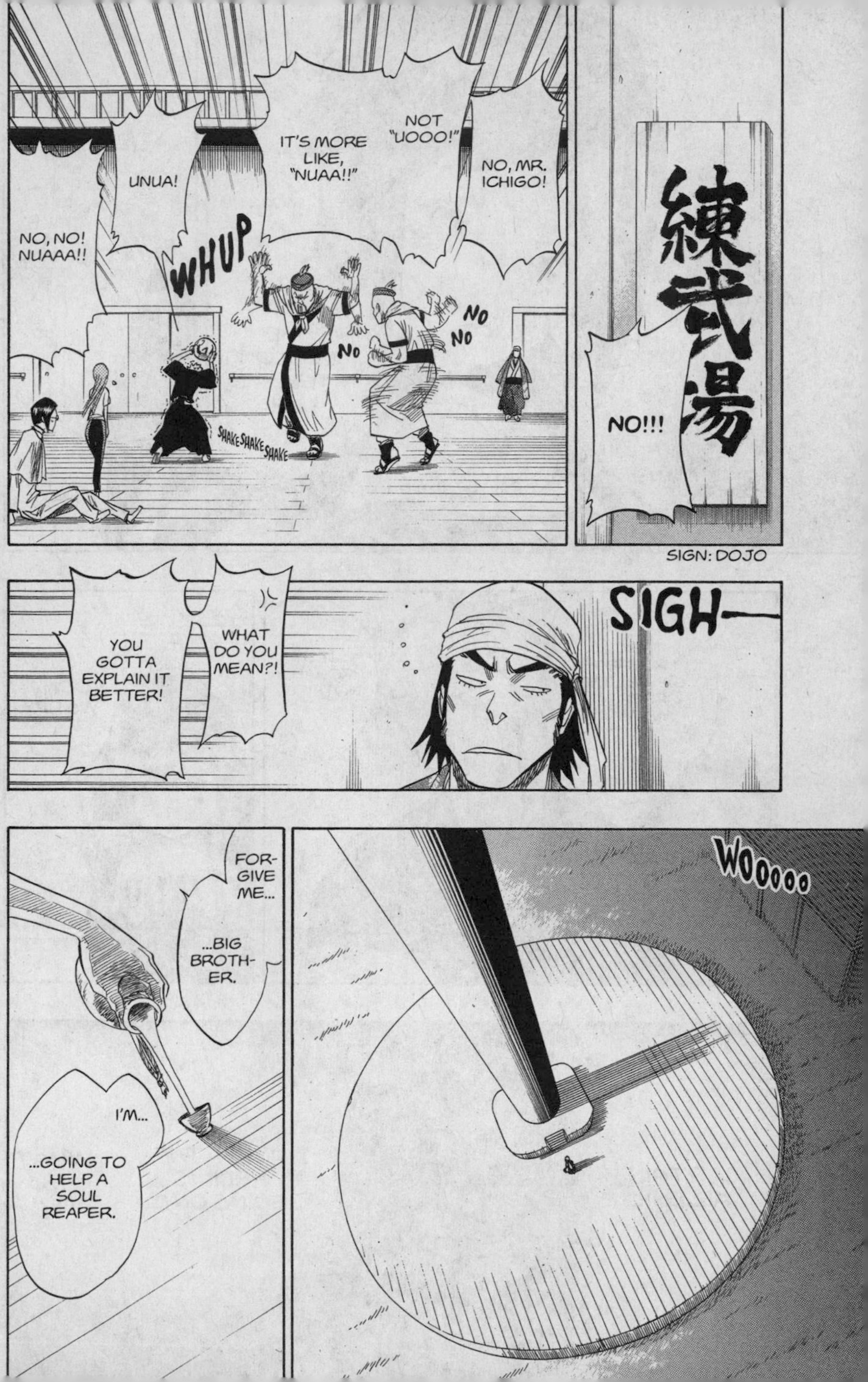
練武場
NO!!!
SIGN: DOJO
NO, MR. ICHIGO!
NOT "UOOO!"
IT'S MORE LIKE, "NUAA!!"
UNUA!
WHUP
NO, NO! NUAAA!!
NO NO
NO
SHAKE SHAKE SHAKE
SIGH—
WHAT DO YOU MEAN?!
YOU GOTTA EXPLAIN IT BETTER!
WOOOOO
FORGIVE ME...
...BIG BROTHER.
I'M...
...GOING TO HELP A SOUL REAPER.

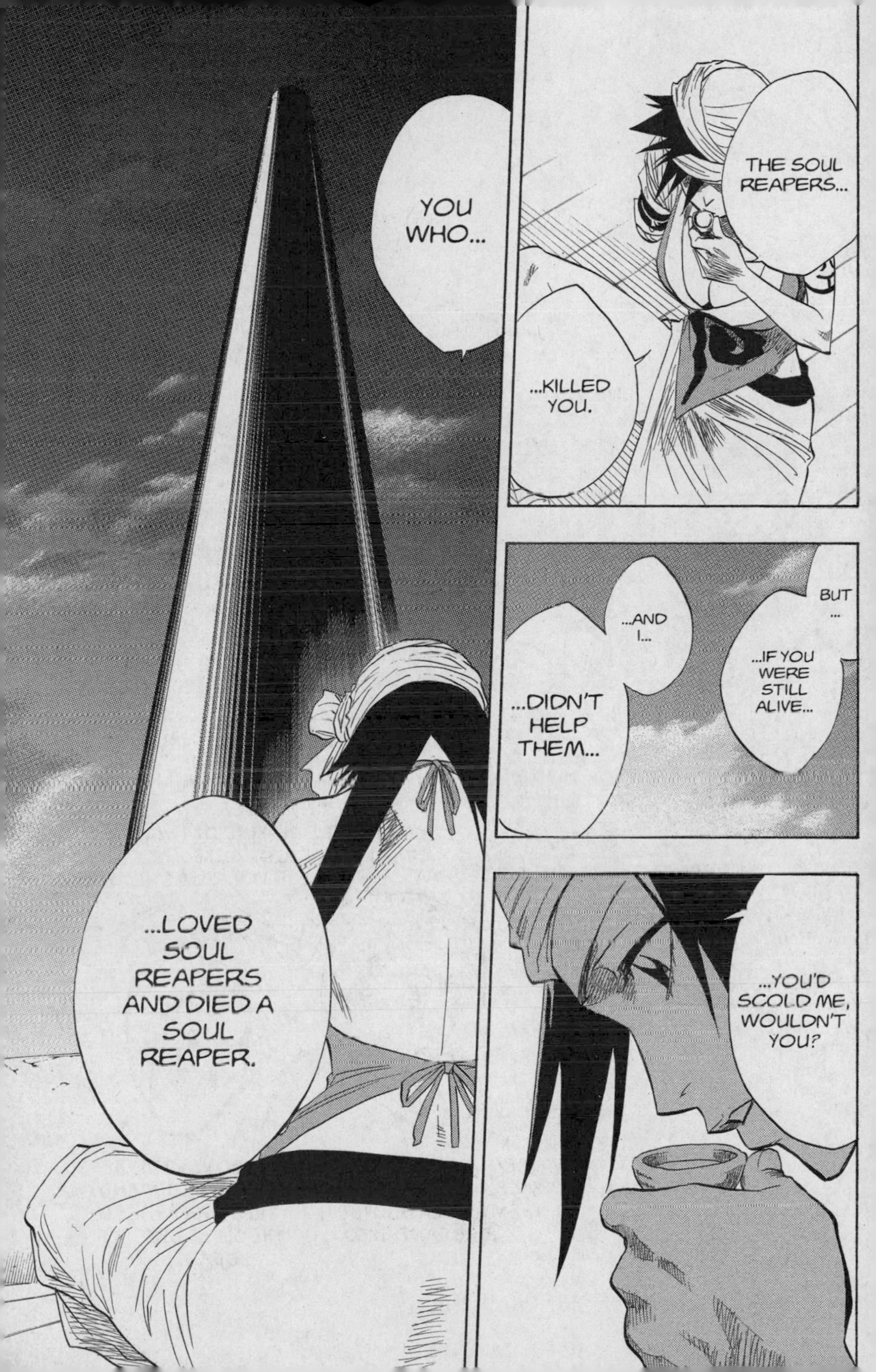
THE SOUL REAPERS...
...KILLED YOU.
BUT...
...IF YOU WERE STILL ALIVE...
...AND I...
...DIDN'T HELP THEM...
...YOU'D SCOLD ME, WOULDN'T YOU?
YOU WHO...
...LOVED SOUL REAPERS AND DIED A SOUL REAPER.

HOW TO DISTINGUISH KOGANEHIKO
FROM SHIROGANEHIKO.
LOTS OF PEOPLE CAN'T TELL
THE DIFFERENCE.
I THINK THEY'RE THE KIND OF TWINS
THAT DON'T LOOK ALIKE...

THE ONE WITH A SQUARE
FACE AND A SPLIT CHIN IS
THE YOUNGER BROTHER,
SHIROGANEHIKO.

THE ONE WITH THE
NARROW CHIN AND
THE LONGER FACE IS
THE OLDER BROTHER,
KOGANEHIKO.

81. Twelve Tone Rendezvous

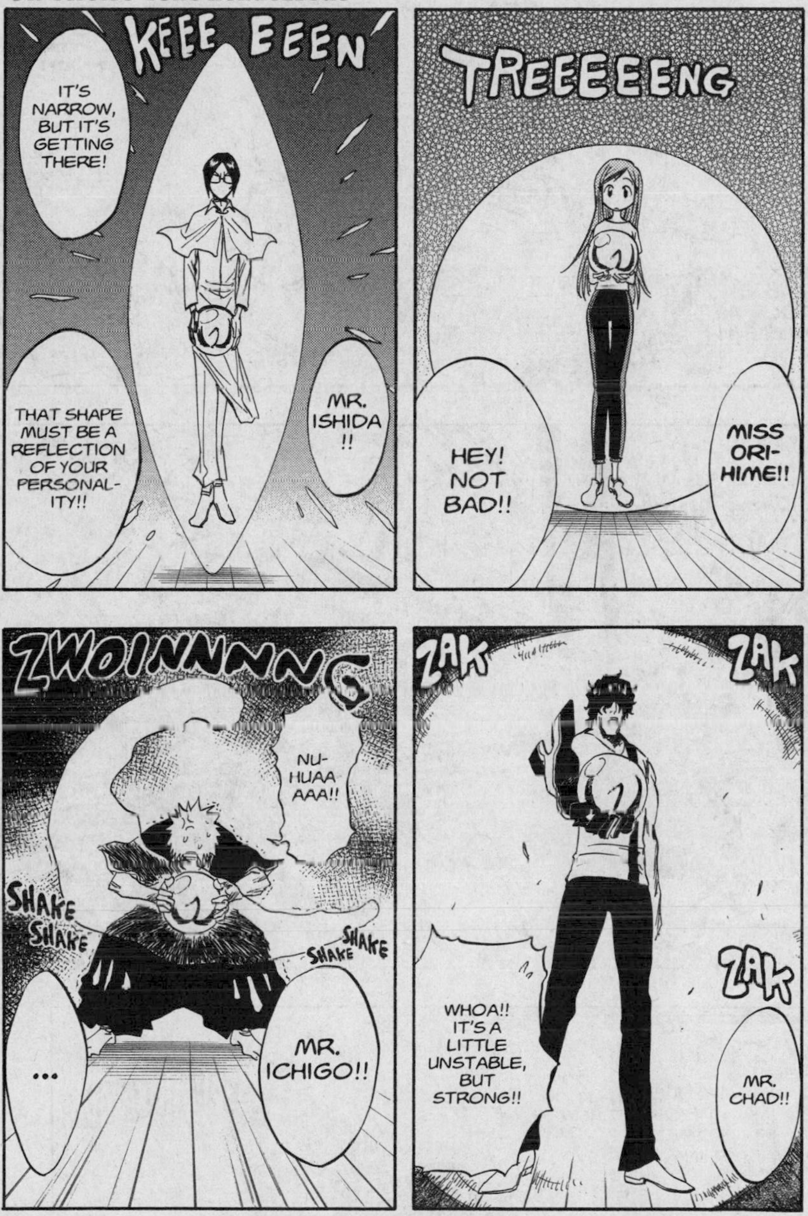
TREEEEENG
MISS ORI-HIME!!
HEY! NOT BAD!!
KEEE EEEN
IT'S NARROW, BUT IT'S GETTING THERE!
MR. ISHIDA!!
THAT SHAPE MUST BE A REFLECTION OF YOUR PERSONAL-ITY!!
ZAK
ZAK
ZAK
MR. CHAD!!
WHOA!! IT'S A LITTLE UNSTABLE, BUT STRONG!!
ZWOINNNNG
NU-HUAA AAA!!
SHAKE SHAKE
SHAKE SHAKE
MR. ICHIGO!!
...

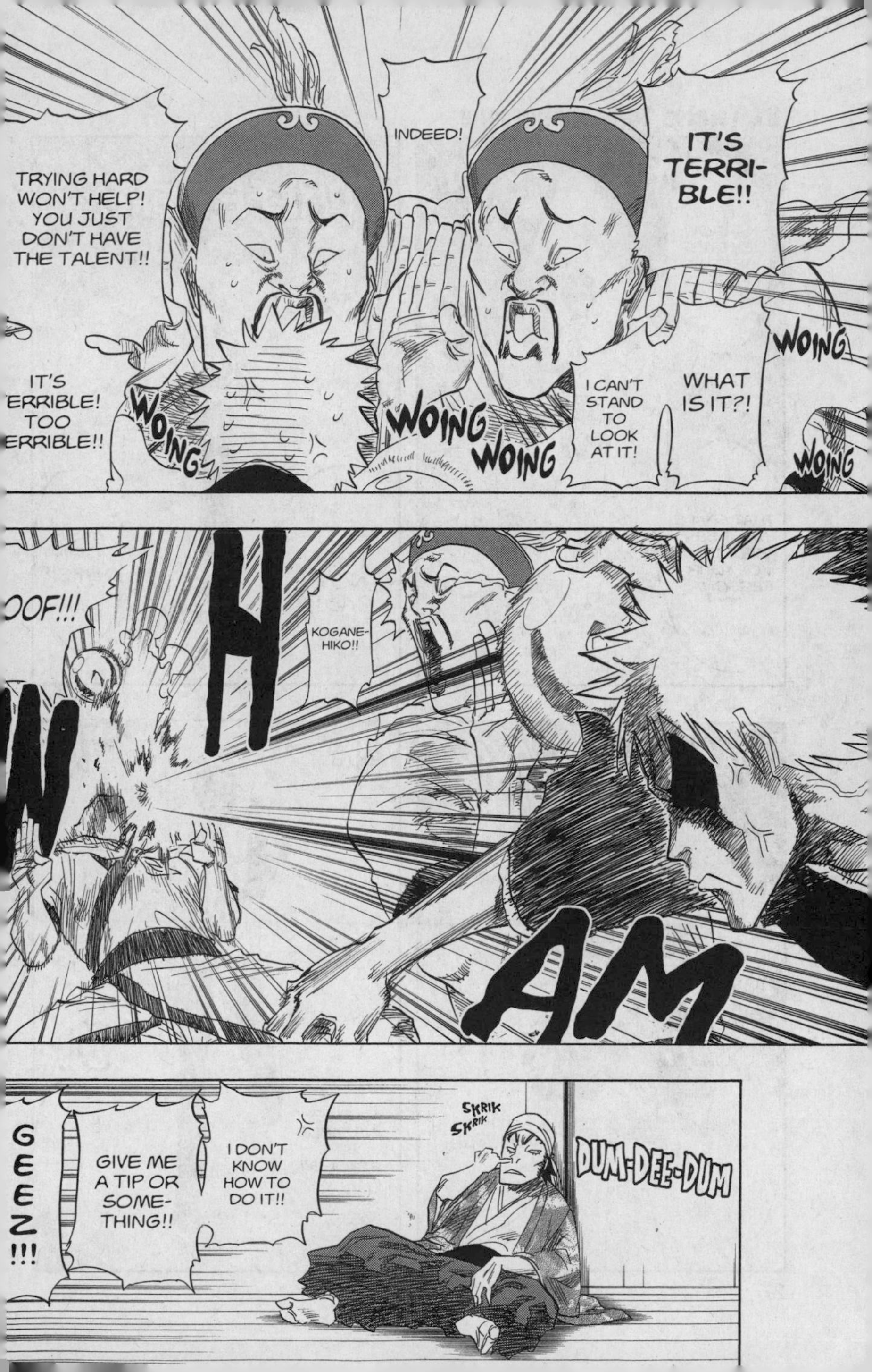
IT'S TERRIBLE!!
WHAT IS IT?!
WOING
WOING
I CAN'T STAND TO LOOK AT IT!
INDEED!
WOING
WOING
TRYING HARD WON'T HELP! YOU JUST DON'T HAVE THE TALENT!!
WOING
IT'S ERRIBLE! TOO ERRIBLE!!
AM
KOGANE-HIKO!!
H
OOF!!!
W
DUM-DEE-DUM
SKRIK SKRIK
I DON'T KNOW HOW TO DO IT!!
GIVE ME A TIP OR SOME-THING!!
GEEZ!!!

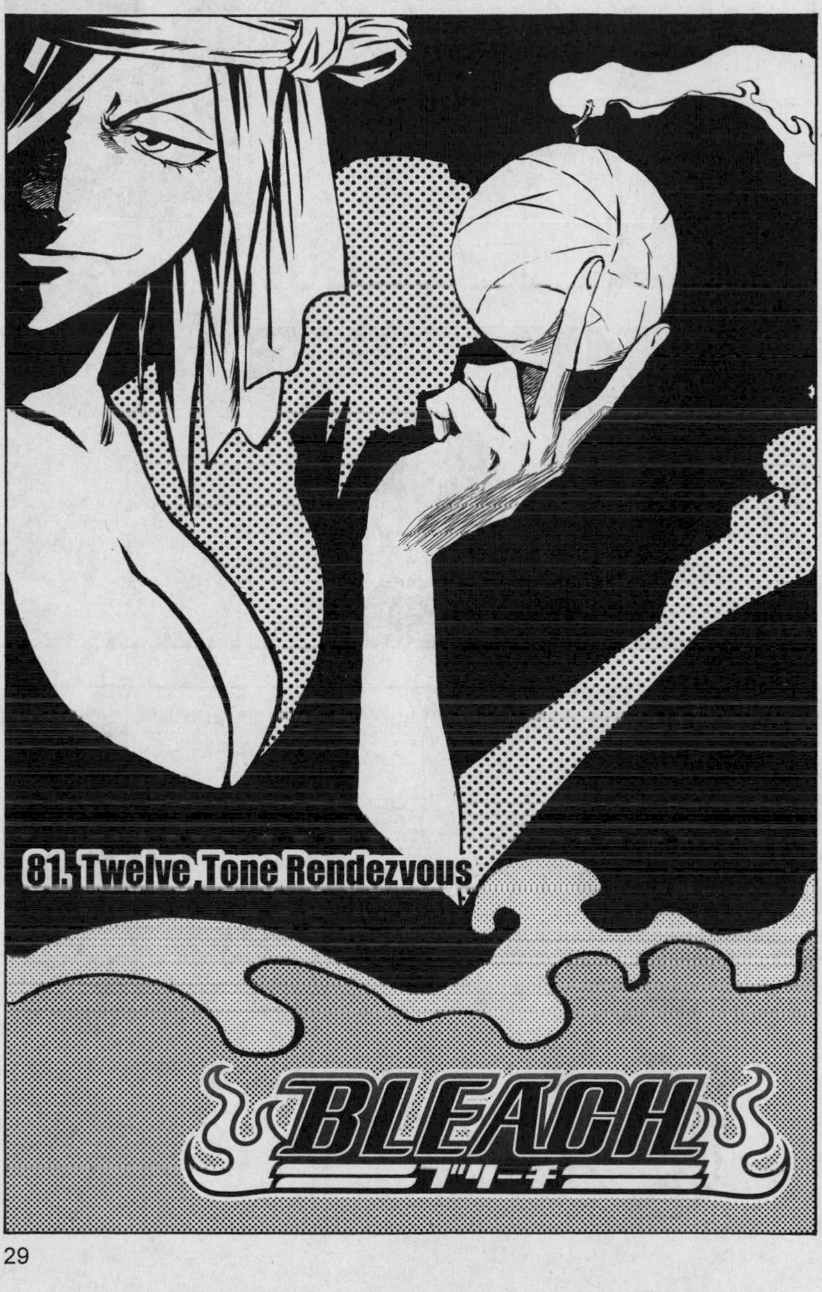
81. Twelve Tone Rendezvous
BLEACH
ブリーチ

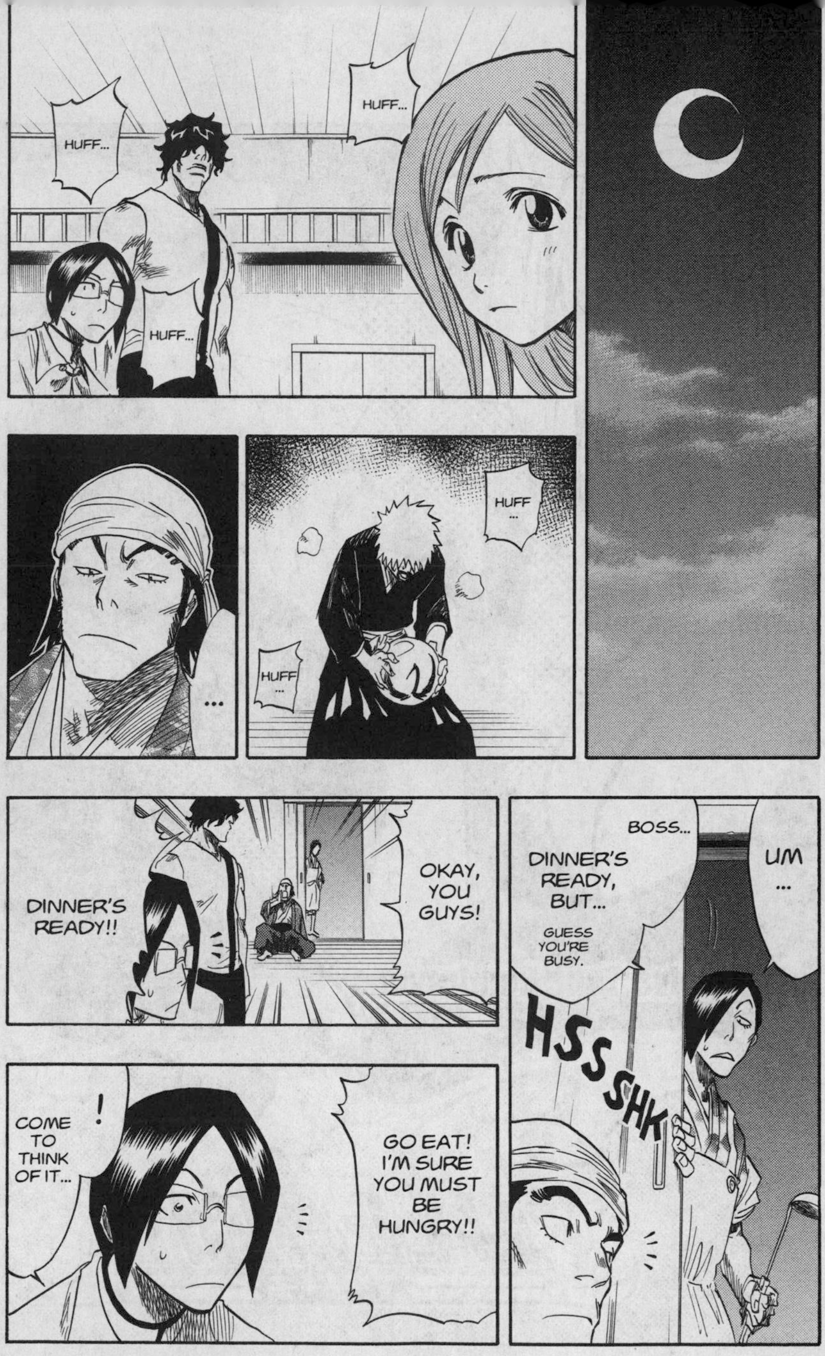
HUFF...
HUFF...
HUFF...
HUFF ...
HUFF ...
...
UM ...
BOSS...
DINNER'S READY, BUT...
GUESS YOU'RE BUSY.
HSS SHK
OKAY, YOU GUYS!
DINNER'S READY!!
GO EAT! I'M SURE YOU MUST BE HUNGRY!!
!
COME TO THINK OF IT...

READ THIS WAY

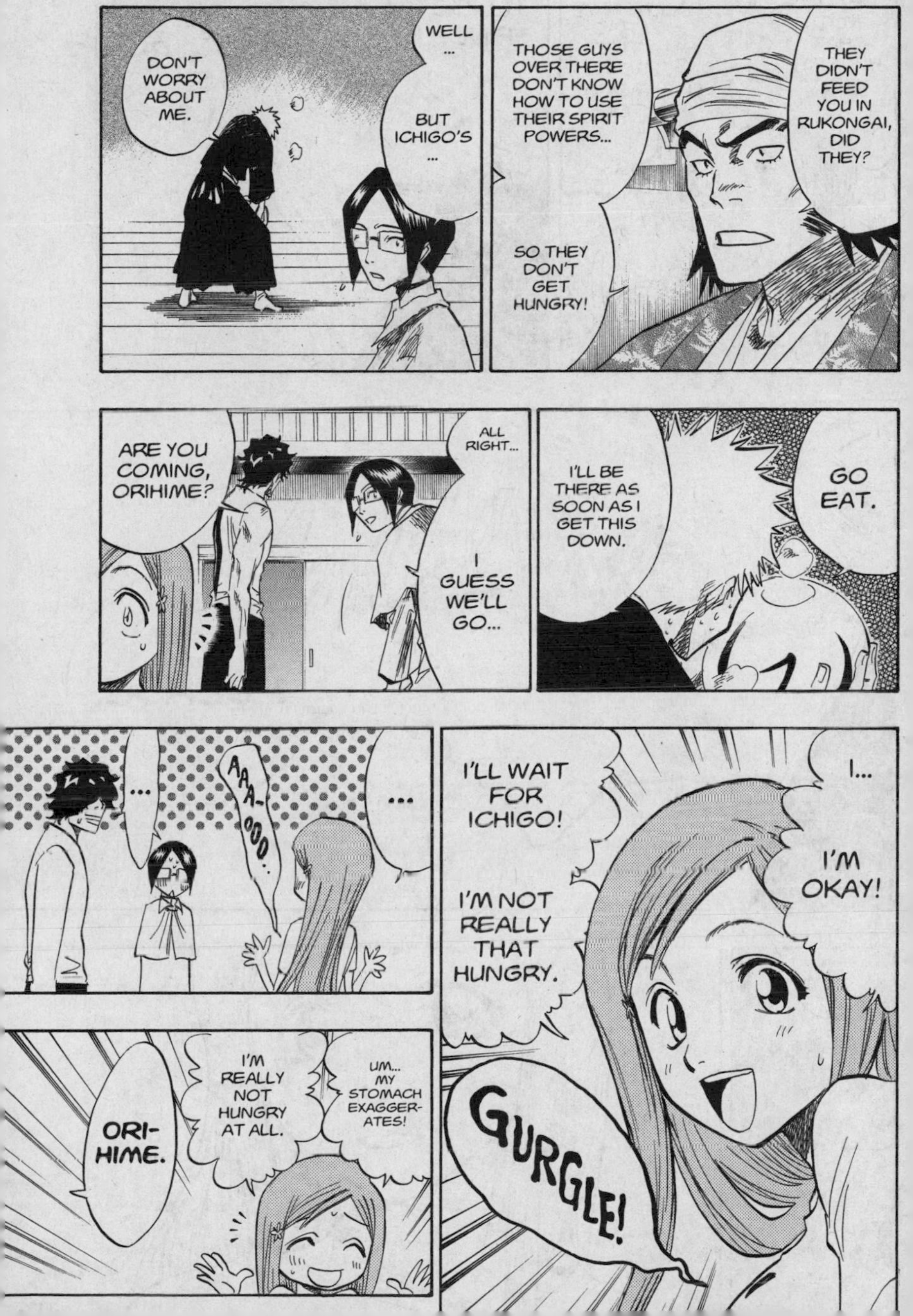
THEY DIDN'T FEED YOU IN RUKONGAI, DID THEY?
THOSE GUYS OVER THERE DON'T KNOW HOW TO USE THEIR SPIRIT POWERS...
SO THEY DON'T GET HUNGRY!
WELL ... BUT ICHIGO'S ...
DON'T WORRY ABOUT ME.
GO EAT.
I'LL BE THERE AS SOON AS I GET THIS DOWN.
ALL RIGHT... I GUESS WE'LL GO...
ARE YOU COMING, ORIHIME?
I... I'M OKAY!
I'LL WAIT FOR ICHIGO!
I'M NOT REALLY THAT HUNGRY.
GURGLE!
...
AAA-OOO...
...
UM... MY STOMACH EXAGGER-ATES!
I'M REALLY NOT HUNGRY AT ALL.
ORI-HIME.

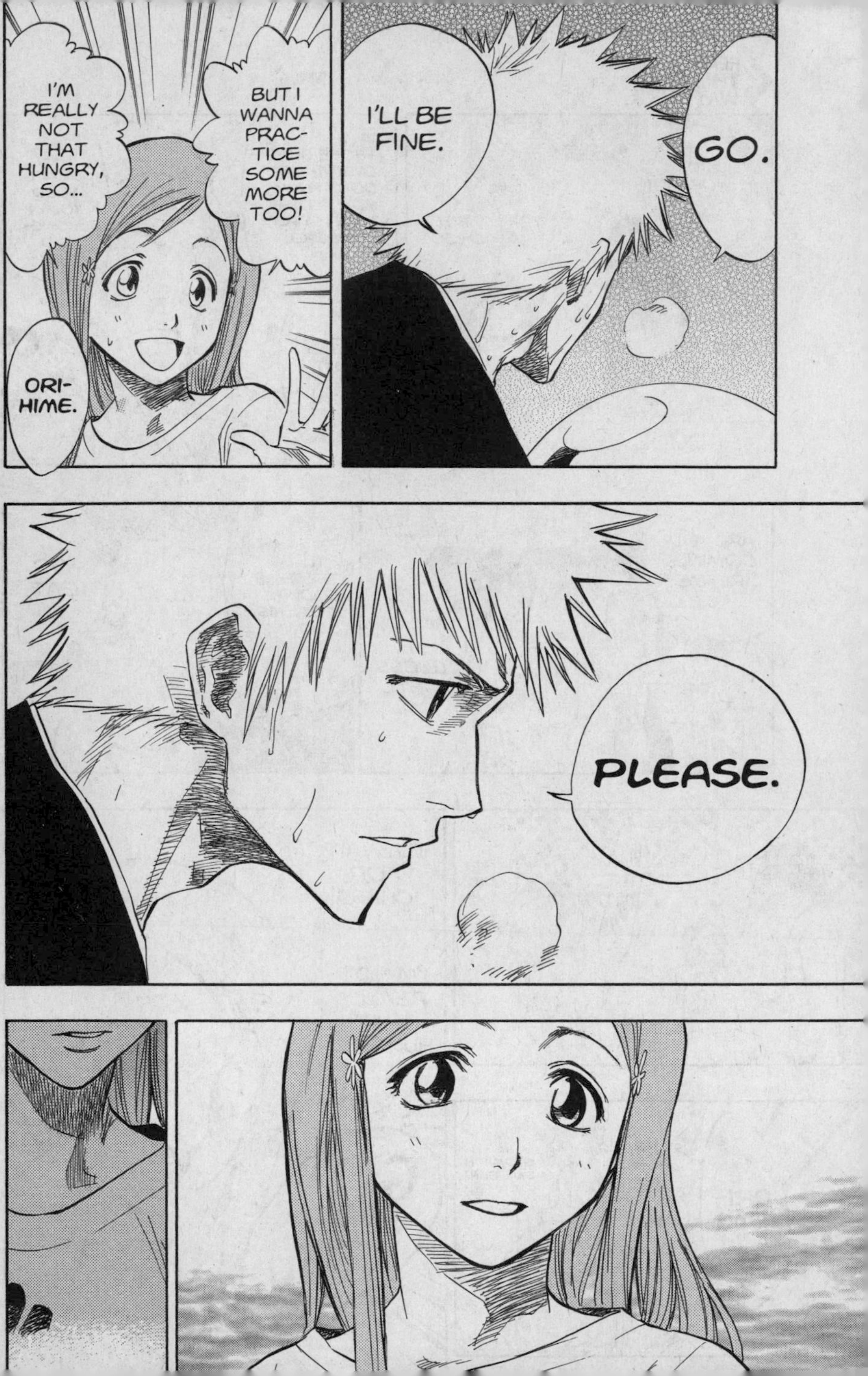
GO.
I'LL BE FINE.
BUT I WANNA PRAC-TICE SOME MORE TOO!
I'M REALLY NOT THAT HUNGRY, SO...
ORI-HIME.
PLEASE.

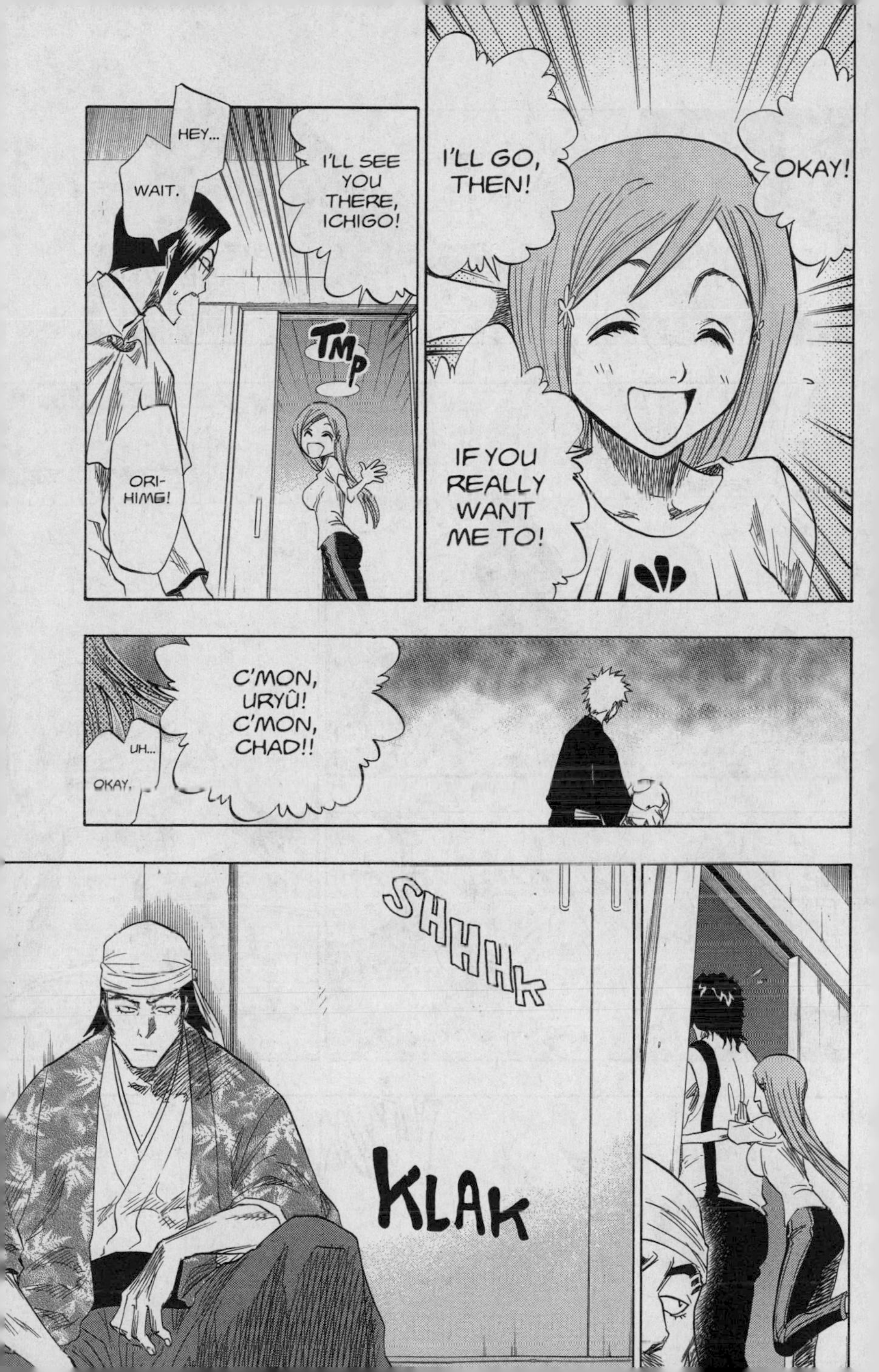
OKAY!
I'LL GO, THEN!
IF YOU REALLY WANT ME TO!
I'LL SEE YOU THERE, ICHIGO!
TMP
HEY...
WAIT.
ORI-HIME!
C'MON, URYÛ! C'MON, CHAD!!
UH...
OKAY.
SHHHK
KLAK

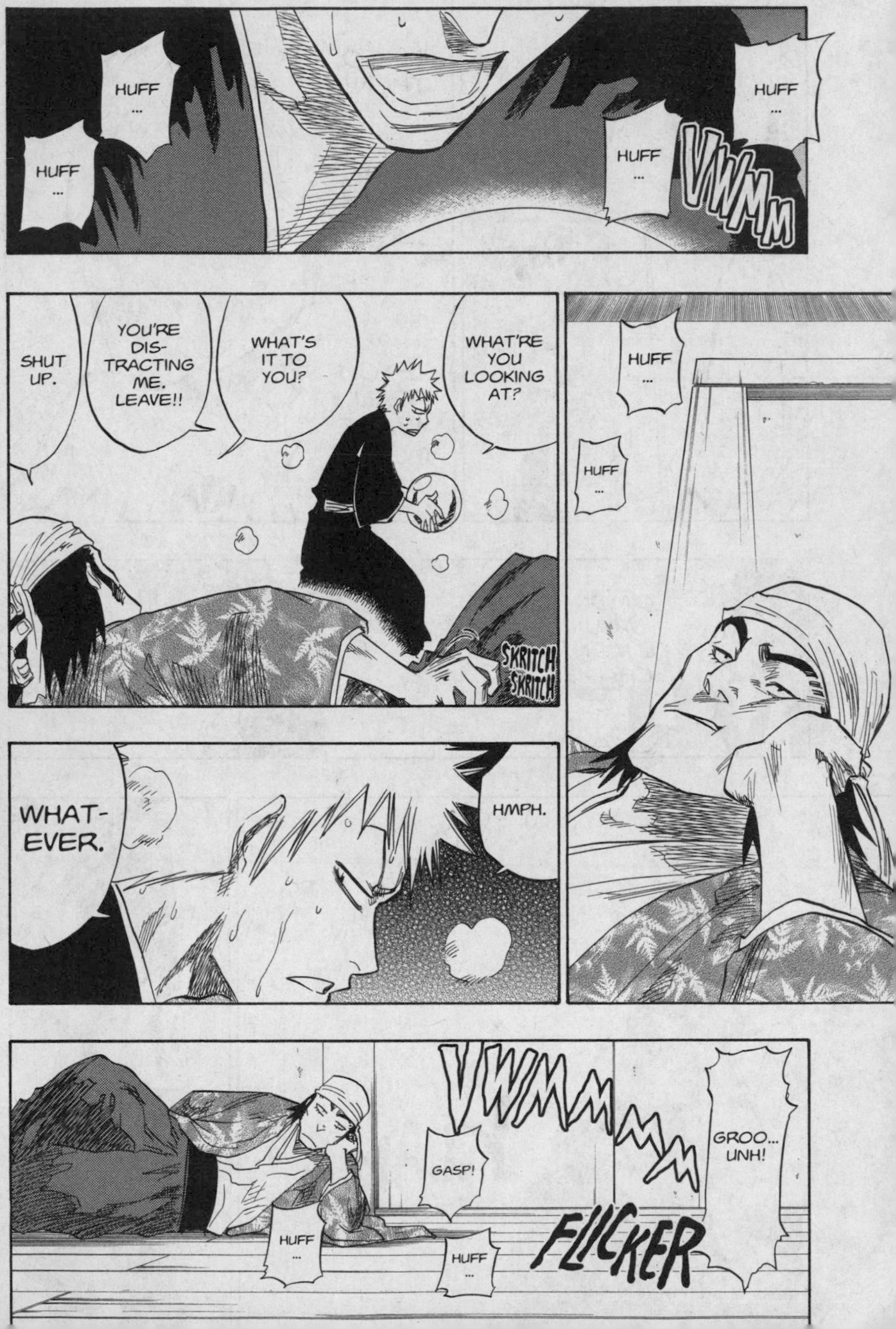
HUFF ...
HUFF ...
VWMM
HUFF ...
HUFF ...
HUFF ...
HUFF ...
WHAT'RE YOU LOOKING AT?
WHAT'S IT TO YOU?
YOU'RE DIS-TRACTING ME. LEAVE!!
SHUT UP.
SKRITCH SKRITCH
HMPH.
WHAT-EVER.
GROO... UNH!
VWMMMMM
GASP!
FLICKER
HUFF ...
HUFF ...

READ THIS WAY

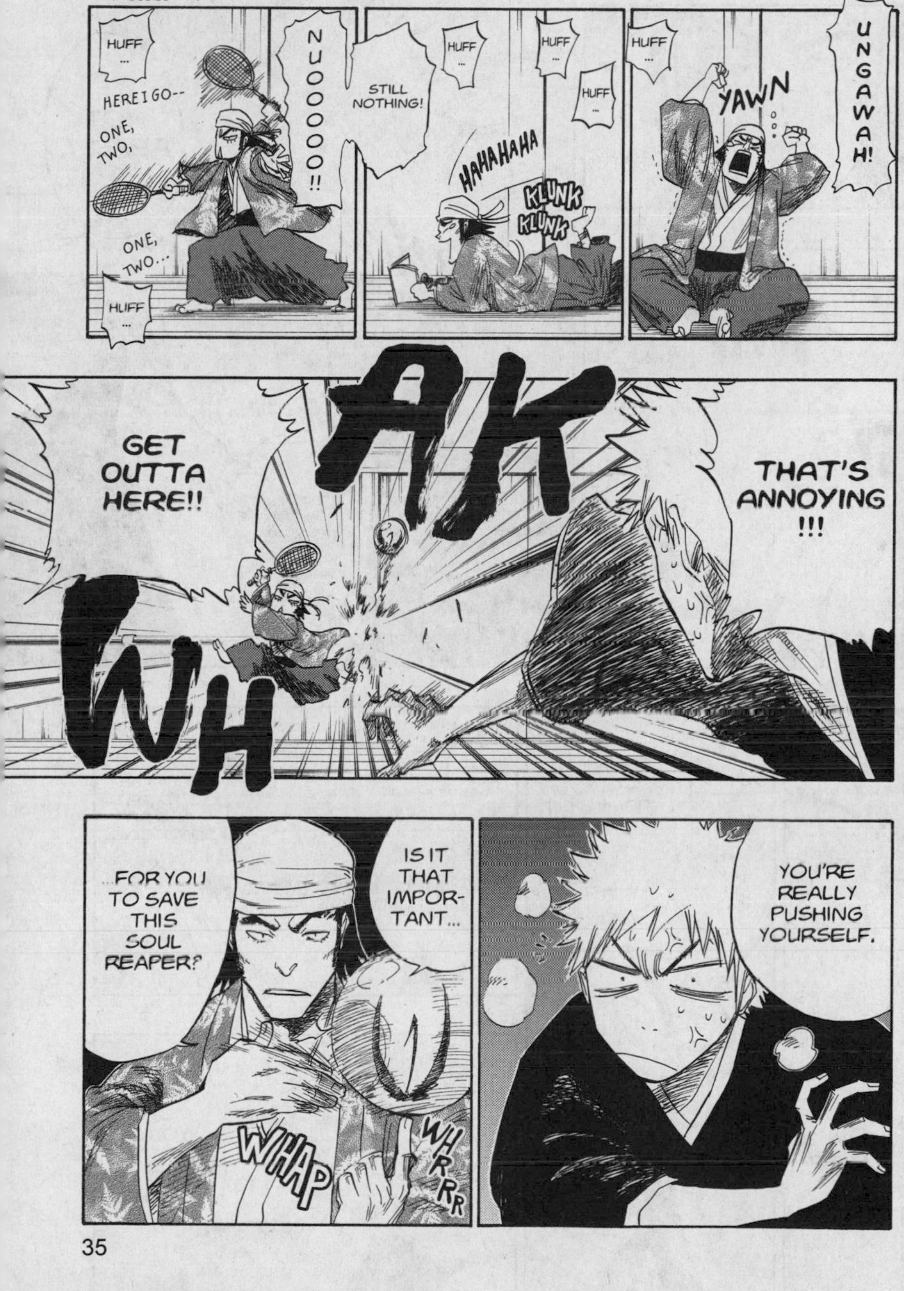
UNGAWAH!
YAWN...
HUFF...
HUFF...
HUFF...
HUFF...
STILL NOTHING!
HAHAHAHA
KLUNK KLUNK
NUOOOOOO!!
HUFF...
HERE I GO--
ONE, TWO,
ONE, TWO...
HUFF...
THAT'S ANNOYING!!!
WH
AK
GET OUTTA HERE!!
YOU'RE REALLY PUSHING YOURSELF.
IS IT THAT IMPORTANT...
...FOR YOU TO SAVE THIS SOUL REAPER?
WHAP
WHRRR

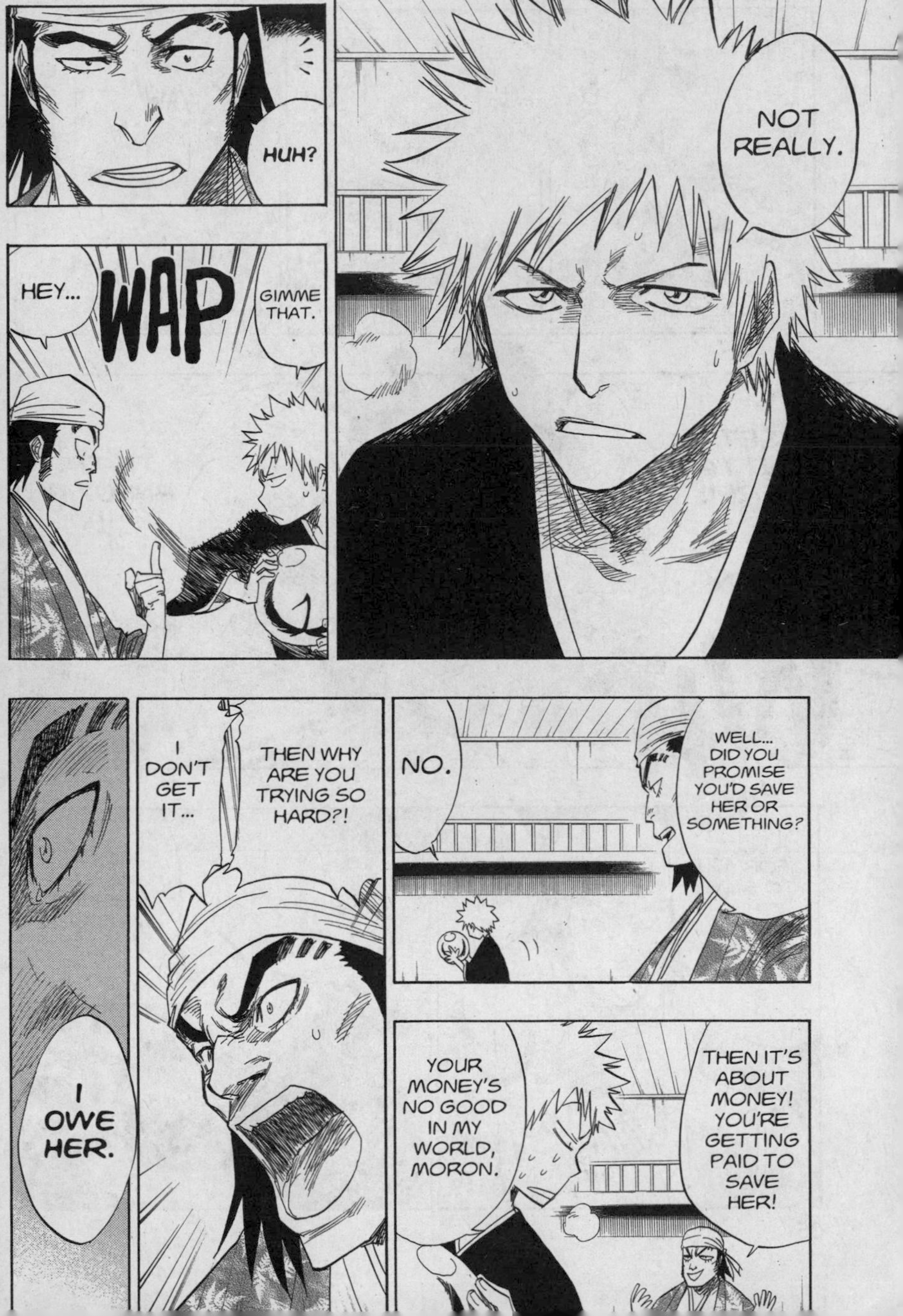
NOT REALLY.
HUH?
HEY...
WAP
GIMME THAT.
WELL... DID YOU PROMISE YOU'D SAVE HER OR SOMETHING?
NO.
THEN IT'S ABOUT MONEY! YOU'RE GETTING PAID TO SAVE HER!
YOUR MONEY'S NO GOOD IN MY WORLD, MORON.
THEN WHY ARE YOU TRYING SO HARD?!
I DON'T GET IT...
I OWE HER.

READ THIS WAY

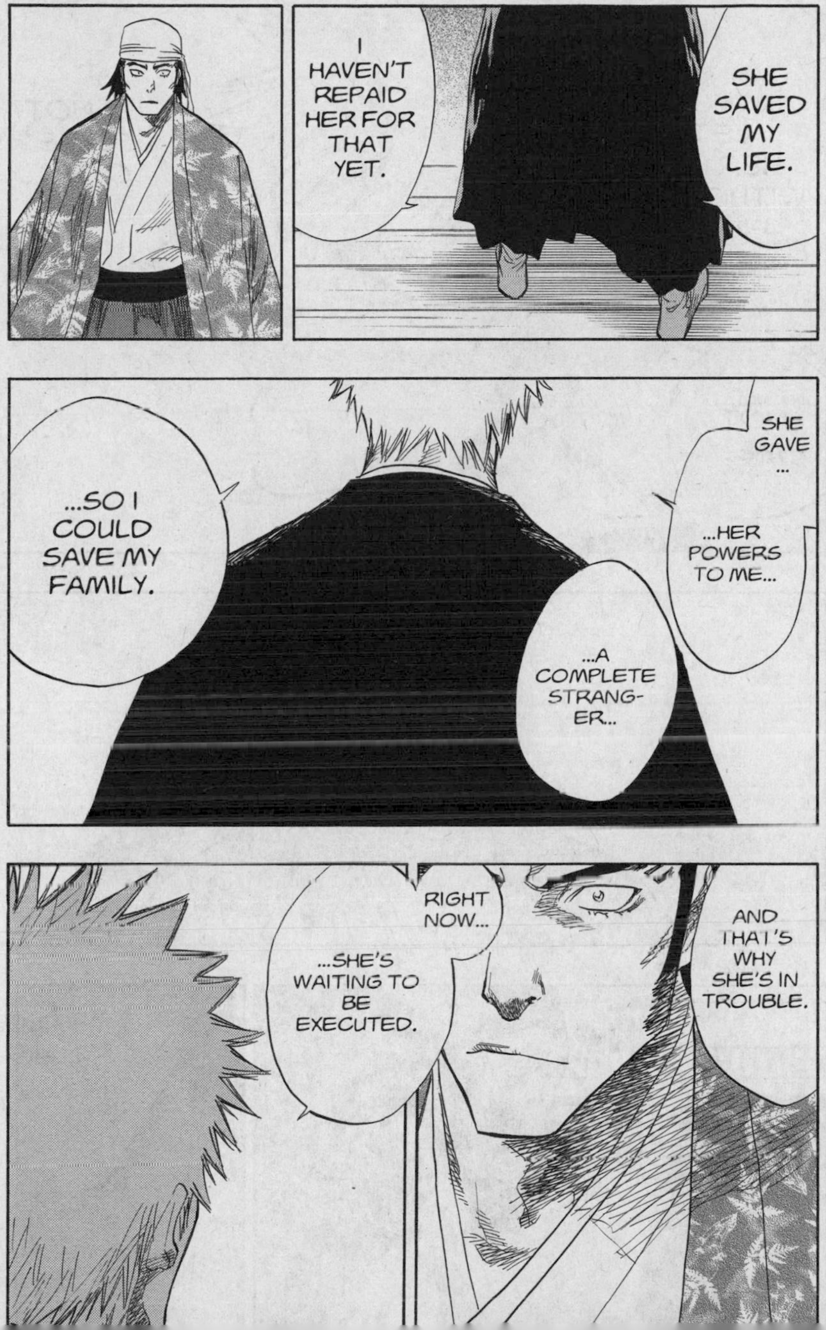
SHE SAVED MY LIFE.
I HAVEN'T REPAID HER FOR THAT YET.
SHE GAVE...
...HER POWERS TO ME...
...A COMPLETE STRANGER...
...SO I COULD SAVE MY FAMILY.
AND THAT'S WHY SHE'S IN TROUBLE.
RIGHT NOW...
...SHE'S WAITING TO BE EXECUTED.

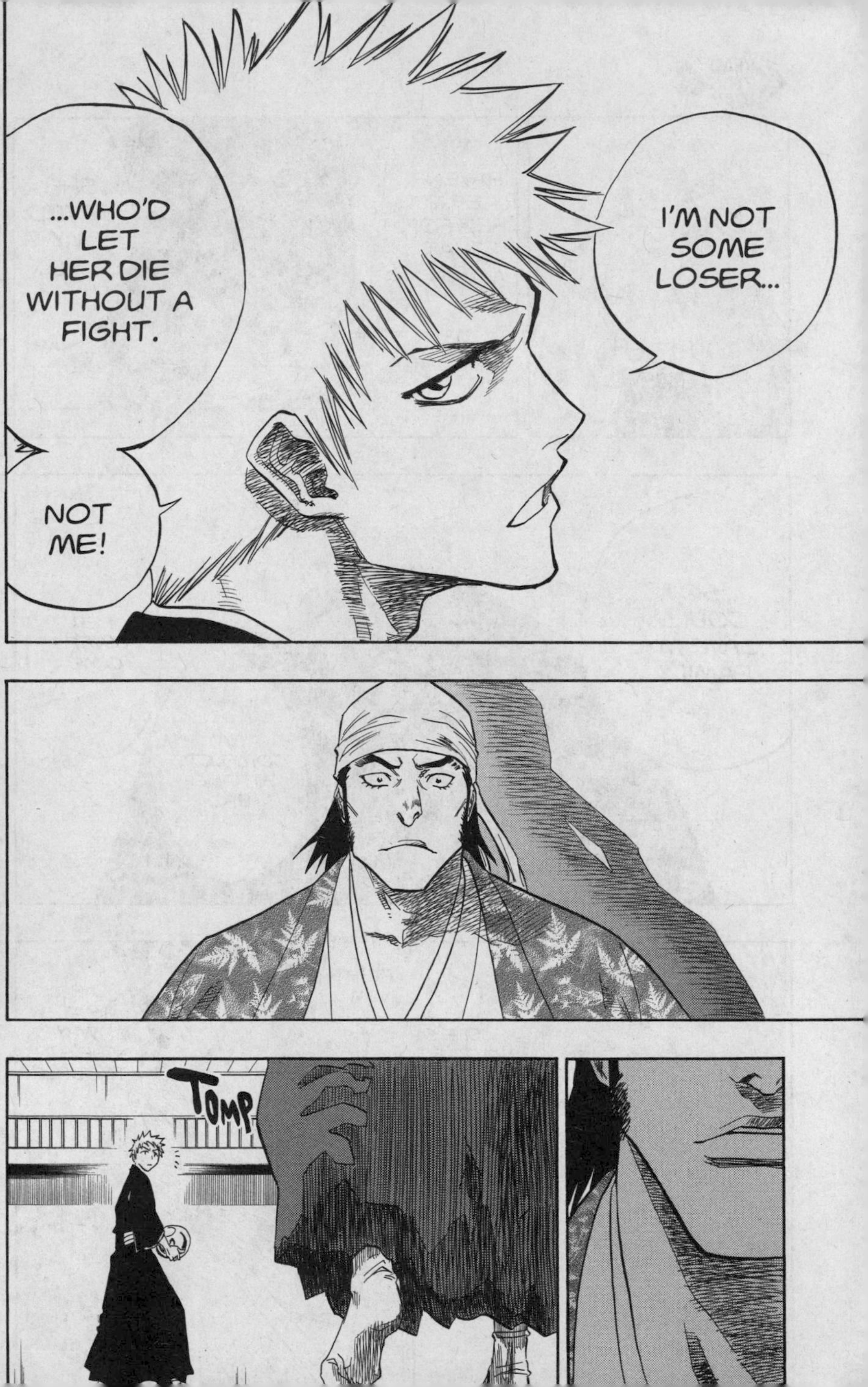
I'M NOT SOME LOSER...
...WHO'D LET HER DIE WITHOUT A FIGHT.
NOT ME!
TOMP

READ THIS WAY

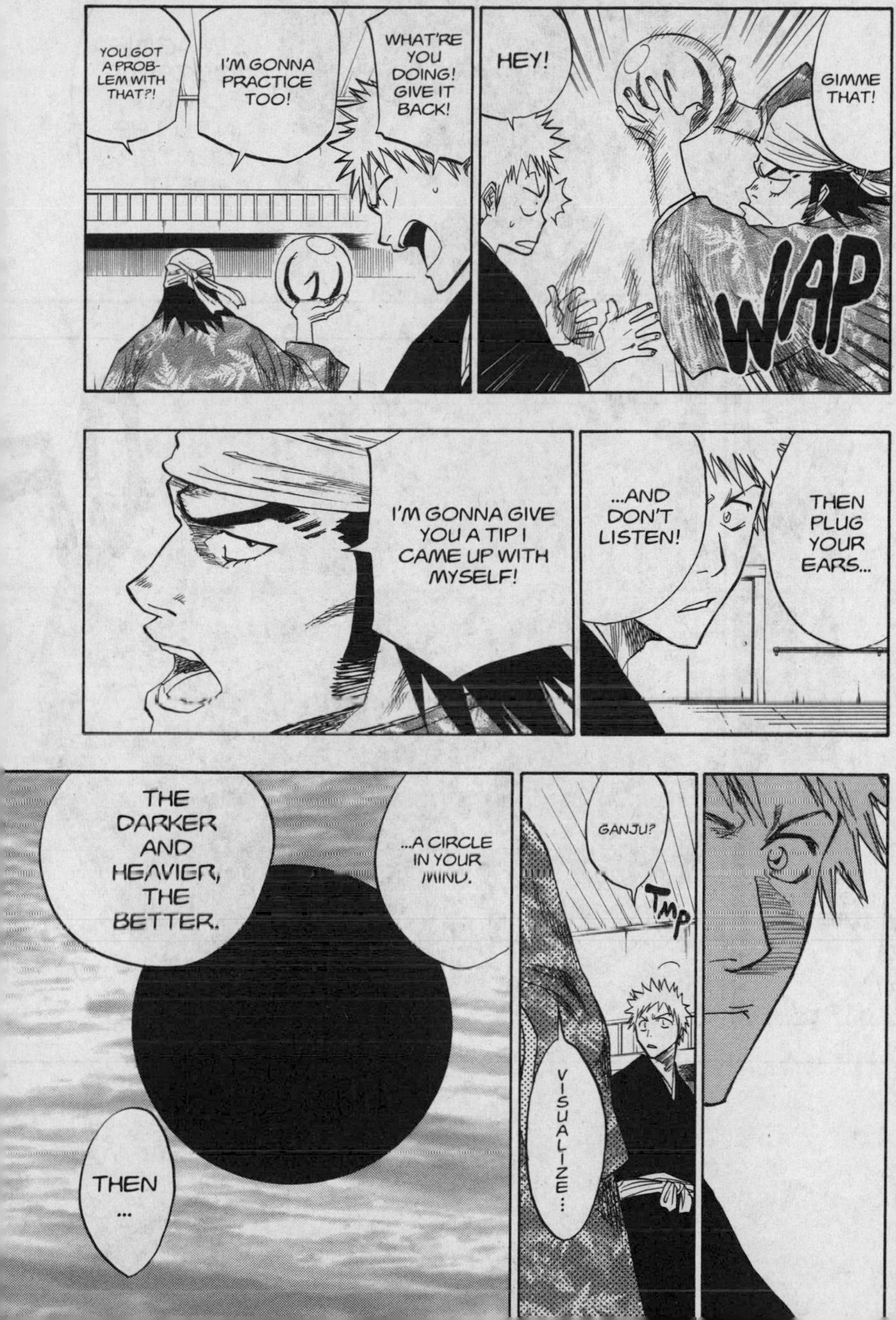
GIMME THAT!
WAP
HEY!
WHAT'RE YOU DOING! GIVE IT BACK!
I'M GONNA PRACTICE TOO!
YOU GOT A PROB-LEM WITH THAT?!
THEN PLUG YOUR EARS...
...AND DON'T LISTEN!
I'M GONNA GIVE YOU A TIP I CAME UP WITH MYSELF!
GANJU?
TMP
VISUALIZE...
...A CIRCLE IN YOUR MIND.
THE DARKER AND HEAVIER, THE BETTER.
THEN...

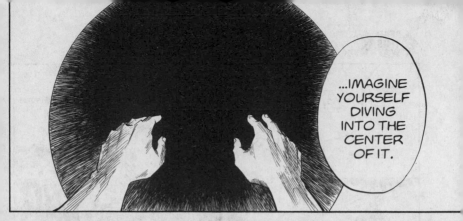

...IMAGINE YOURSELF DIVING INTO THE CENTER OF IT.

THIS IS...

THE BASIC FORM OF ALL SPELLS.

PO

OF

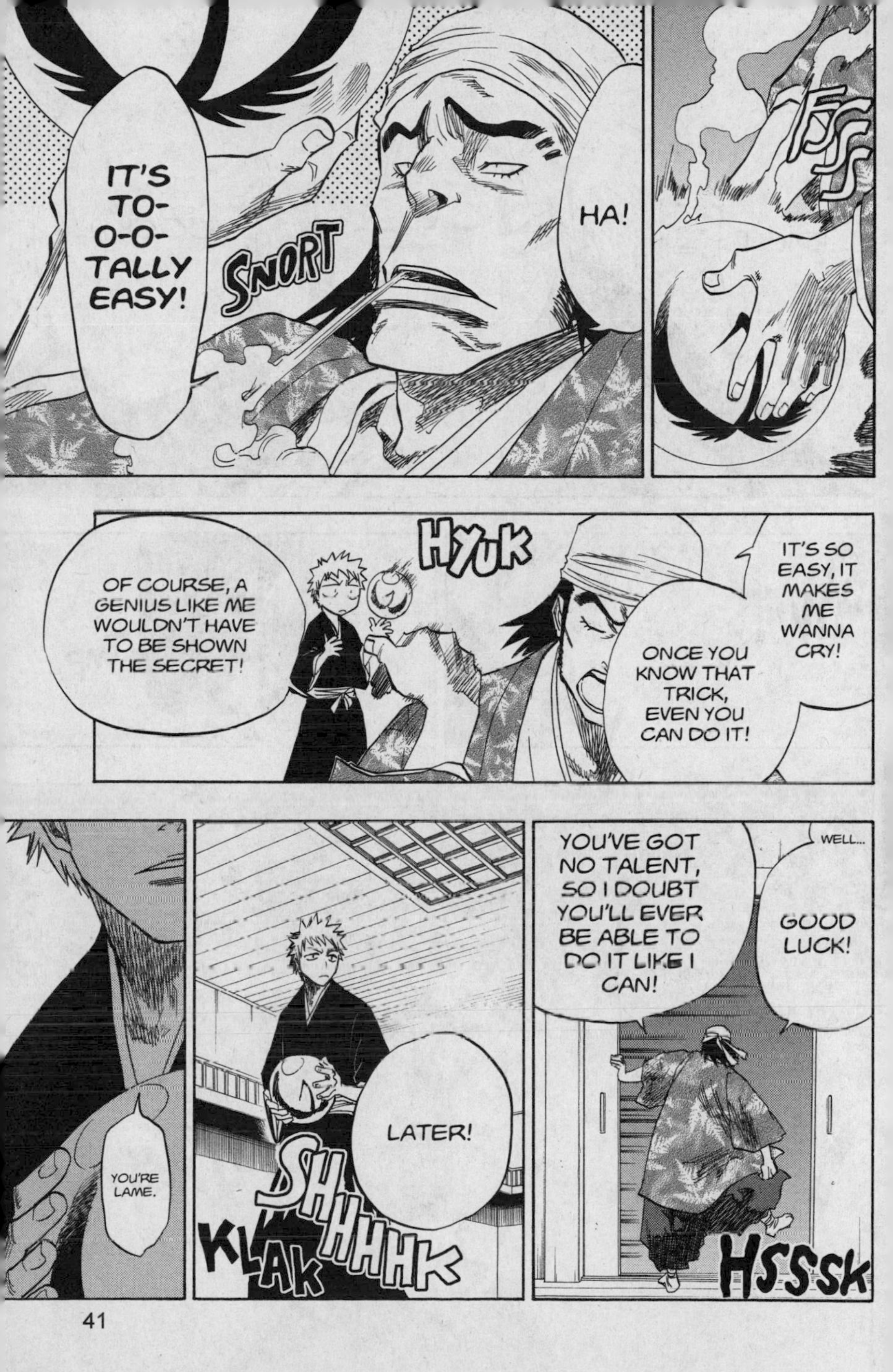
FSSS
HA!
IT'S TO-O-O-TALLY EASY!
SNORT
IT'S SO EASY, IT MAKES ME WANNA CRY!
ONCE YOU KNOW THAT TRICK, EVEN YOU CAN DO IT!
HYUK
OF COURSE, A GENIUS LIKE ME WOULDN'T HAVE TO BE SHOWN THE SECRET!
WELL...
GOOD LUCK!
YOU'VE GOT NO TALENT, SO I DOUBT YOU'LL EVER BE ABLE TO DO IT LIKE I CAN!
HSSSK
LATER!
SHHHHHK
KLAK
YOU'RE LAME.

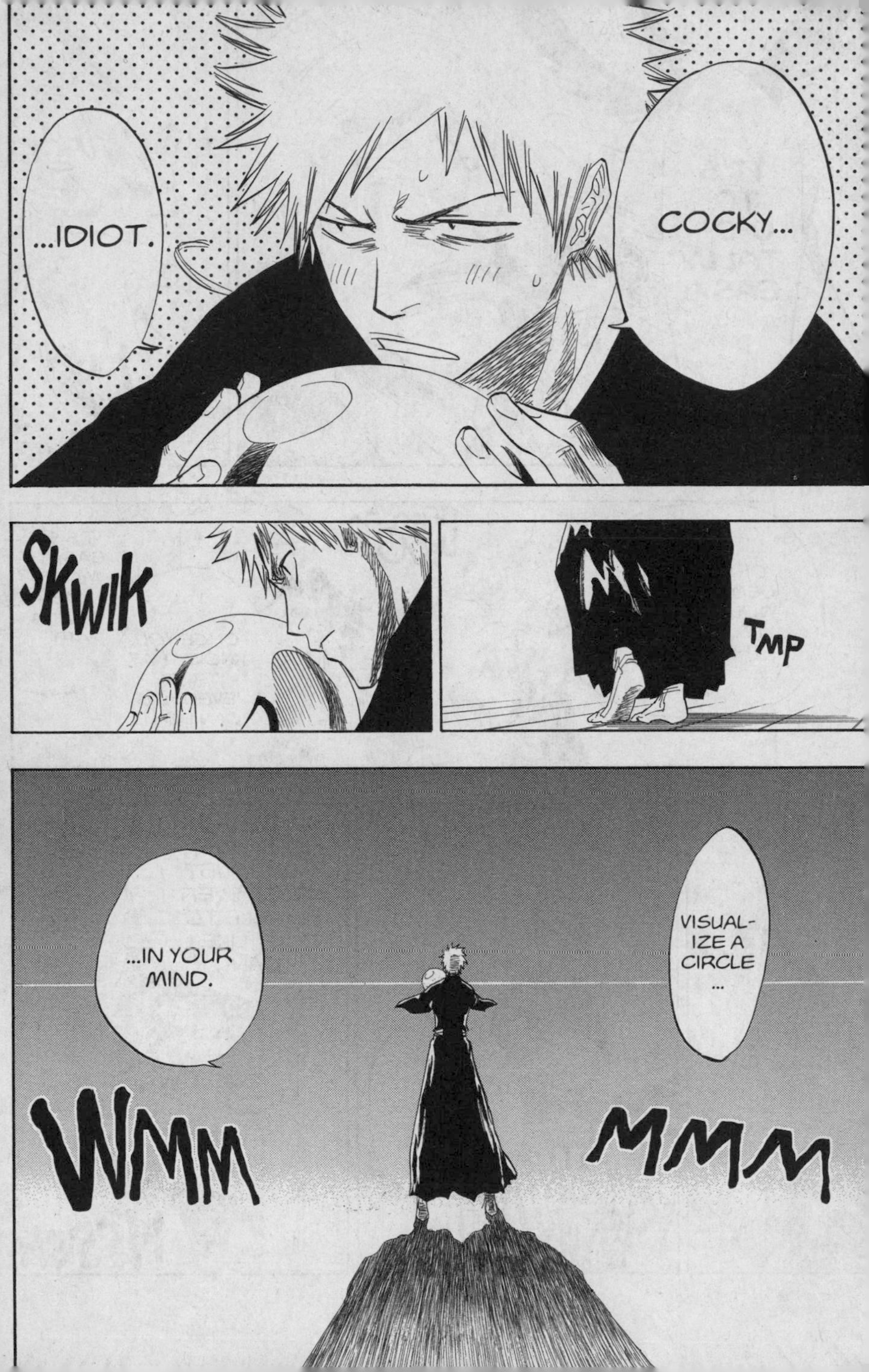
COCKY...
...IDIOT.
TMP
SKWIK
VISUALIZE A CIRCLE ...
...IN YOUR MIND.
WMM MMM

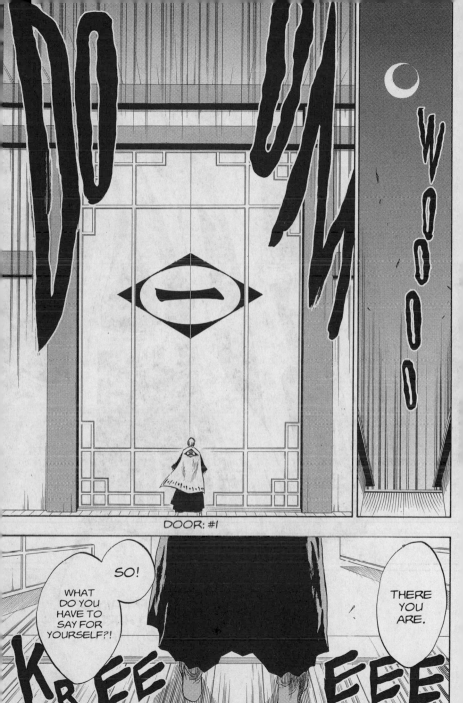

DOOM

WOOOO

DOOR: #1

SO!
WHAT DO YOU HAVE TO SAY FOR YOURSELF?!

THERE YOU ARE.

KREE EEE

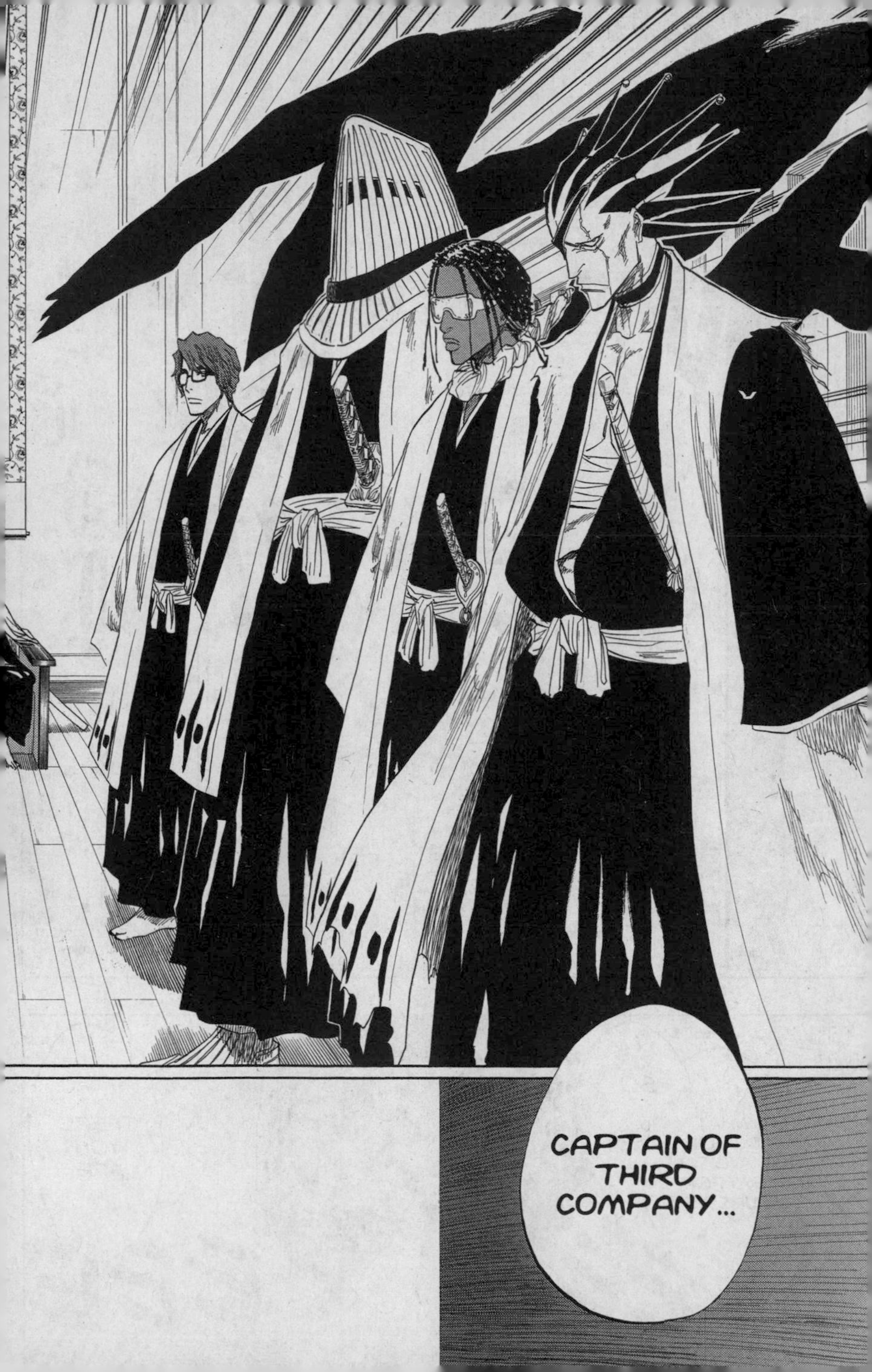
CAPTAIN OF THIRD COMPANY...

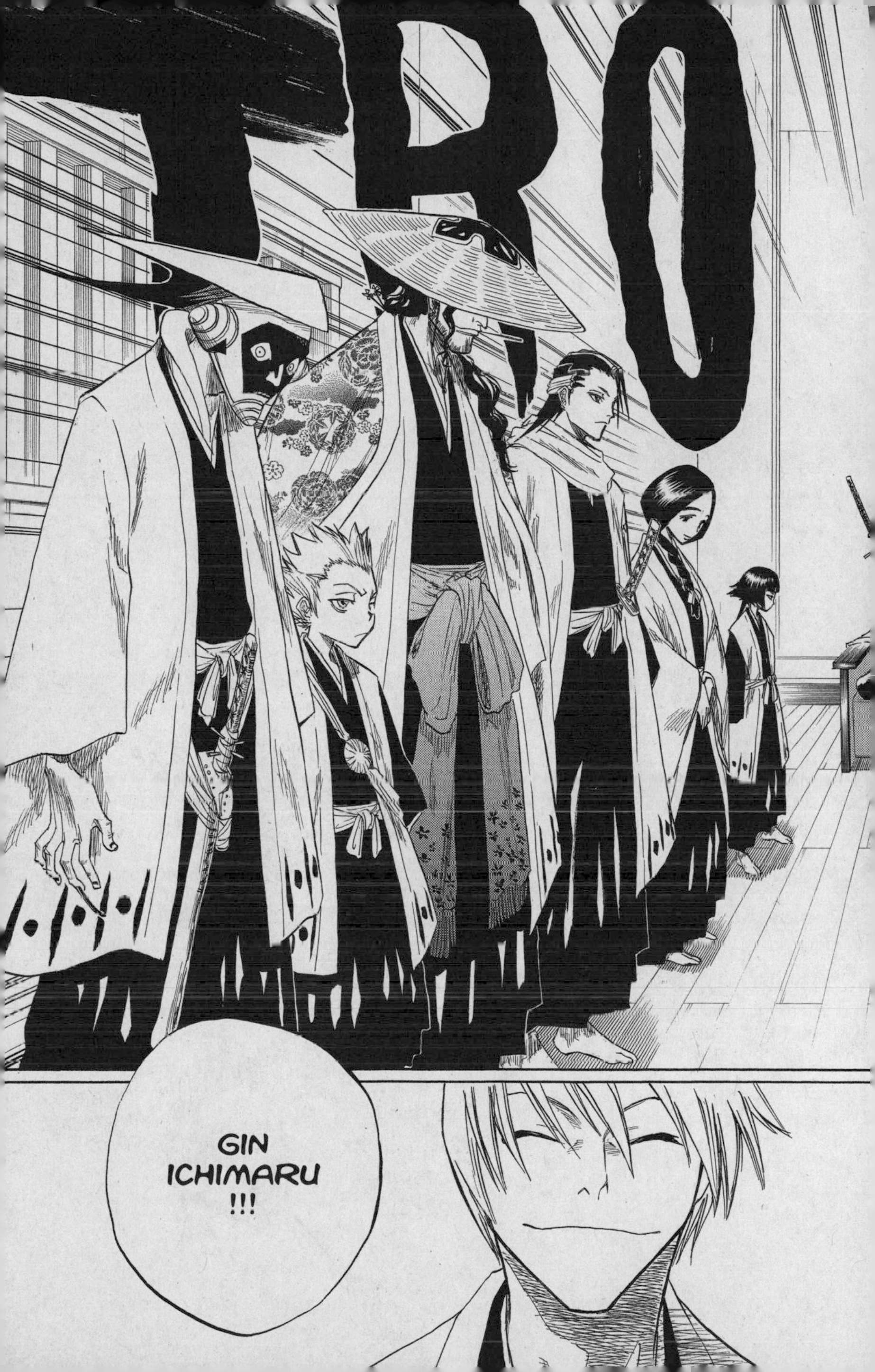
GIN ICHIMARU !!!

FWAP
FWAP
FWAP
DOPPLER EFFECT
FWAP
FWAP
FWAP
HEY!
THERE'S ANOTHER ONE!
I'VE BEEN SEEING THOSE THINGS A LOT LATELY.
I WONDER WHY?
IS IT THE GHOST OF SOME ANIMAL?

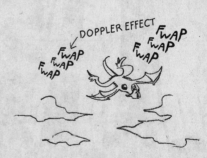

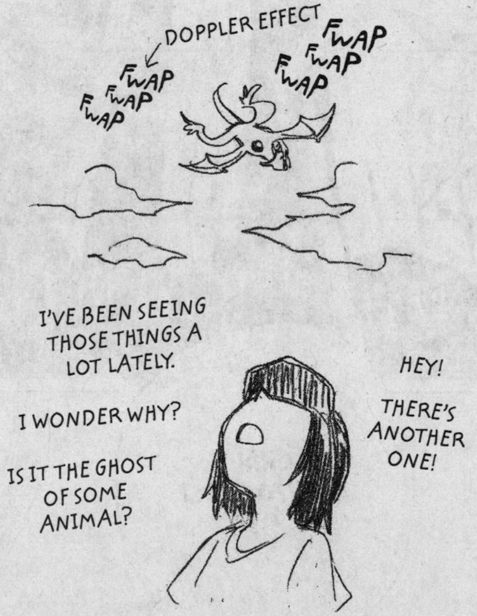

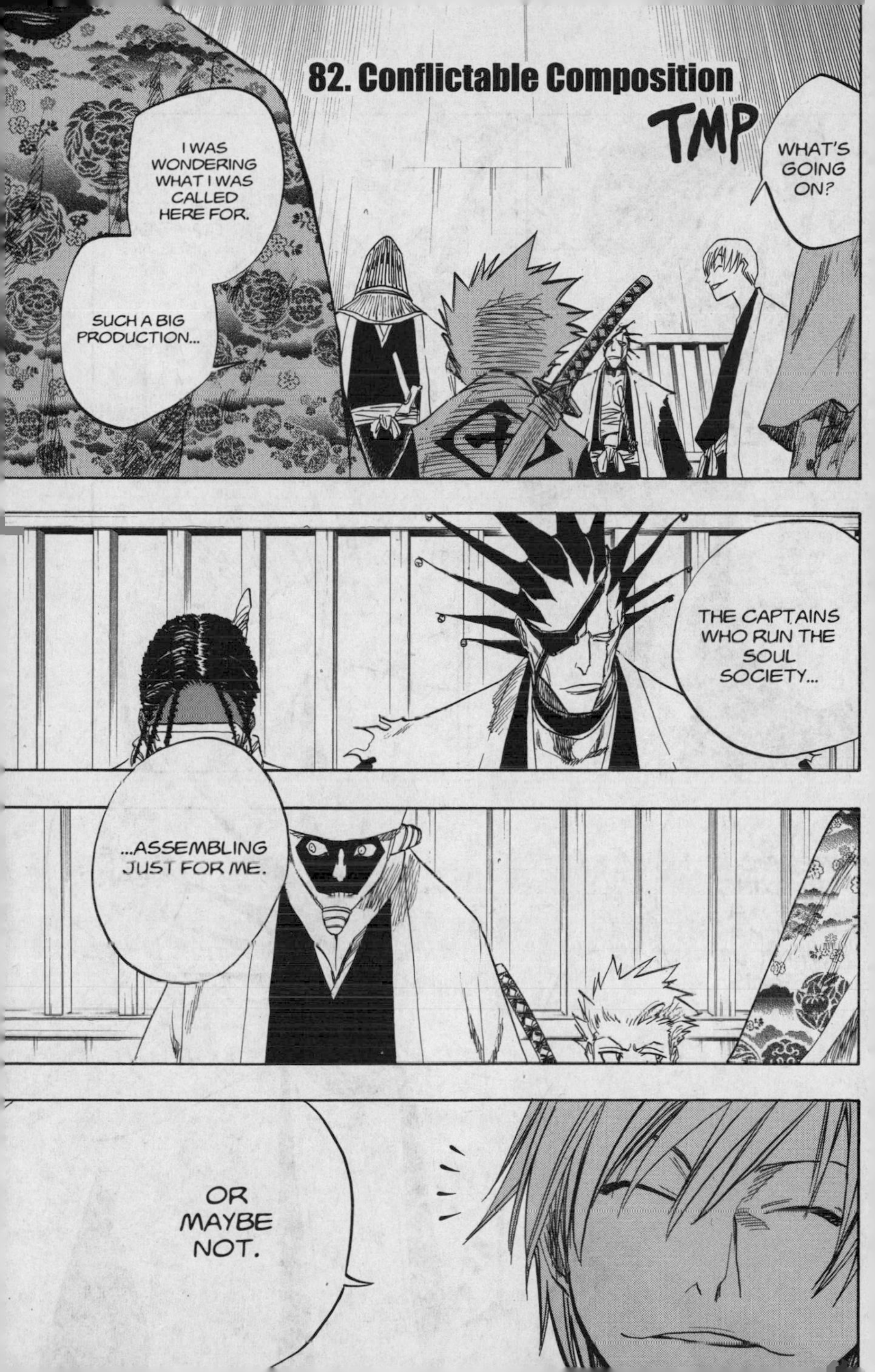
82. Conflictable Composition
TMP
WHAT'S GOING ON?
I WAS WONDERING WHAT I WAS CALLED HERE FOR.
SUCH A BIG PRODUCTION...
THE CAPTAINS WHO RUN THE SOUL SOCIETY...
...ASSEMBLING JUST FOR ME.
OR MAYBE NOT.

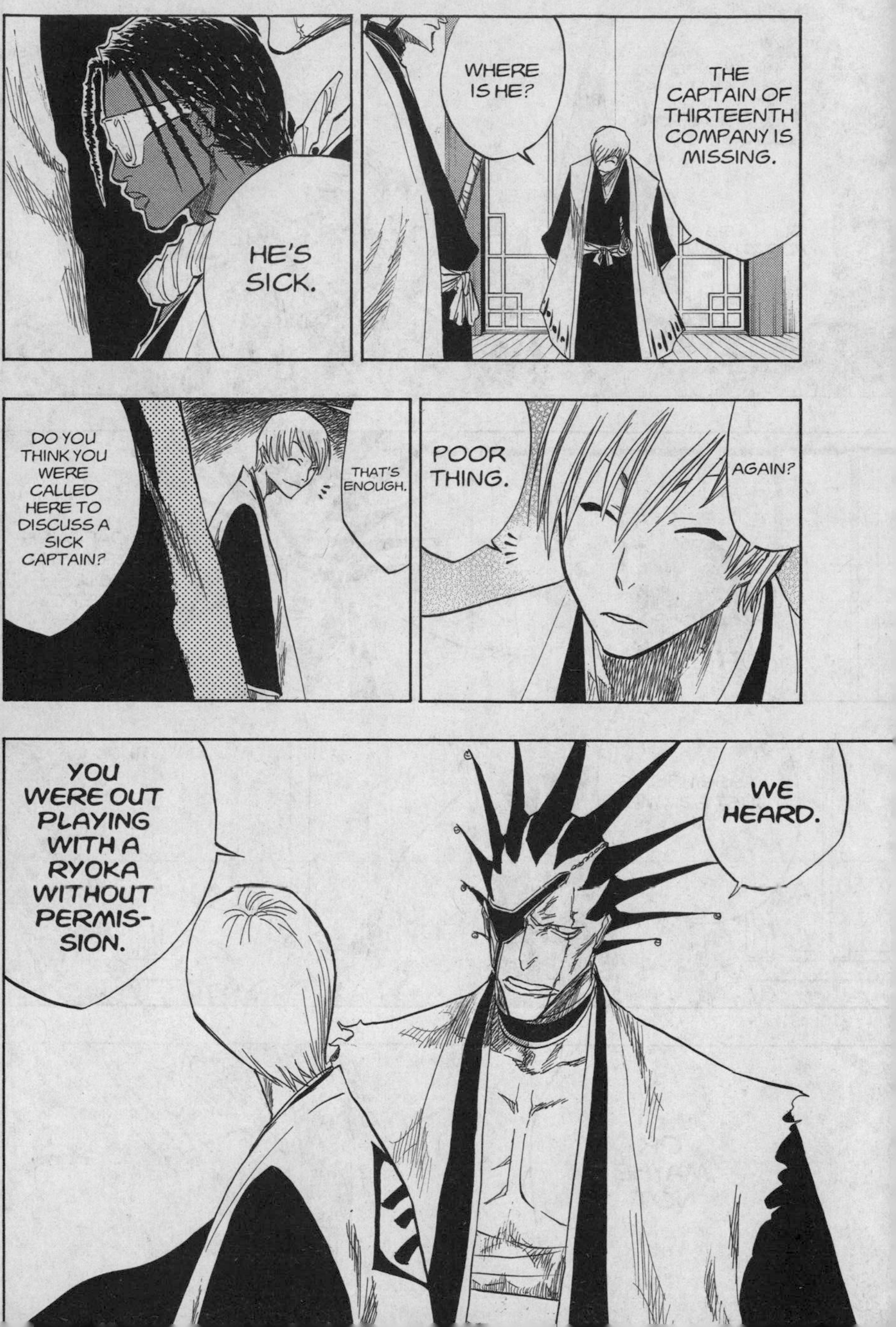
THE CAPTAIN OF THIRTEENTH COMPANY IS MISSING.
WHERE IS HE?
HE'S SICK.
AGAIN?
POOR THING.
THAT'S ENOUGH.
DO YOU THINK YOU WERE CALLED HERE TO DISCUSS A SICK CAPTAIN?
WE HEARD.
YOU WERE OUT PLAYING WITH A RYOKA WITHOUT PERMIS-SION.

READ THIS WAY

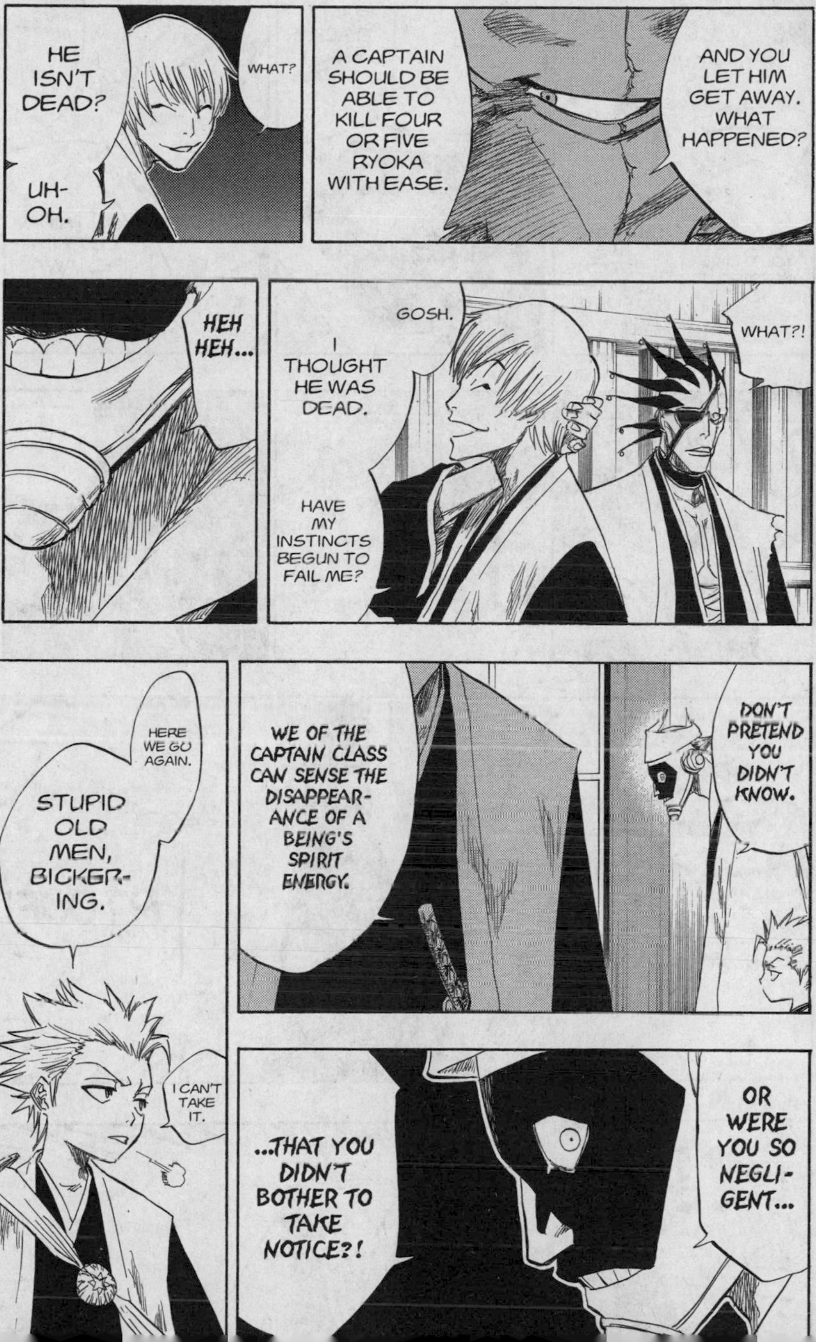
AND YOU LET HIM GET AWAY. WHAT HAPPENED?
A CAPTAIN SHOULD BE ABLE TO KILL FOUR OR FIVE RYOKA WITH EASE.
WHAT?
HE ISN'T DEAD?
UH-OH.
WHAT?!
GOSH.
I THOUGHT HE WAS DEAD.
HAVE MY INSTINCTS BEGUN TO FAIL ME?
HEH HEH...
DON'T PRETEND YOU DIDN'T KNOW.
WE OF THE CAPTAIN CLASS CAN SENSE THE DISAPPEARANCE OF A BEING'S SPIRIT ENERGY.
OR WERE YOU SO NEGLIGENT...
...THAT YOU DIDN'T BOTHER TO TAKE NOTICE?!
HERE WE GO AGAIN.
STUPID OLD MEN, BICKERING.
I CAN'T TAKE IT.

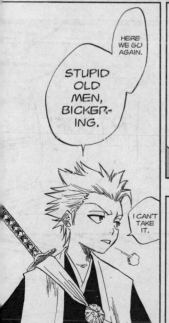

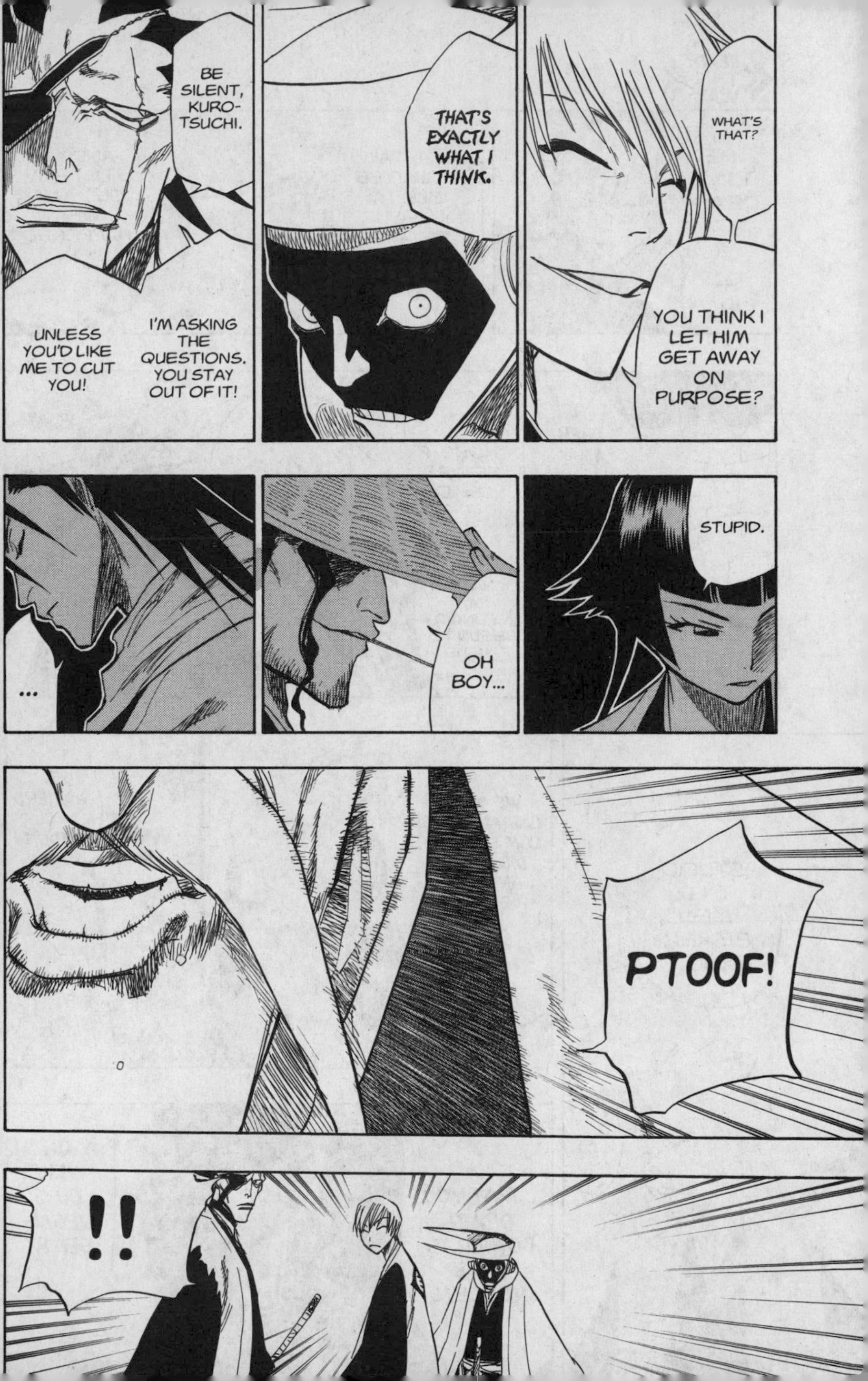
WHAT'S THAT?
YOU THINK I LET HIM GET AWAY ON PURPOSE?
THAT'S EXACTLY WHAT I THINK.
BE SILENT, KURO-TSUCHI.
I'M ASKING THE QUESTIONS. YOU STAY OUT OF IT!
UNLESS YOU'D LIKE ME TO CUT YOU!
STUPID.
OH BOY...
...
PTOOF!
!!

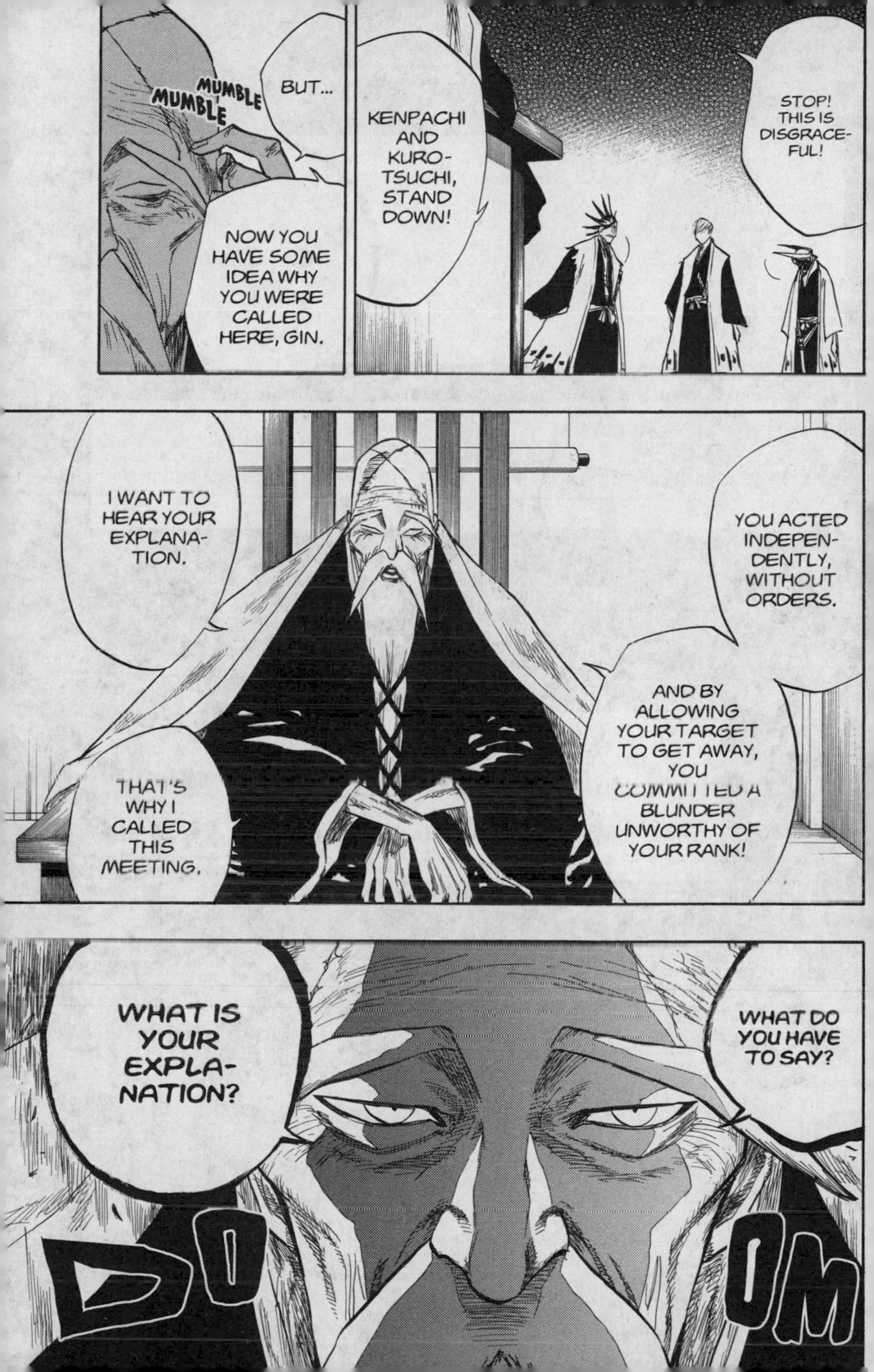

STOP! THIS IS DISGRACE-FUL!
KENPACHI AND KURO-TSUCHI, STAND DOWN!
BUT...
MUMBLE MUMBLE
NOW YOU HAVE SOME IDEA WHY YOU WERE CALLED HERE, GIN.
YOU ACTED INDEPEN-DENTLY, WITHOUT ORDERS.
AND BY ALLOWING YOUR TARGET TO GET AWAY, YOU COMMITTED A BLUNDER UNWORTHY OF YOUR RANK!
THAT'S WHY I CALLED THIS MEETING.
I WANT TO HEAR YOUR EXPLANA-TION.
WHAT DO YOU HAVE TO SAY?
WHAT IS YOUR EXPLA-NATION?
DOOM

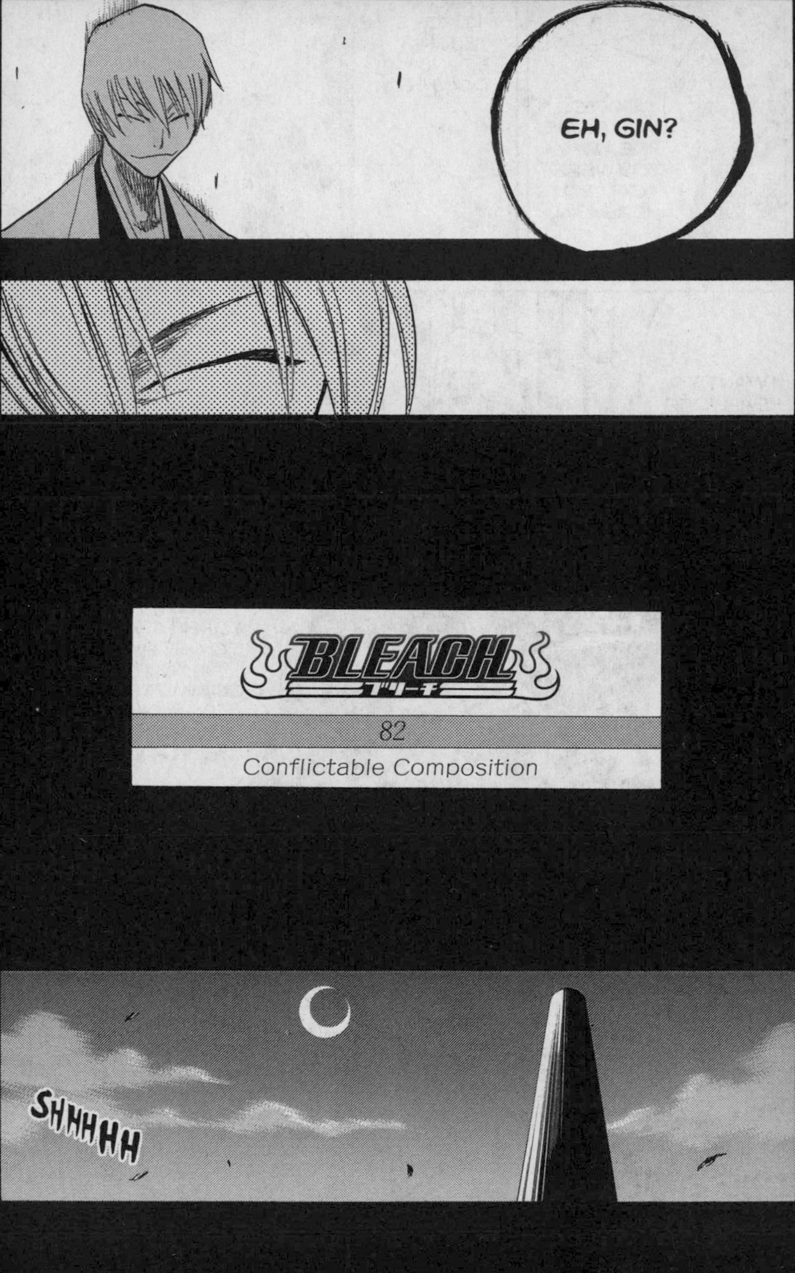
EH, GIN?
82
Conflictable Composition
SHHHHH

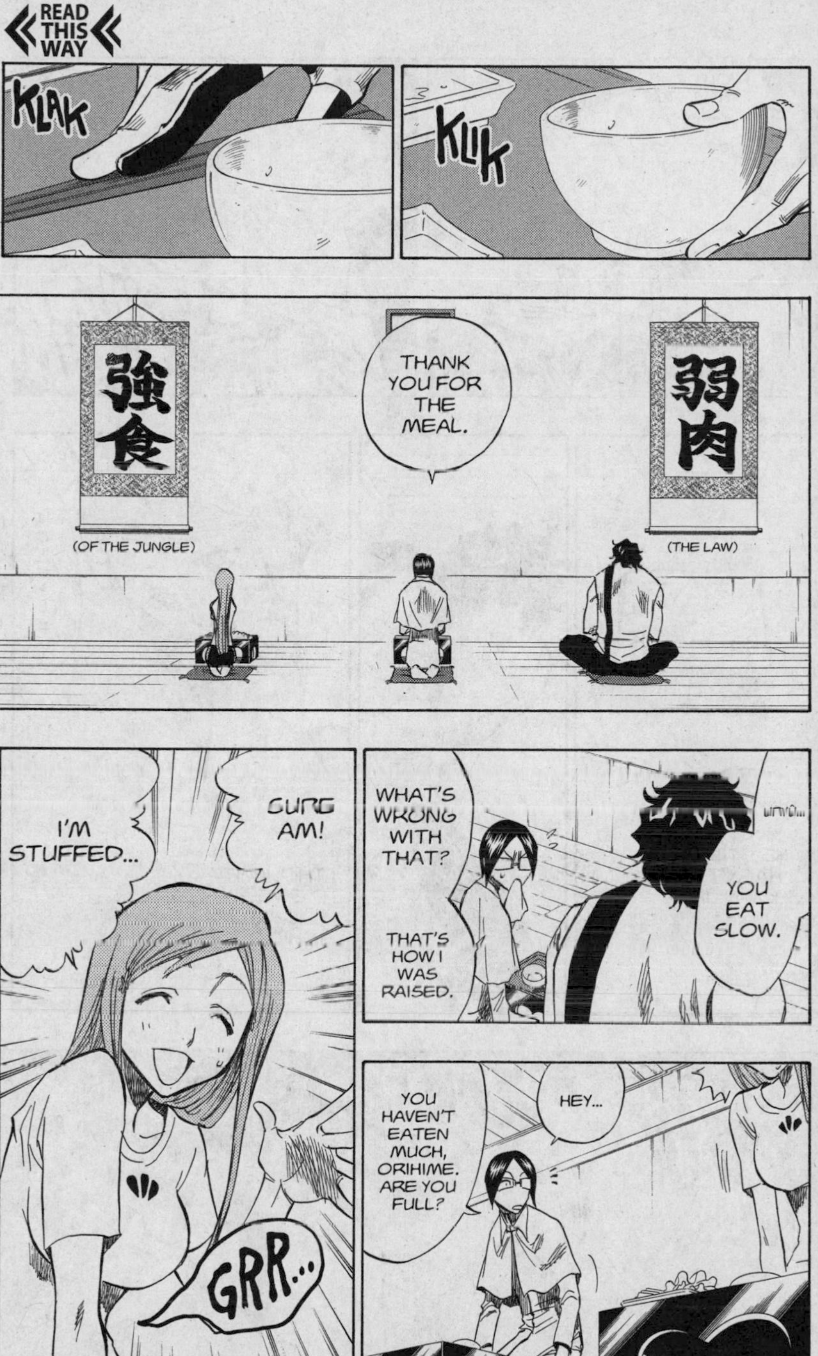
READ THIS WAY
KLIK
KLAK
THANK YOU FOR THE MEAL.
弱肉
(THE LAW)
強食
(OF THE JUNGLE)
YOU EAT SLOW.
WHAT'S WRONG WITH THAT?
THAT'S HOW I WAS RAISED.
HEY...
YOU HAVEN'T EATEN MUCH, ORIHIME. ARE YOU FULL?
SURE AM!
I'M STUFFED...
GRR...

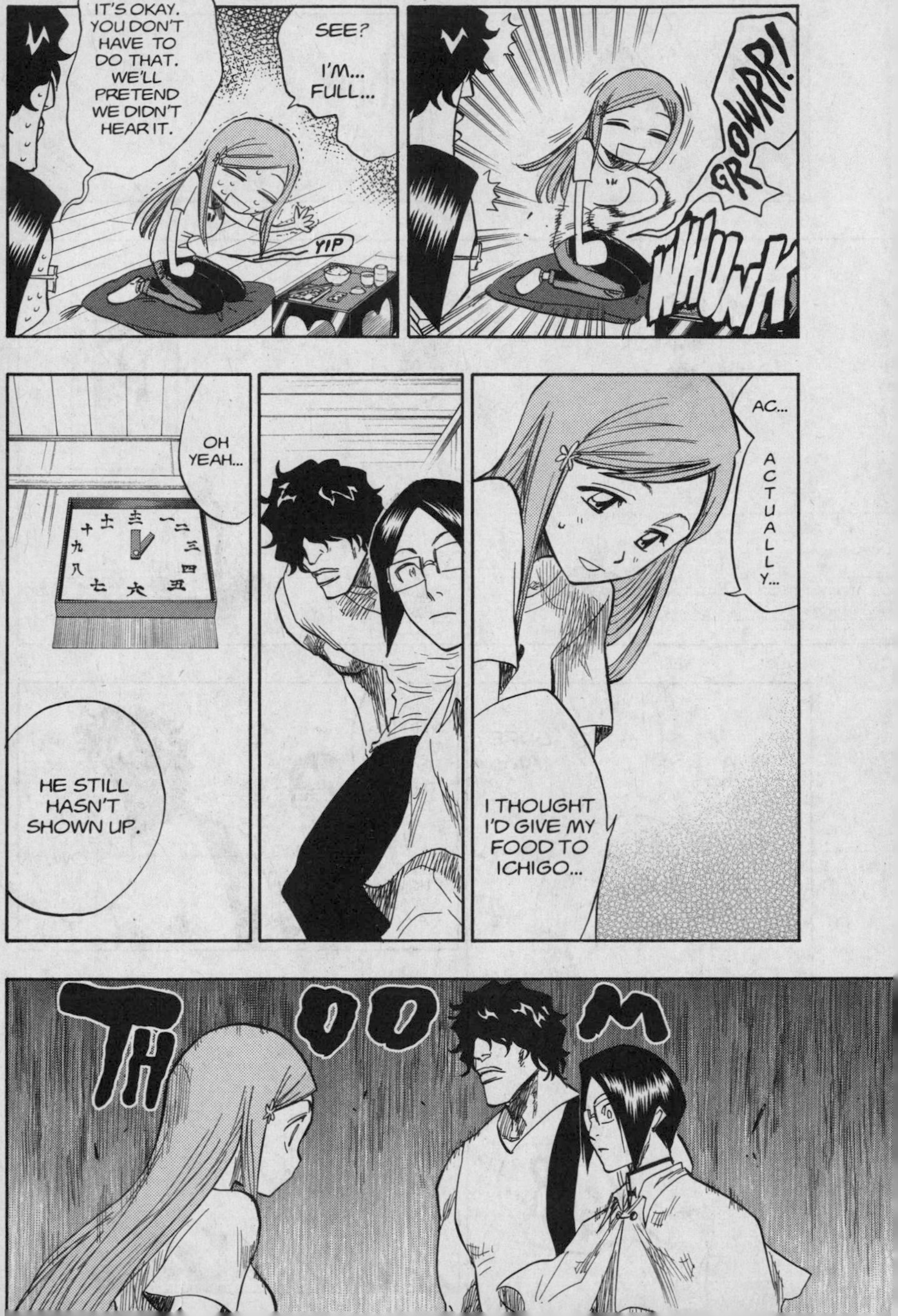
GROWRR!
WHUNK
SEE?
I'M... FULL...
IT'S OKAY. YOU DON'T HAVE TO DO THAT. WE'LL PRETEND WE DIDN'T HEAR IT.
YIP
AC...
ACTUALLY...
I THOUGHT I'D GIVE MY FOOD TO ICHIGO...
OH YEAH...
HE STILL HASN'T SHOWN UP.
THOOM

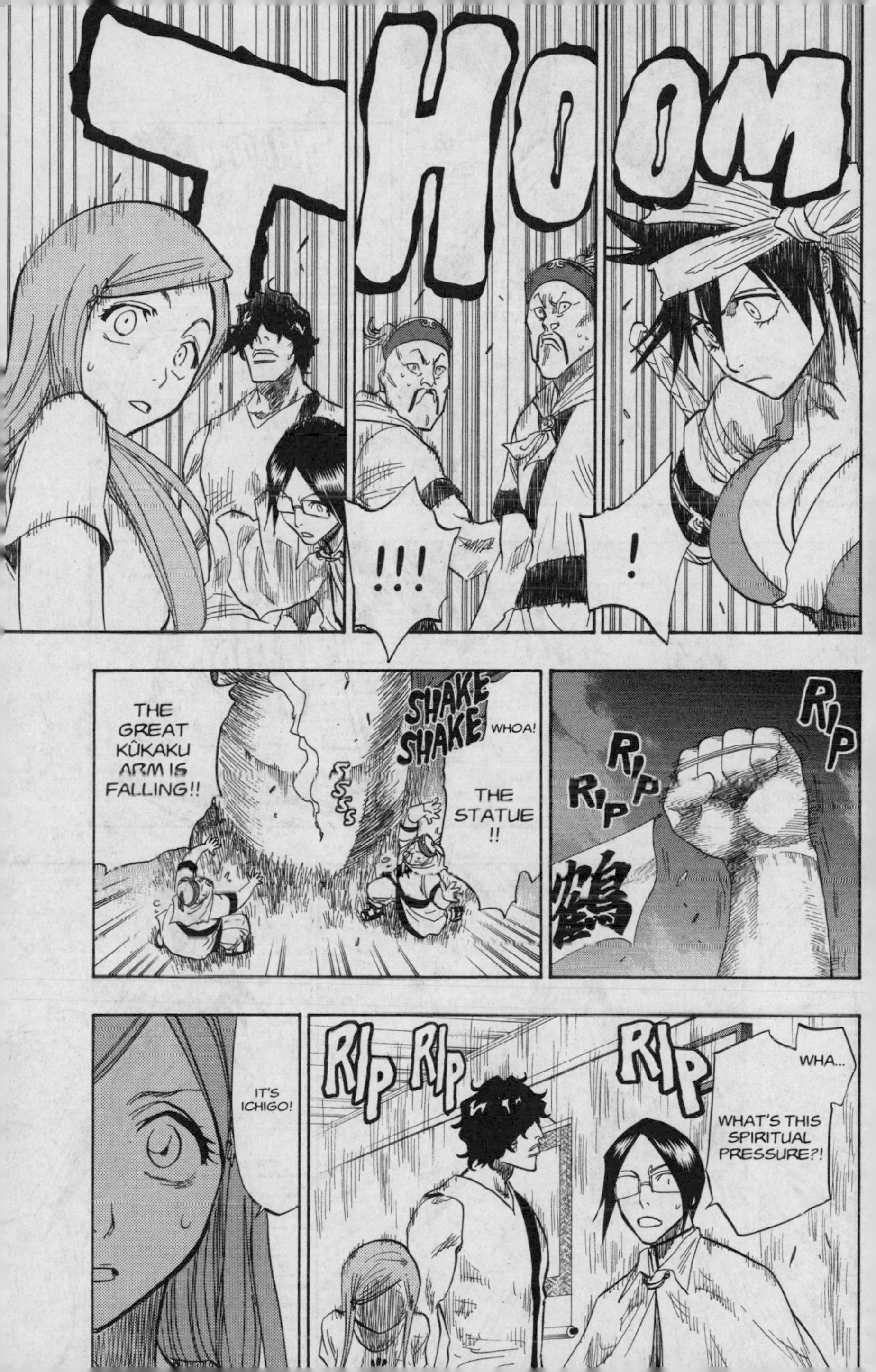
THOOM
!
!!!
RIP
RIP
RIP
鶴
SHAKE SHAKE
WHOA!
THE STATUE!!
THE GREAT KÛKAKU ARM IS FALLING!!
RIP
WHA...
WHAT'S THIS SPIRITUAL PRESSURE?!
RIP RIP
IT'S ICHIGO!

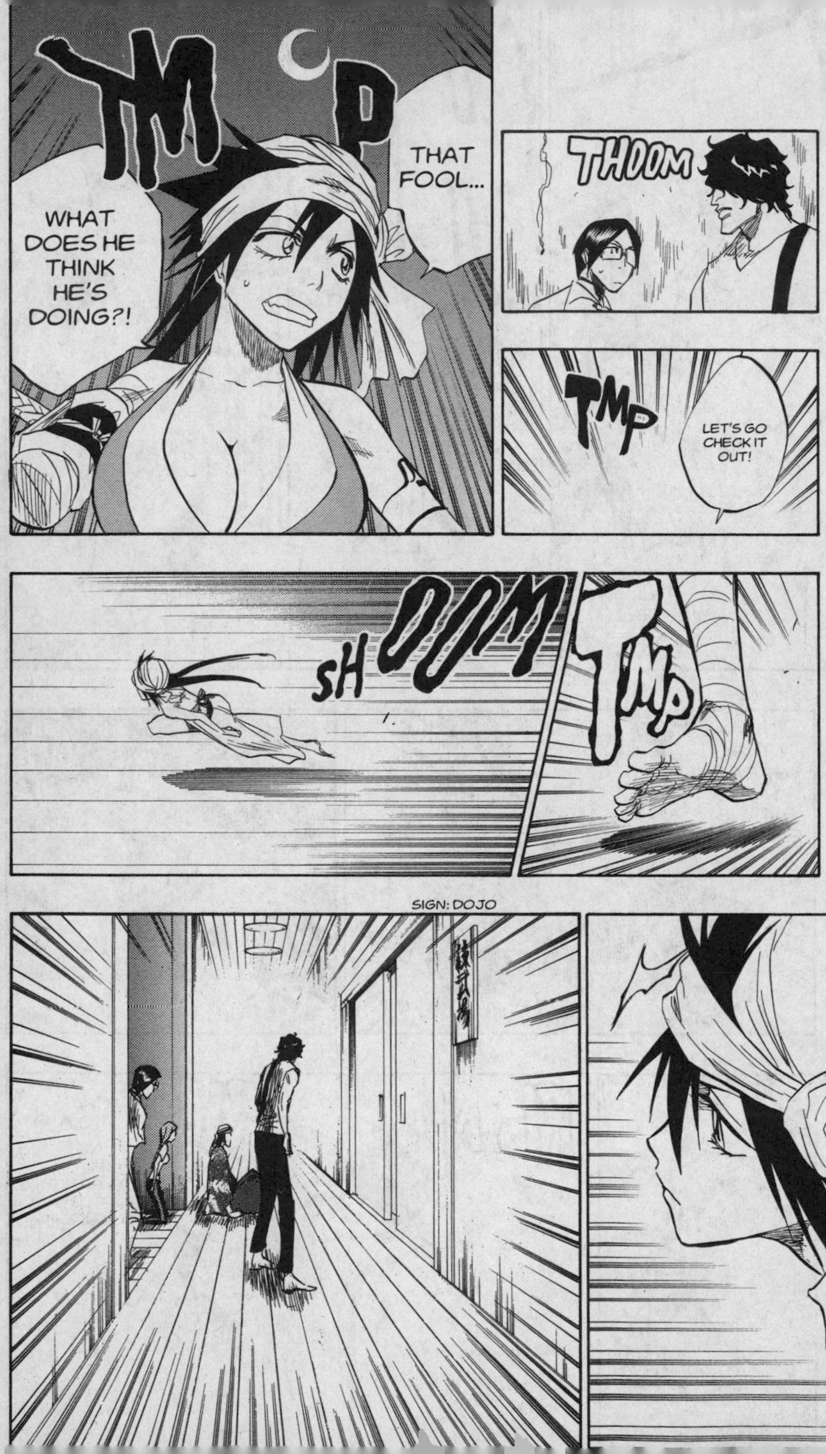
THOOM
TMP
LET'S GO CHECK IT OUT!
TMP
THAT FOOL...
WHAT DOES HE THINK HE'S DOING?!
TMP
SHOOM
SIGN: DOJO

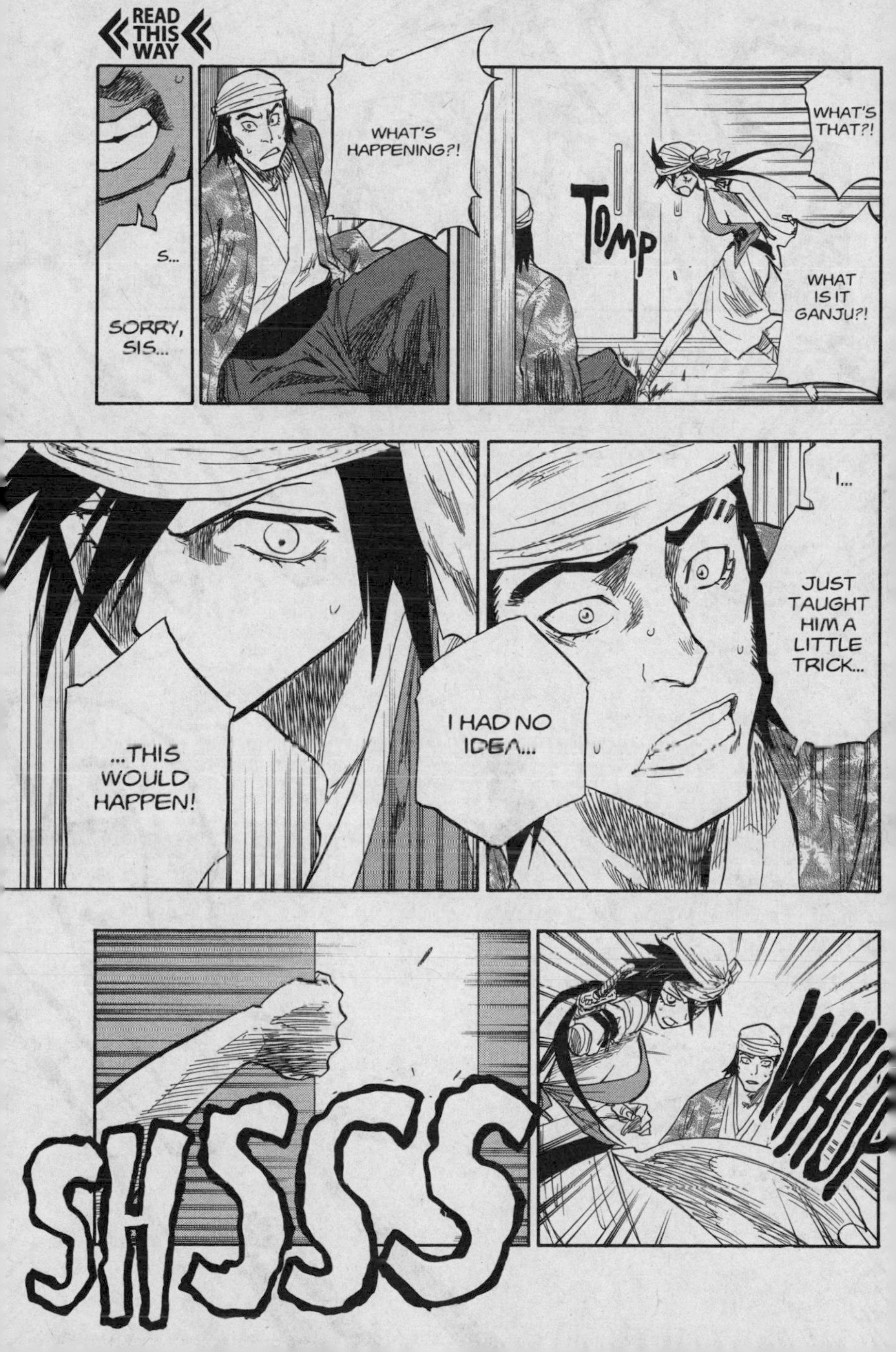
READ THIS WAY
WHAT'S THAT?!
TOMP
WHAT IS IT GANJU?!
WHAT'S HAPPENING?!
S...
SORRY, SIS...
I...
JUST TAUGHT HIM A LITTLE TRICK...
I HAD NO IDEA...
...THIS WOULD HAPPEN!
WHUP
SHSSS

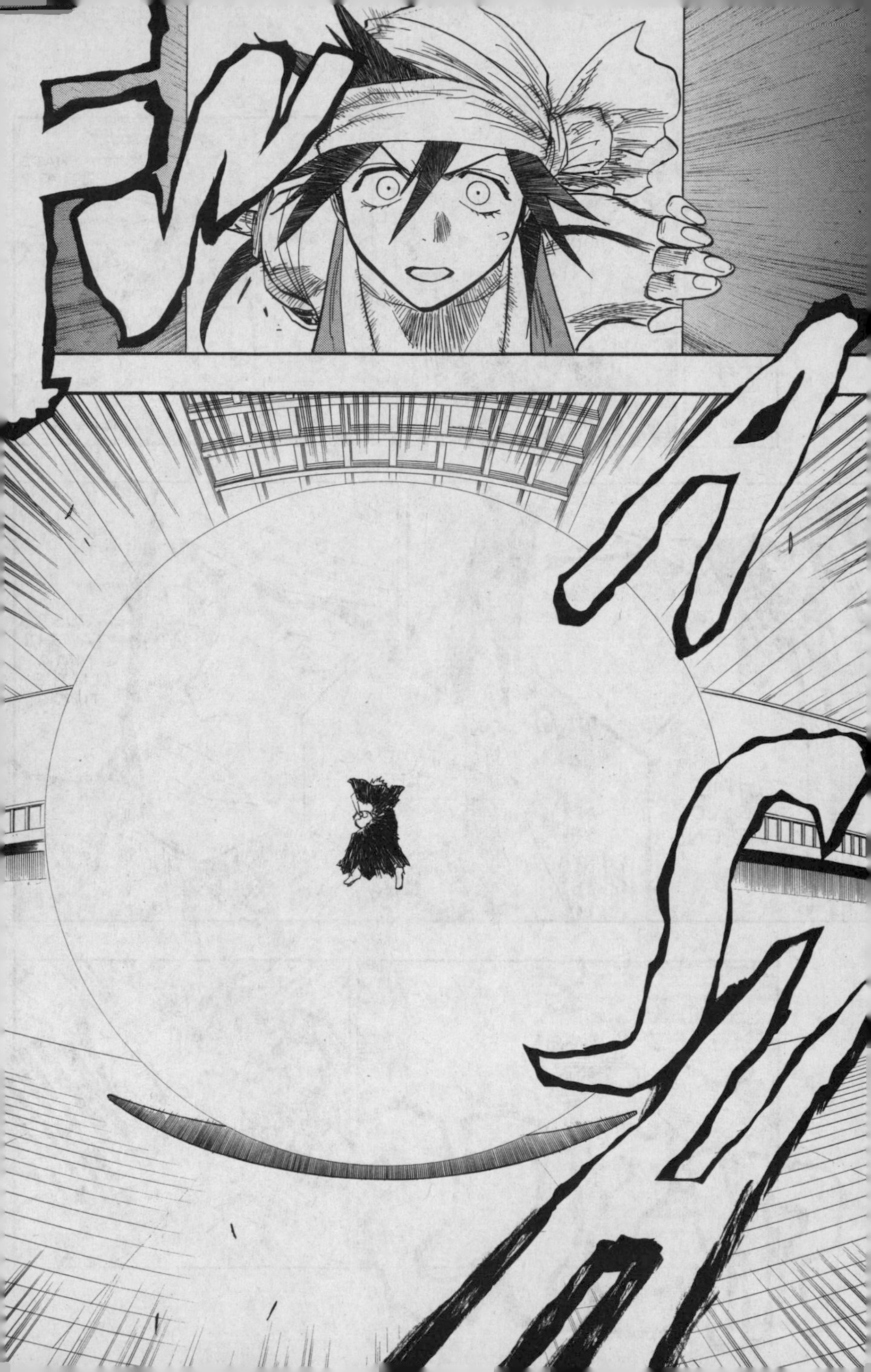

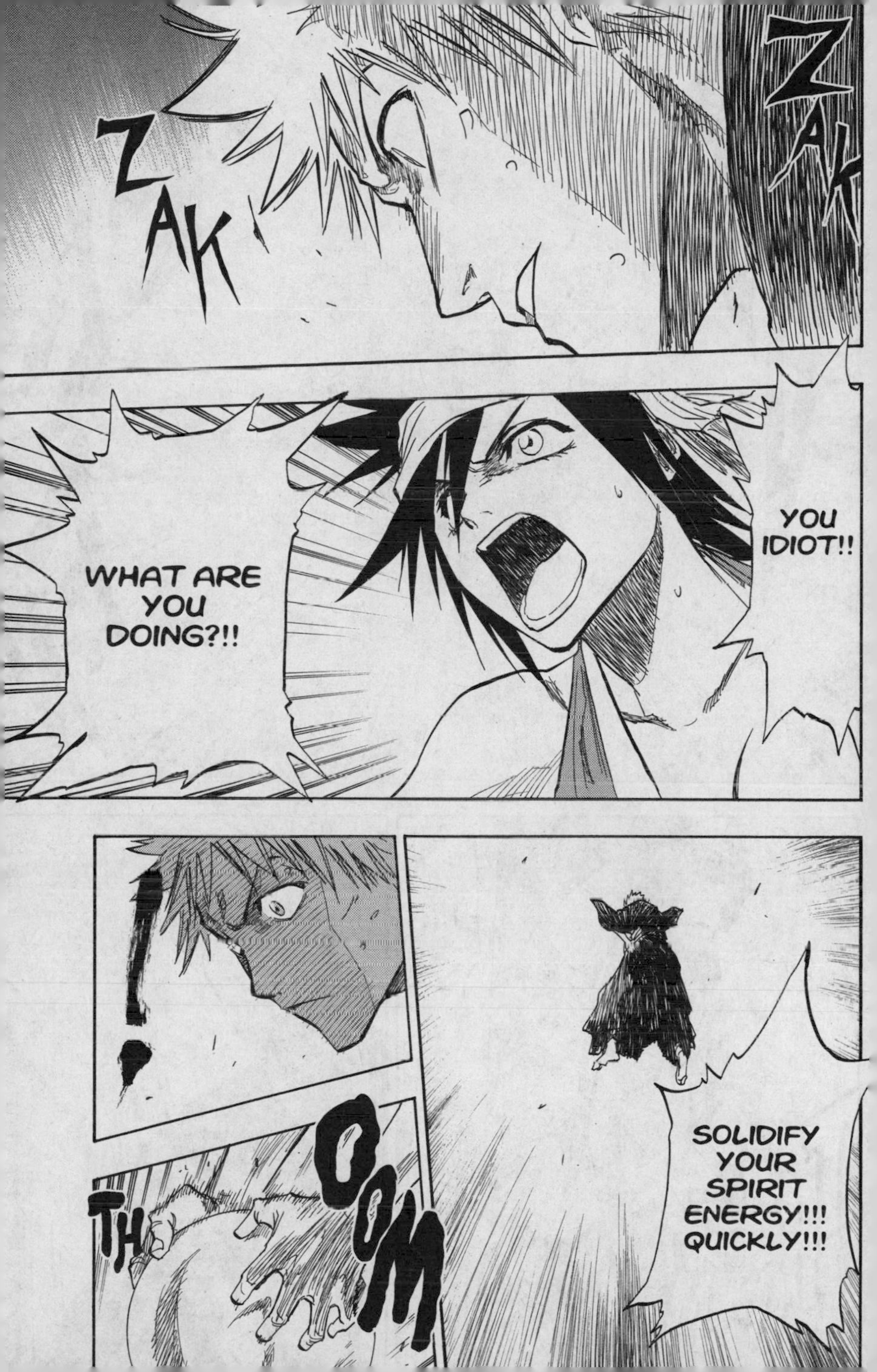
ZAK
ZAK
YOU IDIOT!!
WHAT ARE YOU DOING?!!
SOLIDIFY YOUR SPIRIT ENERGY!!! QUICKLY!!!
!
THOOM

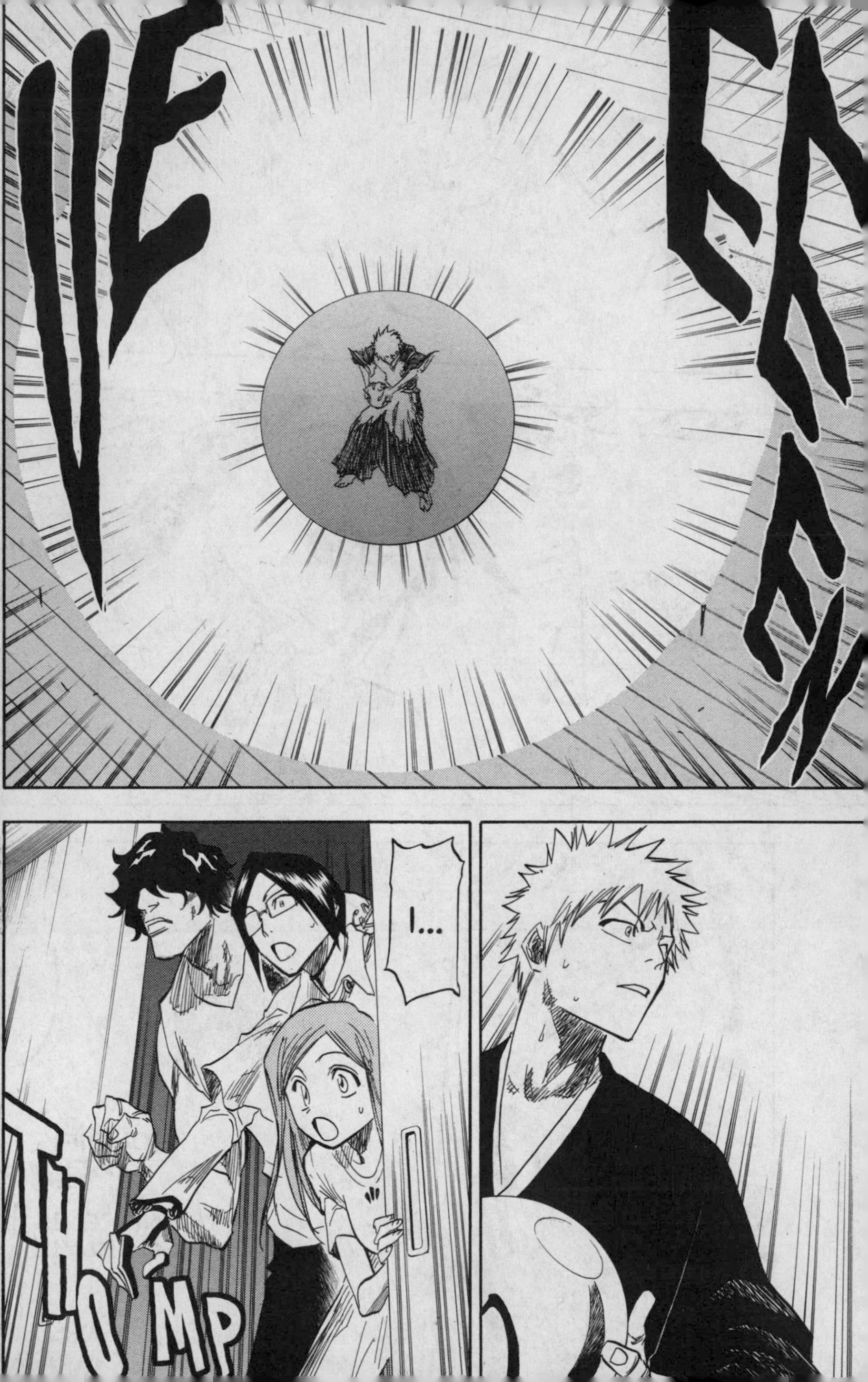
VEEEEN
I...
THOMP

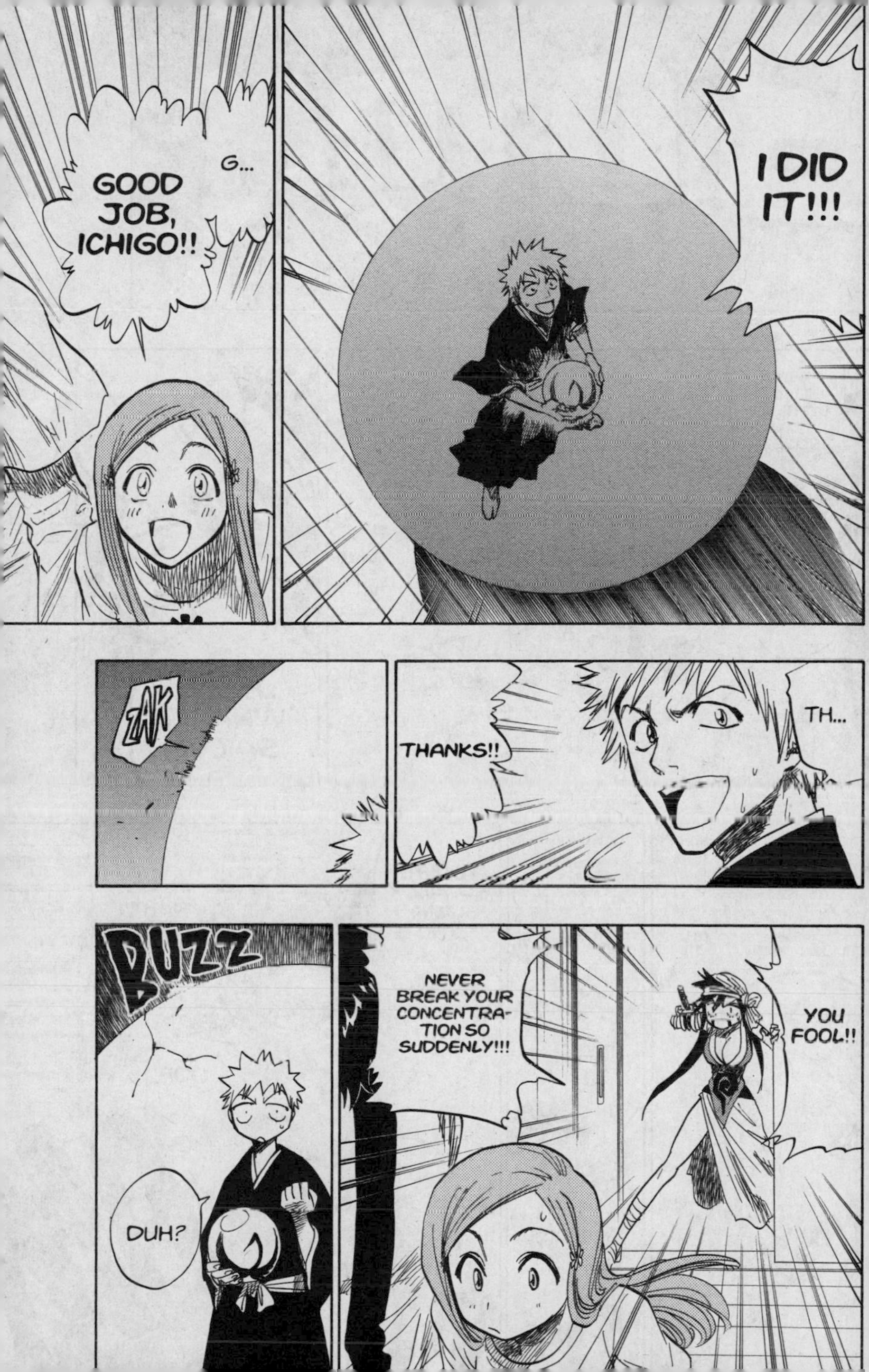
I DID IT!!!
G...
GOOD JOB, ICHIGO!!
TH...
THANKS!!
ZAK
YOU FOOL!!
NEVER BREAK YOUR CONCENTRA-TION SO SUDDENLY!!!
BUZZ
DUH?

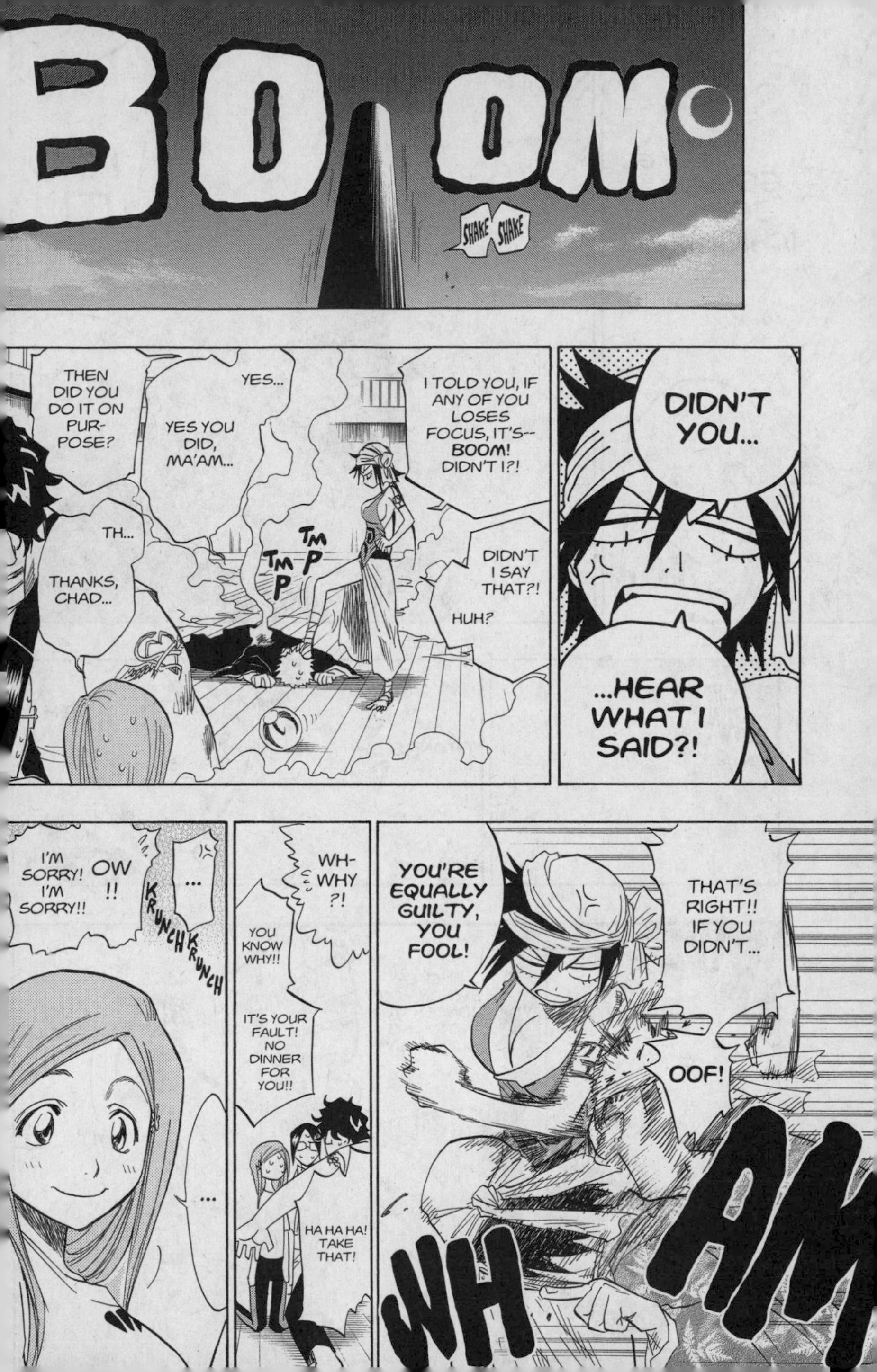
BOOM
SHAKE SHAKE
DIDN'T YOU...
...HEAR WHAT I SAID?!
I TOLD YOU, IF ANY OF YOU LOSES FOCUS, IT'S-- BOOM! DIDN'T I?!
DIDN'T I SAY THAT?!
HUH?
YES...
THEN DID YOU DO IT ON PUR-POSE?
YES YOU DID, MA'AM...
TMP TMP
TH...
THANKS, CHAD...
THAT'S RIGHT!! IF YOU DIDN'T...
YOU'RE EQUALLY GUILTY, YOU FOOL!
OOF!
WHAM
WH- WHY ?!
YOU KNOW WHY!!
IT'S YOUR FAULT! NO DINNER FOR YOU!!
HA HA HA! TAKE THAT!
...
OW !!
I'M SORRY! I'M SORRY!!
KRUNCH KRUNCH
...

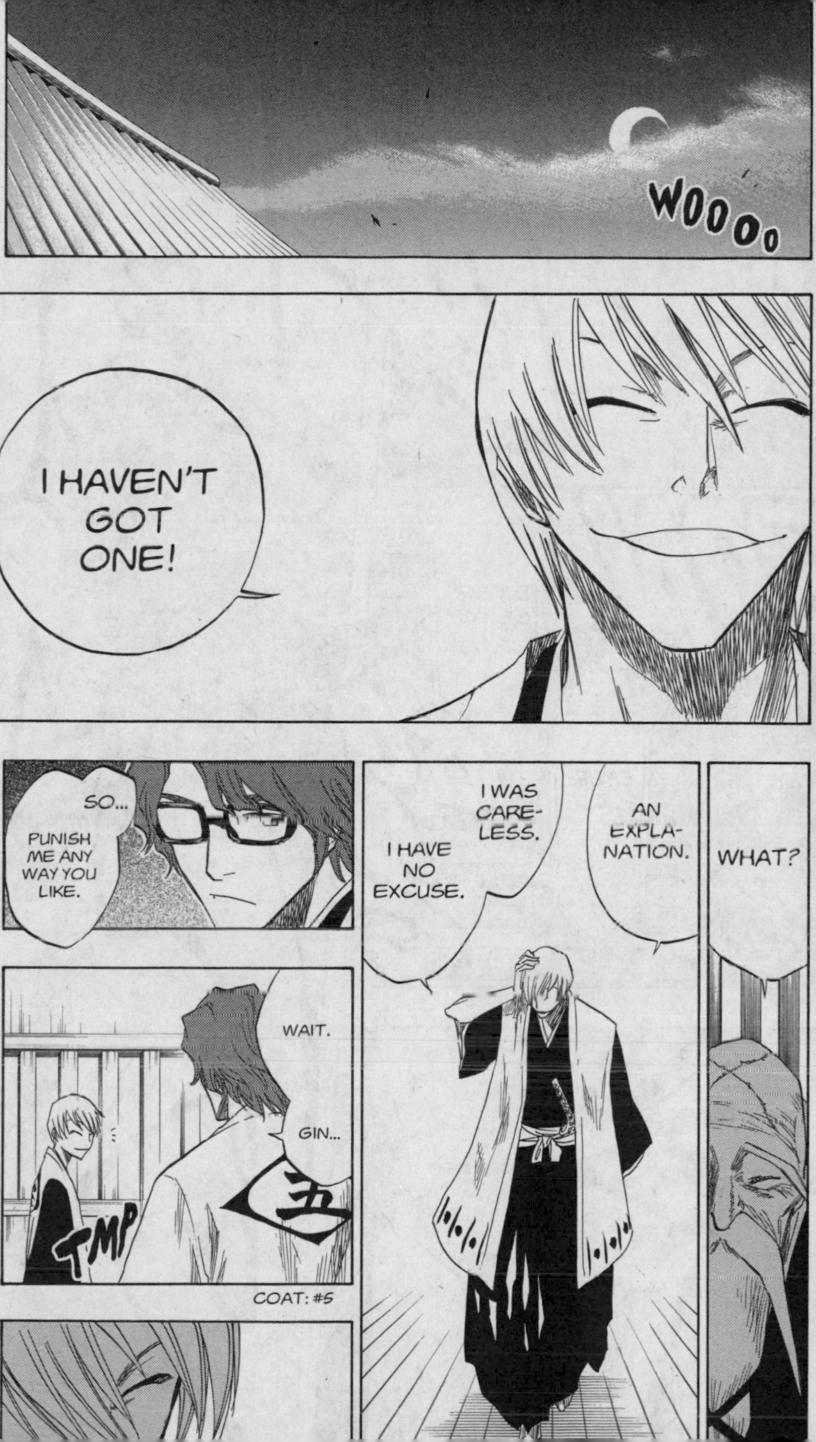
WOOOO
I HAVEN'T GOT ONE!
WHAT?
AN EXPLANATION.
I WAS CARELESS.
I HAVE NO EXCUSE.
SO...
PUNISH ME ANY WAY YOU LIKE.
WAIT.
GIN...
TMP
COAT: #5

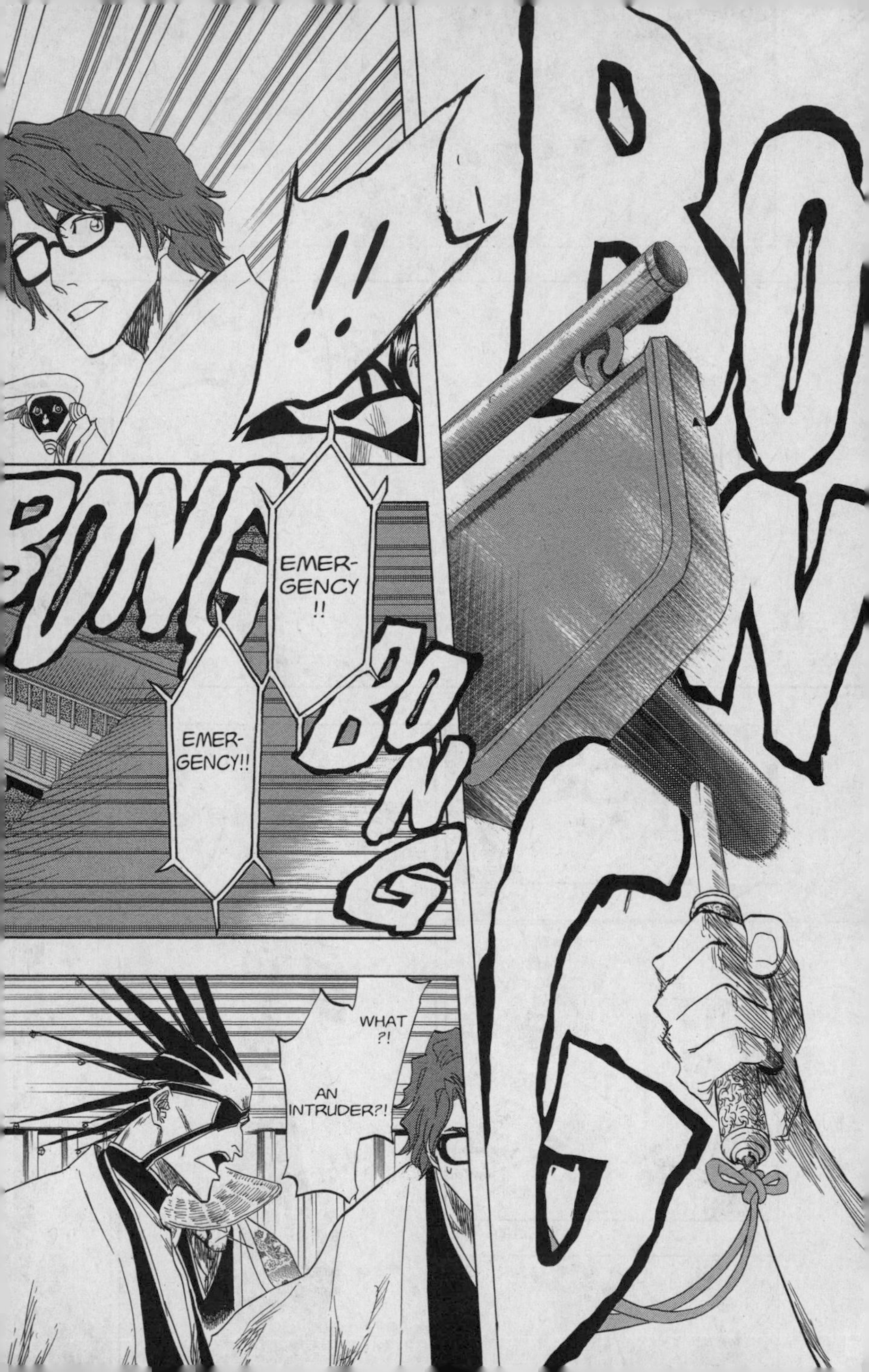
BONG
!!
EMERGENCY!!
BONG
EMERGENCY!!
BONG
WHAT?!
AN INTRUDER?!

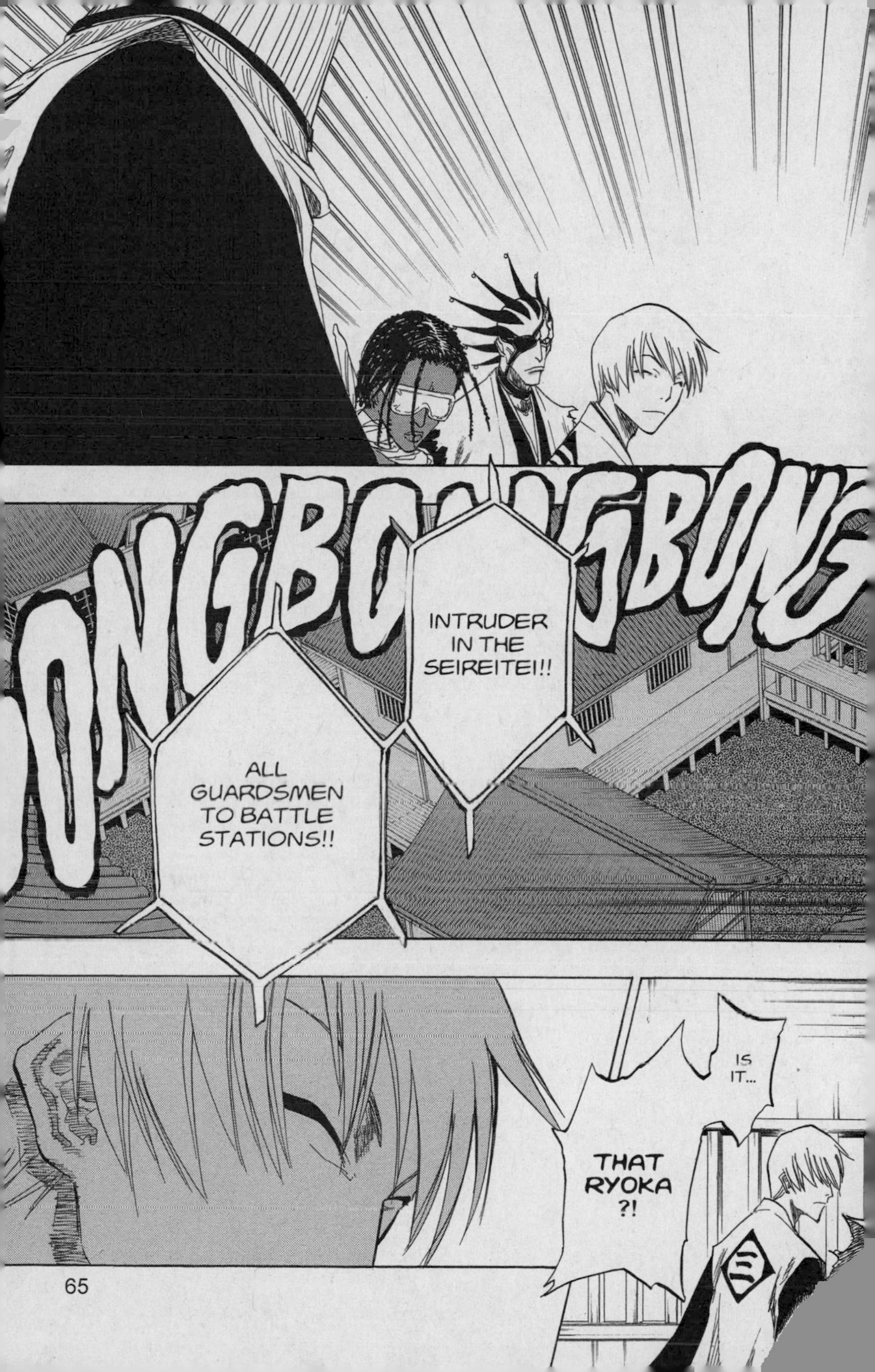
INTRUDER IN THE SEIREITEI!!
ALL GUARDSMEN TO BATTLE STATIONS!!
IS IT...
THAT RYOKA ?!

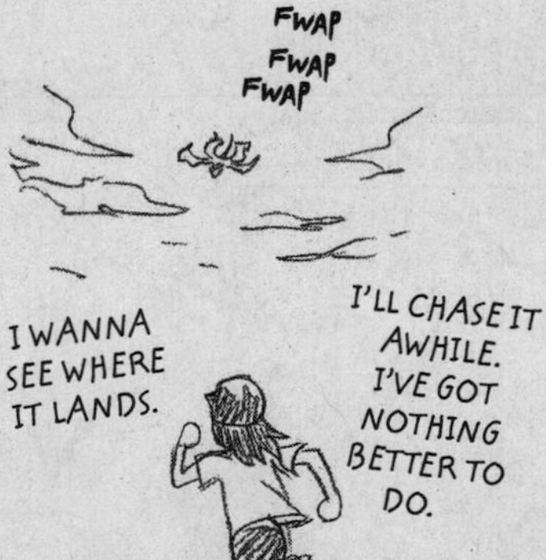
FWAP
FWAP
FWAP
I'LL CHASE IT AWHILE. I'VE GOT NOTHING BETTER TO DO.
I WANNA SEE WHERE IT LANDS.

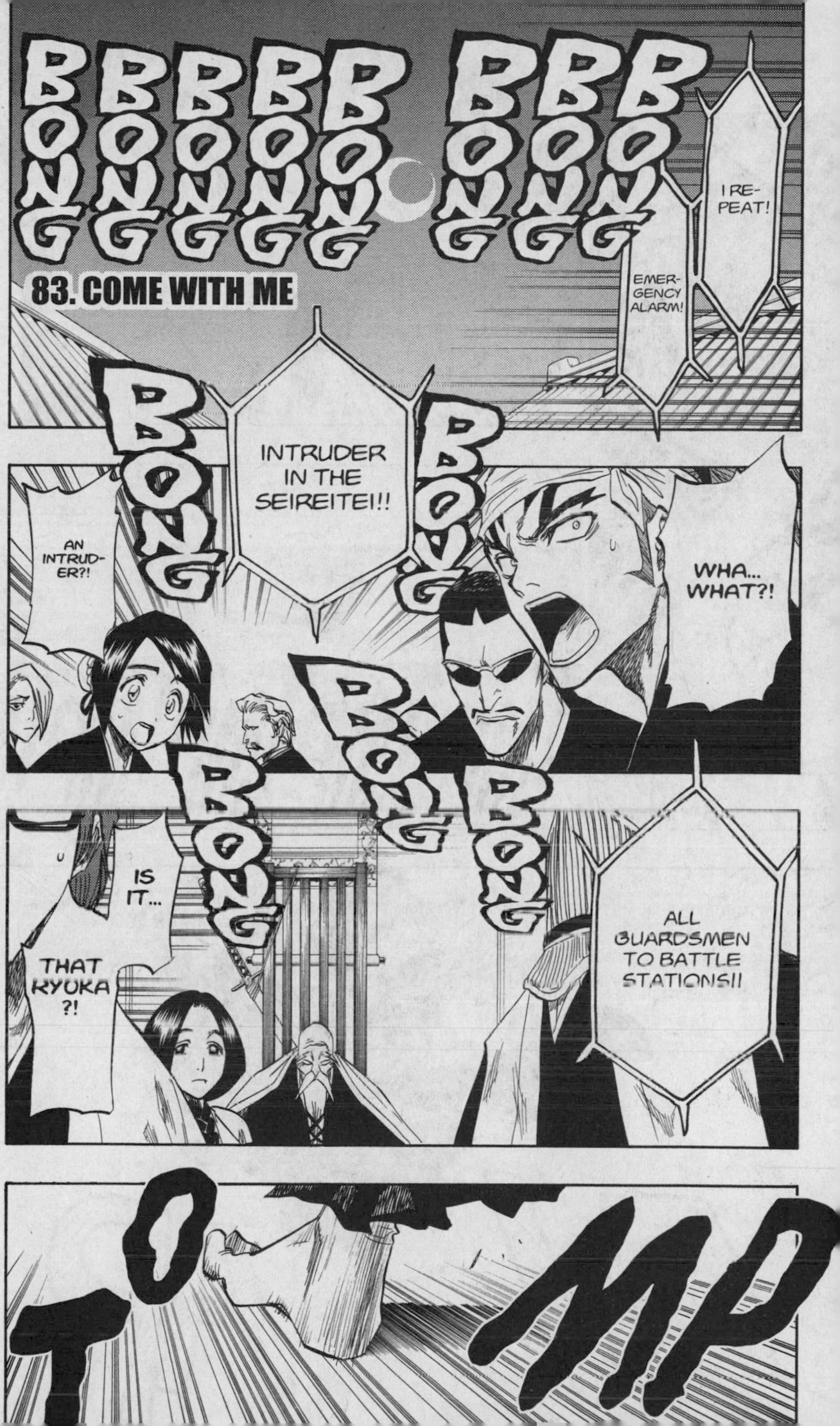
BBBBB BBB
BONG BONG BONG BONG BONG BONG BONG BONG
83. COME WITH ME
I RE-PEAT!
EMERGENCY ALARM!
BONG
INTRUDER IN THE SEIREITEI!!!
BONG
WHA... WHAT?!
AN INTRUDER?!
BONG BONG BONG
ALL GUARDSMEN TO BATTLE STATIONS!!
IS IT...
THAT RYUKA ?!
TOMP

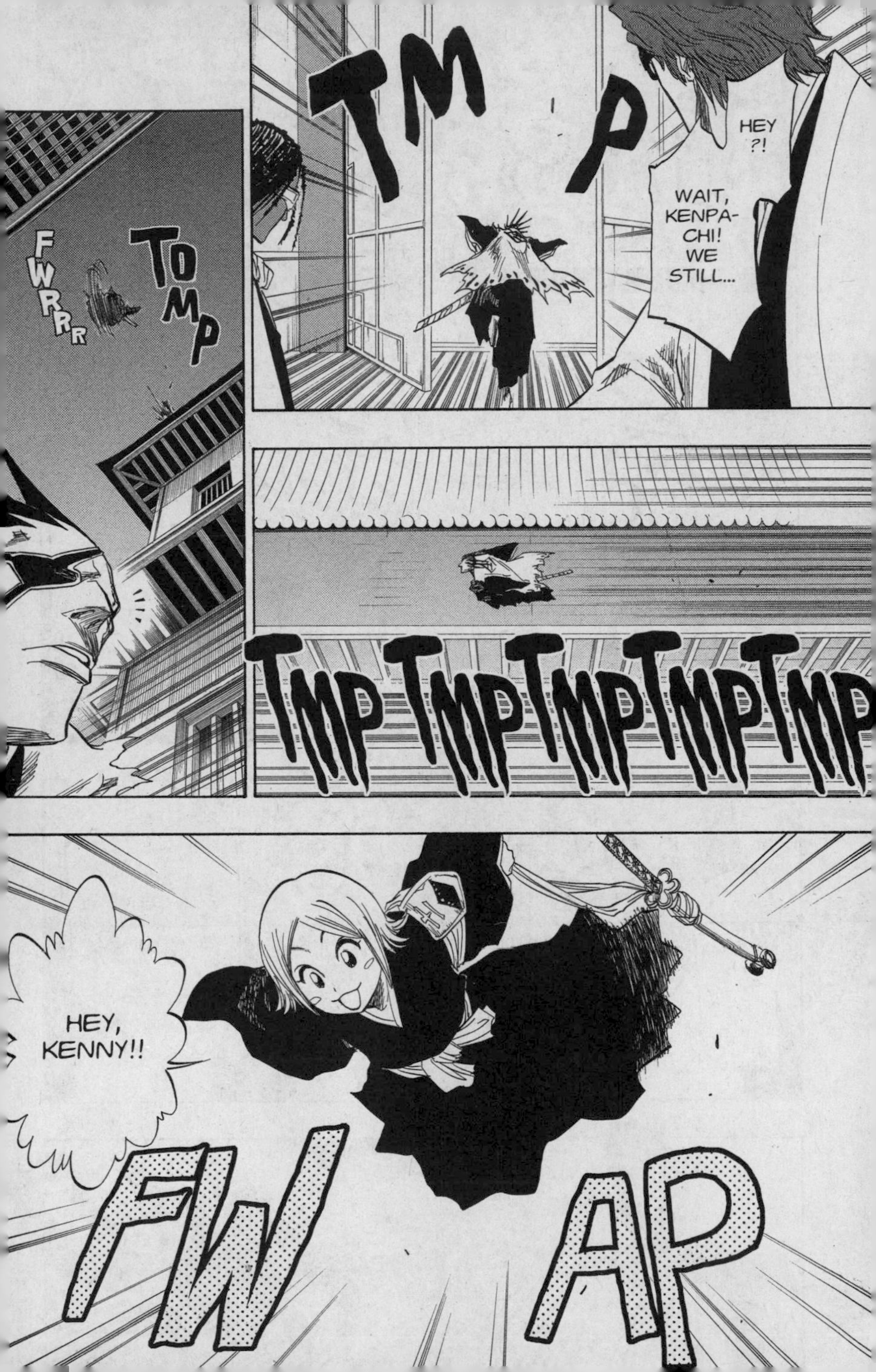
HEY ?!
WAIT, KENPA-CHI! WE STILL...
TMP
TMP TMP TMP TMP TMP
FWRRR
TOMP
HEY, KENNY!!
FWAP

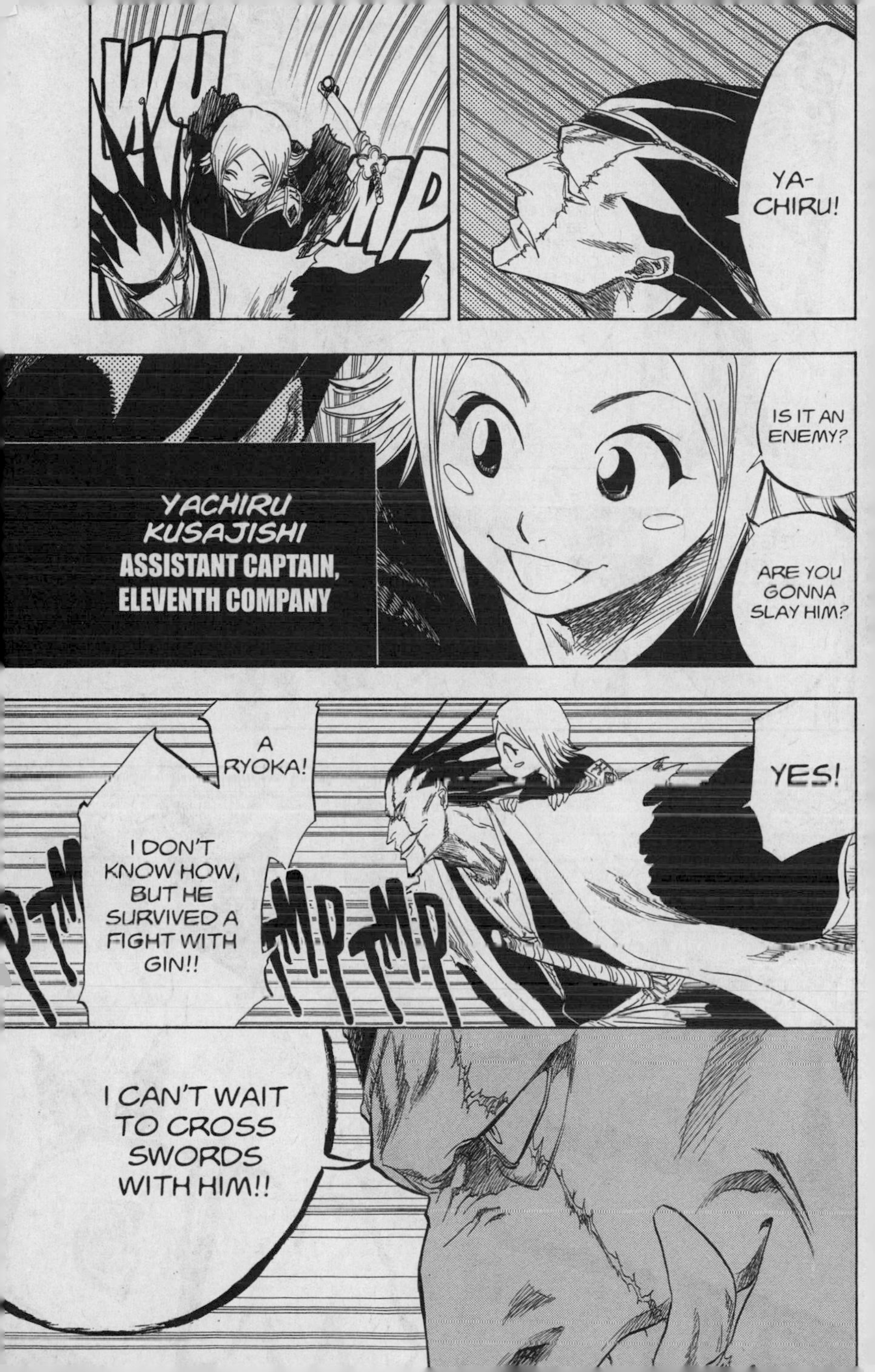
YA-CHIRU!
WUMP
IS IT AN ENEMY?
ARE YOU GONNA SLAY HIM?
YACHIRU KUSAJISHI
ASSISTANT CAPTAIN, ELEVENTH COMPANY
YES!
A RYOKA!
I DON'T KNOW HOW, BUT HE SURVIVED A FIGHT WITH GIN!!
TMP TMP TMP
I CAN'T WAIT TO CROSS SWORDS WITH HIM!!

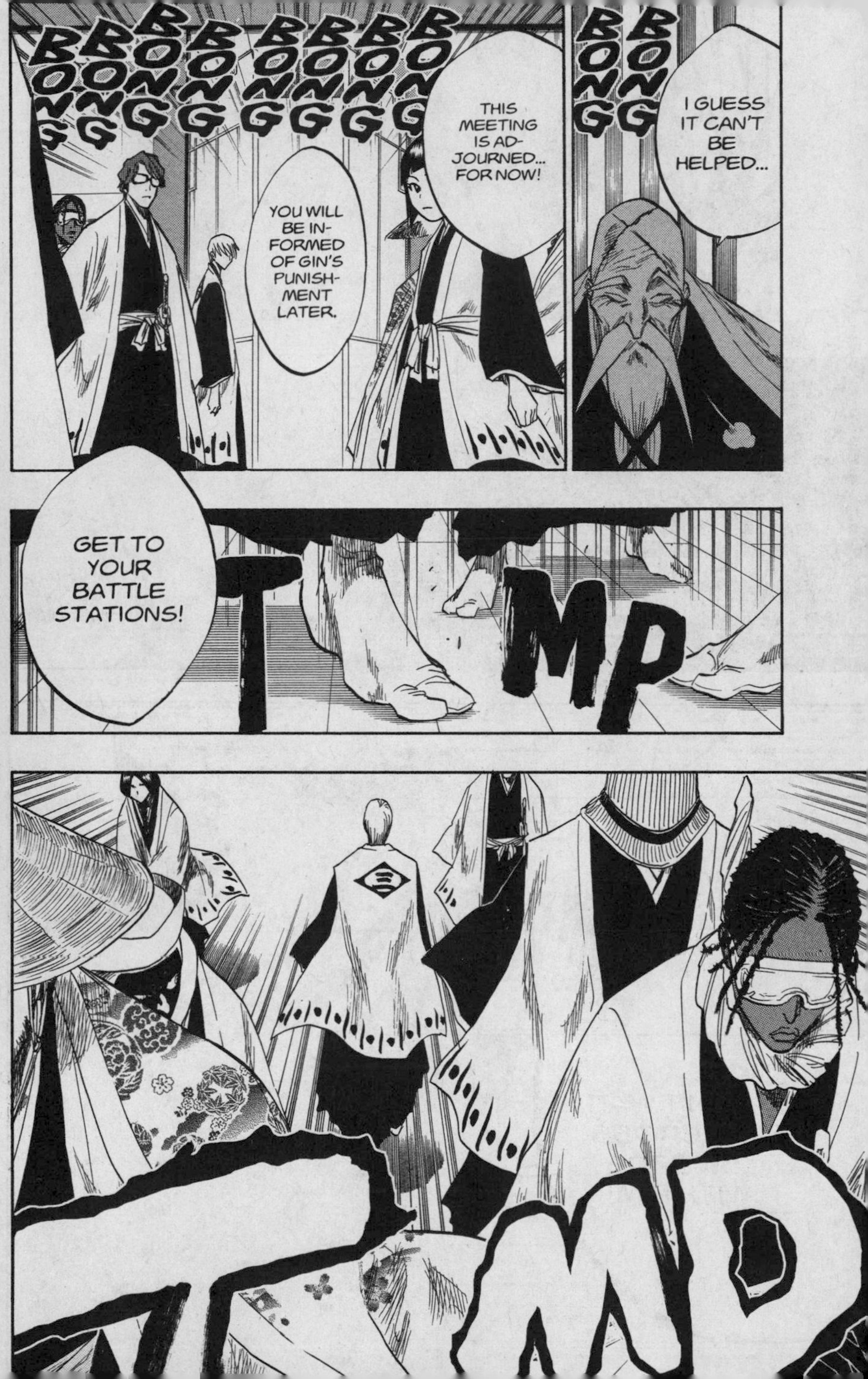
BONG BONG
I GUESS IT CAN'T BE HELPED...
BOONG BOONG BOONG BOONG BOONG BOONG
THIS MEETING IS AD-JOURNED... FOR NOW!
YOU WILL BE IN-FORMED OF GIN'S PUNISH-MENT LATER.
GET TO YOUR BATTLE STATIONS!
TMP
TMP

READ THIS WAY

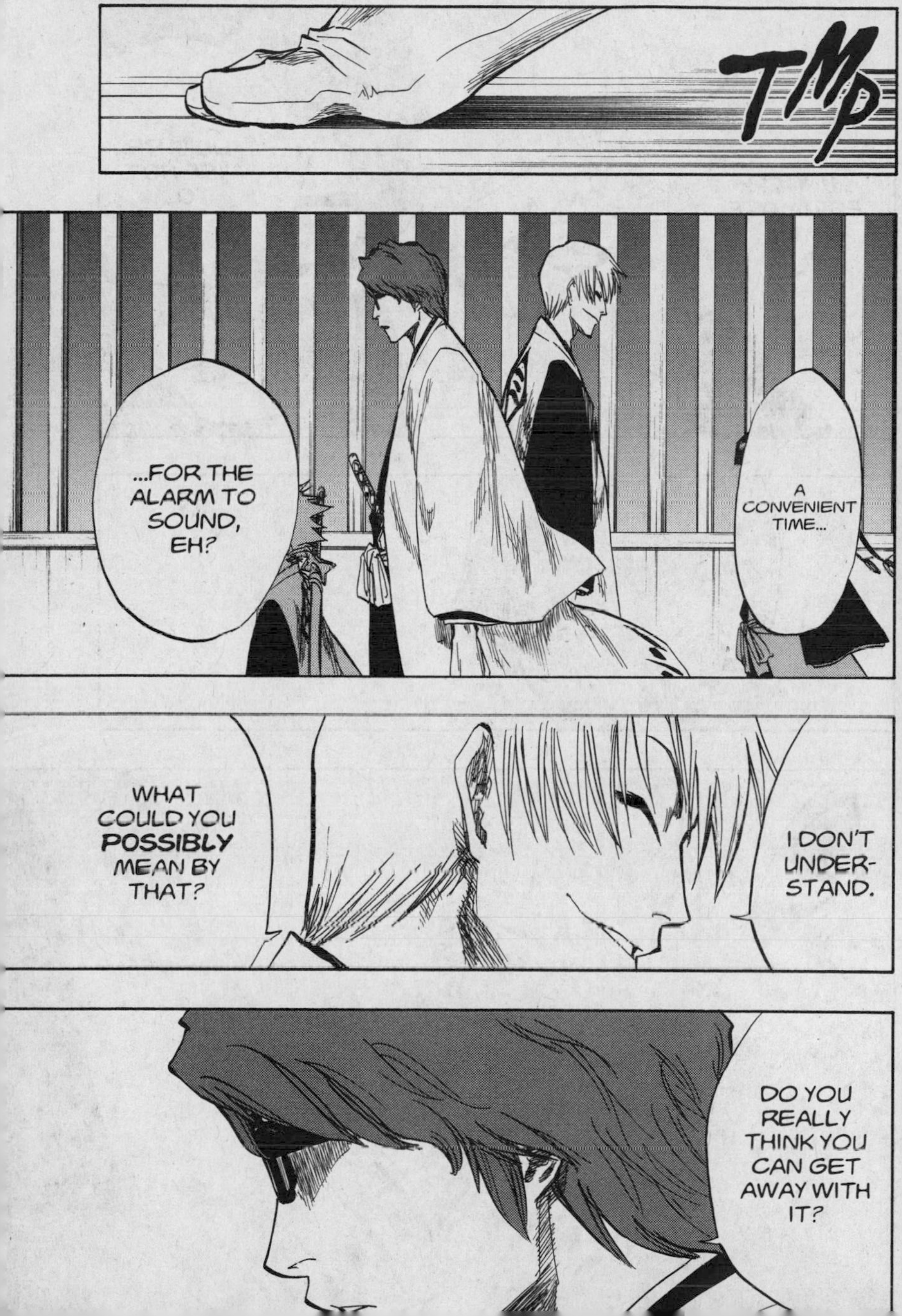
TMP
A CONVENIENT TIME...
...FOR THE ALARM TO SOUND, EH?
I DON'T UNDER-STAND.
WHAT COULD YOU **POSSIBLY** MEAN BY THAT?
DO YOU REALLY THINK YOU CAN GET AWAY WITH IT?

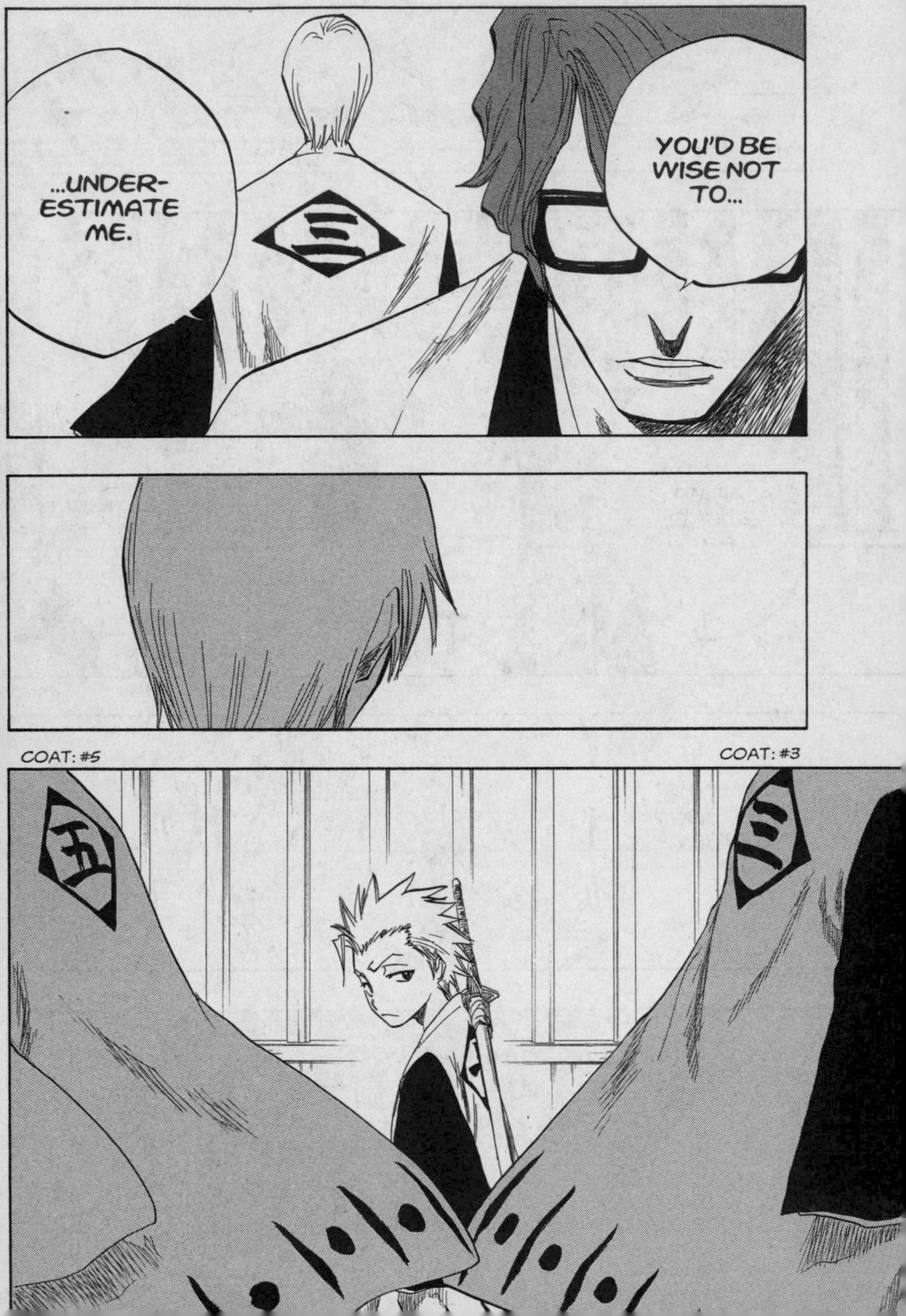
YOU'D BE WISE NOT TO...
...UNDER-ESTIMATE ME.
COAT: #3
COAT: #5

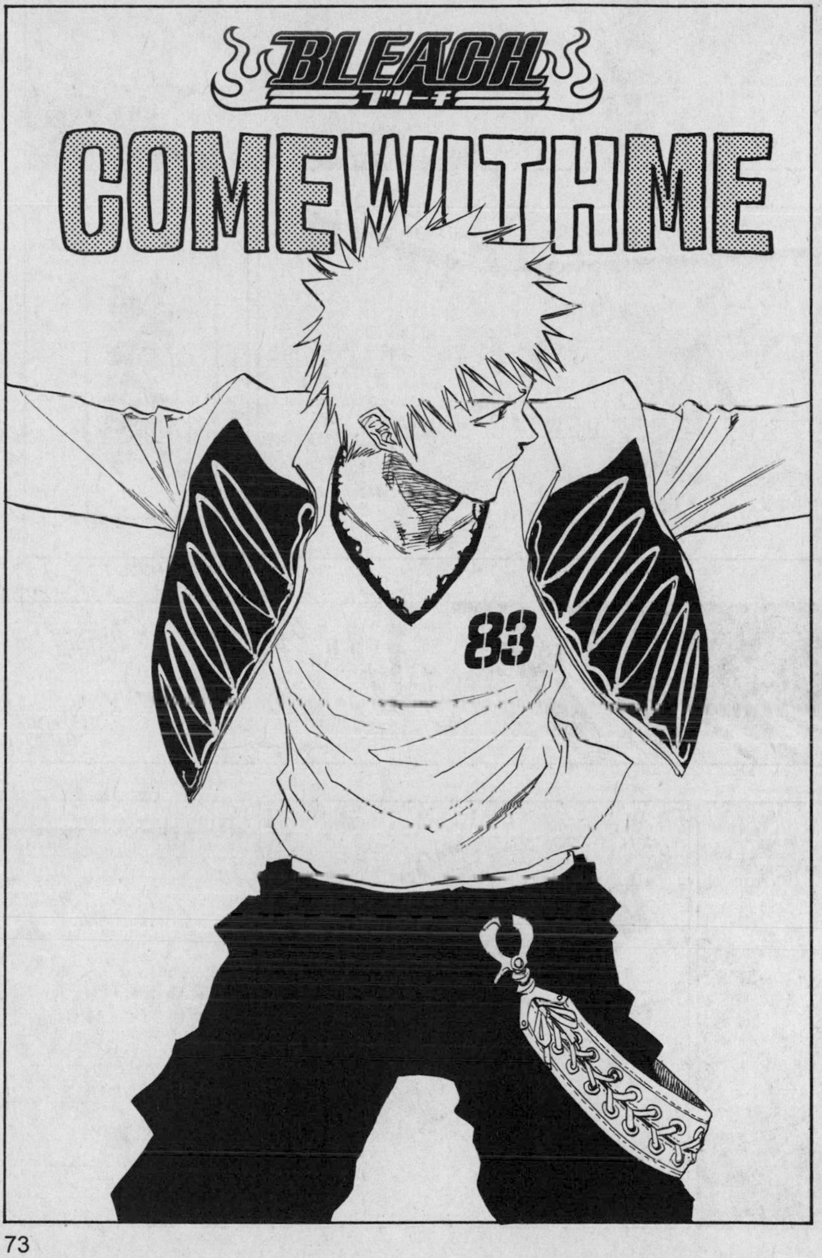
BLEACH
ブリーチ
COME WITH ME
83

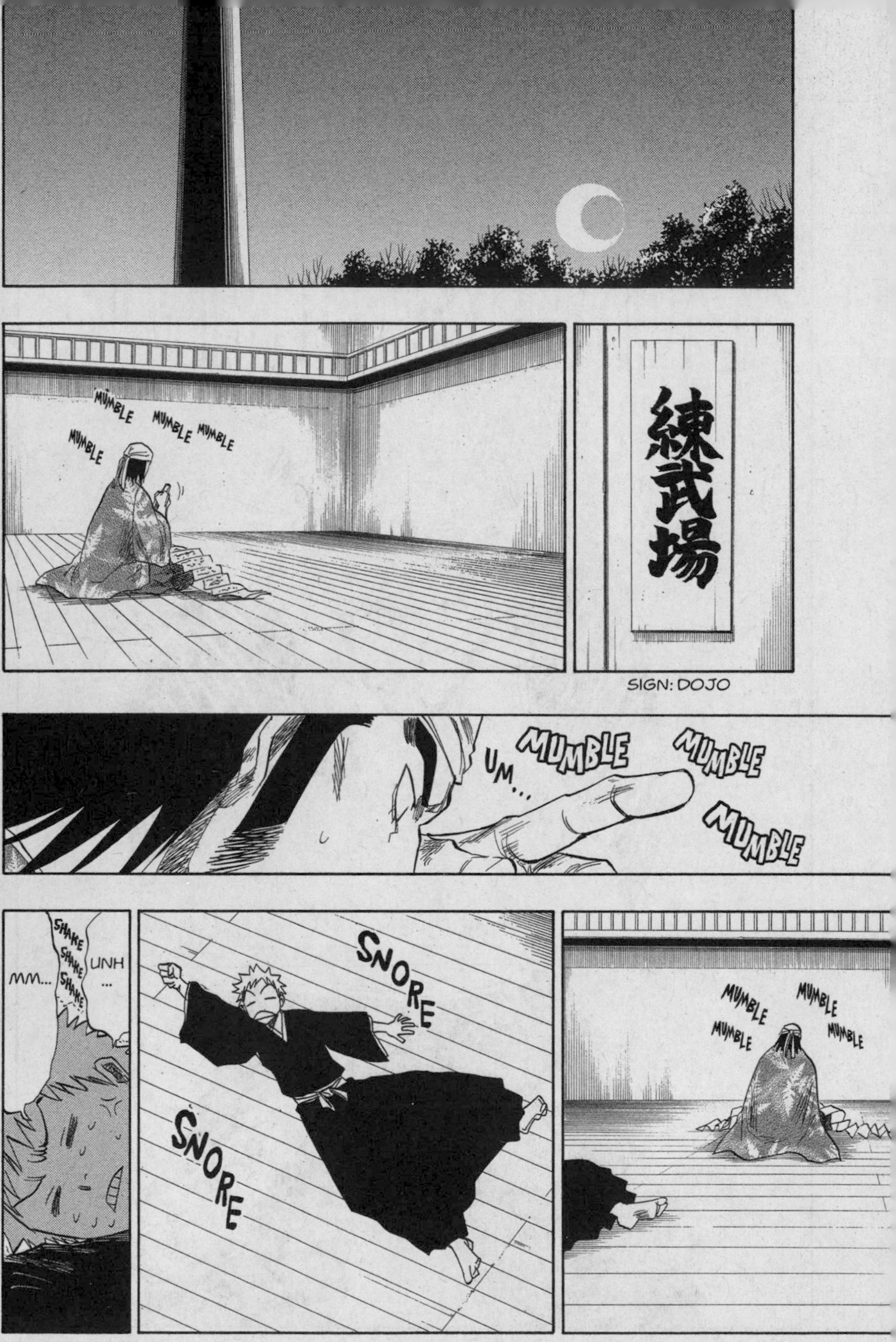

練武場
SIGN: DOJO
MUMBLE
MUMBLE
MUMBLE
MUMBLE
MUMBLE
MUMBLE
UM...
MUMBLE
MUMBLE
MUMBLE
MUMBLE
MUMBLE
SNORE
SNORE
SHAKE SHAKE SHAKE
UNH ...
MM...

READ THIS WAY

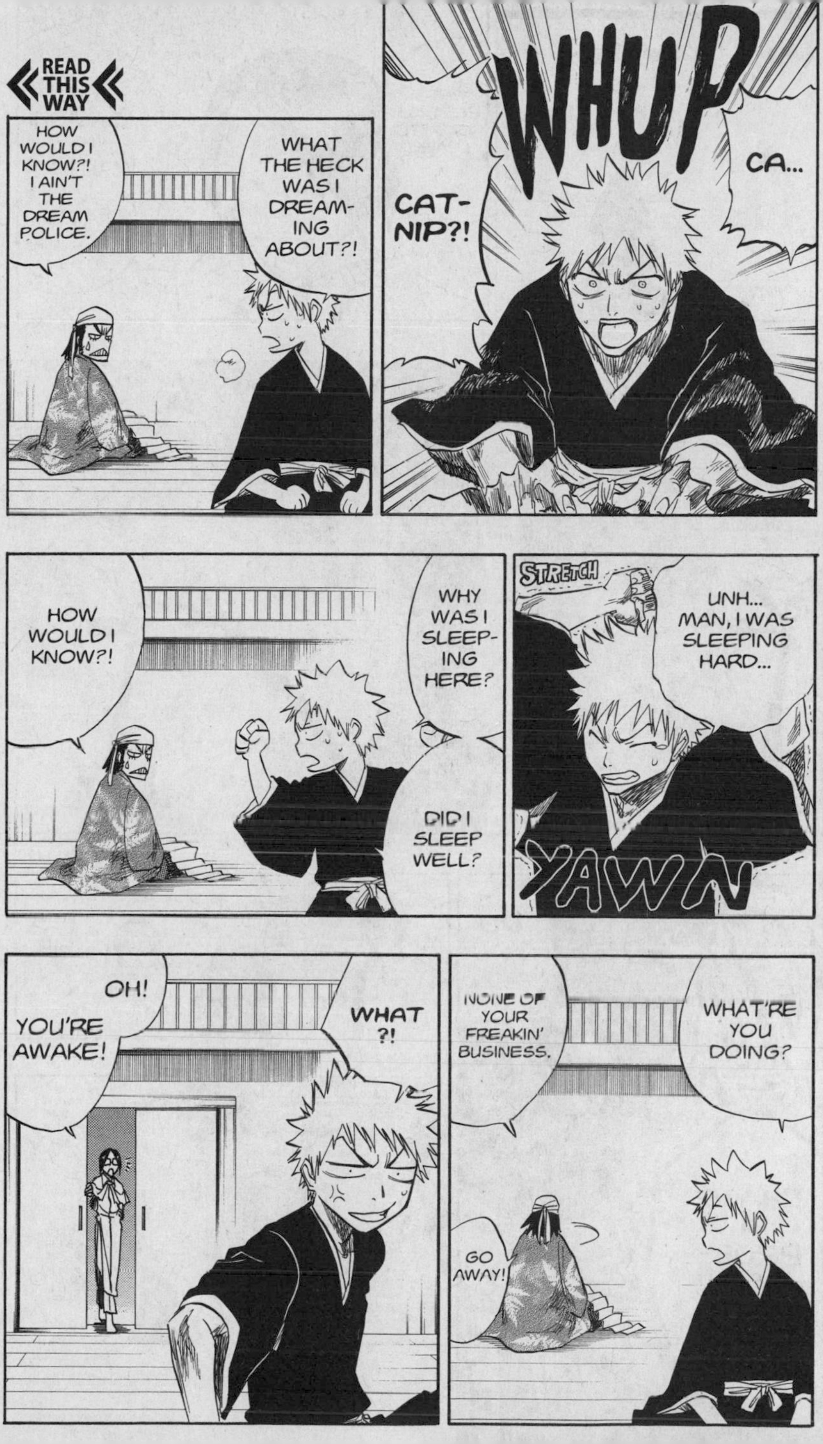
WHUP
CA...
CAT-NIP?!
WHAT THE HECK WAS I DREAMING ABOUT?!
HOW WOULD I KNOW?! I AIN'T THE DREAM POLICE.
STRETCH
UNH... MAN, I WAS SLEEPING HARD...
YAWN
WHY WAS I SLEEPING HERE?
DID I SLEEP WELL?
HOW WOULD I KNOW?!
WHAT'RE YOU DOING?
NONE OF YOUR FREAKIN' BUSINESS.
GO AWAY!
WHAT ?!
OH! YOU'RE AWAKE!

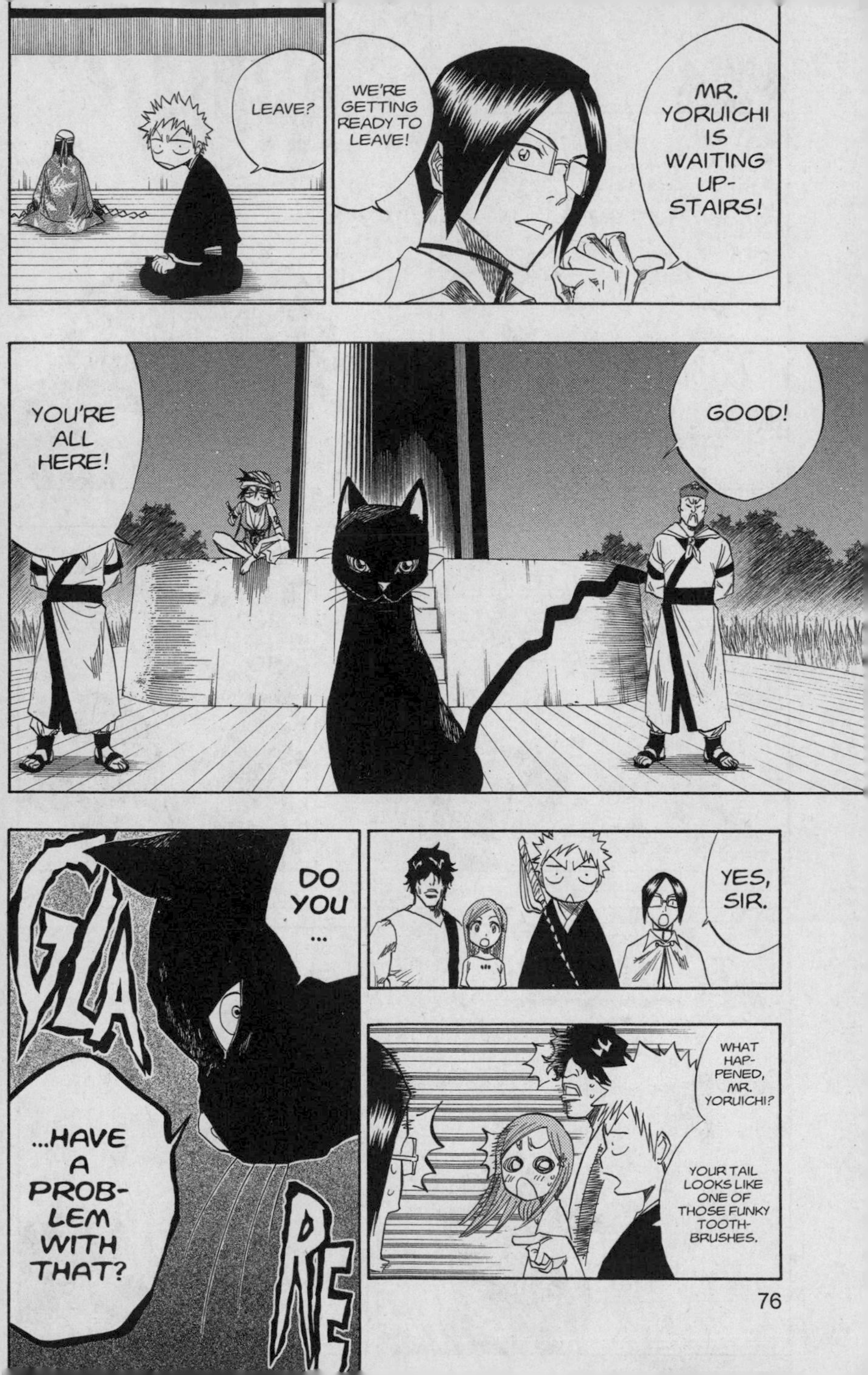
MR. YORUICHI IS WAITING UP-STAIRS!
WE'RE GETTING READY TO LEAVE!
LEAVE?
GOOD!
YOU'RE ALL HERE!
YES, SIR.
WHAT HAP-PENED, MR. YORUICHI?
YOUR TAIL LOOKS LIKE ONE OF THOSE FUNKY TOOTH-BRUSHES.
DO YOU ...
...HAVE A PROB-LEM WITH THAT?
GLA
RE

READ THIS WAY

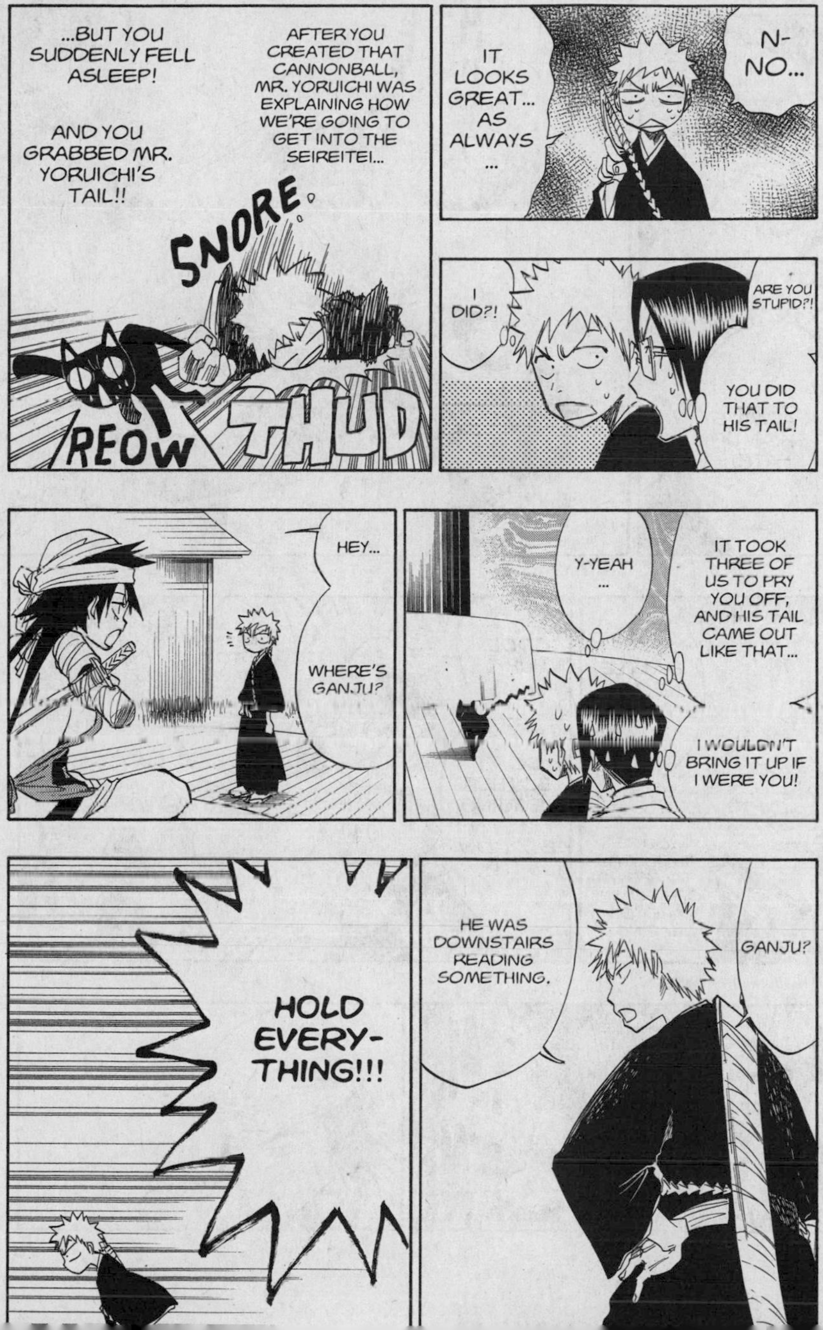
N-NO...
IT LOOKS GREAT... AS ALWAYS ...
ARE YOU STUPID?!
YOU DID THAT TO HIS TAIL!
I DID?!
AFTER YOU CREATED THAT CANNONBALL, MR. YORUICHI WAS EXPLAINING HOW WE'RE GOING TO GET INTO THE SEIREITEI...
...BUT YOU SUDDENLY FELL ASLEEP!
AND YOU GRABBED MR. YORUICHI'S TAIL!!
SNORE
THUD
REOW
IT TOOK THREE OF US TO PRY YOU OFF, AND HIS TAIL CAME OUT LIKE THAT...
Y-YEAH ...
I WOULDN'T BRING IT UP IF I WERE YOU!
HEY...
WHERE'S GANJU?
GANJU?
HE WAS DOWNSTAIRS READING SOMETHING.
HOLD EVERY-THING!!!

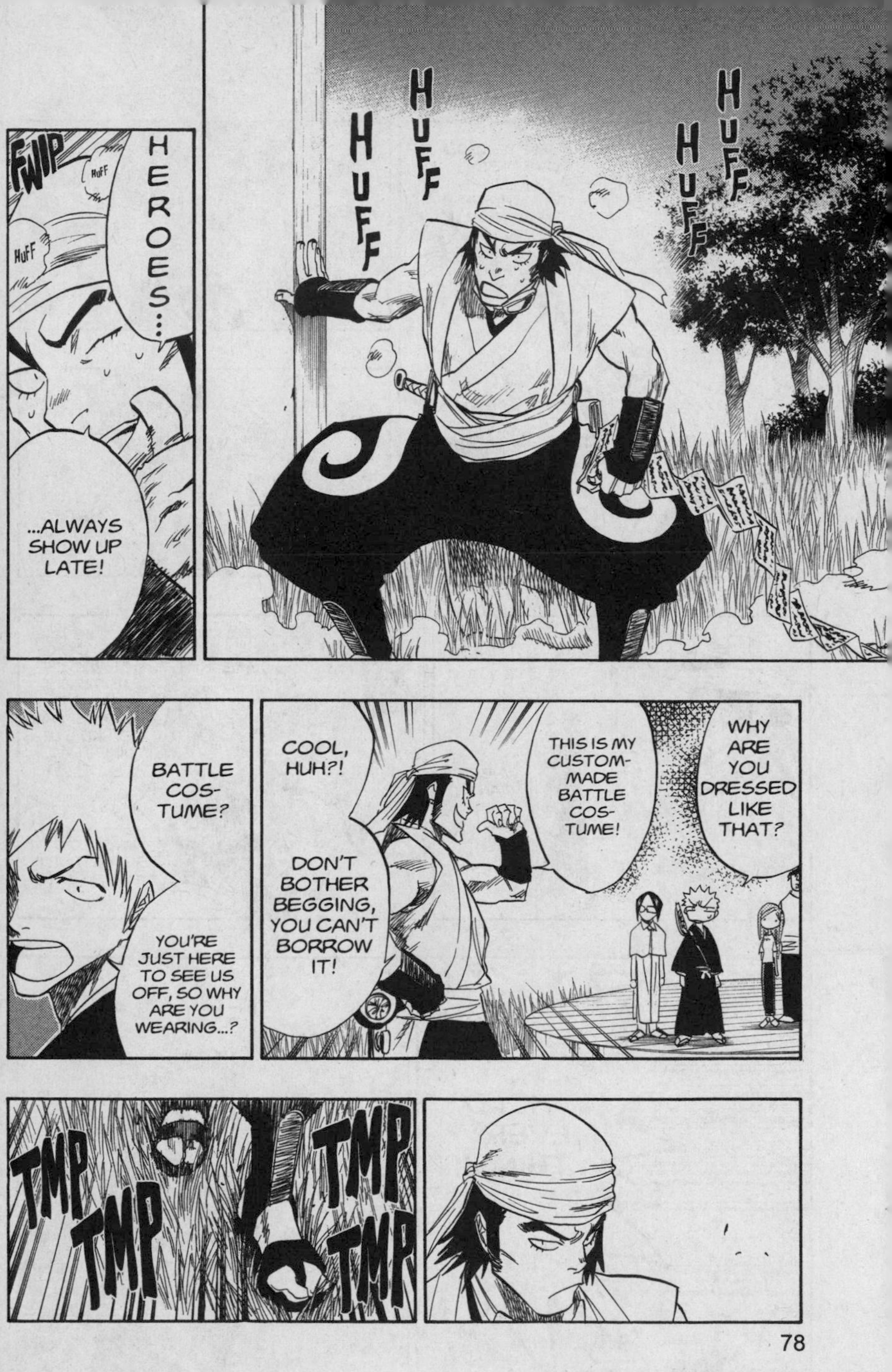
HUFF HUFF
HUFF HUFF
FWIP
HUFF
HUFF
HEROES...
...ALWAYS SHOW UP LATE!
WHY ARE YOU DRESSED LIKE THAT?
THIS IS MY CUSTOM-MADE BATTLE COS-TUME!
COOL, HUH?!
DON'T BOTHER BEGGING, YOU CAN'T BORROW IT!
BATTLE COS-TUME?
YOU'RE JUST HERE TO SEE US OFF, SO WHY ARE YOU WEARING...?
TMP TMP
TMP TMP

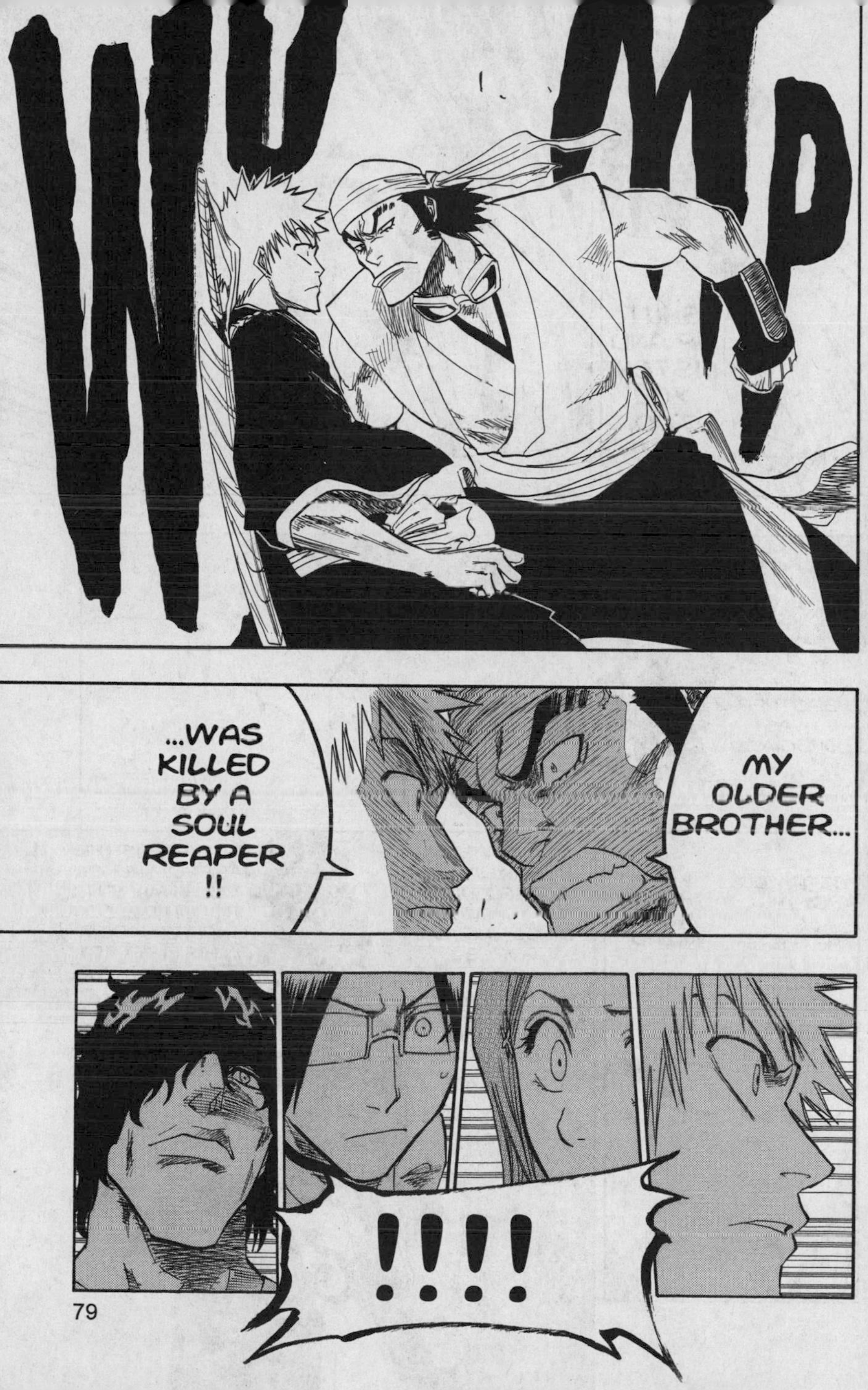
WHUMP
MY OLDER BROTHER...
...WAS KILLED BY A SOUL REAPER!!
!!!!

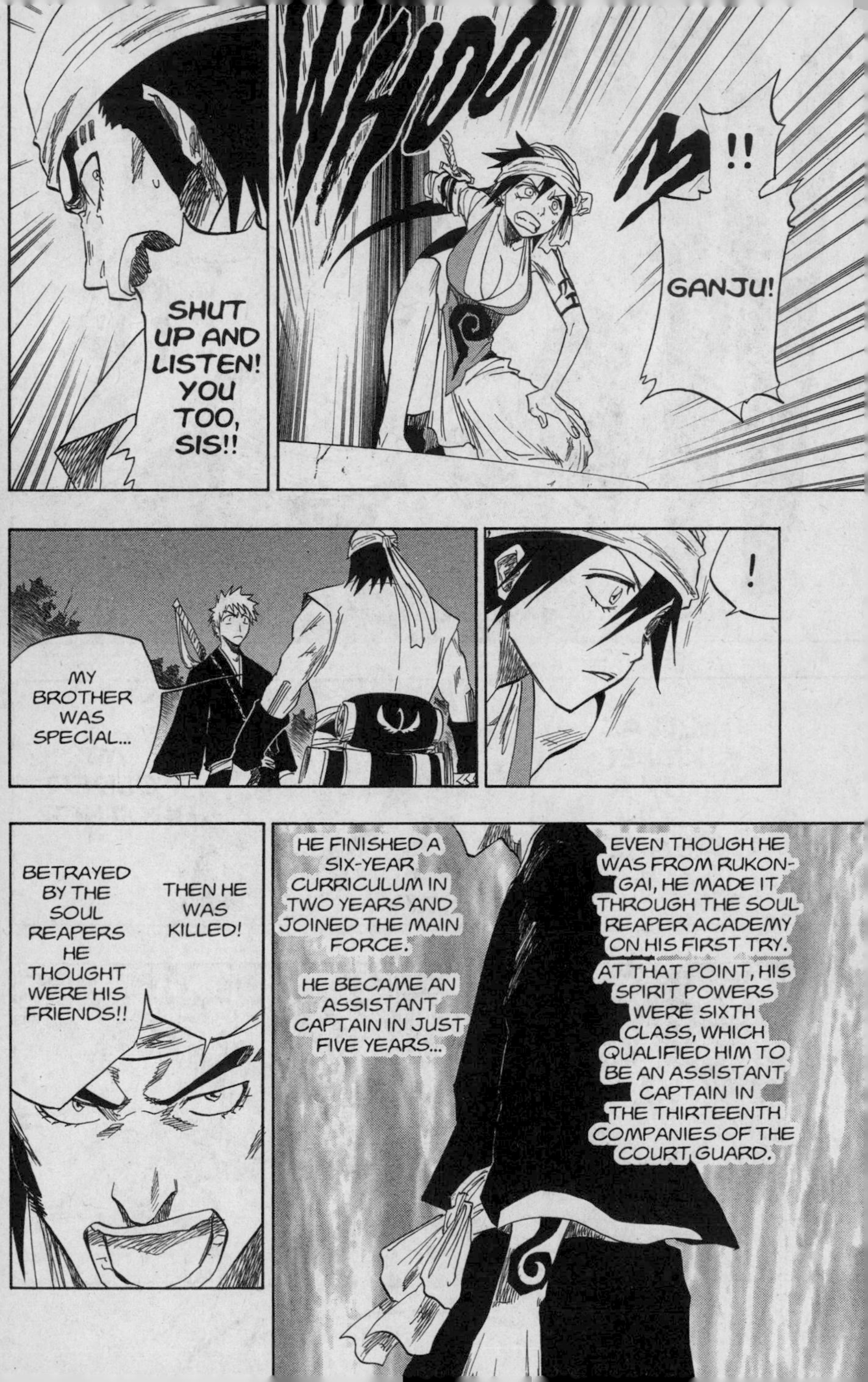
WHOOM!!
GANJU!
SHUT UP AND LISTEN! YOU TOO, SIS!!
!
MY BROTHER WAS SPECIAL...
EVEN THOUGH HE WAS FROM RUKON-GAI, HE MADE IT THROUGH THE SOUL REAPER ACADEMY ON HIS FIRST TRY.
AT THAT POINT, HIS SPIRIT POWERS WERE SIXTH CLASS, WHICH QUALIFIED HIM TO BE AN ASSISTANT CAPTAIN IN THE THIRTEENTH COMPANIES OF THE COURT GUARD.
HE FINISHED A SIX-YEAR CURRICULUM IN TWO YEARS AND JOINED THE MAIN FORCE.
HE BECAME AN ASSISTANT CAPTAIN IN JUST FIVE YEARS...
THEN HE WAS KILLED!
BETRAYED BY THE SOUL REAPERS HE THOUGHT WERE HIS FRIENDS!!

READ THIS WAY

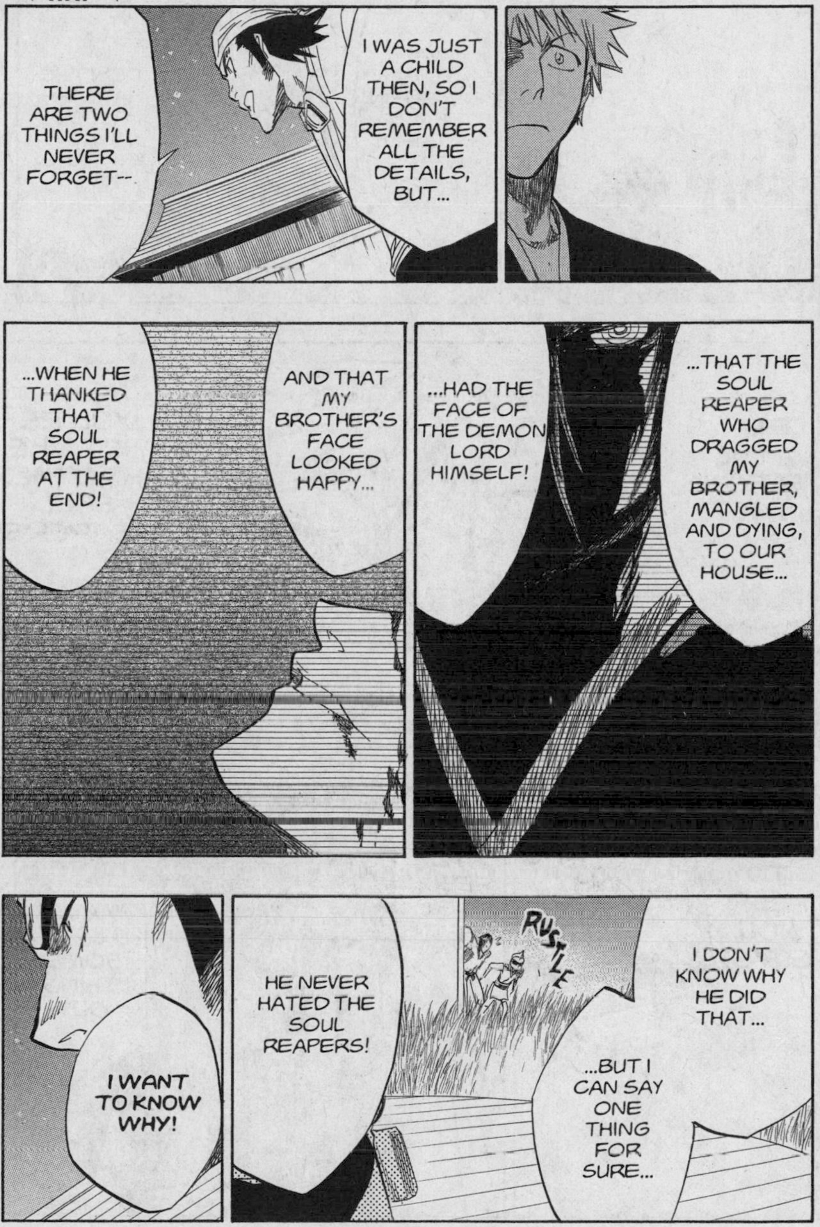

I WAS JUST A CHILD THEN, SO I DON'T REMEMBER ALL THE DETAILS, BUT...
THERE ARE TWO THINGS I'LL NEVER FORGET--
...THAT THE SOUL REAPER WHO DRAGGED MY BROTHER, MANGLED AND DYING, TO OUR HOUSE...
...HAD THE FACE OF THE DEMON LORD HIMSELF!
AND THAT MY BROTHER'S FACE LOOKED HAPPY...
...WHEN HE THANKED THAT SOUL REAPER AT THE END!
I DON'T KNOW WHY HE DID THAT...
RUSTLE
...BUT I CAN SAY ONE THING FOR SURE...
HE NEVER HATED THE SOUL REAPERS!
I WANT TO KNOW WHY!

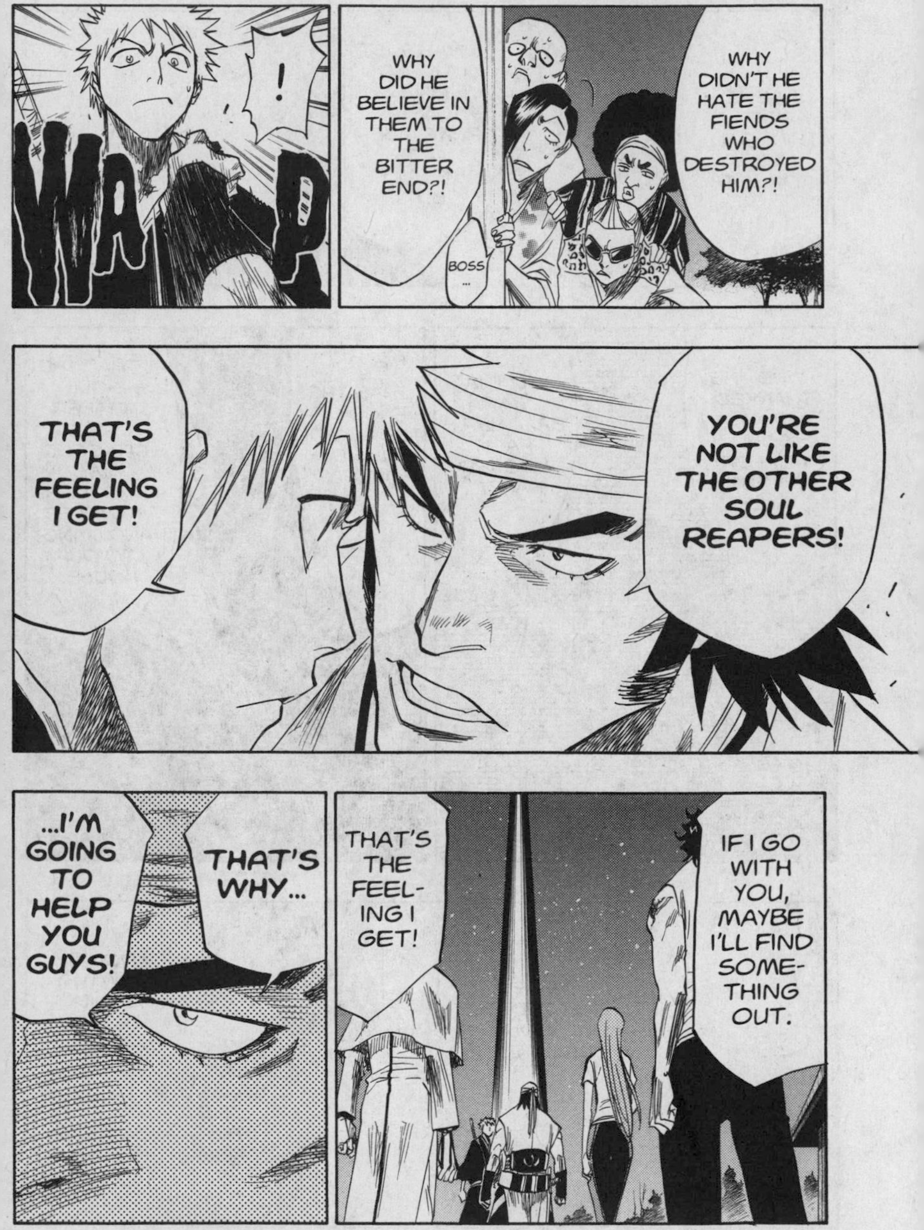
WHY DIDN'T HE HATE THE FIENDS WHO DESTROYED HIM?!
WHY DID HE BELIEVE IN THEM TO THE BITTER END?!
BOSS ...
!
WAP
YOU'RE NOT LIKE THE OTHER SOUL REAPERS!
THAT'S THE FEELING I GET!
IF I GO WITH YOU, MAYBE I'LL FIND SOME-THING OUT.
THAT'S THE FEEL-ING I GET!
THAT'S WHY...
...I'M GOING TO HELP YOU GUYS!

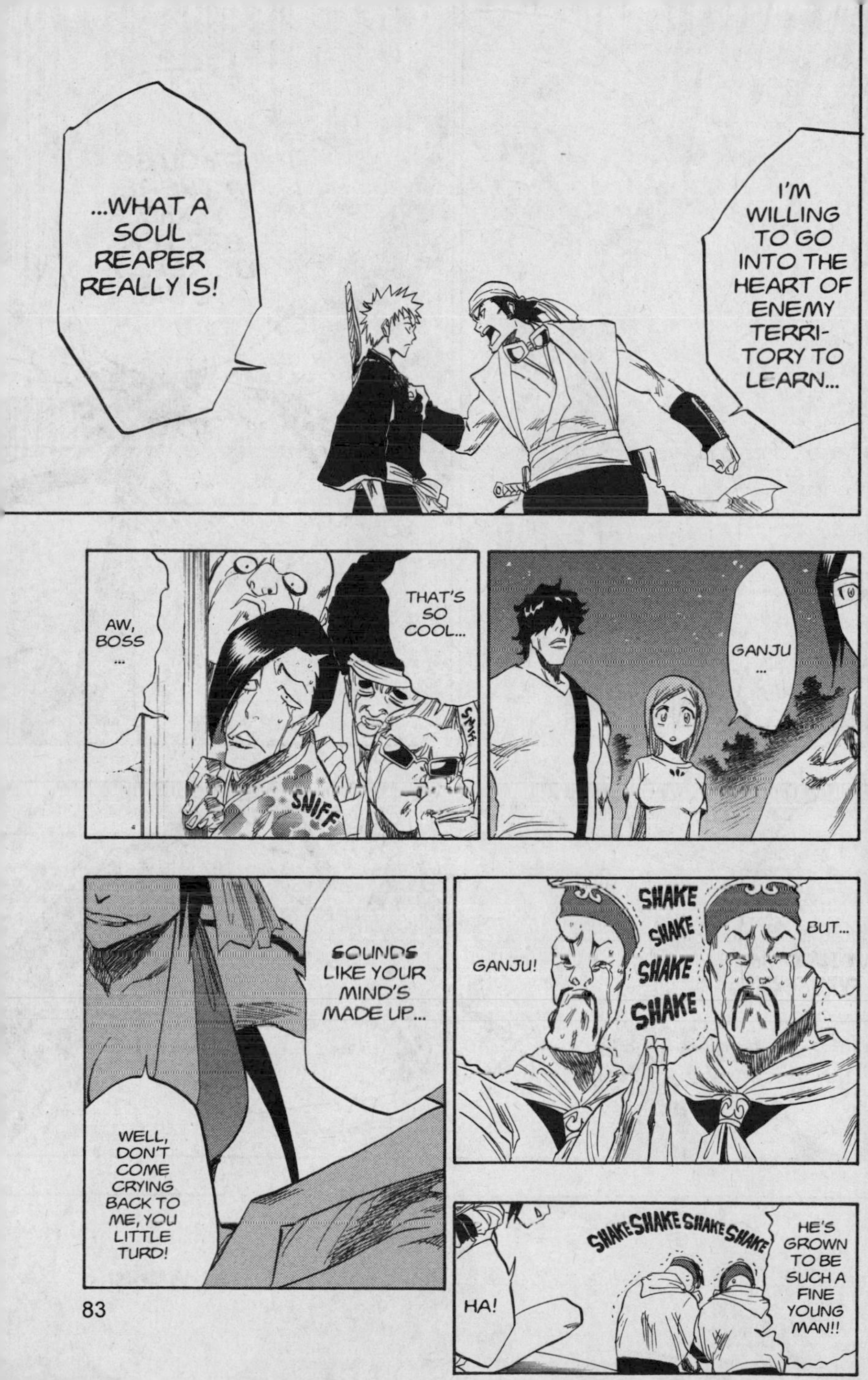
I'M WILLING TO GO INTO THE HEART OF ENEMY TERRITORY TO LEARN...
...WHAT A SOUL REAPER REALLY IS!
GANJU...
THAT'S SO COOL...
SNIFF
SNIFF
AW, BOSS...
BUT...
SHAKE
SHAKE
SHAKE
SHAKE
GANJU!
HE'S GROWN TO BE SUCH A FINE YOUNG MAN!!
SHAKE SHAKE SHAKE SHAKE
HA!
SOUNDS LIKE YOUR MIND'S MADE UP...
WELL, DON'T COME CRYING BACK TO ME, YOU LITTLE TURD!

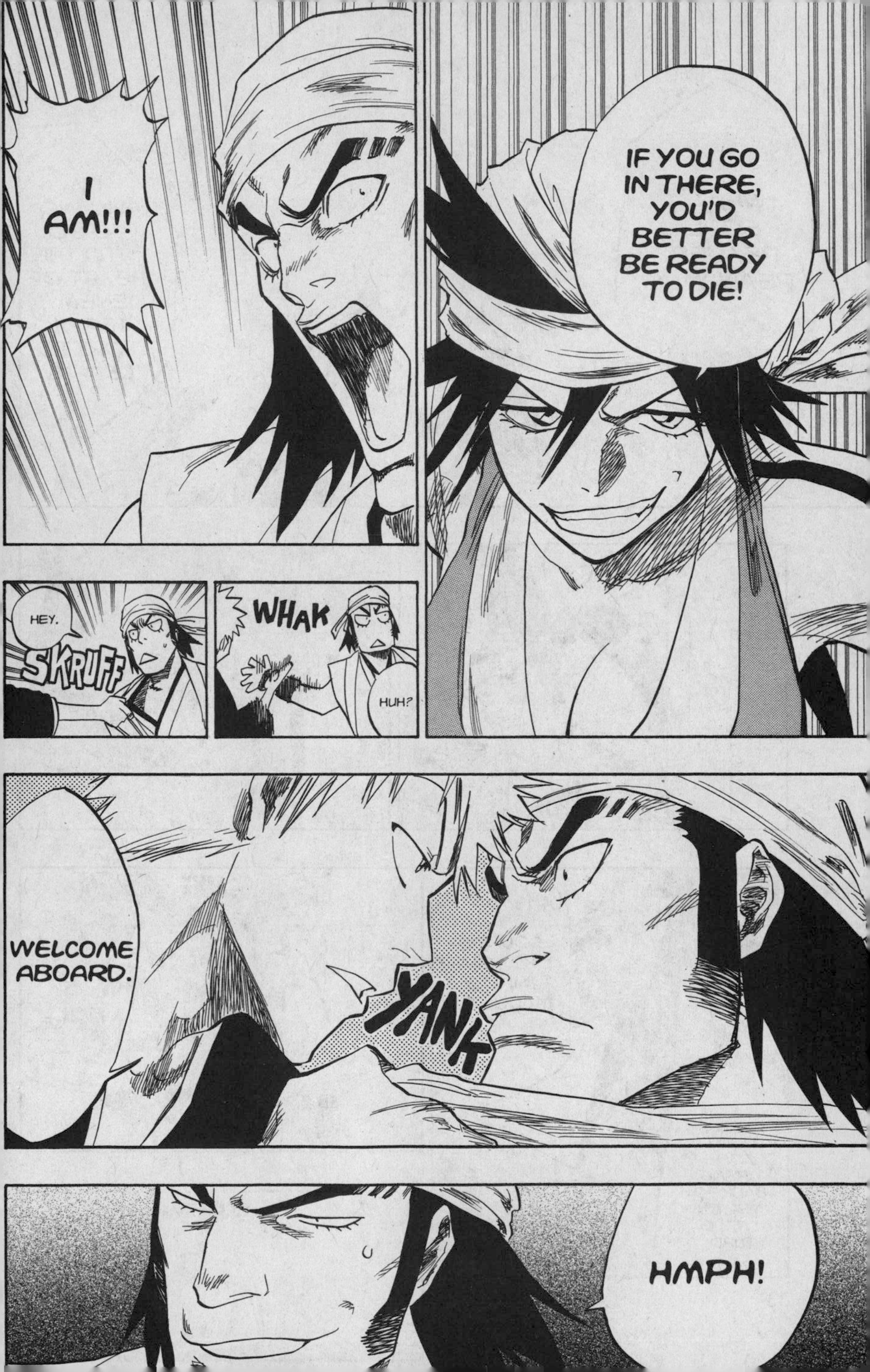
IF YOU GO IN THERE, YOU'D BETTER BE READY TO DIE!
I AM!!!
WHAK
HUH?
HEY.
SKRUFF
YANK
WELCOME ABOARD.
HMPH!

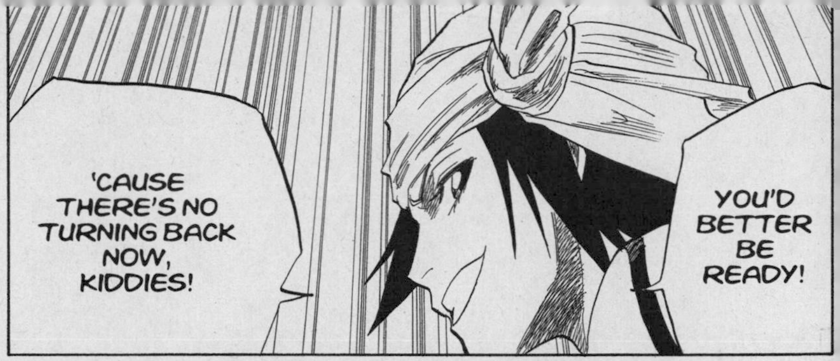
YOU'D BETTER BE READY!
'CAUSE THERE'S NO TURNING BACK NOW, KIDDIES!

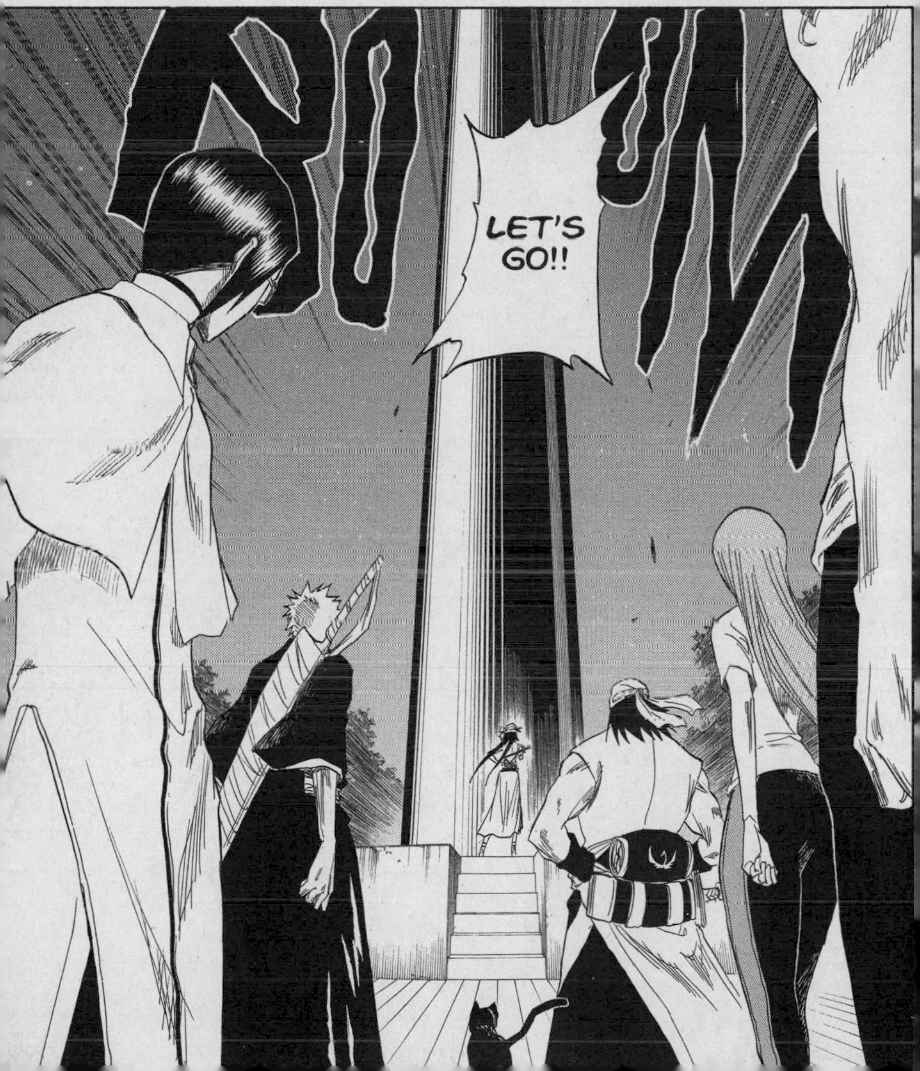
LET'S GO!!

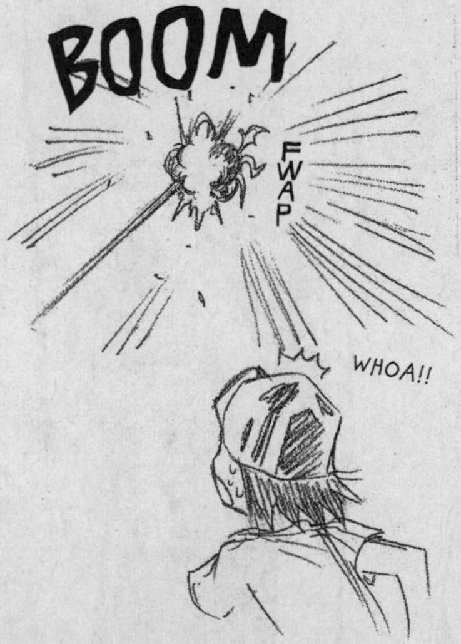
BOOM
FWAP
WHOA!!

84. The Shooting Star Project 2 (Tattoo on the Sky)

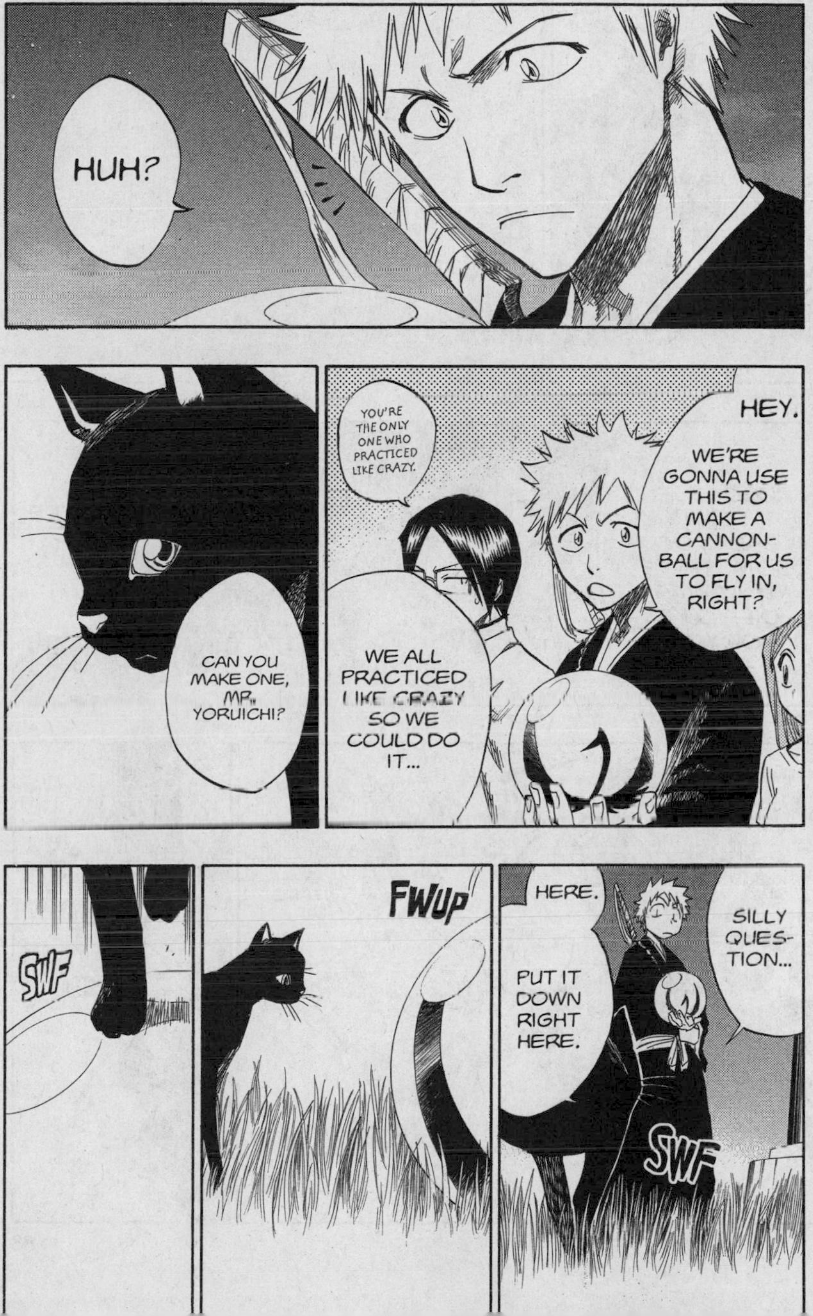
HUH?
HEY.
WE'RE GONNA USE THIS TO MAKE A CANNON-BALL FOR US TO FLY IN, RIGHT?
WE ALL PRACTICED LIKE CRAZY SO WE COULD DO IT...
YOU'RE THE ONLY ONE WHO PRACTICED LIKE CRAZY.
CAN YOU MAKE ONE, MR. YORUICHI?
SILLY QUES-TION...
HERE.
PUT IT DOWN RIGHT HERE.
SWF
FWUP
SWF

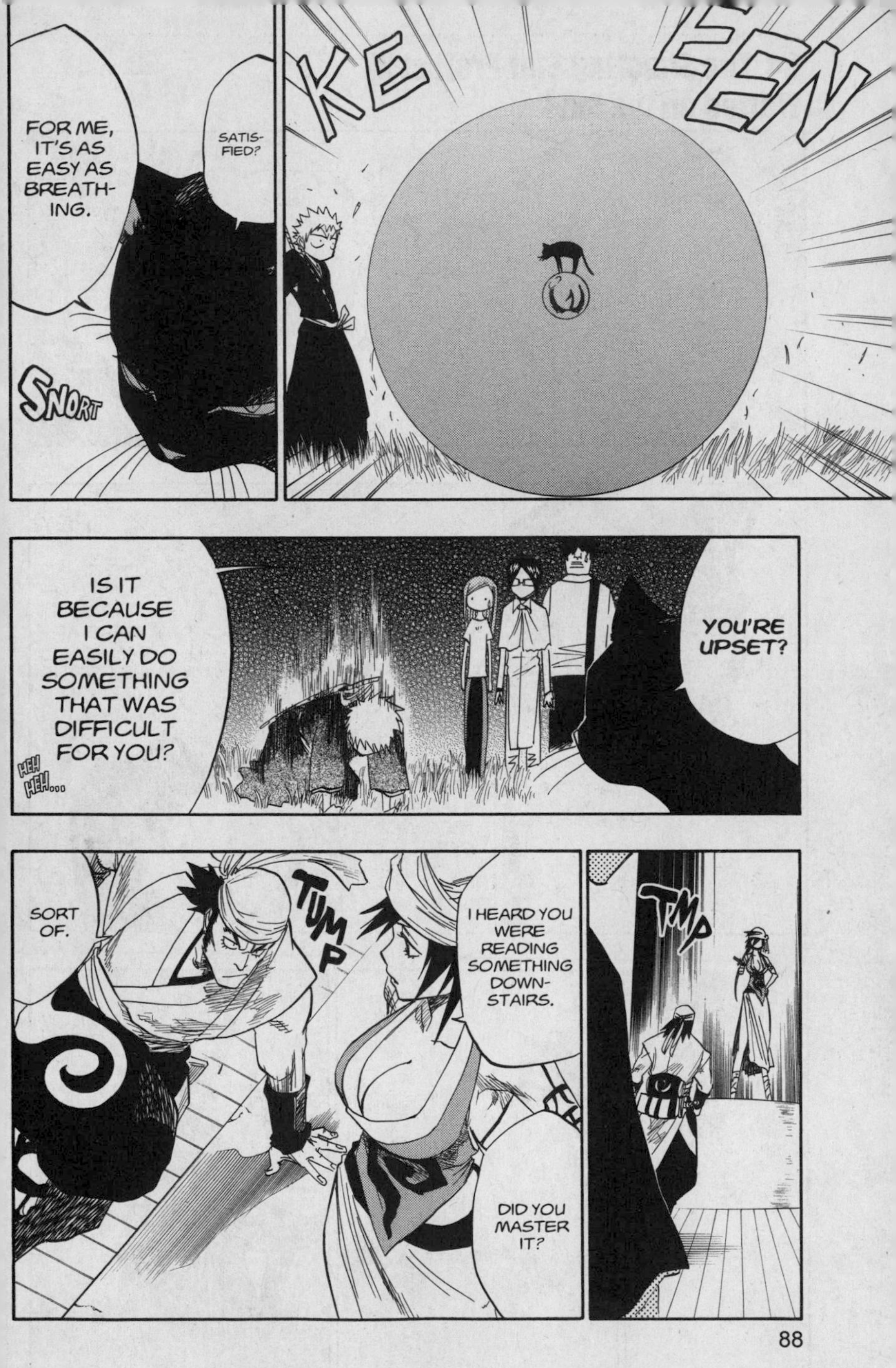
KE
EEN
SATIS-FIED?
FOR ME, IT'S AS EASY AS BREATHING.
SNORT
YOU'RE UPSET?
IS IT BECAUSE I CAN EASILY DO SOMETHING THAT WAS DIFFICULT FOR YOU?
HEH HEH...
TMP
I HEARD YOU WERE READING SOMETHING DOWN-STAIRS.
DID YOU MASTER IT?
TUMP
SORT OF.

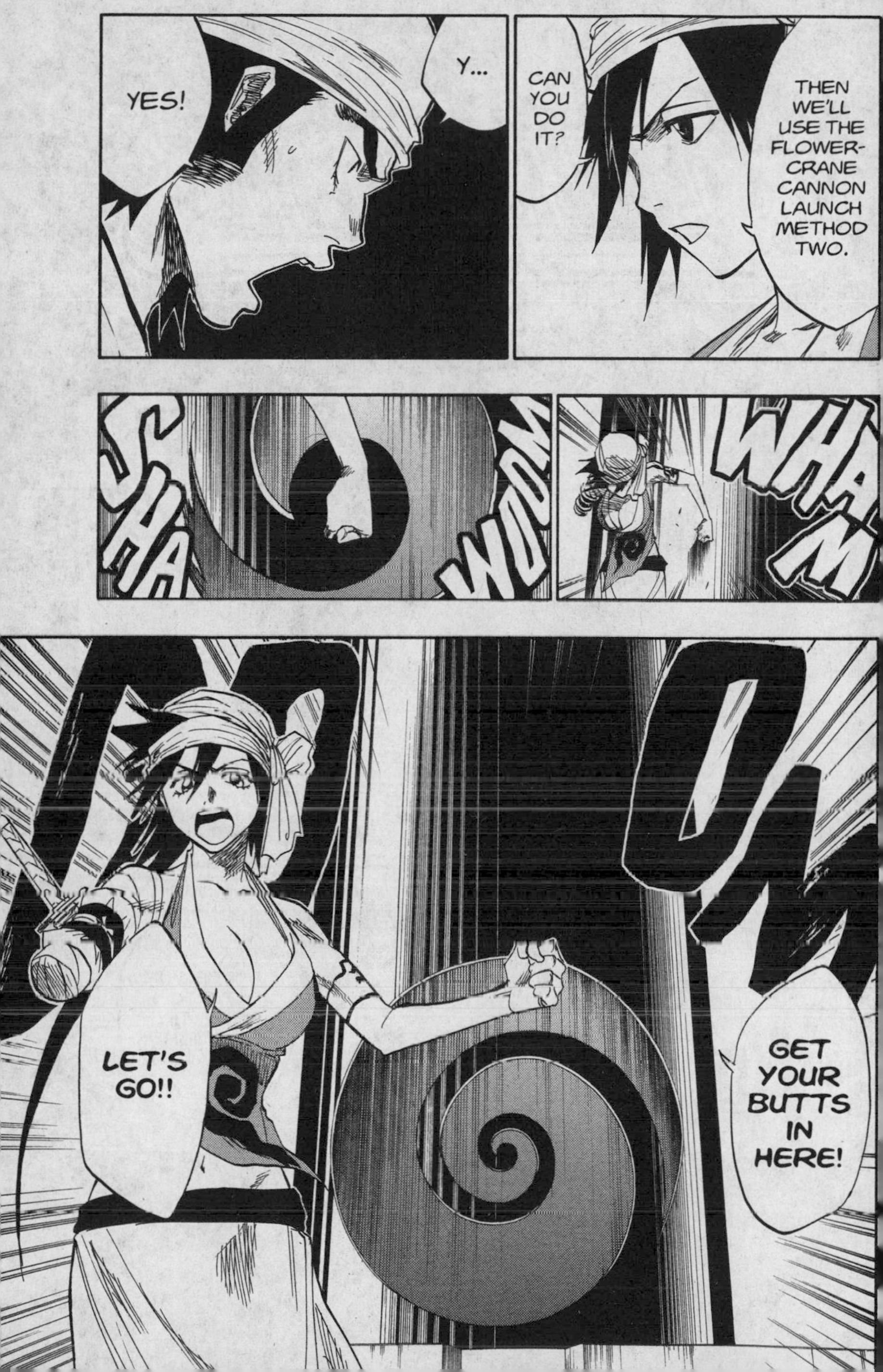
THEN WE'LL USE THE FLOWER-CRANE CANNON LAUNCH METHOD TWO.
CAN YOU DO IT?
Y...
YES!
WHAM
SHA
WOOM
GET YOUR BUTTS IN HERE!
LET'S GO!!

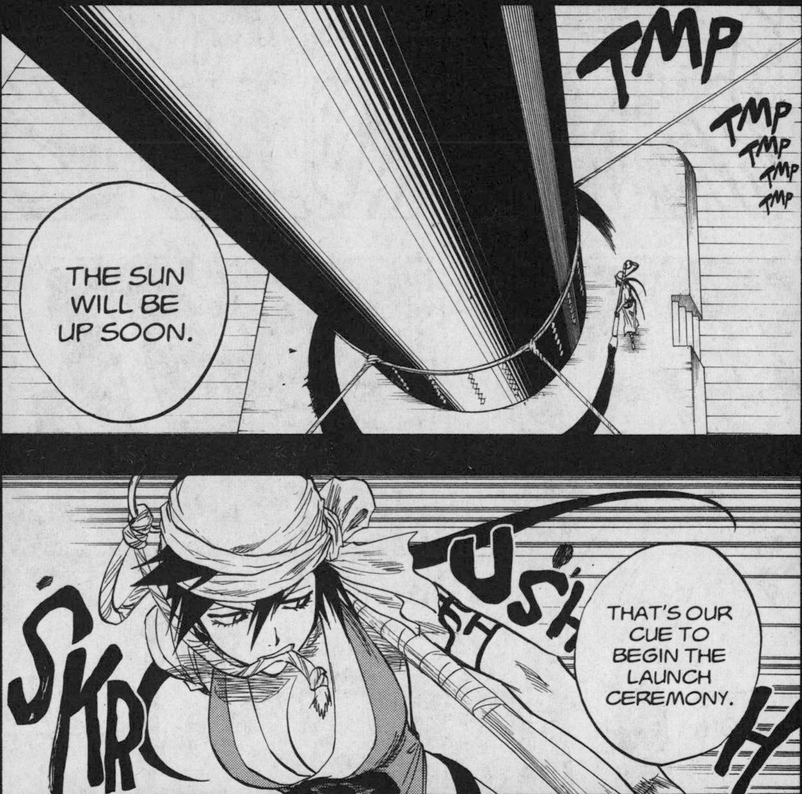
TMP
TMP TMP TMP TMP
THE SUN WILL BE UP SOON.
THAT'S OUR CUE TO BEGIN THE LAUNCH CEREMONY.

84. The Shooting Star Project 2 (Tattoo on the Sky)

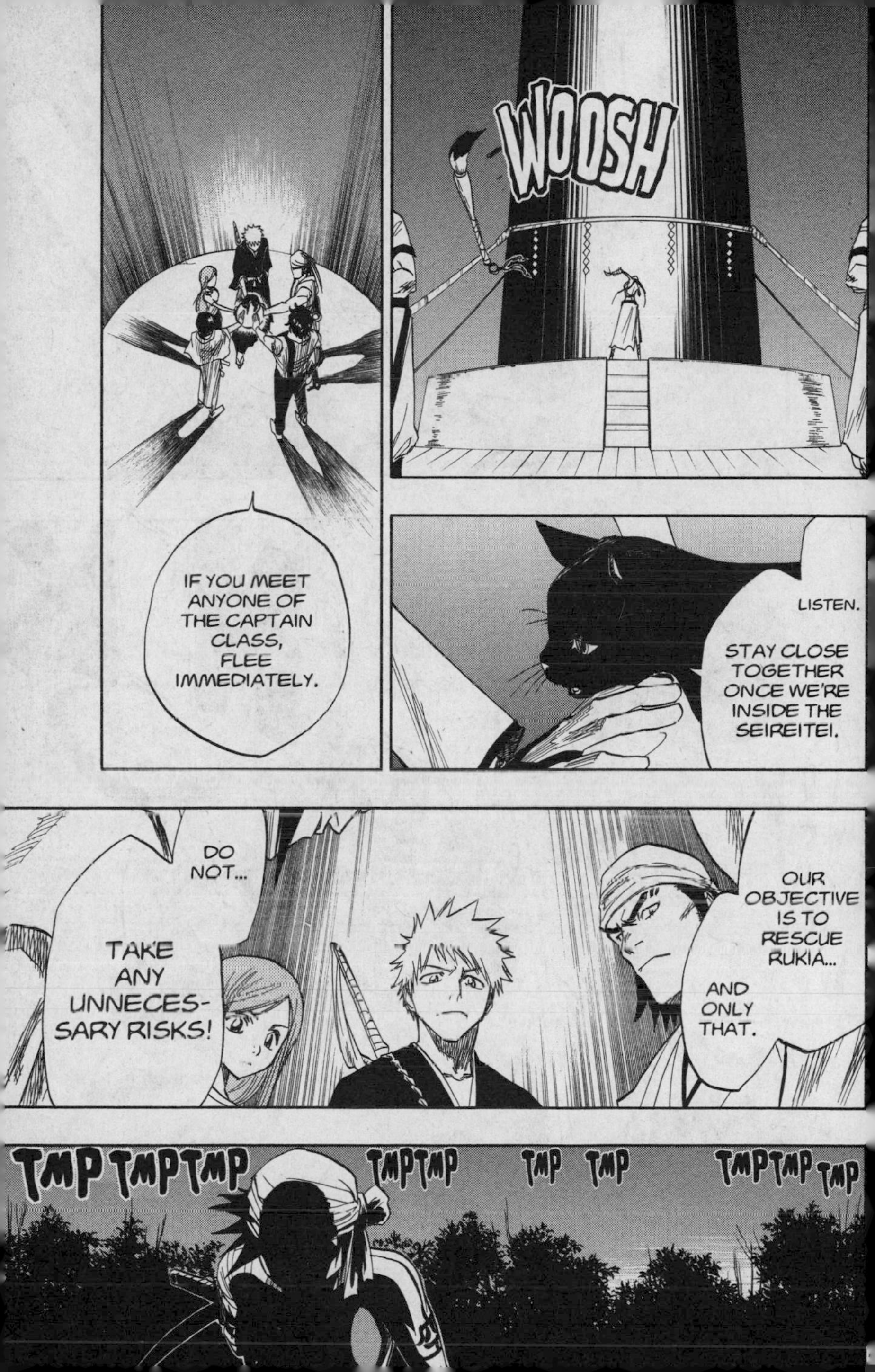
WOOSH
LISTEN.
STAY CLOSE TOGETHER ONCE WE'RE INSIDE THE SEIREITEI.
IF YOU MEET ANYONE OF THE CAPTAIN CLASS, FLEE IMMEDIATELY.
OUR OBJECTIVE IS TO RESCUE RUKIA...
AND ONLY THAT.
DO NOT...
TAKE ANY UNNECES-SARY RISKS!
TMPTMP TMP
TMP
TMP
TMPTMP
TMP TMPTMP

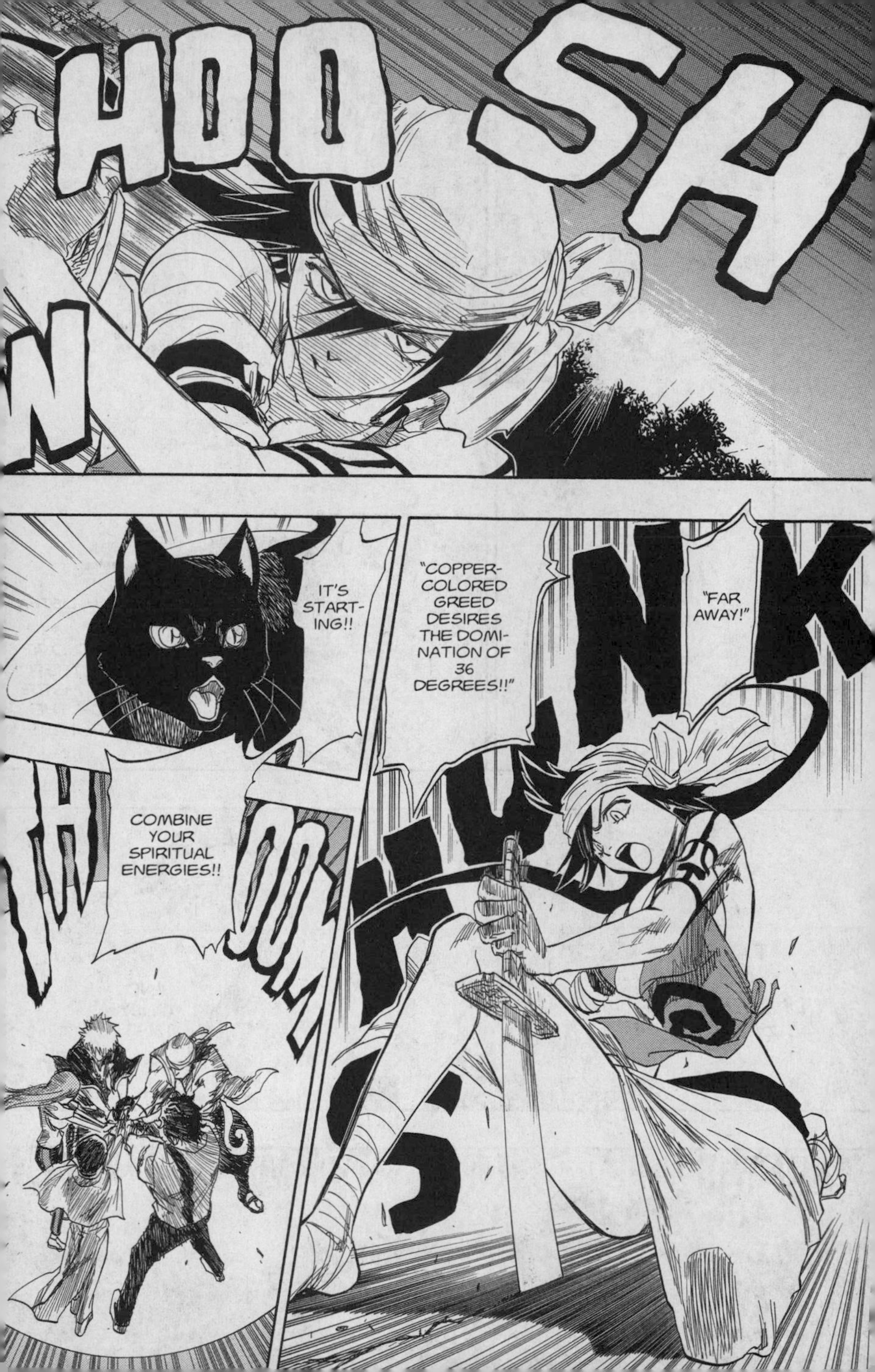
HOO SH
"FAR AWAY!"
"COPPER-COLORED GREED DESIRES THE DOMINATION OF 36 DEGREES!!"
IT'S STARTING!!
COMBINE YOUR SPIRITUAL ENERGIES!!

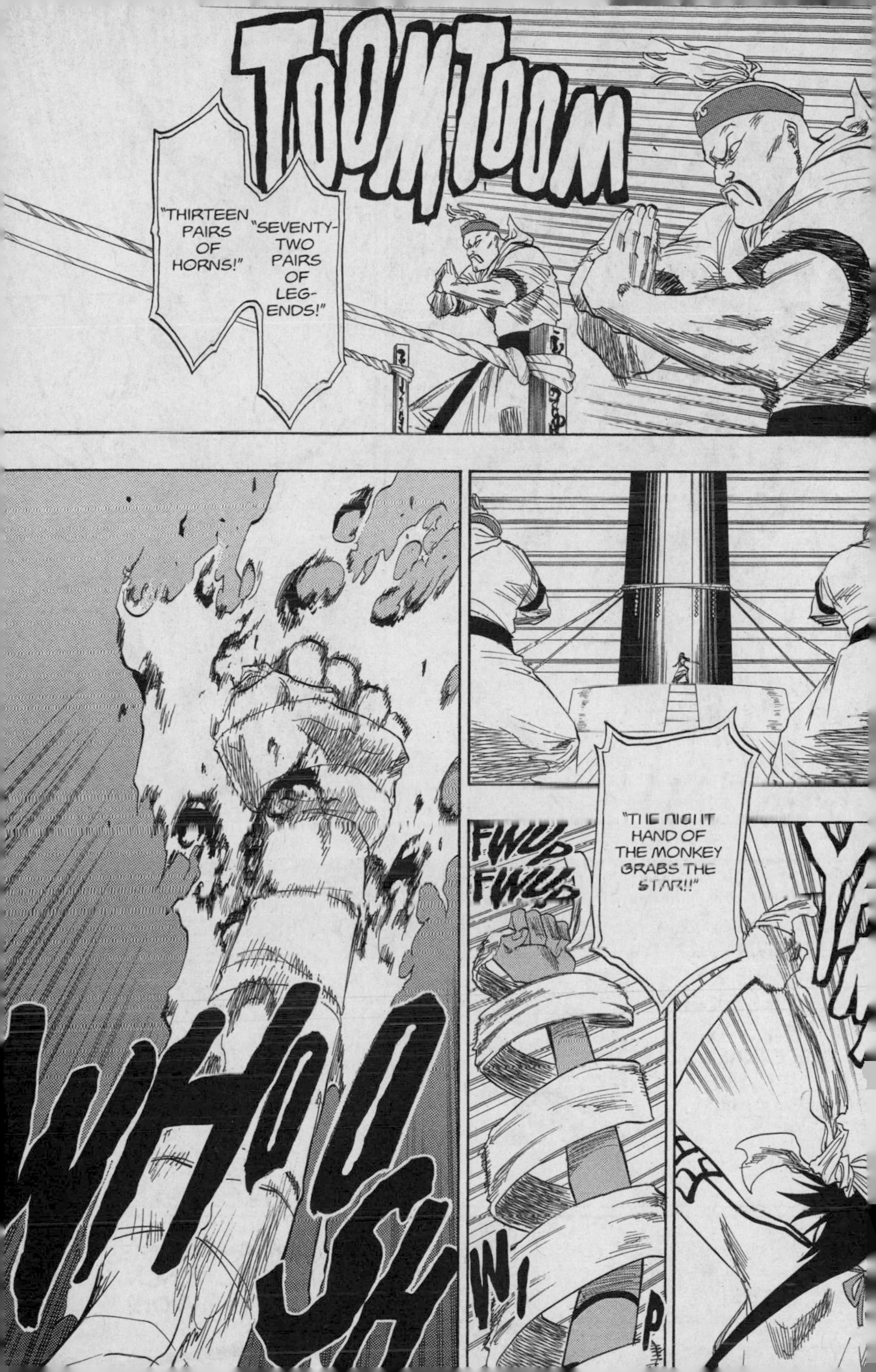
TOOM TOOM
"THIRTEEN PAIRS OF HORNS!"
"SEVENTY-TWO PAIRS OF LEG-ENDS!"
"THE RIGHT HAND OF THE MONKEY GRABS THE STAR!!"
FWUP FWUP
WIP
WHOOSH

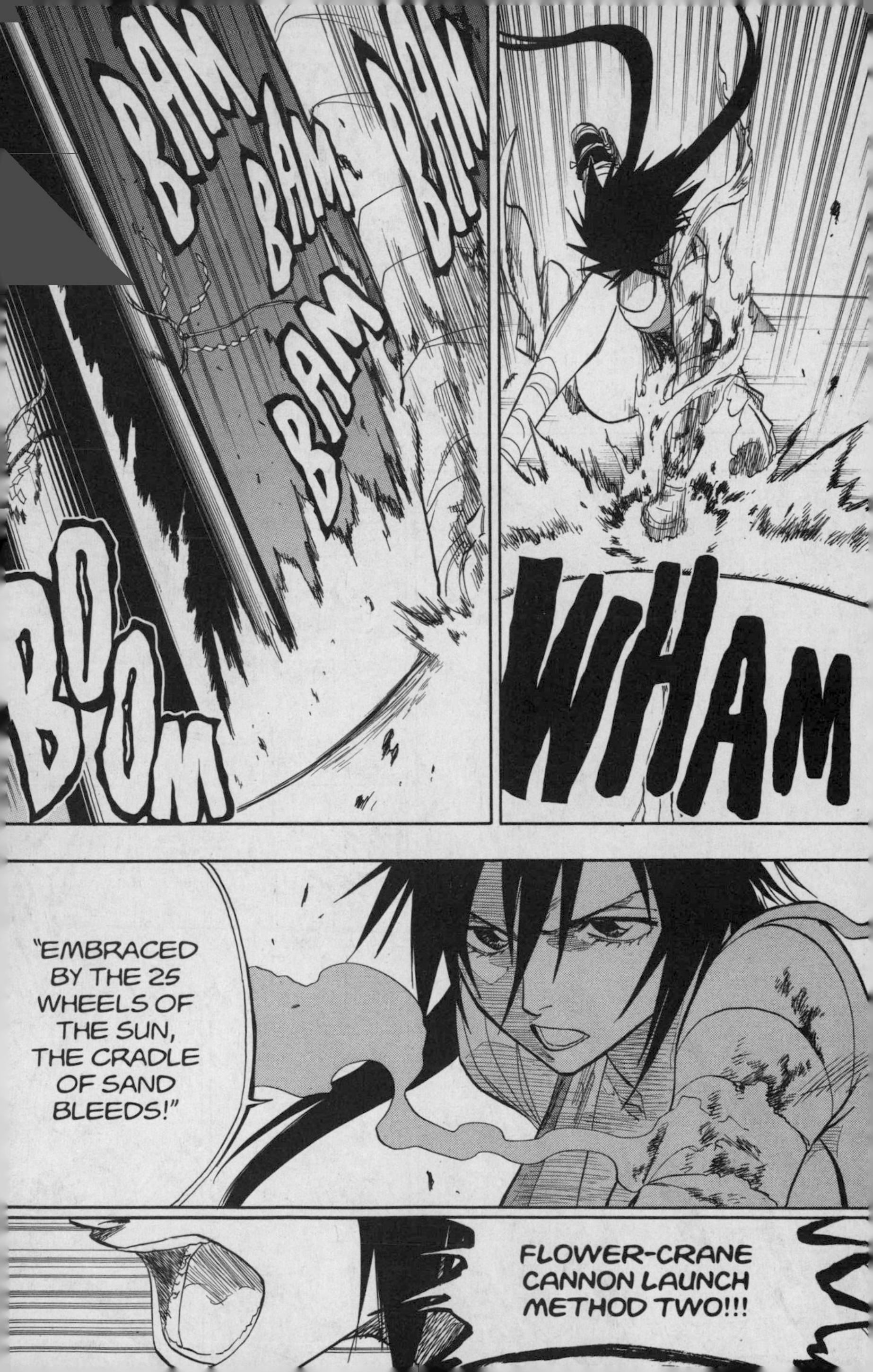
WHAM
BAM BAM BAM BAM
BOOM
"EMBRACED BY THE 25 WHEELS OF THE SUN, THE CRADLE OF SAND BLEEDS!"
FLOWER-CRANE CANNON LAUNCH METHOD TWO!!!

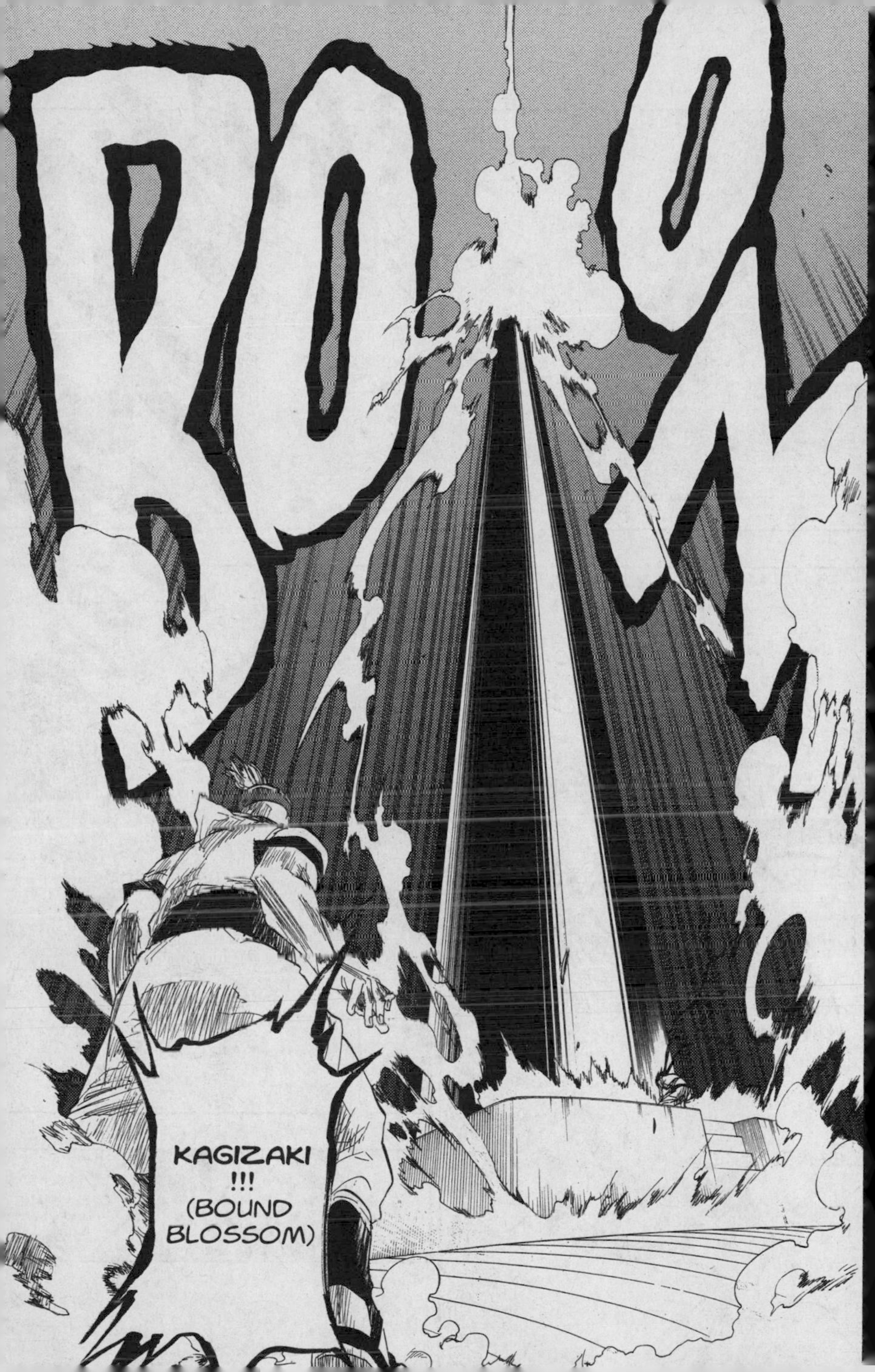
DOO
KAGIZAKI !!! (BOUND BLOSSOM)

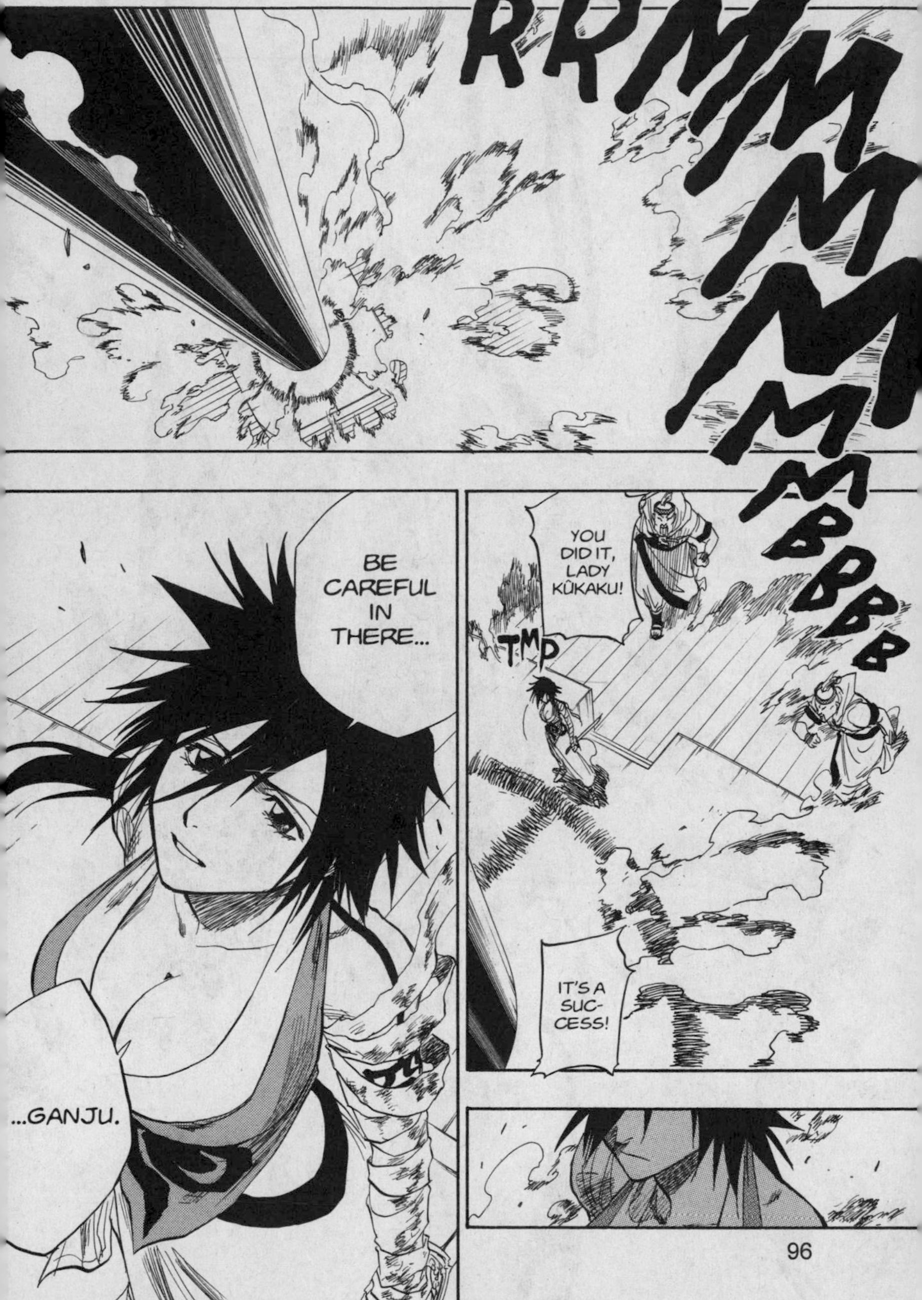
RRMMMMMMBBBB
YOU DID IT, LADY KÛKAKU!
TMP
IT'S A SUC-CESS!
BE CAREFUL IN THERE...
...GANJU.

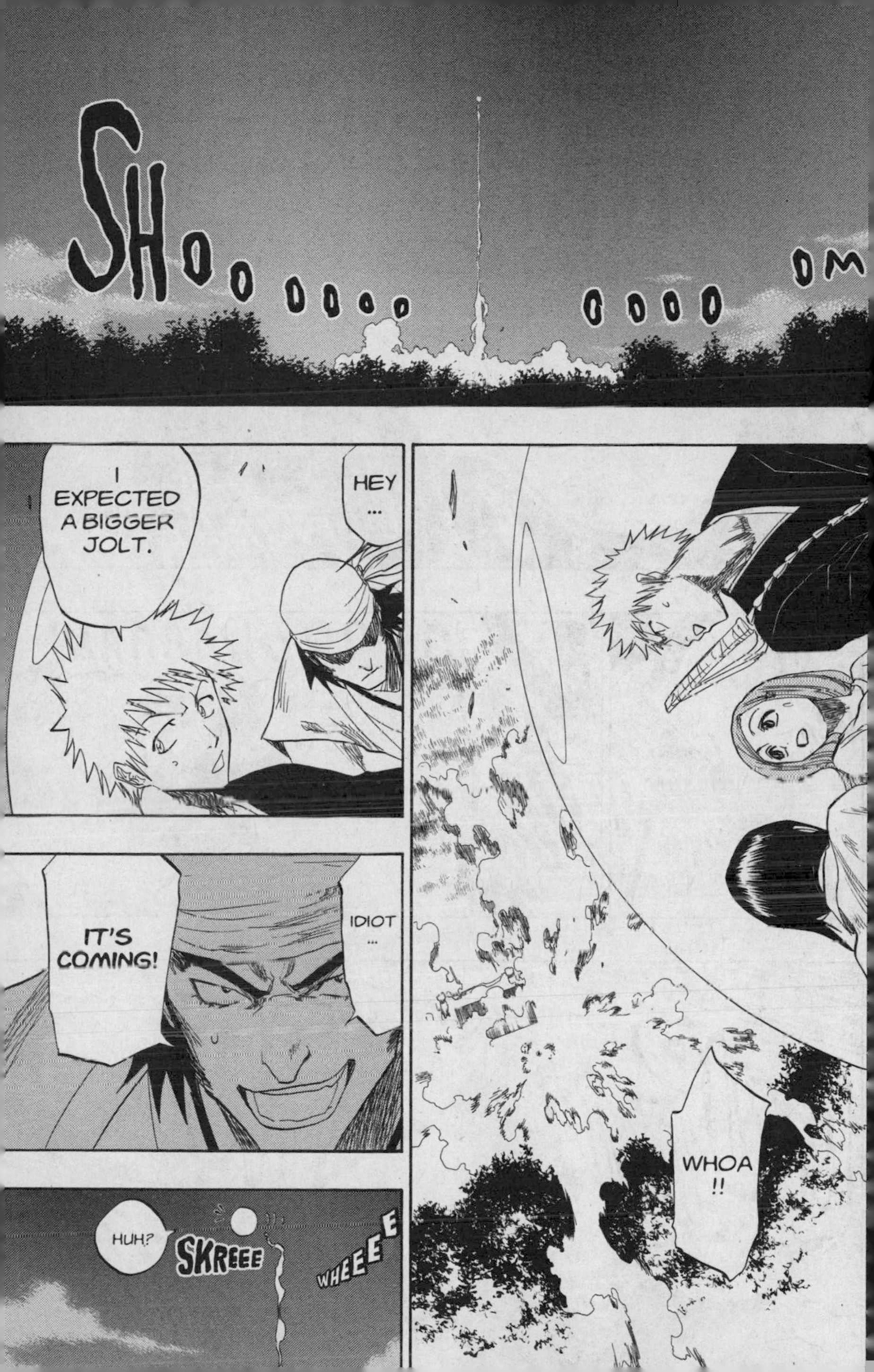
SHOOOOOOOOOOOM
WHOA!!
HEY...
I EXPECTED A BIGGER JOLT.
IDIOT...
IT'S COMING!
HUH?
SKREEE
WHEEEE

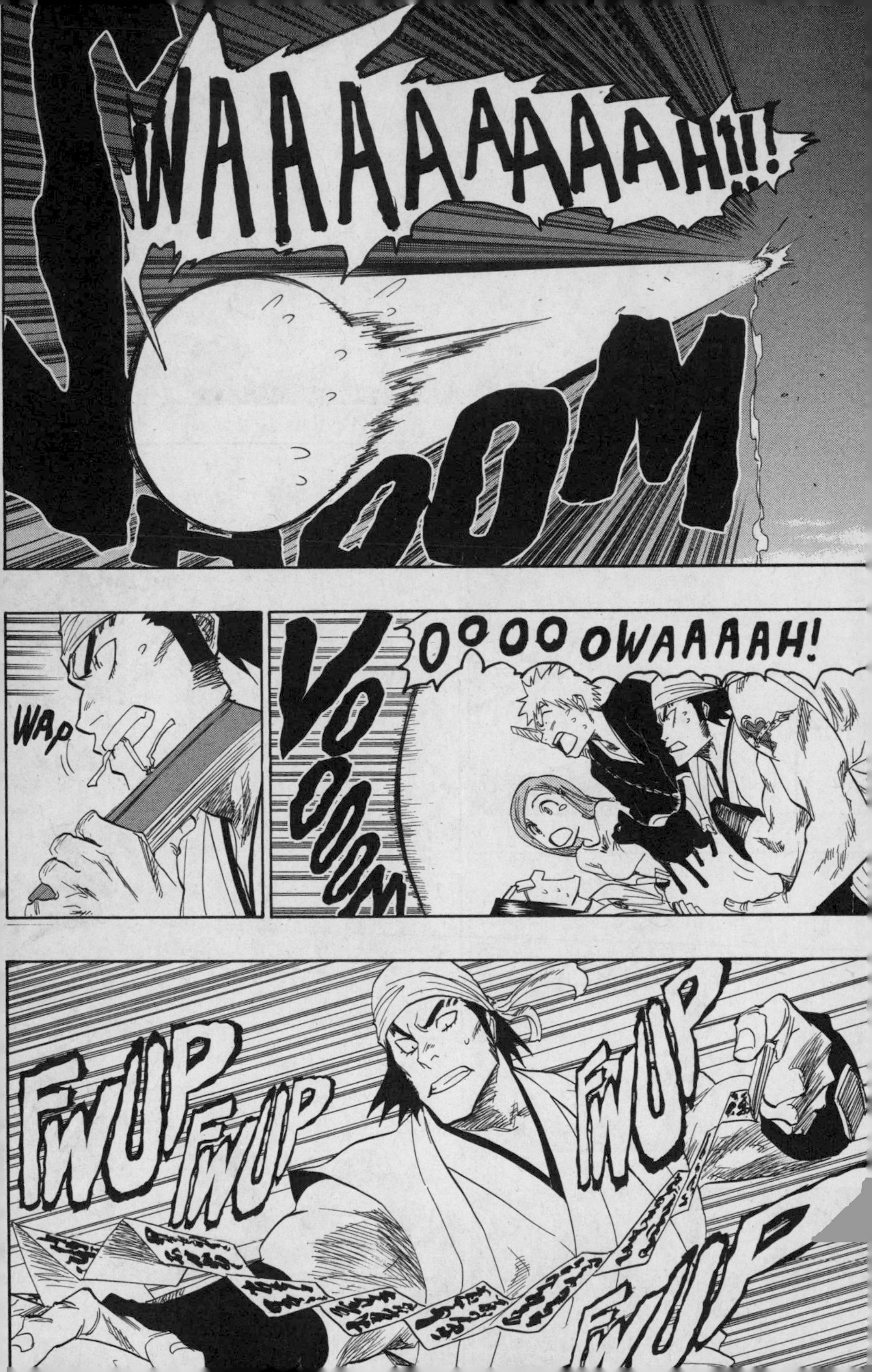
WAAAAAAAAH!!!
OOM
VOOOOOM
OOOOOWAAAAAH!
WAP
FWUP
FWUP
FWUP
FWUP

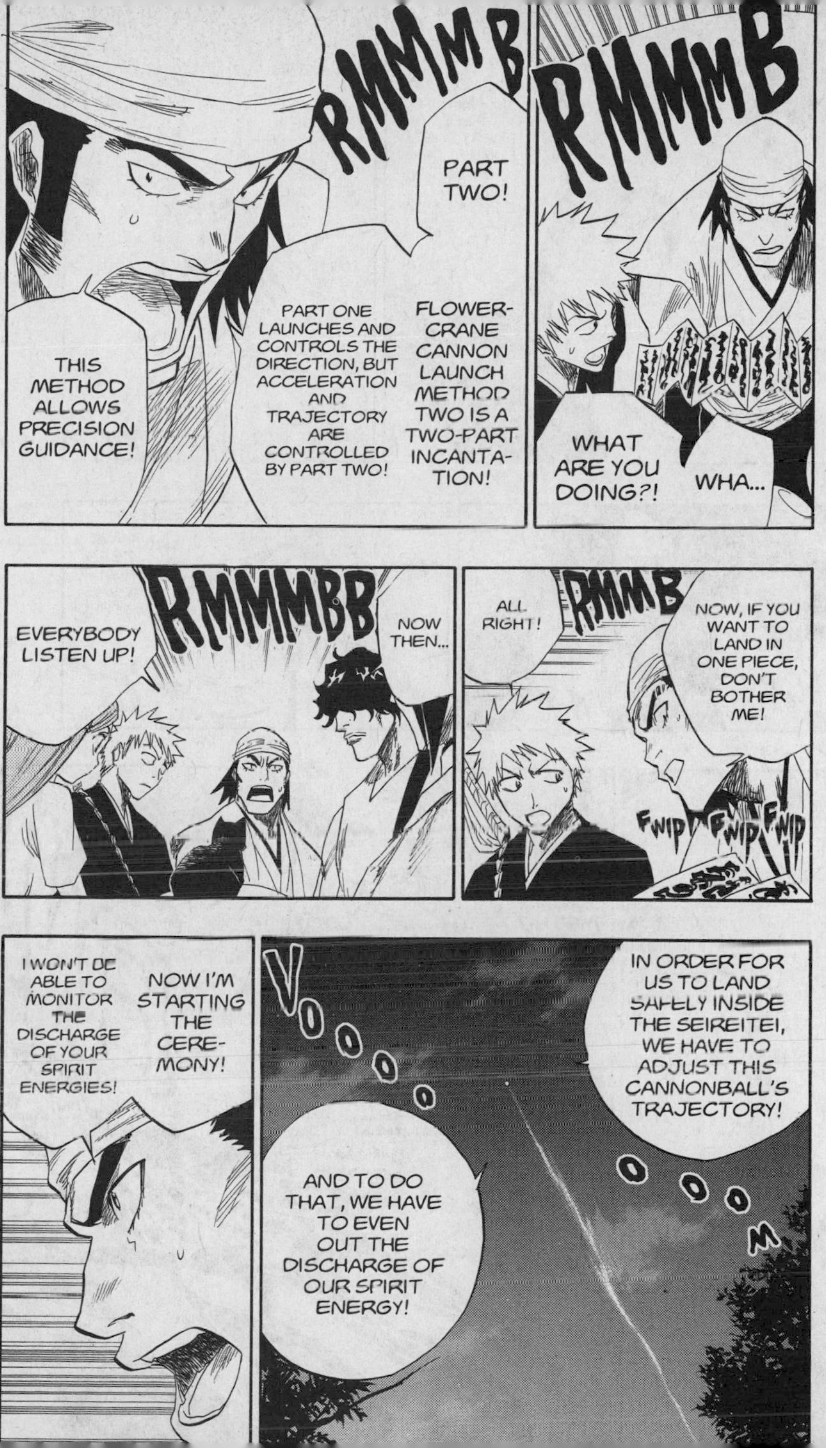
RMMMB
WHA...
WHAT ARE YOU DOING?!
RMMMB
PART TWO!
FLOWER-CRANE CANNON LAUNCH METHOD TWO IS A TWO-PART INCANTATION!
PART ONE LAUNCHES AND CONTROLS THE DIRECTION, BUT ACCELERATION AND TRAJECTORY ARE CONTROLLED BY PART TWO!
THIS METHOD ALLOWS PRECISION GUIDANCE!
RMMB
NOW, IF YOU WANT TO LAND IN ONE PIECE, DON'T BOTHER ME!
ALL RIGHT!
FWIP FWIP FWIP
NOW THEN...
RMMMBB
EVERYBODY LISTEN UP!
IN ORDER FOR US TO LAND SAFELY INSIDE THE SEIREITEI, WE HAVE TO ADJUST THIS CANNONBALL'S TRAJECTORY!
VOOOOOOOOOM
AND TO DO THAT, WE HAVE TO EVEN OUT THE DISCHARGE OF OUR SPIRIT ENERGY!
NOW I'M STARTING THE CEREMONY!
I WON'T BE ABLE TO MONITOR THE DISCHARGE OF YOUR SPIRIT ENERGIES!

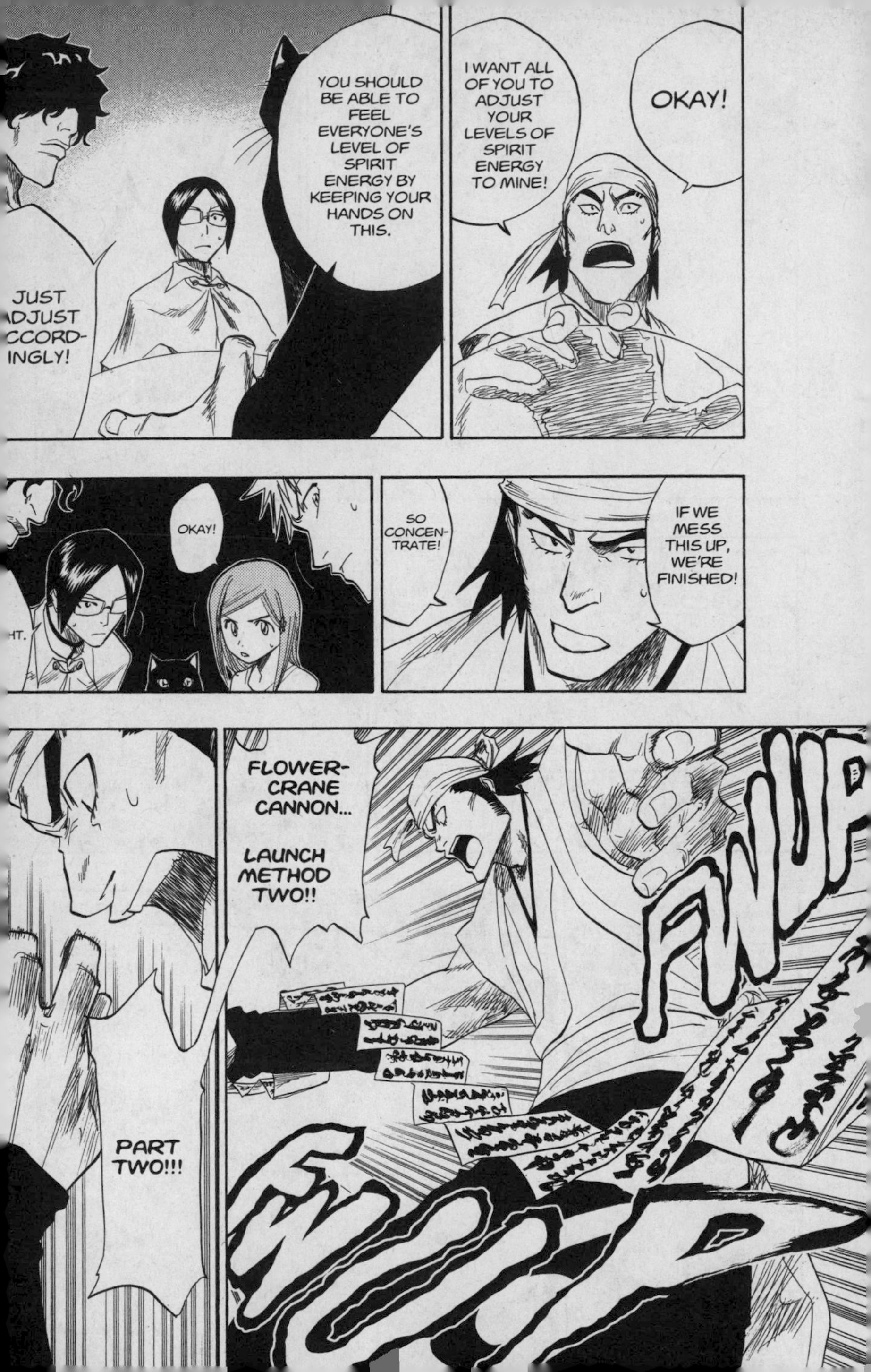
OKAY!
I WANT ALL OF YOU TO ADJUST YOUR LEVELS OF SPIRIT ENERGY TO MINE!
YOU SHOULD BE ABLE TO FEEL EVERYONE'S LEVEL OF SPIRIT ENERGY BY KEEPING YOUR HANDS ON THIS.
JUST ADJUST ACCORDINGLY!
IF WE MESS THIS UP, WE'RE FINISHED!
SO CONCENTRATE!
OKAY!
FWUP
FLOWER-CRANE CANNON...
LAUNCH METHOD TWO!!
PART TWO!!!

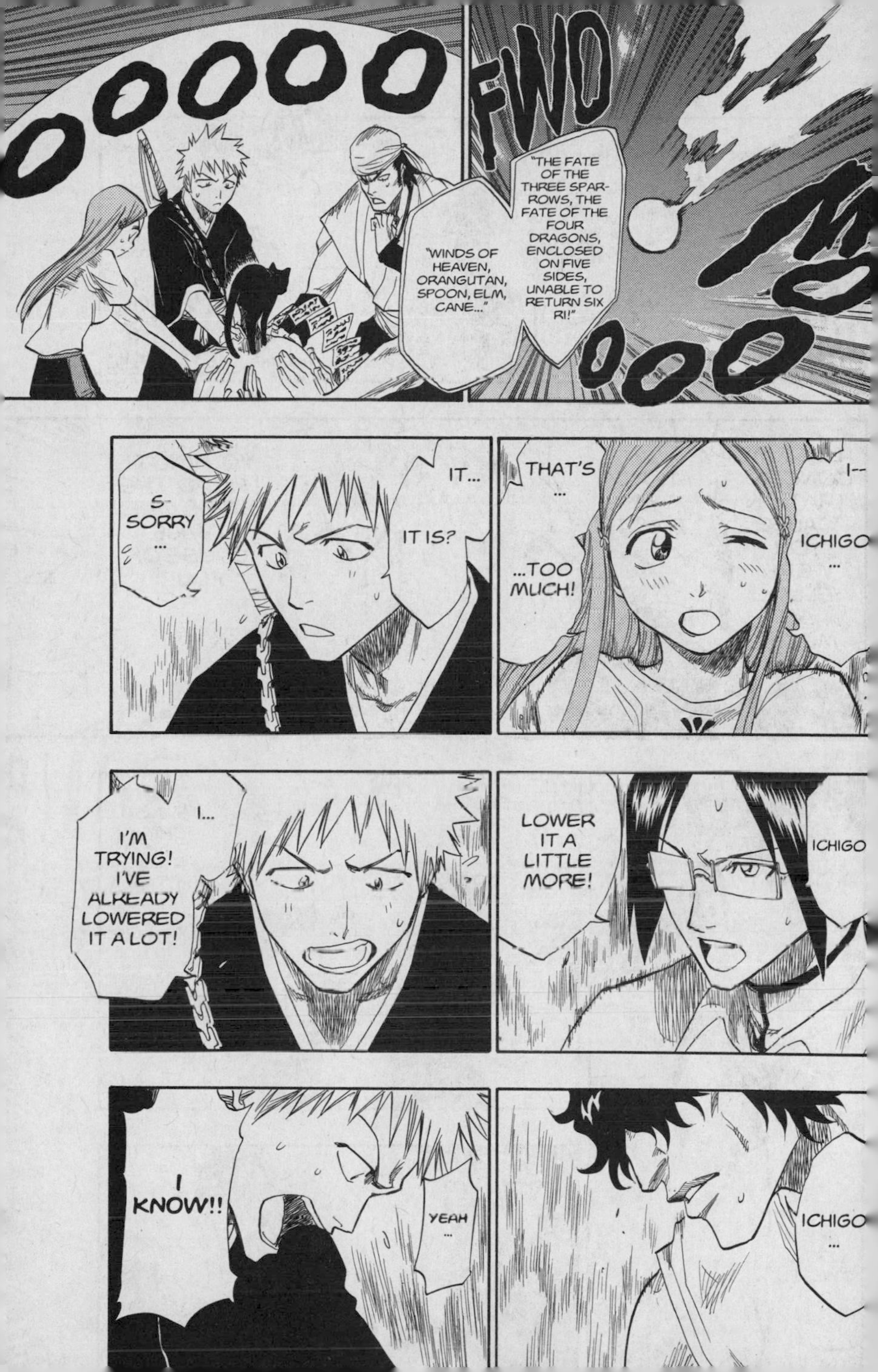
FWO
MO
OOO
"THE FATE OF THE THREE SPARROWS, THE FATE OF THE FOUR DRAGONS, ENCLOSED ON FIVE SIDES, UNABLE TO RETURN SIX RI!"
"WINDS OF HEAVEN, ORANGUTAN, SPOON, ELM, CANE..."
OOOOOO
I-- ICHIGO ...
THAT'S ... ...TOO MUCH!
IT... IT IS?
S-SORRY ...
ICHIGO
LOWER IT A LITTLE MORE!
I... I'M TRYING! I'VE ALREADY LOWERED IT A LOT!
ICHIGO ...
YEAH ...
I KNOW!!

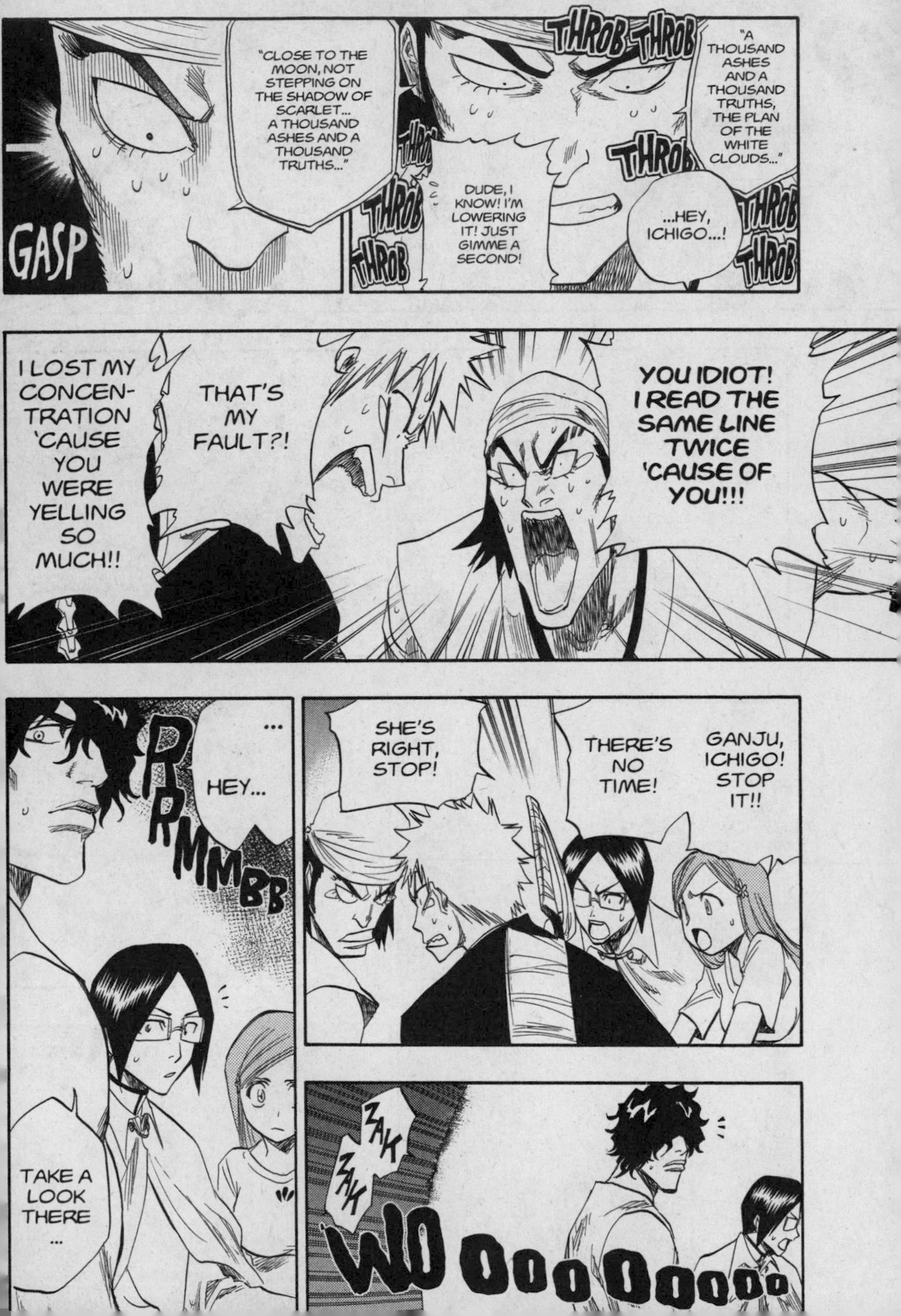
THROB THROB
"A THOUSAND ASHES AND A THOUSAND TRUTHS, THE PLAN OF THE WHITE CLOUDS..."
THROB
...HEY, ICHIGO...!
THROB THROB
DUDE, I KNOW! I'M LOWERING IT! JUST GIMME A SECOND!
THROB THROB THROB
"CLOSE TO THE MOON, NOT STEPPING ON THE SHADOW OF SCARLET... A THOUSAND ASHES AND A THOUSAND TRUTHS..."
GASP
YOU IDIOT! I READ THE SAME LINE TWICE 'CAUSE OF YOU!!!
THAT'S MY FAULT?!
I LOST MY CONCENTRATION 'CAUSE YOU WERE YELLING SO MUCH!!
GANJU, ICHIGO! STOP IT!!
THERE'S NO TIME!
SHE'S RIGHT, STOP!
ZAK ZAK
WOOOOOOOOOO
...
HEY...
RRMMBB
TAKE A LOOK THERE ...

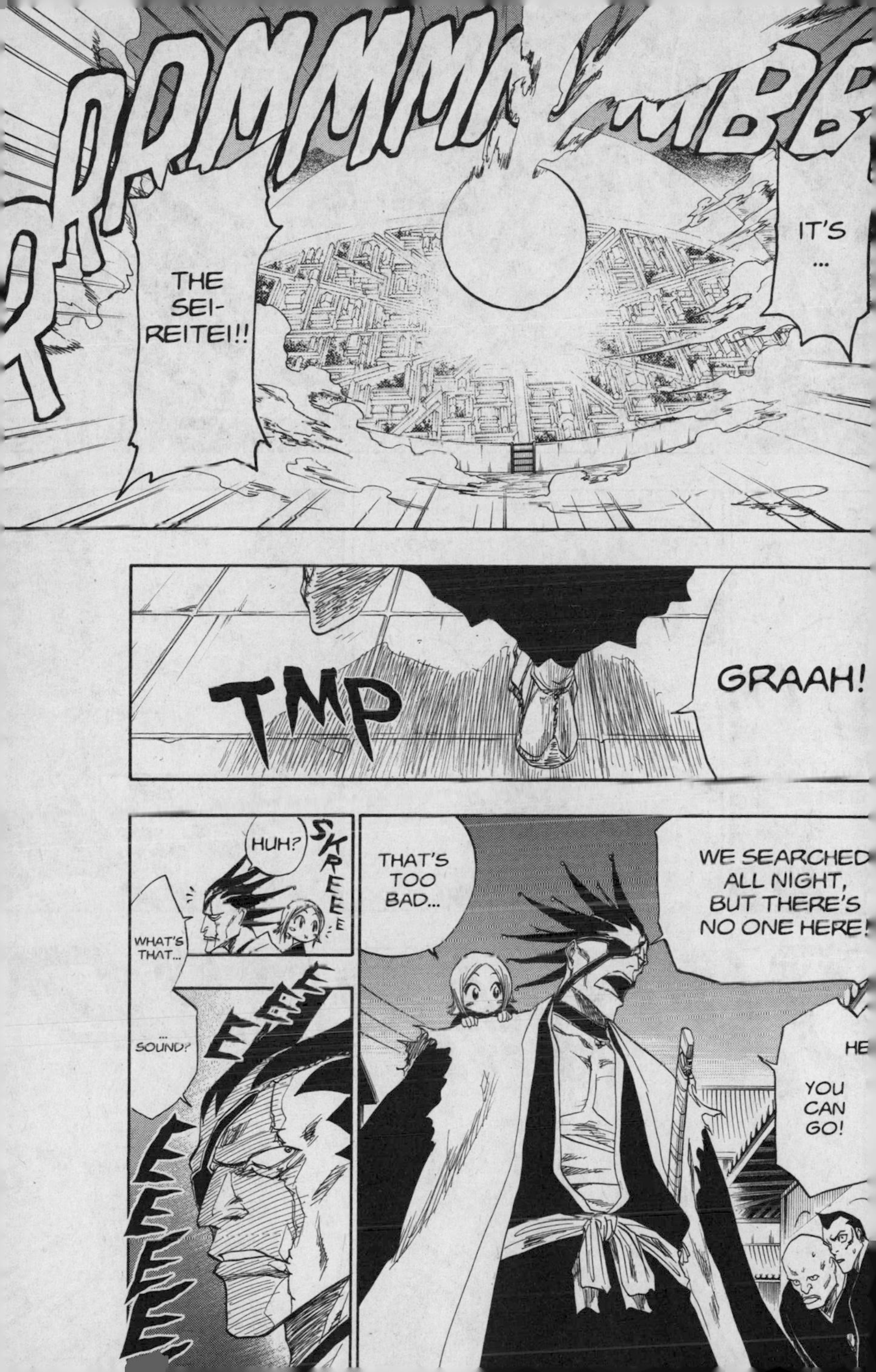
IT'S ...
THE SEI-REITEI!!
GRAAH!
TMP
HE
YOU CAN GO!
WE SEARCHED ALL NIGHT, BUT THERE'S NO ONE HERE!
THAT'S TOO BAD...
SKREEEE
HUH?
WHAT'S THAT...
... SOUND?
EEEEEE

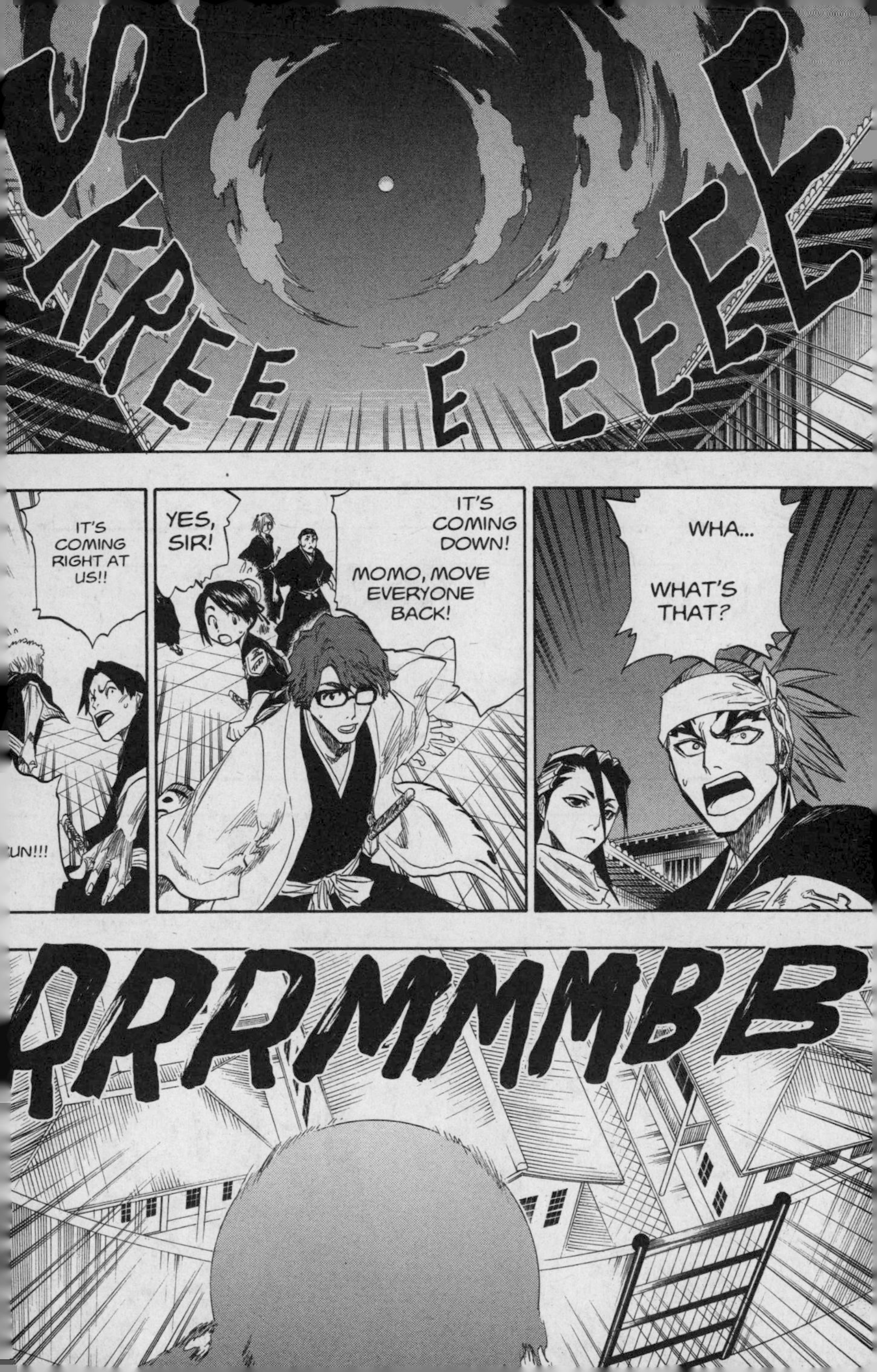
SKREEEEEEE
WHA...
WHAT'S THAT?
IT'S COMING DOWN!
MOMO, MOVE EVERYONE BACK!
YES, SIR!
IT'S COMING RIGHT AT US!!
RRRMMMBB

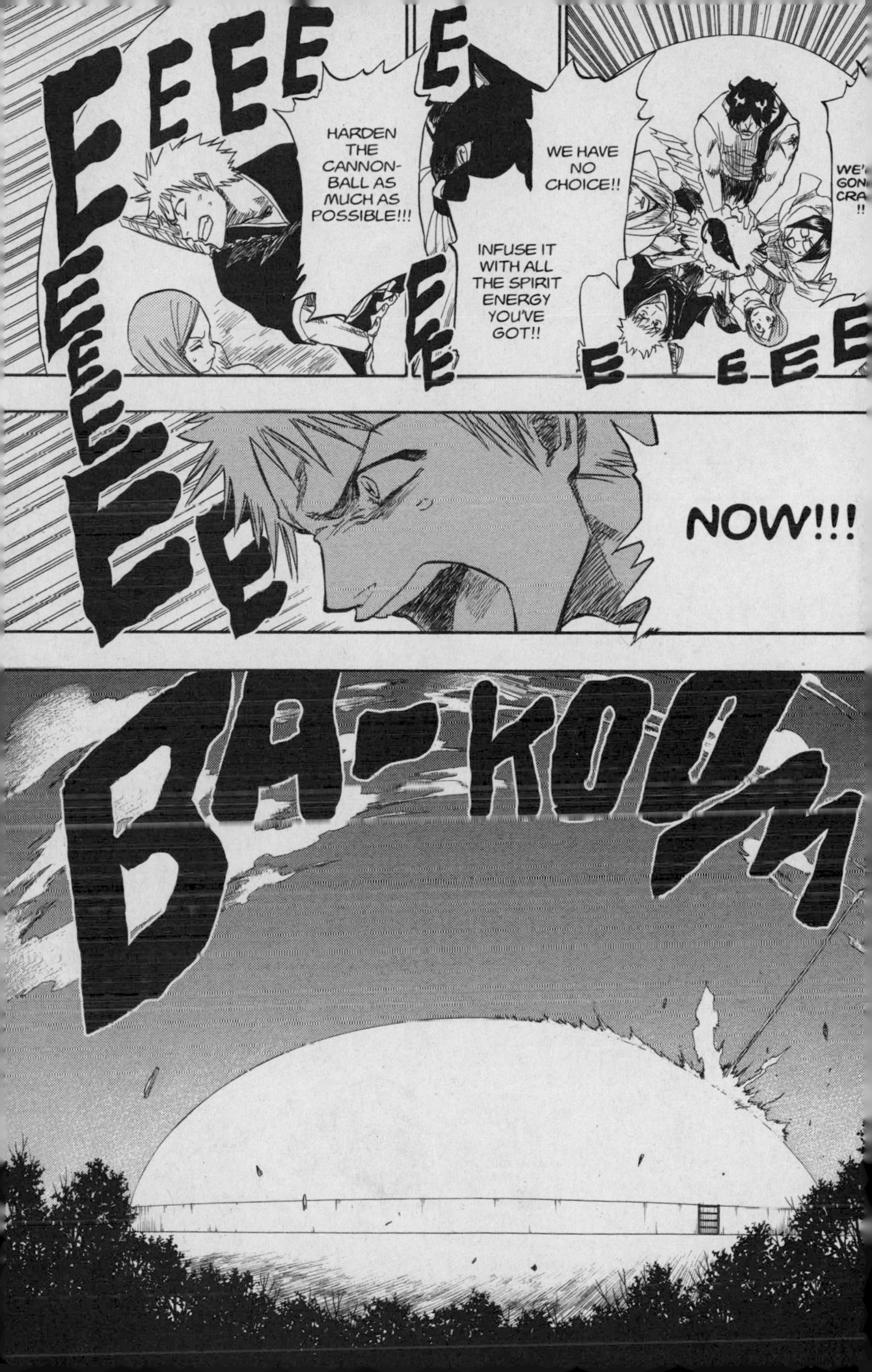
EEE EEEE
WE'
GON
CRA
!!
WE HAVE NO CHOICE!!
INFUSE IT WITH ALL THE SPIRIT ENERGY YOU'VE GOT!!
HARDEN THE CANNON-BALL AS MUCH AS POSSIBLE!!!
EEEE E EEEEEEEE
NOW!!!
BA-KOOM

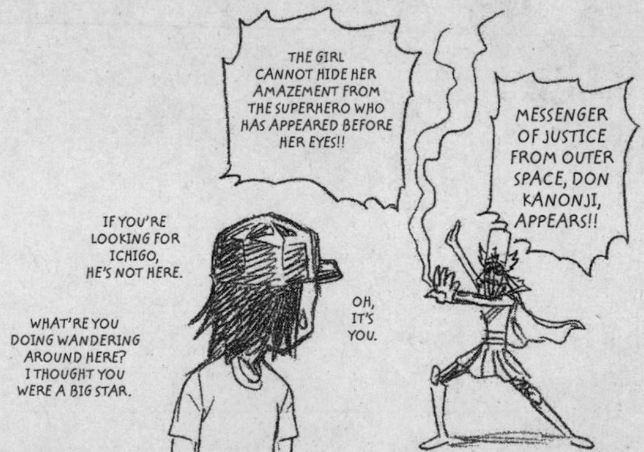
MESSENGER OF JUSTICE FROM OUTER SPACE, DON KANONJI, APPEARS!!
THE GIRL CANNOT HIDE HER AMAZEMENT FROM THE SUPERHERO WHO HAS APPEARED BEFORE HER EYES!!
OH, IT'S YOU.
IF YOU'RE LOOKING FOR ICHIGO, HE'S NOT HERE.
WHAT'RE YOU DOING WANDERING AROUND HERE? I THOUGHT YOU WERE A BIG STAR.

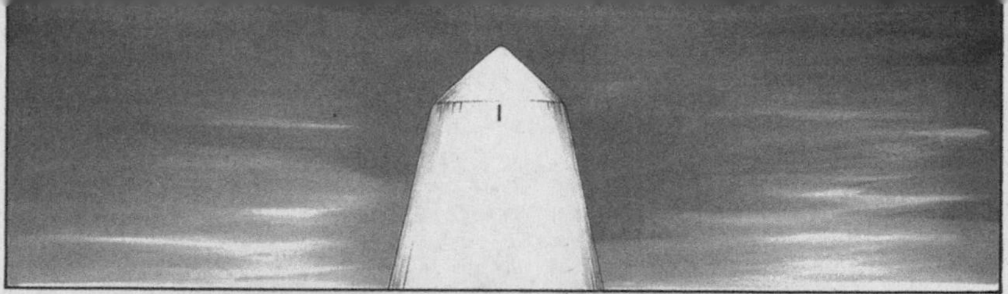

85.INTRUDERZ 2 (Breakthrough the roof mix)

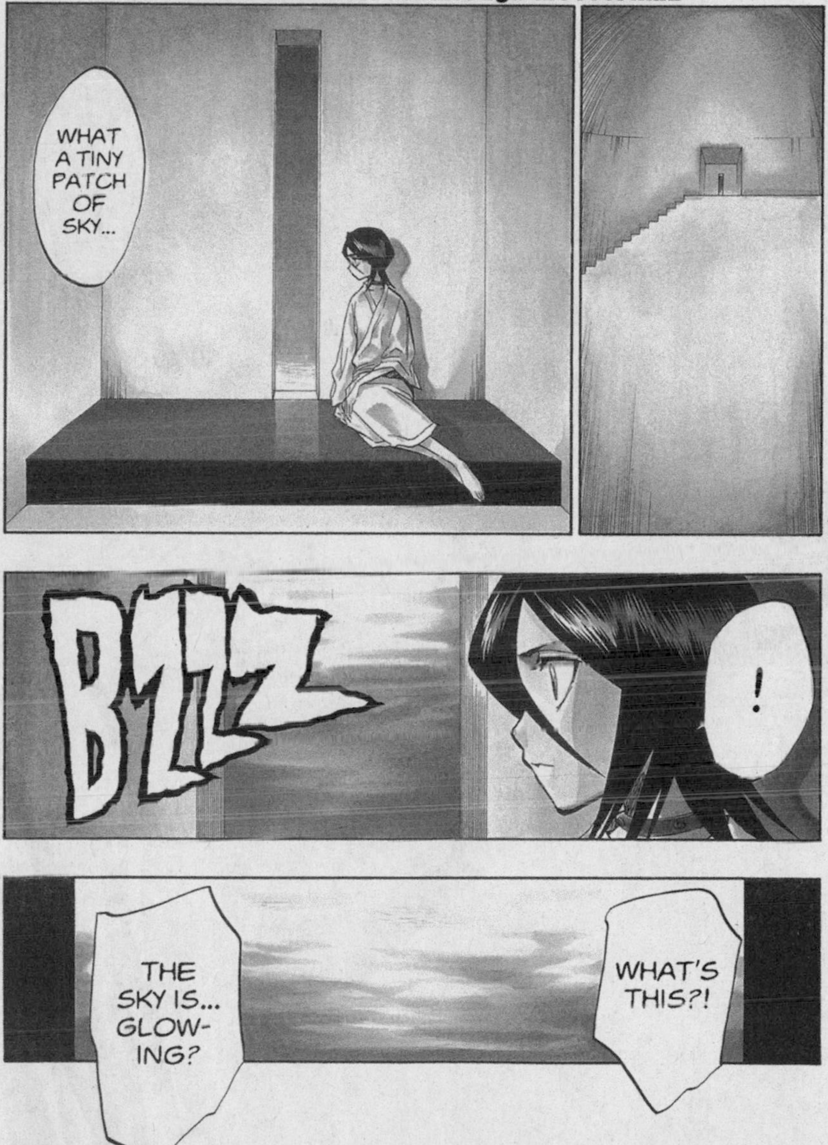
WHAT A TINY PATCH OF SKY...
!
BZZZ
WHAT'S THIS?!
THE SKY IS... GLOWING?

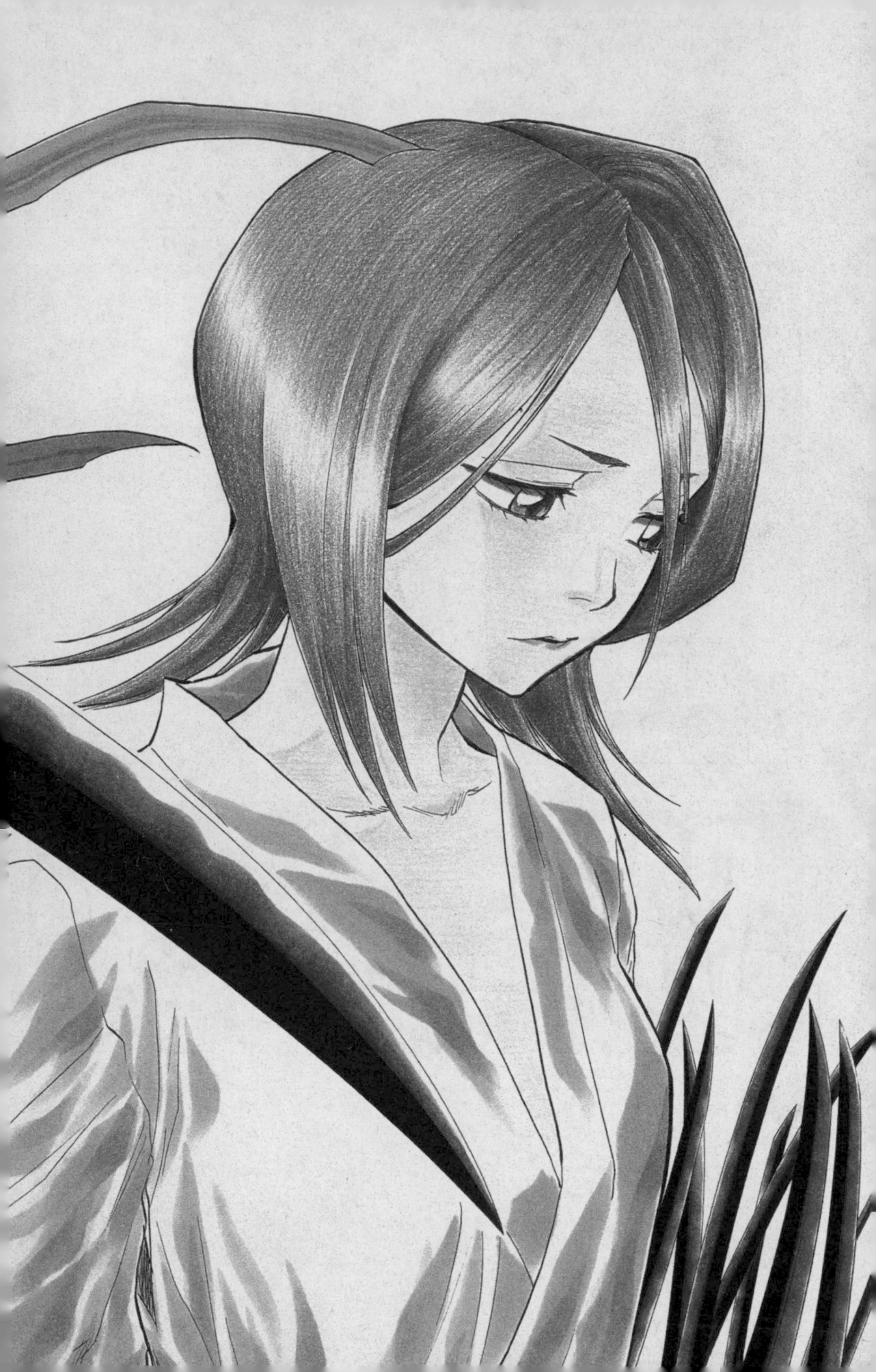

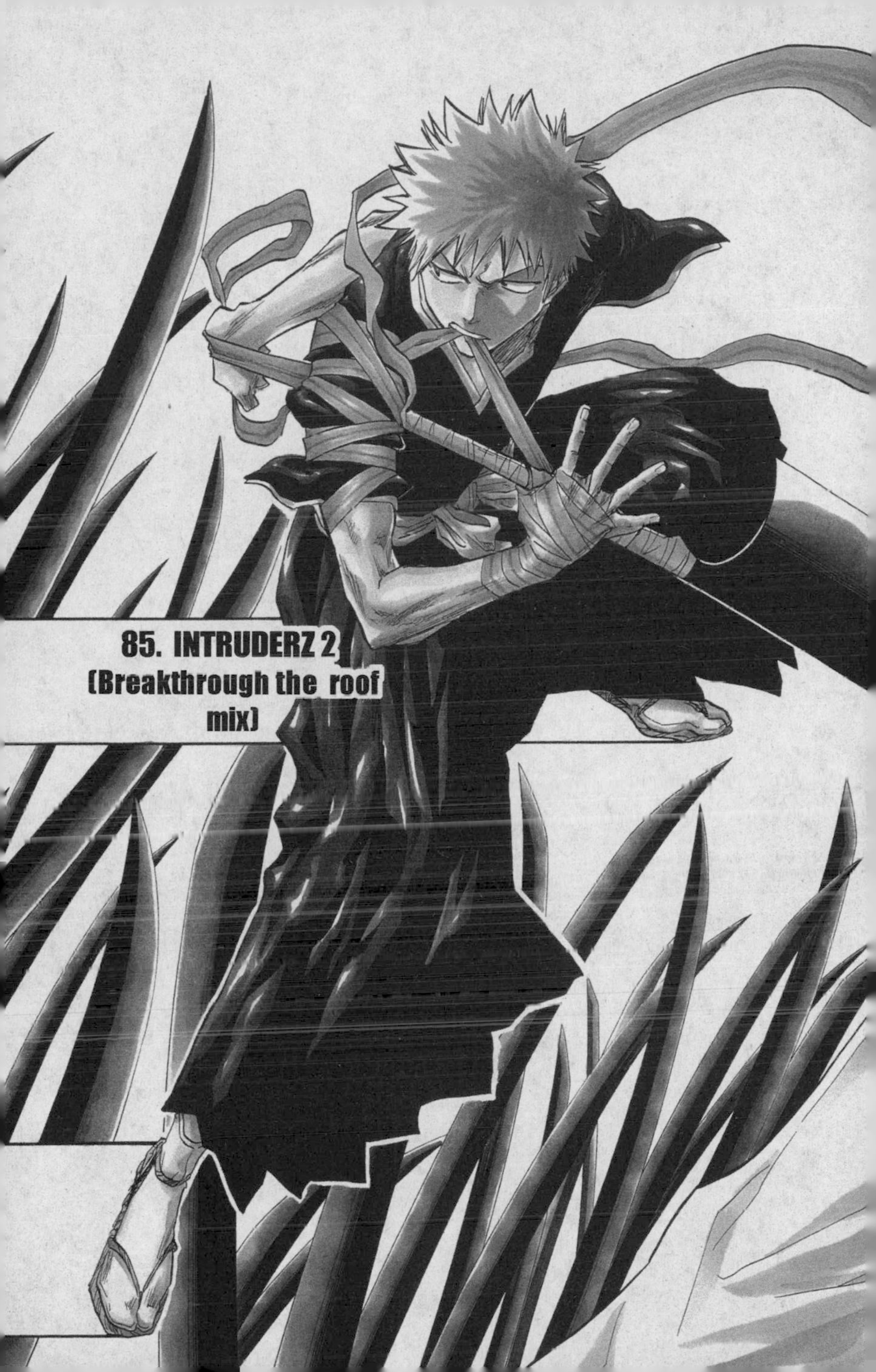
85. INTRUDERZ 2
(Breakthrough the roof mix)

BLEACH
ブリーチ

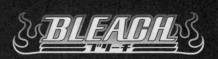

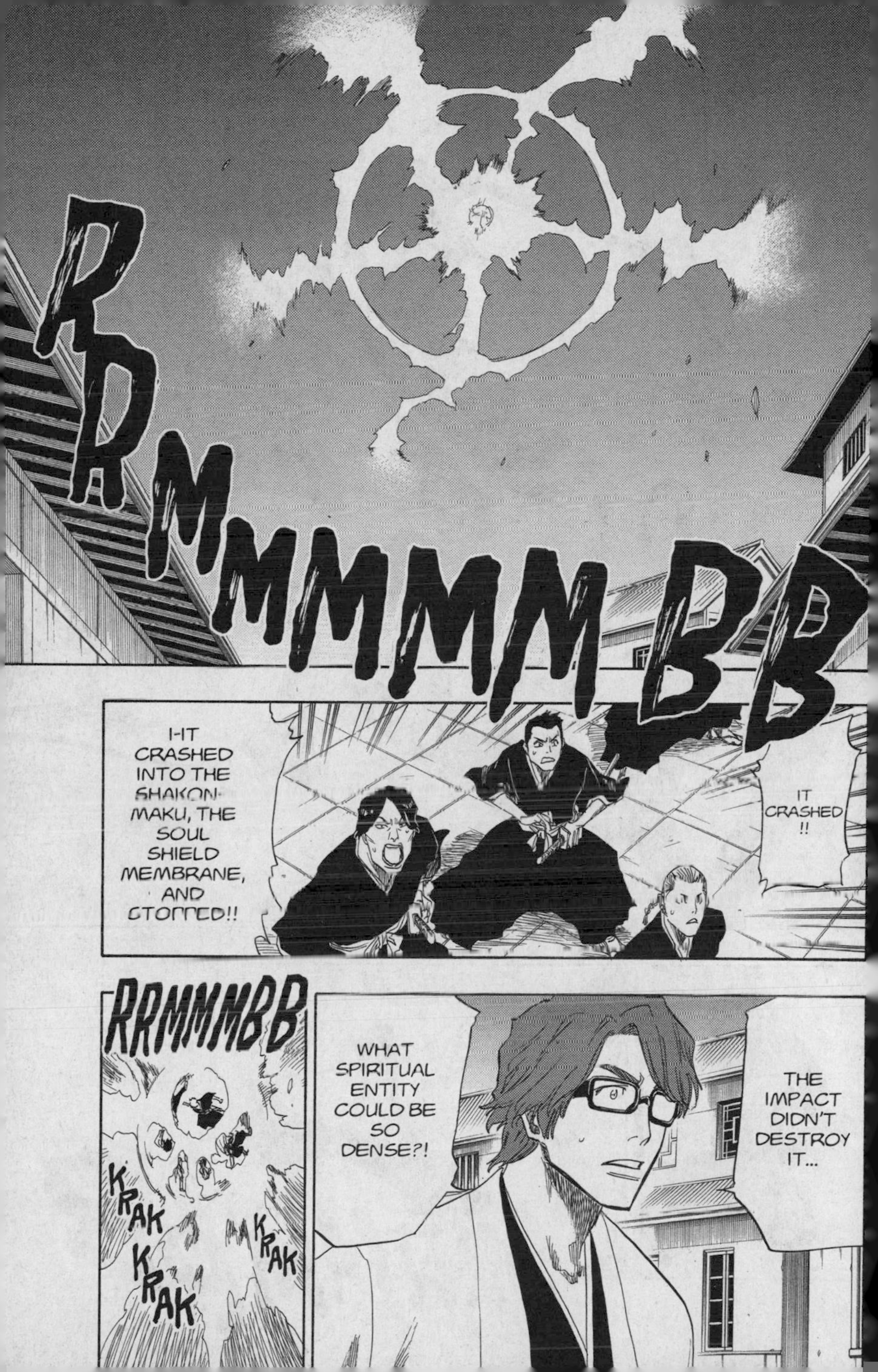
RRMMMMMMBB
IT CRASHED!!
I-IT CRASHED INTO THE SHAKONMAKU, THE SOUL SHIELD MEMBRANE, AND STOPPED!!
THE IMPACT DIDN'T DESTROY IT...
WHAT SPIRITUAL ENTITY COULD BE SO DENSE?!
RRMMMBB
KRAK KRAK
KRAK

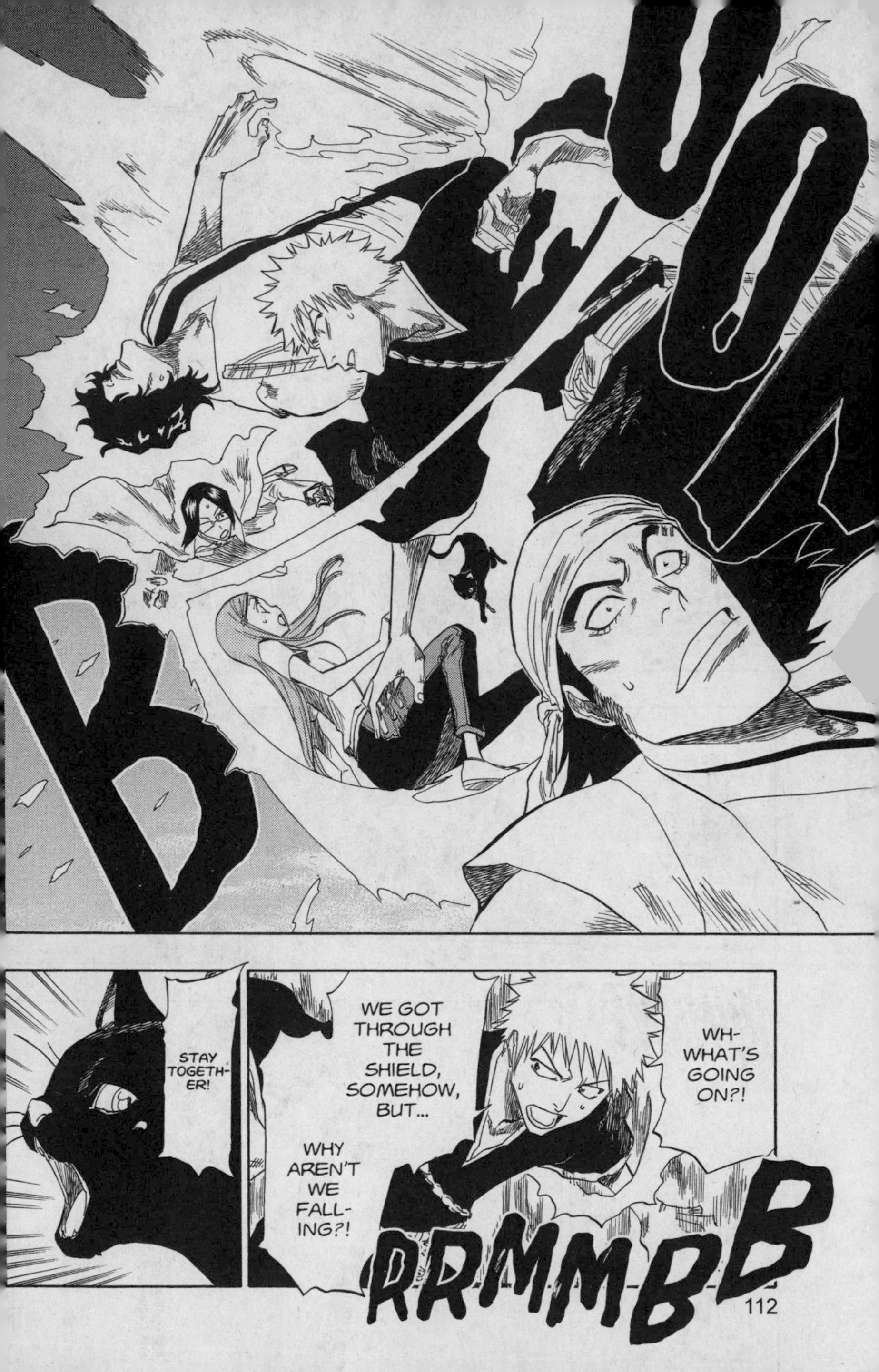
WH- WHAT'S GOING ON?!
WE GOT THROUGH THE SHIELD, SOMEHOW, BUT...
WHY AREN'T WE FALLING?!
RRMMBB
STAY TOGETHER!

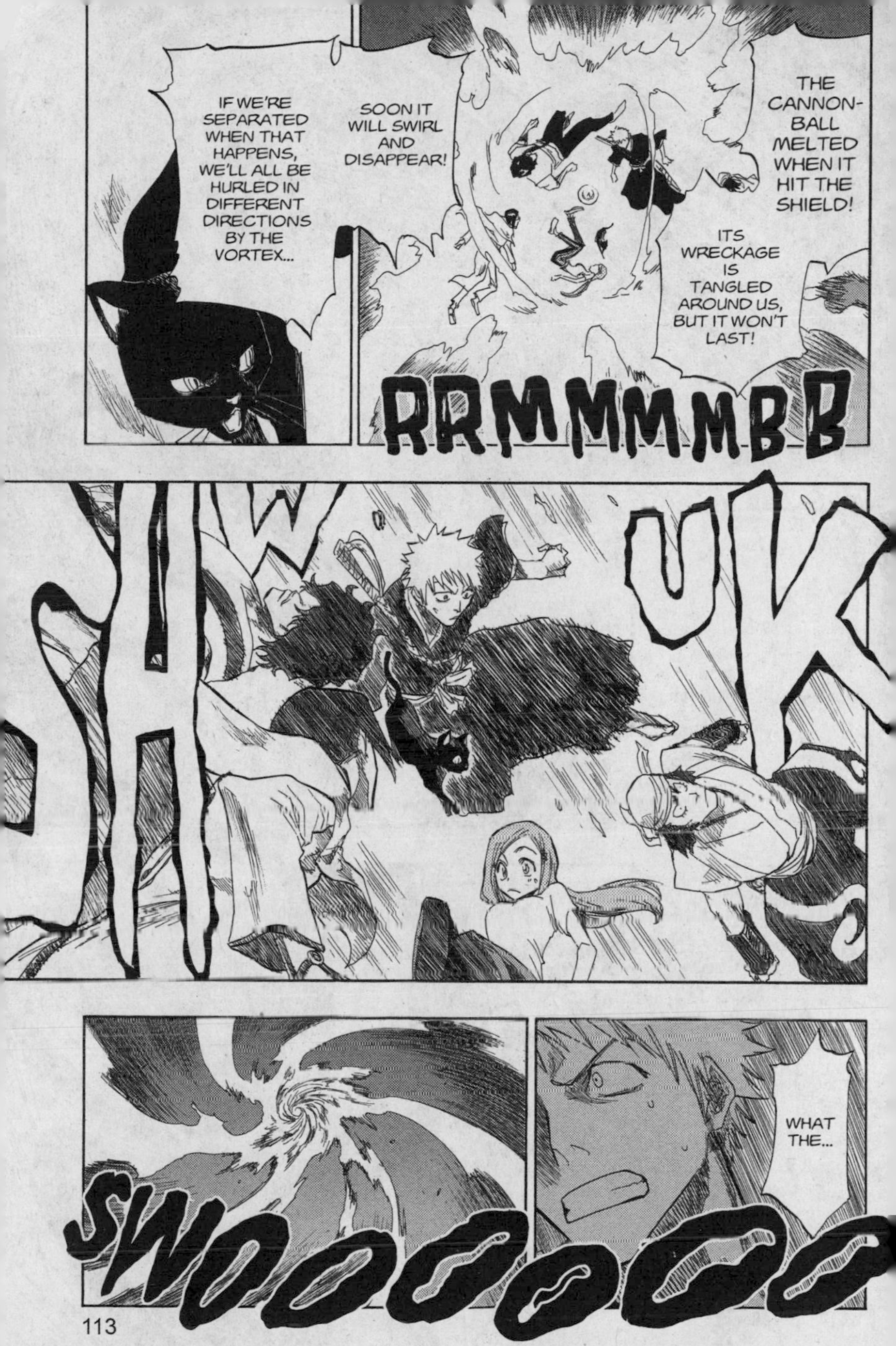
THE CANNONBALL MELTED WHEN IT HIT THE SHIELD!
ITS WRECKAGE IS TANGLED AROUND US, BUT IT WON'T LAST!
SOON IT WILL SWIRL AND DISAPPEAR!
RRMMMMBB
IF WE'RE SEPARATED WHEN THAT HAPPENS, WE'LL ALL BE HURLED IN DIFFERENT DIRECTIONS BY THE VORTEX...
SHWUK
WHAT THE...
SWOOOOOO

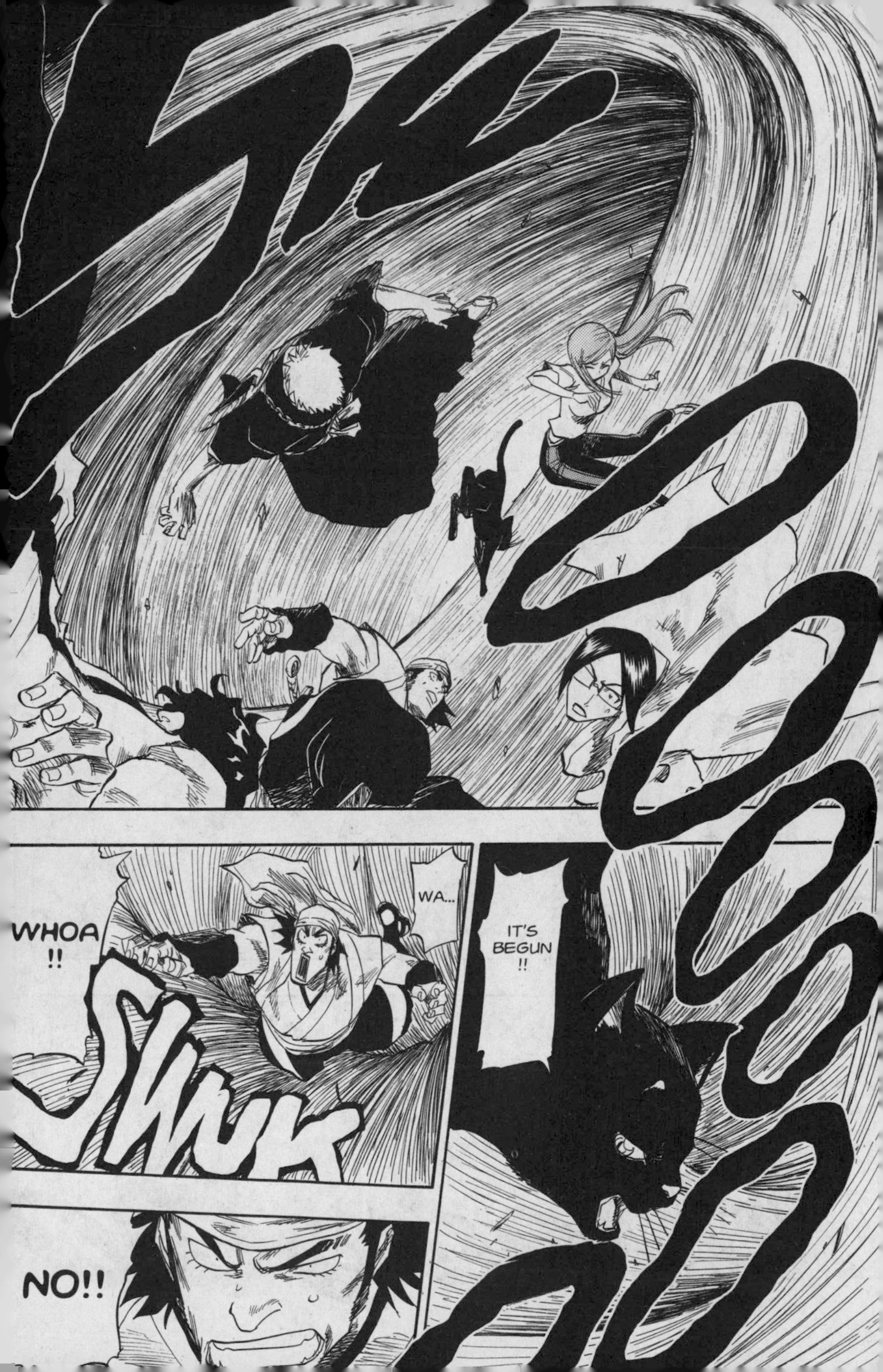
IT'S BEGUN!!
WA...
WHOA!!
NO!!

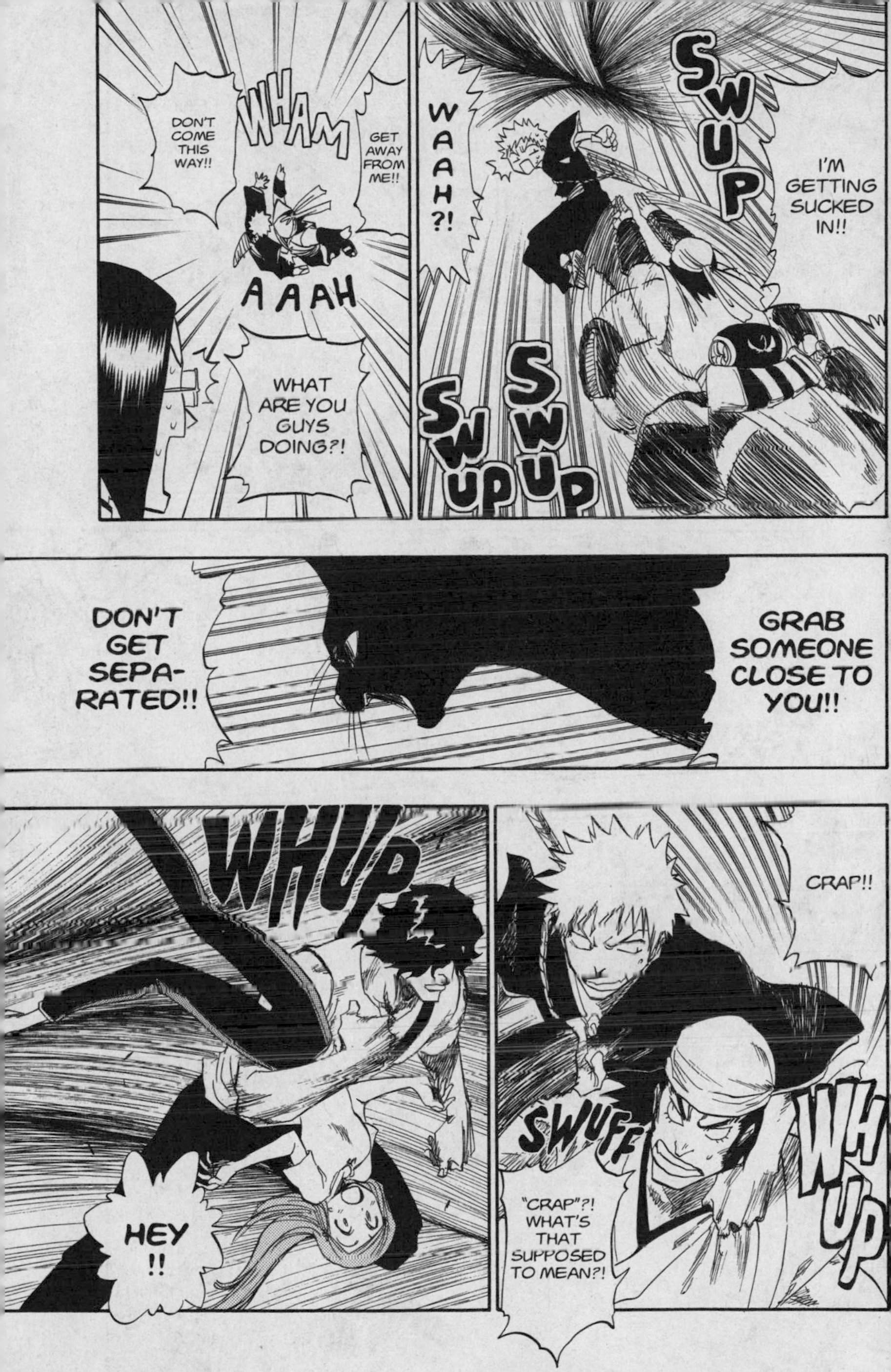
SWUP
I'M GETTING SUCKED IN!!
WAAAH?!
SWUP
SWUP
GET AWAY FROM ME!!
WHAM
DON'T COME THIS WAY!!
AAAH
WHAT ARE YOU GUYS DOING?!
GRAB SOMEONE CLOSE TO YOU!!
DON'T GET SEPA-RATED!!
CRAP!!
WHUP
SWUFF
"CRAP"?! WHAT'S THAT SUPPOSED TO MEAN?!
WHUP
HEY !!

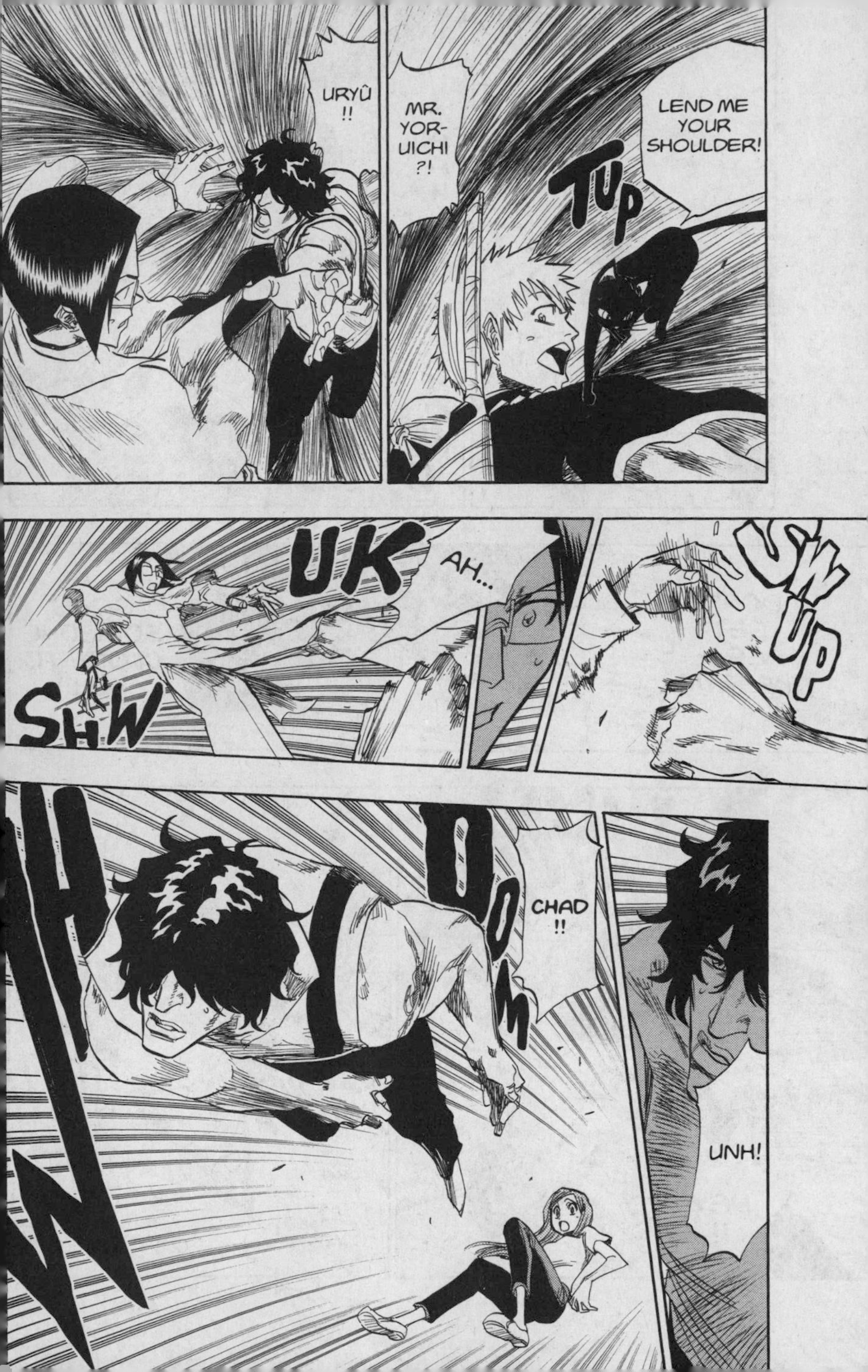

LEND ME YOUR SHOULDER!
MR. YOR-UICHI ?!
TUP
URYÛ !!
SWUP
AH...
UK
SHW
UNH!
CHAD !!
DOOM

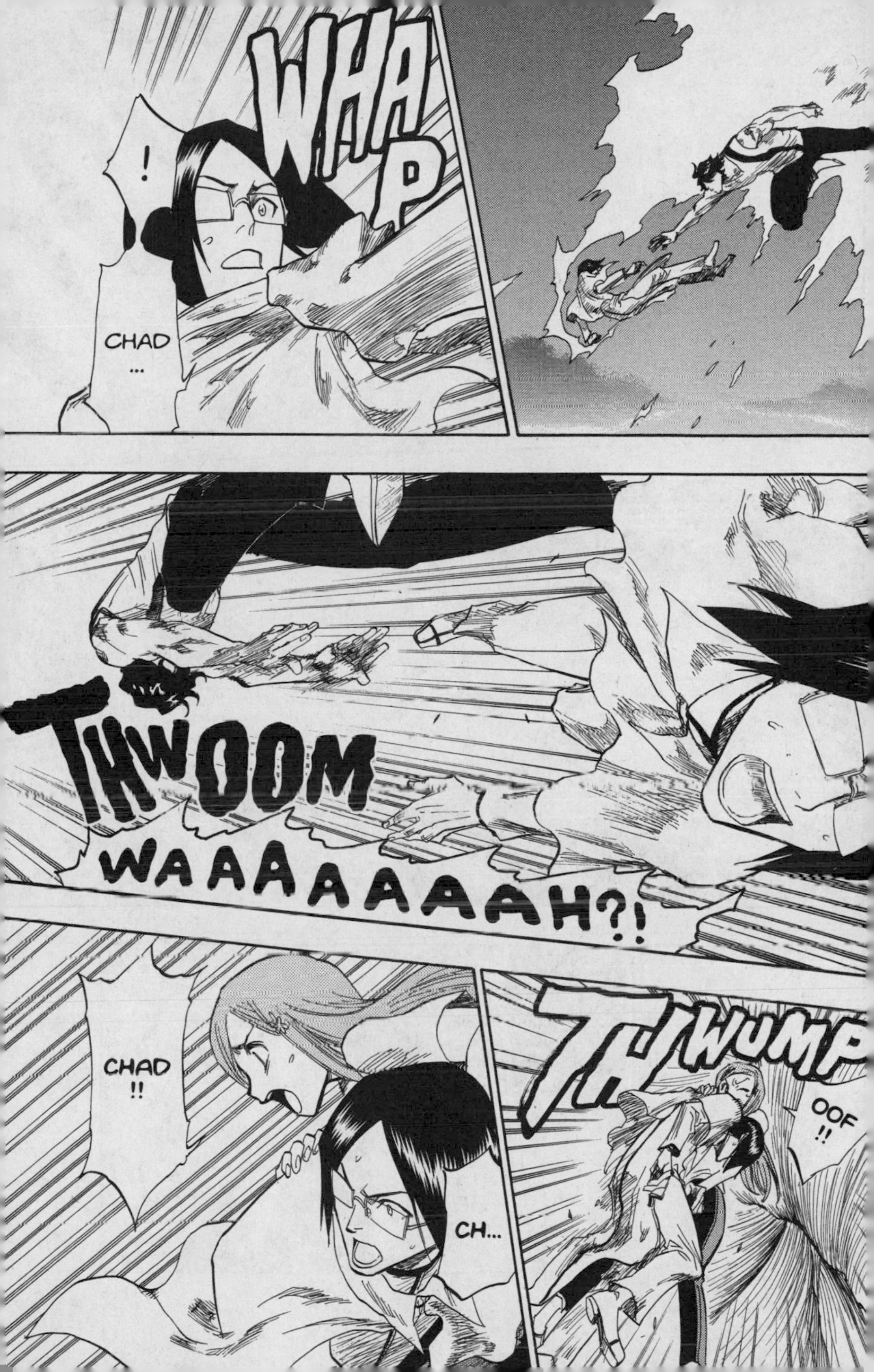
WHAP
!
CHAD ...
THWOOM
WAAAAAAAAH?!
THWUMP
OOF !!
CHAD !!
CH...

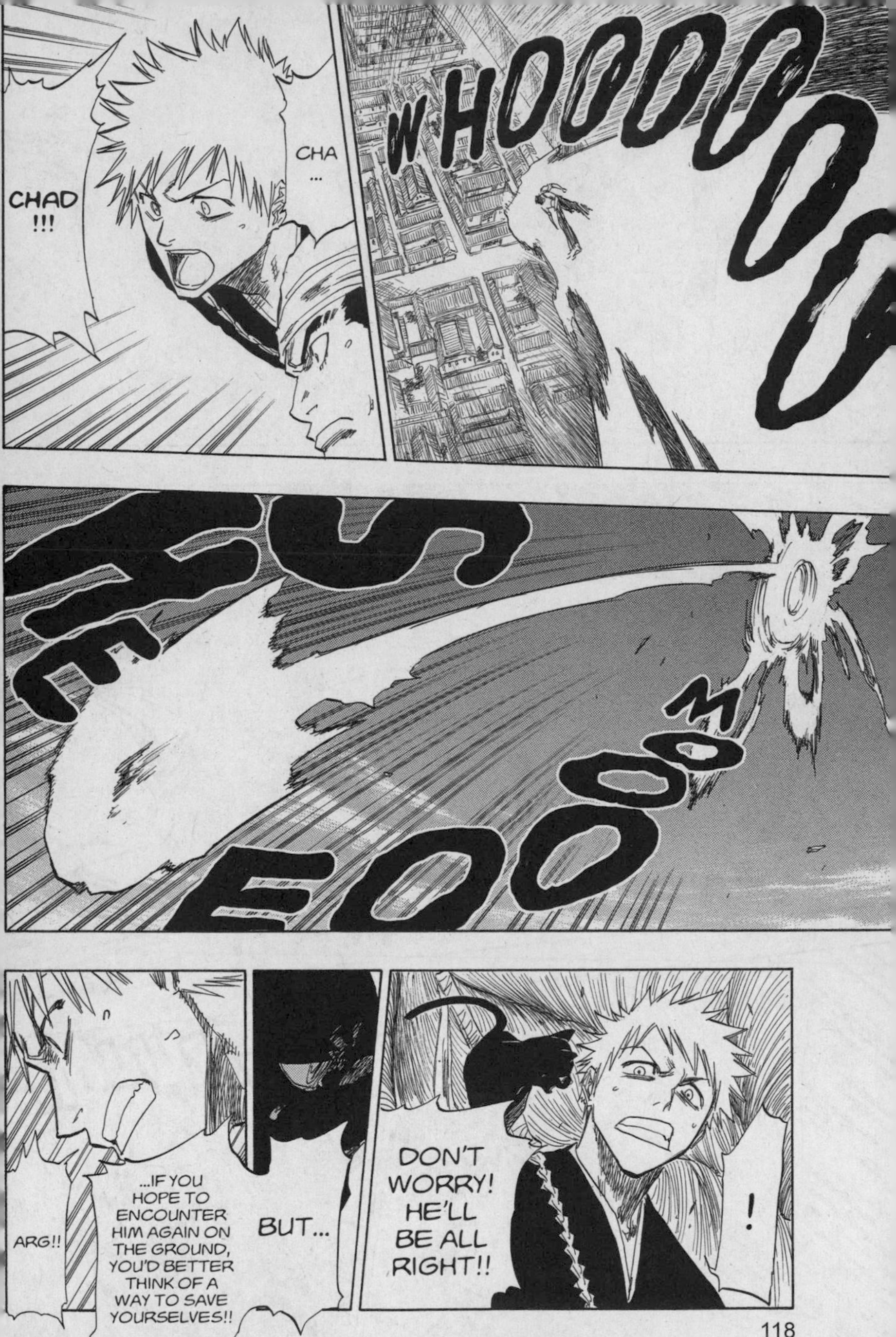
WHOOOOOOO
CHA ...
CHAD !!!
!
DON'T WORRY! HE'LL BE ALL RIGHT!!
BUT...
...IF YOU HOPE TO ENCOUNTER HIM AGAIN ON THE GROUND, YOU'D BETTER THINK OF A WAY TO SAVE YOURSELVES!!
ARG!!

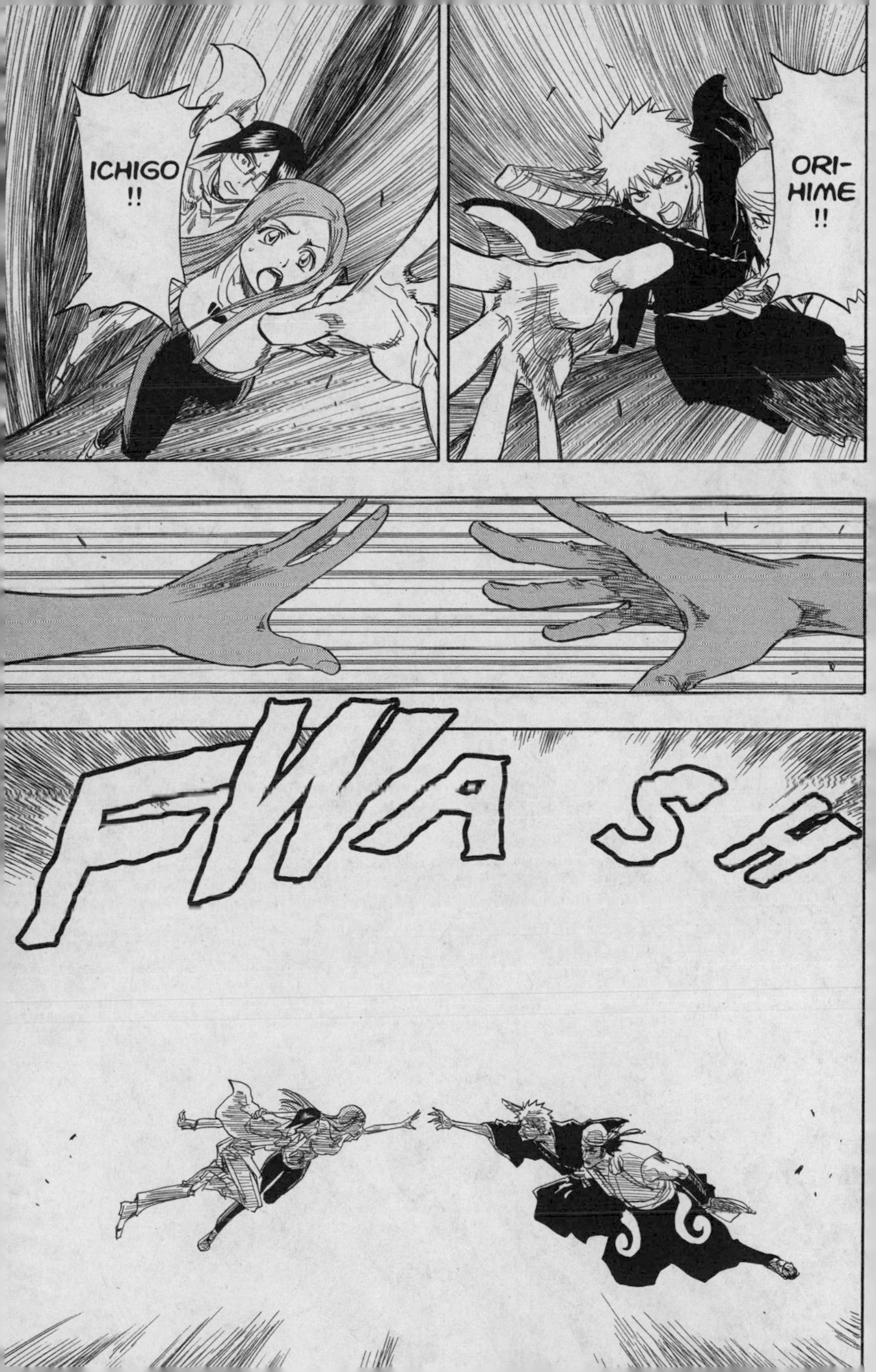
ORI-HIME !!
ICHIGO !!
FWA SH

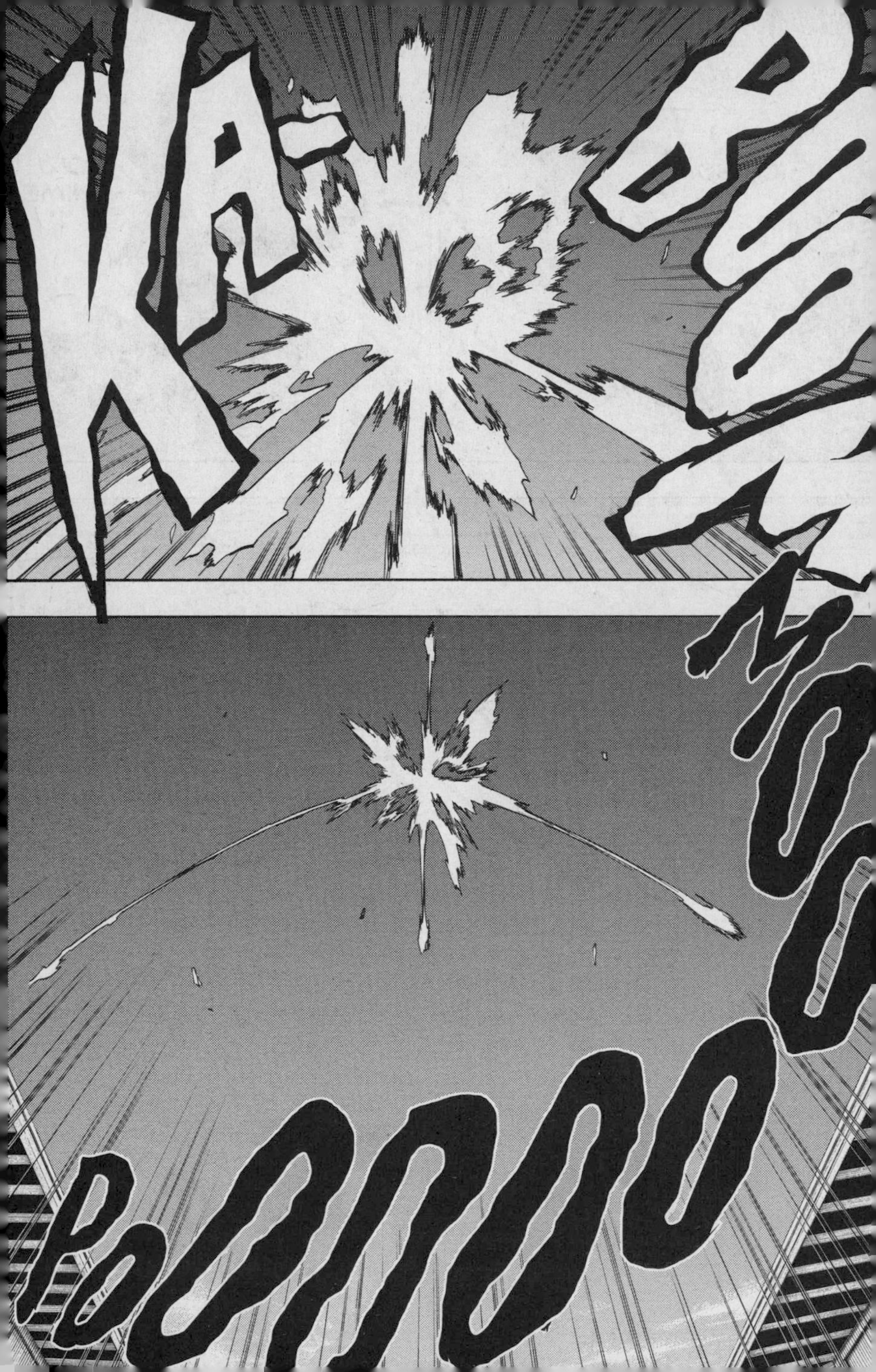

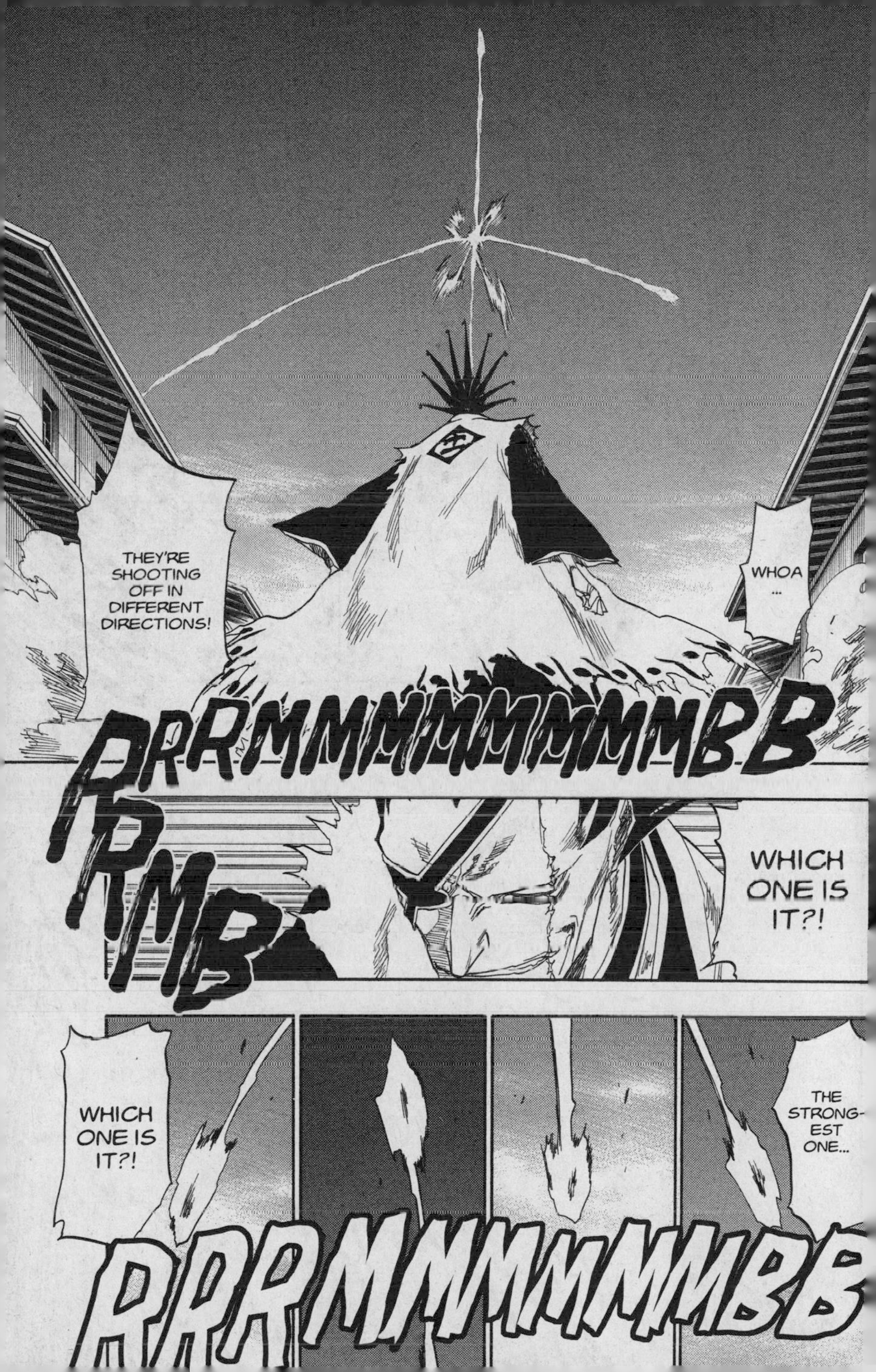
WHOA ...
THEY'RE SHOOTING OFF IN DIFFERENT DIRECTIONS!
RRRMMMMMMMMMMBB
RMB
WHICH ONE IS IT?!
THE STRONGEST ONE...
WHICH ONE IS IT?!
RRRMMMMMMMBB

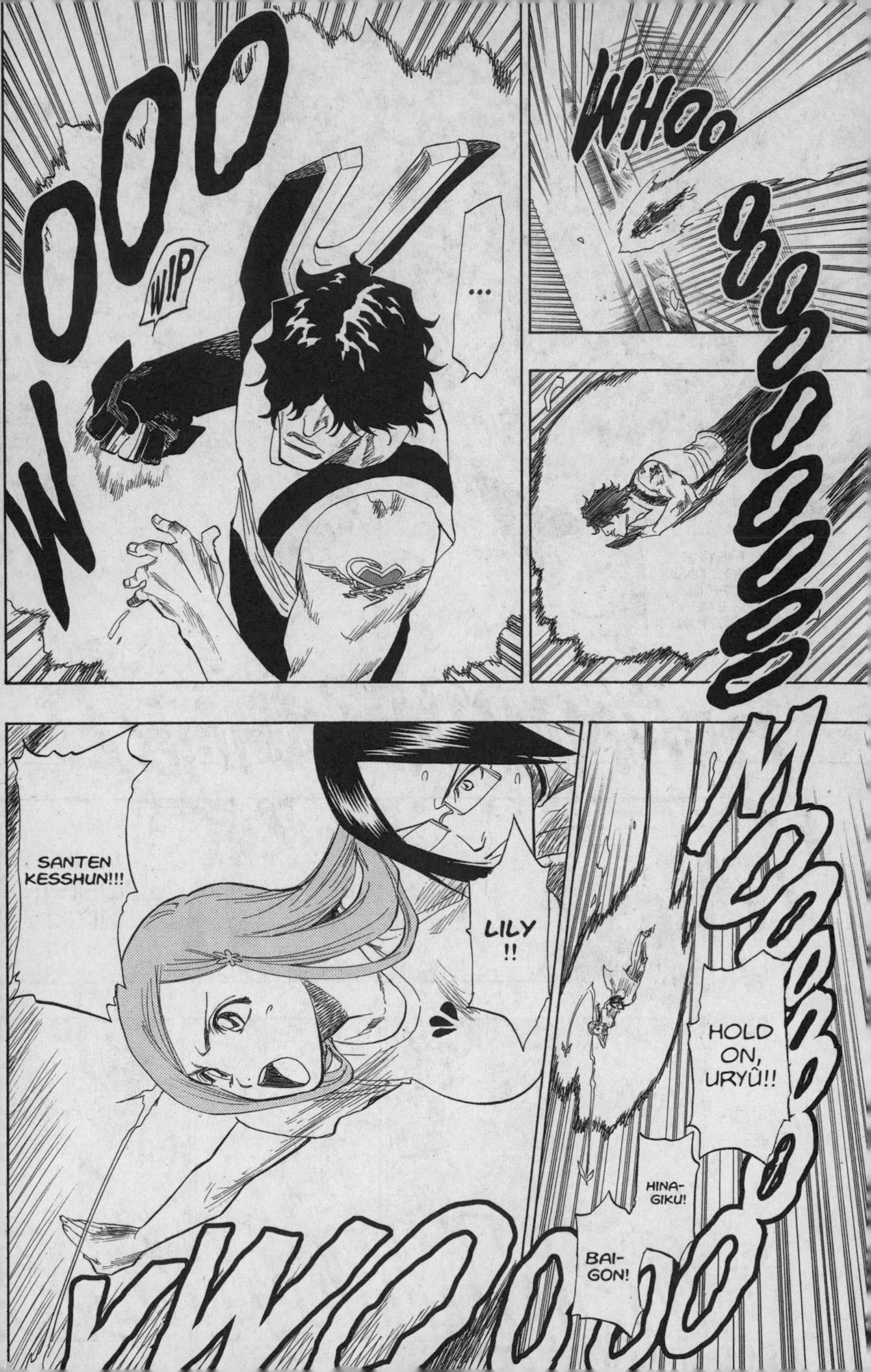
WHOOOOOOOOOOOO
WOOOO
WIP
...
MOOOOOOOOO
HOLD ON, URYÛ!!
HINA-GIKU!
BAI-GON!
LILY !!
SANTEN KESSHUN!!!
WHOOOOOO

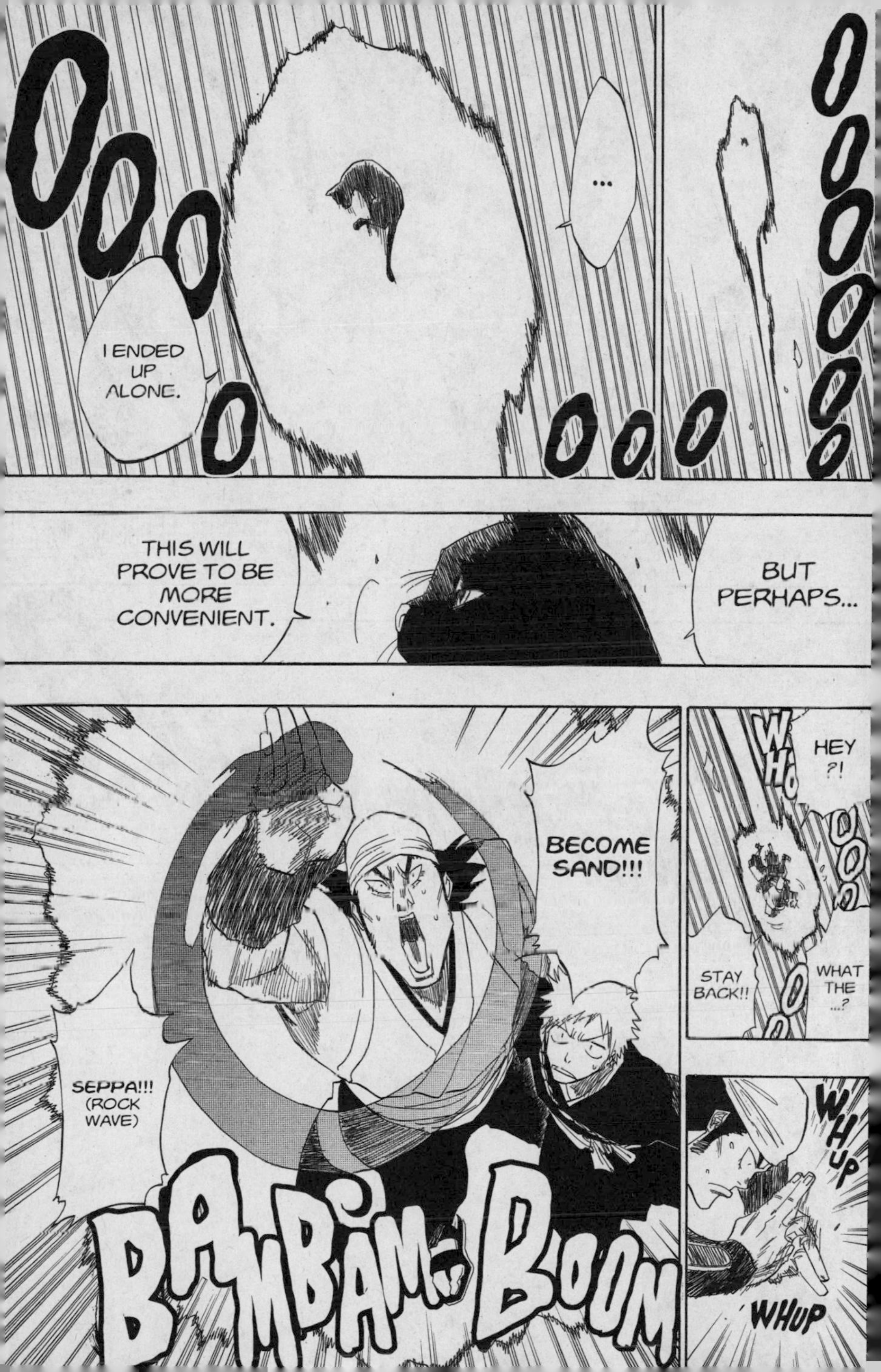
OOOOOOOOOO
...
I ENDED UP ALONE.
OOOOOOOO
BUT PERHAPS...
THIS WILL PROVE TO BE MORE CONVENIENT.
HEY ?!
WHOOOO
WHAT THE ...?
STAY BACK!!
WHUP
WHUP
BECOME SAND!!!
SEPPA!!! (ROCK WAVE)
BAMBAM-BOOM

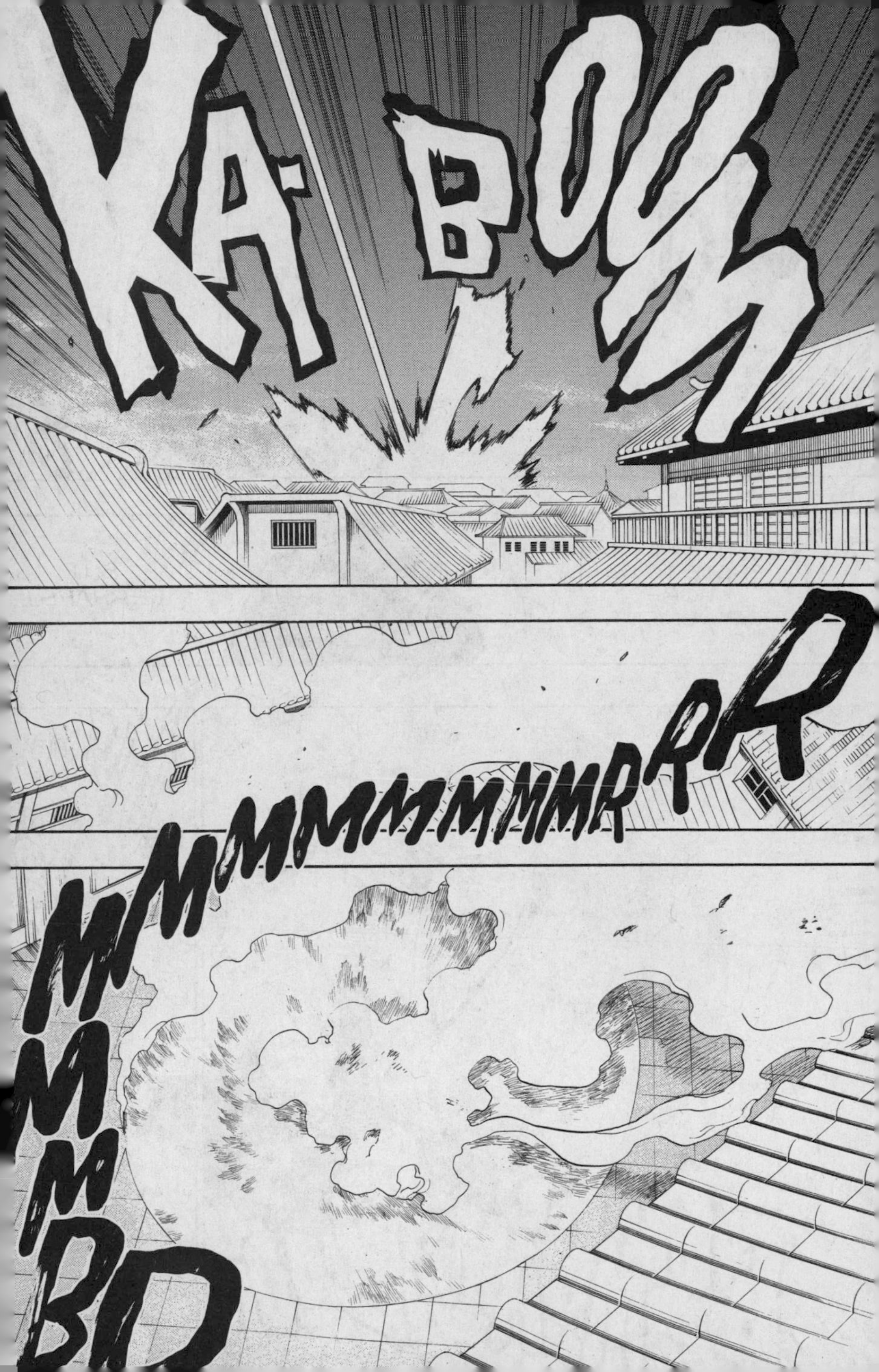
KA-BOOM

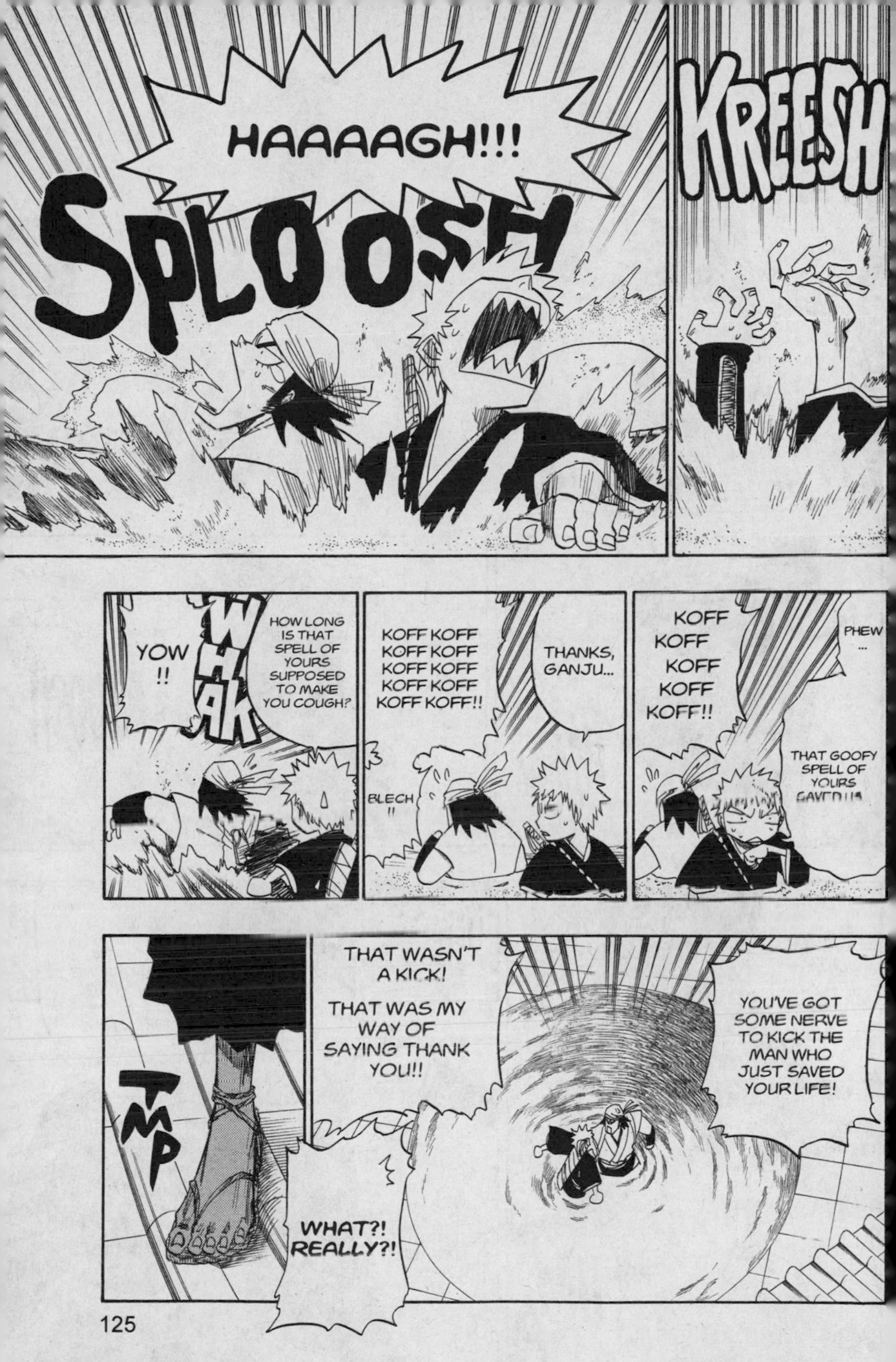
KREESH
HAAAAGH!!!
SPLOOSH
KOFF KOFF KOFF KOFF KOFF!!
PHEW ...
THAT GOOFY SPELL OF YOURS
THANKS, GANJU...
KOFF KOFF KOFF KOFF KOFF KOFF KOFF KOFF KOFF KOFF!!
BLECH !!
HOW LONG IS THAT SPELL OF YOURS SUPPOSED TO MAKE YOU COUGH?
WHAK
YOW !!
YOU'VE GOT SOME NERVE TO KICK THE MAN WHO JUST SAVED YOUR LIFE!
THAT WASN'T A KICK!
THAT WAS MY WAY OF SAYING THANK YOU!!
WHAT?! REALLY?!
TMP

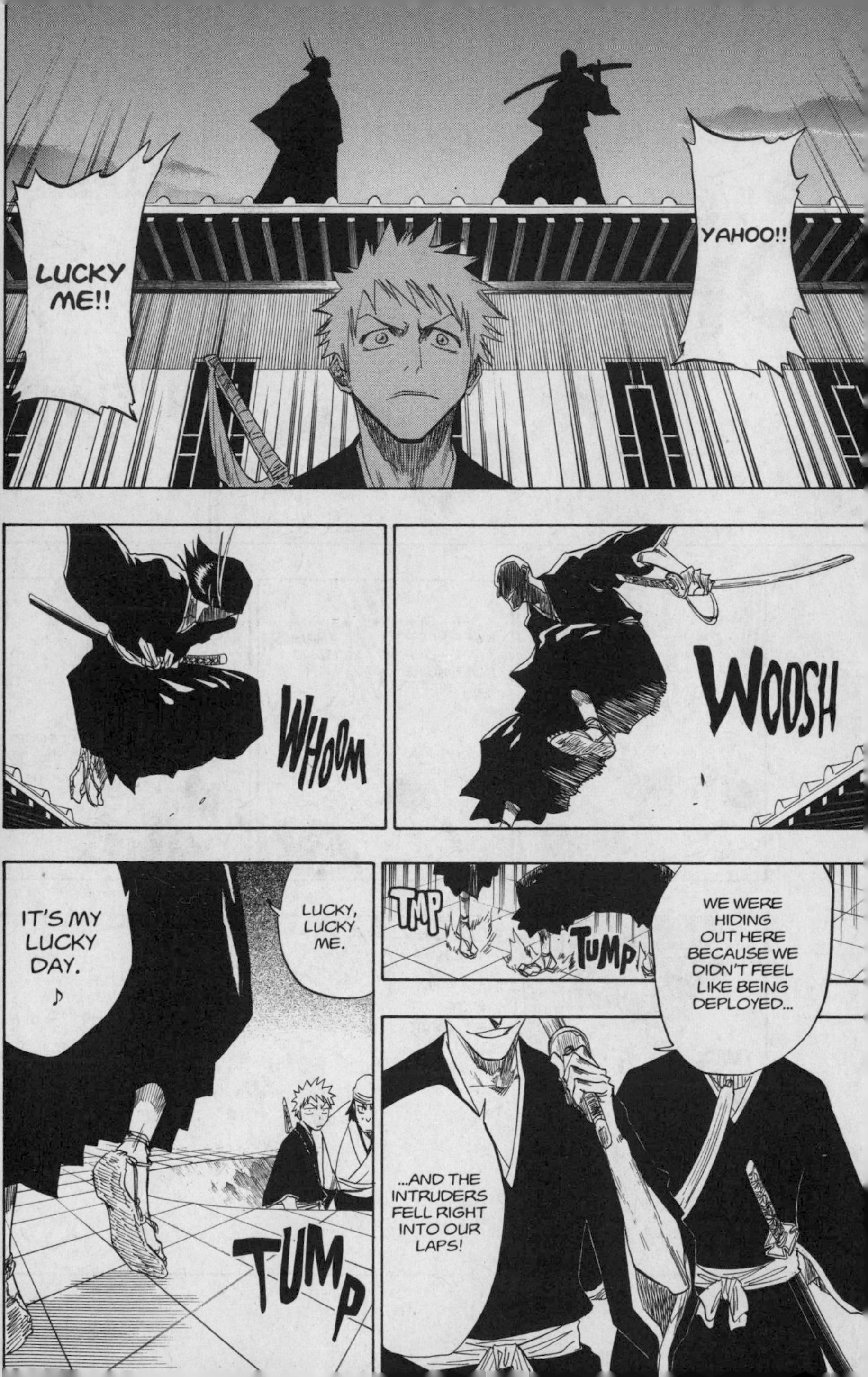
YAHOO!!
LUCKY ME!!
WOOSH
WHOOM
TMP
TUMP
WE WERE HIDING OUT HERE BECAUSE WE DIDN'T FEEL LIKE BEING DEPLOYED...
...AND THE INTRUDERS FELL RIGHT INTO OUR LAPS!
LUCKY, LUCKY ME.
IT'S MY LUCKY DAY. ♪
TUMP

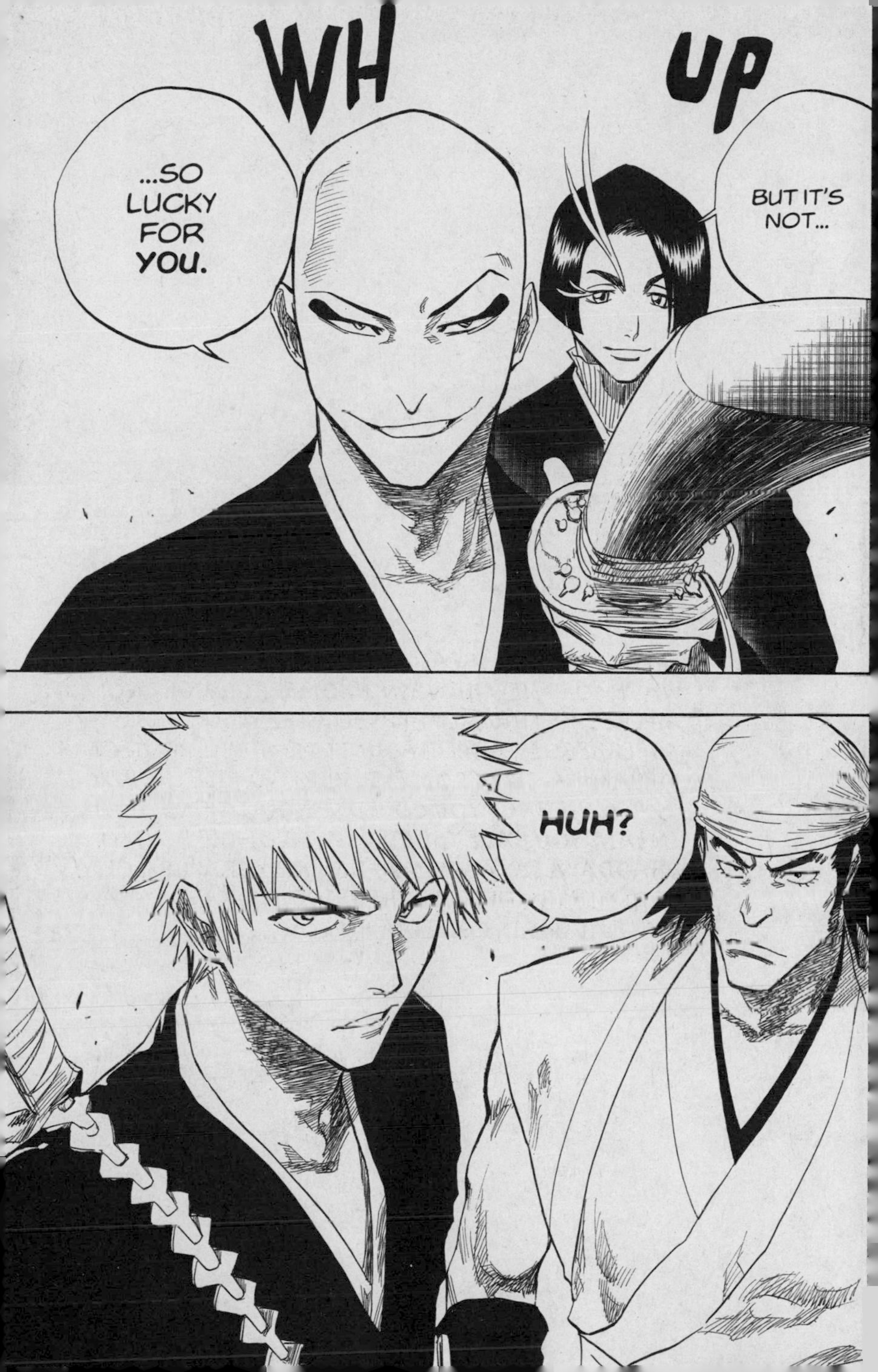
WH UP
BUT IT'S NOT...
...SO LUCKY FOR YOU.
HUH?

HEH HEH... I'D ALREADY DETECTED THE BOY'S SOUL WAVE, SO I KNEW HE WASN'T HOME! BUT RIGHT NOW I'M RECRUITING MEMBERS FOR THE KARAKURA SUPERHEROES, A SPECIAL UNIT THAT WILL PROTECT KARAKURA CITY FROM EVIL SPIRITS WHILE THE BOY IS AWAY!! SINCE YOU COULD SEE THAT THING, THAT MEANS YOU HAVE THE GIFT, SISTER OF THE BOY! SO, WHADDAYA SAY? WILL YOU DEFEND KARAKURA CITY WITH ME?! BY THE WAY, THE THING YOU SAW WAS AN EVIL SPIRIT, CALLED A HOLLOW...

WHAT? EVIL SPIRIT?

SUPER- HEROES?

SOUNDS LAME...

GEEZ, ARE YOU DONE YET?

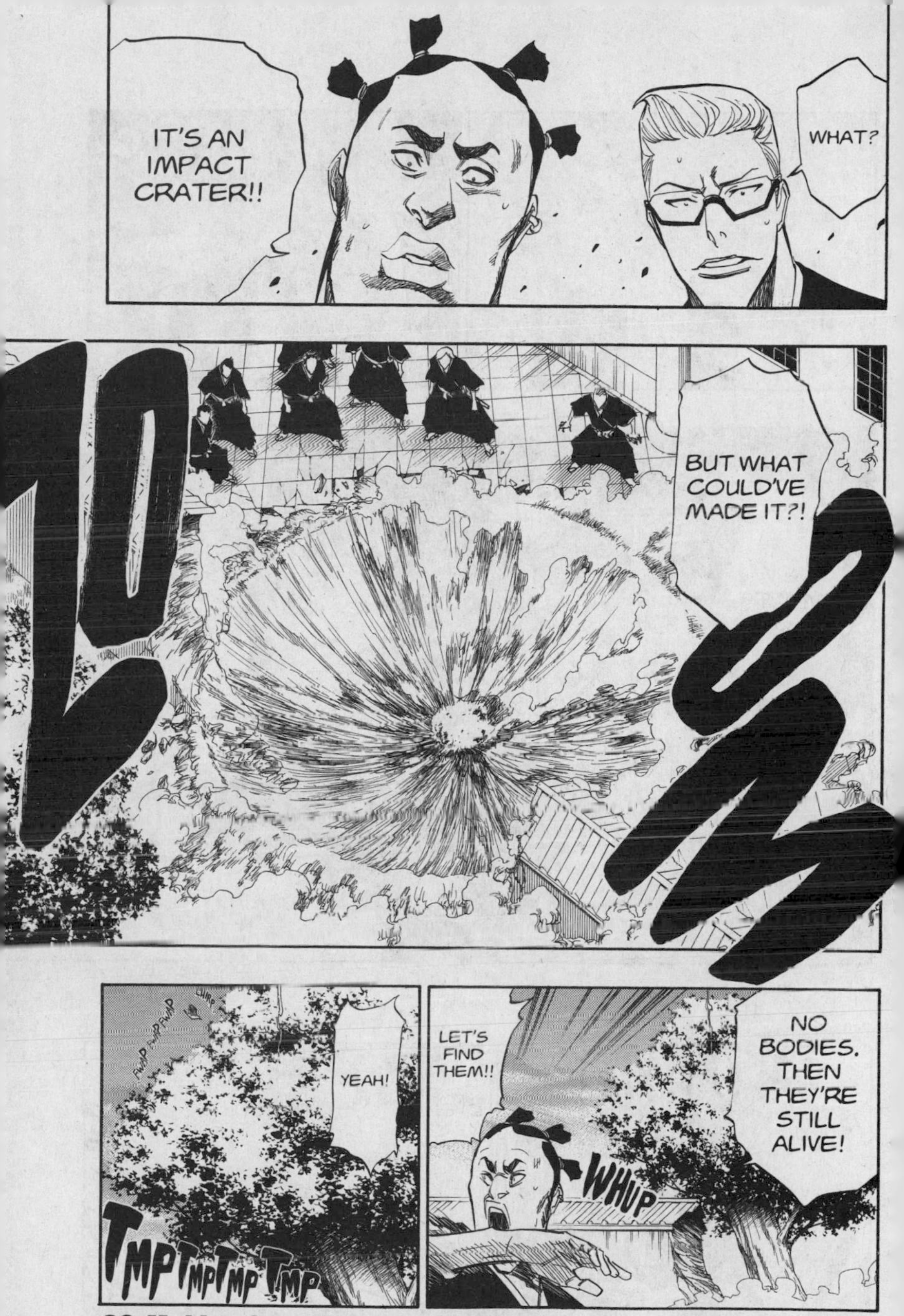
WHAT?
IT'S AN IMPACT CRATER!!
BUT WHAT COULD'VE MADE IT?!
NO BODIES. THEN THEY'RE STILL ALIVE!
LET'S FIND THEM!!
WHUP
YEAH!
TMP TMP TMP TMP

86. Making Good Relations, OK?

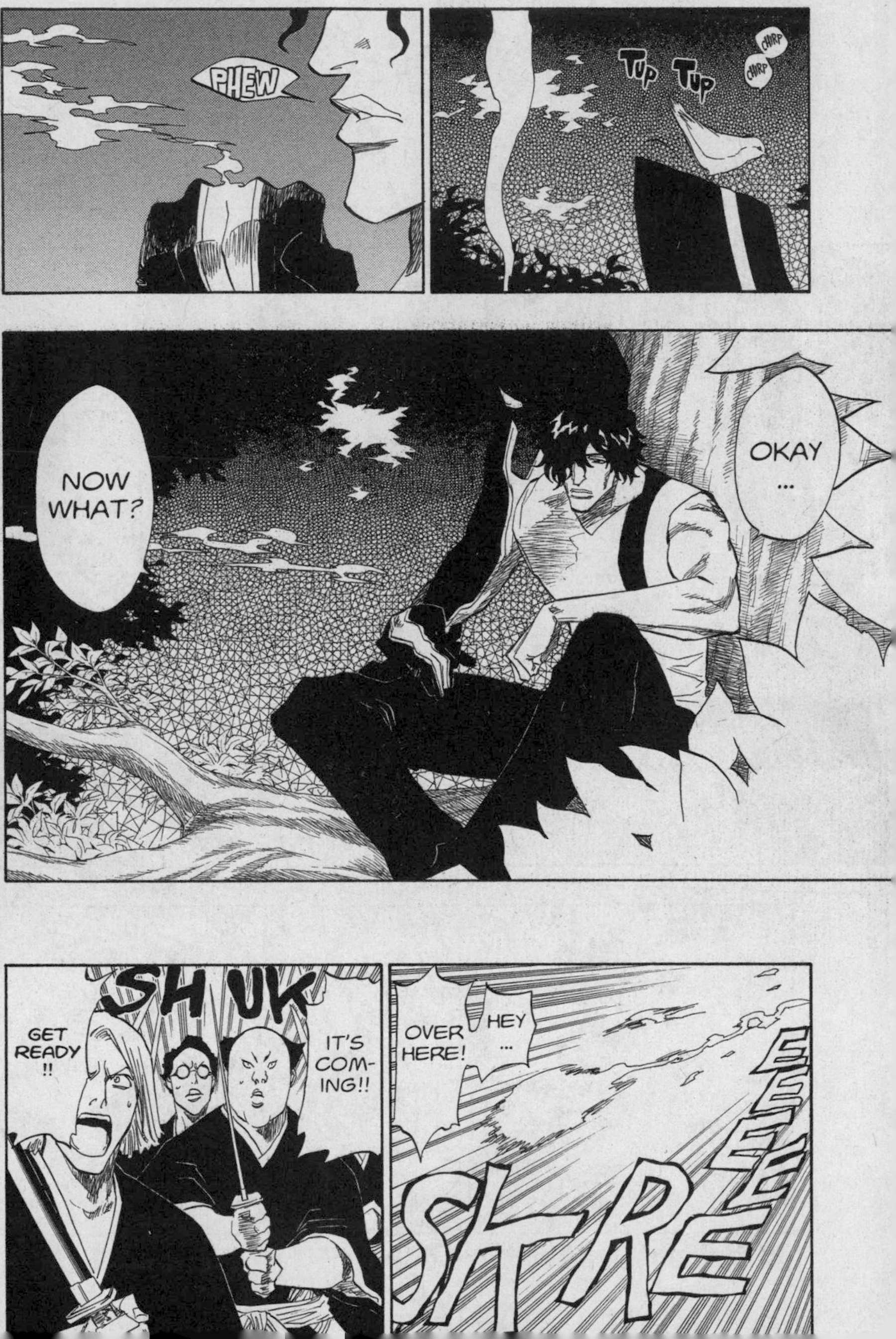
TUP TUP
CHIRP
CHIRP
PHEW
OKAY ...
NOW WHAT?
HEY ...
OVER HERE!
SHREEEEE
SHUK
IT'S COMING!!
GET READY !!

READ THIS WAY

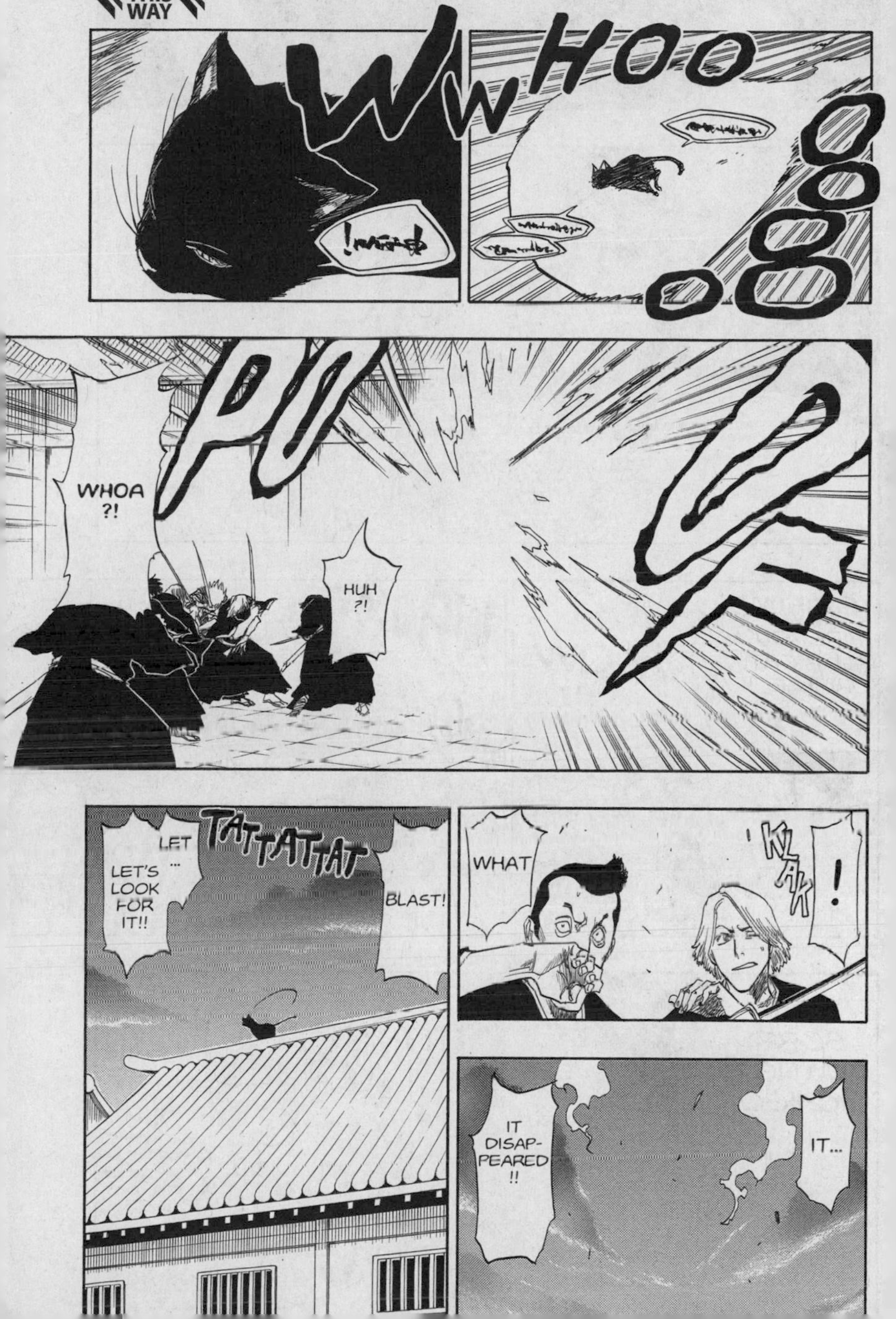
WWHOOOOOO
PO
HUH ?!
WHOA ?!
KLAK
!
WHAT
IT...
IT DISAPPEARED!!
BLAST!
TATTATTAT
LET ... LET'S LOOK FOR IT!!

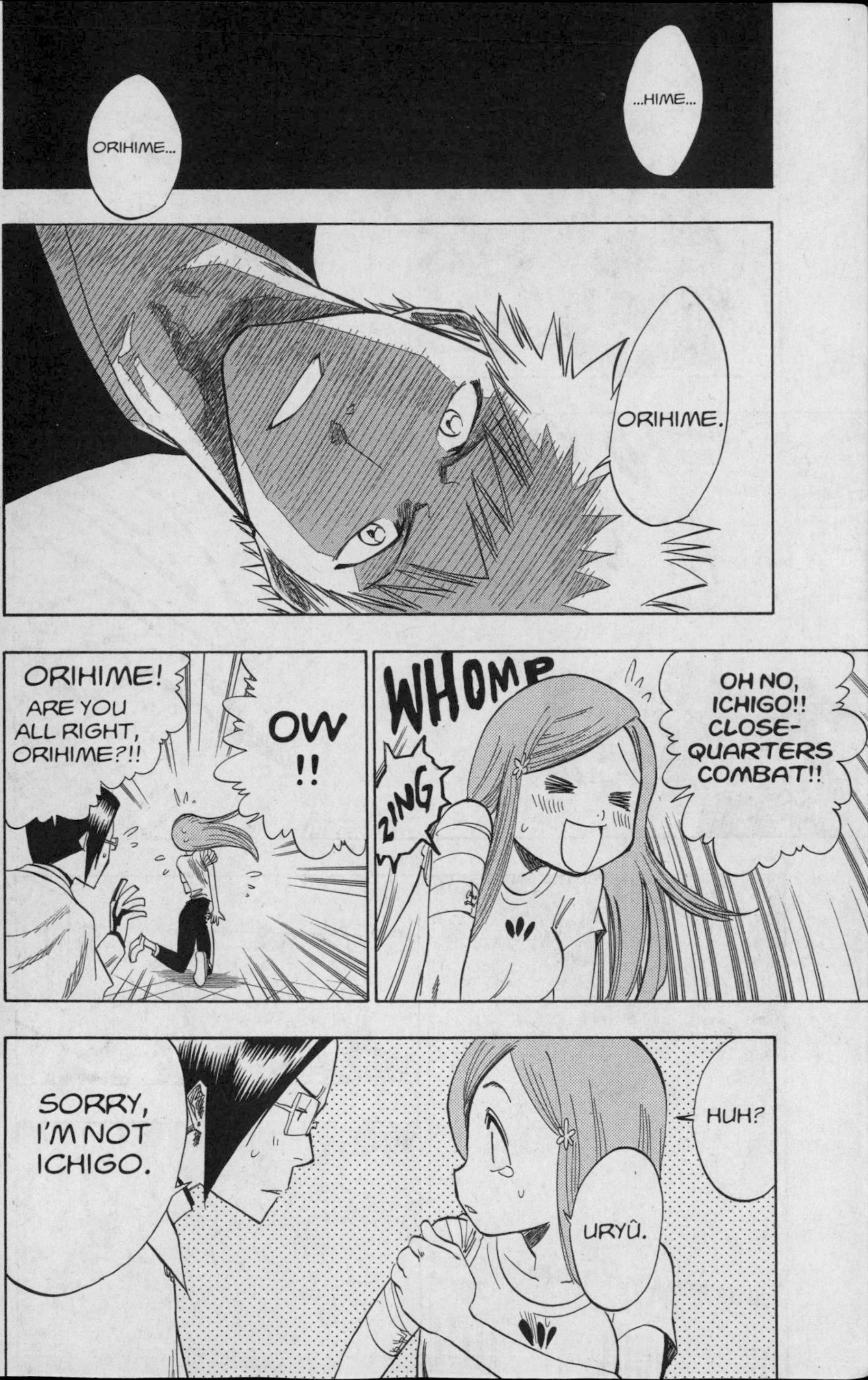
...HIME...
ORIHIME...
ORIHIME.
OH NO, ICHIGO!! CLOSE-QUARTERS COMBAT!!
WHOMP
ZING
OW !!
ORIHIME! ARE YOU ALL RIGHT, ORIHIME?!!
HUH?
URYÛ.
SORRY, I'M NOT ICHIGO.

READ THIS WAY

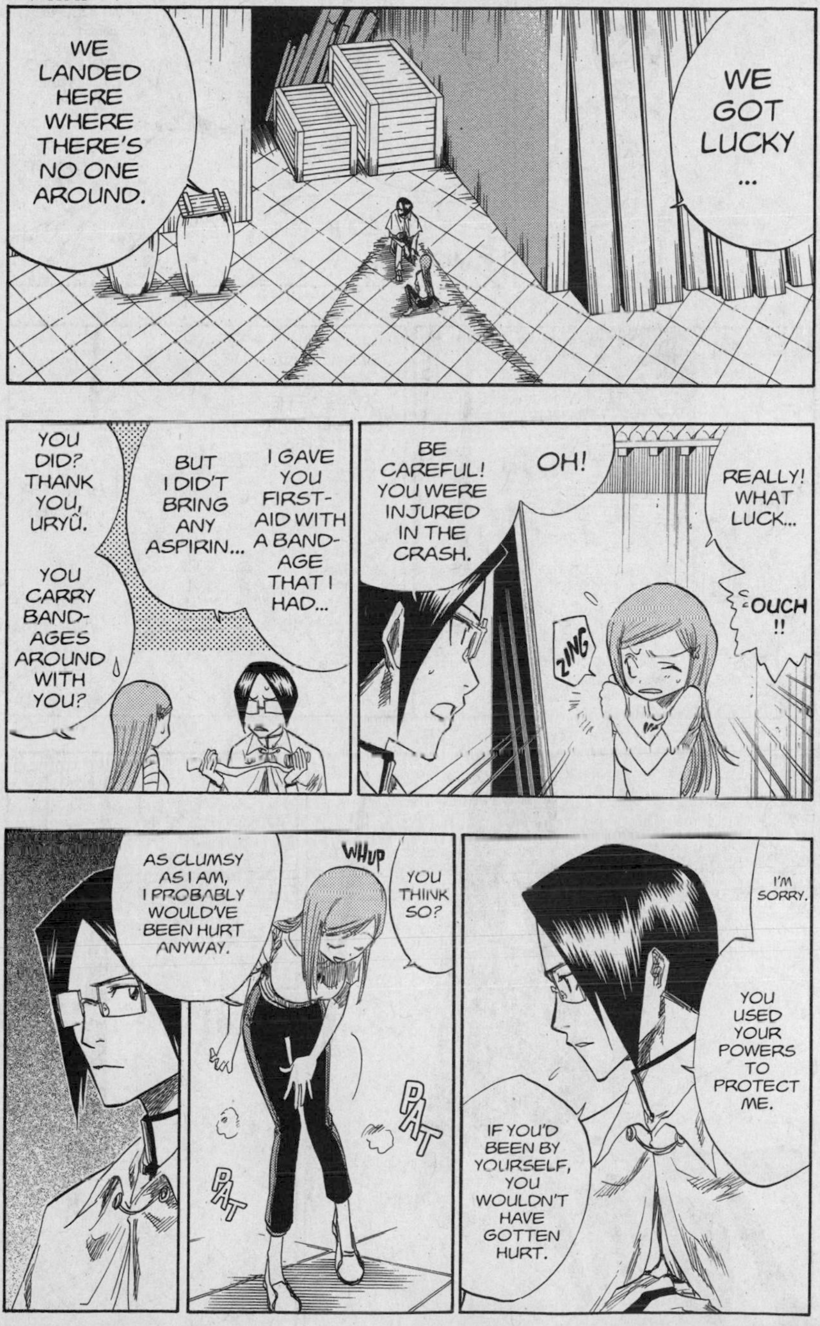

WE GOT LUCKY ...
WE LANDED HERE WHERE THERE'S NO ONE AROUND.
REALLY! WHAT LUCK...
OUCH!!
ZING
OH!
BE CAREFUL! YOU WERE INJURED IN THE CRASH.
I GAVE YOU FIRST-AID WITH A BAND-AGE THAT I HAD...
BUT I DIDN'T BRING ANY ASPIRIN...
YOU DID? THANK YOU, URYŪ.
YOU CARRY BAND-AGES AROUND WITH YOU?
I'M SORRY.
YOU USED YOUR POWERS TO PROTECT ME.
IF YOU'D BEEN BY YOURSELF, YOU WOULDN'T HAVE GOTTEN HURT.
WHUP
YOU THINK SO?
PAT
PAT
AS CLUMSY AS I AM, I PROBABLY WOULD'VE BEEN HURT ANYWAY.

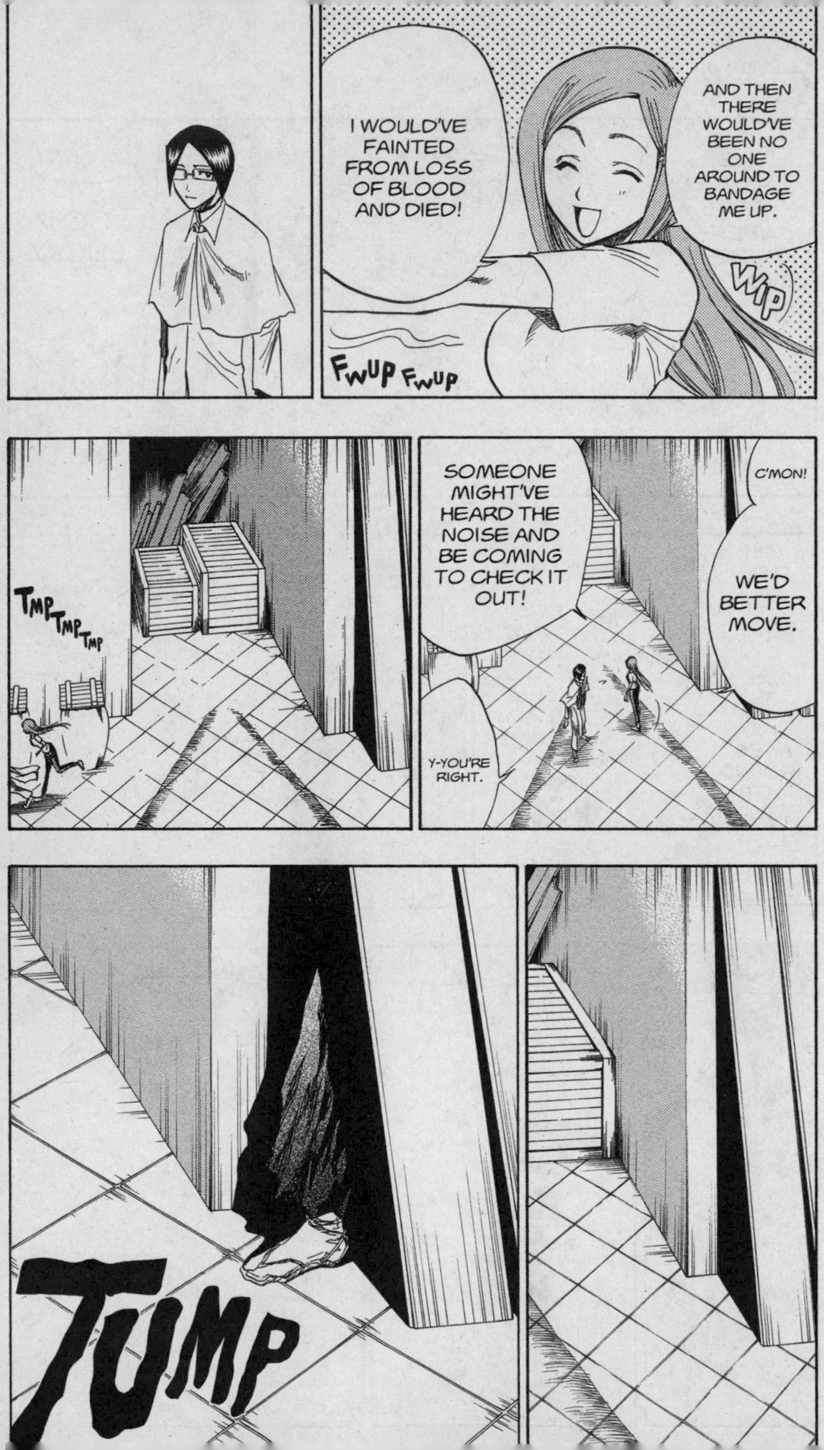
AND THEN THERE WOULD'VE BEEN NO ONE AROUND TO BANDAGE ME UP.
I WOULD'VE FAINTED FROM LOSS OF BLOOD AND DIED!
WIP
FWUP FWUP
C'MON!
WE'D BETTER MOVE.
SOMEONE MIGHT'VE HEARD THE NOISE AND BE COMING TO CHECK IT OUT!
Y-YOU'RE RIGHT.
TMP TMP TMP
TUMP

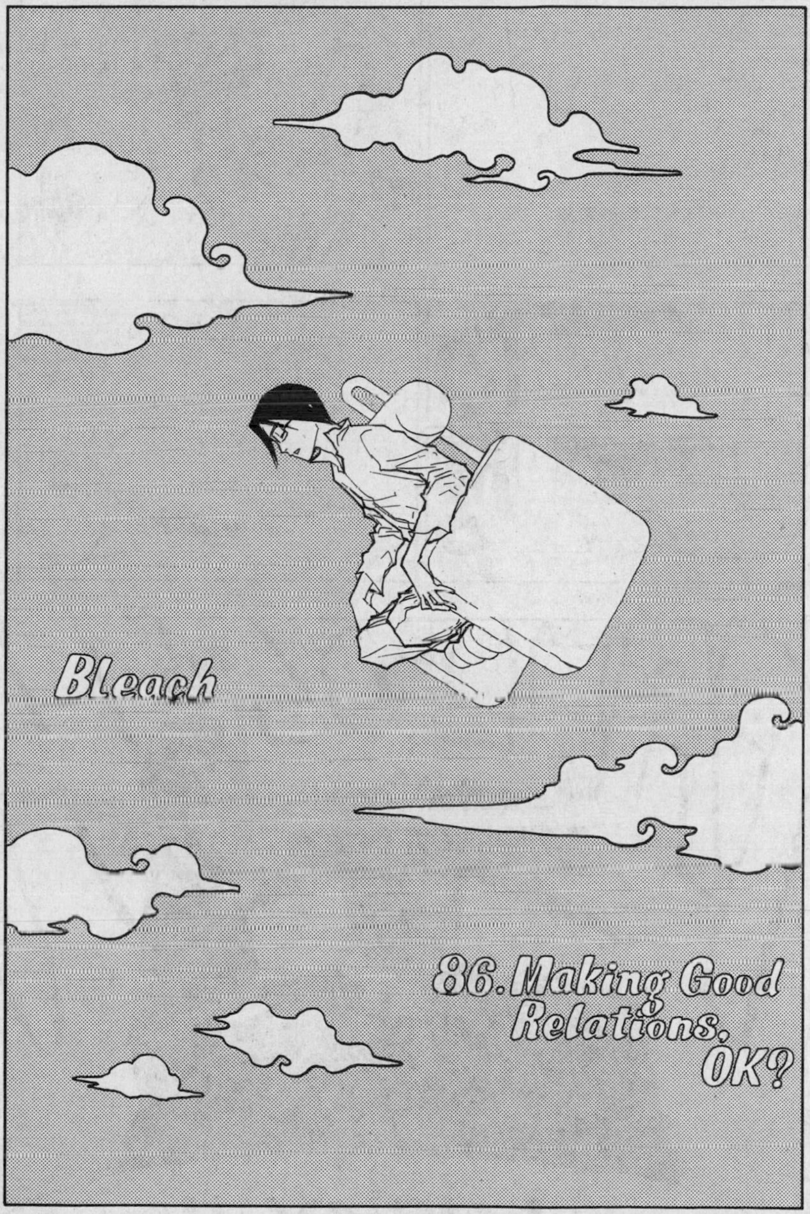
Bleach
86. Making Good Relations, OK?

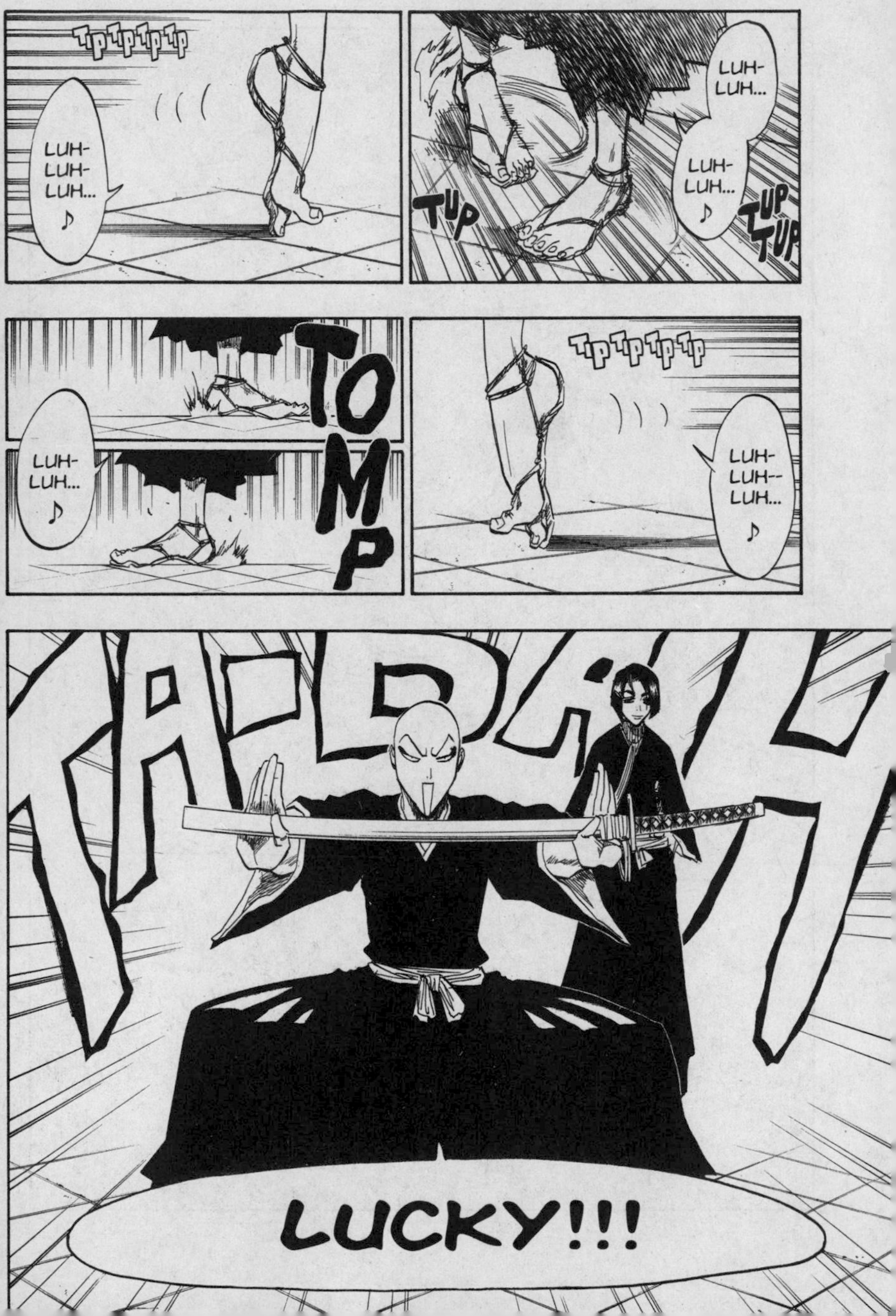
LUH-LUH...
LUH-LUH... ♪
TUP TUP
TUP
TIP TIP TIP TIP
LUH-LUH-LUH... ♪
TIP TIP TIP TIP
LUH-LUH--LUH... ♪
TOMP
LUH-LUH... ♪
LUCKY!!!

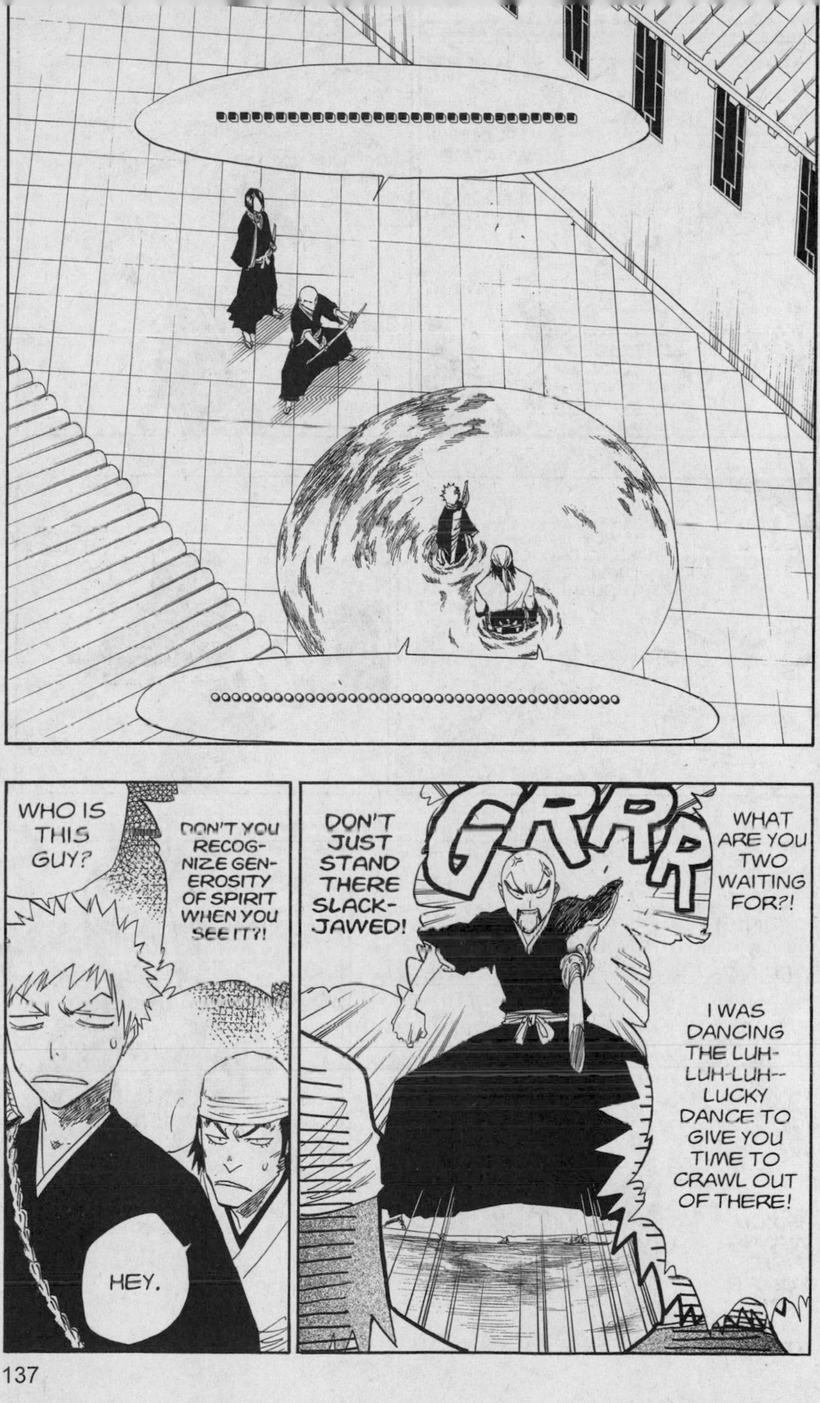

....
....
WHAT ARE YOU TWO WAITING FOR?!
GRRR
DON'T JUST STAND THERE SLACK-JAWED!
I WAS DANCING THE LUH-LUH-LUH--LUCKY DANCE TO GIVE YOU TIME TO CRAWL OUT OF THERE!
DON'T YOU RECOGNIZE GENEROSITY OF SPIRIT WHEN YOU SEE IT?!
WHO IS THIS GUY?
HEY.

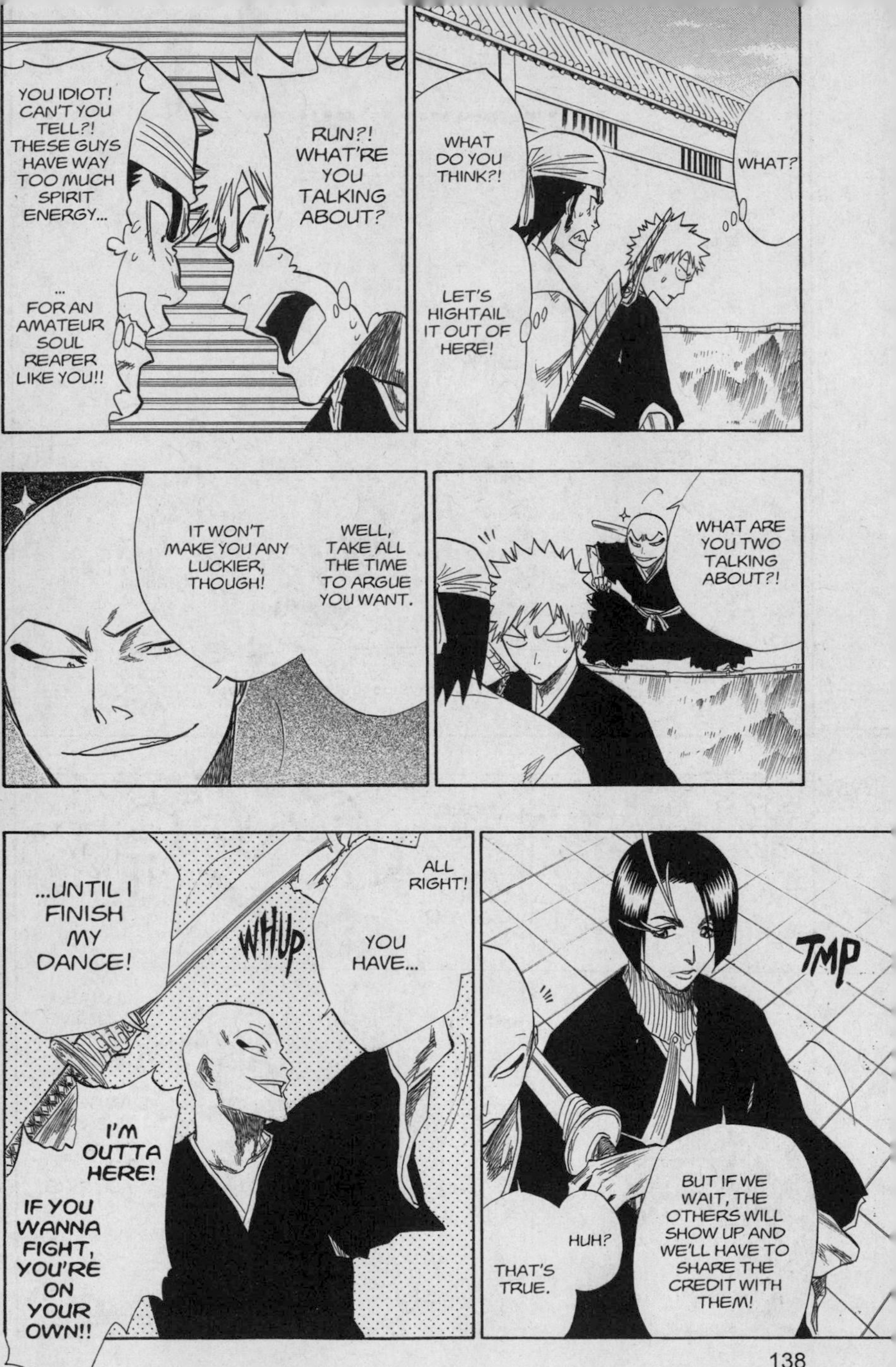
WHAT?
WHAT DO YOU THINK?!
LET'S HIGHTAIL IT OUT OF HERE!
RUN?! WHAT'RE YOU TALKING ABOUT?
YOU IDIOT! CAN'T YOU TELL?! THESE GUYS HAVE WAY TOO MUCH SPIRIT ENERGY...
...FOR AN AMATEUR SOUL REAPER LIKE YOU!!
WHAT ARE YOU TWO TALKING ABOUT?!
WELL, TAKE ALL THE TIME TO ARGUE YOU WANT.
IT WON'T MAKE YOU ANY LUCKIER, THOUGH!
TMP
BUT IF WE WAIT, THE OTHERS WILL SHOW UP AND WE'LL HAVE TO SHARE THE CREDIT WITH THEM!
HUH?
THAT'S TRUE.
ALL RIGHT!
YOU HAVE...
...UNTIL I FINISH MY DANCE!
WHUP
I'M OUTTA HERE!
IF YOU WANNA FIGHT, YOU'RE ON YOUR OWN!!

READ THIS WAY

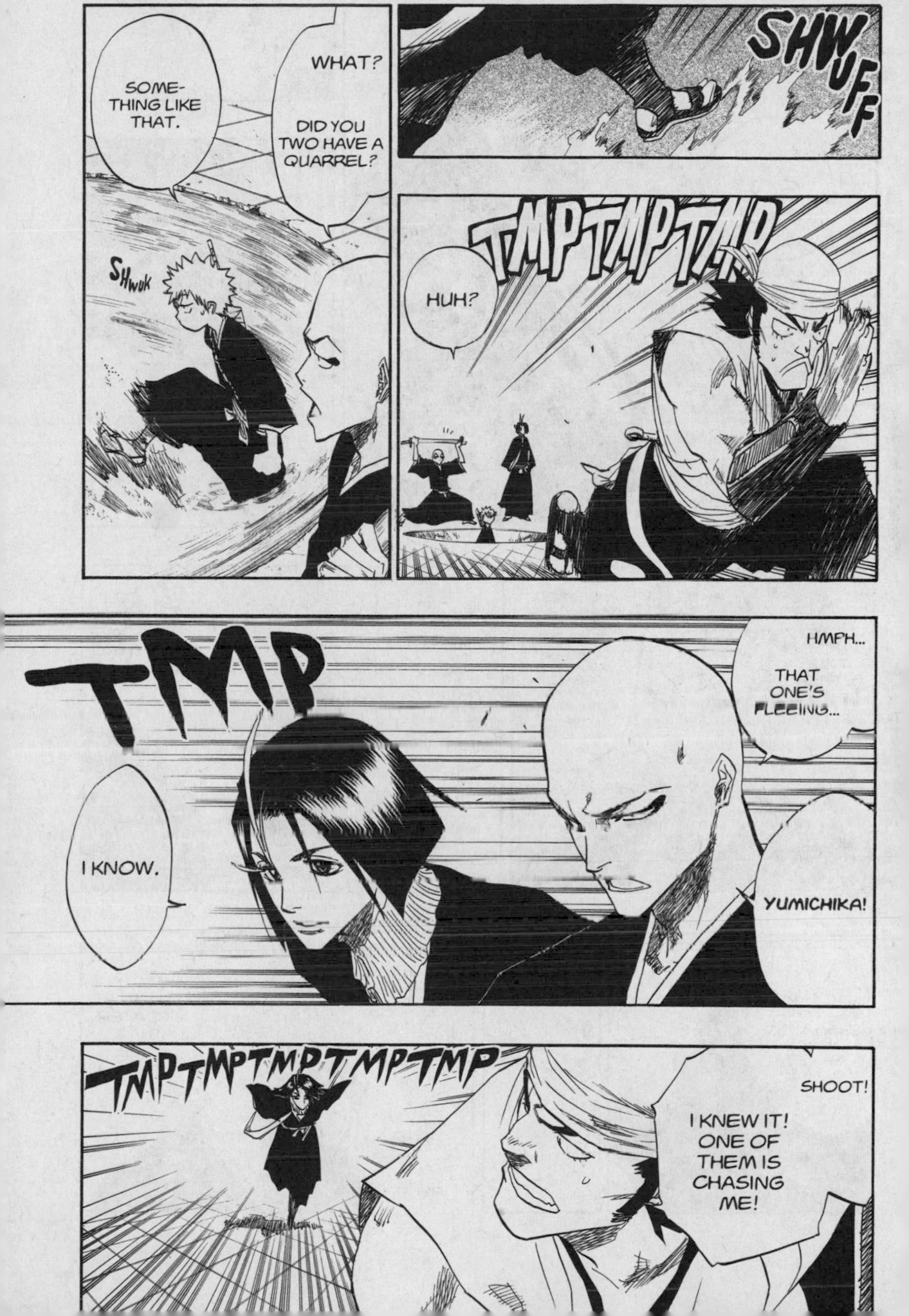

SHWUFF
TMPTMPTMP
HUH?
WHAT?
DID YOU TWO HAVE A QUARREL?
SOME-THING LIKE THAT.
SHWUK
HMPH...
THAT ONE'S FLEEING...
YUMICHIKA!
TMP
I KNOW.
SHOOT!
I KNEW IT! ONE OF THEM IS CHASING ME!
TMPTMPTMPTMPTMP

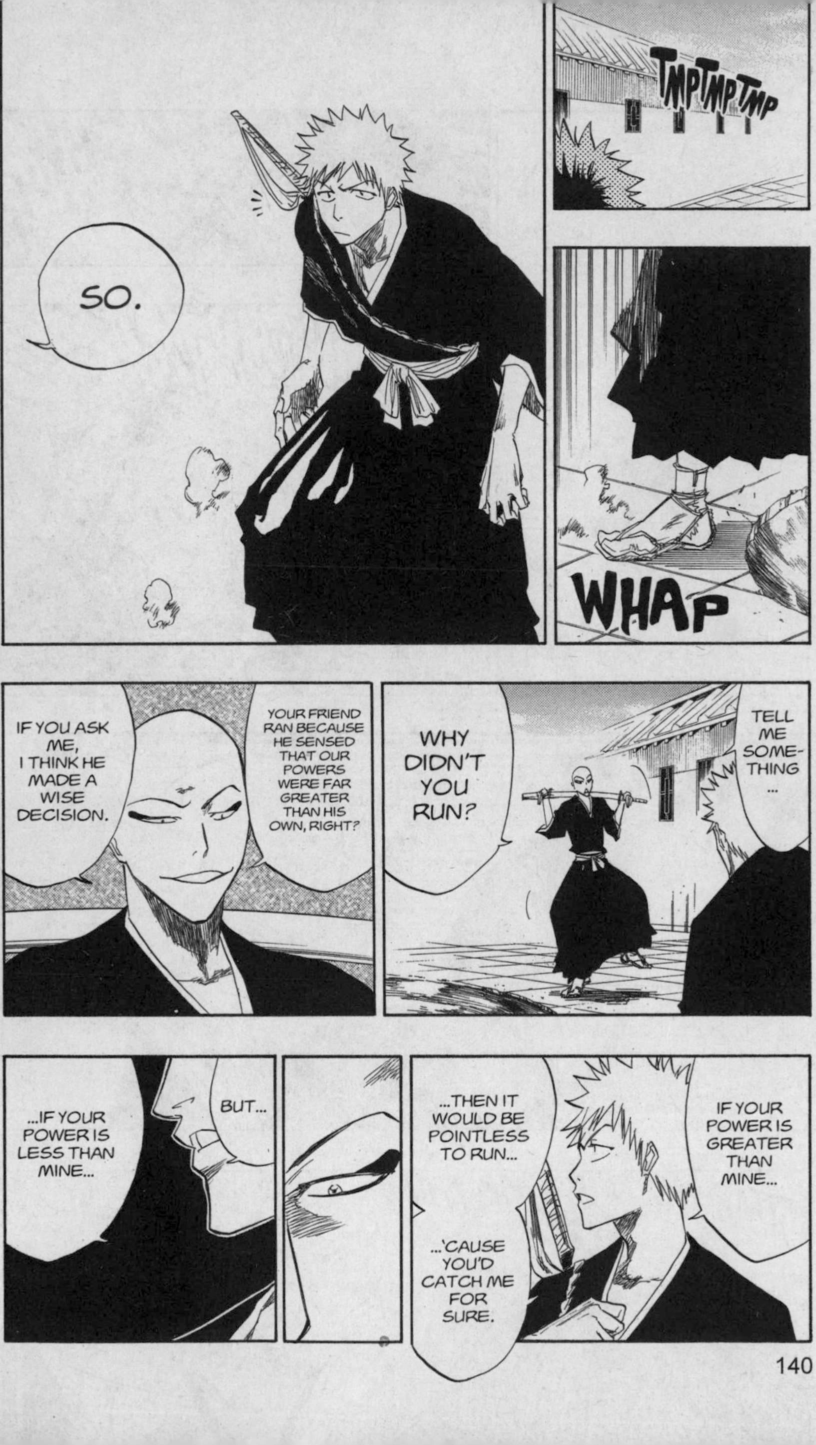
TMPTMPTMP
WHAP
SO.
TELL ME SOMETHING...
WHY DIDN'T YOU RUN?
YOUR FRIEND RAN BECAUSE HE SENSED THAT OUR POWERS WERE FAR GREATER THAN HIS OWN, RIGHT?
IF YOU ASK ME, I THINK HE MADE A WISE DECISION.
IF YOUR POWER IS GREATER THAN MINE...
...THEN IT WOULD BE POINTLESS TO RUN...
...'CAUSE YOU'D CATCH ME FOR SURE.
BUT...
...IF YOUR POWER IS LESS THAN MINE...

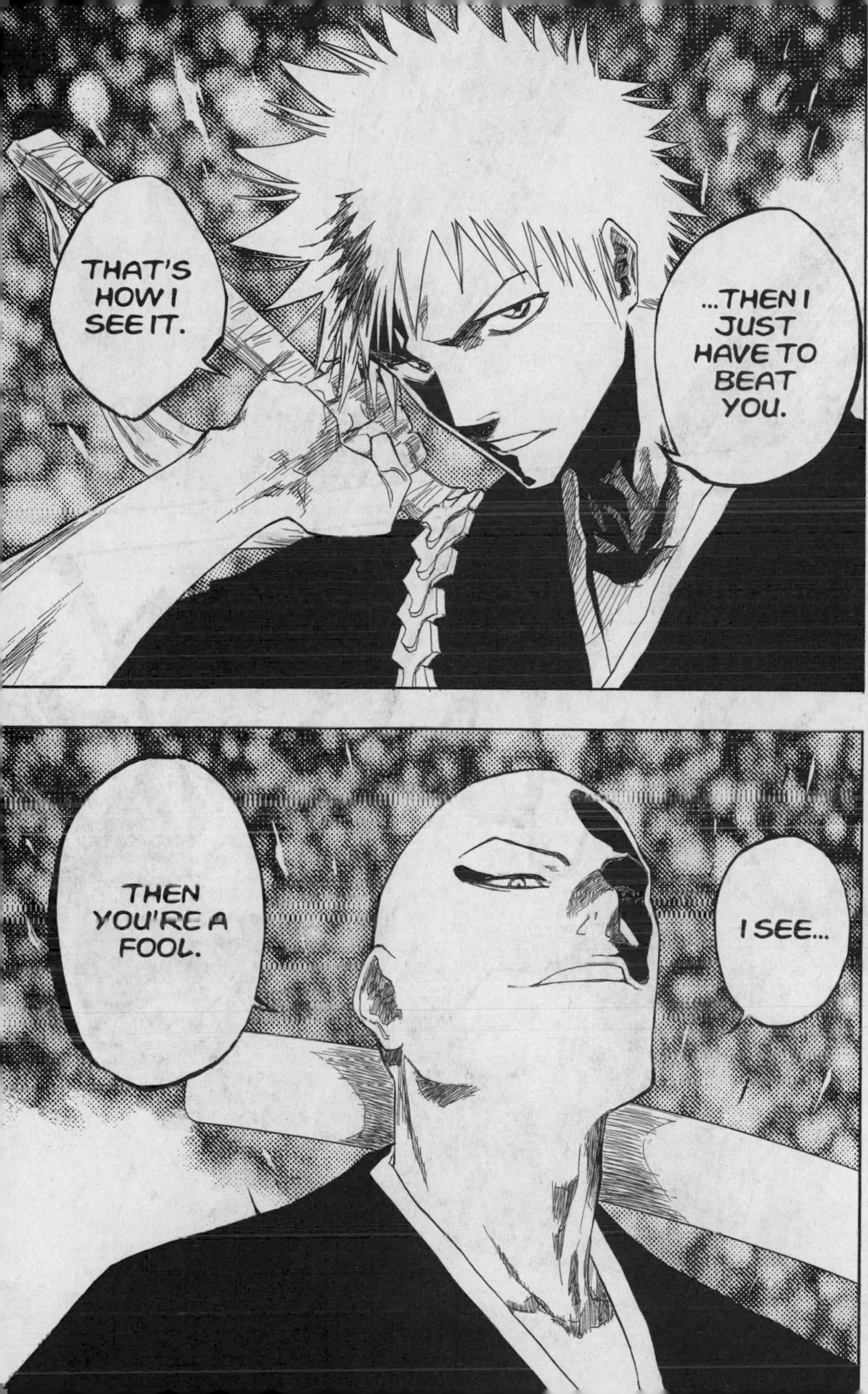
...THEN I JUST HAVE TO BEAT YOU.
THAT'S HOW I SEE IT.
I SEE...
THEN YOU'RE A FOOL.

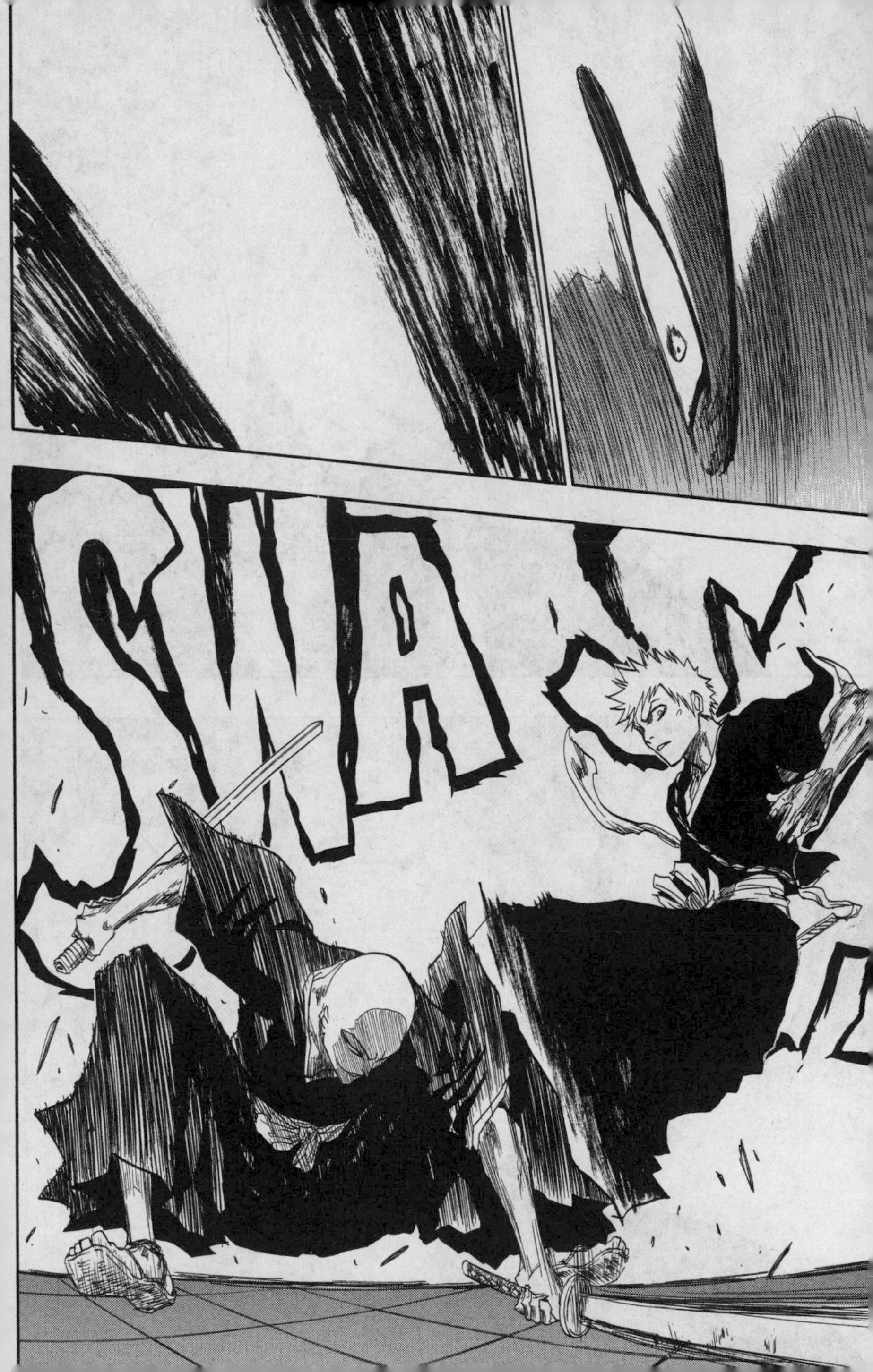
SWA

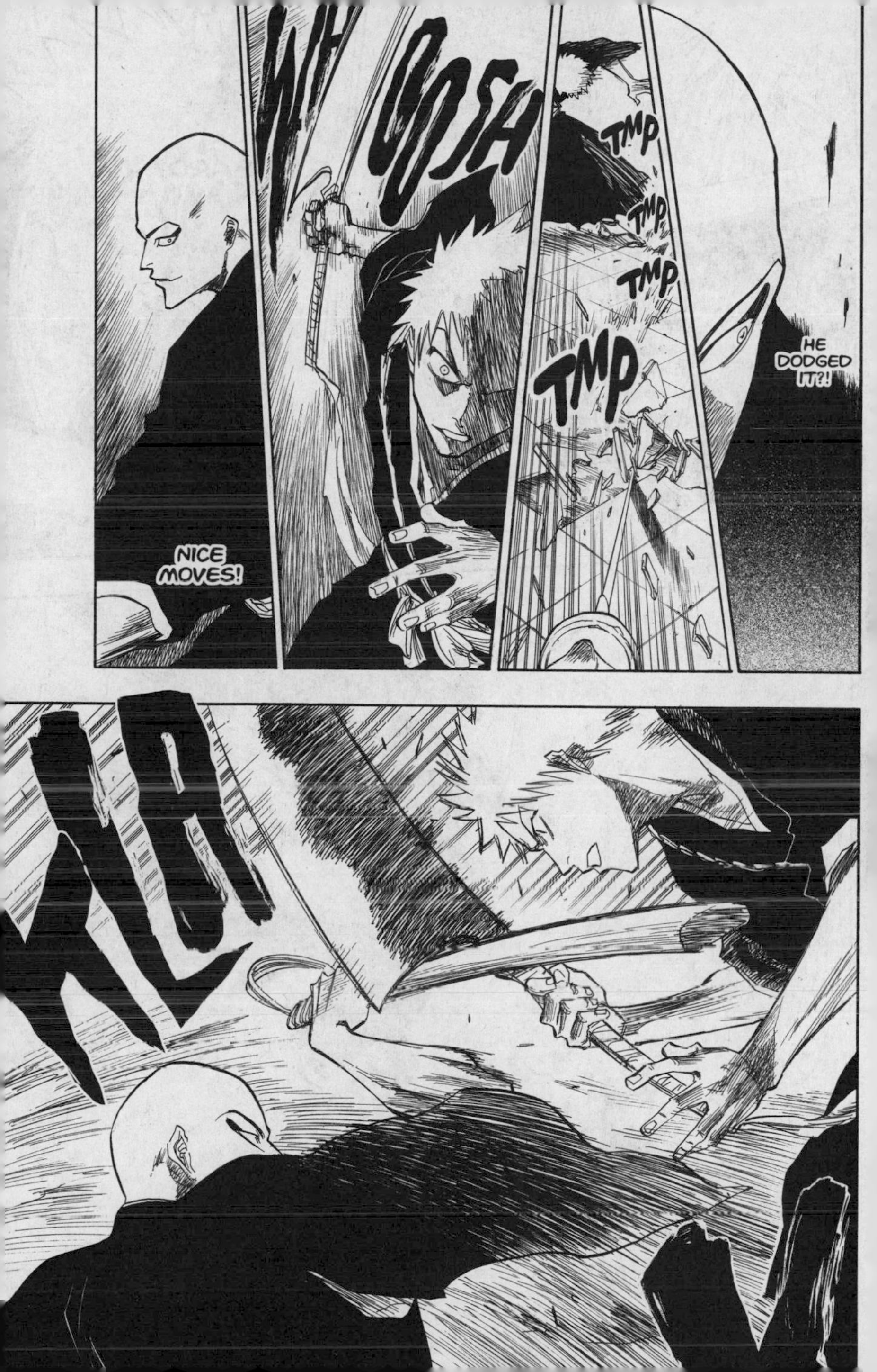
HE DODGED IT?!
TMP
TMP
TMP
TMP
WHOOSH
NICE MOVES!

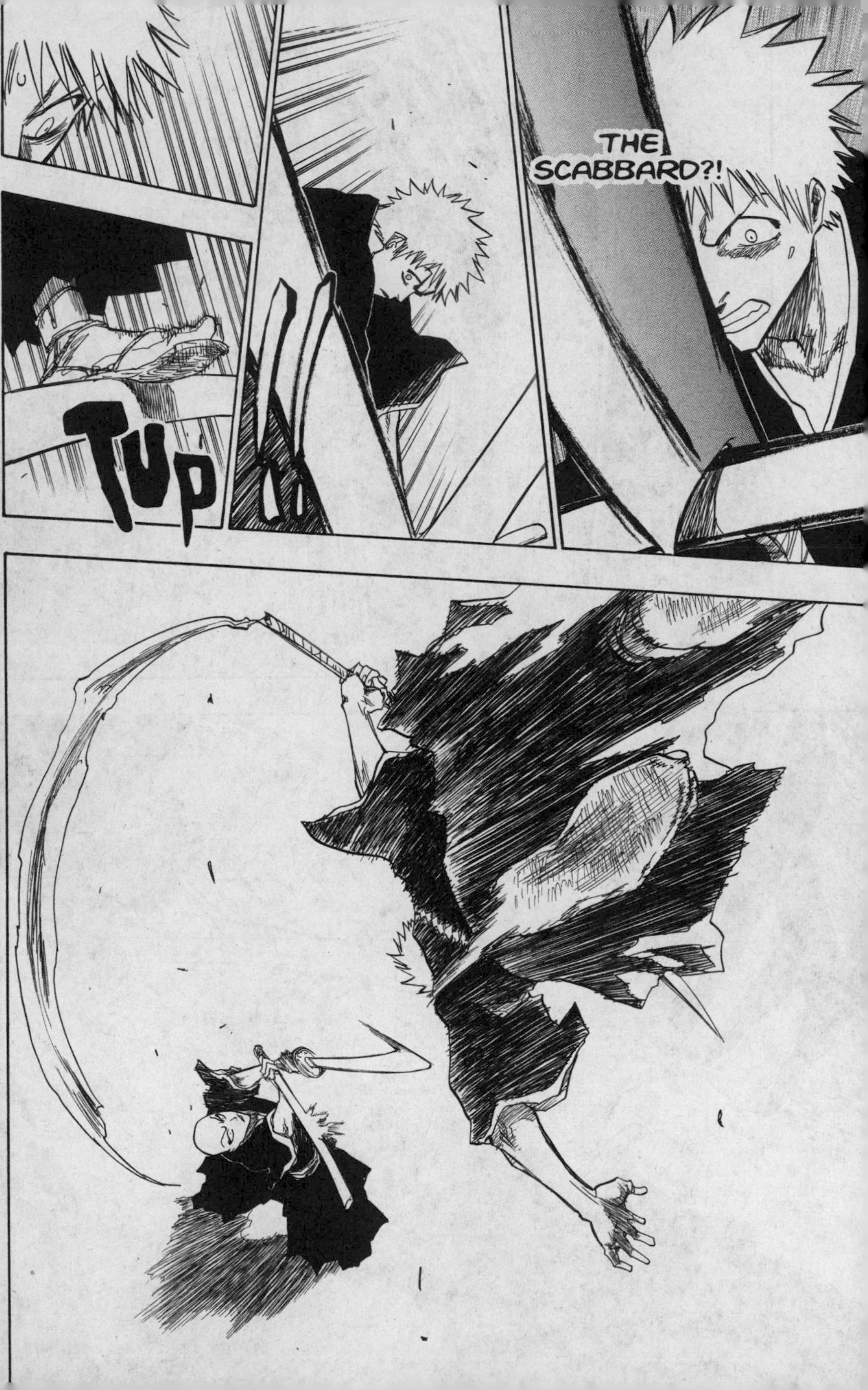
THE SCABBARD?!
TUP

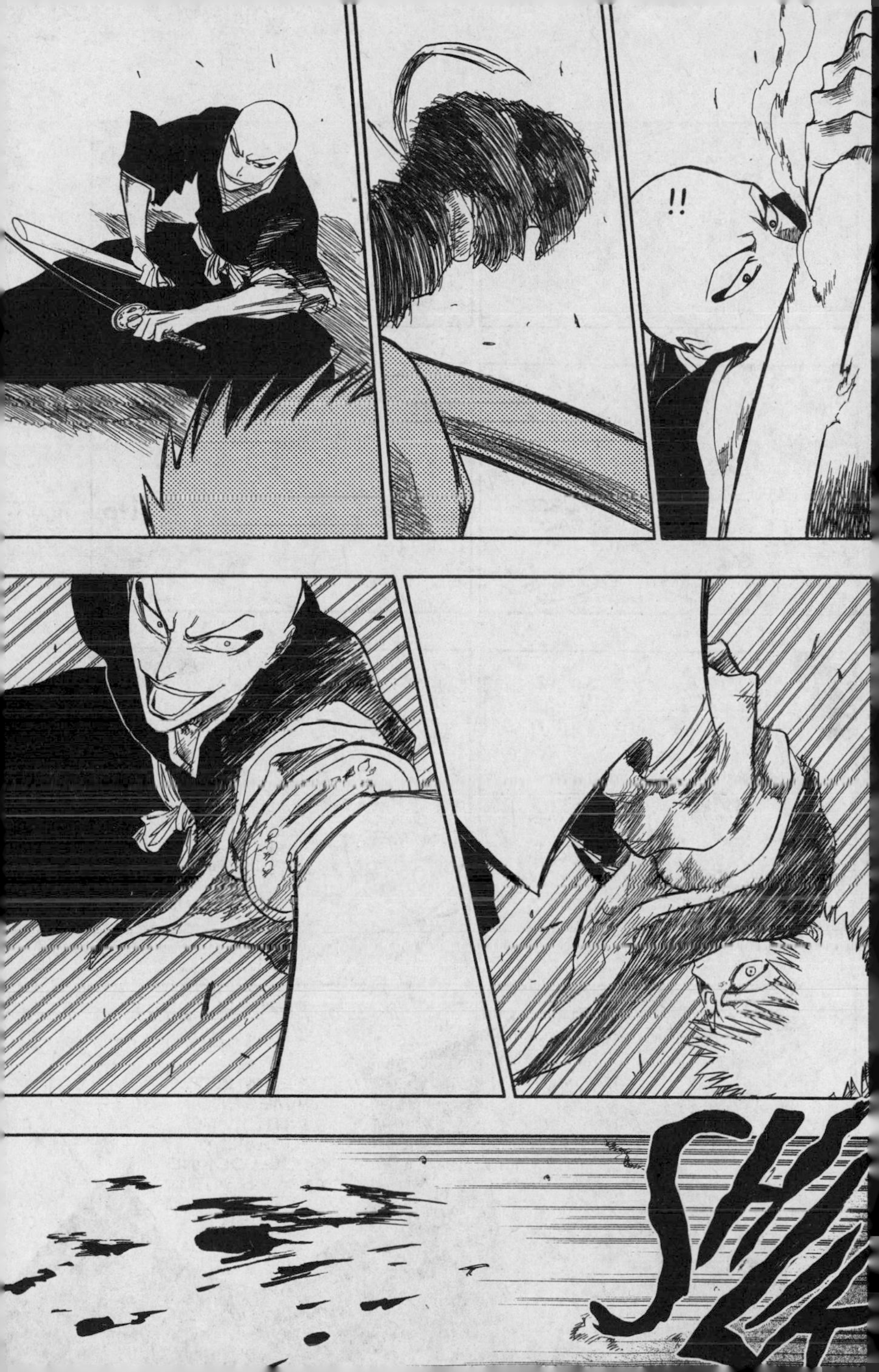
!!
SHA

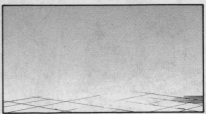

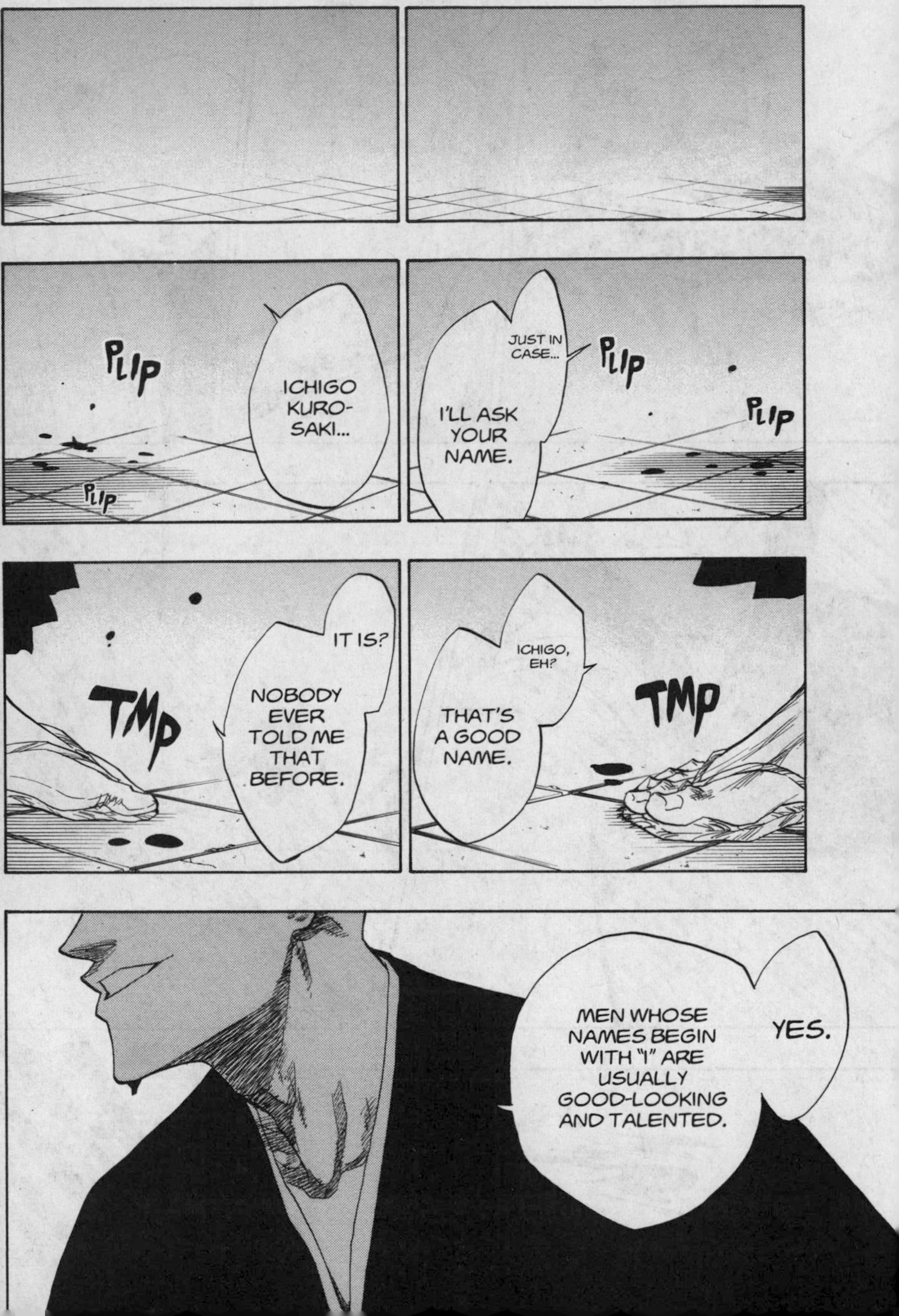
PLIP
JUST IN CASE...
I'LL ASK YOUR NAME.
PLIP
PLIP
ICHIGO KURO-SAKI...
PLIP
TMP
ICHIGO, EH?
THAT'S A GOOD NAME.
IT IS?
NOBODY EVER TOLD ME THAT BEFORE.
TMP
YES.
MEN WHOSE NAMES BEGIN WITH "I" ARE USUALLY GOOD-LOOKING AND TALENTED.

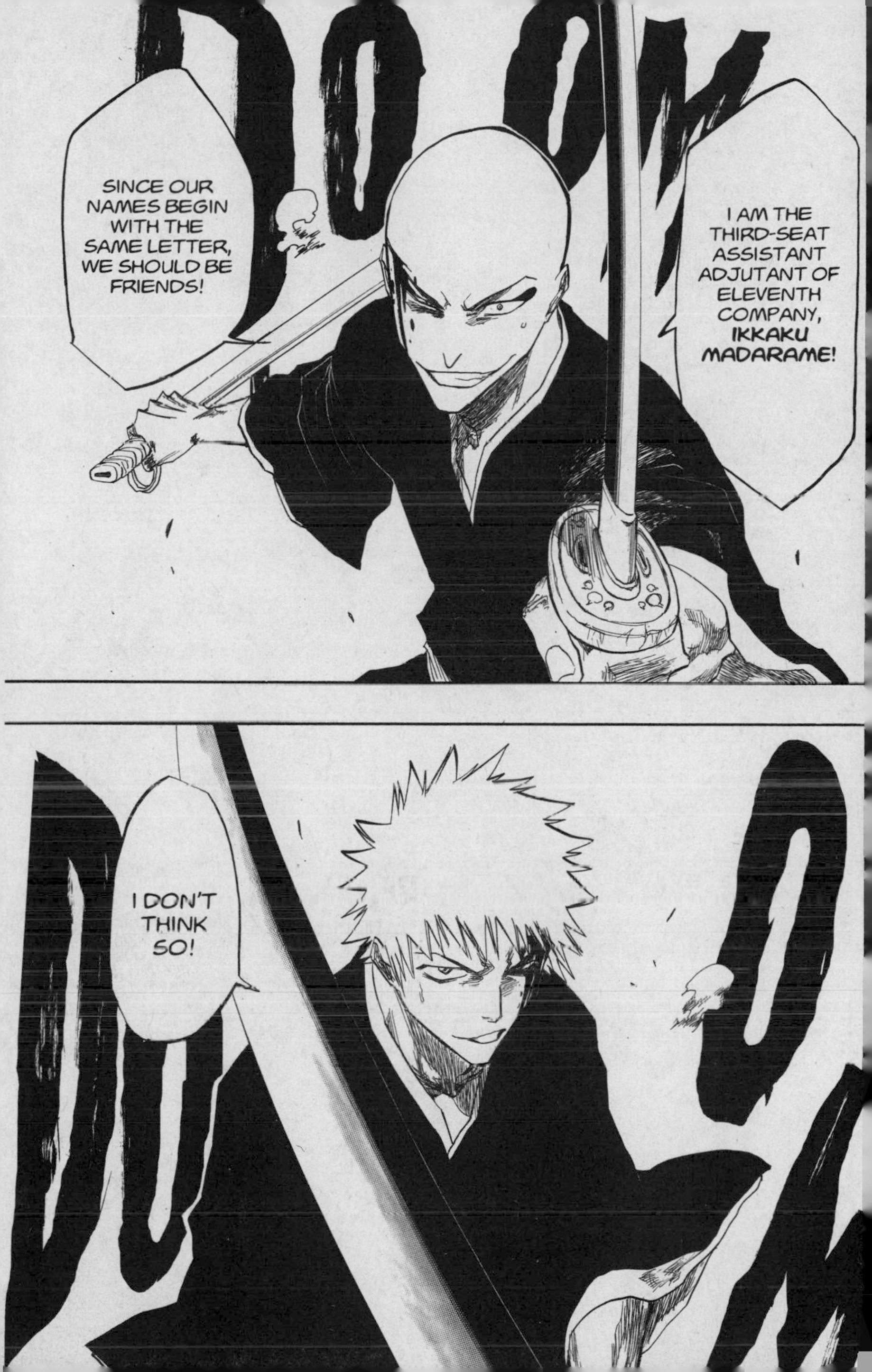
DOOM
I AM THE THIRD-SEAT ASSISTANT ADJUTANT OF ELEVENTH COMPANY, **IKKAKU MADARAME!**
SINCE OUR NAMES BEGIN WITH THE SAME LETTER, WE SHOULD BE FRIENDS!
I DON'T THINK SO!

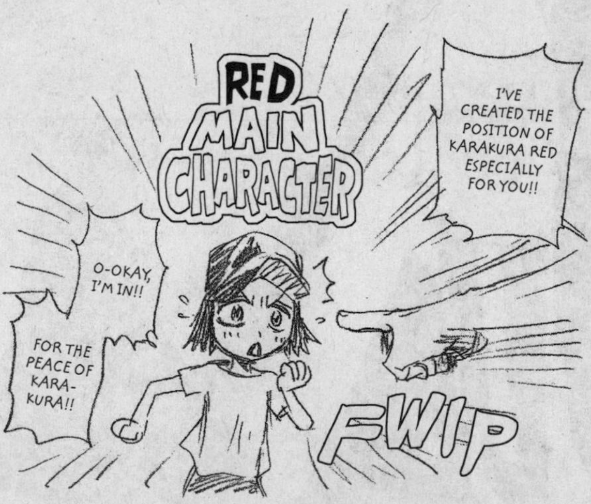
I'VE CREATED THE POSITION OF KARAKURA RED ESPECIALLY FOR YOU!!
RED MAIN CHARACTER
O-OKAY, I'M IN!!
FOR THE PEACE OF KARA-KURA!!
FWIP

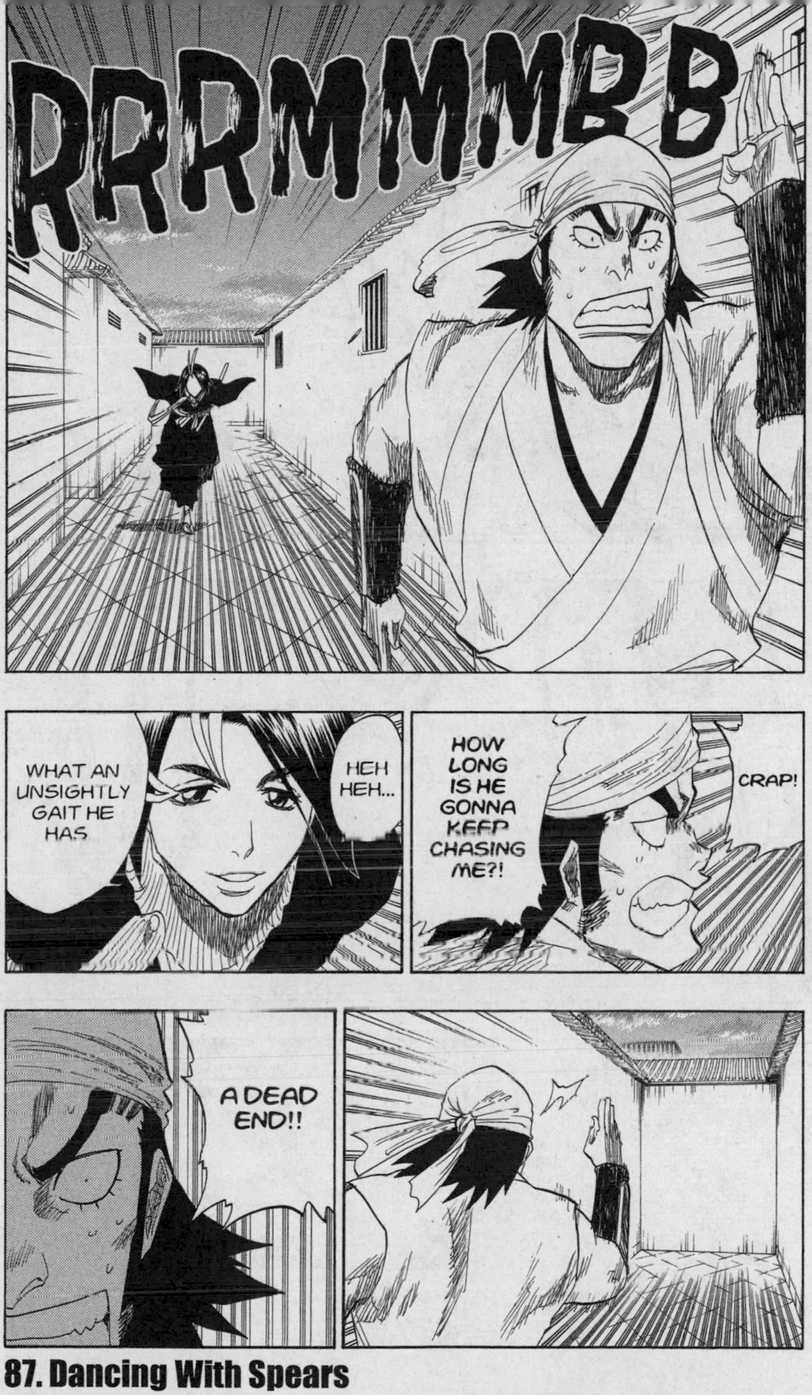
RRRMMMBB
CRAP!
HOW LONG IS HE GONNA KEEP CHASING ME?!
HEH HEH...
WHAT AN UNSIGHTLY GAIT HE HAS...
A DEAD END!!

87. Dancing With Spears

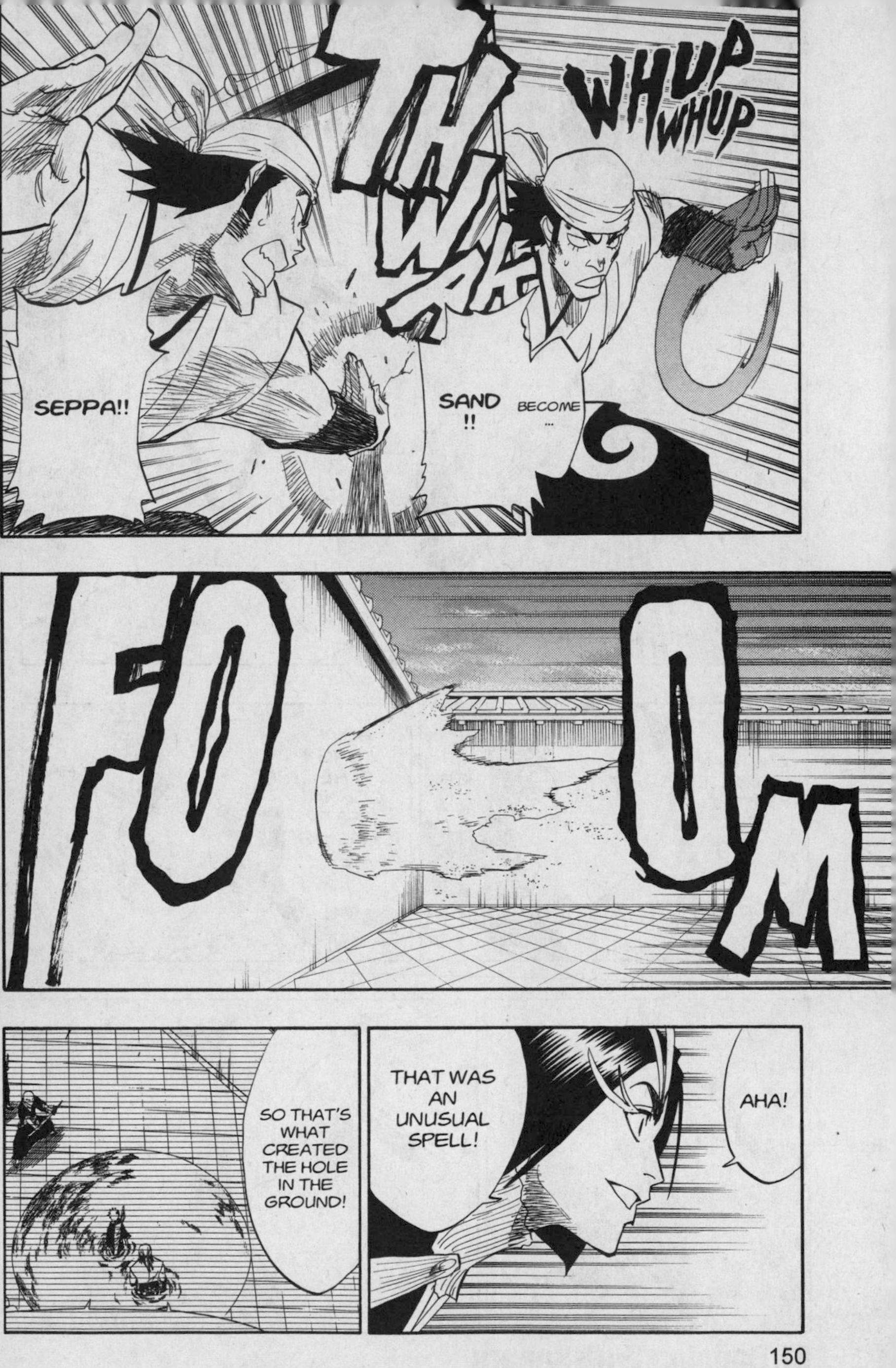
WHUP WHUP
WHAK
BECOME...
SAND!!
SEPPA!!
FOOM
AHA!
THAT WAS AN UNUSUAL SPELL!
SO THAT'S WHAT CREATED THE HOLE IN THE GROUND!

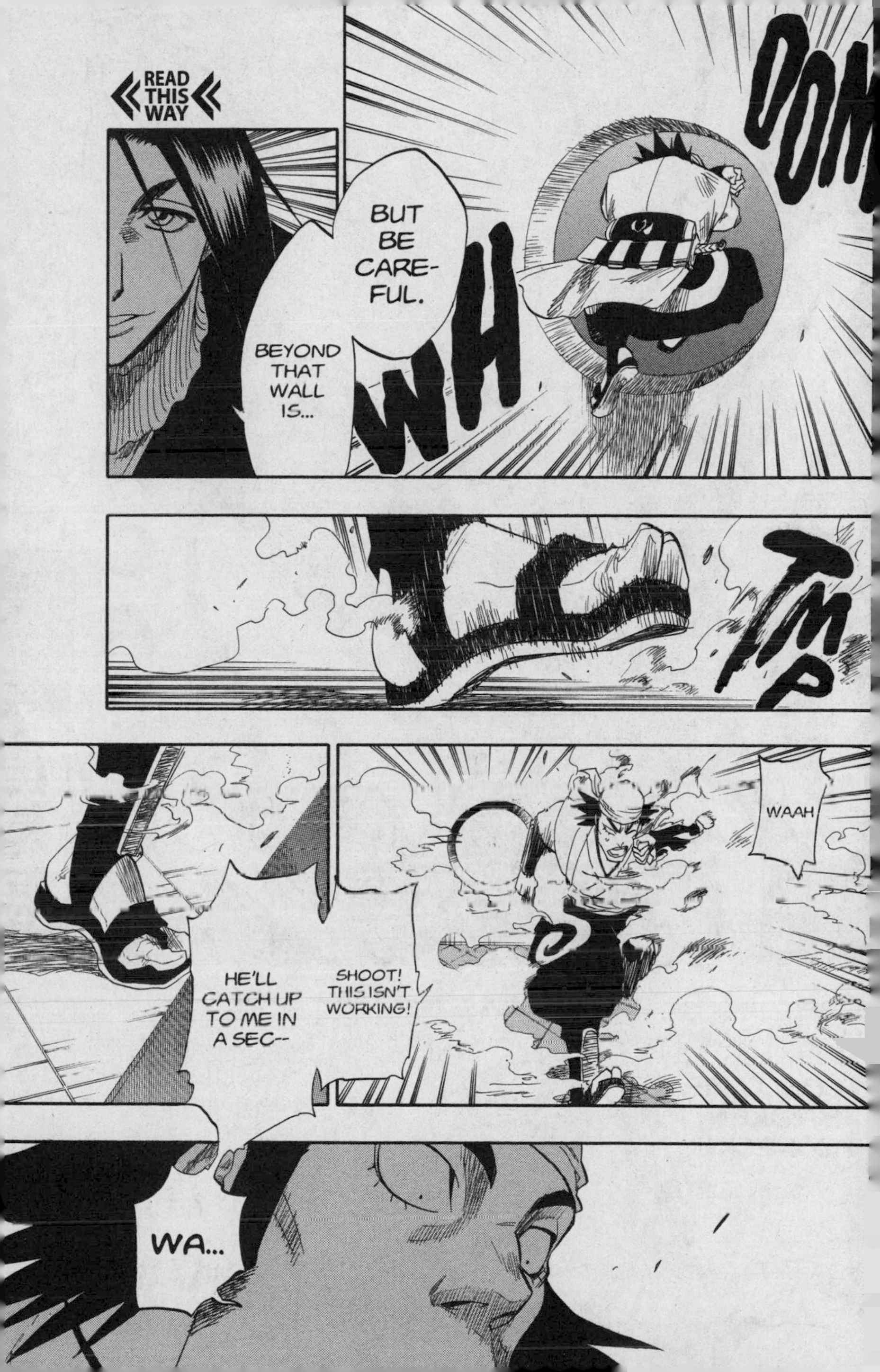
READ THIS WAY
WH
OOM
BUT BE CAREFUL.
BEYOND THAT WALL IS...
TMP
WAAH
SHOOT! THIS ISN'T WORKING!
HE'LL CATCH UP TO ME IN A SEC--
WA...

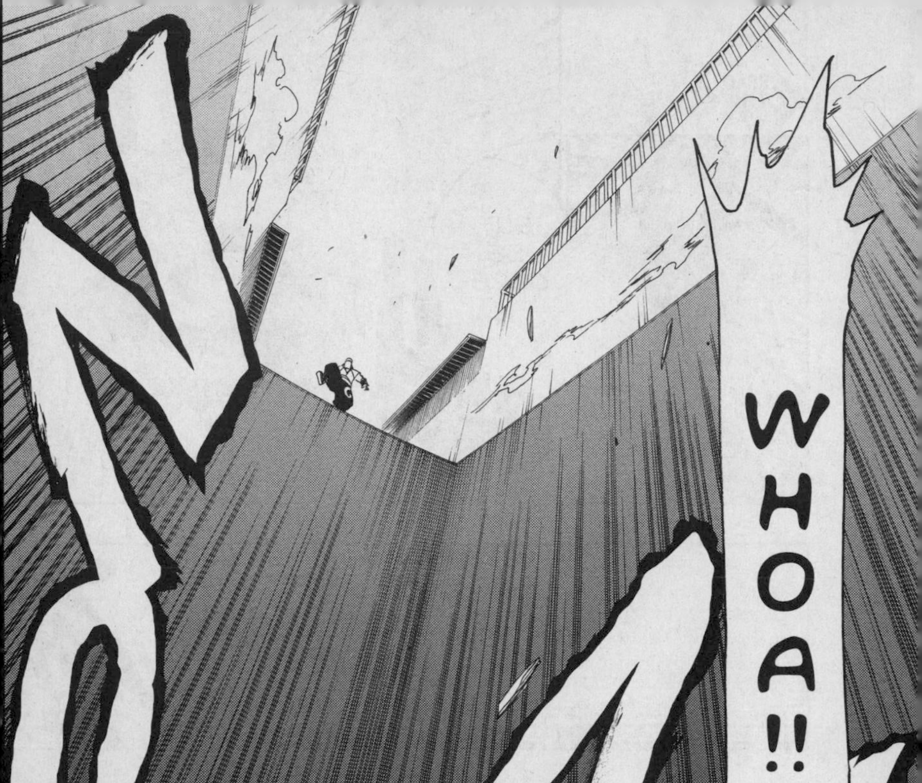
WHOA!!
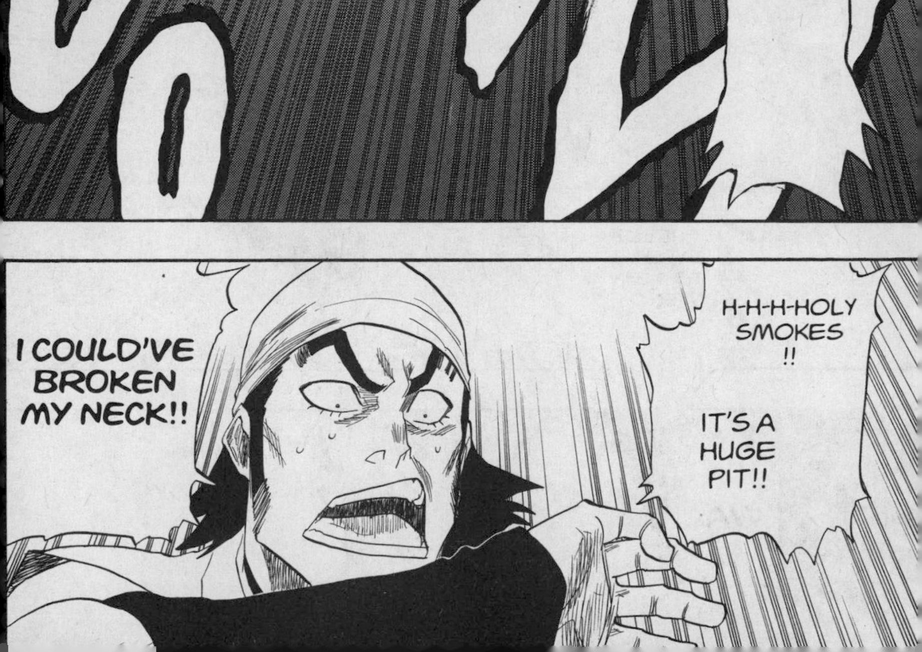
H-H-H-HOLY SMOKES!!
IT'S A HUGE PIT!!
I COULD'VE BROKEN MY NECK!!

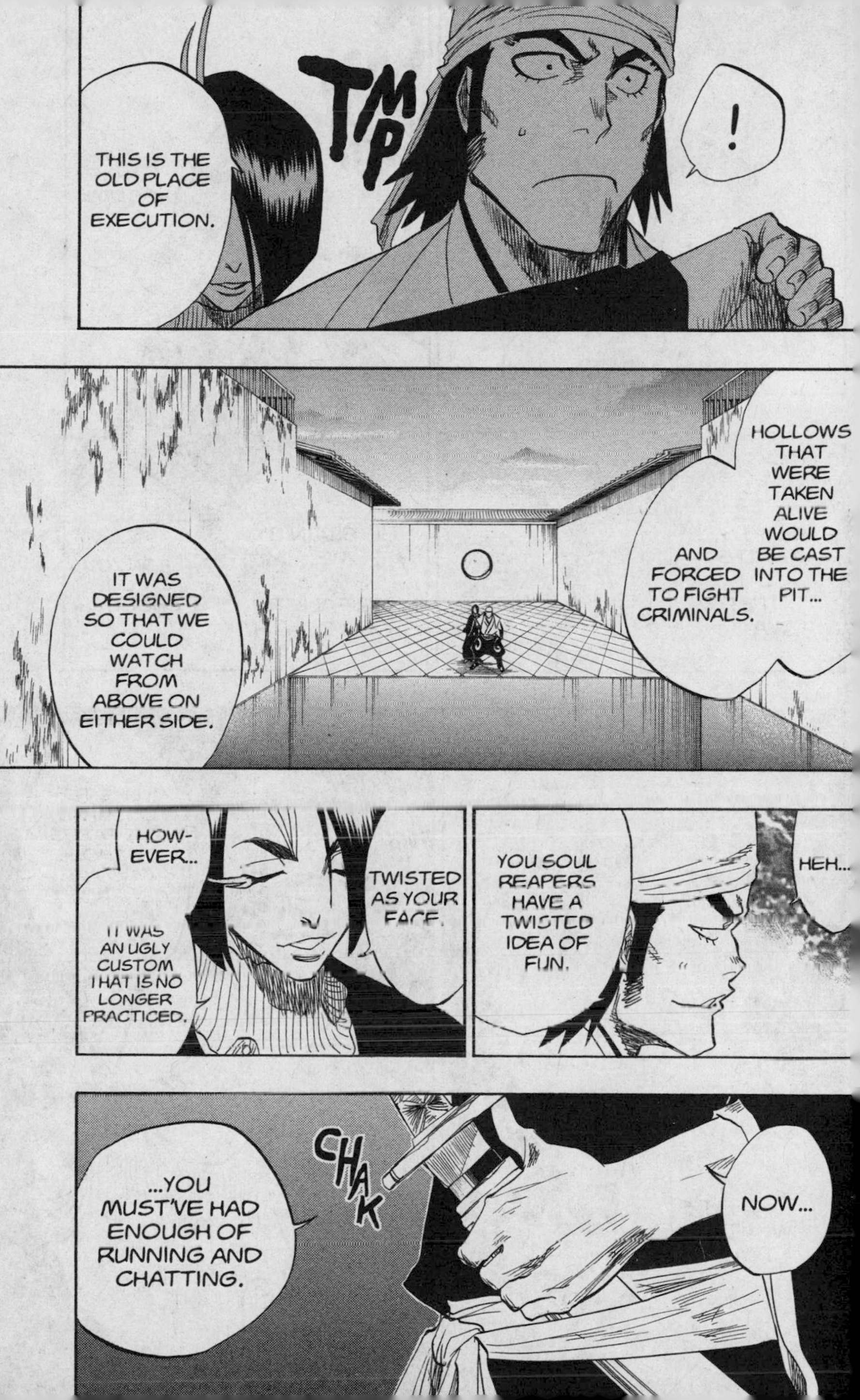
!
TMP
THIS IS THE OLD PLACE OF EXECUTION.
HOLLOWS THAT WERE TAKEN ALIVE WOULD BE CAST INTO THE PIT...
AND FORCED TO FIGHT CRIMINALS.
IT WAS DESIGNED SO THAT WE COULD WATCH FROM ABOVE ON EITHER SIDE.
HEH...
YOU SOUL REAPERS HAVE A TWISTED IDEA OF FUN.
TWISTED AS YOUR FACE.
HOW-EVER...
IT WAS AN UGLY CUSTOM THAT IS NO LONGER PRACTICED.
NOW...
CHAK
...YOU MUST'VE HAD ENOUGH OF RUNNING AND CHATTING.

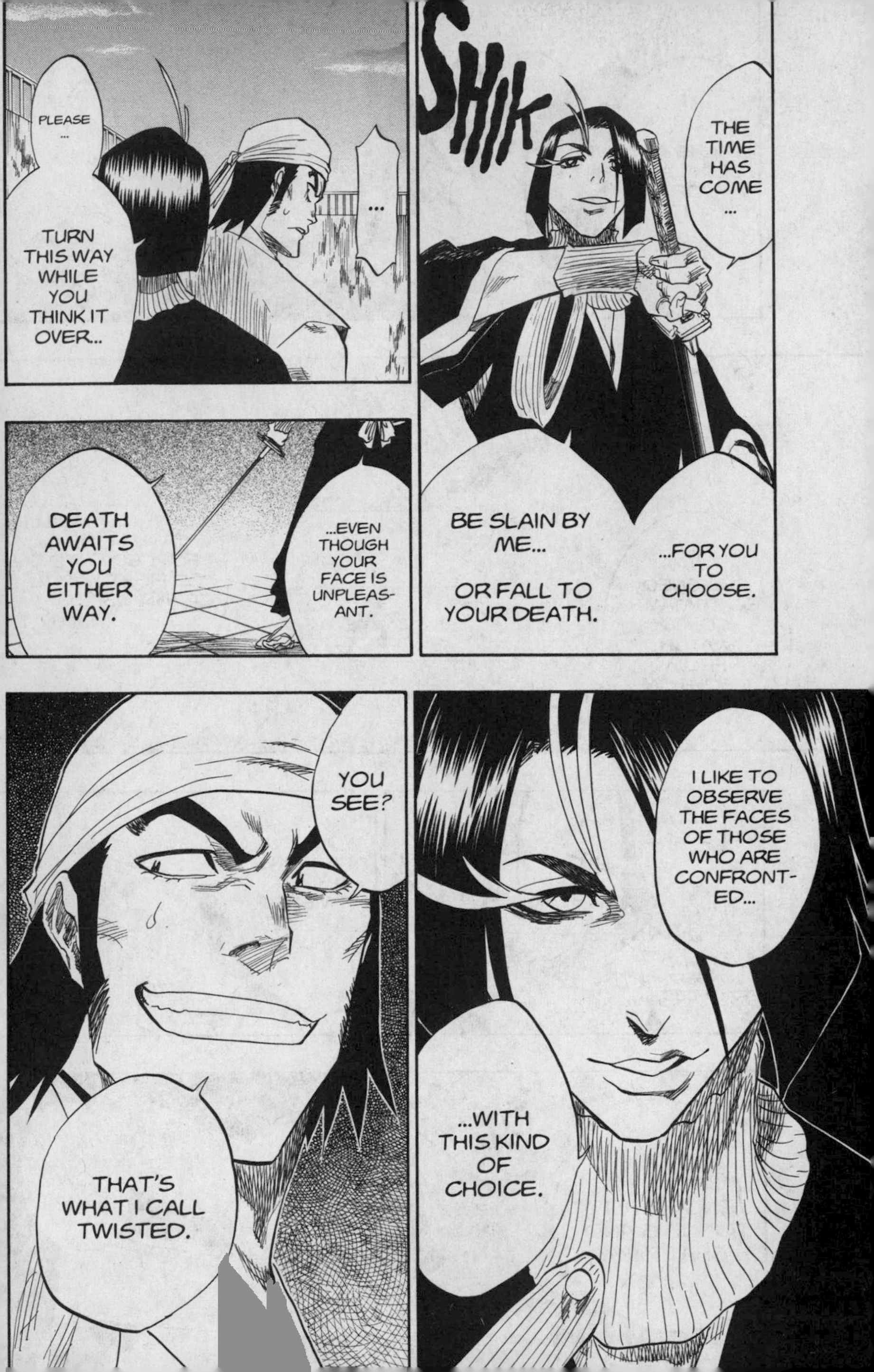
SHIK
THE TIME HAS COME...
BE SLAIN BY ME... OR FALL TO YOUR DEATH.
...FOR YOU TO CHOOSE.
PLEASE...
TURN THIS WAY WHILE YOU THINK IT OVER...
...
...EVEN THOUGH YOUR FACE IS UNPLEASANT.
DEATH AWAITS YOU EITHER WAY.
I LIKE TO OBSERVE THE FACES OF THOSE WHO ARE CONFRONTED...
...WITH THIS KIND OF CHOICE.
YOU SEE?
THAT'S WHAT I CALL TWISTED.

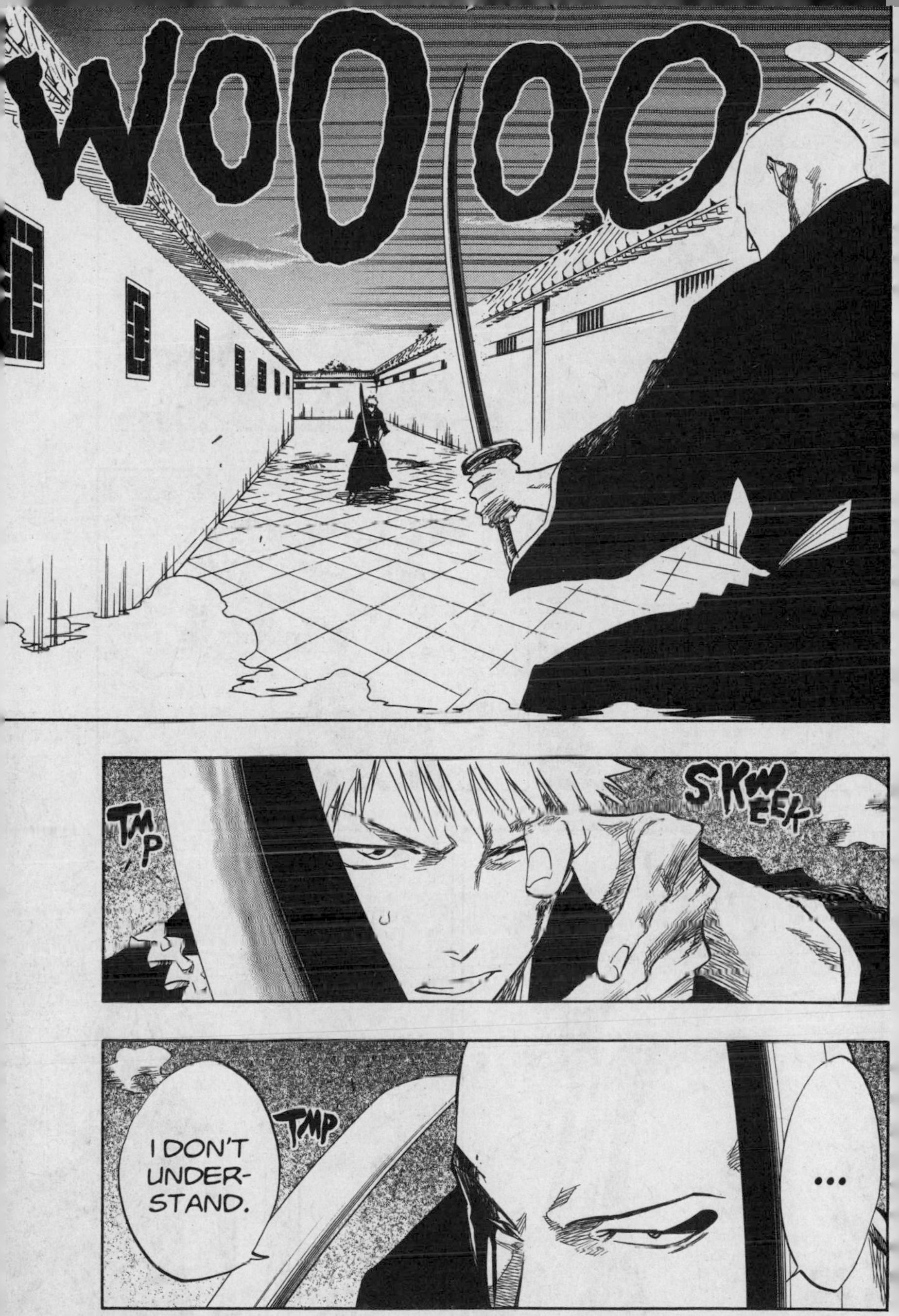
WOOOO
SKWEEK
TMP
...
TMP
I DON'T UNDER-STAND.

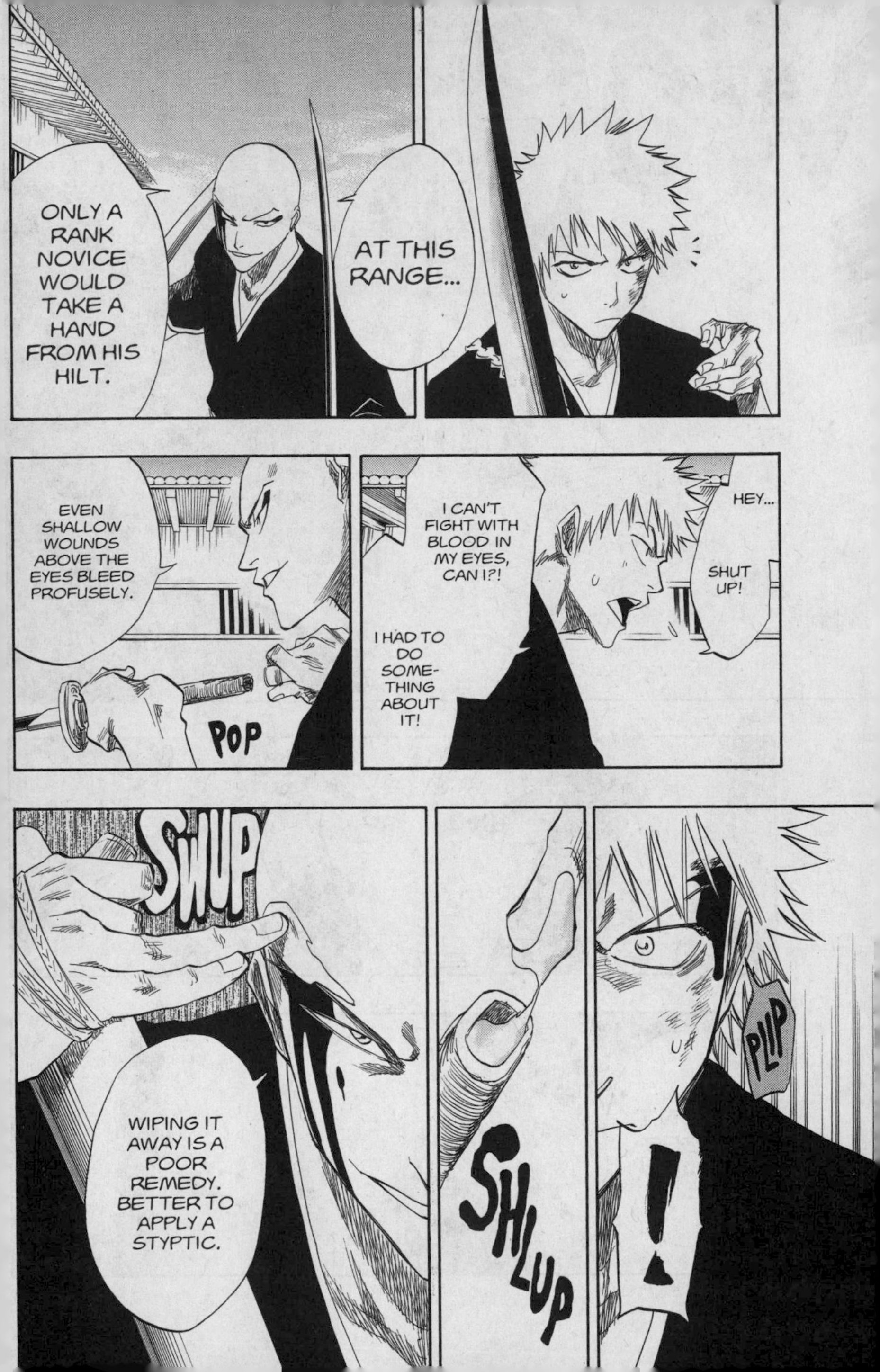
AT THIS RANGE...
ONLY A RANK NOVICE WOULD TAKE A HAND FROM HIS HILT.
HEY...
SHUT UP!
I CAN'T FIGHT WITH BLOOD IN MY EYES, CAN I?!
I HAD TO DO SOME-THING ABOUT IT!
EVEN SHALLOW WOUNDS ABOVE THE EYES BLEED PROFUSELY.
POP
PLIP
!
SHLUP
SWUP
WIPING IT AWAY IS A POOR REMEDY. BETTER TO APPLY A STYPTIC.

READ THIS WAY

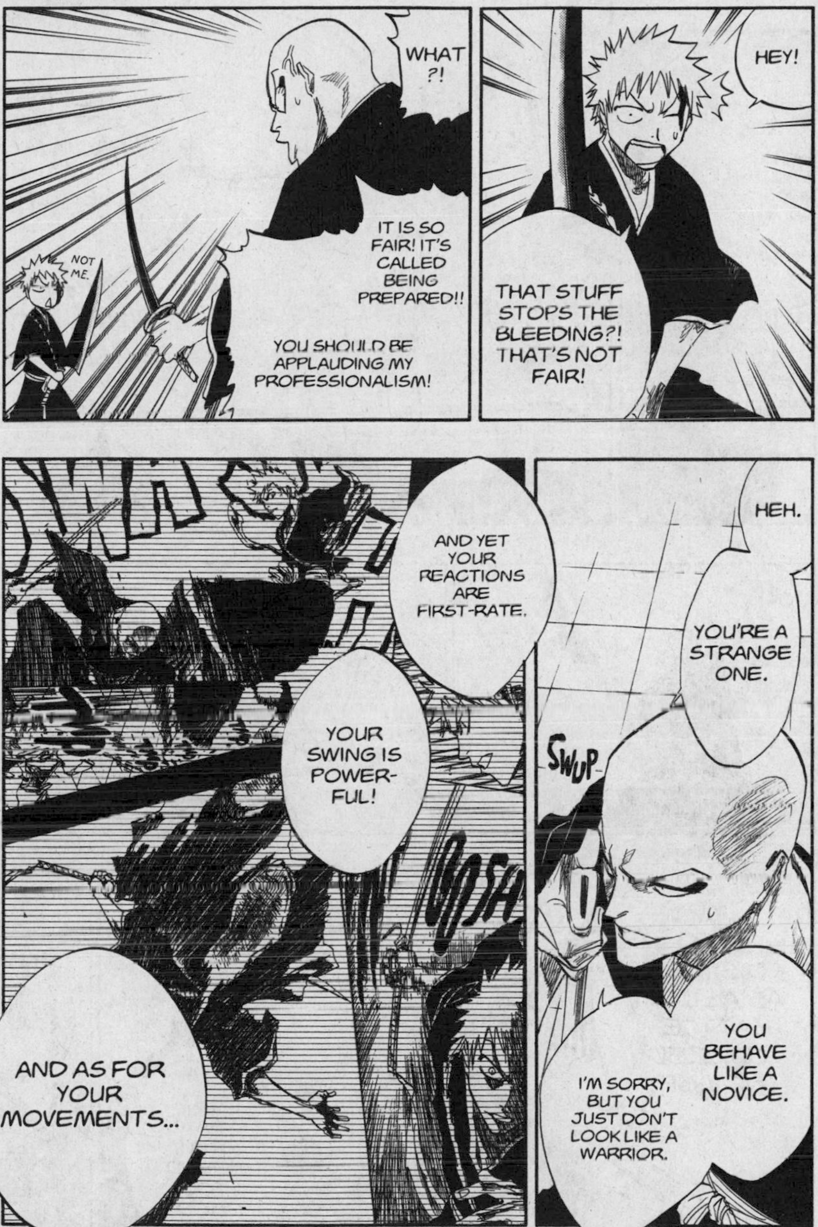
HEY!
THAT STUFF STOPS THE BLEEDING?! THAT'S NOT FAIR!
WHAT ?!
IT IS SO FAIR! IT'S CALLED BEING PREPARED!!
YOU SHOULD BE APPLAUDING MY PROFESSIONALISM!
NOT ME.
HEH.
YOU'RE A STRANGE ONE.
SWUP
YOU BEHAVE LIKE A NOVICE.
I'M SORRY, BUT YOU JUST DON'T LOOK LIKE A WARRIOR.
AND YET YOUR REACTIONS ARE FIRST-RATE.
YOUR SWING IS POWER-FUL!
AND AS FOR YOUR MOVEMENTS...

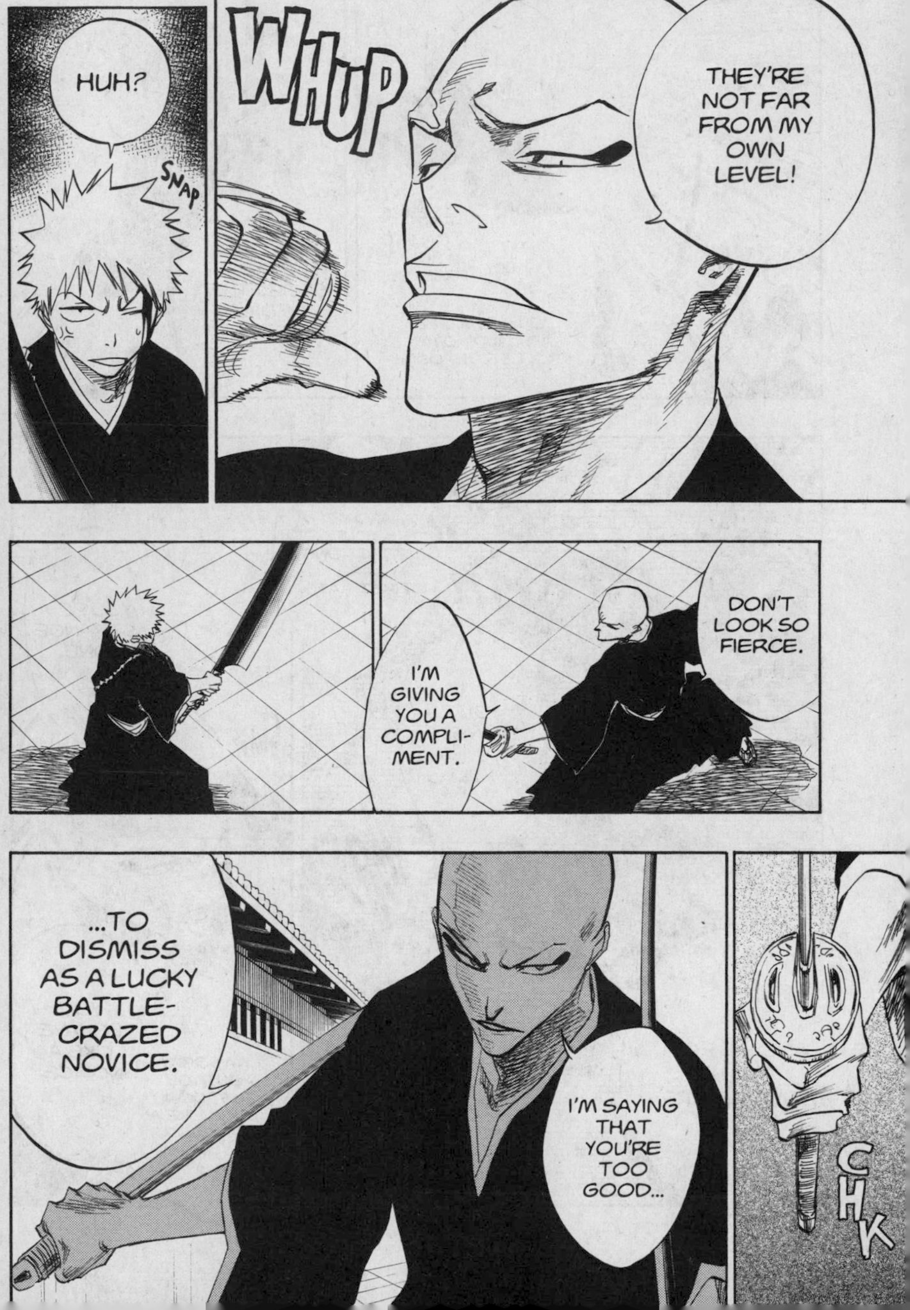
THEY'RE NOT FAR FROM MY OWN LEVEL!
WHUP
HUH?
SNAP
DON'T LOOK SO FIERCE.
I'M GIVING YOU A COMPLIMENT.
CHK
I'M SAYING THAT YOU'RE TOO GOOD...
...TO DISMISS AS A LUCKY BATTLE-CRAZED NOVICE.

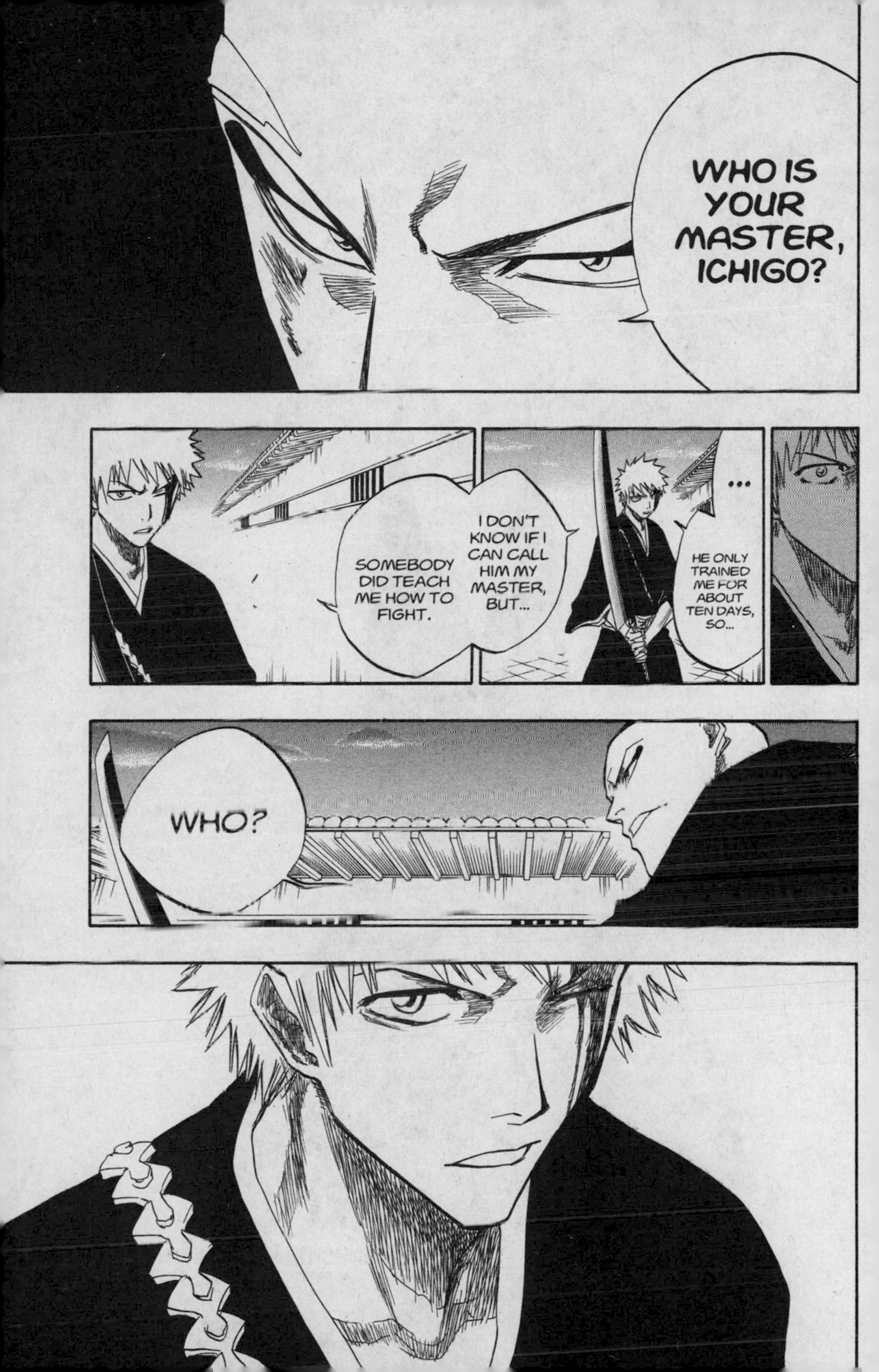
WHO IS YOUR MASTER, ICHIGO?
...
HE ONLY TRAINED ME FOR ABOUT TEN DAYS, SO...
I DON'T KNOW IF I CAN CALL HIM MY MASTER, BUT...
SOMEBODY DID TEACH ME HOW TO FIGHT.
WHO?

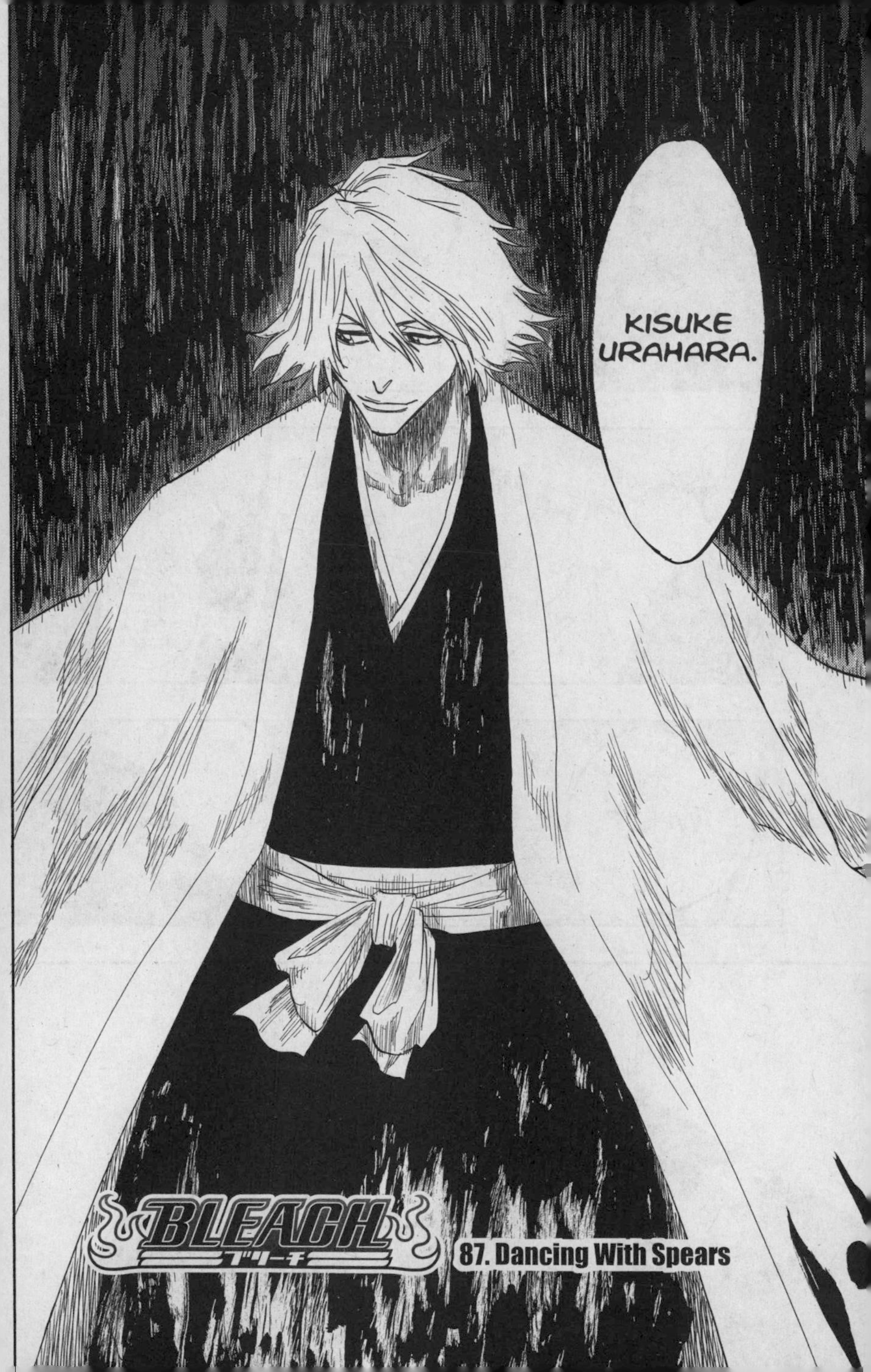
KISUKE URAHARA.
BLEACH
ブリーチ
87. Dancing With Spears

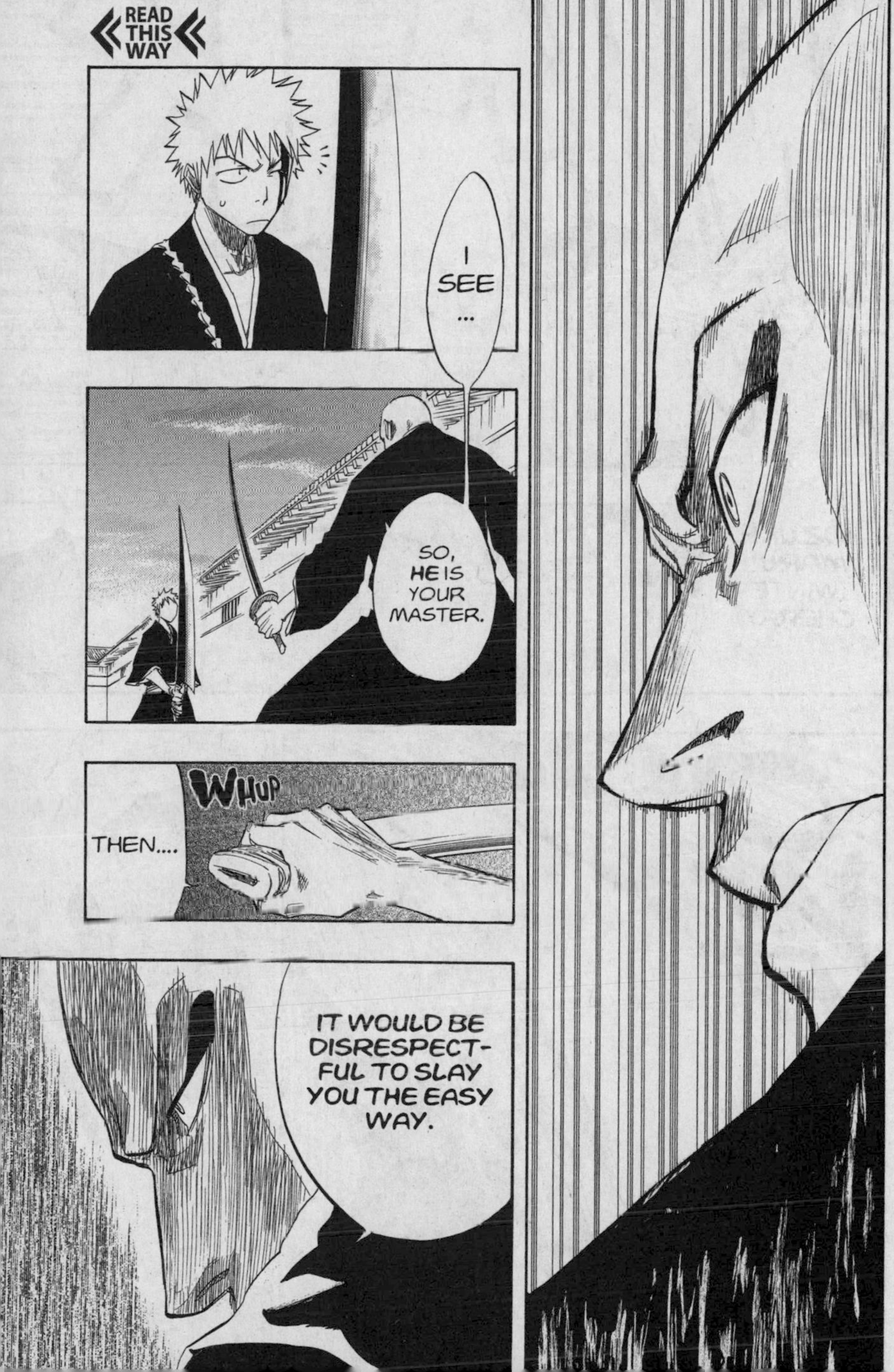
READ THIS WAY
I SEE ...
SO, HE IS YOUR MASTER.
WHUP
THEN....
IT WOULD BE DISRESPECTFUL TO SLAY YOU THE EASY WAY.

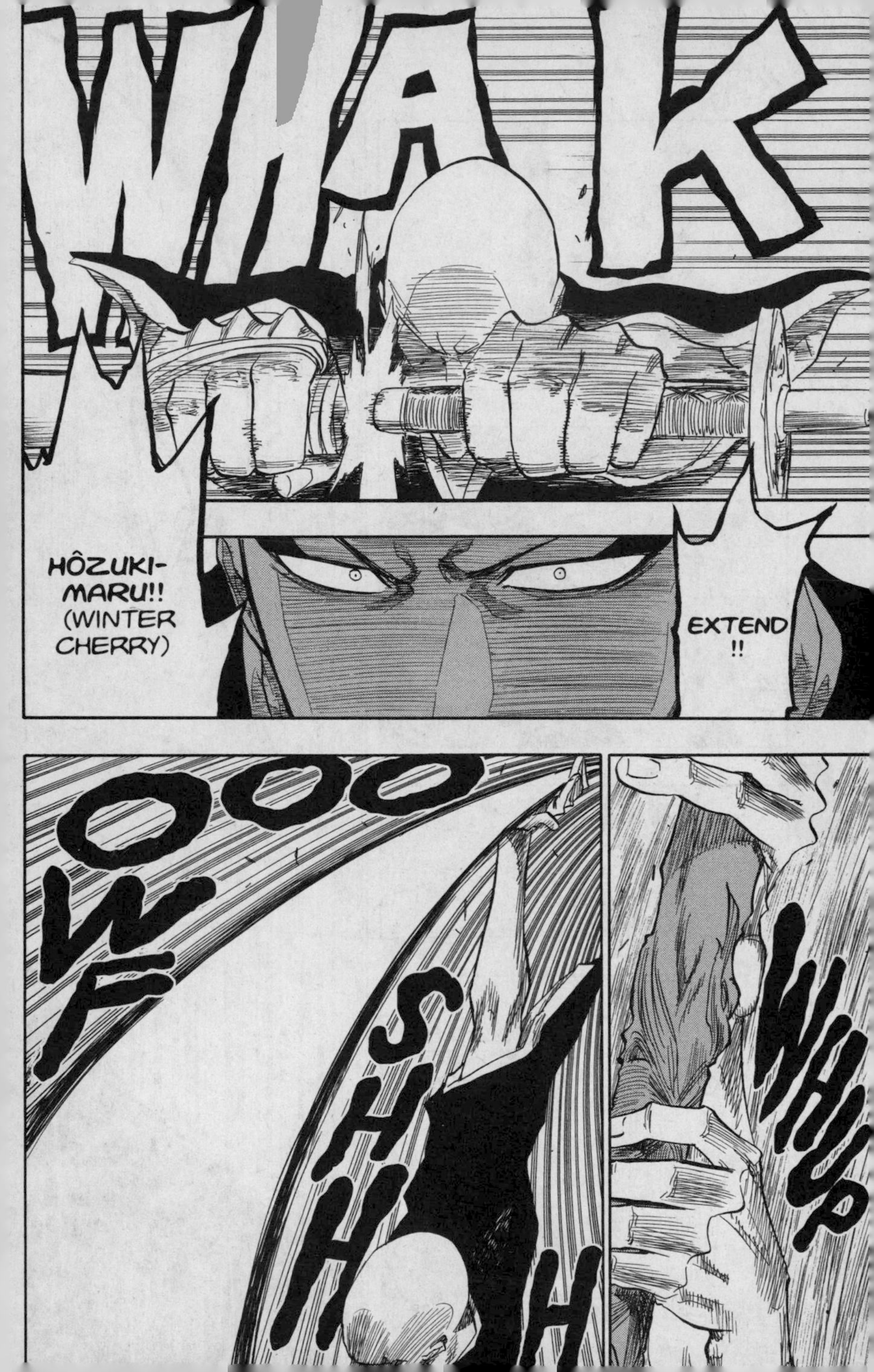
WHAK
EXTEND !!
HÔZUKI-MARU!! (WINTER CHERRY)
WHUP
FWOOOO
SHHHH

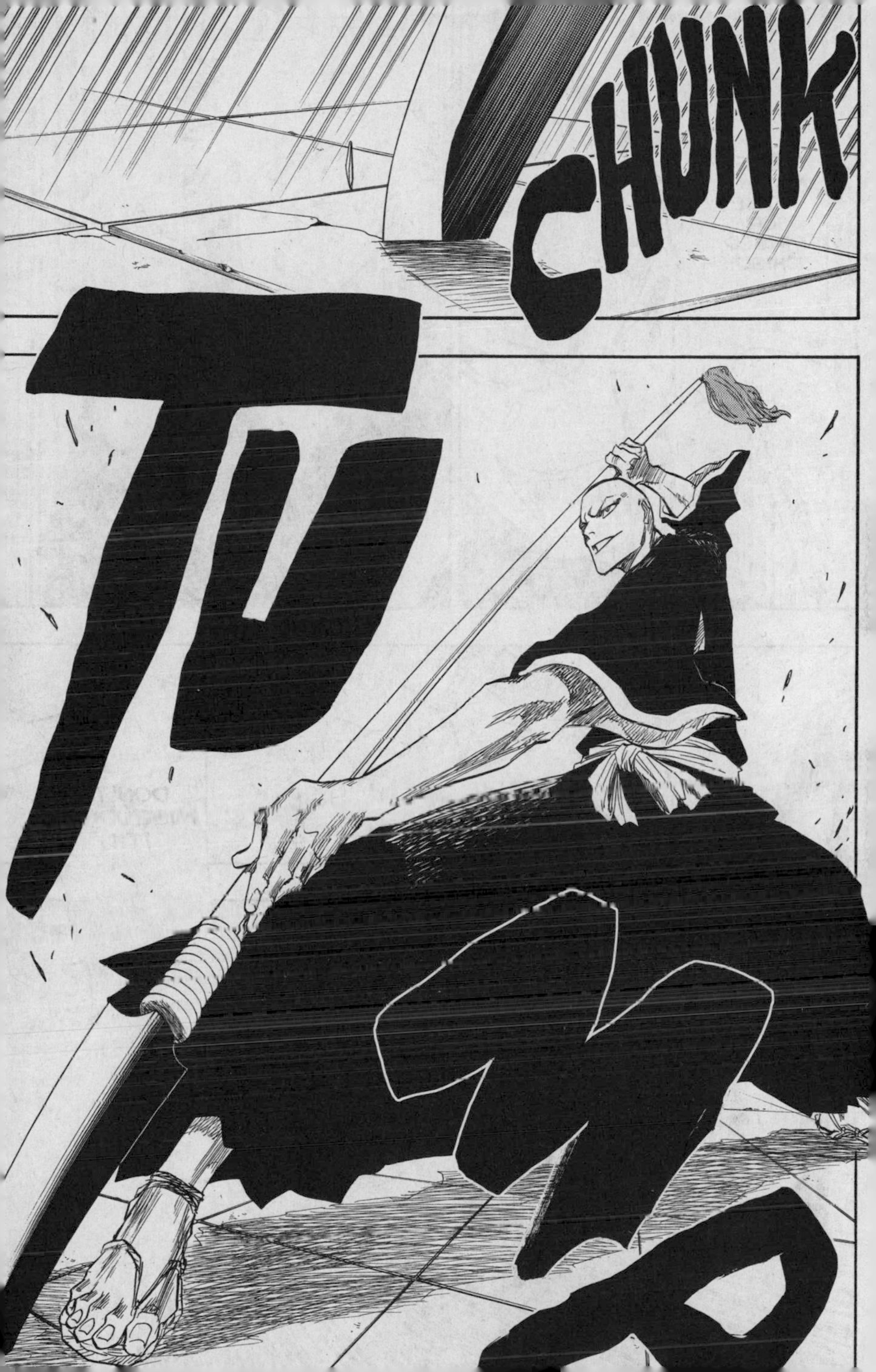
CHUNK

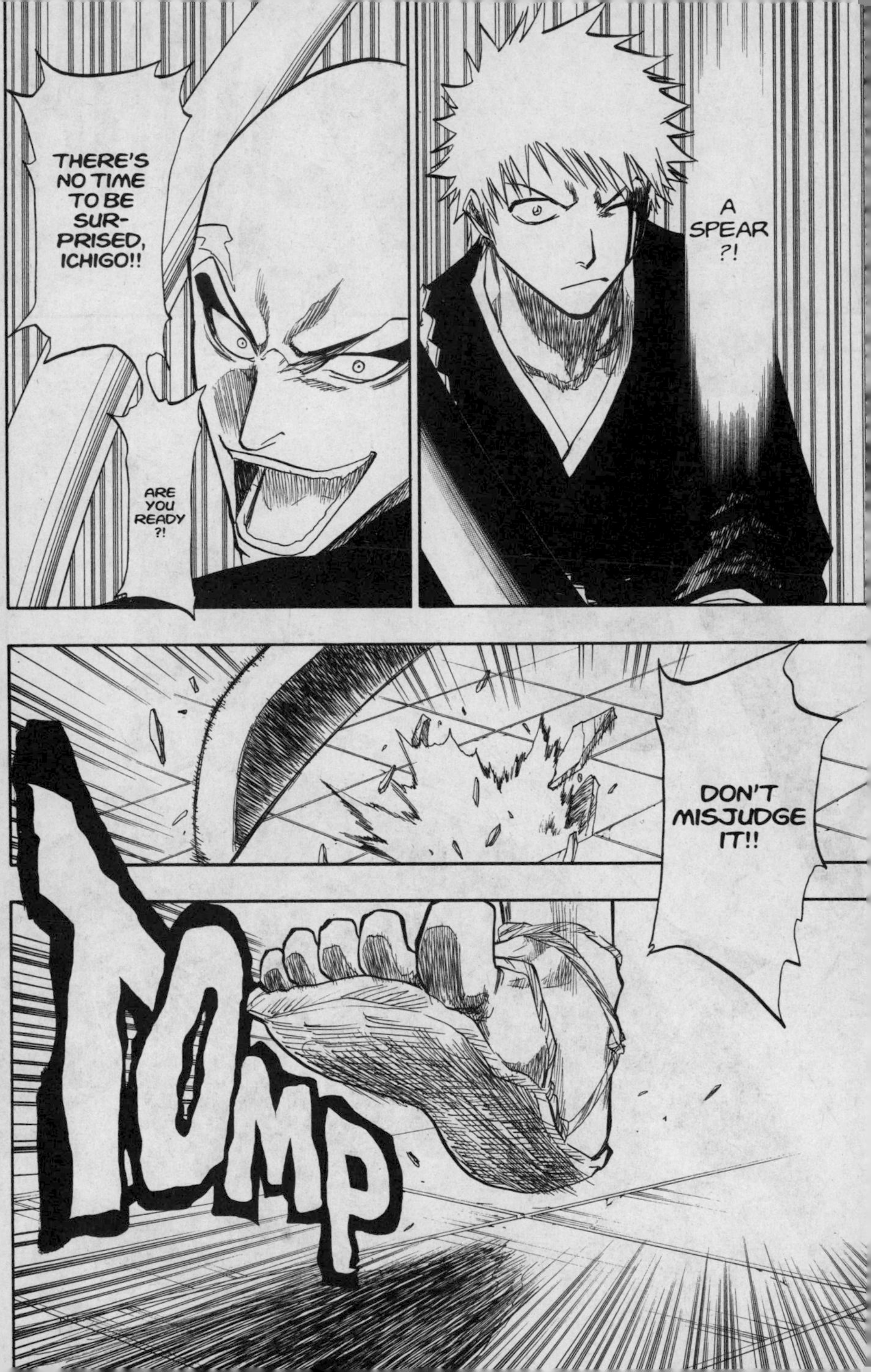
A SPEAR ?!
THERE'S NO TIME TO BE SUR-PRISED, ICHIGO!!
ARE YOU READY ?!
DON'T MISJUDGE IT!!
TOMP

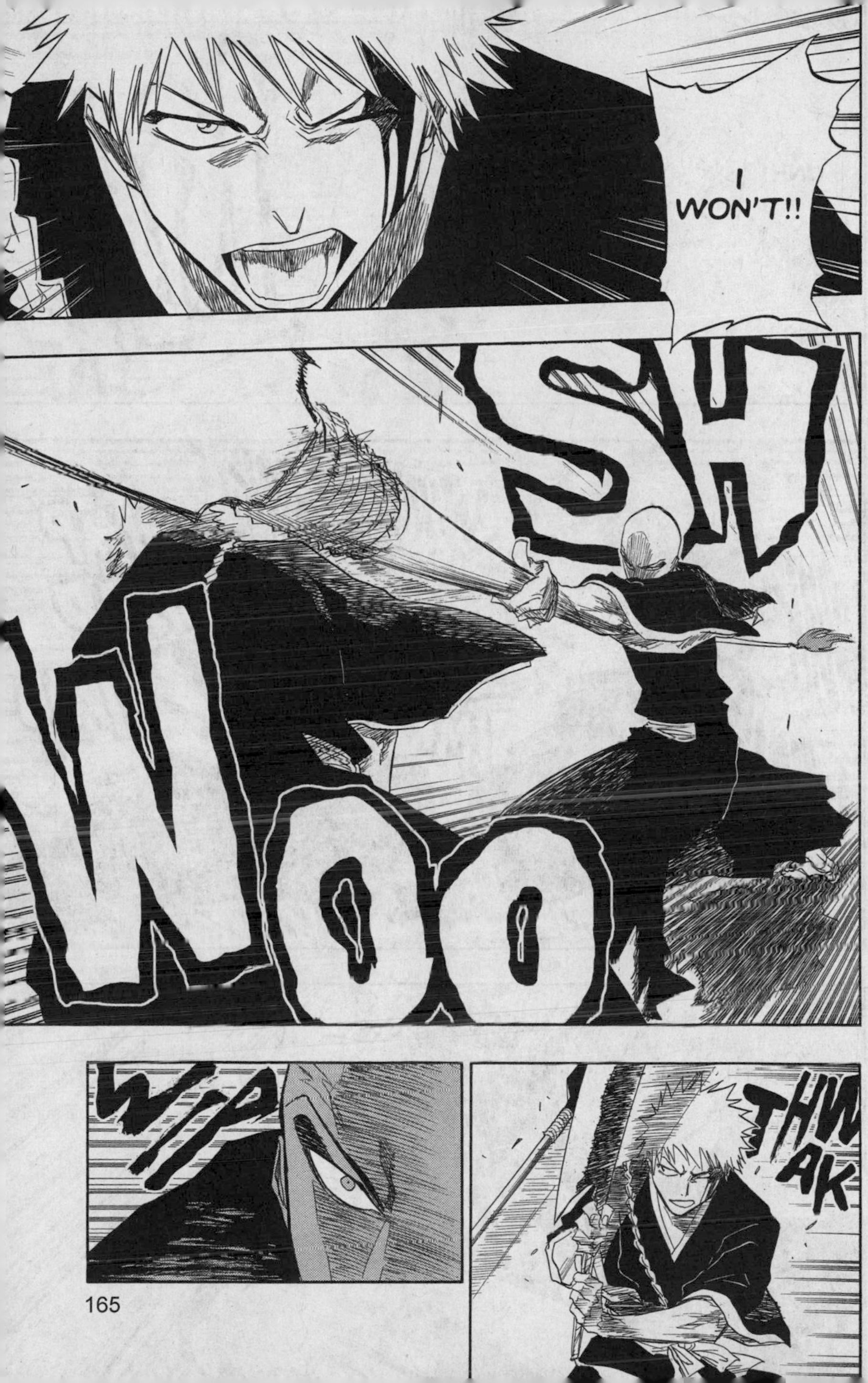
I WON'T!!
SHWOOO
THWAK
WIP

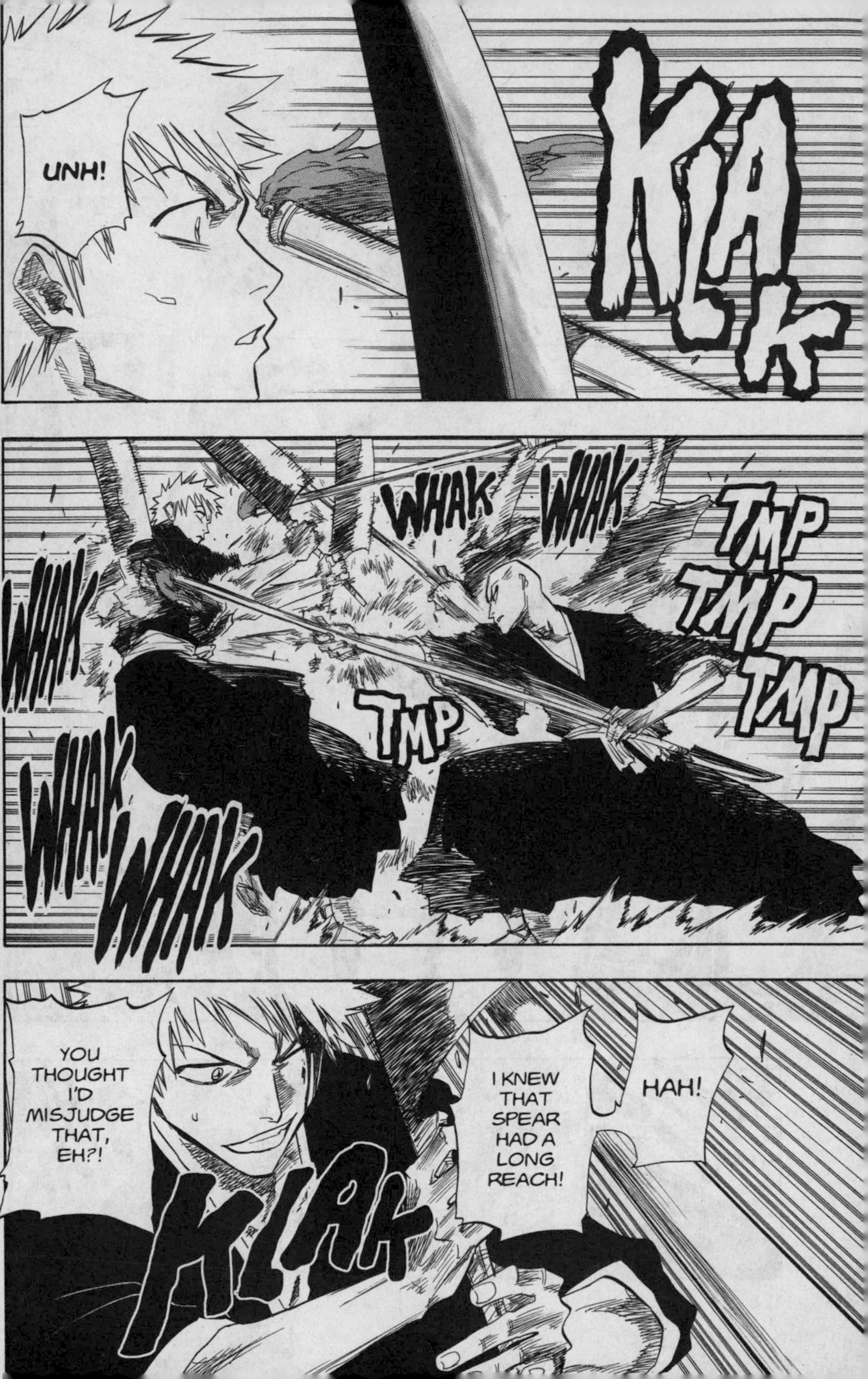
KLAK
UNH!
TMP TMP TMP
WHAK WHAK
TMP
WHAK
WHAK WHAK
HAH!
I KNEW THAT SPEAR HAD A LONG REACH!
YOU THOUGHT I'D MISJUDGE THAT, EH?!
KLAK

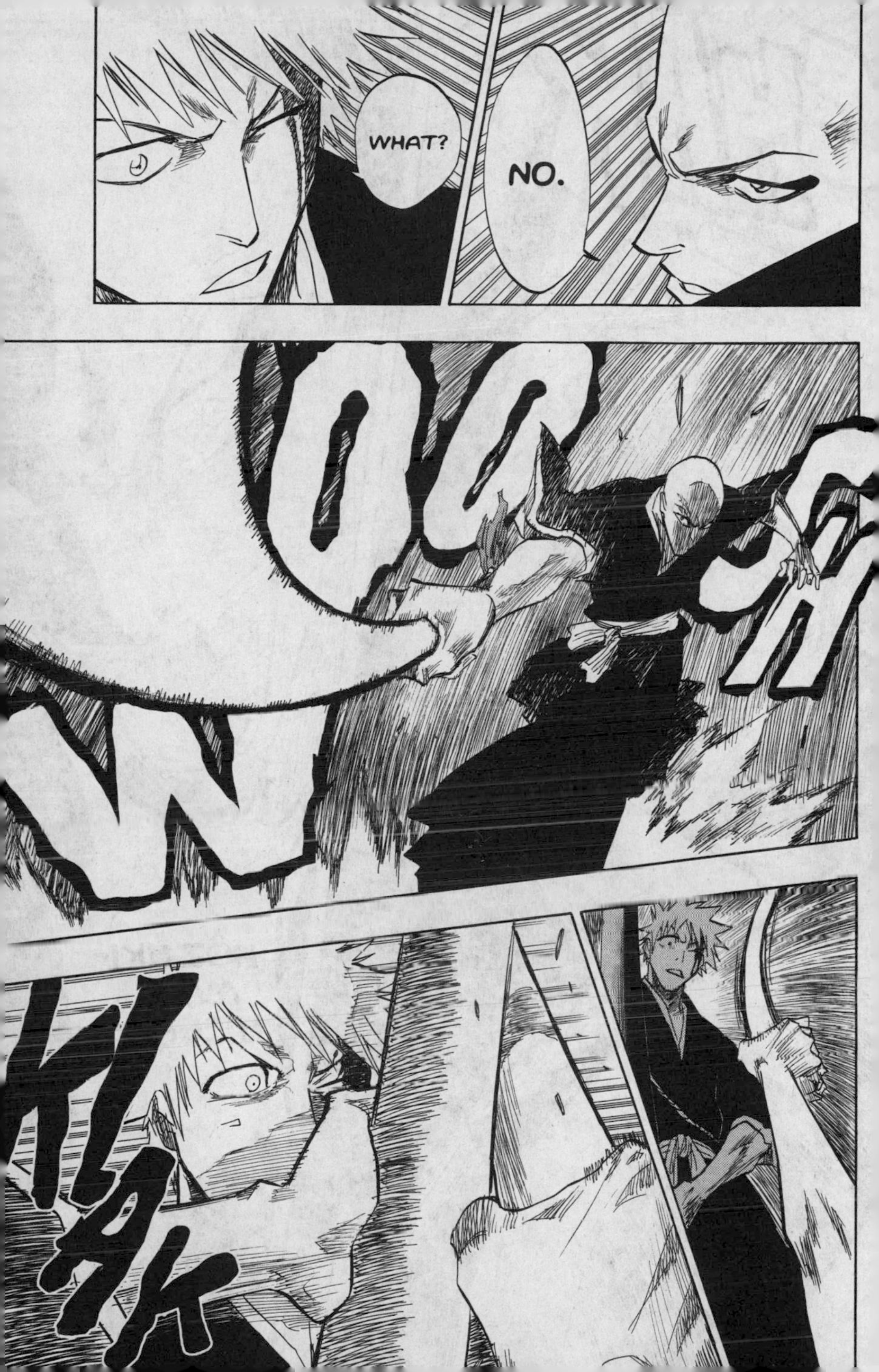
NO.
WHAT?

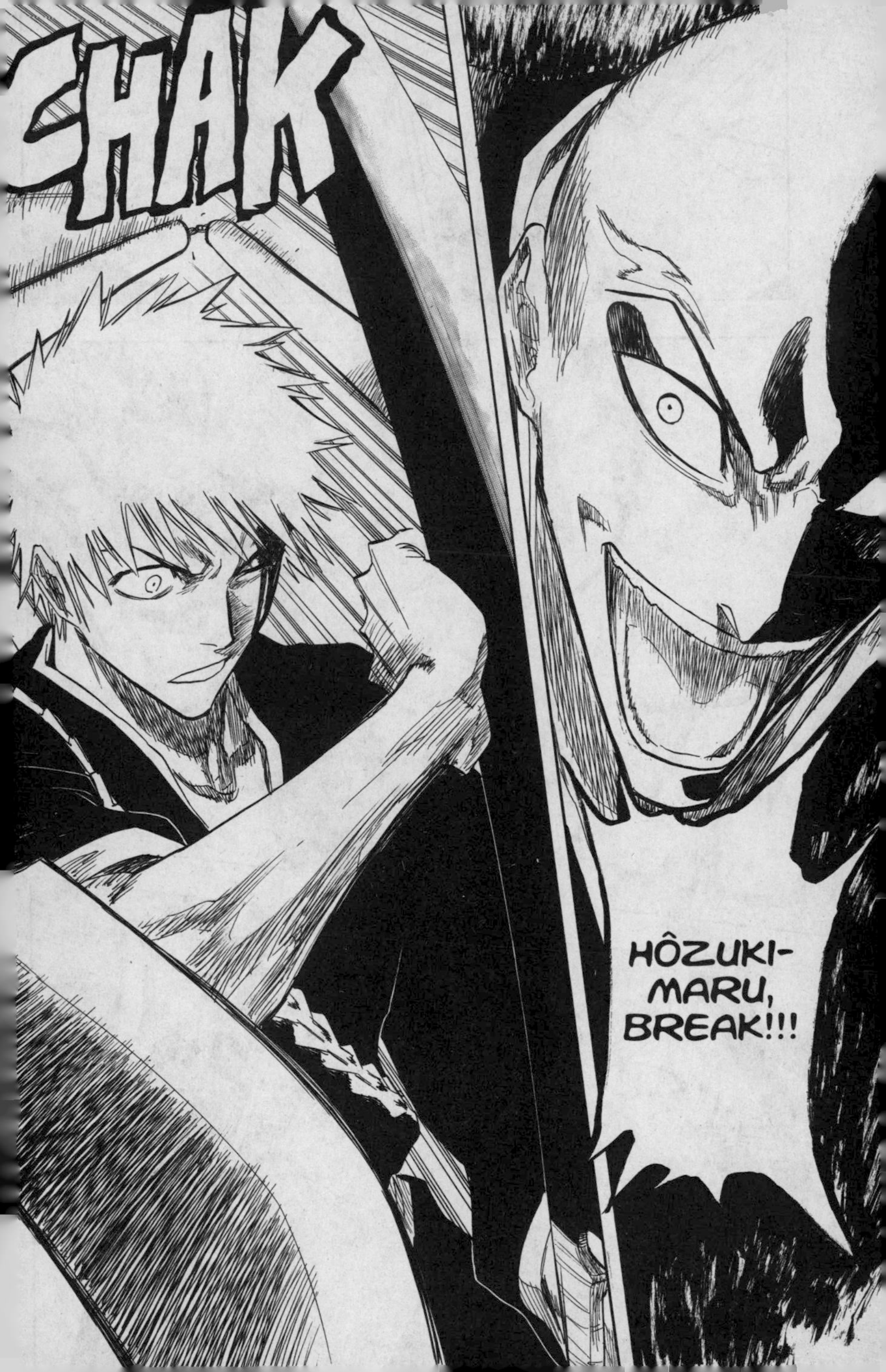
CHAK
HÔZUKI-
MARU,
BREAK!!!

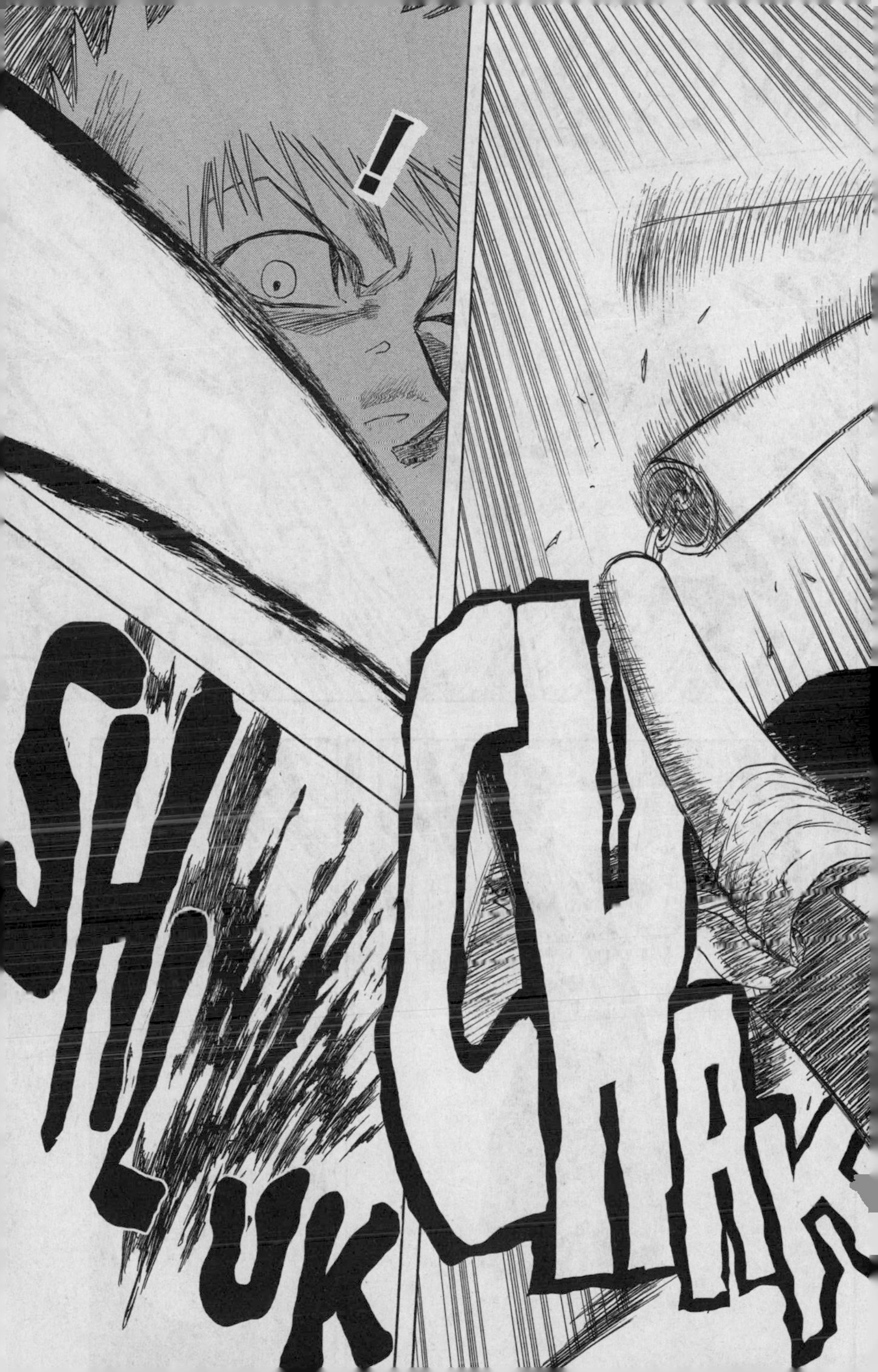
CHAK
!
SHUK

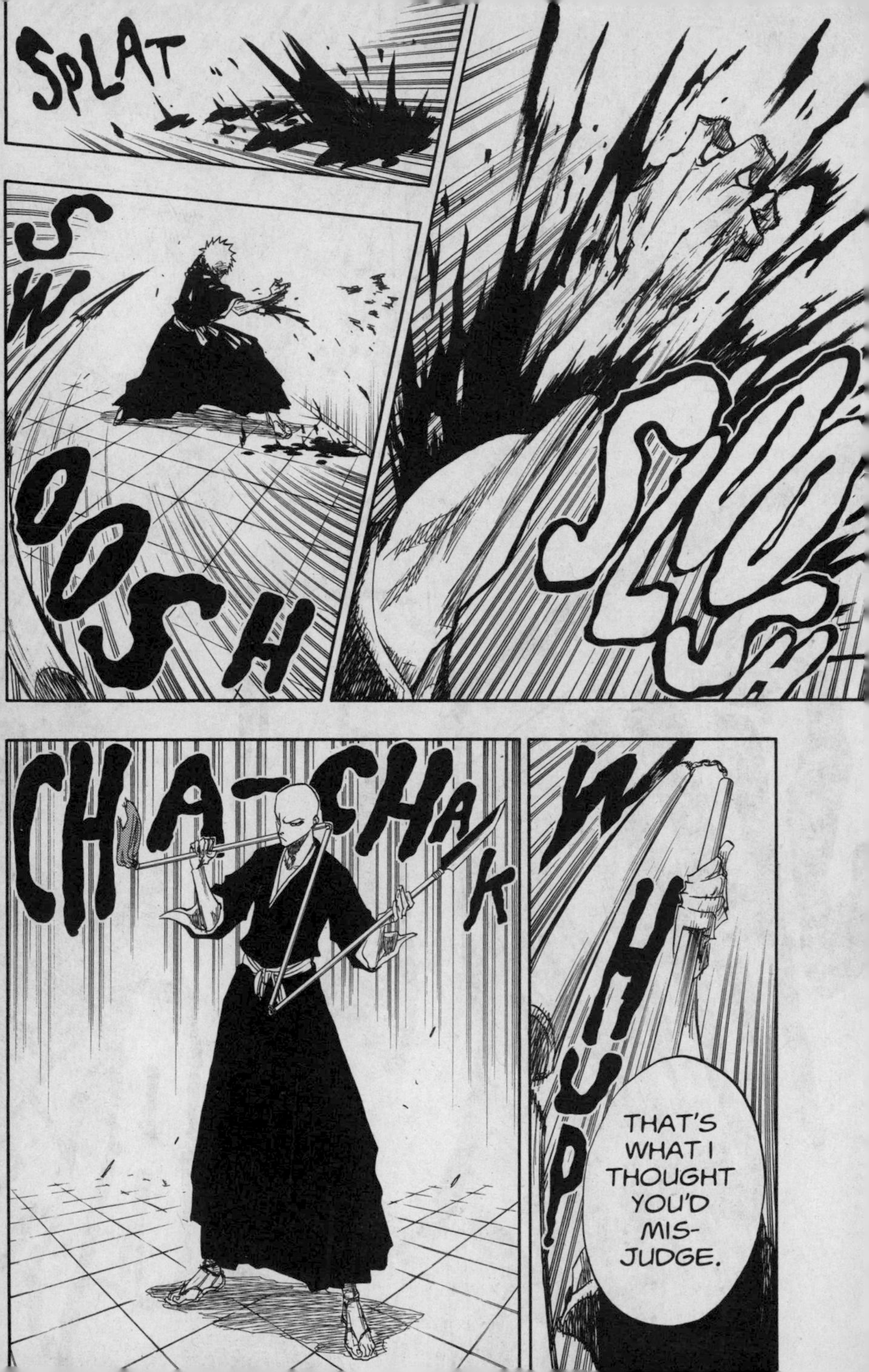
SPLAT
WHOOSH
WHUP!
THAT'S WHAT I THOUGHT YOU'D MIS-JUDGE.
CHA-CHAK

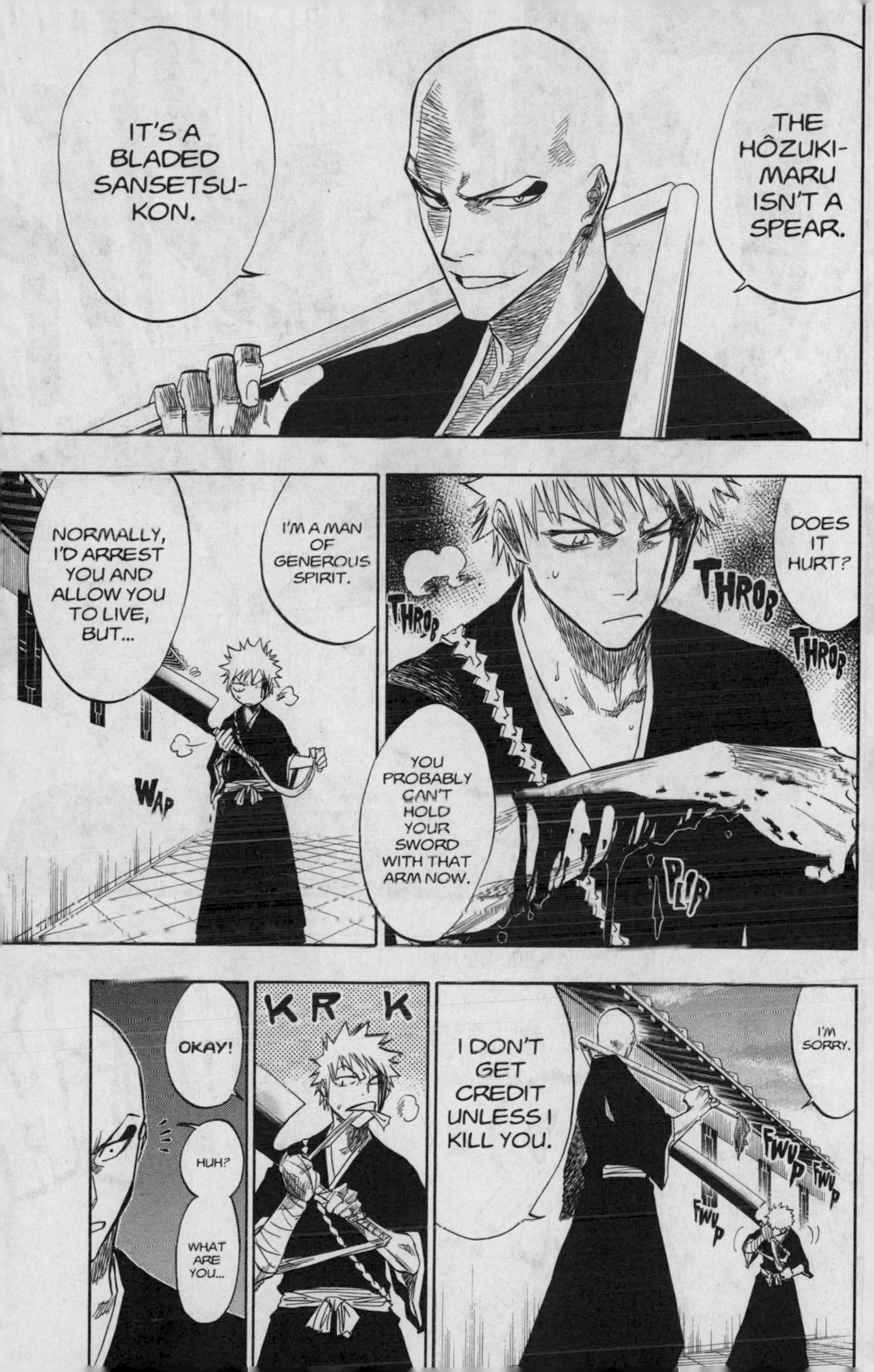
THE HÔZUKI-MARU ISN'T A SPEAR.
IT'S A BLADED SANSETSU-KON.
DOES IT HURT?
THROB
THROB
THROB
YOU PROBABLY CAN'T HOLD YOUR SWORD WITH THAT ARM NOW.
PLOP
I'M A MAN OF GENEROUS SPIRIT.
NORMALLY, I'D ARREST YOU AND ALLOW YOU TO LIVE, BUT...
WAP
I'M SORRY.
I DON'T GET CREDIT UNLESS I KILL YOU.
FWUP
FWUP
FWUP
KR K
OKAY!
HUH?
WHAT ARE YOU...

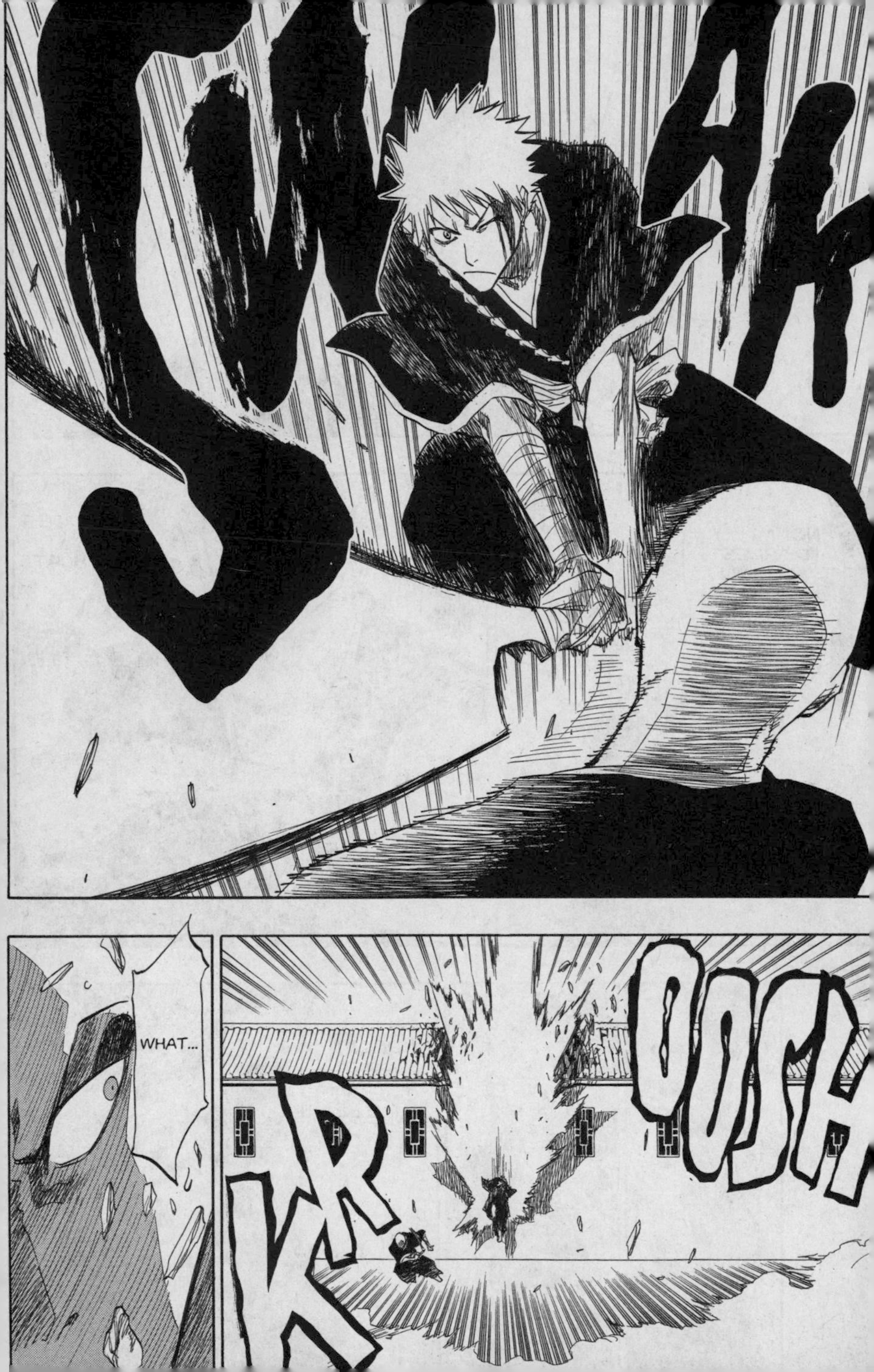
WHAT...

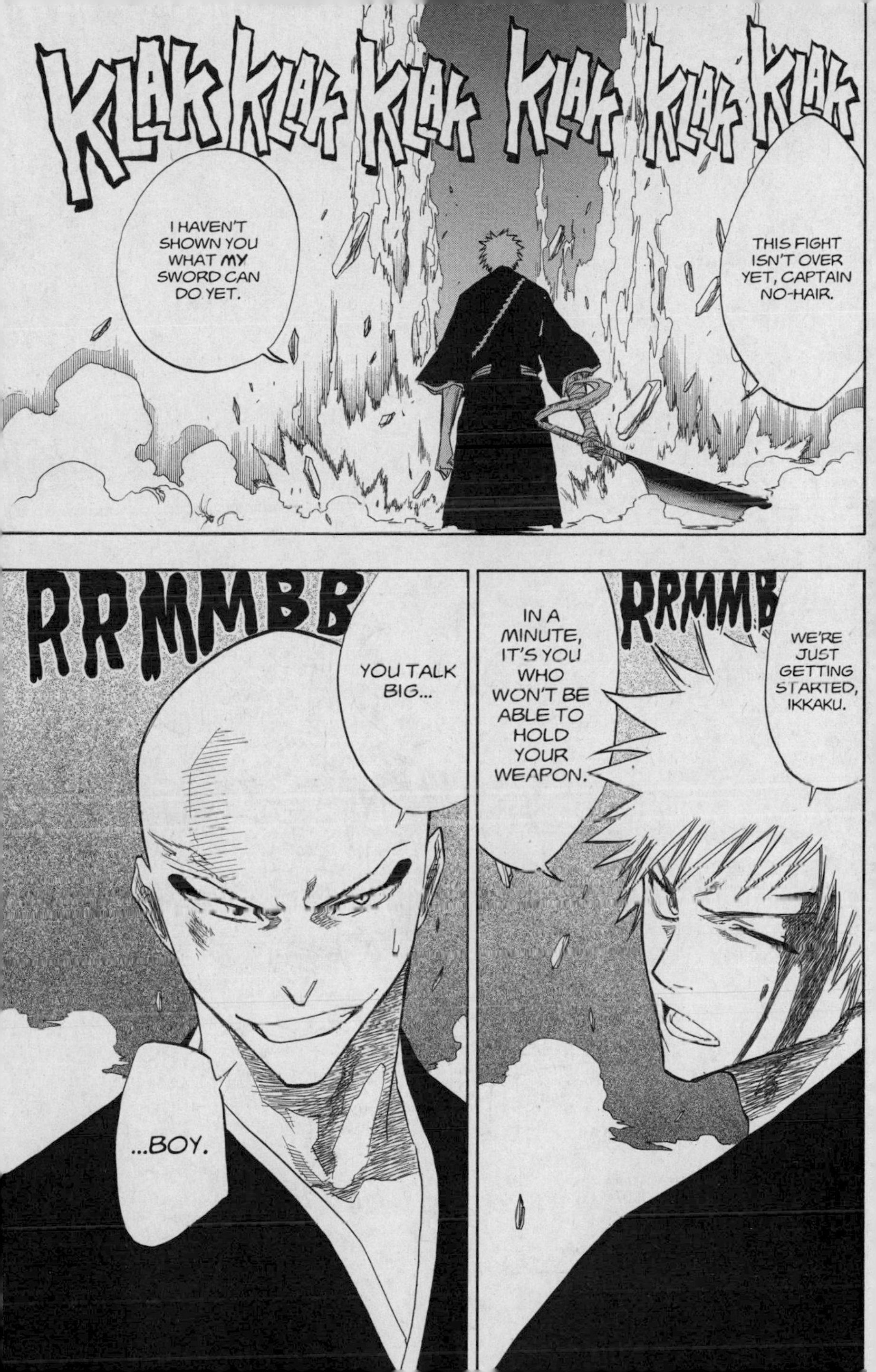
KLAK KLAK KLAK KLAK KLAK KLAK
THIS FIGHT ISN'T OVER YET, CAPTAIN NO-HAIR.
I HAVEN'T SHOWN YOU WHAT MY SWORD CAN DO YET.
RRMMB
WE'RE JUST GETTING STARTED, IKKAKU.
IN A MINUTE, IT'S YOU WHO WON'T BE ABLE TO HOLD YOUR WEAPON.
RRMMBB
YOU TALK BIG...
...BOY.

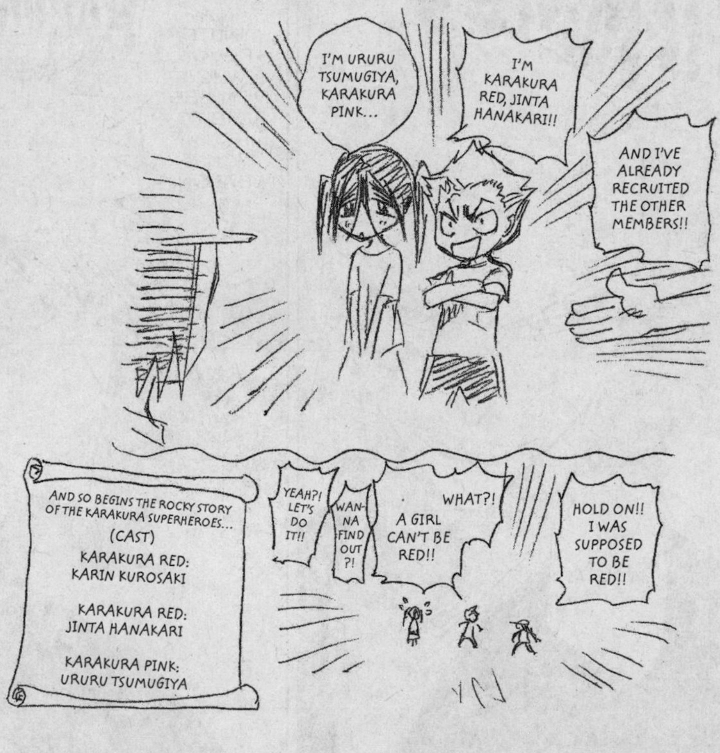
I'M KARAKURA RED, JINTA HANAKARI!!
AND I'VE ALREADY RECRUITED THE OTHER MEMBERS!!
I'M URURU TSUMUGIYA, KARAKURA PINK...
HOLD ON!! I WAS SUPPOSED TO BE RED!!
WHAT?!
A GIRL CAN'T BE RED!!
WAN-NA FIND OUT?!
YEAH?! LET'S DO IT!!
AND SO BEGINS THE ROCKY STORY OF THE KARAKURA SUPERHEROES...
(CAST)
KARAKURA RED: KARIN KUROSAKI
KARAKURA RED: JINTA HANAKARI
KARAKURA PINK: URURU TSUMUGIYA

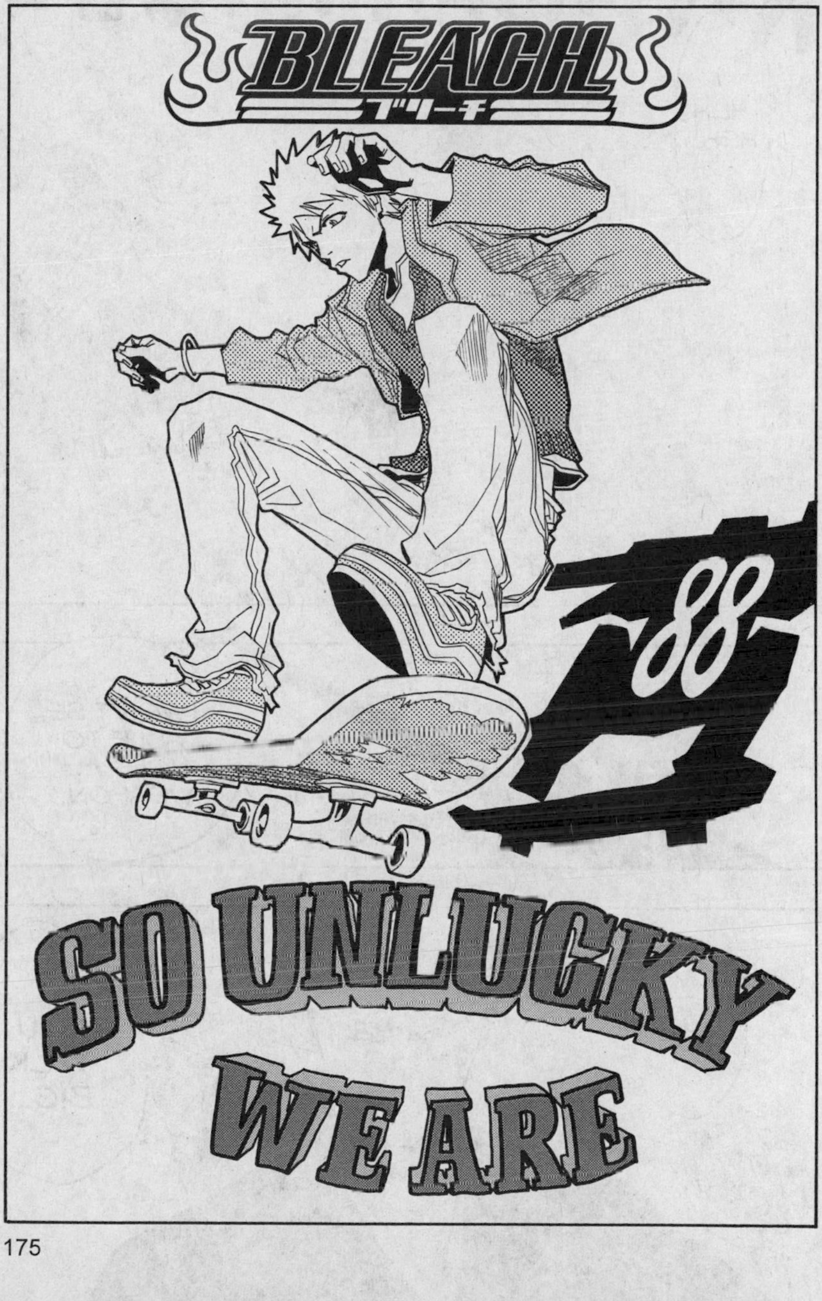
BLEACH
ブリーチ
-88-
SO UNLUCKY WE ARE

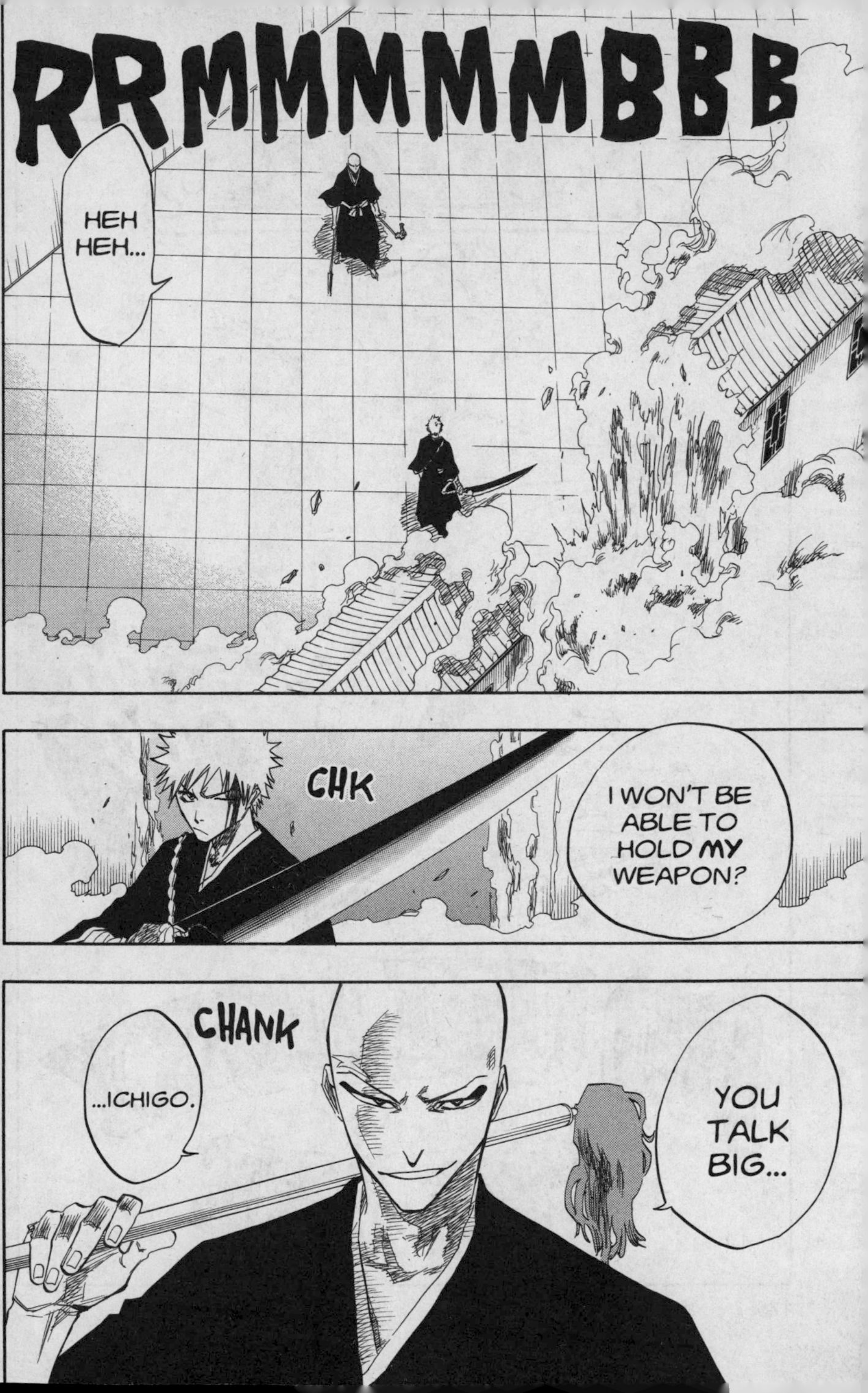
RRMMMMMBBB
HEH HEH...
I WON'T BE ABLE TO HOLD MY WEAPON?
CHK
YOU TALK BIG...
CHANK
...ICHIGO.

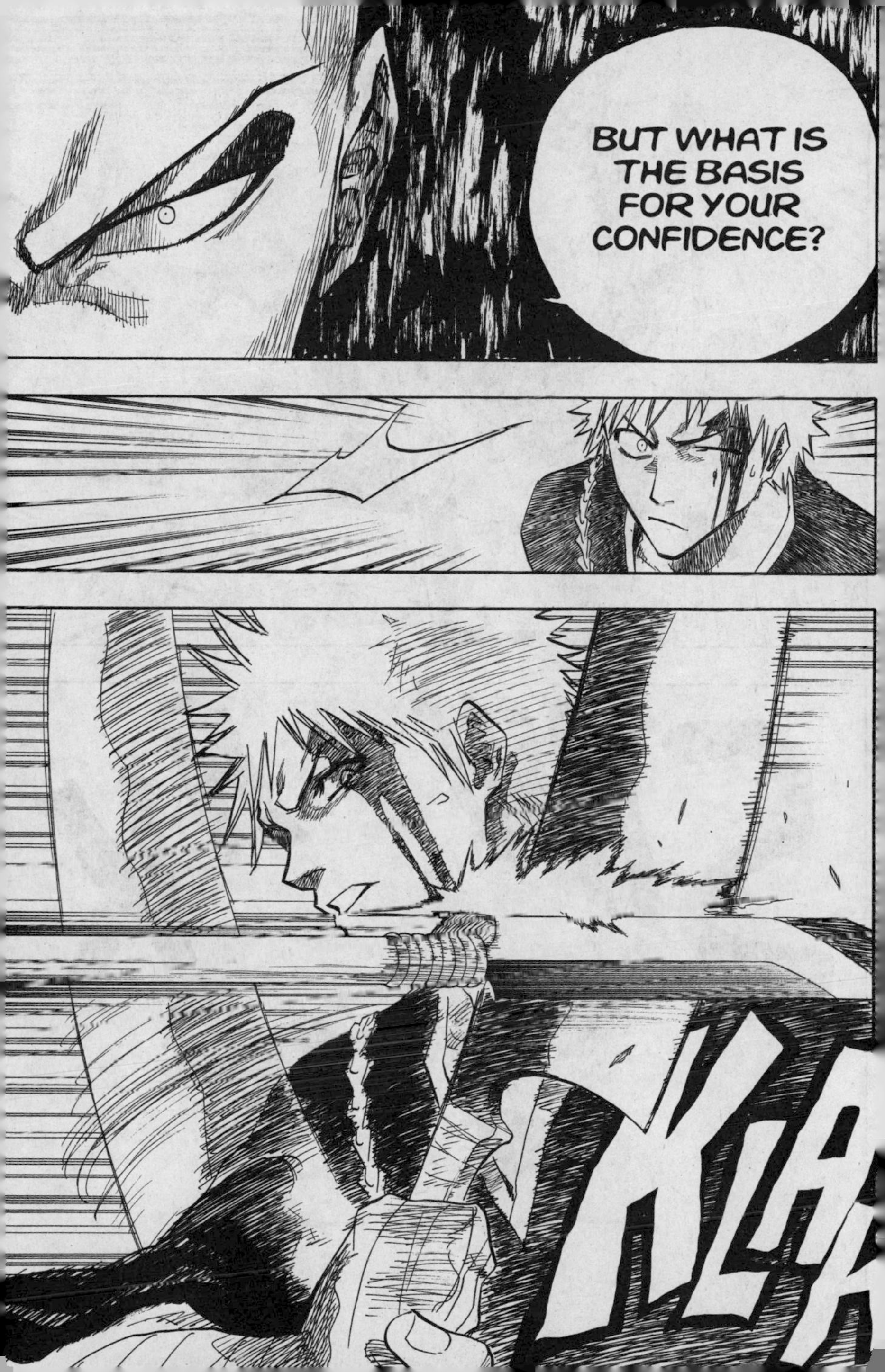
BUT WHAT IS THE BASIS FOR YOUR CONFIDENCE?

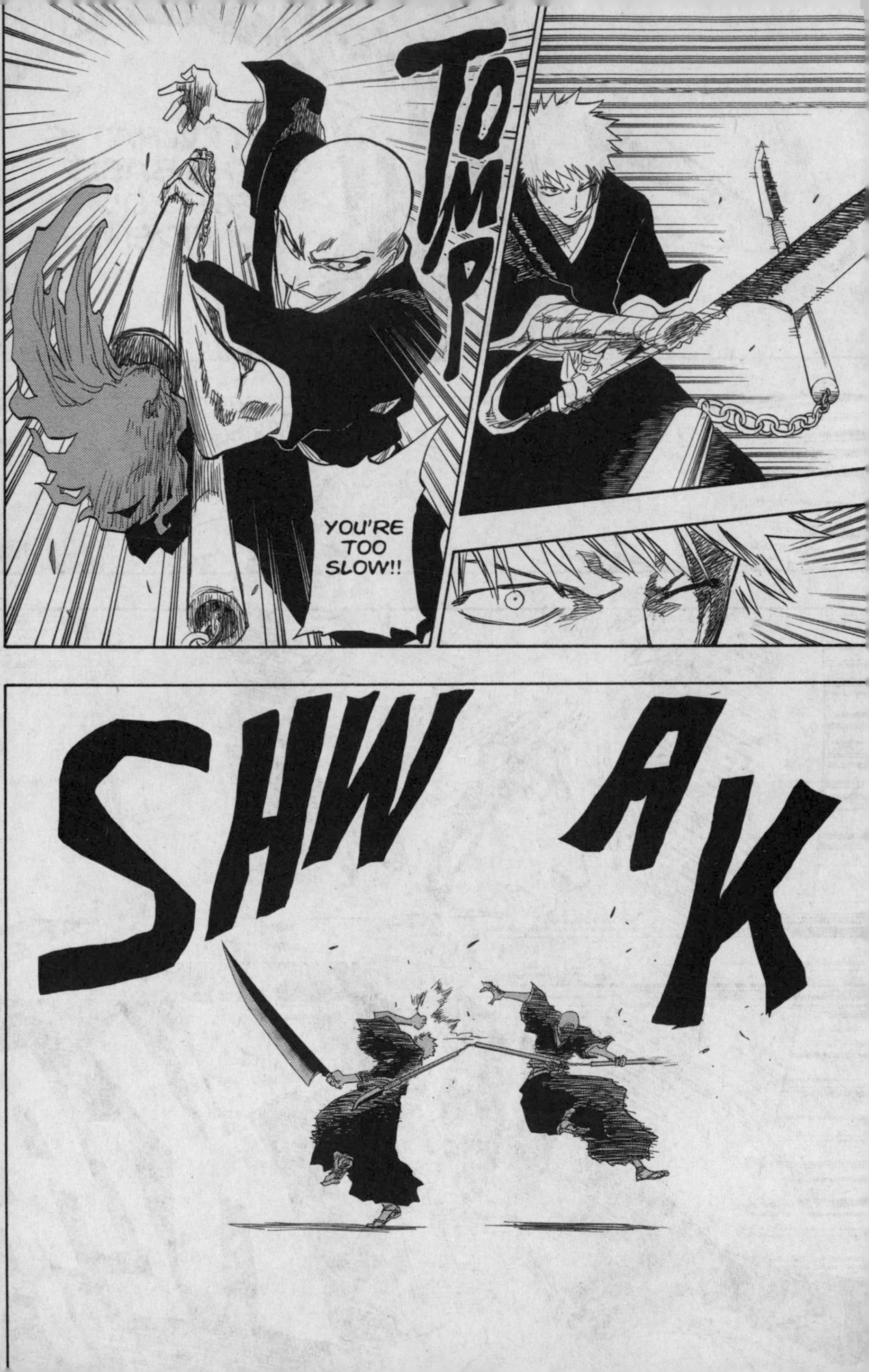
TOMP
YOU'RE TOO SLOW!!
SHWAK

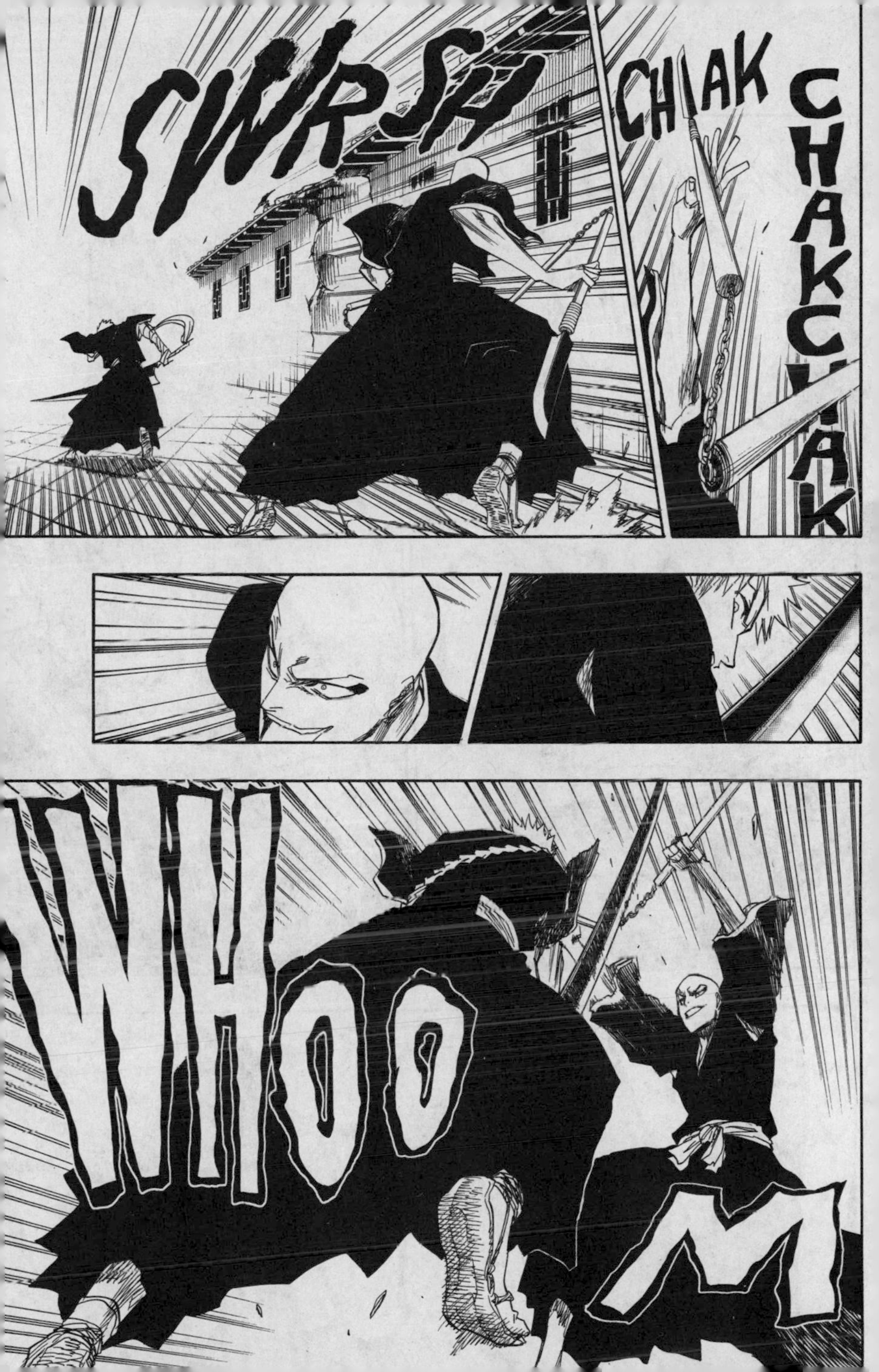
CHAK
CHAKCHAK
SWRSH
WHOOM

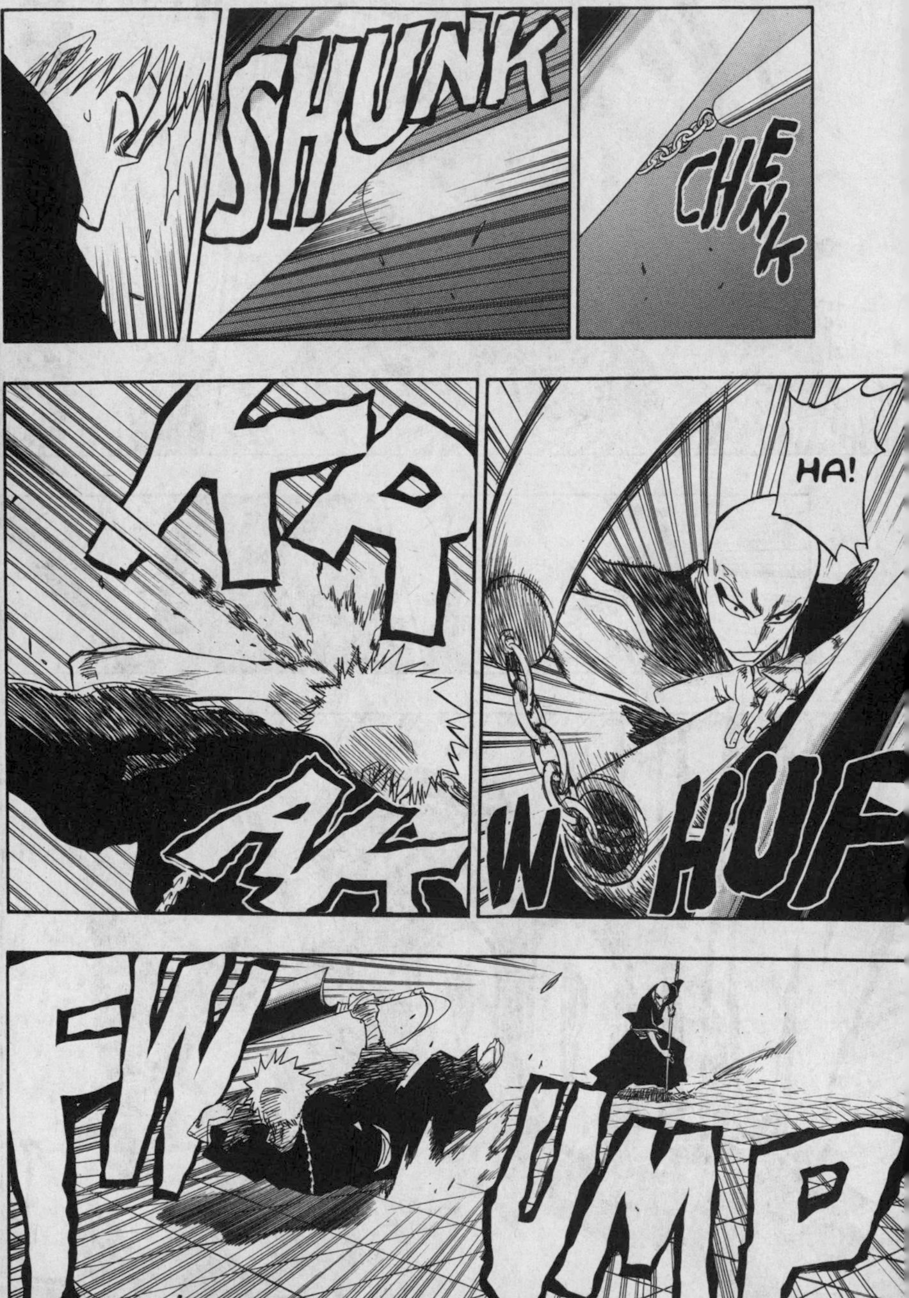
CHENK
SHUNK
HA!
WHUP
KRAK
FWUMP

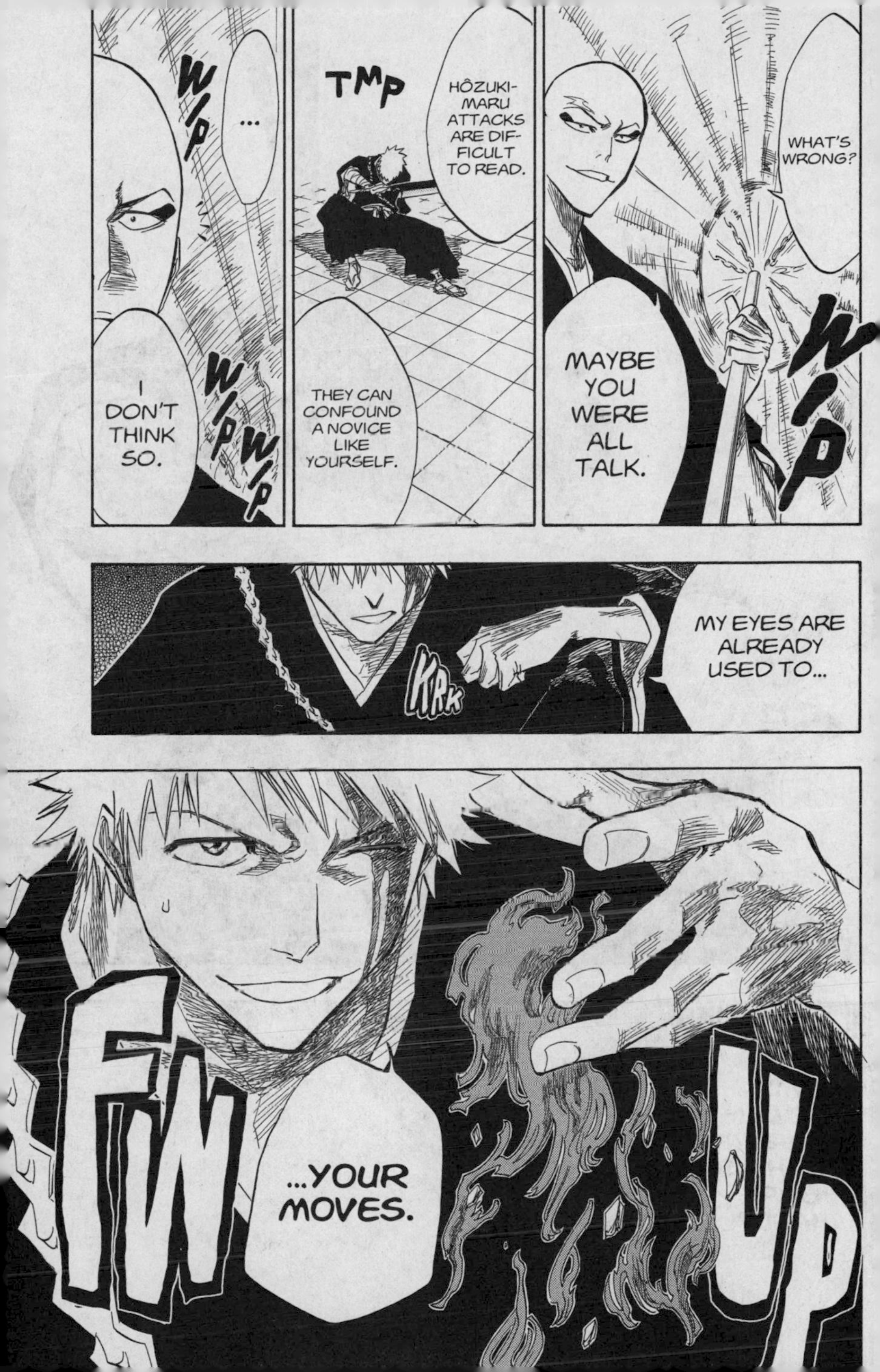
WHAT'S WRONG?
WIP
MAYBE YOU WERE ALL TALK.
TMP
HÔZUKI-MARU ATTACKS ARE DIF-FICULT TO READ.
THEY CAN CONFOUND A NOVICE LIKE YOURSELF.
WIP
...
I DON'T THINK SO.
WIPWIP
MY EYES ARE ALREADY USED TO...
KRK
...YOUR MOVES.
FWUP

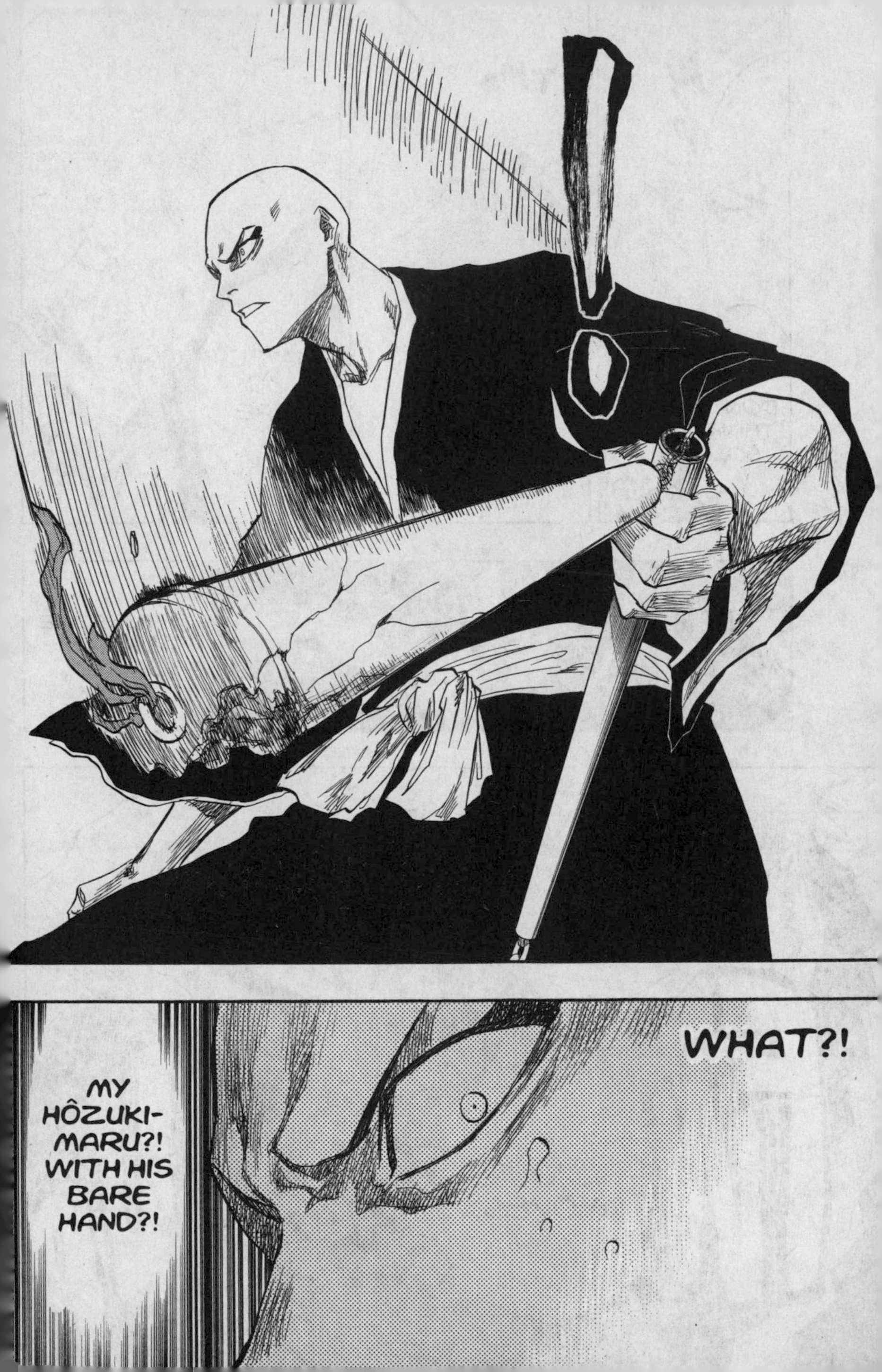
WHAT?!
MY HÔZUKI-MARU?! WITH HIS BARE HAND?!

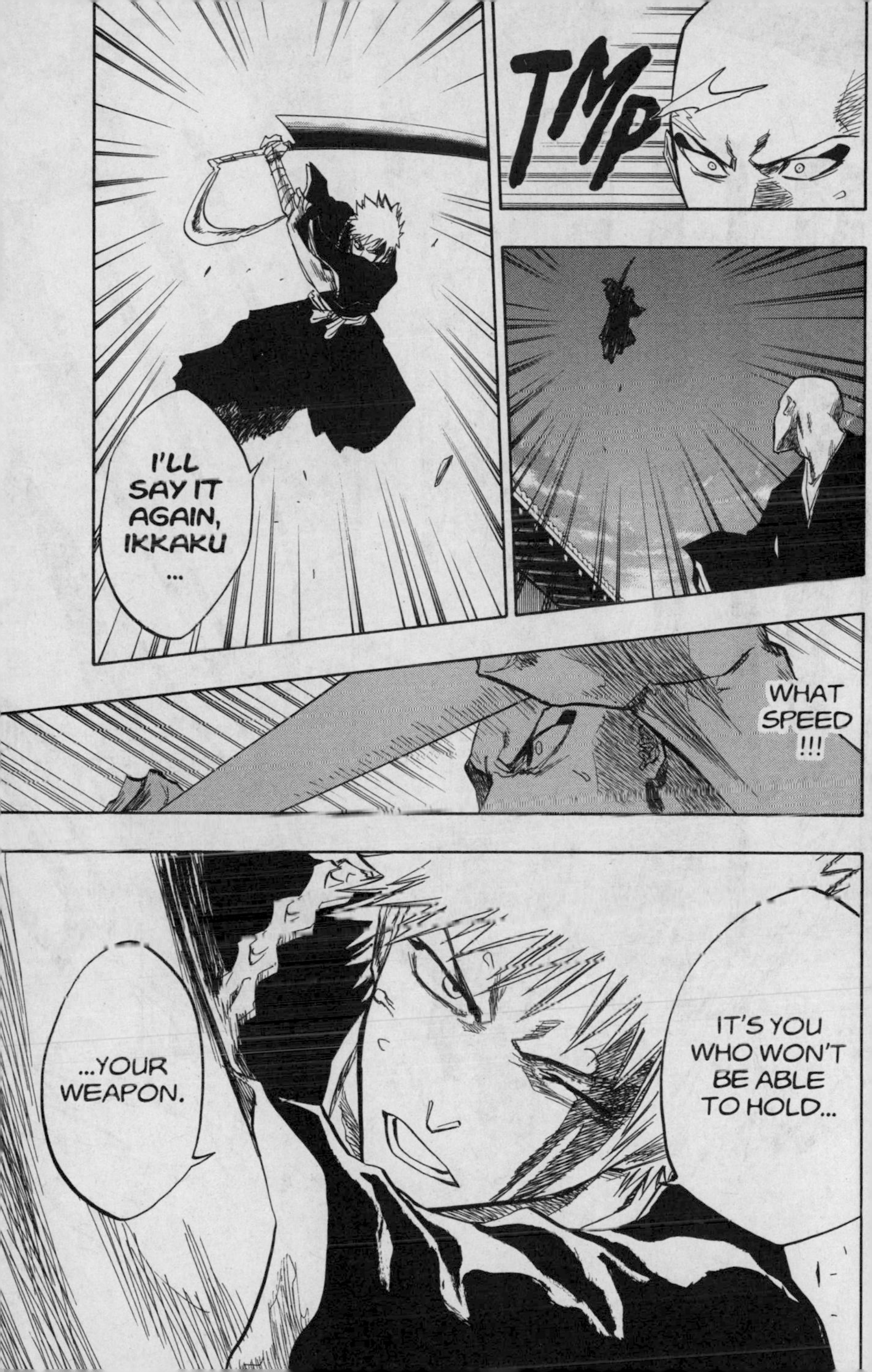
TMP
I'LL SAY IT AGAIN, IKKAKU ...
WHAT SPEED !!!
IT'S YOU WHO WON'T BE ABLE TO HOLD...
...YOUR WEAPON.

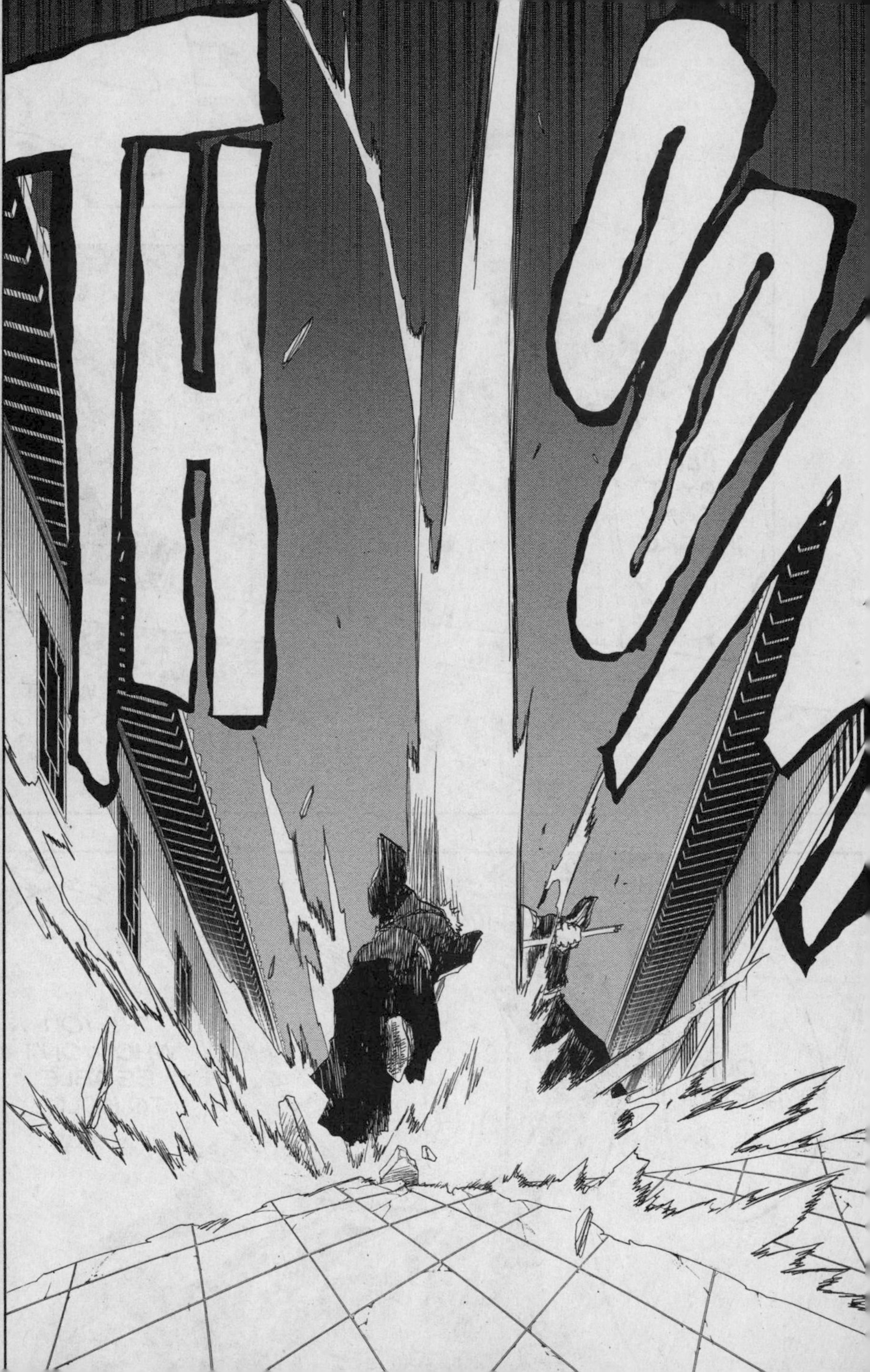
THOO

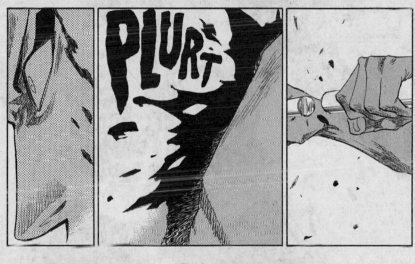

PLURT

PLUP
PLU P
PLUP
PLUP
PLUP

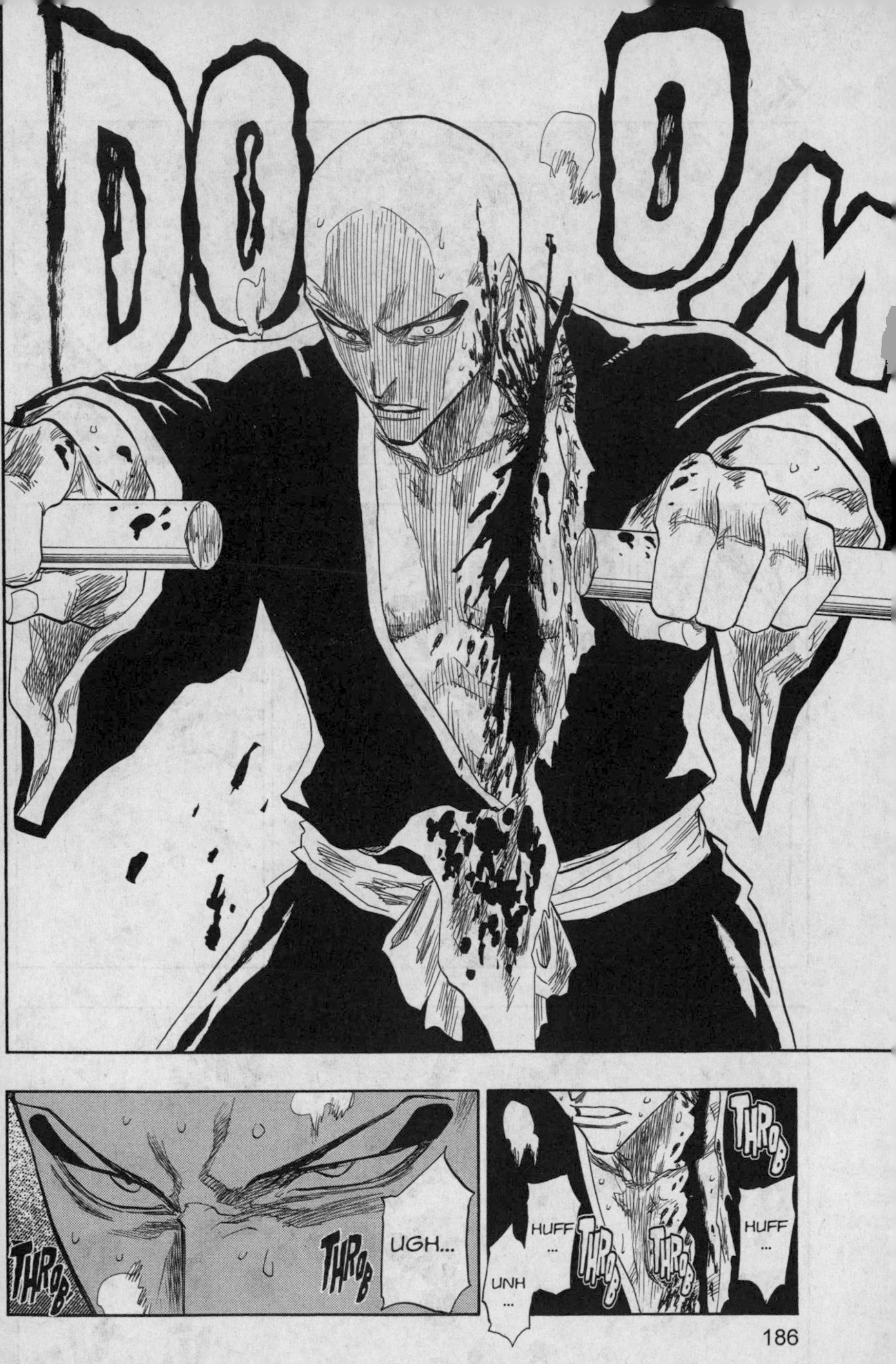
DOOM
THROB
HUFF ...
THROB
THROB
HUFF ...
UNH ...
UGH...
THROB
THROB

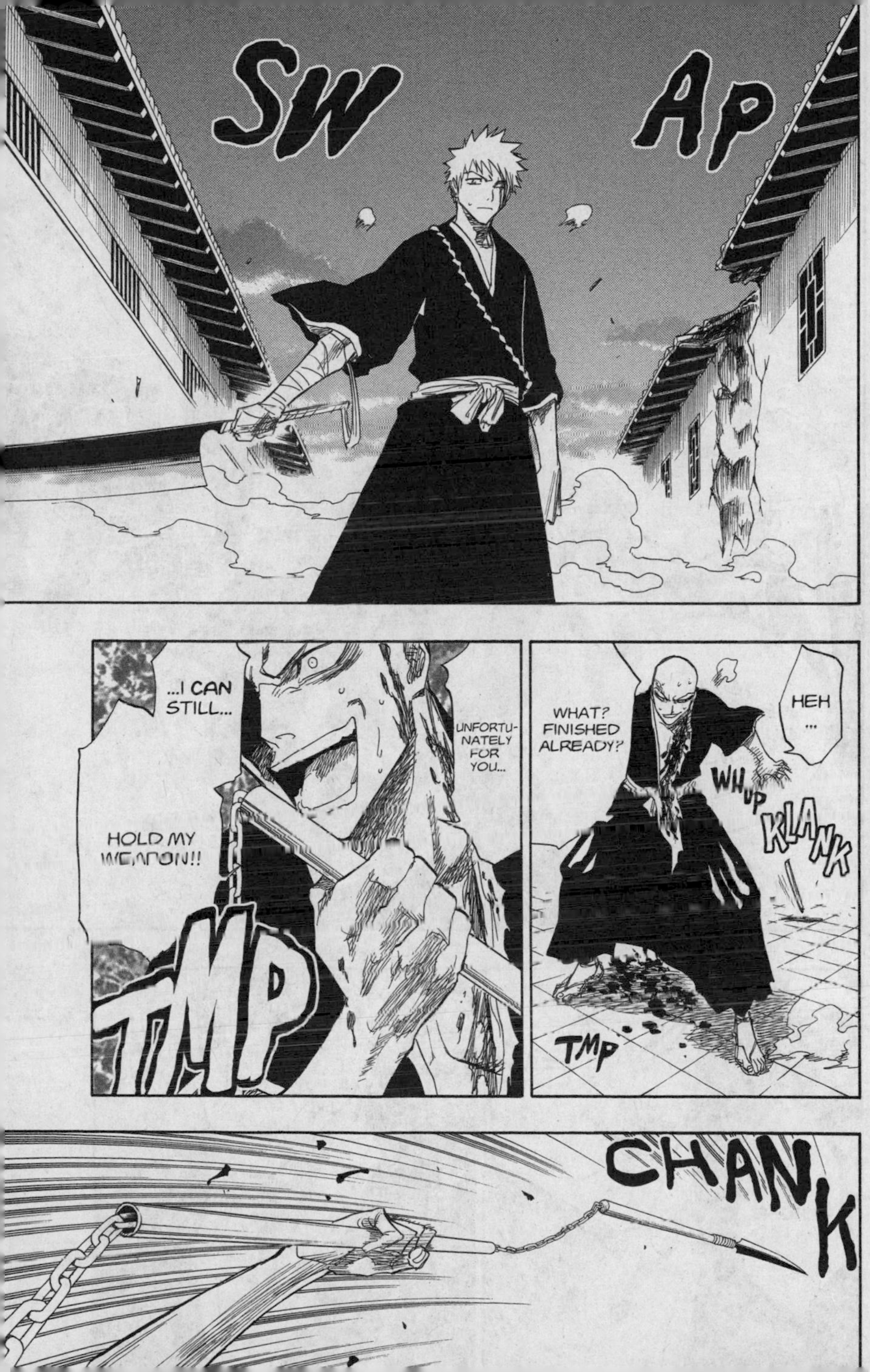
SW
AP
HEH
...
WHAT? FINISHED ALREADY?
WHUP
KLANK
TMP
UNFORTU-NATELY FOR YOU...
...I CAN STILL...
HOLD MY WEAPON!!
TMP
CHANK

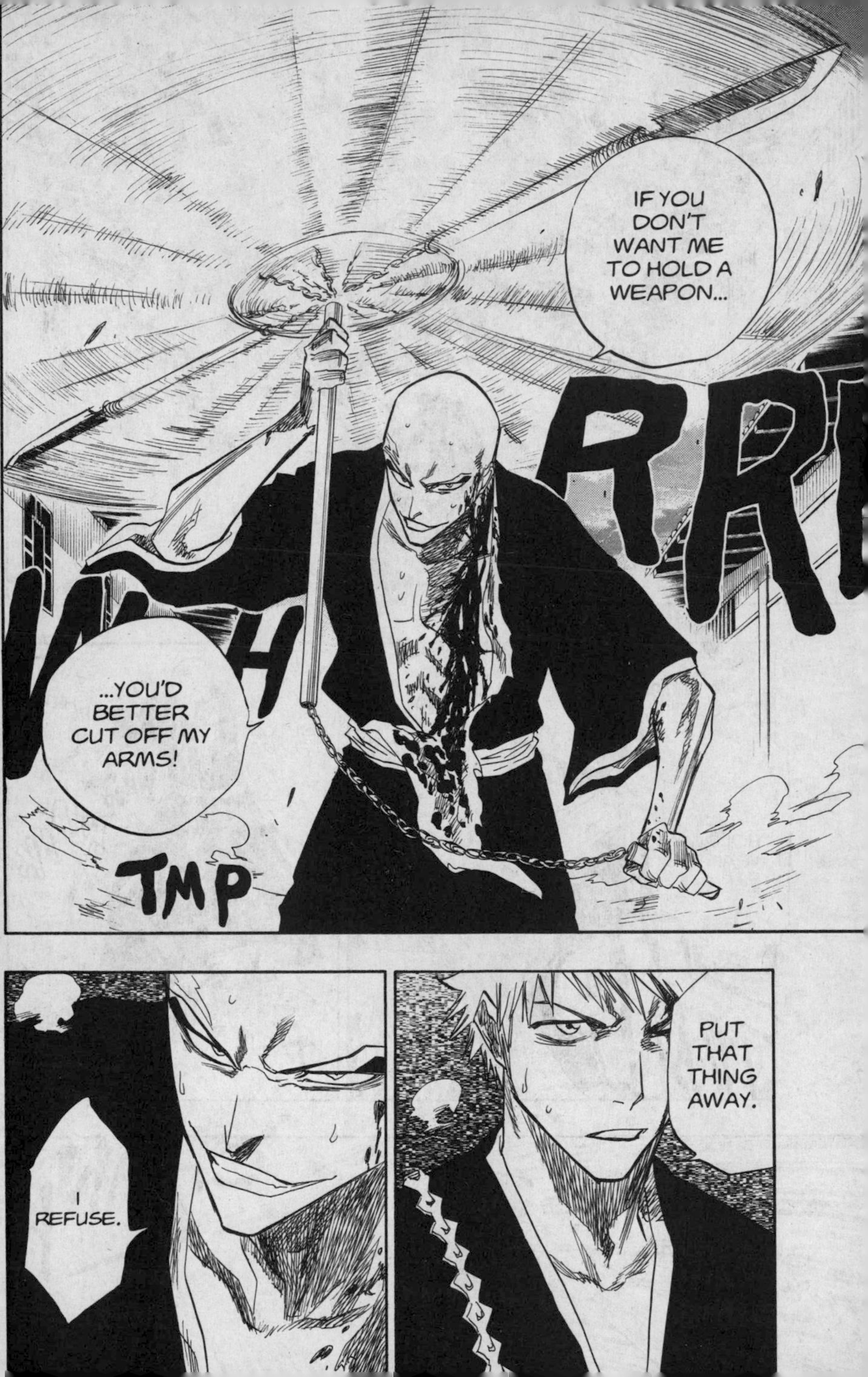
IF YOU DON'T WANT ME TO HOLD A WEAPON...
...YOU'D BETTER CUT OFF MY ARMS!
TMP
PUT THAT THING AWAY.
I REFUSE.

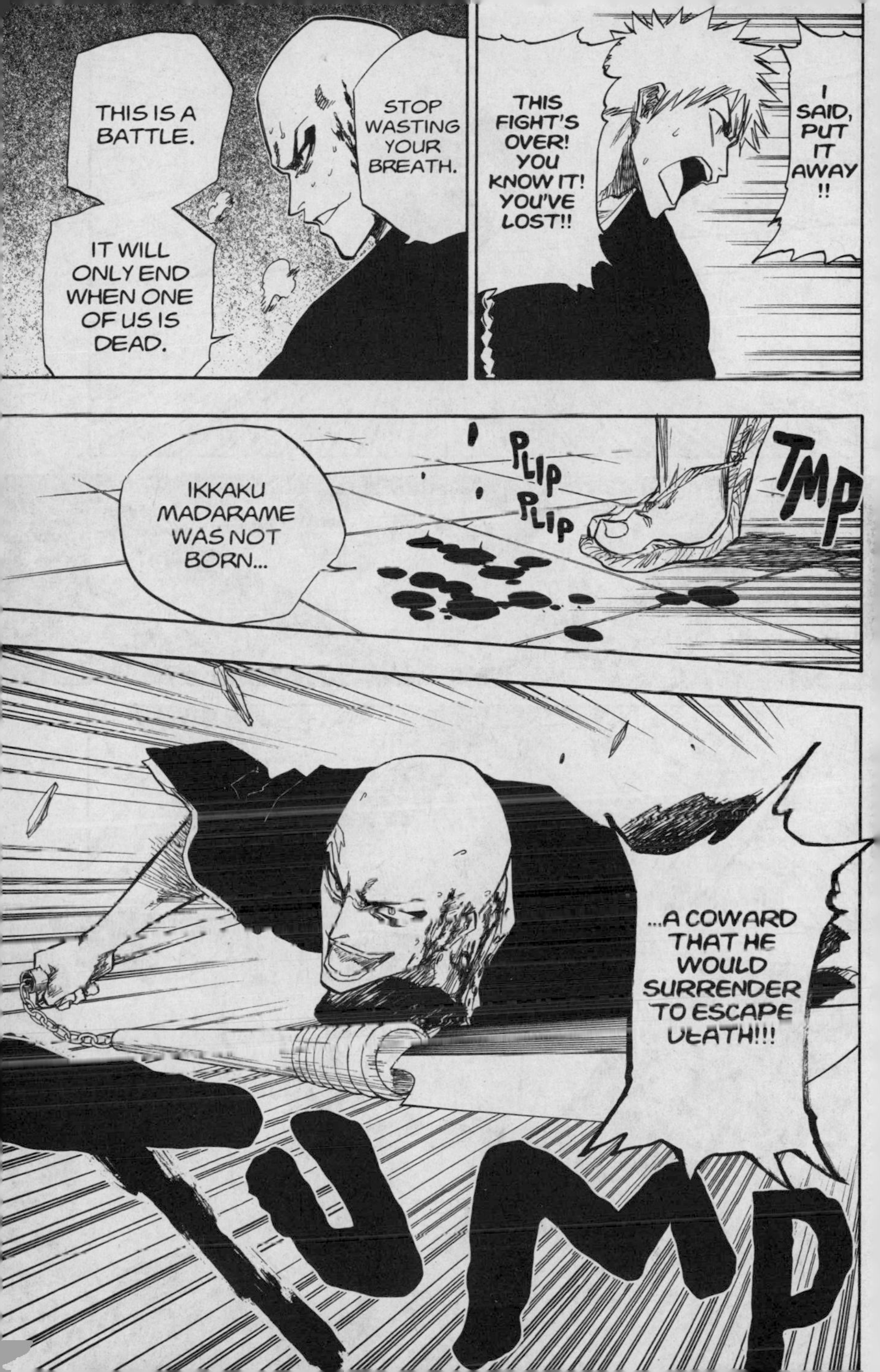
I SAID, PUT IT AWAY!!
THIS FIGHT'S OVER! YOU KNOW IT! YOU'VE LOST!!
STOP WASTING YOUR BREATH.
THIS IS A BATTLE.
IT WILL ONLY END WHEN ONE OF US IS DEAD.
TMP
PLIP PLIP
IKKAKU MADARAME WAS NOT BORN...
...A COWARD THAT HE WOULD SURRENDER TO ESCAPE DEATH!!!
TMP

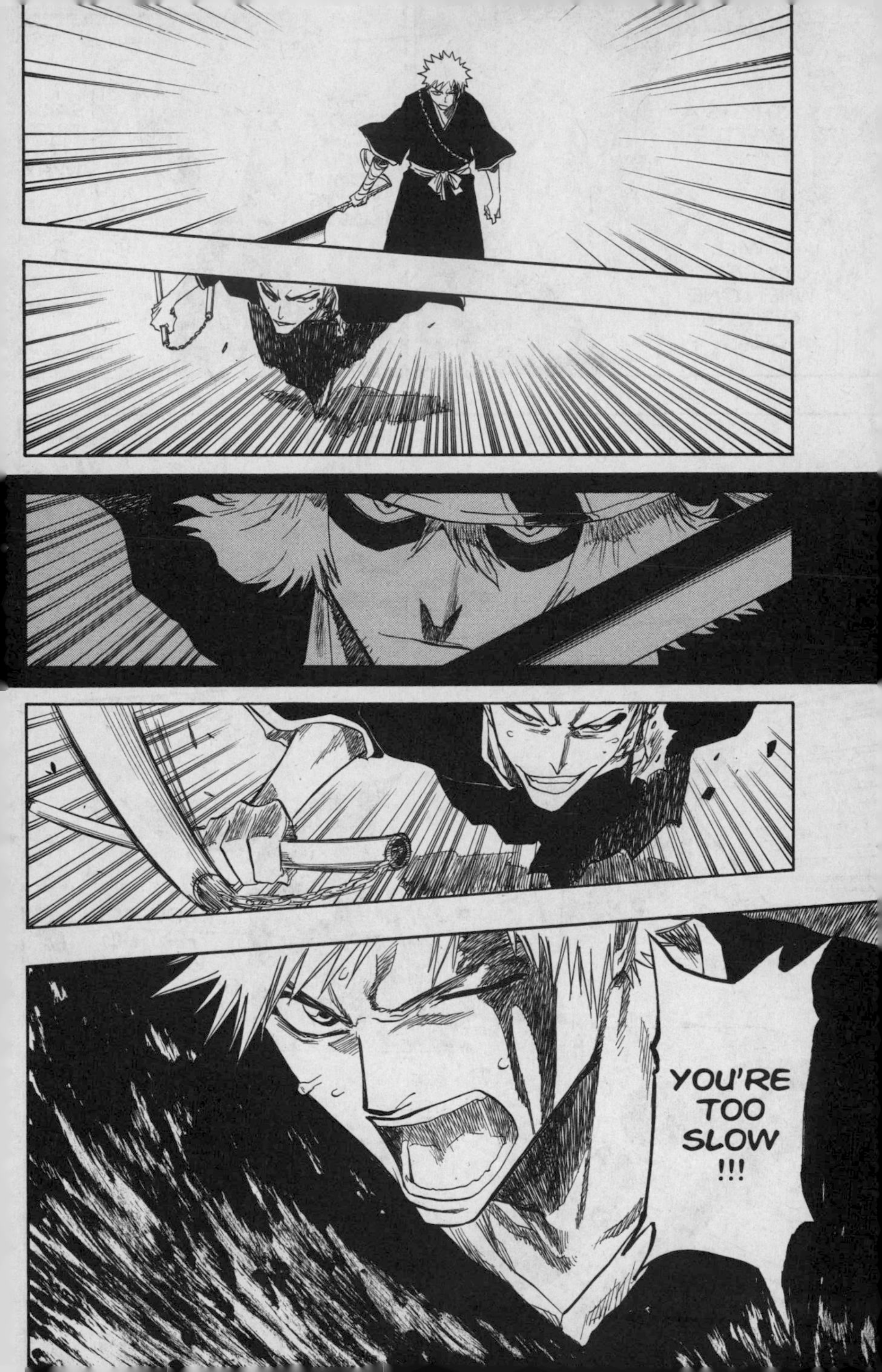
YOU'RE TOO SLOW !!!

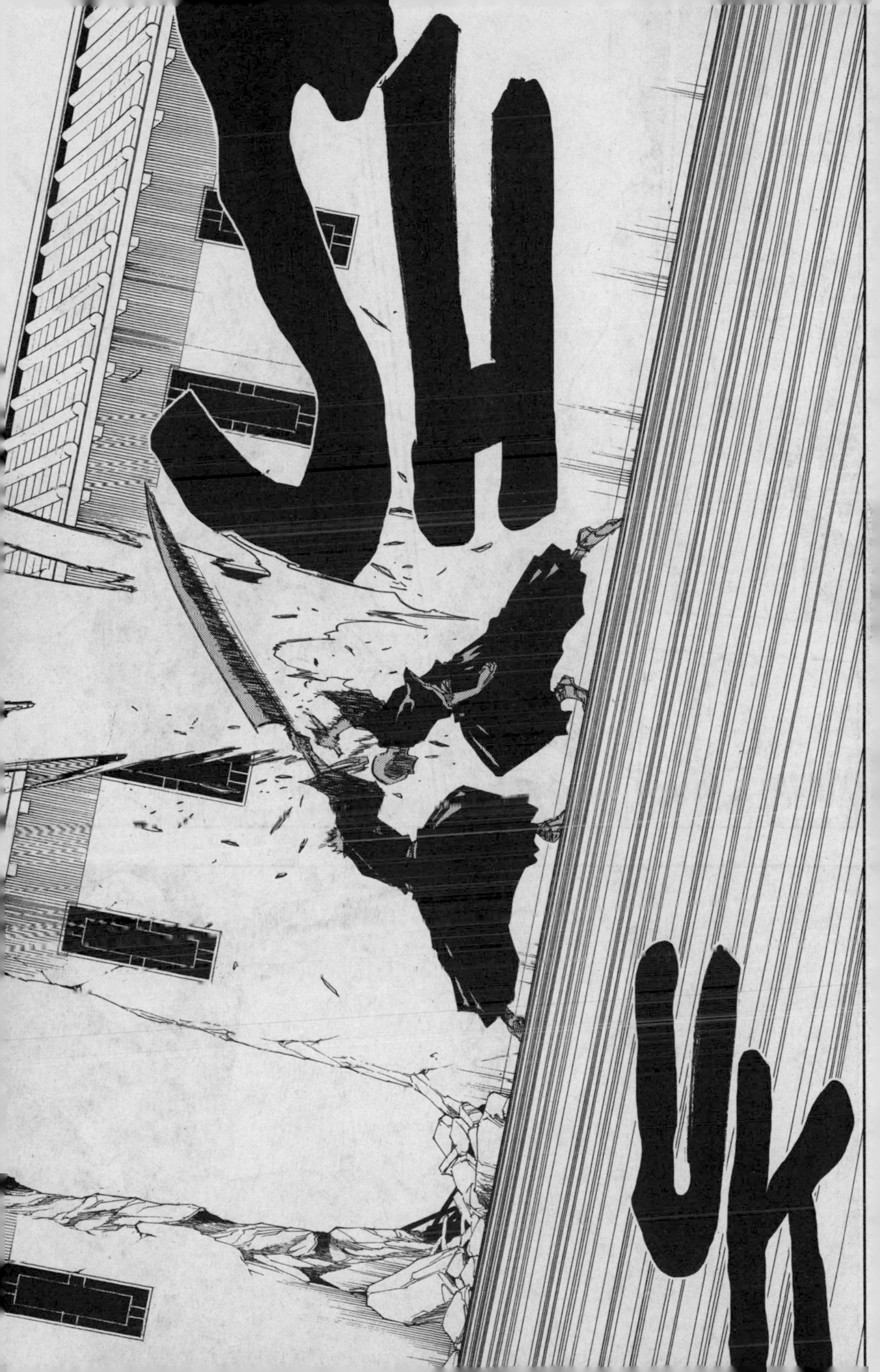
SHUK

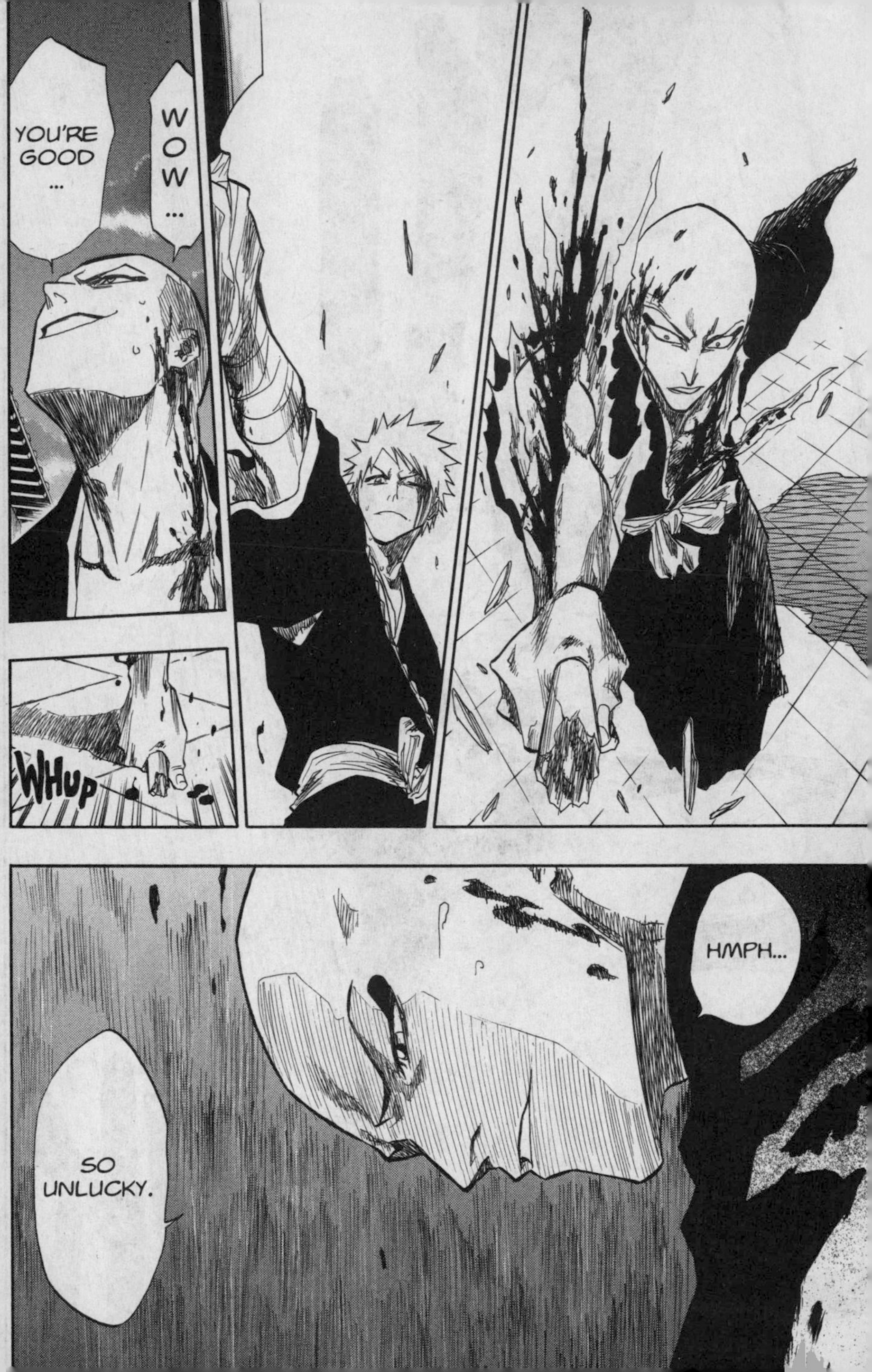
WOW...
YOU'RE GOOD...
WHUP
HMPH...
SO UNLUCKY.

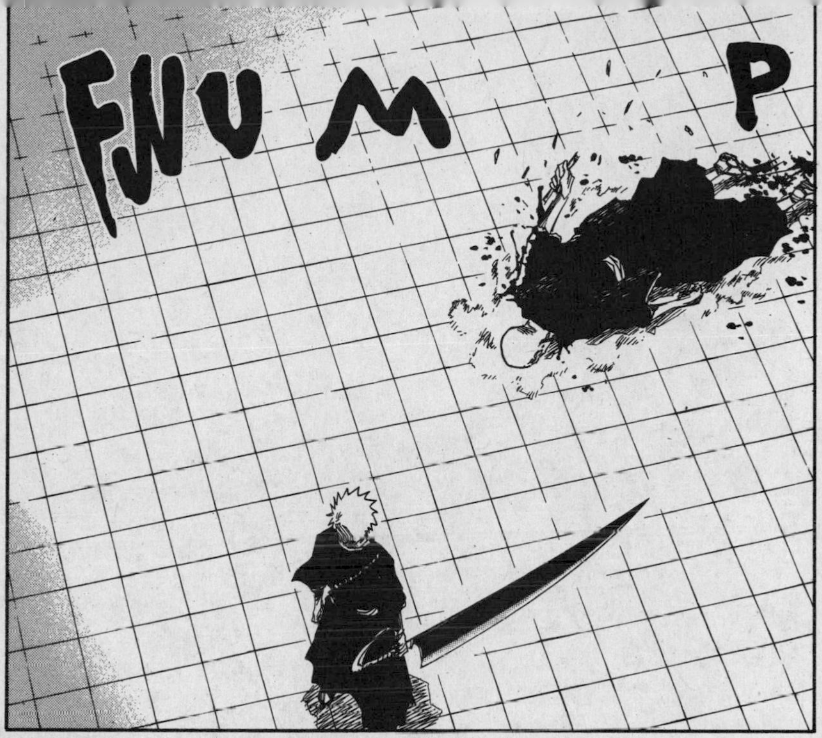
FWUMP
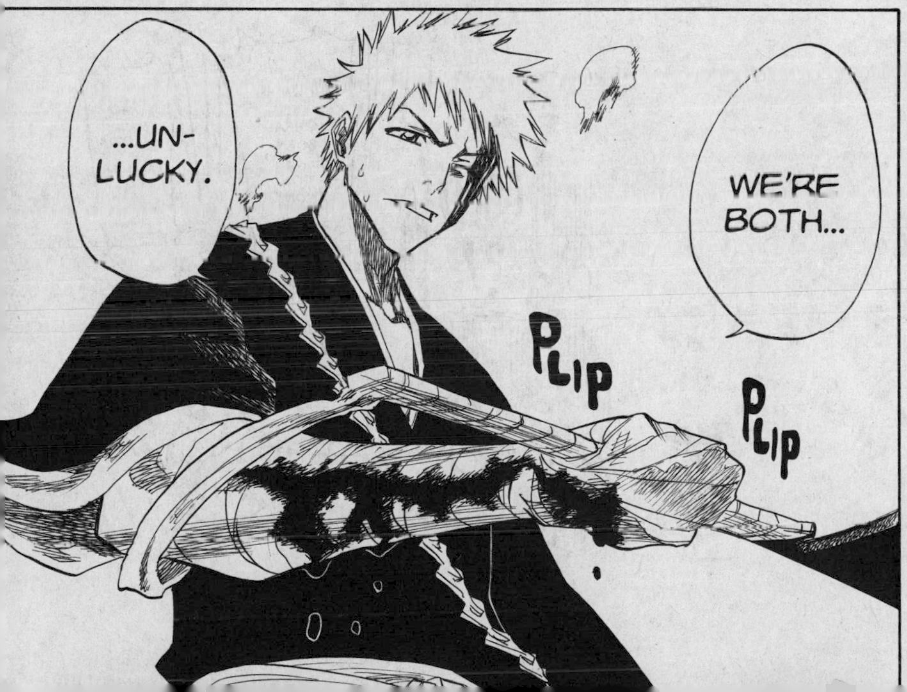
WE'RE BOTH...
...UN-LUCKY.
PLIP
PLIP

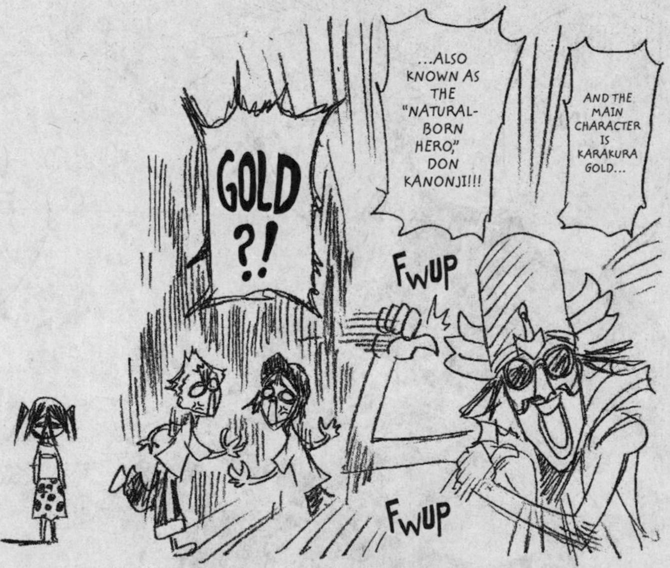
AND THE MAIN CHARACTER IS KARAKURA GOLD...
...ALSO KNOWN AS THE "NATURAL-BORN HERO," DON KANONJI!!!
FWUP
FWUP
GOLD?!

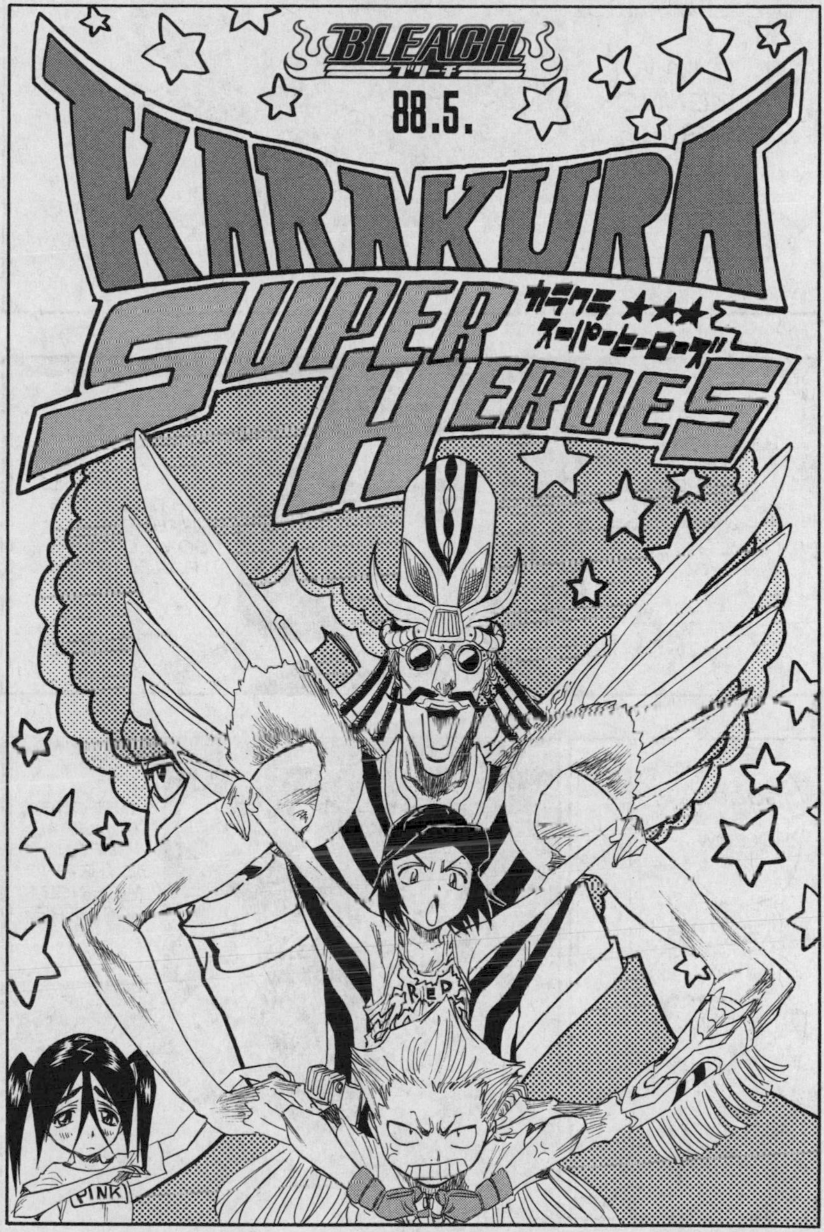
BLEACH
ブリーチ
88.5.
KARAKURA SUPER HEROES
カラクラ★★★スーパーヒーローズ
RED
PINK

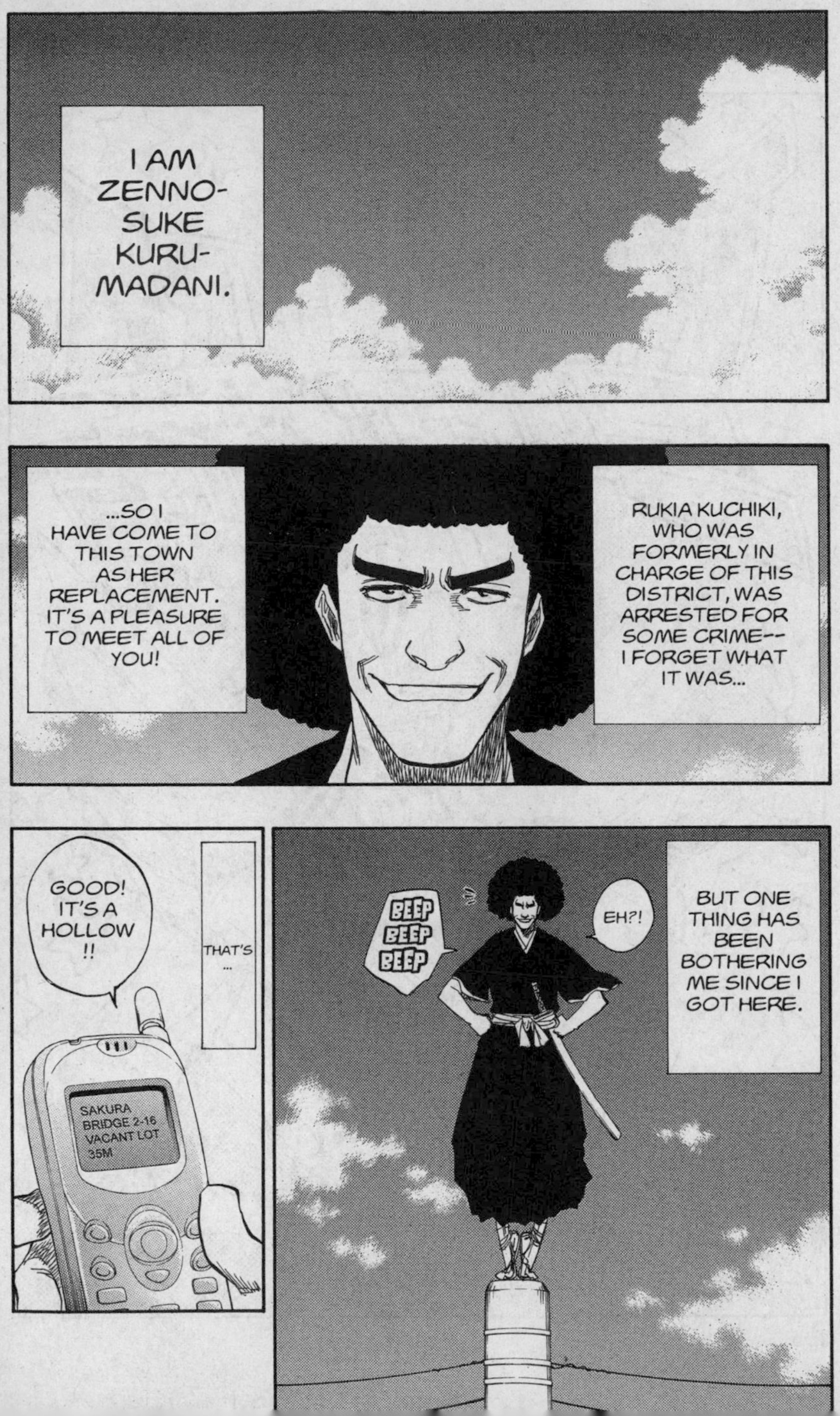
I AM ZENNOSUKE KURUMADANI.
RUKIA KUCHIKI, WHO WAS FORMERLY IN CHARGE OF THIS DISTRICT, WAS ARRESTED FOR SOME CRIME-- I FORGET WHAT IT WAS...
...SO I HAVE COME TO THIS TOWN AS HER REPLACEMENT. IT'S A PLEASURE TO MEET ALL OF YOU!
BUT ONE THING HAS BEEN BOTHERING ME SINCE I GOT HERE.
EH?!
BEEP BEEP BEEP
THAT'S ...
GOOD! IT'S A HOLLOW !!
SAKURA BRIDGE 2-16 VACANT LOT 35M

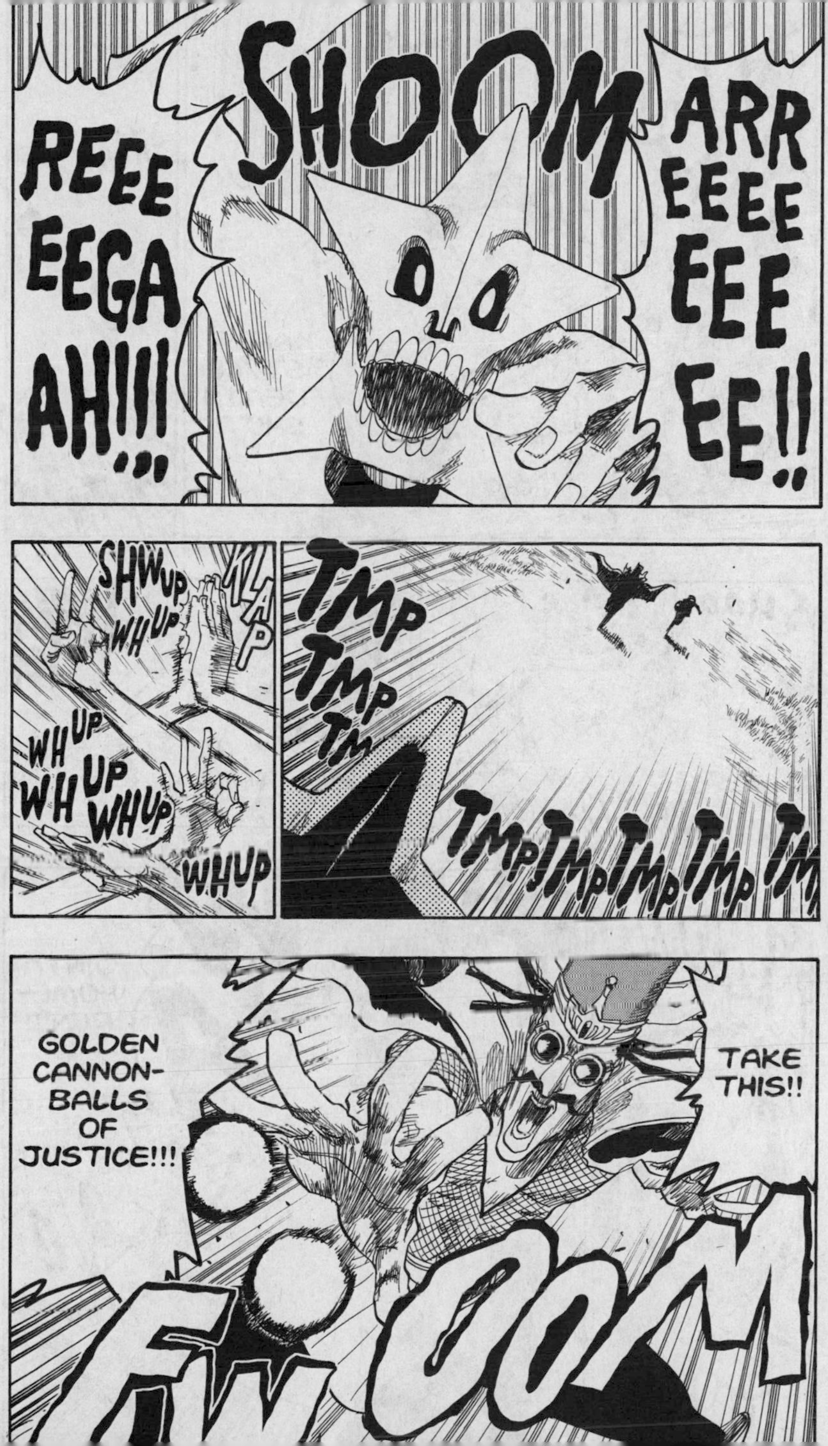
ARR
EEEE
EEE
EE!!
SHOOM
REEEE
EEGA
AH!!!
TMP
TMP
TM
TMP TMP TMP TMP TM
SHWUP
KLAP
WHUP
WHUP
WHUP
WHUP
WHUP
TAKE THIS!!
GOLDEN CANNON-BALLS OF JUSTICE!!!
FWOOM

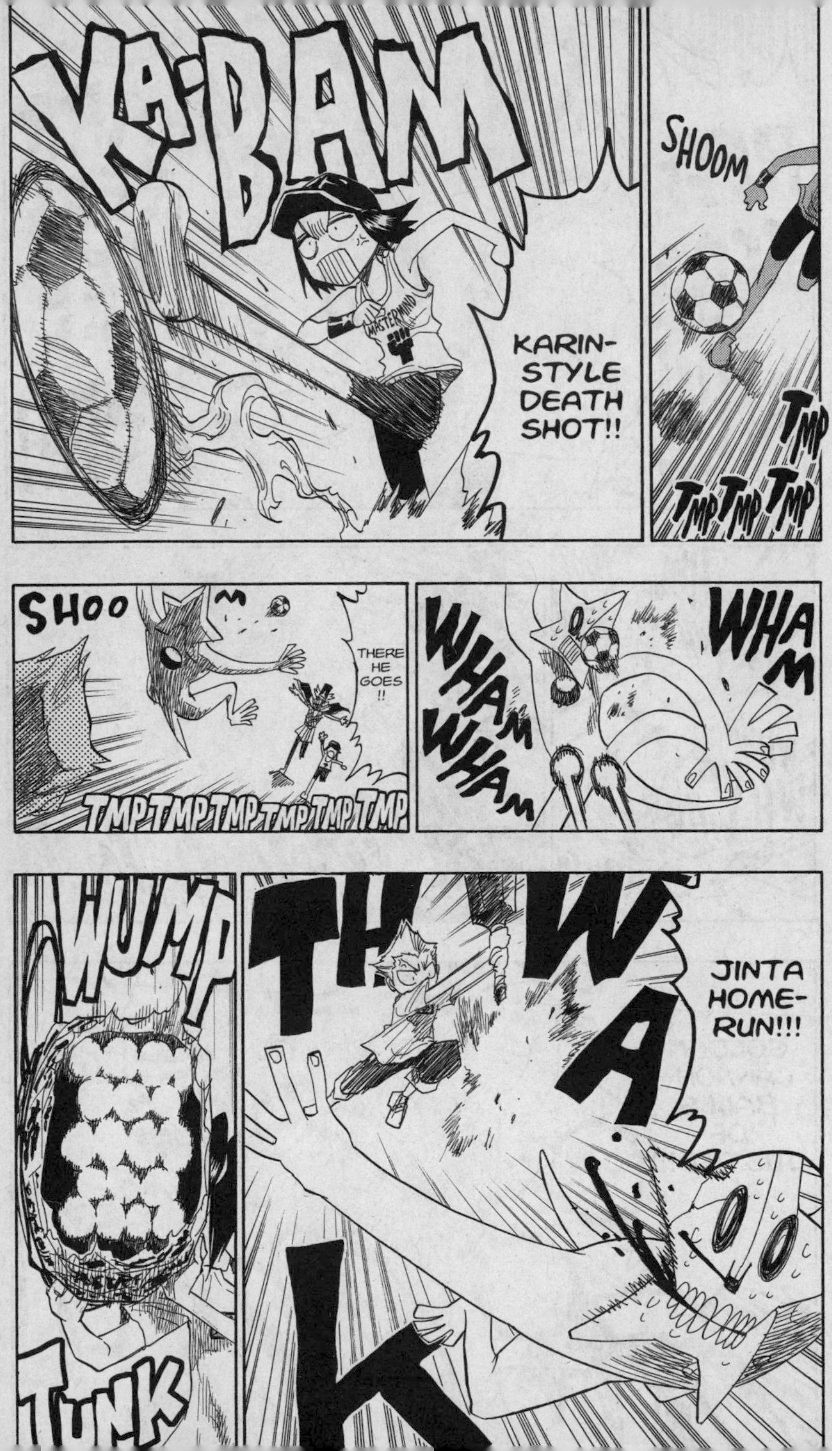
SHOOM
TMP TMP TMP TMP TMP
KA-BAM
MASTERMIND
KARIN-STYLE DEATH SHOT!!
WHAM
WHAM WHAM
WHAM
SHOOM
THERE HE GOES!!
TMP TMP TMP TMP TMP TMP
THWAK
JINTA HOME-RUN!!!
WUMP
TUNK

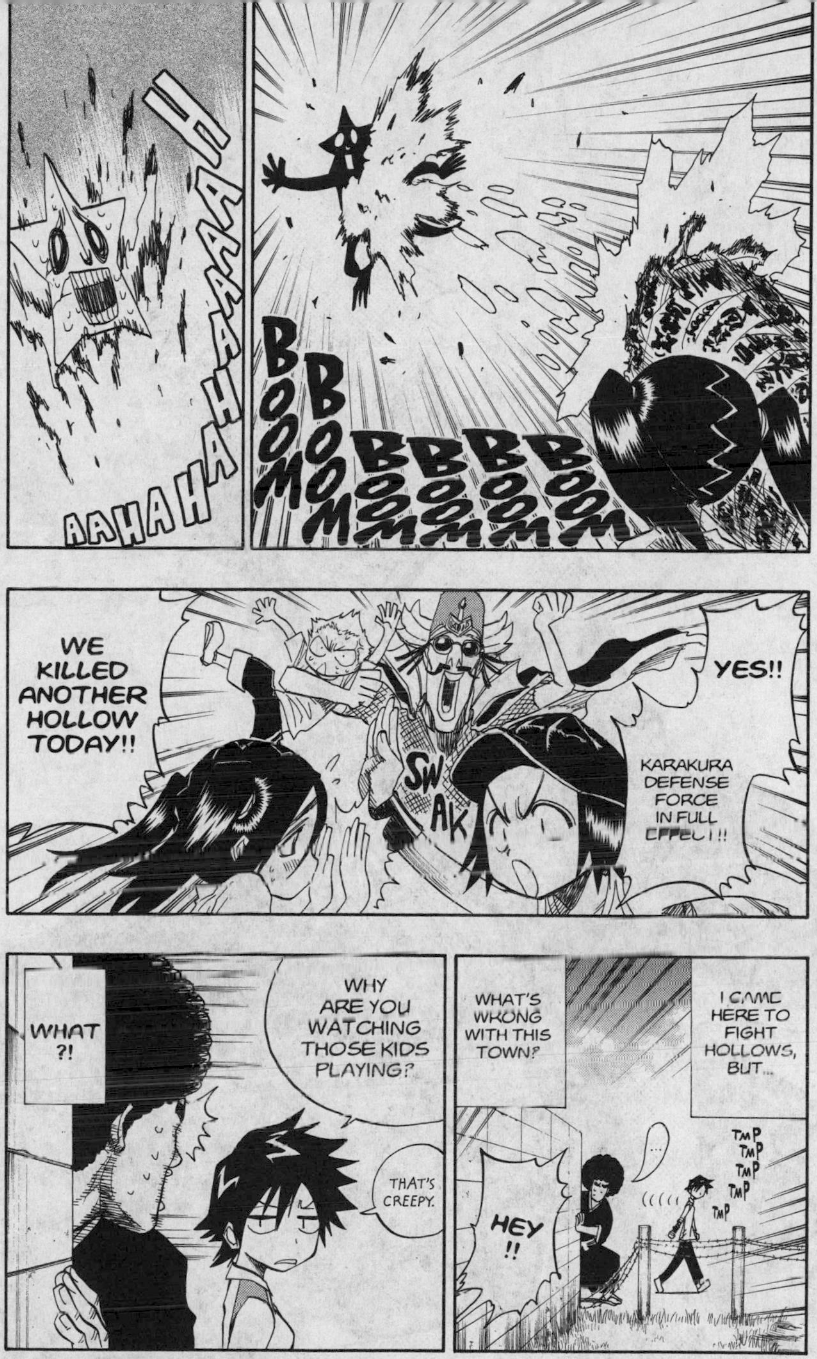
BOOM BOOM BOOM BOOM BOOM BOOM
AAHAHAHAHAAAAA!!
YES!!
KARAKURA DEFENSE FORCE IN FULL EFFECT!!
SWAK
WE KILLED ANOTHER HOLLOW TODAY!!
I CAME HERE TO FIGHT HOLLOWS, BUT...
WHAT'S WRONG WITH THIS TOWN?
...
TMP TMP TMP TMP TMP
HEY!!
WHY ARE YOU WATCHING THOSE KIDS PLAYING?
THAT'S CREEPY.
WHAT?!

TO BE CONTINUED IN VOL. 11!

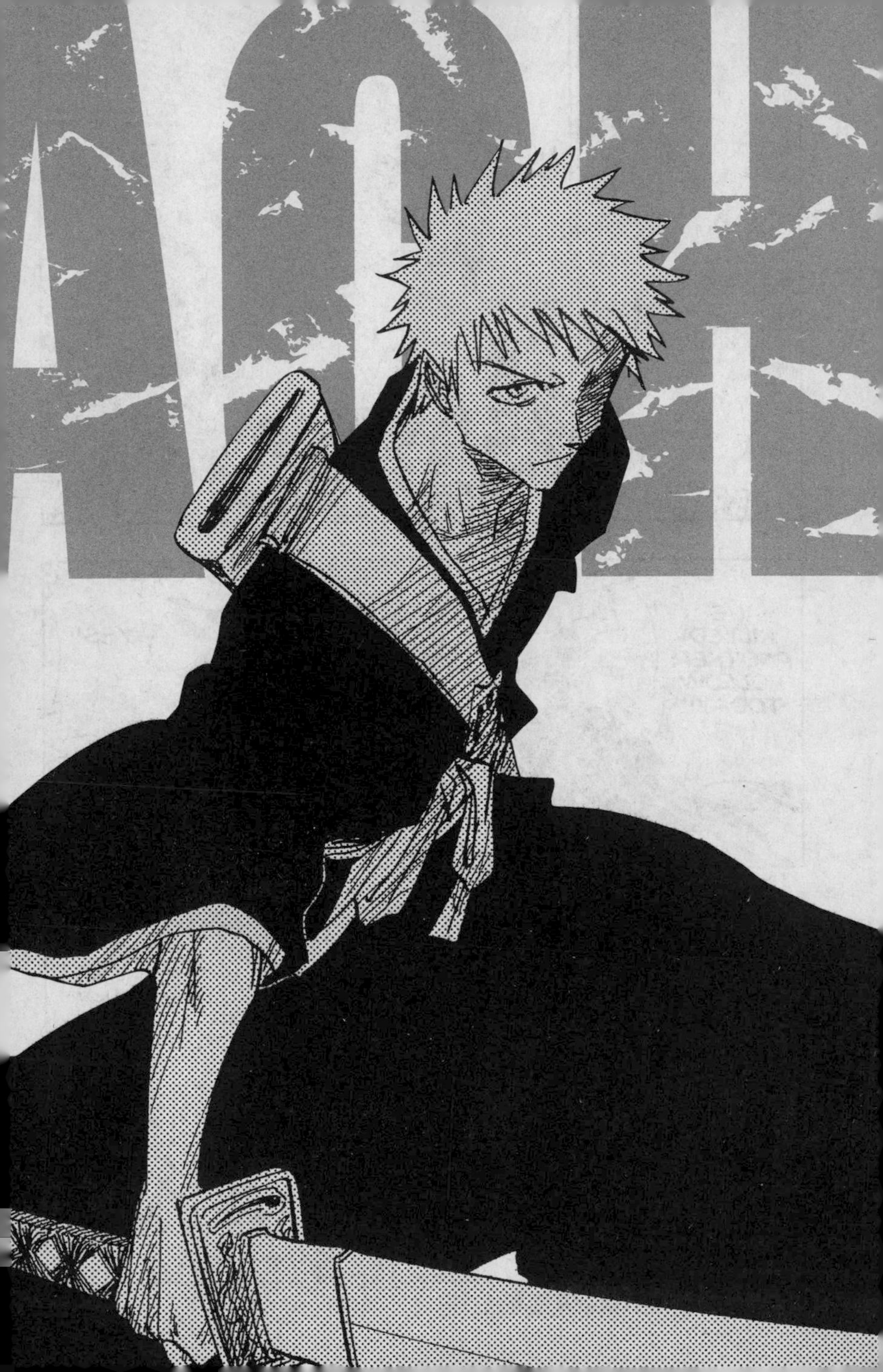

Maybe it's because I've been so busy lately, but I constantly find myself thinking, "I wish I could draw without worrying about time." But in reality, when I do get some free time, I'll probably piddle around and do nothing. I guess you always want what you don't have.

-Tite Kubo, 2003

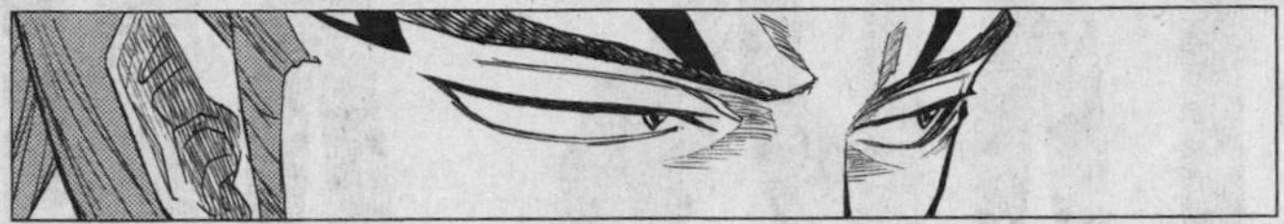

Light a fire to the fang that cannot be reached
So that I do not have to see that star
So that I do not slit this throat

BLEACH 11

A STAR AND A STRAY DOG

Shonen Jump Manga

STARS AND

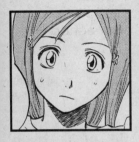

志波岩鷲

Ganju Shiba

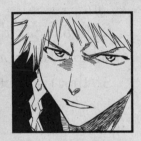

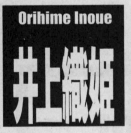

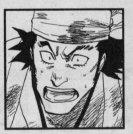

Ichigo Kurosaki

黒崎一護

Orihime Inoue

井上織姫

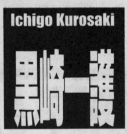

plot

While Rukia awaits execution in a Soul Society cell, Ichigo and the others try to rescue her. They manage to penetrate the shield that protects the inner city of the Soul Reapers but are hurled in different directions by the impact. They find themselves scattered and hunted by an army of Soul Reapers. Ichigo fights and defeats Ikkaku Madarame, a Sansetsukon user! Meanwhile, Ganju faces off with a pursuer of his own...

BLEACH ALL

Renji Abarai

Uryû Ishida

Yumichika Ayasegawa

STORIES

BLEACH 11

A STAR AND A STRAY DOG

Contents

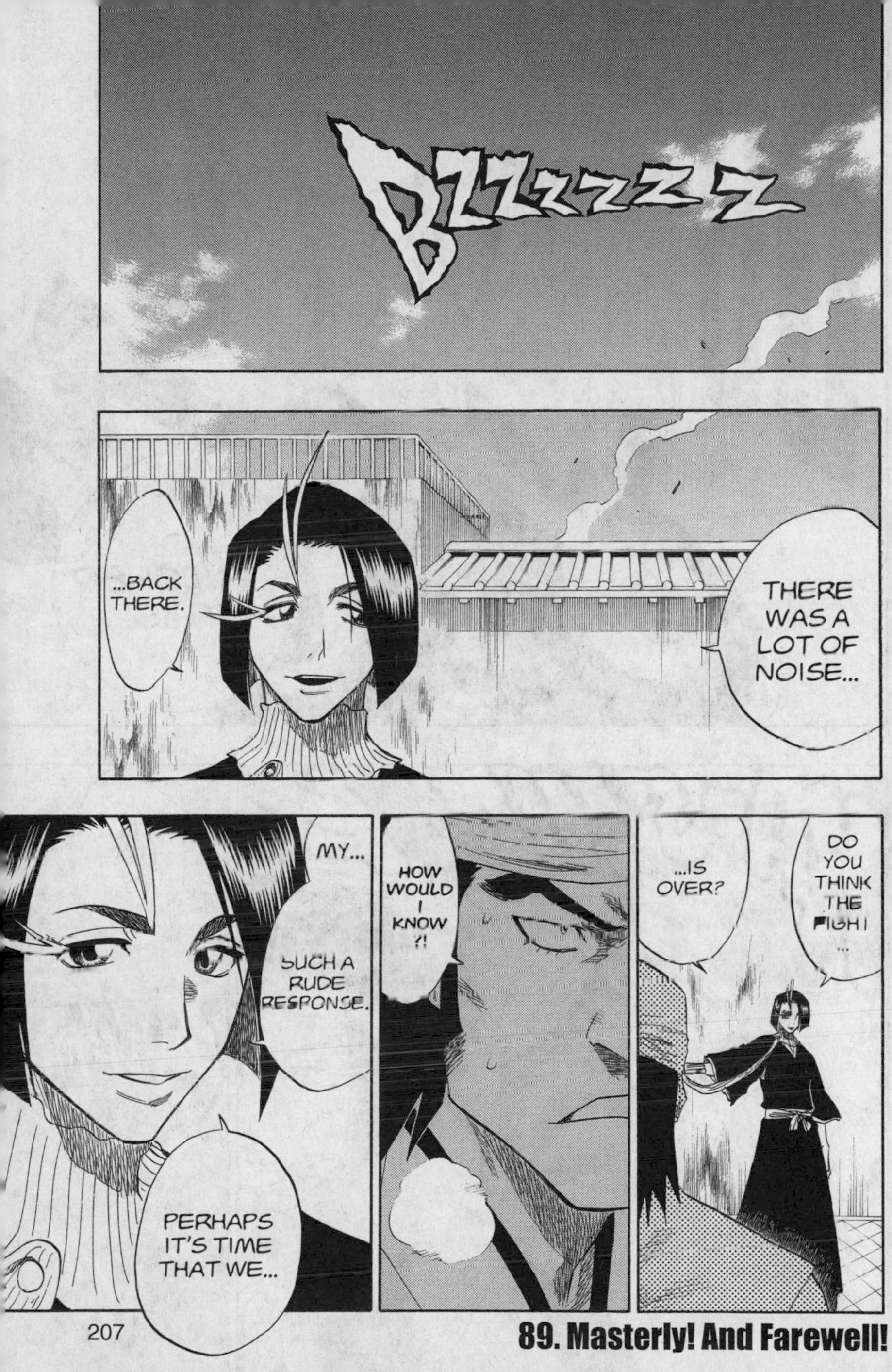
BZZZZZZ
THERE WAS A LOT OF NOISE...
...BACK THERE.
DO YOU THINK THE FIGHT...
...IS OVER?
HOW WOULD I KNOW ?!
MY...
SUCH A RUDE RESPONSE.
PERHAPS IT'S TIME THAT WE...

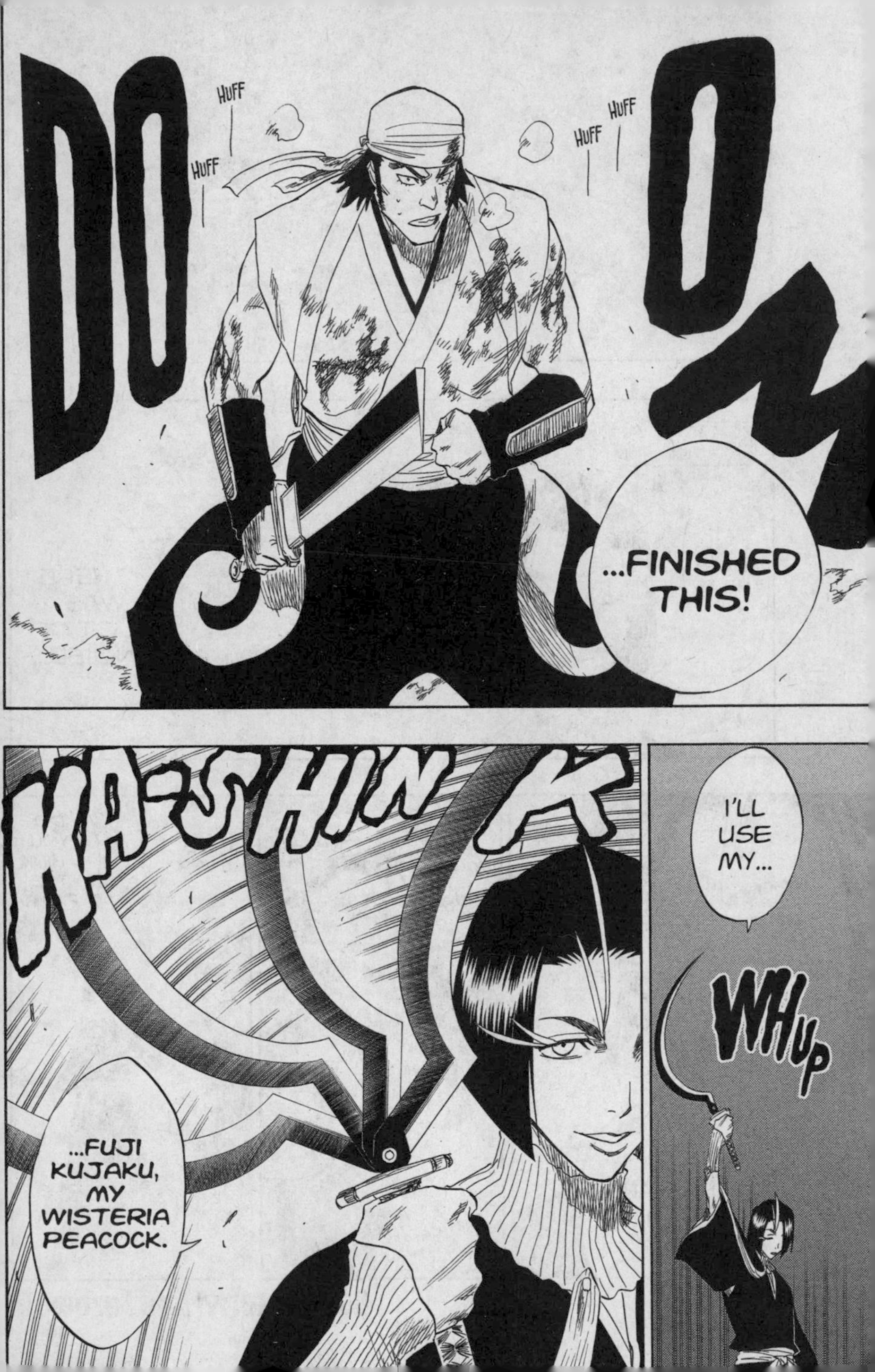
DO OM
HUFF
HUFF
HUFF
HUFF
...FINISHED THIS!
I'LL USE MY...
WHUP
KA-SHINK
...FUJI KUJAKU, MY WISTERIA PEACOCK.

READ THIS WAY

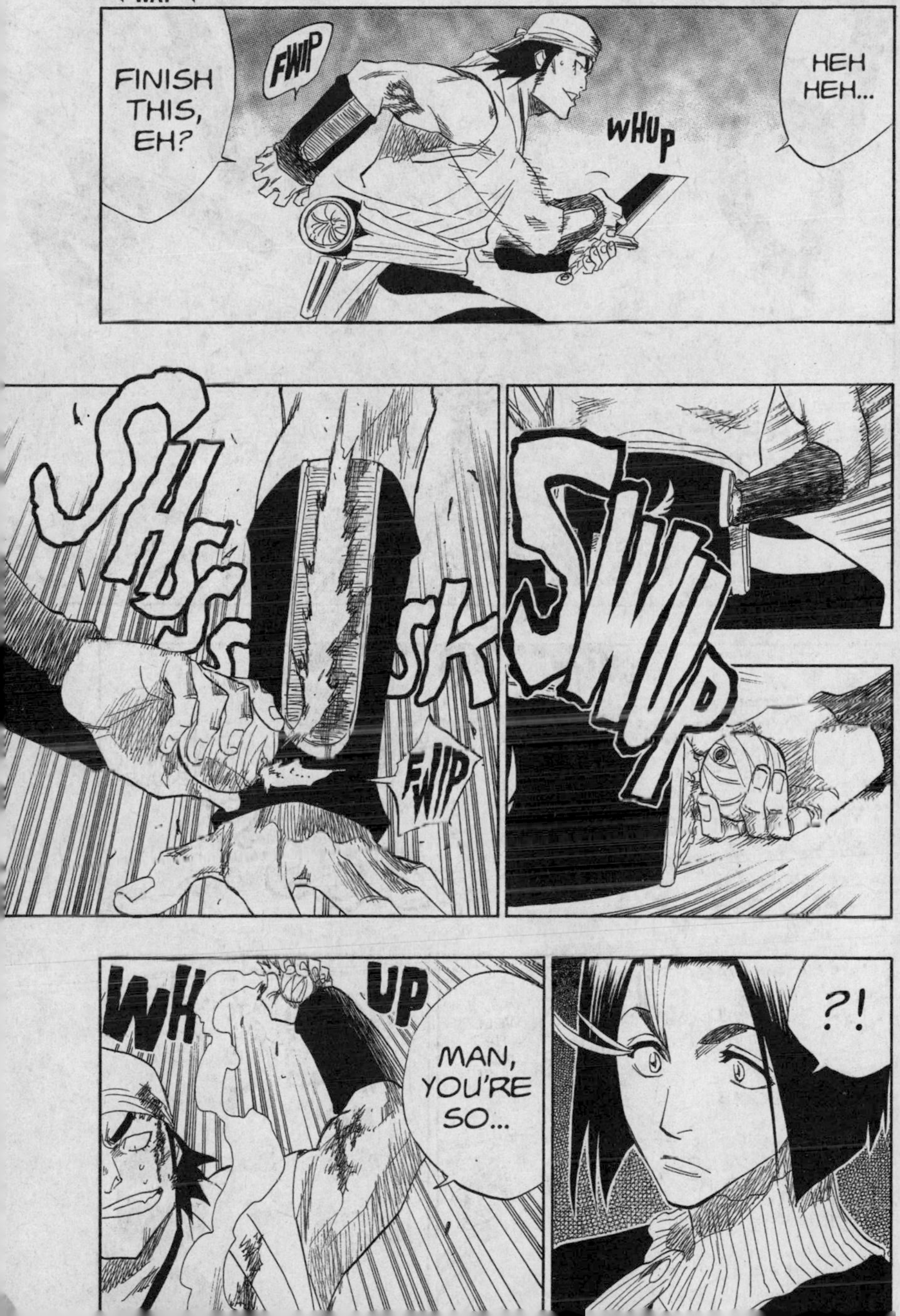
HEH HEH...
FWIP
FINISH THIS, EH?
WHUP
SWIP
SHSSSK
FWIP
?!
WHUP
MAN, YOU'RE SO...

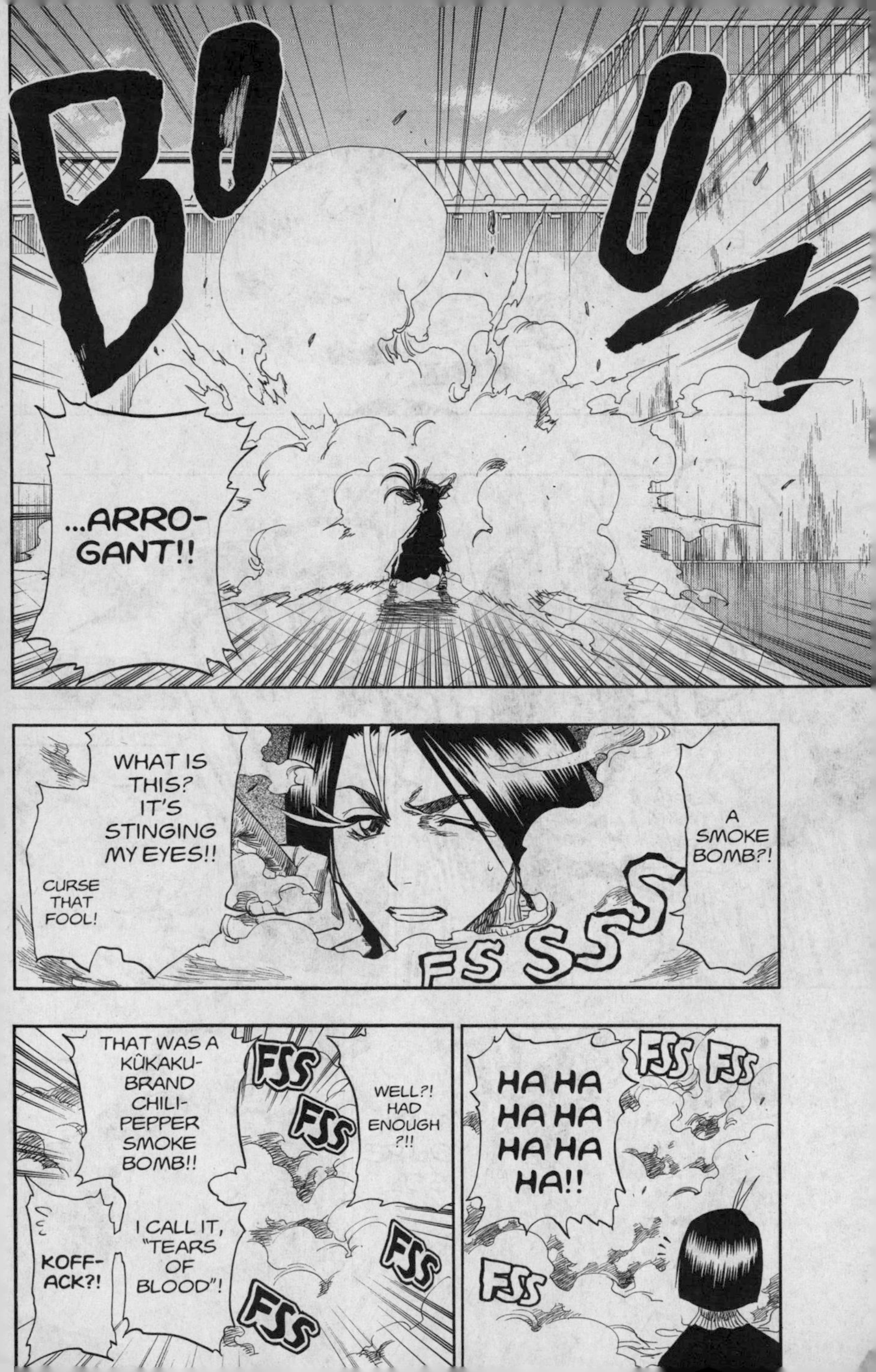
BOOM
...ARRO-GANT!!
A SMOKE BOMB?!
FSSSSS
WHAT IS THIS? IT'S STINGING MY EYES!!
CURSE THAT FOOL!
FSS FSS
HA HA HA HA HA HA HA!!
FSS
WELL?! HAD ENOUGH?!!
FSS FSS
THAT WAS A KÛKAKU-BRAND CHILI-PEPPER SMOKE BOMB!!
I CALL IT, "TEARS OF BLOOD"!
FSS FSS
KOFF-ACK?!

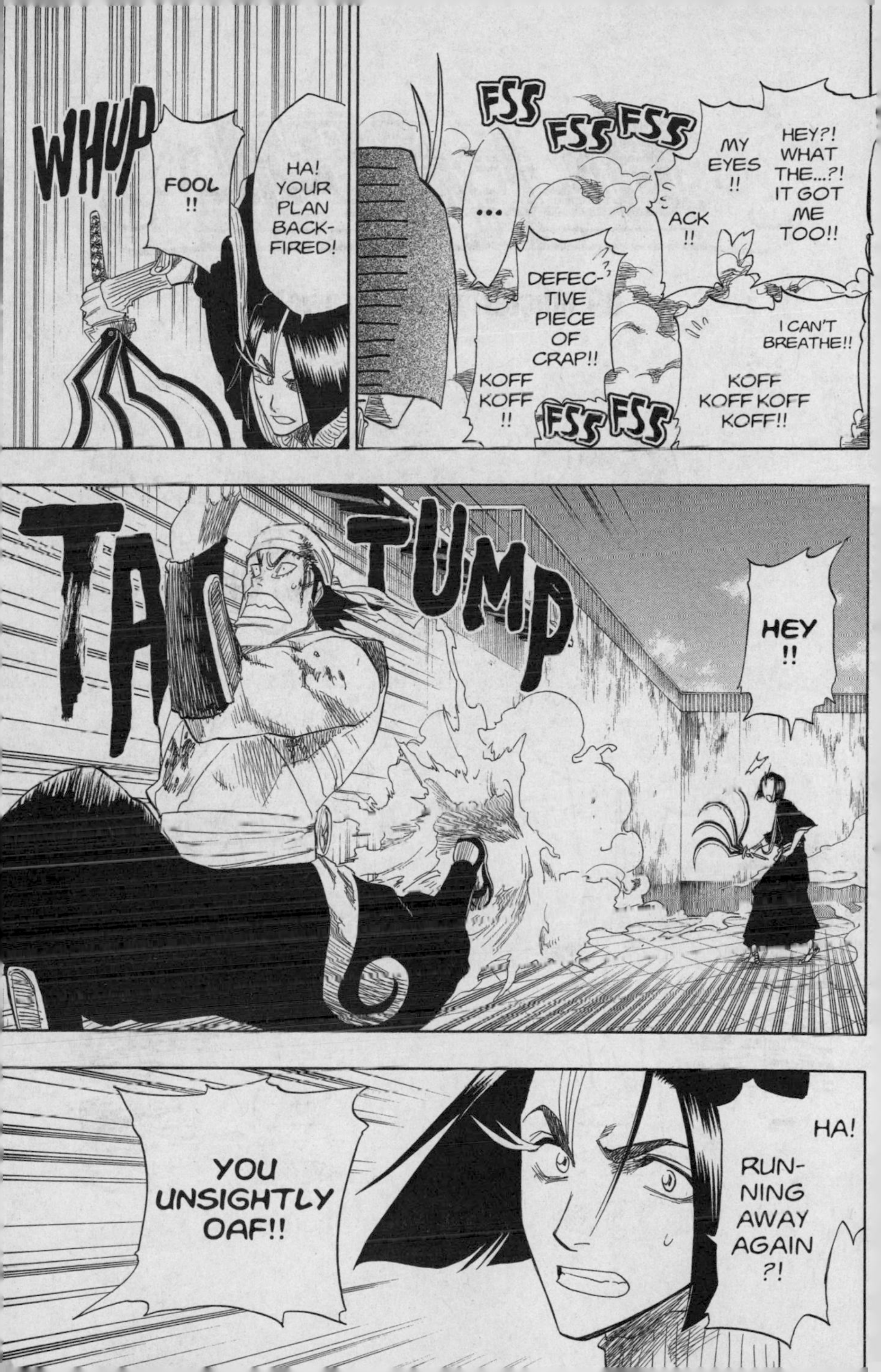
HEY?! WHAT THE...?! IT GOT ME TOO!!
MY EYES !!
ACK !!
FSS FSS FSS
I CAN'T BREATHE!!
KOFF KOFF KOFF KOFF!!
...
DEFECTIVE PIECE OF CRAP!!
FSS FSS
KOFF KOFF !!
HA! YOUR PLAN BACKFIRED!
FOOL !!
WHUP
HEY !!
TA
TUMP
HA!
RUNNING AWAY AGAIN ?!
YOU UNSIGHTLY OAF!!

BLEACH
ブリーチ

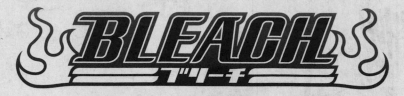

89. Masterly! And Farewell!

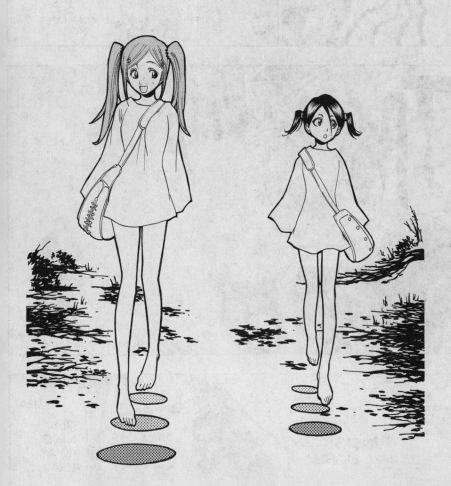

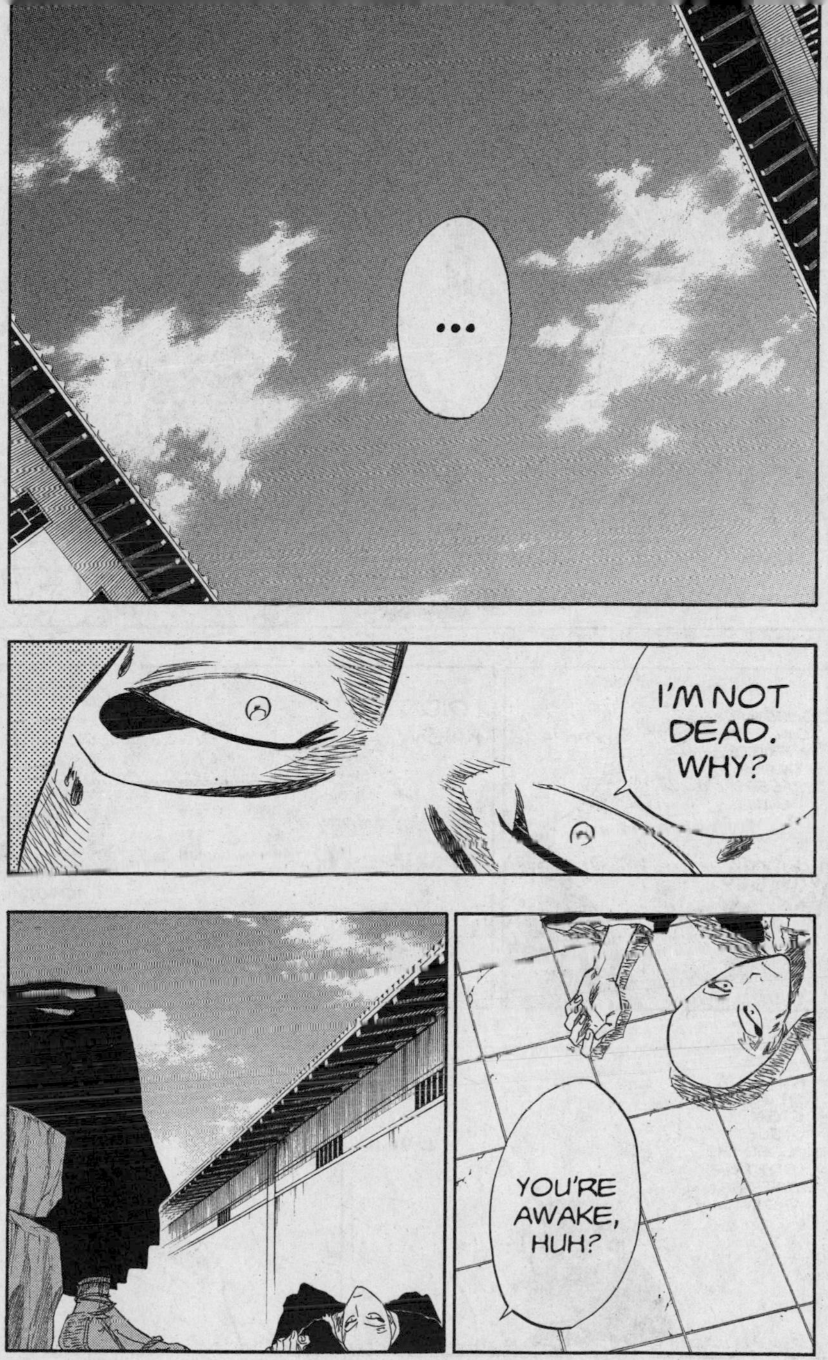
...
I'M NOT DEAD. WHY?
YOU'RE AWAKE, HUH?

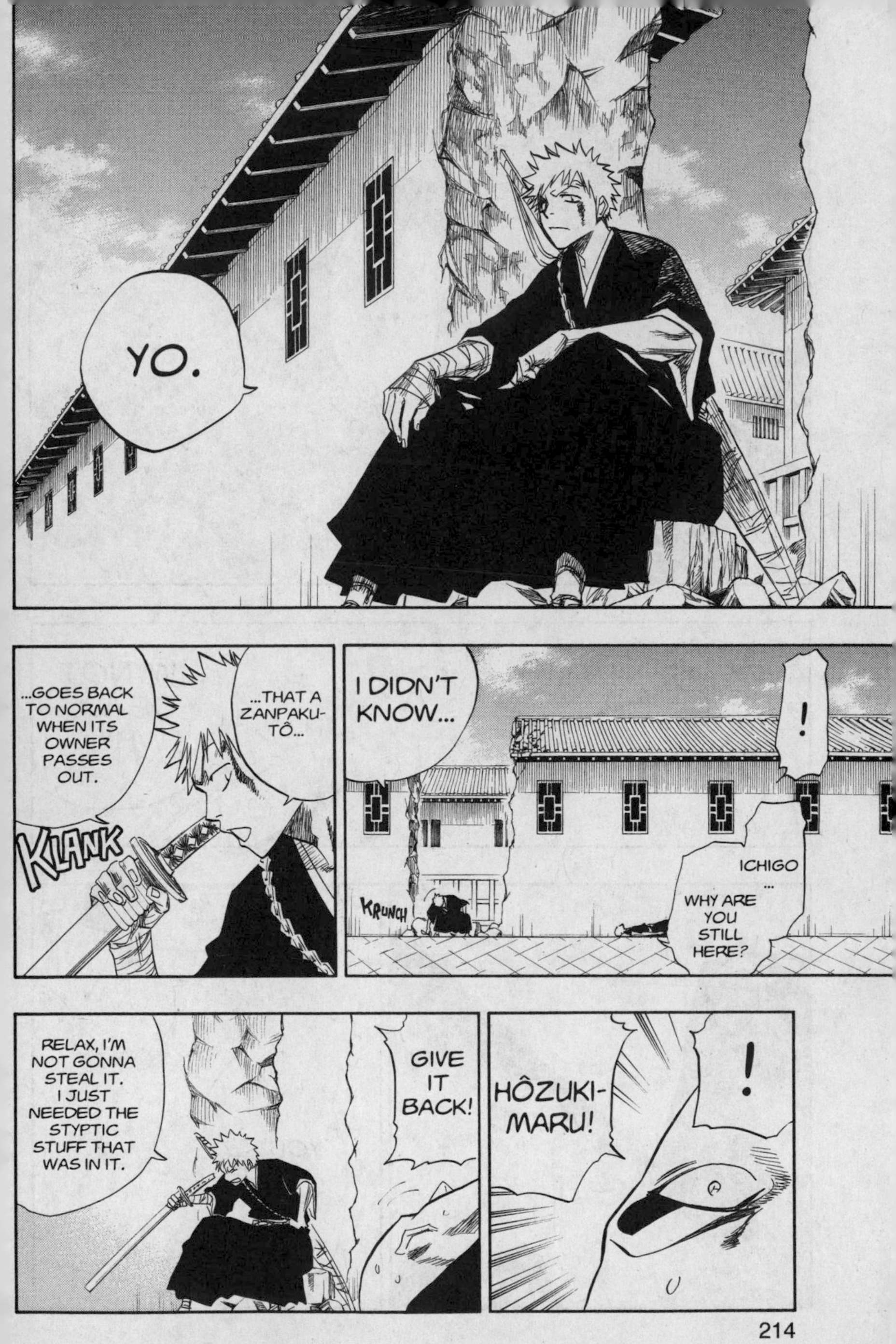
YO.
!
I DIDN'T KNOW...
ICHIGO ... WHY ARE YOU STILL HERE?
KRUNCH
...THAT A ZANPAKU-TÔ...
...GOES BACK TO NORMAL WHEN ITS OWNER PASSES OUT.
KLANK
!
HÔZUKI-MARU!
GIVE IT BACK!
RELAX, I'M NOT GONNA STEAL IT. I JUST NEEDED THE STYPTIC STUFF THAT WAS IN IT.

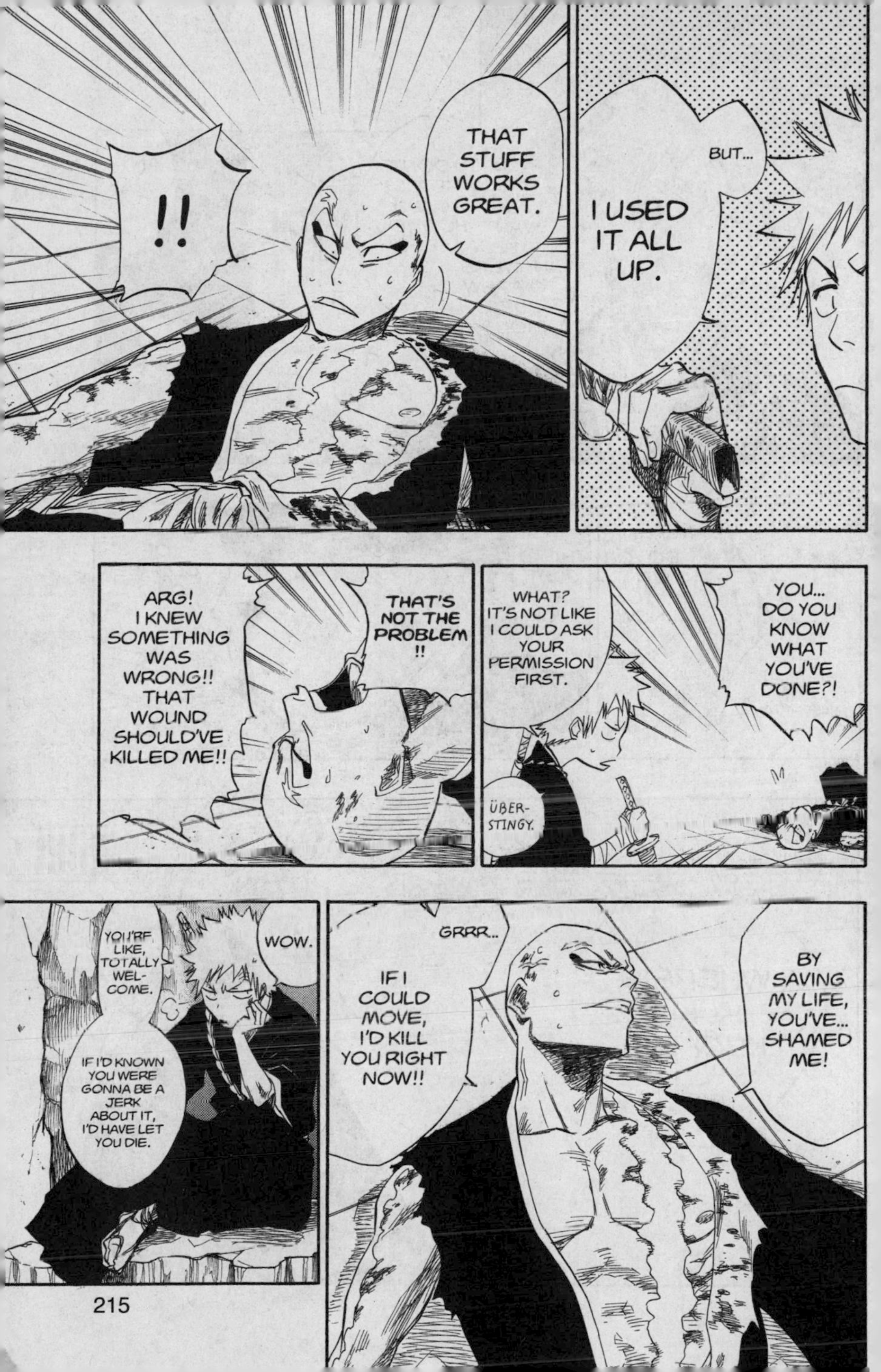
BUT...
I USED IT ALL UP.
THAT STUFF WORKS GREAT.
!!
YOU... DO YOU KNOW WHAT YOU'VE DONE?!
WHAT? IT'S NOT LIKE I COULD ASK YOUR PERMISSION FIRST.
ÜBER-STINGY.
THAT'S NOT THE PROBLEM!!
ARG! I KNEW SOMETHING WAS WRONG!! THAT WOUND SHOULD'VE KILLED ME!!
BY SAVING MY LIFE, YOU'VE... SHAMED ME!
GRRR...
IF I COULD MOVE, I'D KILL YOU RIGHT NOW!!
WOW.
YOU'RE LIKE, TOTALLY WEL-COME.
IF I'D KNOWN YOU WERE GONNA BE A JERK ABOUT IT, I'D HAVE LET YOU DIE.

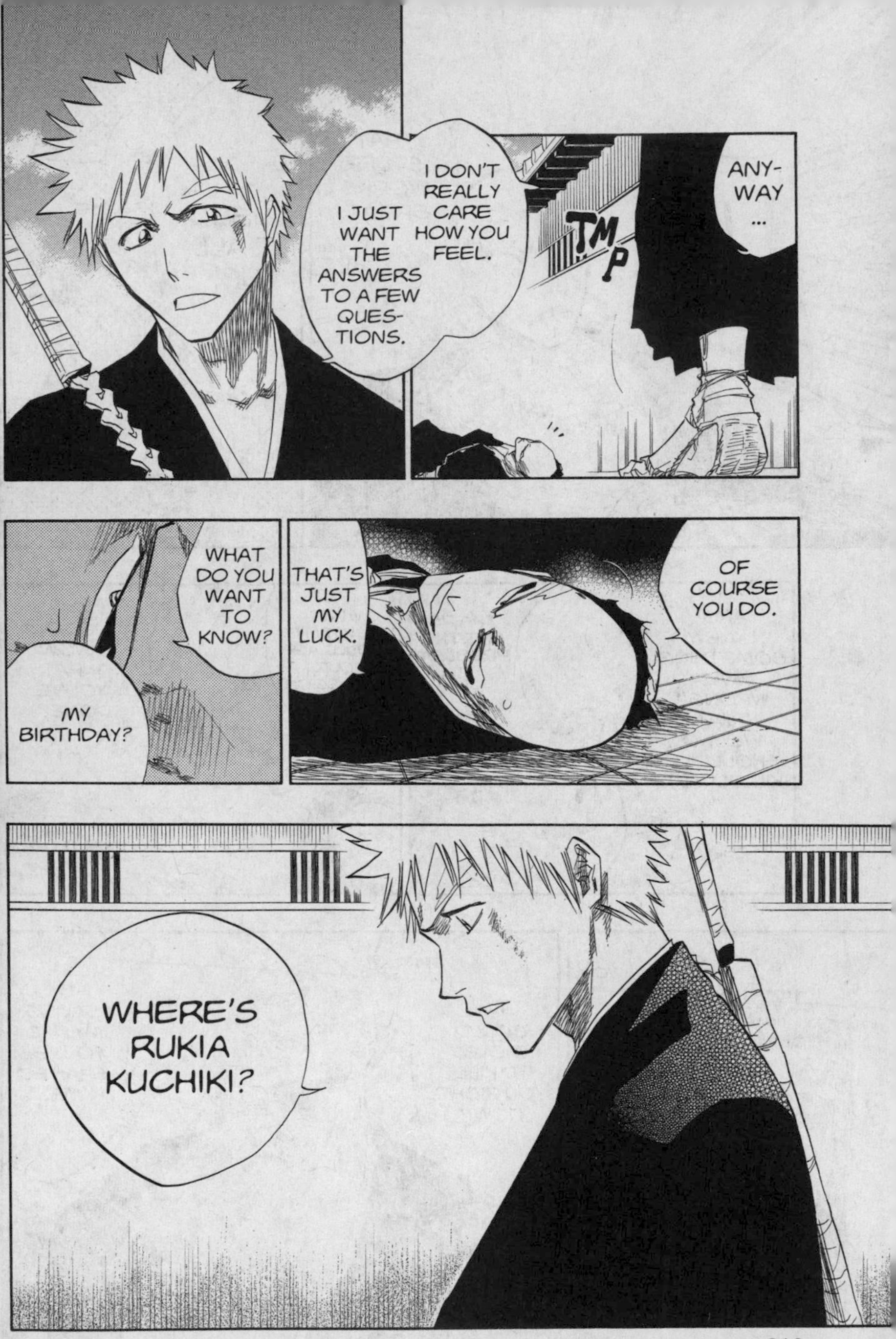
ANY-WAY ...
TMP
I DON'T REALLY CARE HOW YOU FEEL.
I JUST WANT THE ANSWERS TO A FEW QUES-TIONS.
OF COURSE YOU DO.
THAT'S JUST MY LUCK.
WHAT DO YOU WANT TO KNOW?
MY BIRTHDAY?
WHERE'S RUKIA KUCHIKI?

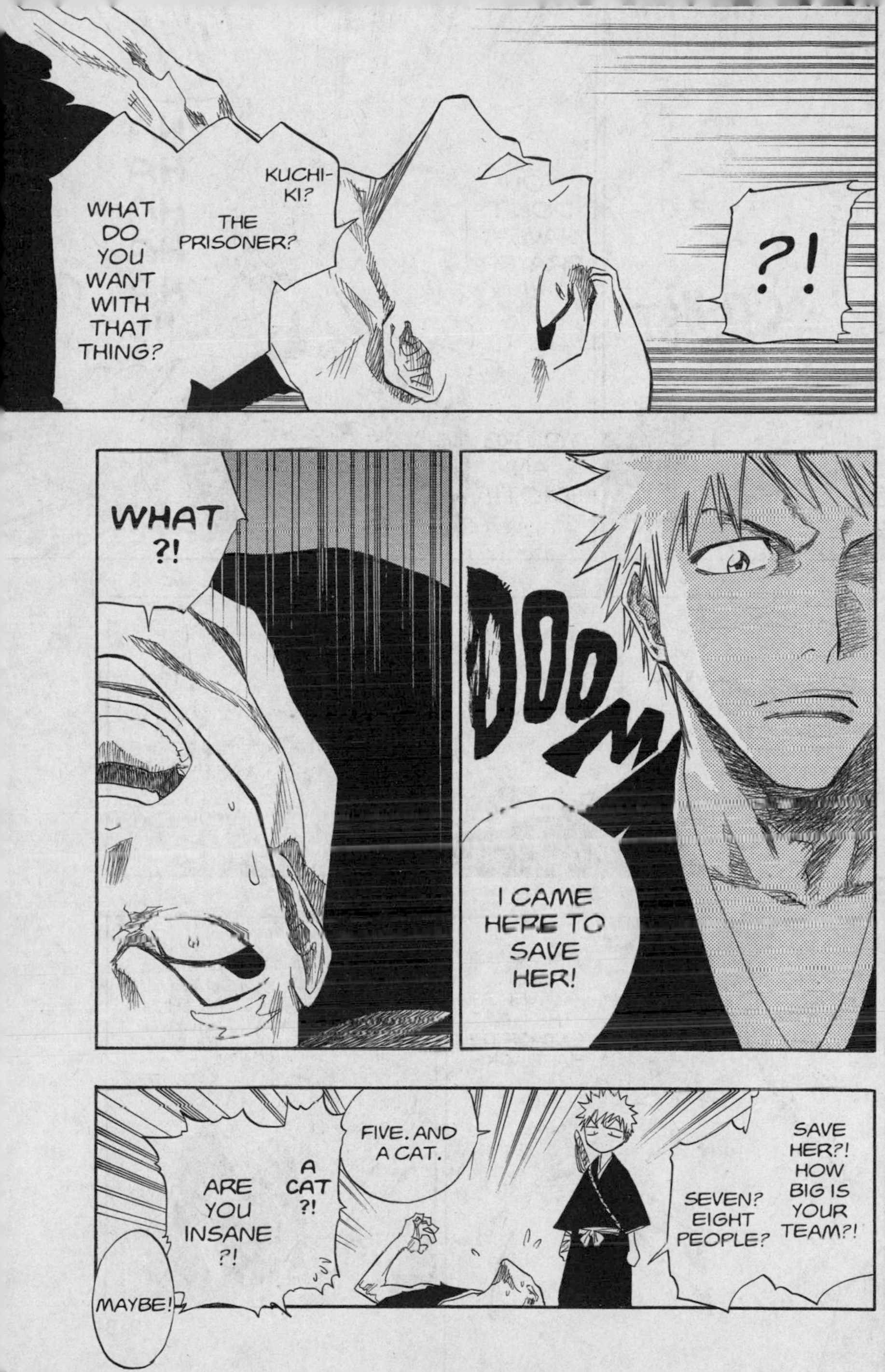
?!
KUCHIKI? THE PRISONER?
WHAT DO YOU WANT WITH THAT THING?
DOOM
I CAME HERE TO SAVE HER!
WHAT?!
SAVE HER?! HOW BIG IS YOUR TEAM?!
SEVEN? EIGHT PEOPLE?
FIVE. AND A CAT.
A CAT?!
ARE YOU INSANE?!
MAYBE!

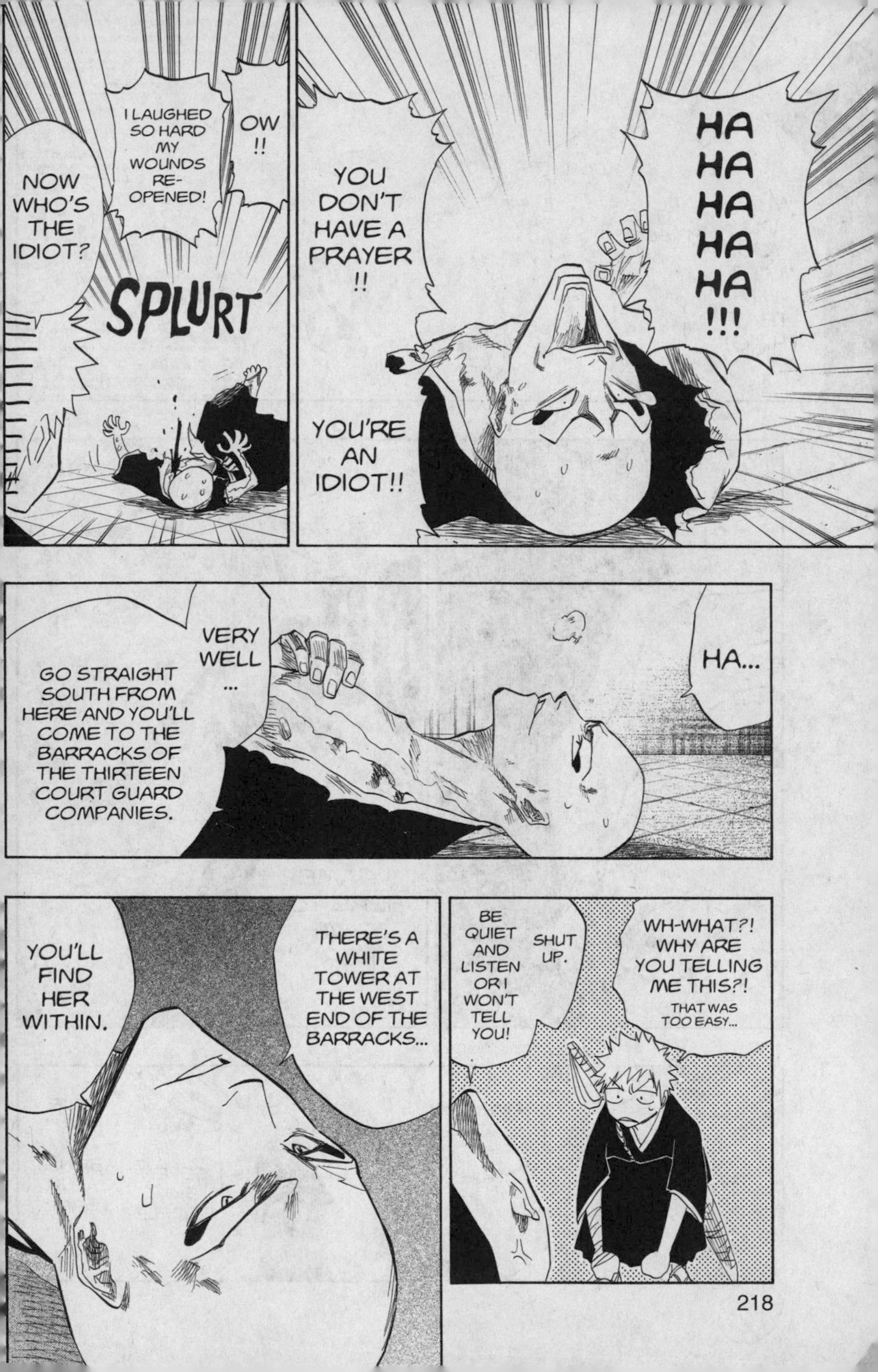
HA HA HA HA HA HA!!!
YOU DON'T HAVE A PRAYER!!
YOU'RE AN IDIOT!!
OW!!
I LAUGHED SO HARD MY WOUNDS RE-OPENED!
NOW WHO'S THE IDIOT?
SPLURT
HA...
VERY WELL...
GO STRAIGHT SOUTH FROM HERE AND YOU'LL COME TO THE BARRACKS OF THE THIRTEEN COURT GUARD COMPANIES.
WH-WHAT?! WHY ARE YOU TELLING ME THIS?!
THAT WAS TOO EASY...
SHUT UP.
BE QUIET AND LISTEN OR I WON'T TELL YOU!
THERE'S A WHITE TOWER AT THE WEST END OF THE BARRACKS...
YOU'LL FIND HER WITHIN.

READ THIS WAY

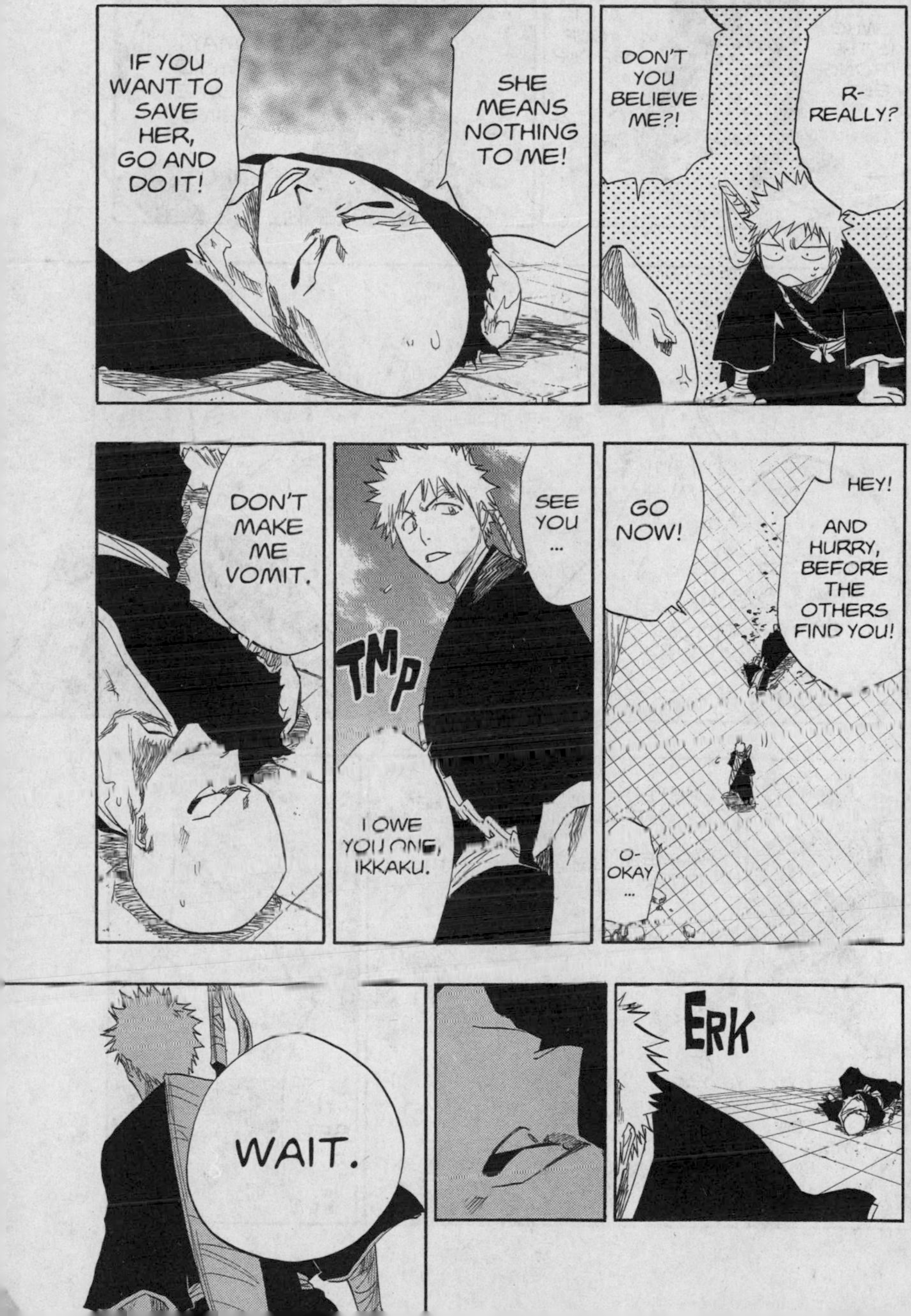

R- REALLY?
DON'T YOU BELIEVE ME?!
SHE MEANS NOTHING TO ME!
IF YOU WANT TO SAVE HER, GO AND DO IT!
HEY!
AND HURRY, BEFORE THE OTHERS FIND YOU!
GO NOW!
O- OKAY ...
SEE YOU ...
TMP
I OWE YOU ONE, IKKAKU.
DON'T MAKE ME VOMIT.
ERK
WAIT.

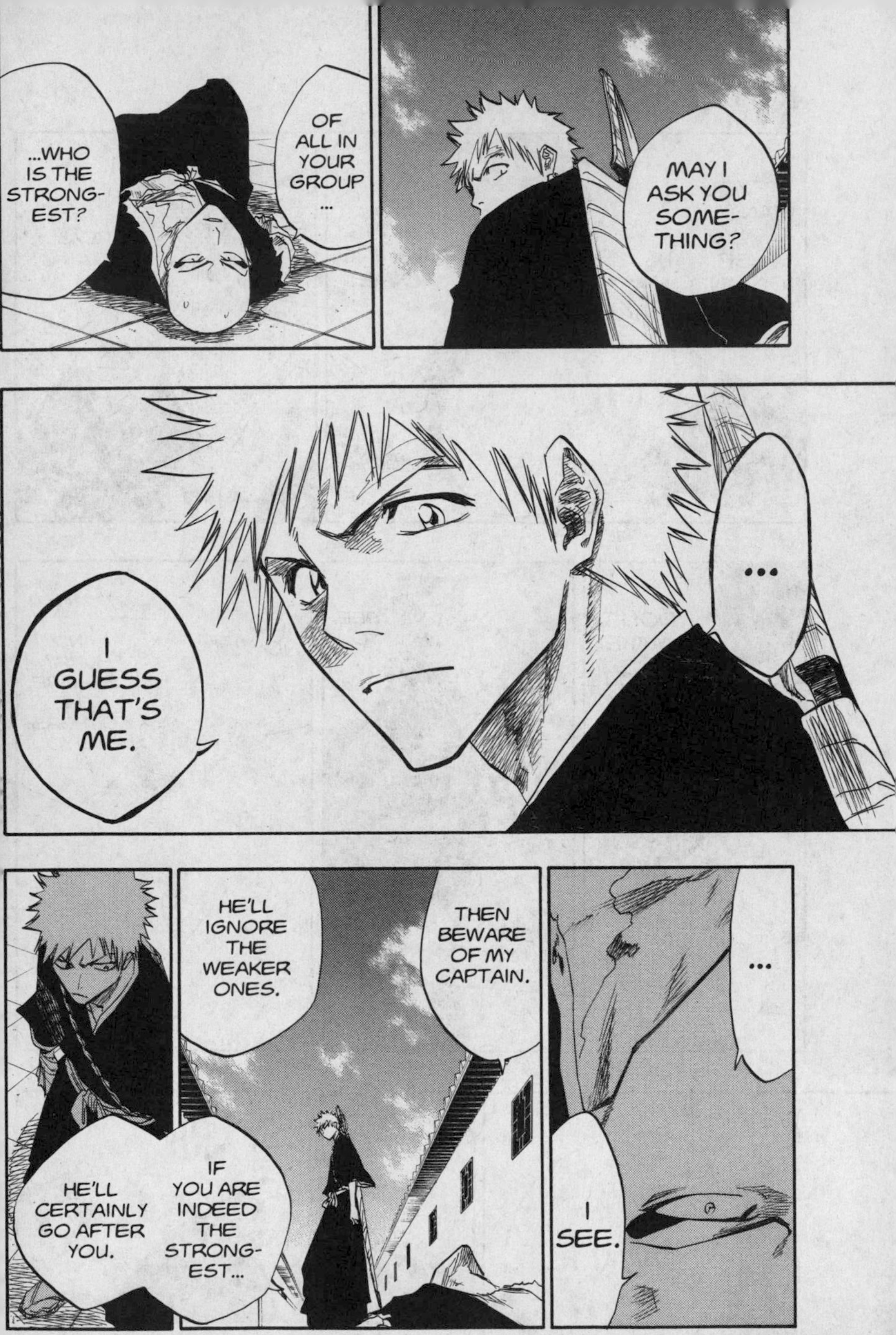
MAY I ASK YOU SOMETHING?
OF ALL IN YOUR GROUP...
...WHO IS THE STRONGEST?
...
I GUESS THAT'S ME.
...
I SEE.
THEN BEWARE OF MY CAPTAIN.
HE'LL IGNORE THE WEAKER ONES.
IF YOU ARE INDEED THE STRONGEST...
HE'LL CERTAINLY GO AFTER YOU.

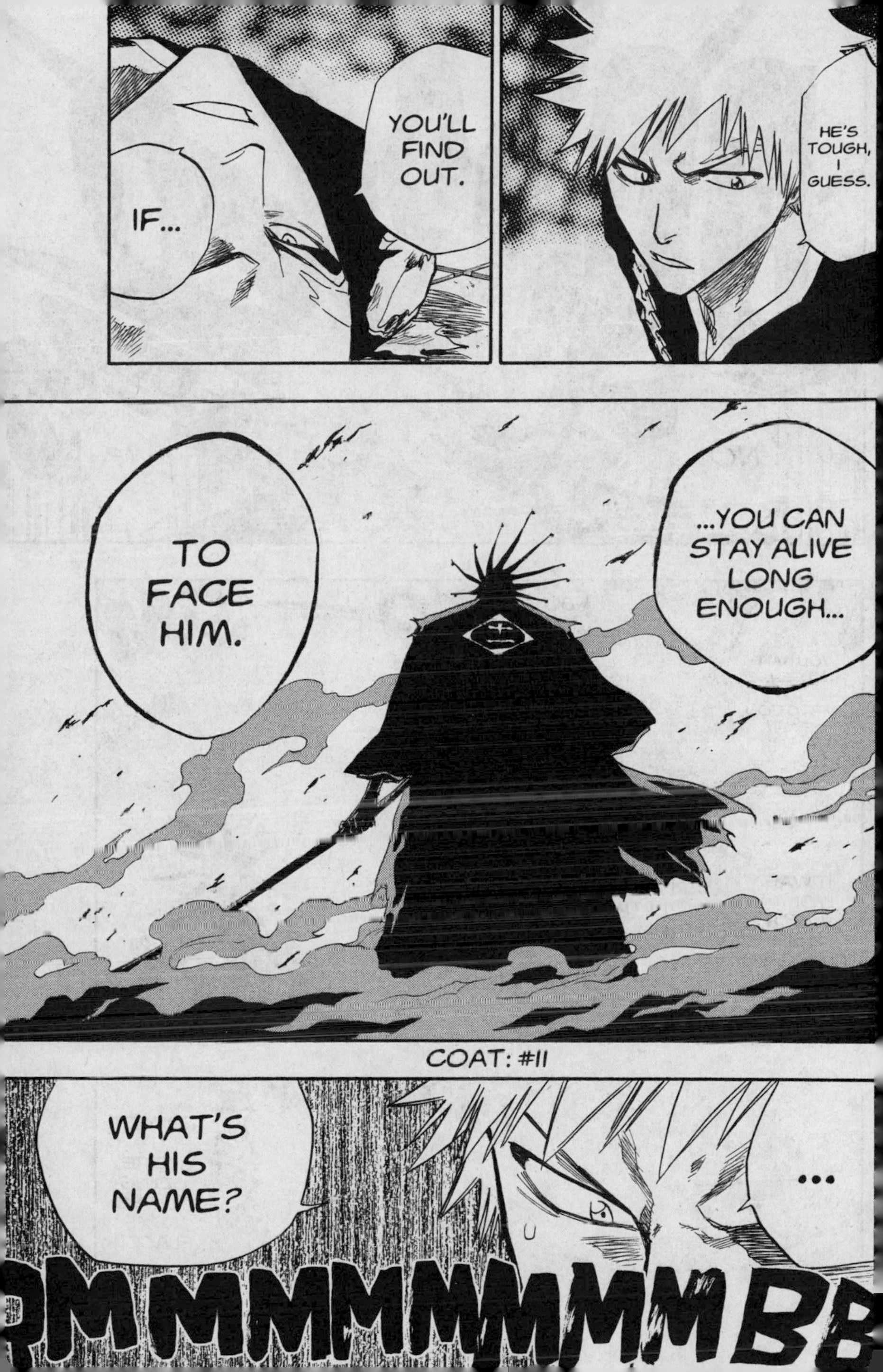
HE'S TOUGH, I GUESS.
YOU'LL FIND OUT.
IF...
...YOU CAN STAY ALIVE LONG ENOUGH...
TO FACE HIM.
COAT: #11
...
WHAT'S HIS NAME?
MMMMMMMMBB

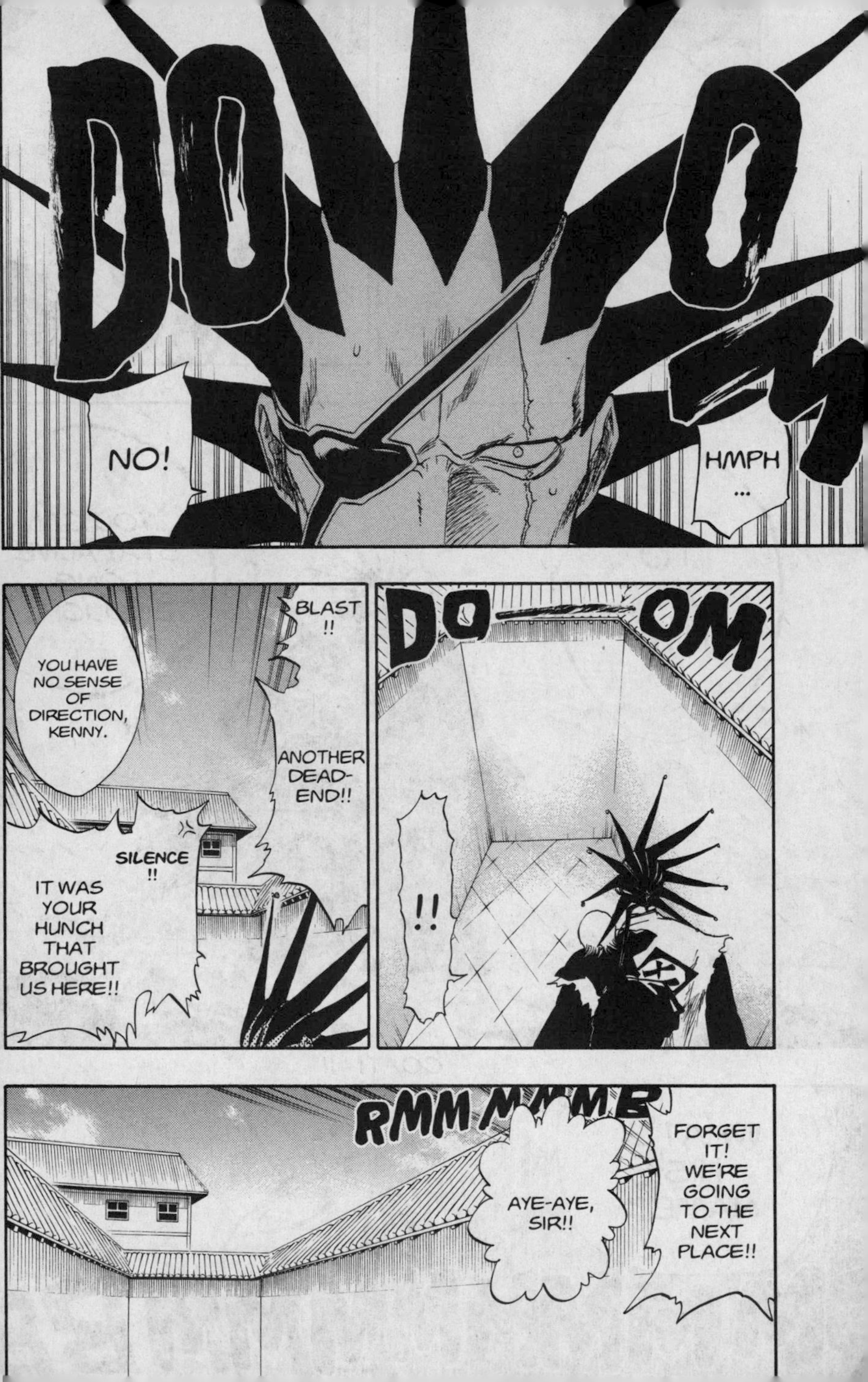
DO-OM
HMPH ...
NO!
DO—OM
!!
BLAST !!
ANOTHER DEAD-END!!
YOU HAVE NO SENSE OF DIRECTION, KENNY.
SILENCE !!
IT WAS YOUR HUNCH THAT BROUGHT US HERE!!
FORGET IT! WE'RE GOING TO THE NEXT PLACE!!
RMM MMMB
AYE-AYE, SIR!!

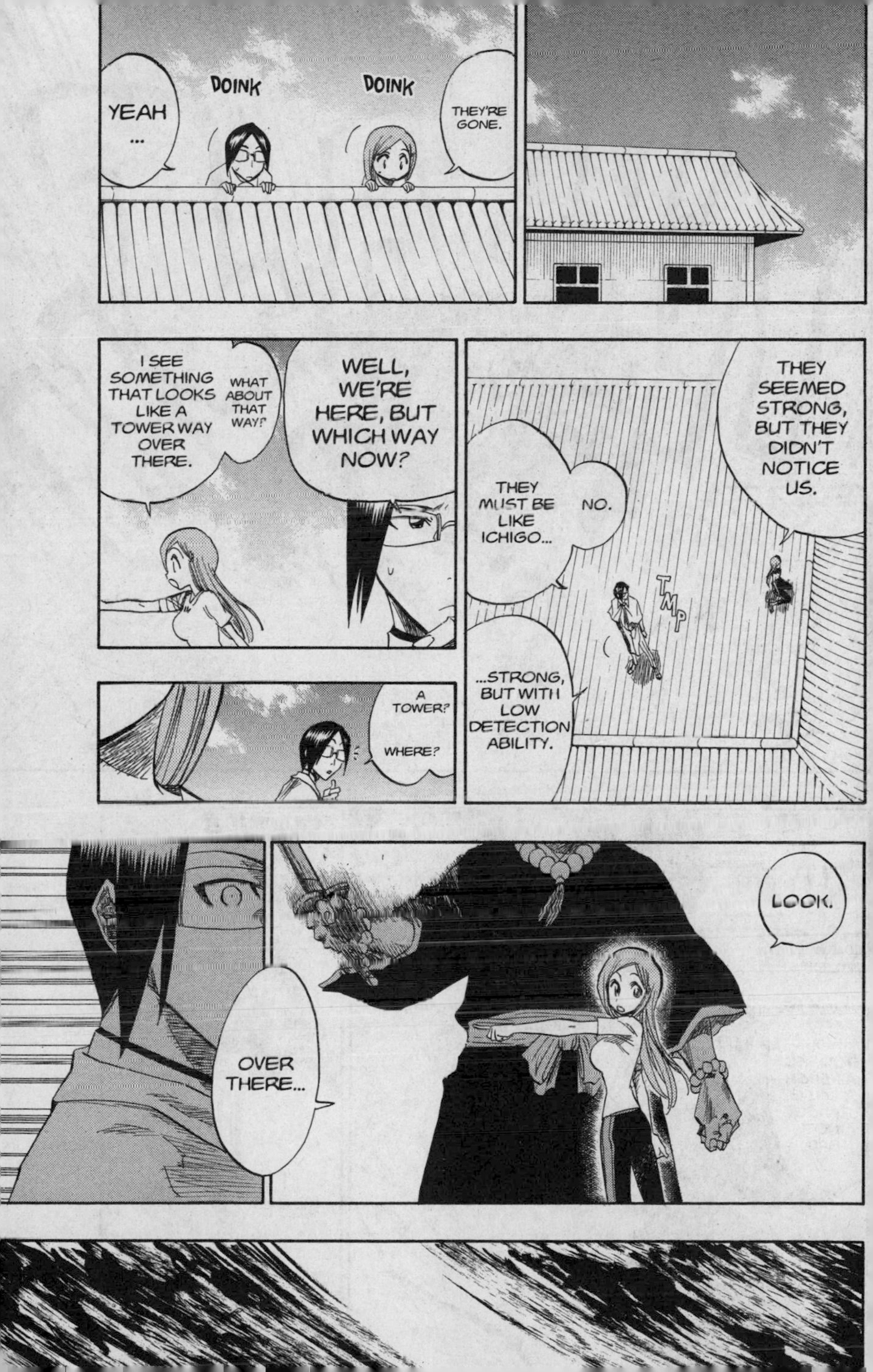
THEY'RE GONE.
DOINK
DOINK
YEAH ...
THEY SEEMED STRONG, BUT THEY DIDN'T NOTICE US.
NO.
THEY MUST BE LIKE ICHIGO...
TMP
...STRONG, BUT WITH LOW DETECTION ABILITY.
WELL, WE'RE HERE, BUT WHICH WAY NOW?
WHAT ABOUT THAT WAY?
I SEE SOMETHING THAT LOOKS LIKE A TOWER WAY OVER THERE.
A TOWER? WHERE?
LOOK.
OVER THERE...

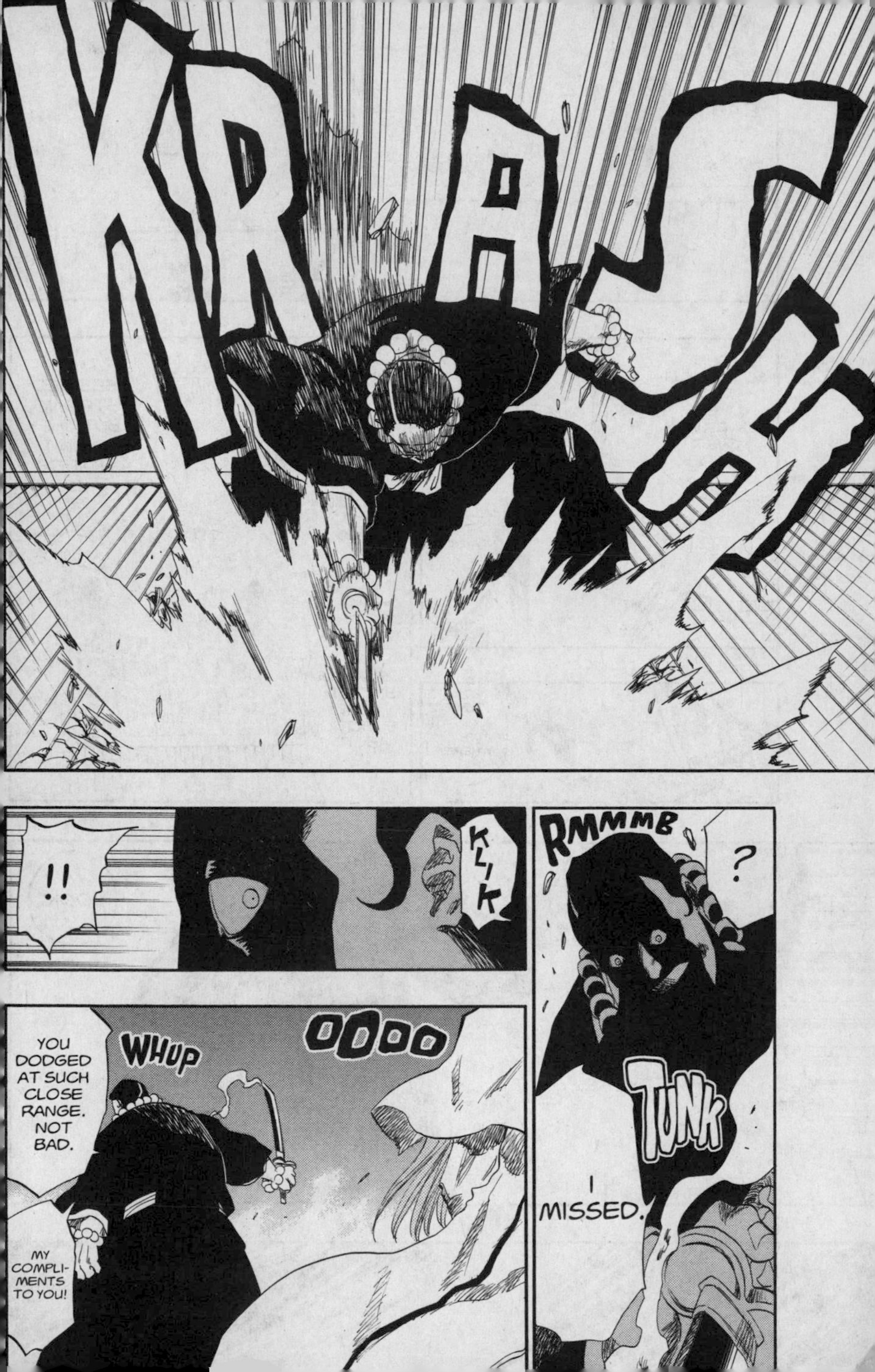
KRASH
RMMMB
?
TUNK
I MISSED.
KLIK
!!
OOOO
WHUP
YOU DODGED AT SUCH CLOSE RANGE. NOT BAD.
MY COMPLIMENTS TO YOU!

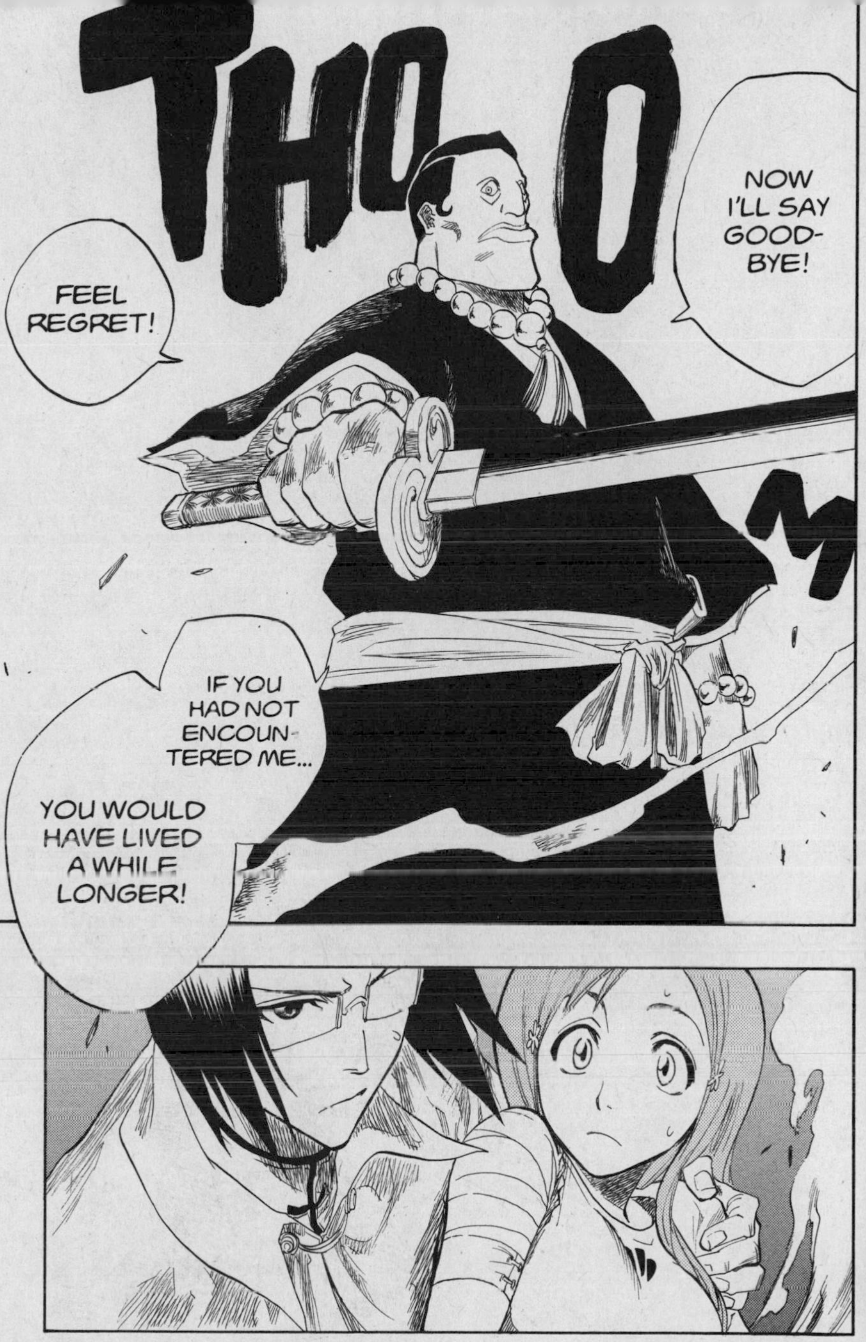
THO O M
NOW I'LL SAY GOOD-BYE!
FEEL REGRET!
IF YOU HAD NOT ENCOUN-TERED ME...
YOU WOULD HAVE LIVED A WHILE LONGER!

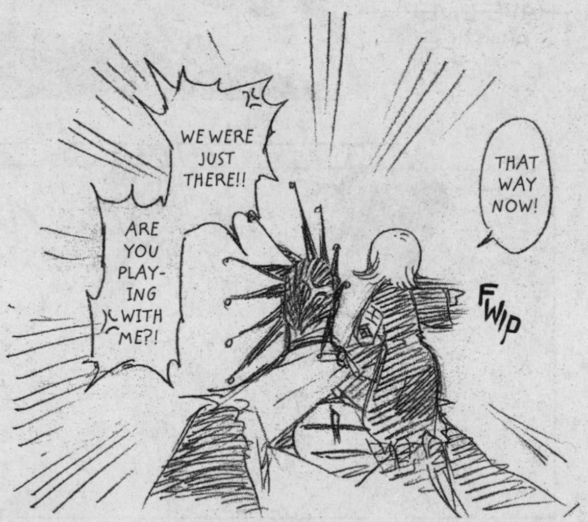
THAT WAY NOW!
WE WERE JUST THERE!!
FWIP
ARE YOU PLAY-ING WITH ME?!

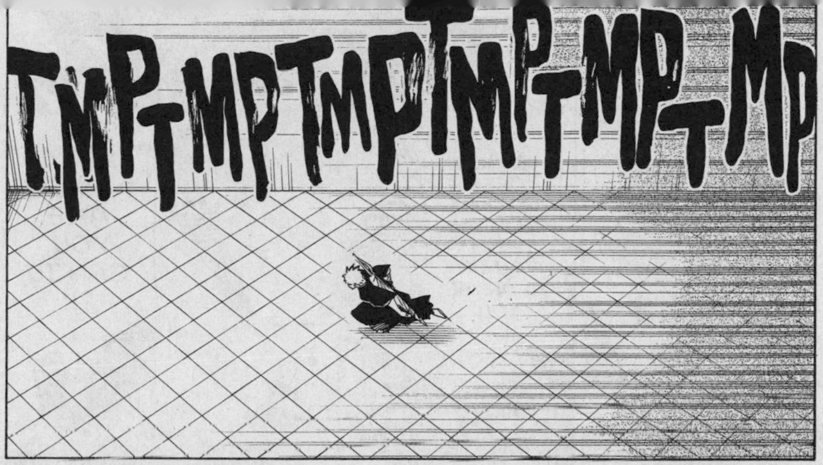
TMP TMP TMP TMP TMP TMP

90. See You Under a Firework

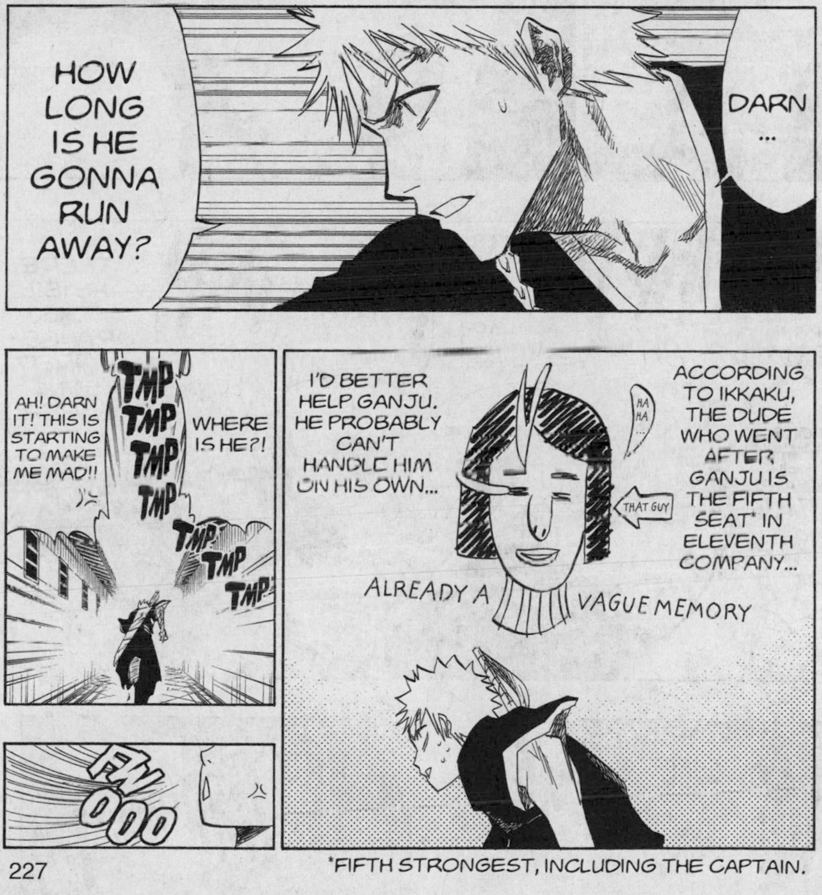
DARN ...
HOW LONG IS HE GONNA RUN AWAY?
ACCORDING TO IKKAKU, THE DUDE WHO WENT AFTER GANJU IS THE FIFTH SEAT* IN ELEVENTH COMPANY...
HA HA ...
THAT GUY
ALREADY A VAGUE MEMORY
I'D BETTER HELP GANJU. HE PROBABLY CAN'T HANDLE HIM ON HIS OWN...
WHERE IS HE?!
TMP TMP TMP TMP TMP
AH! DARN IT! THIS IS STARTING TO MAKE ME MAD!!
TMP TMP TMP
FWOOO

*FIFTH STRONGEST, INCLUDING THE CAPTAIN.

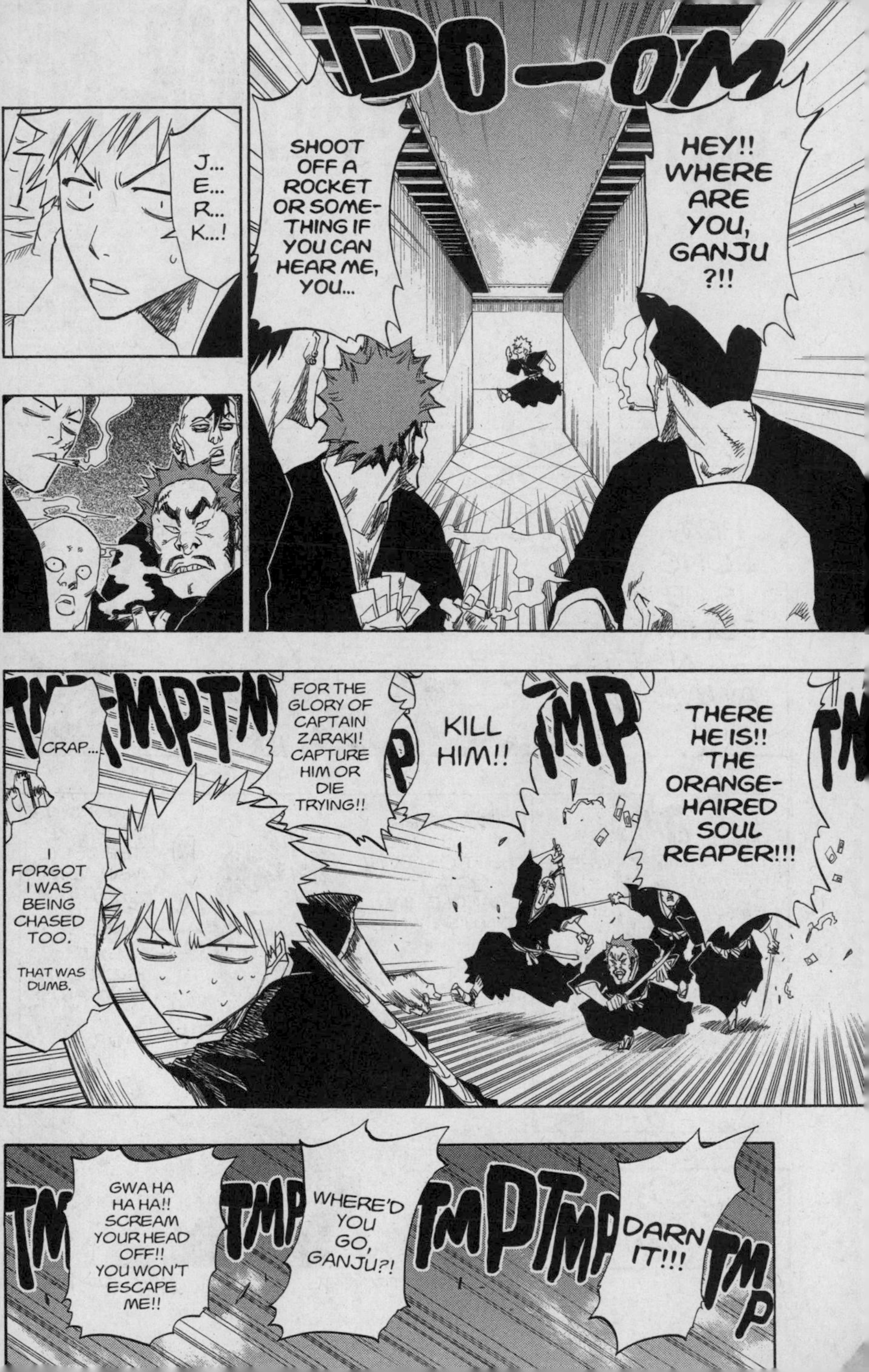
DO-OM
HEY!! WHERE ARE YOU, GANJU?!!
SHOOT OFF A ROCKET OR SOMETHING IF YOU CAN HEAR ME, YOU...
J... E... R... K...!
TMP
THERE HE IS!! THE ORANGE-HAIRED SOUL REAPER!!!
TMP
KILL HIM!!
FOR THE GLORY OF CAPTAIN ZARAKI!! CAPTURE HIM OR DIE TRYING!!
TMPTMPTM
CRAP...
I FORGOT I WAS BEING CHASED TOO.
THAT WAS DUMB.
TMP
DARN IT!!!
TMPTMP
WHERE'D YOU GO, GANJU?!
TMP
GWA HA HA HA!! SCREAM YOUR HEAD OFF!! YOU WON'T ESCAPE ME!!
TM

90. See You Under a Firework

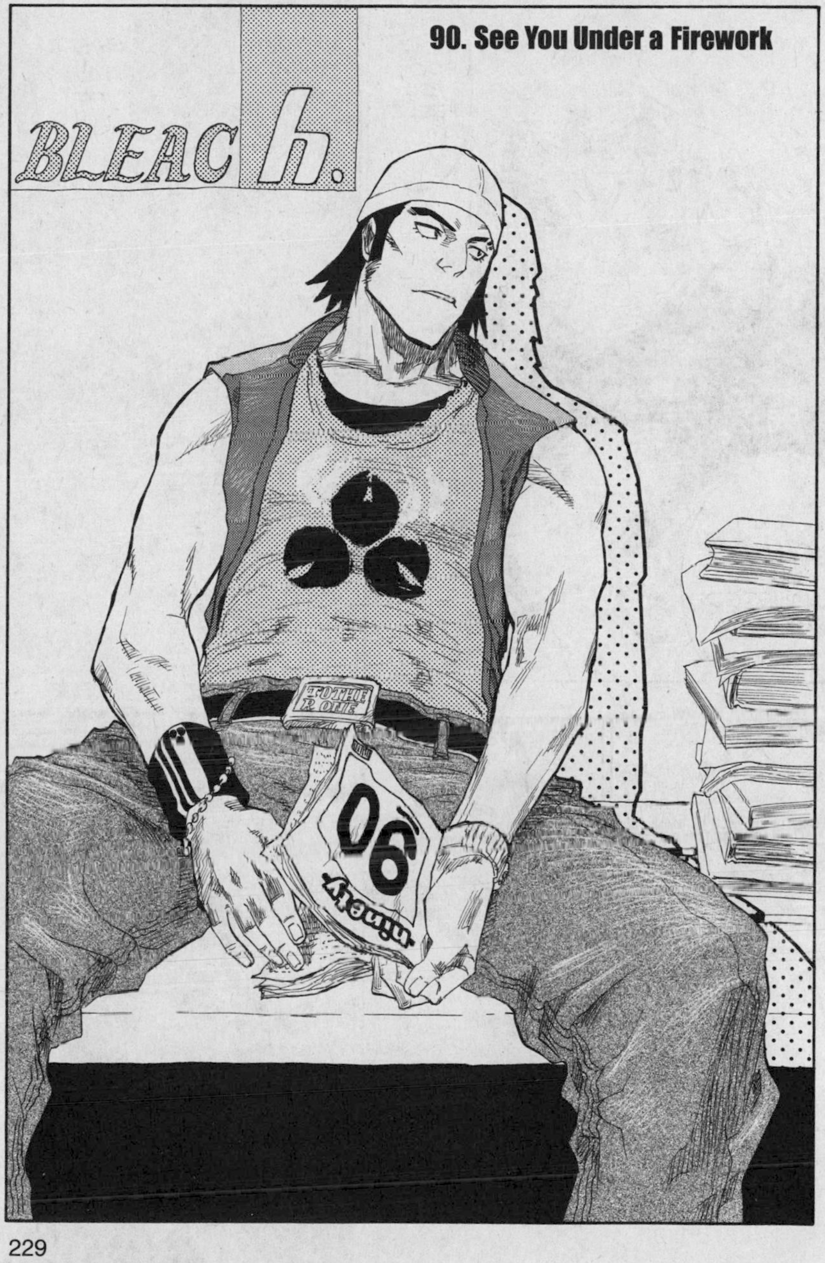
BLEACH
90
ninety

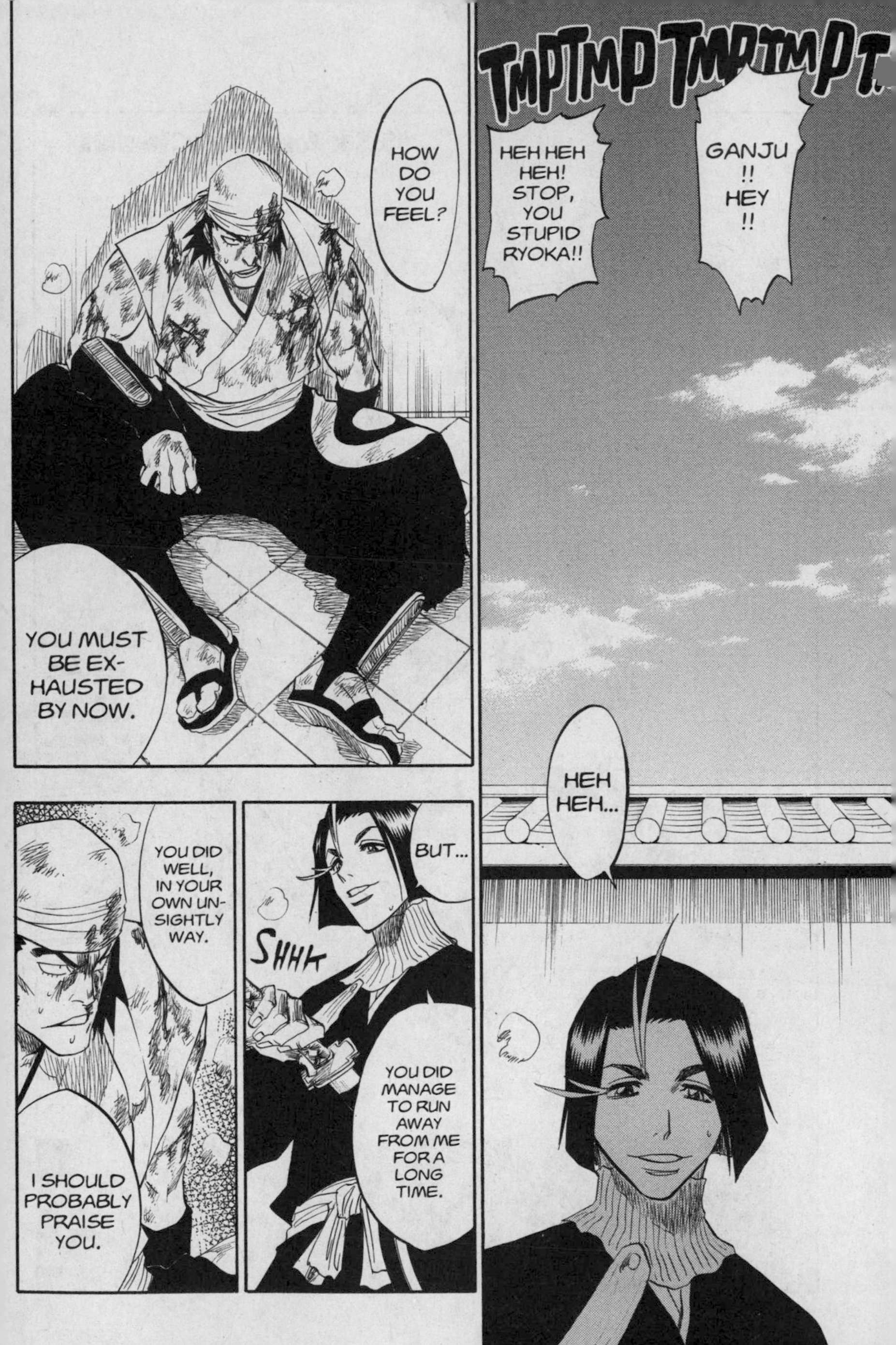
TMPTMP TMPTMP T
GANJU!! HEY!!
HEH HEH HEH! STOP, YOU STUPID RYOKA!!
HEH HEH...
HOW DO YOU FEEL?
YOU MUST BE EX-HAUSTED BY NOW.
BUT...
SHHK
YOU DID MANAGE TO RUN AWAY FROM ME FOR A LONG TIME.
YOU DID WELL, IN YOUR OWN UN-SIGHTLY WAY.
I SHOULD PROBABLY PRAISE YOU.

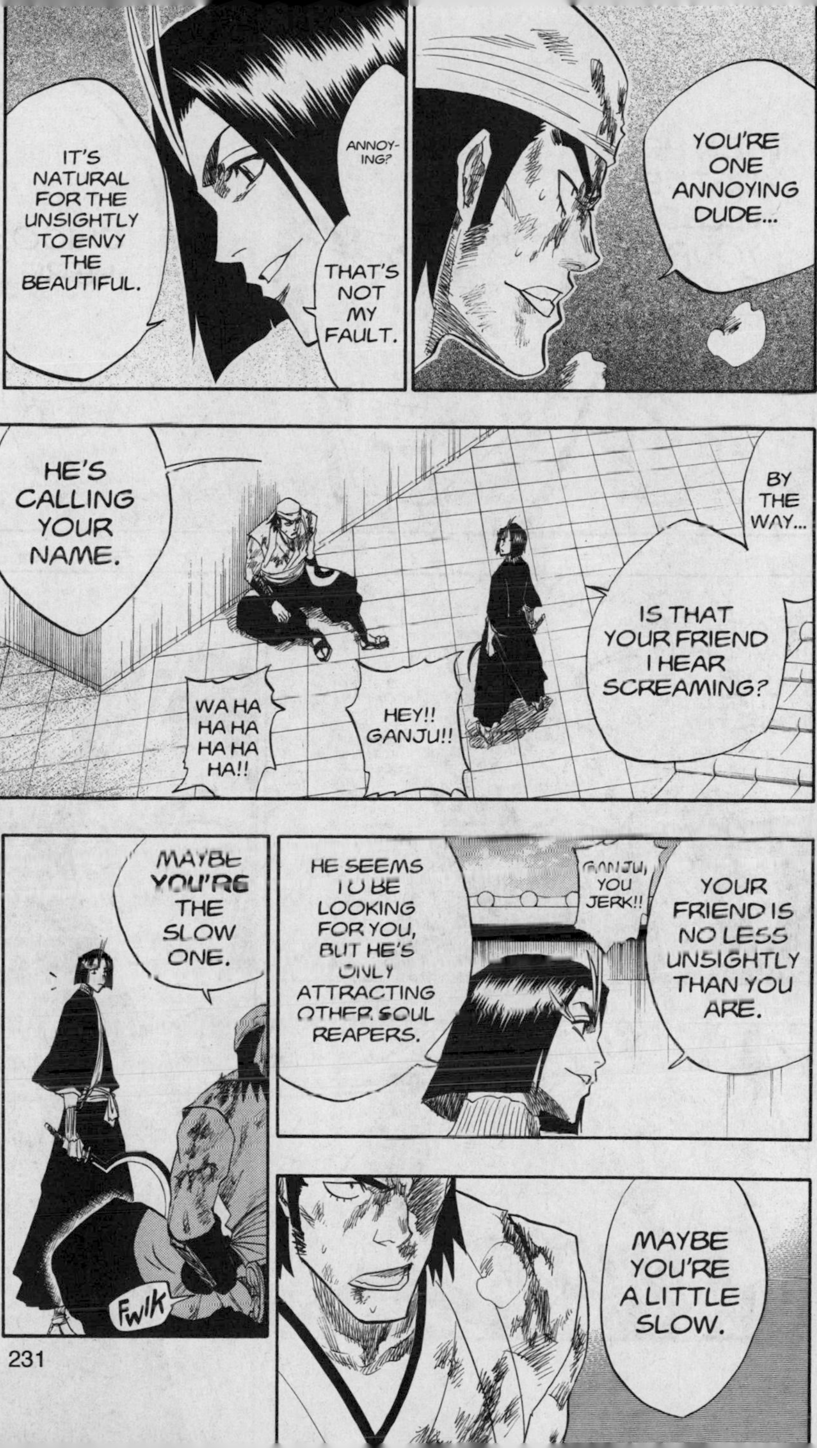
YOU'RE ONE ANNOYING DUDE...
ANNOY-ING?
THAT'S NOT MY FAULT.
IT'S NATURAL FOR THE UNSIGHTLY TO ENVY THE BEAUTIFUL.
BY THE WAY...
IS THAT YOUR FRIEND I HEAR SCREAMING?
HEY!! GANJU!!
WA HA HA HA HA HA HA!!
HE'S CALLING YOUR NAME.
GANJU, YOU JERK!!
YOUR FRIEND IS NO LESS UNSIGHTLY THAN YOU ARE.
HE SEEMS TO BE LOOKING FOR YOU, BUT HE'S ONLY ATTRACTING OTHER SOUL REAPERS.
MAYBE YOU'RE A LITTLE SLOW.
MAYBE YOU'RE THE SLOW ONE.
FWIK

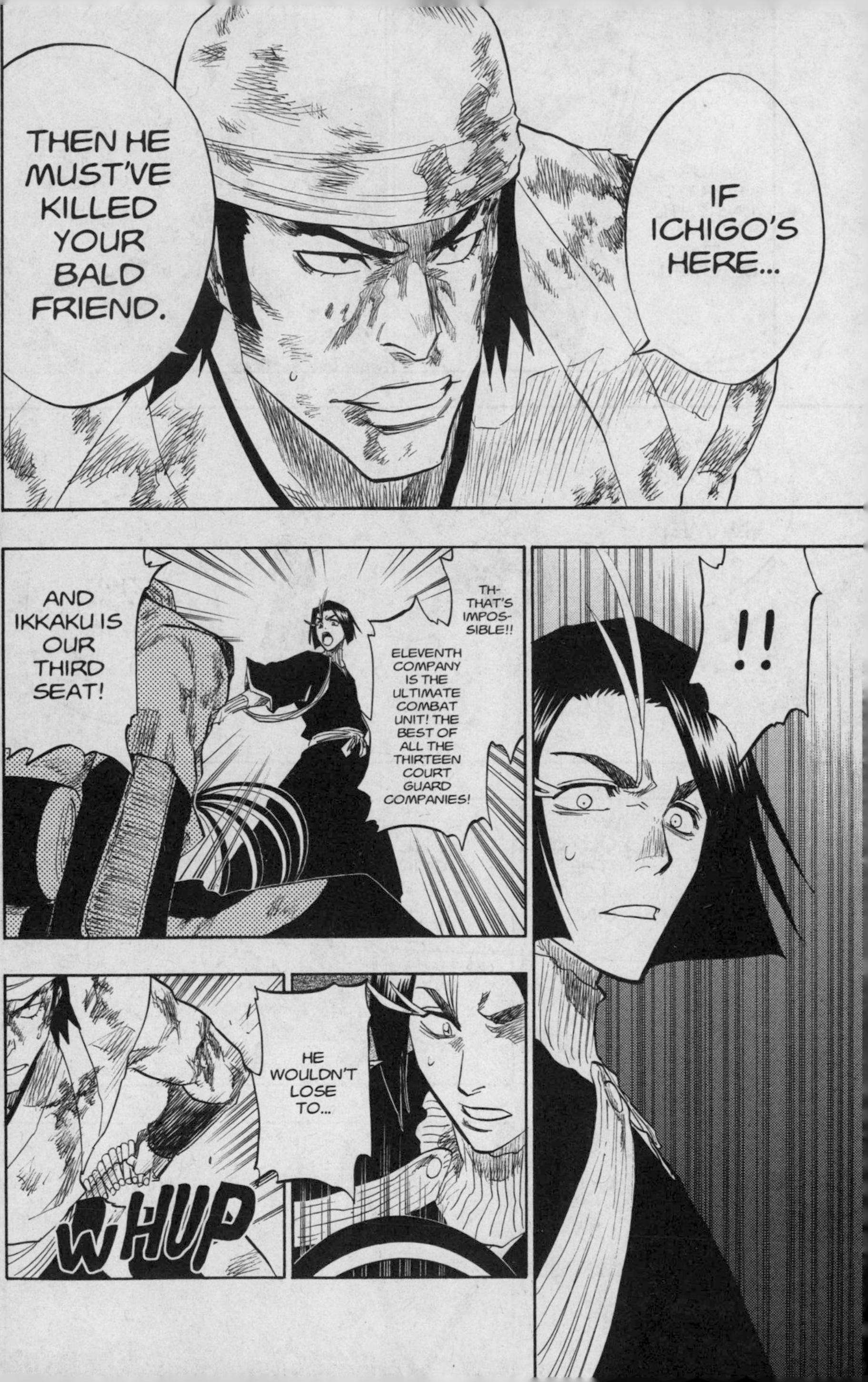
IF ICHIGO'S HERE...
THEN HE MUST'VE KILLED YOUR BALD FRIEND.
!!
TH-THAT'S IMPOSSIBLE!!
ELEVENTH COMPANY IS THE ULTIMATE COMBAT UNIT! THE BEST OF ALL THE THIRTEEN COURT GUARD COMPANIES!
AND IKKAKU IS OUR THIRD SEAT!
HE WOULDN'T LOSE TO...
WHUP

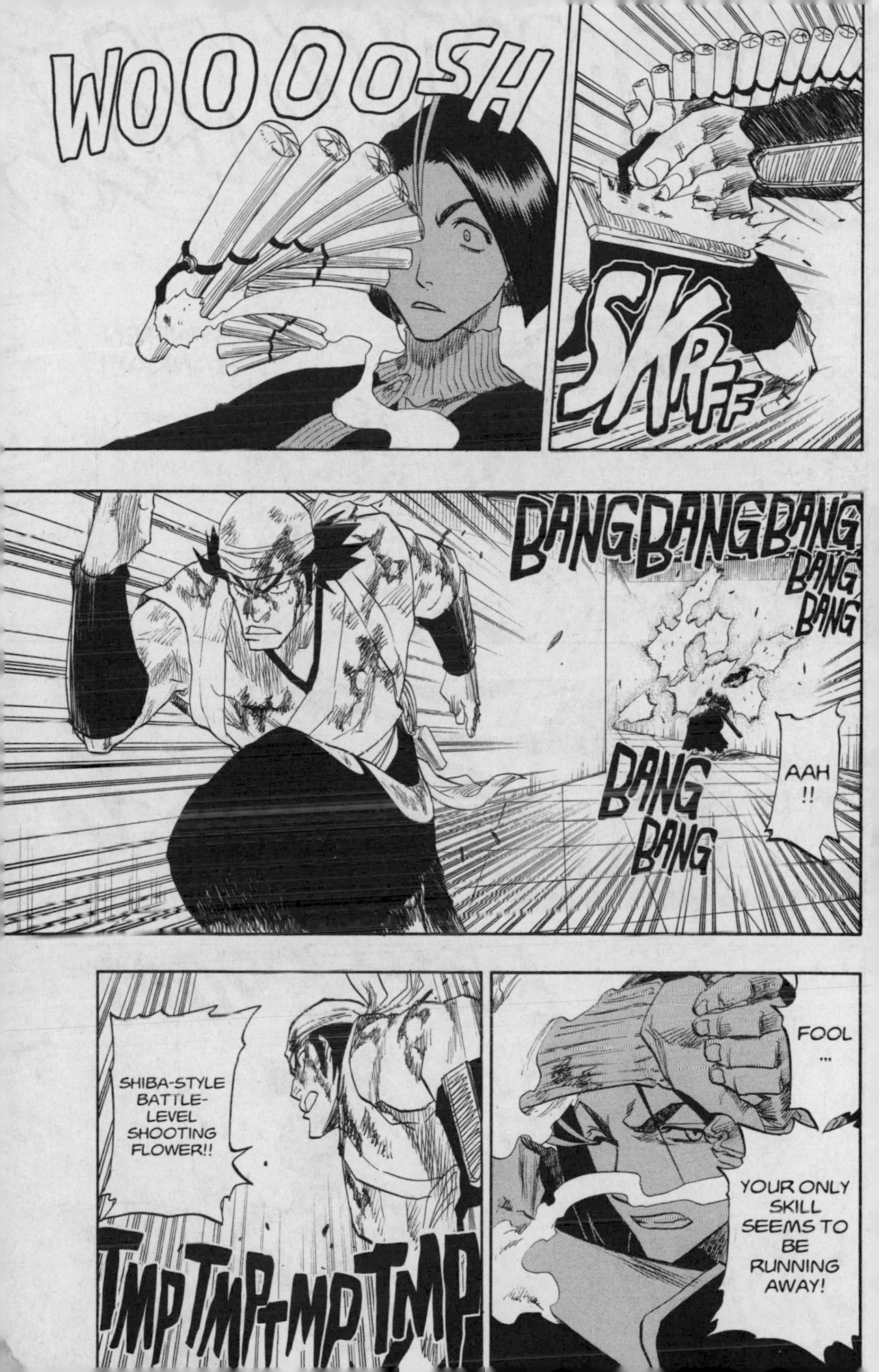
SKRFFF
WOOOOSH
BANG BANG BANG BANG BANG
AAH !!
BANG BANG
FOOL ...
YOUR ONLY SKILL SEEMS TO BE RUNNING AWAY!
SHIBA-STYLE BATTLE-LEVEL SHOOTING FLOWER!!
TMP TMP-TMP TMP

SHWOOOOOOOOMMM

SENPEN BANKA!!!

(TEN THOUSAND SPINNING FLOWERS)

DON'T UNDER- ESTIMATE ME!

KIINK

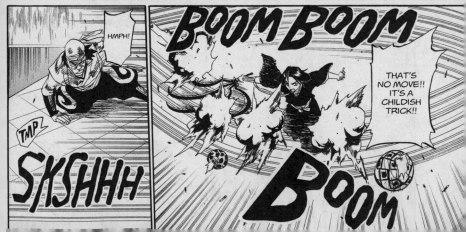

HMPH!

TMP

SKSHHH

BOOM BOOM

THAT'S NO MOVE!! IT'S A CHILDISH TRICK!!

BOOM

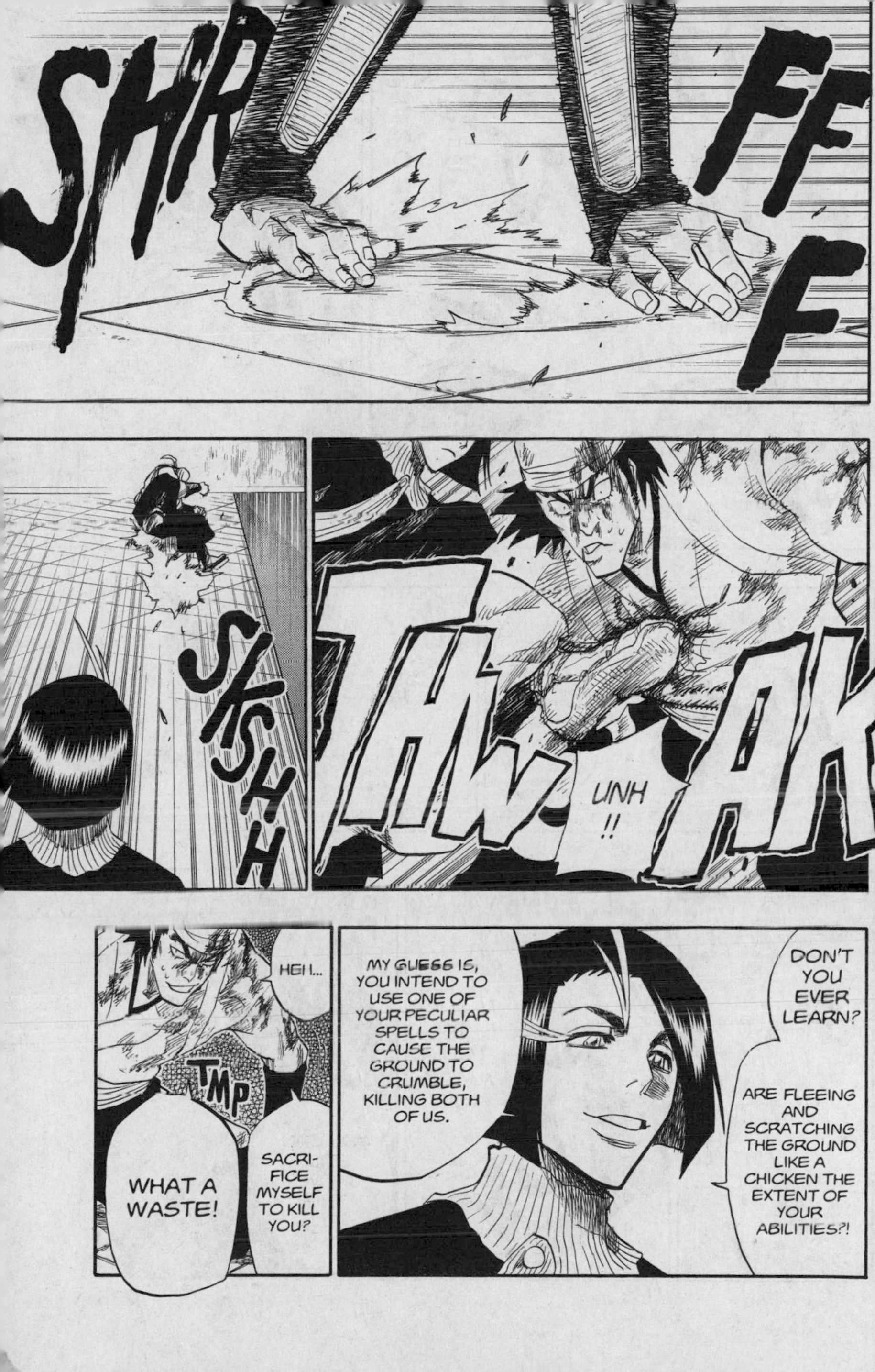
SHRFFF
THWAK
UNH !!
SKSHH
DON'T YOU EVER LEARN?
ARE FLEEING AND SCRATCHING THE GROUND LIKE A CHICKEN THE EXTENT OF YOUR ABILITIES?!
MY GUESS IS, YOU INTEND TO USE ONE OF YOUR PECULIAR SPELLS TO CAUSE THE GROUND TO CRUMBLE, KILLING BOTH OF US.
HEH...
TMP
SACRI-FICE MYSELF TO KILL YOU?
WHAT A WASTE!

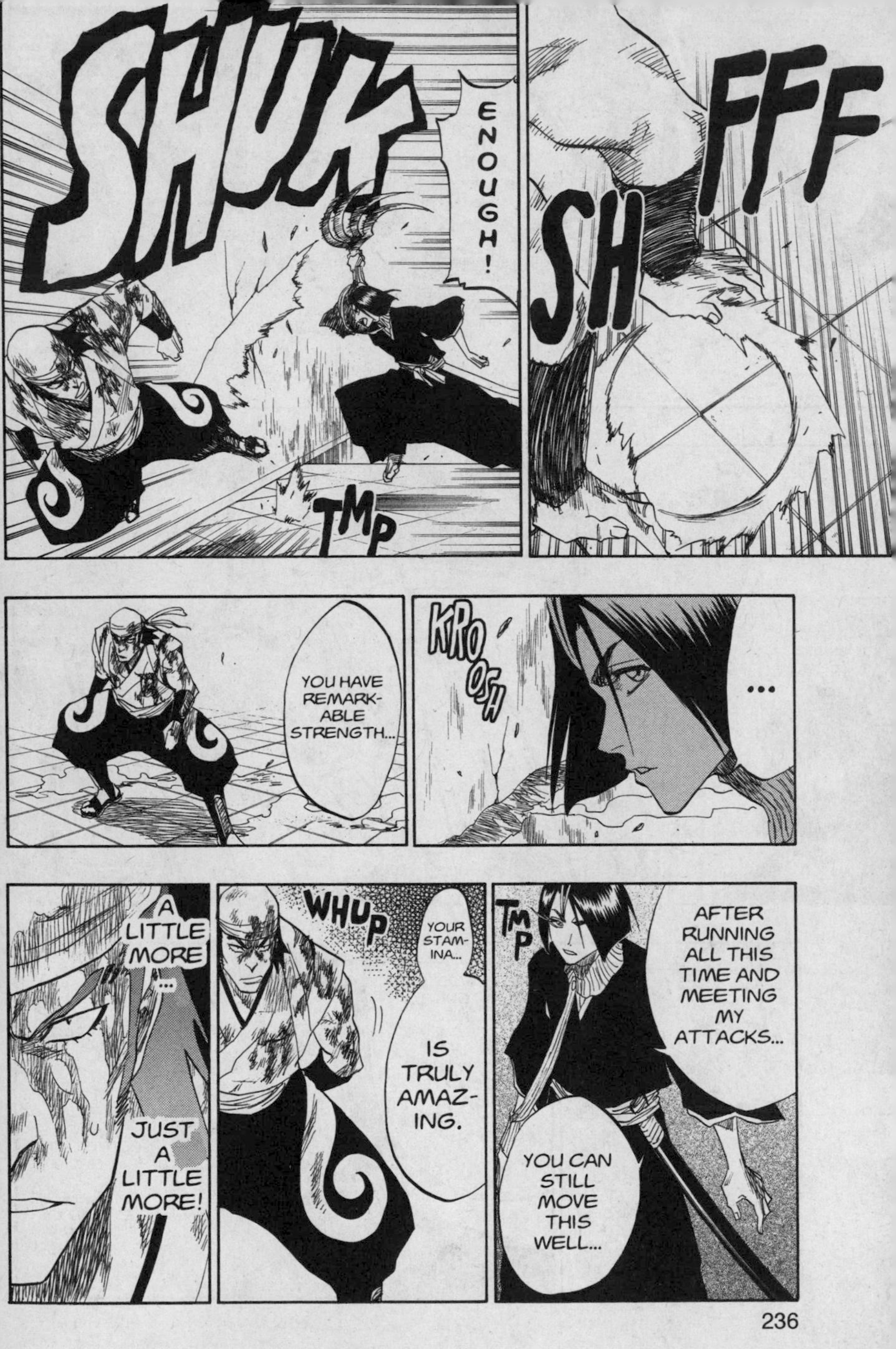
SHFFF
ENOUGH!
SHUK
TMP
KROOSH
...
YOU HAVE REMARKABLE STRENGTH...
TMP
AFTER RUNNING ALL THIS TIME AND MEETING MY ATTACKS...
YOU CAN STILL MOVE THIS WELL...
WHUP
YOUR STAMINA...
IS TRULY AMAZING.
A LITTLE MORE...
JUST A LITTLE MORE!

READ THIS WAY

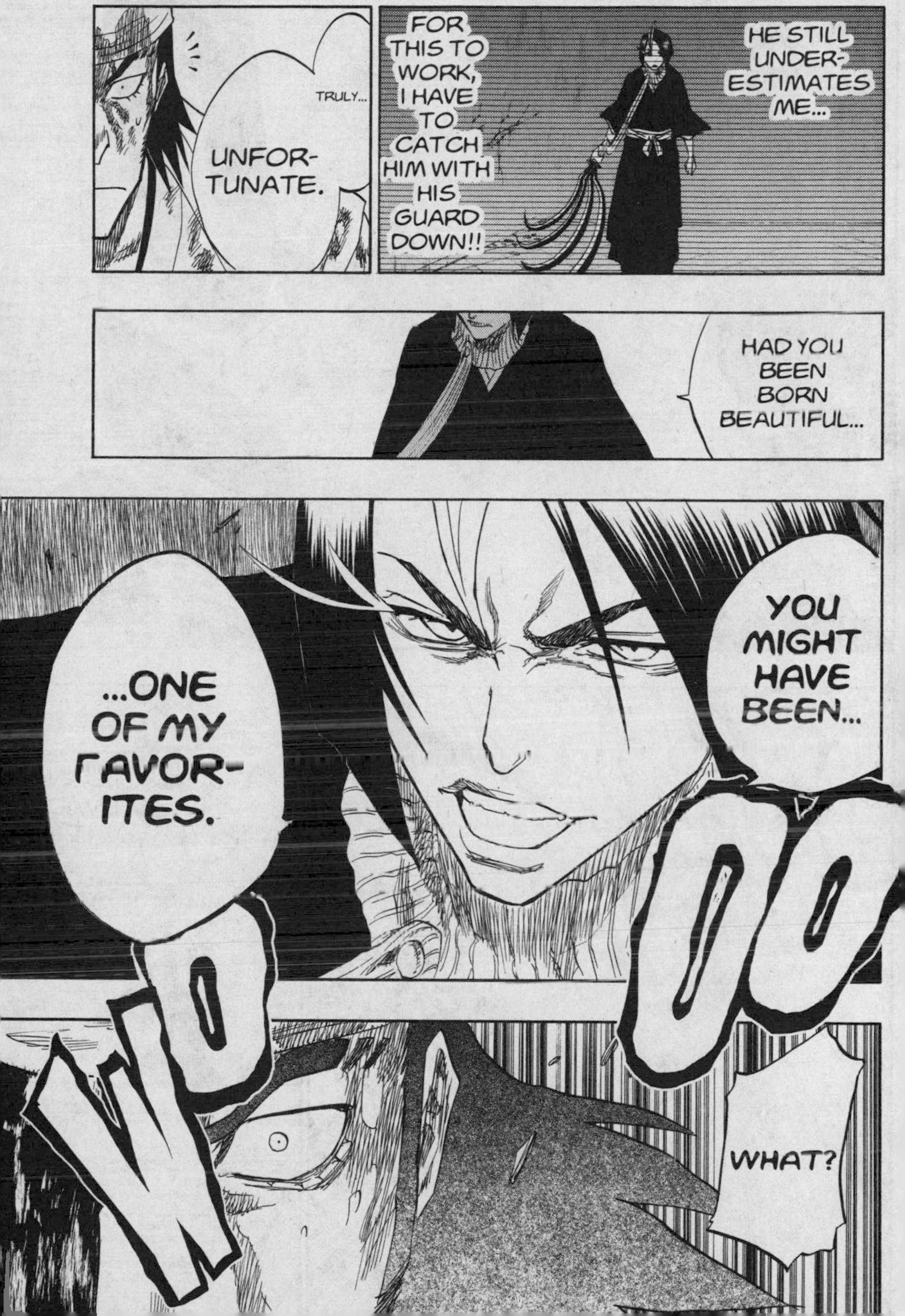
HE STILL UNDER-ESTIMATES ME...
FOR THIS TO WORK, I HAVE TO CATCH HIM WITH HIS GUARD DOWN!!
TRULY...
UNFOR-TUNATE.
HAD YOU BEEN BORN BEAUTIFUL...
YOU MIGHT HAVE BEEN...
...ONE OF MY FAVOR-ITES.
WHAT?

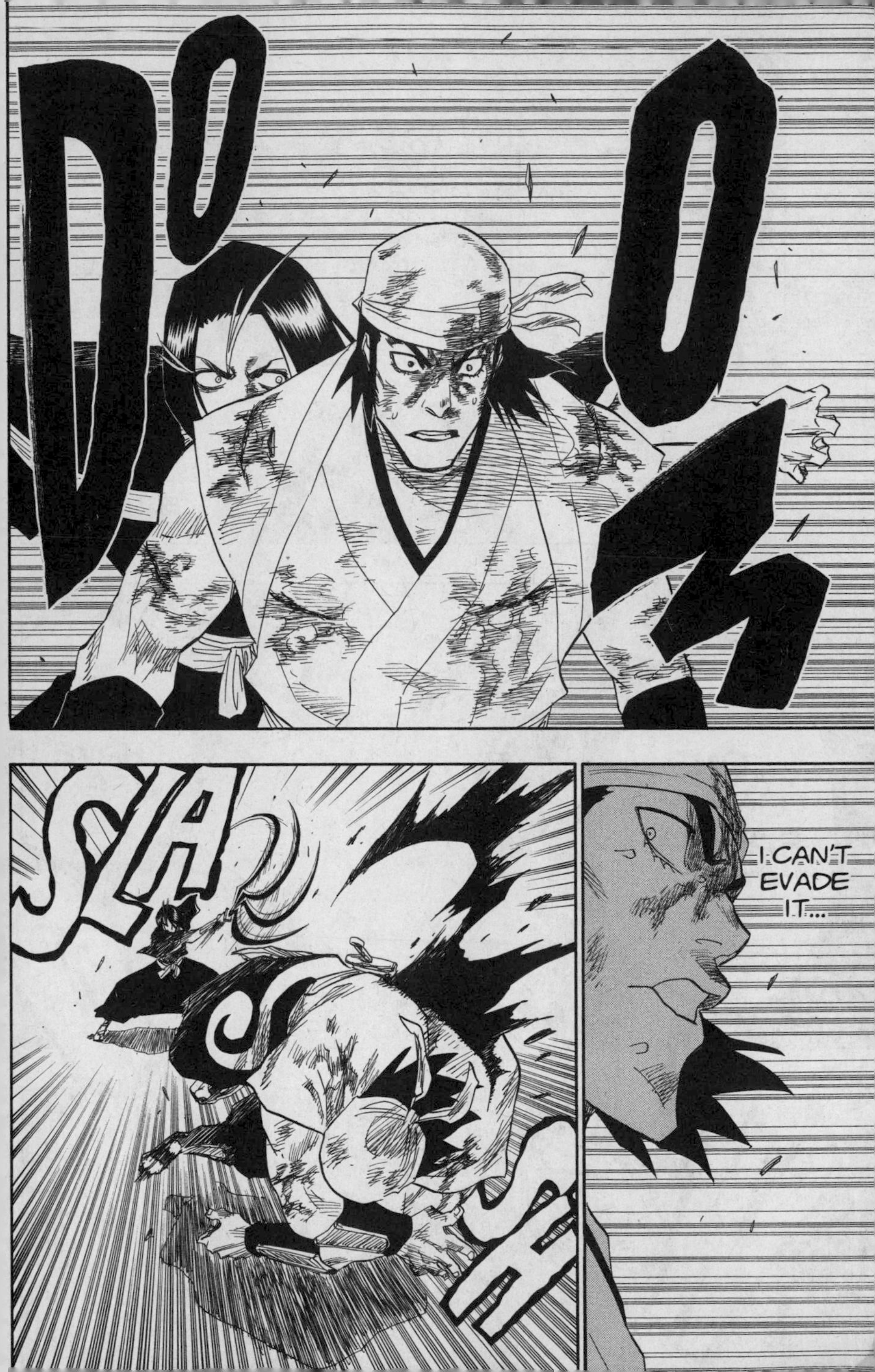
DOOM
I CAN'T EVADE IT...
SLASH

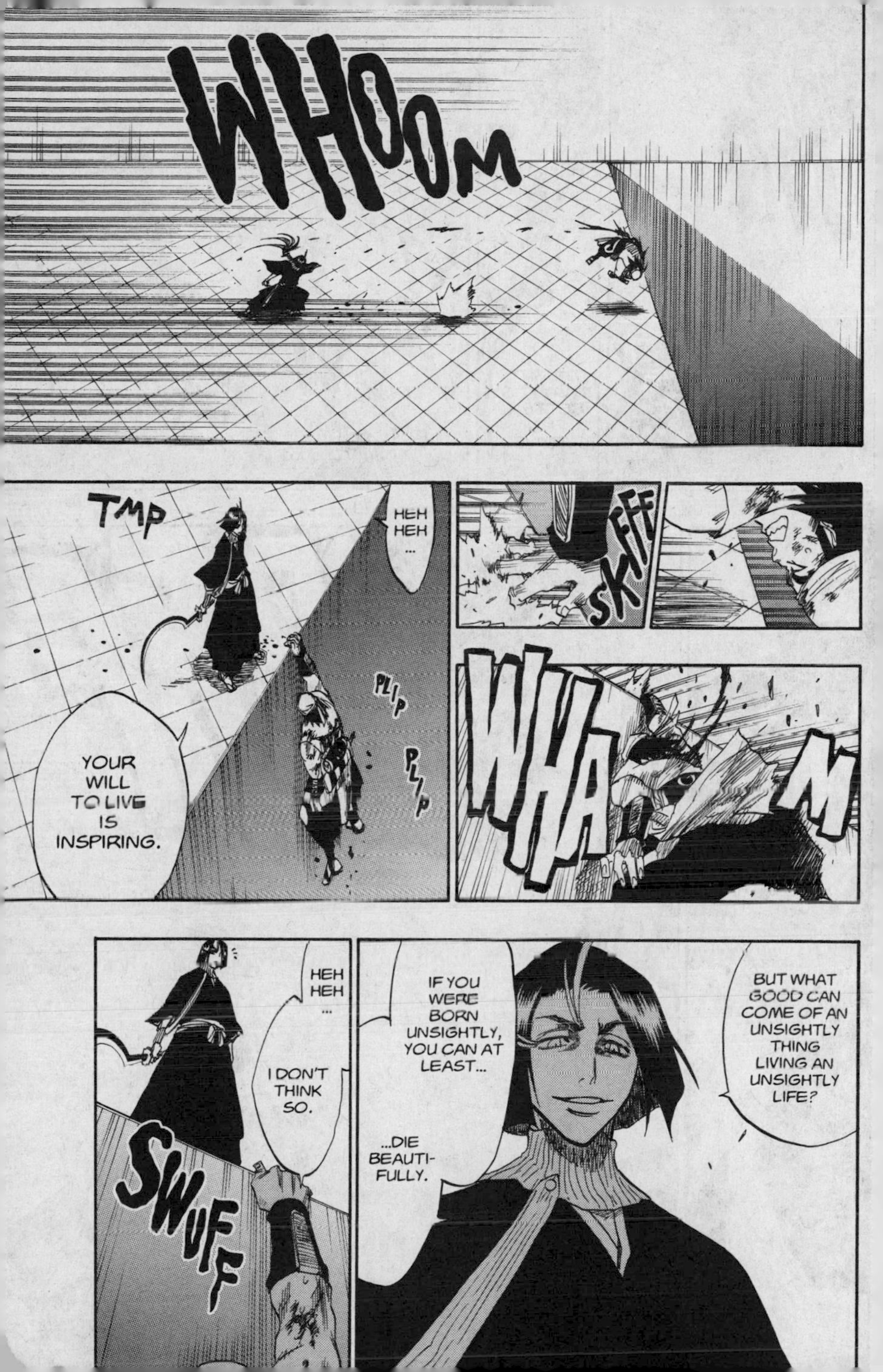
WHOOM
SKIFFF
WHAM
HEH HEH ...
TMP
PLIP
PLIP
YOUR WILL TO LIVE IS INSPIRING.
BUT WHAT GOOD CAN COME OF AN UNSIGHTLY THING LIVING AN UNSIGHTLY LIFE?
IF YOU WERE BORN UNSIGHTLY, YOU CAN AT LEAST...
...DIE BEAUTIFULLY.
HEH HEH ...
I DON'T THINK SO.
SWUFF

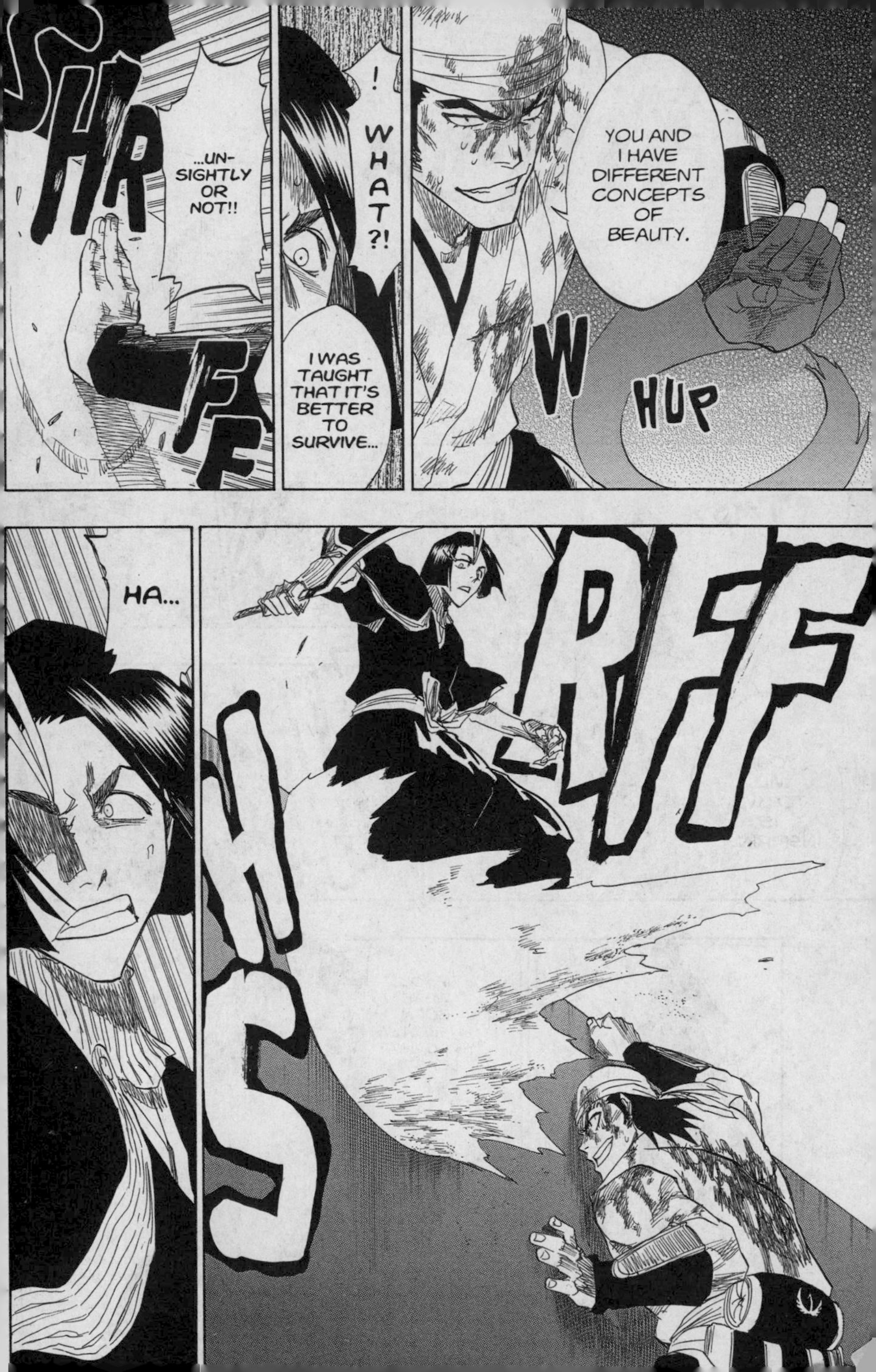
YOU AND I HAVE DIFFERENT CONCEPTS OF BEAUTY.
WHUP
!
WHAT?!
I WAS TAUGHT THAT IT'S BETTER TO SURVIVE...
SHR
...UN-SIGHTLY OR NOT!!
FF
RFF
HS
HA...

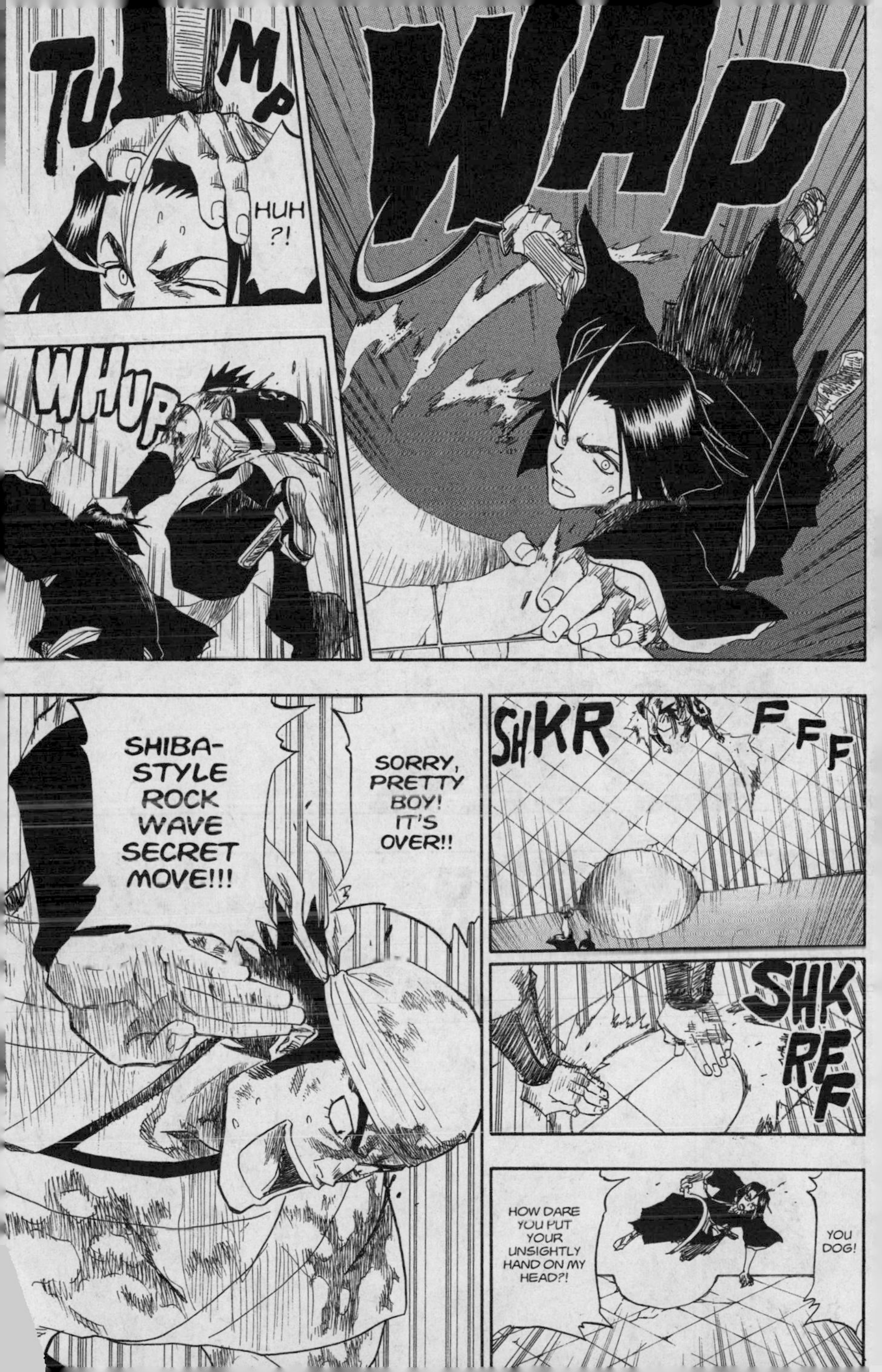
WAP
TUMP
HUH ?!
WHUP
SHKR FFF
SHK RFF
YOU DOG!
HOW DARE YOU PUT YOUR UNSIGHTLY HAND ON MY HEAD?!
SORRY, PRETTY BOY! IT'S OVER!!
SHIBA-STYLE ROCK WAVE SECRET MOVE!!!

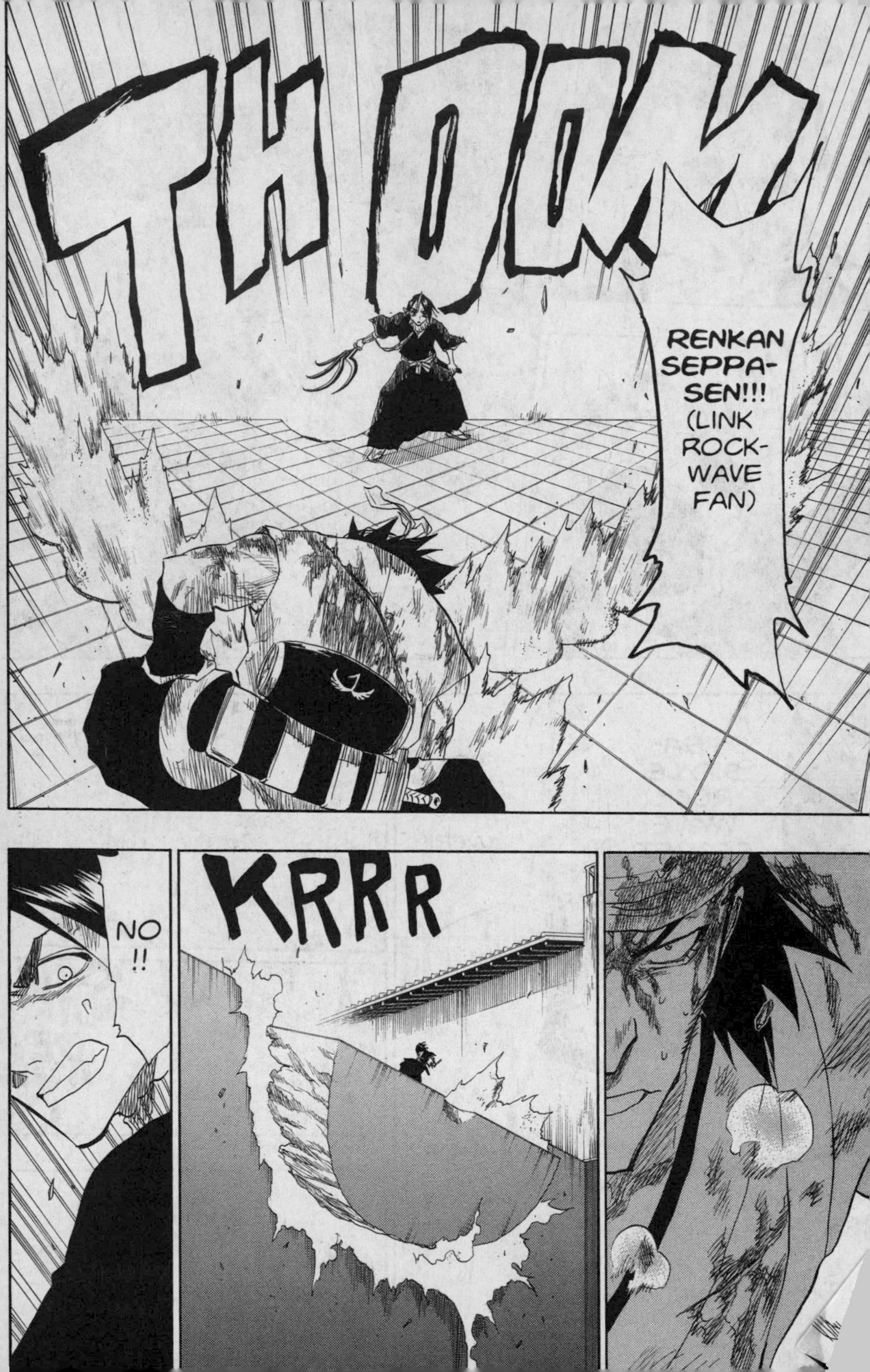
THOOM
RENKAN SEPPA-SEN!!! (LINK ROCK-WAVE FAN)
KRRR
NO !!

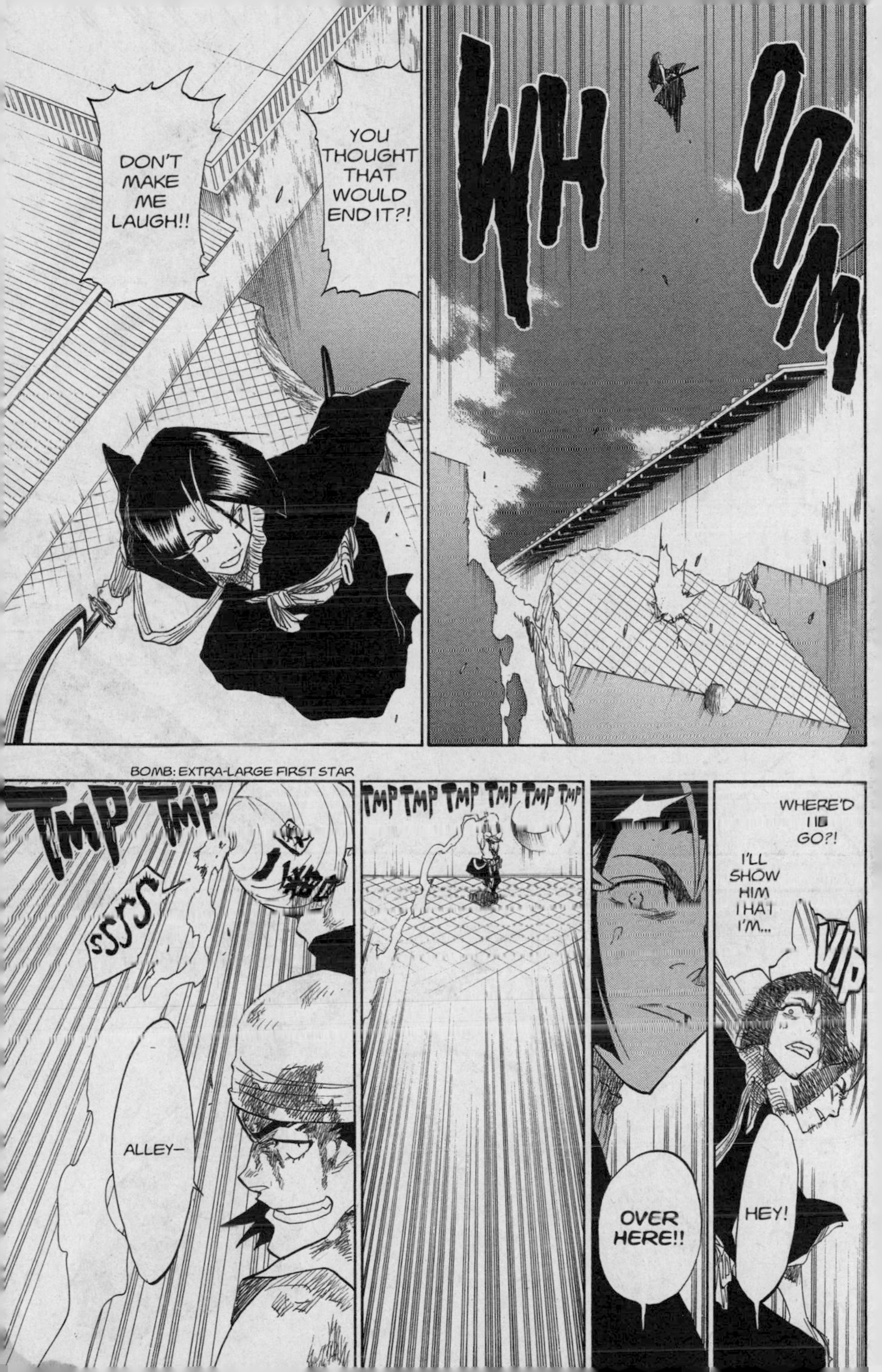
WHOOOM
YOU THOUGHT THAT WOULD END IT?!
DON'T MAKE ME LAUGH!!
WHERE'D HE GO?!
I'LL SHOW HIM THAT I'M...
VIP
HEY!
OVER HERE!!
TMP TMP TMP TMP TMP TMP
BOMB: EXTRA-LARGE FIRST STAR
TMP TMP
SSSS
ALLEY-

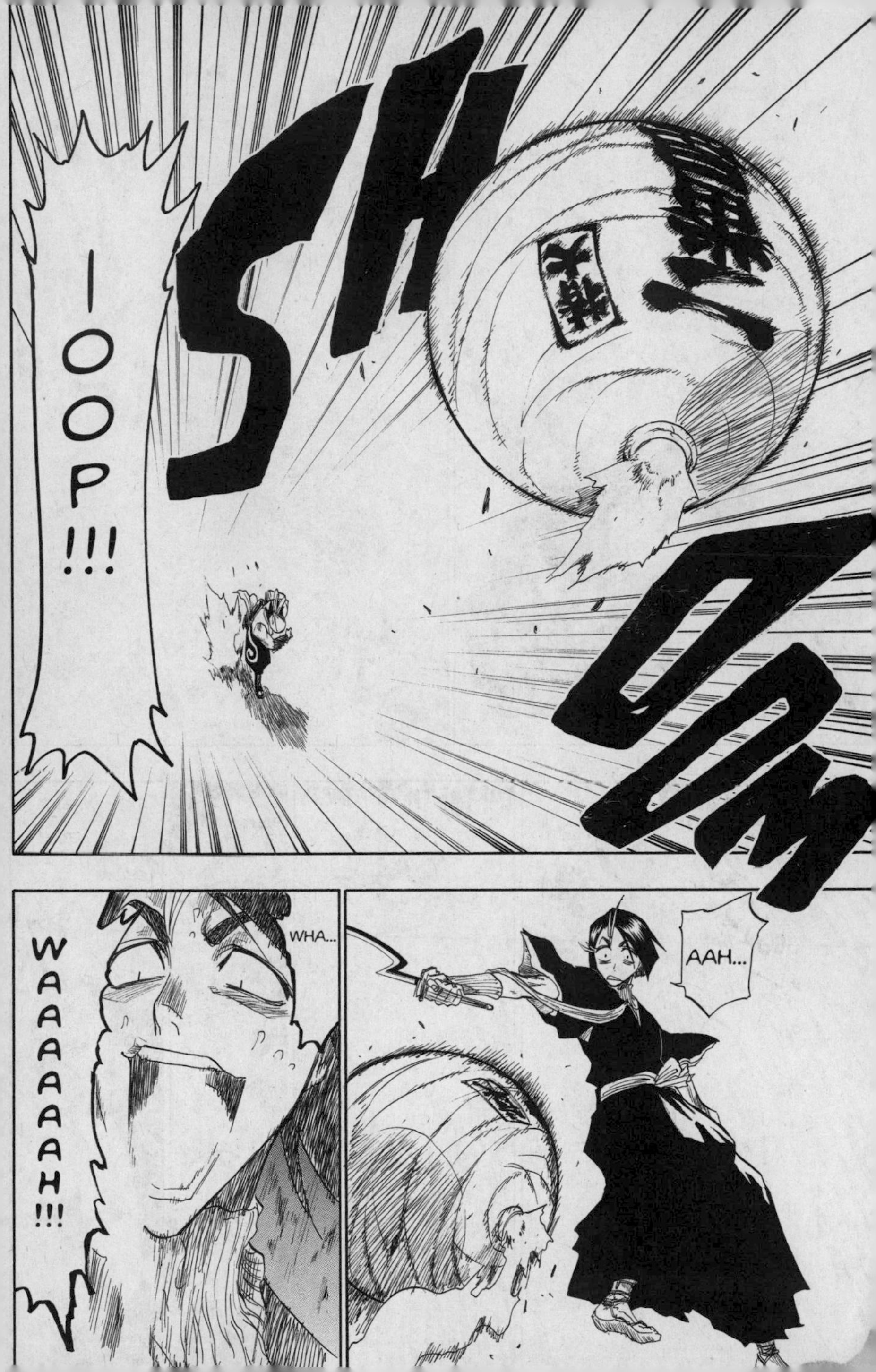
SHOOM
IOOP!!!
AAH...
WHA...
WAAAAAAH!!!

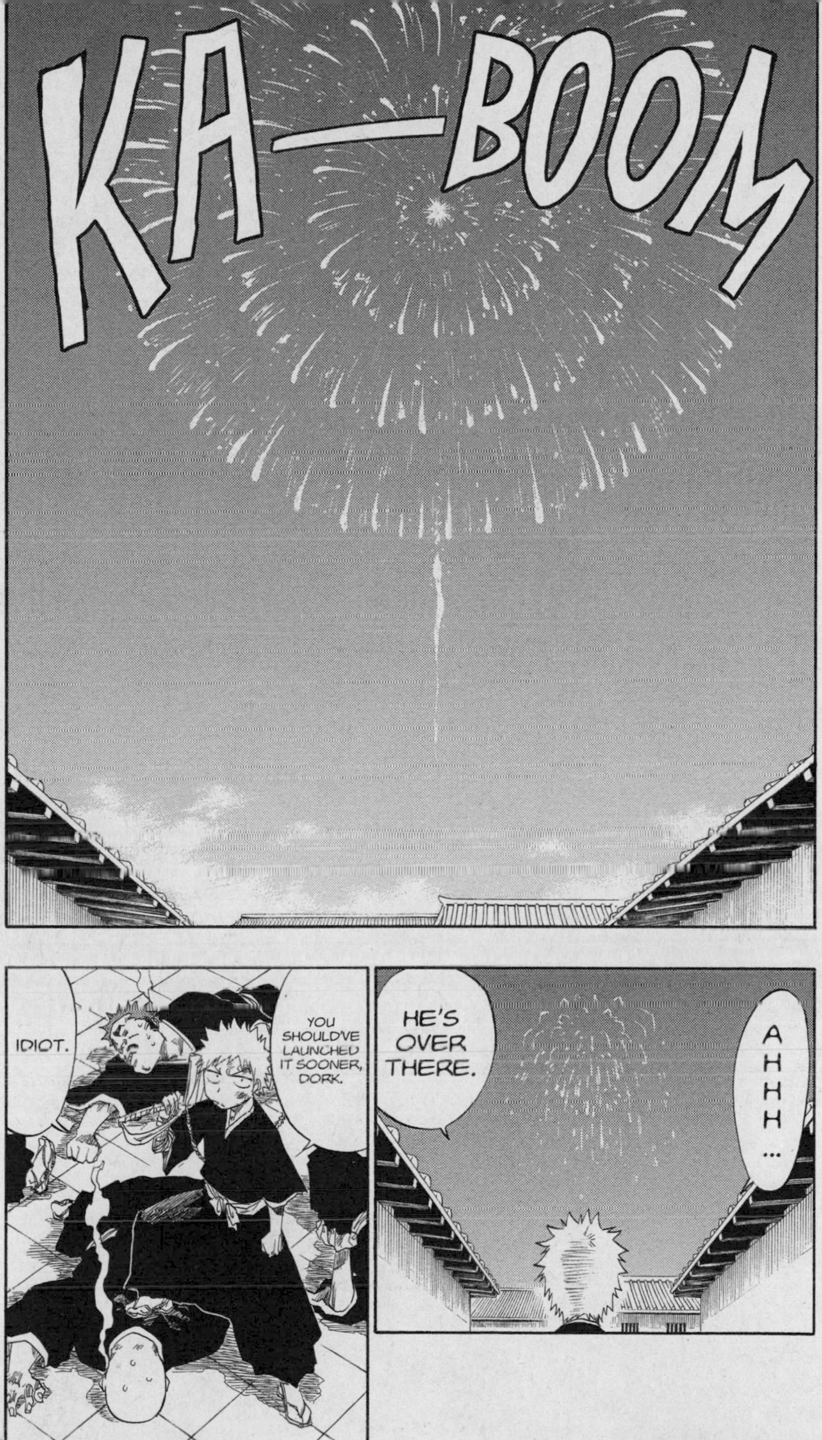
KA-BOOM
AHHH...
HE'S OVER THERE.
YOU SHOULD'VE LAUNCHED IT SOONER, DORK.
IDIOT.

AW...

YUMICHIKA
LOST.

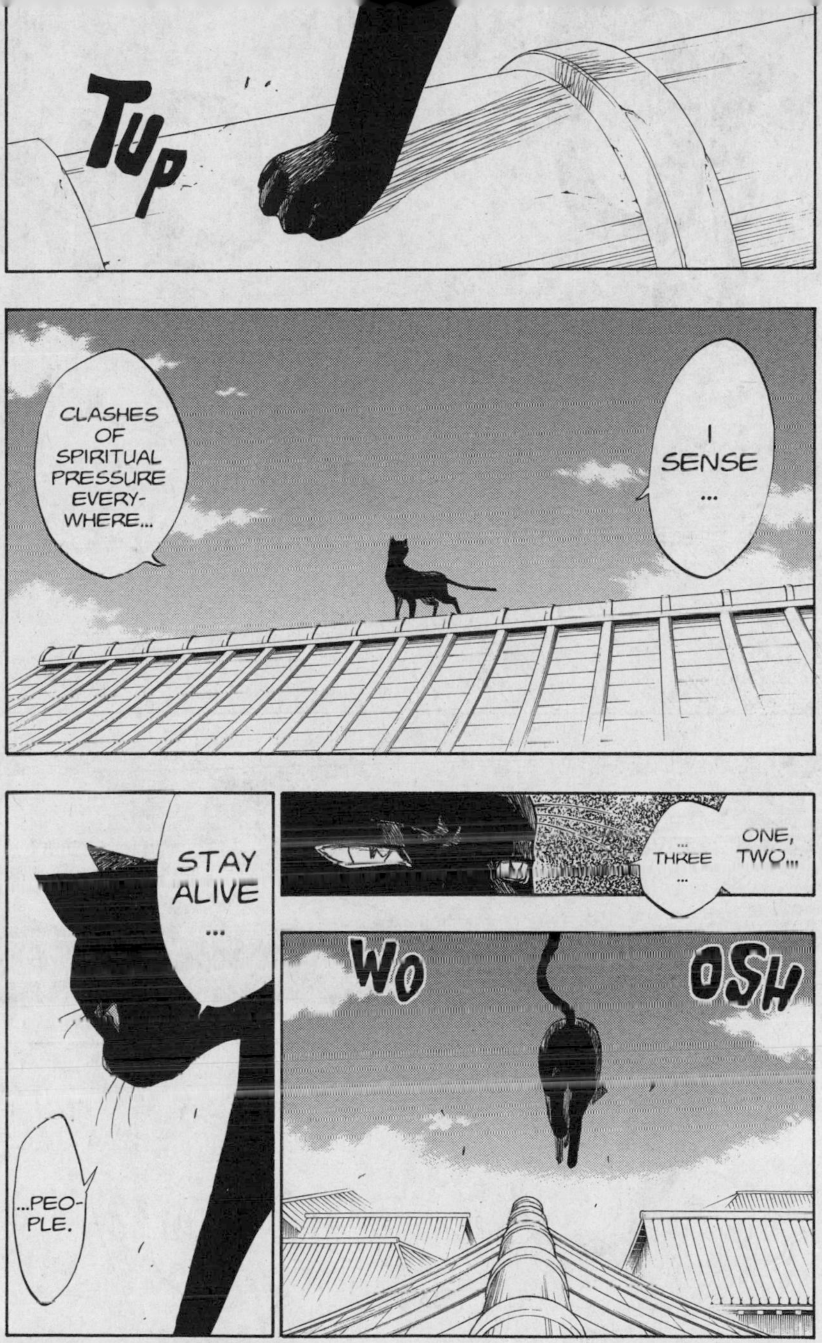
TUP
I SENSE ...
CLASHES OF SPIRITUAL PRESSURE EVERY-WHERE...
ONE, TWO...
... THREE ...
WOOSH
STAY ALIVE ...
...PEO-PLE.

91. King of FREISCHÜTZ

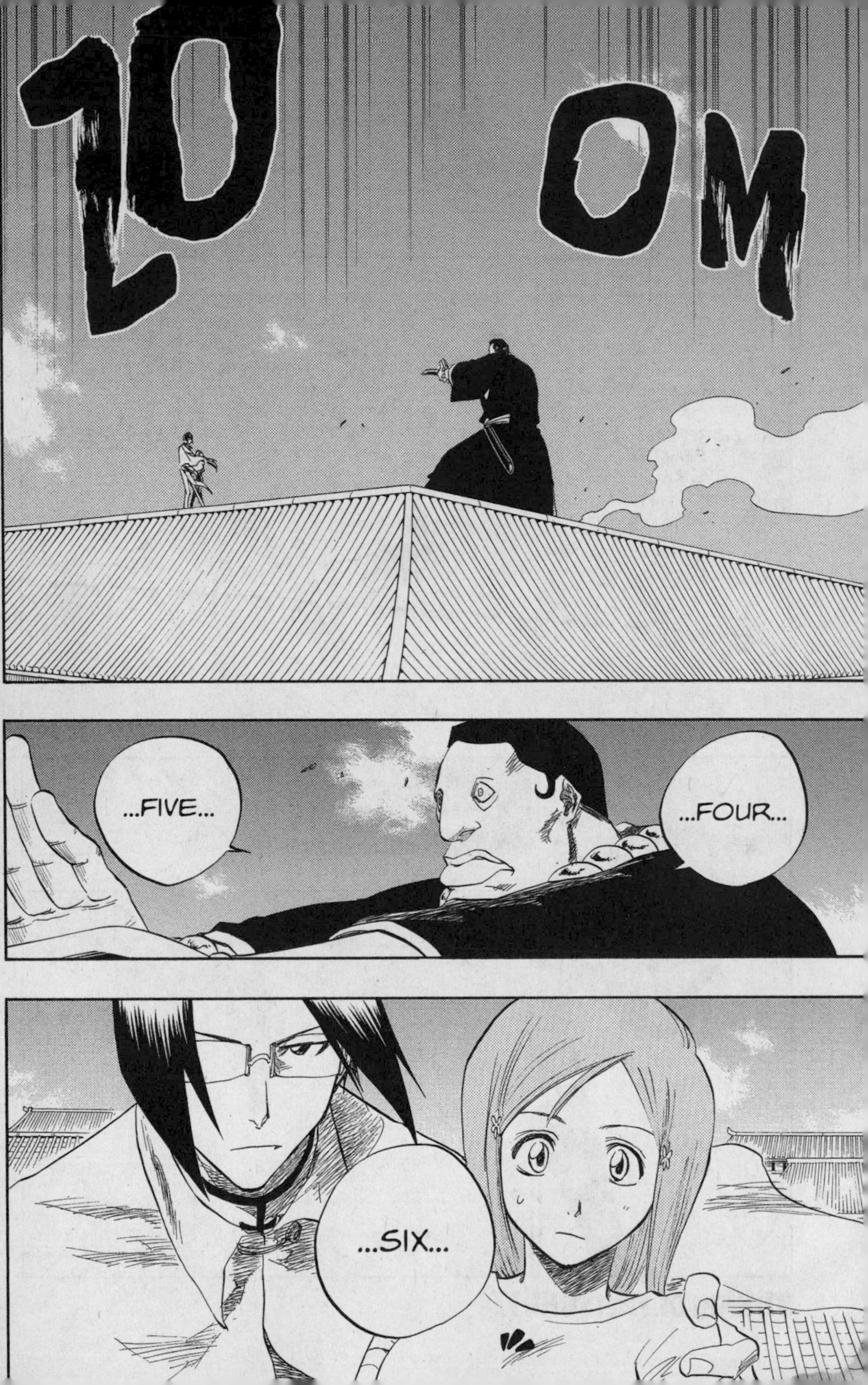
...FOUR...
...FIVE...
...SIX...

READ THIS WAY

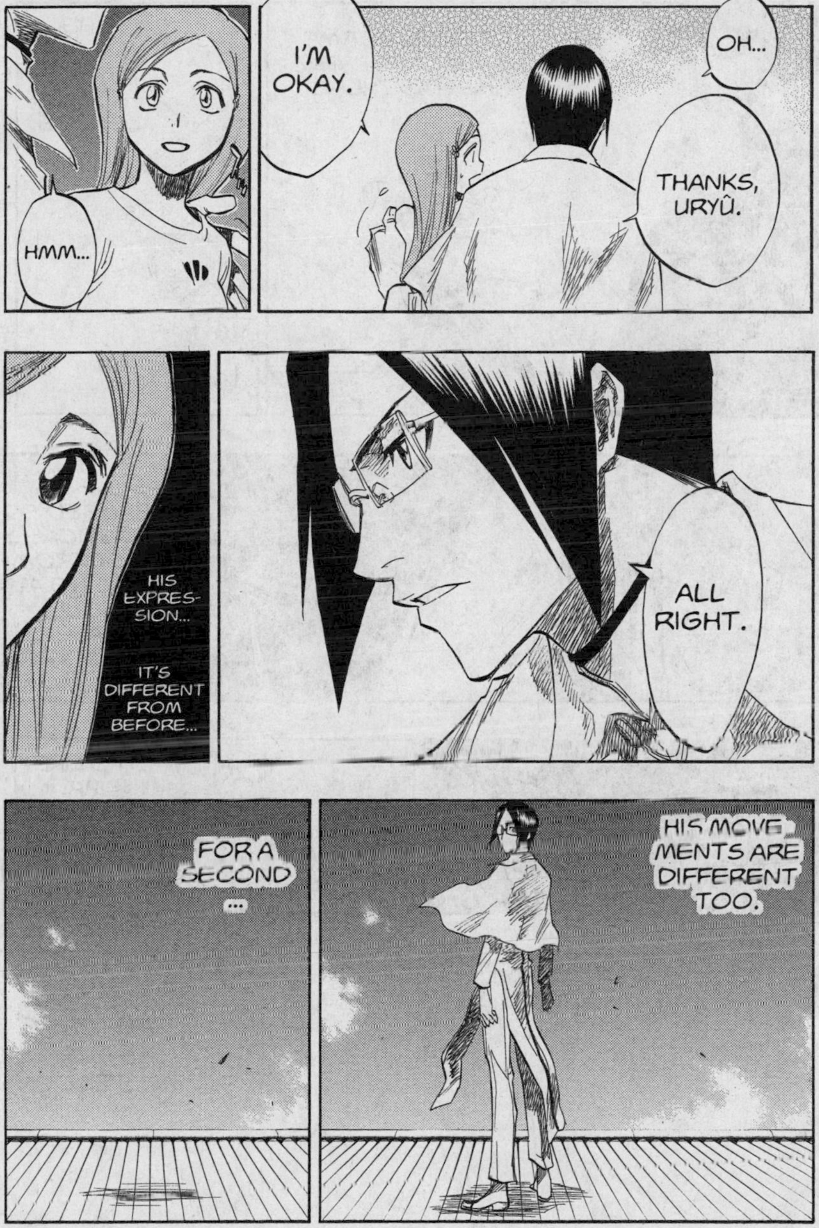
OH...
THANKS, URYÛ.
I'M OKAY.
HMM...
ALL RIGHT.
HIS EXPRES-SION...
IT'S DIFFERENT FROM BEFORE...
HIS MOVE-MENTS ARE DIFFERENT TOO.
FOR A SECOND ...

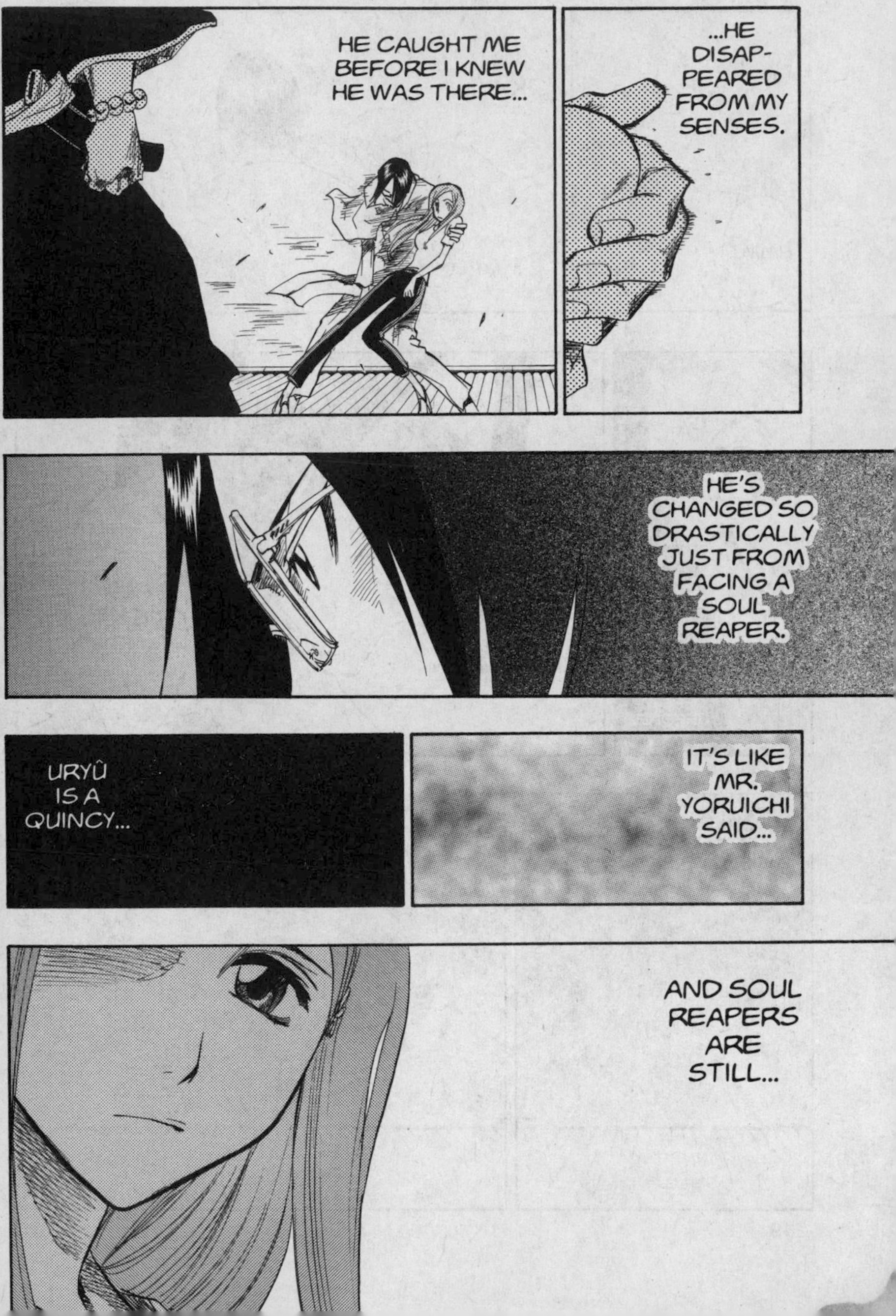
...HE DISAPPEARED FROM MY SENSES.
HE CAUGHT ME BEFORE I KNEW HE WAS THERE...
HE'S CHANGED SO DRASTICALLY JUST FROM FACING A SOUL REAPER.
IT'S LIKE MR. YORUICHI SAID...
URYÛ IS A QUINCY...
AND SOUL REAPERS ARE STILL...

HIS ENEMIES.

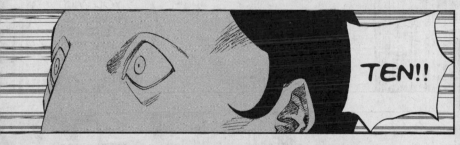

TEN!!

WOUOO

YOUR TIME FOR REGRET IS UP!!

WERE YOU ABLE TO REGRET TO YOUR SATISFAC- TION?!

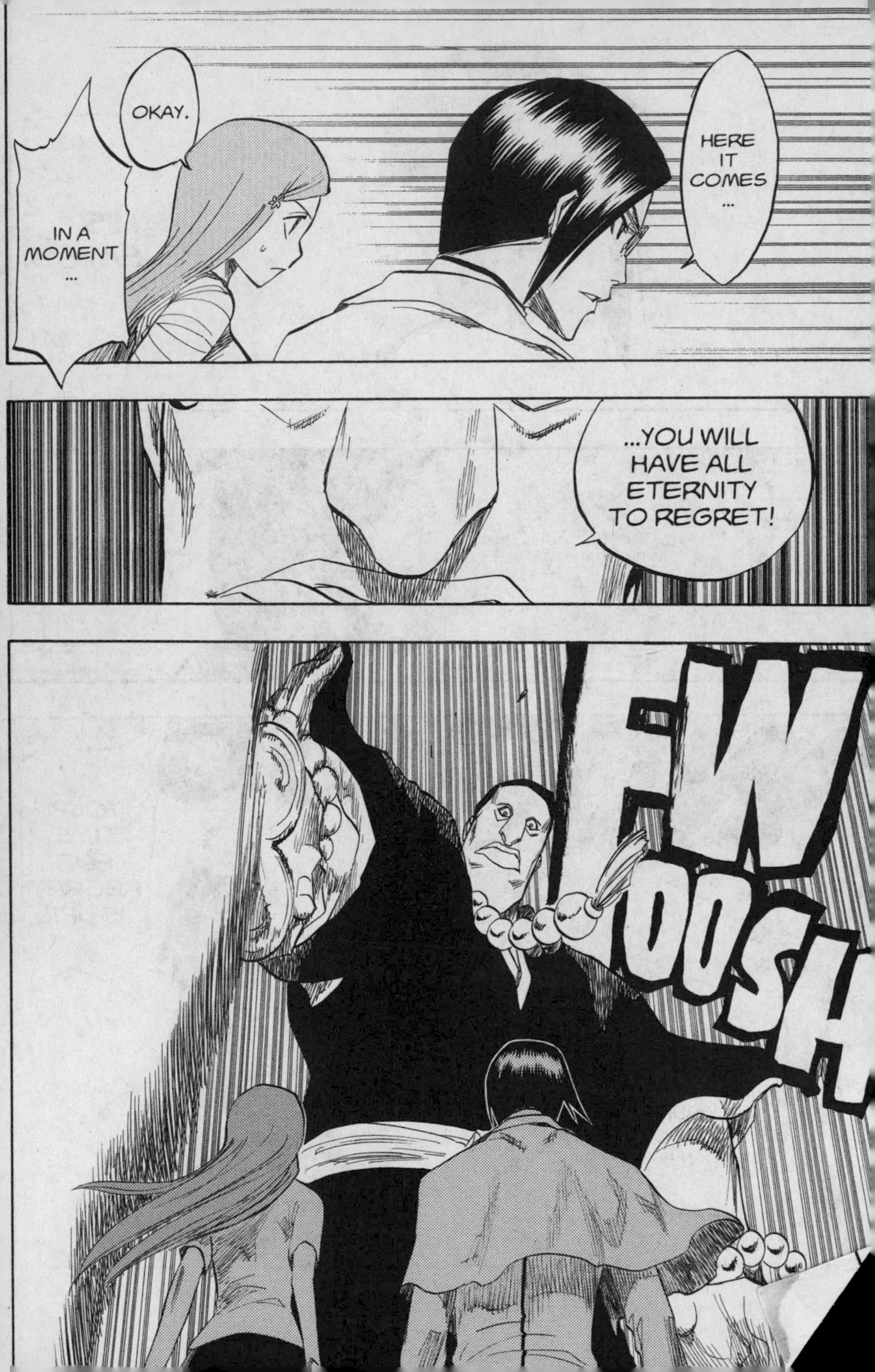
HERE IT COMES ...
OKAY.
IN A MOMENT ...
...YOU WILL HAVE ALL ETERNITY TO REGRET!
FWOOSH

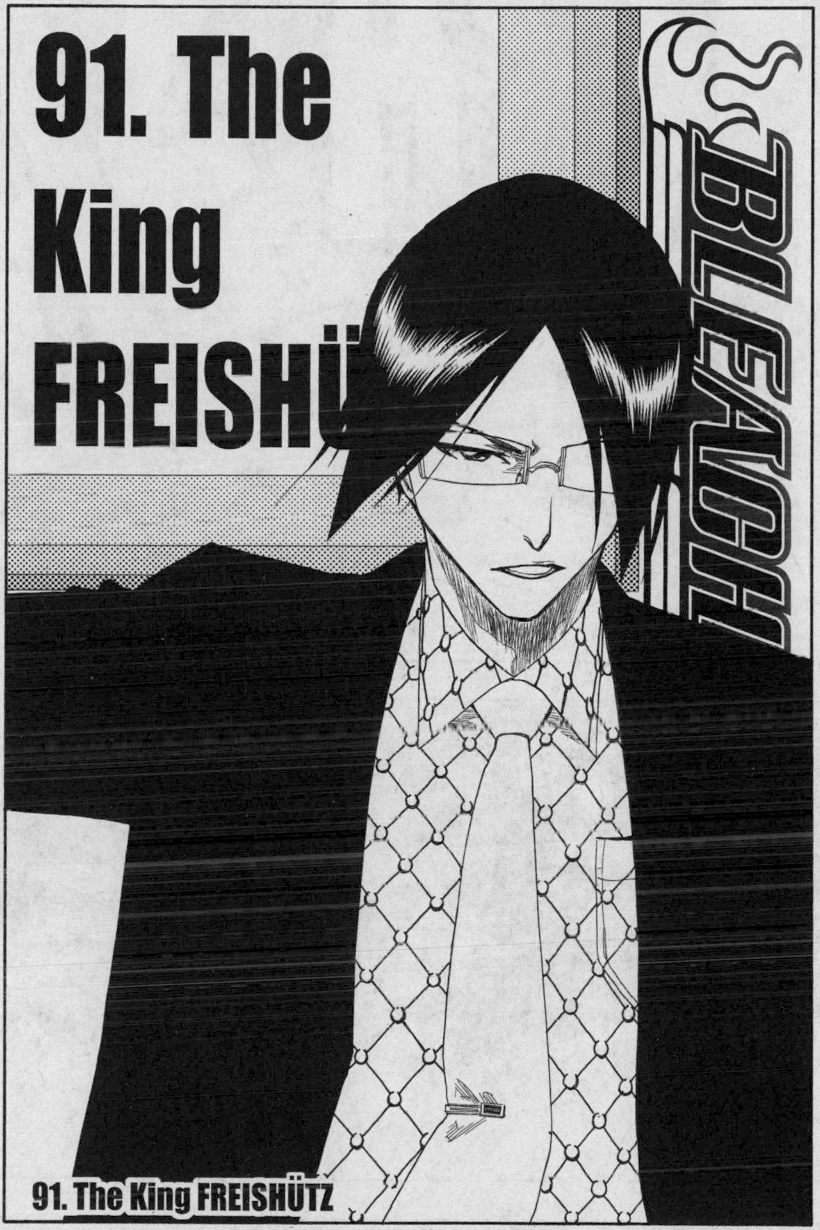
91. The
King
FREISHÜ
91. The King FREISHÜTZ

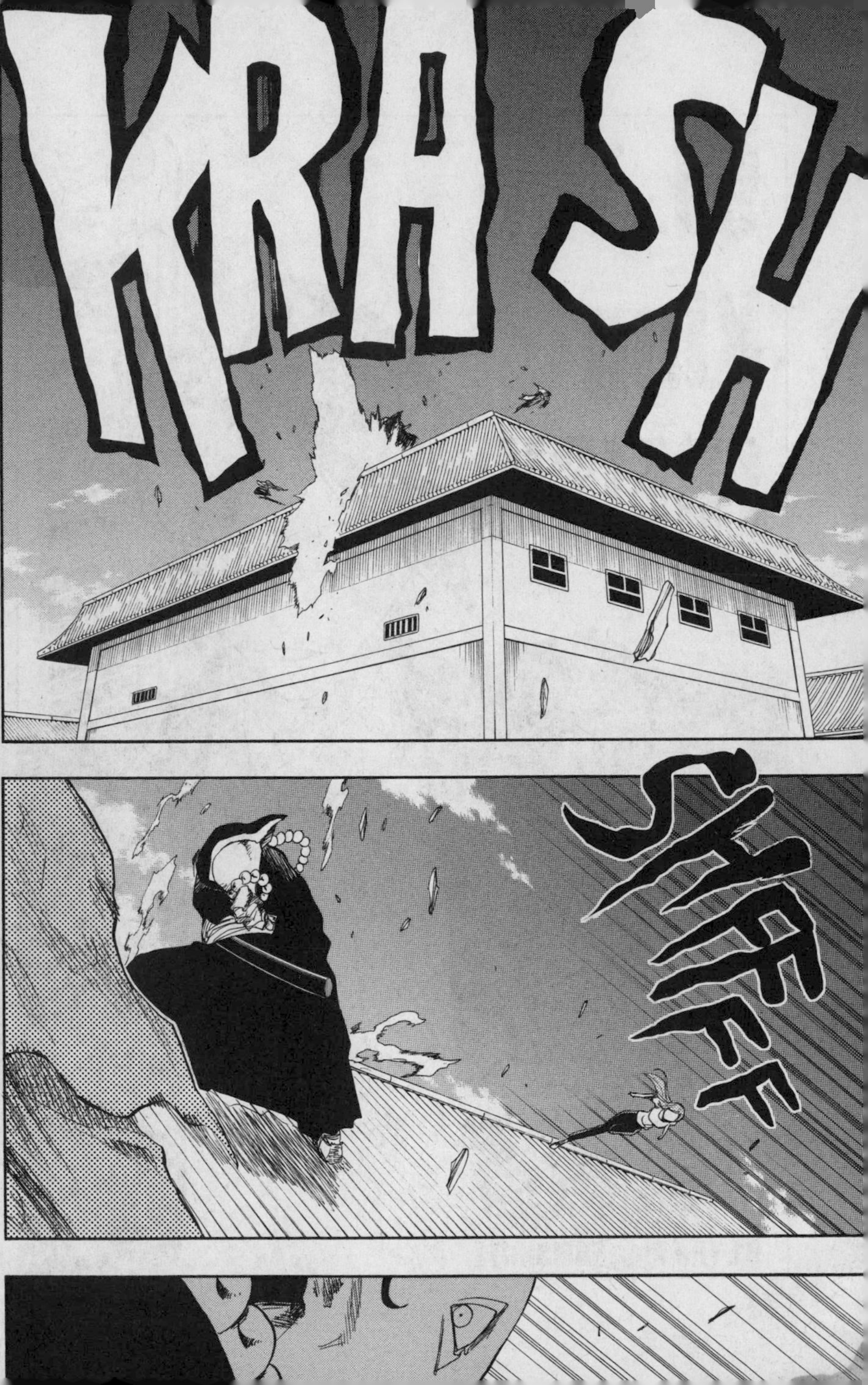
KRASH
SHFFF

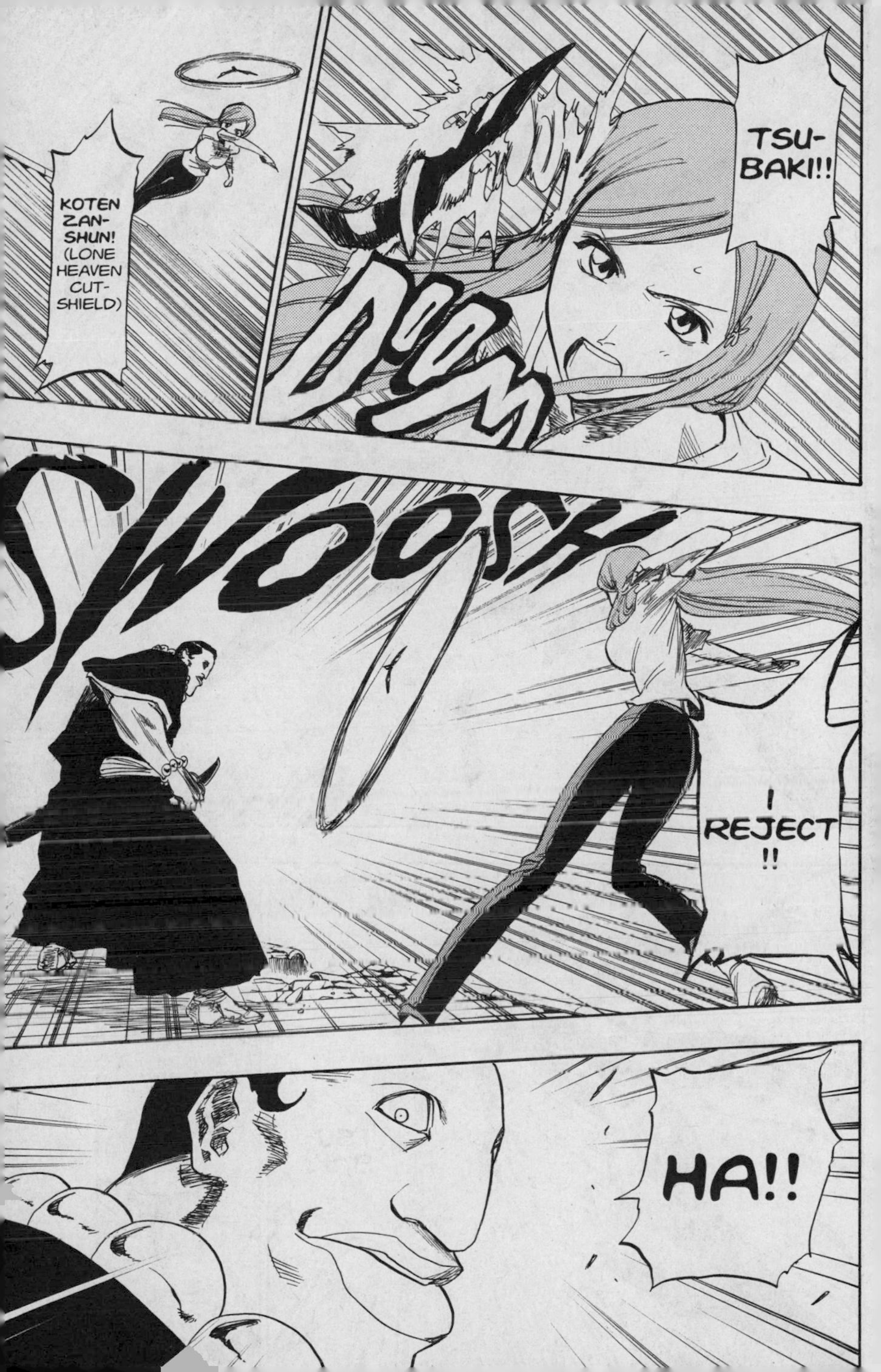
TSU-BAKI!!
DOOM
KOTEN ZAN-SHUN! (LONE HEAVEN CUT-SHIELD)
SWOOSH
I REJECT !!
HA!!

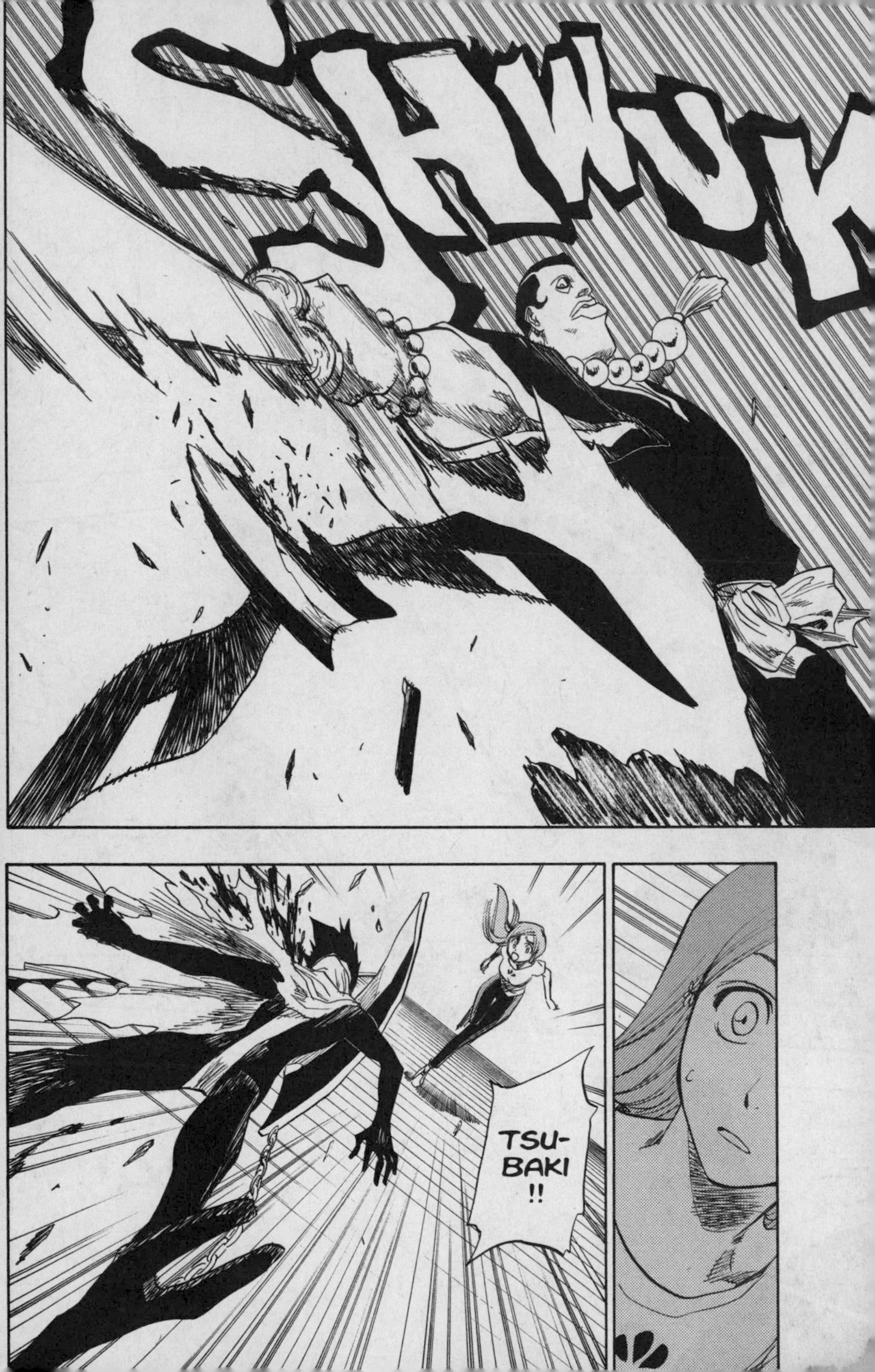
SHWOK
TSU-
BAKI
!!

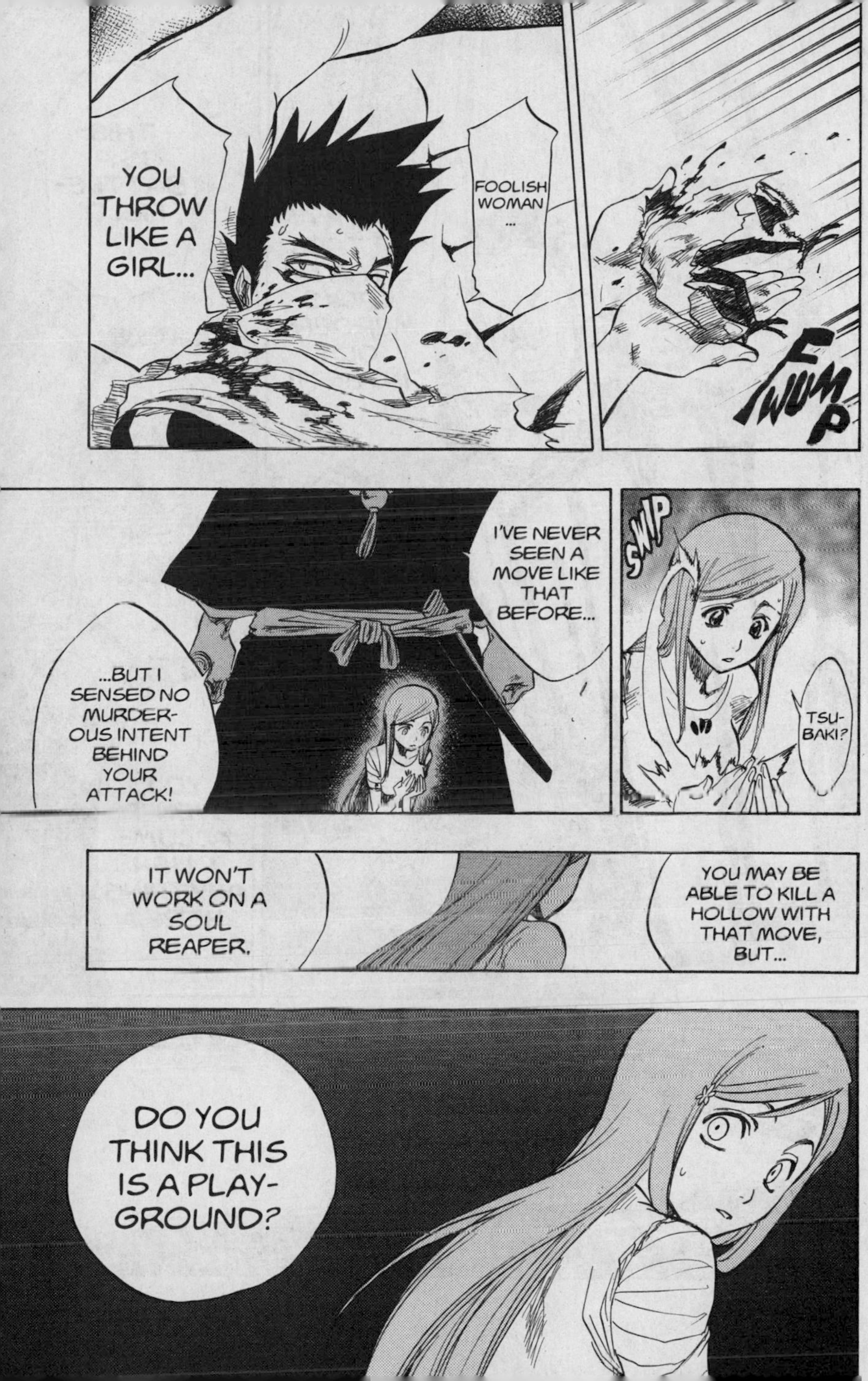
FWUMP
FOOLISH WOMAN...
YOU THROW LIKE A GIRL...
SWIP
TSUBAKI?
I'VE NEVER SEEN A MOVE LIKE THAT BEFORE...
...BUT I SENSED NO MURDEROUS INTENT BEHIND YOUR ATTACK!
YOU MAY BE ABLE TO KILL A HOLLOW WITH THAT MOVE, BUT...
IT WON'T WORK ON A SOUL REAPER.
DO YOU THINK THIS IS A PLAYGROUND?

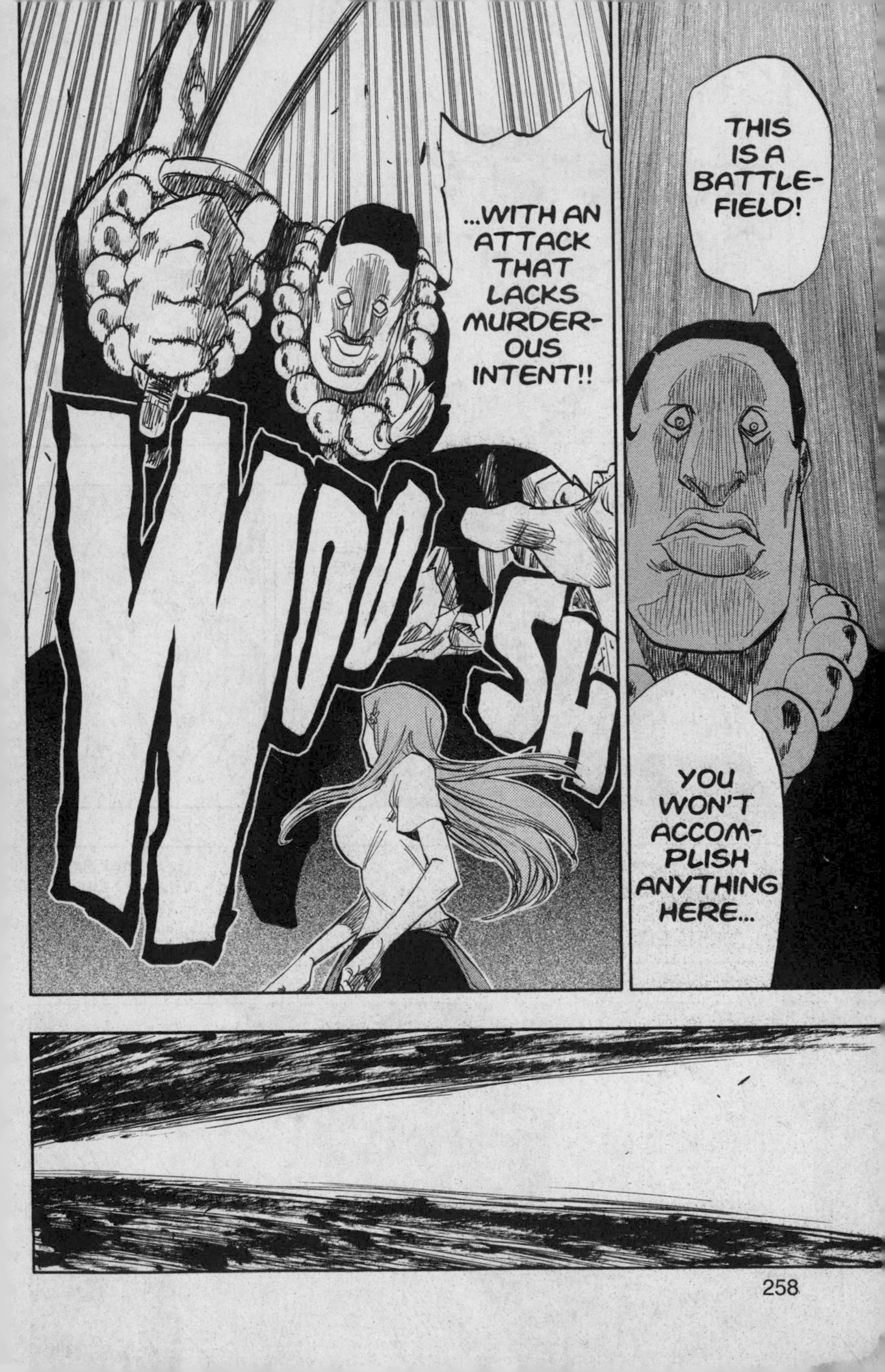
THIS IS A BATTLE-FIELD!
YOU WON'T ACCOMPLISH ANYTHING HERE...
...WITH AN ATTACK THAT LACKS MURDER-OUS INTENT!!
WOOSH

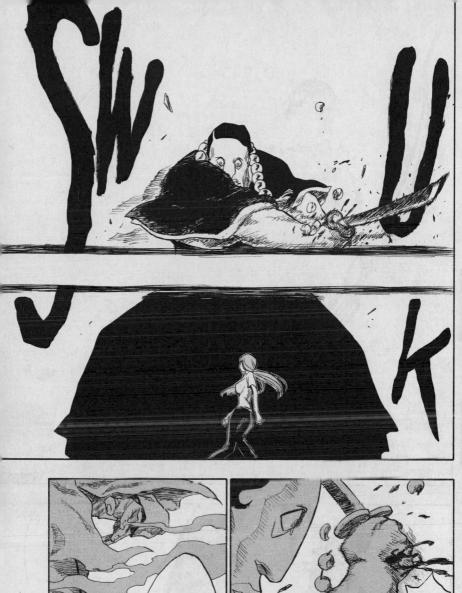

YOU WANT MURDER-OUS INTENT?

WHAT ...

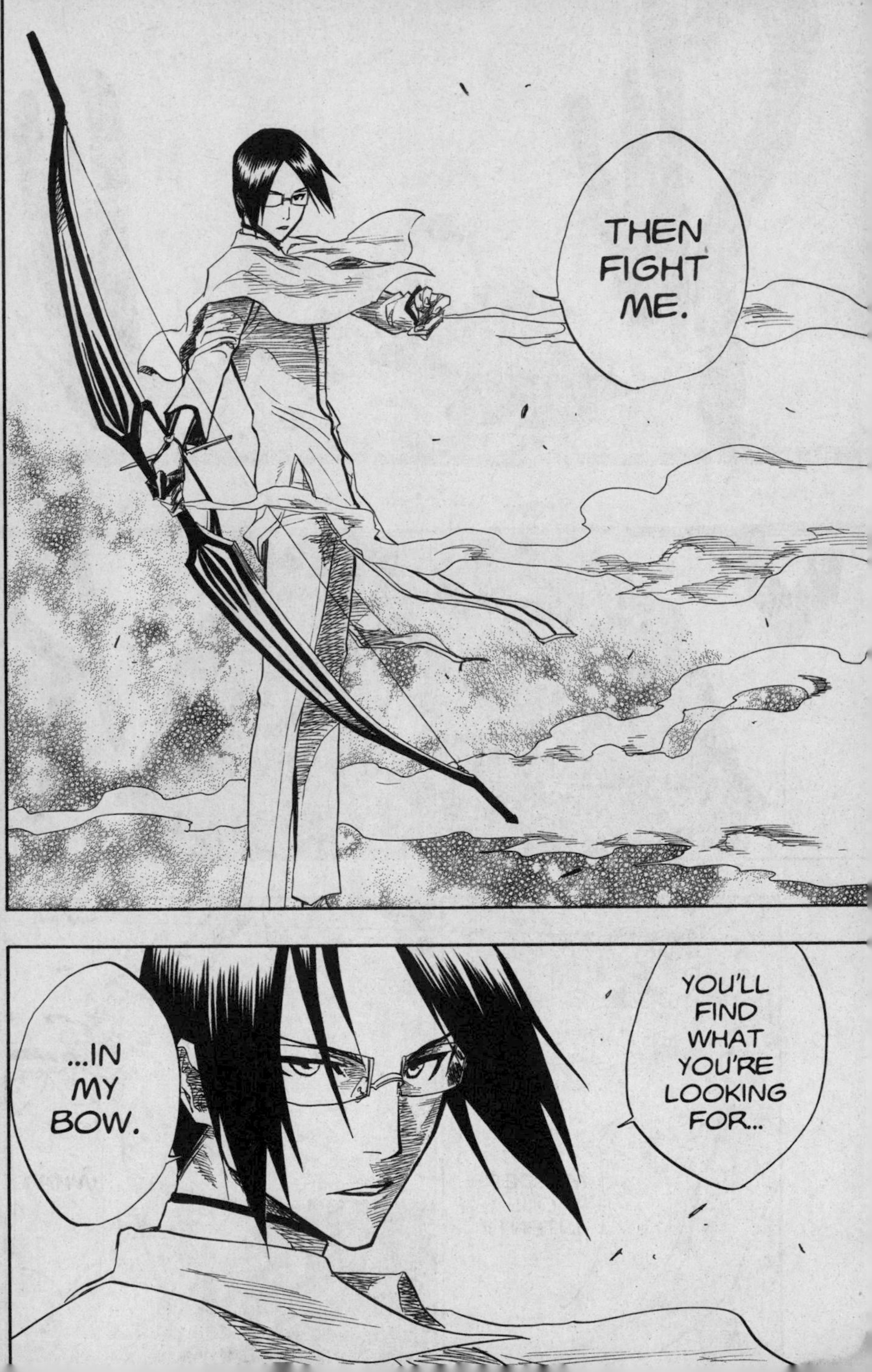
THEN FIGHT ME.
YOU'LL FIND WHAT YOU'RE LOOKING FOR...
...IN MY BOW.

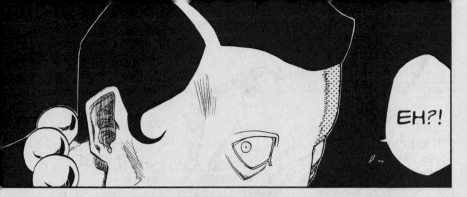

EH?!

I AM.

HOW UNEXPECTED!

YOU WOULDN'T HAPPEN TO BE A QUINCY, WOULD YOU?

PLIP PLIP PLIP

URYÛ'S BOW...

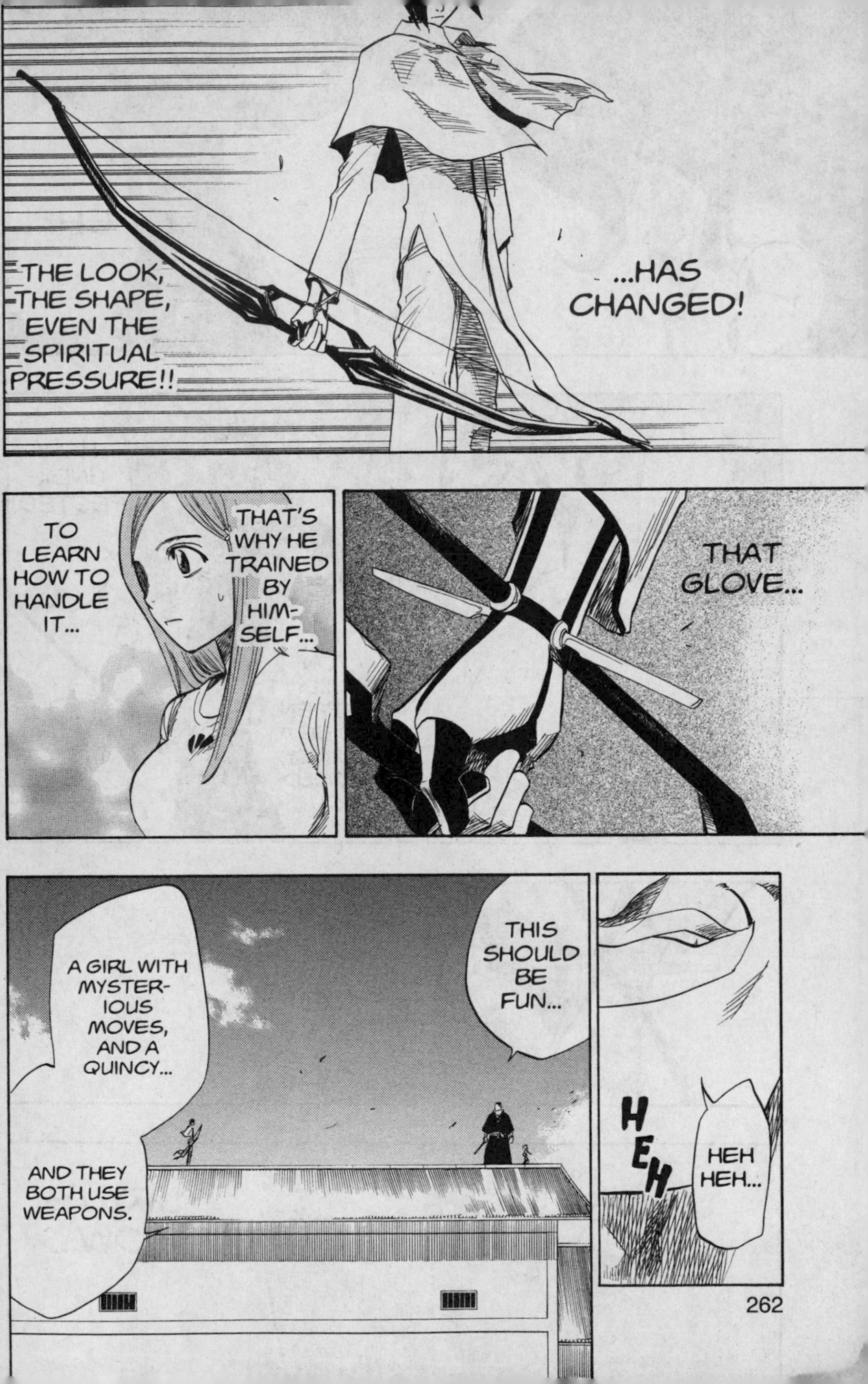
THE LOOK, THE SHAPE, EVEN THE SPIRITUAL PRESSURE!!
...HAS CHANGED!
THAT GLOVE...
THAT'S WHY HE TRAINED BY HIM-SELF...
TO LEARN HOW TO HANDLE IT...
HEH
HEH HEH...
THIS SHOULD BE FUN...
A GIRL WITH MYSTER-IOUS MOVES, AND A QUINCY...
AND THEY BOTH USE WEAPONS.

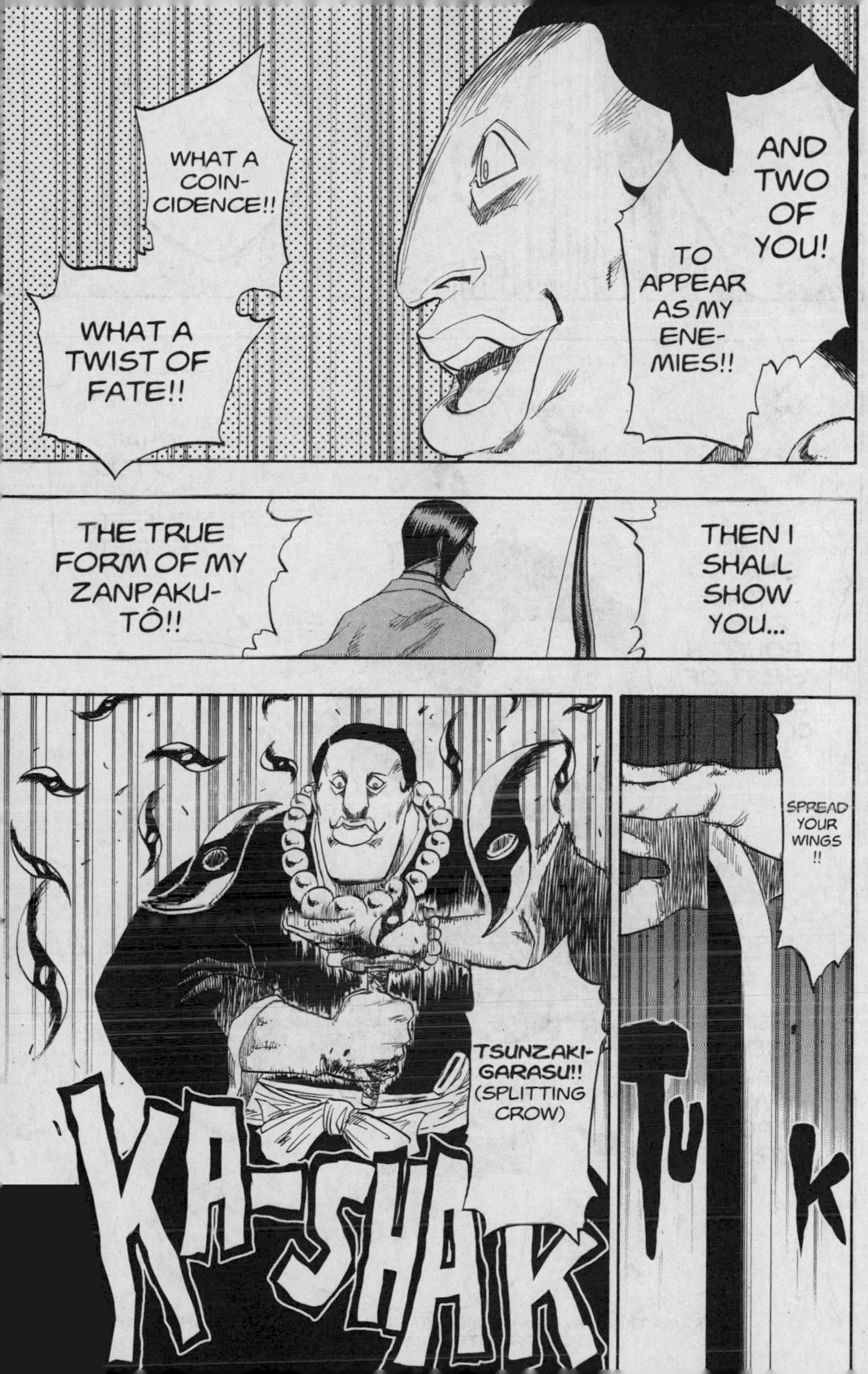
AND TWO OF YOU!
TO APPEAR AS MY ENE-MIES!!
WHAT A COIN-CIDENCE!!
WHAT A TWIST OF FATE!!
THEN I SHALL SHOW YOU...
THE TRUE FORM OF MY ZANPAKU-TÔ!!
SPREAD YOUR WINGS !!
TUK
TSUNZAKI-GARASU!! (SPLITTING CROW)
KA-SHAK

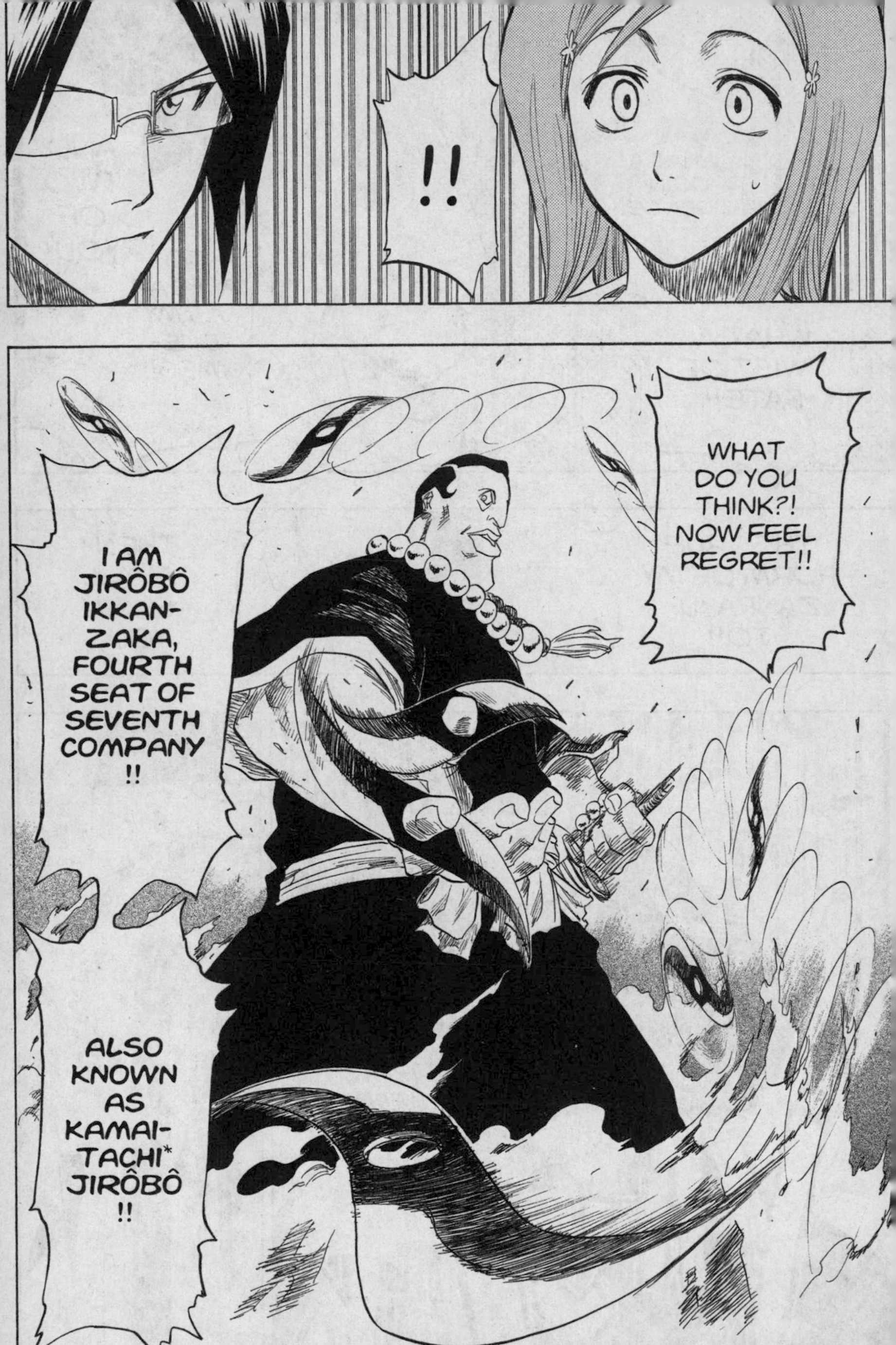
!!
WHAT DO YOU THINK?! NOW FEEL REGRET!!
I AM JIRÔBÔ IKKAN-ZAKA, FOURTH SEAT OF SEVENTH COMPANY!!
ALSO KNOWN AS KAMAI-TACHI* JIRÔBÔ!!

*KAMAITACHI IS AN EXTREMELY FAST AND DEADLY CREATURE OF LEGEND. THE WORD LITERALLY MEANS "SICKLE WEASEL."

READ THIS WAY

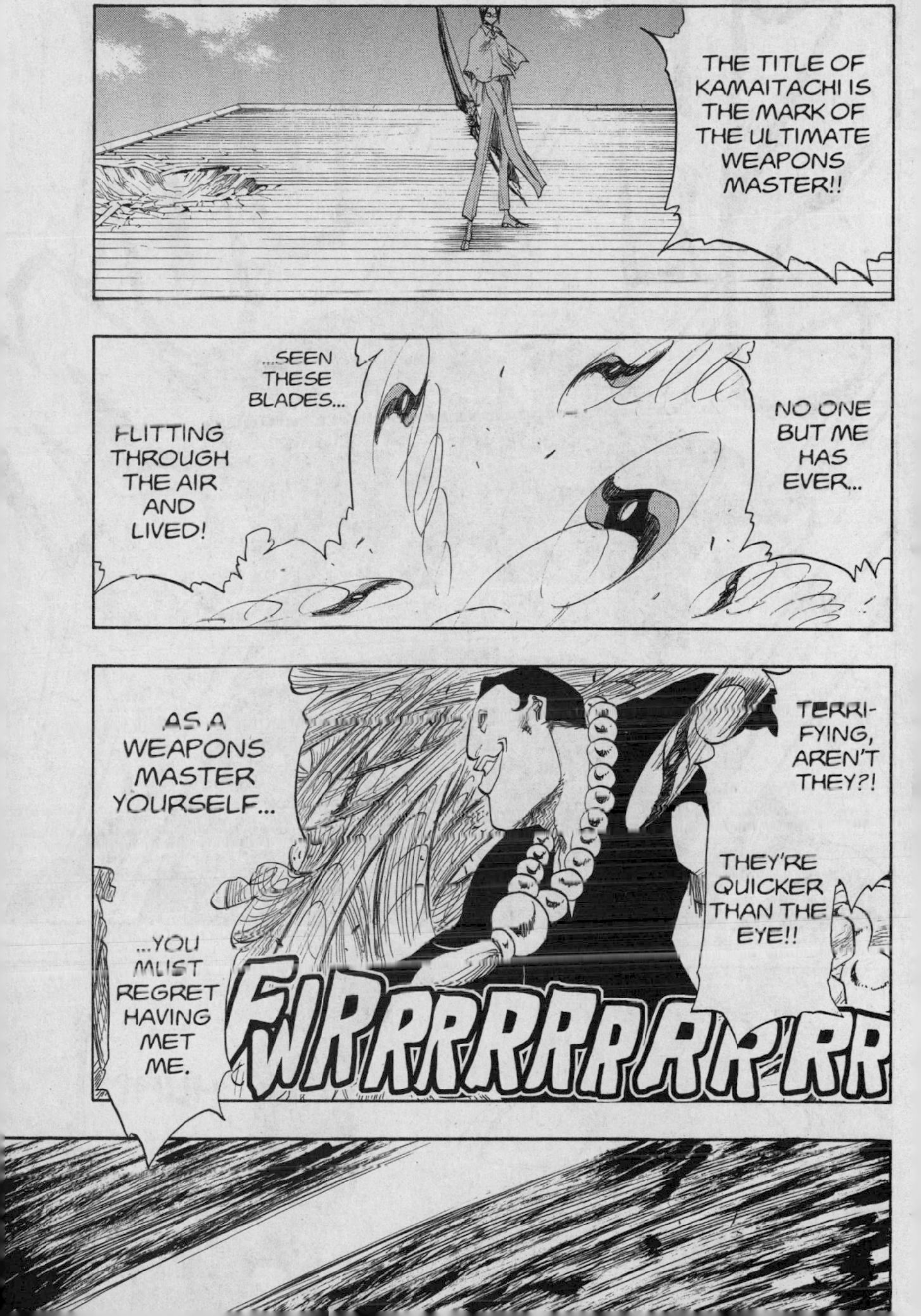

THE TITLE OF KAMAITACHI IS THE MARK OF THE ULTIMATE WEAPONS MASTER!!
NO ONE BUT ME HAS EVER...
...SEEN THESE BLADES...
FLITTING THROUGH THE AIR AND LIVED!
TERRI-FYING, AREN'T THEY?!
THEY'RE QUICKER THAN THE EYE!!
AS A WEAPONS MASTER YOURSELF...
...YOU MUST REGRET HAVING MET ME.
FWRRRRRRRRR

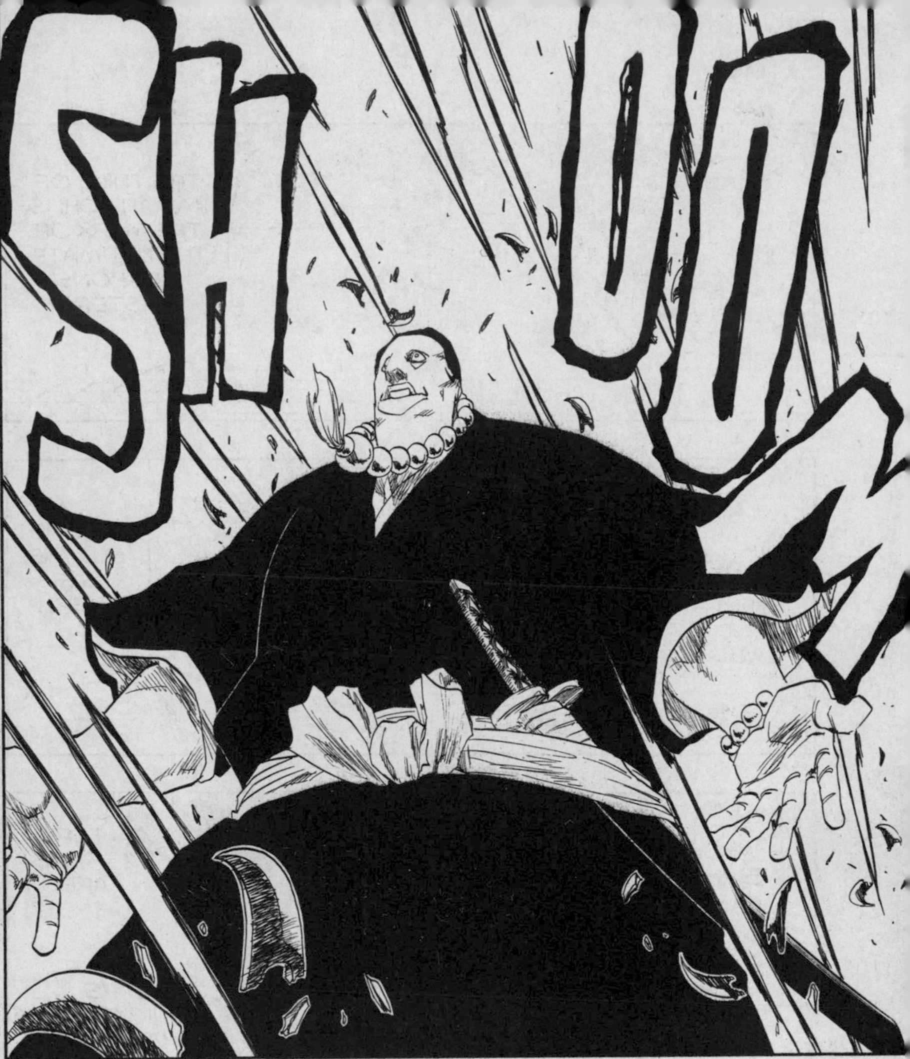
SHOOM
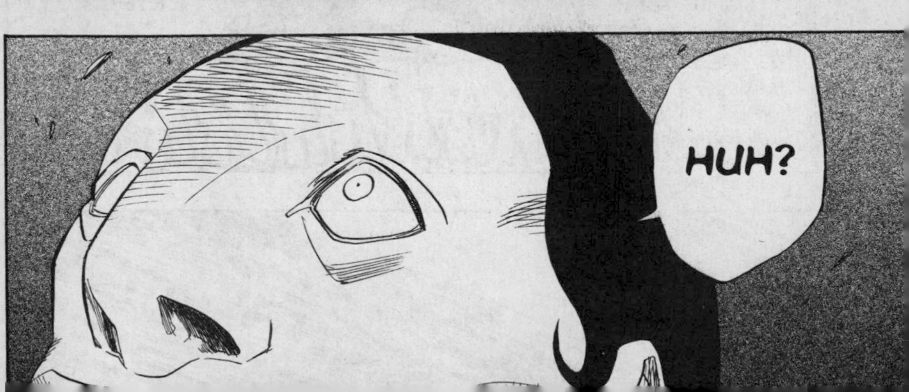
HUH?

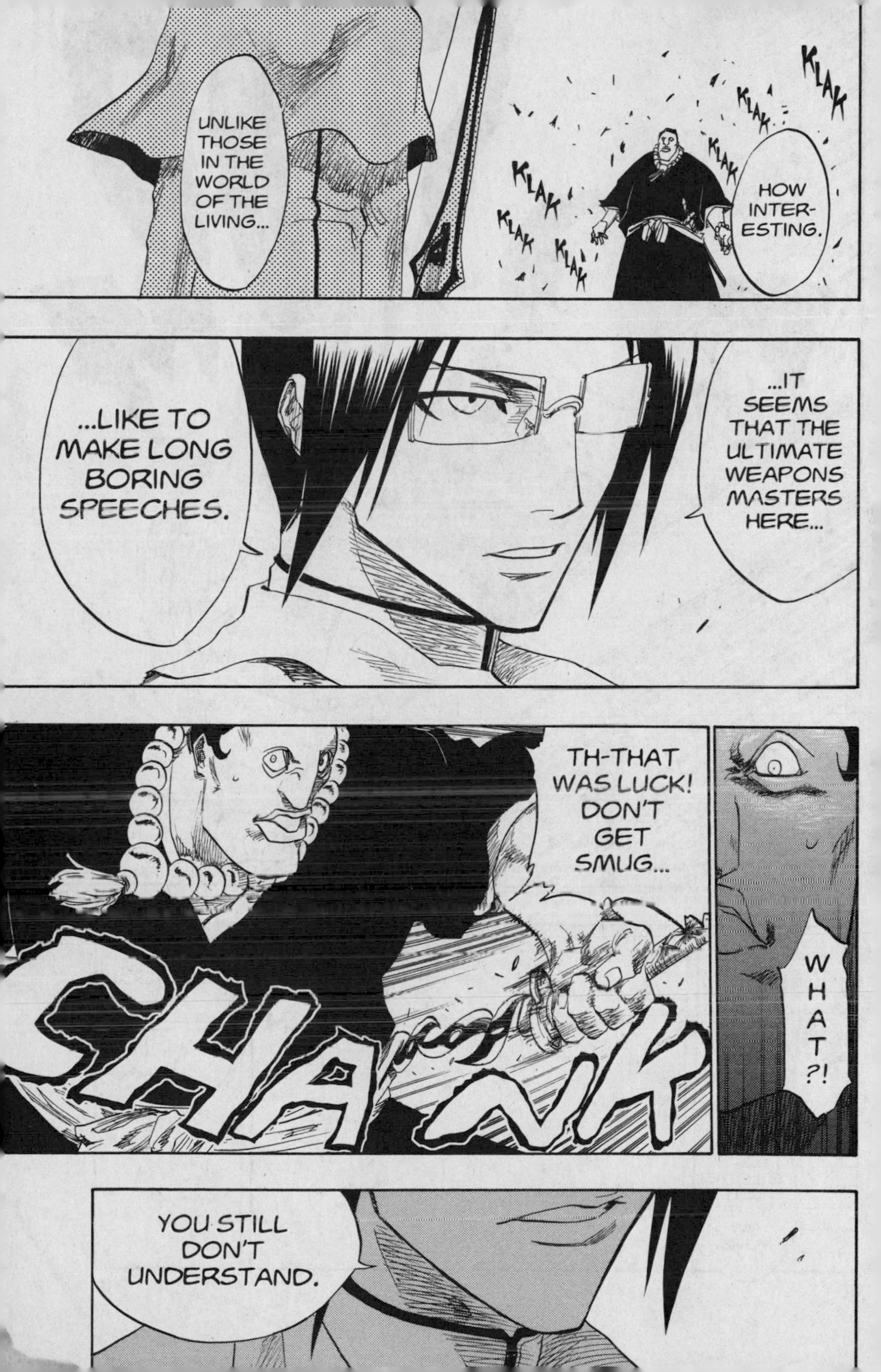
KLAK
KLAK
KLAK
KLAK
KLAK
KLAK
HOW INTER-ESTING.
UNLIKE THOSE IN THE WORLD OF THE LIVING...
...IT SEEMS THAT THE ULTIMATE WEAPONS MASTERS HERE...
...LIKE TO MAKE LONG BORING SPEECHES.
WHAT?!
TH-THAT WAS LUCK! DON'T GET SMUG...
CHANK
YOU STILL DON'T UNDERSTAND.

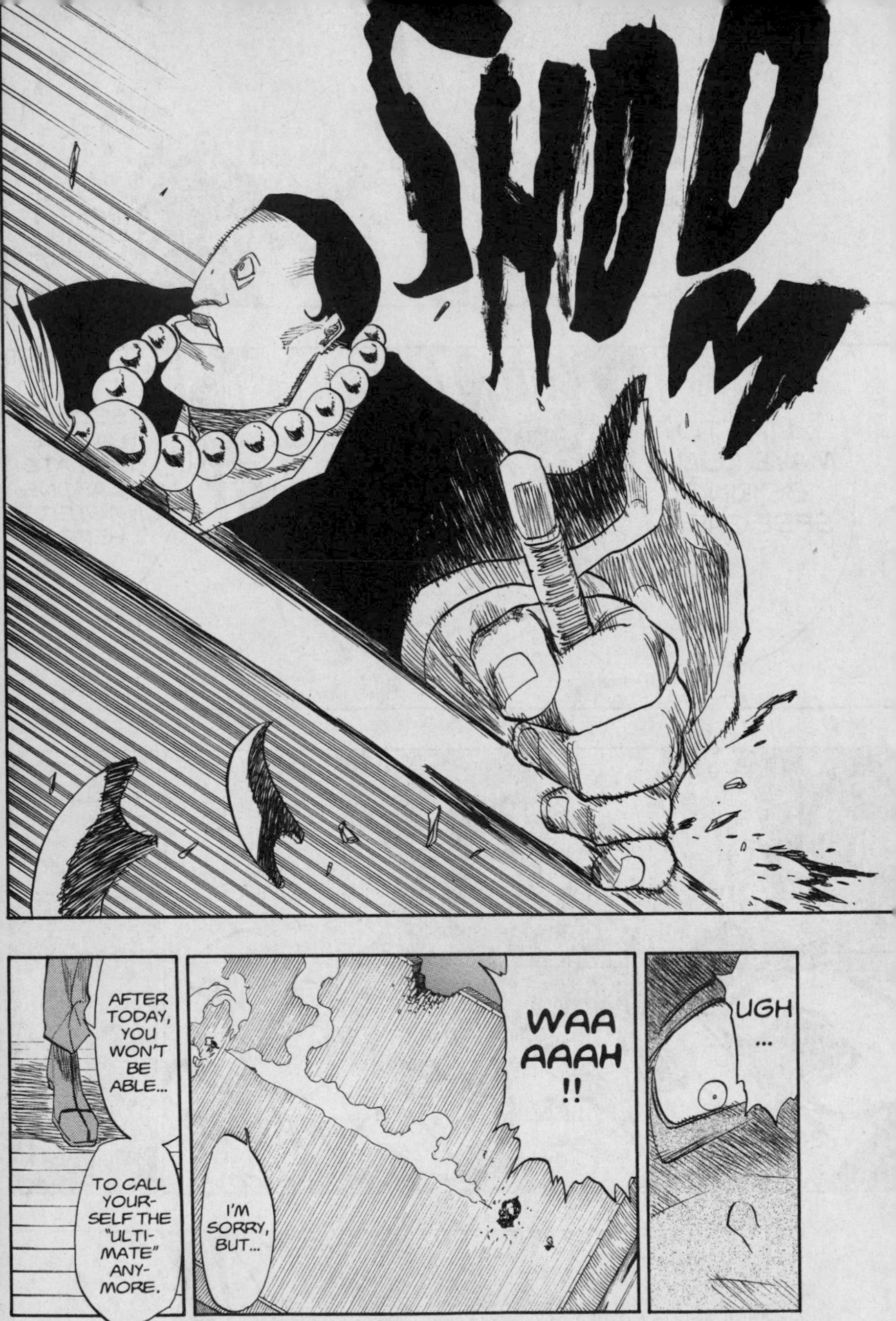
SHOOM
UGH ...
WAA AAAH !!
I'M SORRY, BUT...
AFTER TODAY, YOU WON'T BE ABLE...
TO CALL YOUR-SELF THE "ULTI-MATE" ANY-MORE.

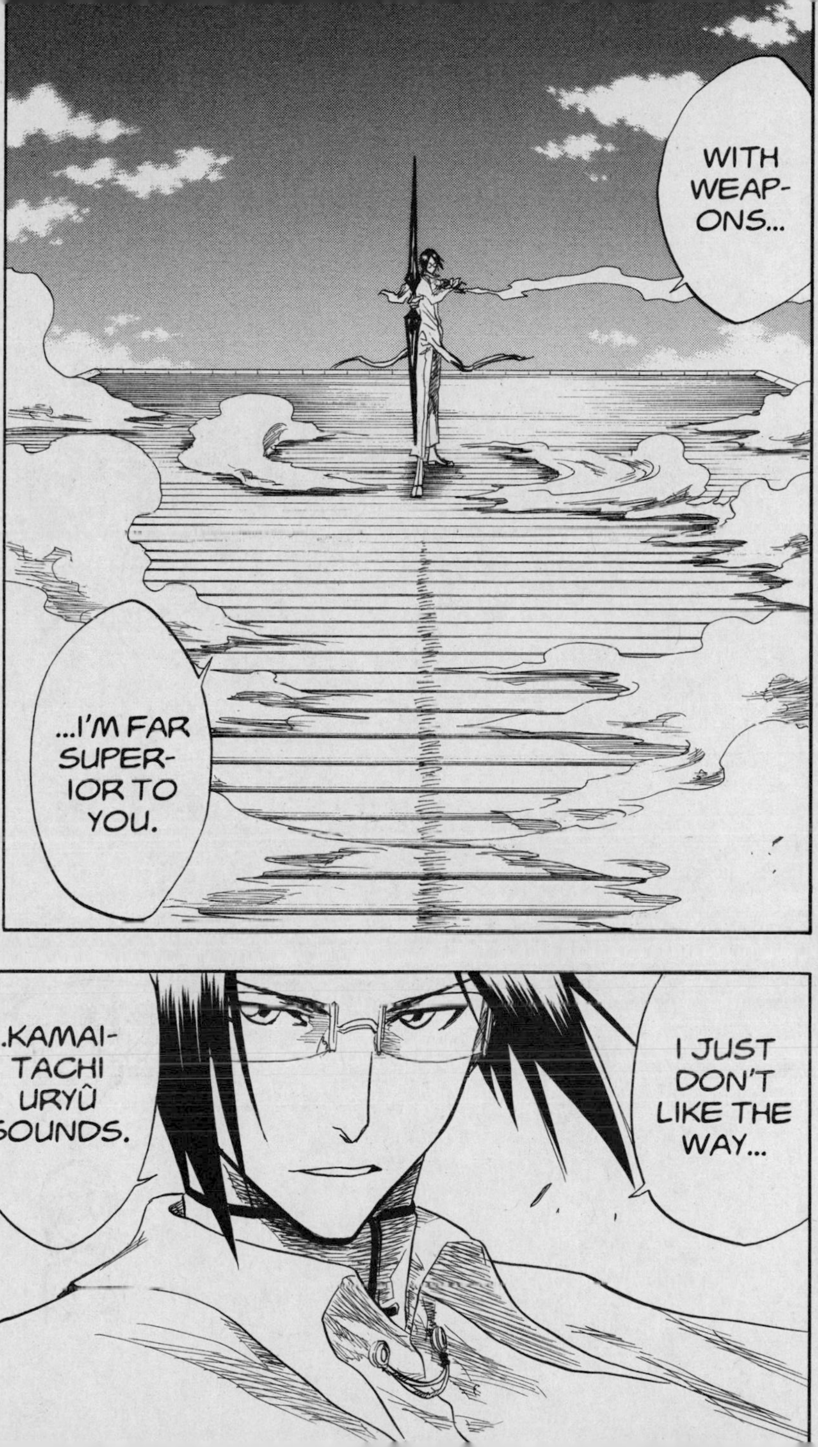
WITH WEAPONS...
...I'M FAR SUPERIOR TO YOU.
I JUST DON'T LIKE THE WAY...
...KAMAITACHI URYÛ SOUNDS.

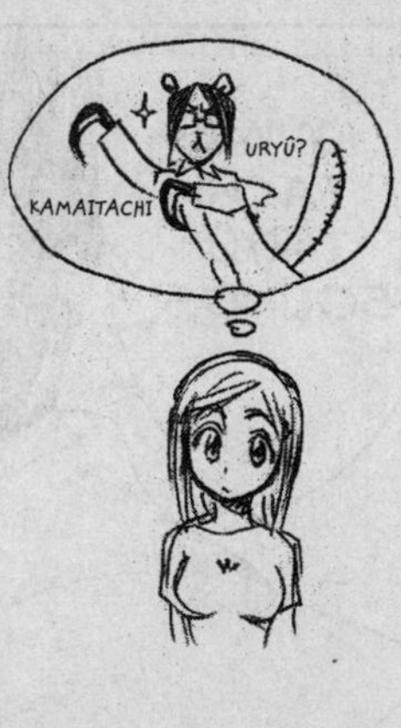
URYŪ?
KAMAITACHI

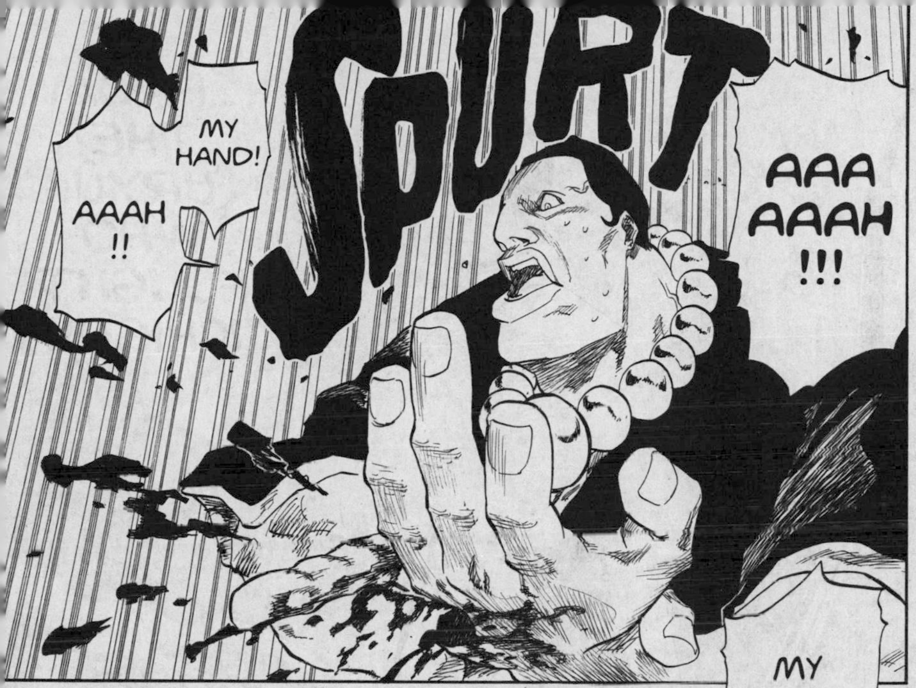
AAA AAAH !!!
SPURT
MY HAND!
AAAH !!
MY HAND !!

92. Masterly! And Farewell! (Reprise)

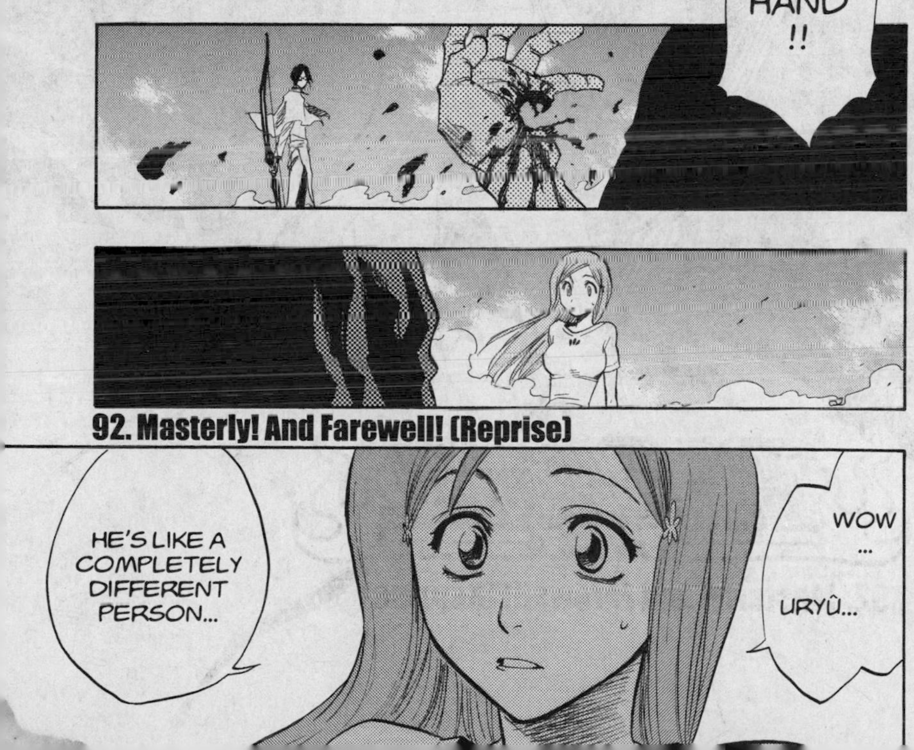
WOW ... URYÛ...
HE'S LIKE A COMPLETELY DIFFERENT PERSON...

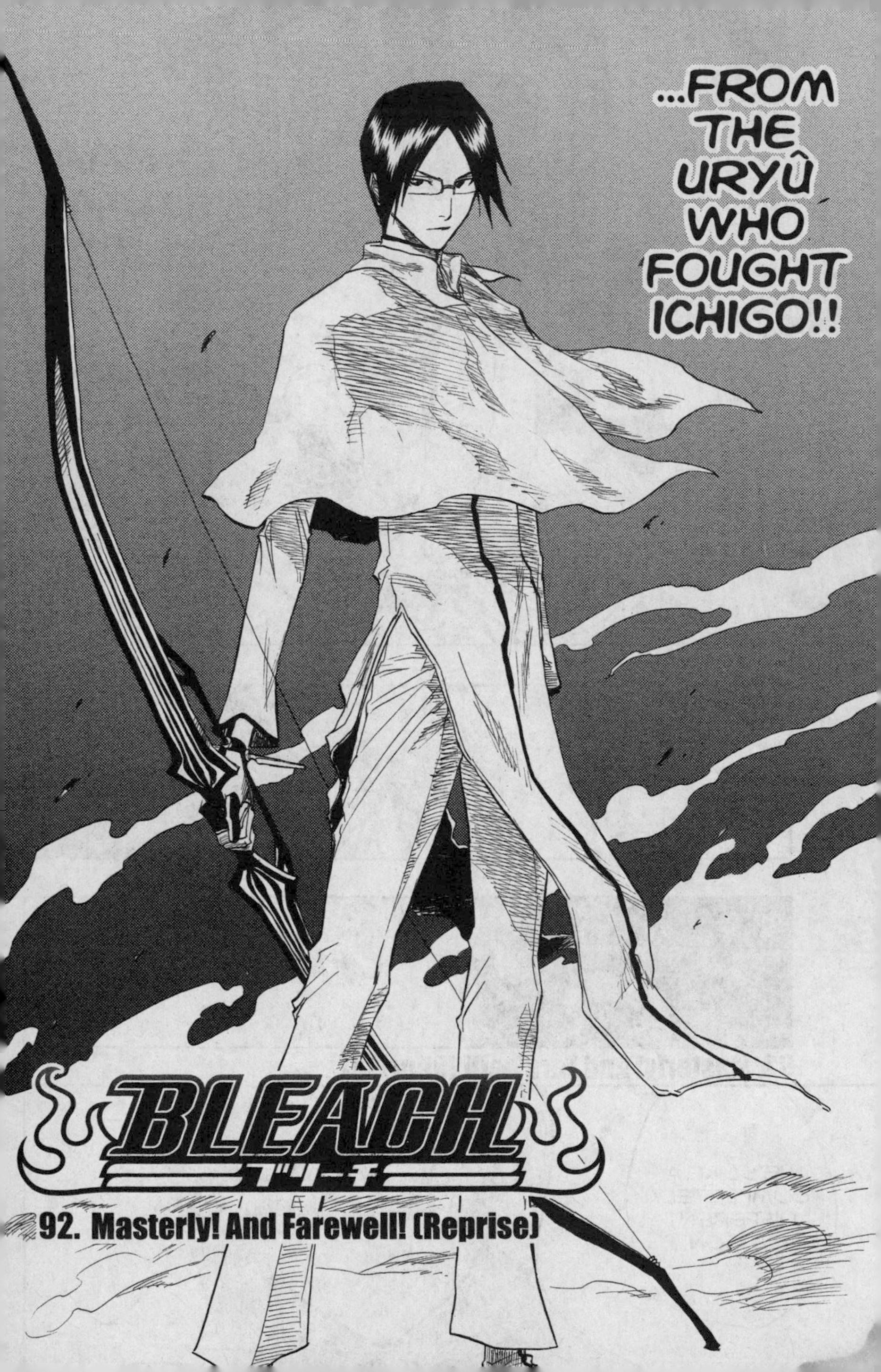
...FROM THE URYÛ WHO FOUGHT ICHIGO!!
BLEACH
ブリーチ
92. Masterly! And Farewell! (Reprise)

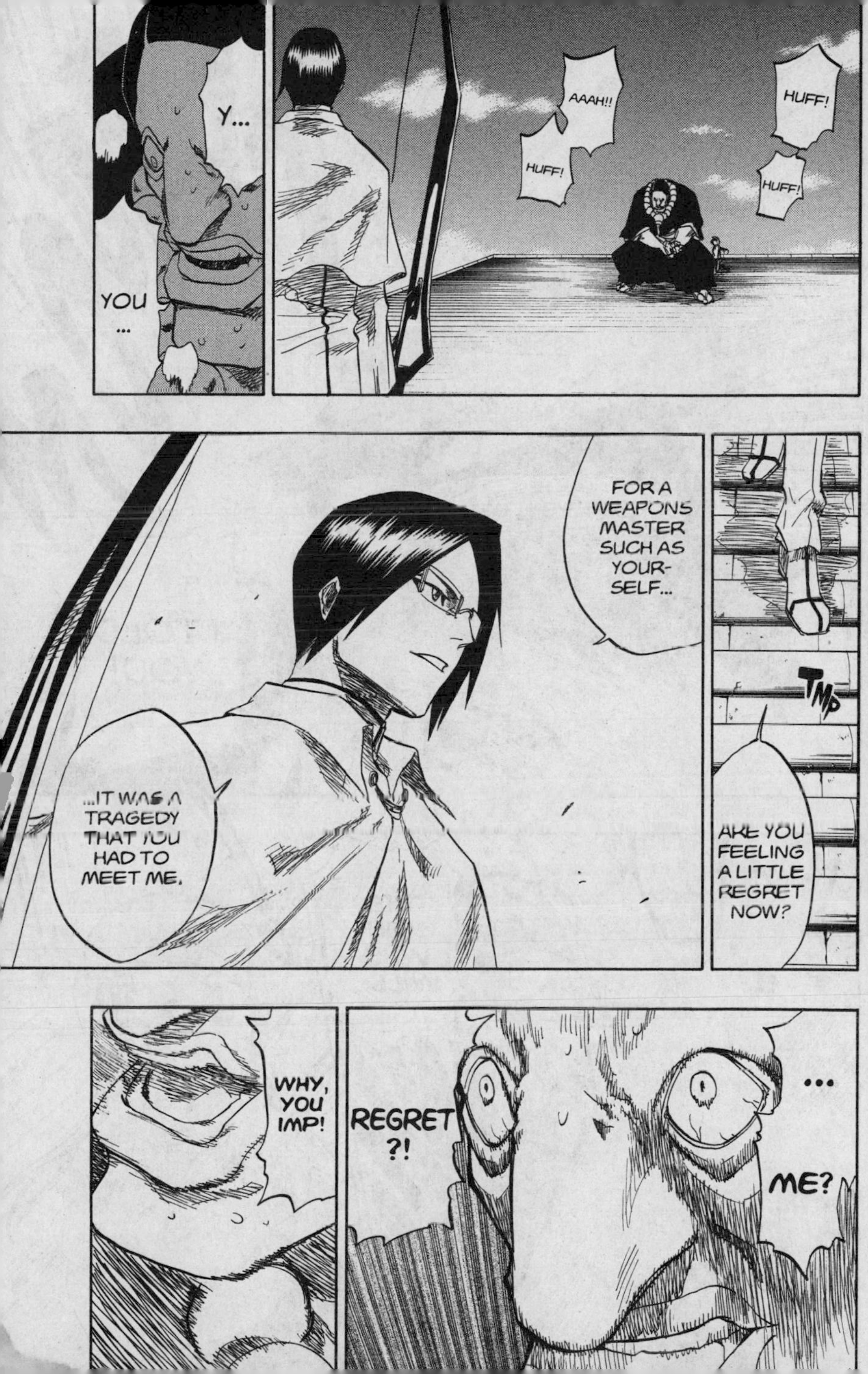
HUFF!
HUFF!
AAAH!!
HUFF!
Y...
YOU ...
TMP
ARE YOU FEELING A LITTLE REGRET NOW?
FOR A WEAPONS MASTER SUCH AS YOURSELF...
...IT WAS A TRAGEDY THAT YOU HAD TO MEET ME.
... ME?
REGRET ?!
WHY, YOU IMP!

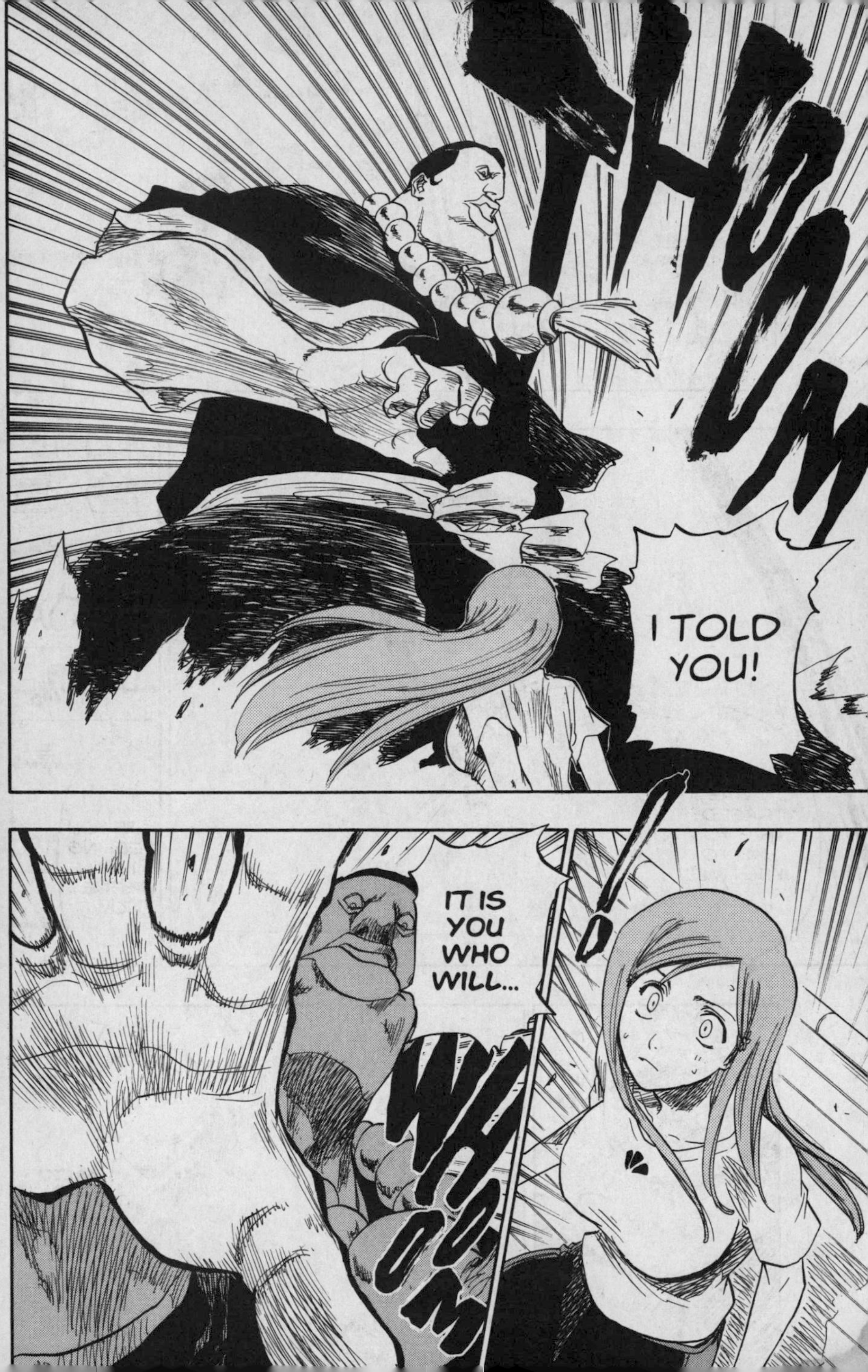
I TOLD YOU!
IT IS YOU WHO WILL...

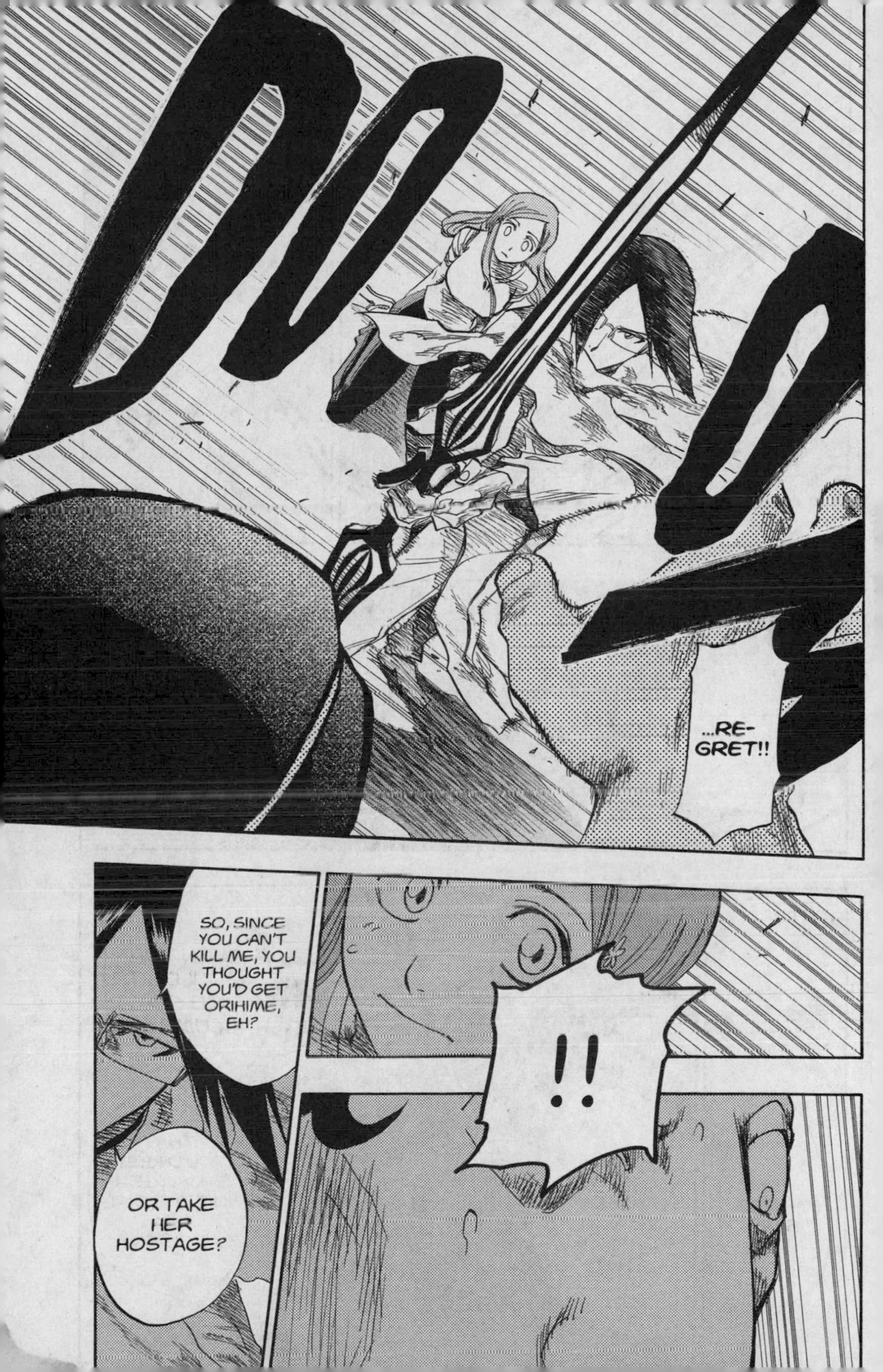
...RE-
GRET!!
!!
SO, SINCE YOU CAN'T KILL ME, YOU THOUGHT YOU'D GET ORIHIME, EH?
OR TAKE HER HOSTAGE?

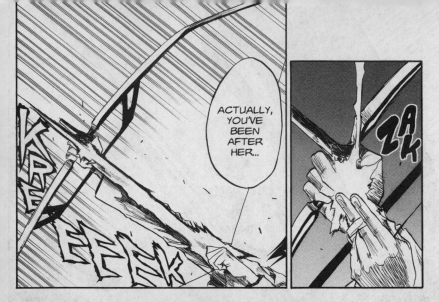

ACTUALLY, YOU'VE BEEN AFTER HER...

...FROM THE VERY BEGINNING.

EVEN YOU COULDN'T BE SO CLUMSY...

THAT YOU'D KEEP ENDANGERING THE GIRL BY ACCIDENT.

NO ONE WITH A SHRED OF HONOR FIGHTS LIKE THAT.

IMPRES-SIVE.

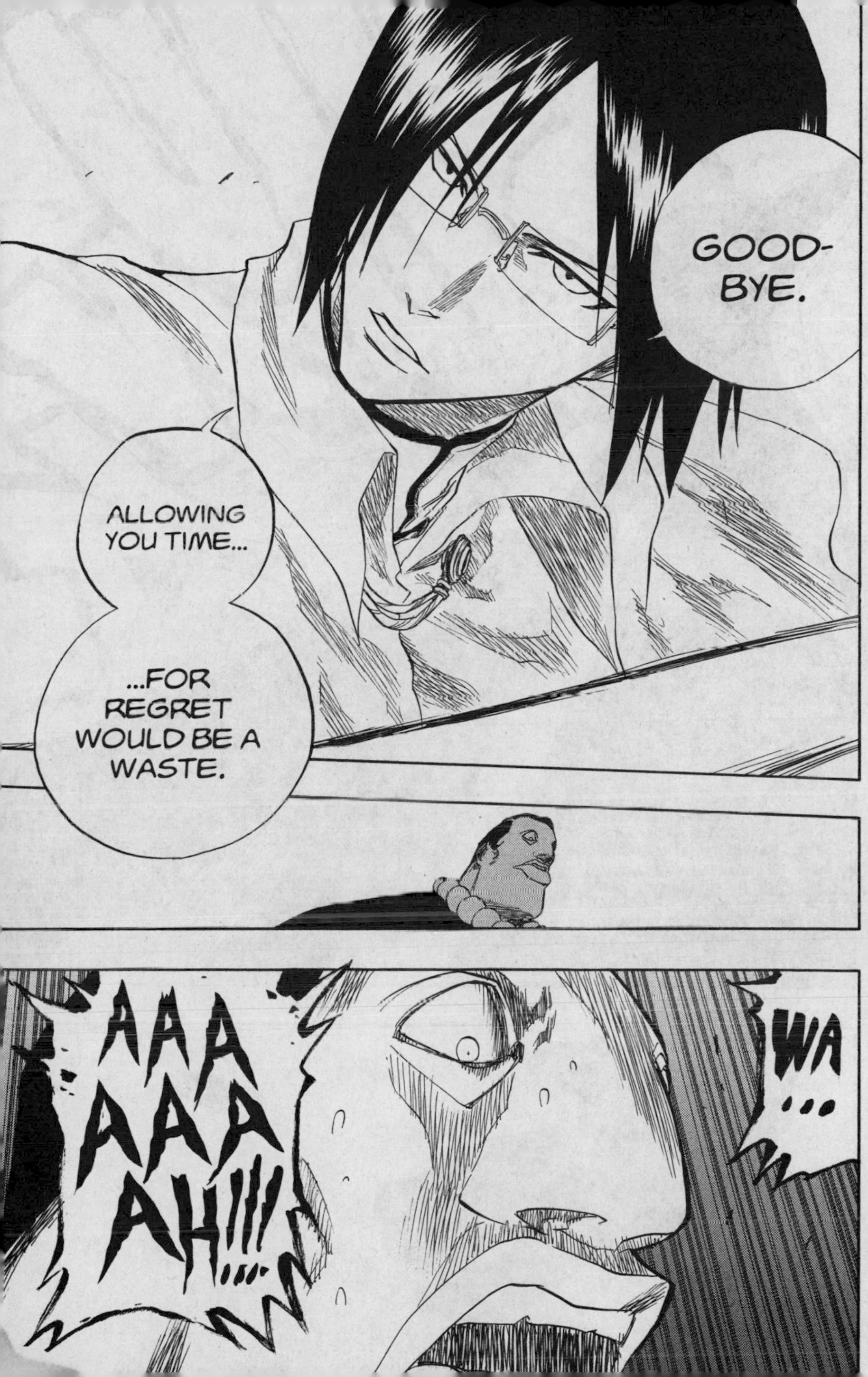
GOOD-BYE.
ALLOWING YOU TIME...
...FOR REGRET WOULD BE A WASTE.
WA...
AAAAAAAH!!!

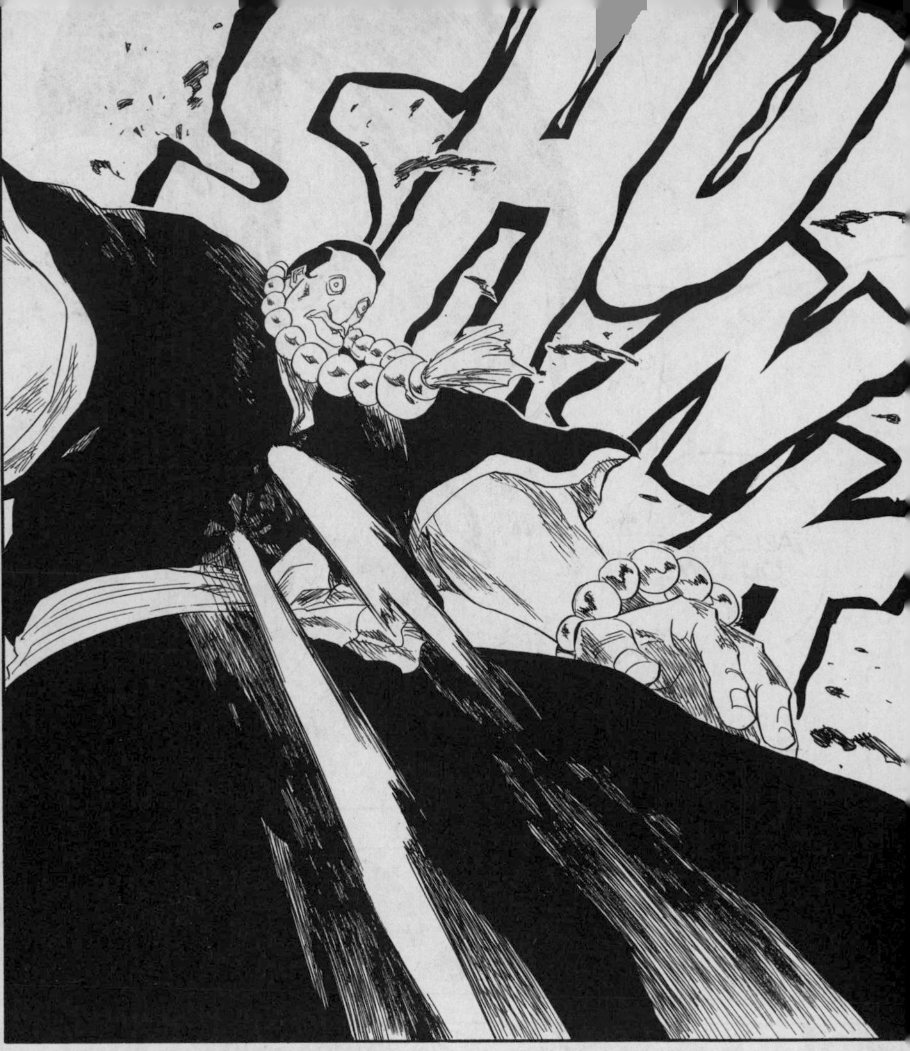

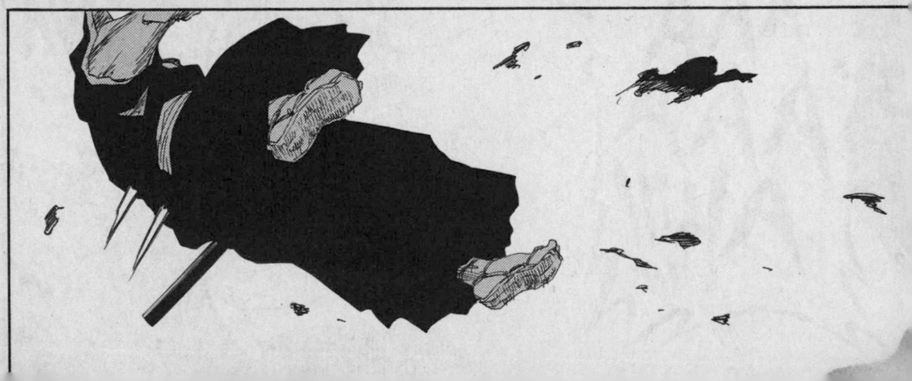

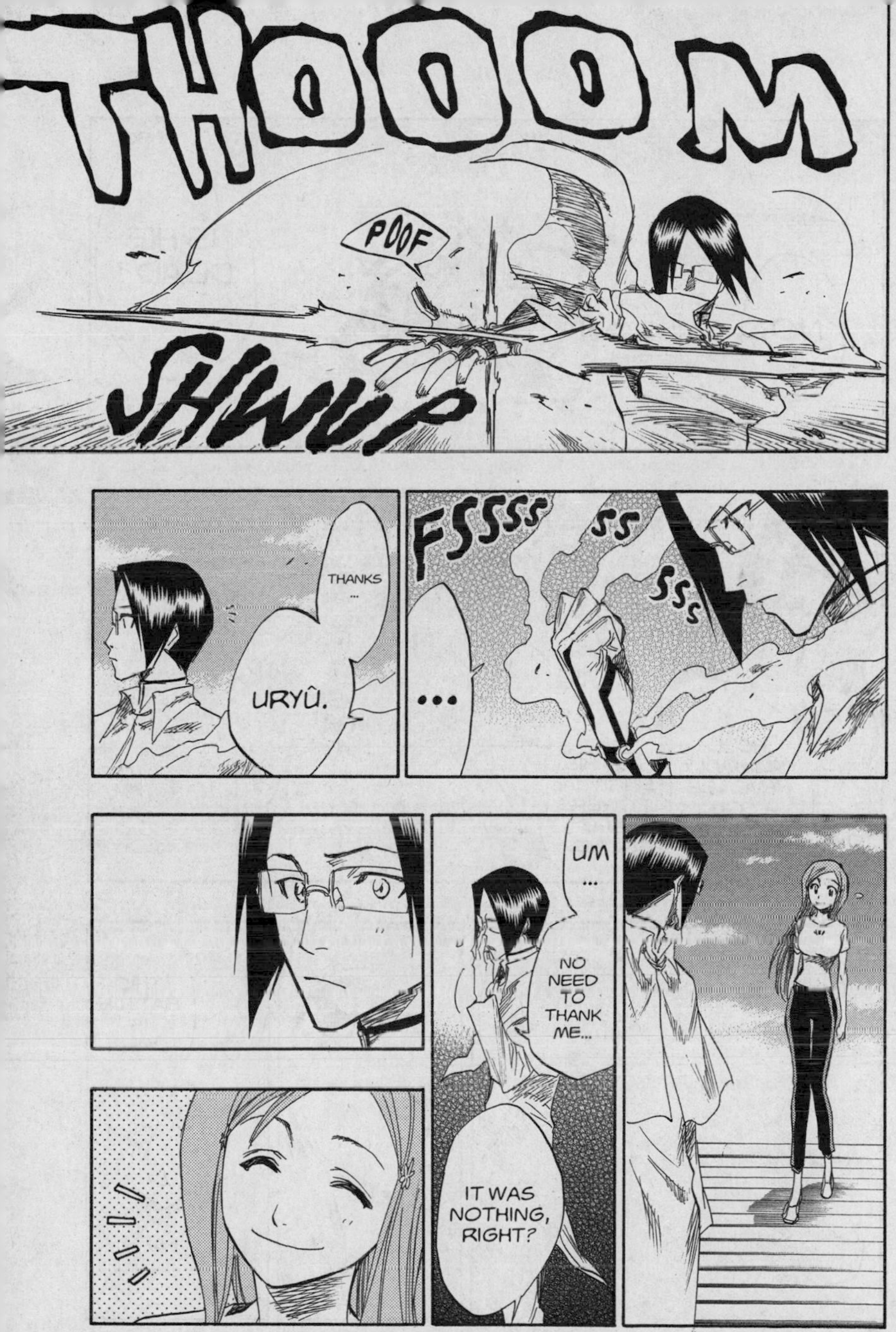
THOOOM
POOF
SHWUP
FSSSSSSSSS
...
THANKS ...
URYÛ.
UM ...
NO NEED TO THANK ME...
IT WAS NOTHING, RIGHT?

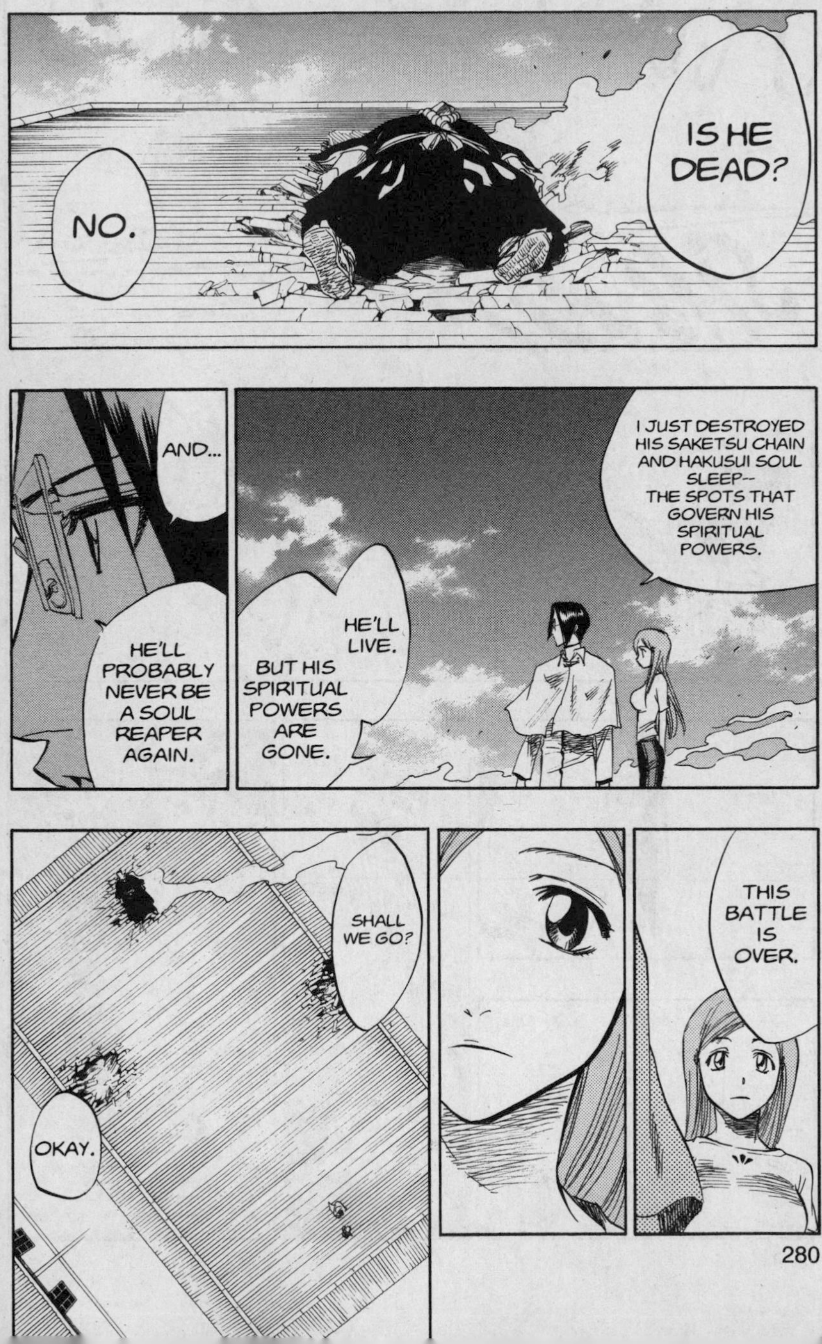
IS HE DEAD?
NO.
I JUST DESTROYED HIS SAKETSU CHAIN AND HAKUSUI SOUL SLEEP-- THE SPOTS THAT GOVERN HIS SPIRITUAL POWERS.
HE'LL LIVE.
BUT HIS SPIRITUAL POWERS ARE GONE.
AND...
HE'LL PROBABLY NEVER BE A SOUL REAPER AGAIN.
THIS BATTLE IS OVER.
SHALL WE GO?
OKAY.

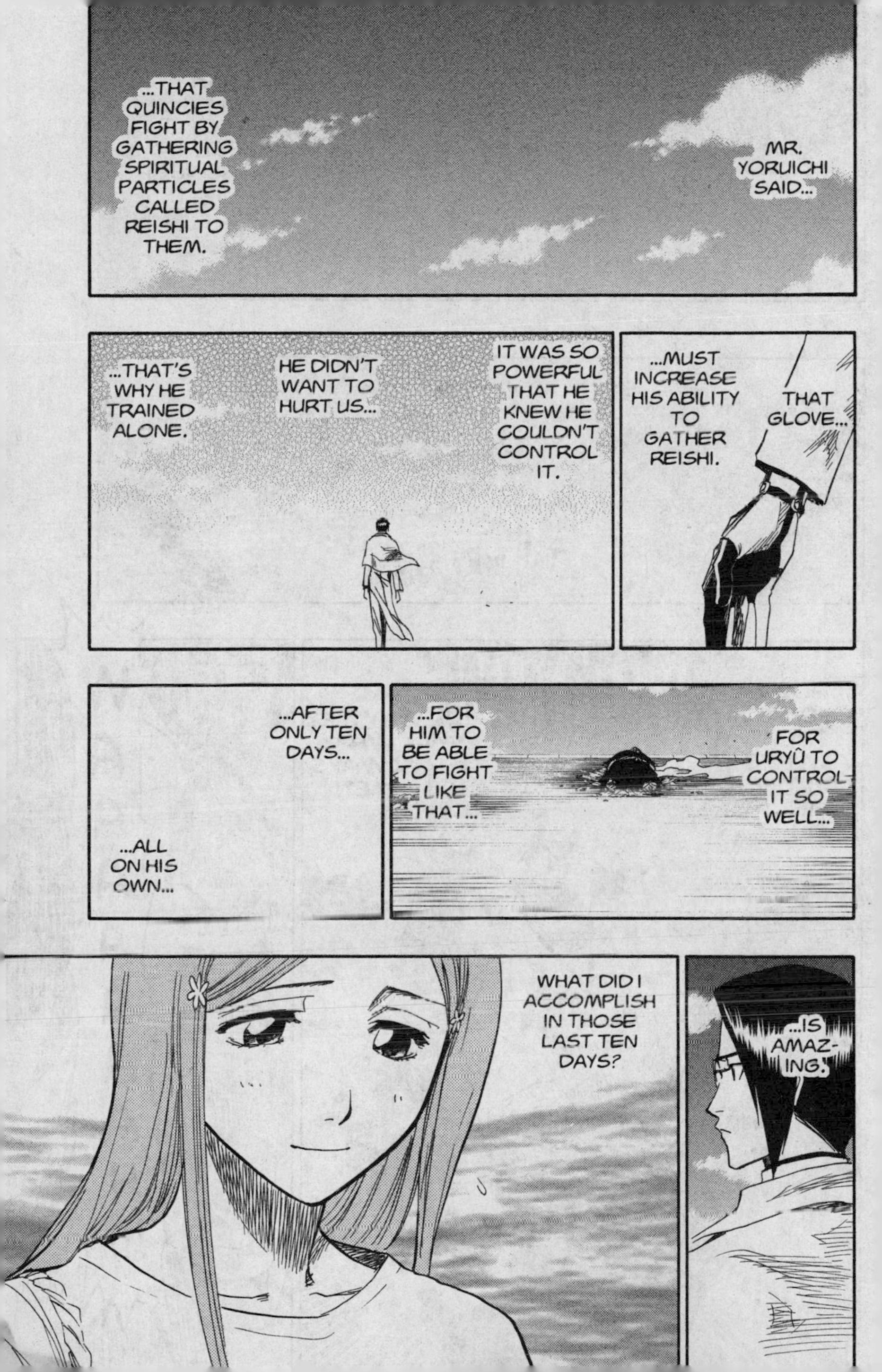
MR. YORUICHI SAID...
...THAT QUINCIES FIGHT BY GATHERING SPIRITUAL PARTICLES CALLED REISHI TO THEM.
THAT GLOVE...
...MUST INCREASE HIS ABILITY TO GATHER REISHI.
IT WAS SO POWERFUL THAT HE KNEW HE COULDN'T CONTROL IT.
HE DIDN'T WANT TO HURT US...
...THAT'S WHY HE TRAINED ALONE.
FOR URYÛ TO CONTROL IT SO WELL...
...FOR HIM TO BE ABLE TO FIGHT LIKE THAT...
...AFTER ONLY TEN DAYS...
...ALL ON HIS OWN...
...IS AMAZ-ING.
WHAT DID I ACCOMPLISH IN THOSE LAST TEN DAYS?

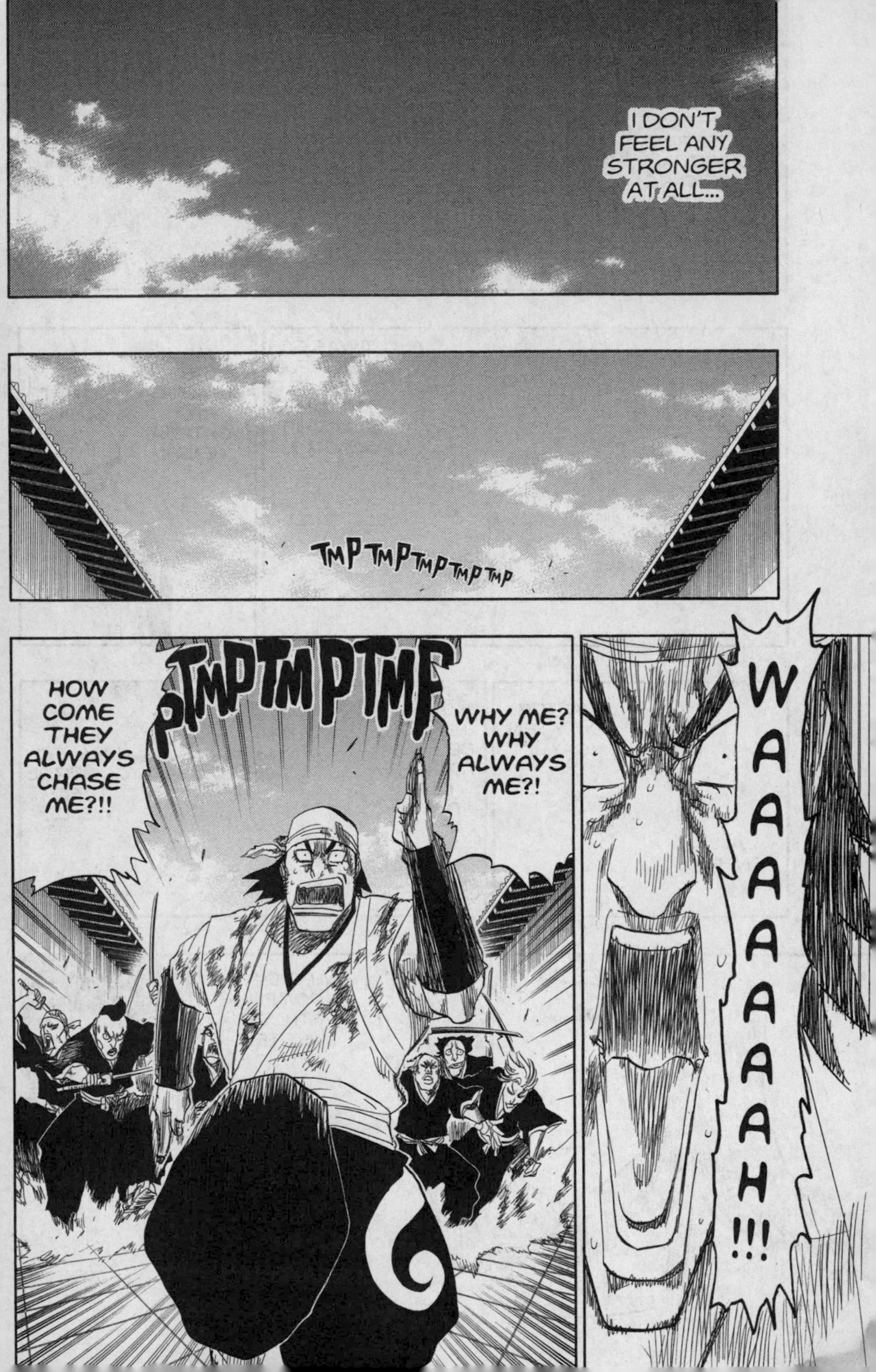
I DON'T FEEL ANY STRONGER AT ALL...
TMP TMP TMP TMP TMP
WAAAAAAAH!!!
PTMPTMPTMP
WHY ME? WHY ALWAYS ME?!
HOW COME THEY ALWAYS CHASE ME?!!

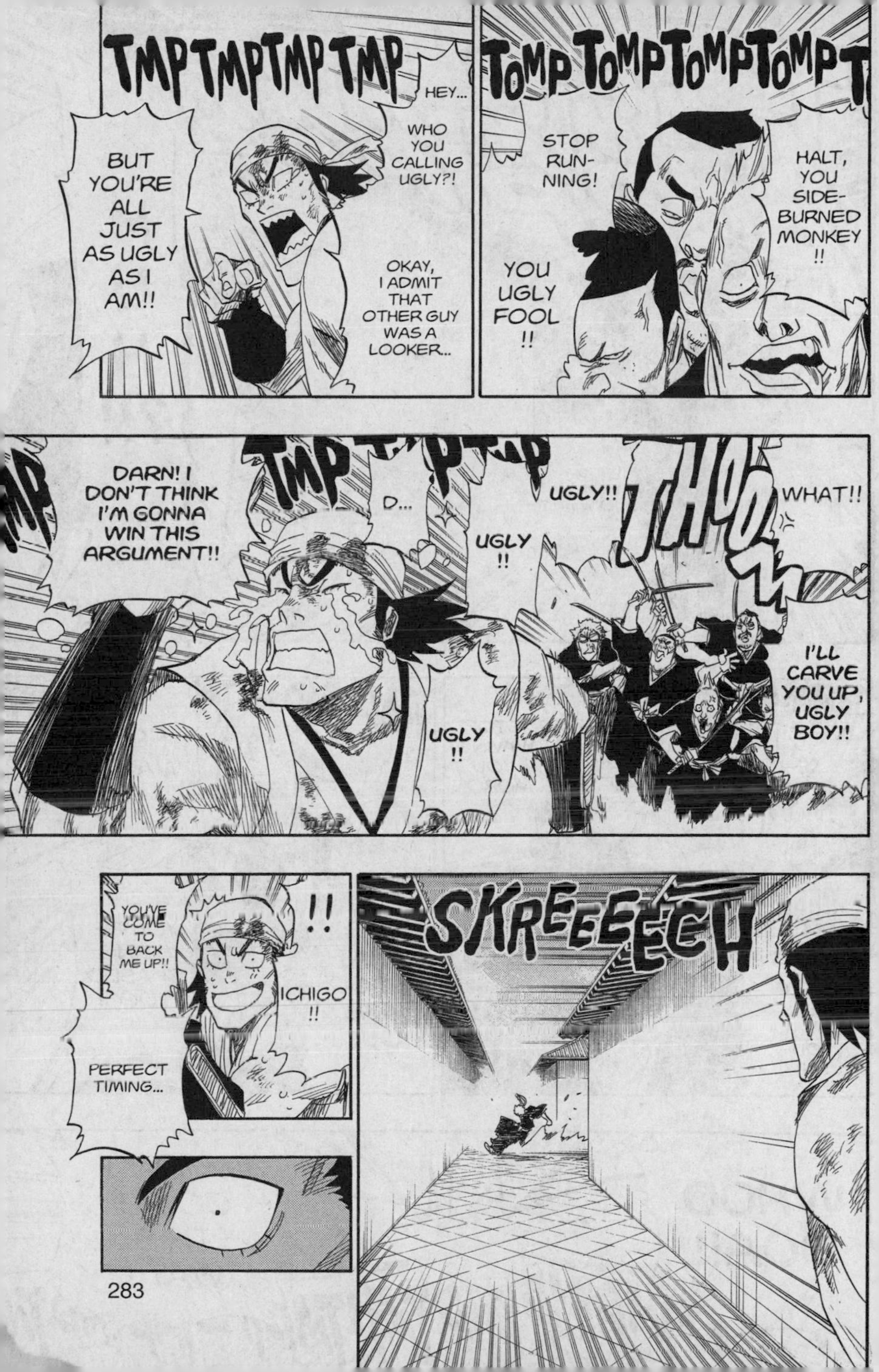
TOMP TOMP TOMP TOMP T
HALT, YOU SIDE-BURNED MONKEY!!
STOP RUN-NING!
YOU UGLY FOOL!!
TMP TMP TMP TMP
HEY...
WHO YOU CALLING UGLY?!
OKAY, I ADMIT THAT OTHER GUY WAS A LOOKER...
BUT YOU'RE ALL JUST AS UGLY AS I AM!!
THOOM
WHAT!!
I'LL CARVE YOU UP, UGLY BOY!!
UGLY!!
UGLY!!
TMP
D...
UGLY!!
DARN! I DON'T THINK I'M GONNA WIN THIS ARGUMENT!!
SKREEEECH
!!
ICHIGO!!
YOU'VE COME TO BACK ME UP!!
PERFECT TIMING...

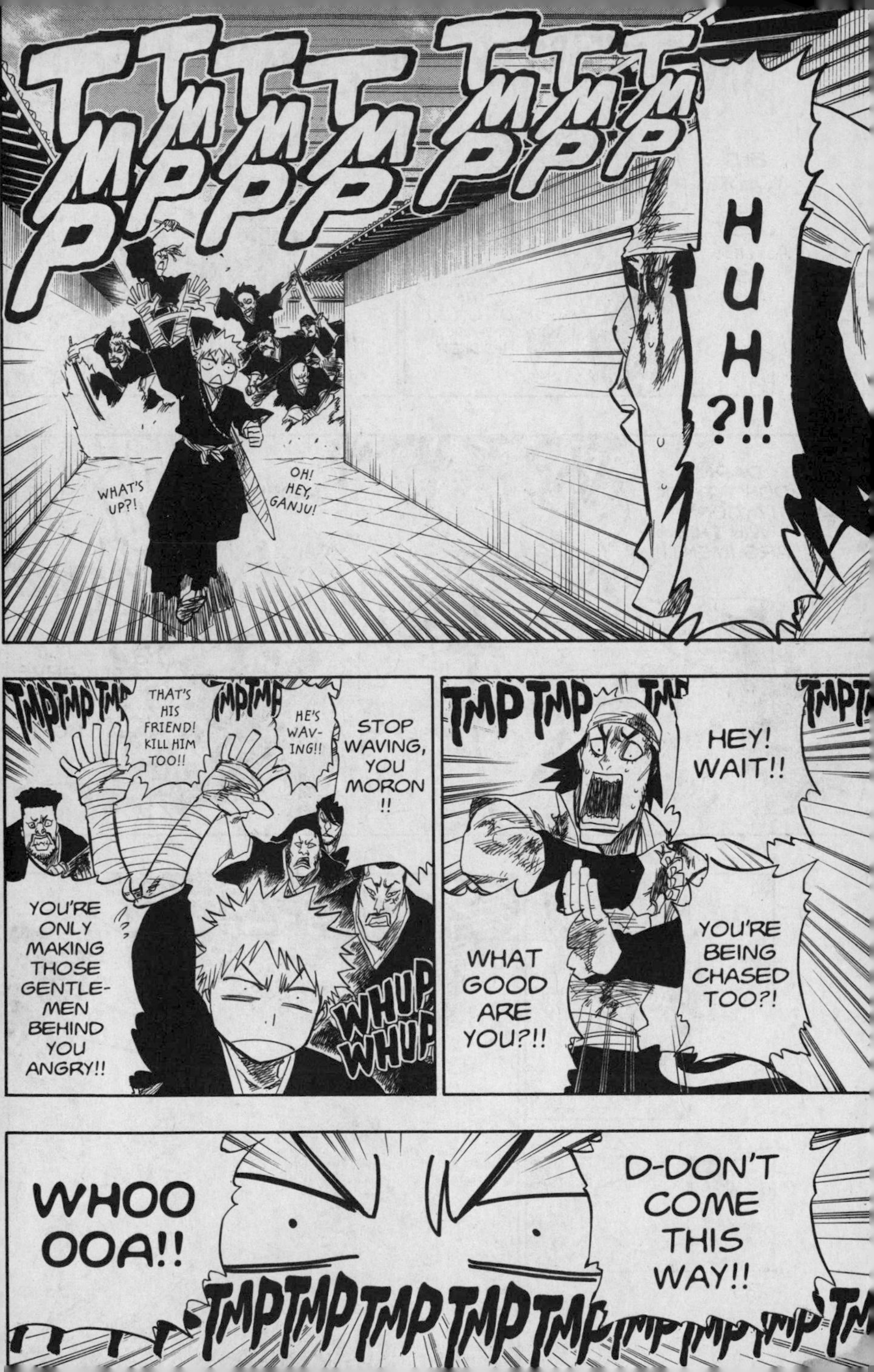
TMP TMP TMP TMP TMP TMP TMP
HUH?!!
OH! HEY, GANJU!
WHAT'S UP?!
TMP TMP
TMPT
HEY! WAIT!!
YOU'RE BEING CHASED TOO?!
WHAT GOOD ARE YOU?!!
TMP TMP TMP
STOP WAVING, YOU MORON!!
TMP TMP
HE'S WAVING!!
THAT'S HIS FRIEND! KILL HIM TOO!!
YOU'RE ONLY MAKING THOSE GENTLEMEN BEHIND YOU ANGRY!!
WHUP WHUP
D-DON'T COME THIS WAY!!
WHOOOOA!!
TMP TMP TMP TMP TMP

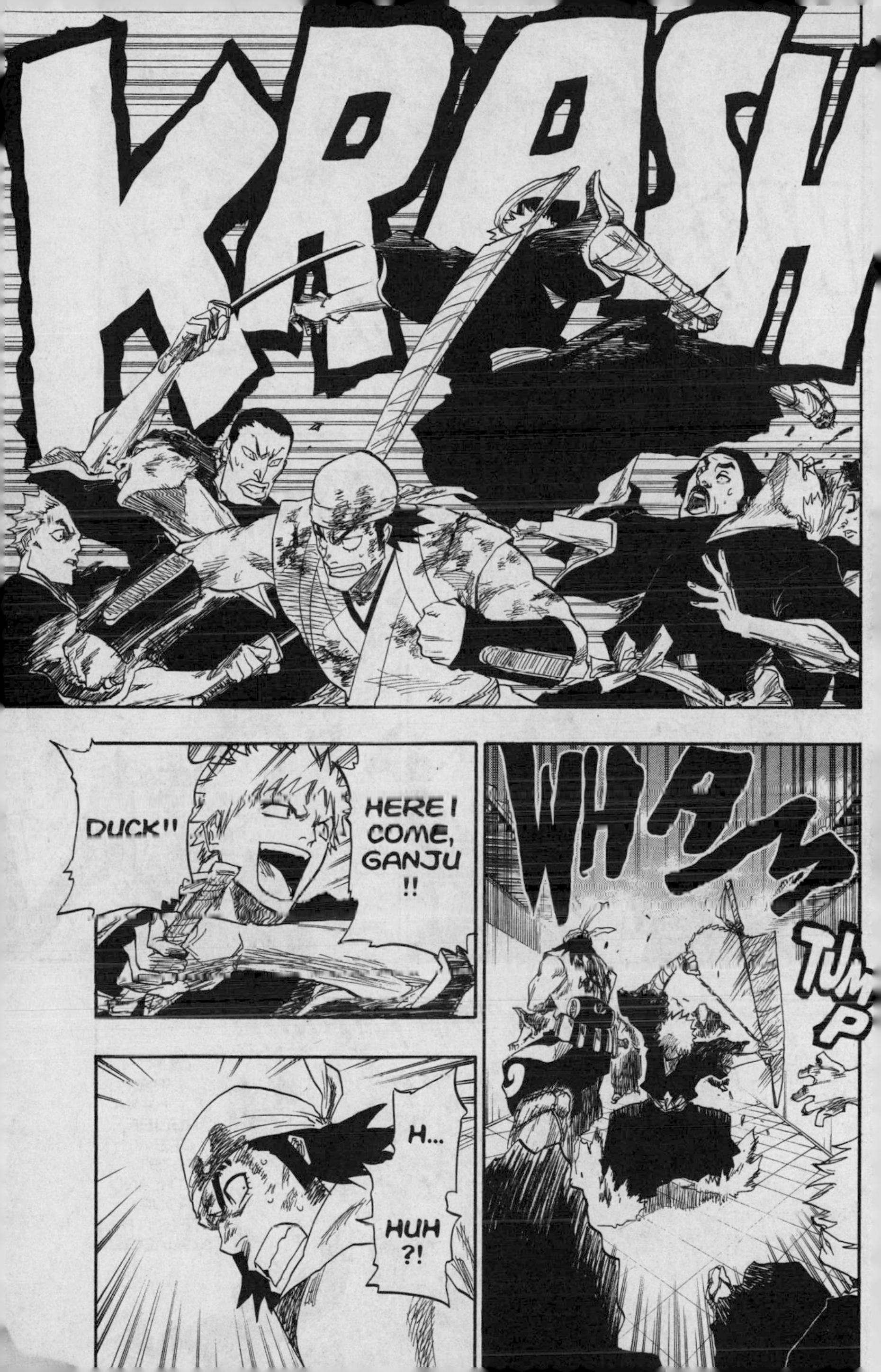
KRASH
TUMP
DUCK!!
HERE I COME, GANJU!!
H...
HUH?!

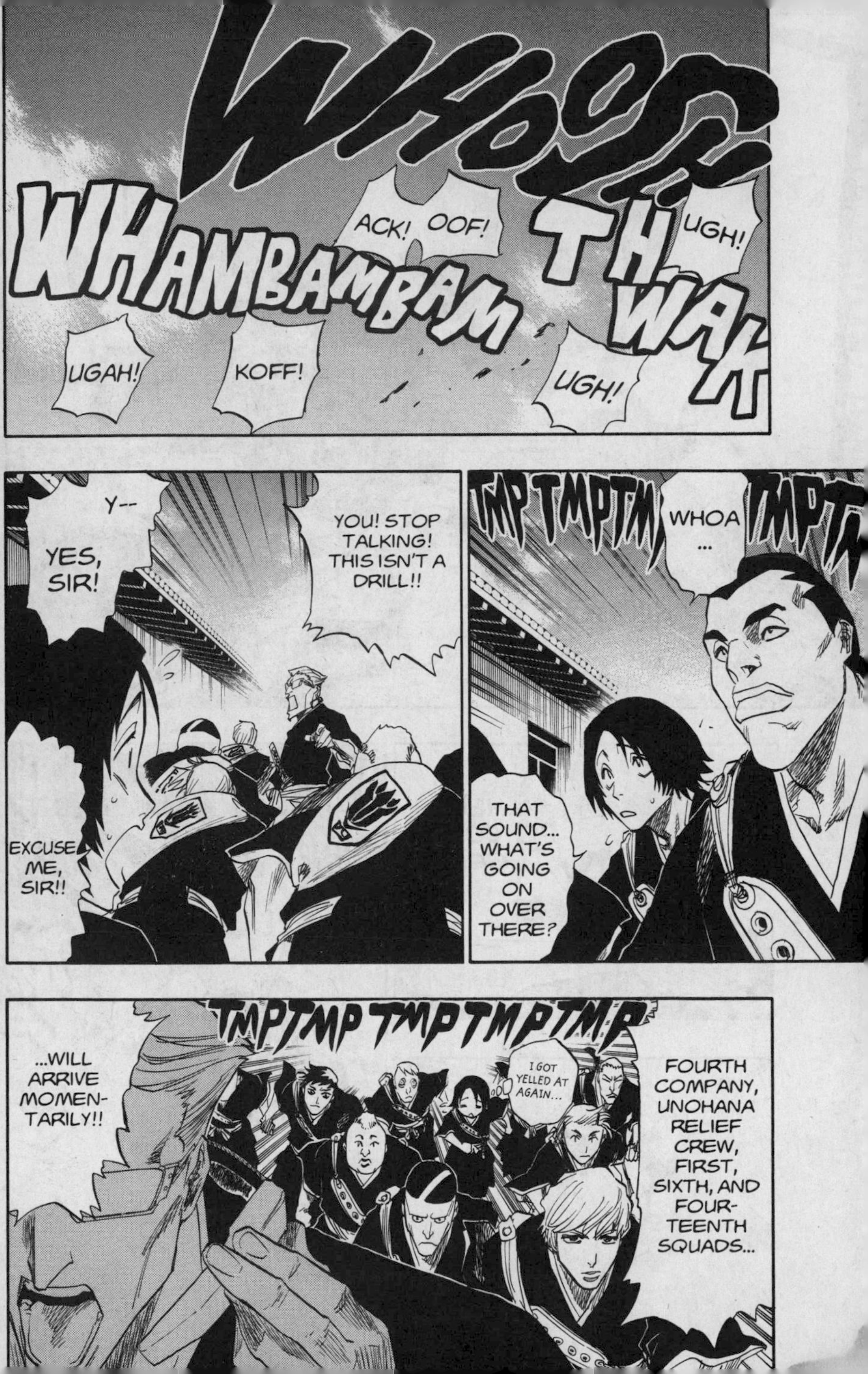
WHOOSH
THWAK
UGH!
OOF!
ACK!
WHAMBAMBAMBAM
UGH!
KOFF!
UGAH!
TMPTMPTMP TMPTMP
WHOA...
THAT SOUND... WHAT'S GOING ON OVER THERE?
YOU! STOP TALKING! THIS ISN'T A DRILL!!
Y-- YES, SIR!
EXCUSE ME, SIR!!
TMPTMP TMPTMPTMP
FOURTH COMPANY, UNOHANA RELIEF CREW, FIRST, SIXTH, AND FOURTEENTH SQUADS...
I GOT YELLED AT AGAIN...
...WILL ARRIVE MOMENTARILY!!

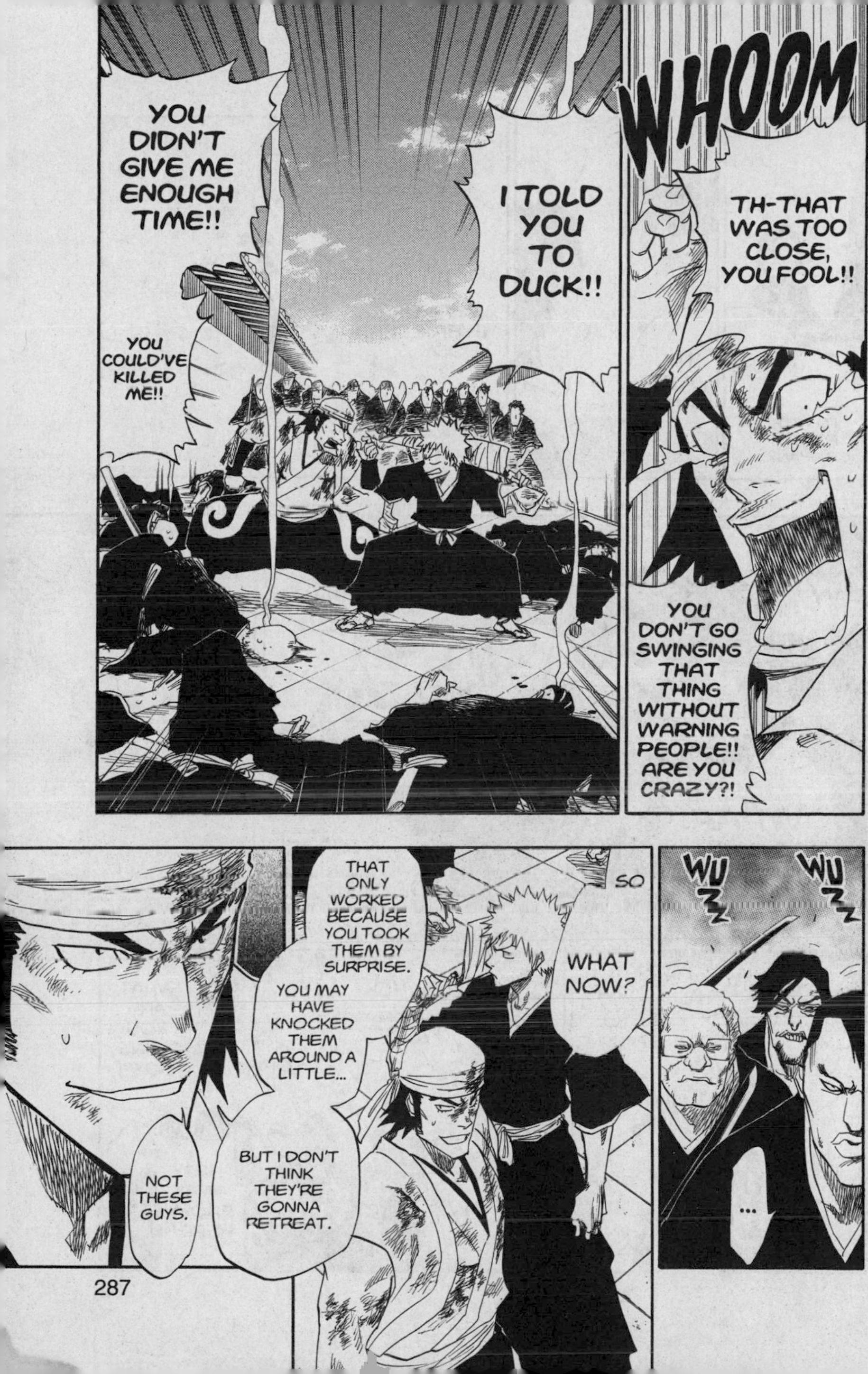
WHOOM
TH-THAT WAS TOO CLOSE, YOU FOOL!!
YOU DON'T GO SWINGING THAT THING WITHOUT WARNING PEOPLE!! ARE YOU CRAZY?!
I TOLD YOU TO DUCK!!
YOU DIDN'T GIVE ME ENOUGH TIME!!
YOU COULD'VE KILLED ME!!
WU WU
...
SO
WHAT NOW?
THAT ONLY WORKED BECAUSE YOU TOOK THEM BY SURPRISE.
YOU MAY HAVE KNOCKED THEM AROUND A LITTLE...
BUT I DON'T THINK THEY'RE GONNA RETREAT.
NOT THESE GUYS.

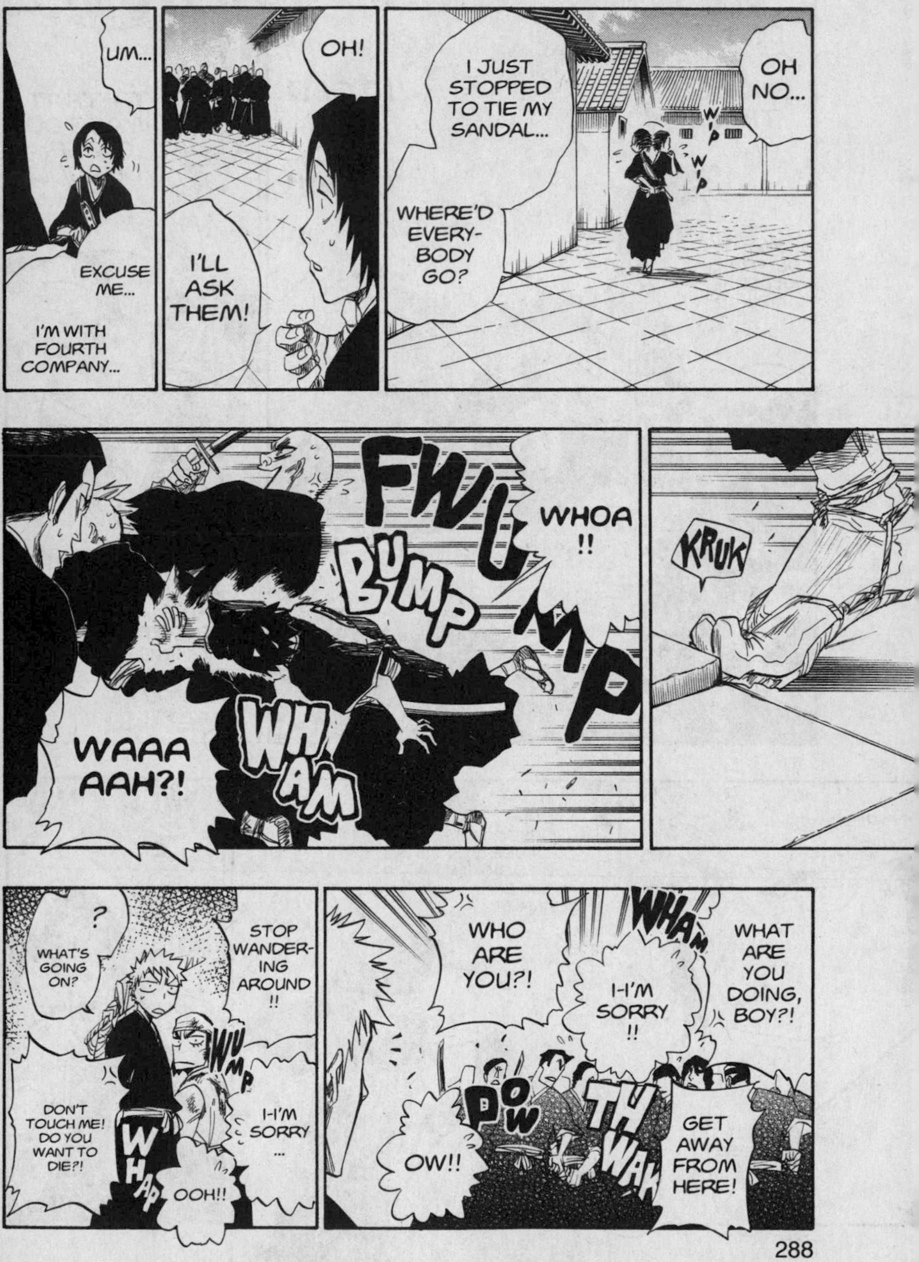
OH NO...
WIP WIP
I JUST STOPPED TO TIE MY SANDAL...
WHERE'D EVERY-BODY GO?
OH!
I'LL ASK THEM!
UM...
EXCUSE ME...
I'M WITH FOURTH COMPANY...
KRUK
FWUMP
WHOA !!
BUMP
WHAM
WAAAAAH?!
WHAT ARE YOU DOING, BOY?!
WHAM
WHO ARE YOU?!
I-I'M SORRY !!
GET AWAY FROM HERE!
THWAK
POW
OW!!
STOP WANDER-ING AROUND !!
?
WHAT'S GOING ON?
WUMP
I-I'M SORRY ...
DON'T TOUCH ME! DO YOU WANT TO DIE?!
WHAP
OOH!!

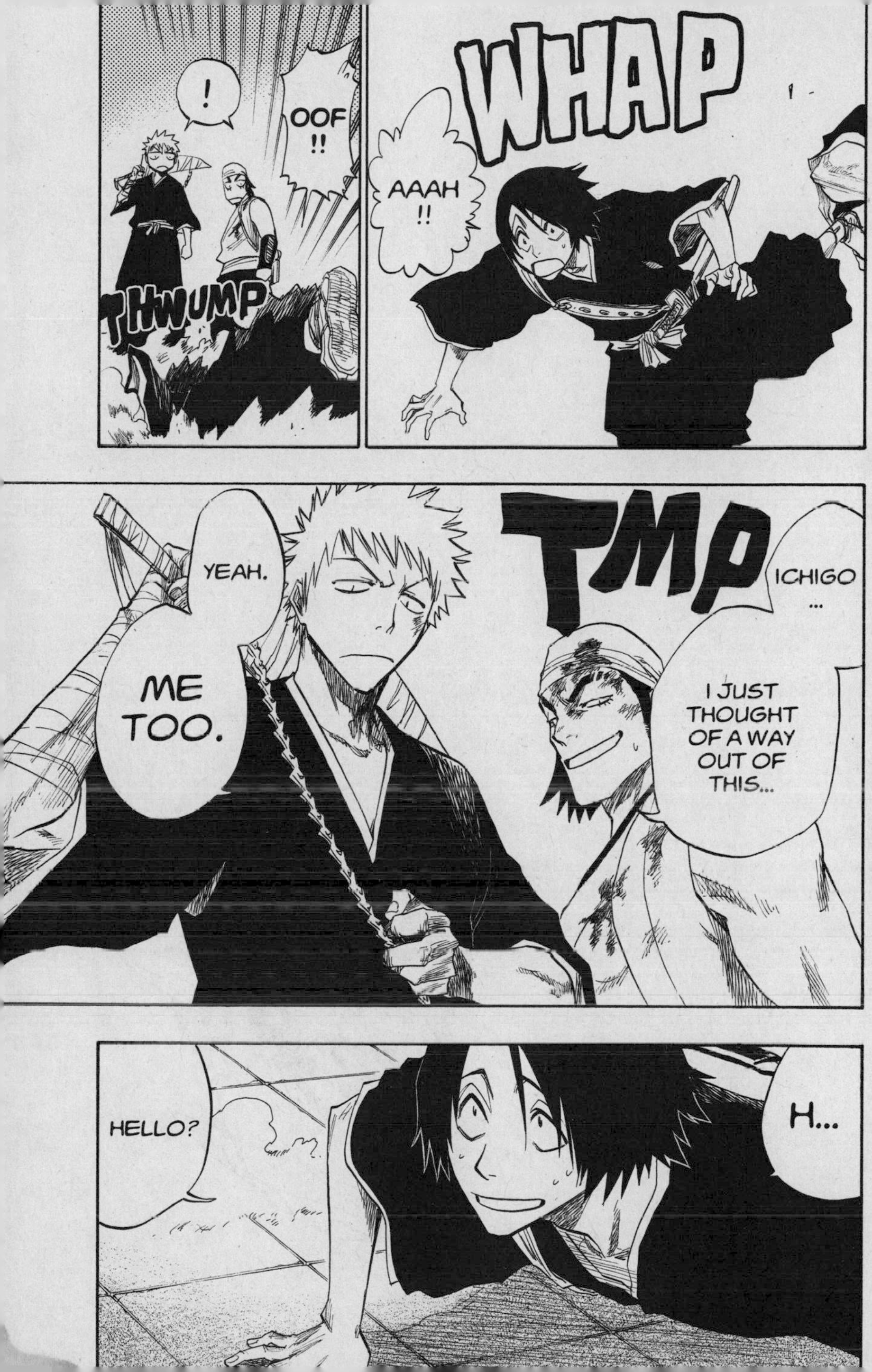
WHAP
AAAH !!
OOF !!
!
THWUMP
ICHIGO ...
TMP
I JUST THOUGHT OF A WAY OUT OF THIS...
YEAH.
ME TOO.
H...
HELLO?

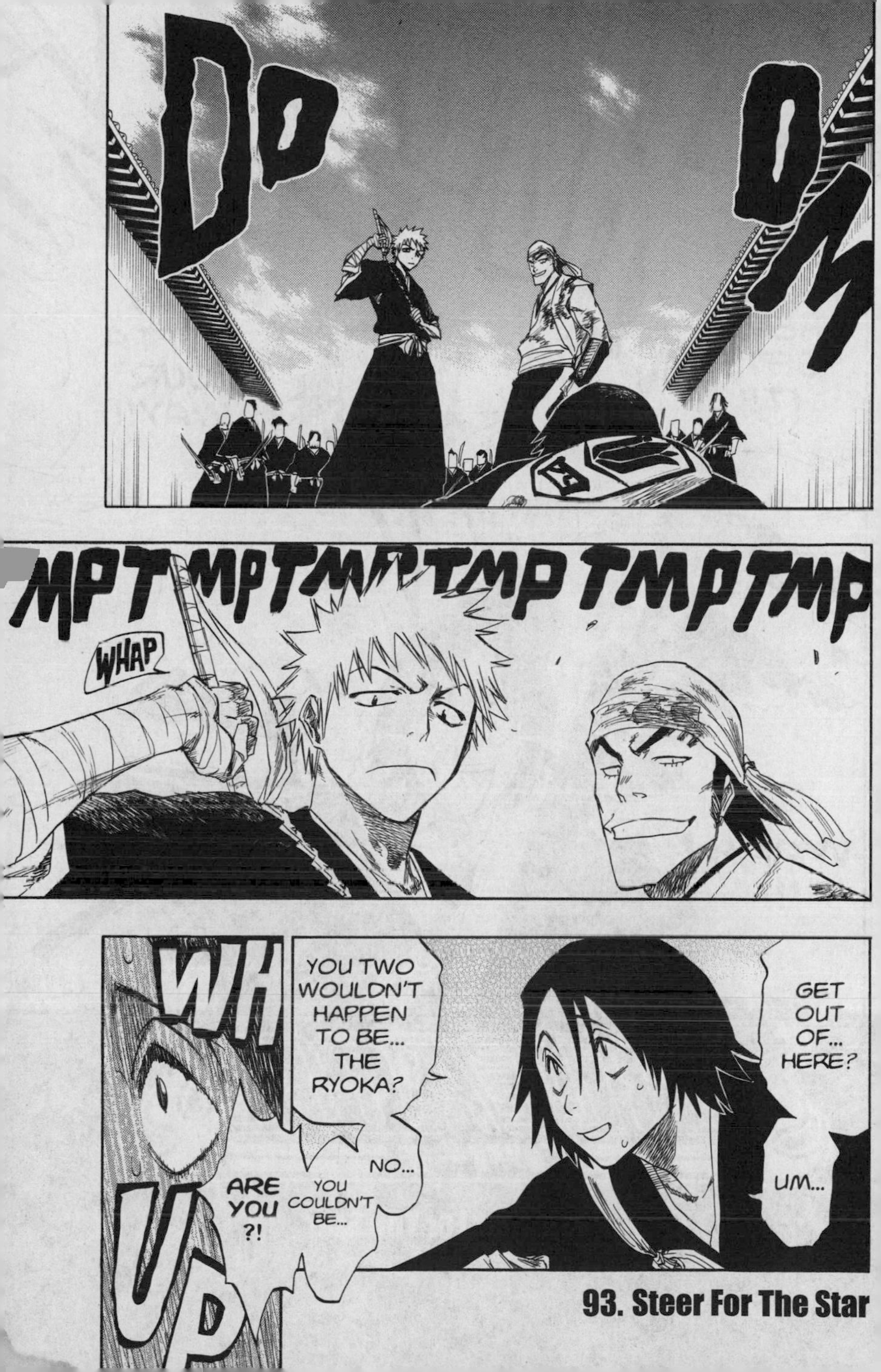
DOOM
MPT MPTMP TMP TMP TMPTMP
WHAP
GET OUT OF... HERE?
UM...
YOU TWO WOULDN'T HAPPEN TO BE... THE RYOKA?
NO... YOU COULDN'T BE...
ARE YOU ?!
WHUD

93. Steer For The Star

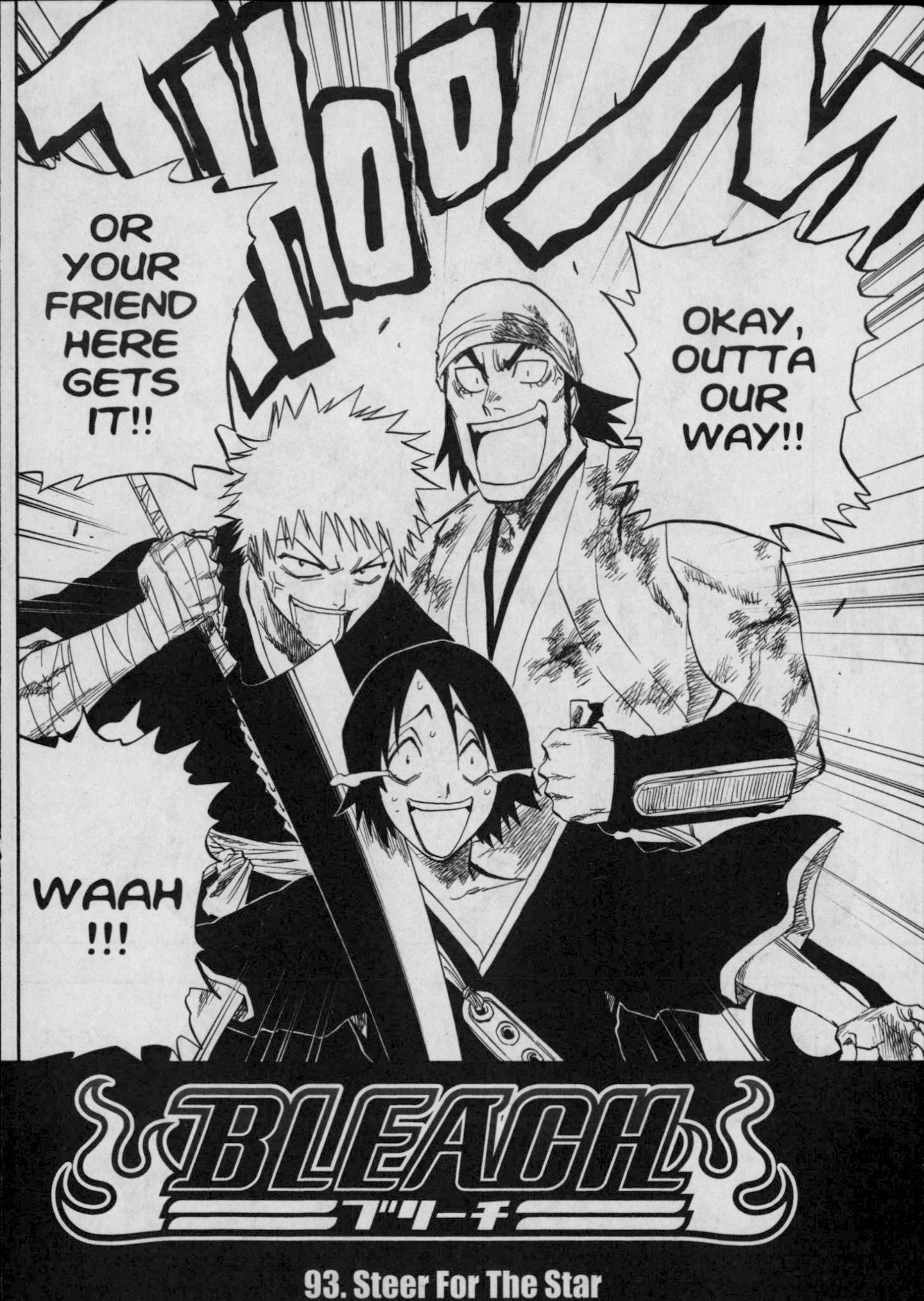
THOOM
OKAY, OUTTA OUR WAY!!
OR YOUR FRIEND HERE GETS IT!!
WAAH !!!

BLEACH
ブリーチ

93. Steer For The Star

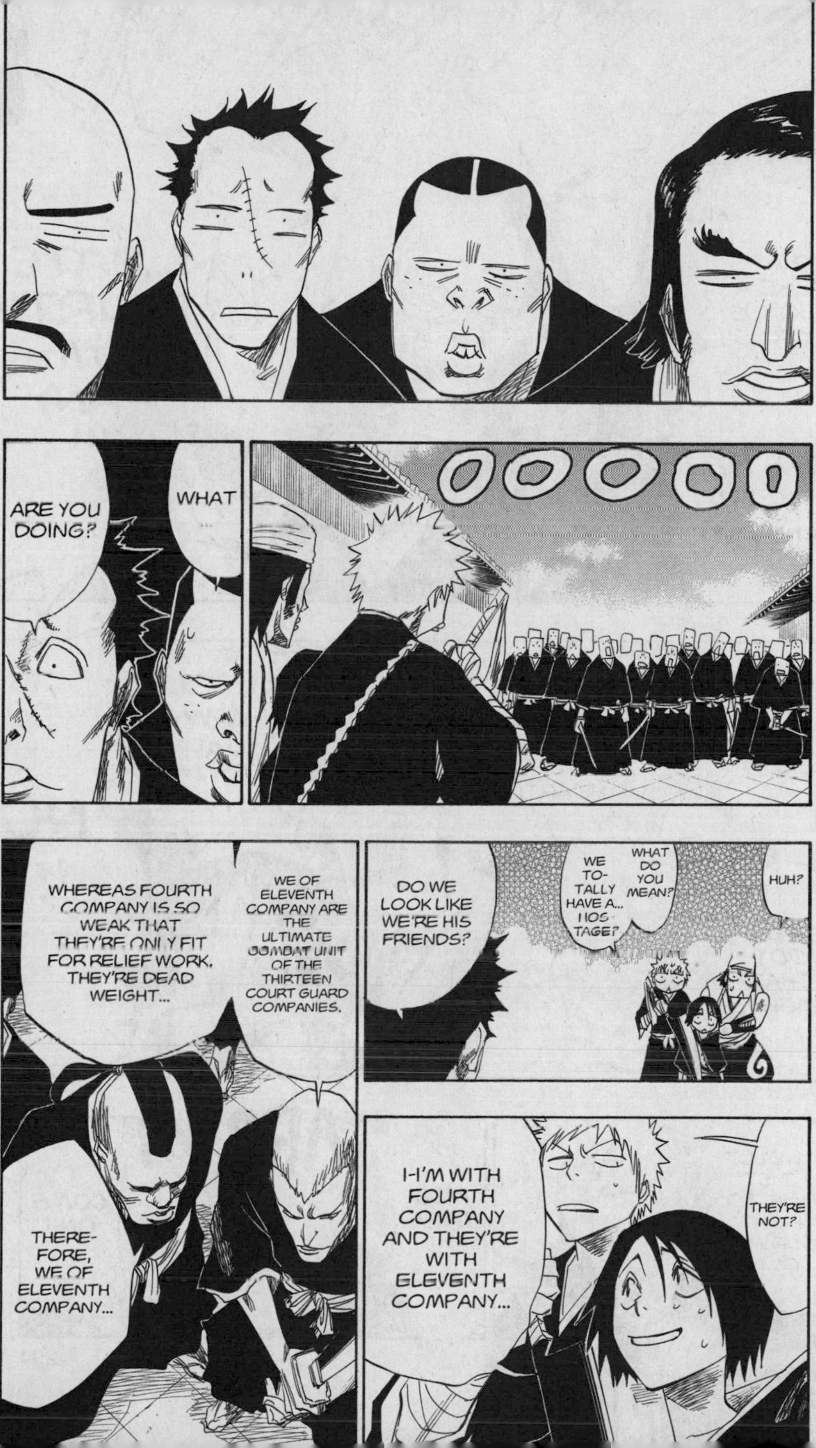
WHAT ...
ARE YOU DOING?
HUH?
WHAT DO YOU MEAN?
WE TOTALLY HAVE A... HOSTAGE?
DO WE LOOK LIKE WE'RE HIS FRIENDS?
THEY'RE NOT?
I-I'M WITH FOURTH COMPANY AND THEY'RE WITH ELEVENTH COMPANY...
WE OF ELEVENTH COMPANY ARE THE ULTIMATE COMBAT UNIT OF THE THIRTEEN COURT GUARD COMPANIES.
WHEREAS FOURTH COMPANY IS SO WEAK THAT THEY'RE ONLY FIT FOR RELIEF WORK. THEY'RE DEAD WEIGHT...
THERE-FORE, WE OF ELEVENTH COMPANY...

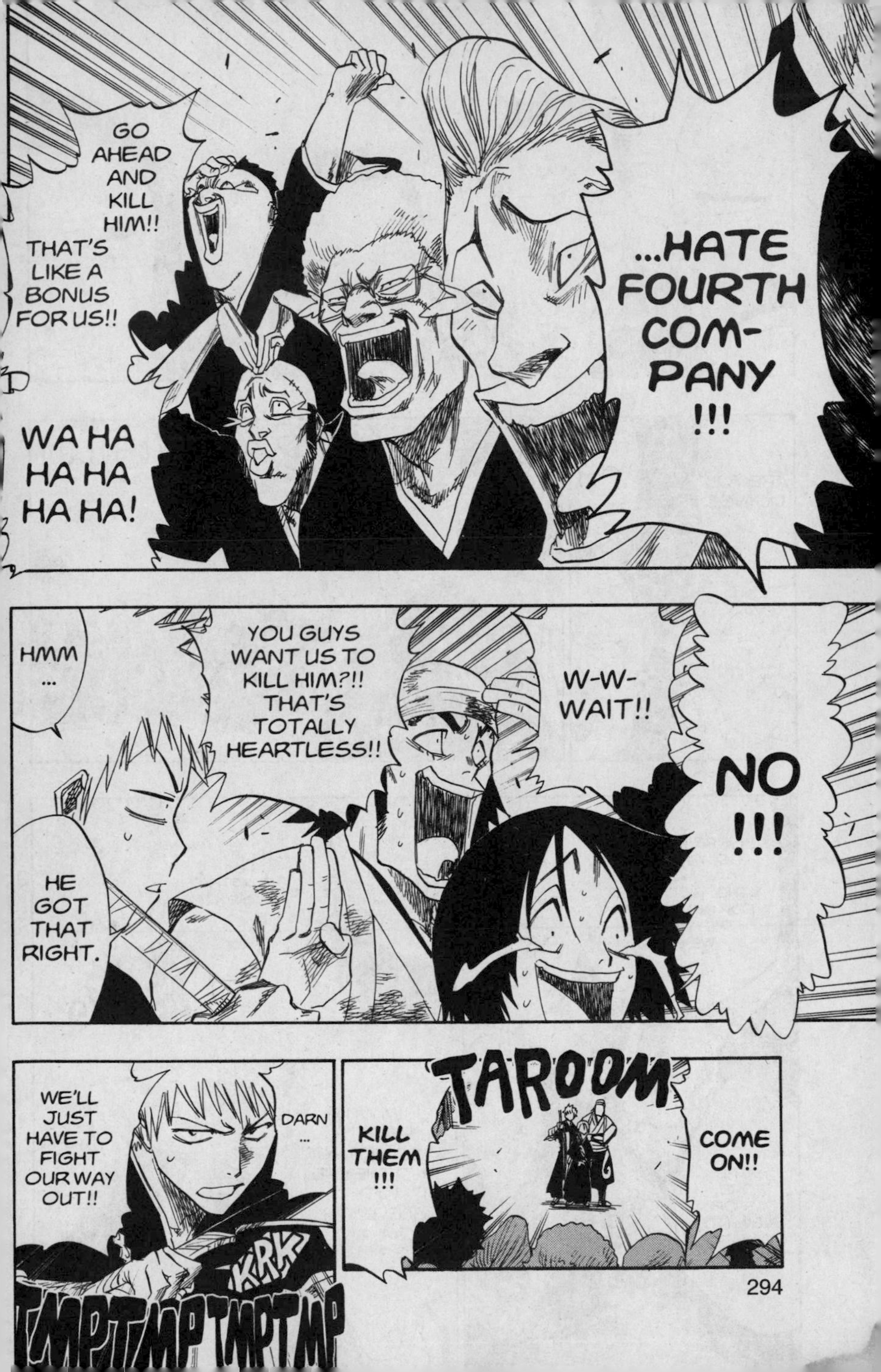
...HATE FOURTH COMPANY!!!
GO AHEAD AND KILL HIM!!
THAT'S LIKE A BONUS FOR US!!
WA HA HA HA HA HA!
NO!!!
W-W-WAIT!!
YOU GUYS WANT US TO KILL HIM?!! THAT'S TOTALLY HEARTLESS!!
HMM ...
HE GOT THAT RIGHT.
TAROOM
COME ON!!
KILL THEM!!!
DARN ...
WE'LL JUST HAVE TO FIGHT OUR WAY OUT!!
KRK
TMPTMP TMPTMP

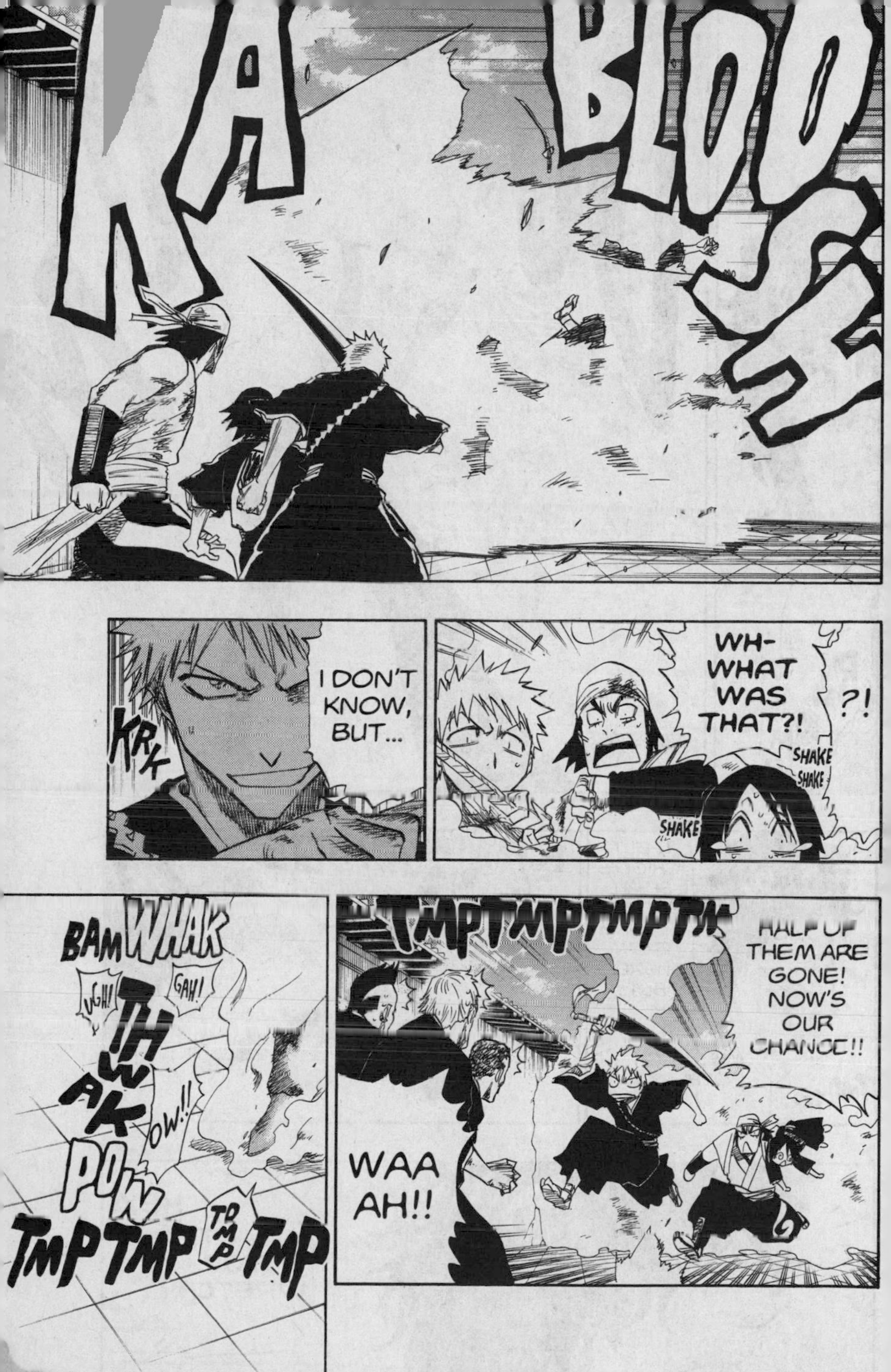
KA BLOO
WH- WHAT WAS THAT?!
?!
SHAKE
SHAKE
SHAKE
I DON'T KNOW, BUT...
KRK
TMPTMPTMPTK
HALF OF THEM ARE GONE! NOW'S OUR CHANCE!!
WAA AH!!
BAM
WHAK
UGH!
GAH!
THWAK
OW!!
POW
TMP TMP
TMP
TMP

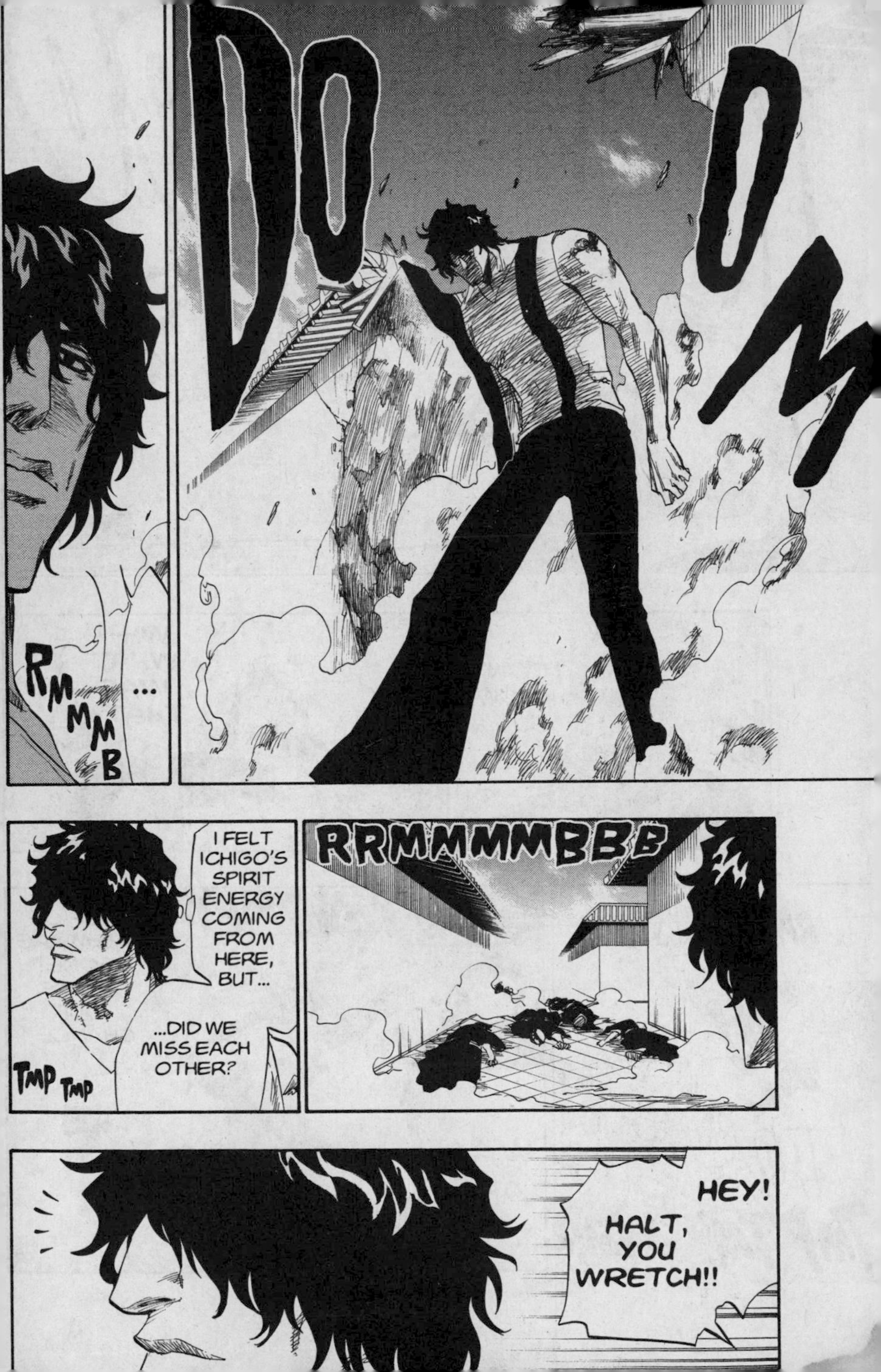
DOOM
RMMMB
...
RRMMMMMBBB
I FELT ICHIGO'S SPIRIT ENERGY COMING FROM HERE, BUT...
...DID WE MISS EACH OTHER?
TMP TMP
HEY!
HALT, YOU WRETCH!!

READ THIS WAY

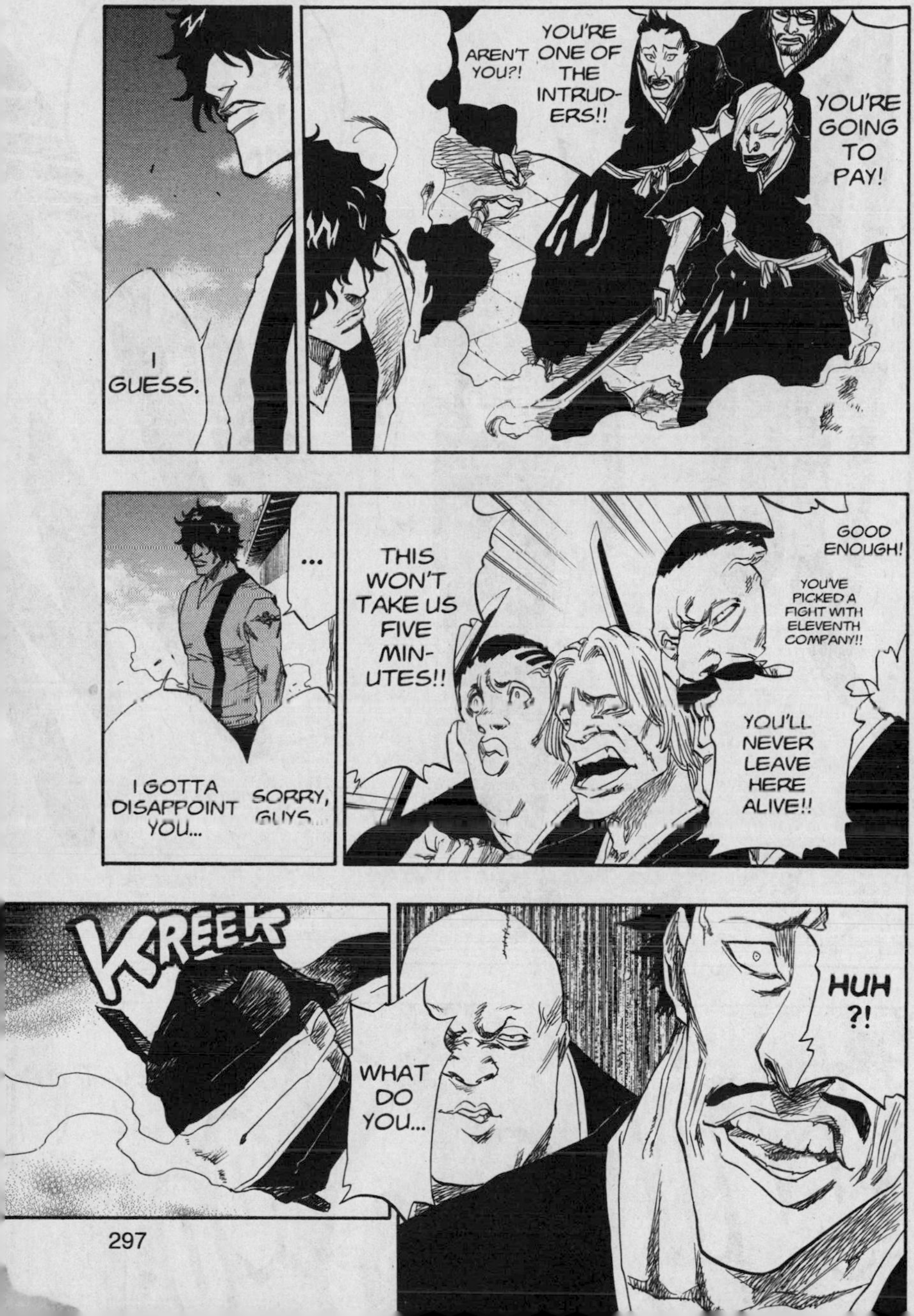

YOU'RE ONE OF THE INTRUDERS!!
AREN'T YOU?!
YOU'RE GOING TO PAY!
I GUESS.
GOOD ENOUGH!
YOU'VE PICKED A FIGHT WITH ELEVENTH COMPANY!!
YOU'LL NEVER LEAVE HERE ALIVE!!
THIS WON'T TAKE US FIVE MINUTES!!
...
SORRY, GUYS...
I GOTTA DISAPPOINT YOU...
HUH ?!
WHAT DO YOU...
KREEK

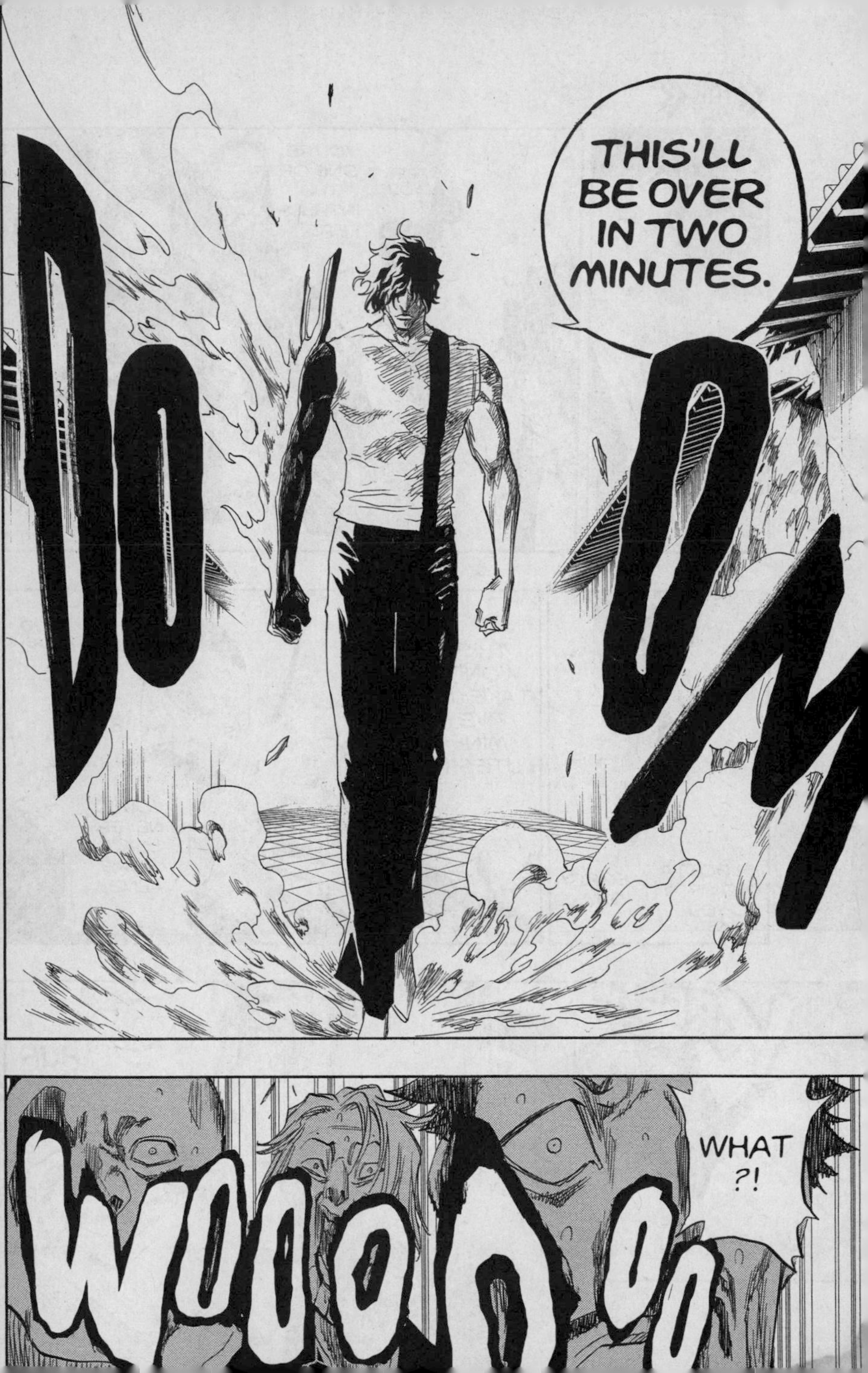
THIS'LL BE OVER IN TWO MINUTES.
DOOM
WHAT ?!

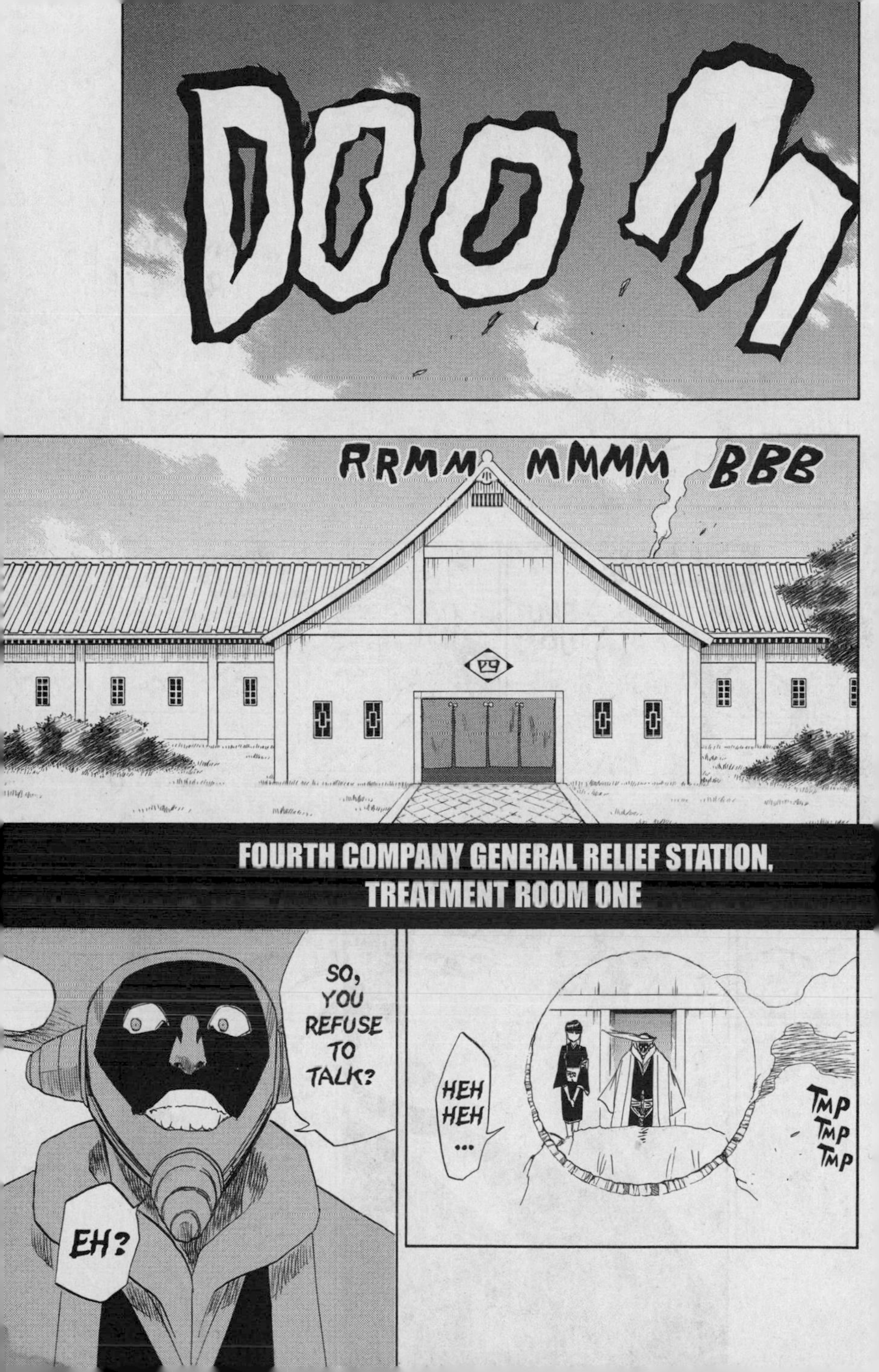
DOOM
RRMM MMMM BBB
FOURTH COMPANY GENERAL RELIEF STATION,
TREATMENT ROOM ONE
TMP TMP TMP
HEH HEH ...
SO, YOU REFUSE TO TALK?
EH?

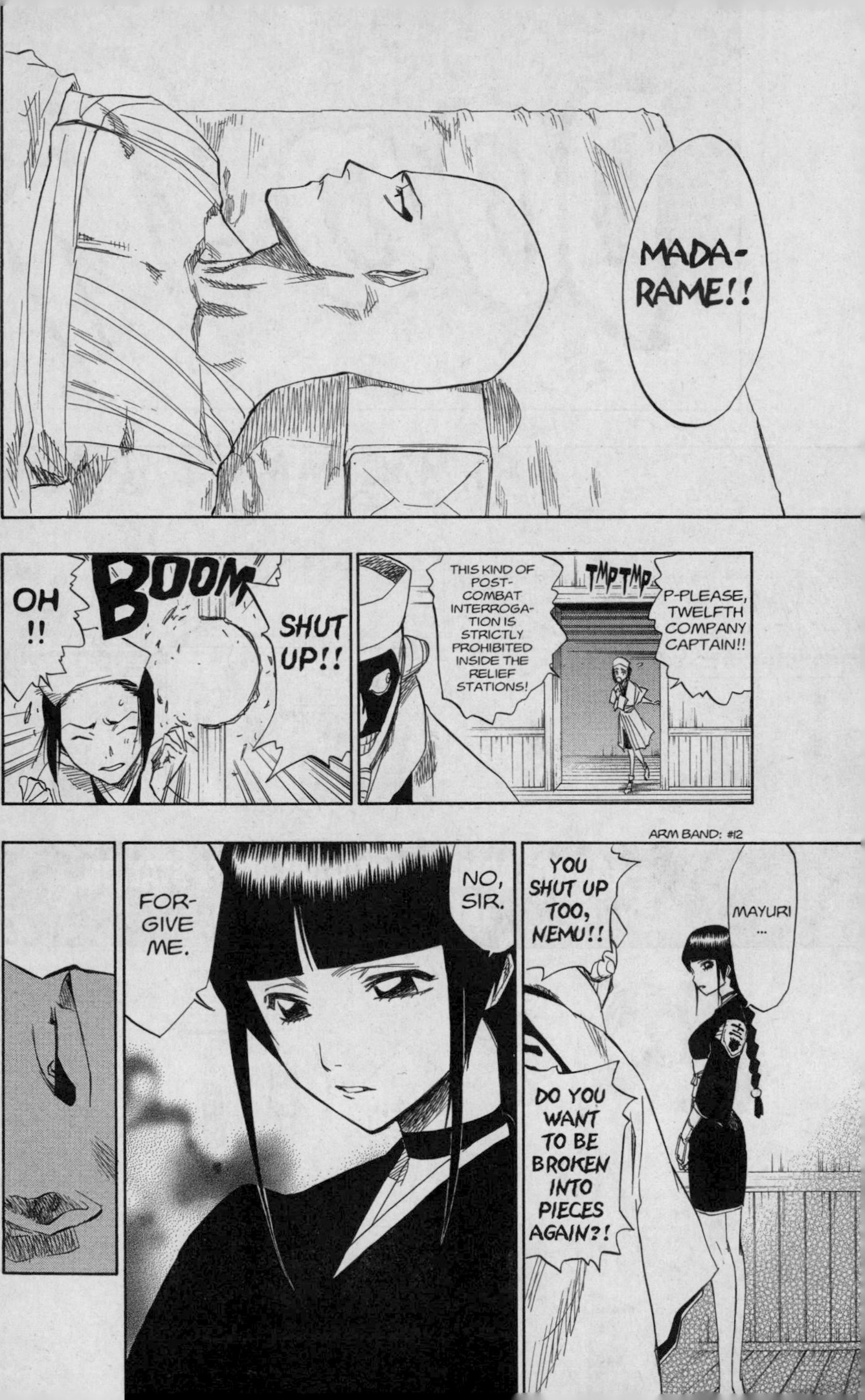
MADA-RAME!!
P-PLEASE, TWELFTH COMPANY CAPTAIN!!
TMP TMP
THIS KIND OF POST-COMBAT INTERROGATION IS STRICTLY PROHIBITED INSIDE THE RELIEF STATIONS!
SHUT UP!!
BOOM
OH !!
ARM BAND: #12
MAYURI ...
YOU SHUT UP TOO, NEMU!!
DO YOU WANT TO BE BROKEN INTO PIECES AGAIN?!
NO, SIR.
FOR-GIVE ME.

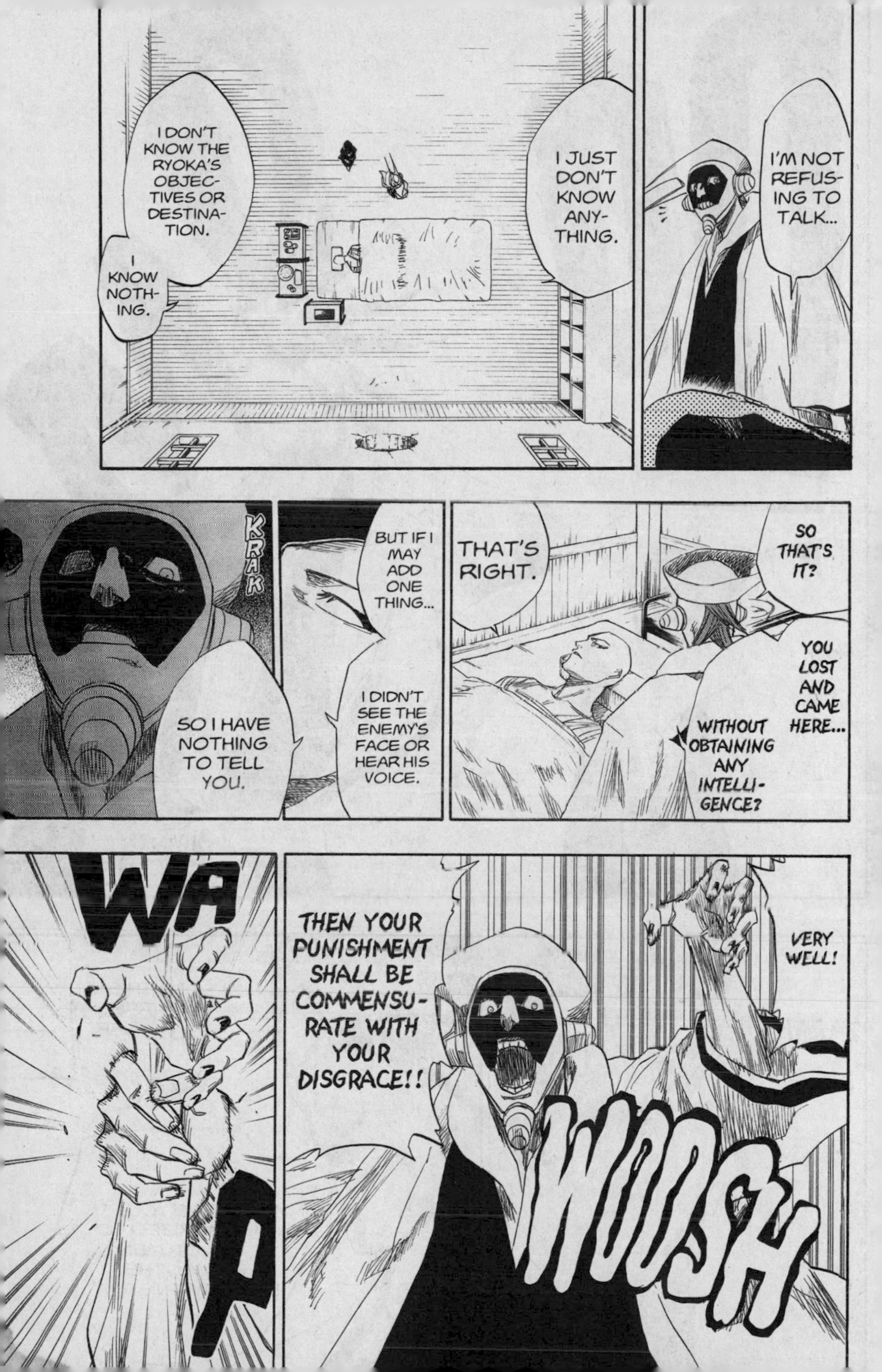
I'M NOT REFUSING TO TALK...
I JUST DON'T KNOW ANYTHING.
I DON'T KNOW THE RYOKA'S OBJECTIVES OR DESTINATION.
I KNOW NOTHING.
SO THAT'S IT?
YOU LOST AND CAME HERE...
WITHOUT OBTAINING ANY INTELLIGENCE?
THAT'S RIGHT.
BUT IF I MAY ADD ONE THING...
I DIDN'T SEE THE ENEMY'S FACE OR HEAR HIS VOICE.
KRAK
SO I HAVE NOTHING TO TELL YOU.
VERY WELL!
THEN YOUR PUNISHMENT SHALL BE COMMENSURATE WITH YOUR DISGRACE!!
WOOSH
WAP

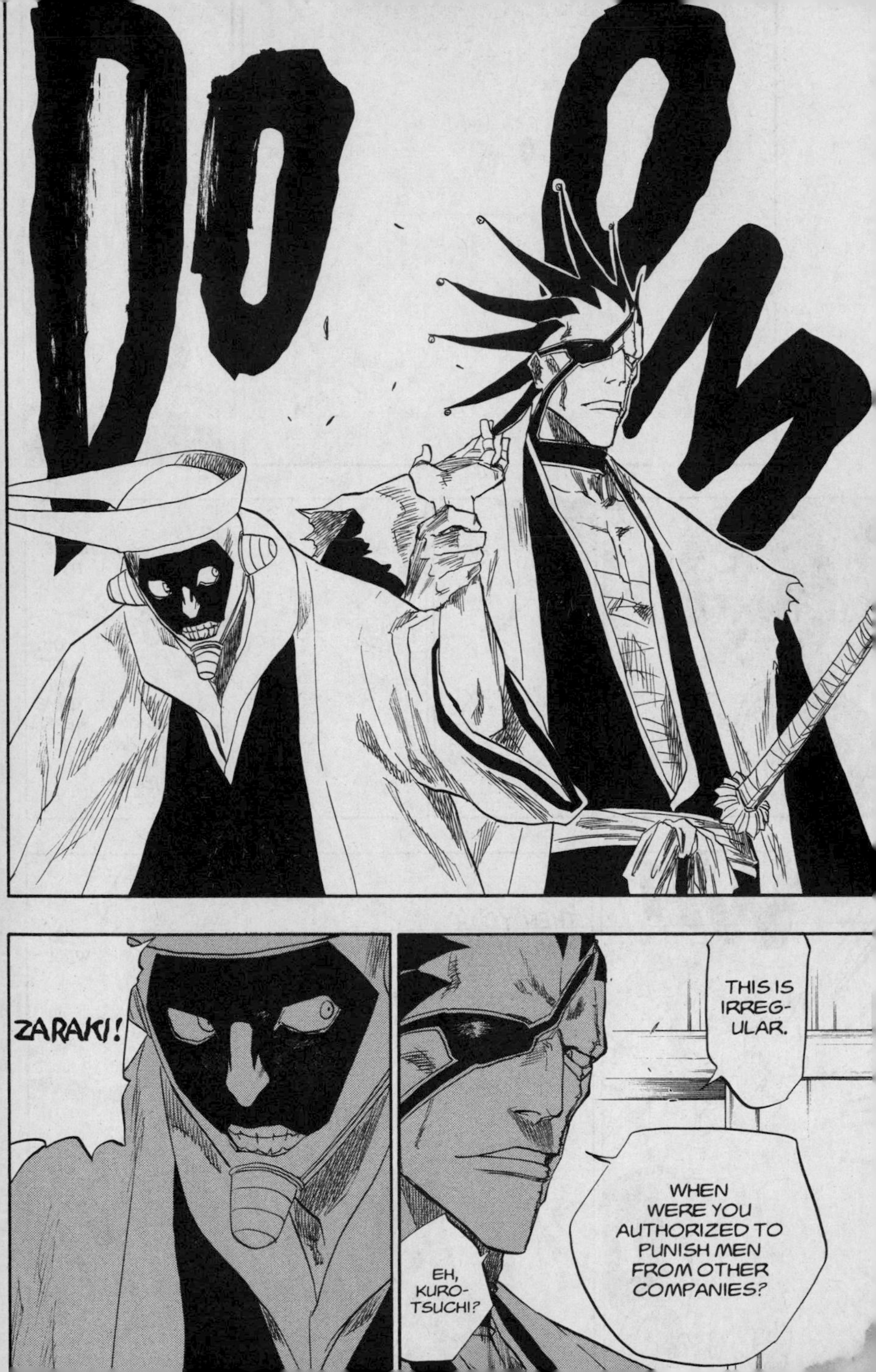
DOOM
THIS IS IRREG-ULAR.
WHEN WERE YOU AUTHORIZED TO PUNISH MEN FROM OTHER COMPANIES?
EH, KURO-TSUCHI?
ZARAKI!

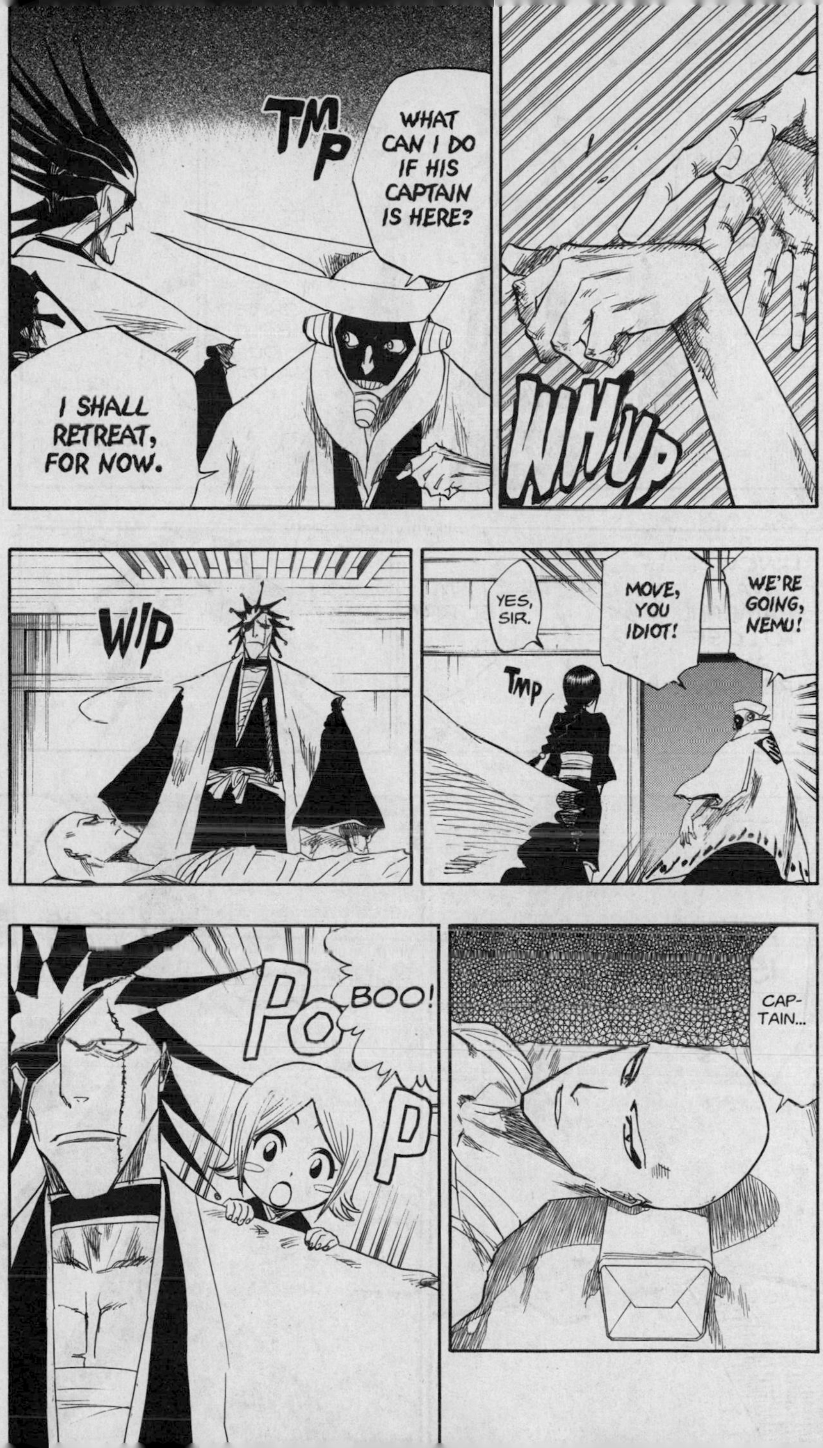
WHUP
WHAT CAN I DO IF HIS CAPTAIN IS HERE?
TMP
I SHALL RETREAT, FOR NOW.
WE'RE GOING, NEMU!
MOVE, YOU IDIOT!
YES, SIR.
TMP
WIP
CAP-TAIN...
POP
BOO!

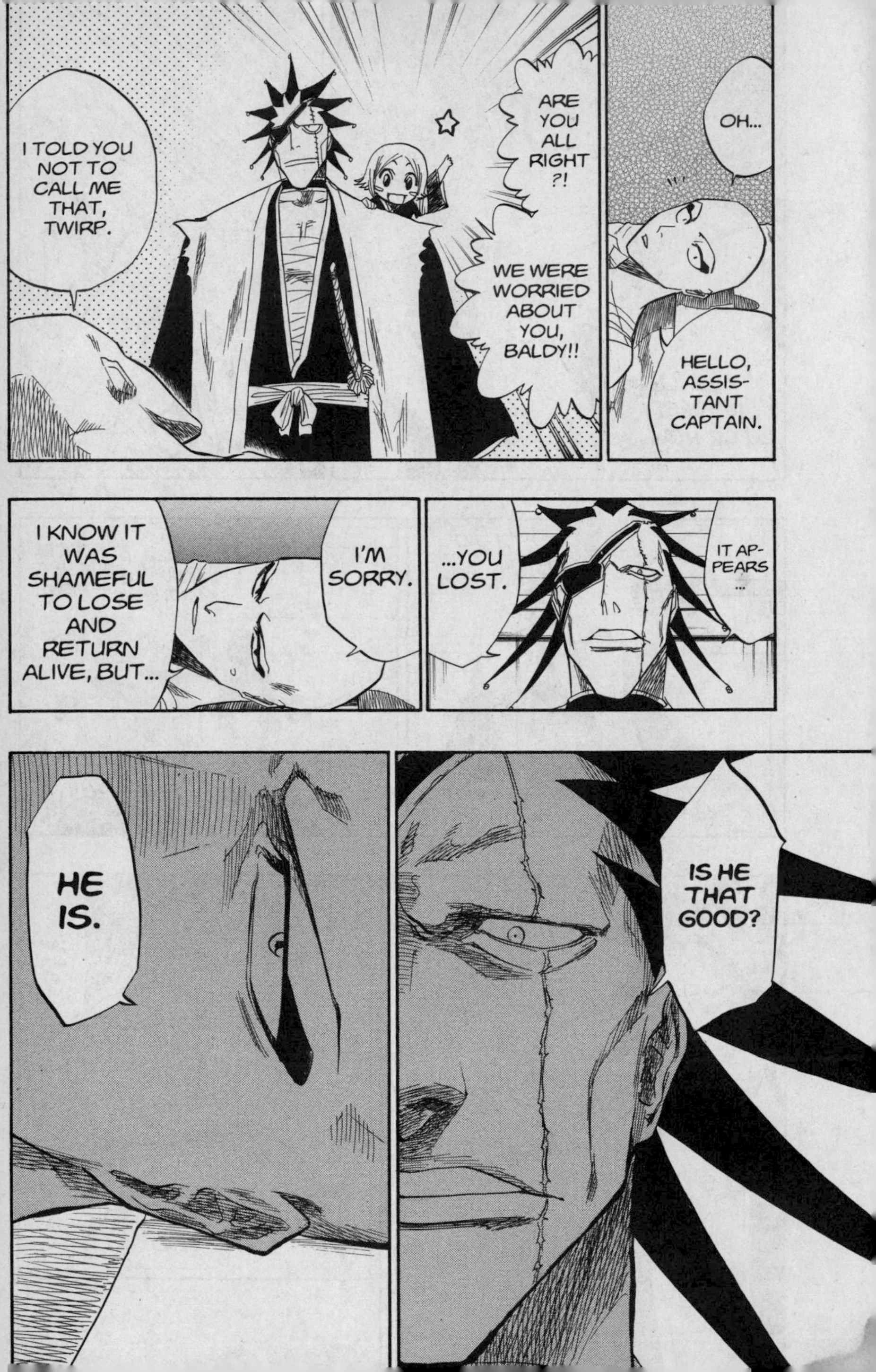
OH...
HELLO, ASSISTANT CAPTAIN.
ARE YOU ALL RIGHT?!
WE WERE WORRIED ABOUT YOU, BALDY!!
I TOLD YOU NOT TO CALL ME THAT, TWIRP.
IT APPEARS...
...YOU LOST.
I'M SORRY.
I KNOW IT WAS SHAMEFUL TO LOSE AND RETURN ALIVE, BUT...
IS HE THAT GOOD?
HE IS.

READ THIS WAY

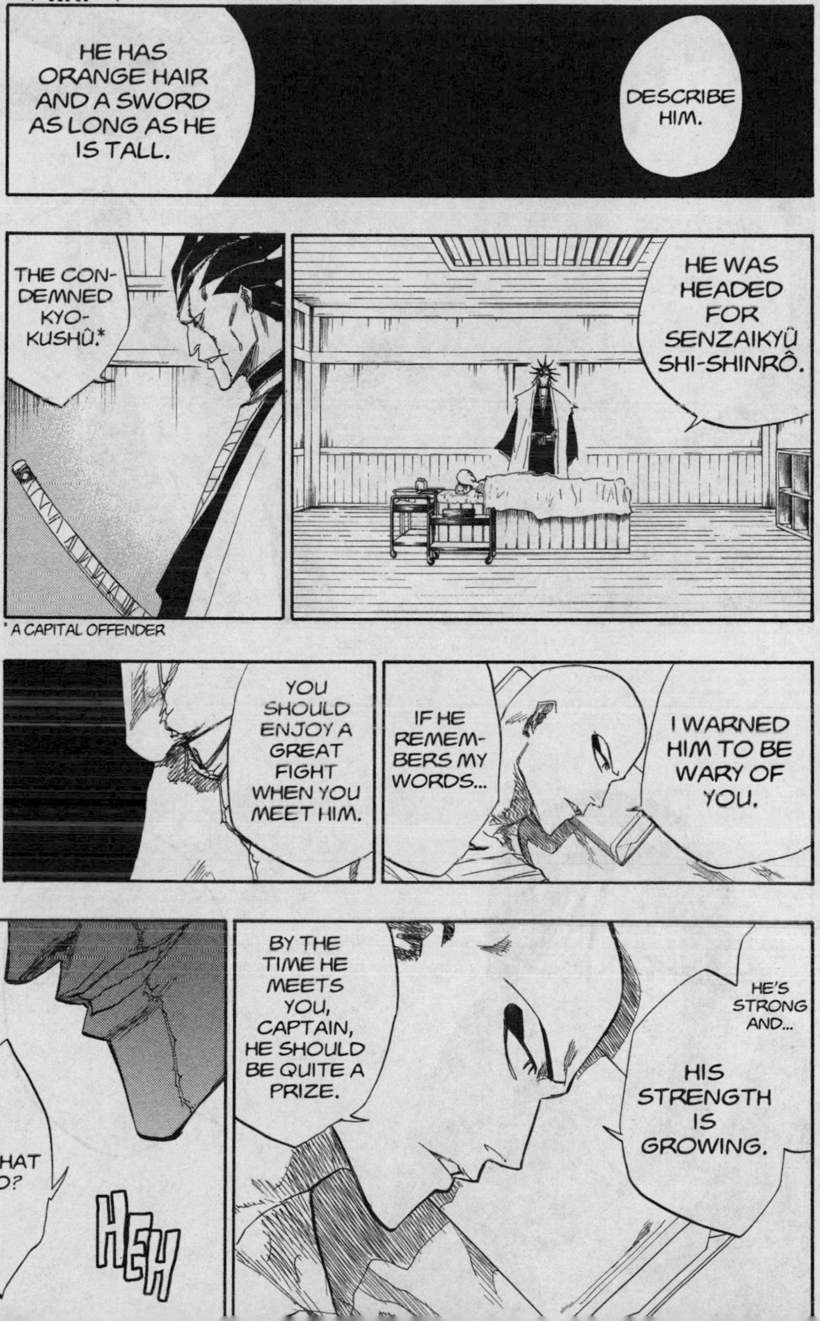
DESCRIBE HIM.
HE HAS ORANGE HAIR AND A SWORD AS LONG AS HE IS TALL.
HE WAS HEADED FOR SENZAIKYŪ SHI-SHINRÔ.
THE CONDEMNED KYOKUSHÛ.*
I WARNED HIM TO BE WARY OF YOU.
IF HE REMEMBERS MY WORDS...
YOU SHOULD ENJOY A GREAT FIGHT WHEN YOU MEET HIM.
HE'S STRONG AND...
HIS STRENGTH IS GROWING.
BY THE TIME HE MEETS YOU, CAPTAIN, HE SHOULD BE QUITE A PRIZE.
IS THAT SO?
HEH

* A CAPITAL OFFENDER

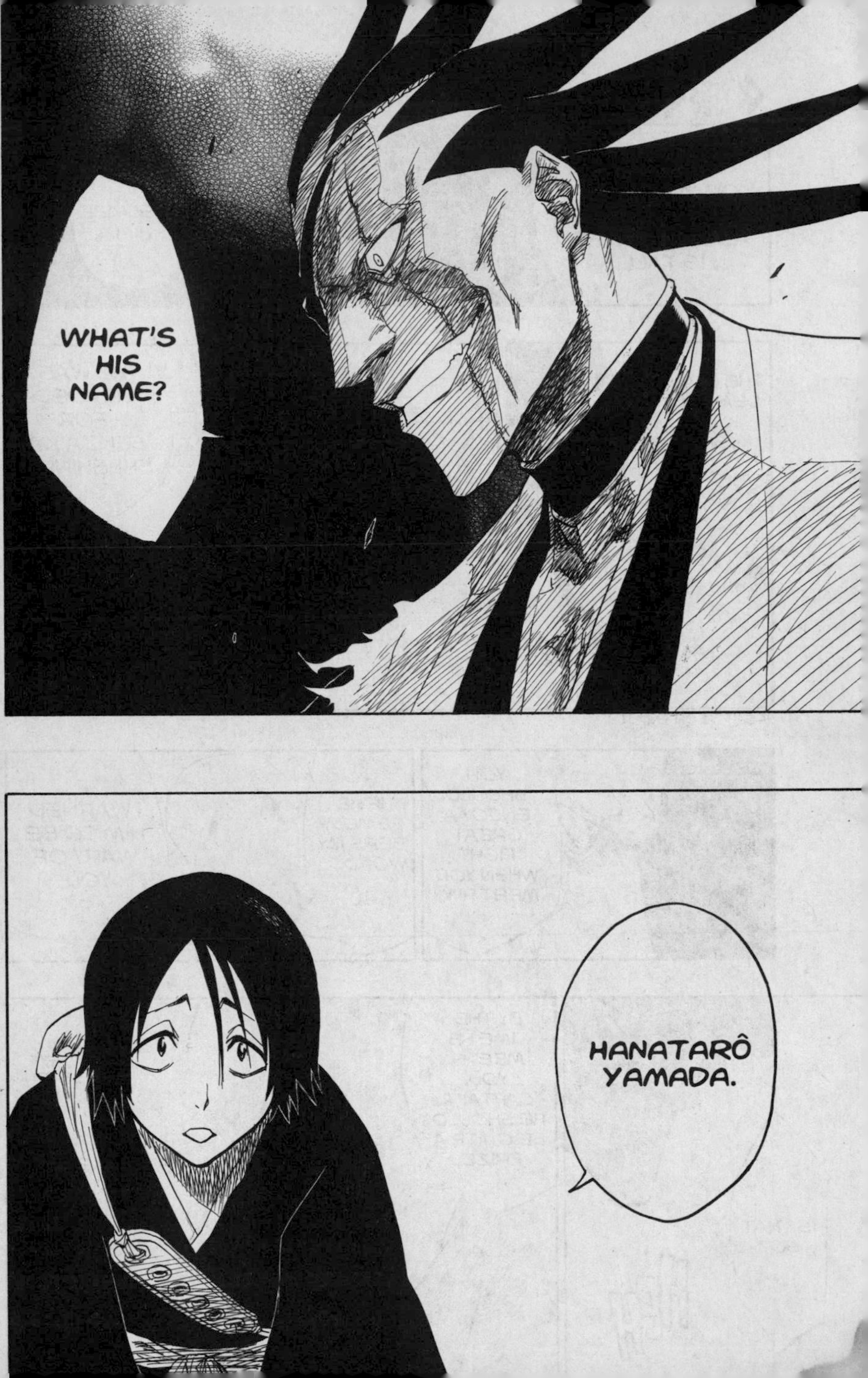
WHAT'S HIS NAME?
HANATARÔ YAMADA.

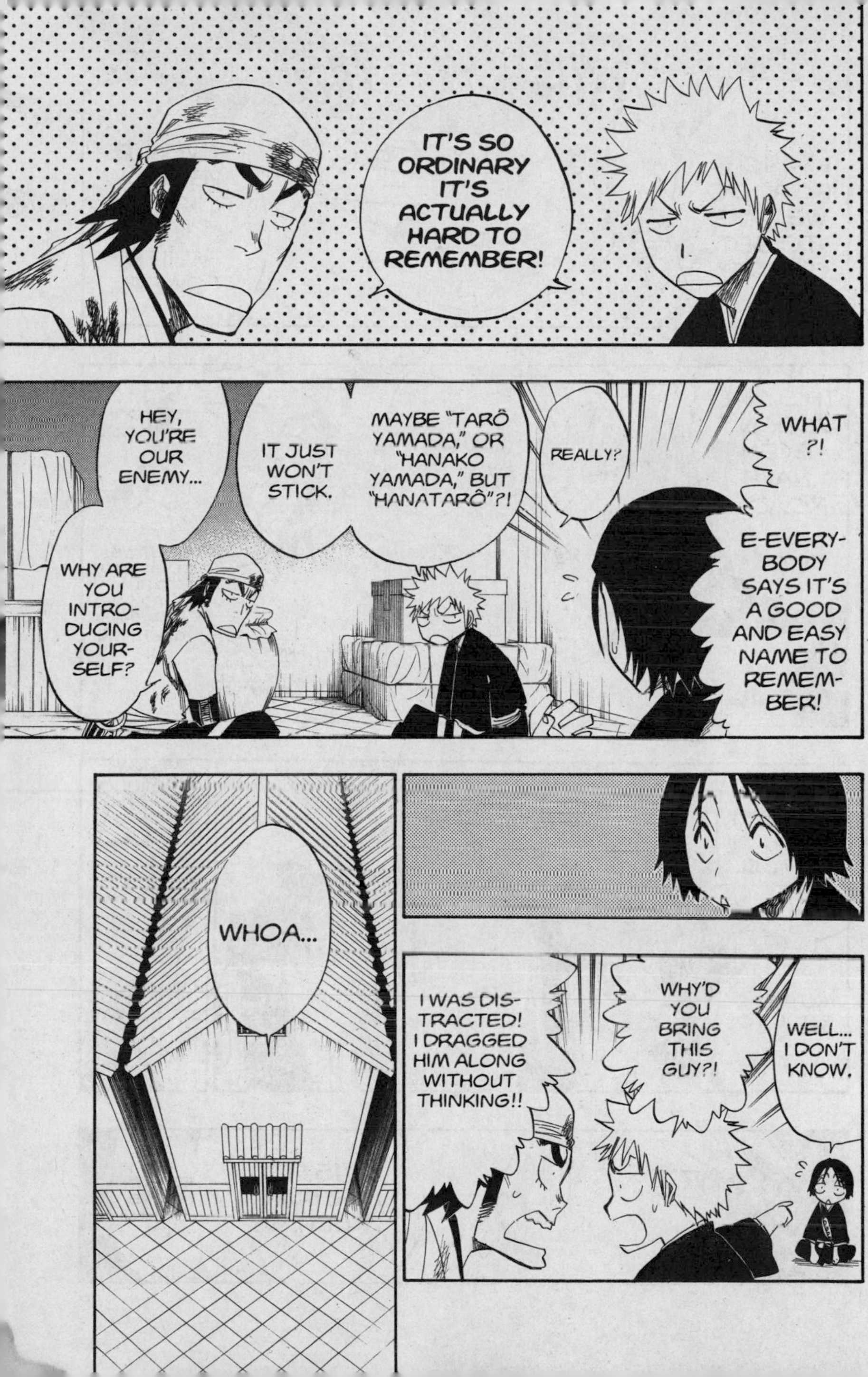
IT'S SO ORDINARY IT'S ACTUALLY HARD TO REMEMBER!
WHAT?!
E-EVERYBODY SAYS IT'S A GOOD AND EASY NAME TO REMEMBER!
REALLY?
MAYBE "TARÔ YAMADA," OR "HANAKO YAMADA," BUT "HANATARÔ"?!
IT JUST WON'T STICK.
HEY, YOU'RE OUR ENEMY...
WHY ARE YOU INTRODUCING YOURSELF?
WELL... I DON'T KNOW.
WHY'D YOU BRING THIS GUY?!
I WAS DISTRACTED! I DRAGGED HIM ALONG WITHOUT THINKING!!
WHOA...

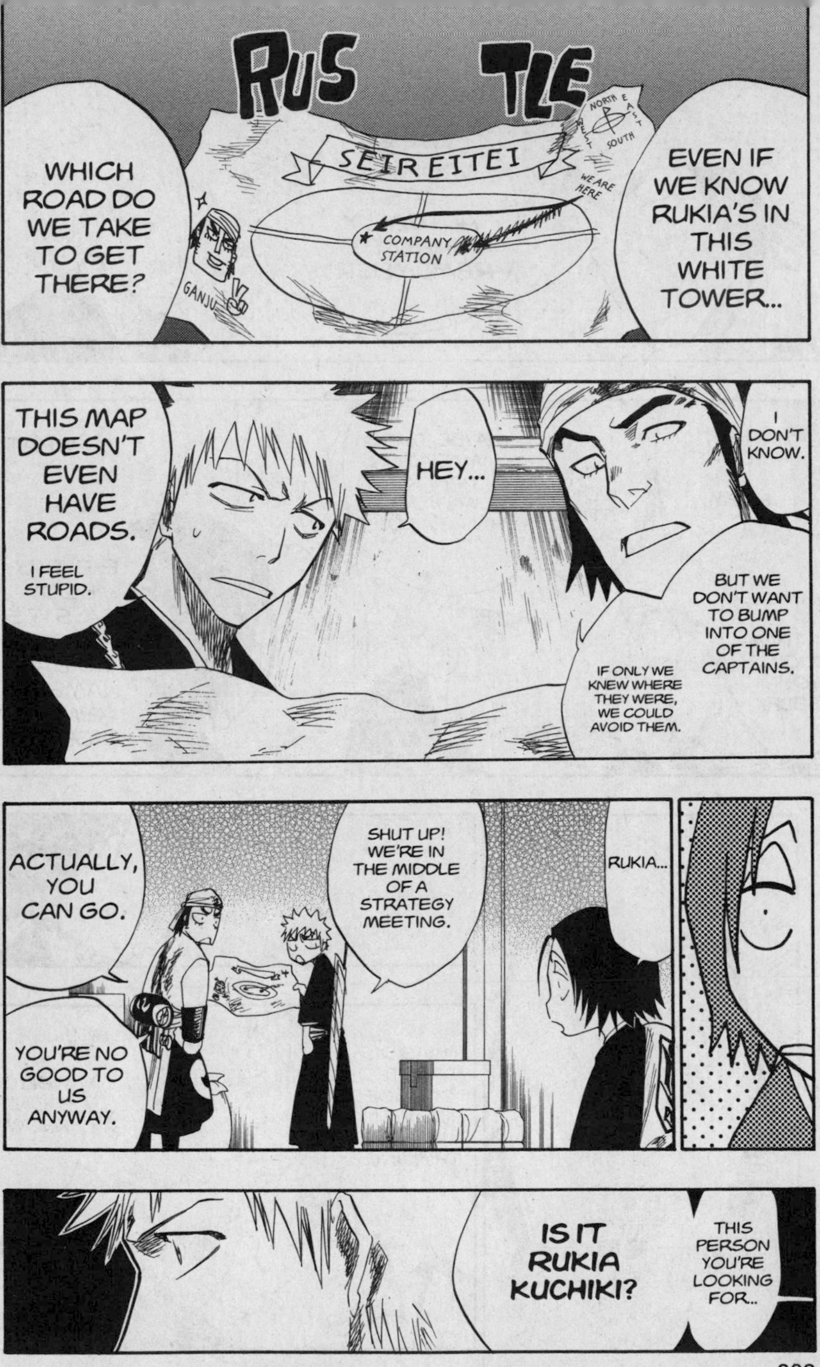
RUSTLE
SEIREITEI
NORTH EAST WEST SOUTH
WE ARE HERE
COMPANY STATION
GANJU
EVEN IF WE KNOW RUKIA'S IN THIS WHITE TOWER...
WHICH ROAD DO WE TAKE TO GET THERE?
I DON'T KNOW.
BUT WE DON'T WANT TO BUMP INTO ONE OF THE CAPTAINS.
IF ONLY WE KNEW WHERE THEY WERE, WE COULD AVOID THEM.
HEY...
THIS MAP DOESN'T EVEN HAVE ROADS.
I FEEL STUPID.
RUKIA...
SHUT UP! WE'RE IN THE MIDDLE OF A STRATEGY MEETING.
ACTUALLY, YOU CAN GO.
YOU'RE NO GOOD TO US ANYWAY.
THIS PERSON YOU'RE LOOKING FOR..
IS IT RUKIA KUCHIKI?

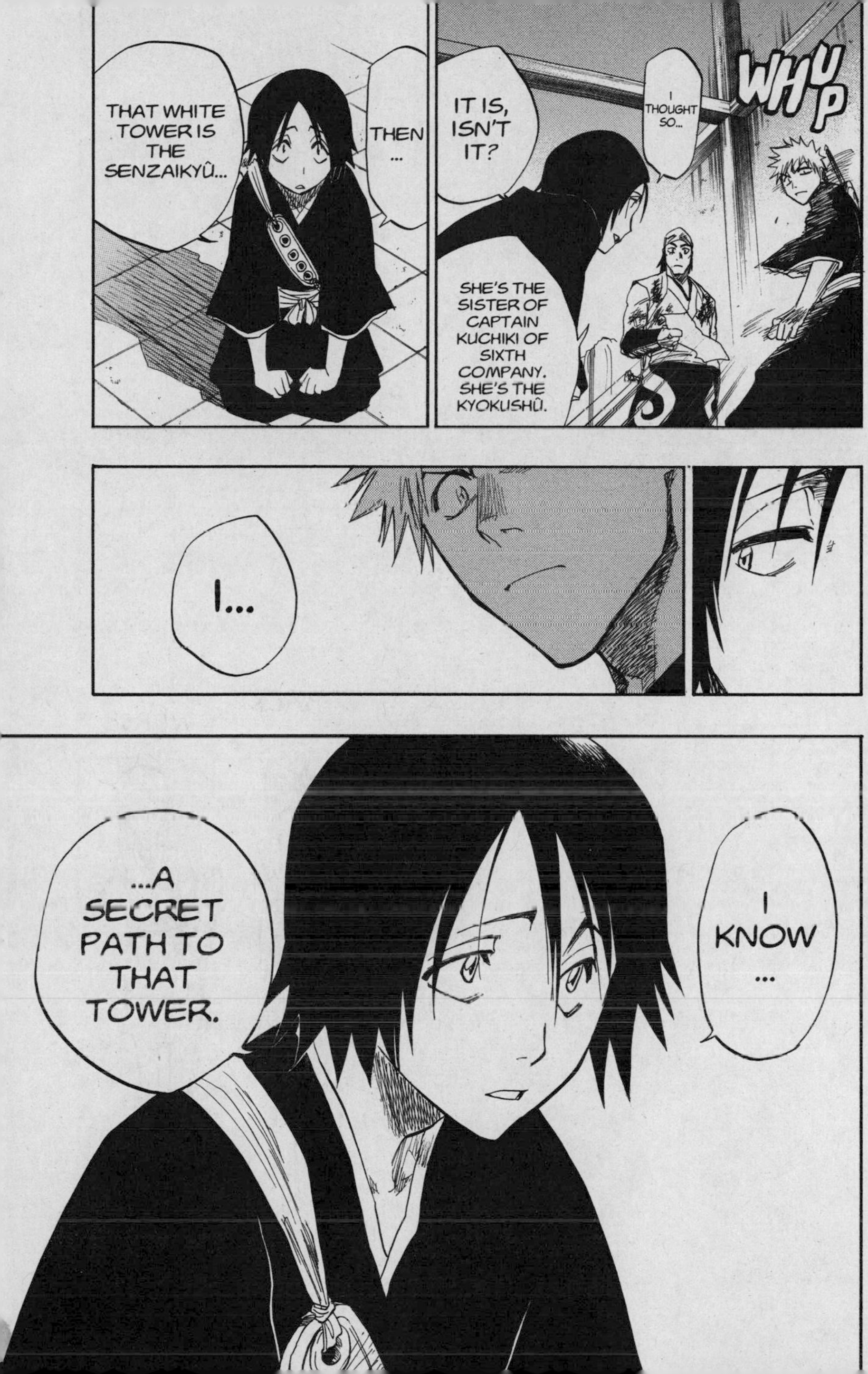
WHUP
I THOUGHT SO...
IT IS, ISN'T IT?
SHE'S THE SISTER OF CAPTAIN KUCHIKI OF SIXTH COMPANY. SHE'S THE KYOKUSHÛ.
THEN...
THAT WHITE TOWER IS THE SENZAIKYÛ...
I...
I KNOW...
...A SECRET PATH TO THAT TOWER.

BACK NURSE

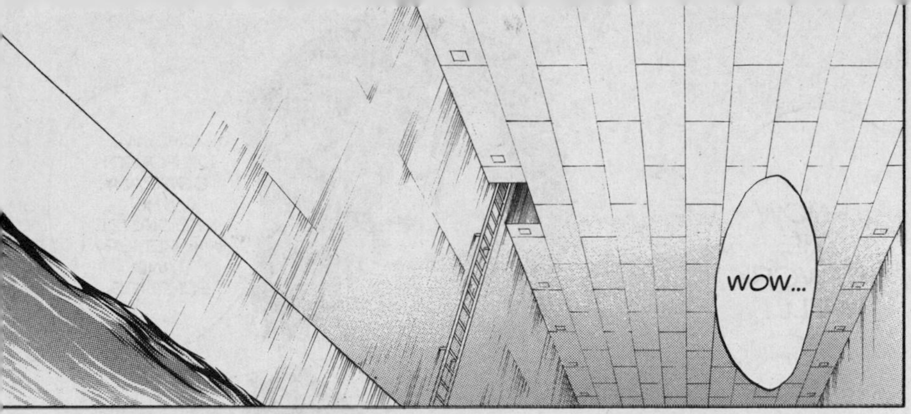
WOW...

94. A Jail Named Remorse

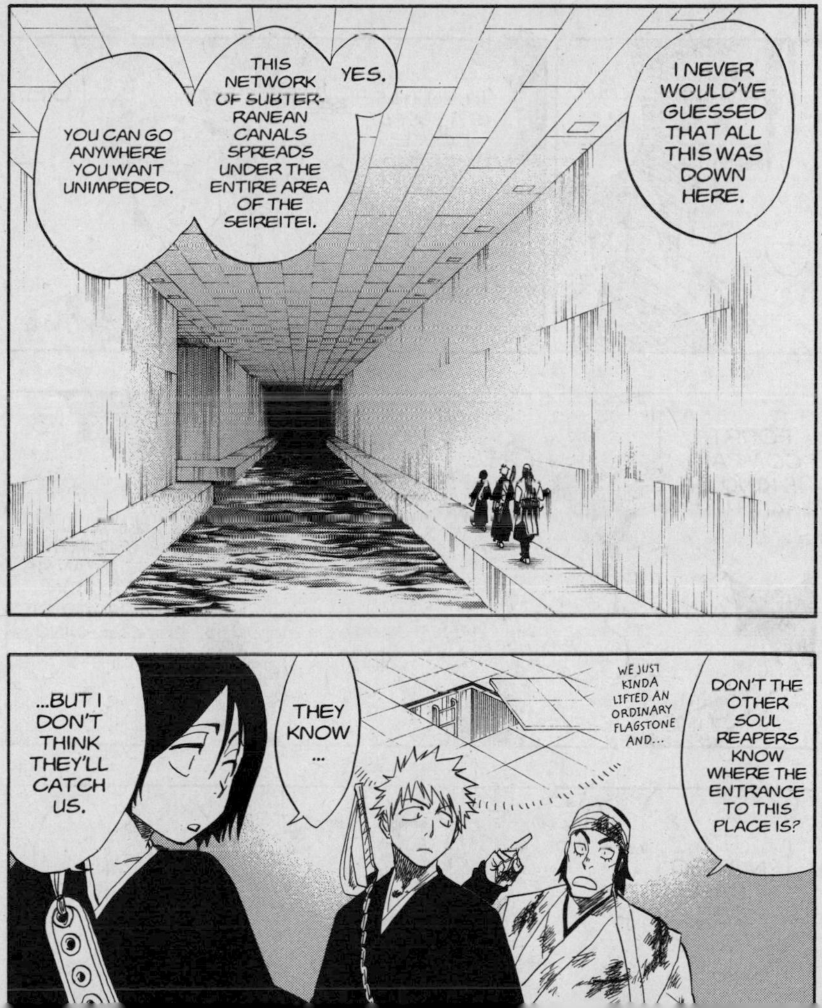
I NEVER WOULD'VE GUESSED THAT ALL THIS WAS DOWN HERE.
YES.
THIS NETWORK OF SUBTER-RANEAN CANALS SPREADS UNDER THE ENTIRE AREA OF THE SEIREITEI.
YOU CAN GO ANYWHERE YOU WANT UNIMPEDED.
DON'T THE OTHER SOUL REAPERS KNOW WHERE THE ENTRANCE TO THIS PLACE IS?
WE JUST KINDA LIFTED AN ORDINARY FLAGSTONE AND...
THEY KNOW...
...BUT I DON'T THINK THEY'LL CATCH US.

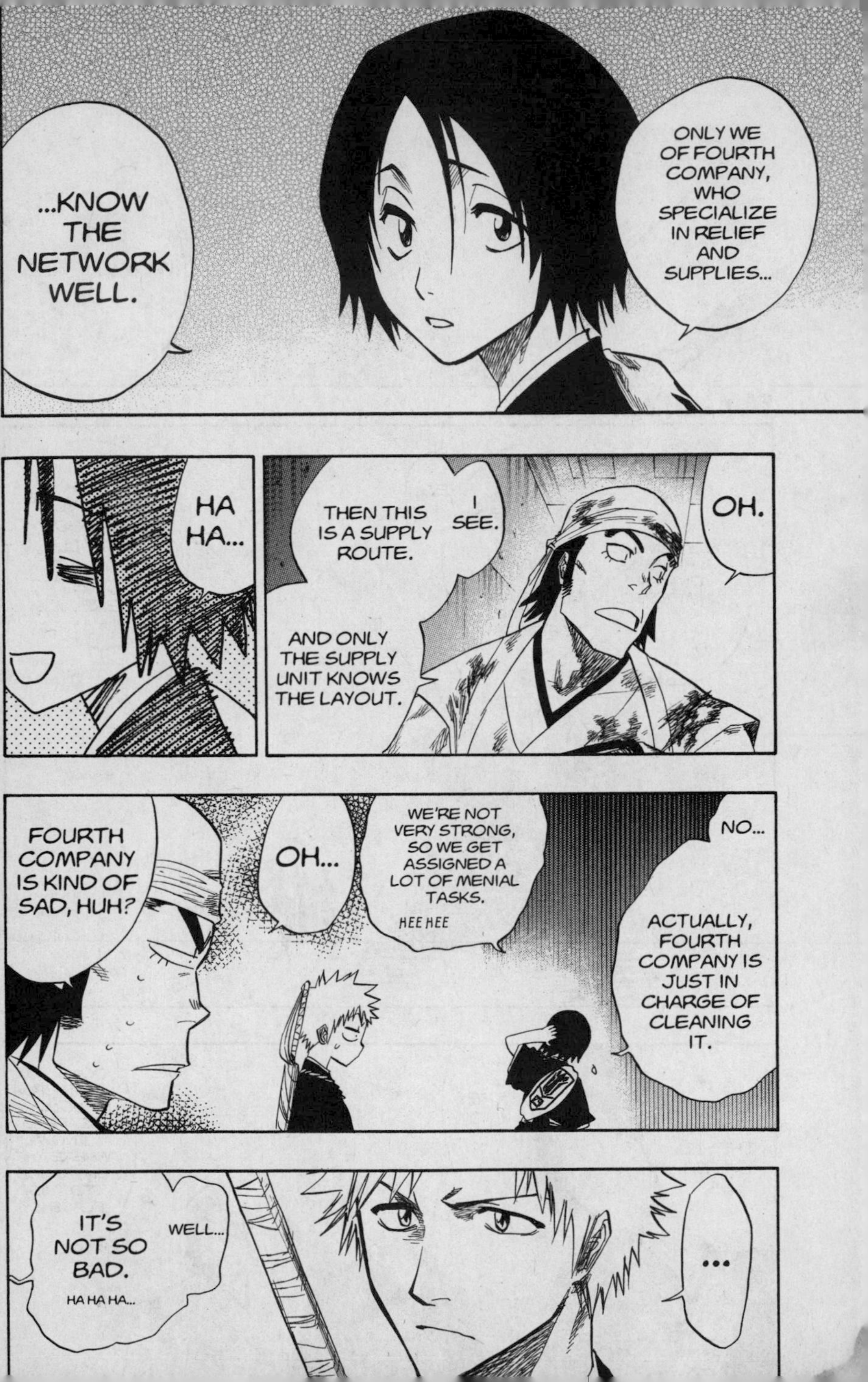
ONLY WE OF FOURTH COMPANY, WHO SPECIALIZE IN RELIEF AND SUPPLIES...
...KNOW THE NETWORK WELL.
OH.
I SEE.
THEN THIS IS A SUPPLY ROUTE.
AND ONLY THE SUPPLY UNIT KNOWS THE LAYOUT.
HA HA...
NO...
ACTUALLY, FOURTH COMPANY IS JUST IN CHARGE OF CLEANING IT.
WE'RE NOT VERY STRONG, SO WE GET ASSIGNED A LOT OF MENIAL TASKS.
HEE HEE
OH...
FOURTH COMPANY IS KIND OF SAD, HUH?
...
WELL...
IT'S NOT SO BAD.
HA HA HA...

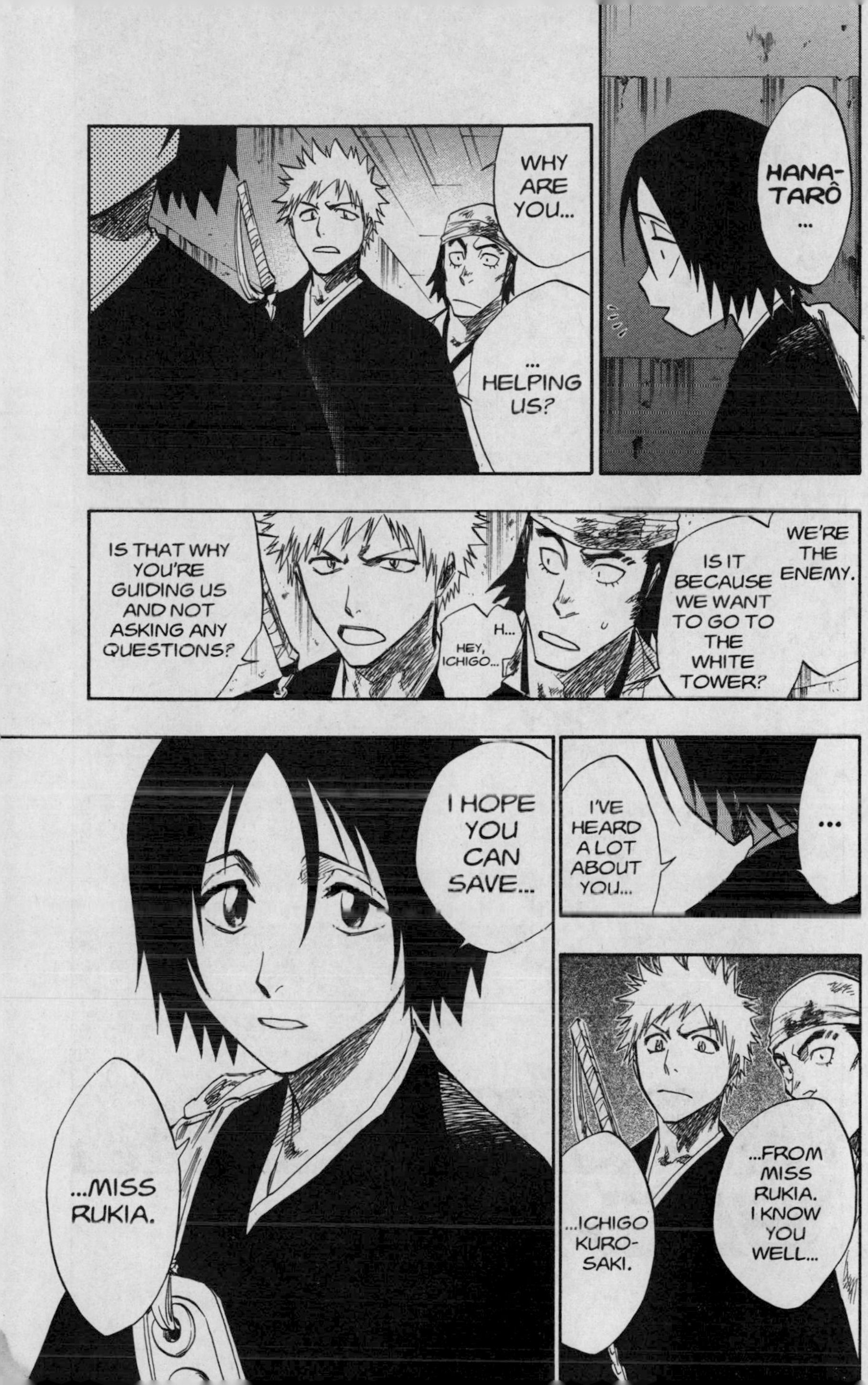
HANA-TARÔ ...
WHY ARE YOU...
... HELPING US?
WE'RE THE ENEMY.
IS IT BECAUSE WE WANT TO GO TO THE WHITE TOWER?
H... HEY, ICHIGO...
IS THAT WHY YOU'RE GUIDING US AND NOT ASKING ANY QUESTIONS?
...
I'VE HEARD A LOT ABOUT YOU...
...FROM MISS RUKIA. I KNOW YOU WELL...
...ICHIGO KUROSAKI.
I HOPE YOU CAN SAVE...
...MISS RUKIA.

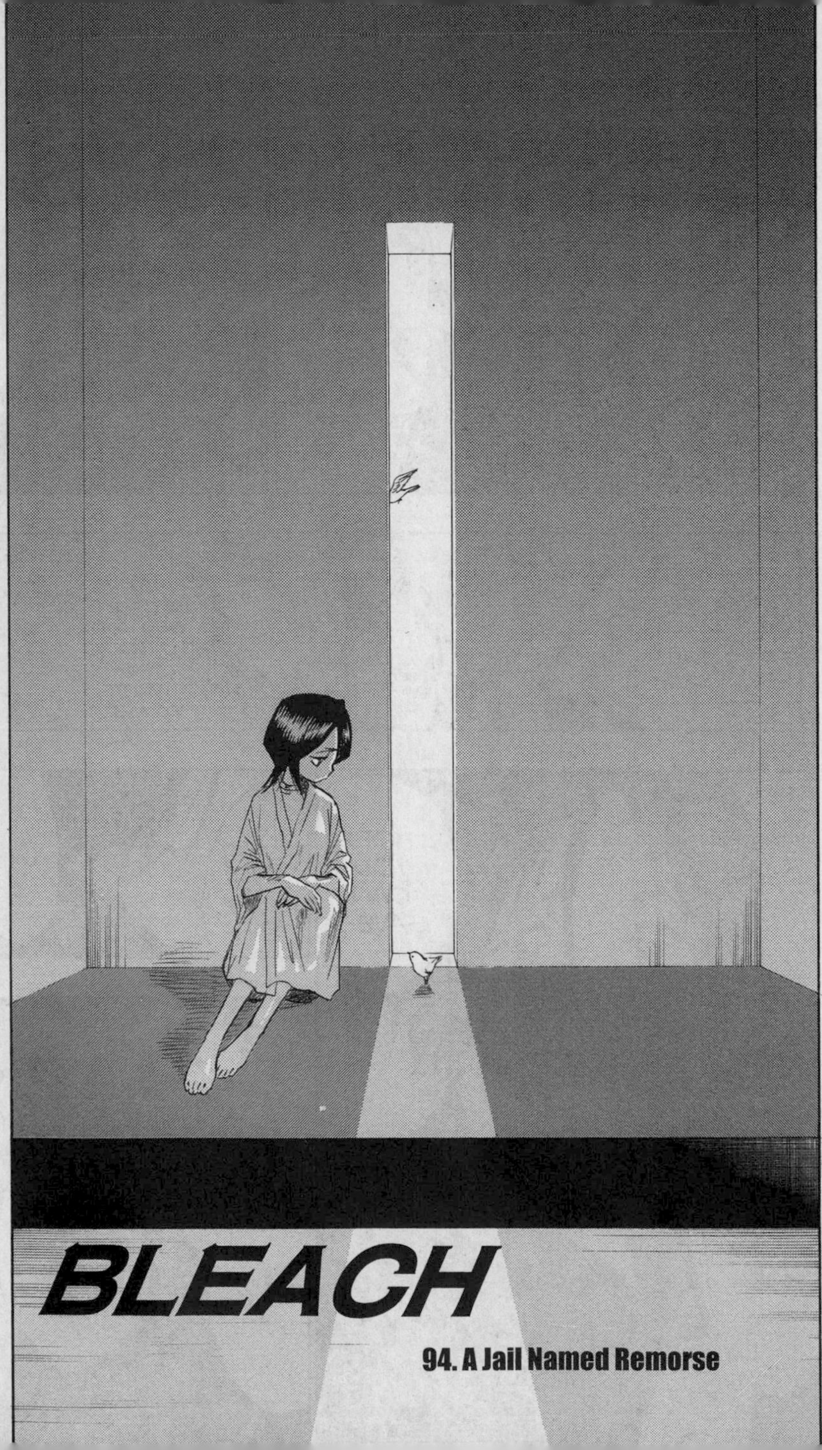
BLEACH
94. A Jail Named Remorse

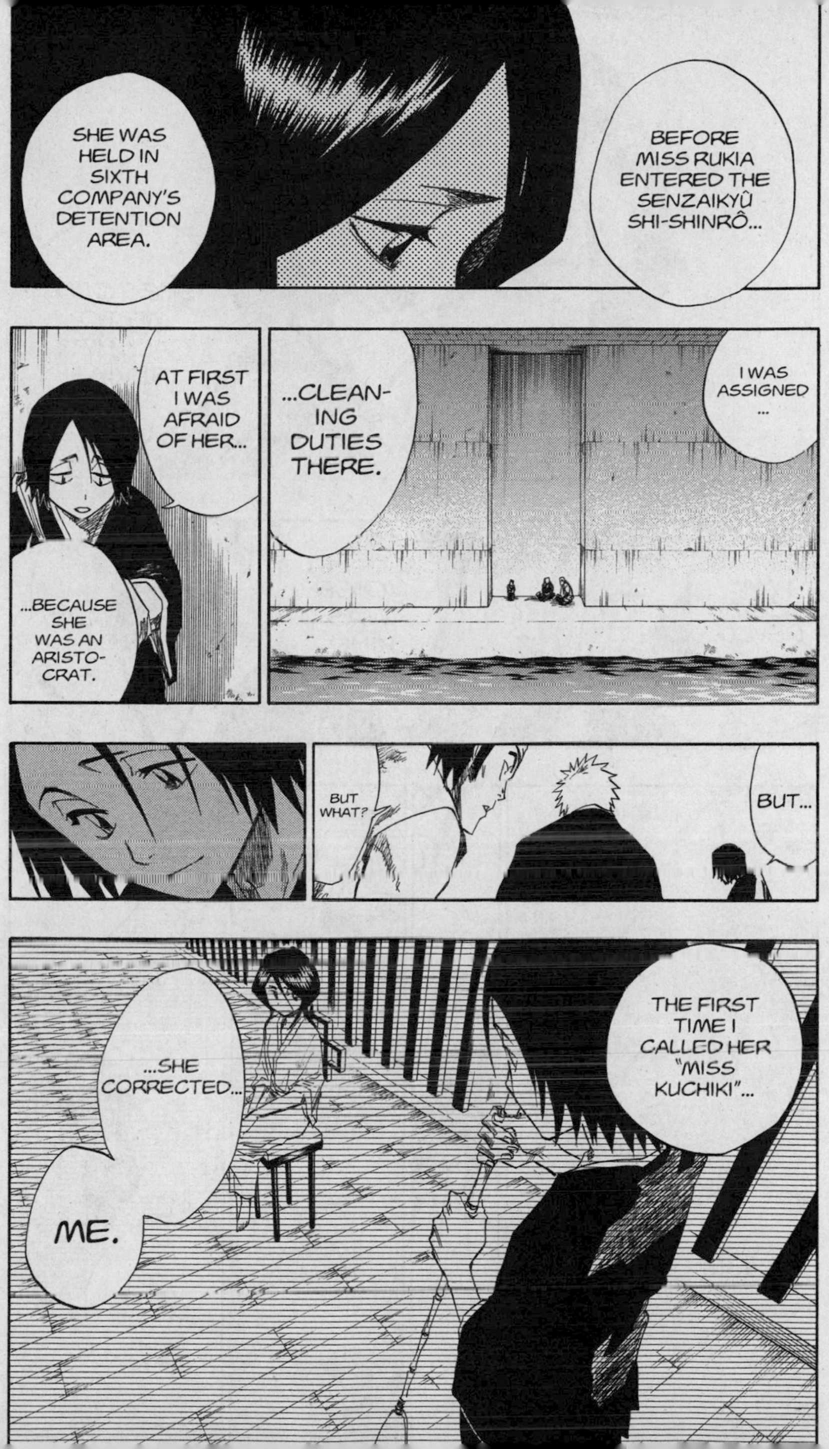
BEFORE MISS RUKIA ENTERED THE SENZAIKYÛ SHI-SHINRÔ...
SHE WAS HELD IN SIXTH COMPANY'S DETENTION AREA.
I WAS ASSIGNED ...
...CLEAN-ING DUTIES THERE.
AT FIRST I WAS AFRAID OF HER...
...BECAUSE SHE WAS AN ARISTO-CRAT.
BUT...
BUT WHAT?
THE FIRST TIME I CALLED HER "MISS KUCHIKI"...
...SHE CORRECTED...
ME.

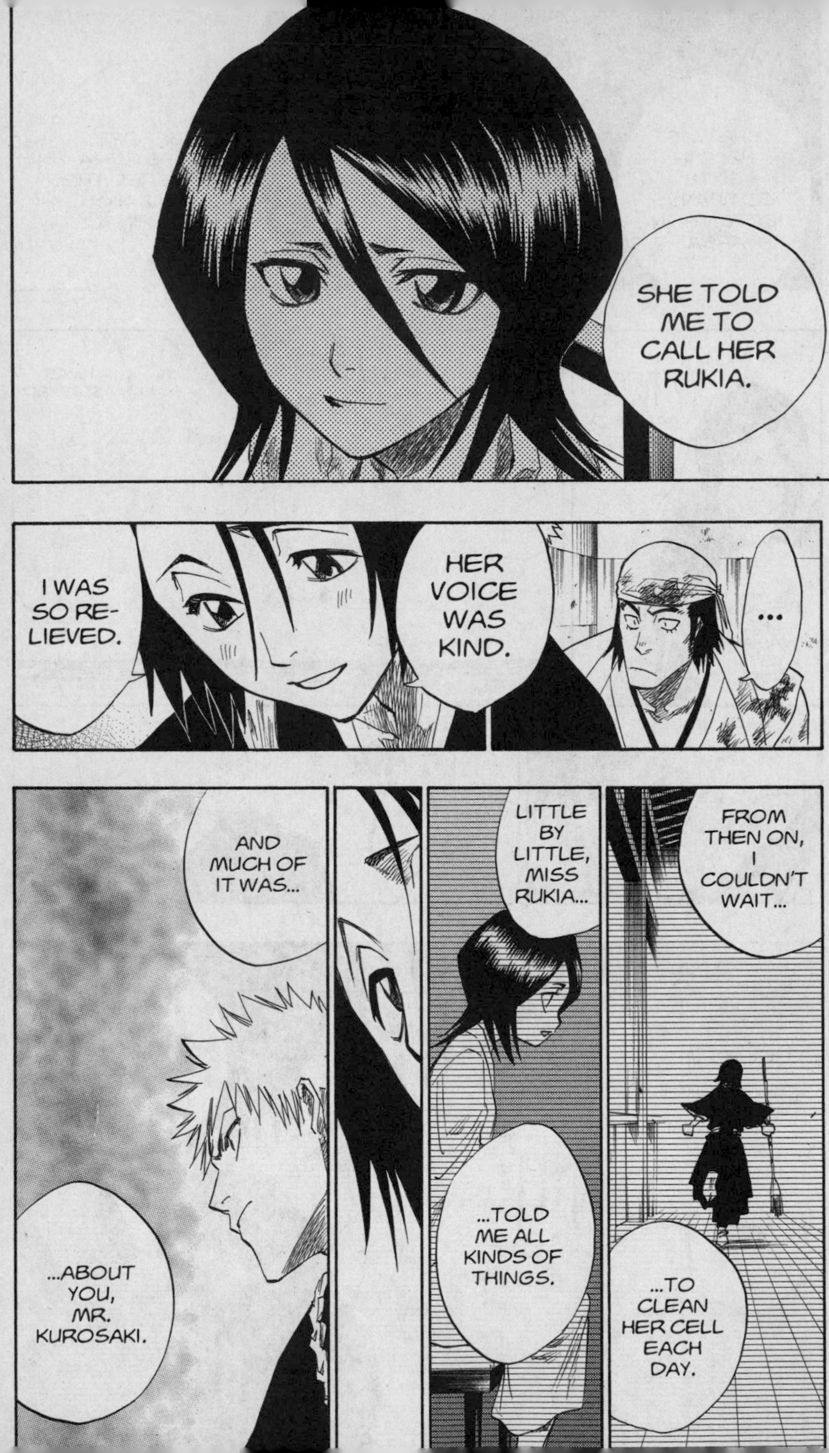
SHE TOLD ME TO CALL HER RUKIA.
...
HER VOICE WAS KIND.
I WAS SO RE-LIEVED.
FROM THEN ON, I COULDN'T WAIT...
...TO CLEAN HER CELL EACH DAY.
LITTLE BY LITTLE, MISS RUKIA...
...TOLD ME ALL KINDS OF THINGS.
AND MUCH OF IT WAS...
...ABOUT YOU, MR. KUROSAKI.

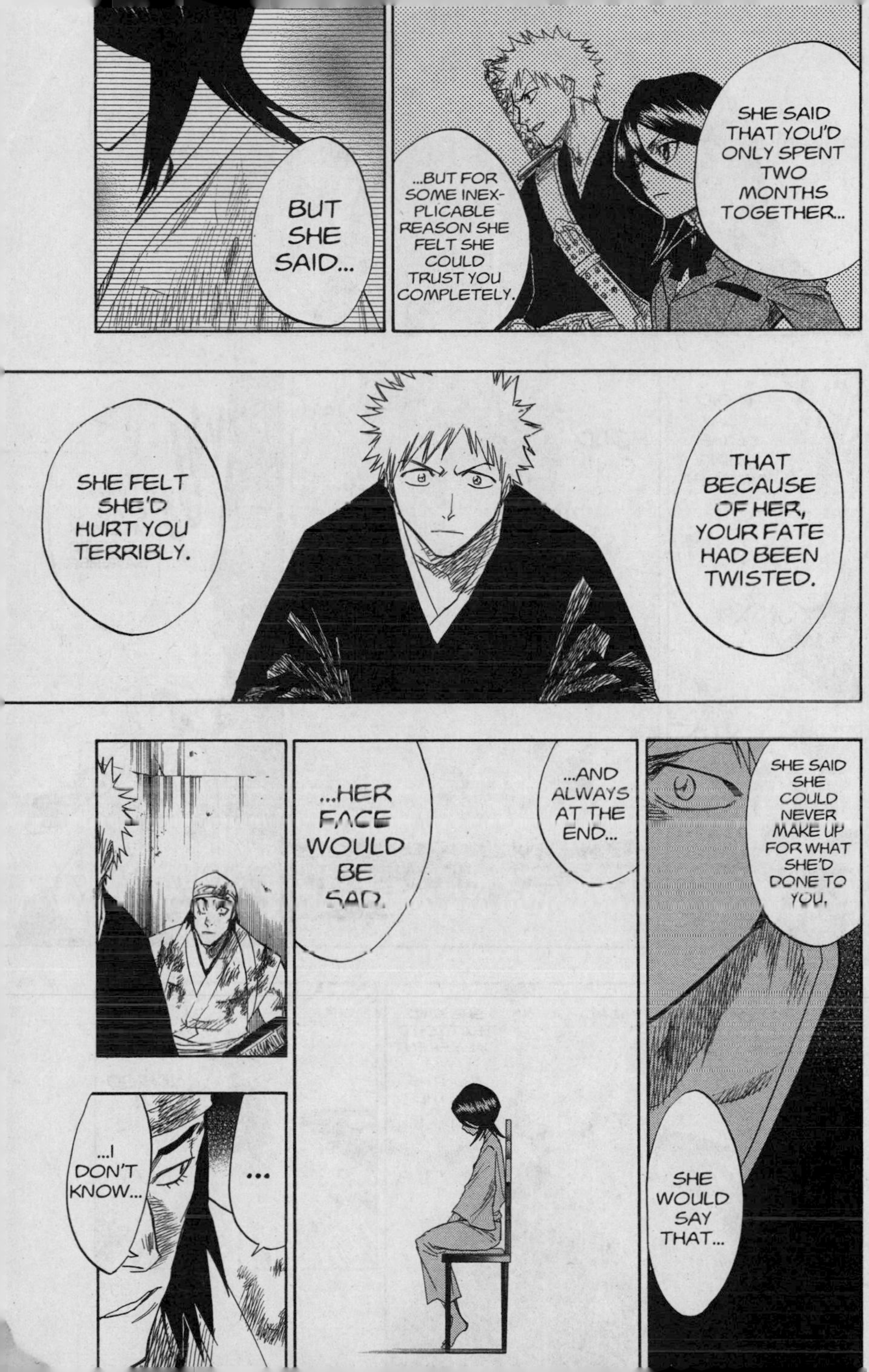
SHE SAID THAT YOU'D ONLY SPENT TWO MONTHS TOGETHER...
...BUT FOR SOME INEXPLICABLE REASON SHE FELT SHE COULD TRUST YOU COMPLETELY.
BUT SHE SAID...
THAT BECAUSE OF HER, YOUR FATE HAD BEEN TWISTED.
SHE FELT SHE'D HURT YOU TERRIBLY.
SHE SAID SHE COULD NEVER MAKE UP FOR WHAT SHE'D DONE TO YOU.
SHE WOULD SAY THAT...
...AND ALWAYS AT THE END...
...HER FACE WOULD BE SAD.
...
...I DON'T KNOW...

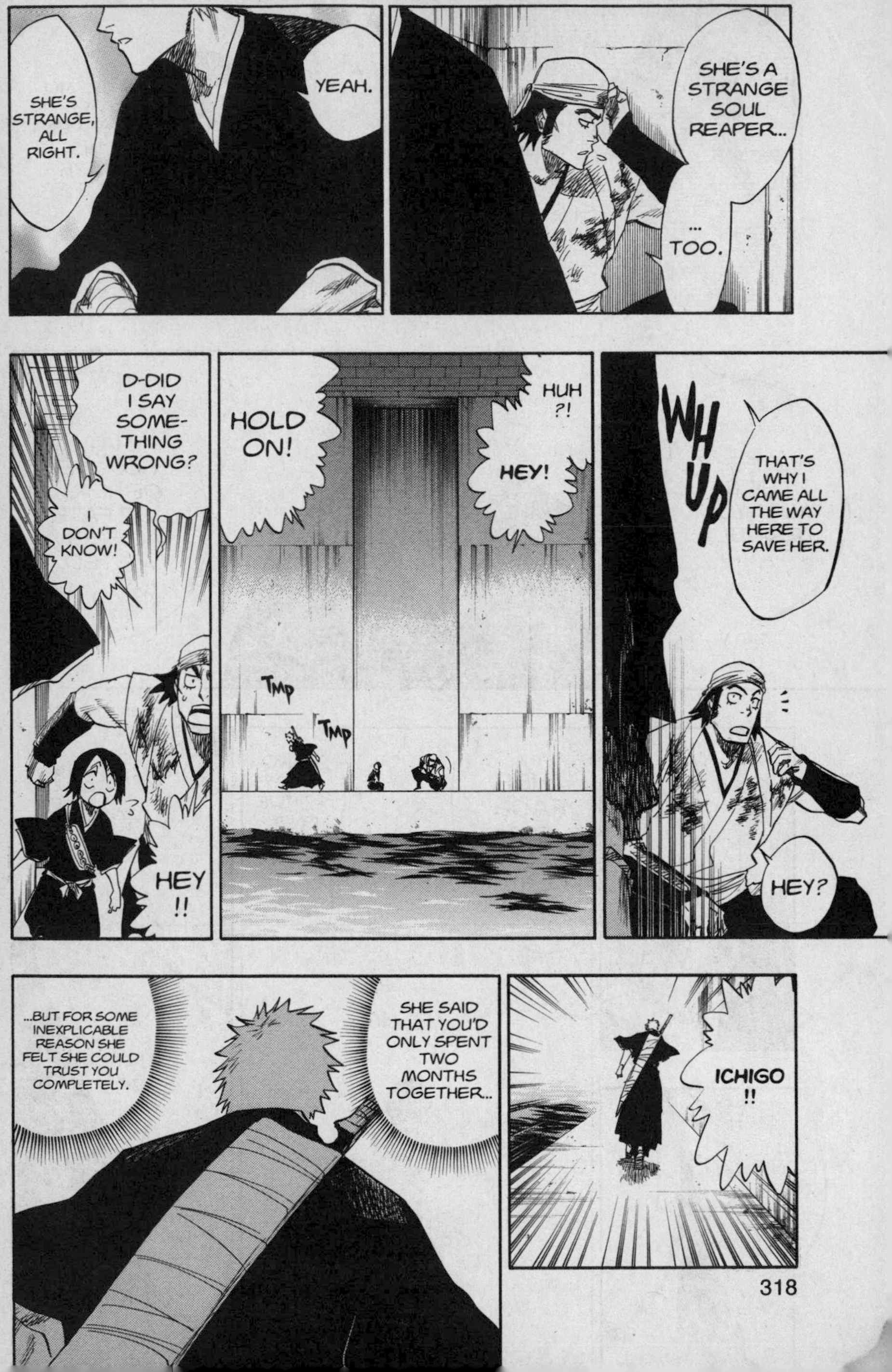
SHE'S A STRANGE SOUL REAPER..
... TOO.
YEAH.
SHE'S STRANGE, ALL RIGHT.
WHUP
THAT'S WHY I CAME ALL THE WAY HERE TO SAVE HER.
HEY?
HUH ?!
HEY!
HOLD ON!
TMP
TMP
D-DID I SAY SOME-THING WRONG?
I DON'T KNOW!
HEY !!
ICHIGO !!
SHE SAID THAT YOU'D ONLY SPENT TWO MONTHS TOGETHER..
...BUT FOR SOME INEXPLICABLE REASON SHE FELT SHE COULD TRUST YOU COMPLETELY.

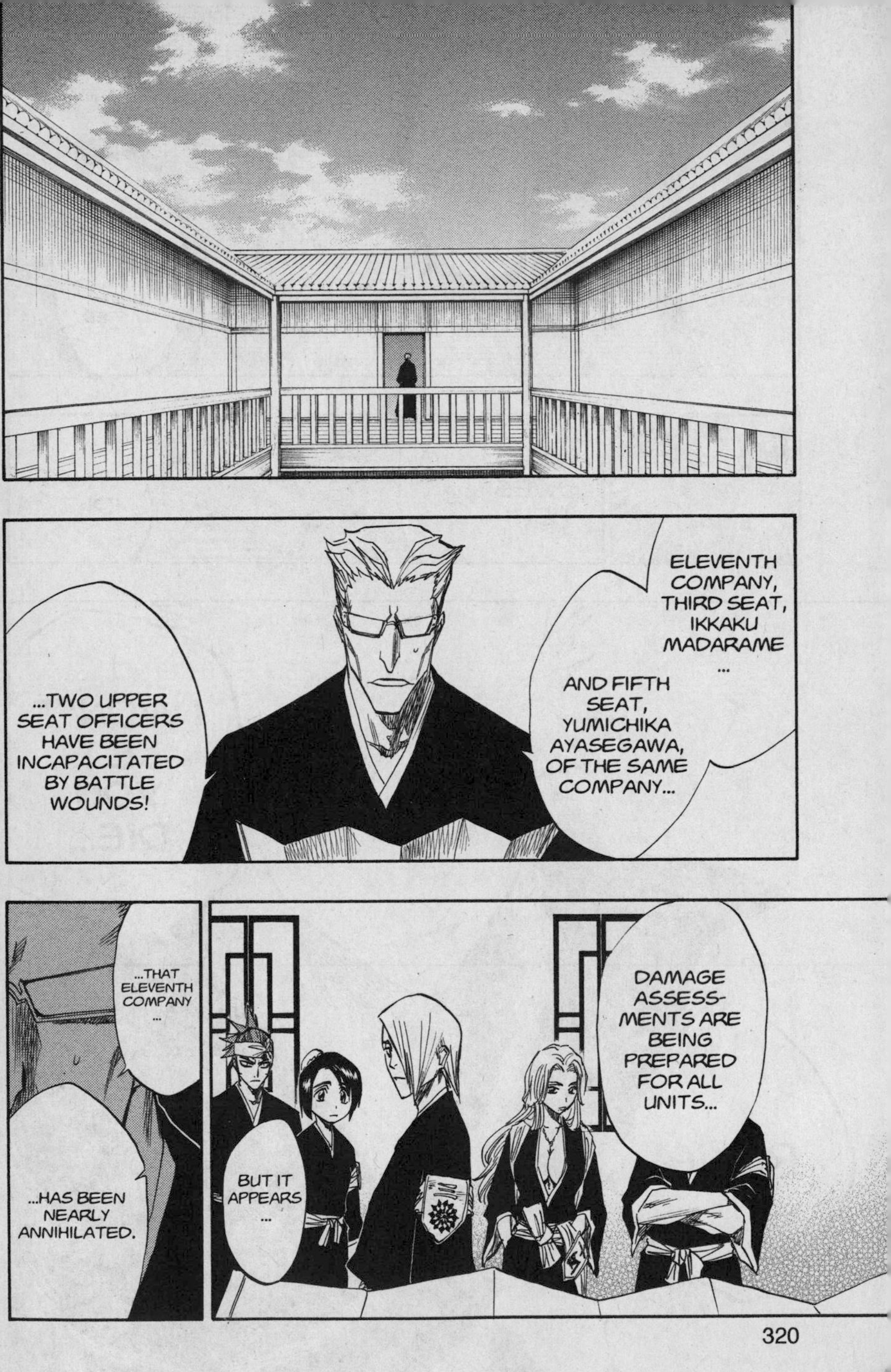
ELEVENTH COMPANY, THIRD SEAT, IKKAKU MADARAME ...
AND FIFTH SEAT, YUMICHIKA AYASEGAWA, OF THE SAME COMPANY...
...TWO UPPER SEAT OFFICERS HAVE BEEN INCAPACITATED BY BATTLE WOUNDS!
DAMAGE ASSESS-MENTS ARE BEING PREPARED FOR ALL UNITS...
BUT IT APPEARS ...
...THAT ELEVENTH COMPANY ...
...HAS BEEN NEARLY ANNIHILATED.

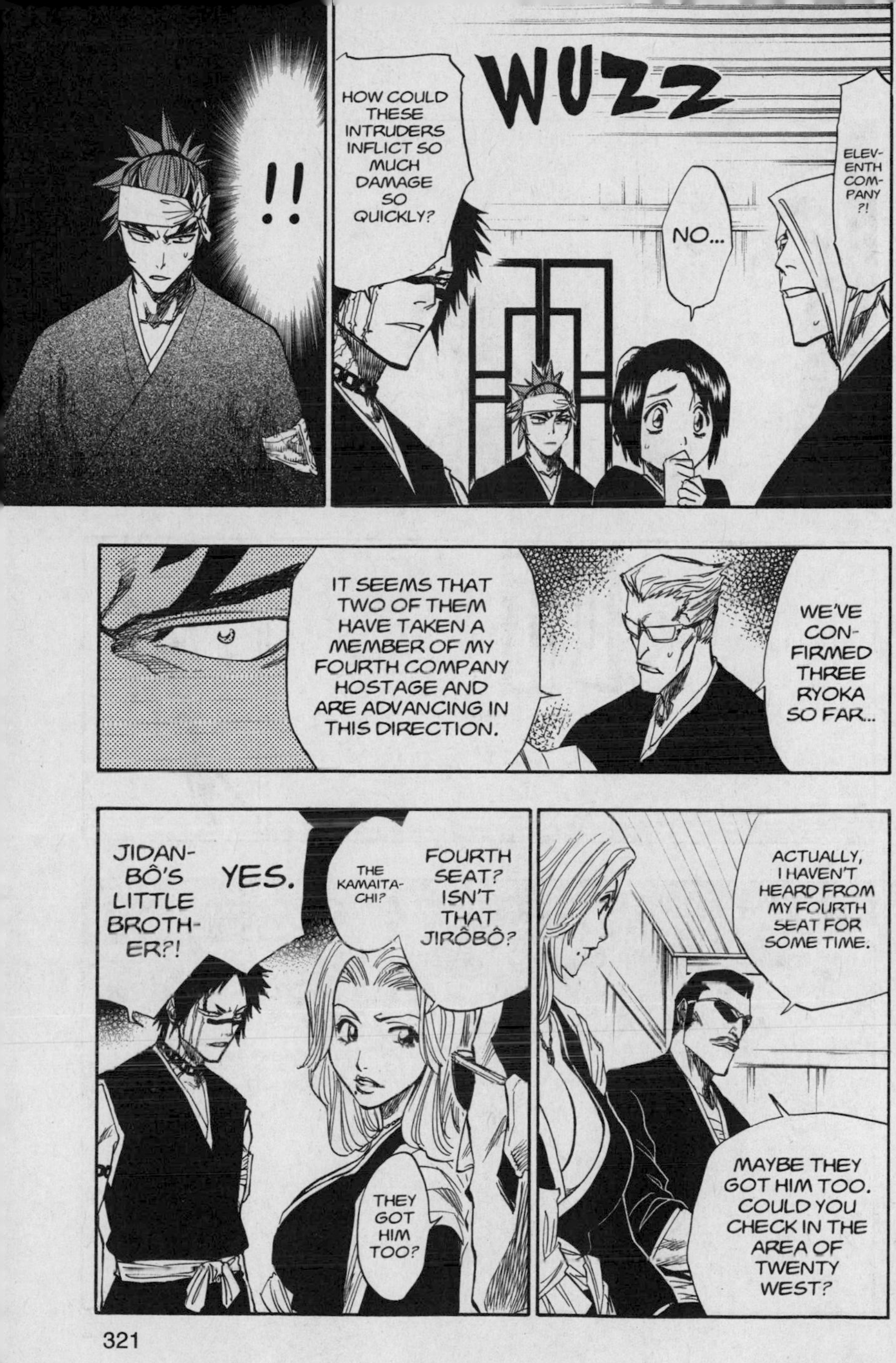
ELEVENTH COMPANY?!
NO...
WUZZ
HOW COULD THESE INTRUDERS INFLICT SO MUCH DAMAGE SO QUICKLY?
!!
WE'VE CONFIRMED THREE RYOKA SO FAR...
IT SEEMS THAT TWO OF THEM HAVE TAKEN A MEMBER OF MY FOURTH COMPANY HOSTAGE AND ARE ADVANCING IN THIS DIRECTION.
ACTUALLY, I HAVEN'T HEARD FROM MY FOURTH SEAT FOR SOME TIME.
MAYBE THEY GOT HIM TOO. COULD YOU CHECK IN THE AREA OF TWENTY WEST?
FOURTH SEAT? ISN'T THAT JIRÔBÔ?
THE KAMAITACHI?
YES.
JIDANBÔ'S LITTLE BROTHER?!
THEY GOT HIM TOO?

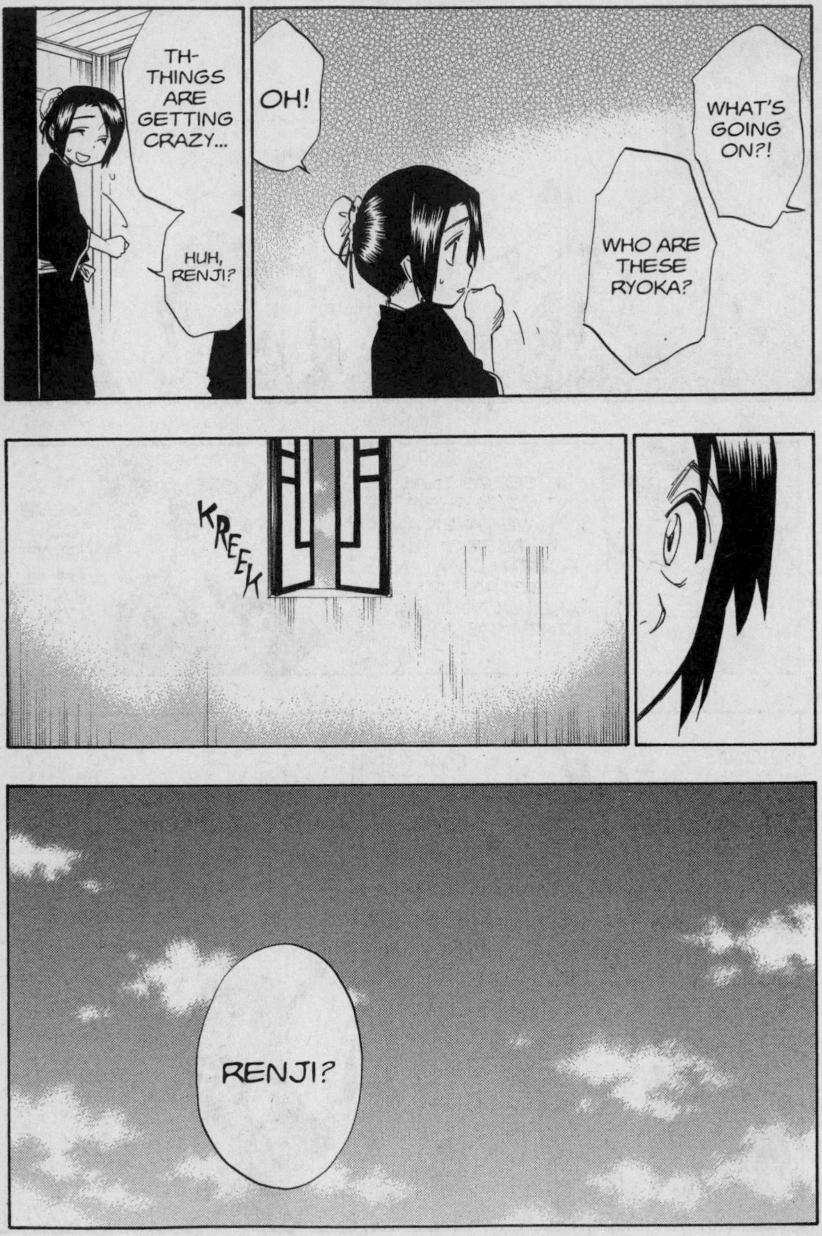
WHAT'S GOING ON?!
WHO ARE THESE RYOKA?
OH!
TH-THINGS ARE GETTING CRAZY...
HUH, RENJI?
KREEEK
RENJI?

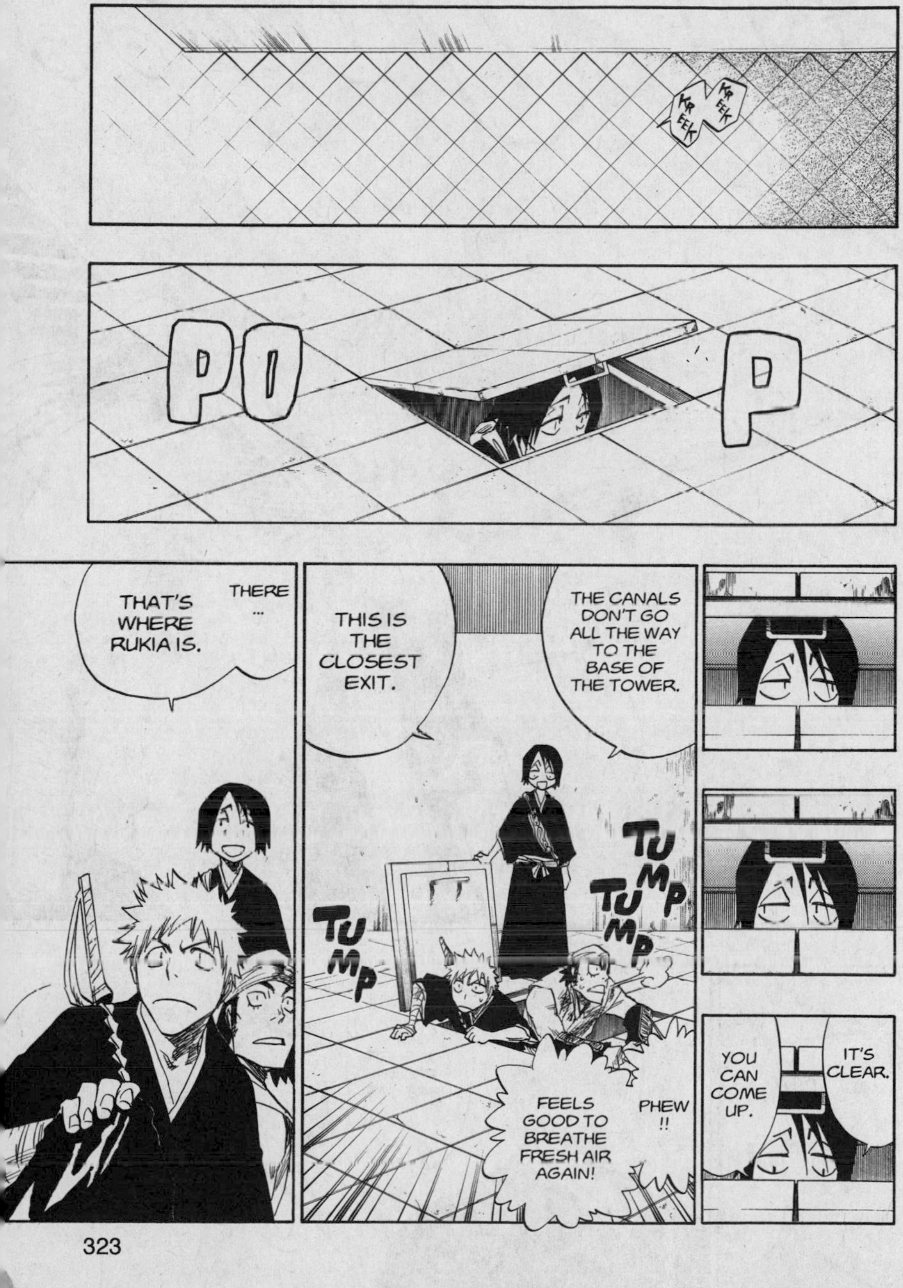
KREEK
KREEK
POP
IT'S CLEAR.
YOU CAN COME UP.
THE CANALS DON'T GO ALL THE WAY TO THE BASE OF THE TOWER.
THIS IS THE CLOSEST EXIT.
TUMP TUMP
TUMP TUMP
PHEW!!
FEELS GOOD TO BREATHE FRESH AIR AGAIN!
THERE...
THAT'S WHERE RUKIA IS.

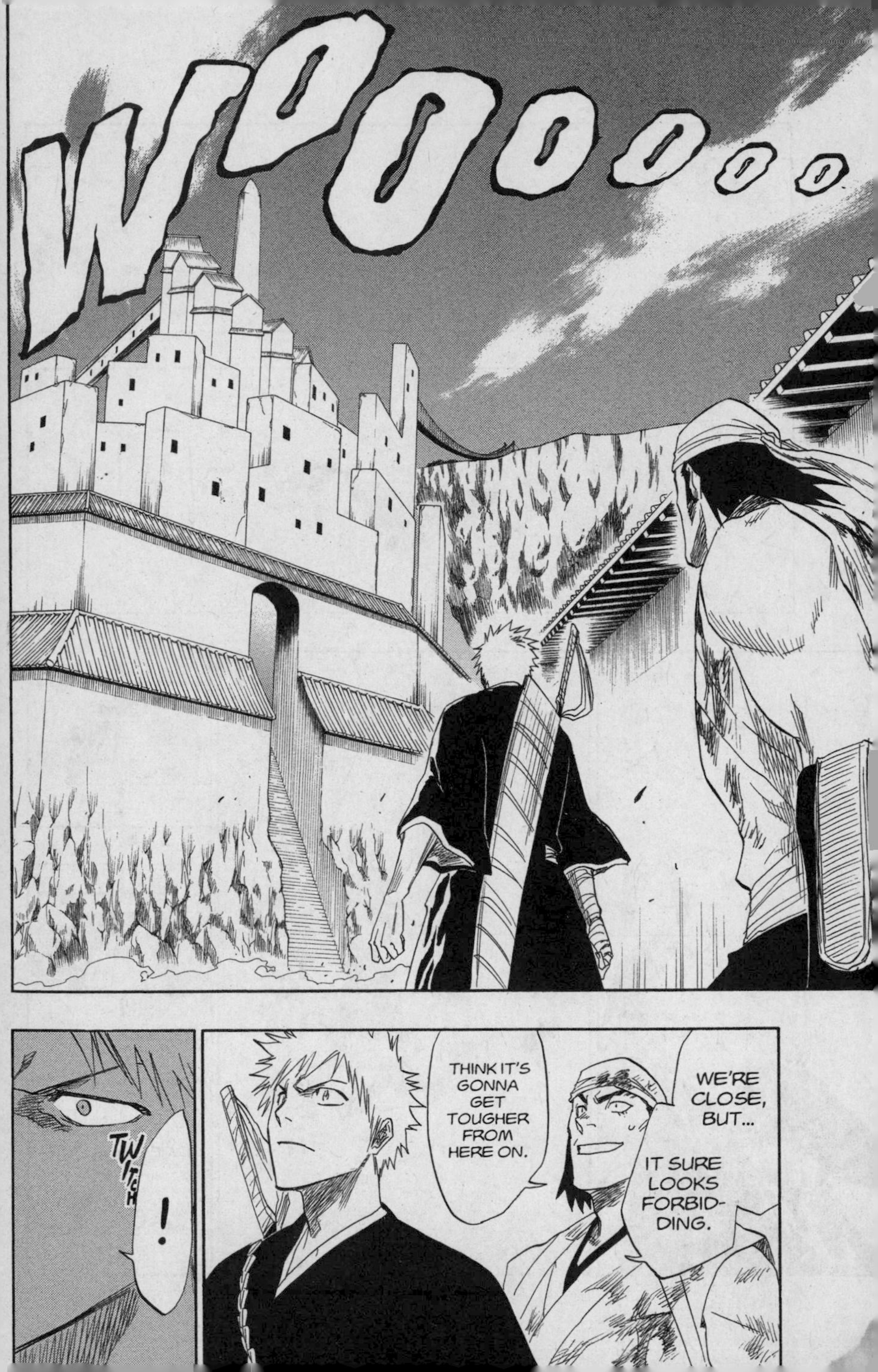
WOOOOOO...
WE'RE CLOSE, BUT...
IT SURE LOOKS FORBIDDING.
THINK IT'S GONNA GET TOUGHER FROM HERE ON.
TWITCH
!

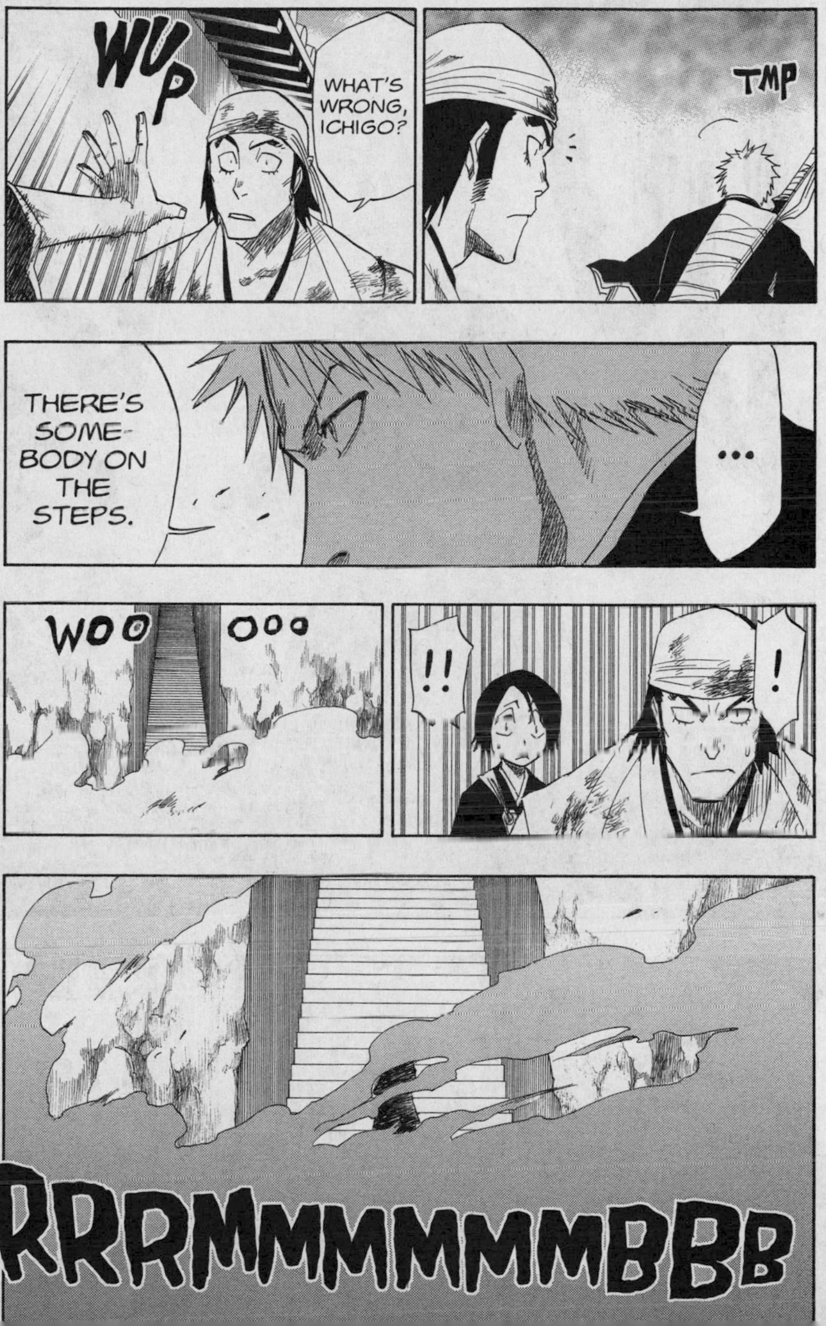
TMP
WHAT'S WRONG, ICHIGO?
WUP
...
THERE'S SOME-BODY ON THE STEPS.
!
!!
WOO OOO
RRRMMMMMMBBB

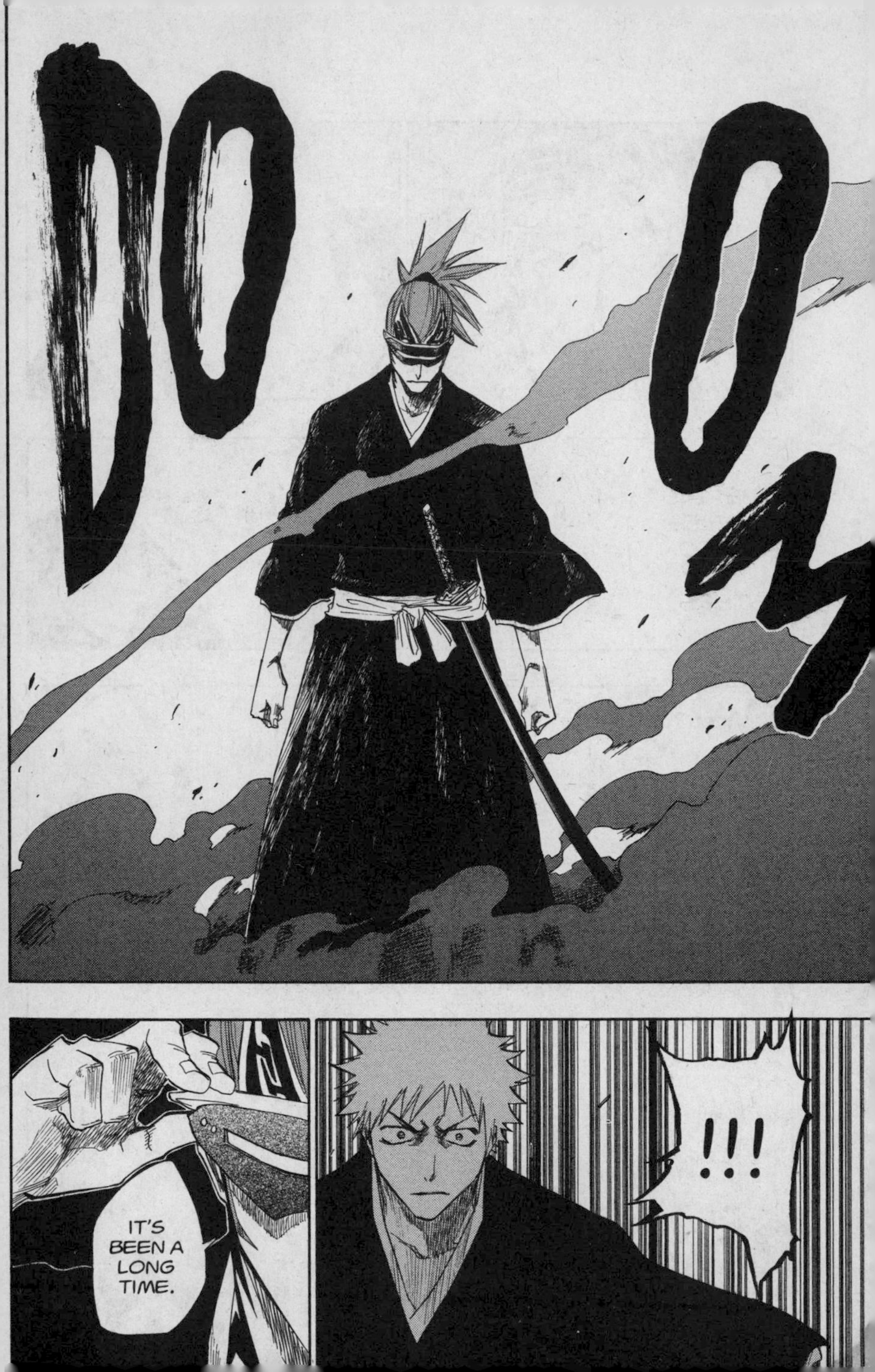
DOOM
!!!
IT'S BEEN A LONG TIME.

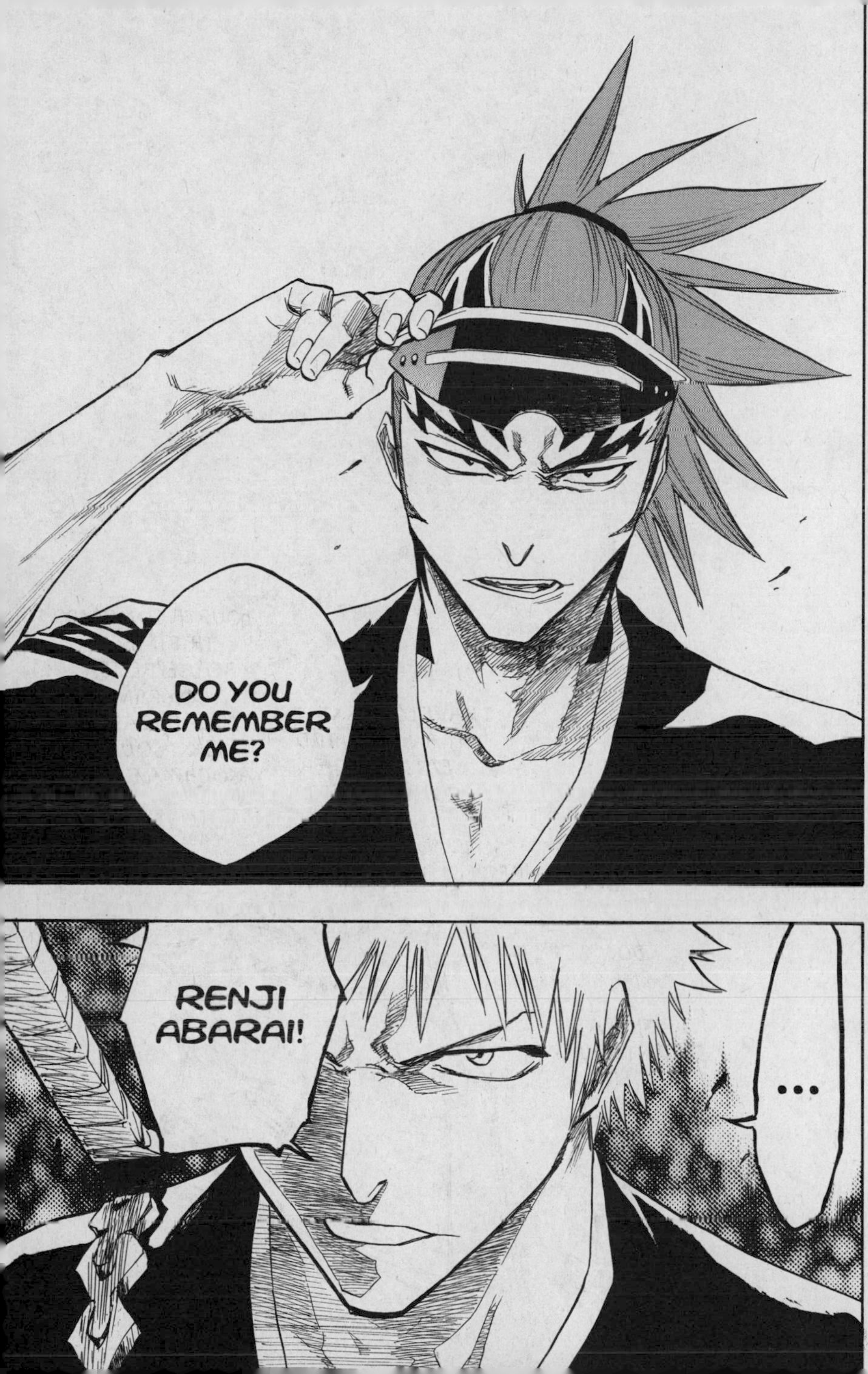
DO YOU REMEMBER ME?
...
RENJI ABARAI!

FOURTH COMPANY,
THIRD SEAT
REFUSE/RELIEF
COMPANY
SQUAD LEADER,
FIRST SQUAD
YASOCHIKA IEMURA.

I HAVE LOWER STATUS
THAN THE THIRD
SEATS OF OTHER
COMPANIES!!

SO I HAVE TO SPEAK
RESPECTFULLY TO THEM.

DON'T CRY, IT'S
EMBARRASSING.

EIGHTH SEAT
ASSISTANT SQUAD
LEADER,
FIRST SQUAD

HARUNOBU
OGIDÔ →

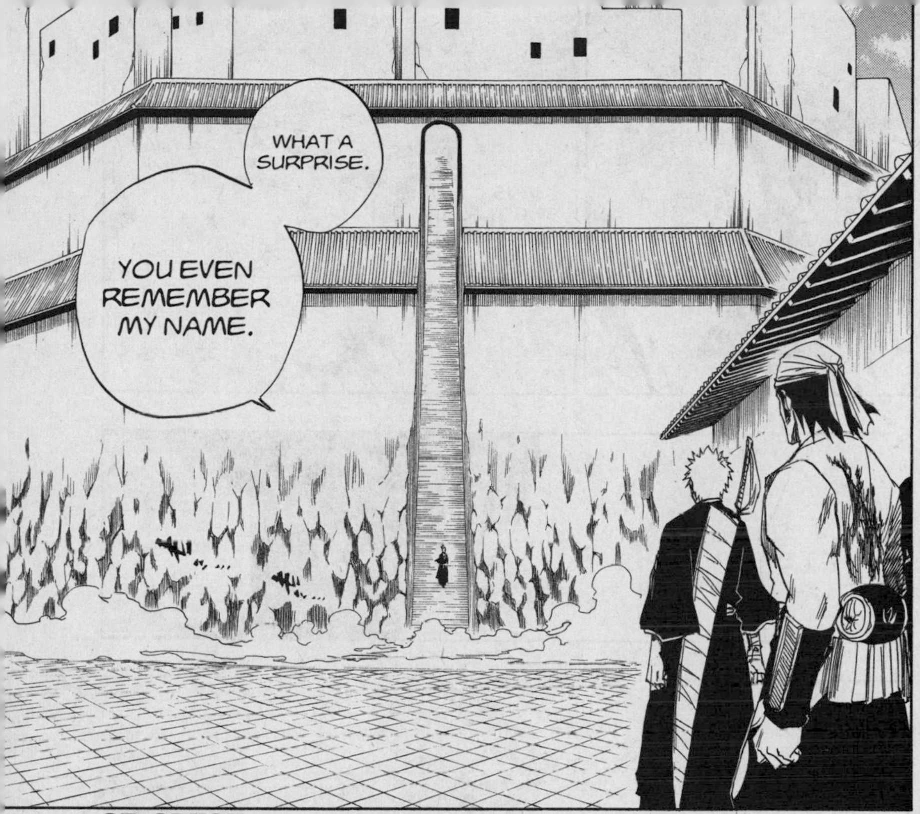
WHAT A SURPRISE.
YOU EVEN REMEMBER MY NAME.

95. CRUSH

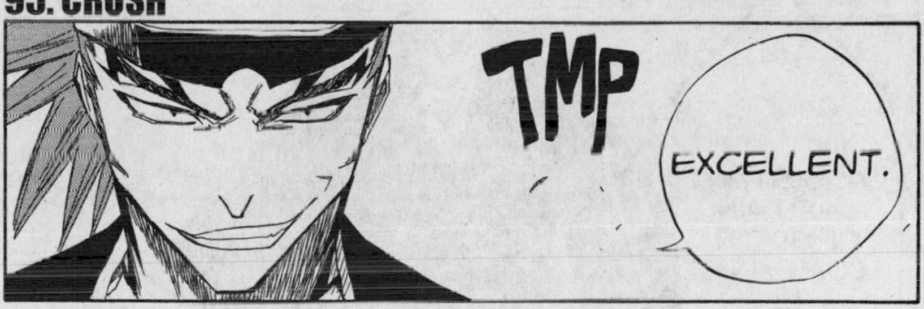
EXCELLENT.
TMP

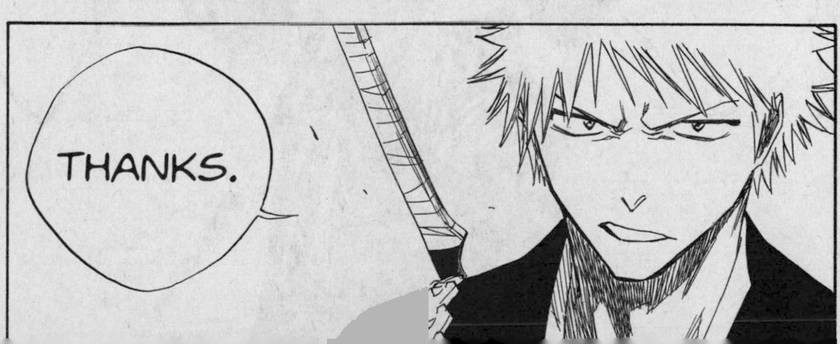
THANKS.

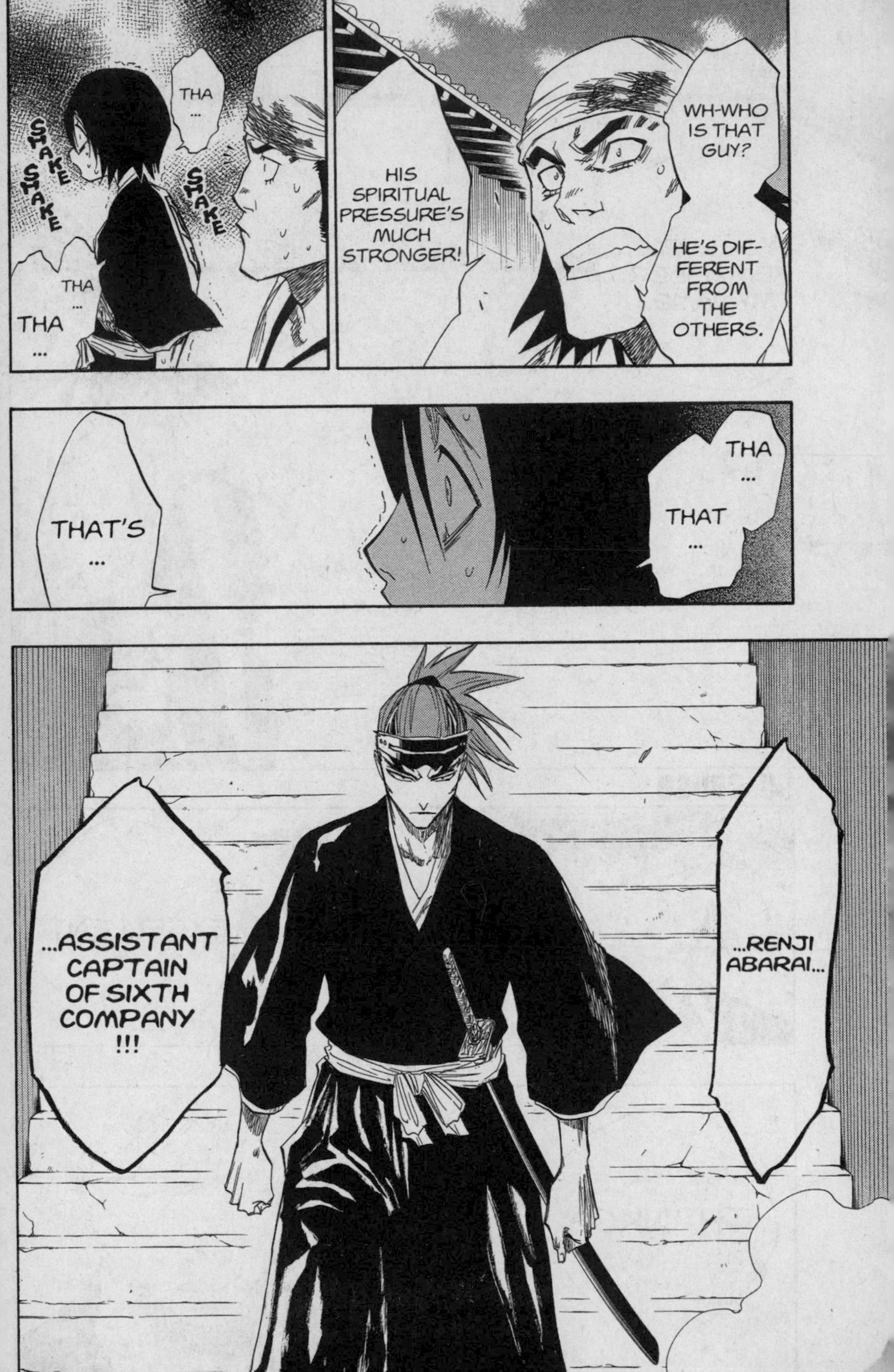
WH-WHO IS THAT GUY?
HE'S DIF-FERENT FROM THE OTHERS.
HIS SPIRITUAL PRESSURE'S MUCH STRONGER!
THA ...
SHAKE
SHAKE SHAKE
THA ...
THA ...
THA ... THAT ...
THAT'S ...
...RENJI ABARAI...
...ASSISTANT CAPTAIN OF SIXTH COMPANY !!!

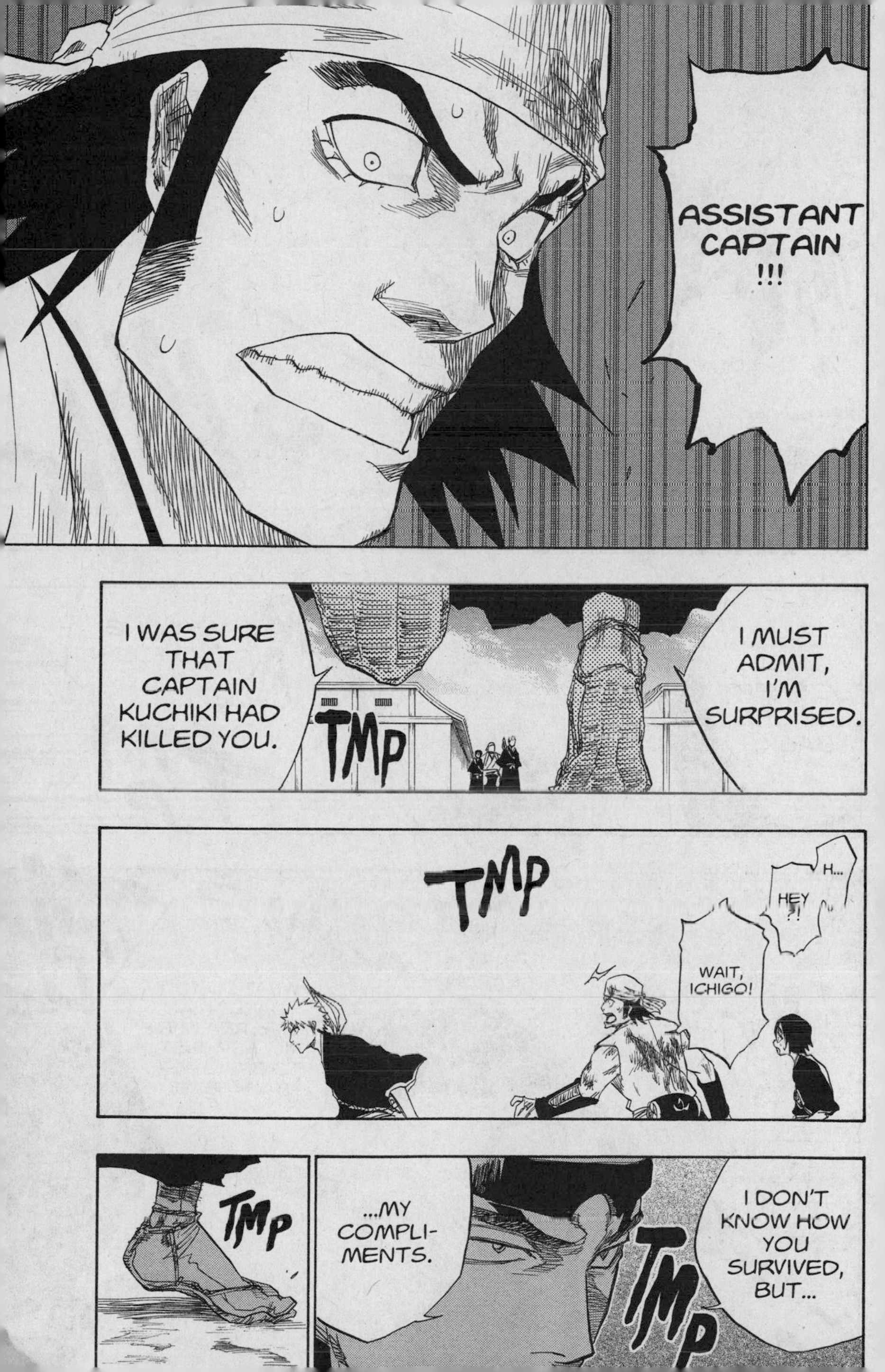
ASSISTANT CAPTAIN !!!
I MUST ADMIT, I'M SURPRISED.
I WAS SURE THAT CAPTAIN KUCHIKI HAD KILLED YOU.
TMP
H... HEY ?!
WAIT, ICHIGO!
TMP
I DON'T KNOW HOW YOU SURVIVED, BUT...
TMP
...MY COMPLIMENTS.
TMP

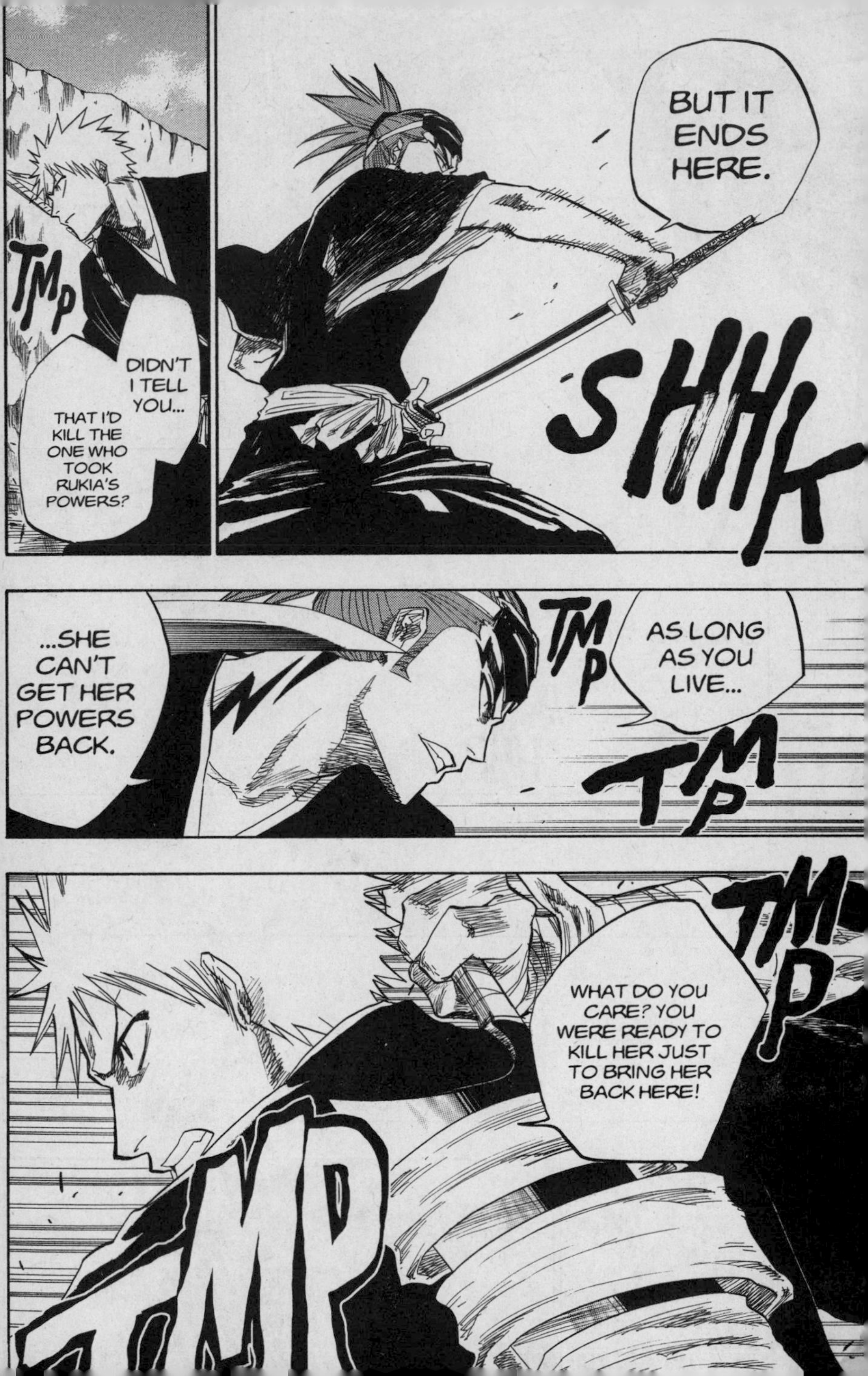
BUT IT ENDS HERE.
SHHK
TMP
DIDN'T I TELL YOU...
THAT I'D KILL THE ONE WHO TOOK RUKIA'S POWERS?
TMP
AS LONG AS YOU LIVE...
TMP
...SHE CAN'T GET HER POWERS BACK.
TMP
WHAT DO YOU CARE? YOU WERE READY TO KILL HER JUST TO BRING HER BACK HERE!
TMP

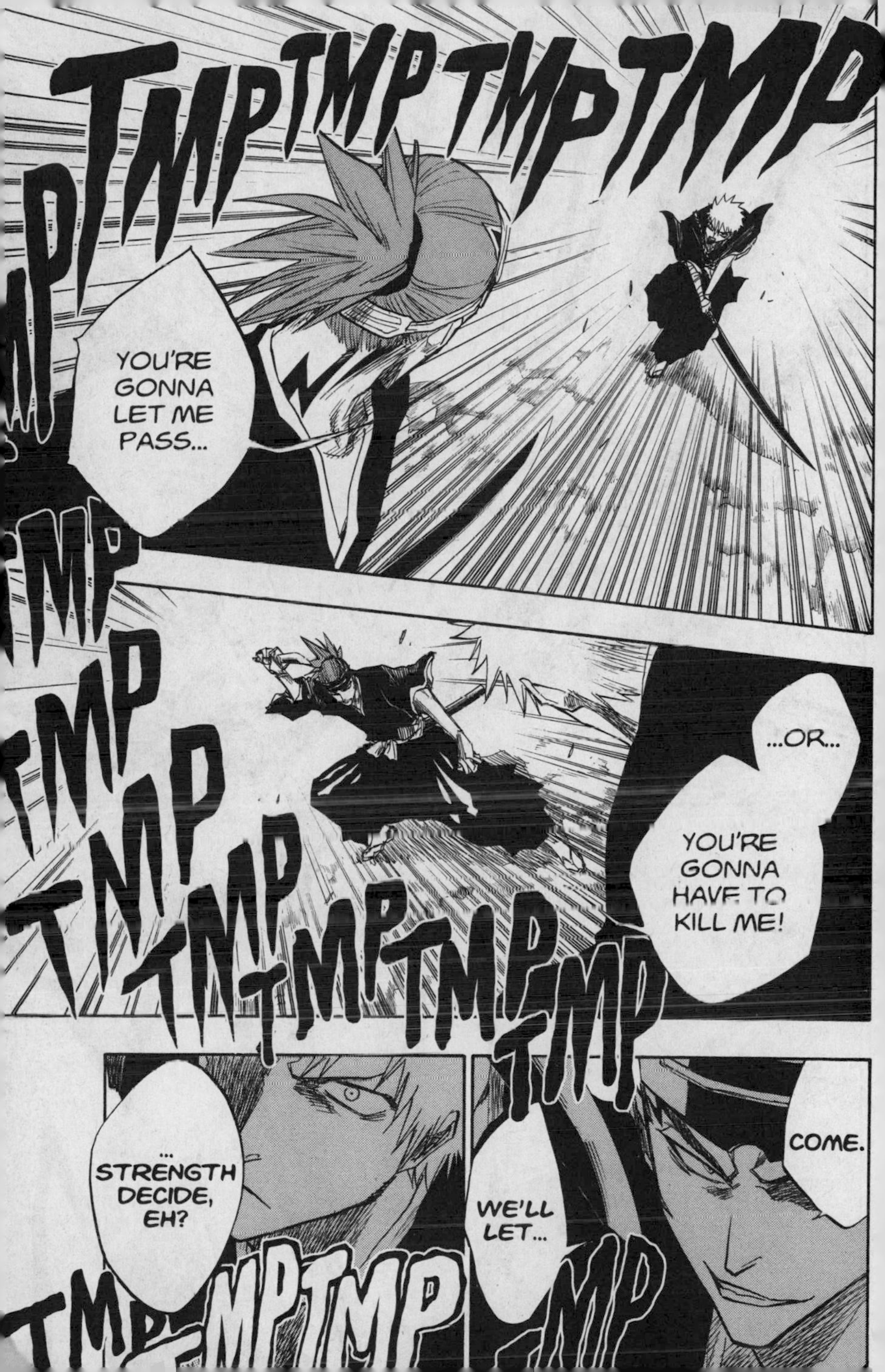
TMP TMP TMP TMP TMP
TMP
YOU'RE GONNA LET ME PASS...
TMP
TMP
TMP TMP TMP TMP TMP TMP
...OR...
YOU'RE GONNA HAVE TO KILL ME!
COME.
WE'LL LET...
... STRENGTH DECIDE, EH?
TMP TMP TMP TMP

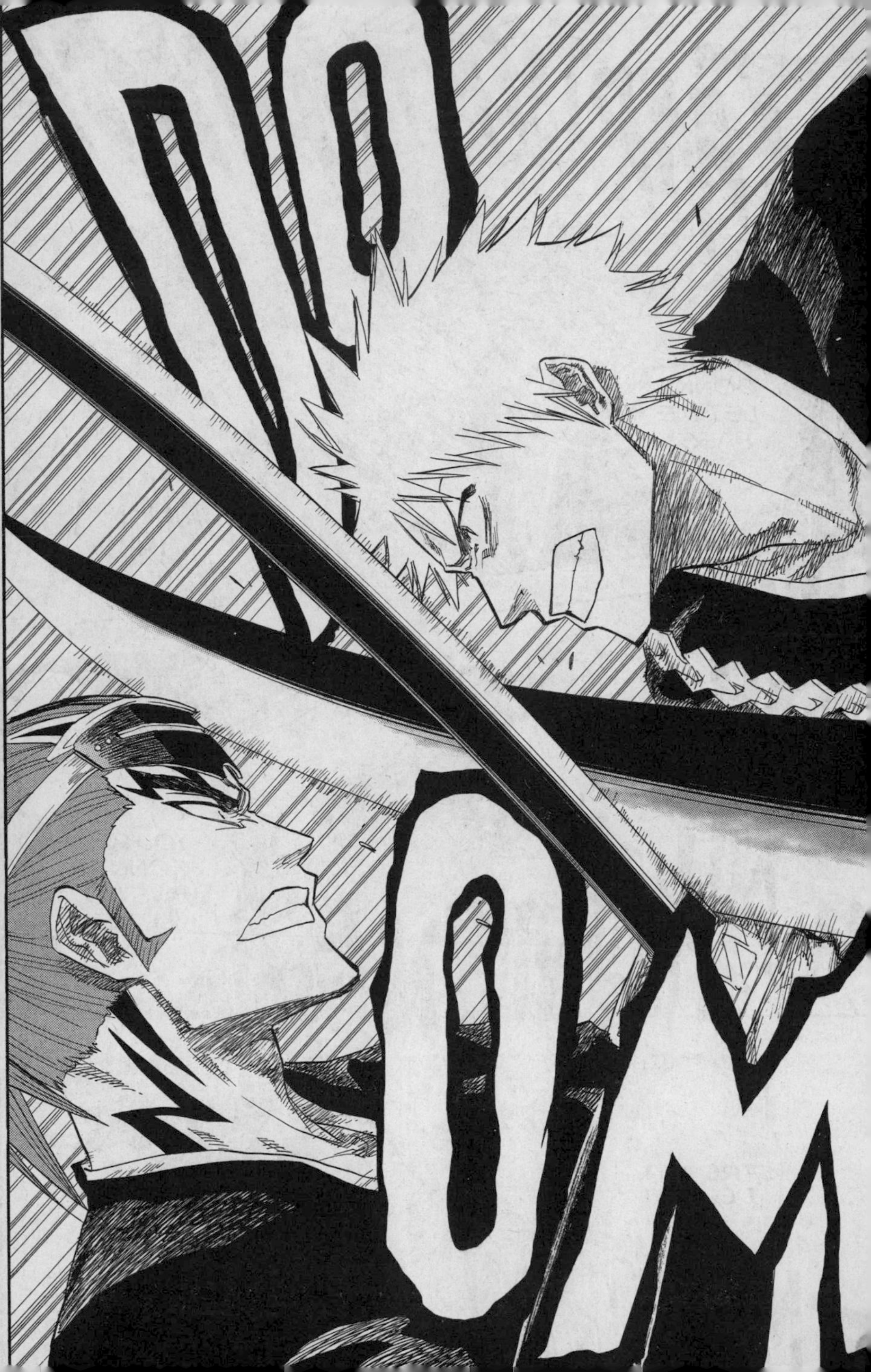

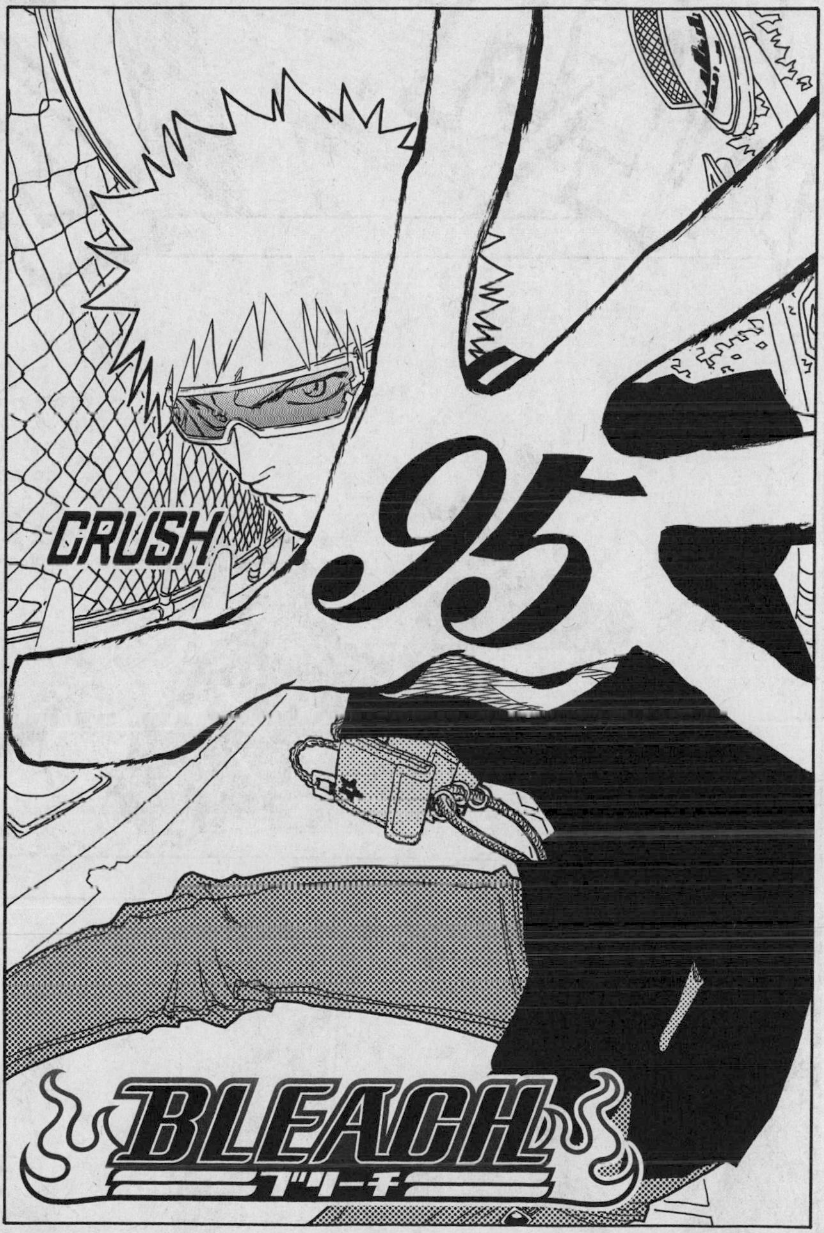
CRUSH
95
BLEACH
ブリーチ

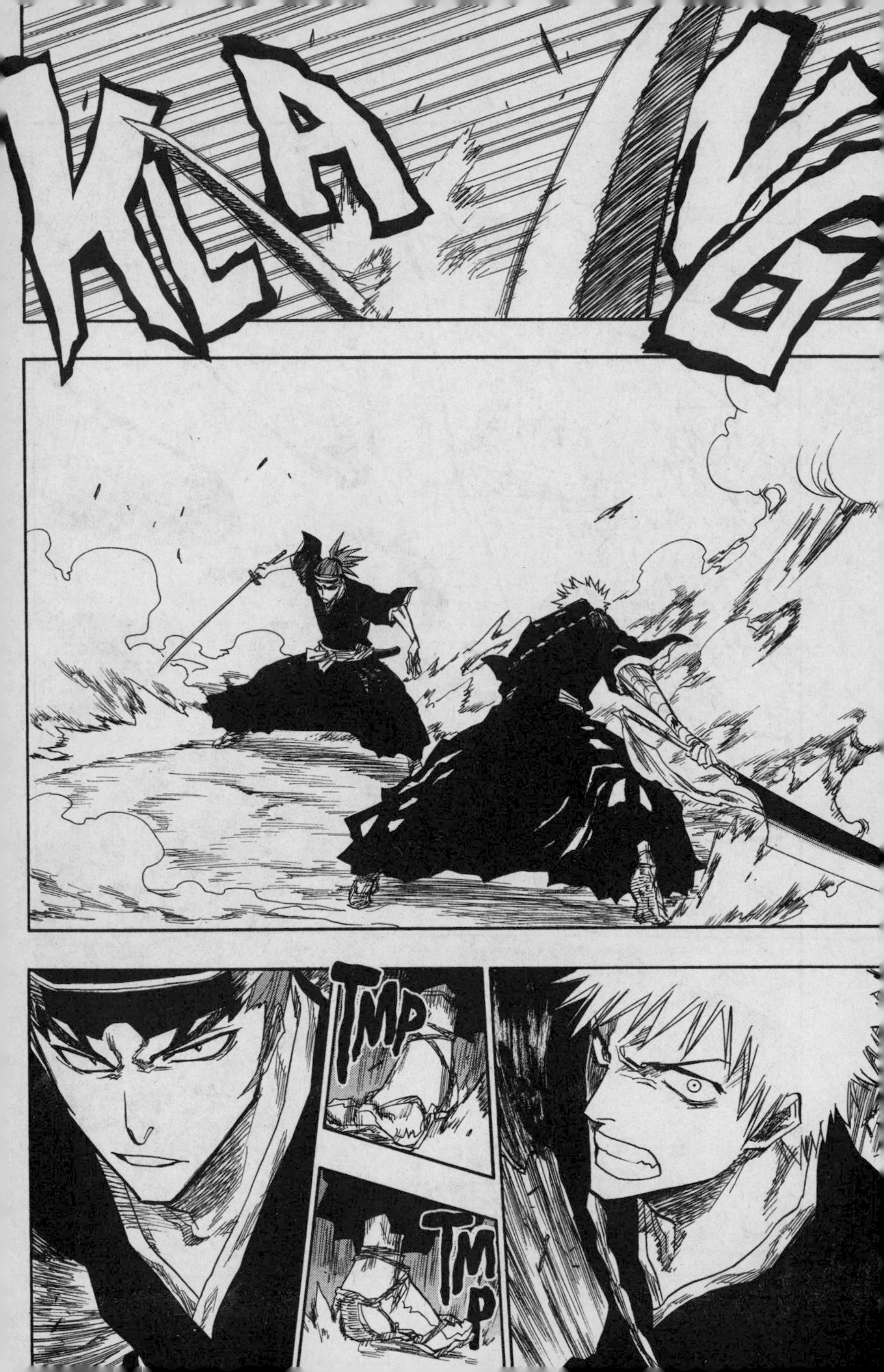
KLANG
TMP
TMP

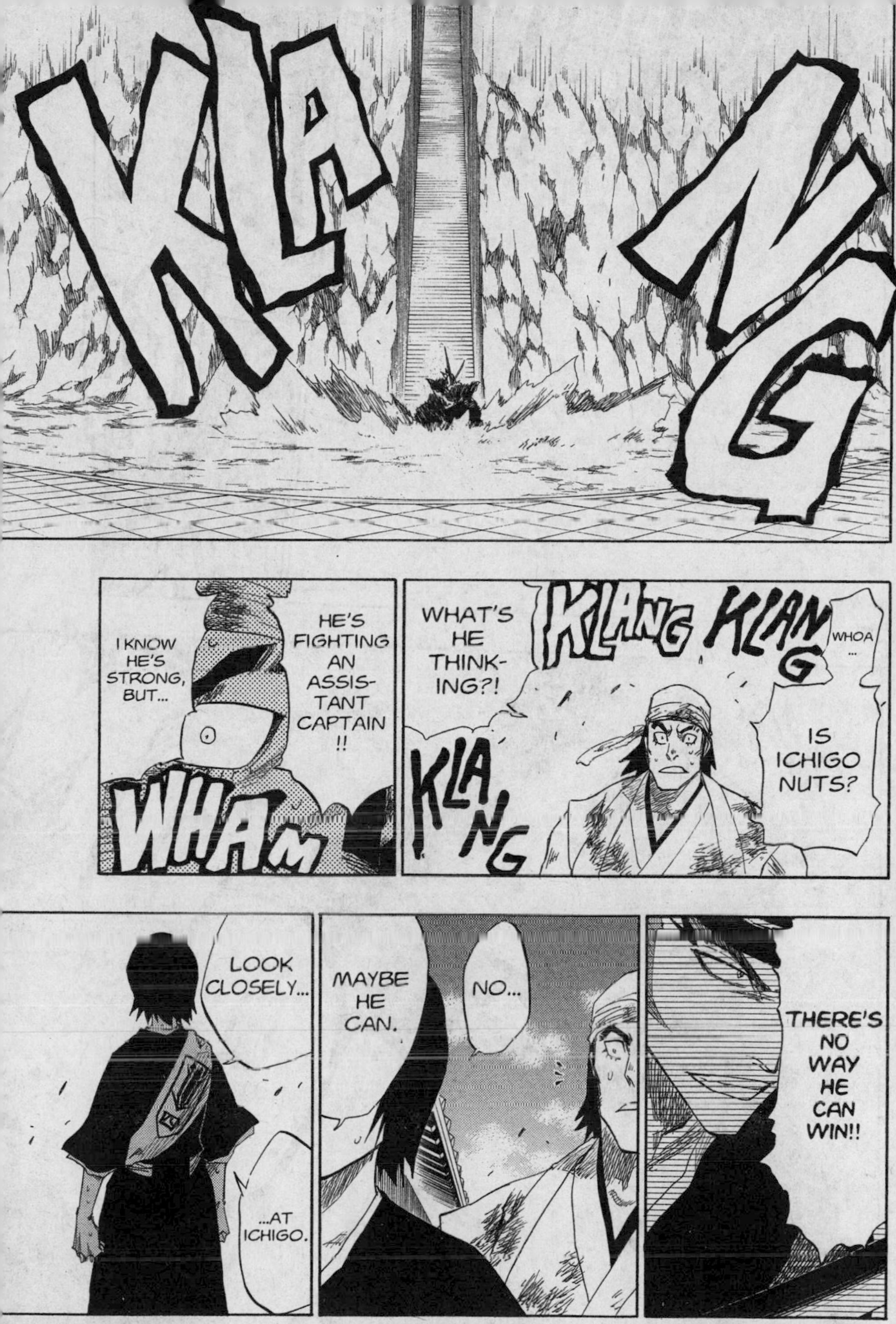
KLANG
WHOA...
KLANG KLANG
WHAT'S HE THINKING?!
IS ICHIGO NUTS?
KLANG
HE'S FIGHTING AN ASSISTANT CAPTAIN!!
I KNOW HE'S STRONG, BUT...
WHAM
THERE'S NO WAY HE CAN WIN!!
NO...
MAYBE HE CAN.
LOOK CLOSELY...
...AT ICHIGO.

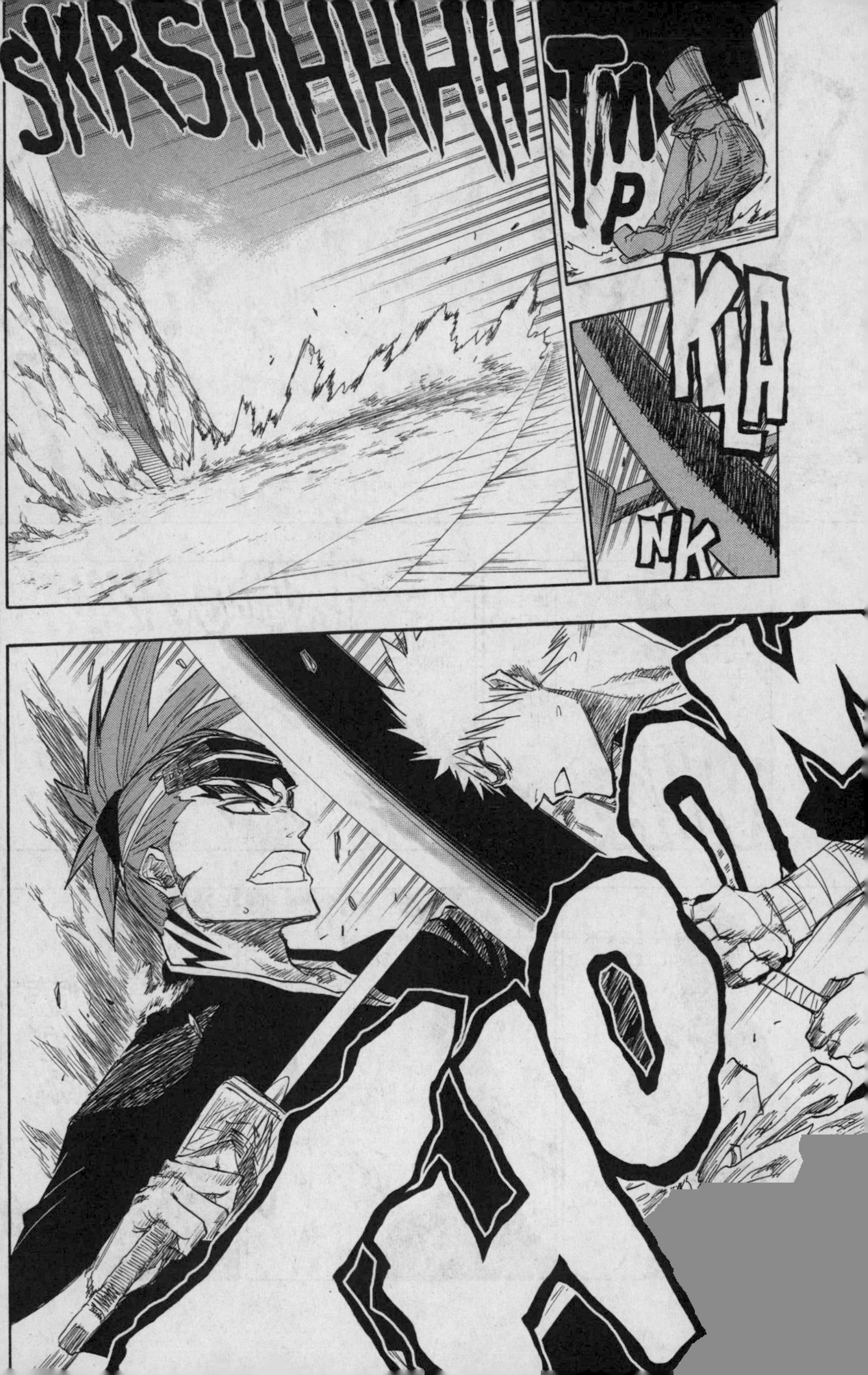
TMP
KLANK
SKRSHHHHH
TOO

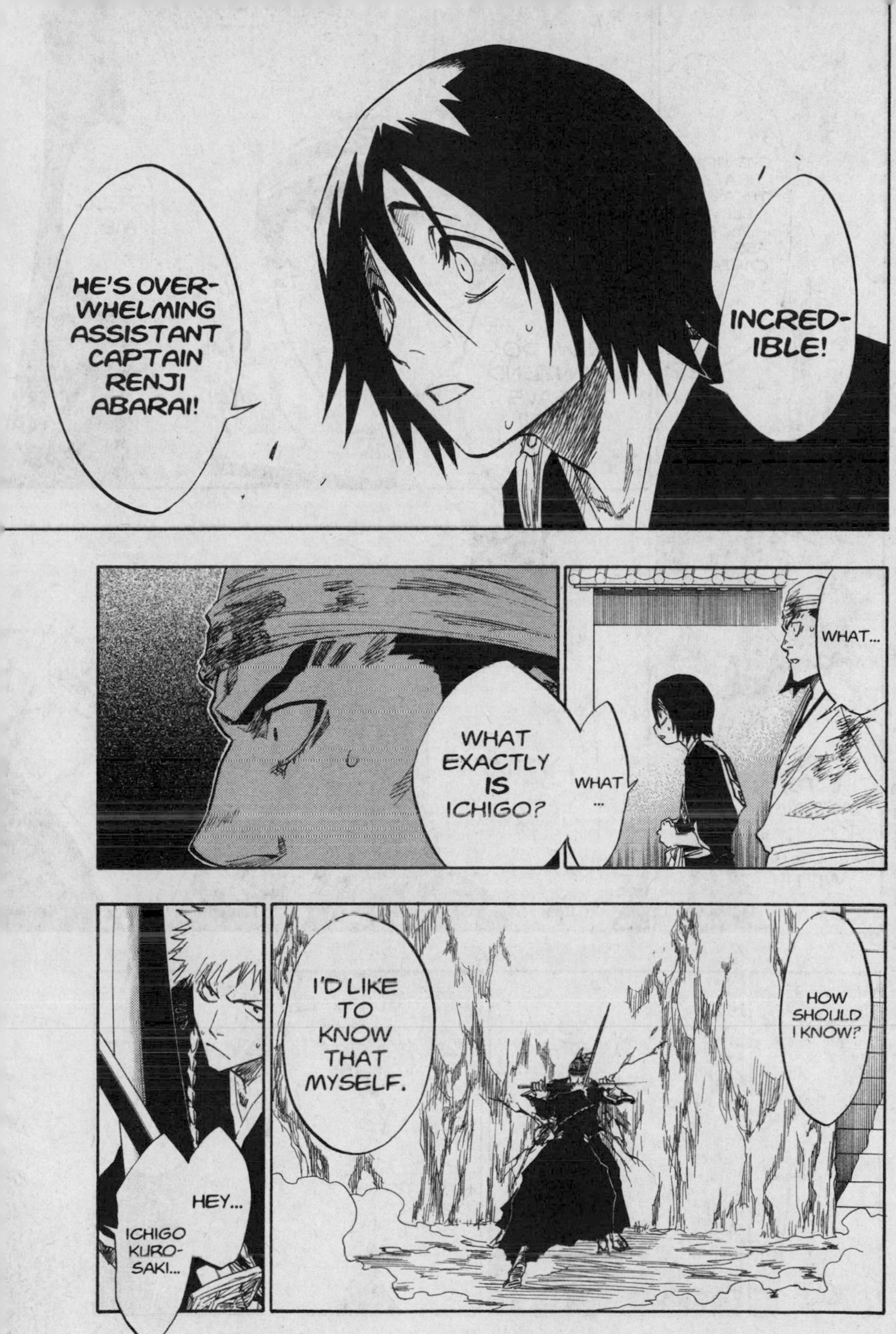
INCRED-IBLE!
HE'S OVER-WHELMING ASSISTANT CAPTAIN RENJI ABARAI!
WHAT...
WHAT ...
WHAT EXACTLY IS ICHIGO?
HOW SHOULD I KNOW?
I'D LIKE TO KNOW THAT MYSELF.
HEY...
ICHIGO KURO-SAKI...

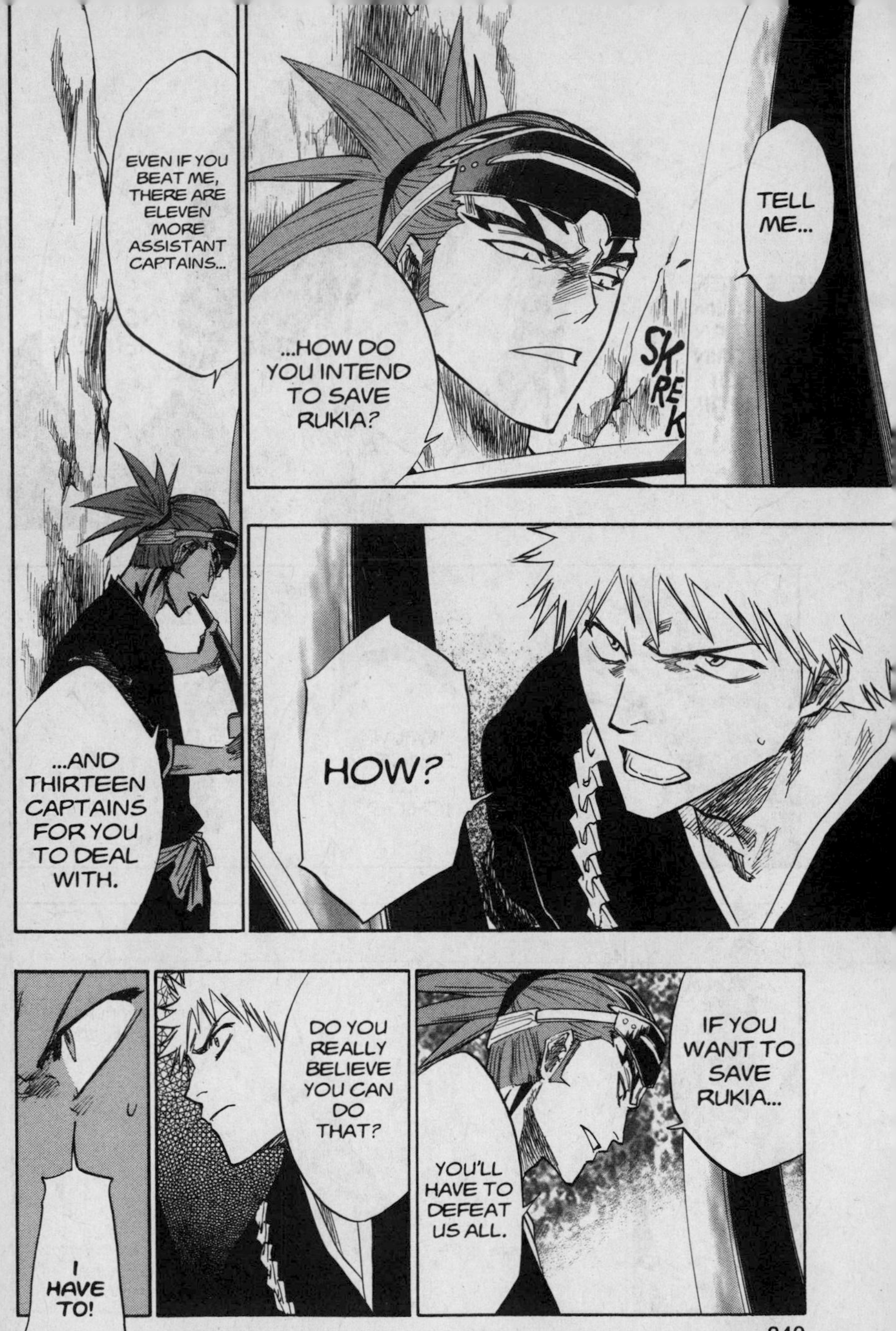
TELL ME...
...HOW DO YOU INTEND TO SAVE RUKIA?
SKREK
HOW?
EVEN IF YOU BEAT ME, THERE ARE ELEVEN MORE ASSISTANT CAPTAINS...
...AND THIRTEEN CAPTAINS FOR YOU TO DEAL WITH.
IF YOU WANT TO SAVE RUKIA...
YOU'LL HAVE TO DEFEAT US ALL.
DO YOU REALLY BELIEVE YOU CAN DO THAT?
I HAVE TO!

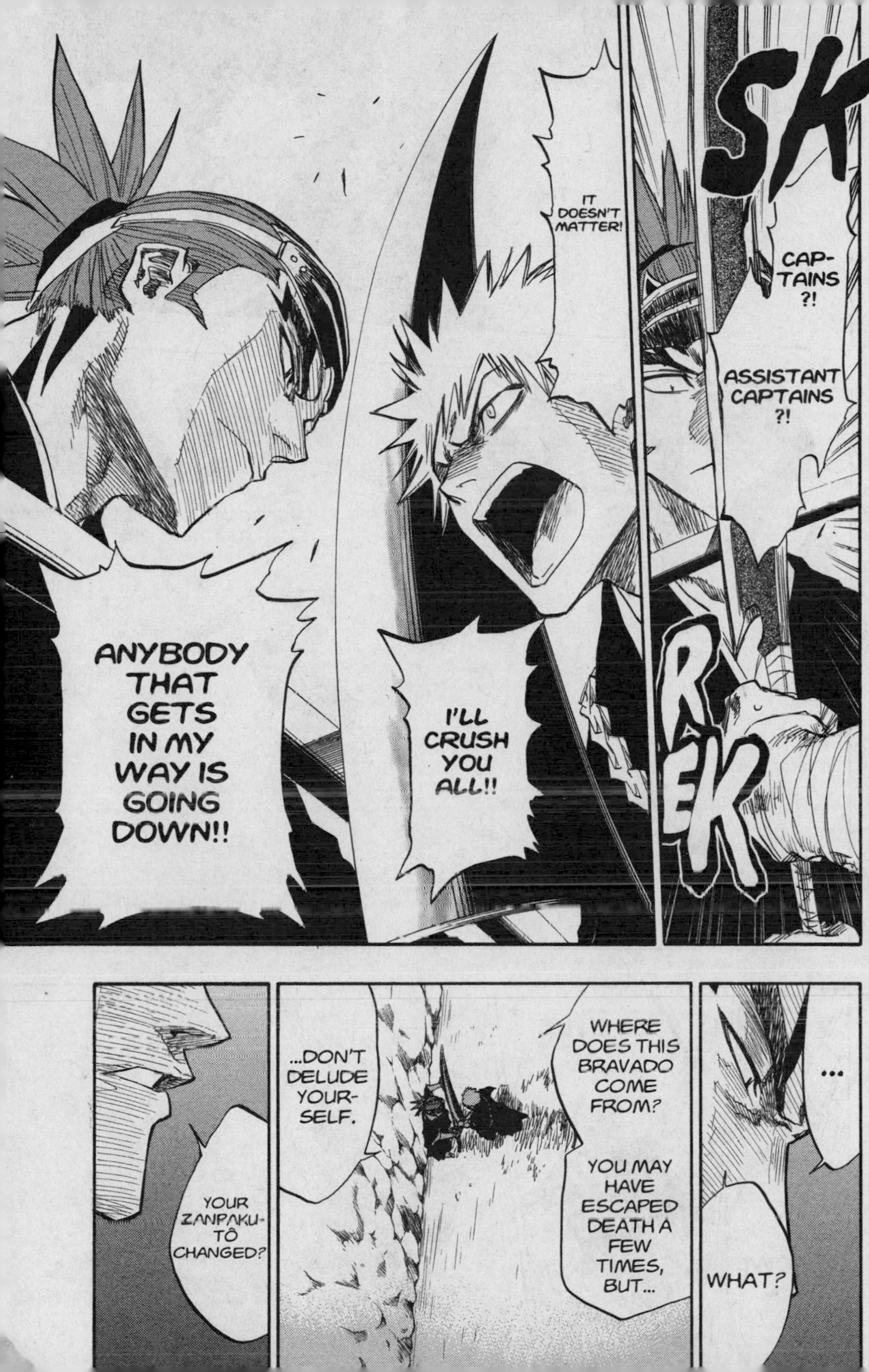
SK
RREK
CAP-TAINS?!
ASSISTANT CAPTAINS?!
IT DOESN'T MATTER!
I'LL CRUSH YOU ALL!!
ANYBODY THAT GETS IN MY WAY IS GOING DOWN!!
...
WHAT?
WHERE DOES THIS BRAVADO COME FROM?
YOU MAY HAVE ESCAPED DEATH A FEW TIMES, BUT...
...DON'T DELUDE YOURSELF.
YOUR ZANPAKU-TÔ CHANGED?

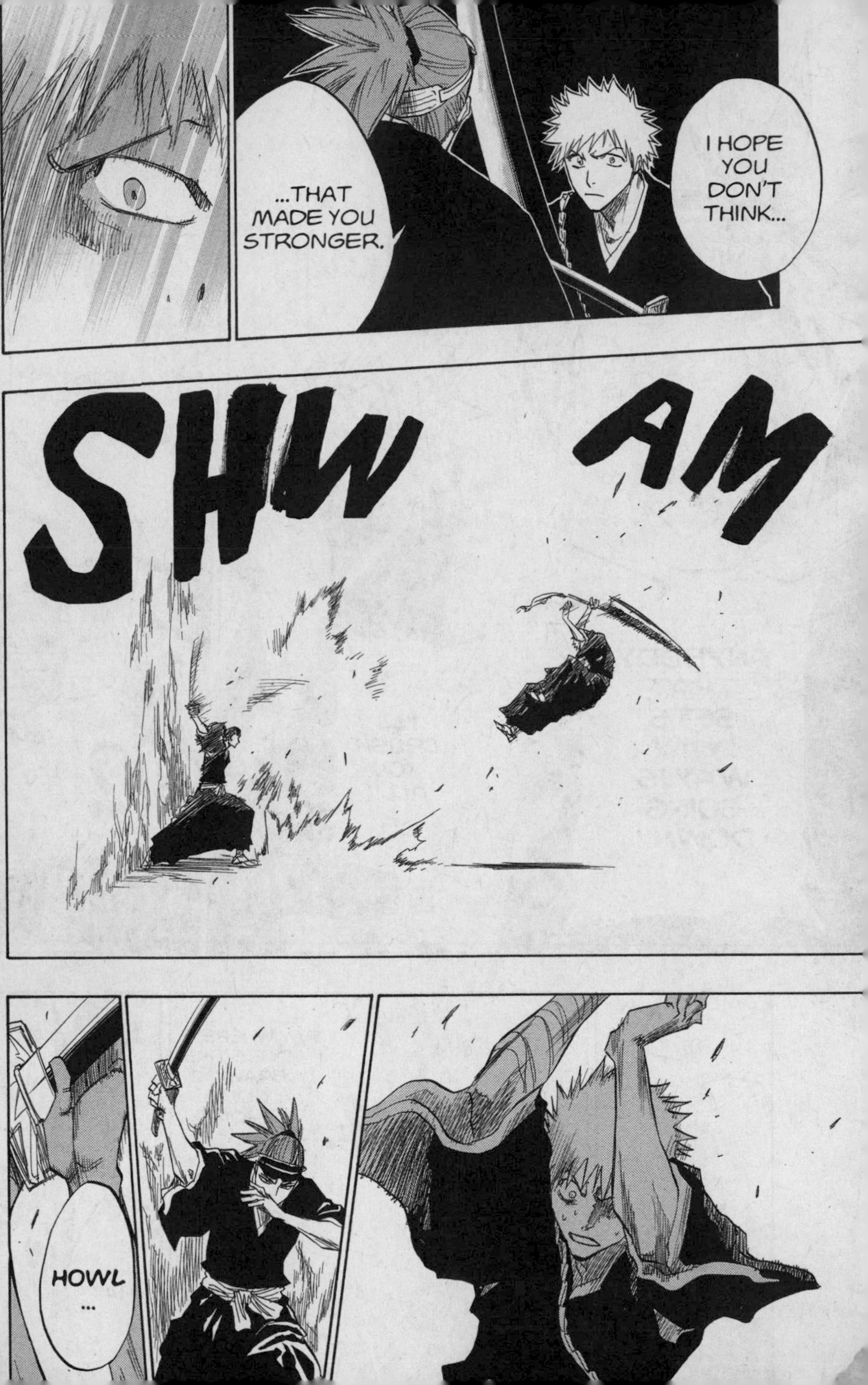
I HOPE YOU DON'T THINK...
...THAT MADE YOU STRONGER.
SHW AM
HOWL ...

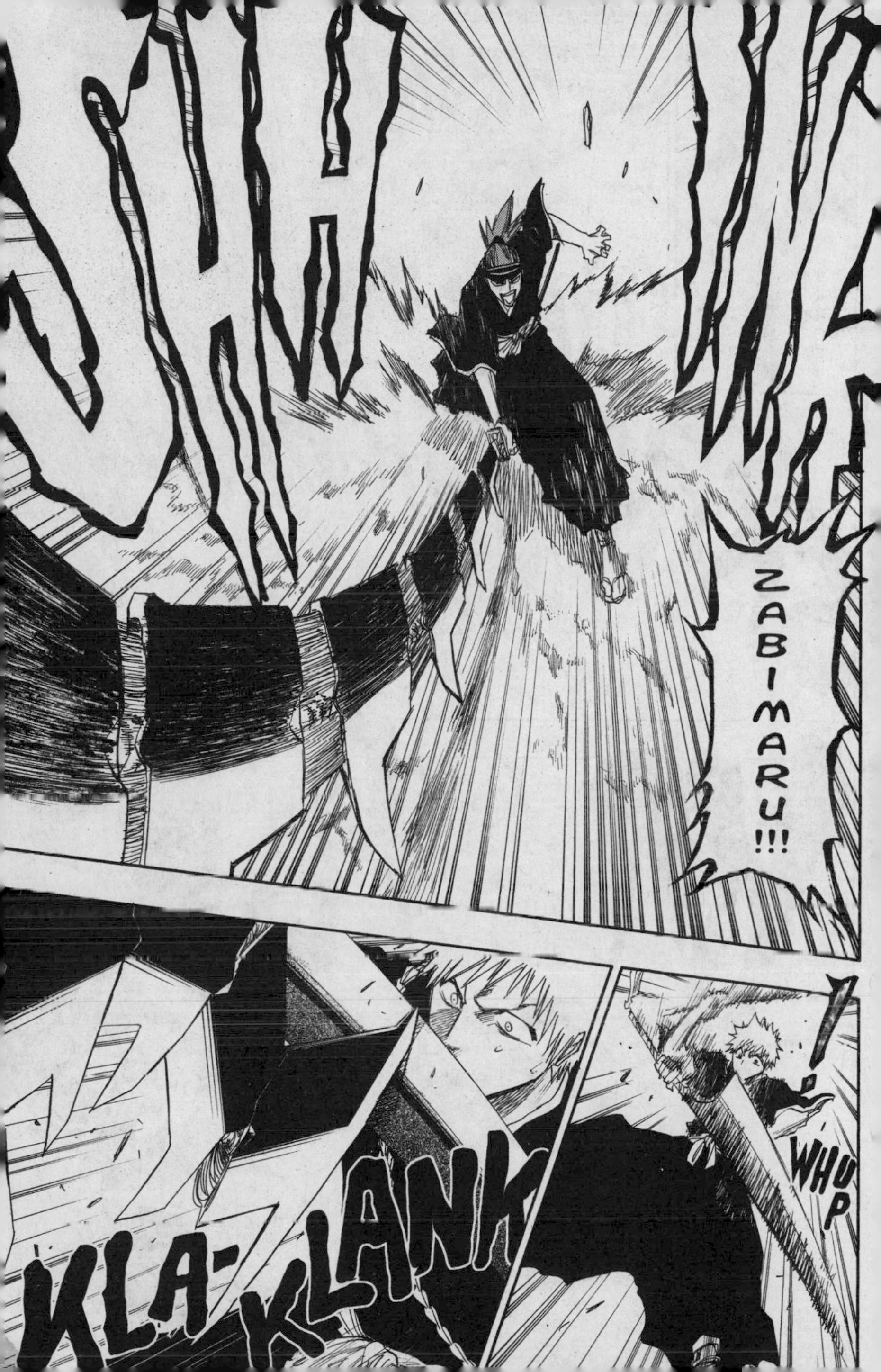
ZABIMARU!!!
!
WHUP
KLA-KLANK

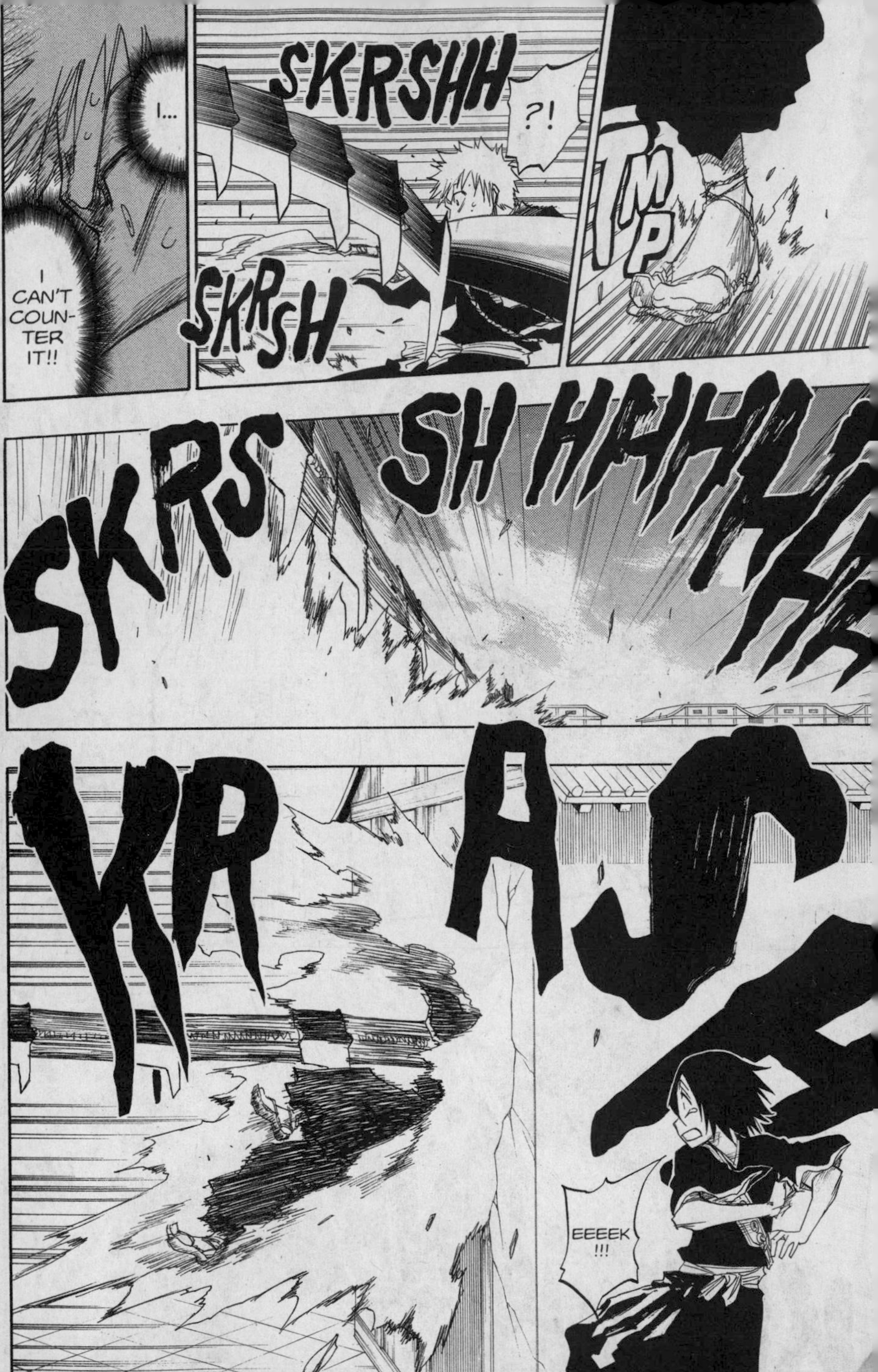
TMP
SKRSHH
?!
SKRSH
I...
I CAN'T COUNTER IT!!
EEEEK !!!

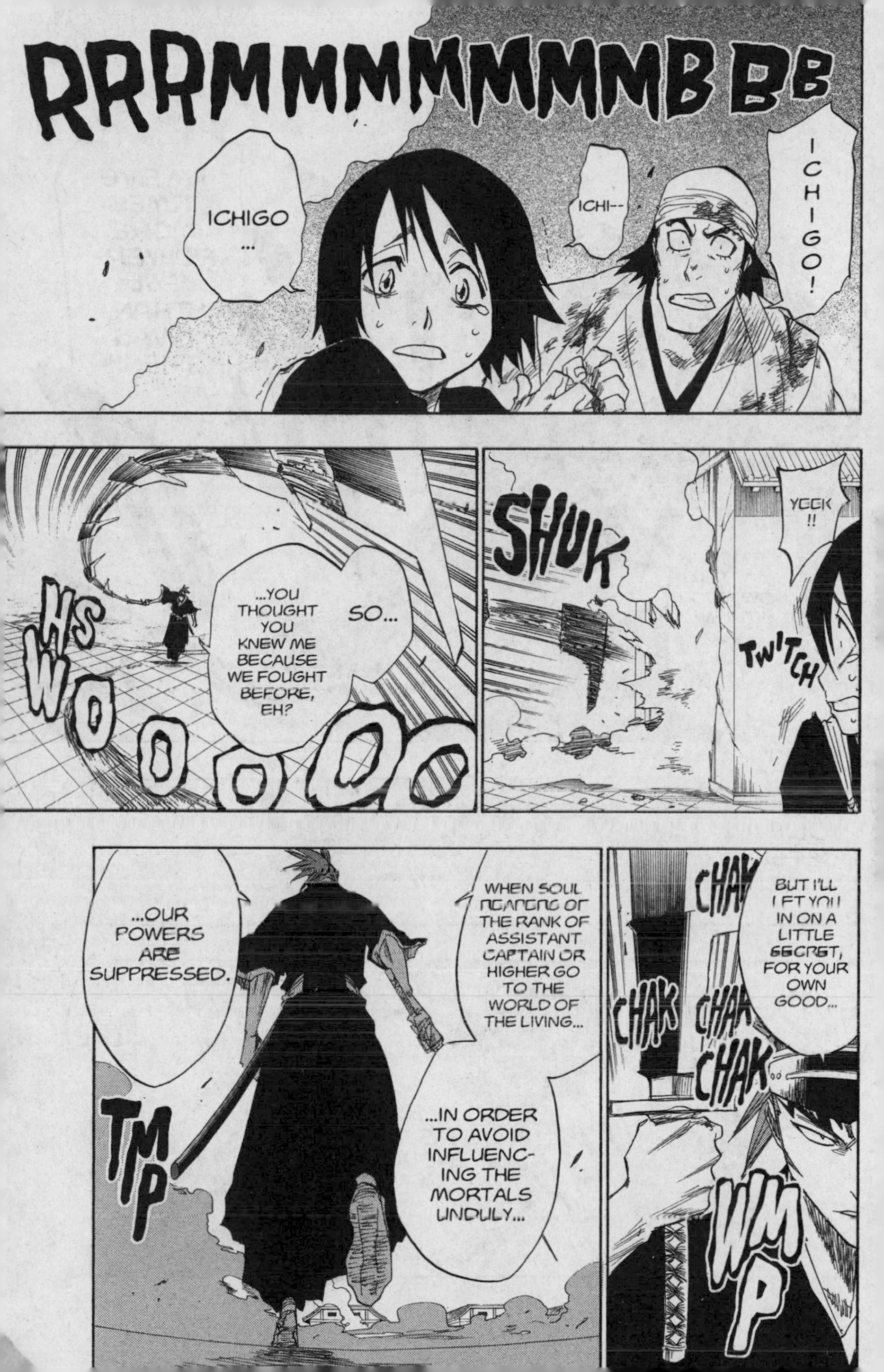
RRRMMMMMMMMB BB
ICHIGO!
ICHI--
ICHIGO ...
YEEK!!
TWITCH
SHUK
SO...
...YOU THOUGHT YOU KNEW ME BECAUSE WE FOUGHT BEFORE, EH?
HSWOOOOOO
BUT I'LL LET YOU IN ON A LITTLE SECRET, FOR YOUR OWN GOOD...
CHAK
CHAK
CHAK
CHAK
WMP
WHEN SOUL REAPERS OF THE RANK OF ASSISTANT CAPTAIN OR HIGHER GO TO THE WORLD OF THE LIVING...
...IN ORDER TO AVOID INFLUENC-ING THE MORTALS UNDULY...
...OUR POWERS ARE SUPPRESSED.
TMP

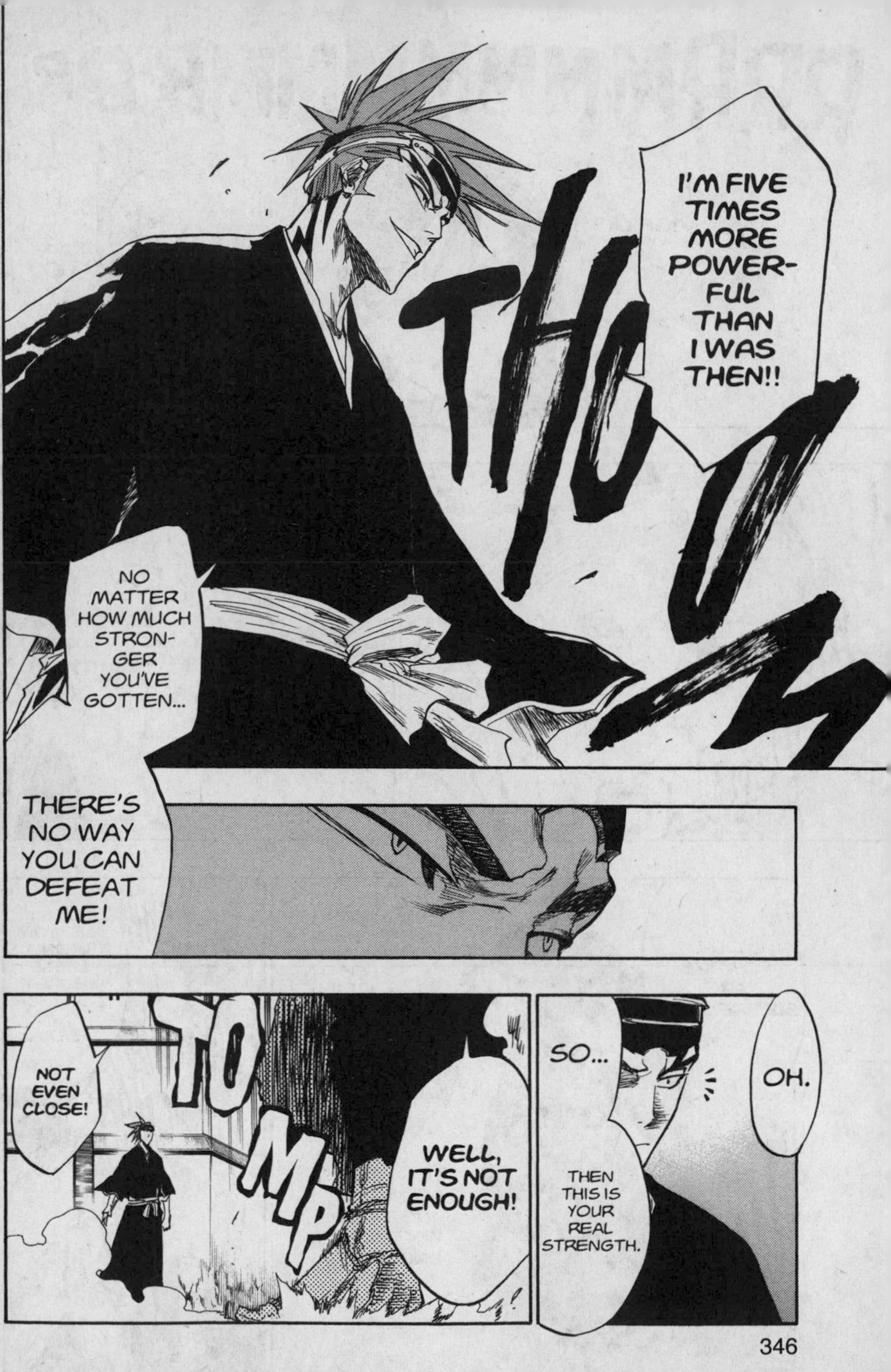
I'M FIVE TIMES MORE POWER-FUL THAN I WAS THEN!!
THOOM
NO MATTER HOW MUCH STRONG-GER YOU'VE GOTTEN...
THERE'S NO WAY YOU CAN DEFEAT ME!
OH.
SO...
THEN THIS IS YOUR REAL STRENGTH.
WELL, IT'S NOT ENOUGH!
TOMP
NOT EVEN CLOSE!

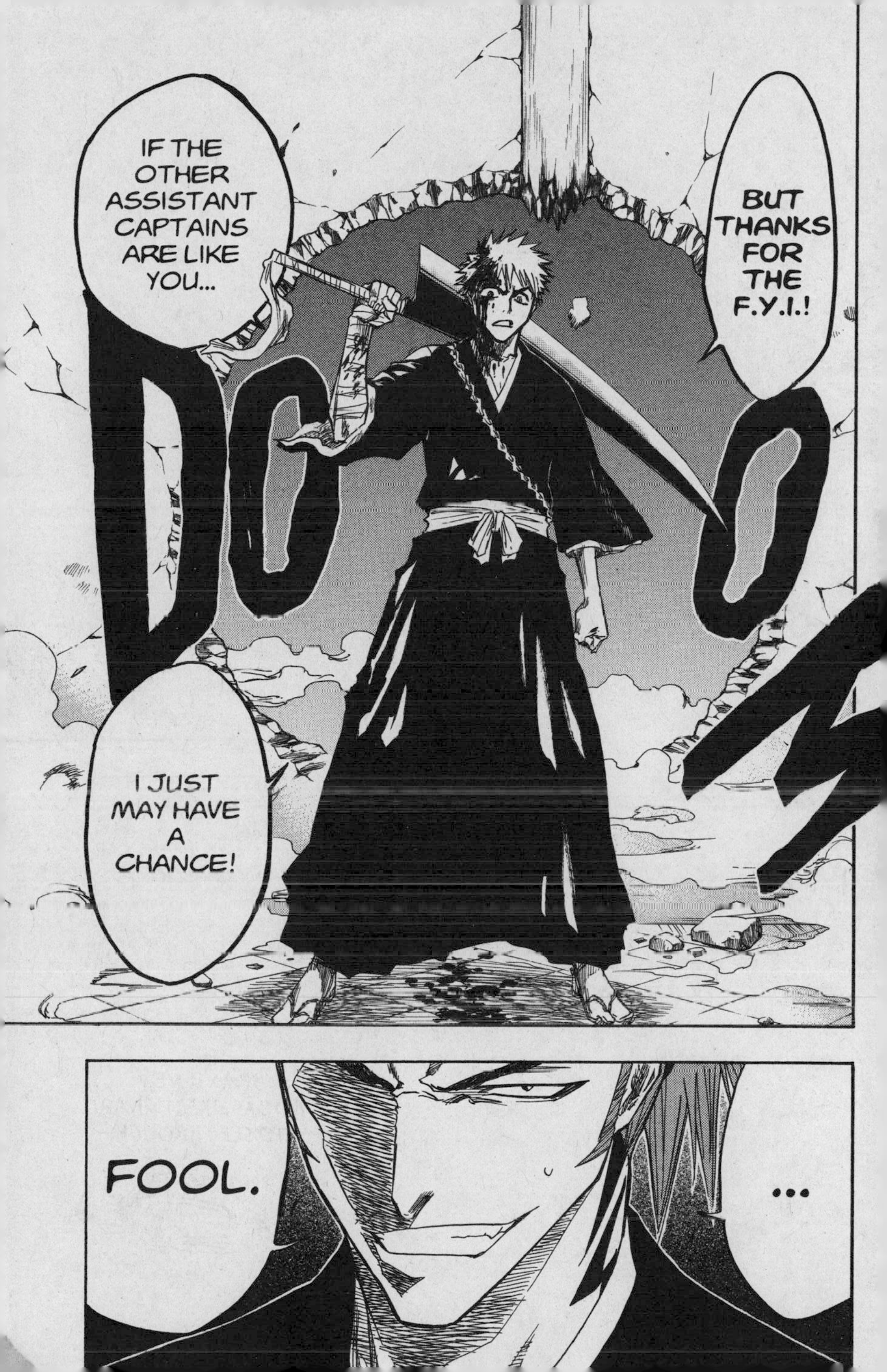
BUT THANKS FOR THE F.Y.I.!
IF THE OTHER ASSISTANT CAPTAINS ARE LIKE YOU...
DOOM
I JUST MAY HAVE A CHANCE!
...
FOOL.

BRAND NEW.
LOOKS LIKE IT'S HARD
TO SEE THROUGH.

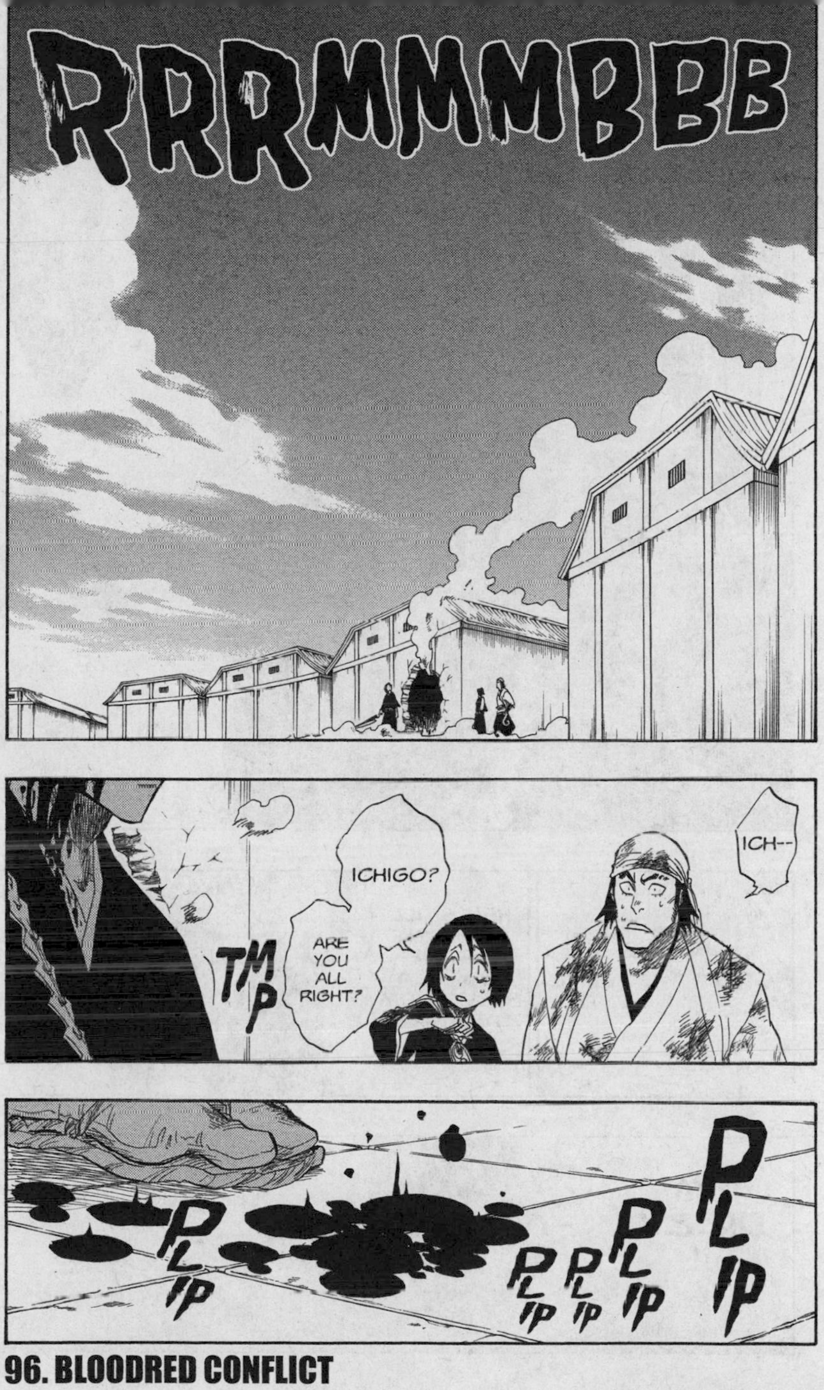
RRRMMMBBB
ICH--
ICHIGO?
ARE YOU ALL RIGHT?
TMP
PLIP
PLIP
PLIP
PLIP
PLIP

96. BLOODRED CONFLICT

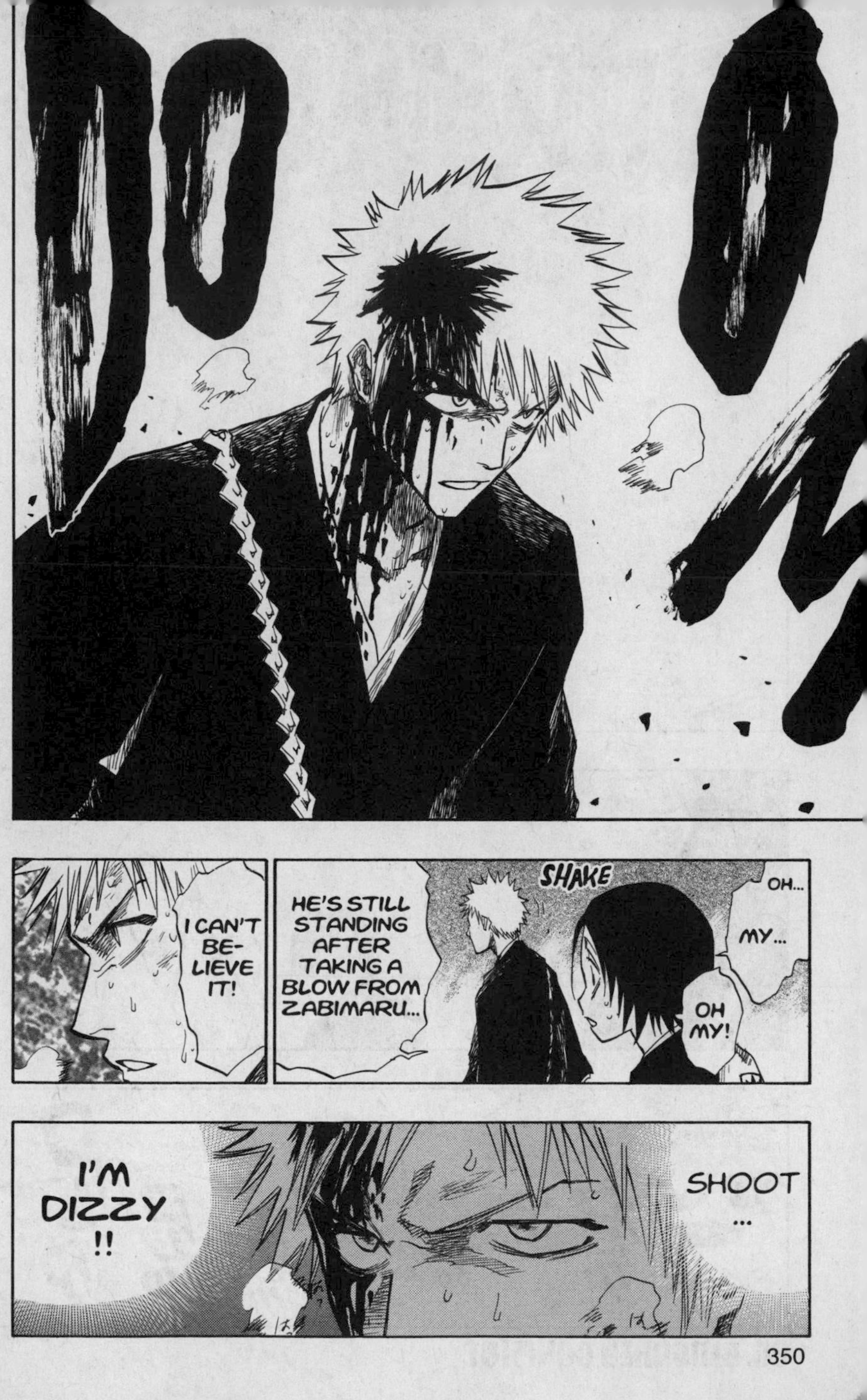
DOOM
SHAKE
OH...
MY...
OH MY!
HE'S STILL STANDING AFTER TAKING A BLOW FROM ZABIMARU...
I CAN'T BE-LIEVE IT!
SHOOT ...
I'M DIZZY !!

READ THIS WAY

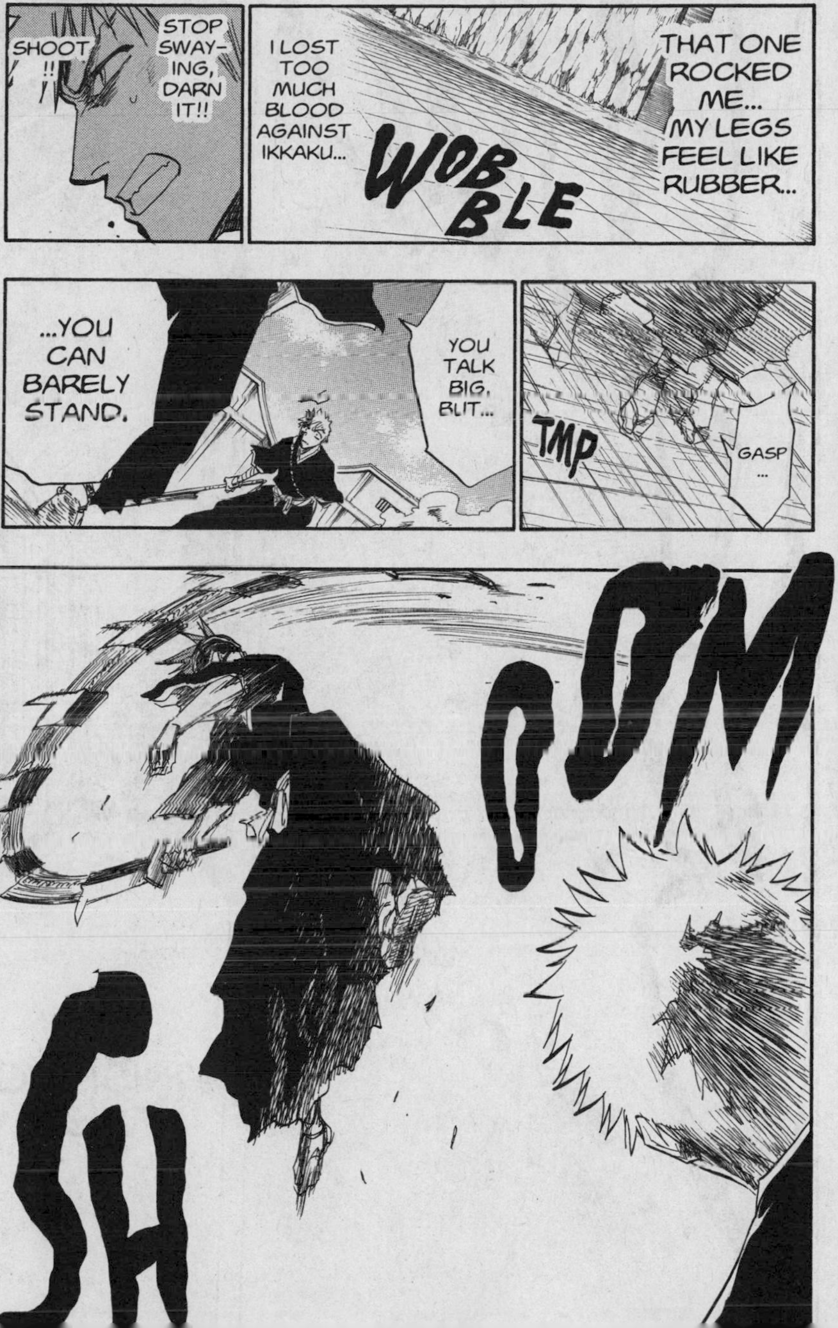
THAT ONE ROCKED ME... MY LEGS FEEL LIKE RUBBER...
I LOST TOO MUCH BLOOD AGAINST IKKAKU...
WOBBLE
STOP SWAYING, DARN IT!!
SHOOT!!
GASP...
TMP
YOU TALK BIG, BUT...
...YOU CAN BARELY STAND.
OOM
SH

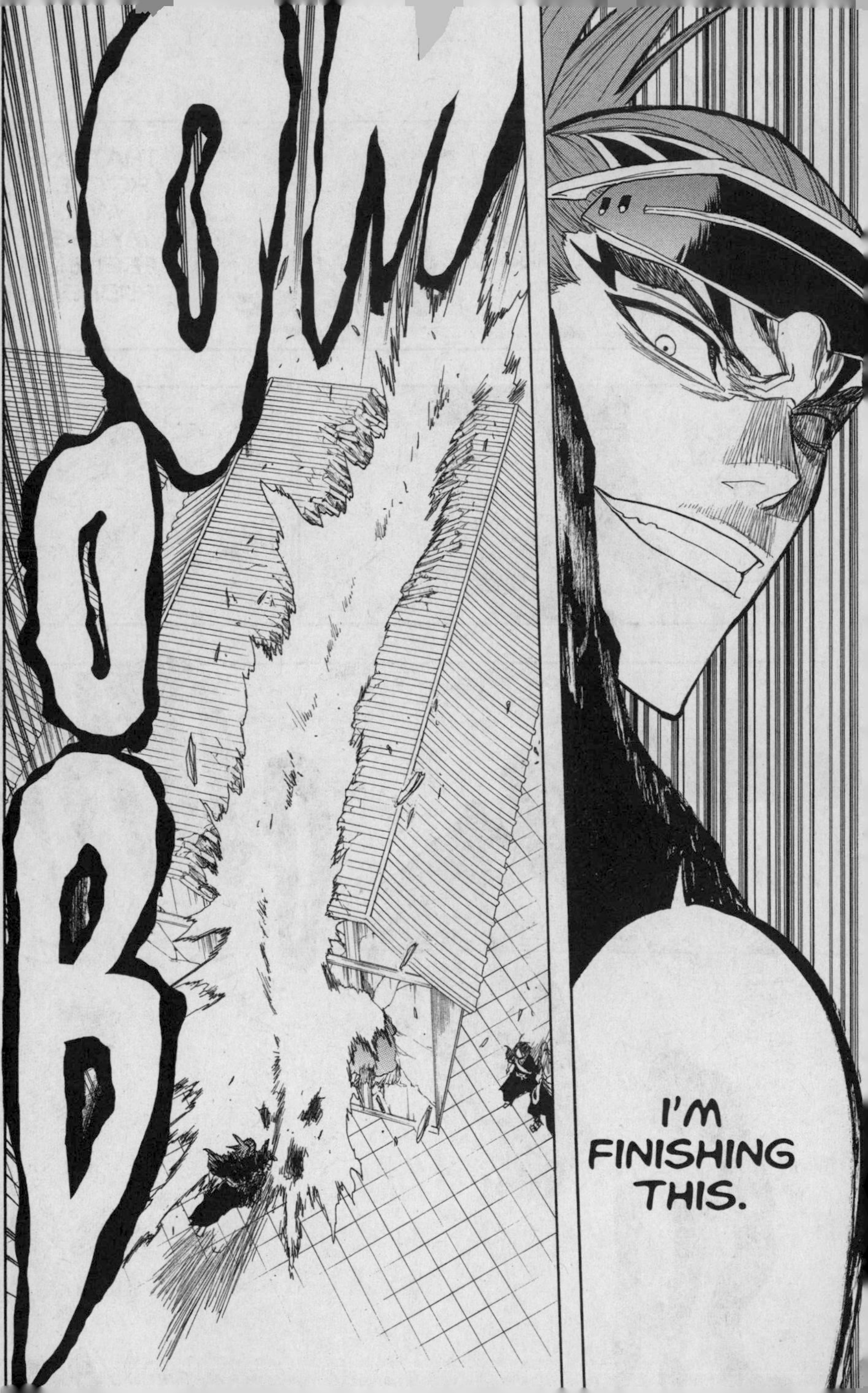
I'M FINISHING THIS.

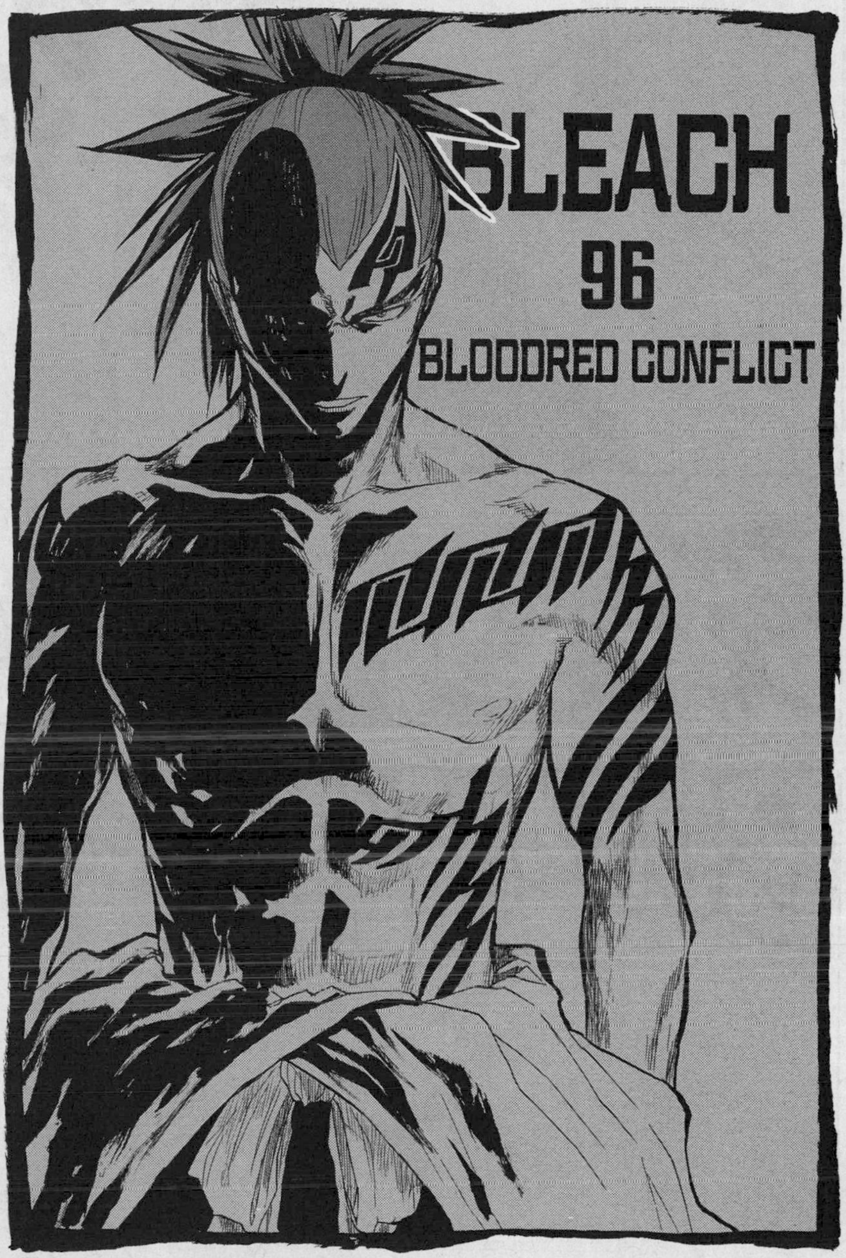
BLEACH
96
BLOODRED CONFLICT

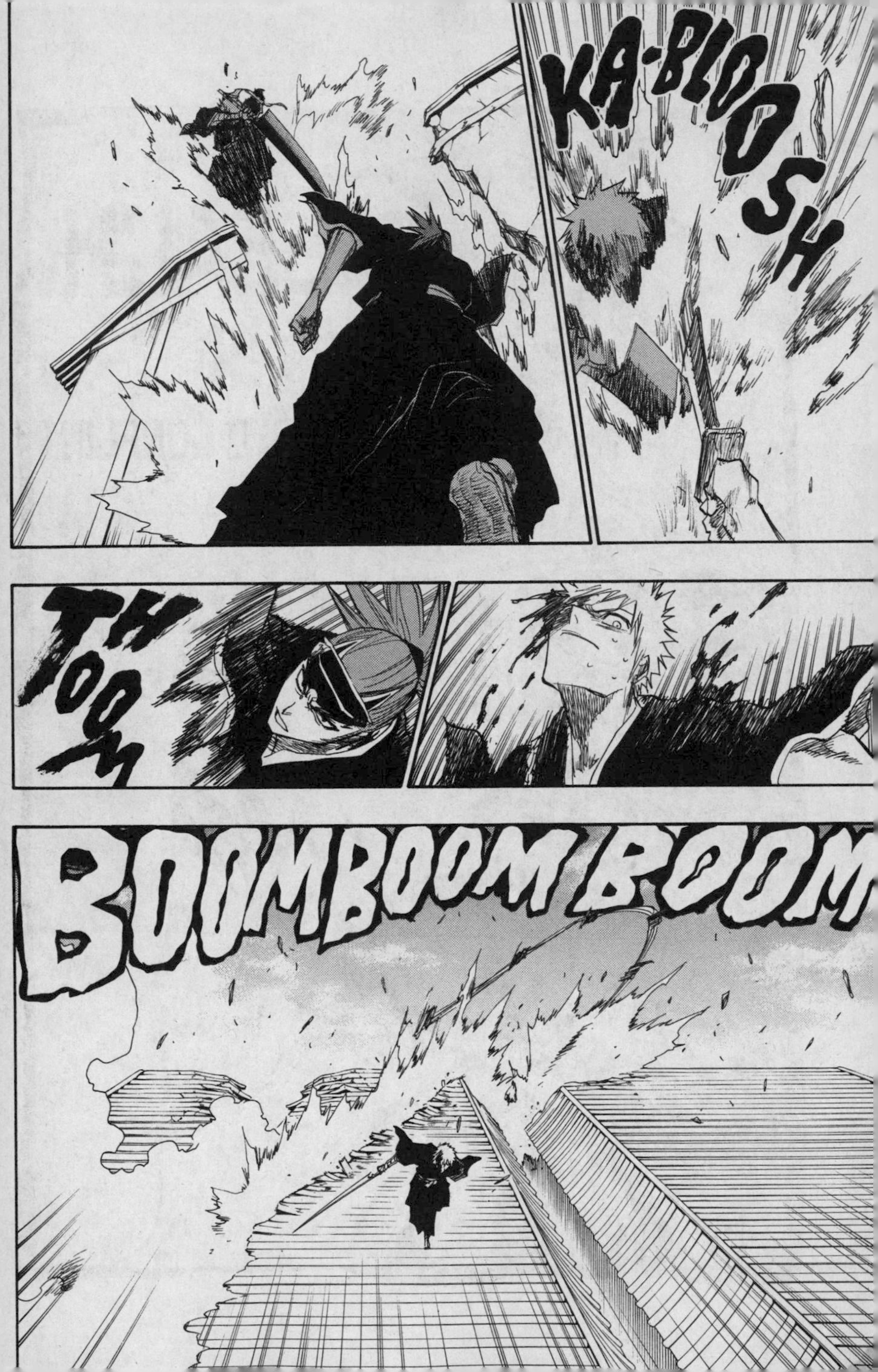
KA-BLOOSH
THOOM
BOOMBOOM BOOM

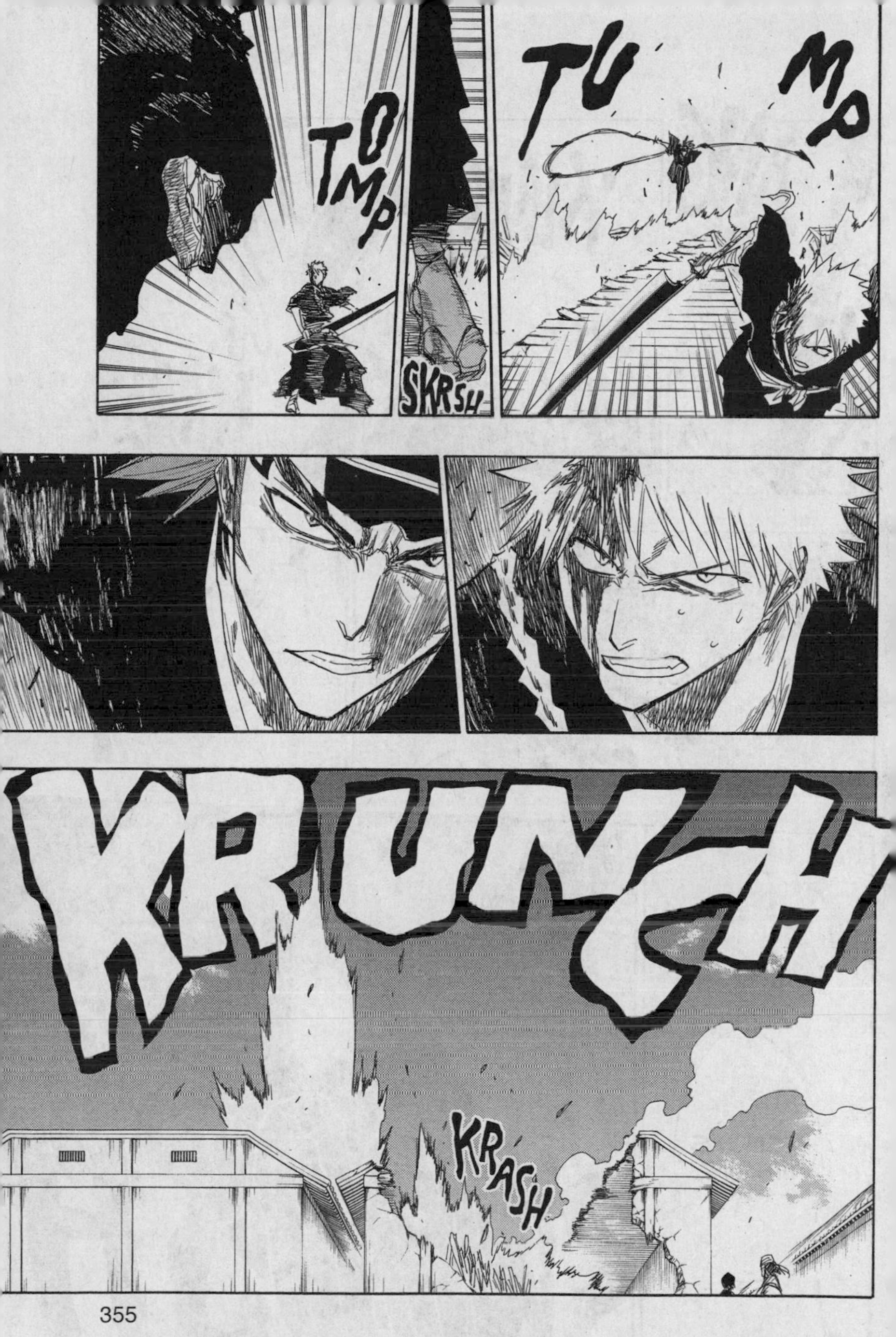
TUMP
SKRSH
TOMP
KRUNCH
KRASH

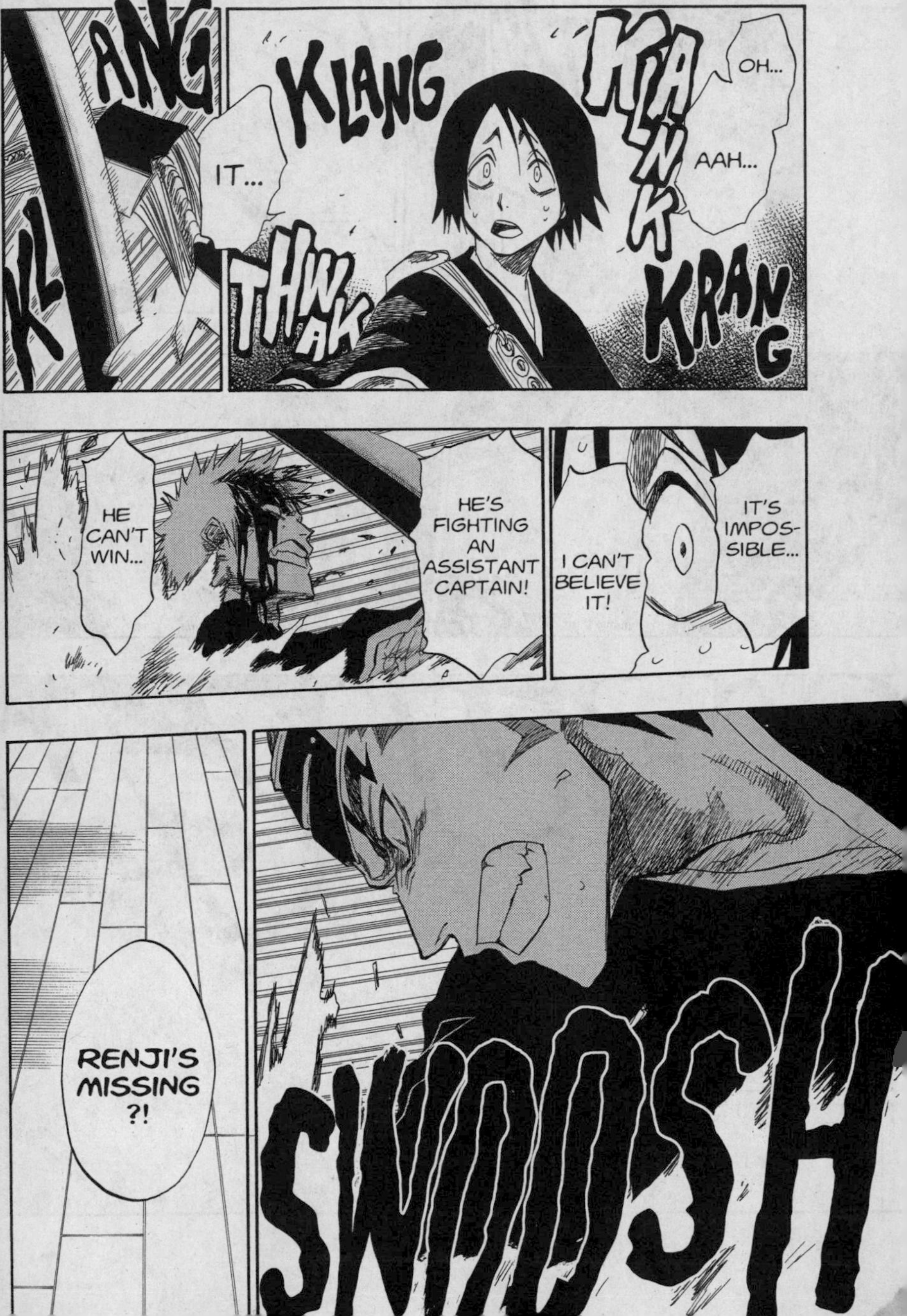
OH...
AAH...
KLANK
KRANG
KLANG
IT...
THWAK
KLANG
IT'S IMPOSSIBLE...
I CAN'T BELIEVE IT!
HE'S FIGHTING AN ASSISTANT CAPTAIN!
HE CAN'T WIN...
SWOOSH
RENJI'S MISSING?!

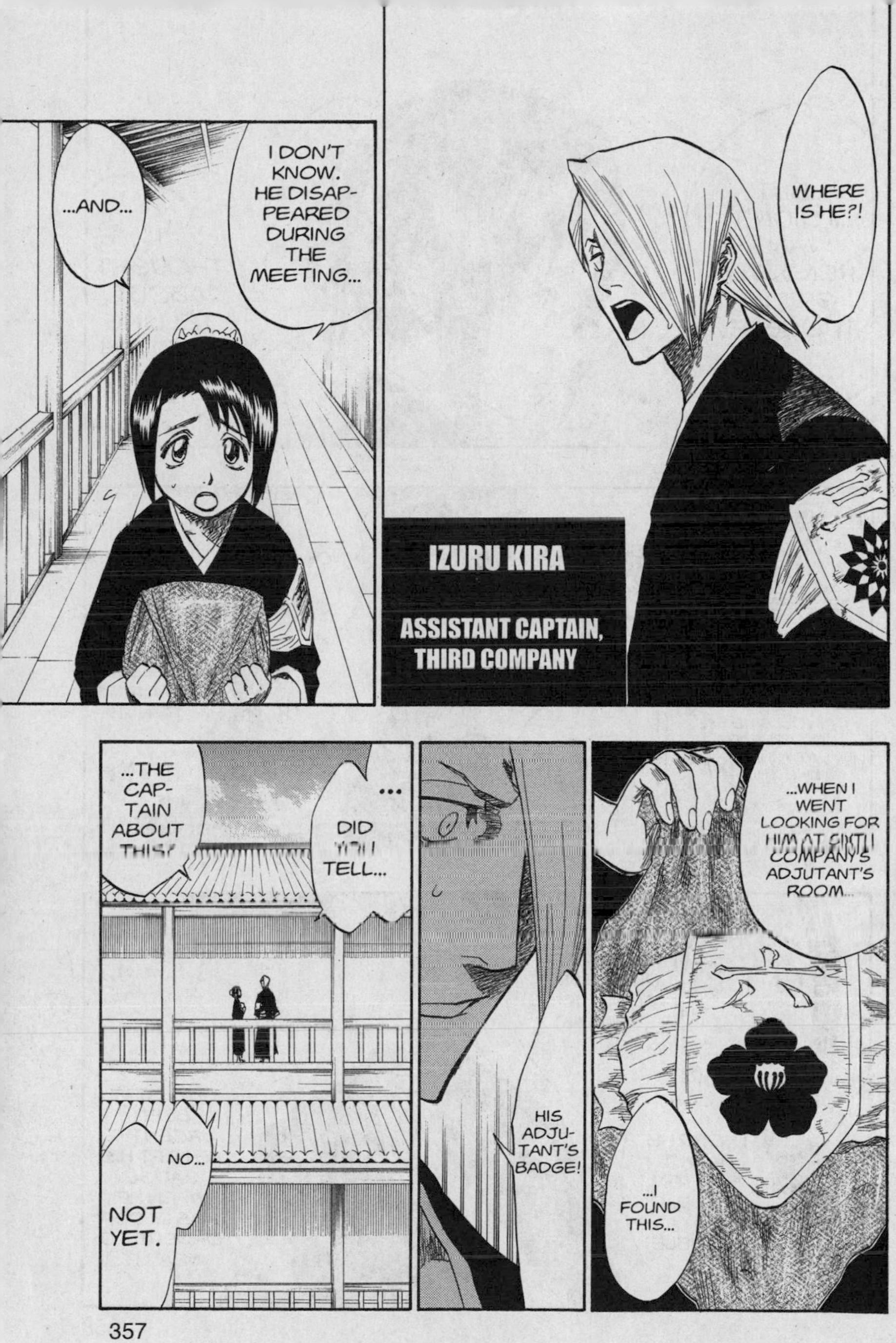
WHERE IS HE?!
IZURU KIRA
ASSISTANT CAPTAIN, THIRD COMPANY
I DON'T KNOW. HE DISAPPEARED DURING THE MEETING...
...AND...
...WHEN I WENT LOOKING FOR HIM AT
COMPANY'S ADJUTANT'S ROOM...
...I FOUND THIS...
HIS ADJUTANT'S BADGE!
...
DID YOU TELL...
...THE CAPTAIN ABOUT THIS?
NO...
NOT YET.

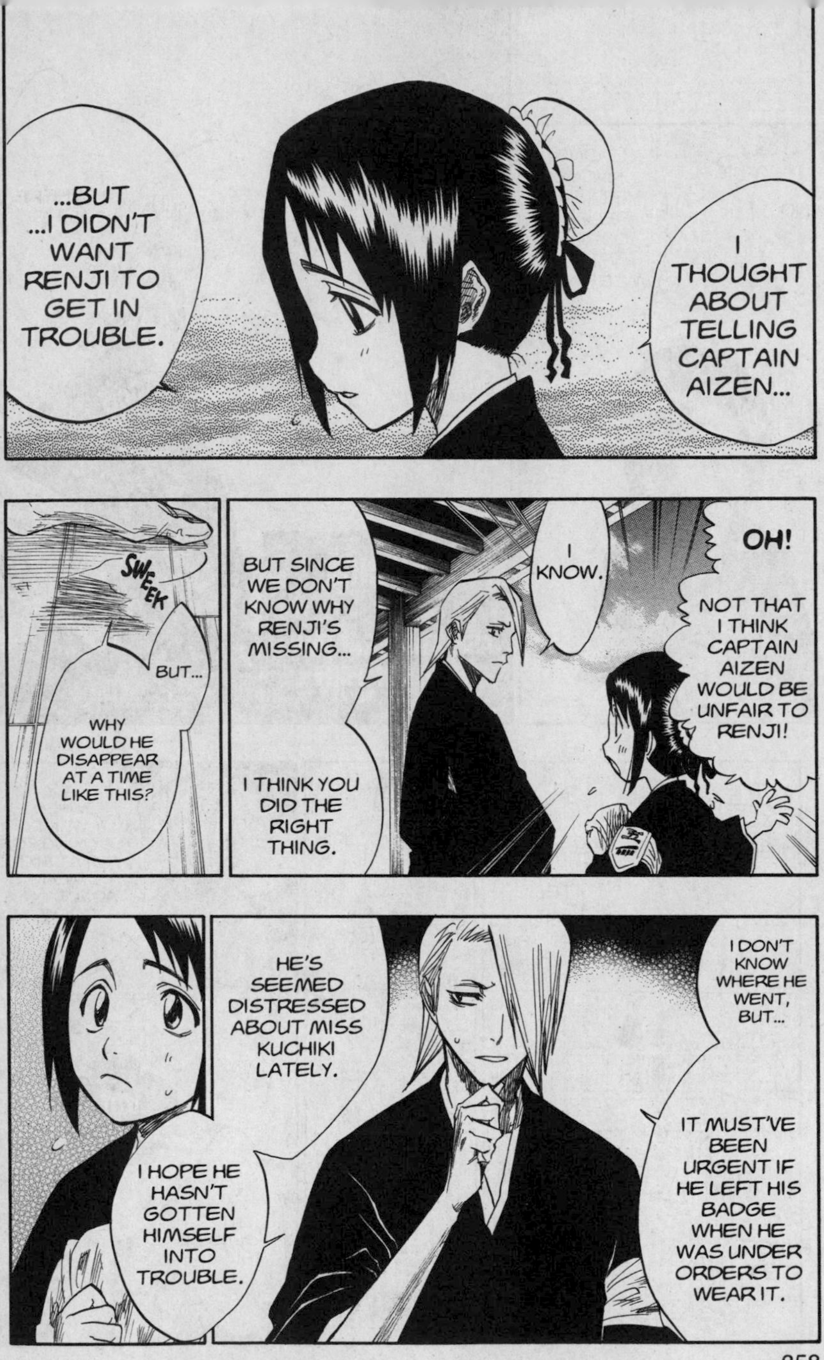

I THOUGHT ABOUT TELLING CAPTAIN AIZEN...
...BUT ...I DIDN'T WANT RENJI TO GET IN TROUBLE.
OH!
NOT THAT I THINK CAPTAIN AIZEN WOULD BE UNFAIR TO RENJI!
I KNOW.
BUT SINCE WE DON'T KNOW WHY RENJI'S MISSING...
I THINK YOU DID THE RIGHT THING.
SWEEK
BUT...
WHY WOULD HE DISAPPEAR AT A TIME LIKE THIS?
I DON'T KNOW WHERE HE WENT, BUT...
IT MUST'VE BEEN URGENT IF HE LEFT HIS BADGE WHEN HE WAS UNDER ORDERS TO WEAR IT.
HE'S SEEMED DISTRESSED ABOUT MISS KUCHIKI LATELY.
I HOPE HE HASN'T GOTTEN HIMSELF INTO TROUBLE.

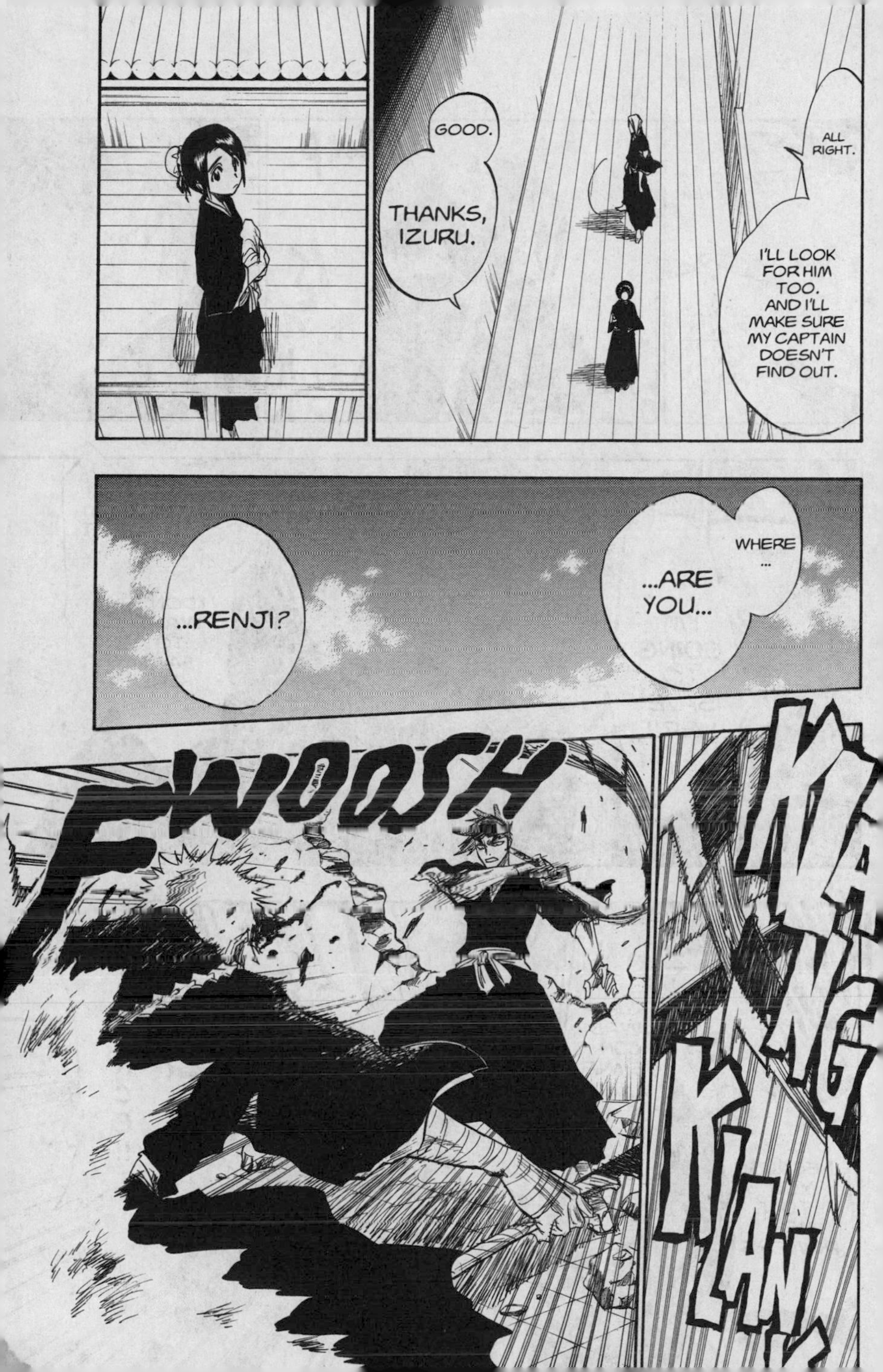
ALL RIGHT.
I'LL LOOK FOR HIM TOO. AND I'LL MAKE SURE MY CAPTAIN DOESN'T FIND OUT.
GOOD.
THANKS, IZURU.
WHERE...
...ARE YOU...
...RENJI?
KANG
KLAN
FWOOSH

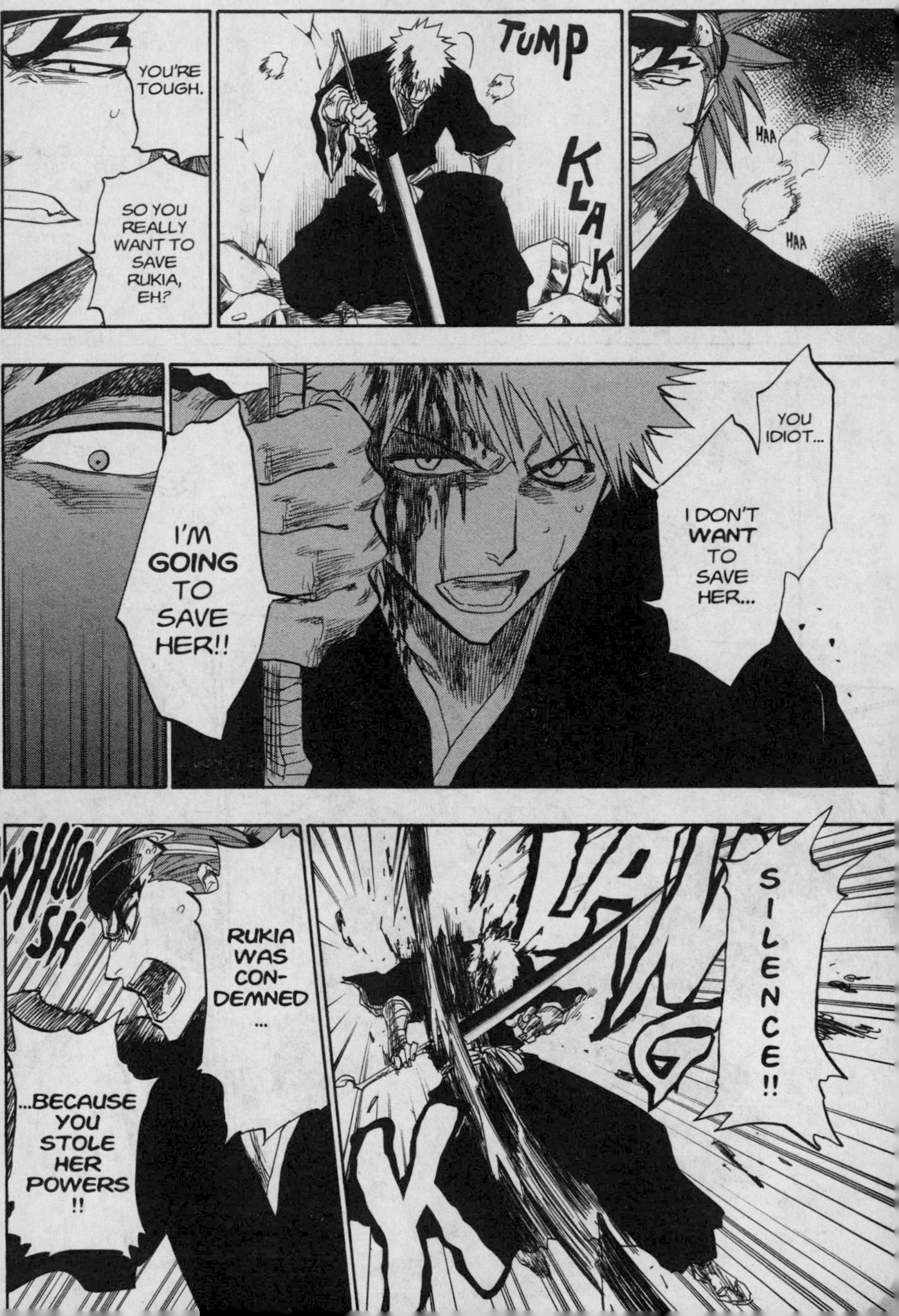
HAA
HAA
TUMP
KLAK
YOU'RE TOUGH.
SO YOU REALLY WANT TO SAVE RUKIA, EH?
YOU IDIOT...
I DON'T WANT TO SAVE HER...
I'M GOING TO SAVE HER!!
SILENCE!!
WHOOSH
RUKIA WAS CON-DEMNED...
...BECAUSE YOU STOLE HER POWERS!!

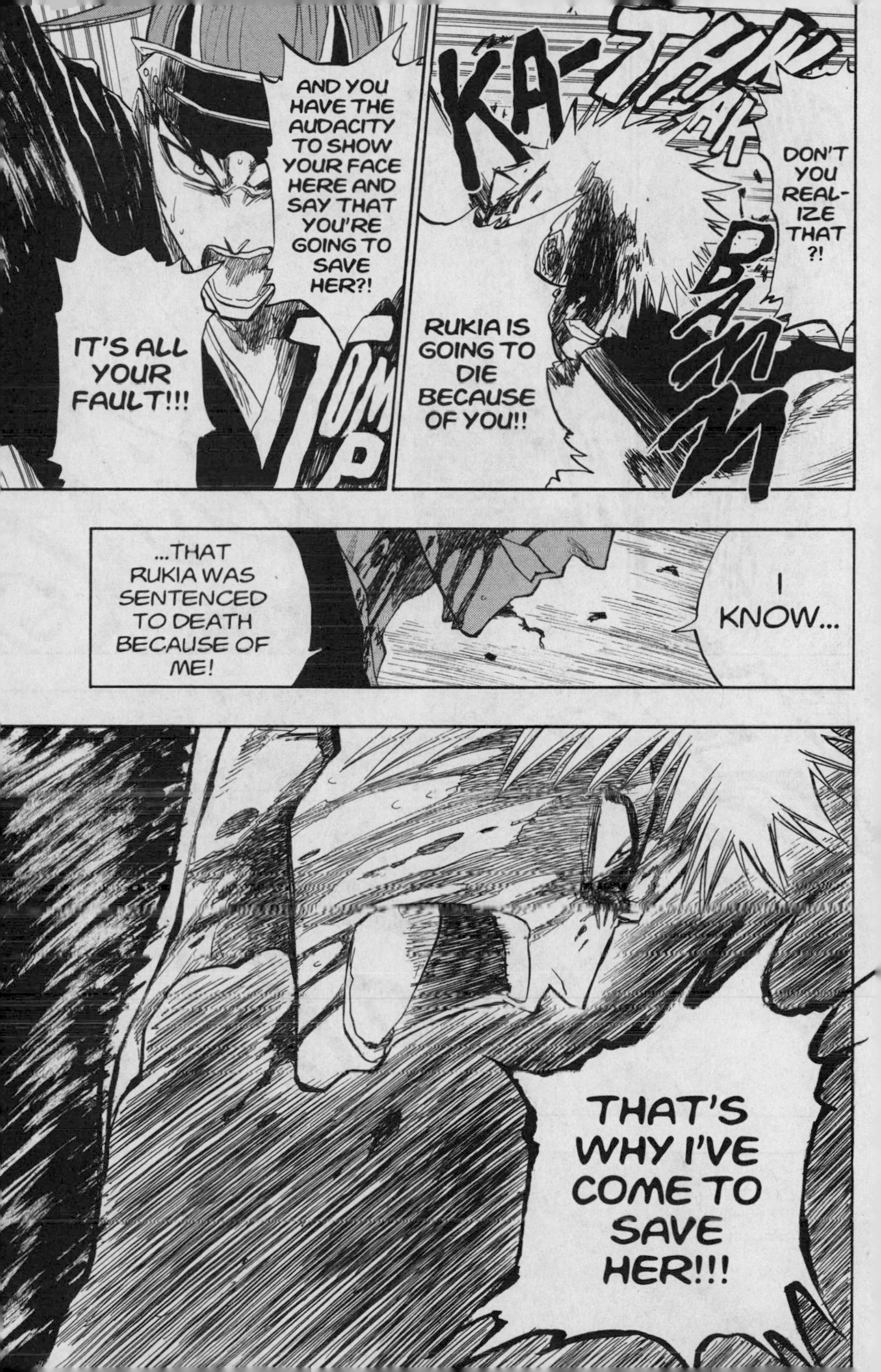
KA-THAK
DON'T YOU REALIZE THAT?!
BAMM
RUKIA IS GOING TO DIE BECAUSE OF YOU!!
AND YOU HAVE THE AUDACITY TO SHOW YOUR FACE HERE AND SAY THAT YOU'RE GOING TO SAVE HER?!
TOMP
IT'S ALL YOUR FAULT!!!
I KNOW...
...THAT RUKIA WAS SENTENCED TO DEATH BECAUSE OF ME!
THAT'S WHY I'VE COME TO SAVE HER!!!

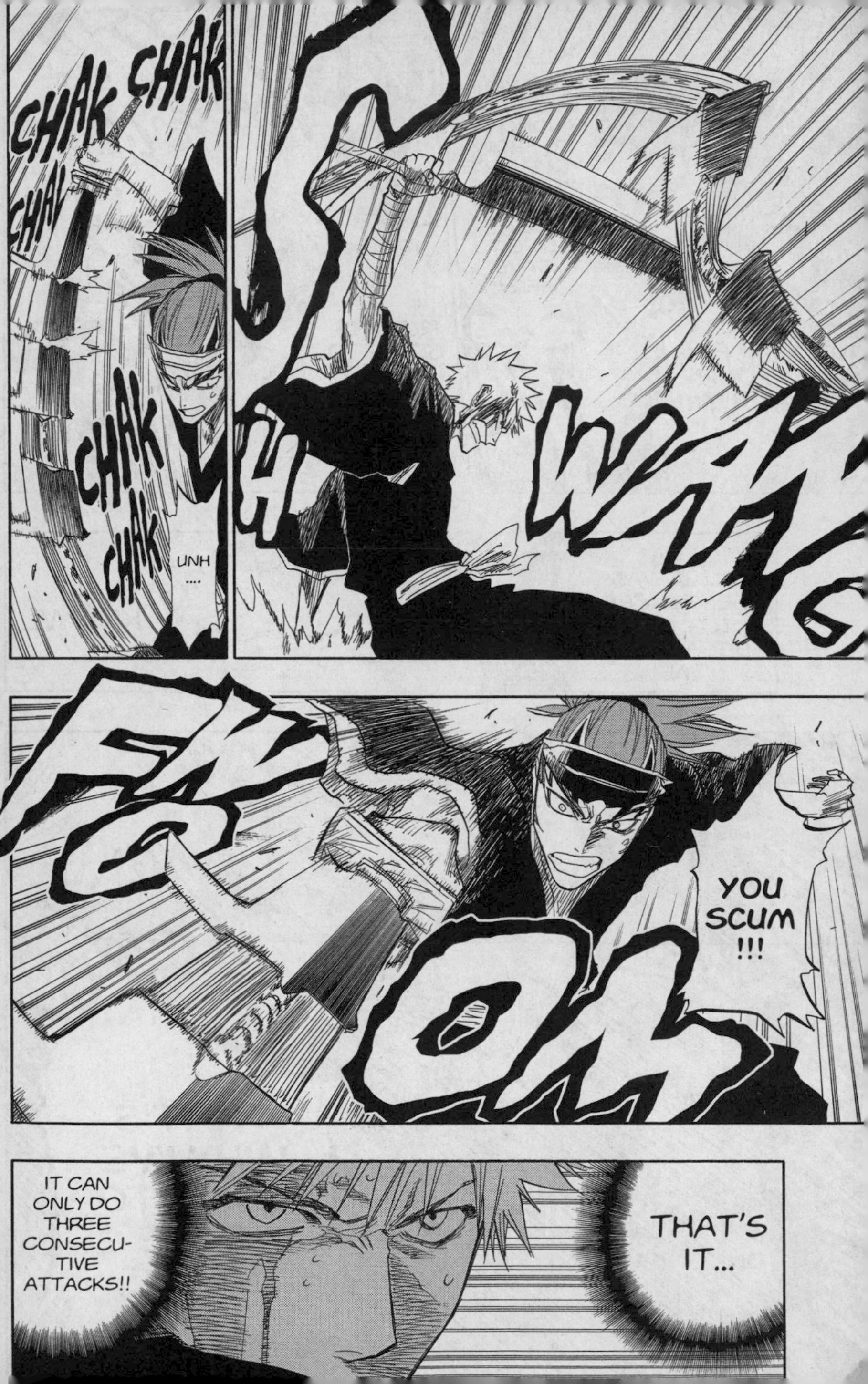
CHAK CHAK
CHAK
CHAK
CHAK
CHAK
UNH
....
YOU SCUM
!!!
THAT'S
IT...
IT CAN ONLY DO THREE CONSECU-TIVE ATTACKS!!

READ THIS WAY

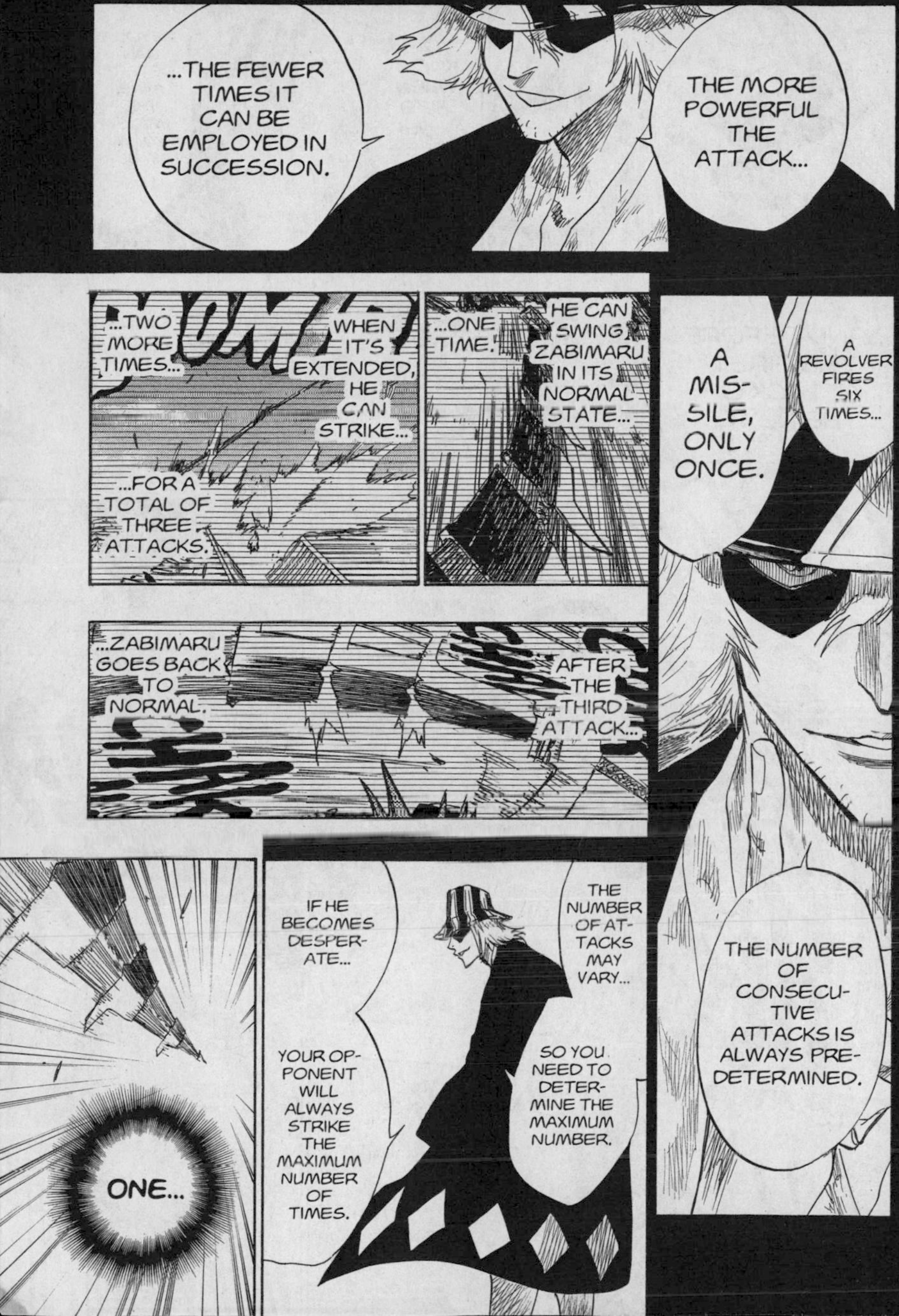
THE MORE POWERFUL THE ATTACK...
...THE FEWER TIMES IT CAN BE EMPLOYED IN SUCCESSION.
A REVOLVER FIRES SIX TIMES...
A MIS-SILE, ONLY ONCE.
THE NUMBER OF CONSECU-TIVE ATTACKS IS ALWAYS PRE-DETERMINED.
HE CAN SWING ZABIMARU IN ITS NORMAL STATE...
...ONE TIME.
WHEN IT'S EXTENDED, HE CAN STRIKE...
...TWO MORE TIMES...
...FOR A TOTAL OF THREE ATTACKS.
AFTER THE THIRD ATTACK...
...ZABIMARU GOES BACK TO NORMAL.
THE NUMBER OF AT-TACKS MAY VARY...
IF HE BECOMES DESPER-ATE...
SO YOU NEED TO DETER-MINE THE MAXIMUM NUMBER.
YOUR OP-PONENT WILL ALWAYS STRIKE THE MAXIMUM NUMBER OF TIMES.
ONE...

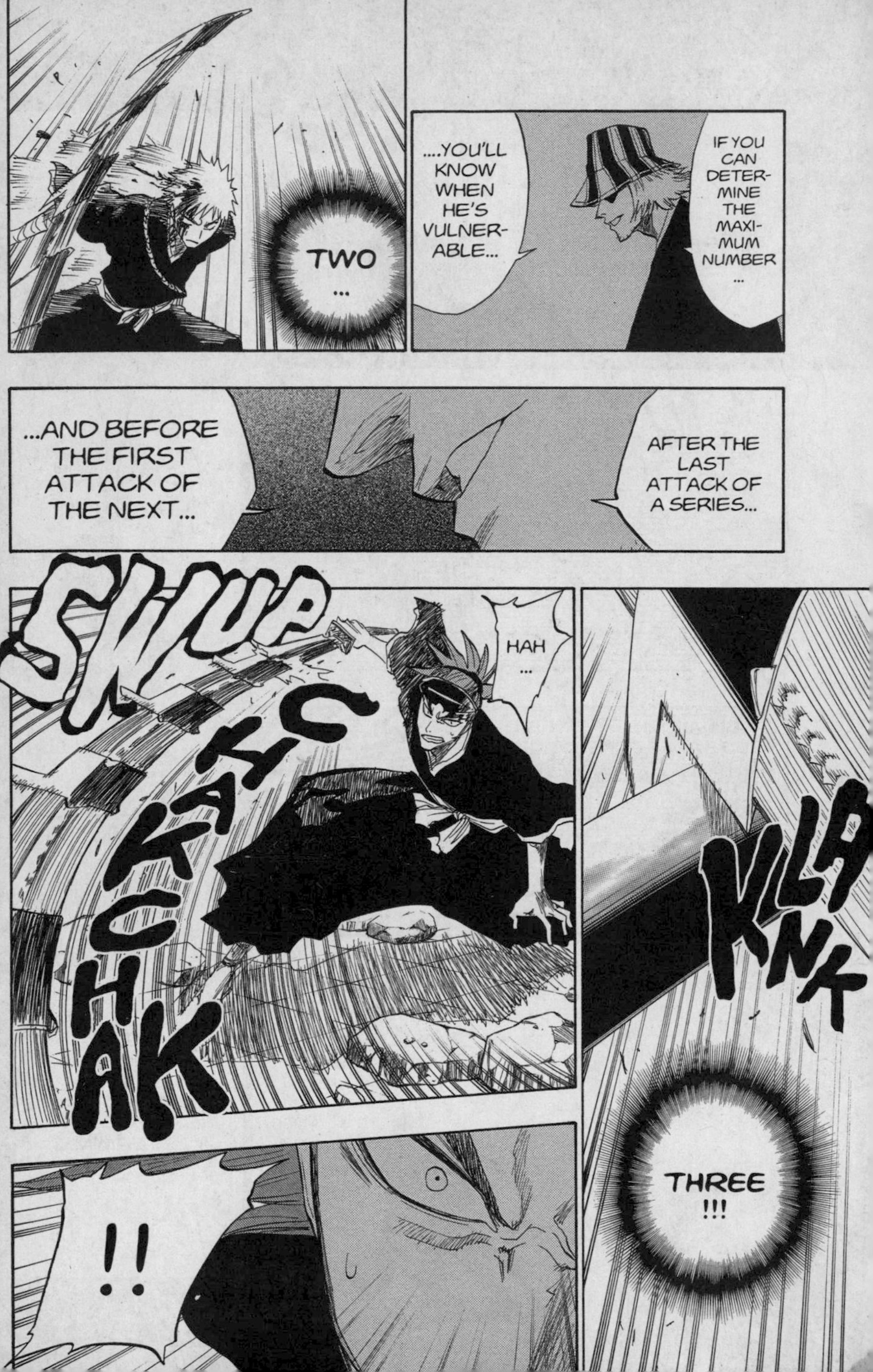
IF YOU CAN DETER-MINE THE MAXI-MUM NUMBER ...
....YOU'LL KNOW WHEN HE'S VULNER-ABLE...
TWO ...
AFTER THE LAST ATTACK OF A SERIES...
...AND BEFORE THE FIRST ATTACK OF THE NEXT...
KLANK
THREE !!!
SHUP
HAH ...
KACHAK
!!

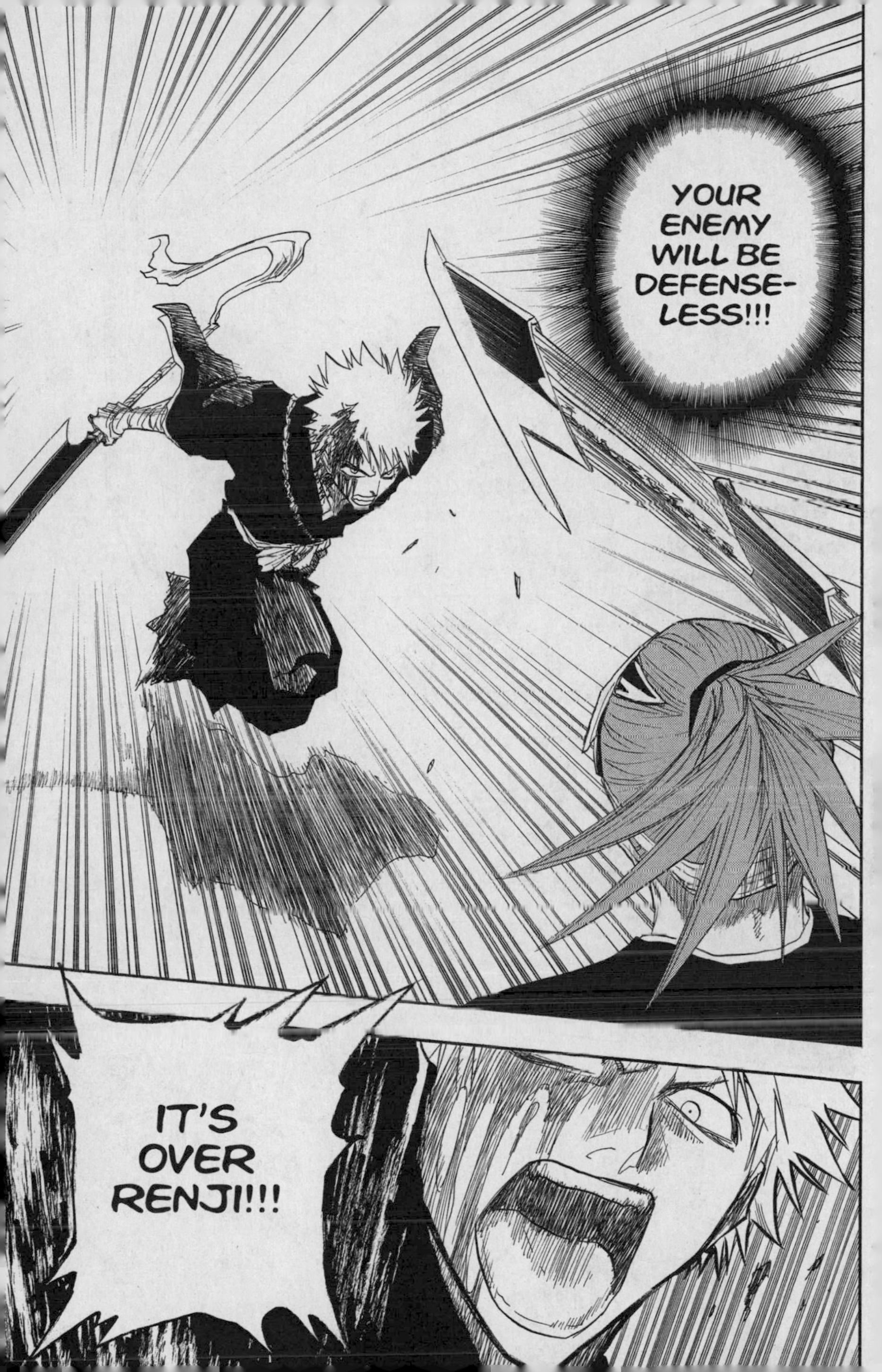
YOUR ENEMY WILL BE DEFENSE-LESS!!!
IT'S OVER RENJI!!!

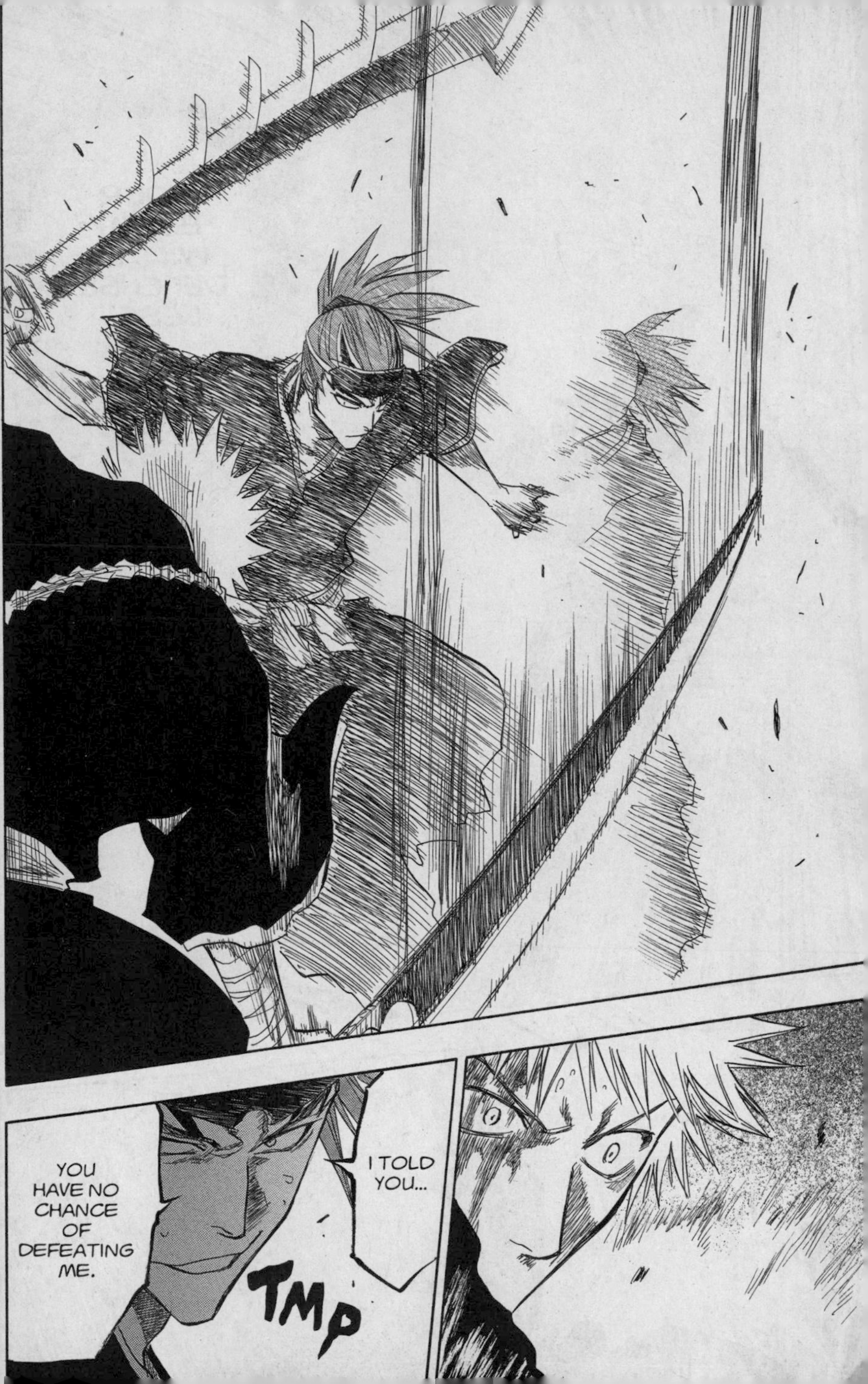
I TOLD YOU...
YOU HAVE NO CHANCE OF DEFEATING ME.
TMP

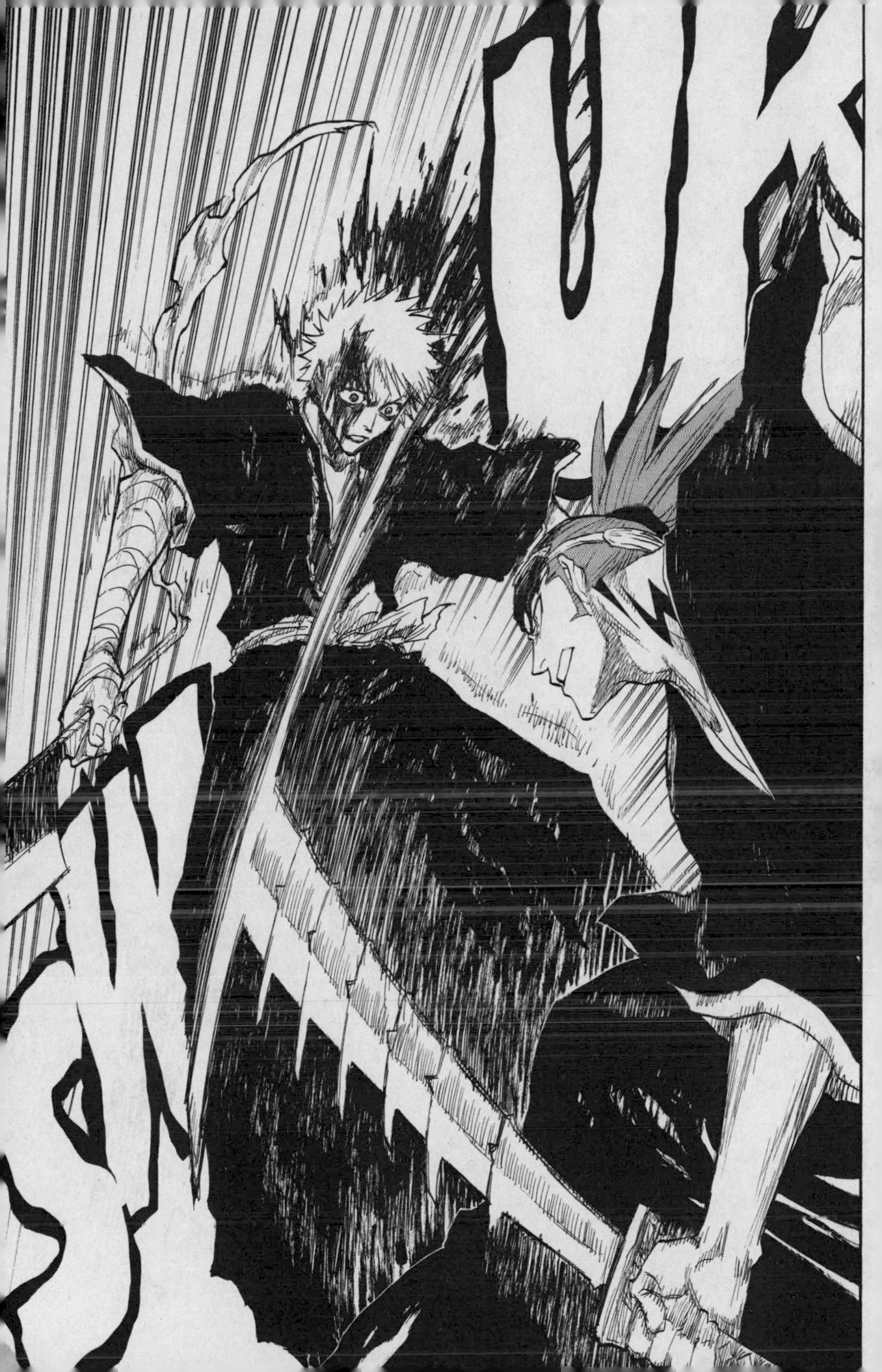

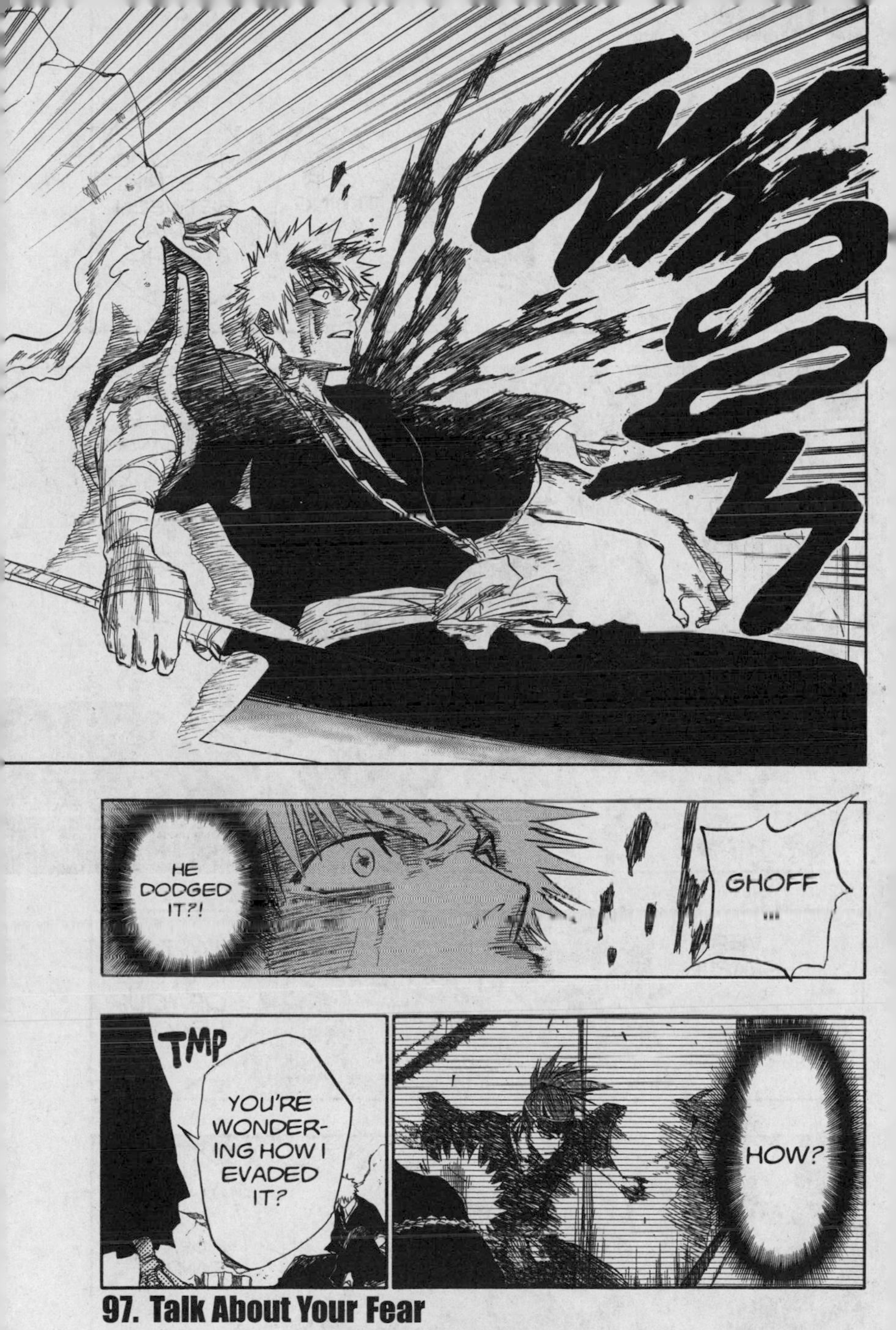
GHOFF ...
HE DODGED IT?!
HOW?
TMP
YOU'RE WONDERING HOW I EVADED IT?

97. Talk About Your Fear

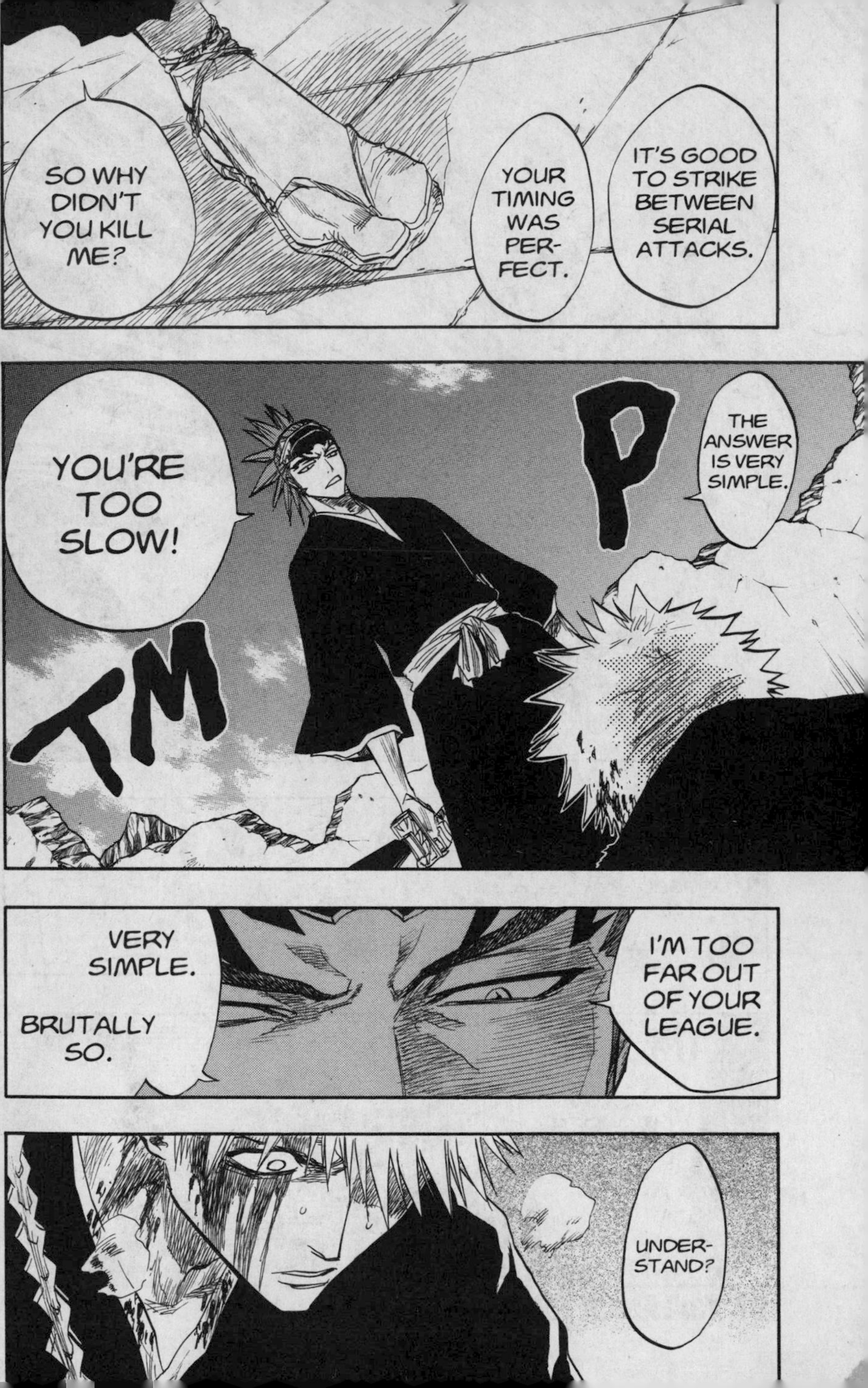
IT'S GOOD TO STRIKE BETWEEN SERIAL ATTACKS.
YOUR TIMING WAS PER-FECT.
SO WHY DIDN'T YOU KILL ME?
THE ANSWER IS VERY SIMPLE.
P
YOU'RE TOO SLOW!
TM
I'M TOO FAR OUT OF YOUR LEAGUE.
VERY SIMPLE.
BRUTALLY SO.
UNDER-STAND?

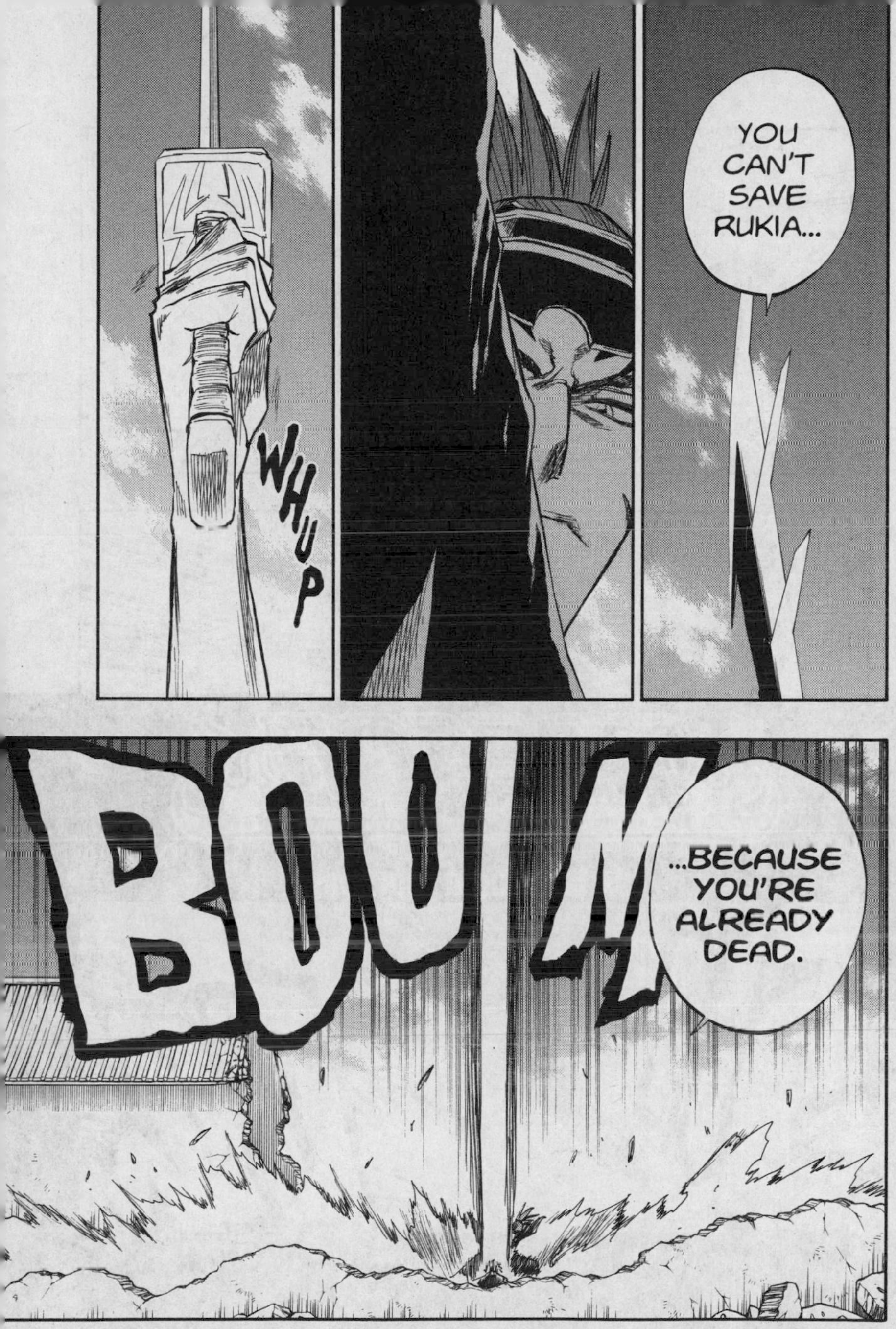
YOU CAN'T SAVE RUKIA...
WHUP
...BECAUSE YOU'RE ALREADY DEAD.
BOOM

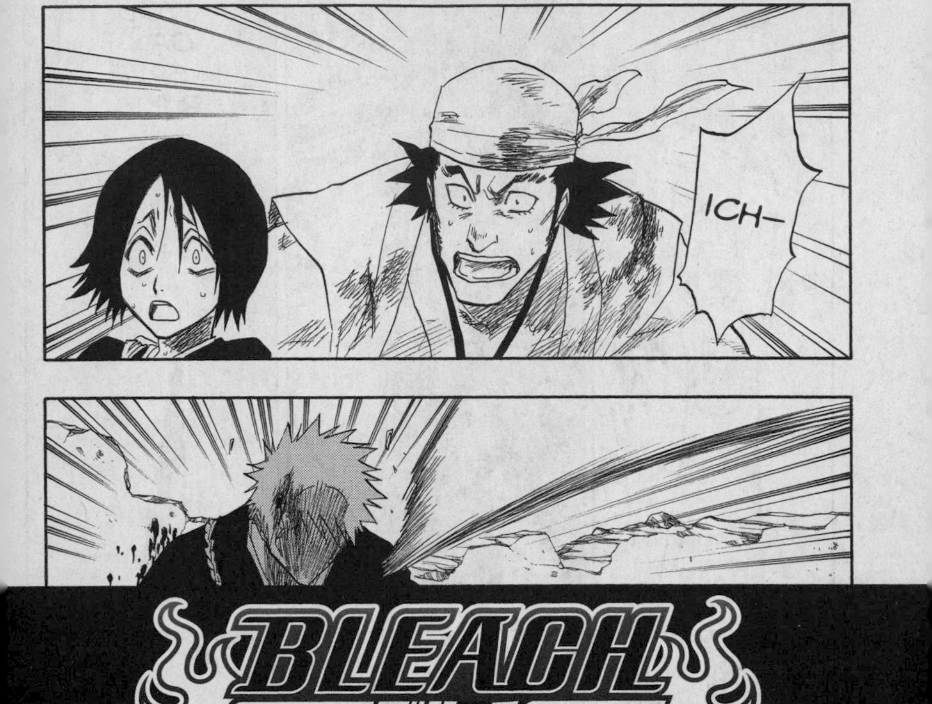
ICH—

BLEACH

97. Talk About Your Fear

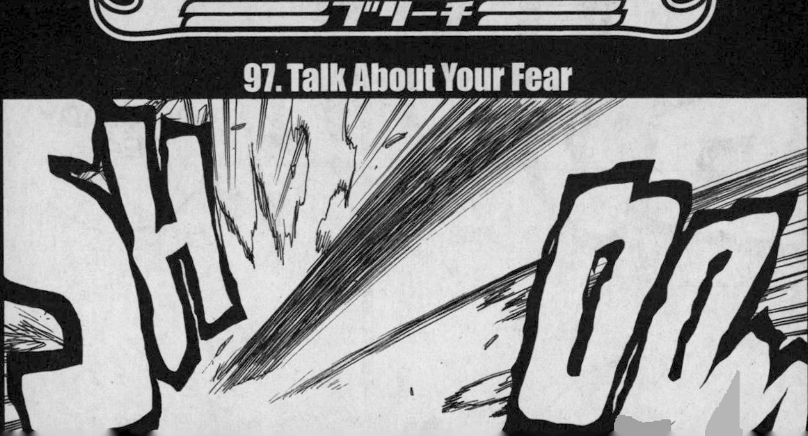

READ THIS WAY

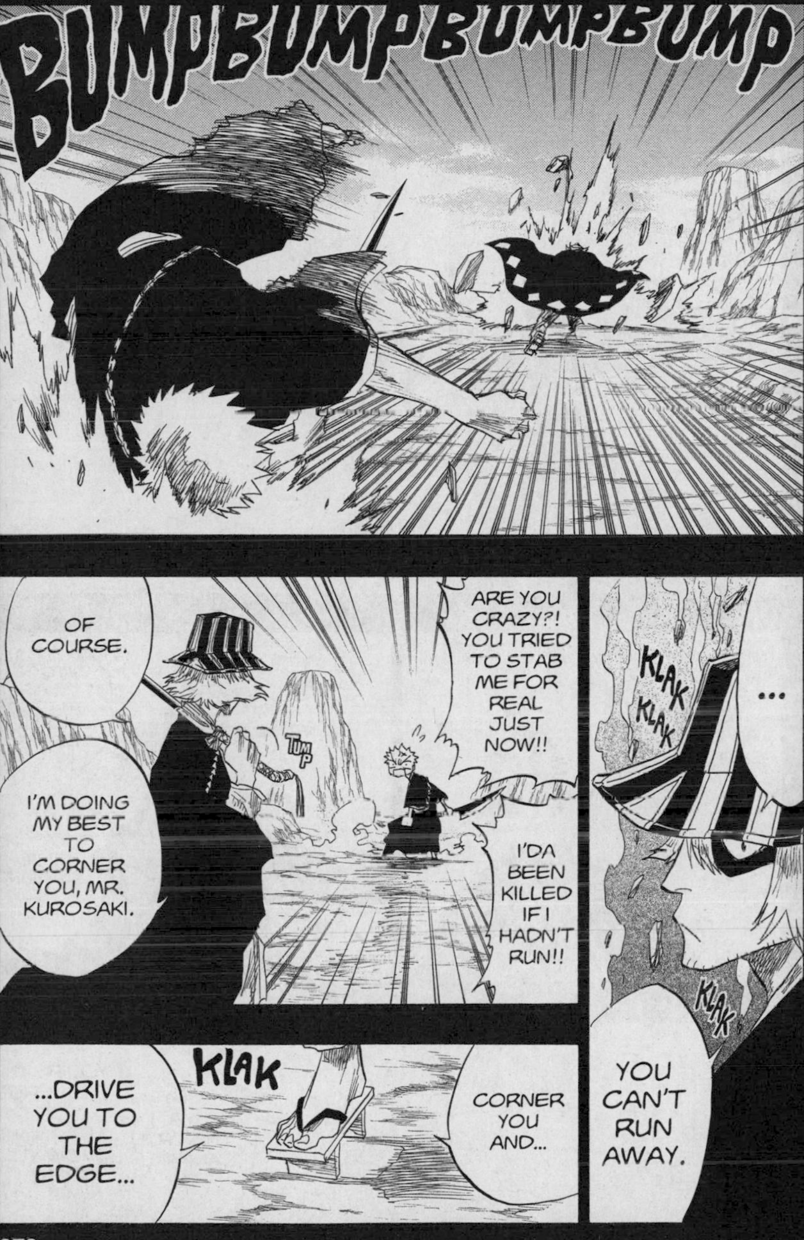
BUMPBUMPBUMPBUMP
...
KLAK KLAK
KLAK
YOU CAN'T RUN AWAY.
ARE YOU CRAZY?! YOU TRIED TO STAB ME FOR REAL JUST NOW!!
I'DA BEEN KILLED IF I HADN'T RUN!!
OF COURSE.
TUMP
I'M DOING MY BEST TO CORNER YOU, MR. KUROSAKI.
CORNER YOU AND...
KLAK
...DRIVE YOU TO THE EDGE...

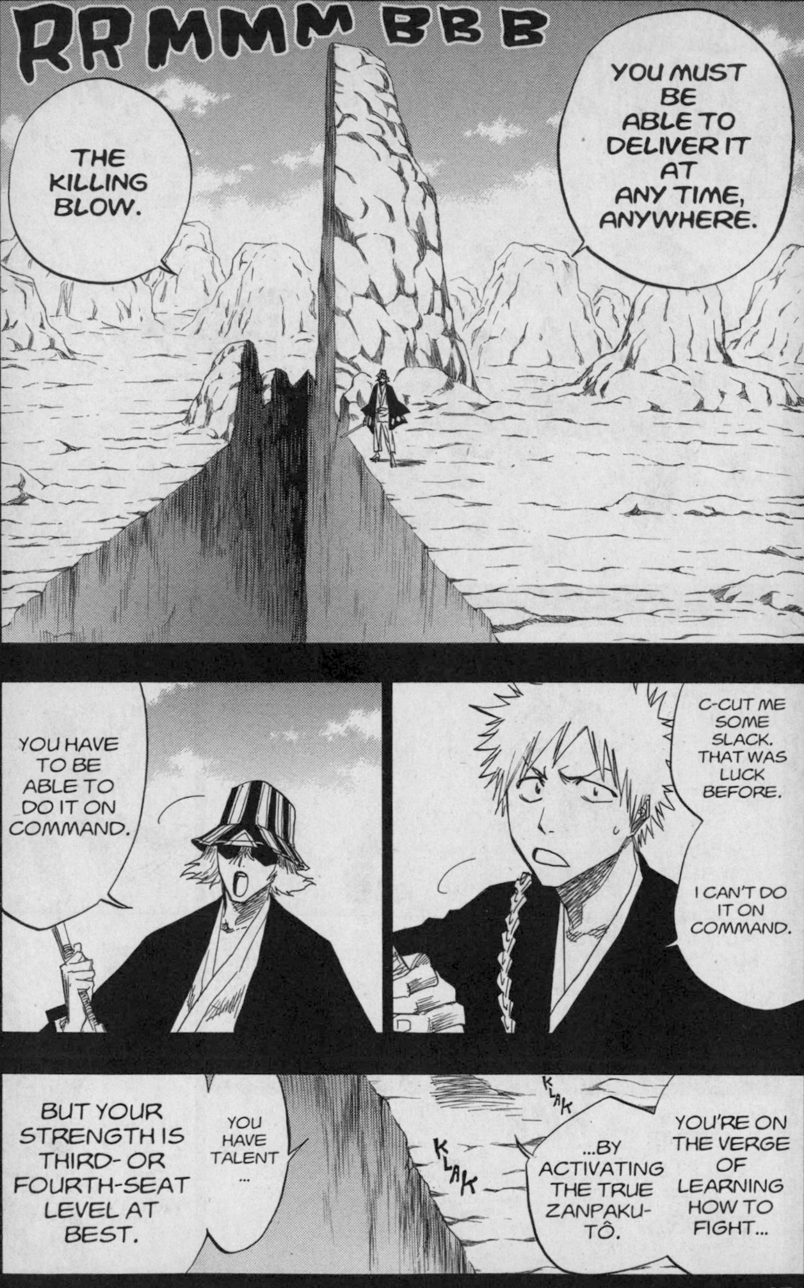
RRMMM BBB
YOU MUST BE ABLE TO DELIVER IT AT ANY TIME, ANYWHERE.
THE KILLING BLOW.
C-CUT ME SOME SLACK. THAT WAS LUCK BEFORE.
I CAN'T DO IT ON COMMAND.
YOU HAVE TO BE ABLE TO DO IT ON COMMAND.
YOU'RE ON THE VERGE OF LEARNING HOW TO FIGHT...
...BY ACTIVATING THE TRUE ZANPAKU-TÔ.
KLAK
KLAK
YOU HAVE TALENT ...
BUT YOUR STRENGTH IS THIRD- OR FOURTH-SEAT LEVEL AT BEST.

READ THIS WAY

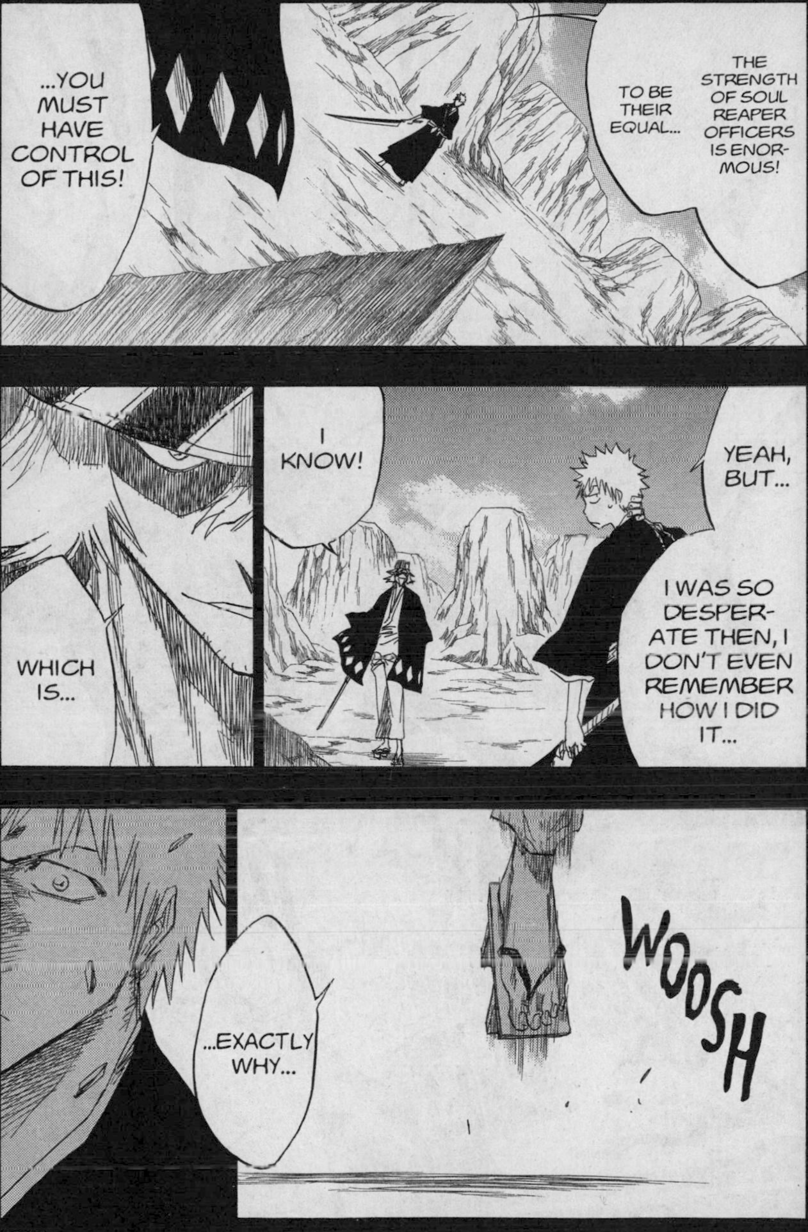

THE STRENGTH OF SOUL REAPER OFFICERS IS ENORMOUS!
TO BE THEIR EQUAL...
...YOU MUST HAVE CONTROL OF THIS!
YEAH, BUT...
I WAS SO DESPERATE THEN, I DON'T EVEN REMEMBER HOW I DID IT...
I KNOW!
WHICH IS...
WOOSH
...EXACTLY WHY...

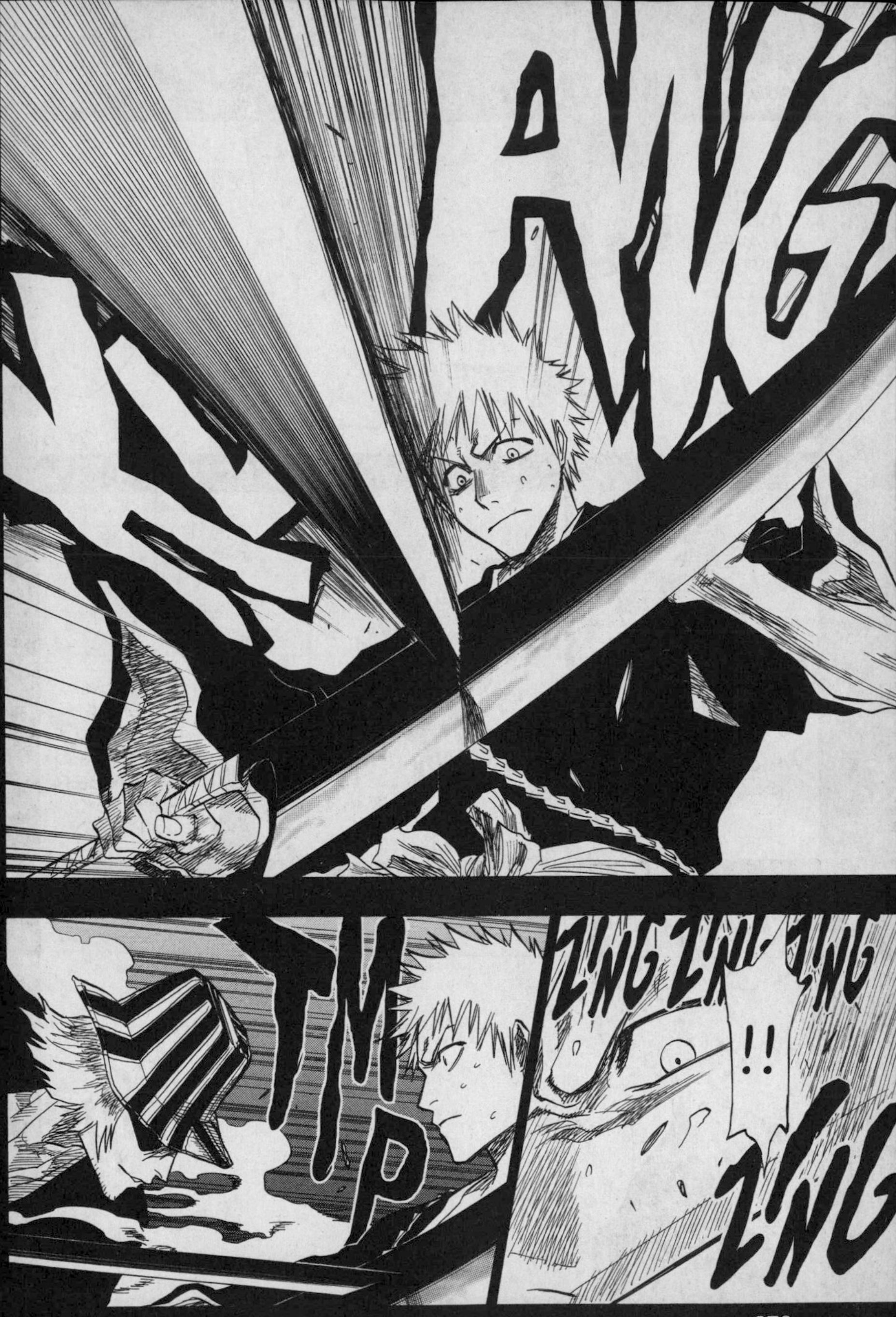
!!

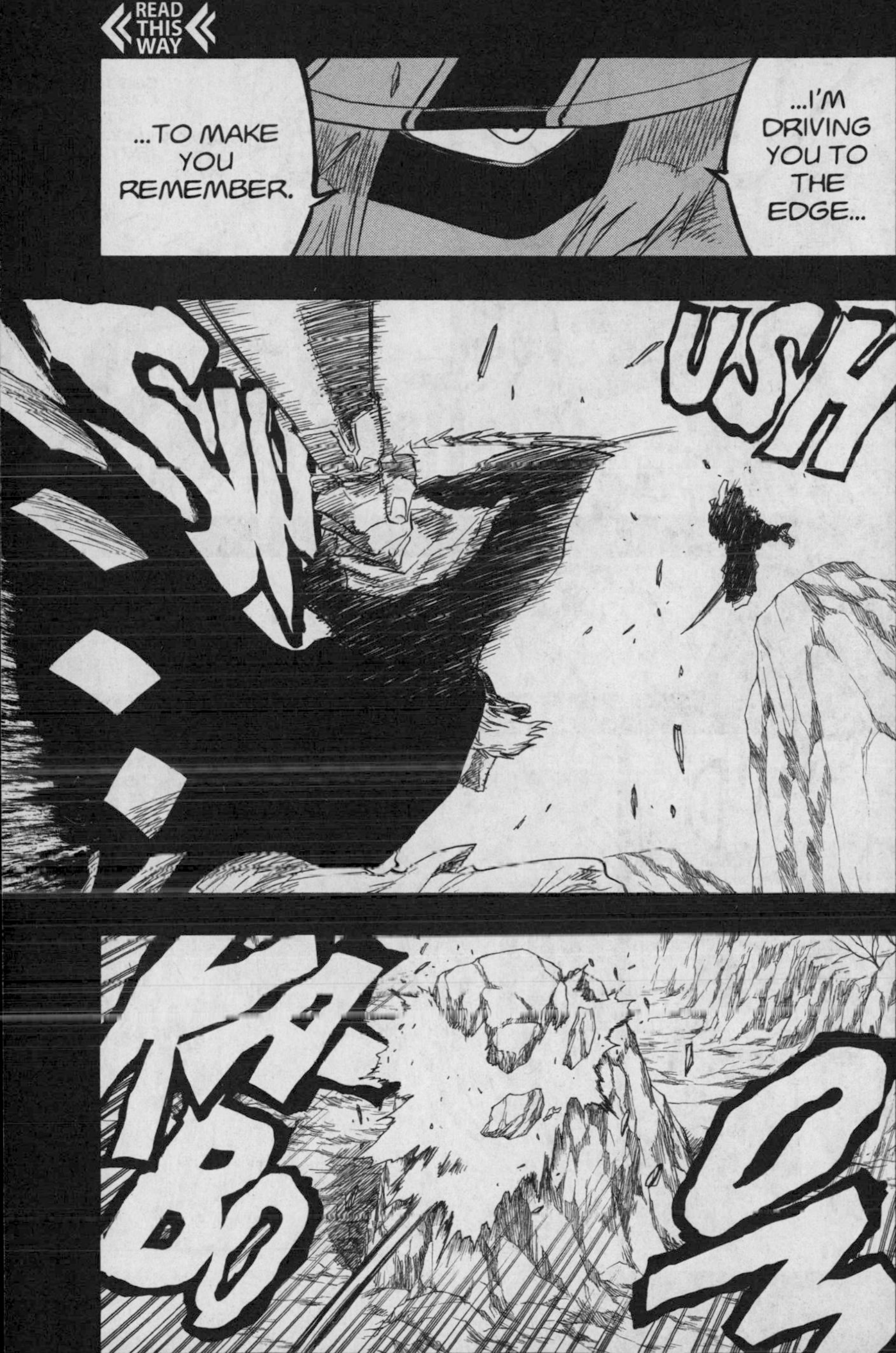
READ THIS WAY
...I'M DRIVING YOU TO THE EDGE...
...TO MAKE YOU REMEMBER.

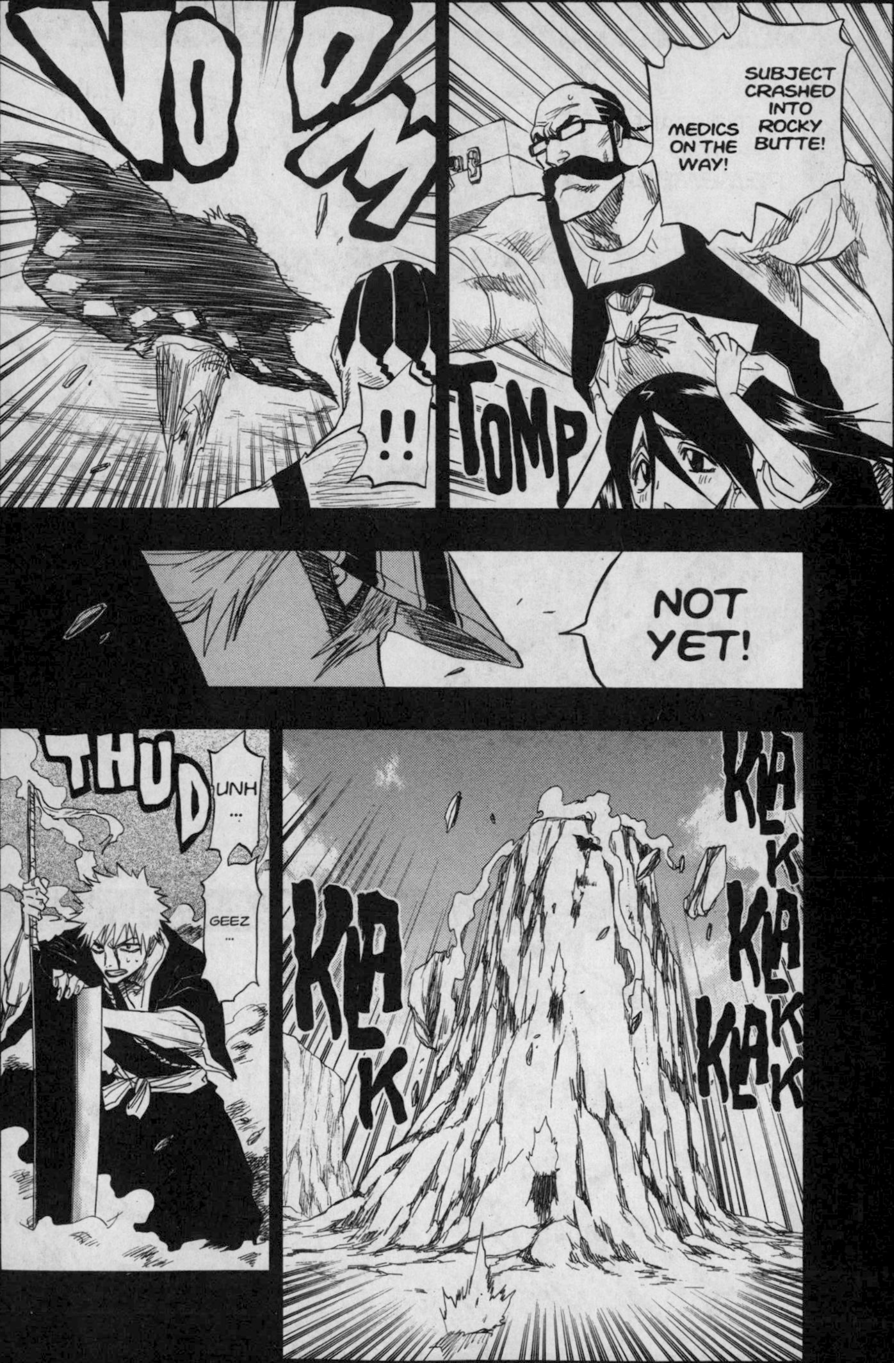
SUBJECT CRASHED INTO ROCKY BUTTE!
MEDICS ON THE WAY!
TOMP
VOOM
!!
NOT YET!
KLAK KLAK KLAK
KLAK
THUD
UNH...
GEEZ...

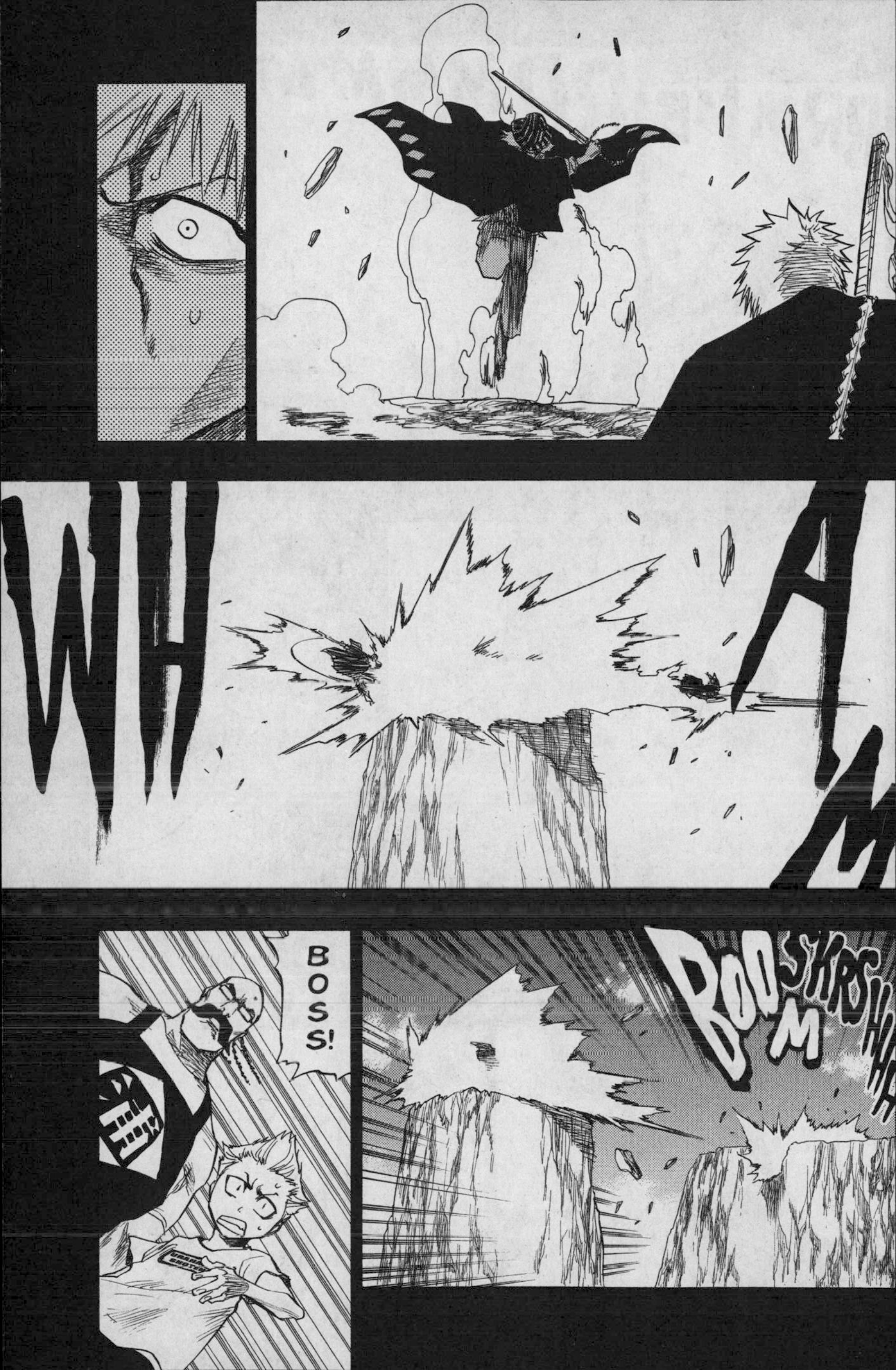
WHAM
SHRSHHHH
BOOM
BOSS!

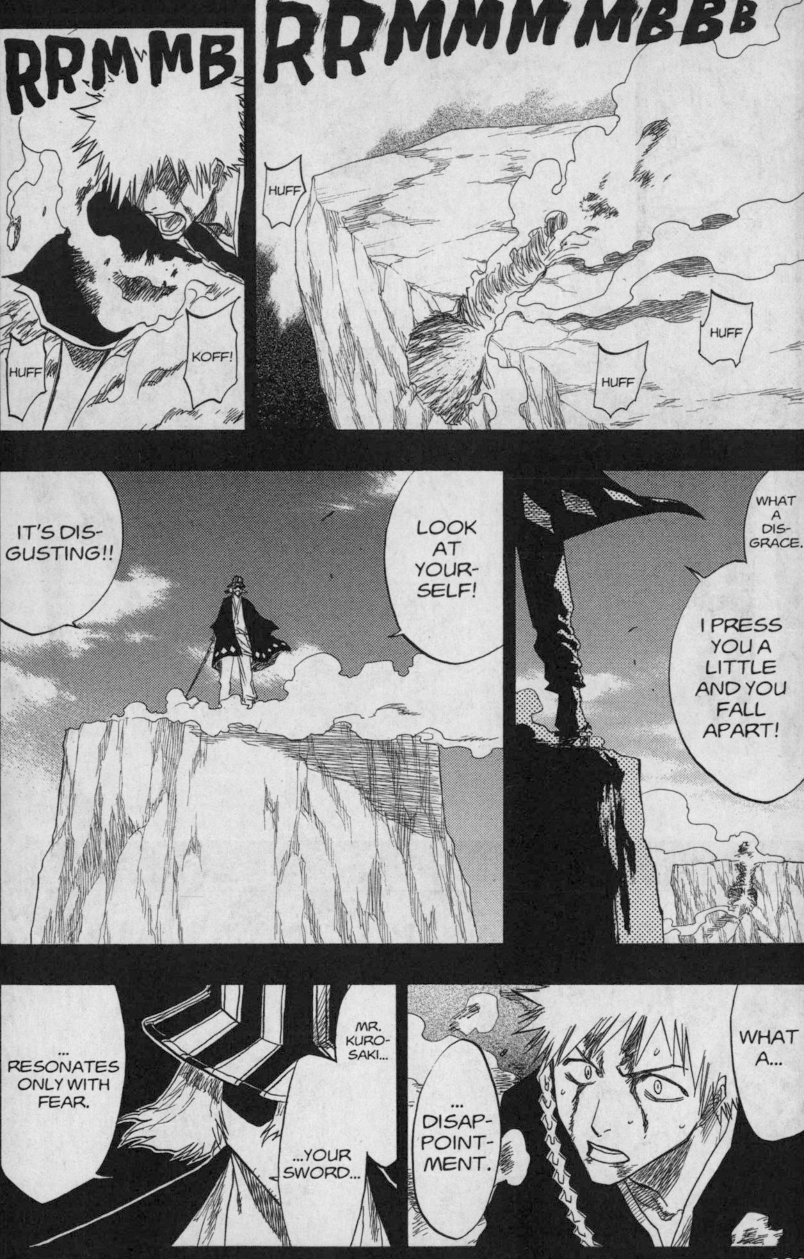
RRMMMMBBB
HUFF
HUFF
HUFF
RRMMB
KOFF!
HUFF
WHAT A DIS-GRACE.
I PRESS YOU A LITTLE AND YOU FALL APART!
LOOK AT YOUR-SELF!
IT'S DIS-GUSTING!!
WHAT A...
...DISAP-POINT-MENT.
MR. KURO-SAKI...
...YOUR SWORD...
...RESONATES ONLY WITH FEAR.

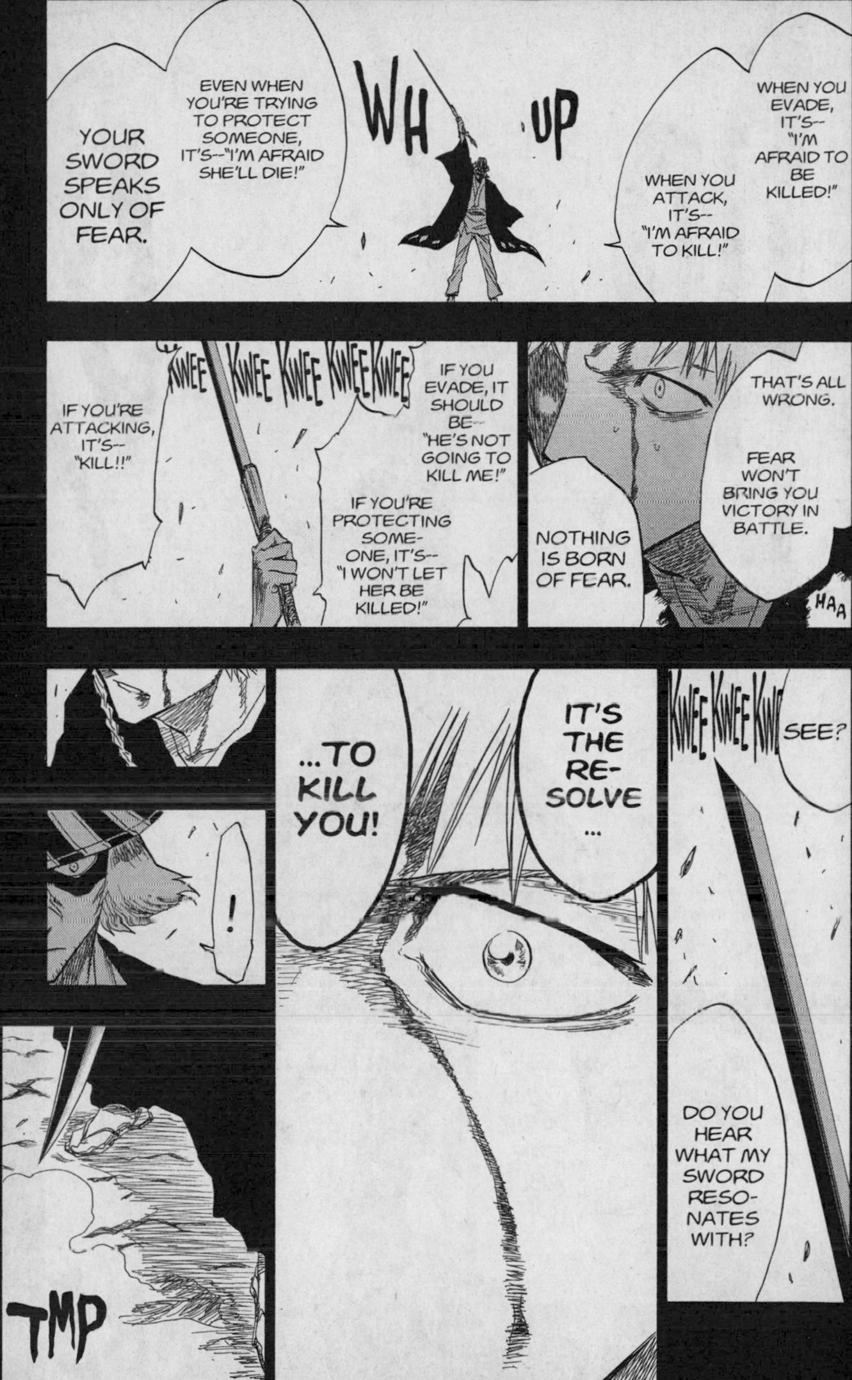
WHEN YOU EVADE, IT'S-- "I'M AFRAID TO BE KILLED!"
WHEN YOU ATTACK, IT'S-- "I'M AFRAID TO KILL!"
WHUP
EVEN WHEN YOU'RE TRYING TO PROTECT SOMEONE, IT'S--"I'M AFRAID SHE'LL DIE!"
YOUR SWORD SPEAKS ONLY OF FEAR.
THAT'S ALL WRONG.
FEAR WON'T BRING YOU VICTORY IN BATTLE.
NOTHING IS BORN OF FEAR.
HAA
KWEE KWEE KWEE KWEE KWEE
IF YOU EVADE, IT SHOULD BE-- "HE'S NOT GOING TO KILL ME!"
IF YOU'RE PROTECTING SOME-ONE, IT'S-- "I WON'T LET HER BE KILLED!"
IF YOU'RE ATTACKING, IT'S-- "KILL!!"
KWEE KWEE KWE
SEE?
DO YOU HEAR WHAT MY SWORD RESO-NATES WITH?
IT'S THE RE-SOLVE ...
...TO KILL YOU!
!
TMP

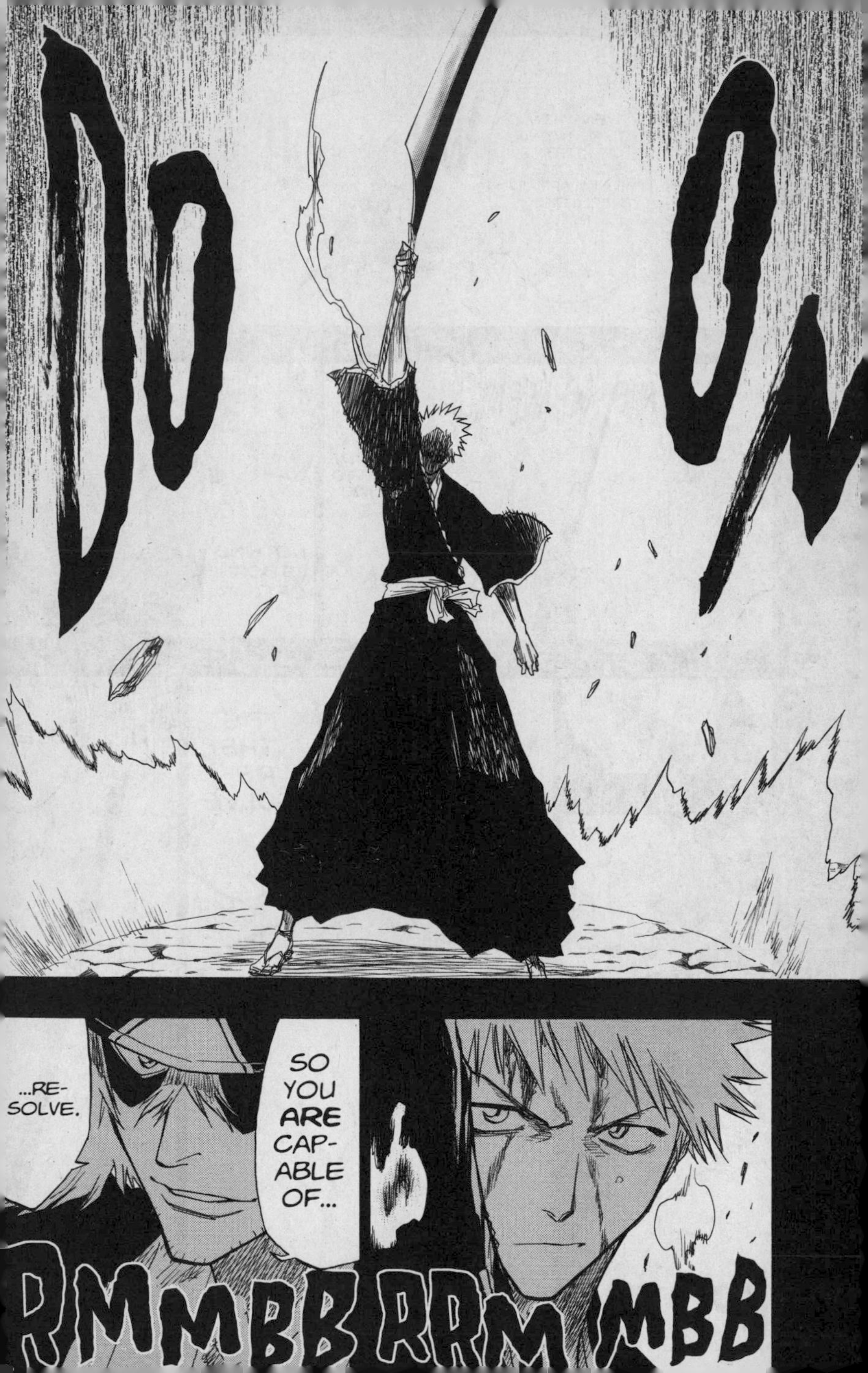
DOON
SO YOU ARE CAP-ABLE OF...
...RE-SOLVE.
RMMBB RRM MBB

READ THIS WAY

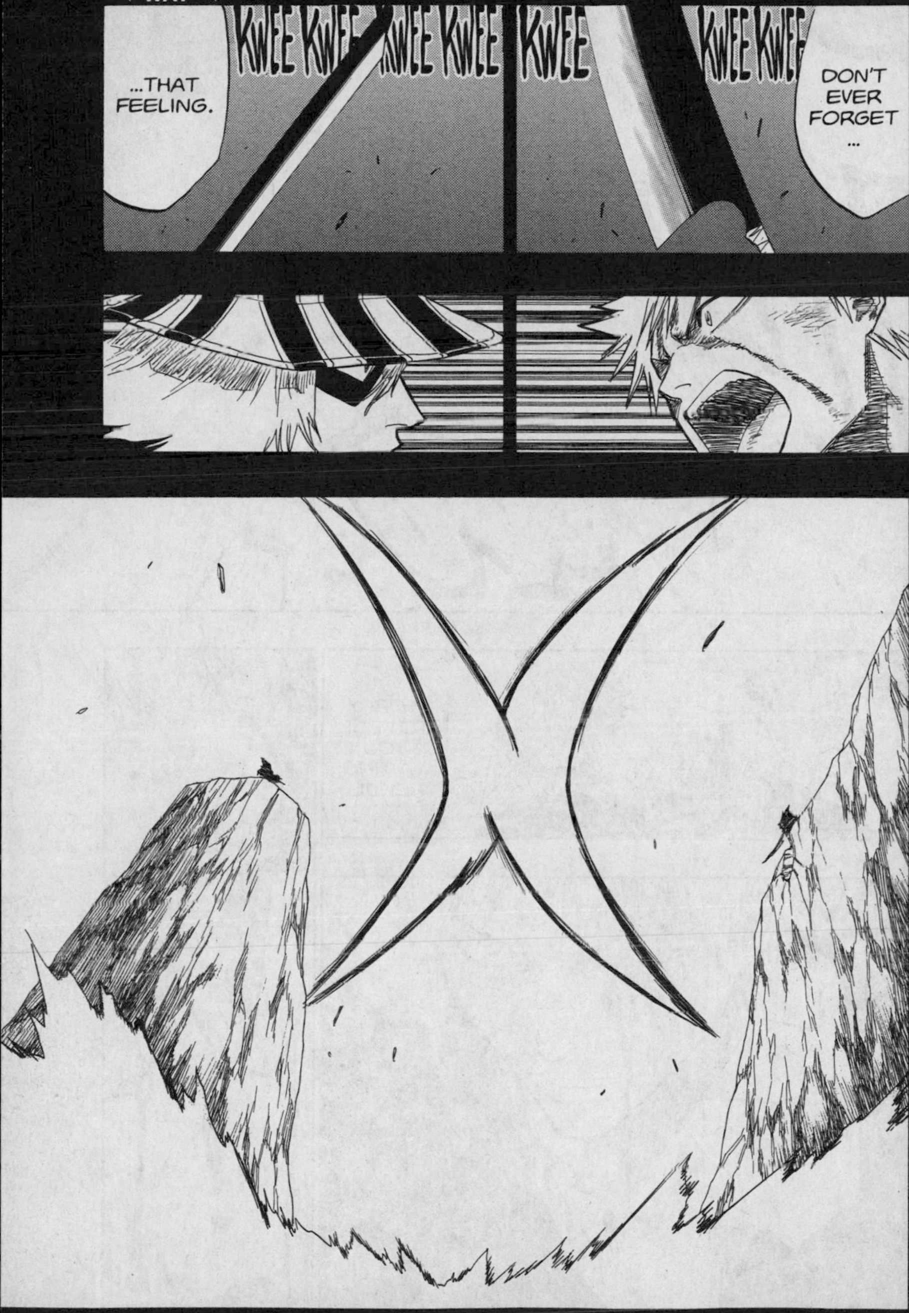
KWEE KWEE
DON'T EVER FORGET ...
KWEE KWEE KWEE KWEE KWEE
...THAT FEELING.

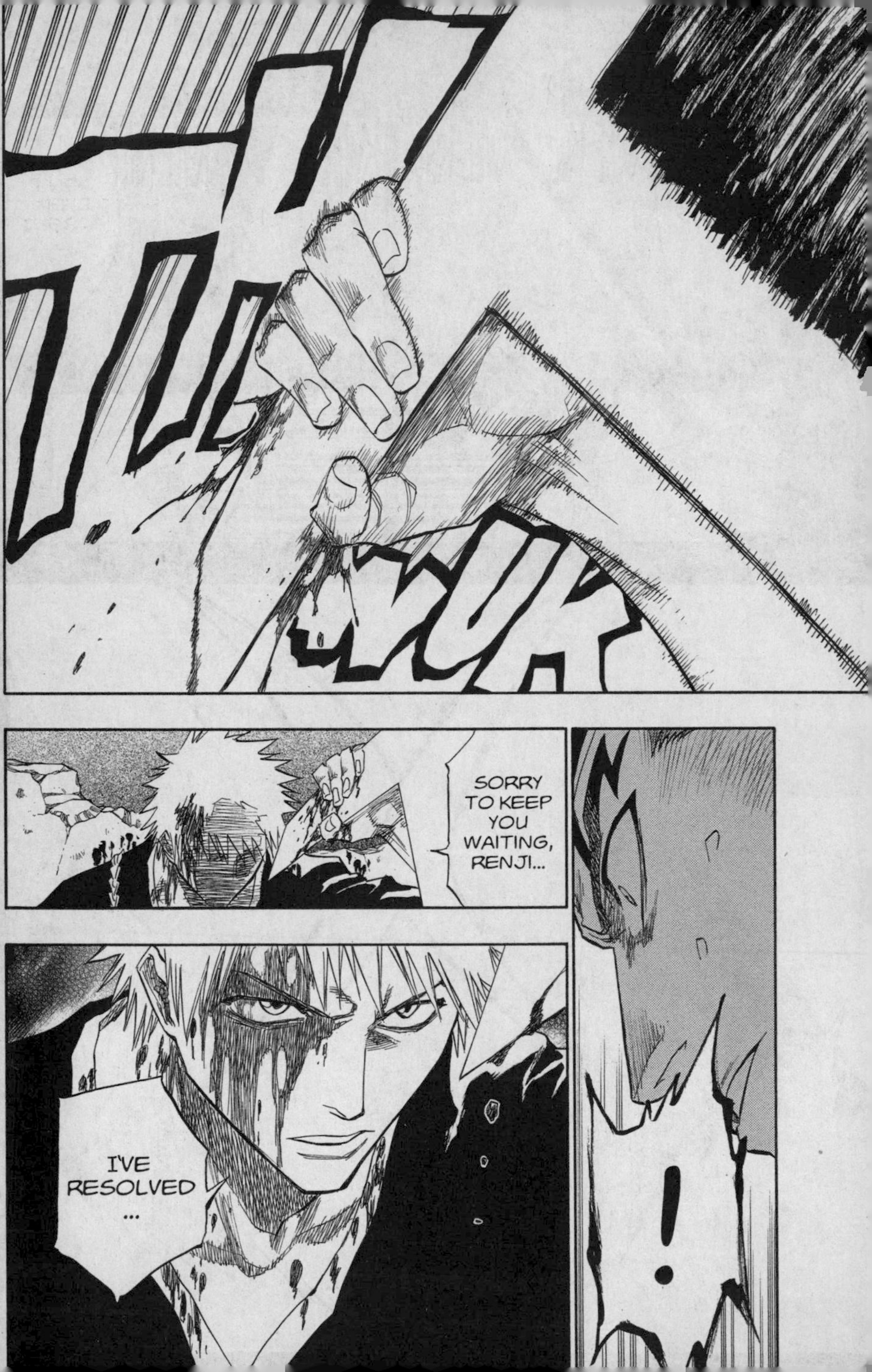
!
SORRY TO KEEP YOU WAITING, RENJI...
I'VE RESOLVED ...

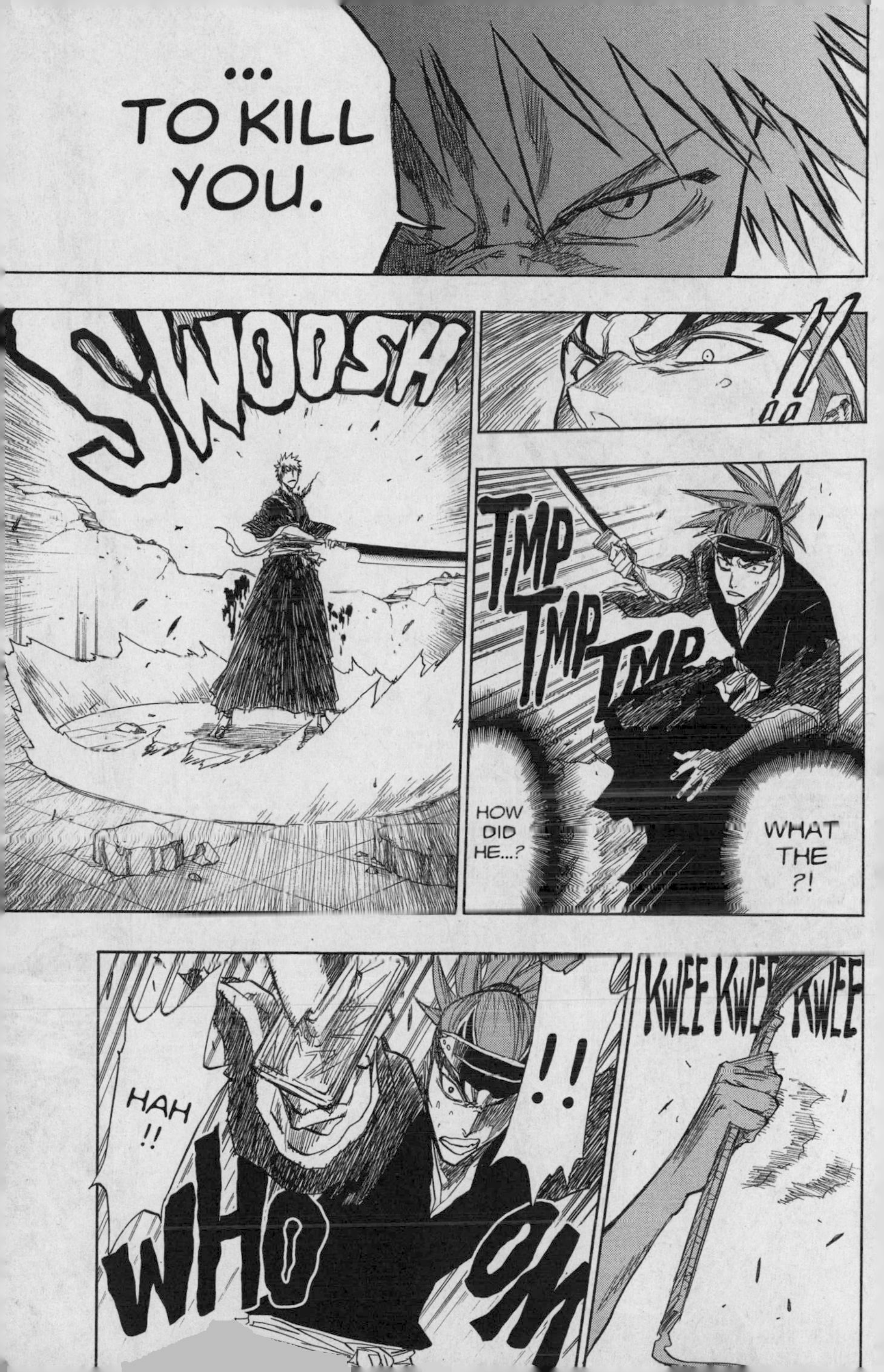
... TO KILL YOU.
!!
TMP TMP TMP
WHAT THE ?!
HOW DID HE...?
SWOOSH
KWEE KWEE KWEE
!!
HAH !!
WHOOM

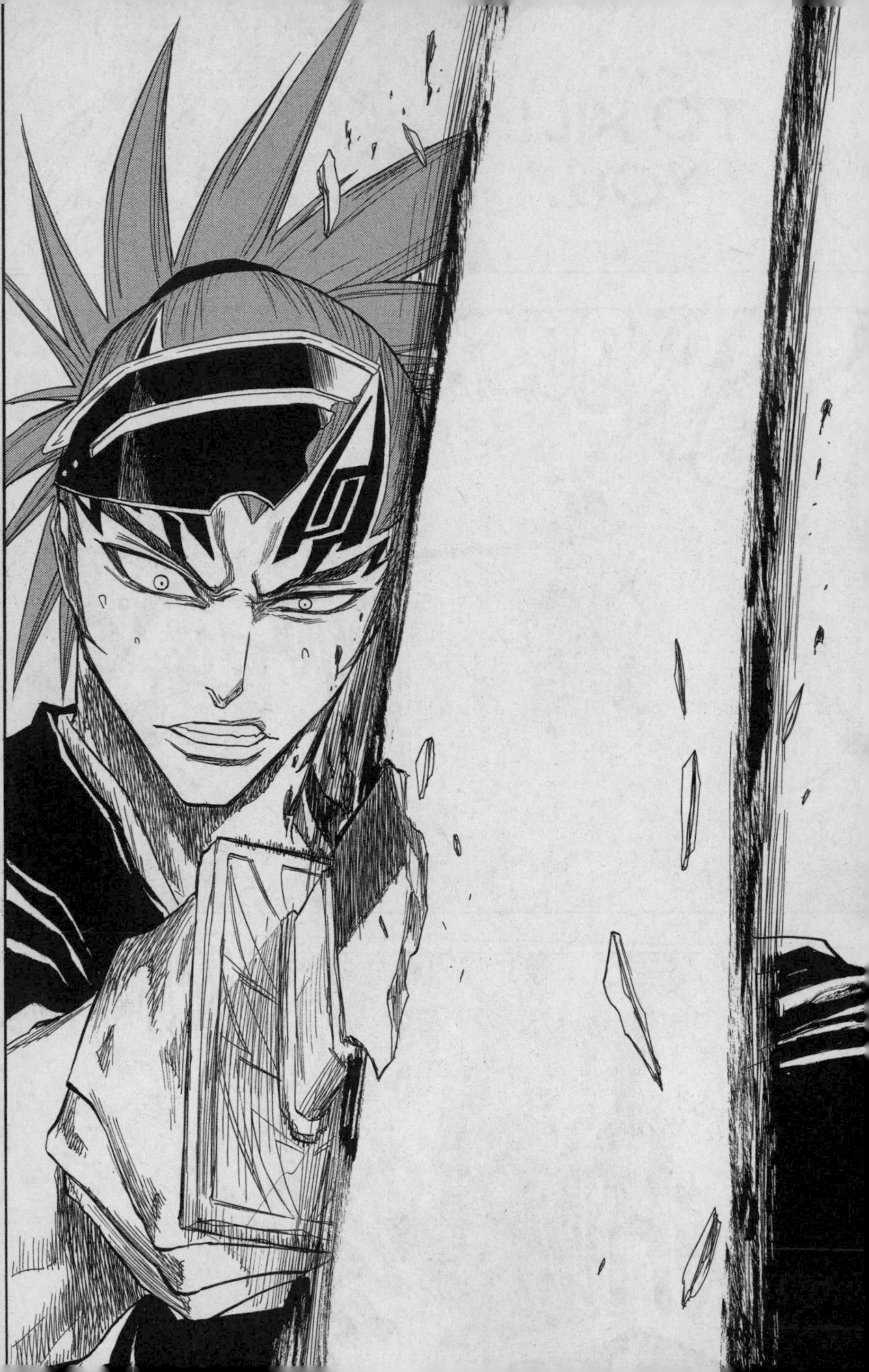

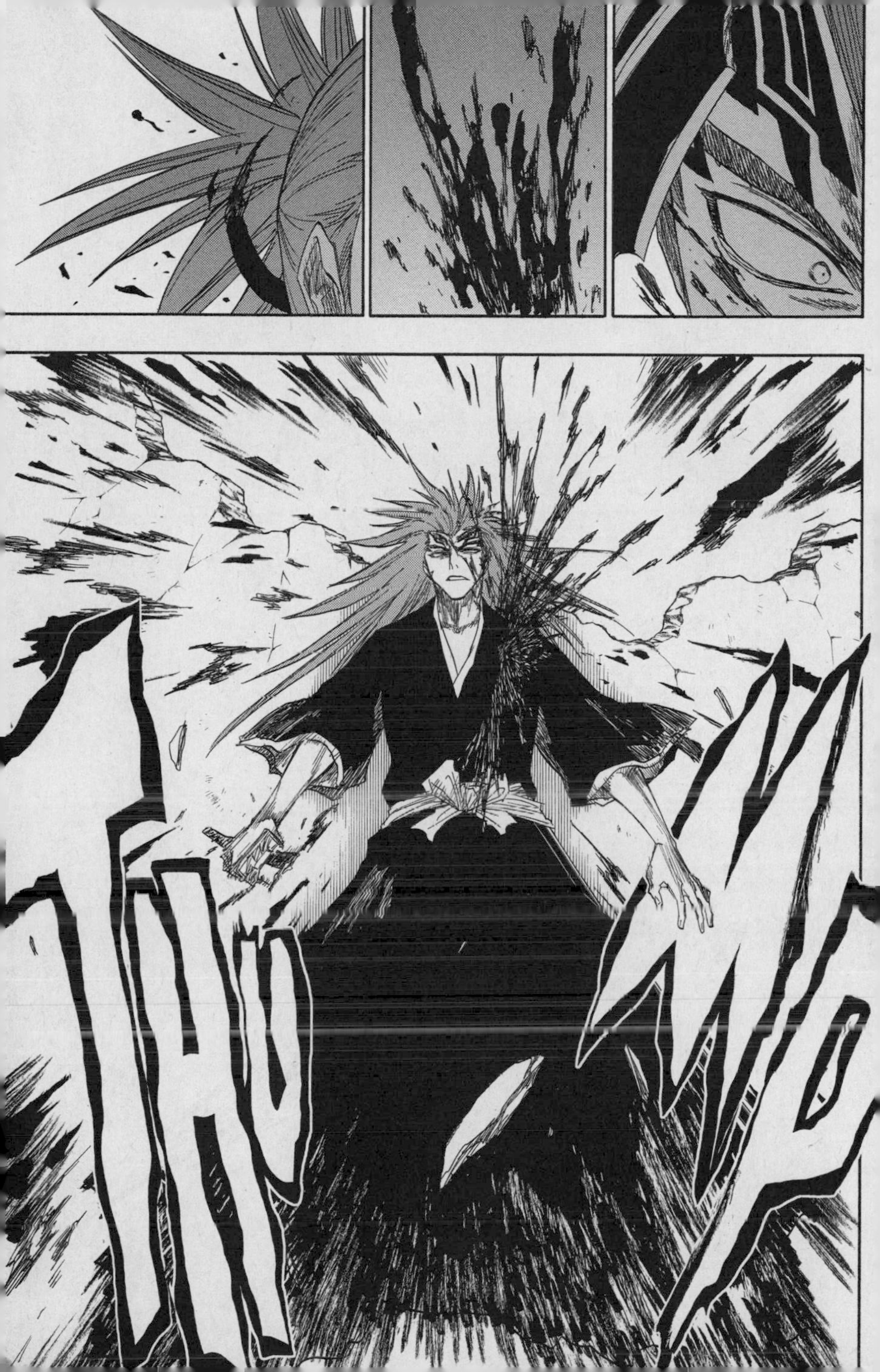

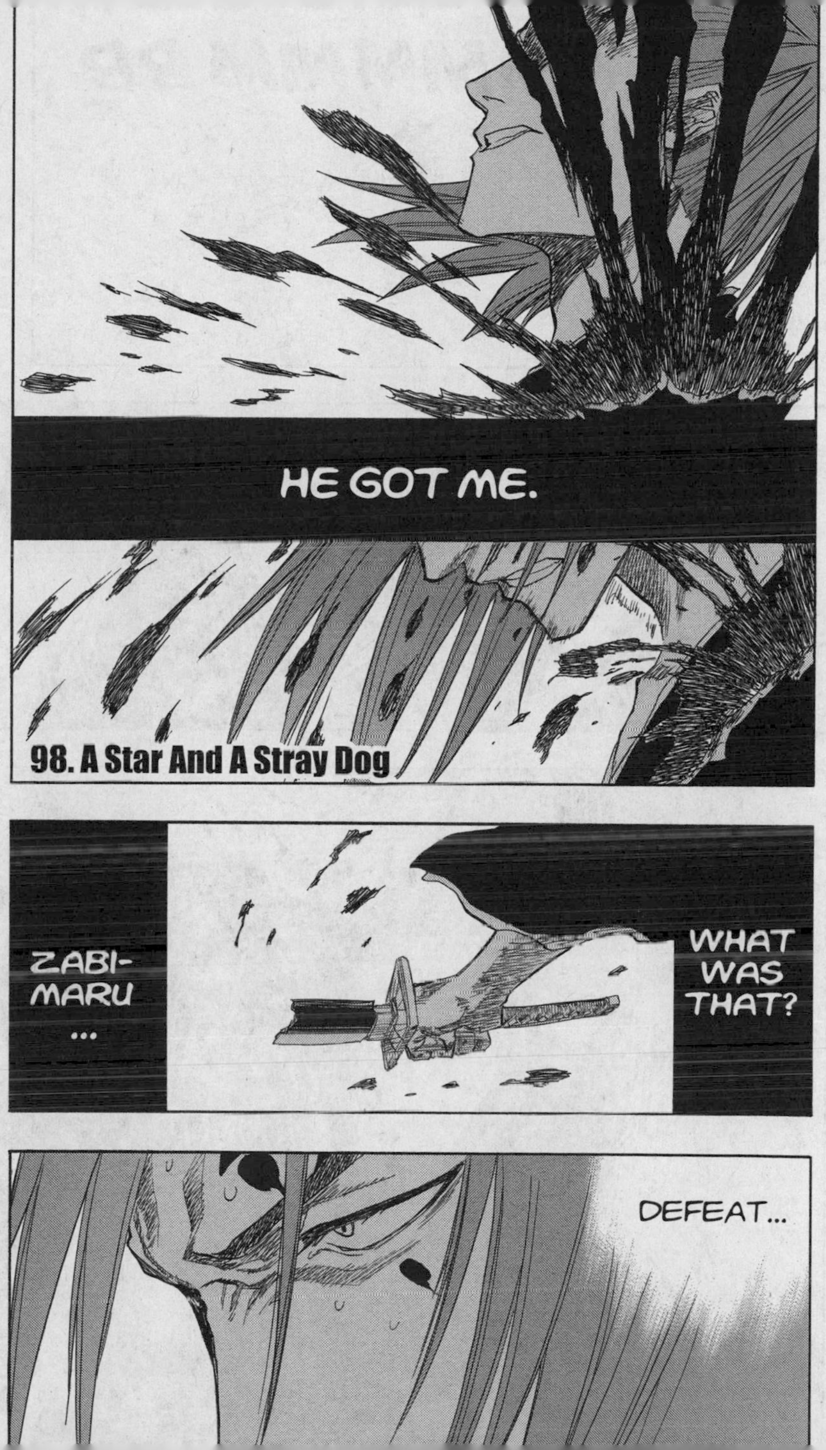
HE GOT ME.
98. A Star And A Stray Dog
WHAT WAS THAT?
ZABI-MARU ...
DEFEAT...

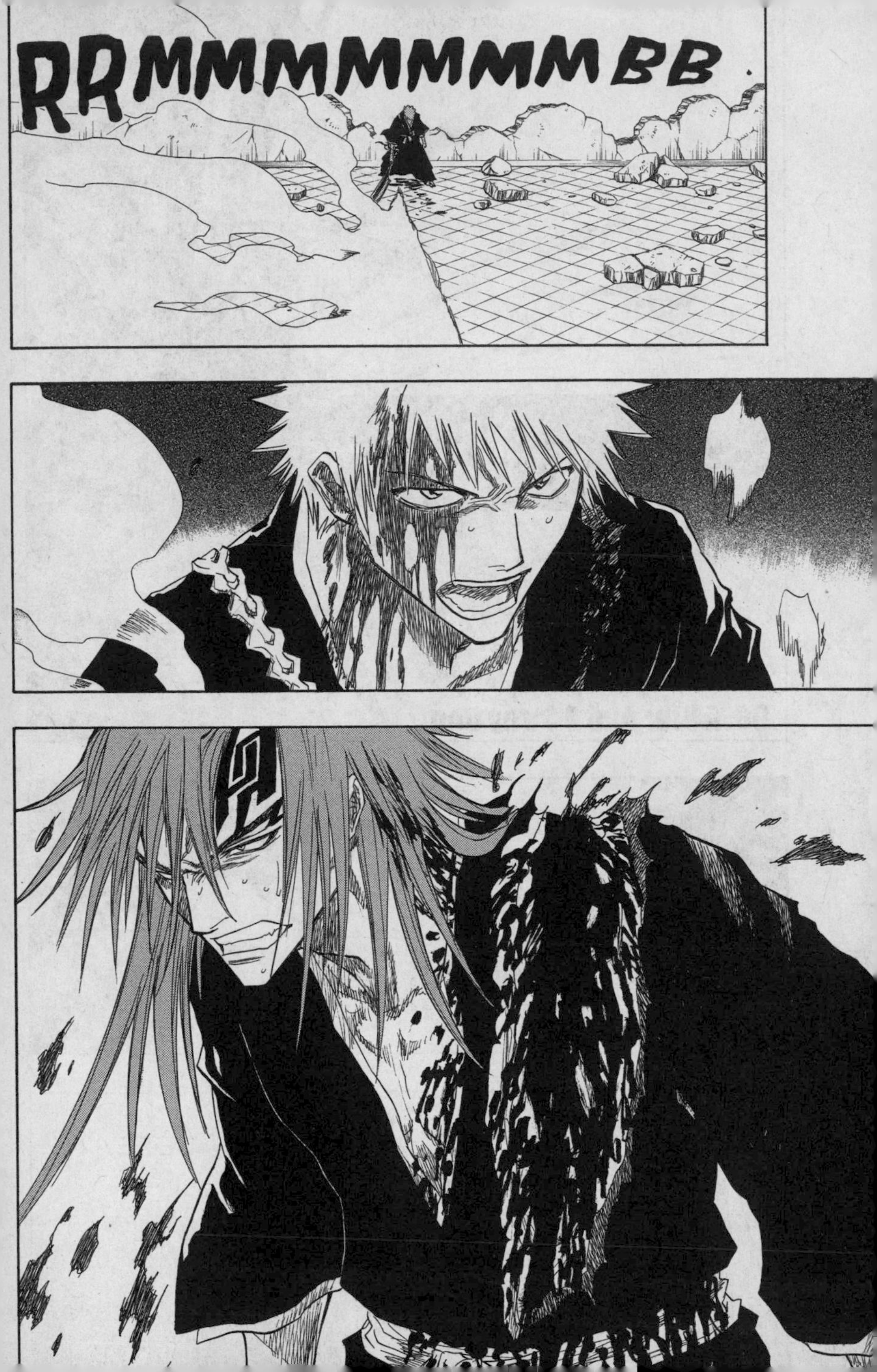
RRMMMMMMMMBB

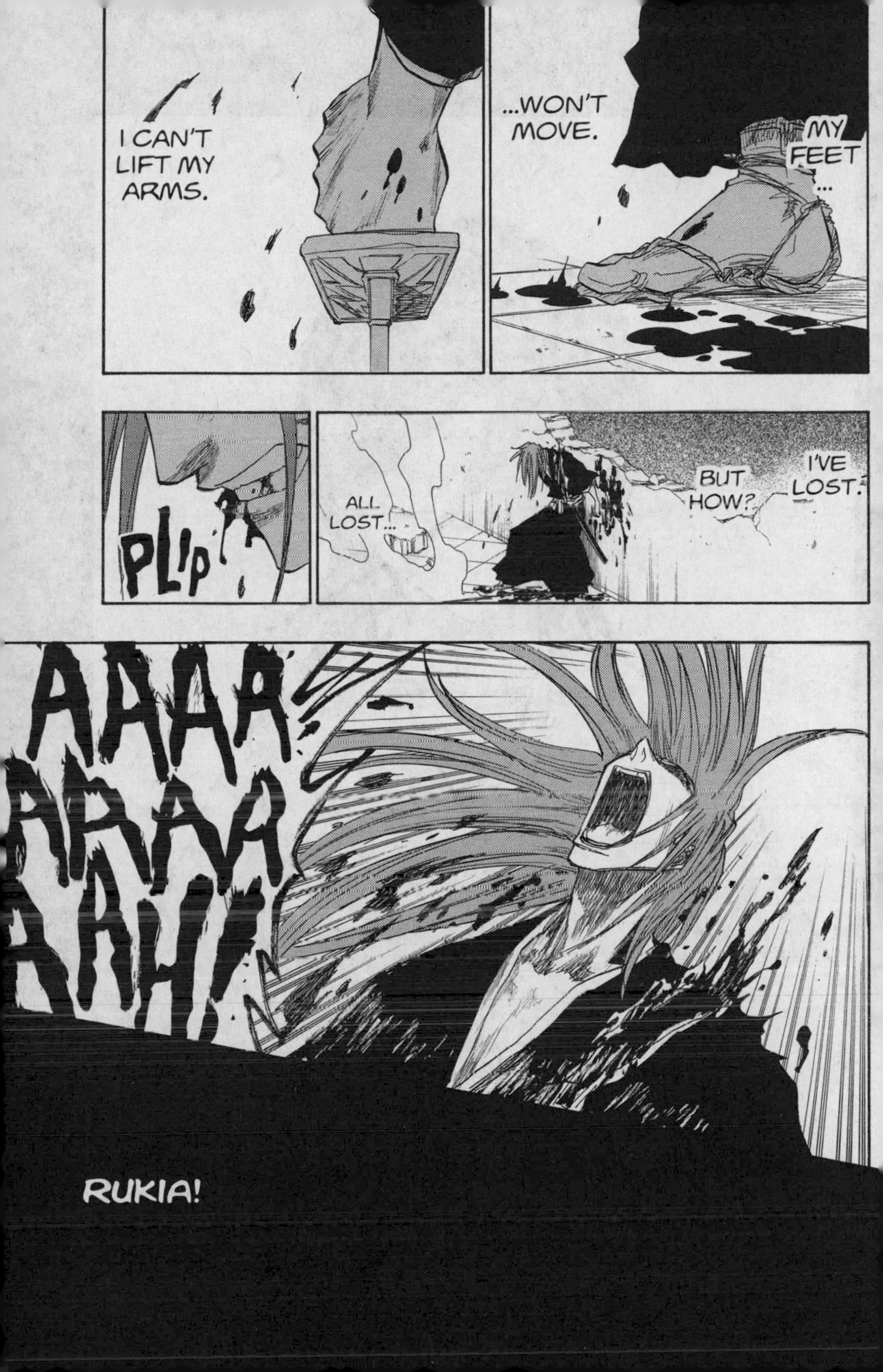
MY FEET...
...WON'T MOVE.
I CAN'T LIFT MY ARMS.
I'VE LOST.
BUT HOW?
ALL LOST...
PLIP
AAARRAARAH!
RUKIA!

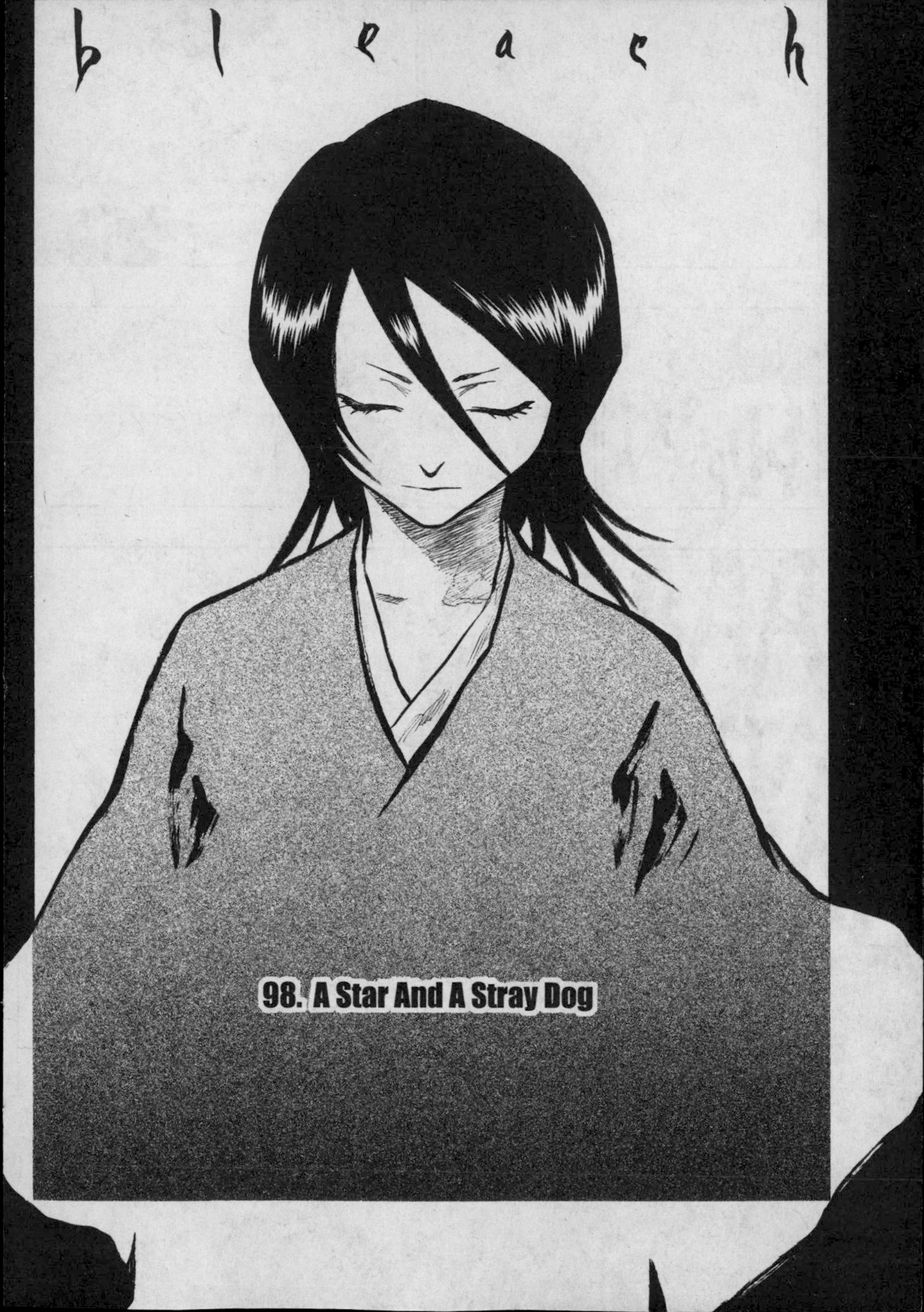
bleach
98. A Star And A Stray Dog

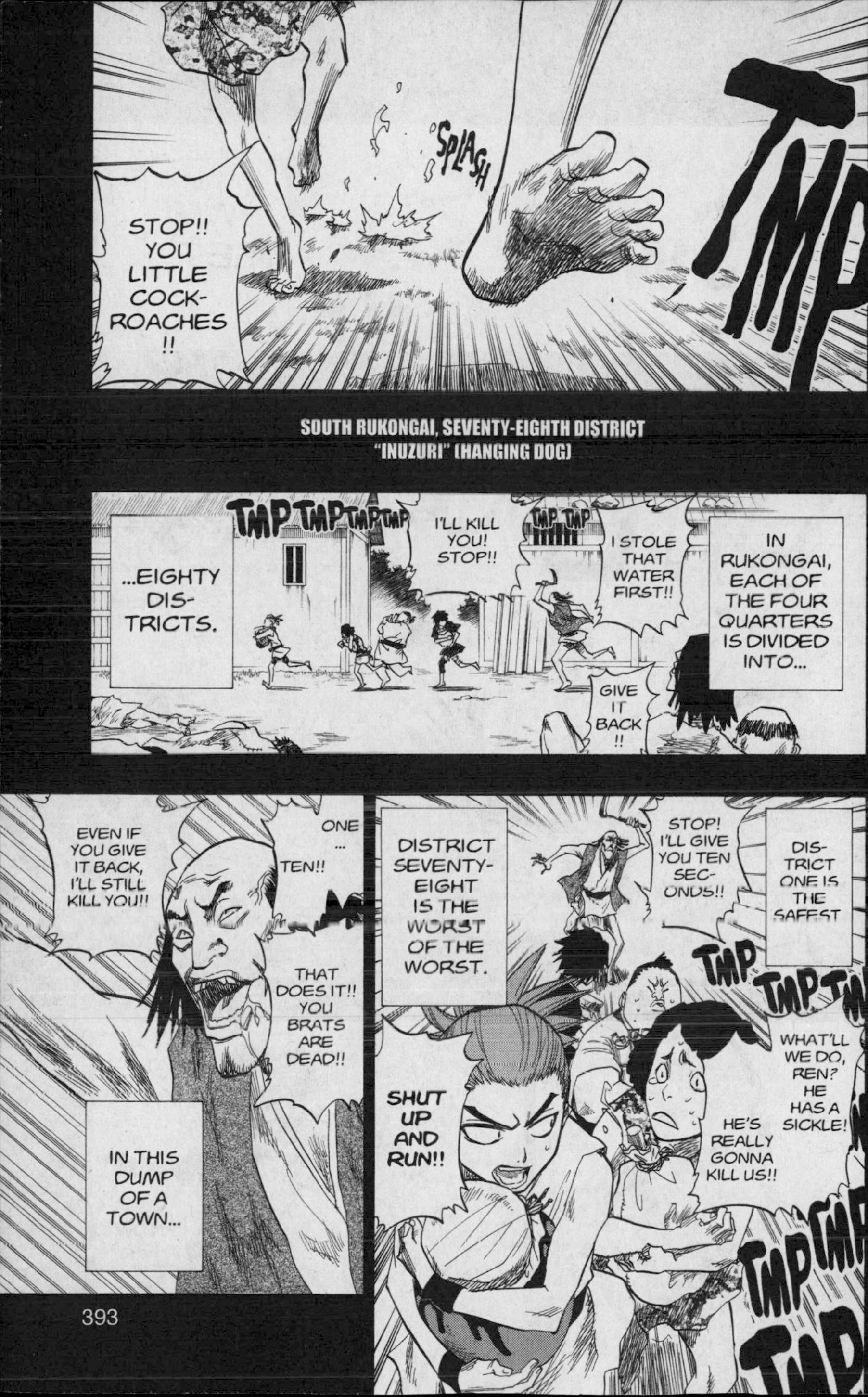
TMP
SPLASH
STOP!! YOU LITTLE COCK-ROACHES!!
SOUTH RUKONGAI, SEVENTY-EIGHTH DISTRICT
"INUZURI" (HANGING DOG)
IN RUKONGAI, EACH OF THE FOUR QUARTERS IS DIVIDED INTO...
GIVE IT BACK!!
I STOLE THAT WATER FIRST!!
TMP TMP
I'LL KILL YOU! STOP!!
TMP TMP TMP TMP
...EIGHTY DIS-TRICTS.
DIS-TRICT ONE IS THE SAFEST
STOP! I'LL GIVE YOU TEN SEC-ONDS!!
DISTRICT SEVENTY-EIGHT IS THE WORST OF THE WORST.
TMP TMP
WHAT'LL WE DO, REN? HE HAS A SICKLE!
HE'S REALLY GONNA KILL US!!
SHUT UP AND RUN!!
TMP TMP
ONE ... TEN!!
EVEN IF YOU GIVE IT BACK, I'LL STILL KILL YOU!!
THAT DOES IT!! YOU BRATS ARE DEAD!!
IN THIS DUMP OF A TOWN...

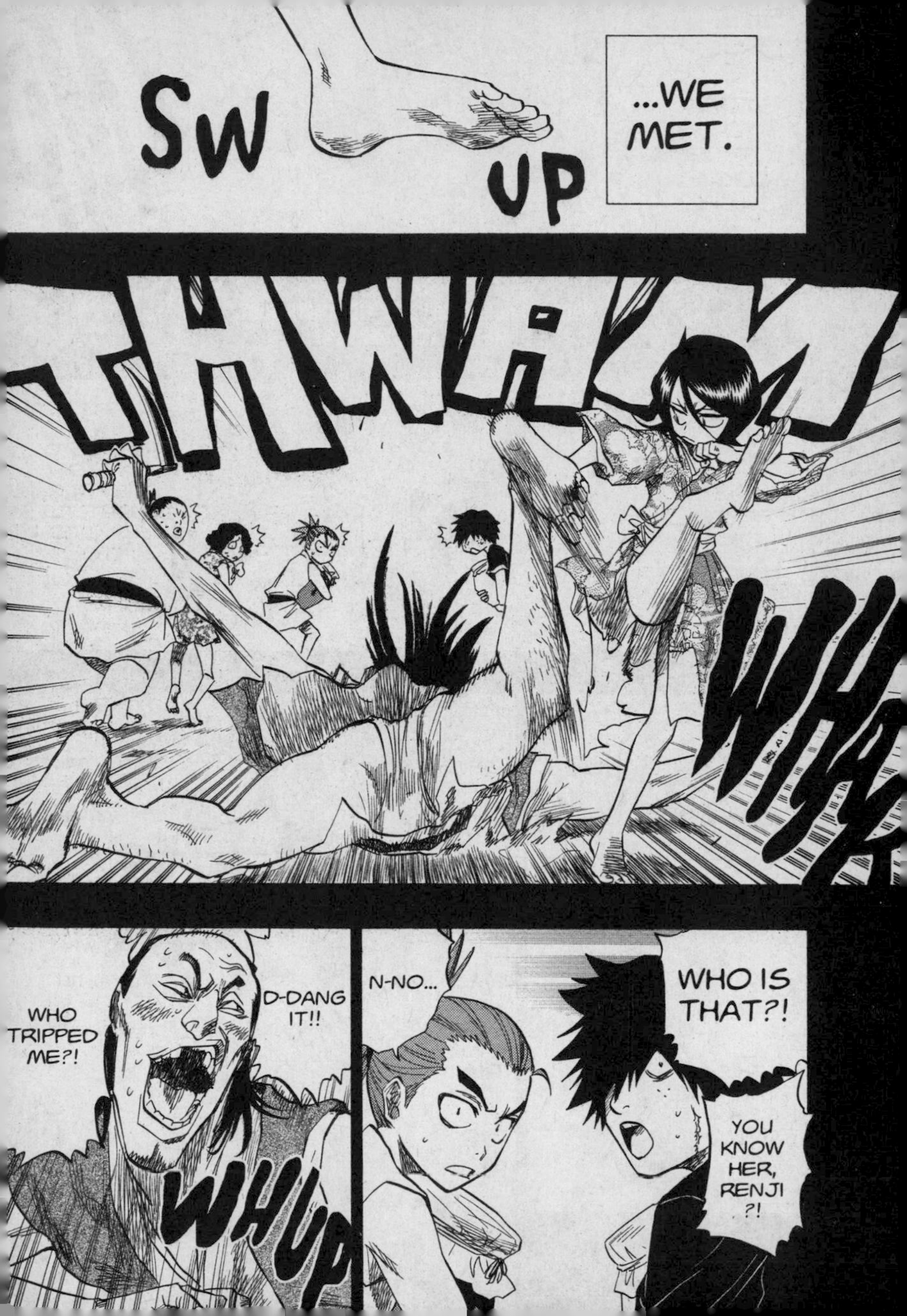
...WE MET.
SW UP
WHO IS THAT?!
YOU KNOW HER, RENJI ?!
N-NO...
D-DANG IT!!
WHO TRIPPED ME?!
WHUP

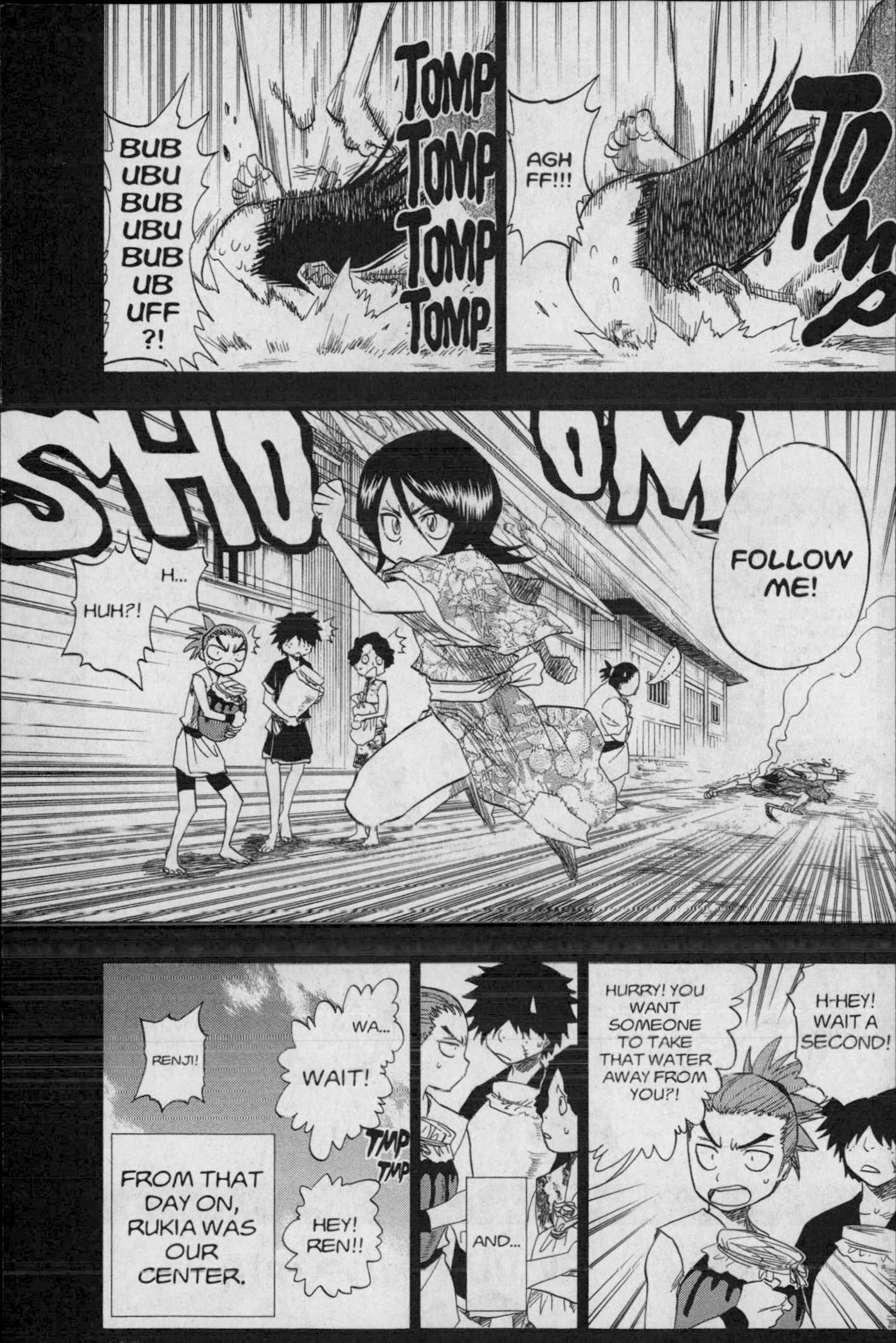
AGH FF!!!
TOMP
BUB UBU BUB UBU BUB UB UFF ?!
TOMP TOMP TOMP TOMP
FOLLOW ME!
H... HUH?!
H-HEY! WAIT A SECOND!
HURRY! YOU WANT SOMEONE TO TAKE THAT WATER AWAY FROM YOU?!
AND...
WA... WAIT!
RENJI!
TMP TMP
HEY! REN!!
FROM THAT DAY ON, RUKIA WAS OUR CENTER.

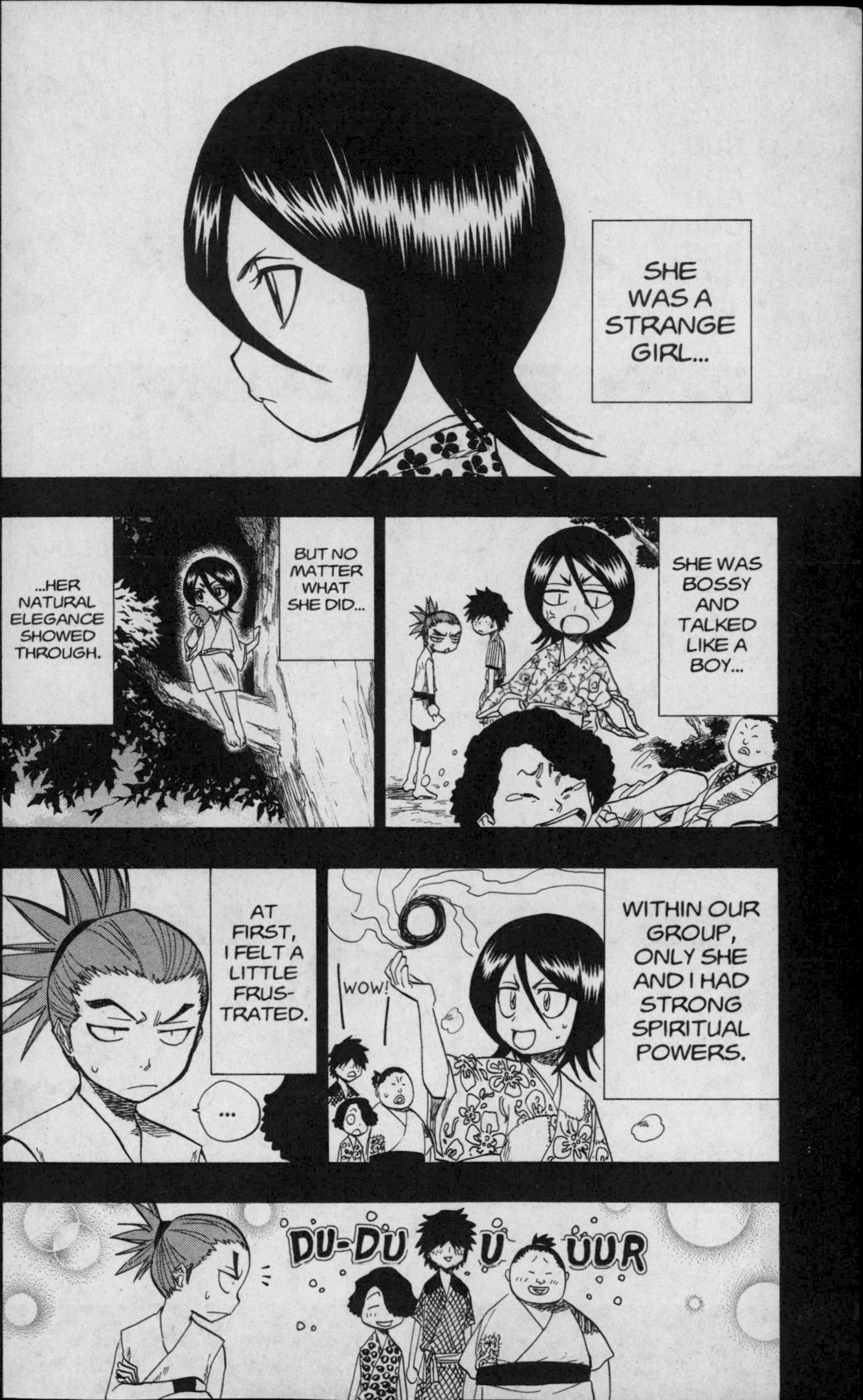
SHE WAS A STRANGE GIRL...
SHE WAS BOSSY AND TALKED LIKE A BOY...
BUT NO MATTER WHAT SHE DID...
...HER NATURAL ELEGANCE SHOWED THROUGH.
WITHIN OUR GROUP, ONLY SHE AND I HAD STRONG SPIRITUAL POWERS.
WOW!
AT FIRST, I FELT A LITTLE FRUS-TRATED.
...
DU-DU U UUR

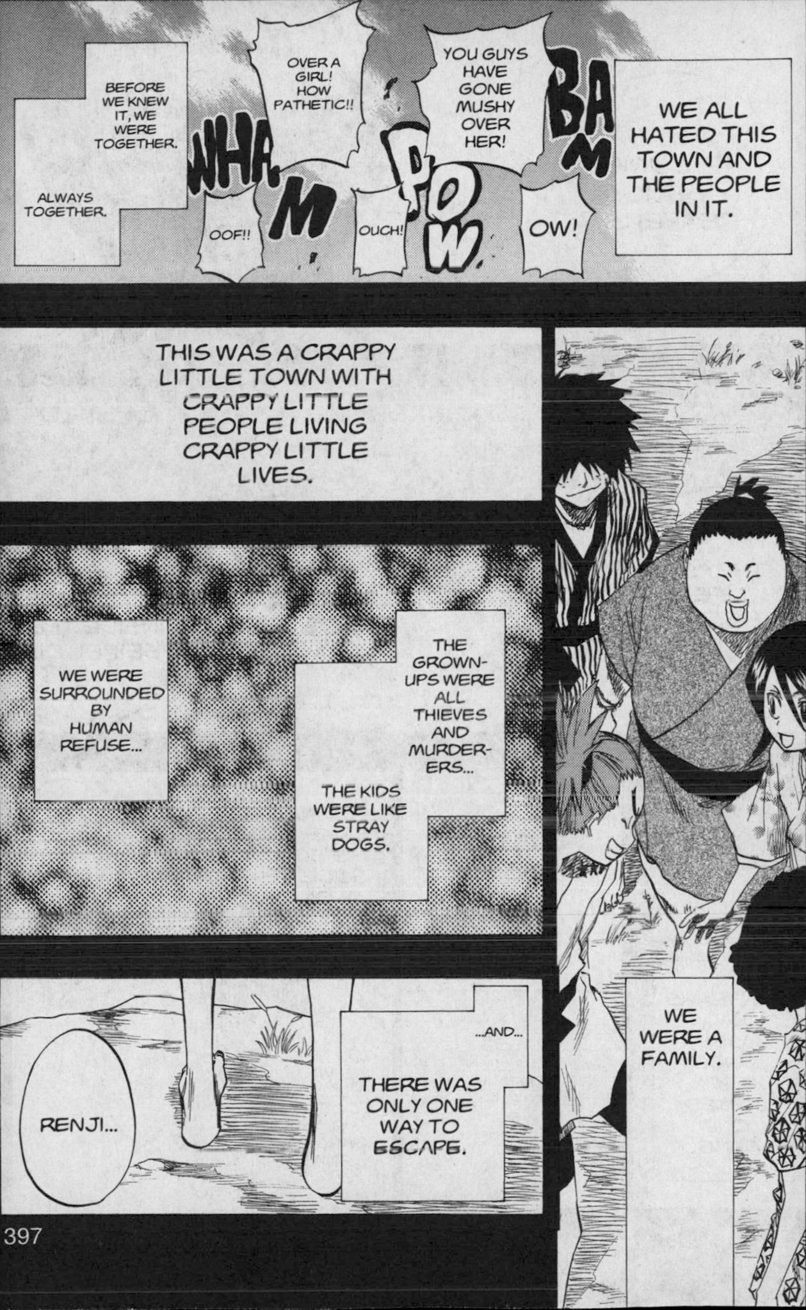
WE ALL HATED THIS TOWN AND THE PEOPLE IN IT.
BAM
OW!
YOU GUYS HAVE GONE MUSHY OVER HER!
POW
OUCH!
OVER A GIRL! HOW PATHETIC!!
WHAM
OOF!!
BEFORE WE KNEW IT, WE WERE TOGETHER.
ALWAYS TOGETHER.
WE WERE A FAMILY.
THIS WAS A CRAPPY LITTLE TOWN WITH CRAPPY LITTLE PEOPLE LIVING CRAPPY LITTLE LIVES.
THE GROWN-UPS WERE ALL THIEVES AND MURDER-ERS...
THE KIDS WERE LIKE STRAY DOGS.
WE WERE SURROUNDED BY HUMAN REFUSE...
...AND...
THERE WAS ONLY ONE WAY TO ESCAPE.
RENJI...

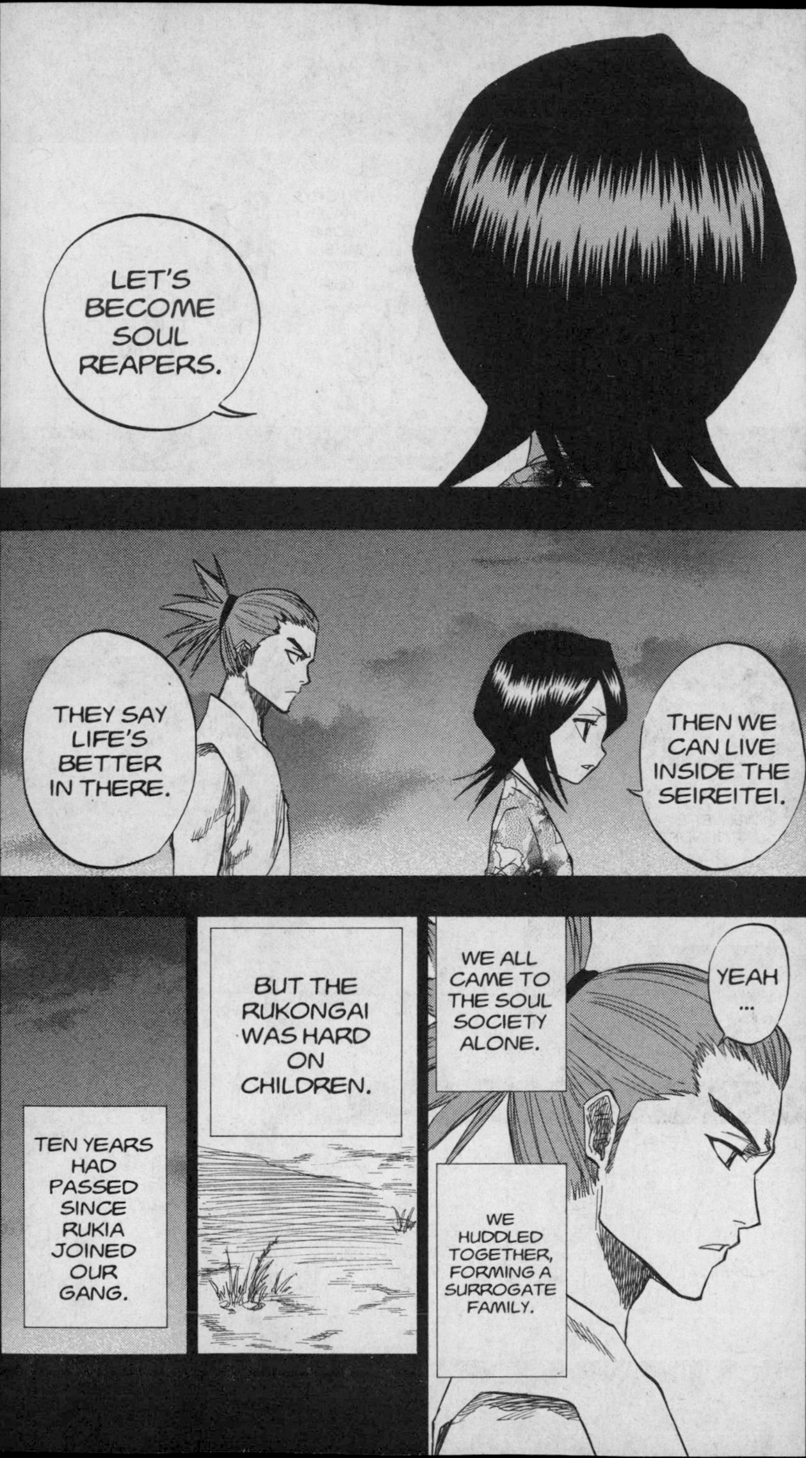
LET'S BECOME SOUL REAPERS.
THEN WE CAN LIVE INSIDE THE SEIREITEI.
THEY SAY LIFE'S BETTER IN THERE.
YEAH ...
WE ALL CAME TO THE SOUL SOCIETY ALONE.
WE HUDDLED TOGETHER, FORMING A SURROGATE FAMILY.
BUT THE RUKONGAI WAS HARD ON CHILDREN.
TEN YEARS HAD PASSED SINCE RUKIA JOINED OUR GANG.

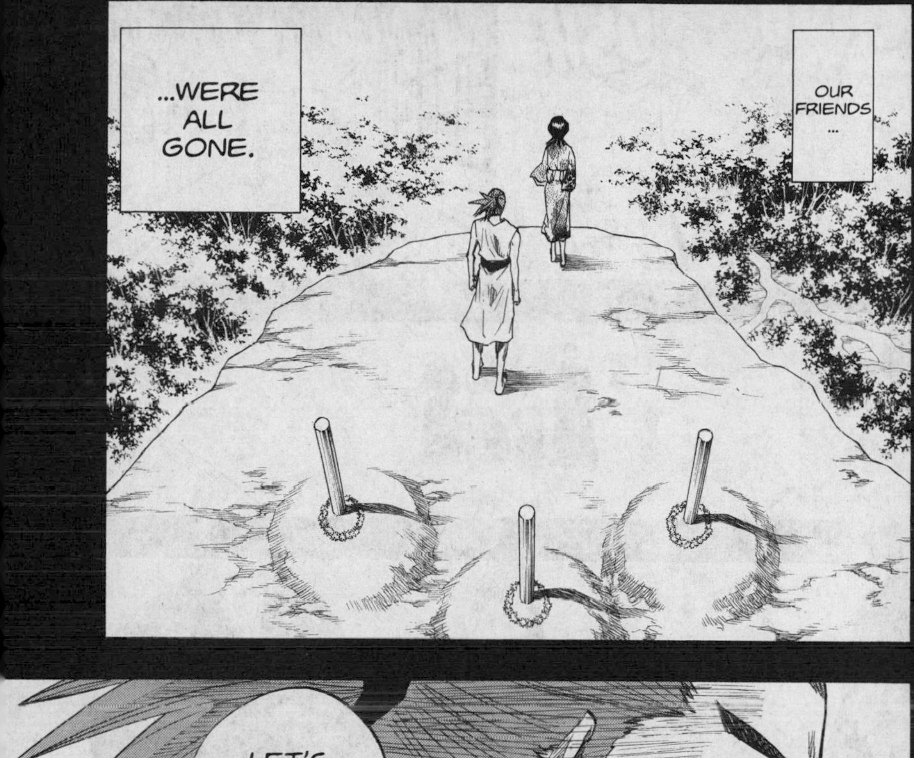
OUR FRIENDS...
...WERE ALL GONE.
LET'S BECOME SOUL REAPERS.
BECAUSE WE HAD SOME TALENT, WE WERE ACCEPTED INTO THE SOUL REAPER ACADEMY.
THOUGH WE WERE SUR-ROUNDED BY ARISTO-CRATIC SNOBS, WE ROSE QUICKLY THROUGH THE RANKS.
AND ONE DAY...

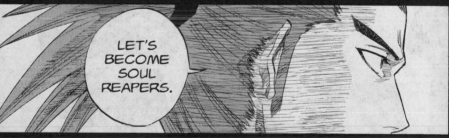

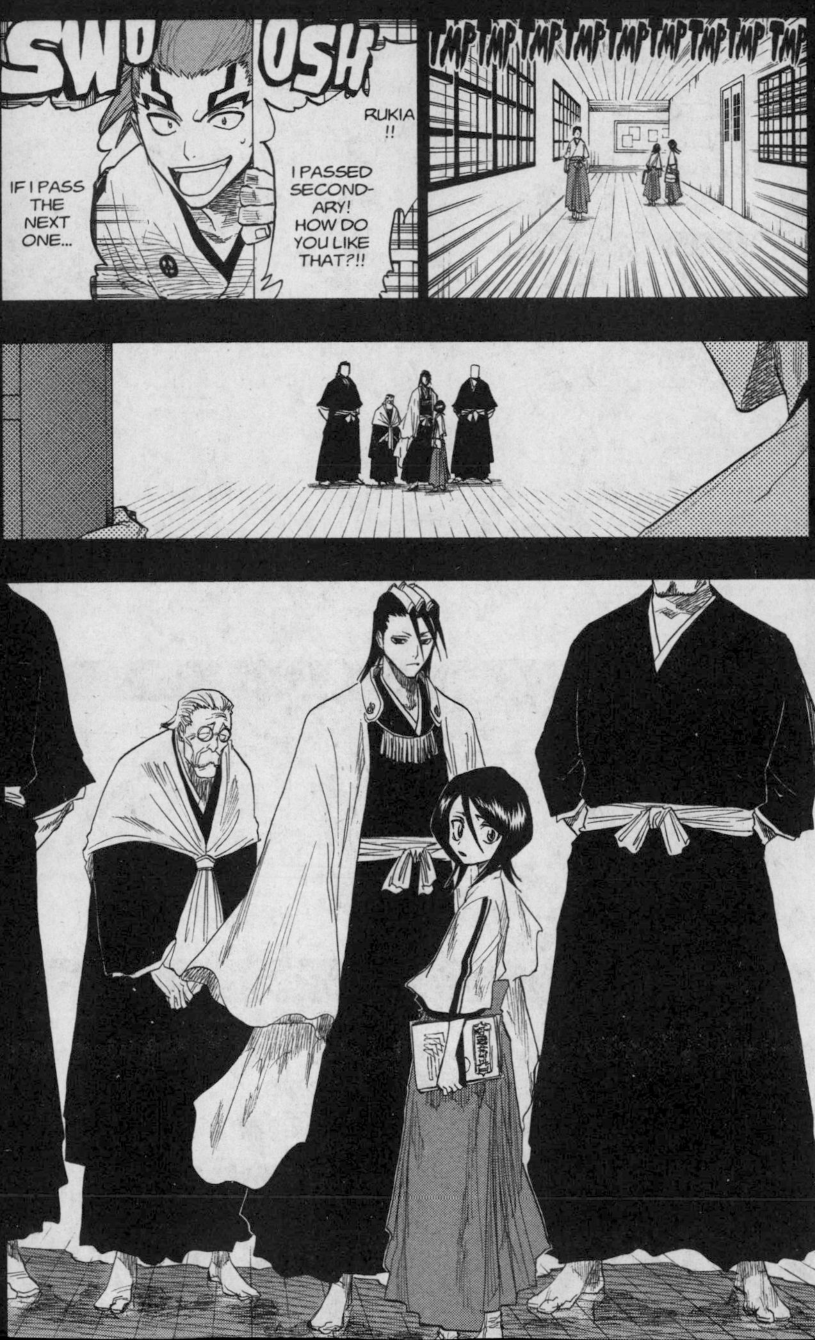
TMP TMP TMP TMP TMP TMP TMP TMP TMP
SWOOSH
RUKIA !!
I PASSED SECOND-ARY! HOW DO YOU LIKE THAT?!!
IF I PASS THE NEXT ONE...

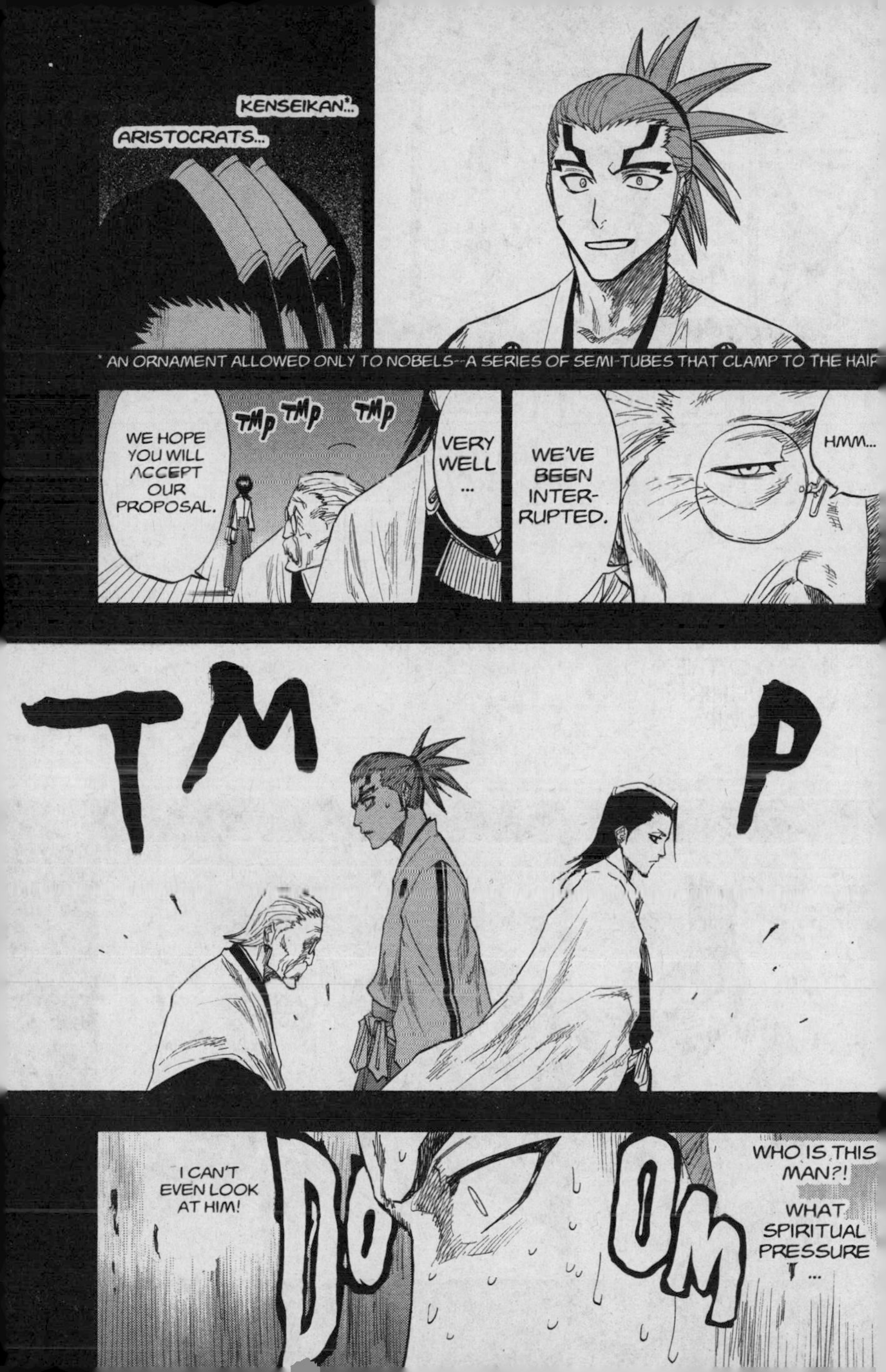
KENSEIKAN*...
ARISTOCRATS...
* AN ORNAMENT ALLOWED ONLY TO NOBELS--A SERIES OF SEMI-TUBES THAT CLAMP TO THE HAIR
HMM...
WE'VE BEEN INTER-RUPTED.
VERY WELL...
TMP TMP TMP
WE HOPE YOU WILL ACCEPT OUR PROPOSAL.
TMP
WHO IS THIS MAN?!
WHAT SPIRITUAL PRESSURE...
DOOM
I CAN'T EVEN LOOK AT HIM!

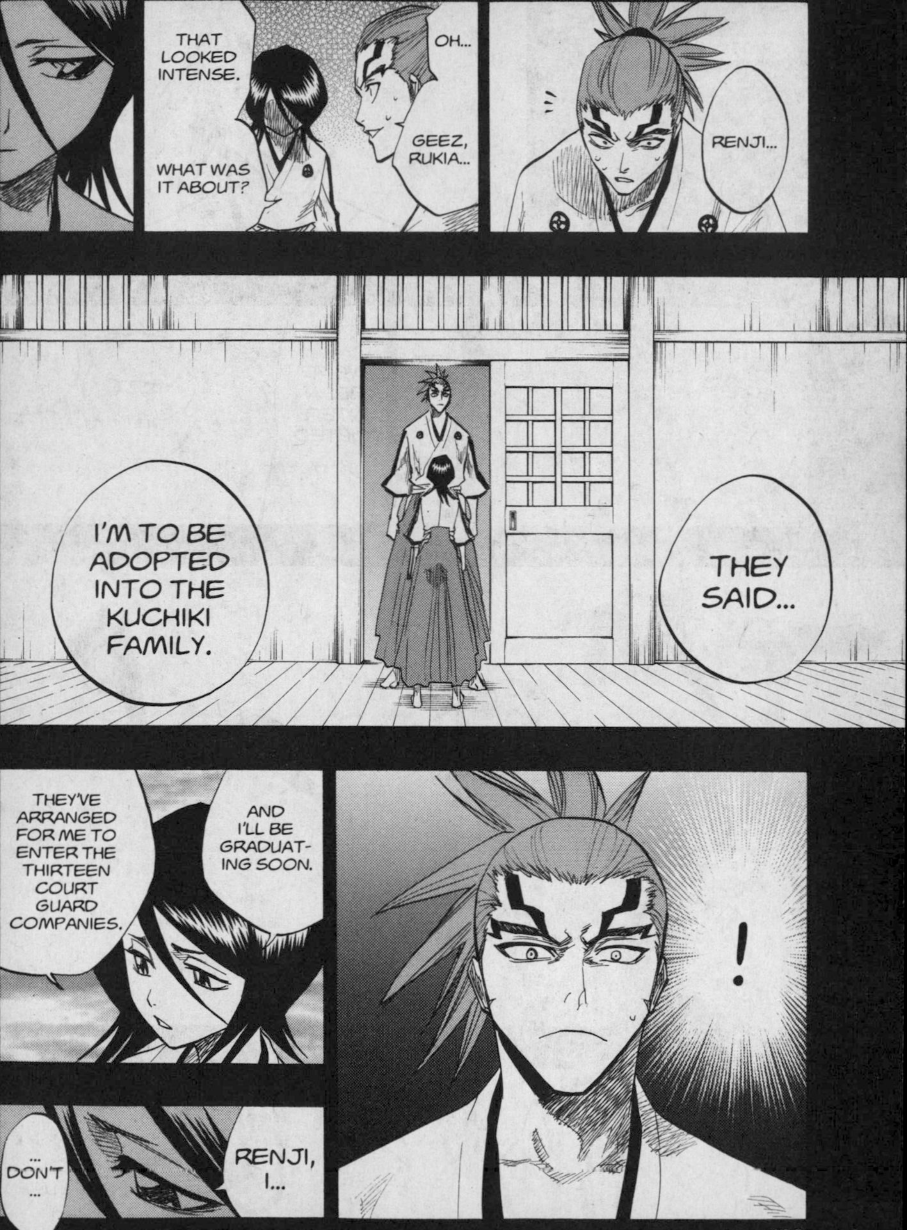
RENJI...
OH...
GEEZ, RUKIA...
THAT LOOKED INTENSE.
WHAT WAS IT ABOUT?
THEY SAID...
I'M TO BE ADOPTED INTO THE KUCHIKI FAMILY.
!
AND I'LL BE GRADUAT-ING SOON.
THEY'VE ARRANGED FOR ME TO ENTER THE THIRTEEN COURT GUARD COMPANIES.
RENJI, I...
... DON'T ...

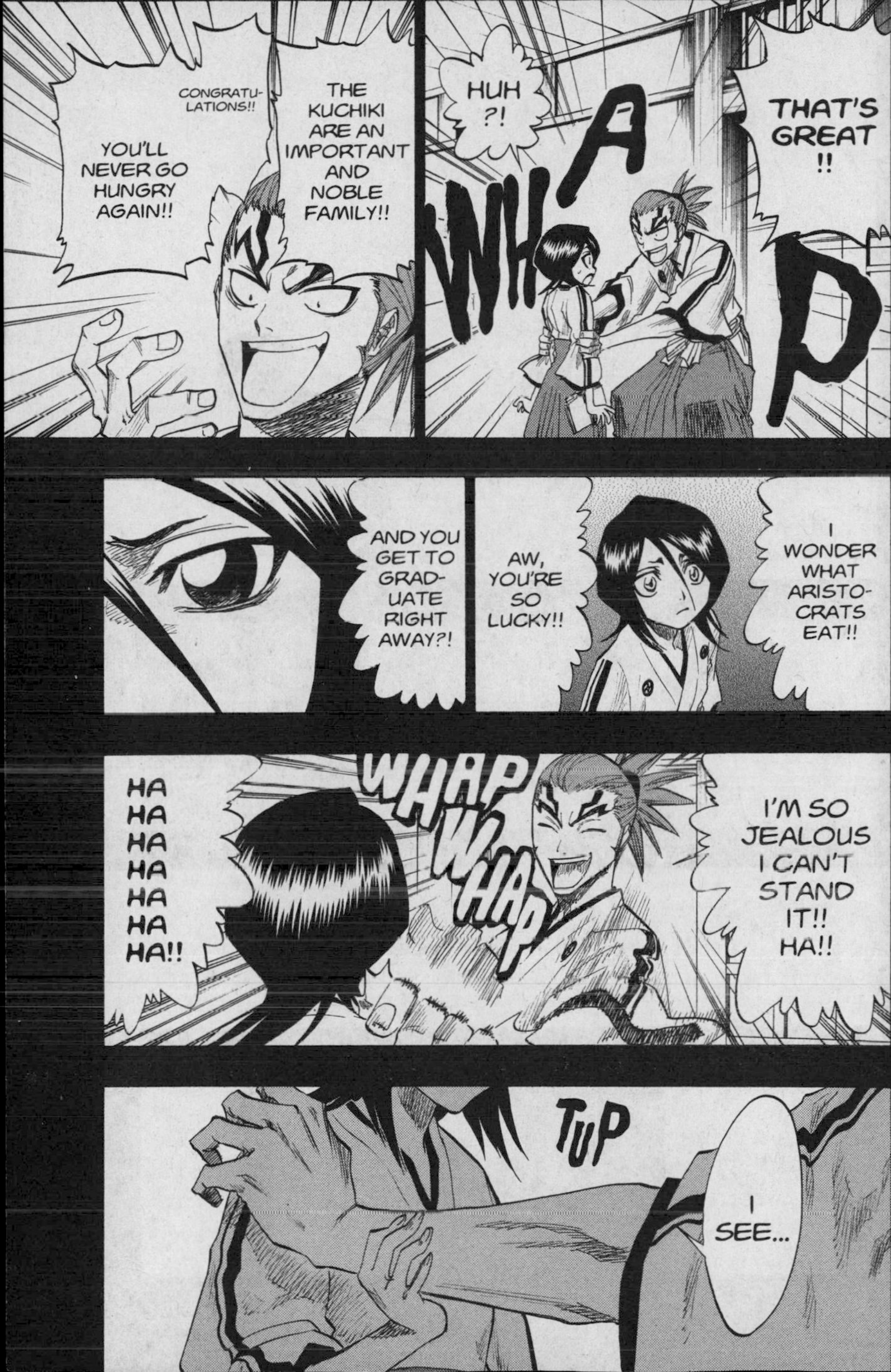
THAT'S GREAT!!
WHAP
HUH?!
THE KUCHIKI ARE AN IMPORTANT AND NOBLE FAMILY!!
CONGRATULATIONS!!
YOU'LL NEVER GO HUNGRY AGAIN!!
I WONDER WHAT ARISTOCRATS EAT!!
AW, YOU'RE SO LUCKY!!
AND YOU GET TO GRADUATE RIGHT AWAY?!
I'M SO JEALOUS I CAN'T STAND IT!! HA!!
WHAP WHAP WHAP
HA HA HA HA HA HA HA!!
TUP
I SEE...

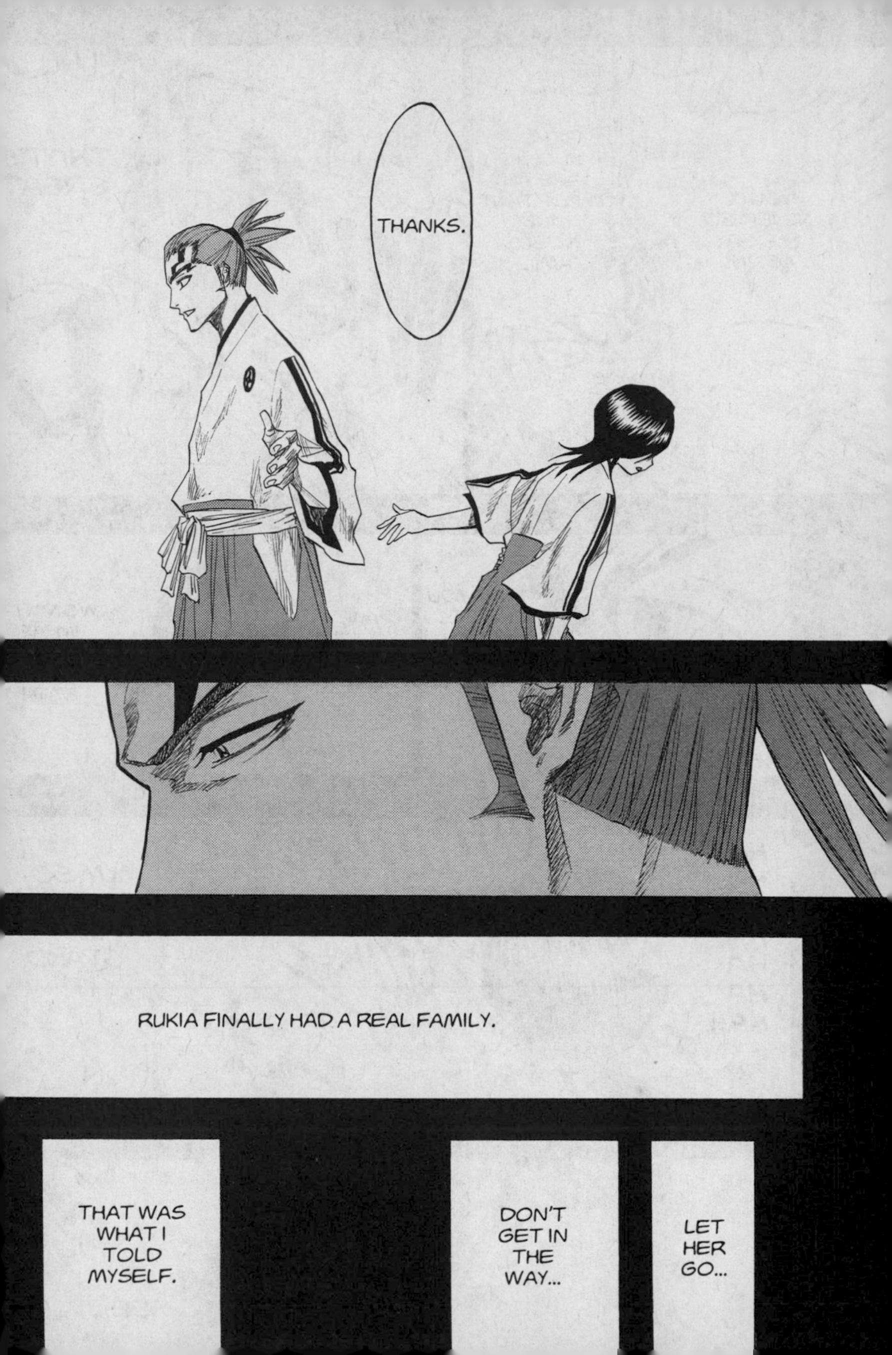
THANKS.
RUKIA FINALLY HAD A REAL FAMILY.
LET HER GO...
DON'T GET IN THE WAY...
THAT WAS WHAT I TOLD MYSELF.

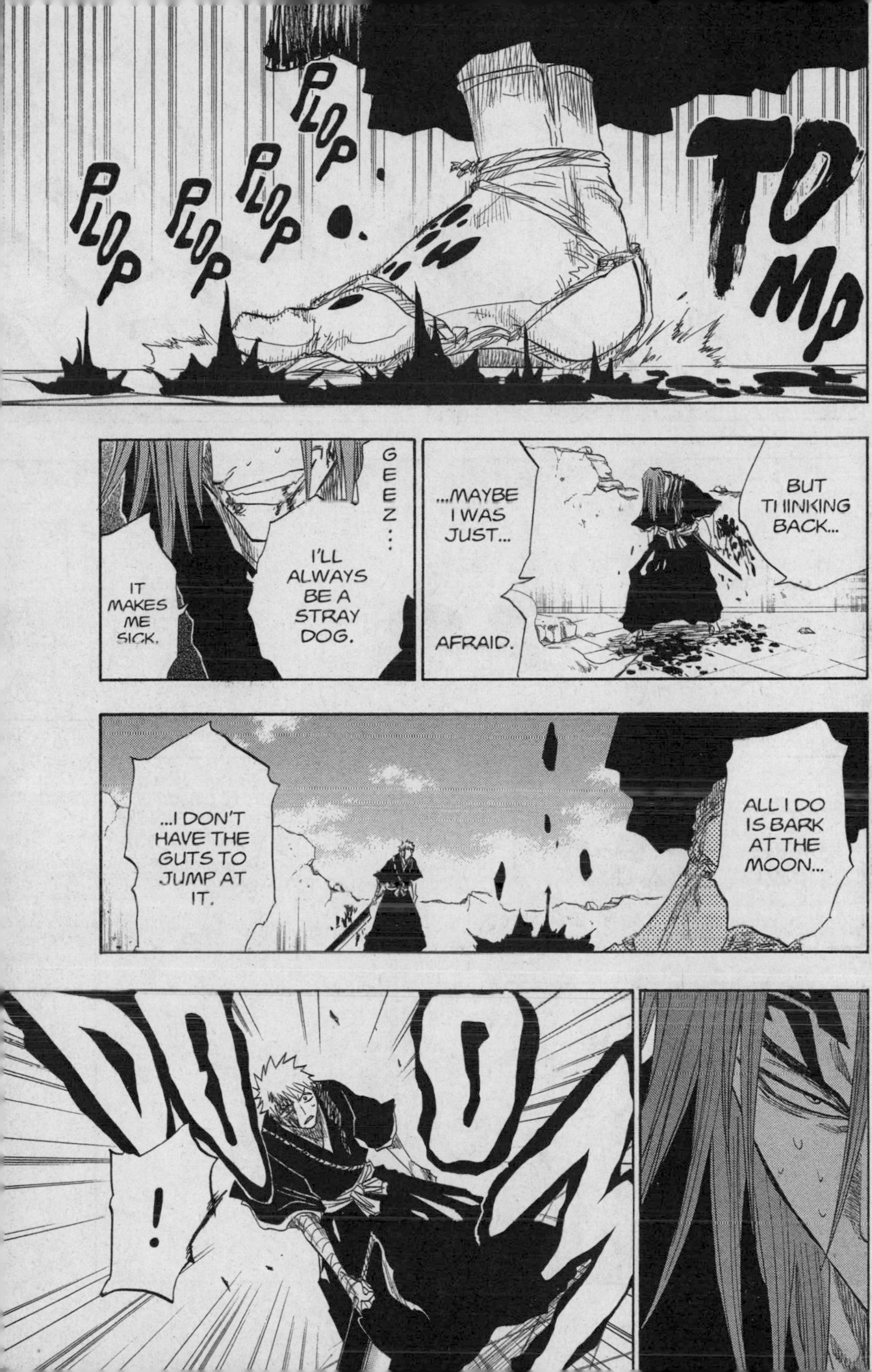
TOMP
PLOP
PLOP
PLOP
PLOP
BUT THINKING BACK...
...MAYBE I WAS JUST...
AFRAID.
GEEZ...
I'LL ALWAYS BE A STRAY DOG.
IT MAKES ME SICK.
ALL I DO IS BARK AT THE MOON...
...I DON'T HAVE THE GUTS TO JUMP AT IT.
!

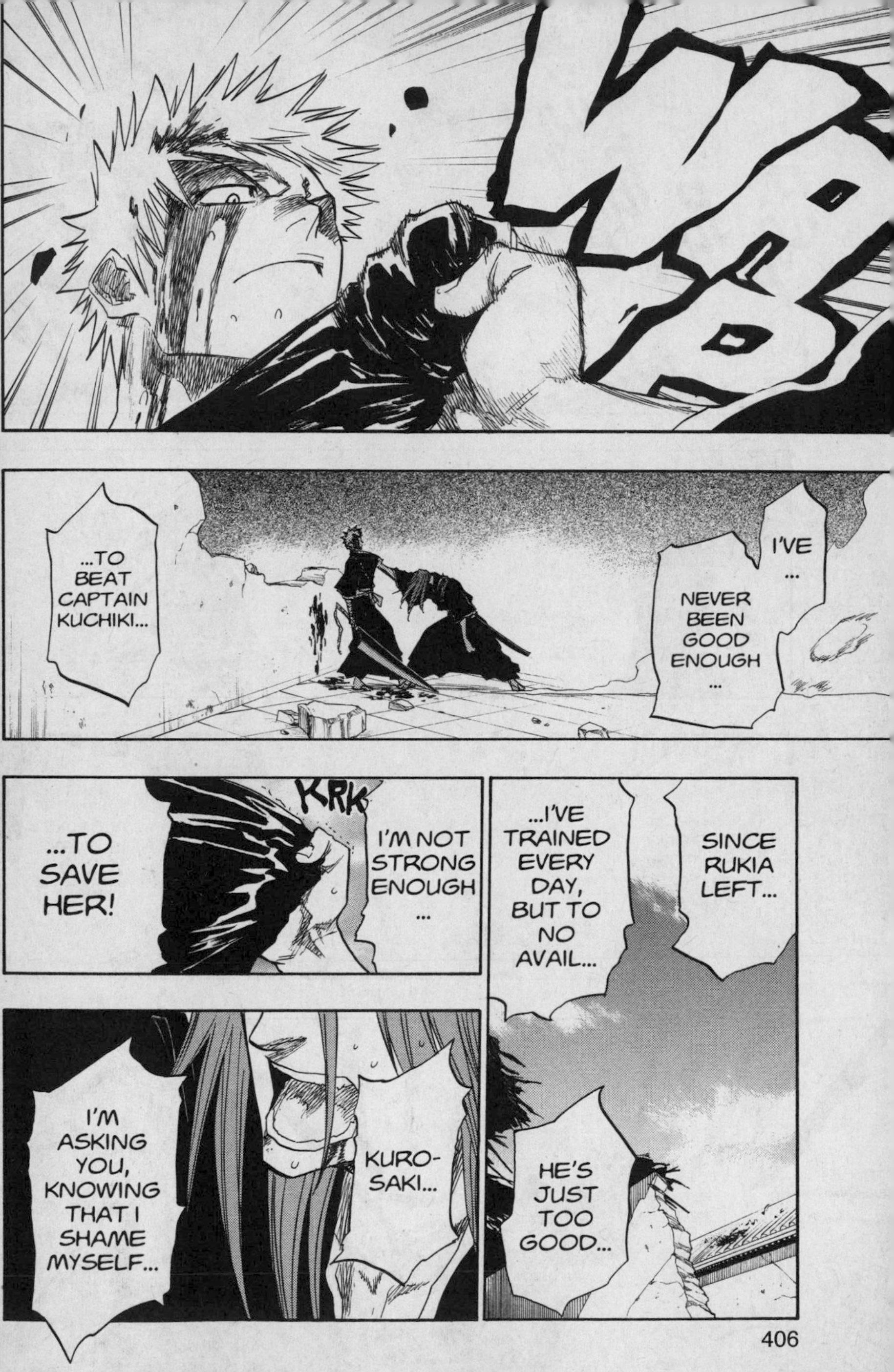
I'VE ... NEVER BEEN GOOD ENOUGH ...
...TO BEAT CAPTAIN KUCHIKI...
SINCE RUKIA LEFT...
...I'VE TRAINED EVERY DAY, BUT TO NO AVAIL...
KRK
I'M NOT STRONG ENOUGH ...
...TO SAVE HER!
HE'S JUST TOO GOOD...
KURO-SAKI...
I'M ASKING YOU, KNOWING THAT I SHAME MYSELF...

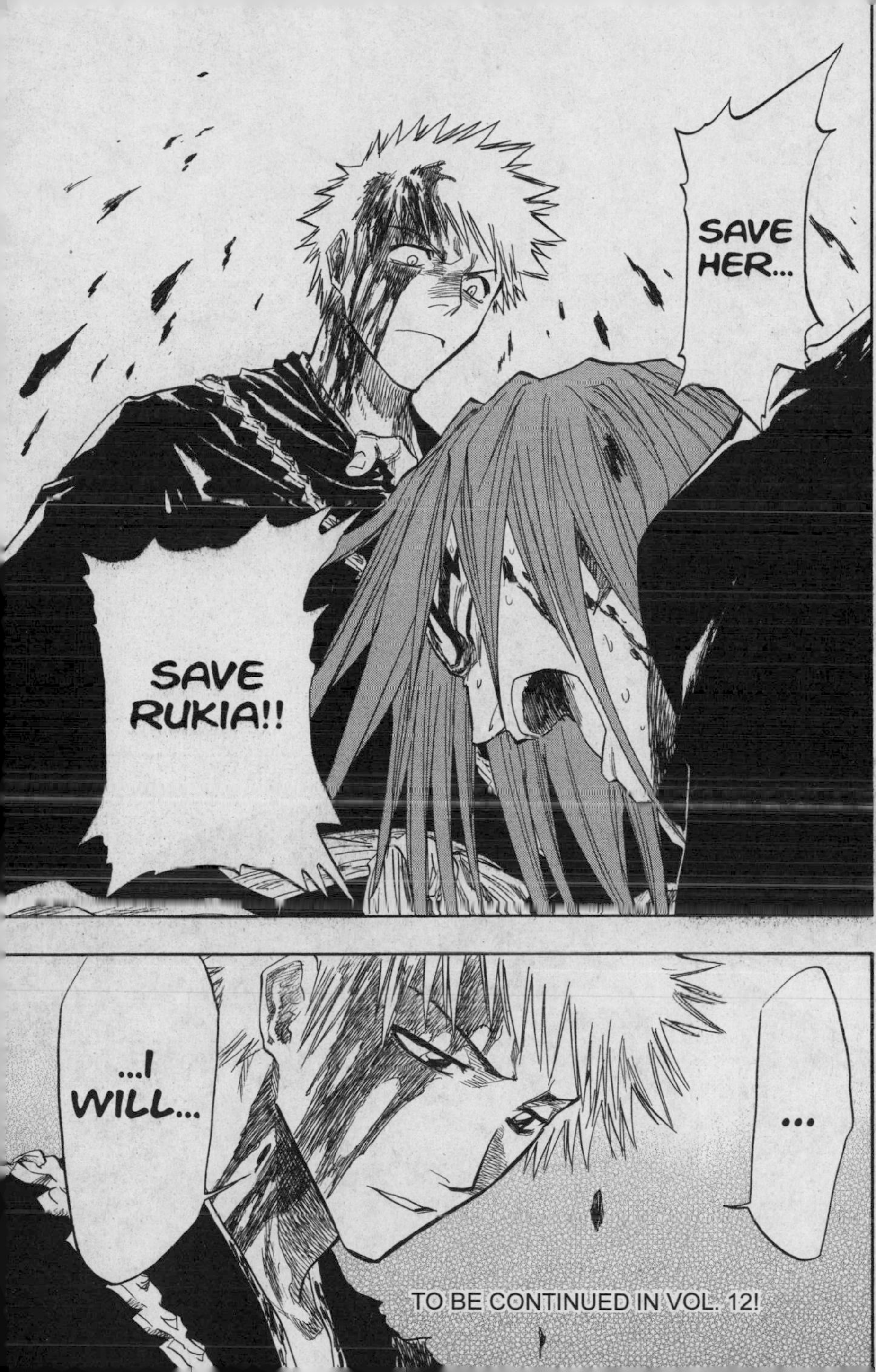
SAVE HER...
SAVE RUKIA!!
...
...I WILL...
TO BE CONTINUED IN VOL. 12!

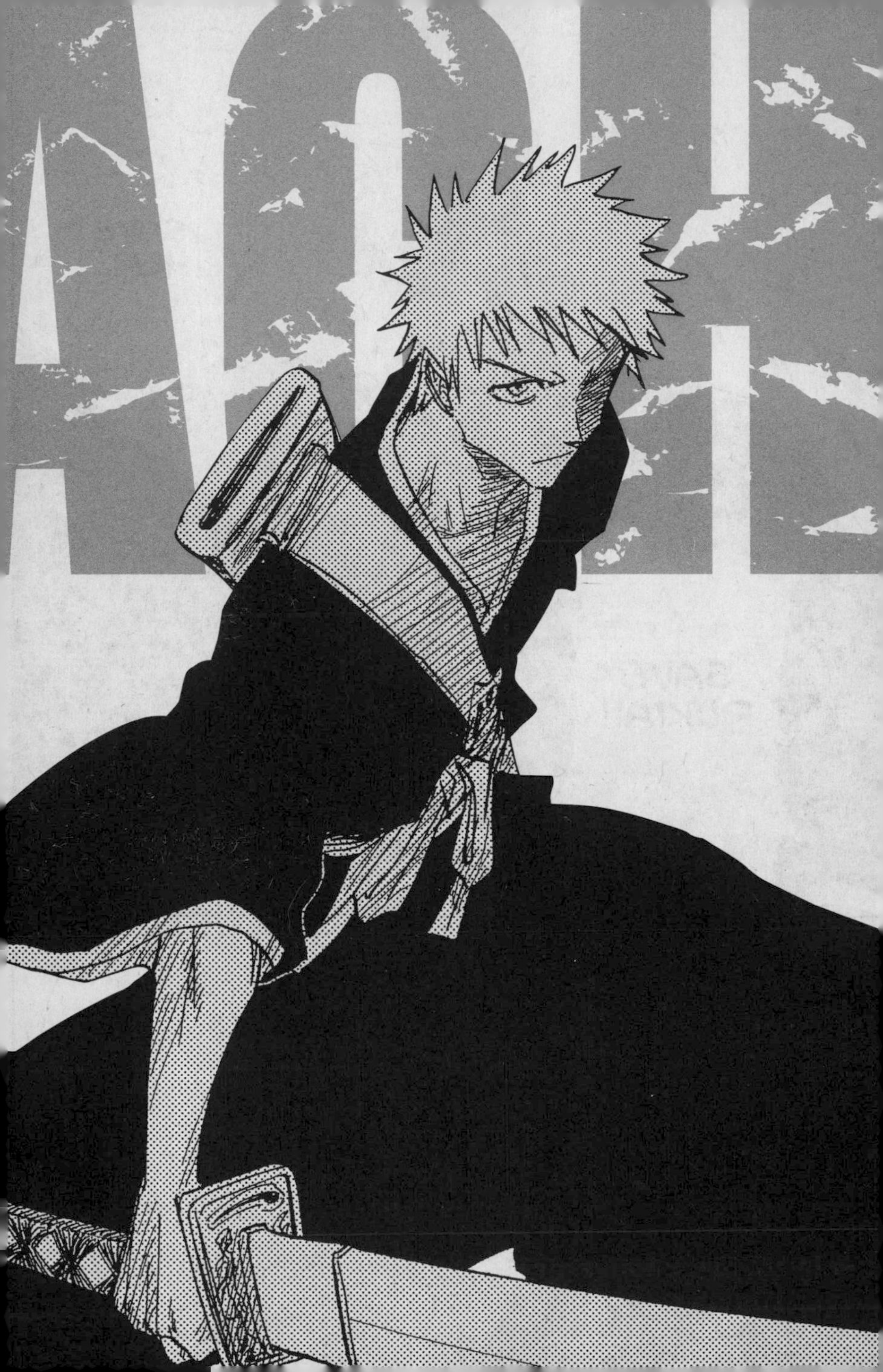

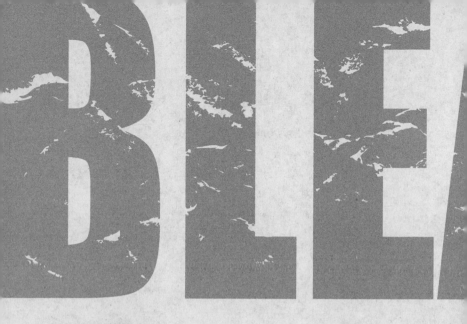

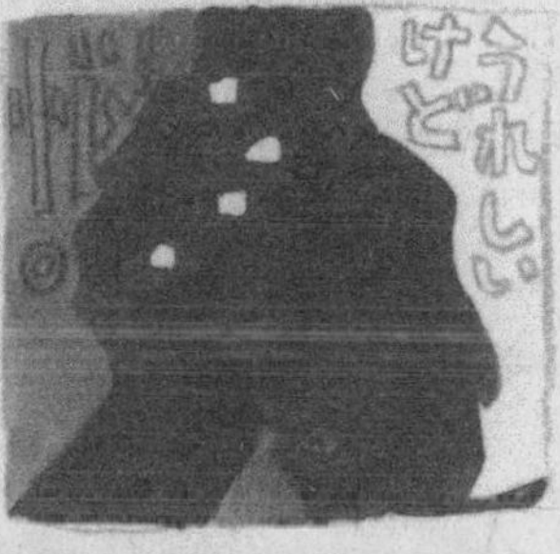
うれしい。
けど
(I'm happy but troubled.)

Every year I participate in *Jump*'s annual JumpFesta event. This year, after leaving the stage, I looked around the convention center for the first time. A lot of fans were cheering me on from behind, but it was kind of embarrassing so I didn't look back.
I really feel bad about that. But what are you supposed to do in a situation like that? Should I have waved? That doesn't seem right either...

-Tite Kubo, 2004

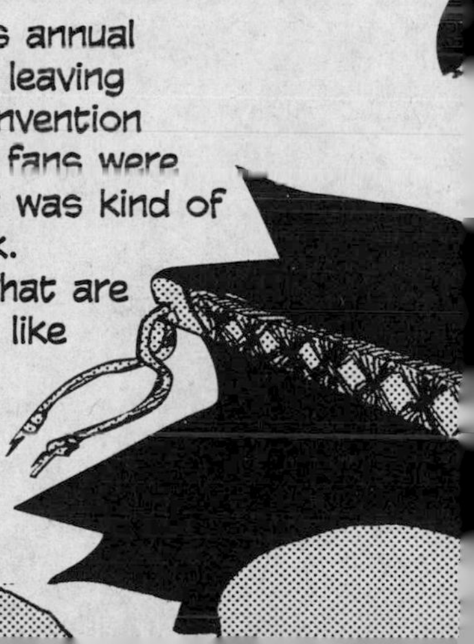

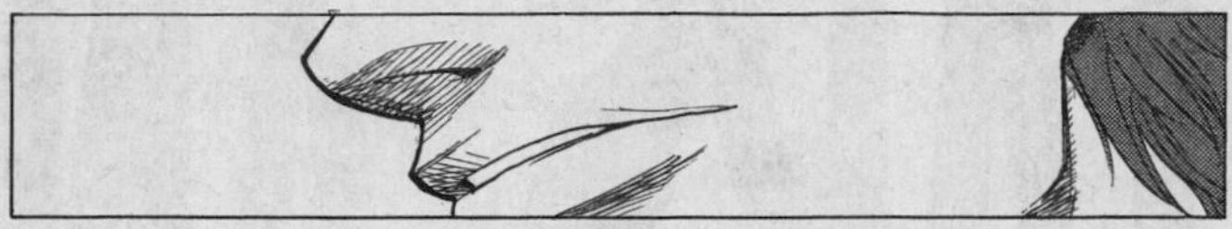

We think a flower on a cliff is beautiful
because we stop our feet at the cliff's edge,
unable to step out into the sky
like that fearless flower.

BLEACH 12 FLOWER ON THE PRECIPICE

Shonen Jump Manga

STARS AND

Yasutora
"Chad" Sado

Ganju Shiba

Ichigo Kurosaki

plot

Having vowed to rescue Rukia, Ichigo and his friends go to the Soul Society and finally infiltrate the Seireitei, the city of the Soul Reapers. With the help of Soul Reaper Hanatarô Yamada, Ichigo eventually reaches the Senzaikyû where Rukia is being held. But before Ichigo can free her, his old enemy Renji arrives on the scene! Despite being terribly wounded, Ichigo defeats Renji, who makes an unexpected plea: "Save Rukia!!"

BLEACH ALL

藍染惣右介

Sôsuke Aizen

雛森桃

Momo Hinamori

Hanatarô Yamada

山田花太郎

STORIES

BLEACH12

FLOWER ON THE PRECIPICE

Contents

99. Dead Black War Cloud

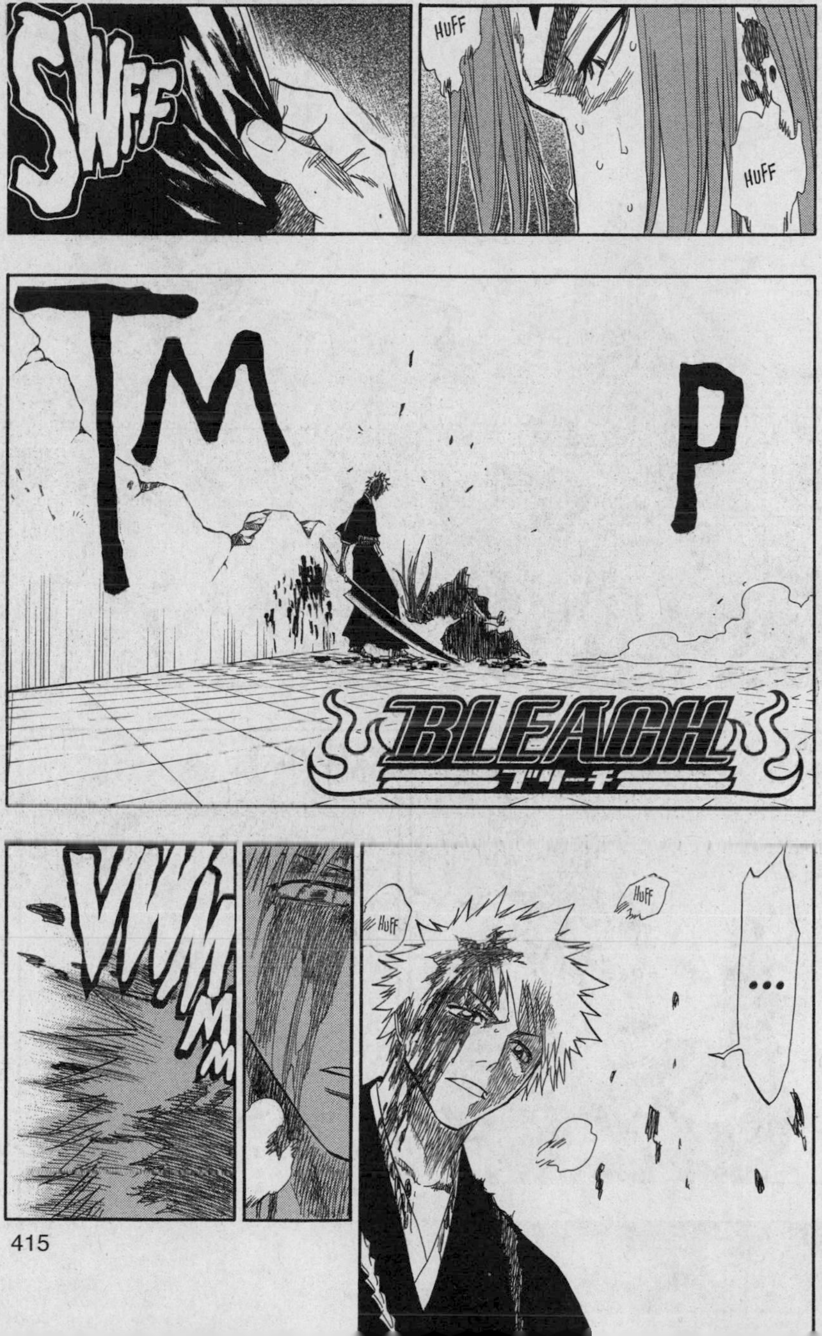
HUFF
HUFF
SWFF
TMP
BLEACH
...
HUFF
HUFF
VWMMM

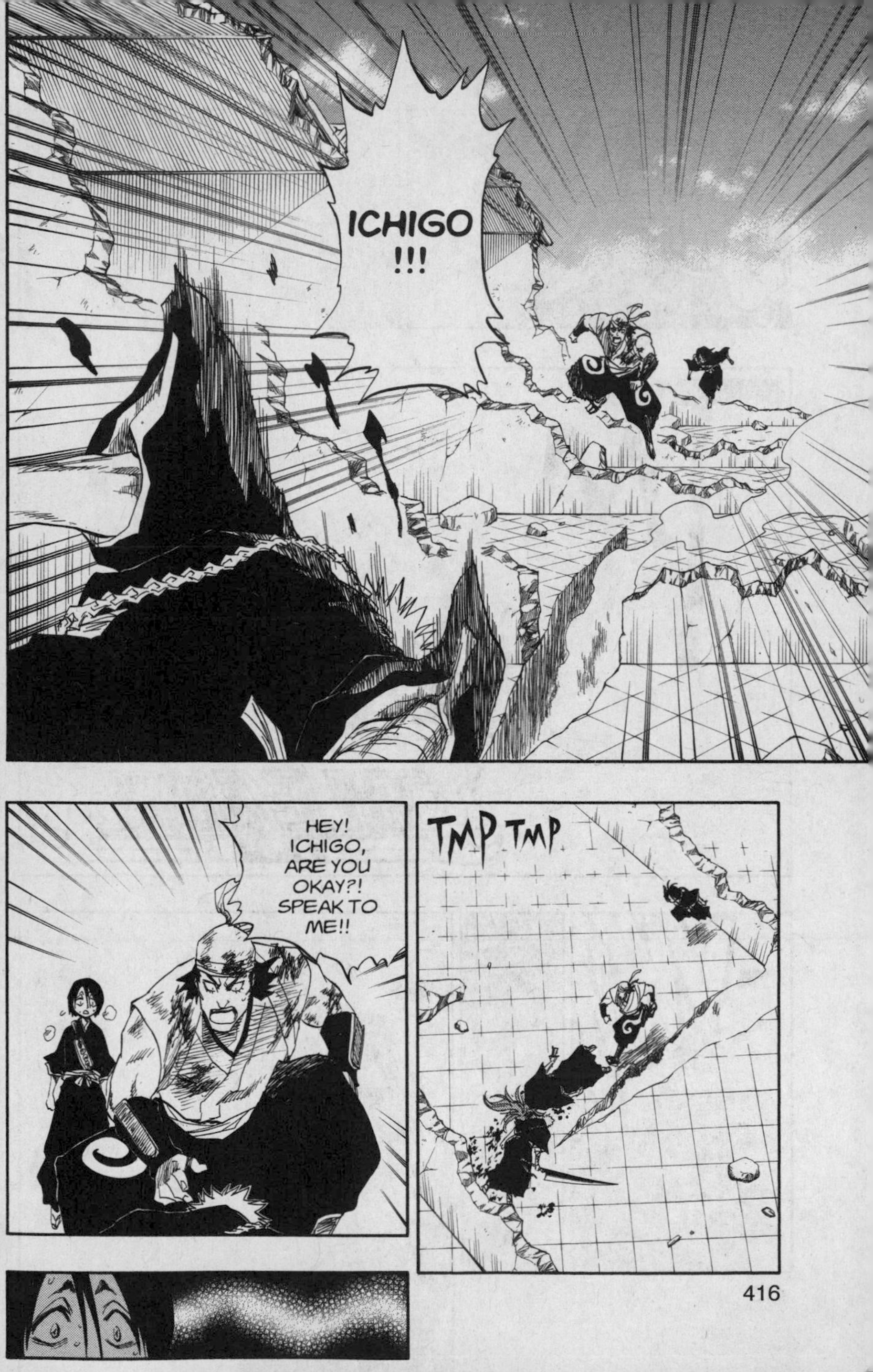
ICHIGO !!!
TMP TMP
HEY! ICHIGO, ARE YOU OKAY?! SPEAK TO ME!!

READ THIS WAY

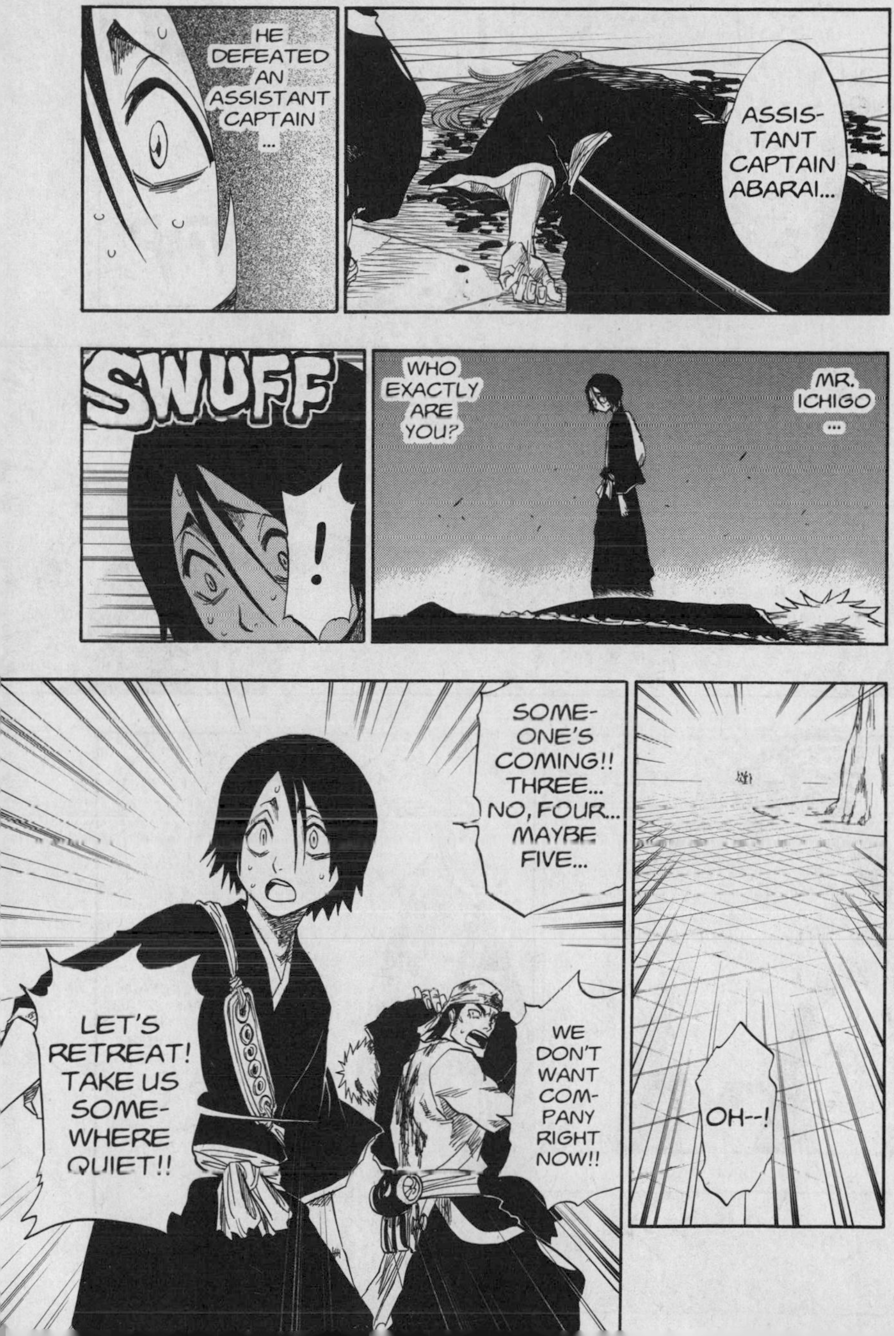
ASSIS-TANT CAPTAIN ABARAI...
HE DEFEATED AN ASSISTANT CAPTAIN...
MR. ICHIGO...
WHO EXACTLY ARE YOU?
SWUFF
!
OH--!
SOME-ONE'S COMING!! THREE... NO, FOUR... MAYBE FIVE...
WE DON'T WANT COM-PANY RIGHT NOW!!
LET'S RETREAT! TAKE US SOME-WHERE QUIET!!

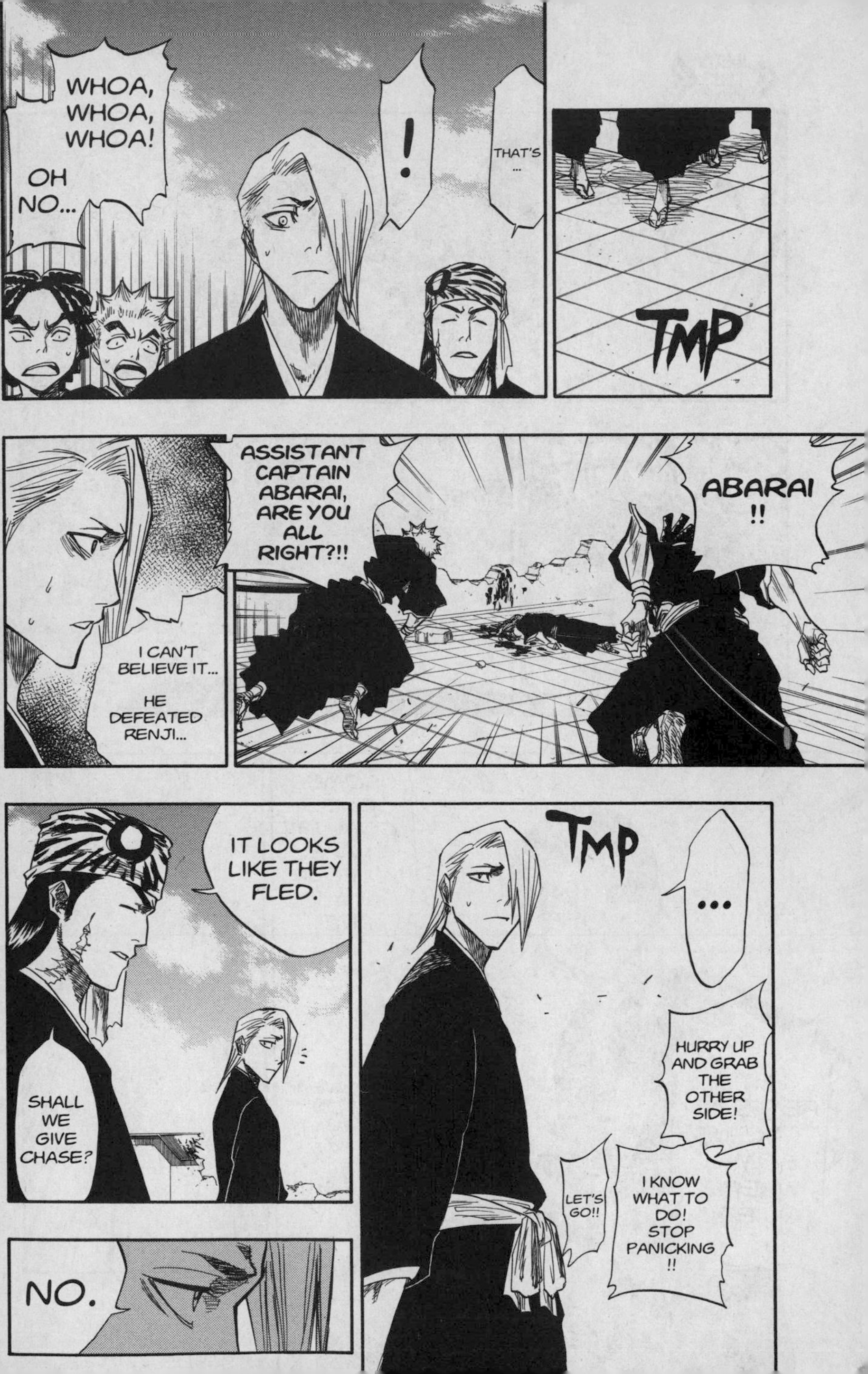
TMP
THAT'S ...
!
WHOA, WHOA, WHOA!
OH NO...
ABARAI !!
ASSISTANT CAPTAIN ABARAI, ARE YOU ALL RIGHT?!!
I CAN'T BELIEVE IT...
HE DEFEATED RENJI...
TMP
...
HURRY UP AND GRAB THE OTHER SIDE!
I KNOW WHAT TO DO! STOP PANICKING !!
LET'S GO!!
IT LOOKS LIKE THEY FLED.
SHALL WE GIVE CHASE?
NO.

READ THIS WAY

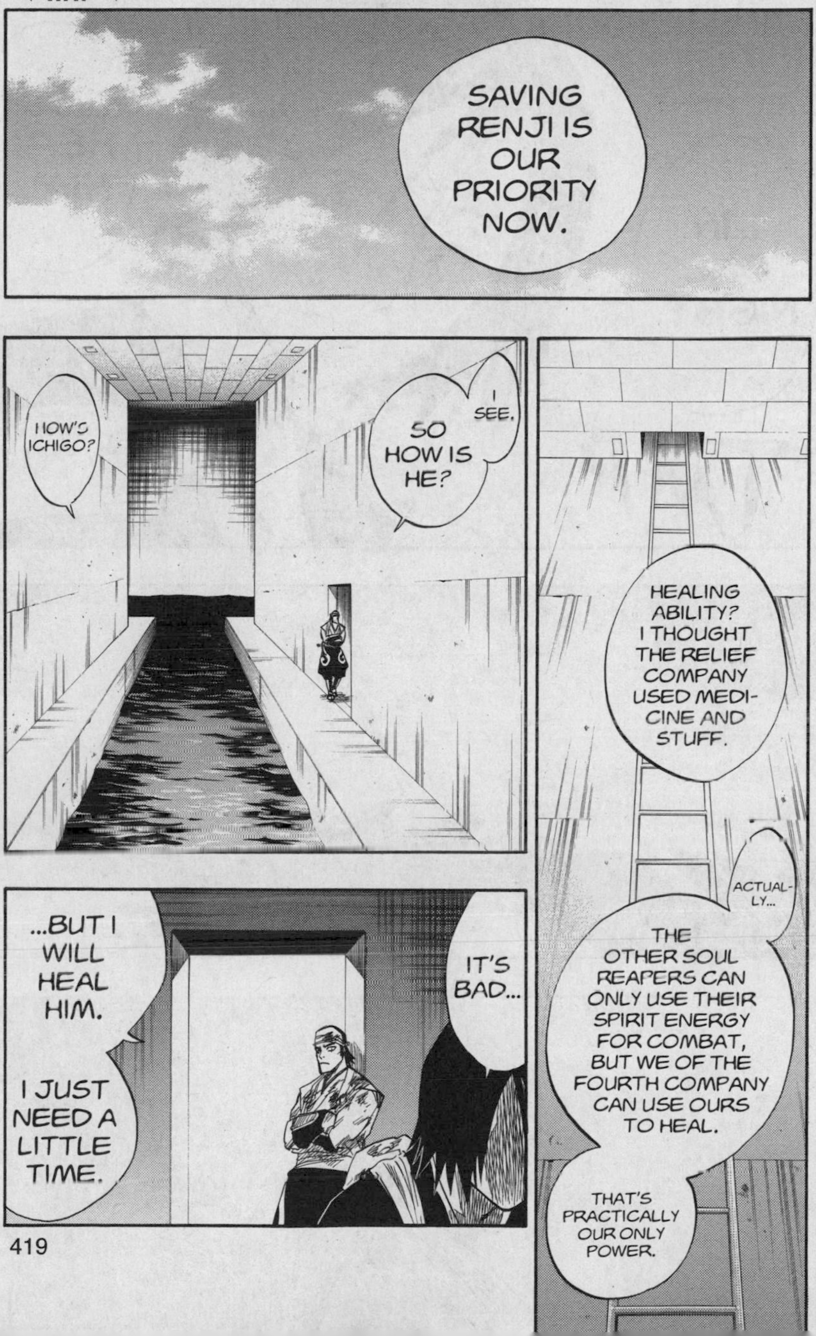
SAVING RENJI IS OUR PRIORITY NOW.
HEALING ABILITY? I THOUGHT THE RELIEF COMPANY USED MEDI-CINE AND STUFF.
ACTUAL-LY...
THE OTHER SOUL REAPERS CAN ONLY USE THEIR SPIRIT ENERGY FOR COMBAT, BUT WE OF THE FOURTH COMPANY CAN USE OURS TO HEAL.
THAT'S PRACTICALLY OUR ONLY POWER.
I SEE.
SO HOW IS HE?
HOW'S ICHIGO?
IT'S BAD...
...BUT I WILL HEAL HIM.
I JUST NEED A LITTLE TIME.

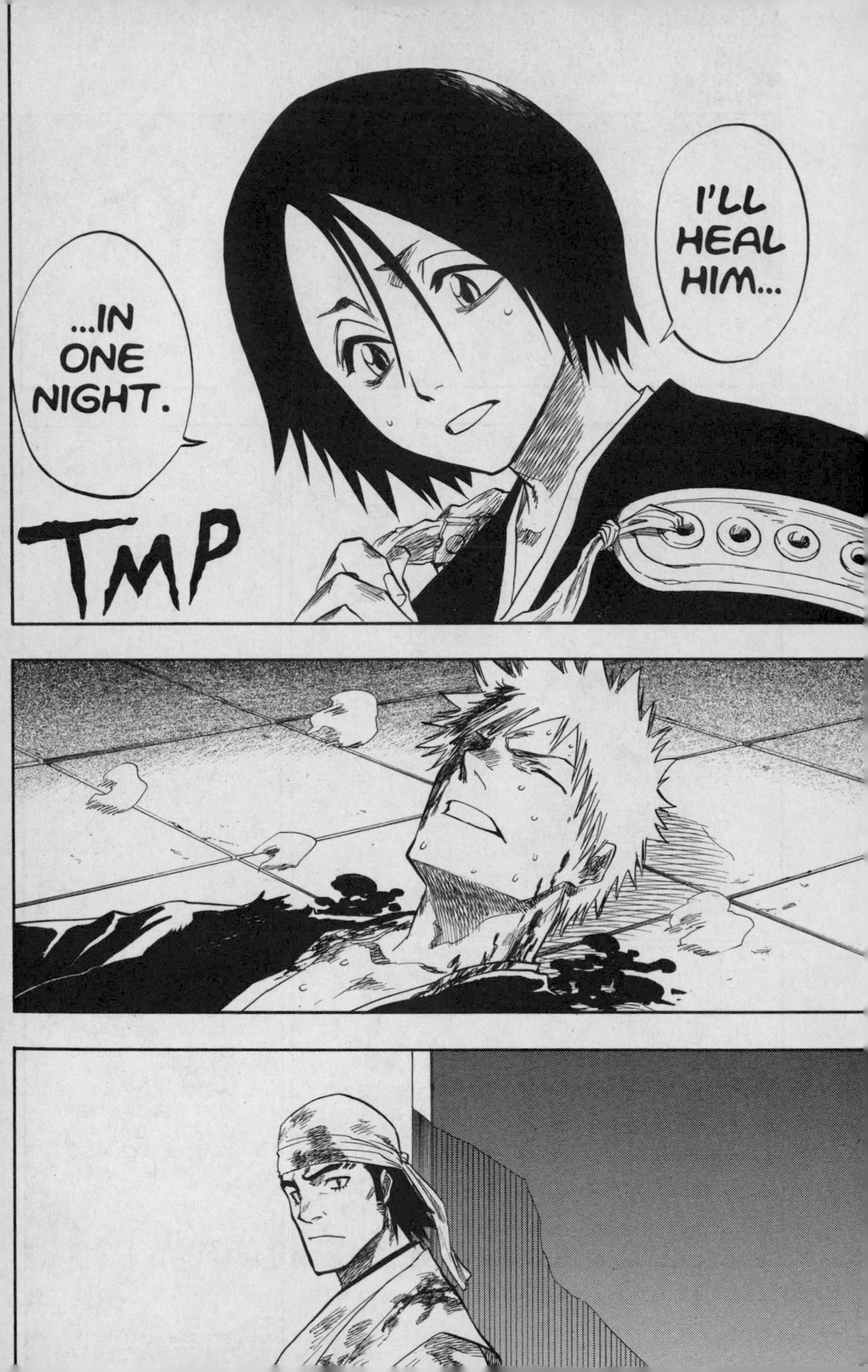
I'LL HEAL HIM...
...IN ONE NIGHT.
TMP

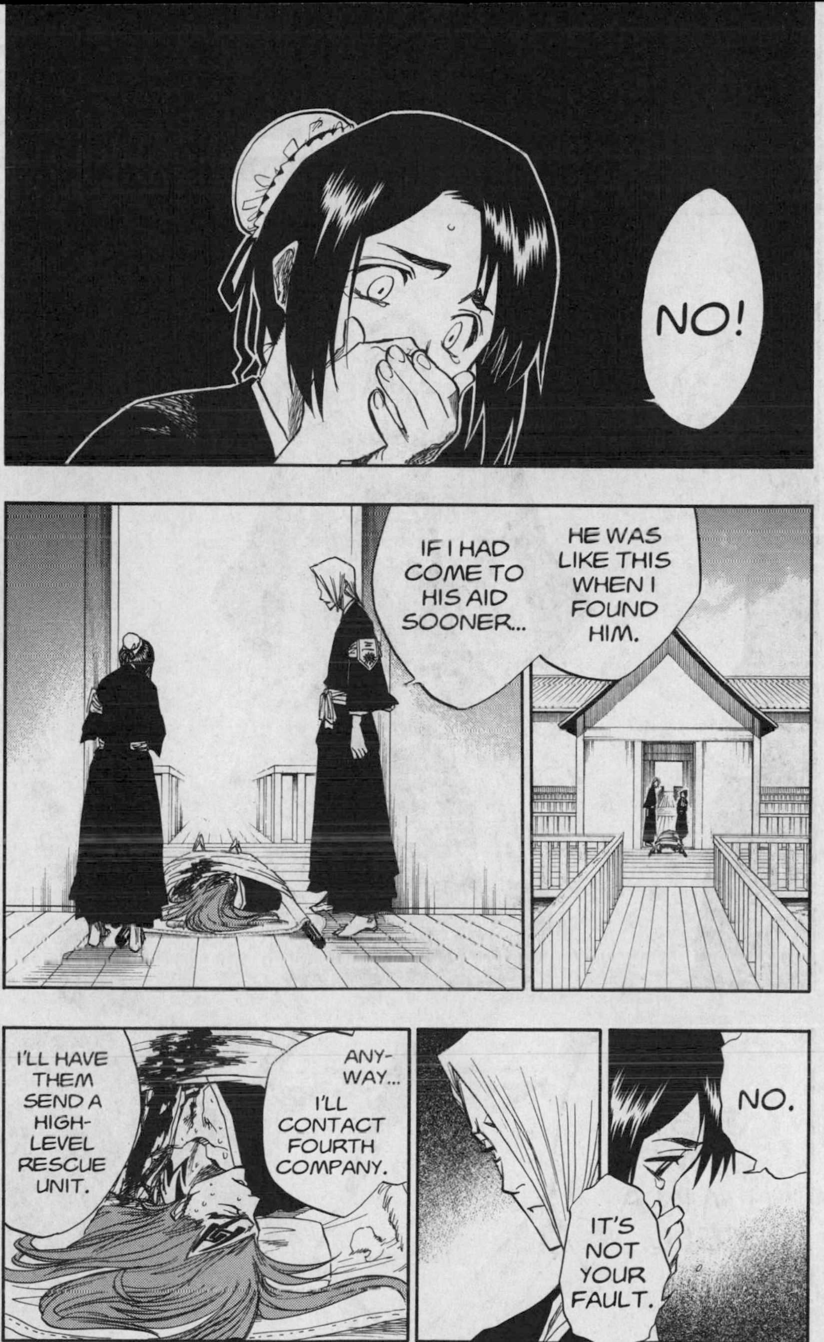
NO!
HE WAS LIKE THIS WHEN I FOUND HIM.
IF I HAD COME TO HIS AID SOONER...
NO.
IT'S NOT YOUR FAULT.
ANY-WAY... I'LL CONTACT FOURTH COMPANY.
I'LL HAVE THEM SEND A HIGH-LEVEL RESCUE UNIT.

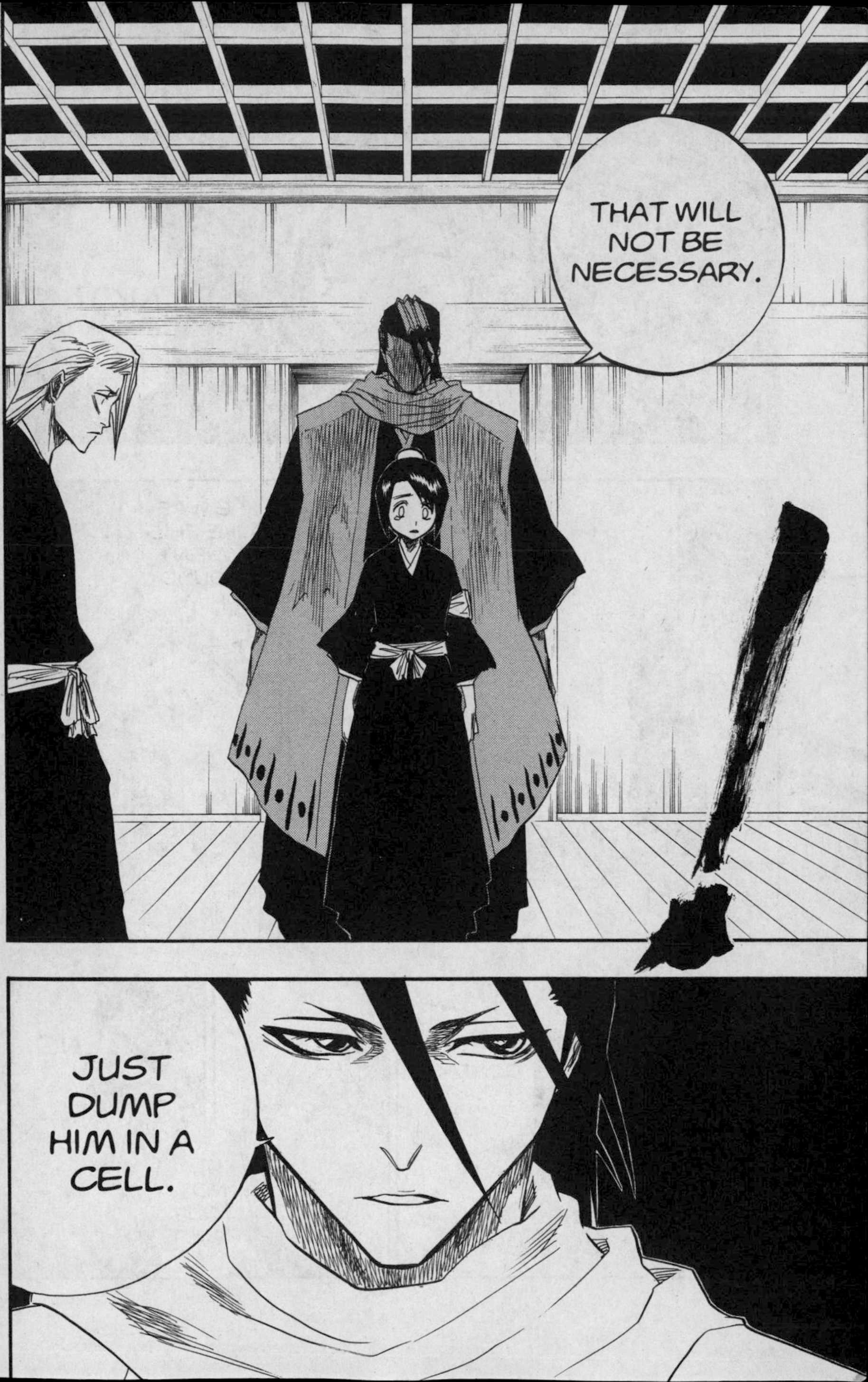
THAT WILL NOT BE NECESSARY.
JUST DUMP HIM IN A CELL.

READ THIS WAY

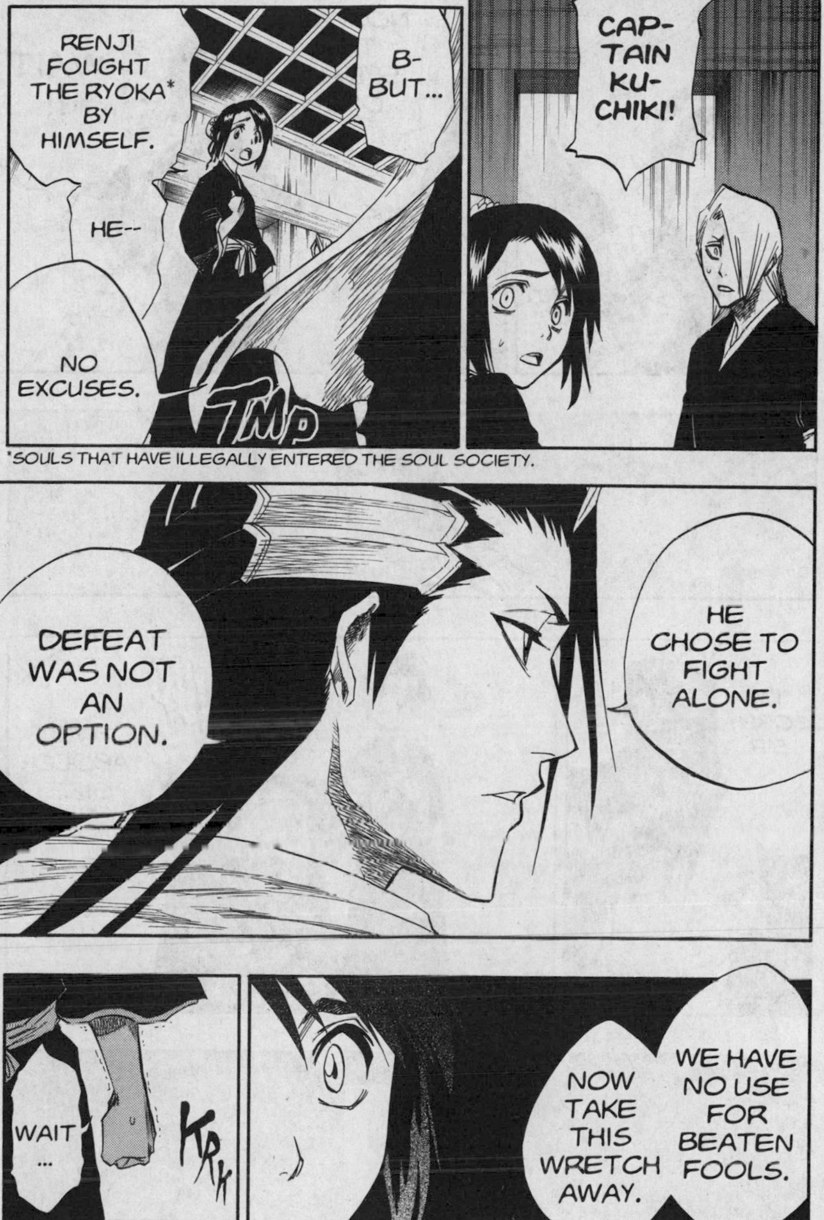
CAPTAIN KUCHIKI!
B-BUT...
RENJI FOUGHT THE RYOKA* BY HIMSELF.
HE--
NO EXCUSES.
TMP
HE CHOSE TO FIGHT ALONE.
DEFEAT WAS NOT AN OPTION.
WE HAVE NO USE FOR BEATEN FOOLS.
NOW TAKE THIS WRETCH AWAY.
KRK
WAIT ...

*SOULS THAT HAVE ILLEGALLY ENTERED THE SOUL SOCIETY.

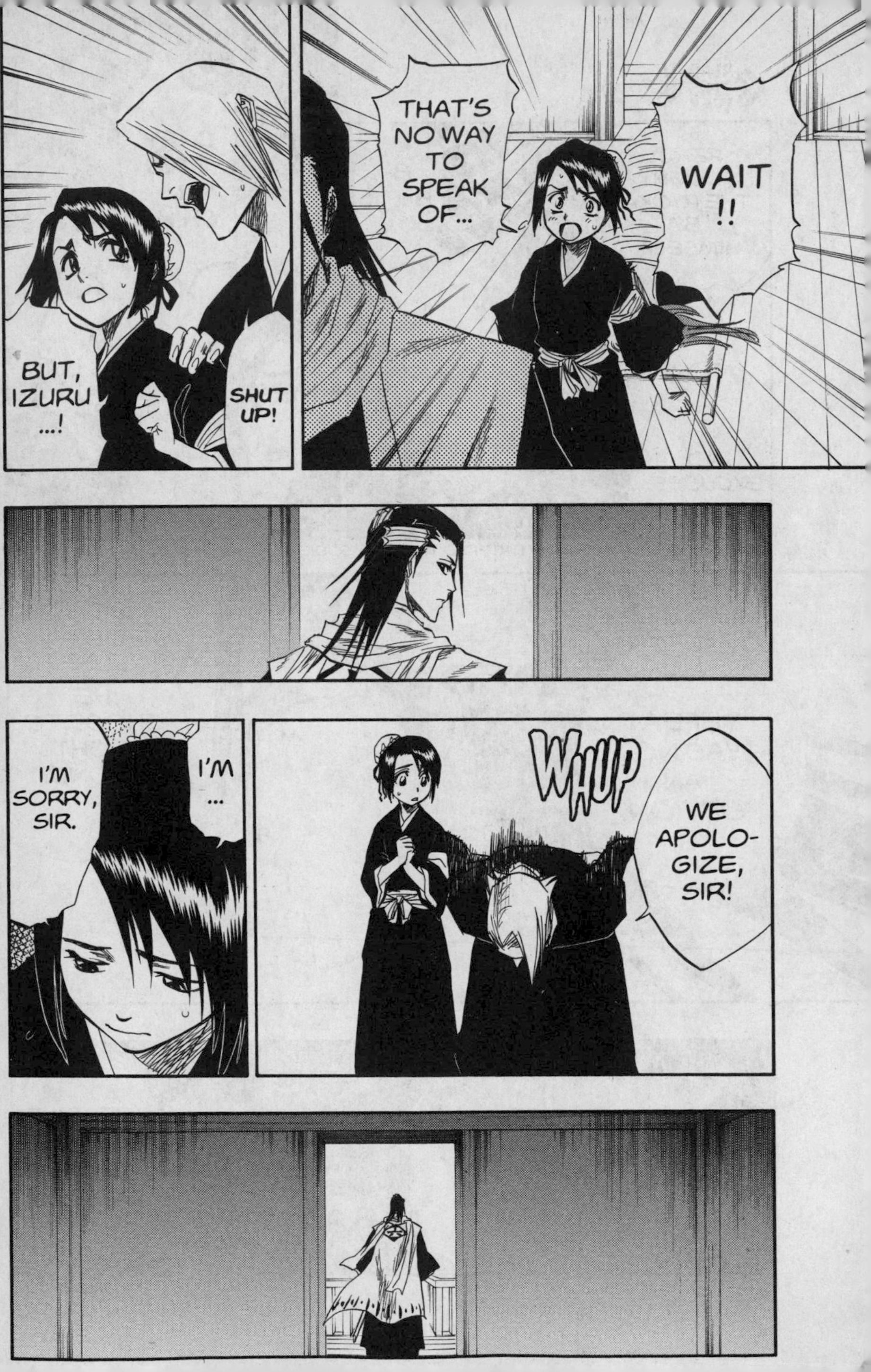
WAIT !!
THAT'S NO WAY TO SPEAK OF...
SHUT UP!
BUT, IZURU ...!
WE APOLOGIZE, SIR!
WHUP
I'M ...
I'M SORRY, SIR.

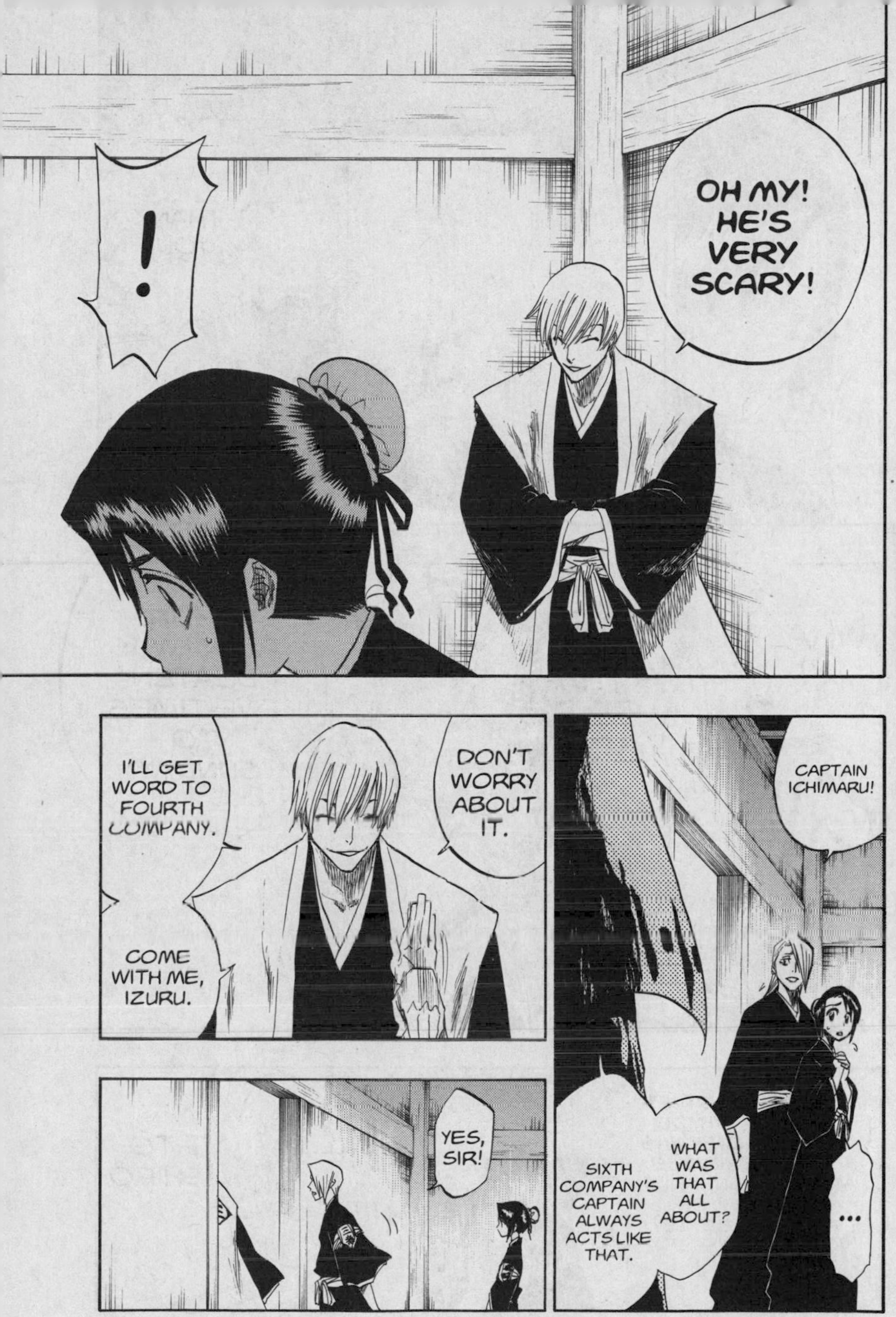
OH MY! HE'S VERY SCARY!
!
CAPTAIN ICHIMARU!
WHAT WAS THAT ALL ABOUT?
SIXTH COMPANY'S CAPTAIN ALWAYS ACTS LIKE THAT.
...
DON'T WORRY ABOUT IT.
I'LL GET WORD TO FOURTH COMPANY.
COME WITH ME, IZURU.
YES, SIR!

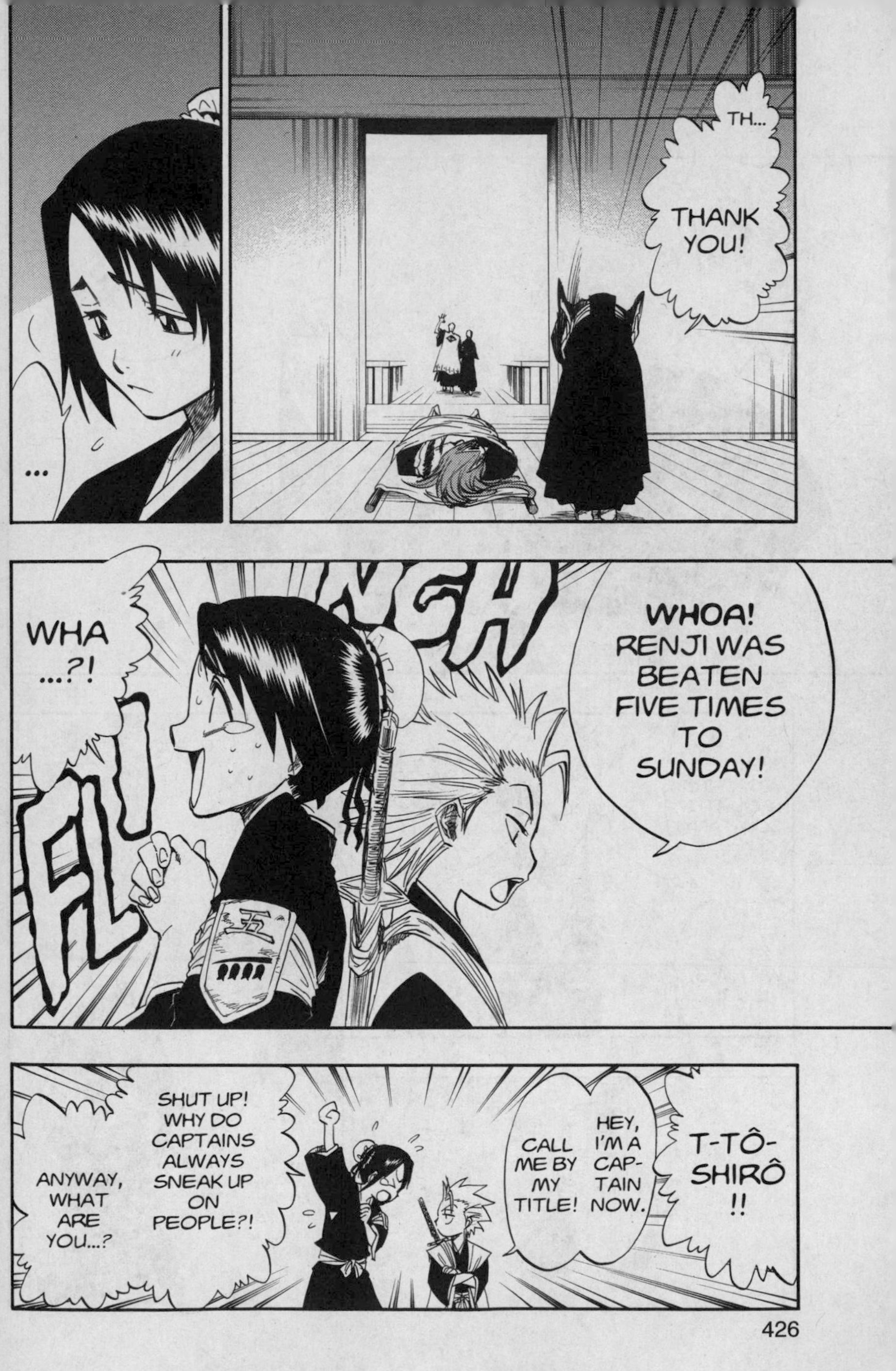
TH...
THANK YOU!
...
WHOA! RENJI WAS BEATEN FIVE TIMES TO SUNDAY!
WHA ...?!
T-TÔ-SHIRÔ !!
HEY, I'M A CAPTAIN NOW.
CALL ME BY MY TITLE!
SHUT UP! WHY DO CAPTAINS ALWAYS SNEAK UP ON PEOPLE?!
ANYWAY, WHAT ARE YOU...?

READ THIS WAY

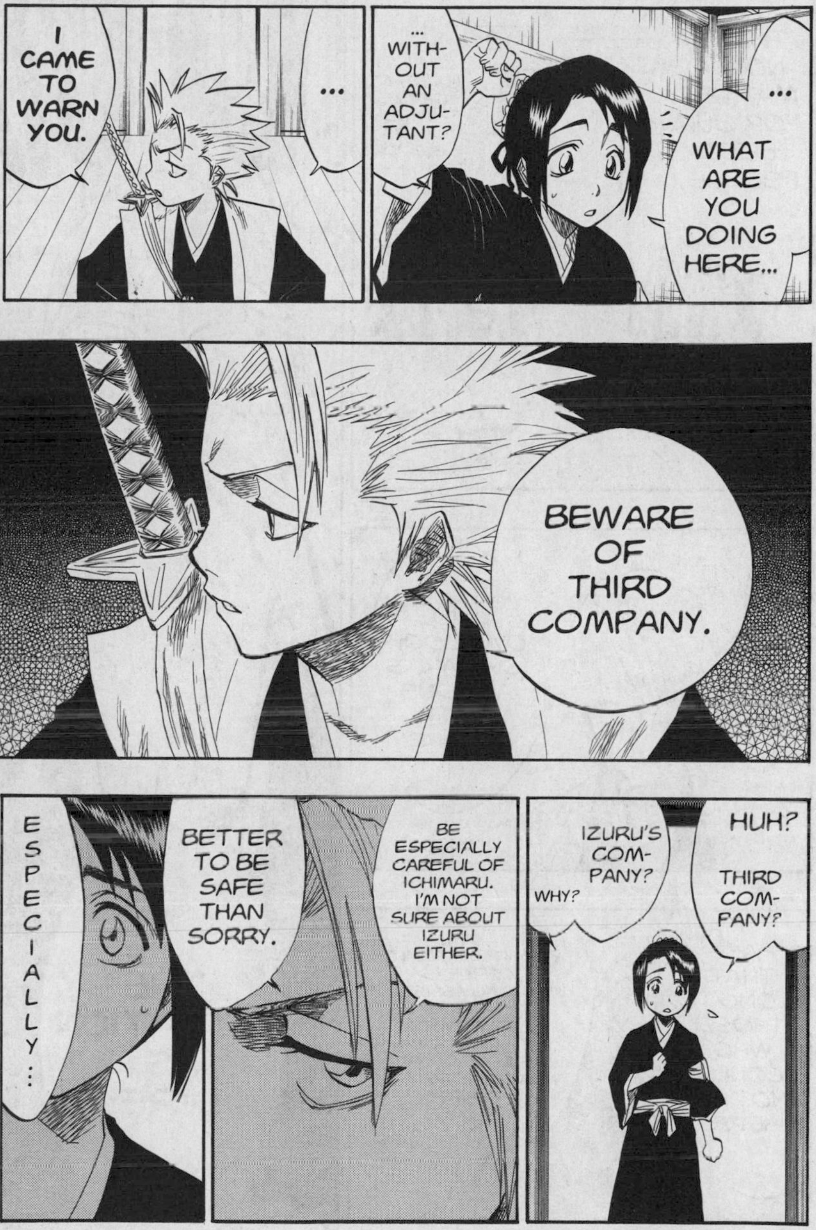
... WHAT ARE YOU DOING HERE...
... WITH-OUT AN ADJU-TANT?
...
I CAME TO WARN YOU.
BEWARE OF THIRD COMPANY.
HUH? THIRD COM-PANY?
IZURU'S COM-PANY?
WHY?
BE ESPECIALLY CAREFUL OF ICHIMARU. I'M NOT SURE ABOUT IZURU EITHER.
BETTER TO BE SAFE THAN SORRY.
ESPECIALLY...

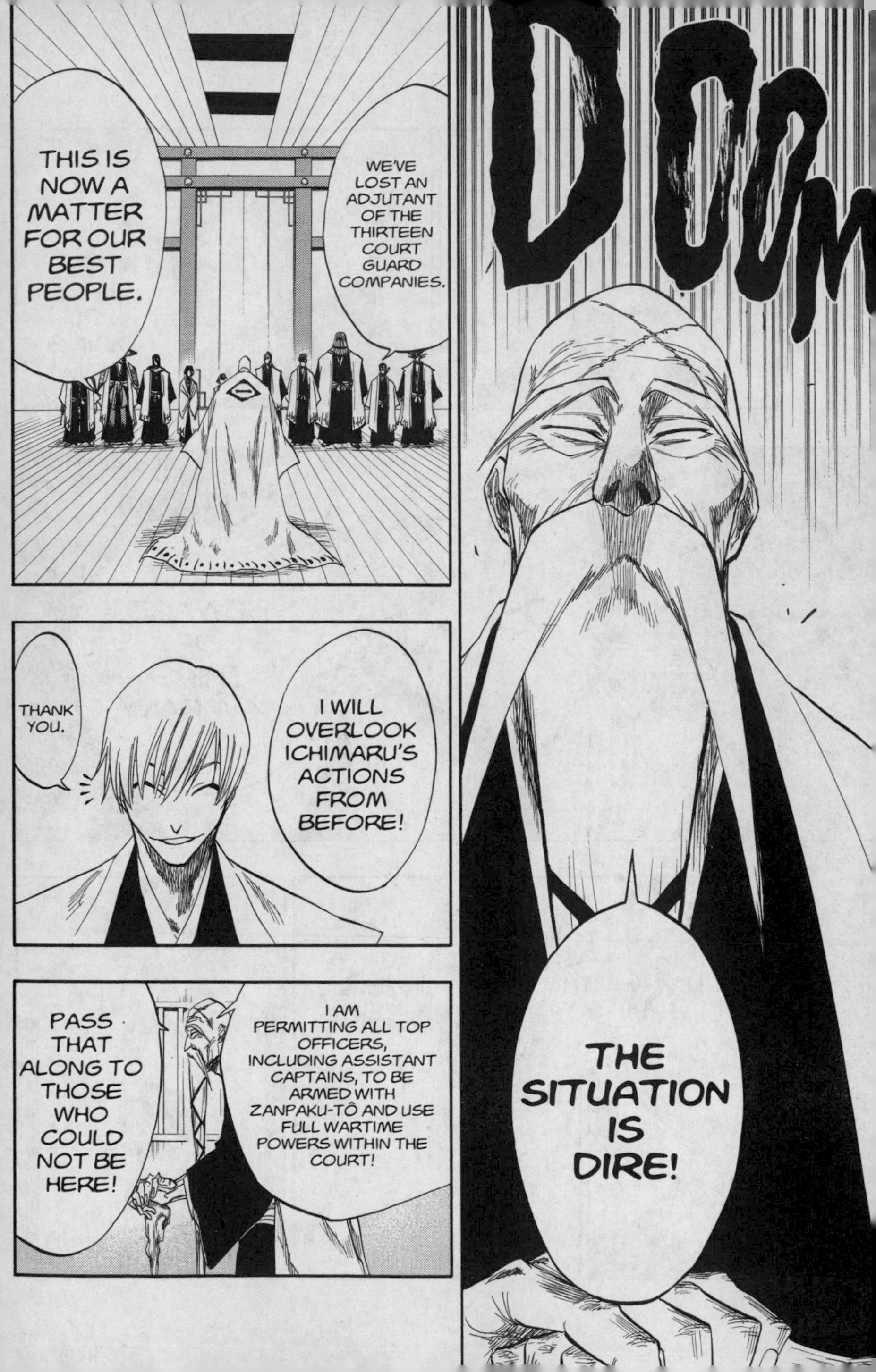
DOOM
THE SITUATION IS DIRE!
WE'VE LOST AN ADJUTANT OF THE THIRTEEN COURT GUARD COMPANIES.
THIS IS NOW A MATTER FOR OUR BEST PEOPLE.
I WILL OVERLOOK ICHIMARU'S ACTIONS FROM BEFORE!
THANK YOU.
I AM PERMITTING ALL TOP OFFICERS, INCLUDING ASSISTANT CAPTAINS, TO BE ARMED WITH ZANPAKU-TÔ AND USE FULL WARTIME POWERS WITHIN THE COURT!
PASS THAT ALONG TO THOSE WHO COULD NOT BE HERE!

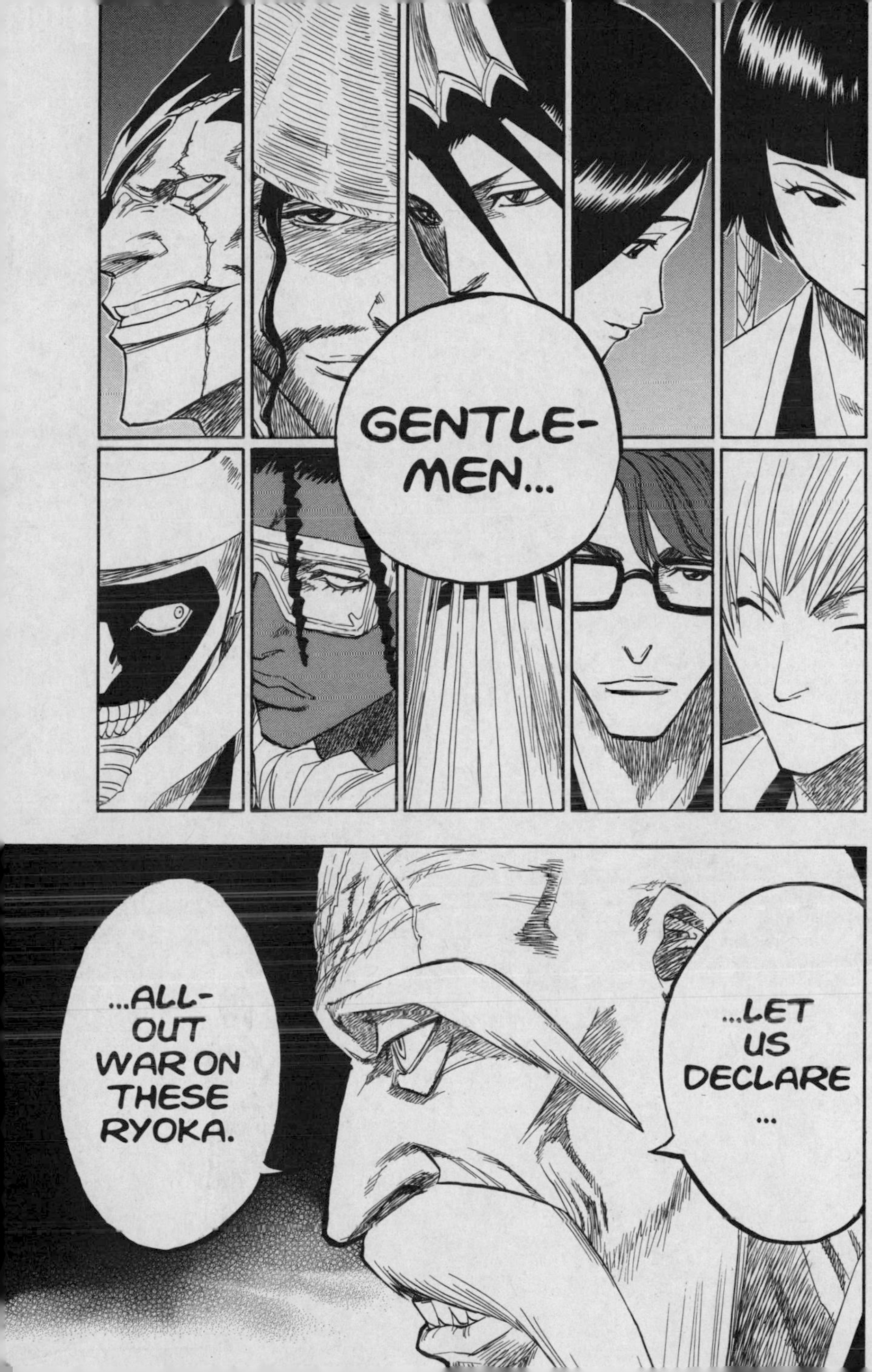
GENTLE-MEN...
...LET US DECLARE ...
...ALL-OUT WAR ON THESE RYOKA.

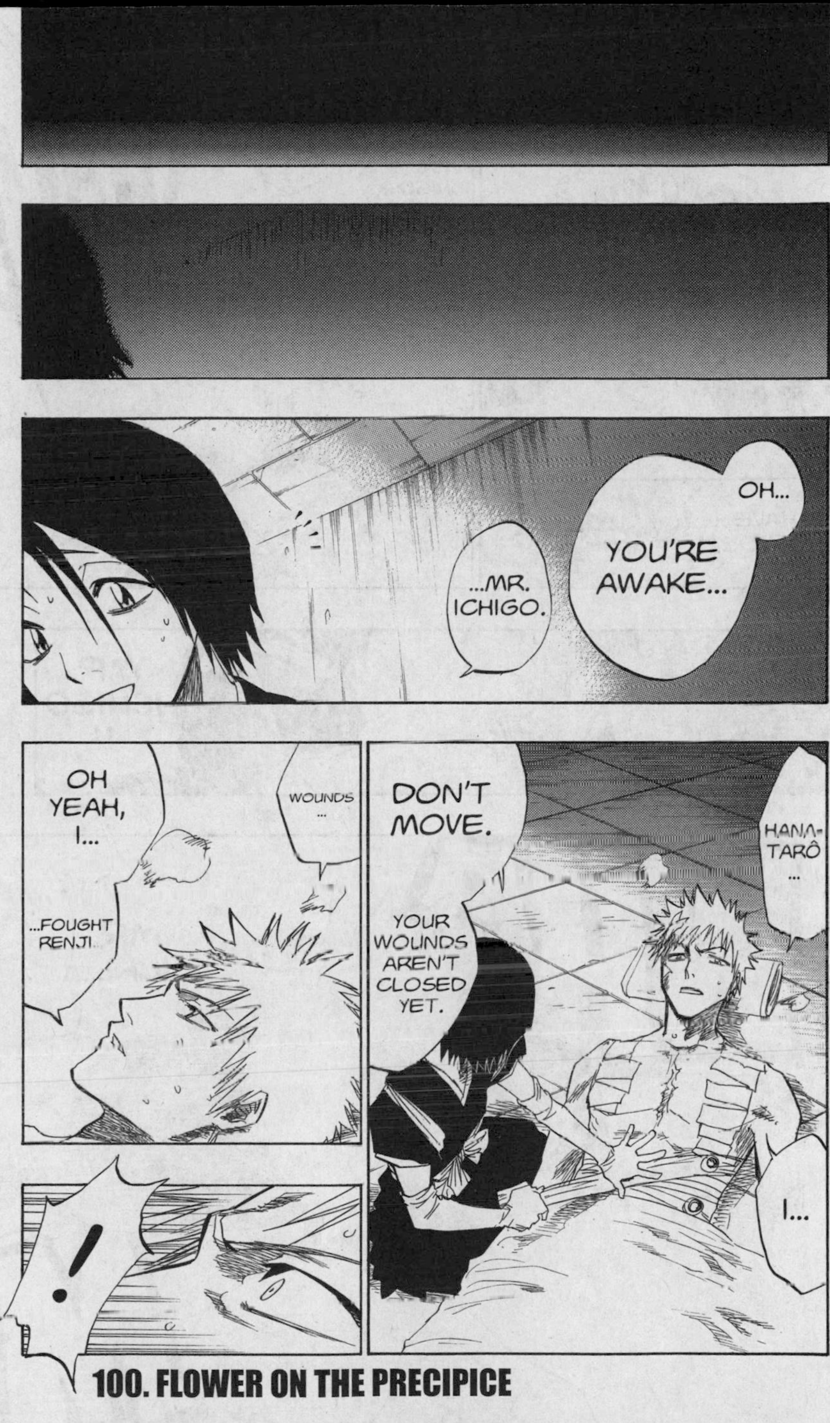
OH...
YOU'RE AWAKE...
...MR. ICHIGO.
HANA-TARÔ ...
DON'T MOVE.
YOUR WOUNDS AREN'T CLOSED YET.
I...
WOUNDS ...
OH YEAH, I...
...FOUGHT RENJI...
!

100. FLOWER ON THE PRECIPICE

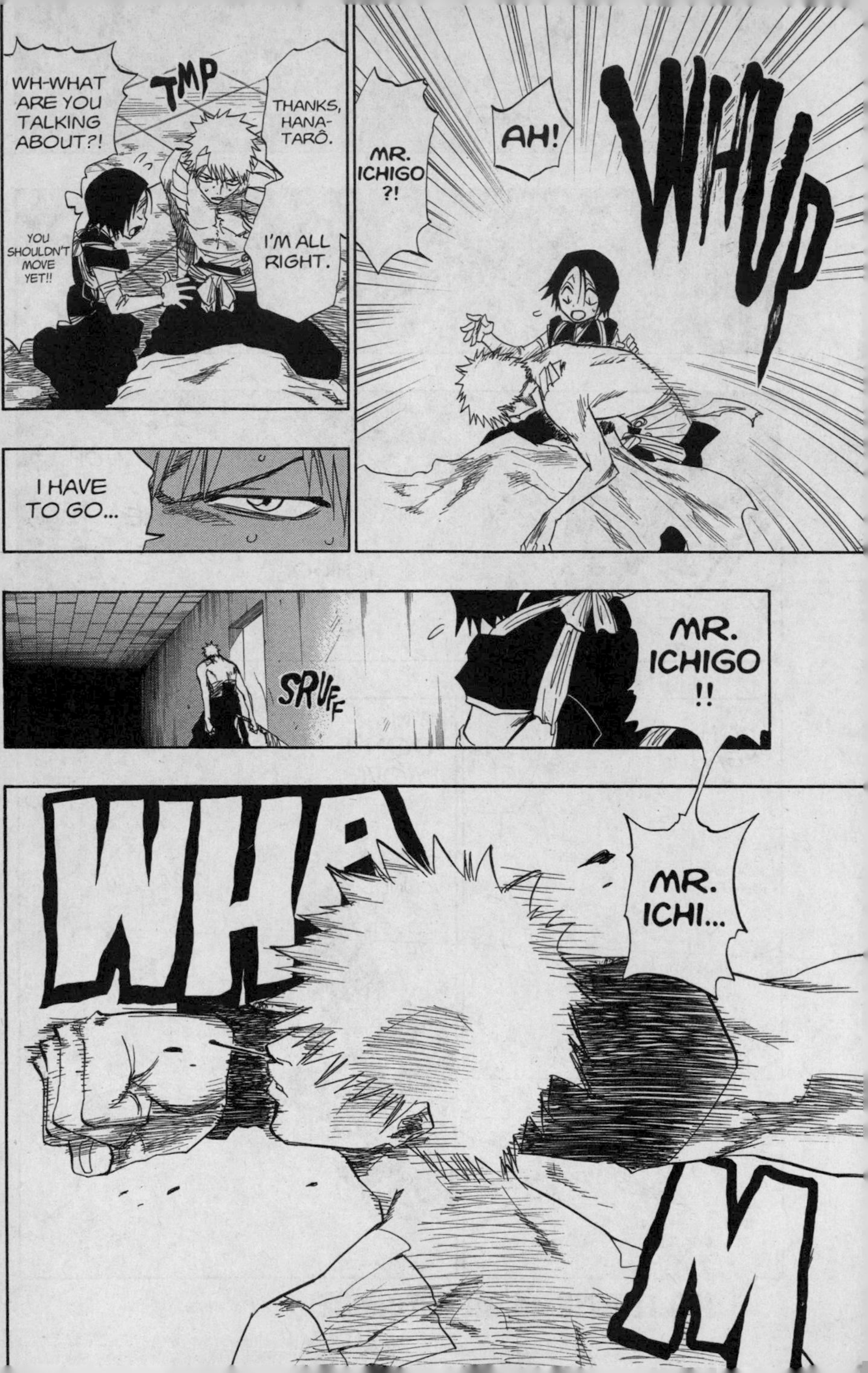
WHUP
AH!
MR. ICHIGO ?!
TMP
THANKS, HANA-TARÔ.
WH-WHAT ARE YOU TALKING ABOUT?!
I'M ALL RIGHT.
YOU SHOULDN'T MOVE YET!!
I HAVE TO GO...
MR. ICHIGO !!
SRUFF
MR. ICHI...
WHAM

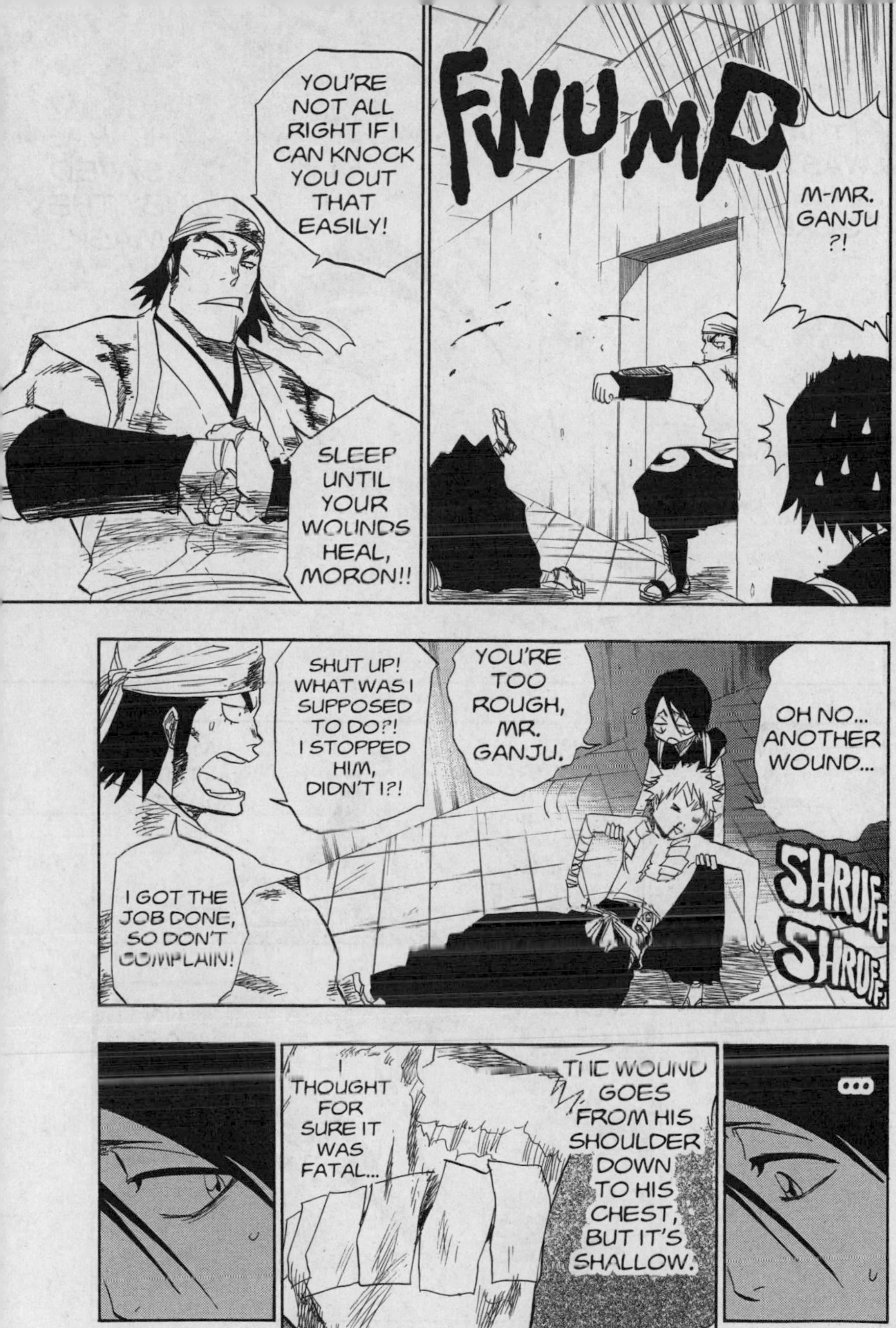
FWUMP
M-MR. GANJU ?!
YOU'RE NOT ALL RIGHT IF I CAN KNOCK YOU OUT THAT EASILY!
SLEEP UNTIL YOUR WOUNDS HEAL, MORON!!
OH NO... ANOTHER WOUND...
SHRUFF
SHRUFF
YOU'RE TOO ROUGH, MR. GANJU.
SHUT UP! WHAT WAS I SUPPOSED TO DO?! I STOPPED HIM, DIDN'T I?!
I GOT THE JOB DONE, SO DON'T COMPLAIN!
...
THE WOUND GOES FROM HIS SHOULDER DOWN TO HIS CHEST, BUT IT'S SHALLOW.
I THOUGHT FOR SURE IT WAS FATAL...

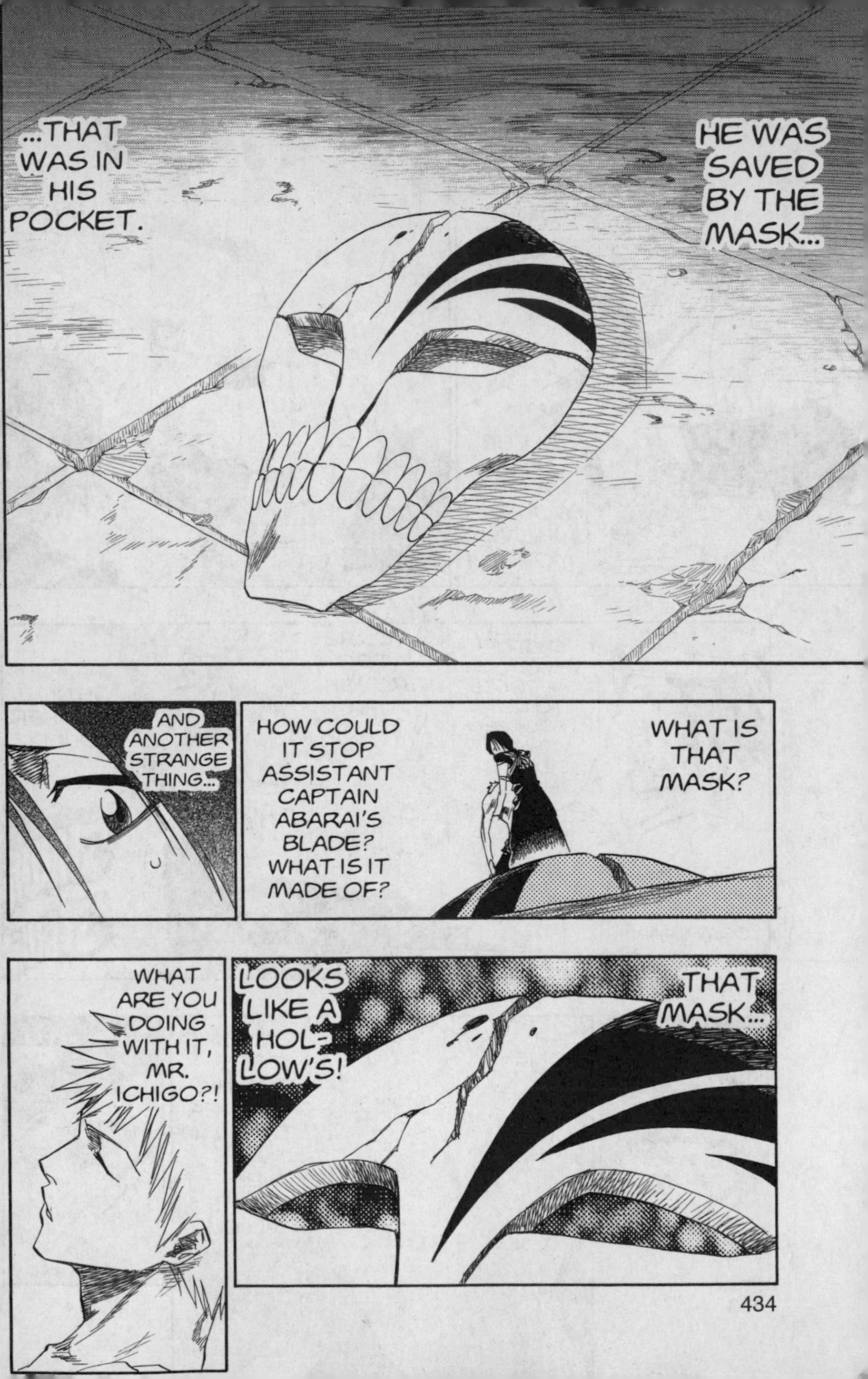
HE WAS SAVED BY THE MASK...
...THAT WAS IN HIS POCKET.
WHAT IS THAT MASK?
HOW COULD IT STOP ASSISTANT CAPTAIN ABARAI'S BLADE? WHAT IS IT MADE OF?
AND ANOTHER STRANGE THING...
THAT MASK...
LOOKS LIKE A HOL-LOW'S!
WHAT ARE YOU DOING WITH IT, MR. ICHIGO?!

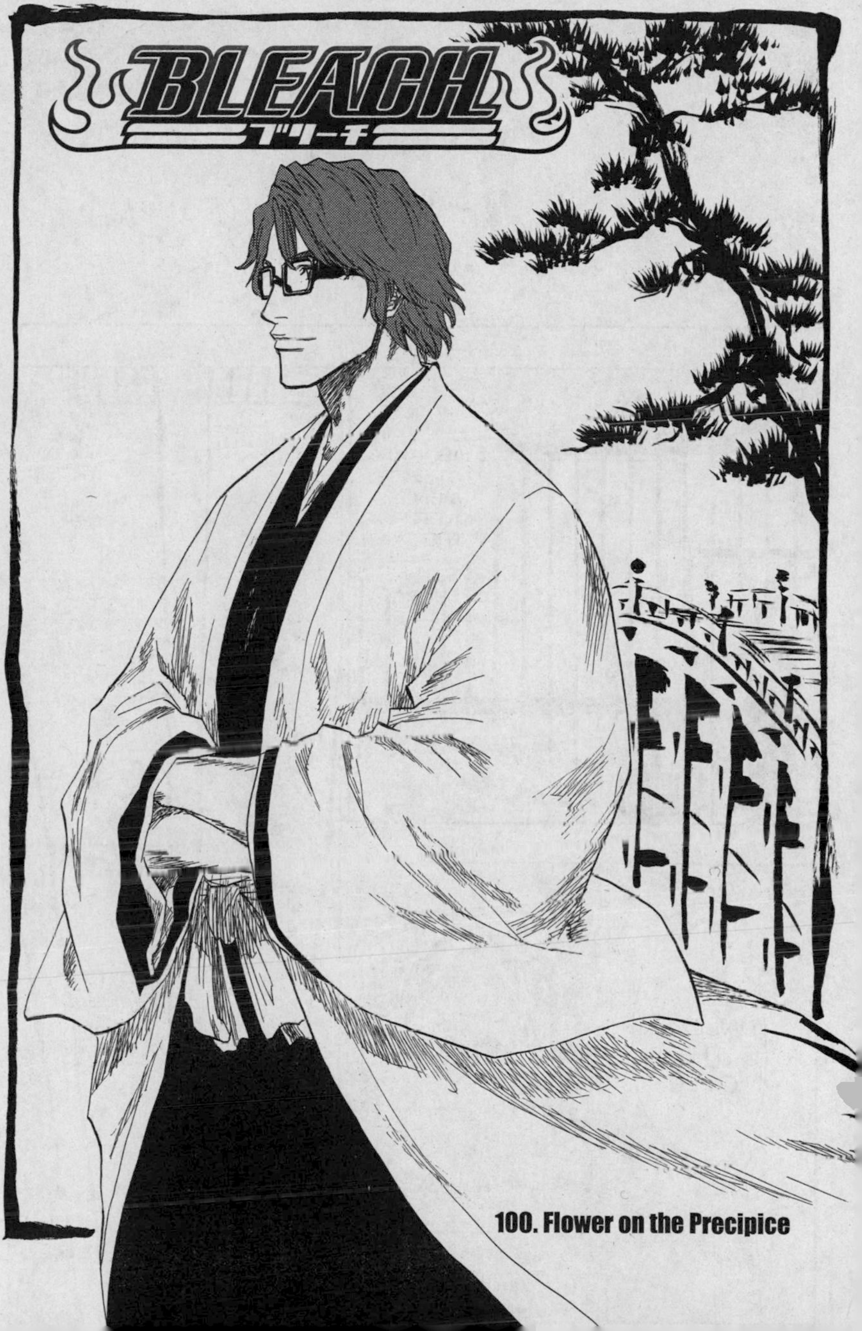
BLEACH
ブリーチ

100. Flower on the Precipice

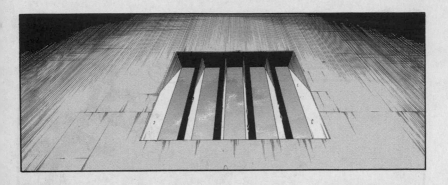

ASSIS-
TANT
CAPTAIN
ABARAI'S
TREAT-
MENT IS
OVER FOR
THE DAY!

UNLOCK
THE
CELL!

SWUP

KLIK

KLIK

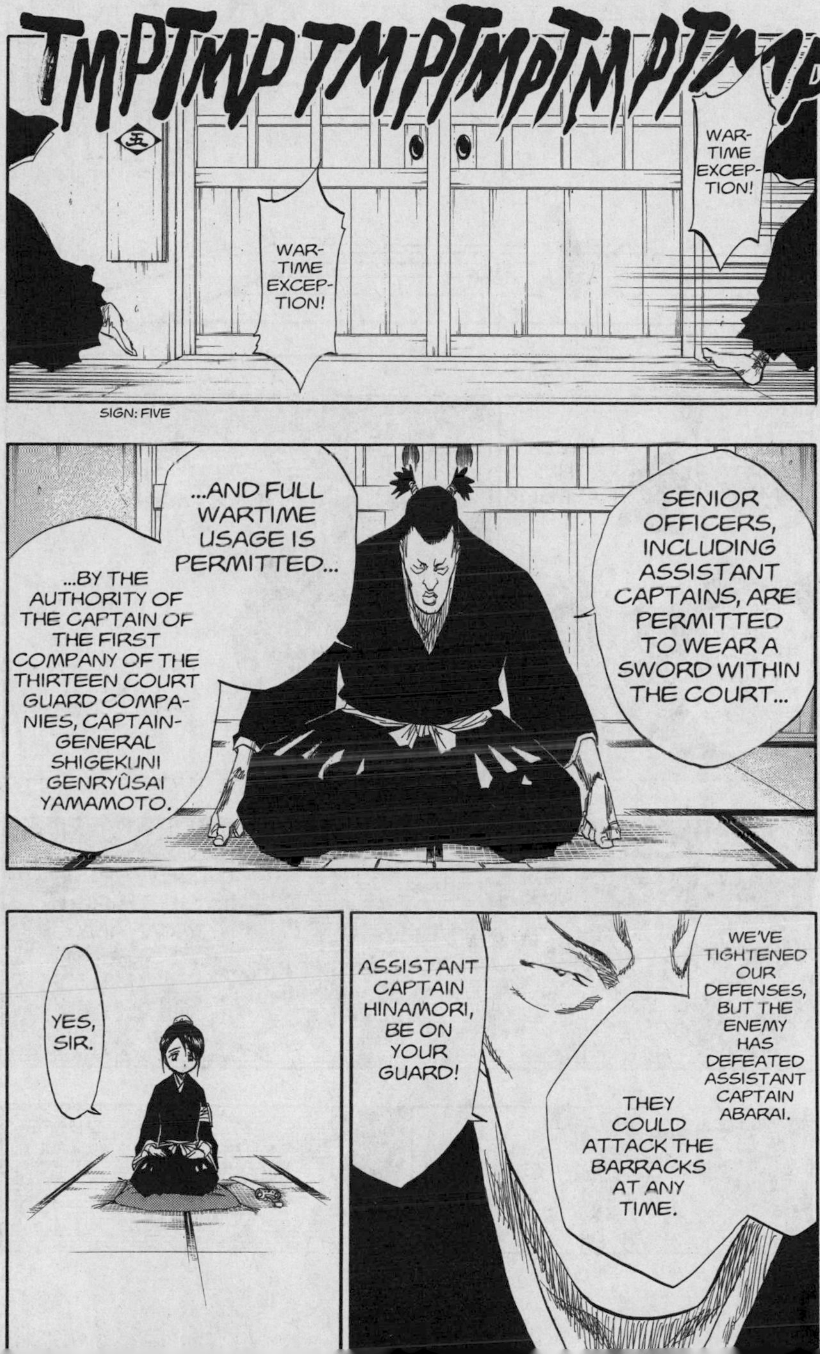
TMPTMPTMPTMPTMPTMP
WARTIME EXCEPTION!
WARTIME EXCEPTION!
SIGN: FIVE
SENIOR OFFICERS, INCLUDING ASSISTANT CAPTAINS, ARE PERMITTED TO WEAR A SWORD WITHIN THE COURT...
...AND FULL WARTIME USAGE IS PERMITTED...
...BY THE AUTHORITY OF THE CAPTAIN OF THE FIRST COMPANY OF THE THIRTEEN COURT GUARD COMPANIES, CAPTAIN-GENERAL SHIGEKUNI GENRYÛSAI YAMAMOTO.
WE'VE TIGHTENED OUR DEFENSES, BUT THE ENEMY HAS DEFEATED ASSISTANT CAPTAIN ABARAI.
THEY COULD ATTACK THE BARRACKS AT ANY TIME.
ASSISTANT CAPTAIN HINAMORI, BE ON YOUR GUARD!
YES, SIR.

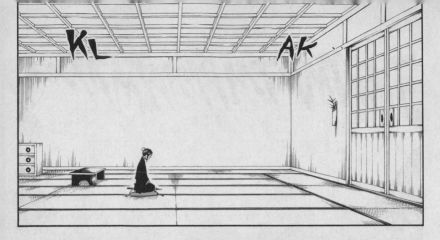

KL AK
WARTIME EXCEPTION?
SWORDS?
RENJI...
HOW DID THIS HAPPEN?
WHY MAKE US CARRY ZANPAKUTÔ?
IS THE THREAT REALLY THAT SERIOUS?
BEWARE OF THIRD COMPANY...
ESPECIALLY...
...CAPTAIN AIZEN...

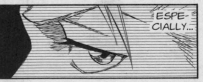

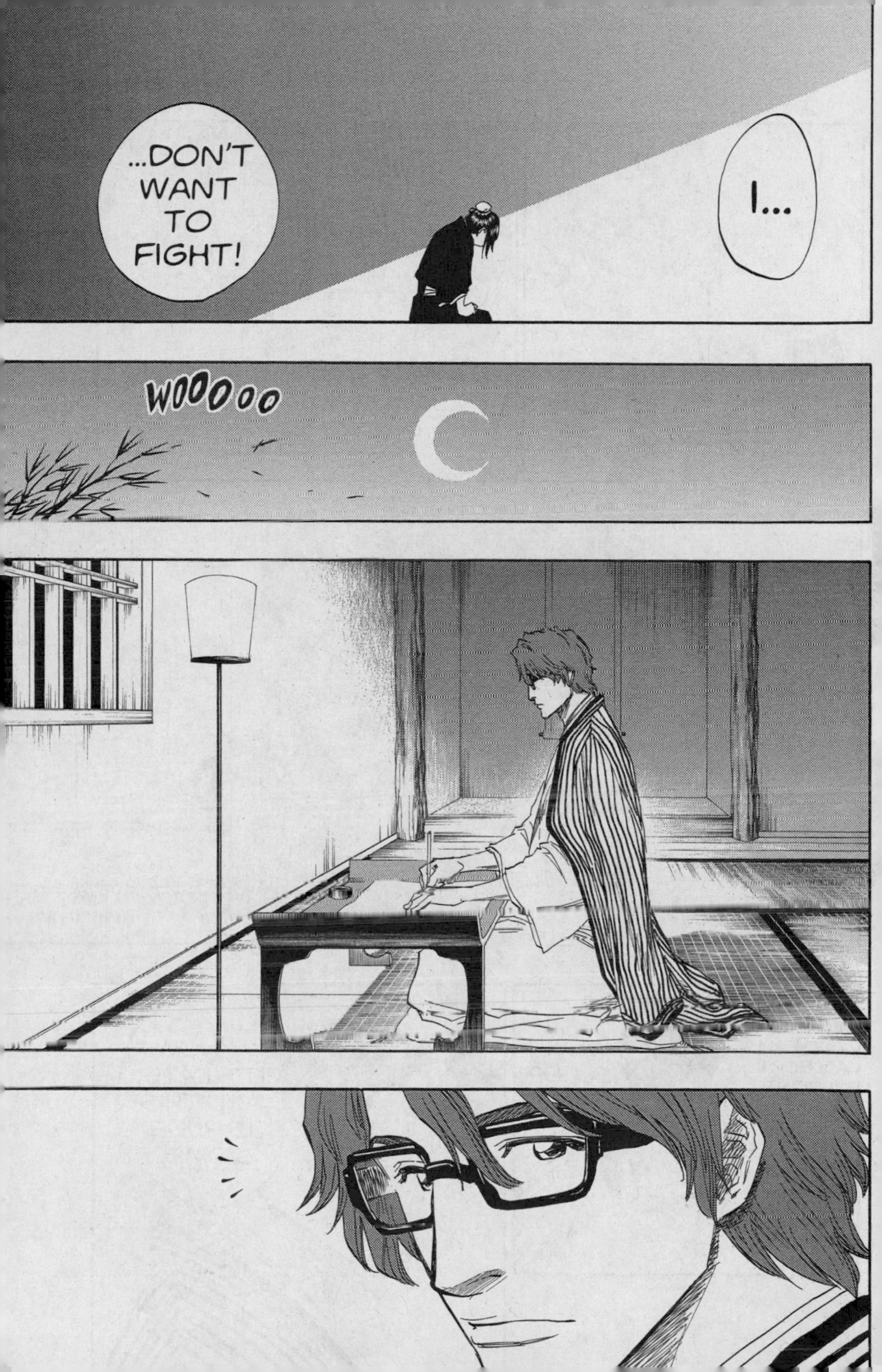
I...
...DON'T WANT TO FIGHT!
WOOOOO

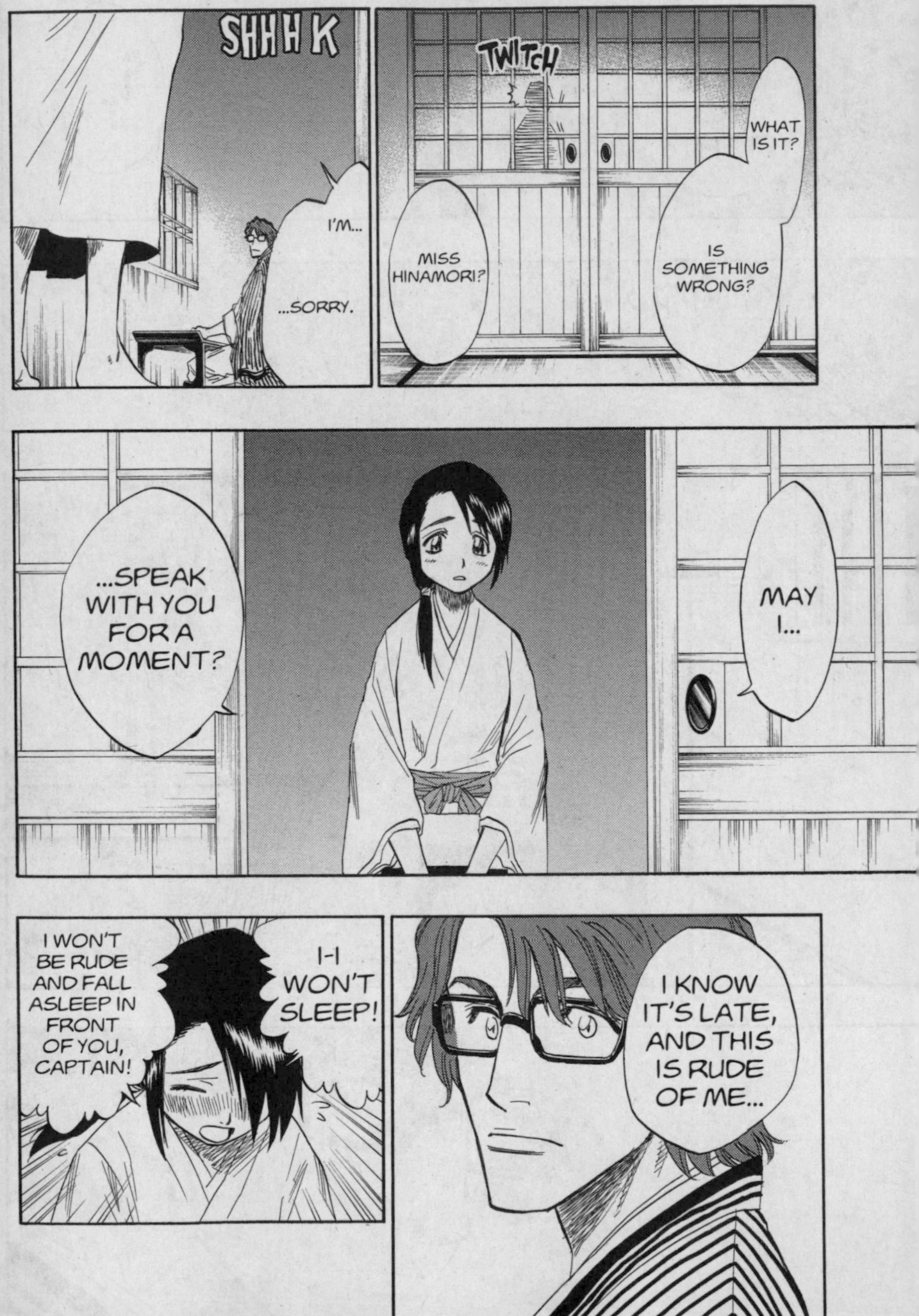
TWITCH
WHAT IS IT?
IS SOMETHING WRONG?
MISS HINAMORI?
SHHHK
I'M...
...SORRY.
MAY I...
...SPEAK WITH YOU FOR A MOMENT?
I KNOW IT'S LATE, AND THIS IS RUDE OF ME...
I-I WON'T SLEEP!
I WON'T BE RUDE AND FALL ASLEEP IN FRONT OF YOU, CAPTAIN!

READ THIS WAY

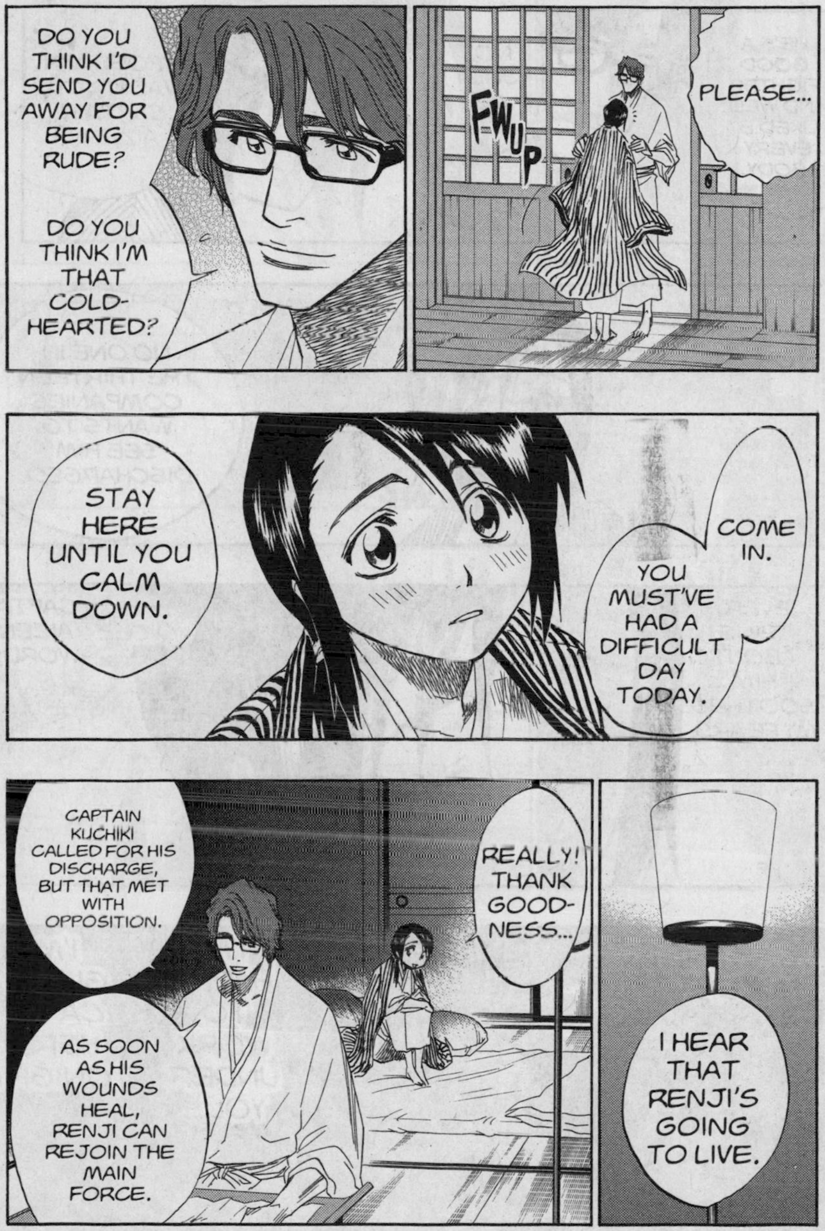
PLEASE...
FWUP
DO YOU THINK I'D SEND YOU AWAY FOR BEING RUDE?
DO YOU THINK I'M THAT COLD-HEARTED?
COME IN.
YOU MUST'VE HAD A DIFFICULT DAY TODAY.
STAY HERE UNTIL YOU CALM DOWN.
I HEAR THAT RENJI'S GOING TO LIVE.
REALLY! THANK GOOD-NESS...
CAPTAIN KUCHIKI CALLED FOR HIS DISCHARGE, BUT THAT MET WITH OPPOSITION.
AS SOON AS HIS WOUNDS HEAL, RENJI CAN REJOIN THE MAIN FORCE.

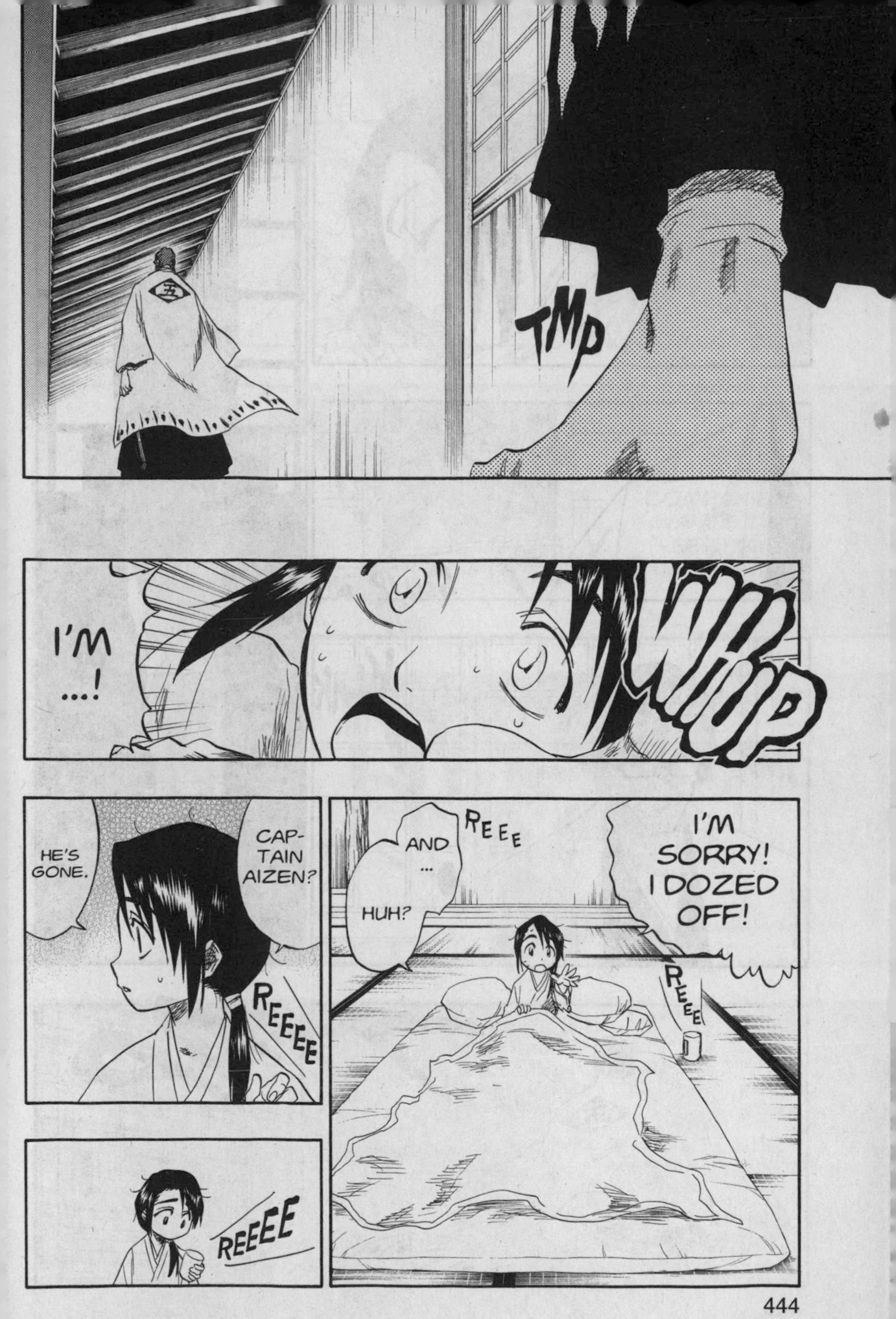
TMP
WHIP
I'M ...!
I'M SORRY! I DOZED OFF!
REEE
AND ...
HUH?
REEE
CAP-TAIN AIZEN?
HE'S GONE.
REEEEE
REEEEE

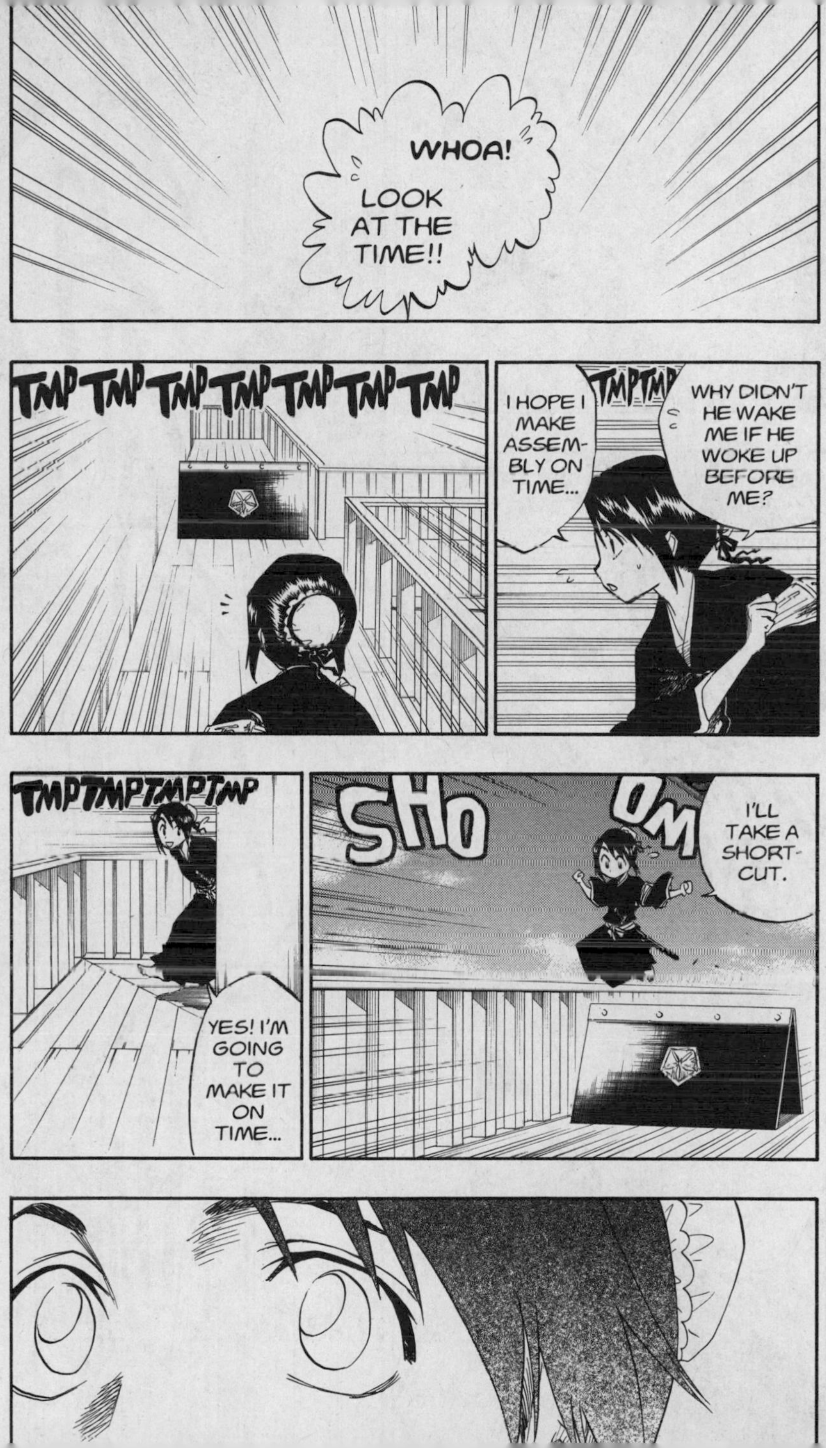
WHOA!
LOOK AT THE TIME!!
TMPTMP
WHY DIDN'T HE WAKE ME IF HE WOKE UP BEFORE ME?
I HOPE I MAKE ASSEMBLY ON TIME...
TMP TMP TMP TMP TMP TMP TMP
SHO OM
I'LL TAKE A SHORTCUT.
TMPTMPTMPTMP
YES! I'M GOING TO MAKE IT ON TIME...

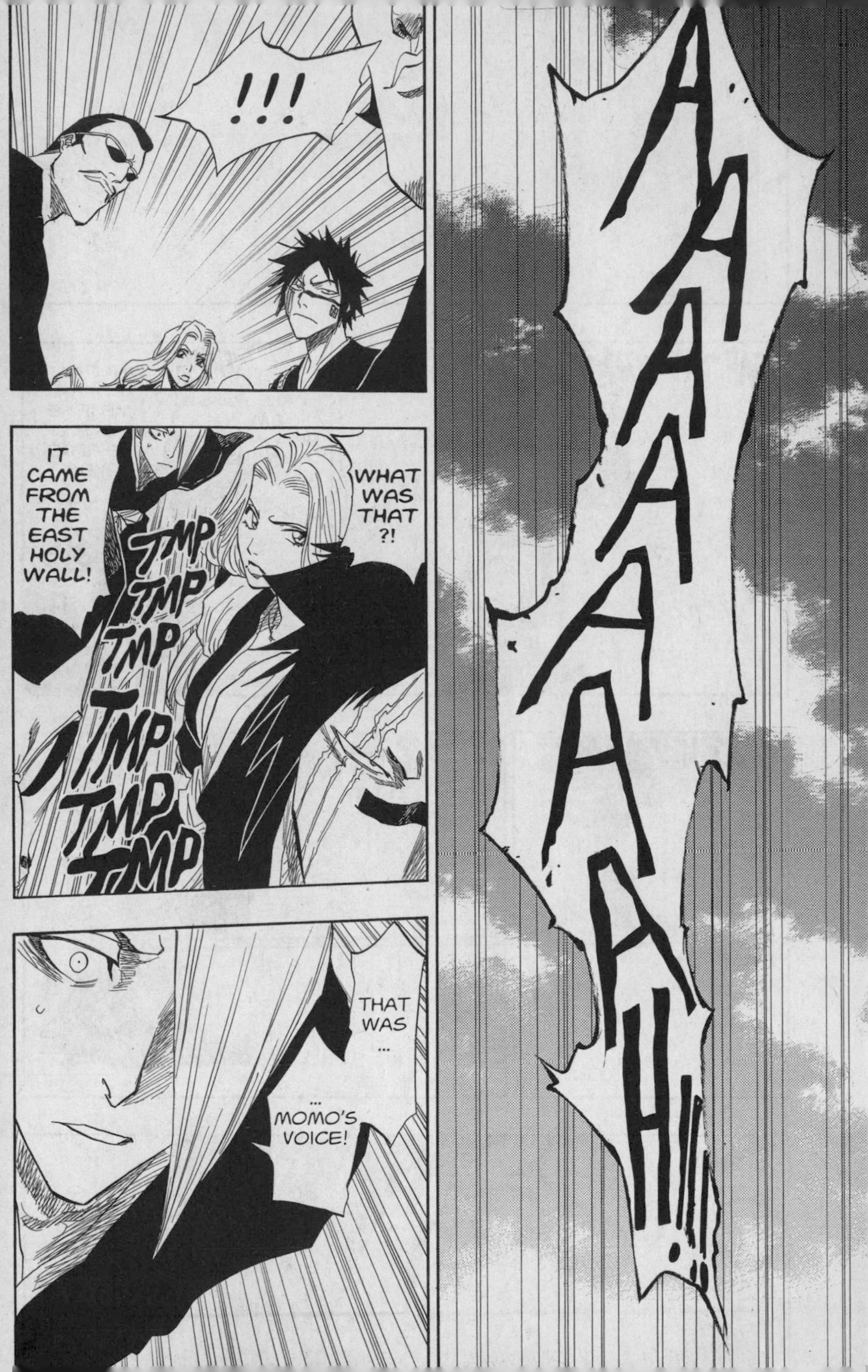
AAAAAAAAH!!!
!!!
WHAT WAS THAT?!
IT CAME FROM THE EAST HOLY WALL!
TMP TMP TMP TMP TMP TMP
THAT WAS...
...MOMO'S VOICE!

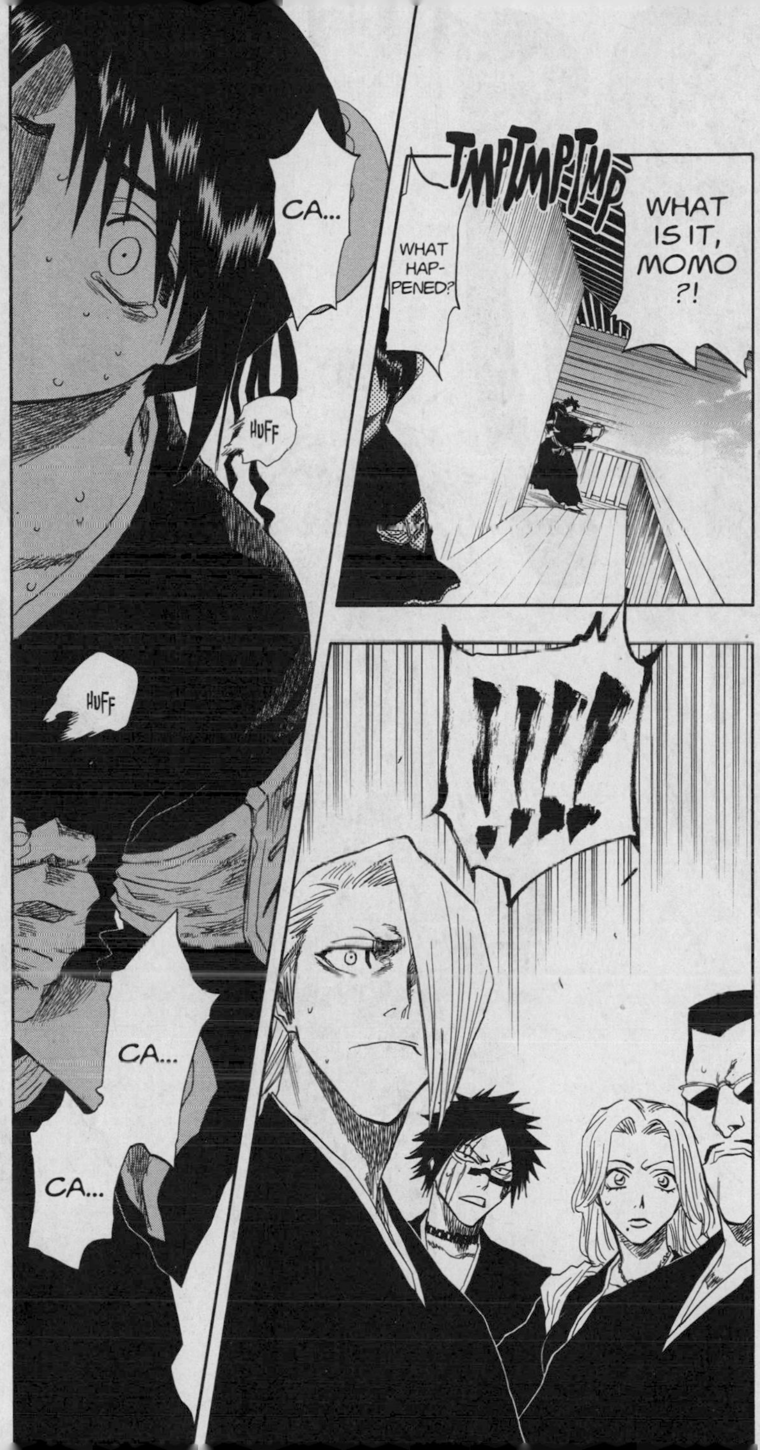
TMP TMP TMP TMP
WHAT IS IT, MOMO?!
WHAT HAP-PENED?
!!!!
CA...
HUFF
HUFF
CA...
CA...

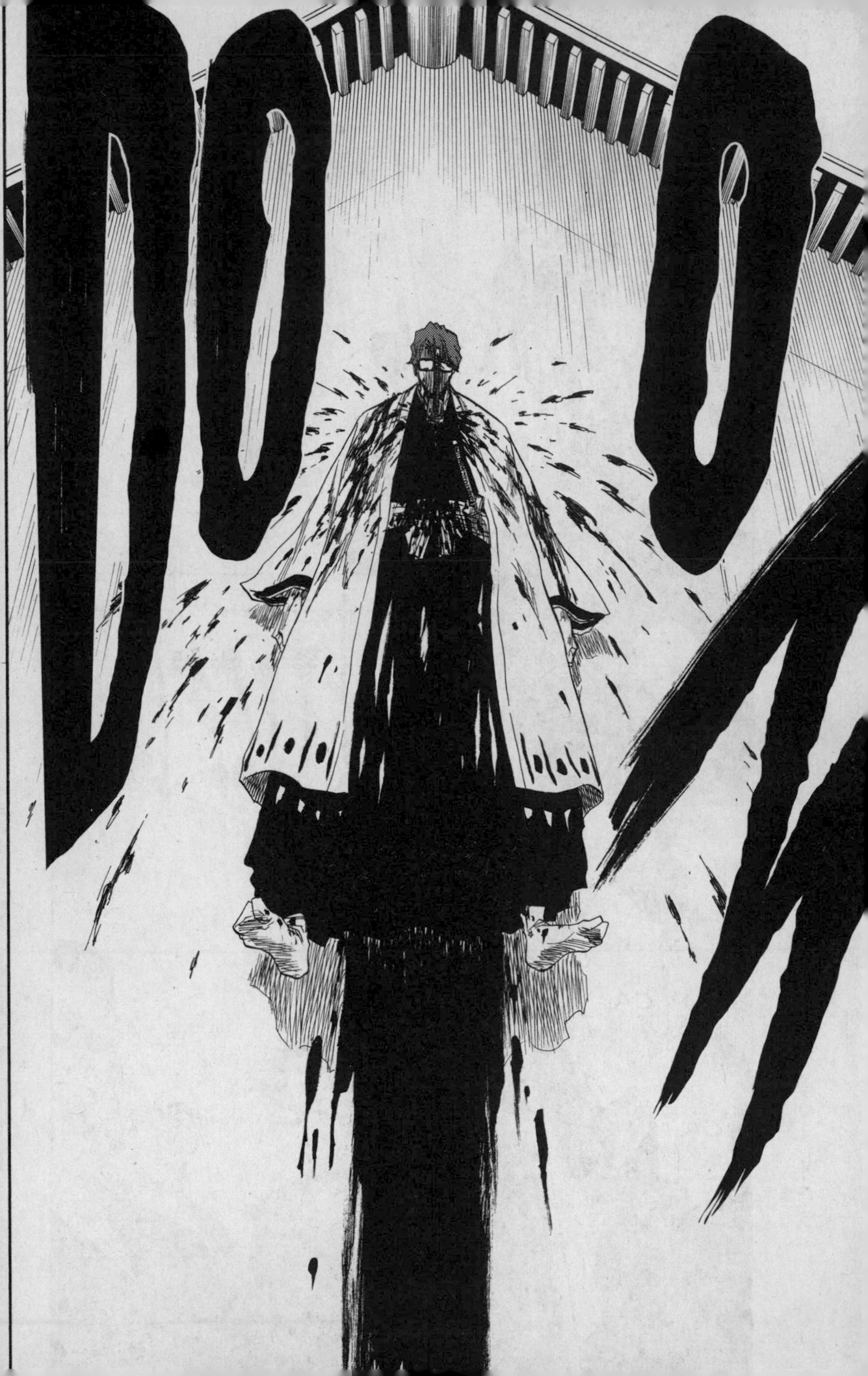
DOO

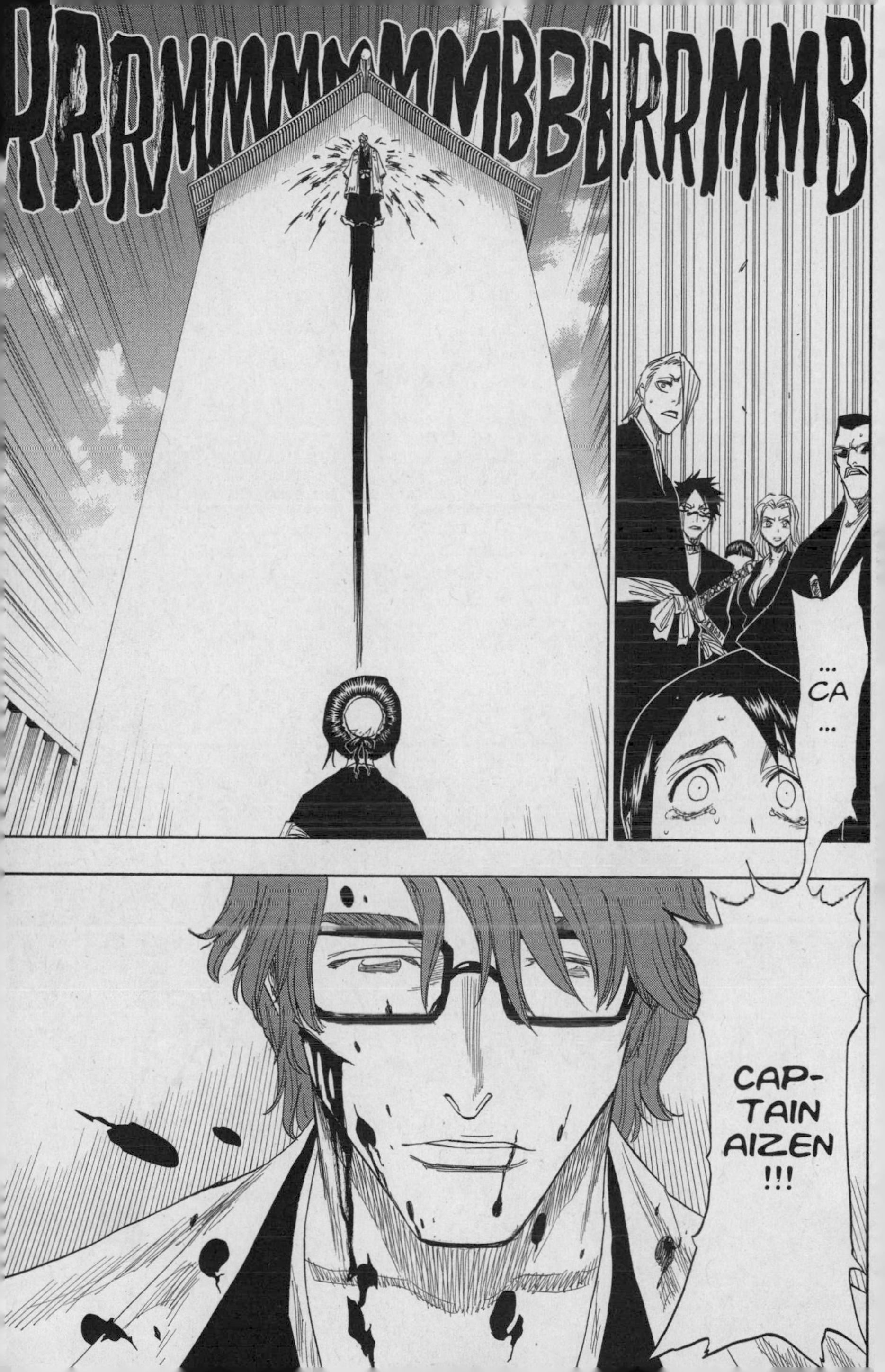
RRRMMMMMMMMMBBBRRRMMB
... CA ...
CAP-TAIN AIZEN !!!

101. Split Under the Red Stalk

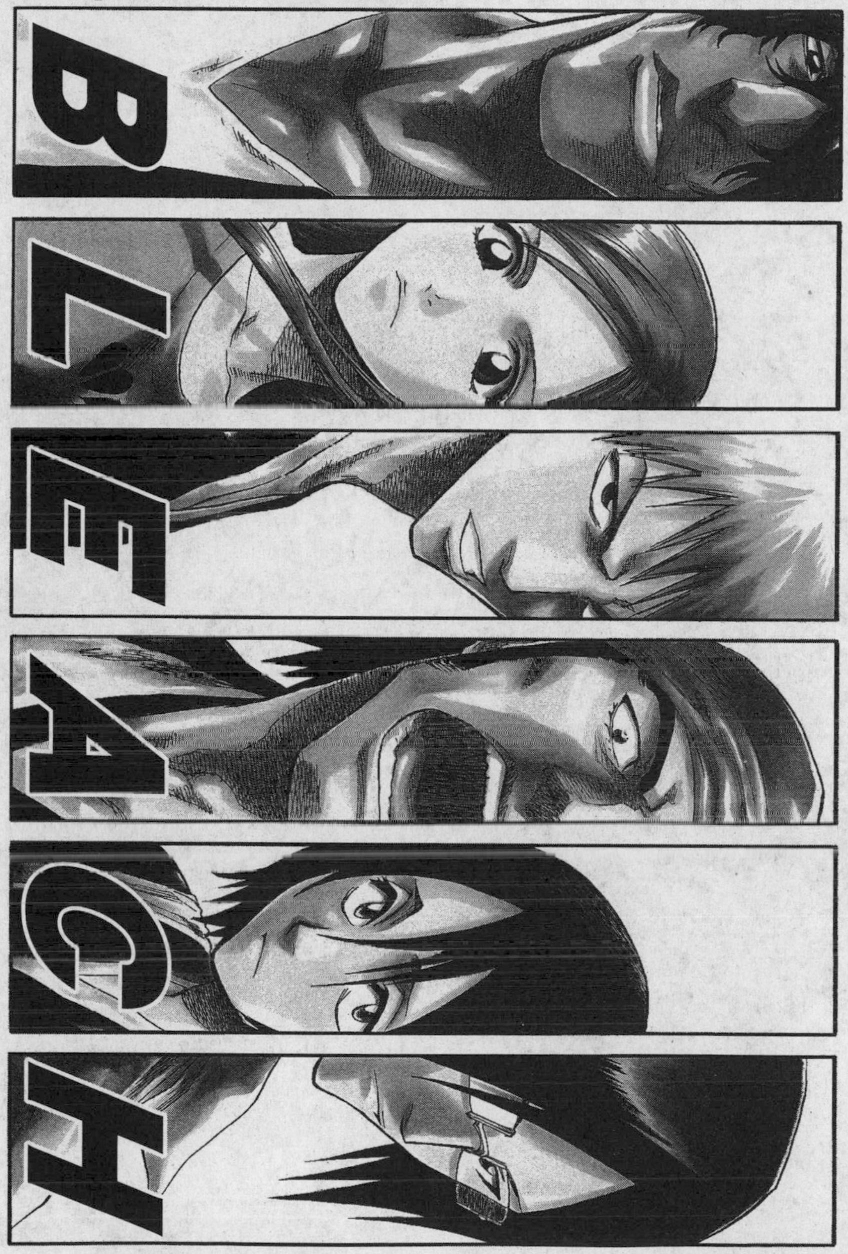
BLEACH

BLEACH
ブリーチ

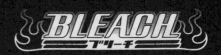

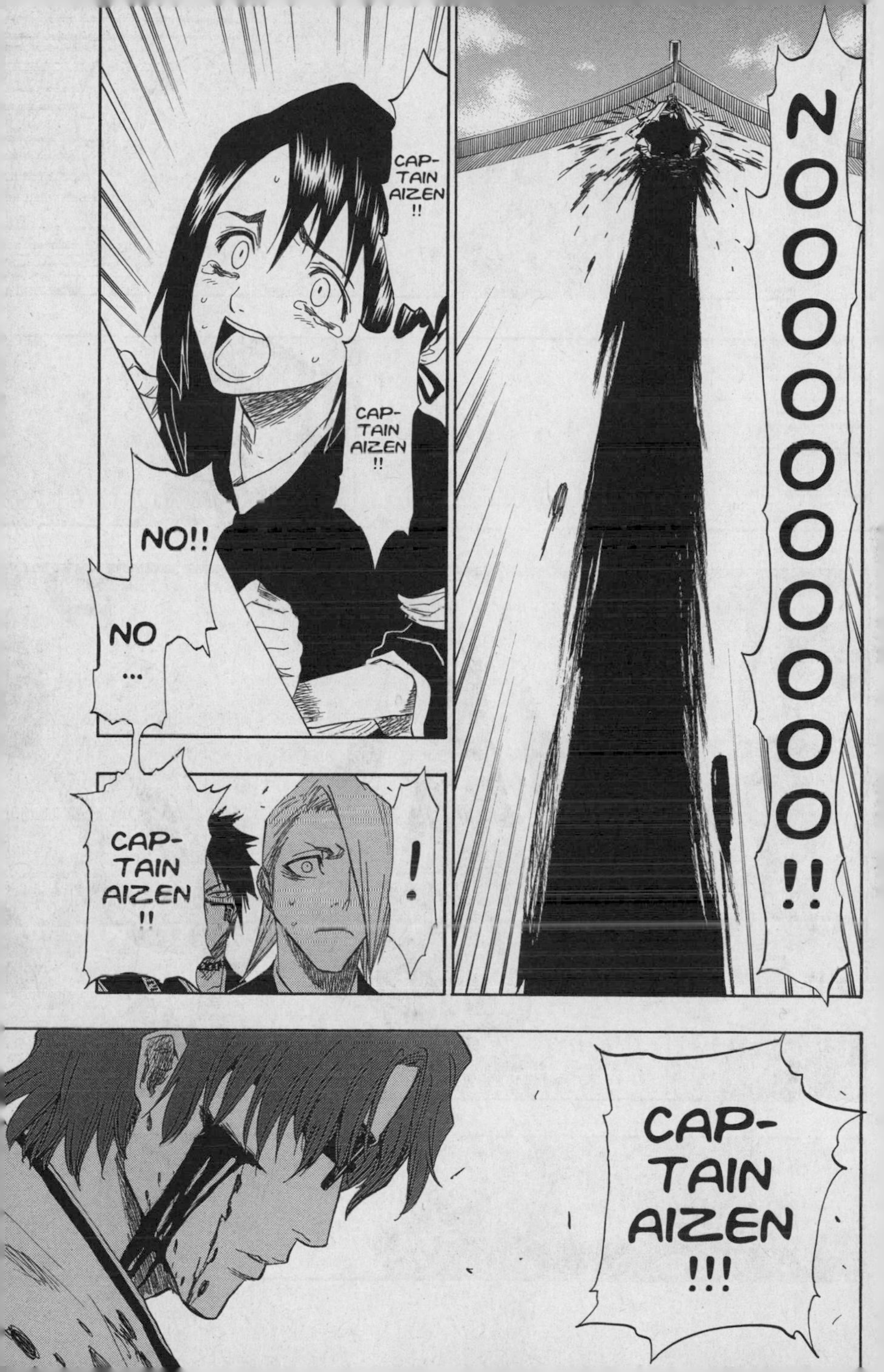

NOOOOOOOOOO!!
CAP-TAIN AIZEN!!
CAP-TAIN AIZEN!!
NO!!
NO...
!
CAP-TAIN AIZEN!!
CAP-TAIN AIZEN!!!

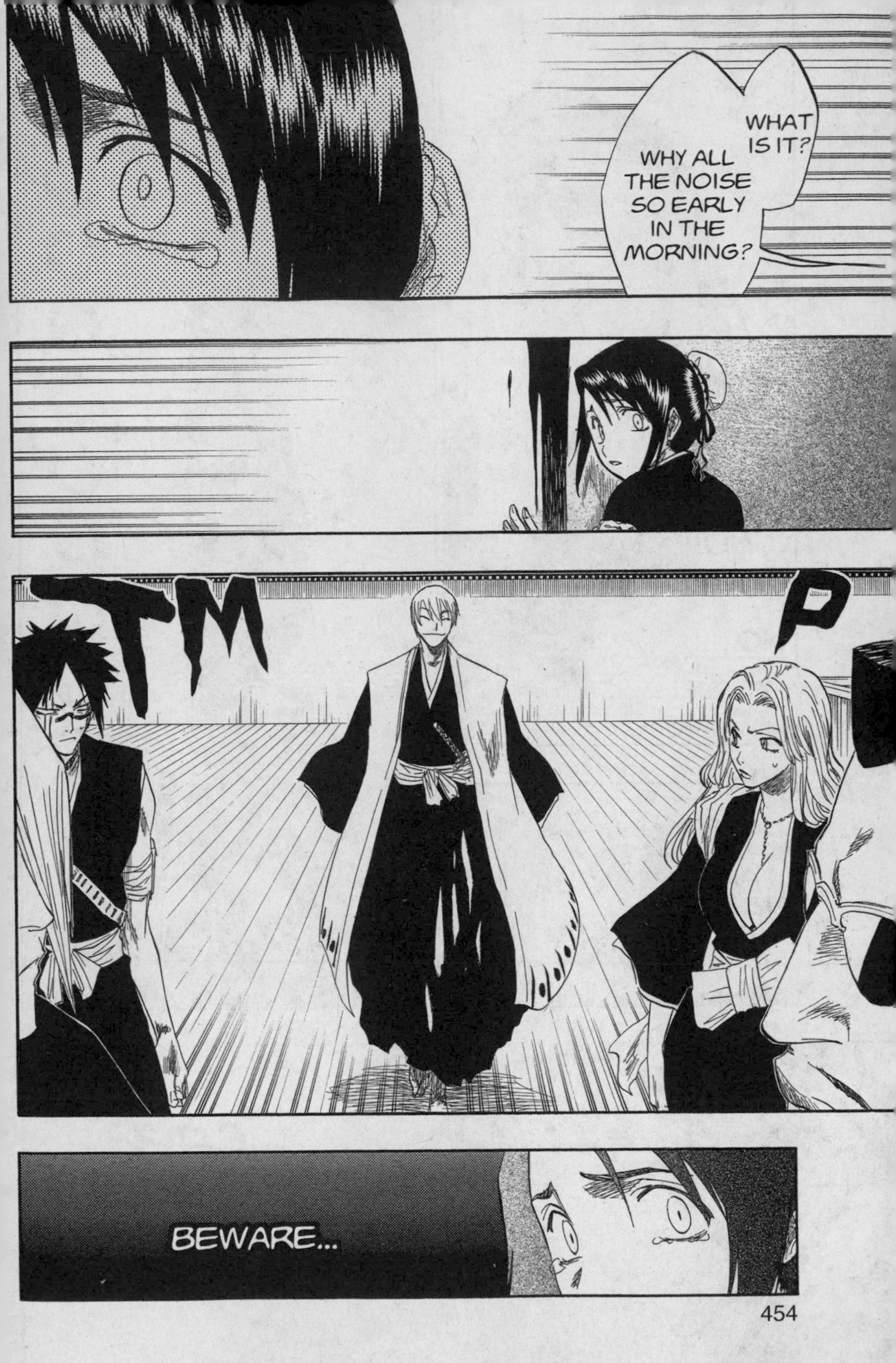
WHAT IS IT?
WHY ALL THE NOISE SO EARLY IN THE MORNING?
P
TM
BEWARE...

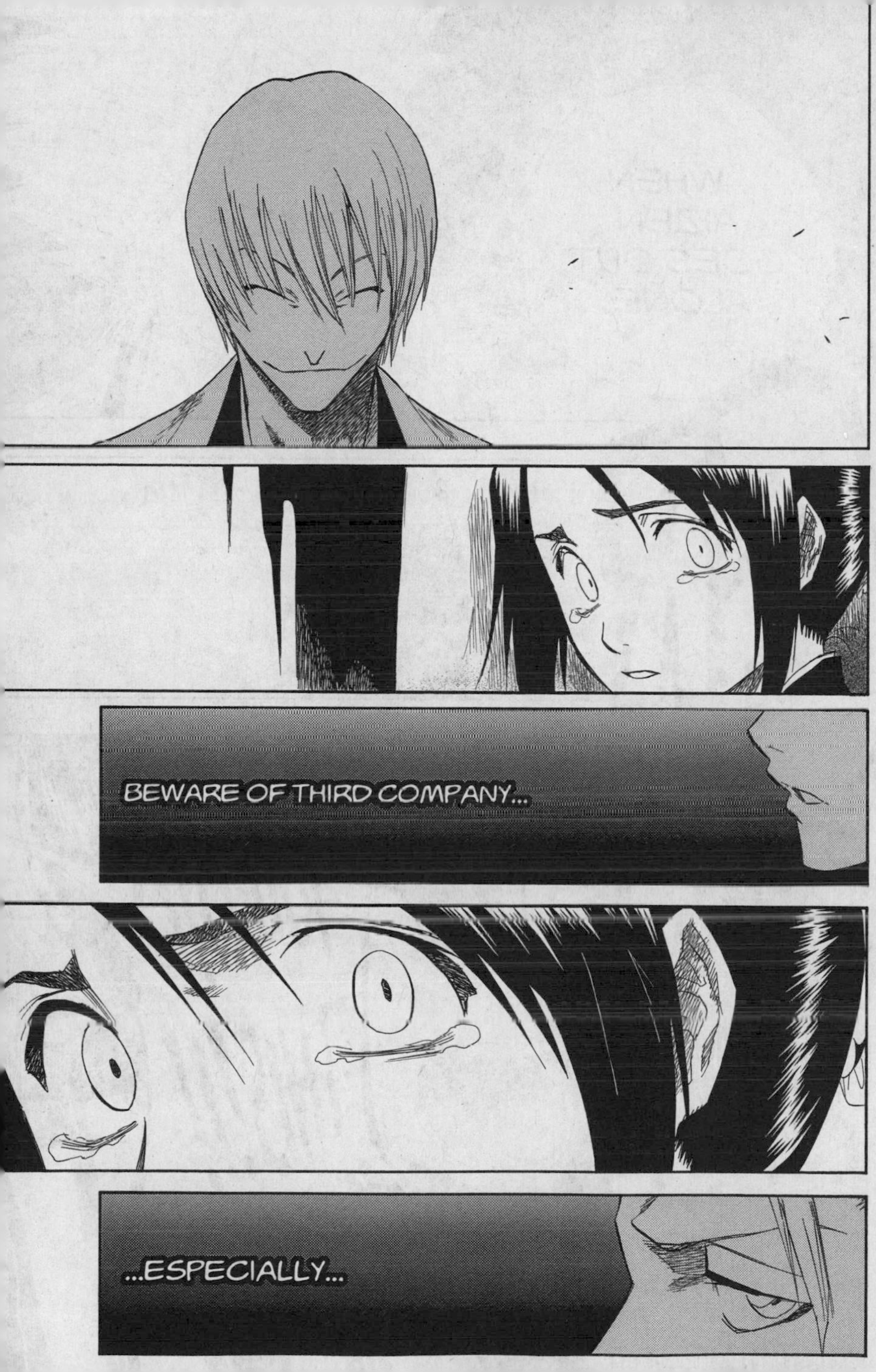
BEWARE OF THIRD COMPANY...
...ESPECIALLY...

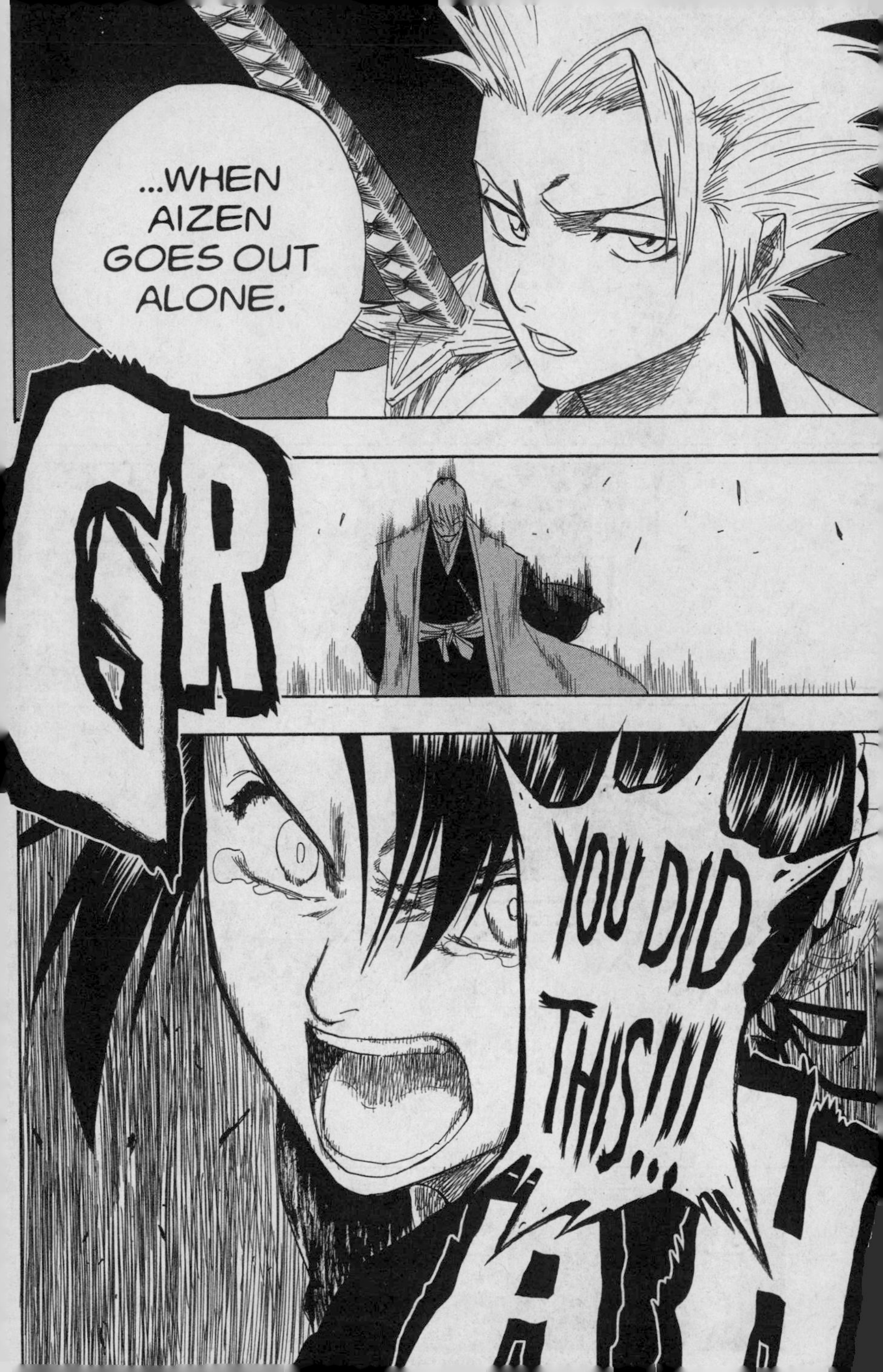
...WHEN AIZEN GOES OUT ALONE.
YOU DID THIS!!

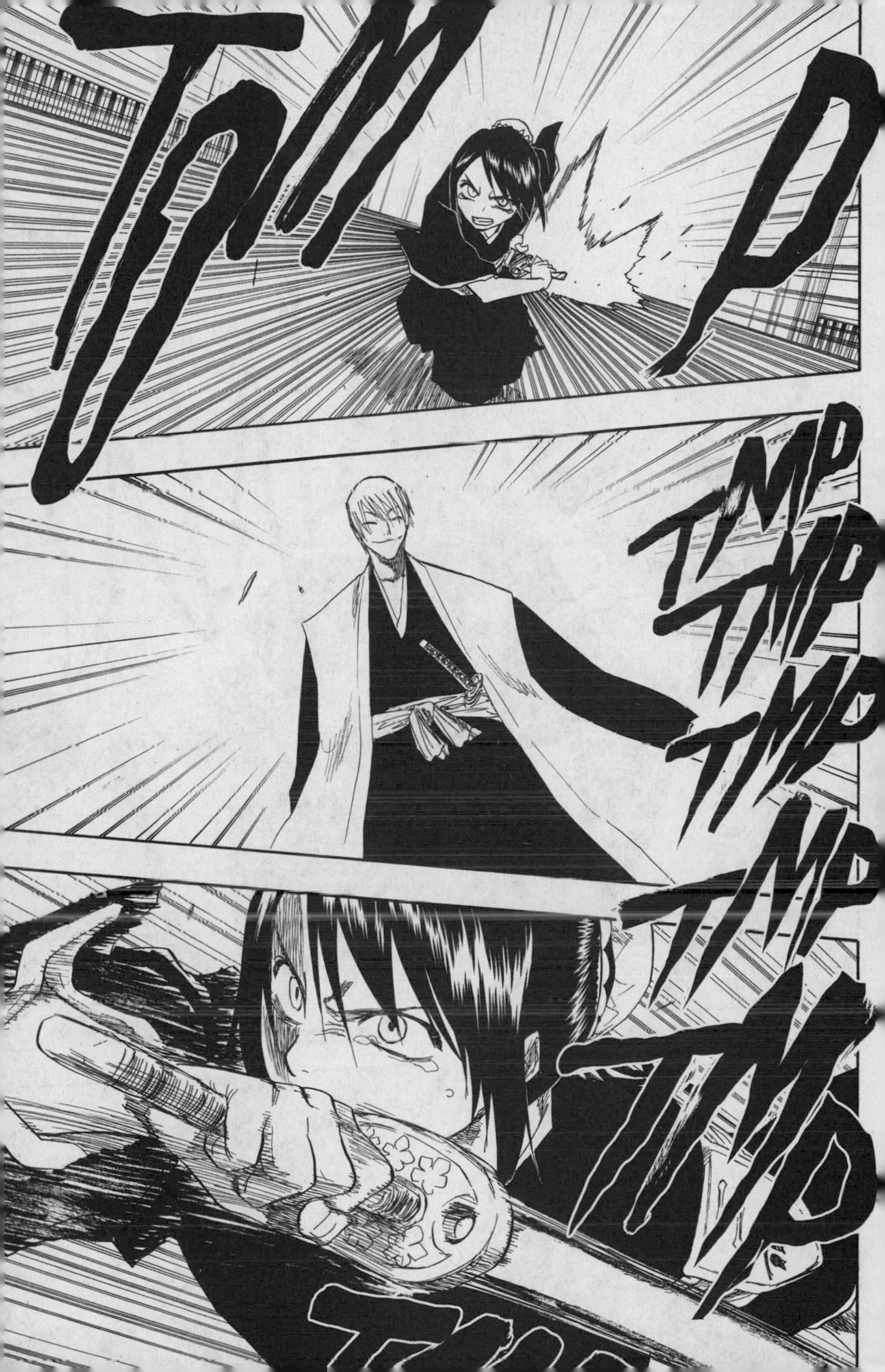
TMMP
TMP
TMP
TMP
TMP
TMP
TMP

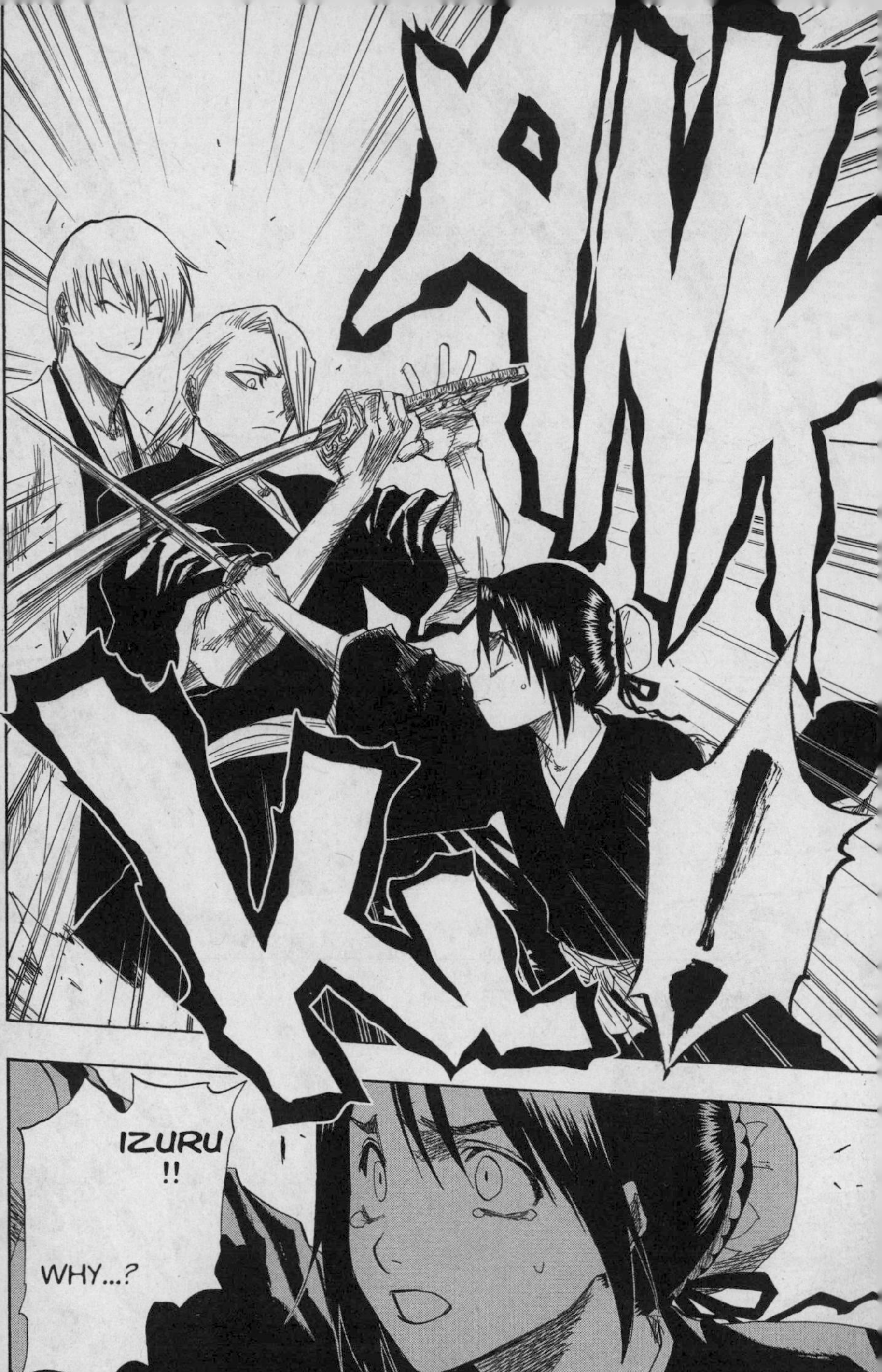
IZURU
!!
WHY...?

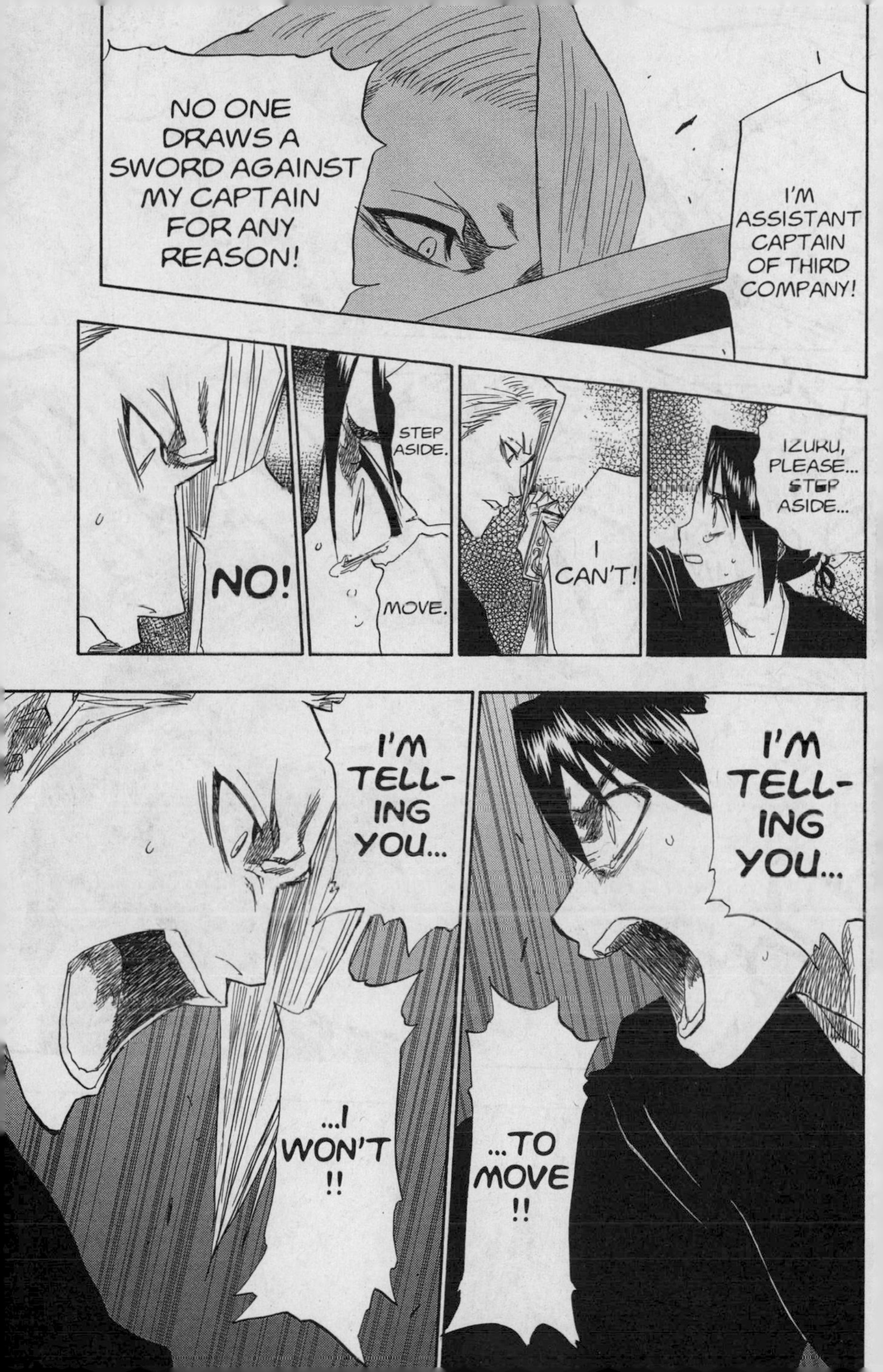
I'M ASSISTANT CAPTAIN OF THIRD COMPANY!
NO ONE DRAWS A SWORD AGAINST MY CAPTAIN FOR ANY REASON!
IZURU, PLEASE... STEP ASIDE...
I CAN'T!
STEP ASIDE.
MOVE.
NO!
I'M TELLING YOU...
...TO MOVE!!
I'M TELLING YOU...
...I WON'T!!

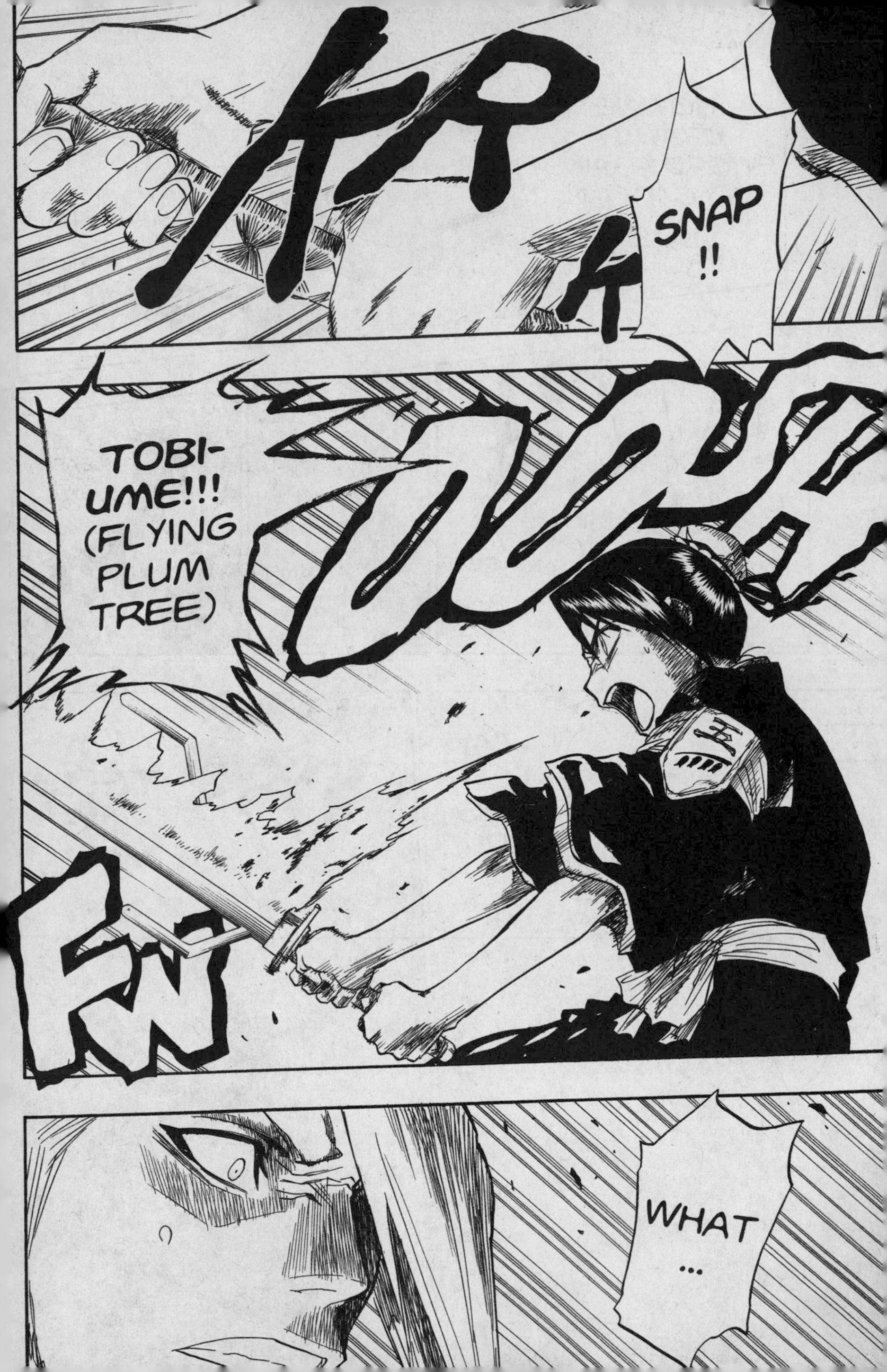
SNAP!!
TOBI-UME!!! (FLYING PLUM TREE)
WHAT...

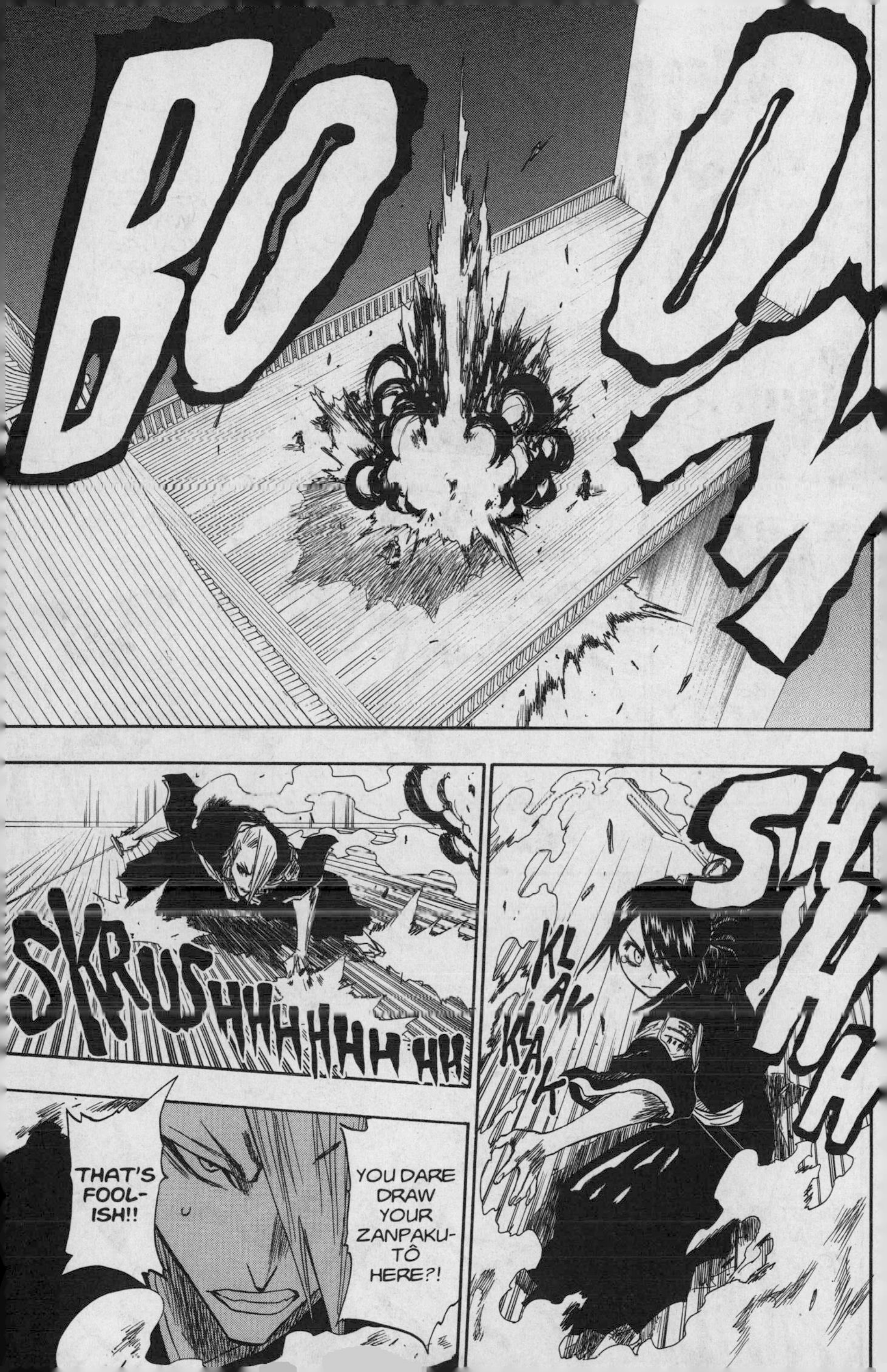
BOOM
SHHH
KLAK
KLAK
SKRUSHHHHHHH HH
YOU DARE DRAW YOUR ZANPAKU-TÔ HERE?!
THAT'S FOOL-ISH!!

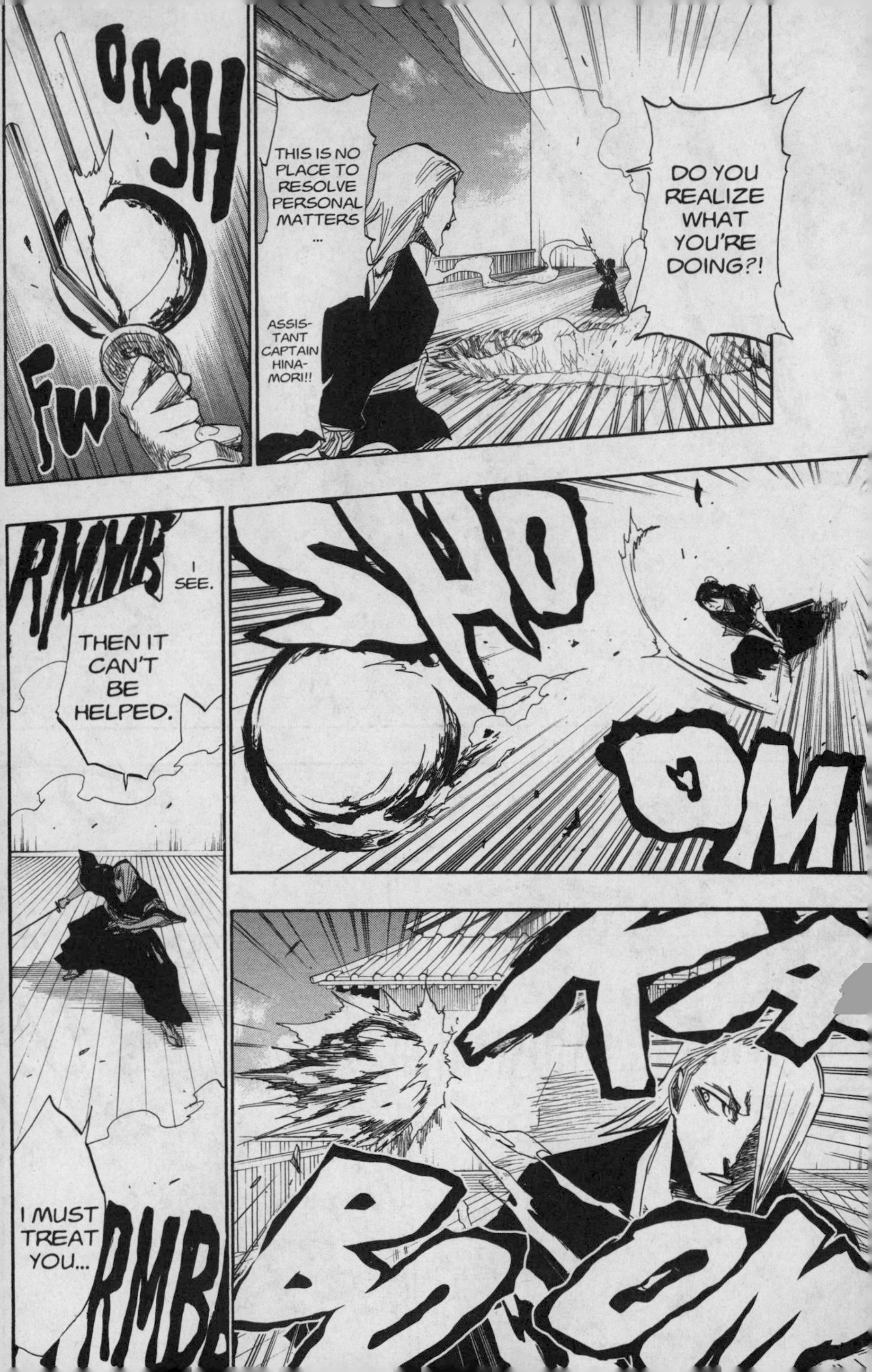
DO YOU REALIZE WHAT YOU'RE DOING?!
THIS IS NO PLACE TO RESOLVE PERSONAL MATTERS ...
ASSISTANT CAPTAIN HINAMORI!!
FWOOSH
SHOOM
RMMB
I SEE.
THEN IT CAN'T BE HELPED.
I MUST TREAT YOU...
RMB

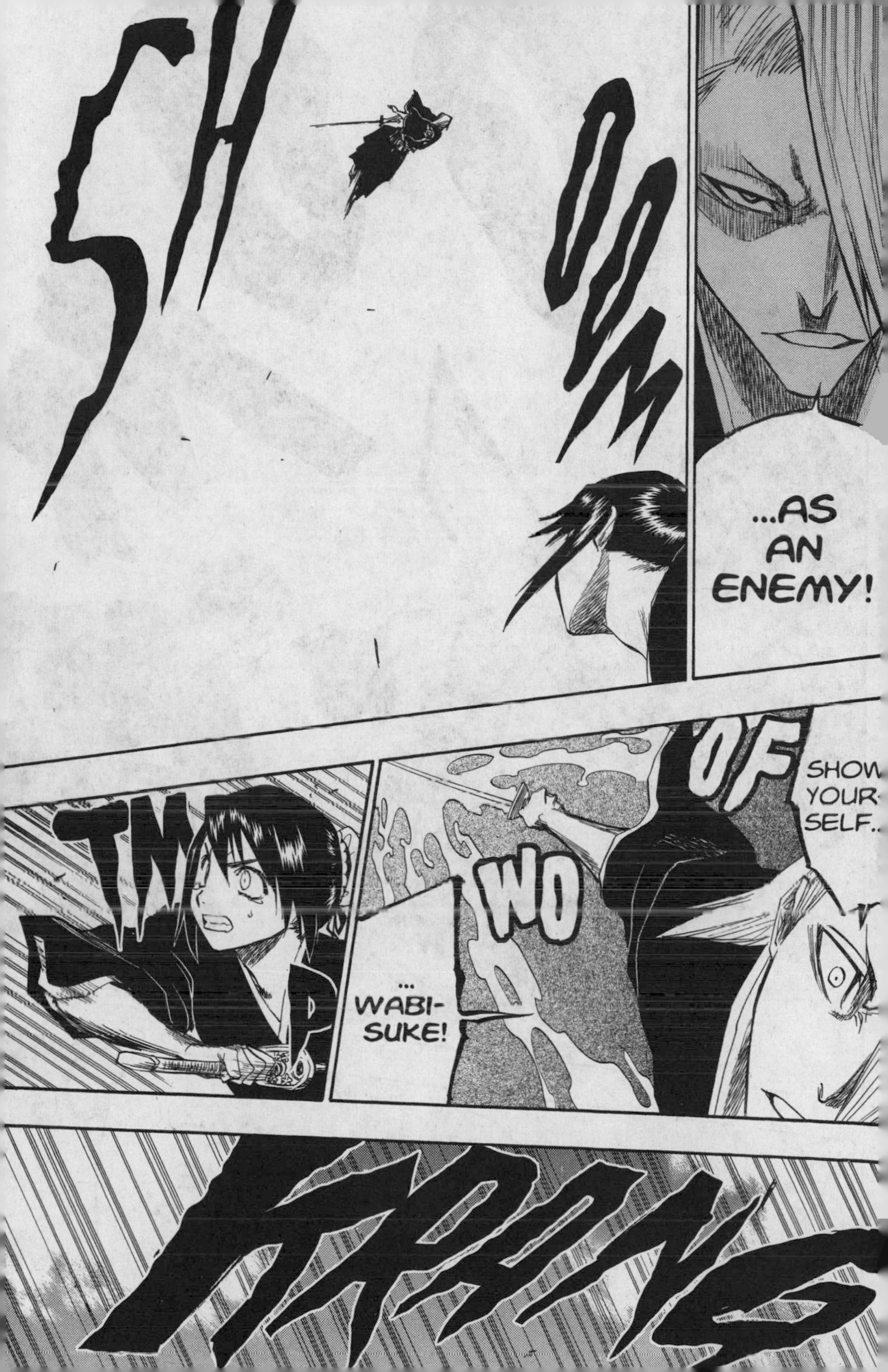
...AS AN ENEMY!
SH
OOOM
SHOW YOUR-SELF...
WO
OF
...WABI-SUKE!
TMP

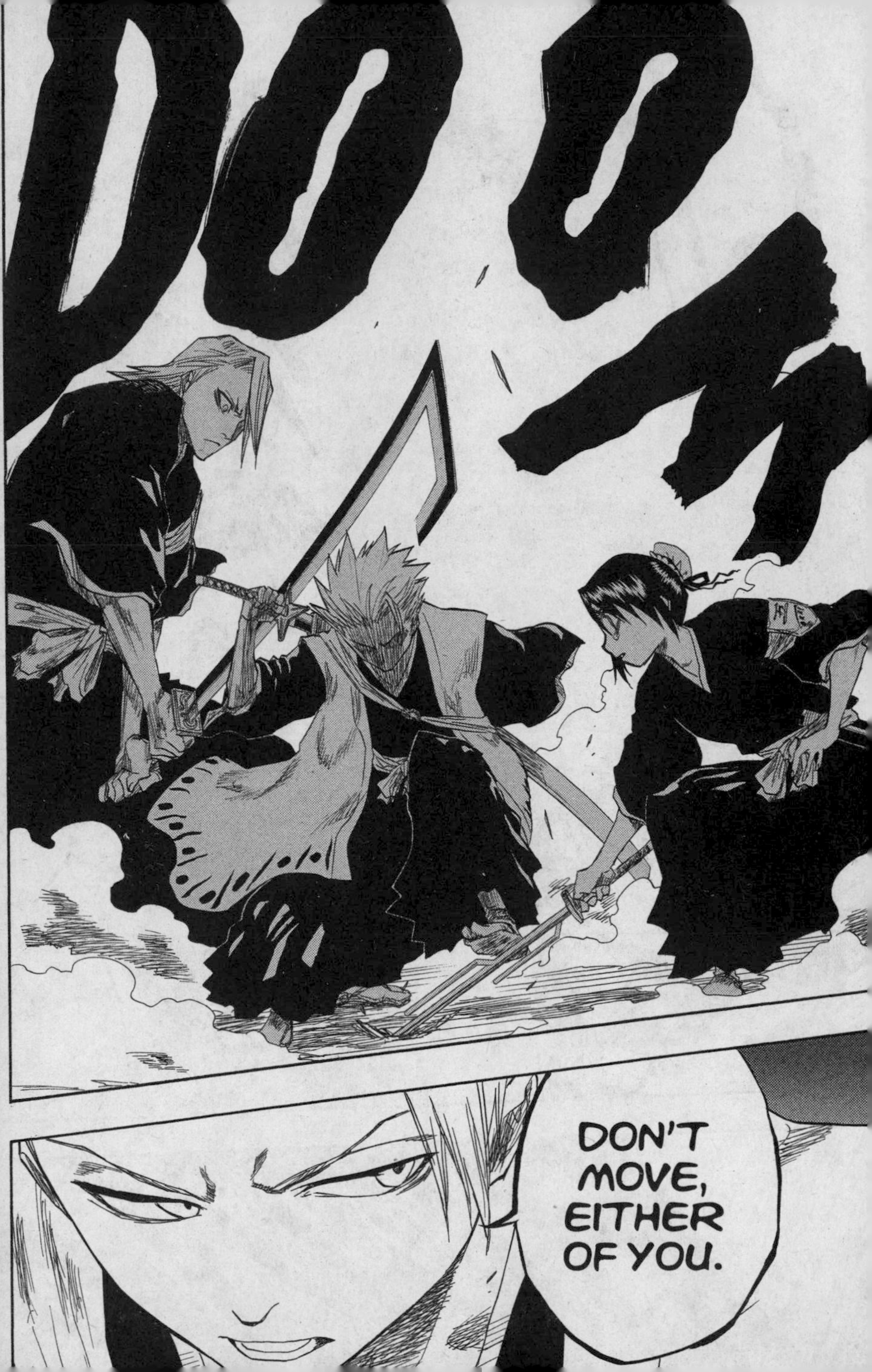
DOOM
DON'T MOVE, EITHER OF YOU.

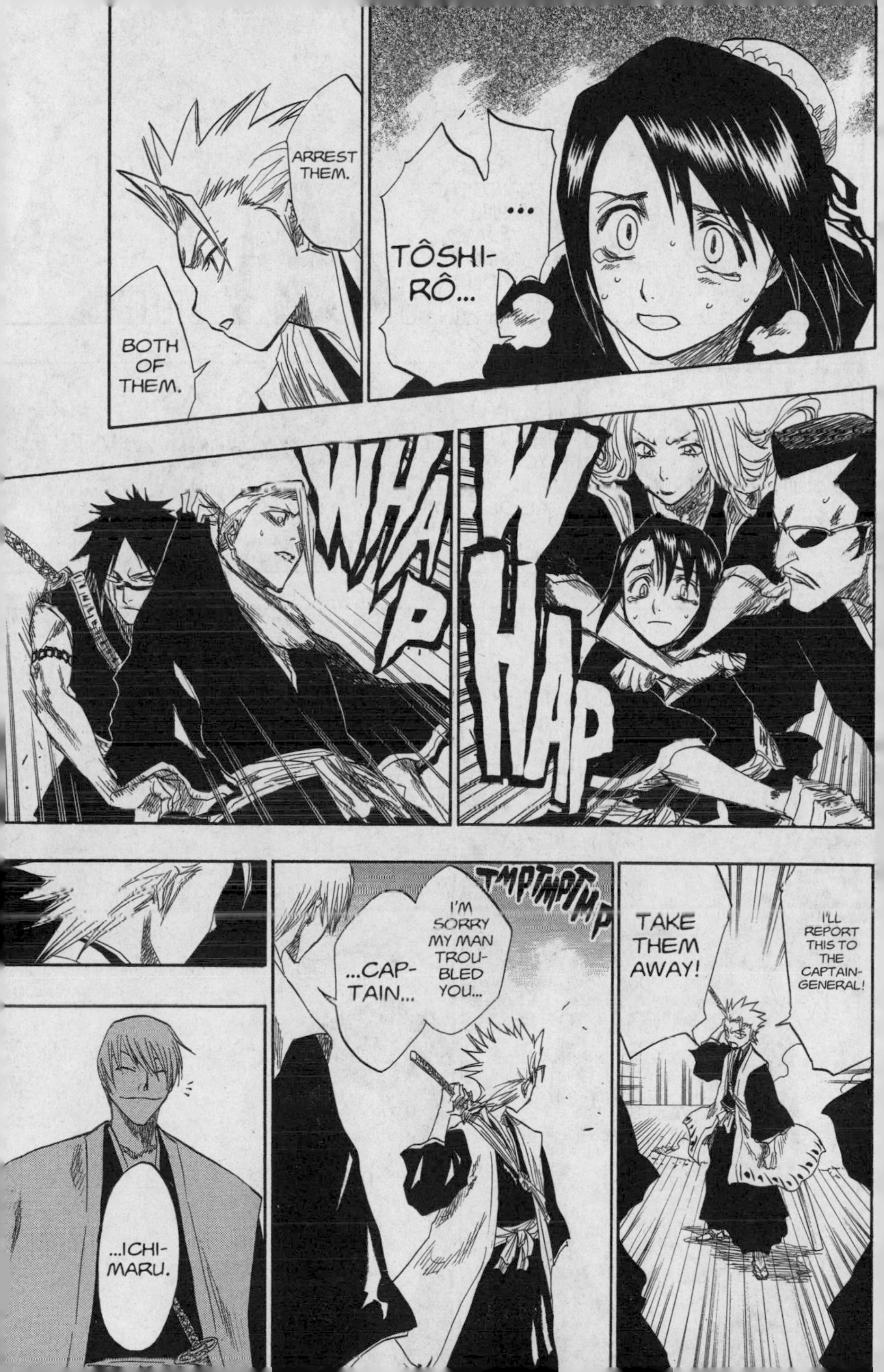
...
TÔSHI-RÔ...
ARREST THEM.
BOTH OF THEM.
WHAP
WHAP
I'LL REPORT THIS TO THE CAPTAIN-GENERAL!
TAKE THEM AWAY!
TMPTMPTMP
I'M SORRY MY MAN TROU-BLED YOU...
...CAP-TAIN...
...ICHI-MARU.

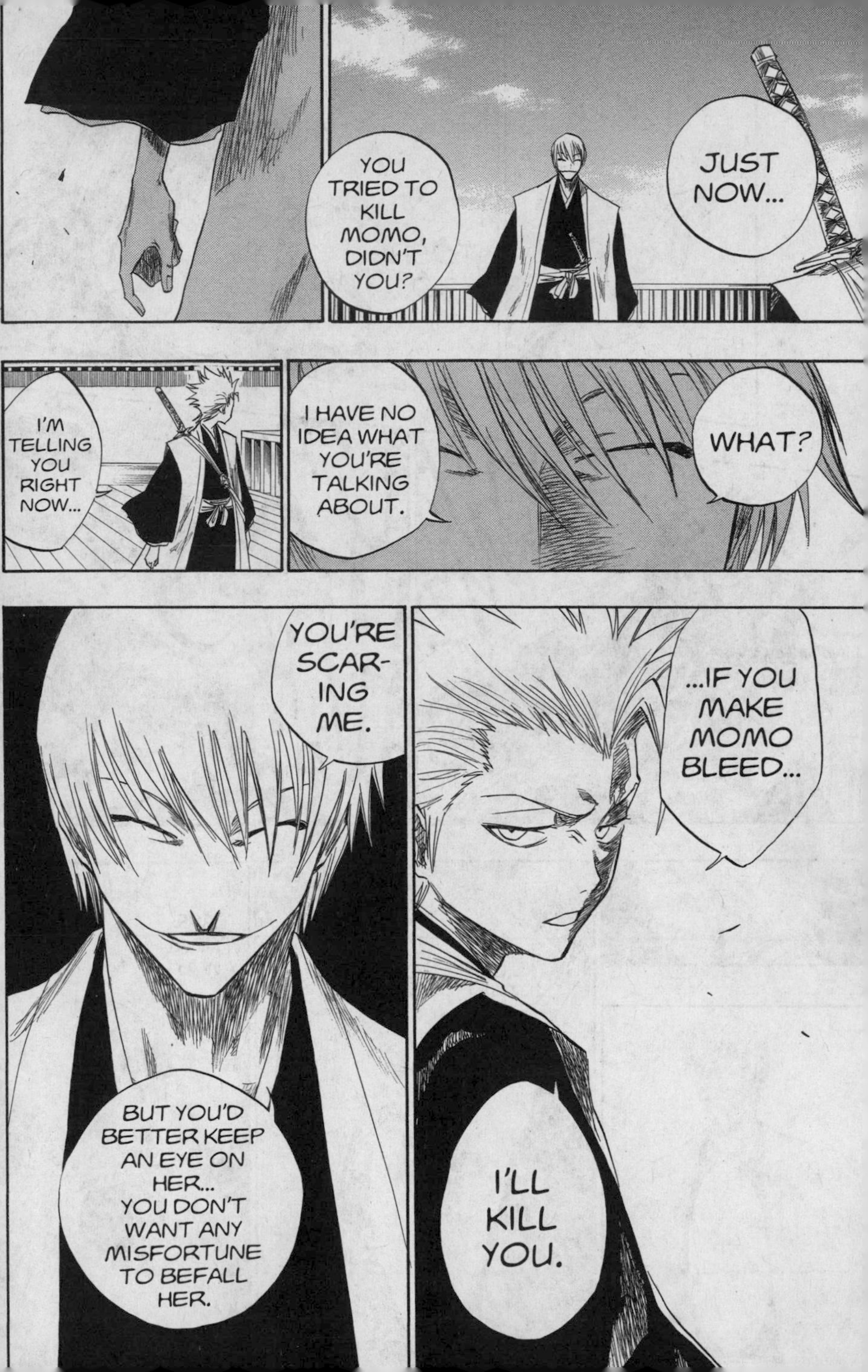
JUST NOW...
YOU TRIED TO KILL MOMO, DIDN'T YOU?
WHAT?
I HAVE NO IDEA WHAT YOU'RE TALKING ABOUT.
I'M TELLING YOU RIGHT NOW...
...IF YOU MAKE MOMO BLEED...
I'LL KILL YOU.
YOU'RE SCAR-ING ME.
BUT YOU'D BETTER KEEP AN EYE ON HER... YOU DON'T WANT ANY MISFORTUNE TO BEFALL HER.

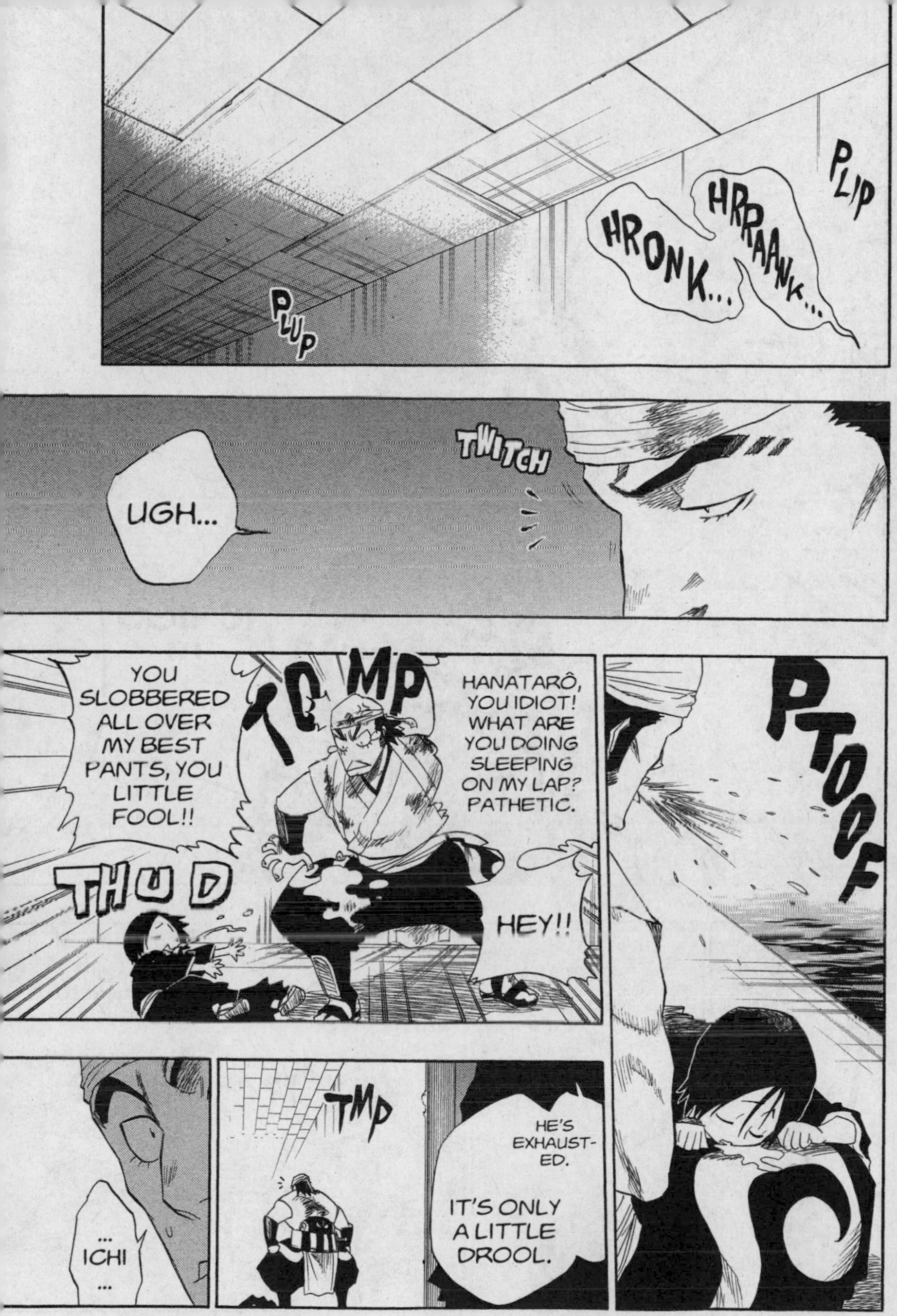
PLIP
HRRAANK...
HRONK...
PLUP
TWITCH
UGH...
PTOOF
HANATARÔ, YOU IDIOT! WHAT ARE YOU DOING SLEEPING ON MY LAP? PATHETIC.
TOMP
YOU SLOBBERED ALL OVER MY BEST PANTS, YOU LITTLE FOOL!!
HEY!!
THUD
HE'S EXHAUST-ED.
IT'S ONLY A LITTLE DROOL.
TMP
...ICHI...

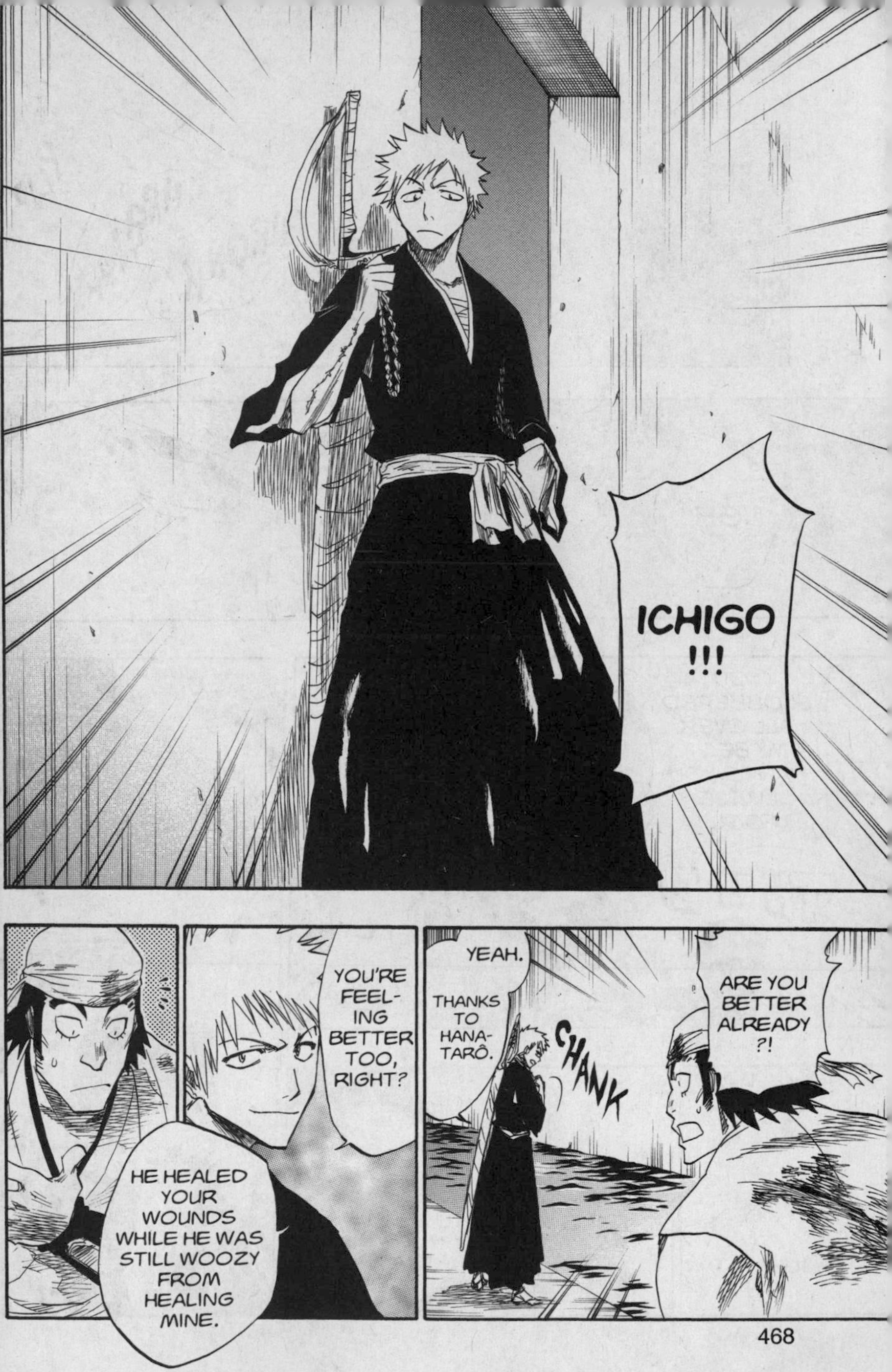
ICHIGO !!!
ARE YOU BETTER ALREADY ?!
CHANK
YEAH.
THANKS TO HANA-TARÔ.
YOU'RE FEEL-ING BETTER TOO, RIGHT?
HE HEALED YOUR WOUNDS WHILE HE WAS STILL WOOZY FROM HEALING MINE.

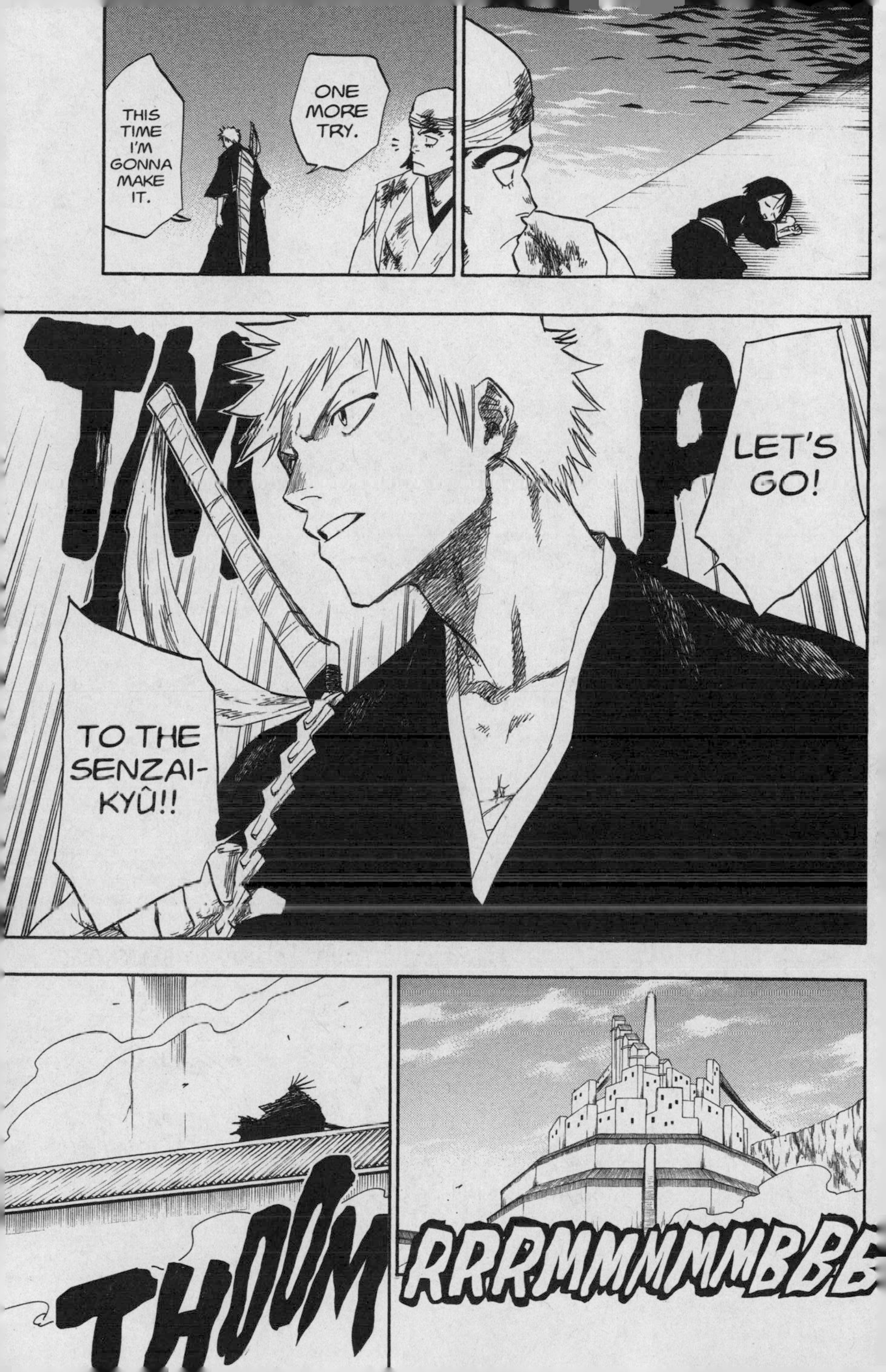
ONE MORE TRY.
THIS TIME I'M GONNA MAKE IT.
TMP
LET'S GO!
TO THE SENZAI-KYÛ!!
RRRMMMMMMBBB
THOOM

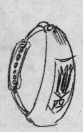

EXCLUSIVE FOURTH COMPANY RELIEF BAG

1
THIS PART DETACHES
2
FASTENER
BECOMES LIKE THIS
FASTENER HEAD

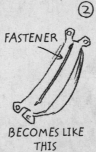

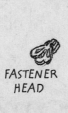

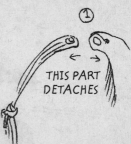

102. Nobody Wins

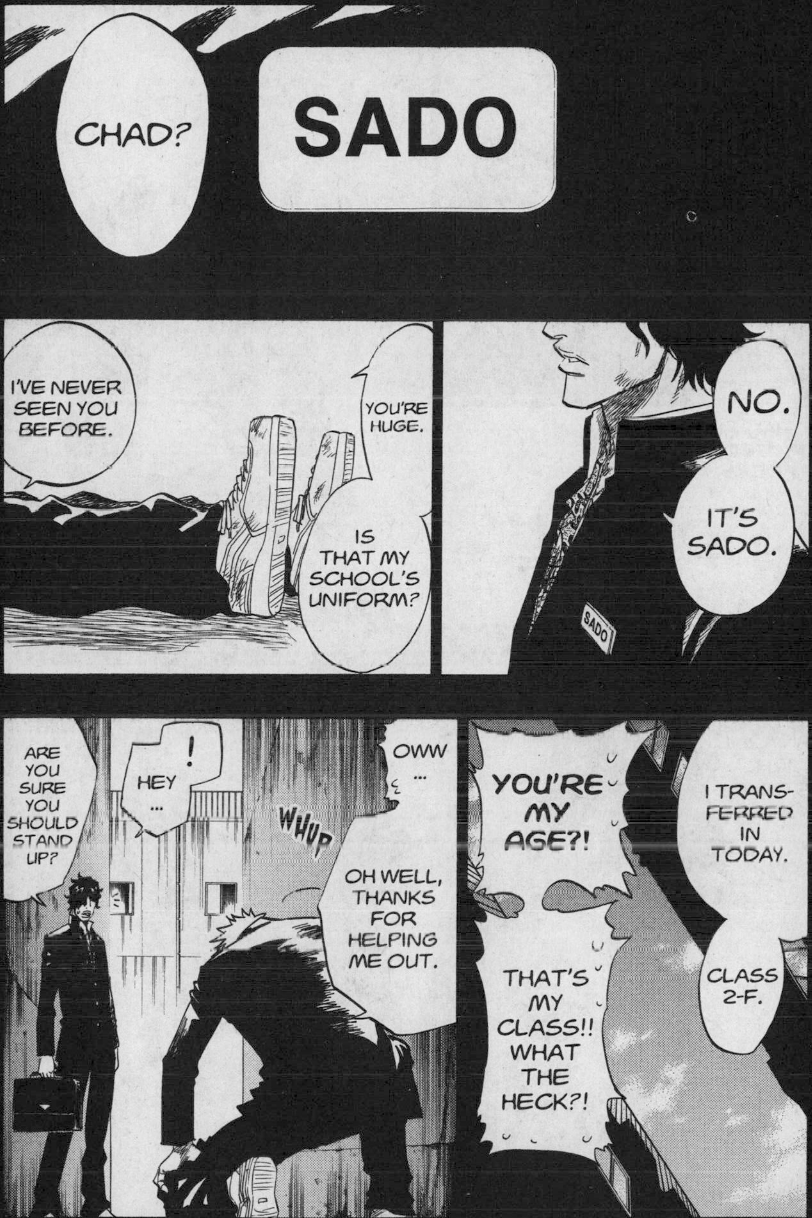

SADO
CHAD?
NO.
IT'S SADO.
SADO
YOU'RE HUGE.
IS THAT MY SCHOOL'S UNIFORM?
I'VE NEVER SEEN YOU BEFORE.
I TRANSFERRED IN TODAY.
CLASS 2-F.
YOU'RE MY AGE?!
THAT'S MY CLASS!! WHAT THE HECK?!
OWW...
WHUP
OH WELL, THANKS FOR HELPING ME OUT.
HEY...
!
ARE YOU SURE YOU SHOULD STAND UP?

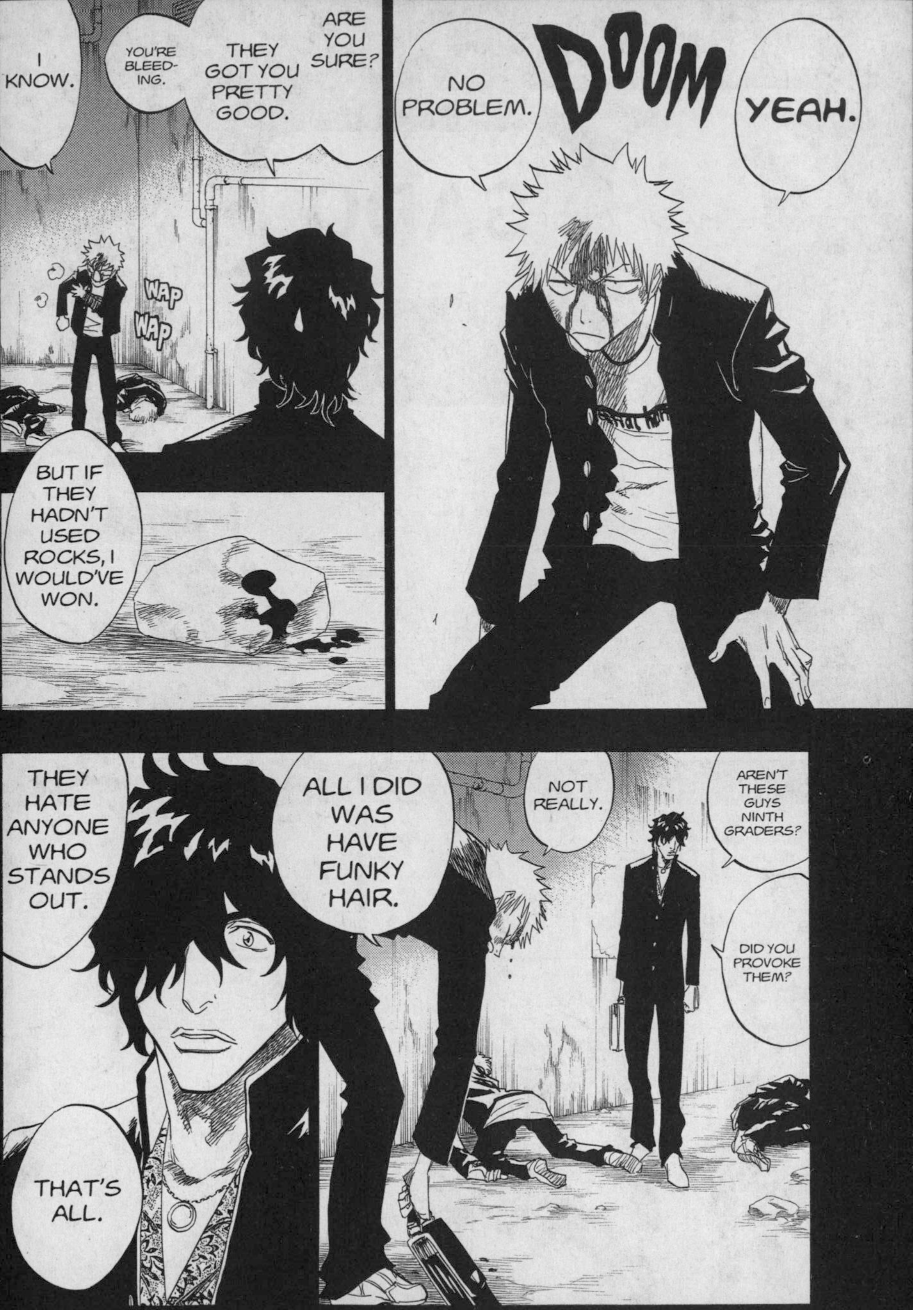
YEAH.
DOOM
NO PROBLEM.
ARE YOU SURE?
THEY GOT YOU PRETTY GOOD.
YOU'RE BLEEDING.
I KNOW.
WAP
WAP
BUT IF THEY HADN'T USED ROCKS, I WOULD'VE WON.
AREN'T THESE GUYS NINTH GRADERS?
DID YOU PROVOKE THEM?
NOT REALLY.
ALL I DID WAS HAVE FUNKY HAIR.
THEY HATE ANYONE WHO STANDS OUT.
THAT'S ALL.

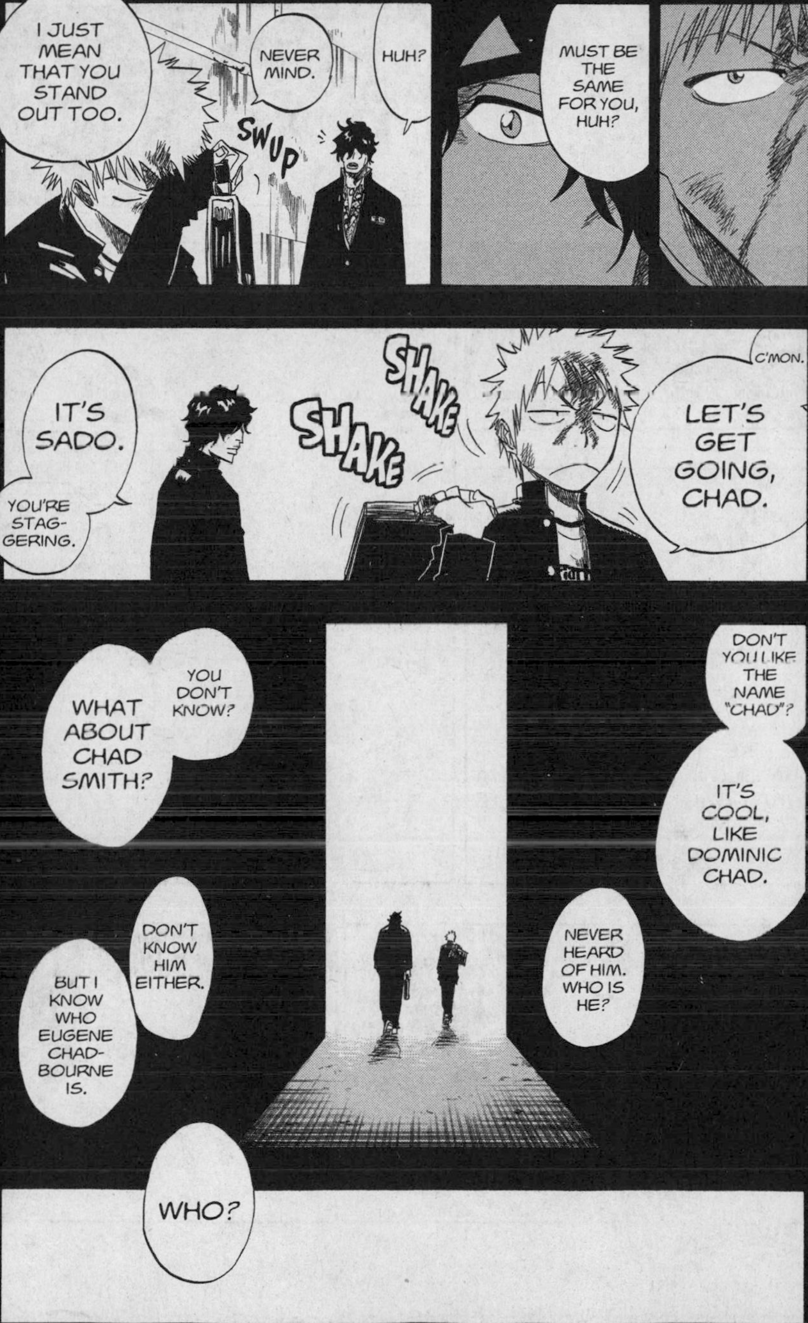
MUST BE THE SAME FOR YOU, HUH?
HUH?
NEVER MIND.
I JUST MEAN THAT YOU STAND OUT TOO.
SWUP
C'MON.
LET'S GET GOING, CHAD.
SHAKE
SHAKE
IT'S SADO.
YOU'RE STAG-GERING.
DON'T YOU LIKE THE NAME "CHAD"?
IT'S COOL, LIKE DOMINIC CHAD.
YOU DON'T KNOW?
WHAT ABOUT CHAD SMITH?
NEVER HEARD OF HIM. WHO IS HE?
DON'T KNOW HIM EITHER.
BUT I KNOW WHO EUGENE CHAD-BOURNE IS.
WHO?

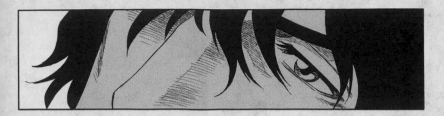

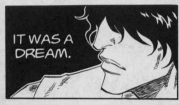

WHUP
IT WAS A DREAM.
TMP
A DREAM ABOUT THE PAST...
...LIKE AN OLD MAN'S DREAM...
TMP TMPTMP TMP
TMPTMP
FIND HIM?!
ALL RIGHT!
THIS WARE-HOUSE IS NEXT!
NO!
SECOND SQUAD, GO AROUND TO THE BACK!!
TMPTMP

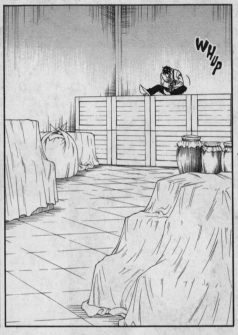

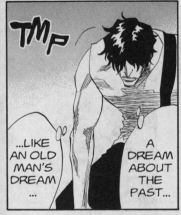

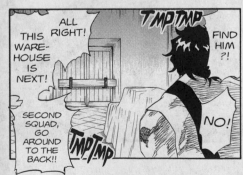

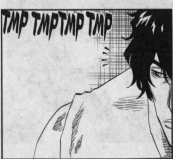

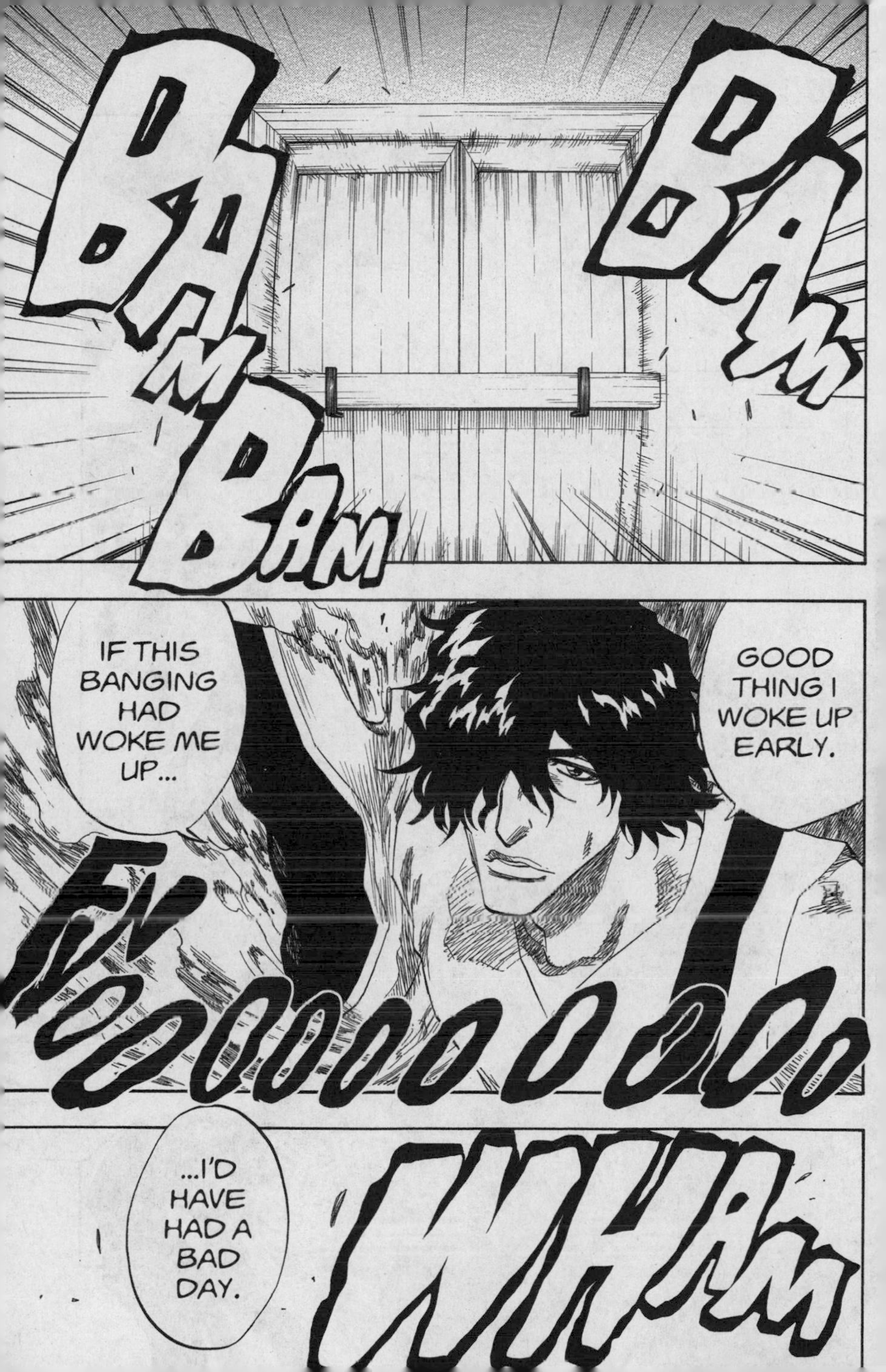
BAM
BAM
BAM
GOOD THING I WOKE UP EARLY.
IF THIS BANGING HAD WOKE ME UP...
FWOOOOOOOOOO
WHAM
...I'D HAVE HAD A BAD DAY.

102. Nobody Wins

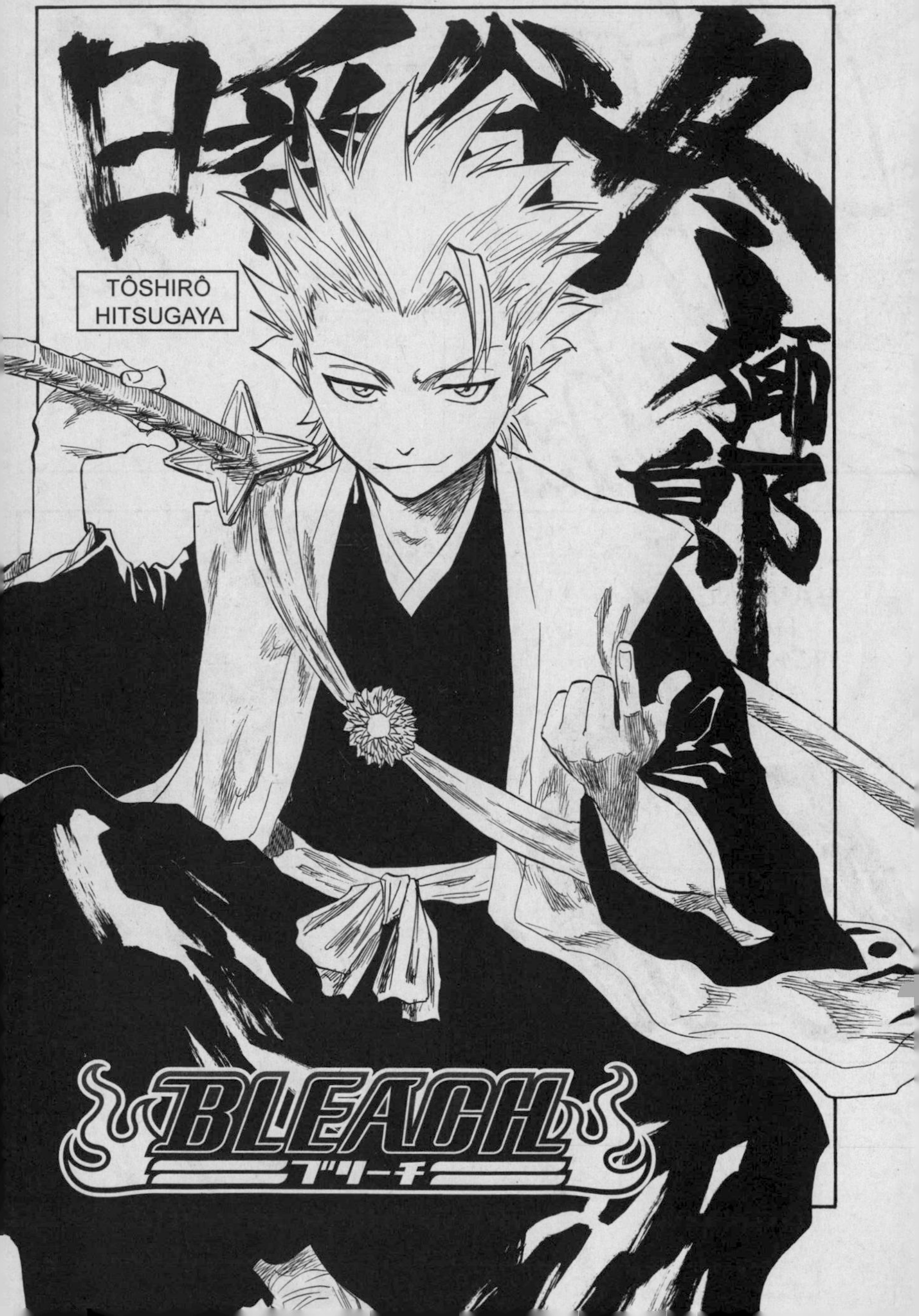
TÔSHIRÔ
HITSUGAYA
BLEACH
ブリーチ

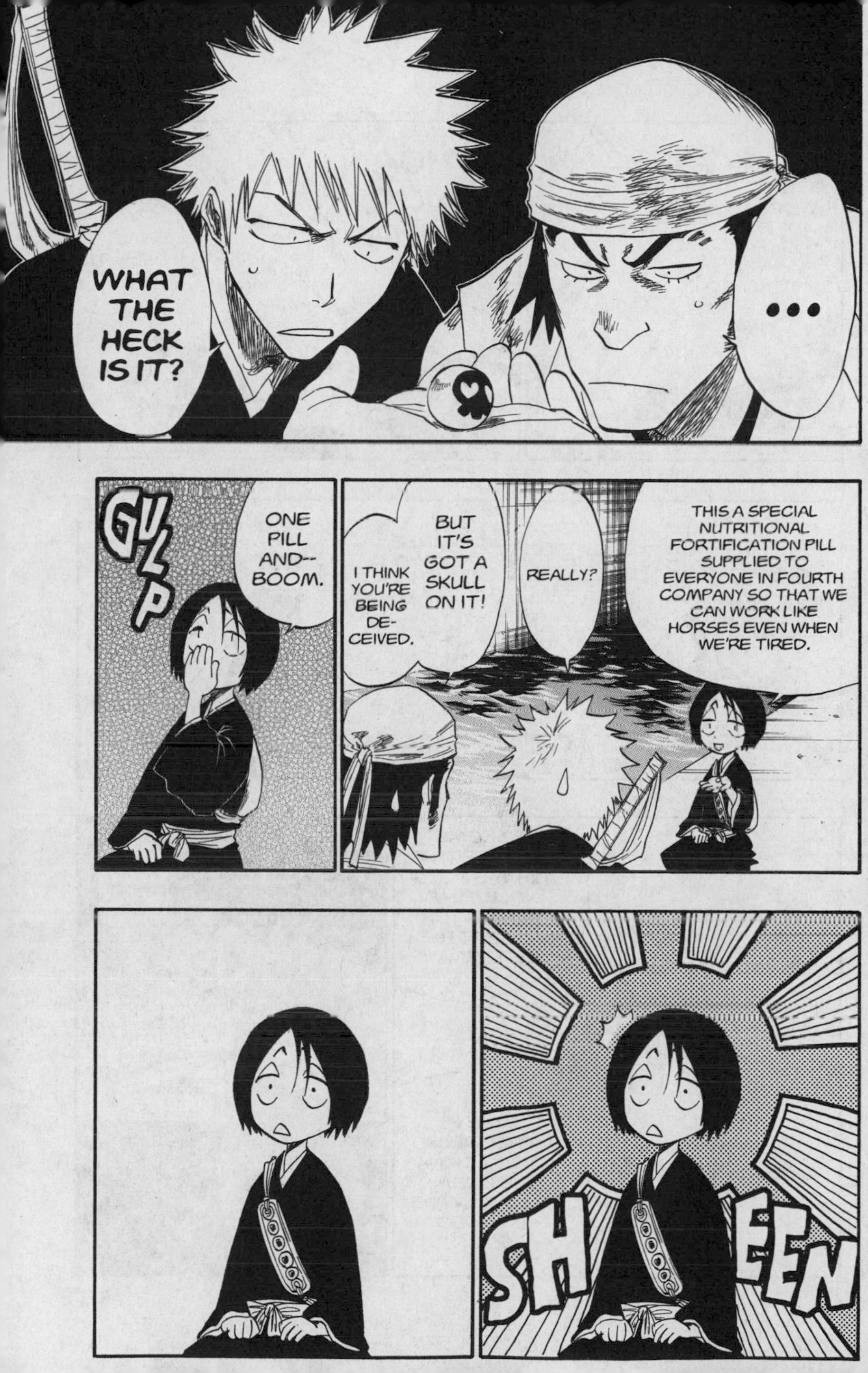

•••
WHAT THE HECK IS IT?
THIS A SPECIAL NUTRITIONAL FORTIFICATION PILL SUPPLIED TO EVERYONE IN FOURTH COMPANY SO THAT WE CAN WORK LIKE HORSES EVEN WHEN WE'RE TIRED.
REALLY?
BUT IT'S GOT A SKULL ON IT!
I THINK YOU'RE BEING DE-CEIVED.
ONE PILL AND-- BOOM.
GULP
SH EEN

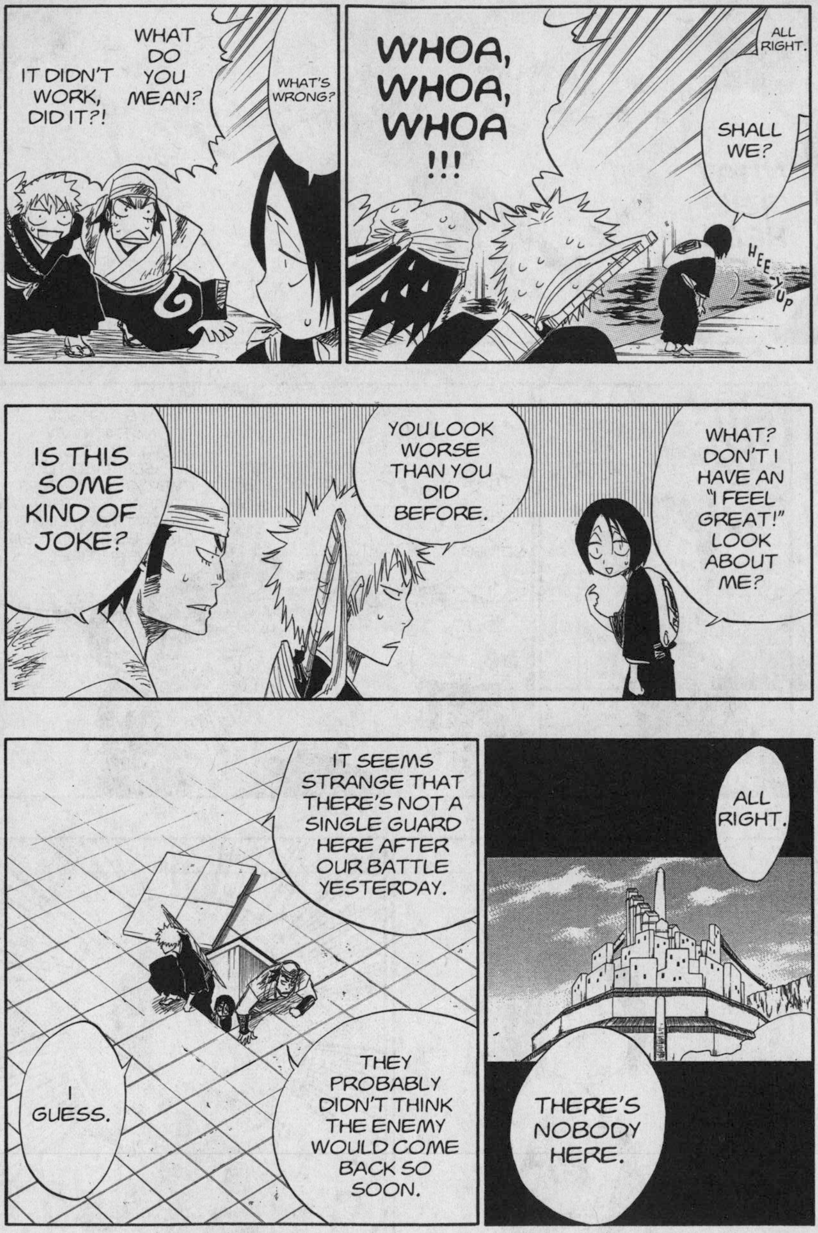
ALL RIGHT.
SHALL WE?
HEE-YUP
WHOA, WHOA, WHOA!!!
WHAT'S WRONG?
WHAT DO YOU MEAN?
IT DIDN'T WORK, DID IT?!
WHAT? DON'T I HAVE AN "I FEEL GREAT!" LOOK ABOUT ME?
YOU LOOK WORSE THAN YOU DID BEFORE.
IS THIS SOME KIND OF JOKE?
ALL RIGHT.
THERE'S NOBODY HERE.
IT SEEMS STRANGE THAT THERE'S NOT A SINGLE GUARD HERE AFTER OUR BATTLE YESTERDAY.
THEY PROBABLY DIDN'T THINK THE ENEMY WOULD COME BACK SO SOON.
I GUESS.

READ THIS WAY

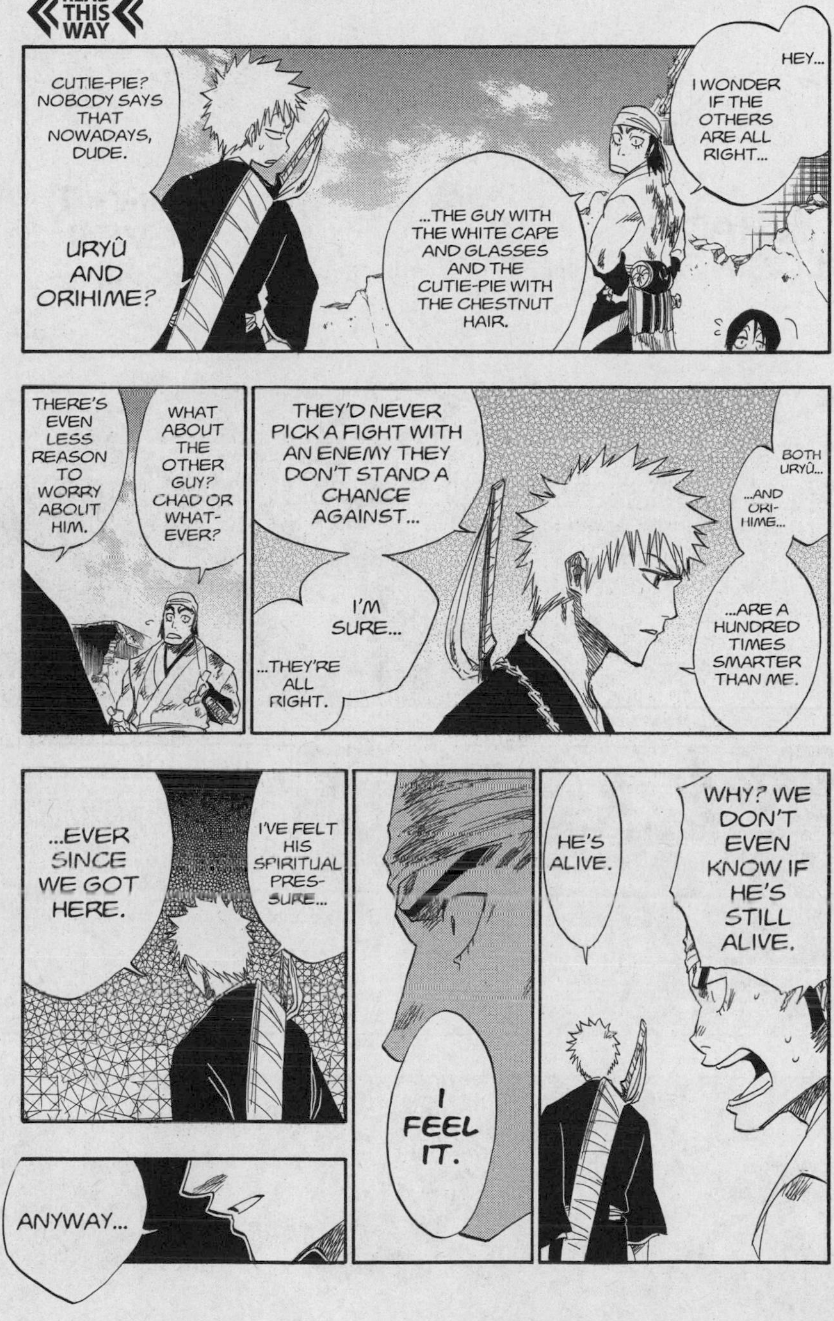
HEY... I WONDER IF THE OTHERS ARE ALL RIGHT...
...THE GUY WITH THE WHITE CAPE AND GLASSES AND THE CUTIE-PIE WITH THE CHESTNUT HAIR.
CUTIE-PIE? NOBODY SAYS THAT NOWADAYS, DUDE.
URYÛ AND ORIHIME?
BOTH URYÛ...
...AND ORIHIME...
...ARE A HUNDRED TIMES SMARTER THAN ME.
THEY'D NEVER PICK A FIGHT WITH AN ENEMY THEY DON'T STAND A CHANCE AGAINST...
I'M SURE...
...THEY'RE ALL RIGHT.
WHAT ABOUT THE OTHER GUY? CHAD OR WHATEVER?
THERE'S EVEN LESS REASON TO WORRY ABOUT HIM.
WHY? WE DON'T EVEN KNOW IF HE'S STILL ALIVE.
HE'S ALIVE.
I FEEL IT.
I'VE FELT HIS SPIRITUAL PRESSURE...
...EVER SINCE WE GOT HERE.
ANYWAY...

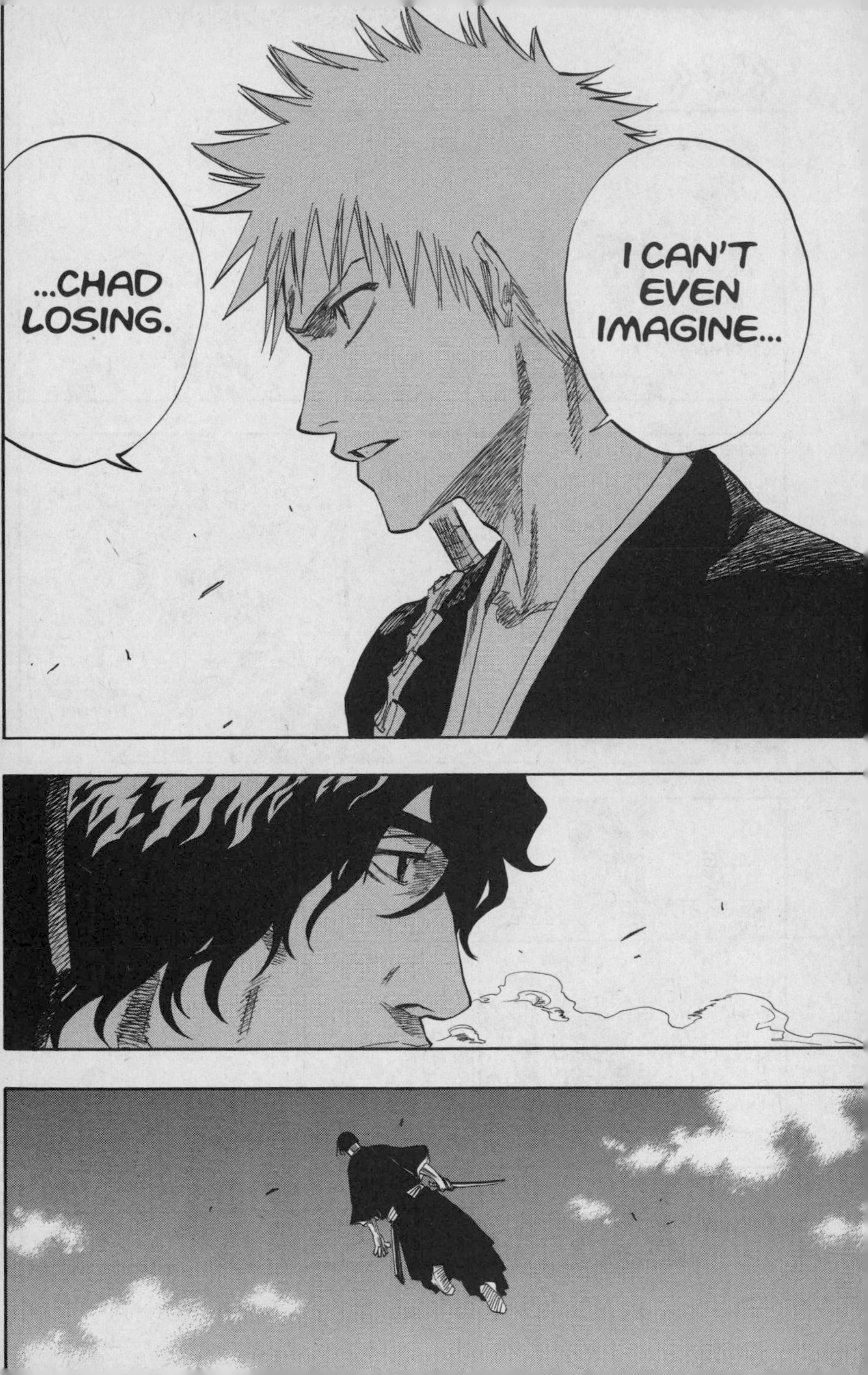
I CAN'T EVEN IMAGINE...
...CHAD LOSING.

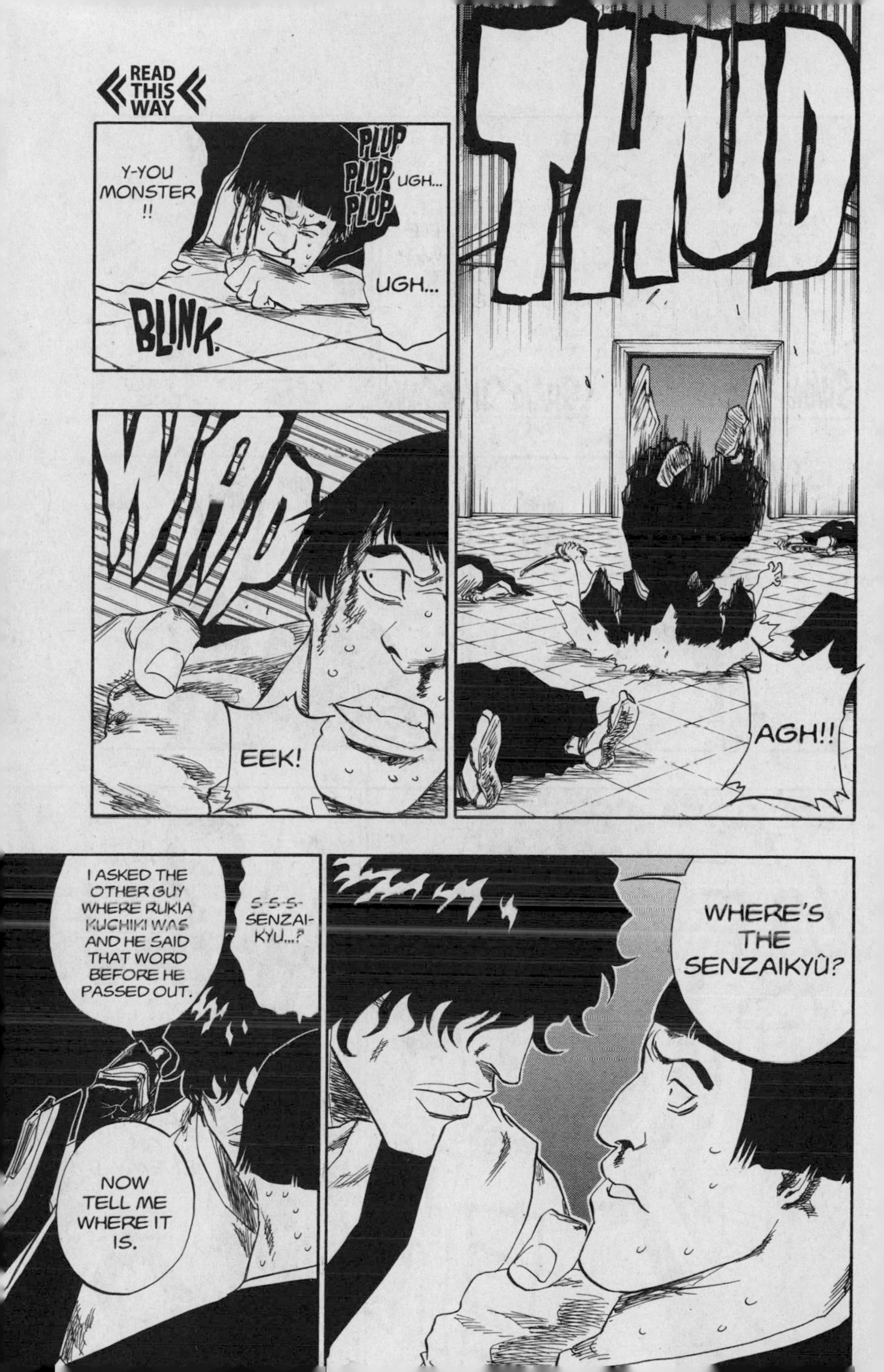
READ THIS WAY
THUD
AGH!!
UGH...
PLUP PLUP PLUP
Y-YOU MONSTER !!
UGH...
BLINK.
WHP
EEK!
WHERE'S THE SENZAIKYÛ?
S-S-S-SENZAI-KYU...?
I ASKED THE OTHER GUY WHERE RUKIA KUCHIKI WAS AND HE SAID THAT WORD BEFORE HE PASSED OUT.
NOW TELL ME WHERE IT IS.

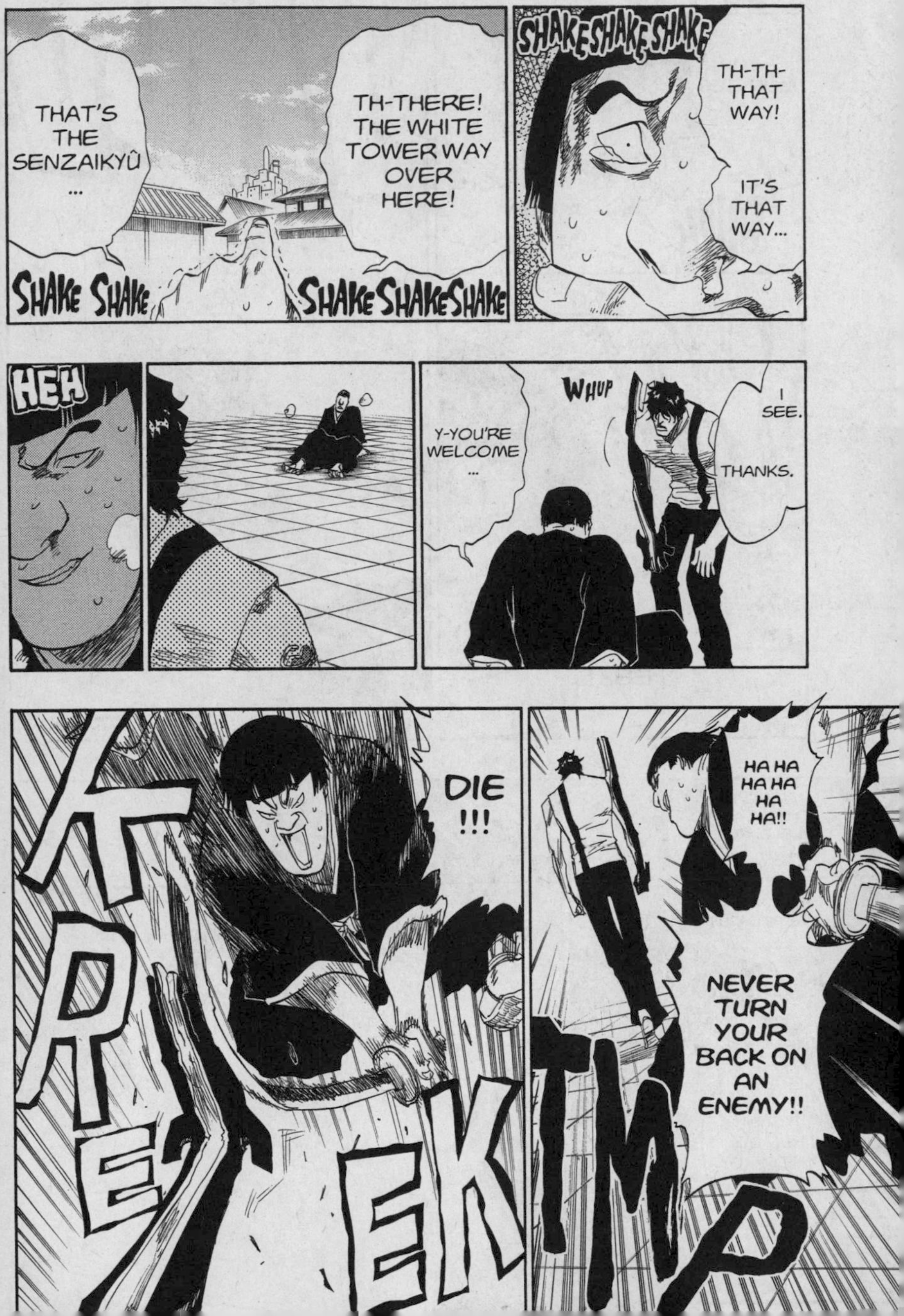
SHAKESHAKESHAKE
TH-TH-THAT WAY!
IT'S THAT WAY...
TH-THERE! THE WHITE TOWER WAY OVER HERE!
SHAKESHAKESHAKE
THAT'S THE SENZAIKYÛ...
SHAKE SHAKE
I SEE.
THANKS.
WHUP
Y-YOU'RE WELCOME...
HEH
HA HA HA HA HA HA!!
NEVER TURN YOUR BACK ON AN ENEMY!!
TMP
DIE!!!
KREEEK

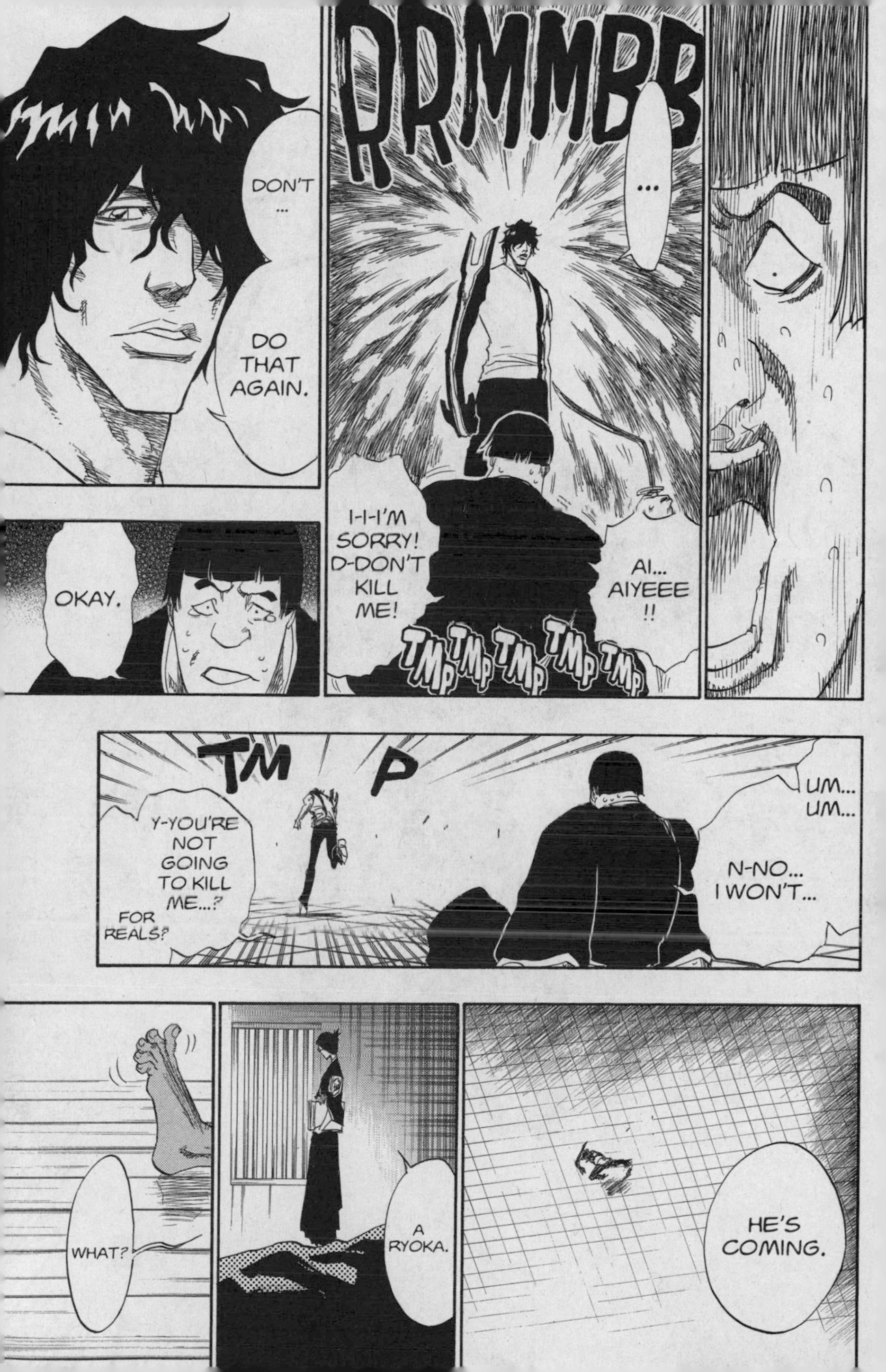
RRMMBB
...
AI... AIYEEE!!
I-I-I'M SORRY! D-DON'T KILL ME!
TMP TMP TMP TMP TMP
DON'T ... DO THAT AGAIN.
OKAY.
UM... UM...
N-NO... I WON'T...
TM P
Y-YOU'RE NOT GOING TO KILL ME...? FOR REALS?
HE'S COMING.
A RYOKA.
WHAT?

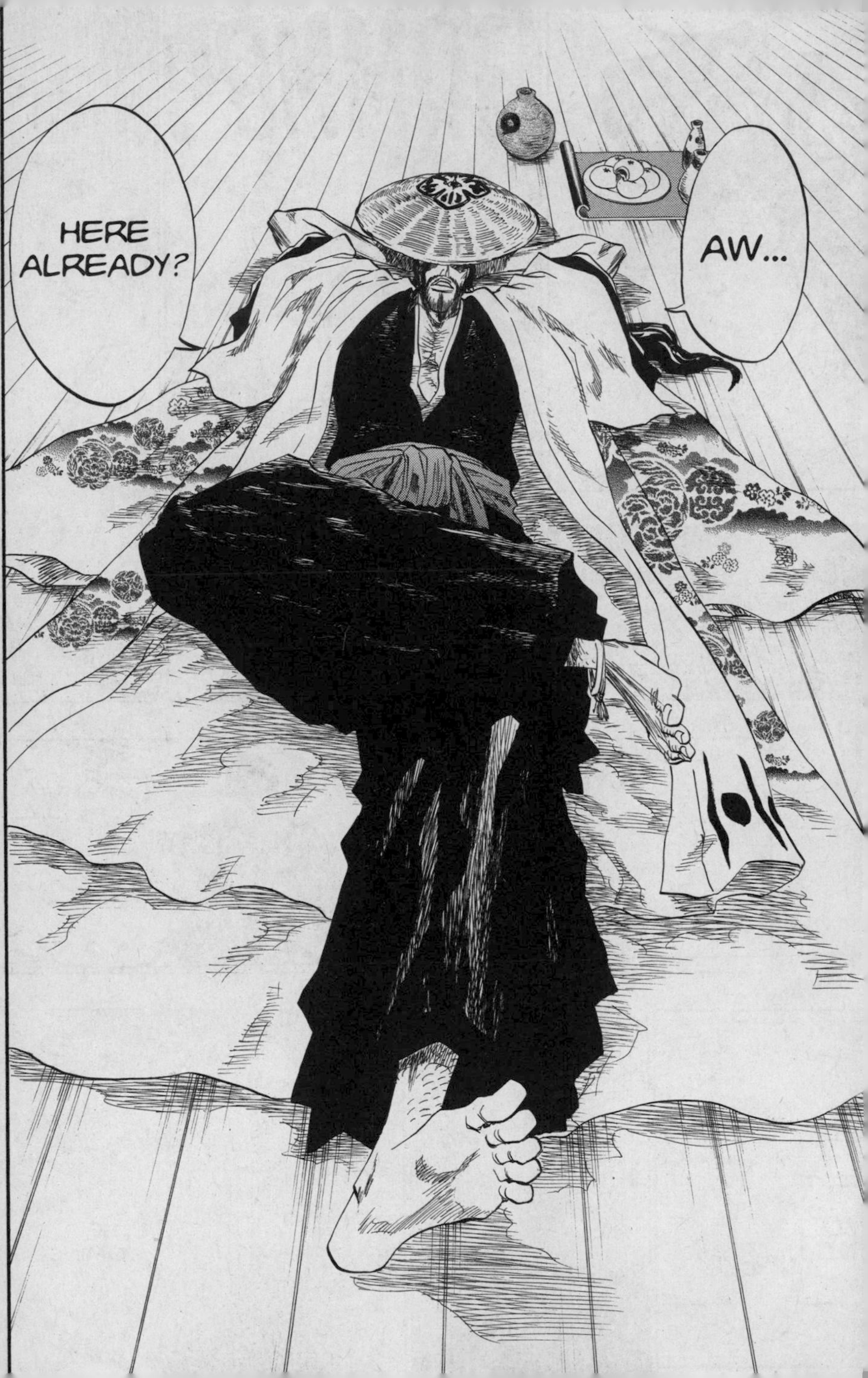
AW...
HERE ALREADY?

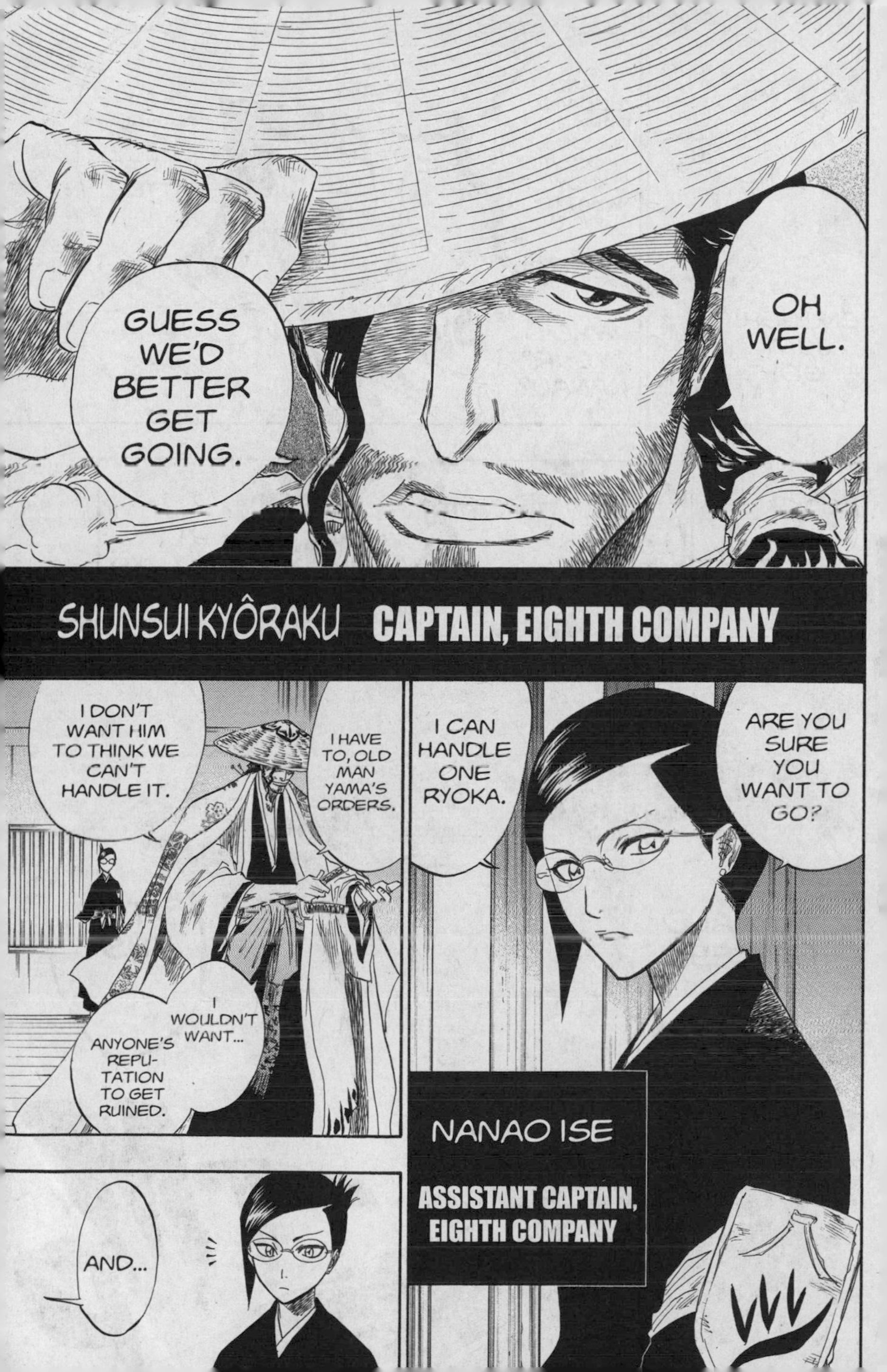
OH WELL.
GUESS WE'D BETTER GET GOING.
SHUNSUI KYÔRAKU CAPTAIN, EIGHTH COMPANY
ARE YOU SURE YOU WANT TO GO?
I CAN HANDLE ONE RYOKA.
NANAO ISE
ASSISTANT CAPTAIN, EIGHTH COMPANY
I HAVE TO, OLD MAN YAMA'S ORDERS.
I DON'T WANT HIM TO THINK WE CAN'T HANDLE IT.
I WOULDN'T WANT...
ANYONE'S REPUTATION TO GET RUINED.
AND...

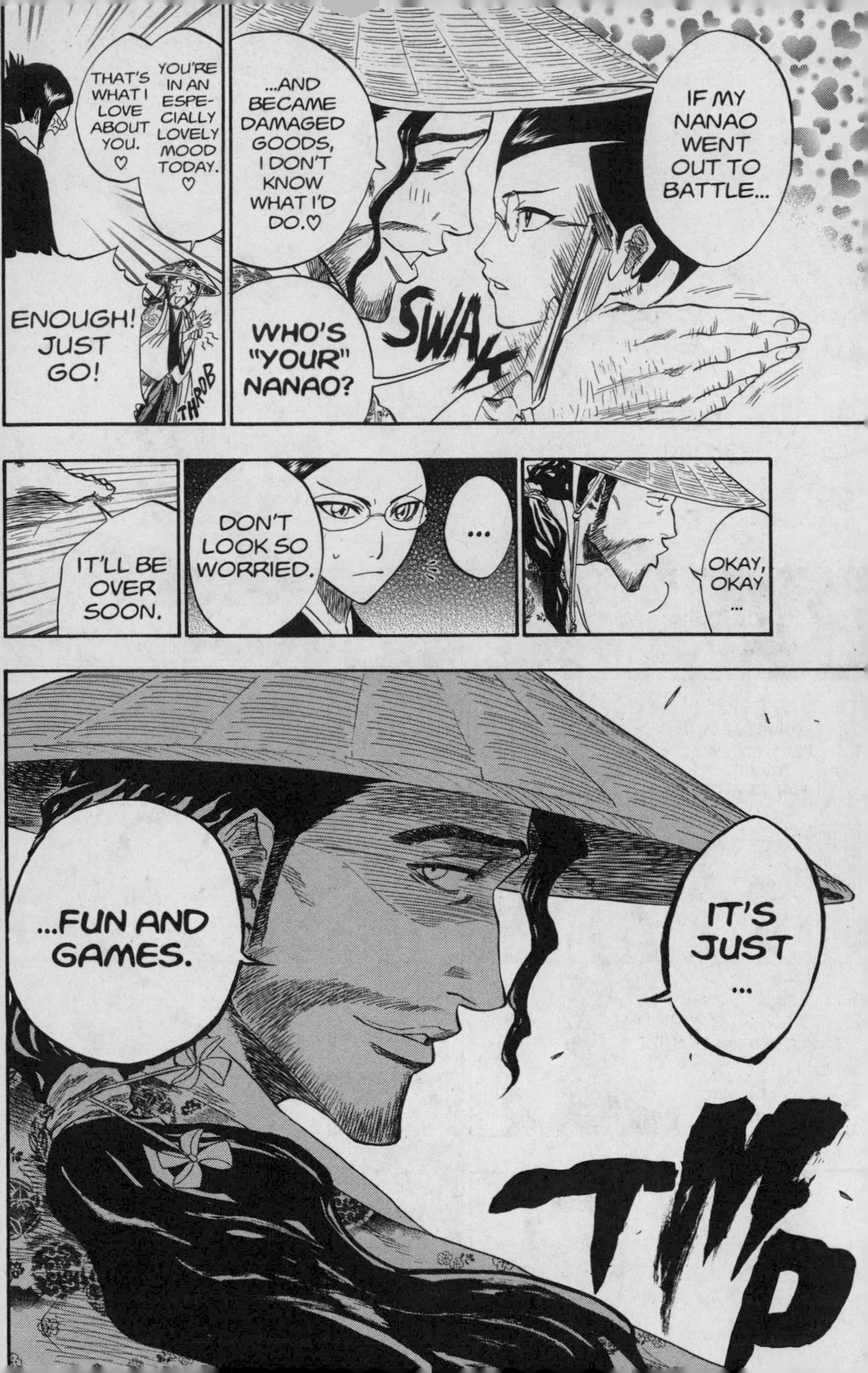
IF MY NANAO WENT OUT TO BATTLE...
...AND BECAME DAMAGED GOODS, I DON'T KNOW WHAT I'D DO.♡
SWAK
WHO'S "YOUR" NANAO?
YOU'RE IN AN ESPE-CIALLY LOVELY MOOD TODAY.♡
THAT'S WHAT I LOVE ABOUT YOU.♡
ENOUGH! JUST GO!
THROB
OKAY, OKAY ...
...
DON'T LOOK SO WORRIED.
IT'LL BE OVER SOON.
IT'S JUST ...
...FUN AND GAMES.
TMP

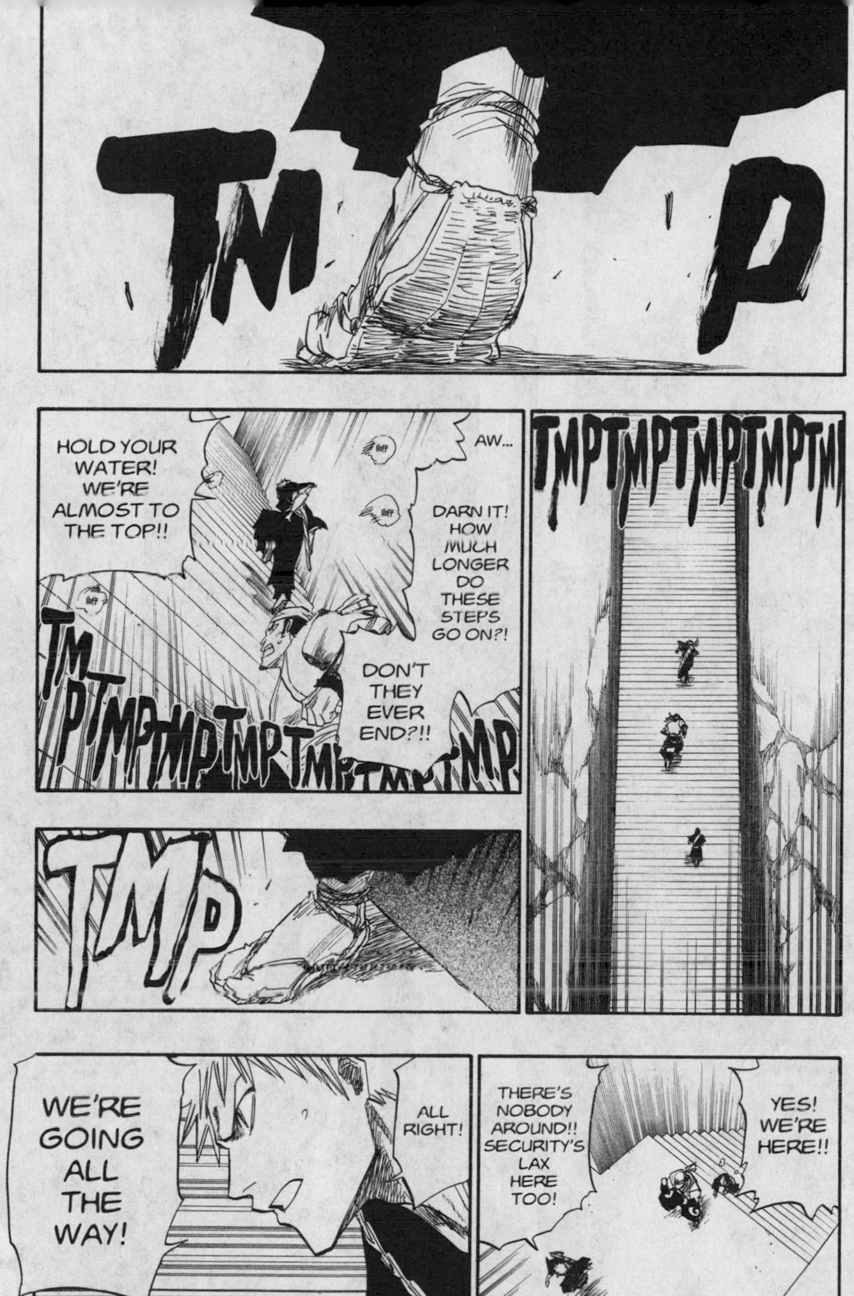
TMP
TMPTMPTMPTMPTM
AW...
DARN IT! HOW MUCH LONGER DO THESE STEPS GO ON?!
DON'T THEY EVER END?!!
HOLD YOUR WATER! WE'RE ALMOST TO THE TOP!!
Huff
Huff
Huff
TMPTMPTMPTMPTMPTMPTMP
TMP
YES! WE'RE HERE!!
THERE'S NOBODY AROUND!! SECURITY'S LAX HERE TOO!
ALL RIGHT!
WE'RE GOING ALL THE WAY!

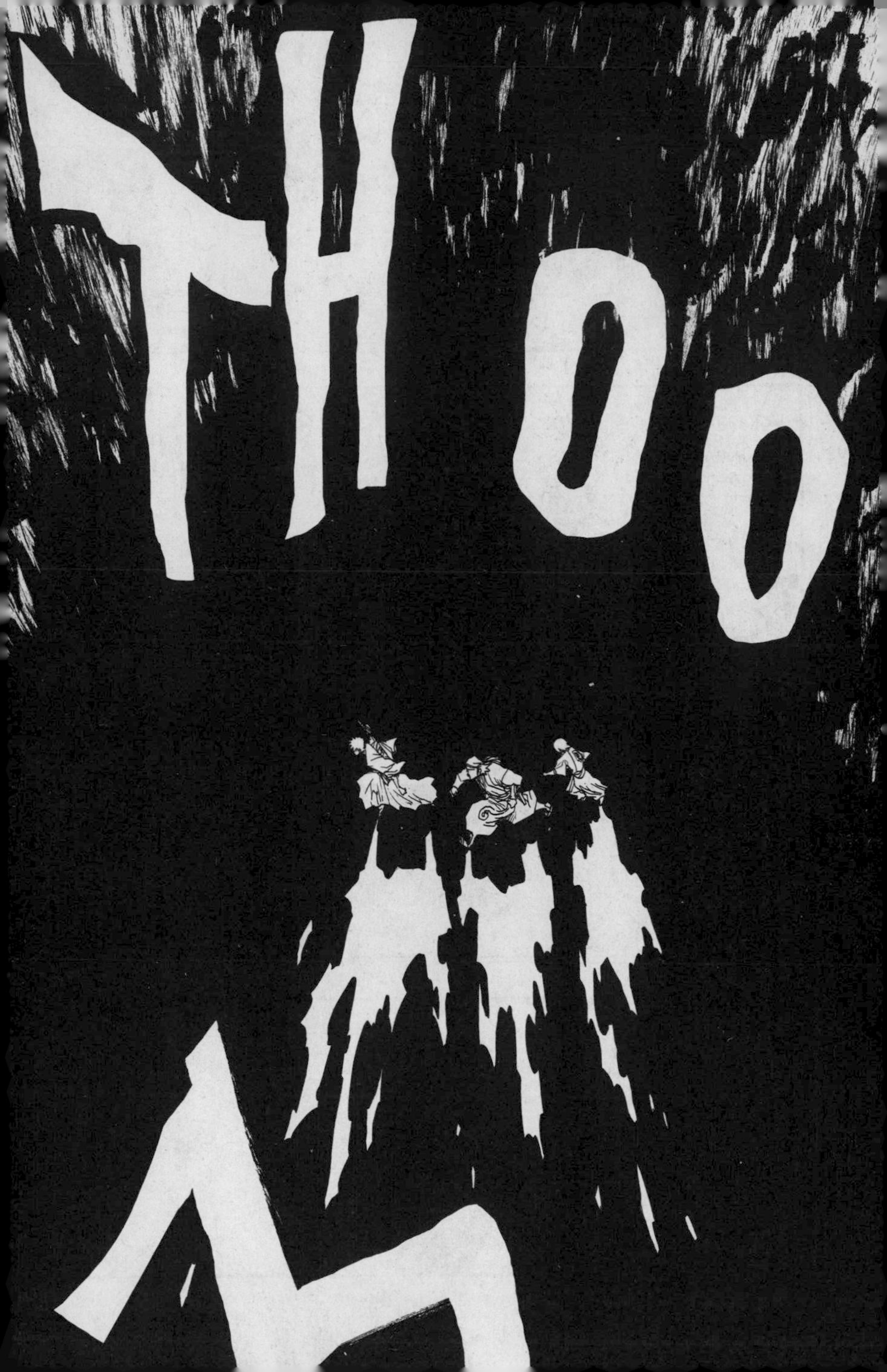
THOO

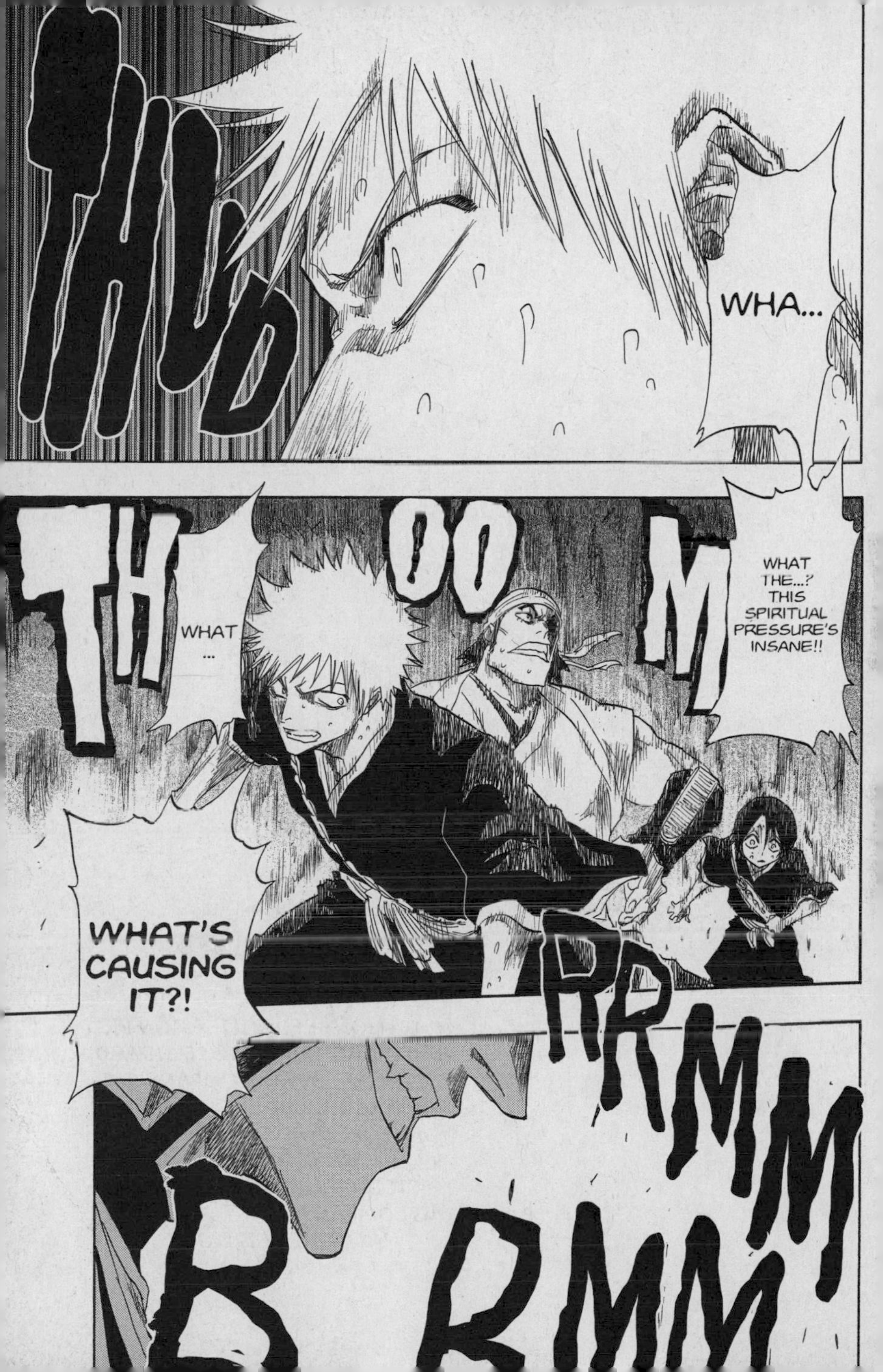
THUD
WHA...
WHAT THE...? THIS SPIRITUAL PRESSURE'S INSANE!!
THOOM
WHAT ...
WHAT'S CAUSING IT?!
RRMM
BRMM

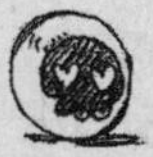

SPECIAL HANATARÔ VERSION NUTRITIONAL FORTIFICATION PILL! HANATARÔ THINKS IT'S STANDARD ISSUE FOR FOURTH COMPANY, BUT WHAT HE'S HOLDING IS SOMETHING HIS SUPERIORS CREATED AS A PRANK. IT'S DIFFERENT FROM THE MEDICINE THE OTHER MEMBERS OF HIS COMPANY CARRY. IT'S ACTIVE INGREDIENT IS FLOUR.

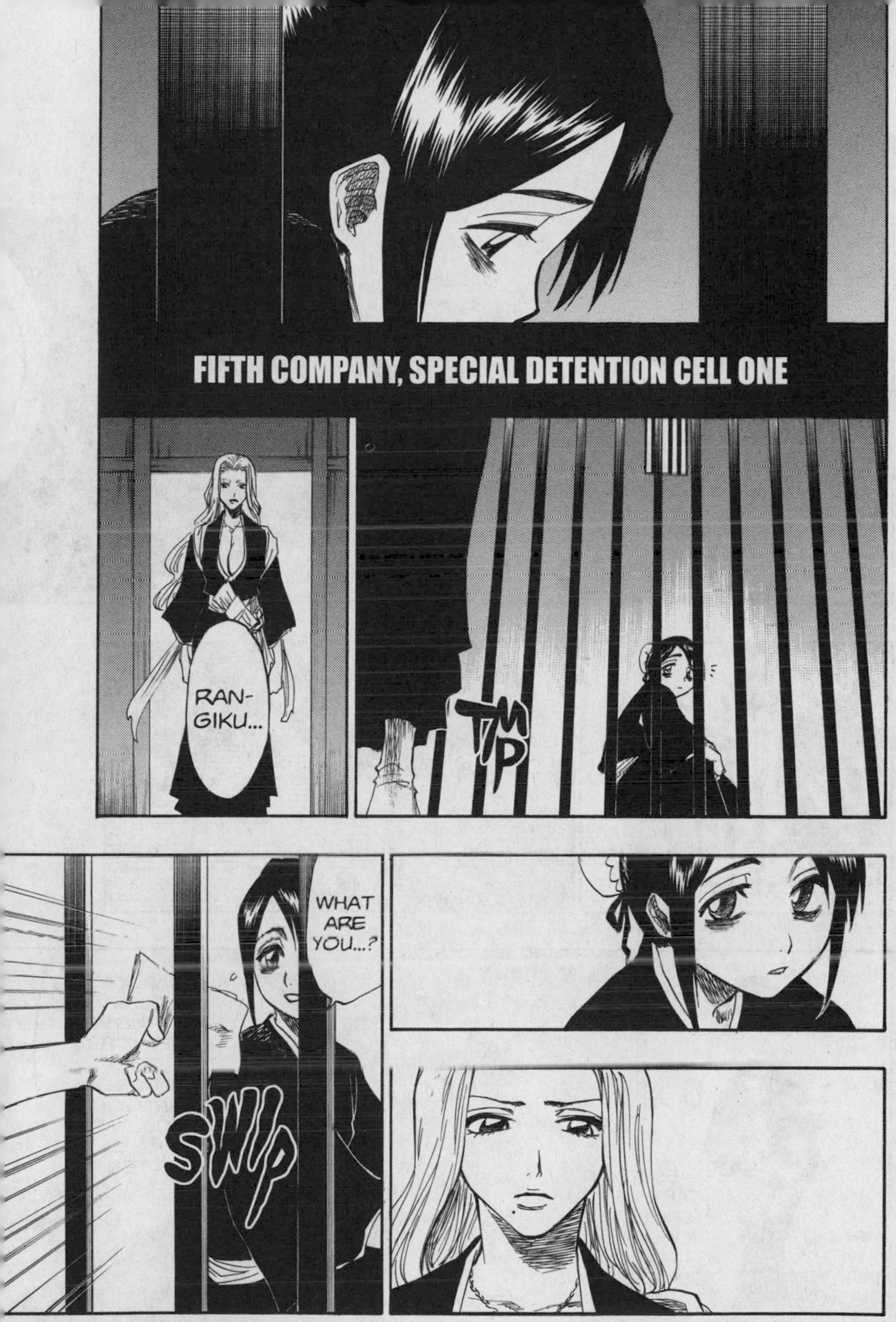
FIFTH COMPANY, SPECIAL DETENTION CELL ONE
TMP
RAN-GIKU...
WHAT ARE YOU...?
SWIP

103. Dominion

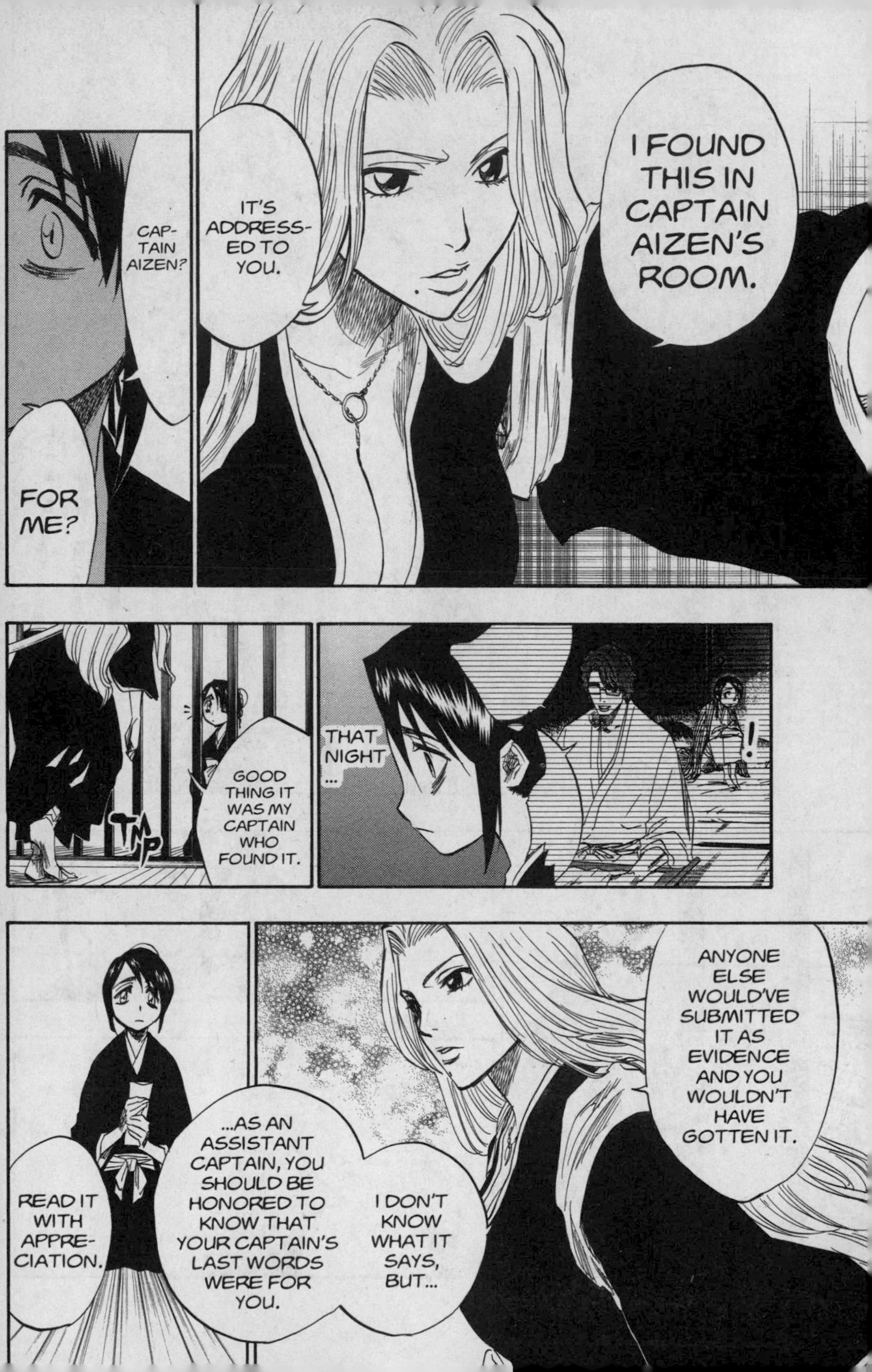
I FOUND THIS IN CAPTAIN AIZEN'S ROOM.
IT'S ADDRESSED TO YOU.
CAPTAIN AIZEN?
FOR ME?
THAT NIGHT...
!
GOOD THING IT WAS MY CAPTAIN WHO FOUND IT.
TMP
ANYONE ELSE WOULD'VE SUBMITTED IT AS EVIDENCE AND YOU WOULDN'T HAVE GOTTEN IT.
I DON'T KNOW WHAT IT SAYS, BUT...
...AS AN ASSISTANT CAPTAIN, YOU SHOULD BE HONORED TO KNOW THAT YOUR CAPTAIN'S LAST WORDS WERE FOR YOU.
READ IT WITH APPRECIATION.

READ THIS WAY

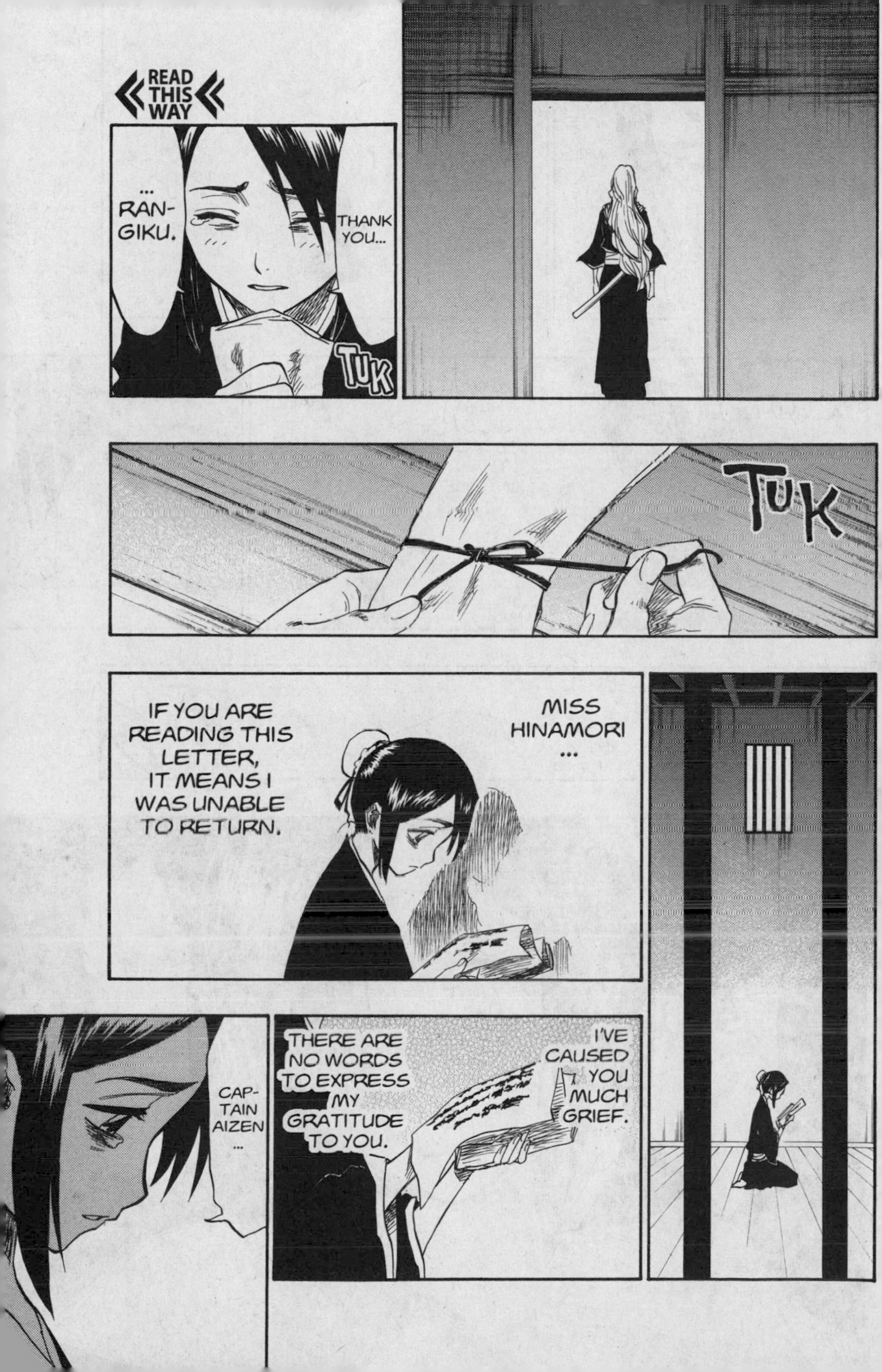
THANK YOU...
... RAN-GIKU.
TUK
TUK
MISS HINAMORI ...
IF YOU ARE READING THIS LETTER, IT MEANS I WAS UNABLE TO RETURN.
I'VE CAUSED YOU MUCH GRIEF.
THERE ARE NO WORDS TO EXPRESS MY GRATITUDE TO YOU.
CAP-TAIN AIZEN ...

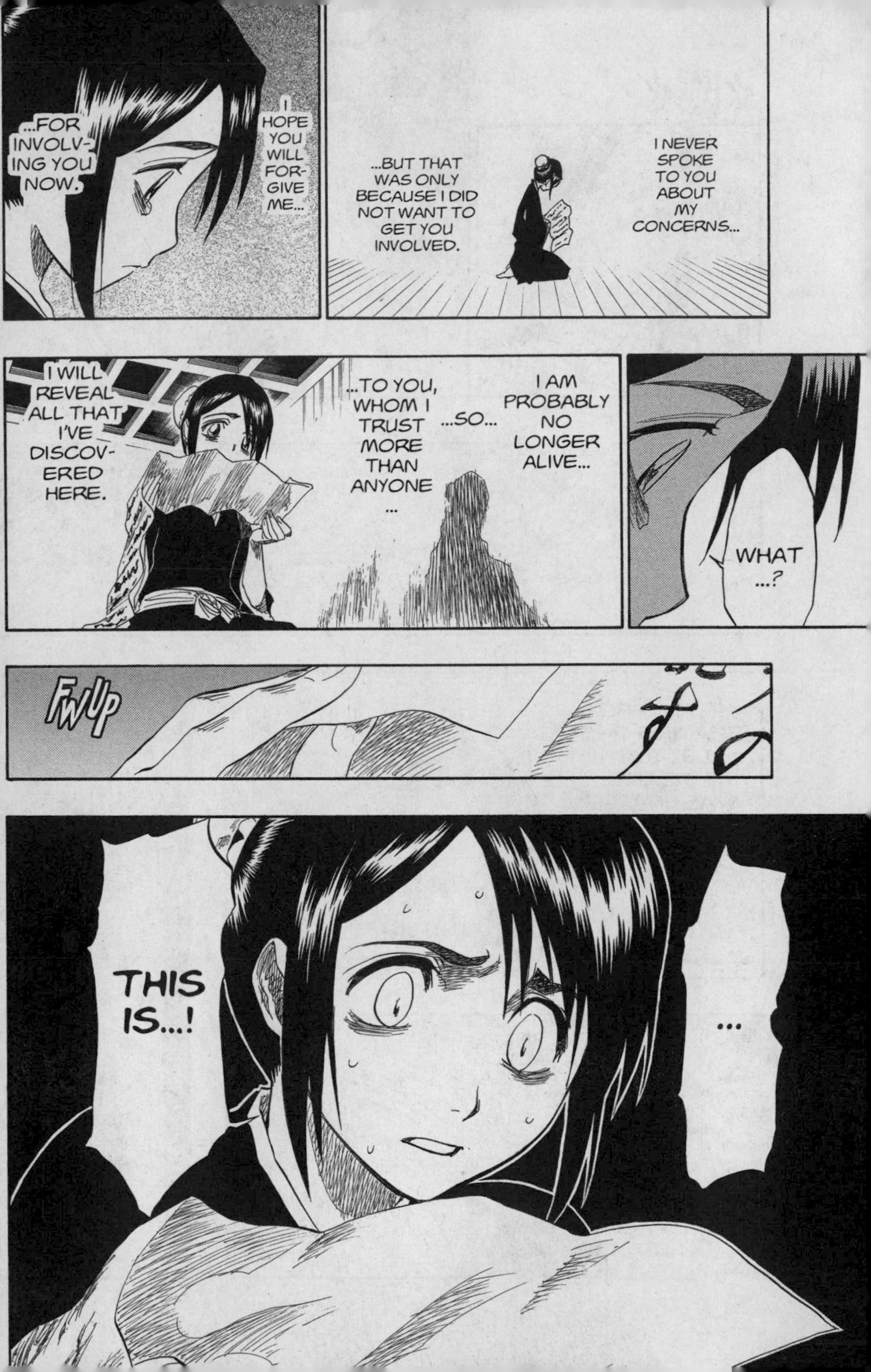
I NEVER SPOKE TO YOU ABOUT MY CONCERNS...
...BUT THAT WAS ONLY BECAUSE I DID NOT WANT TO GET YOU INVOLVED.
I HOPE YOU WILL FOR-GIVE ME...
...FOR INVOLV-ING YOU NOW.
WHAT ...?
I AM PROBABLY NO LONGER ALIVE...
...SO...
...TO YOU, WHOM I TRUST MORE THAN ANYONE ...
I WILL REVEAL ALL THAT I'VE DISCOV-ERED HERE.
FWUP
...
THIS IS...!

103. Dominion

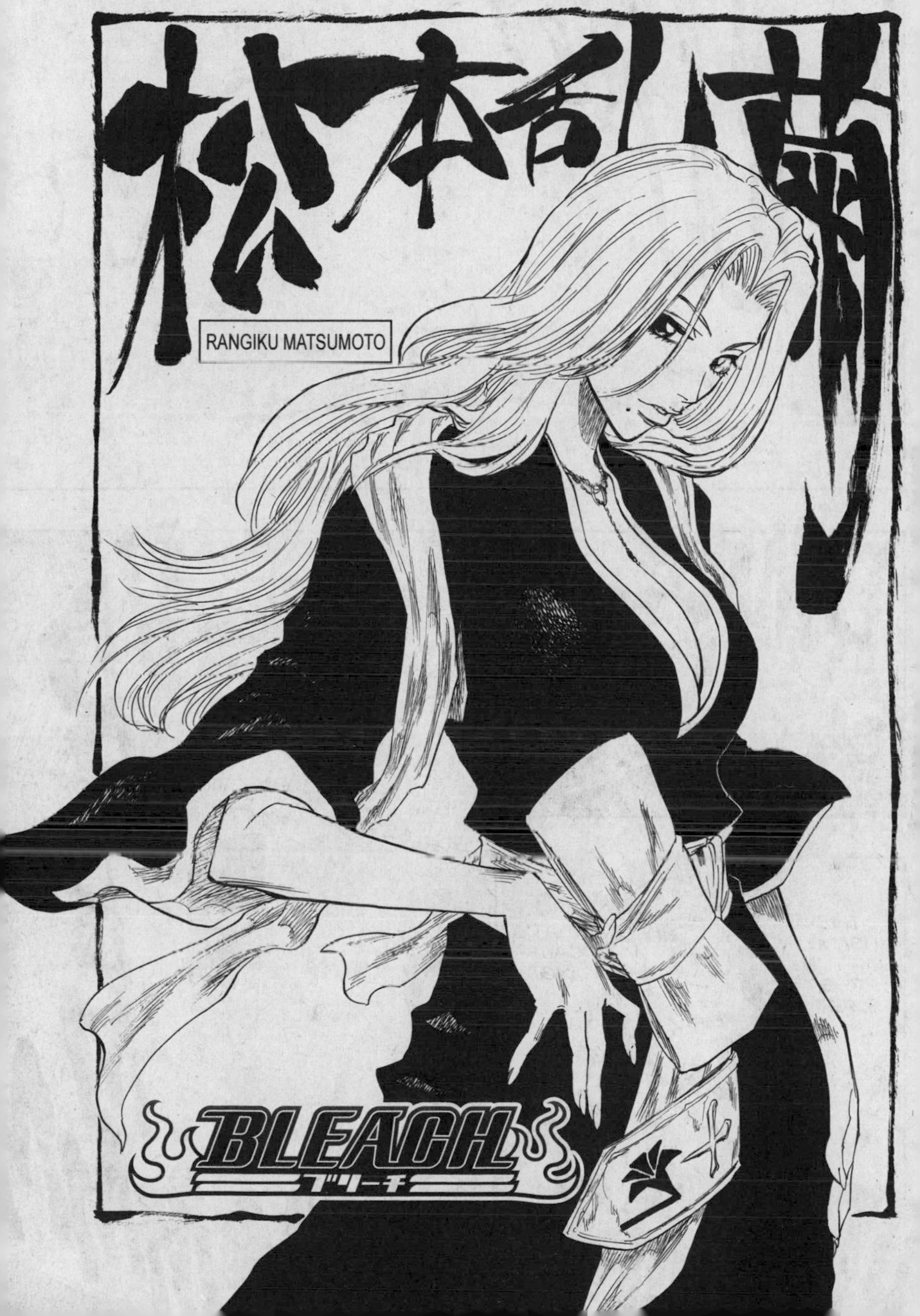
松本乱菊
RANGIKU MATSUMOTO
BLEACH
ブリーチ

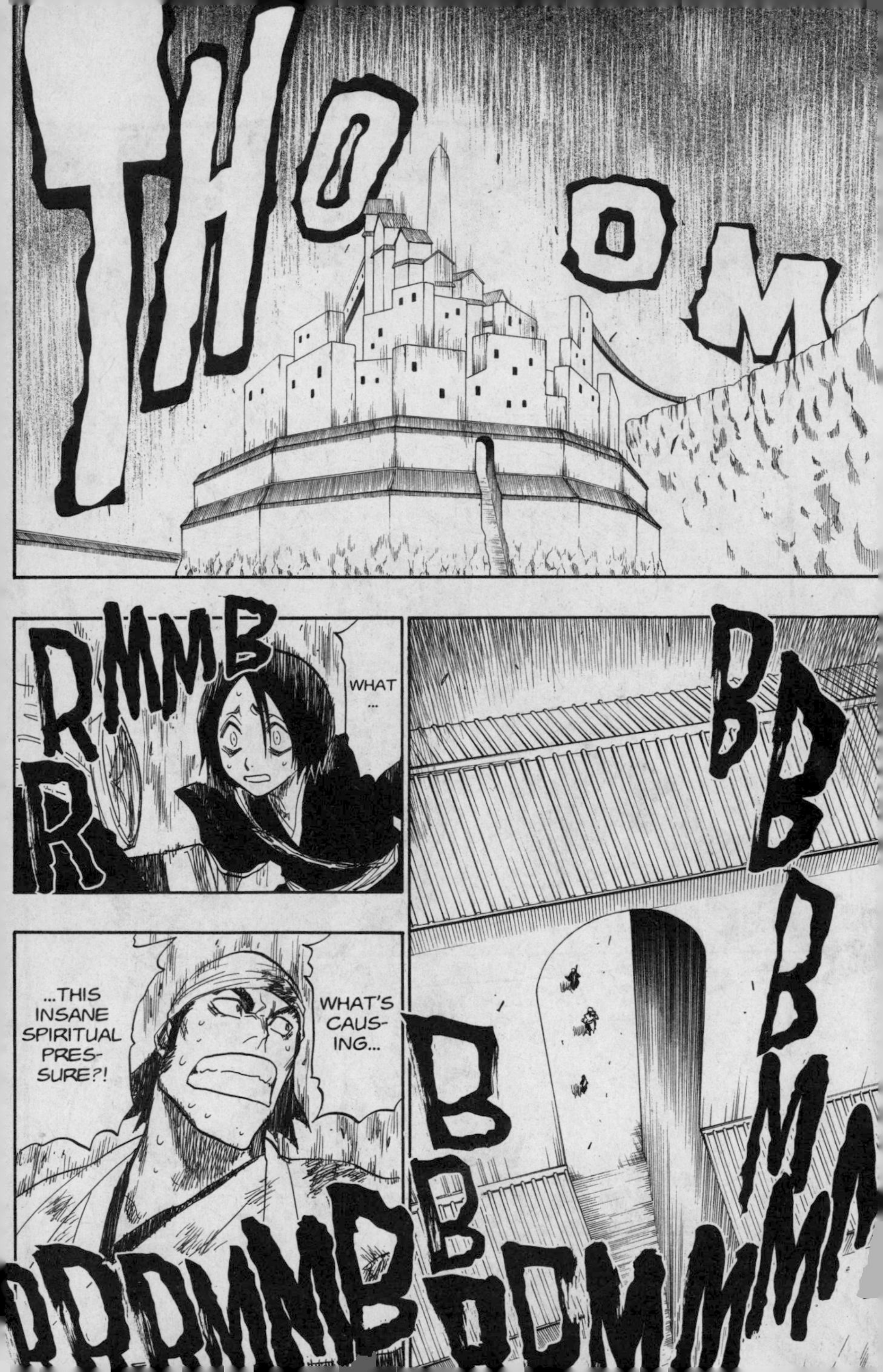
THOOM
WHAT...
WHAT'S CAUSING...
...THIS INSANE SPIRITUAL PRESSURE?!

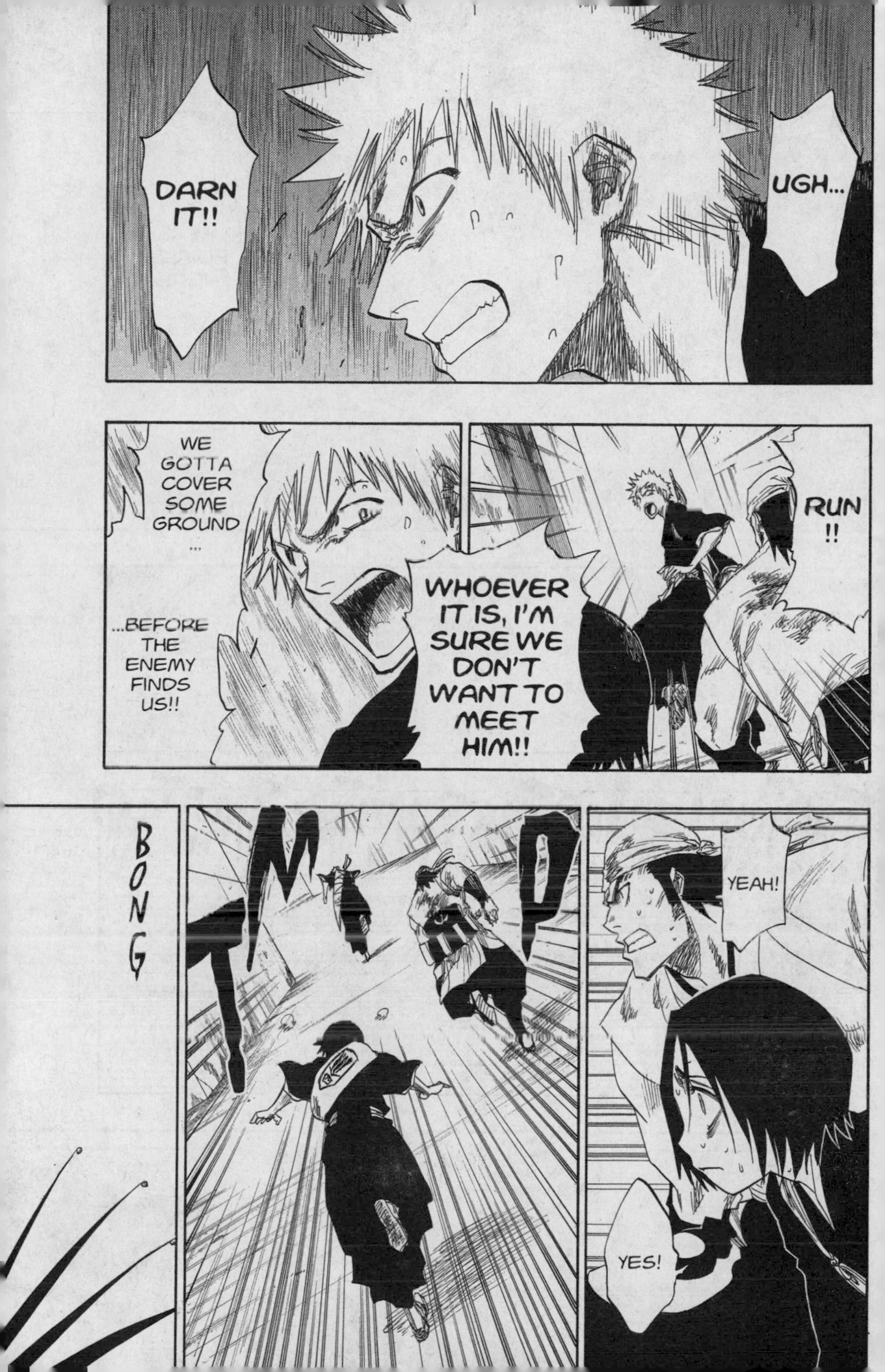
UGH...
DARN IT!!
RUN!!
WHOEVER IT IS, I'M SURE WE DON'T WANT TO MEET HIM!!
WE GOTTA COVER SOME GROUND...
...BEFORE THE ENEMY FINDS US!!
YEAH!
YES!
TMP
BONG

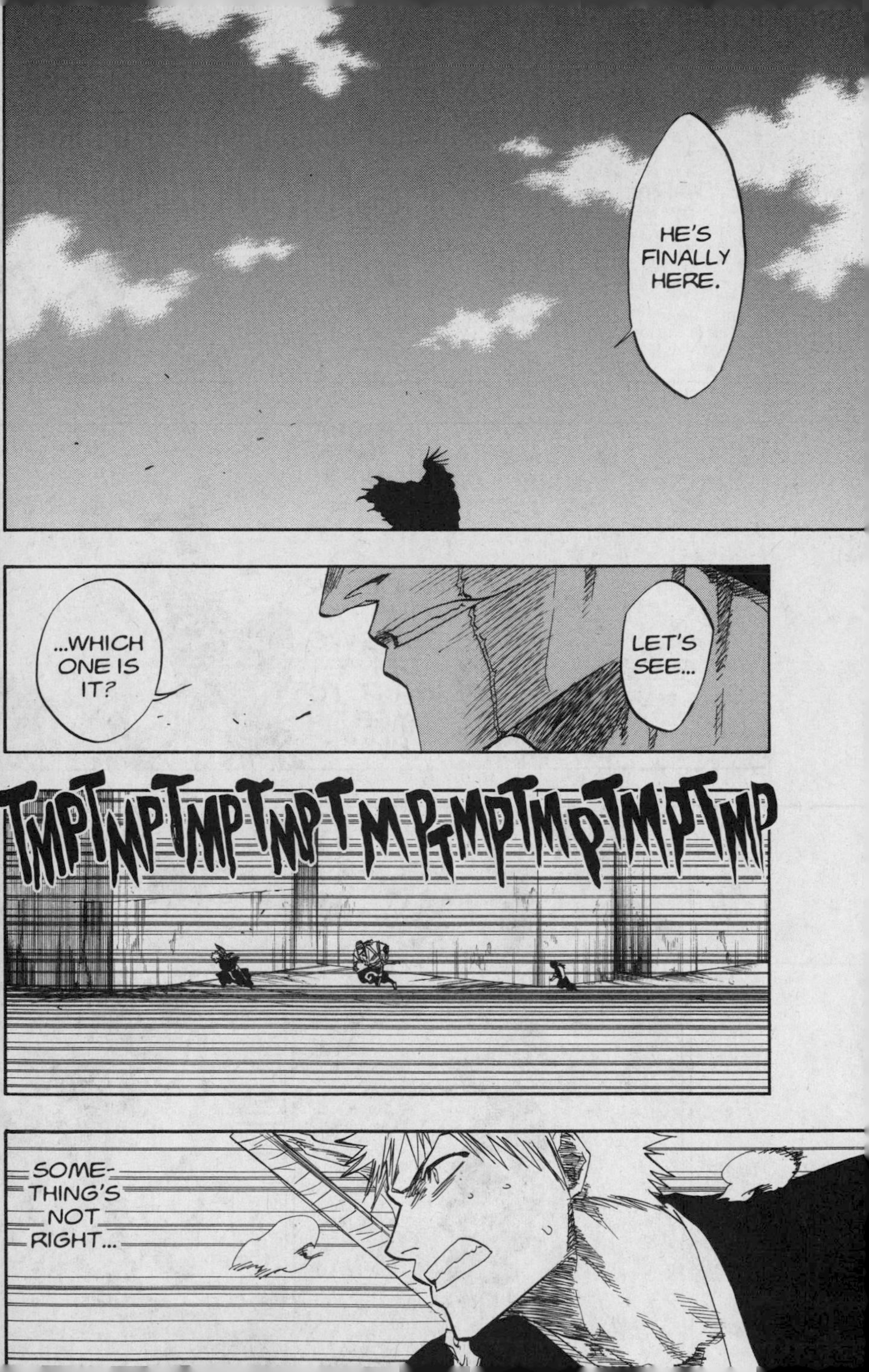
HE'S FINALLY HERE.
LET'S SEE...
...WHICH ONE IS IT?
TMPTMPTMPTMPTMPTMPTMPTMPTMP
SOME-THING'S NOT RIGHT...

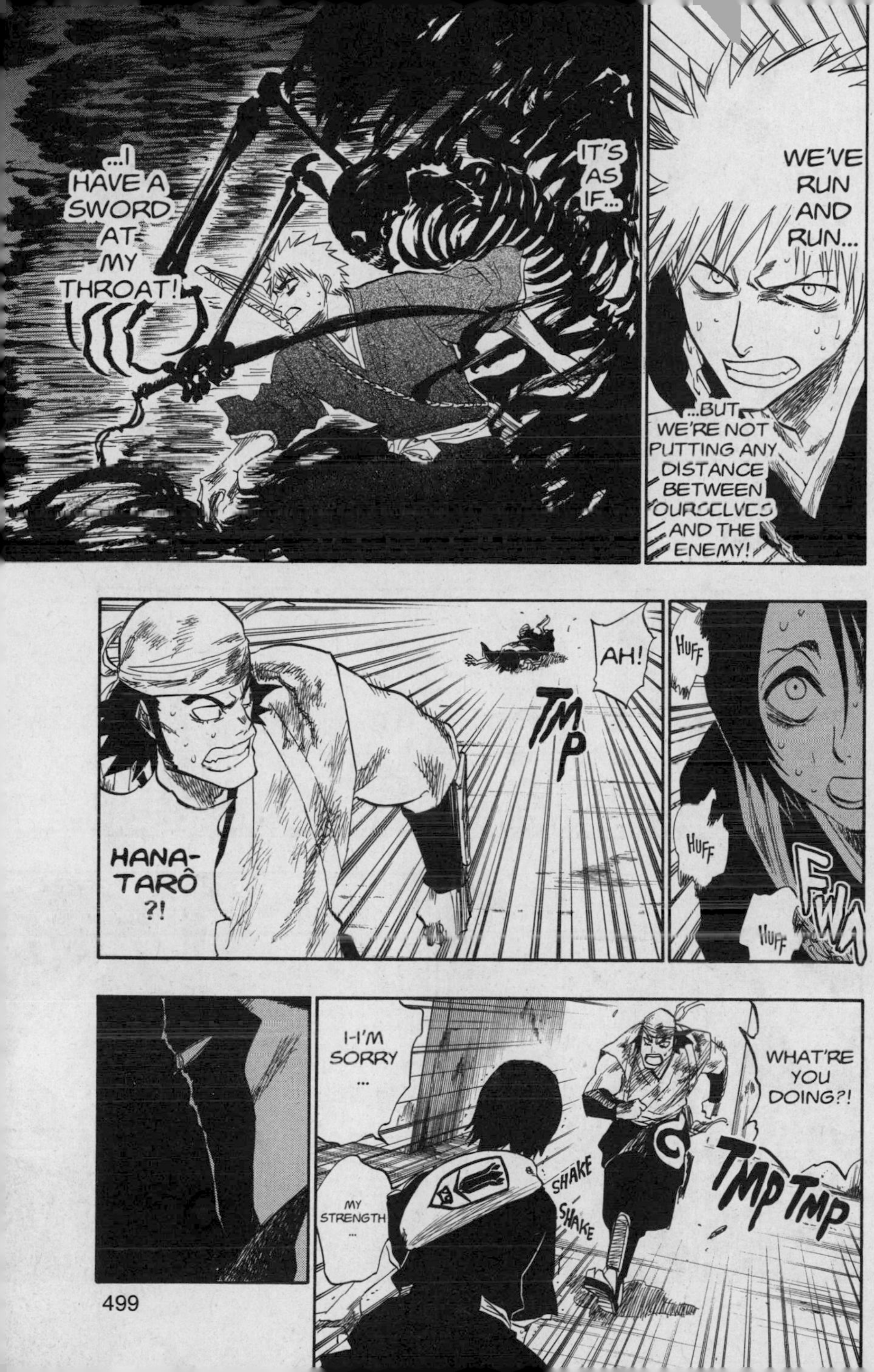
WE'VE RUN AND RUN...
...BUT WE'RE NOT PUTTING ANY DISTANCE BETWEEN OURSELVES AND THE ENEMY!
IT'S AS IF...
...I HAVE A SWORD AT MY THROAT!
HUFF
HUFF
HUFF
FWA
AH!
TMP
HANA-TARÔ?!
WHAT'RE YOU DOING?!
TMP TMP
SHAKE
SHAKE
I-I'M SORRY...
MY STRENGTH...

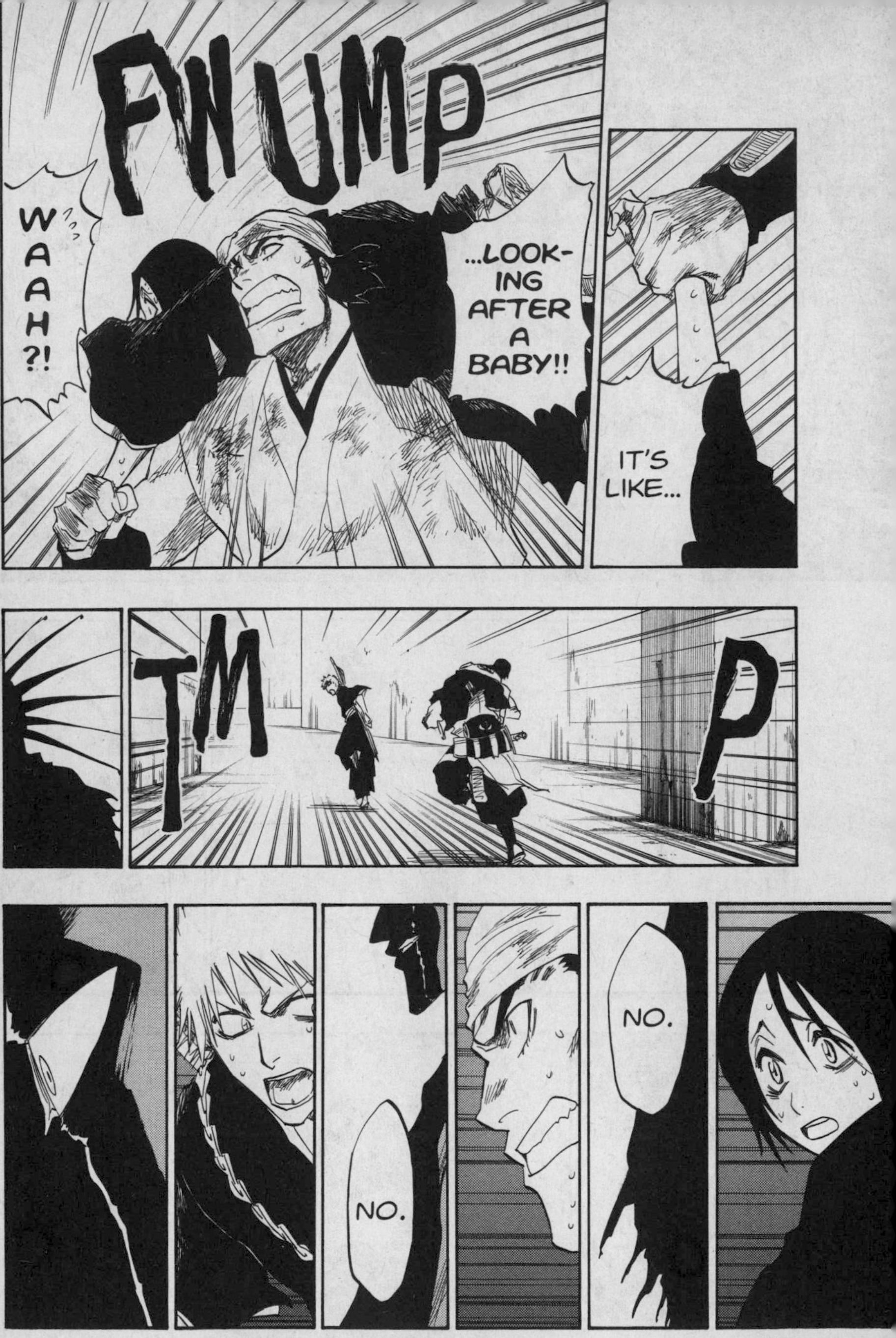
IT'S LIKE...
FWUMP
...LOOKING AFTER A BABY!!
WAAAH?!
TMP
NO.
NO.

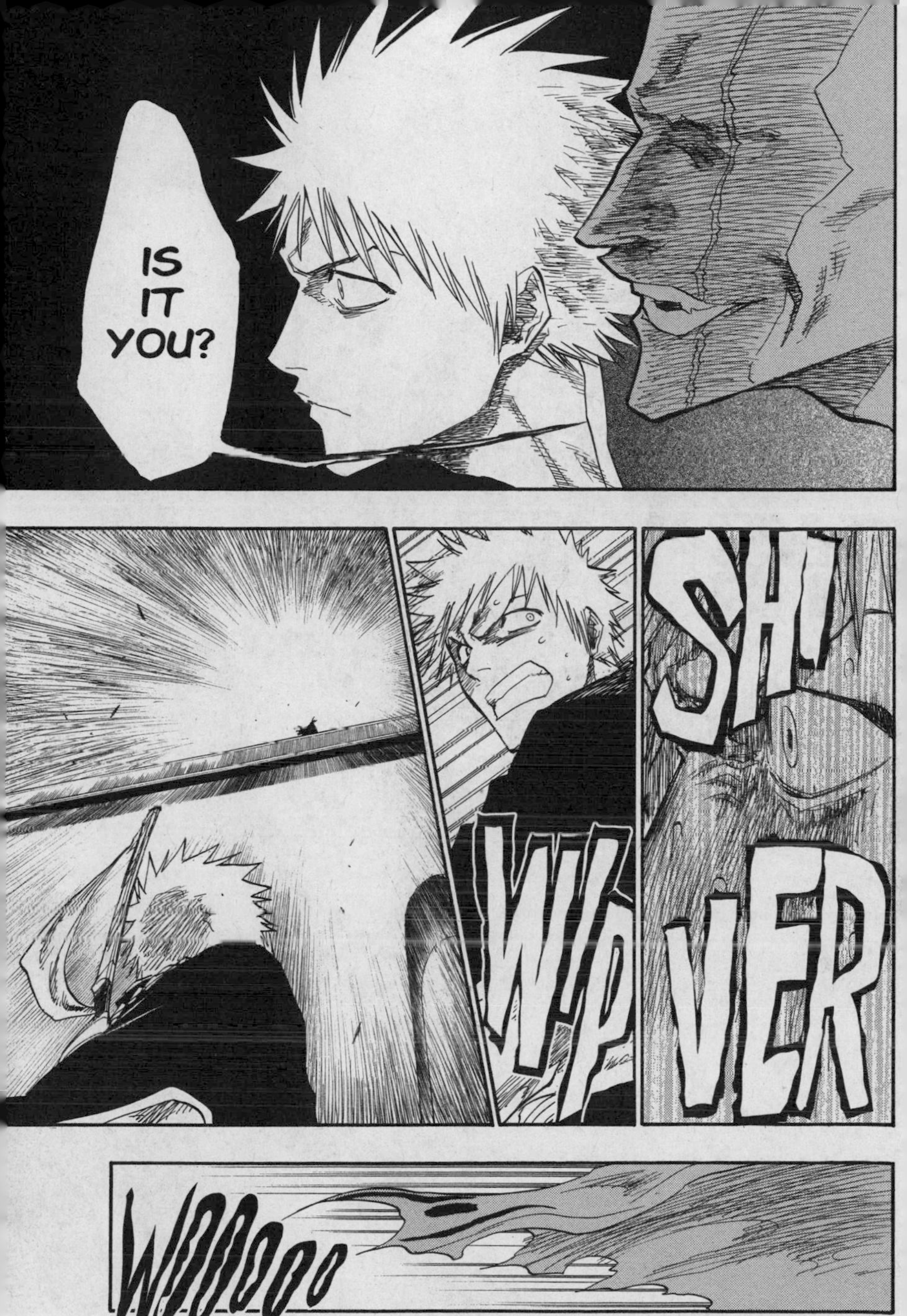

IS IT YOU?
SHIVER
WHIP
WOOOOOO

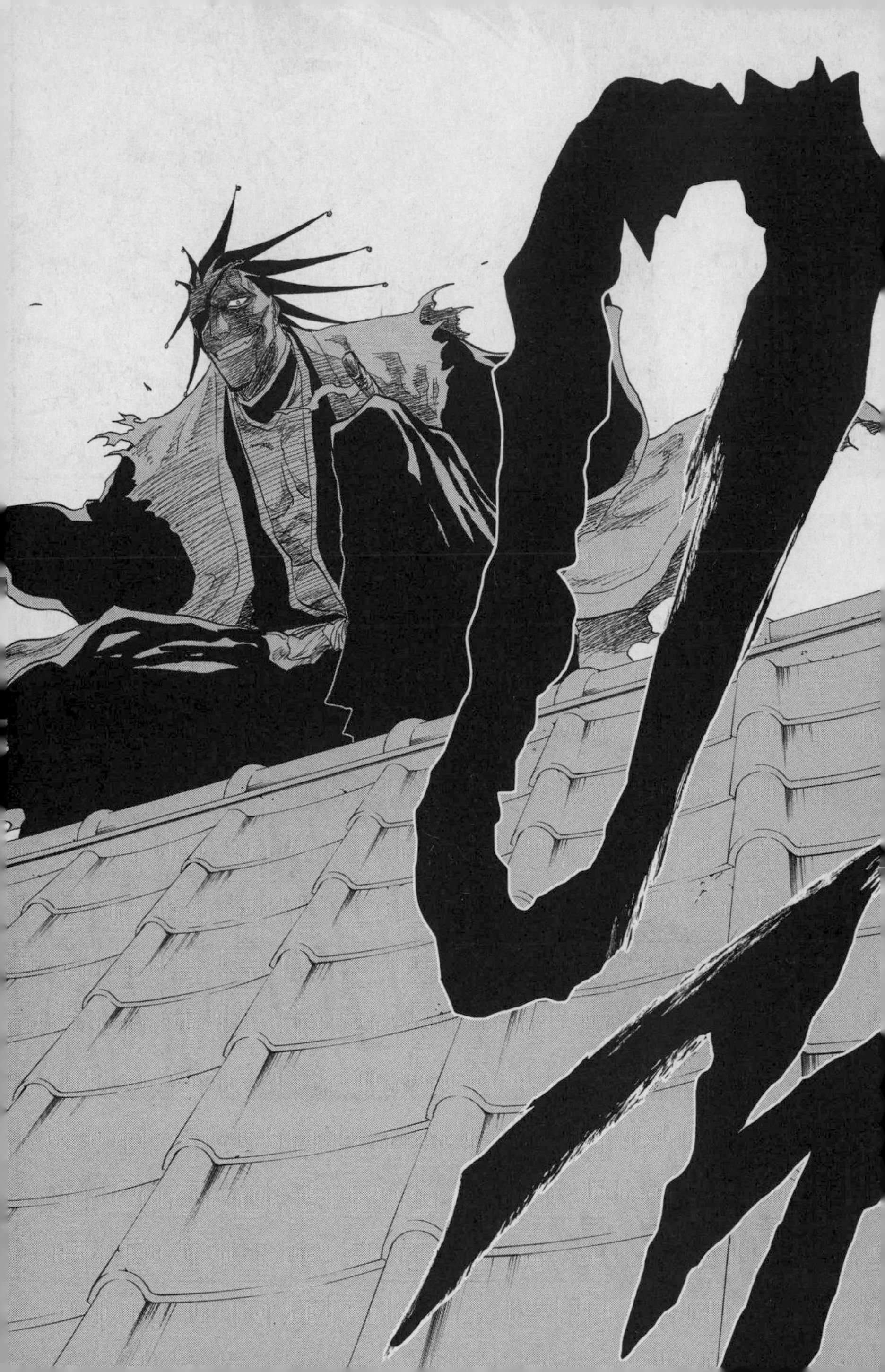

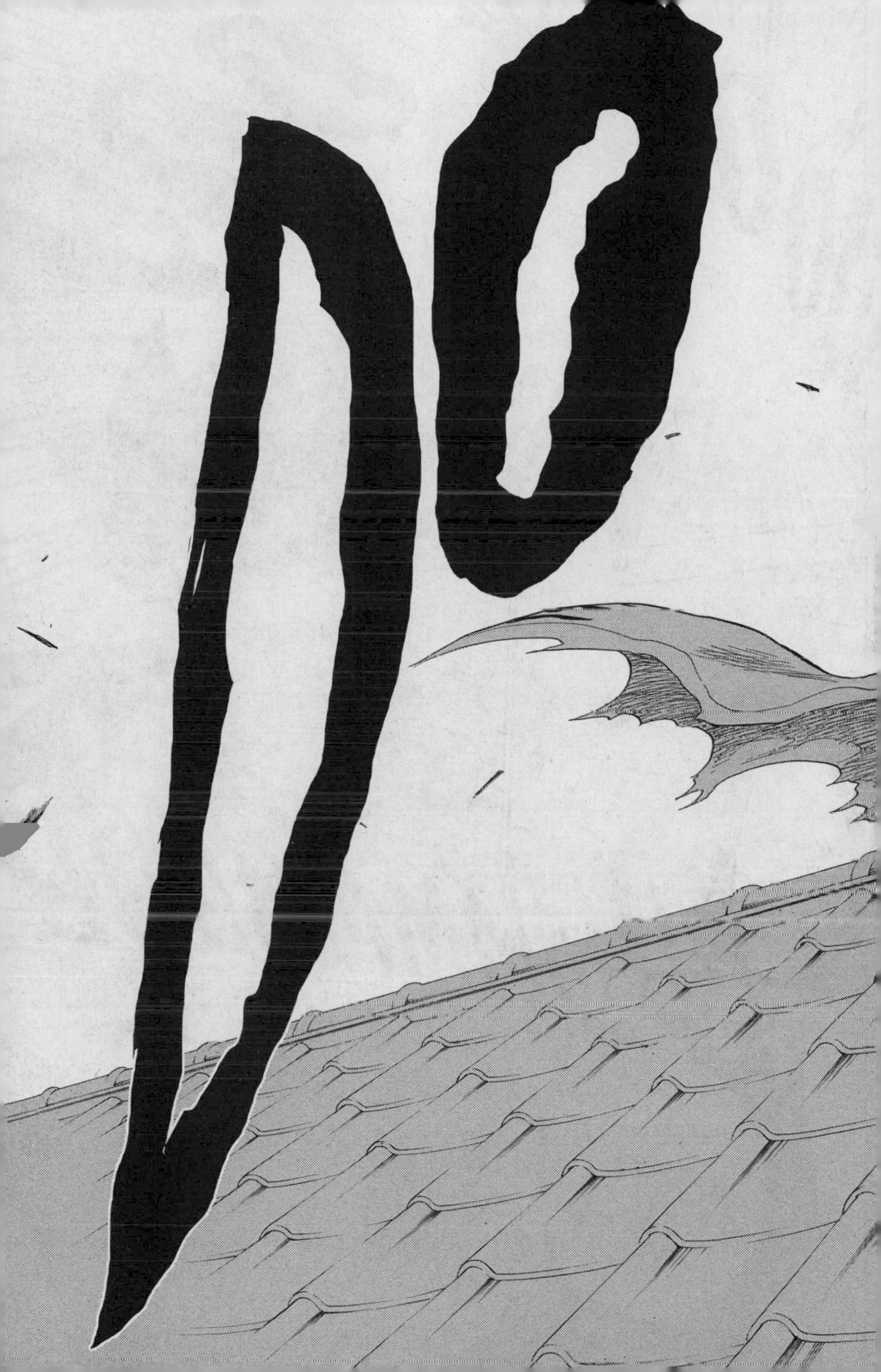

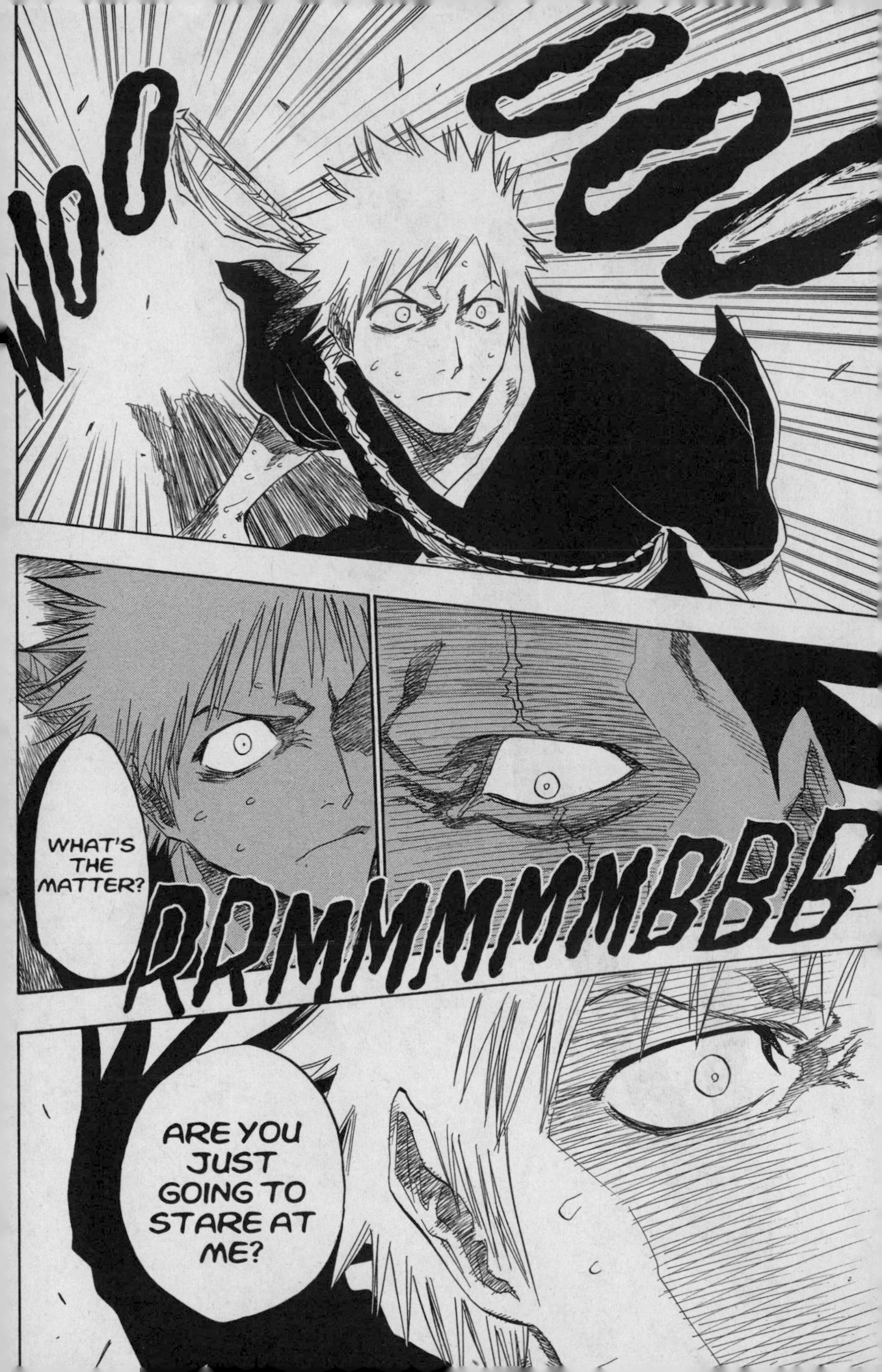
WOOOOOOO
RRMMMMMMBBB
WHAT'S THE MATTER?
ARE YOU JUST GOING TO STARE AT ME?

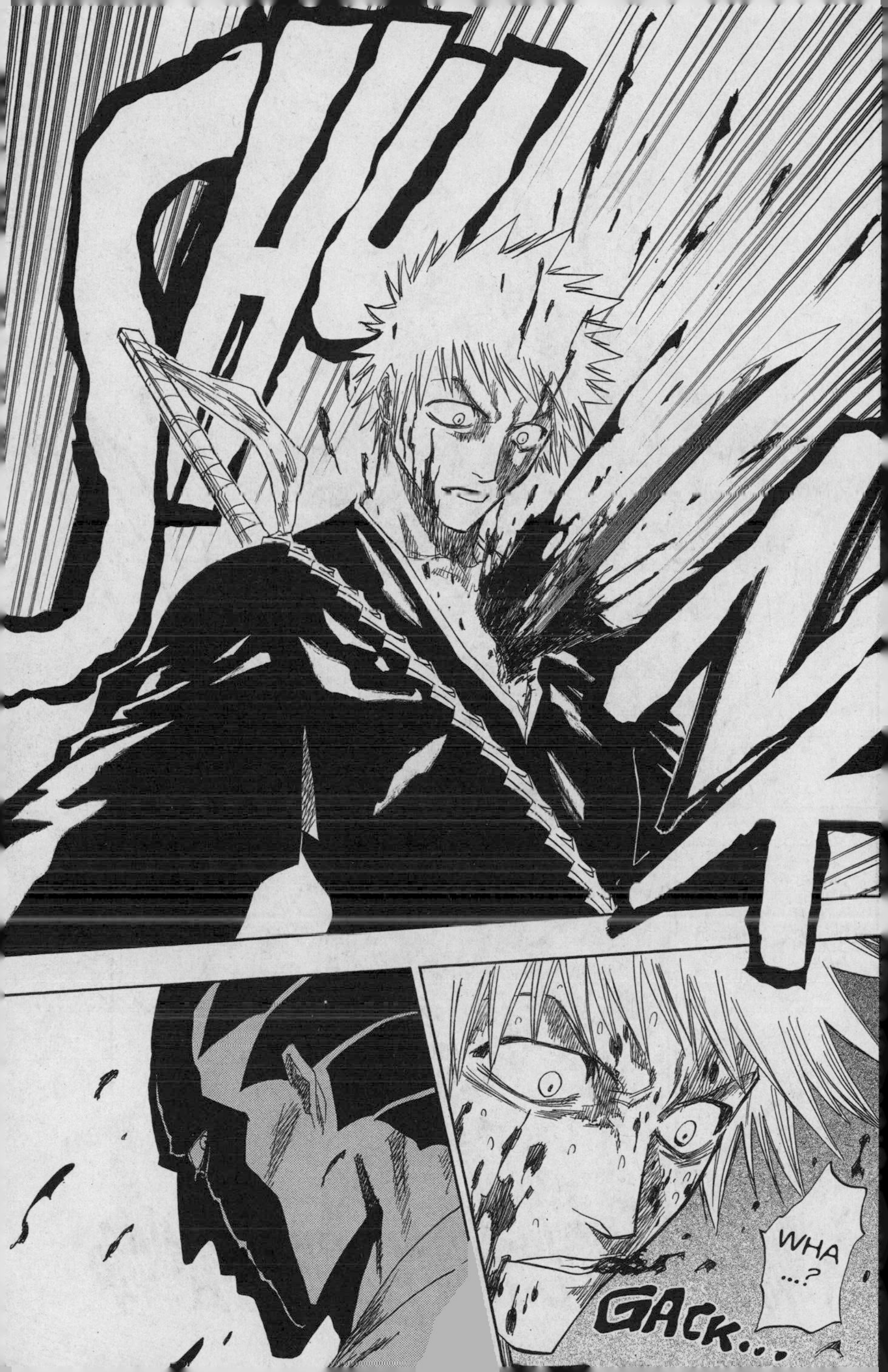
WHA ...?
GACK...

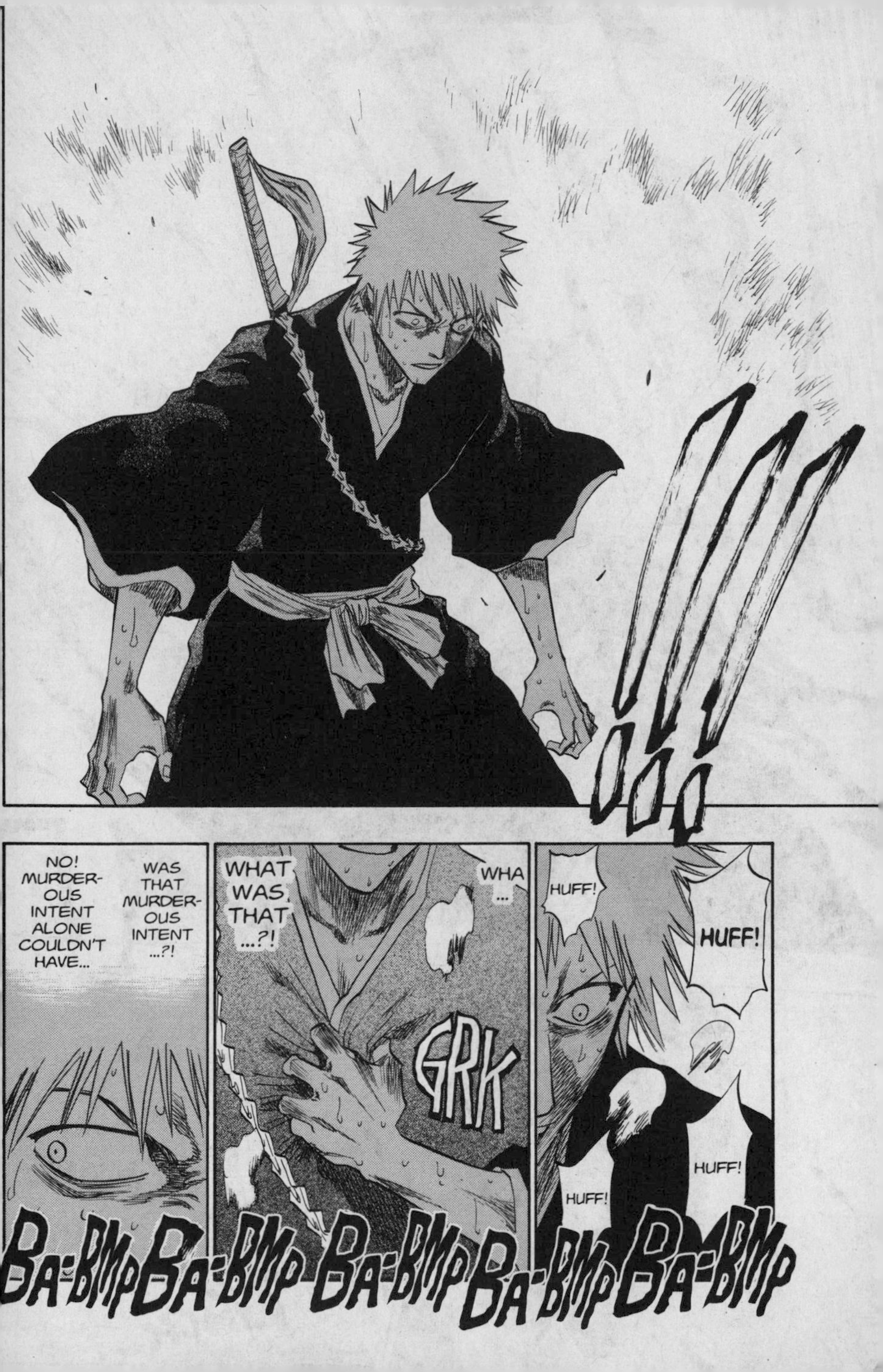
HUFF!
HUFF!
HUFF!
HUFF!
WHA ...
WHAT WAS THAT ...?!
GRK
WAS THAT MURDER-OUS INTENT ...?!
NO! MURDER-OUS INTENT ALONE COULDN'T HAVE...
BA-BMP BA-BMP BA-BMP BA-BMP BA-BMP

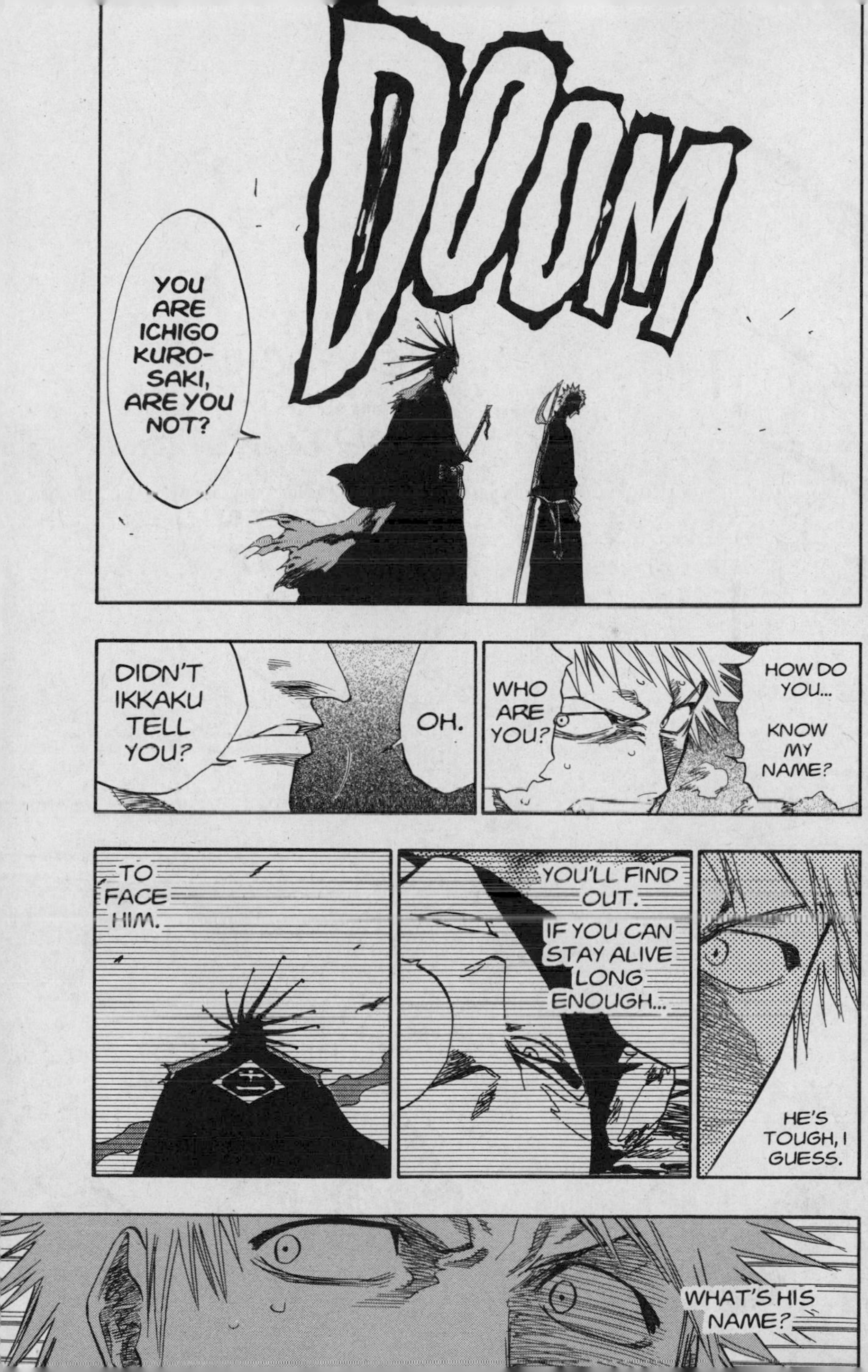
DOOM
YOU ARE ICHIGO KUROSAKI, ARE YOU NOT?
HOW DO YOU... KNOW MY NAME?
WHO ARE YOU?
OH.
DIDN'T IKKAKU TELL YOU?
HE'S TOUGH, I GUESS.
YOU'LL FIND OUT.
IF YOU CAN STAY ALIVE LONG ENOUGH...
TO FACE HIM.
WHAT'S HIS NAME?

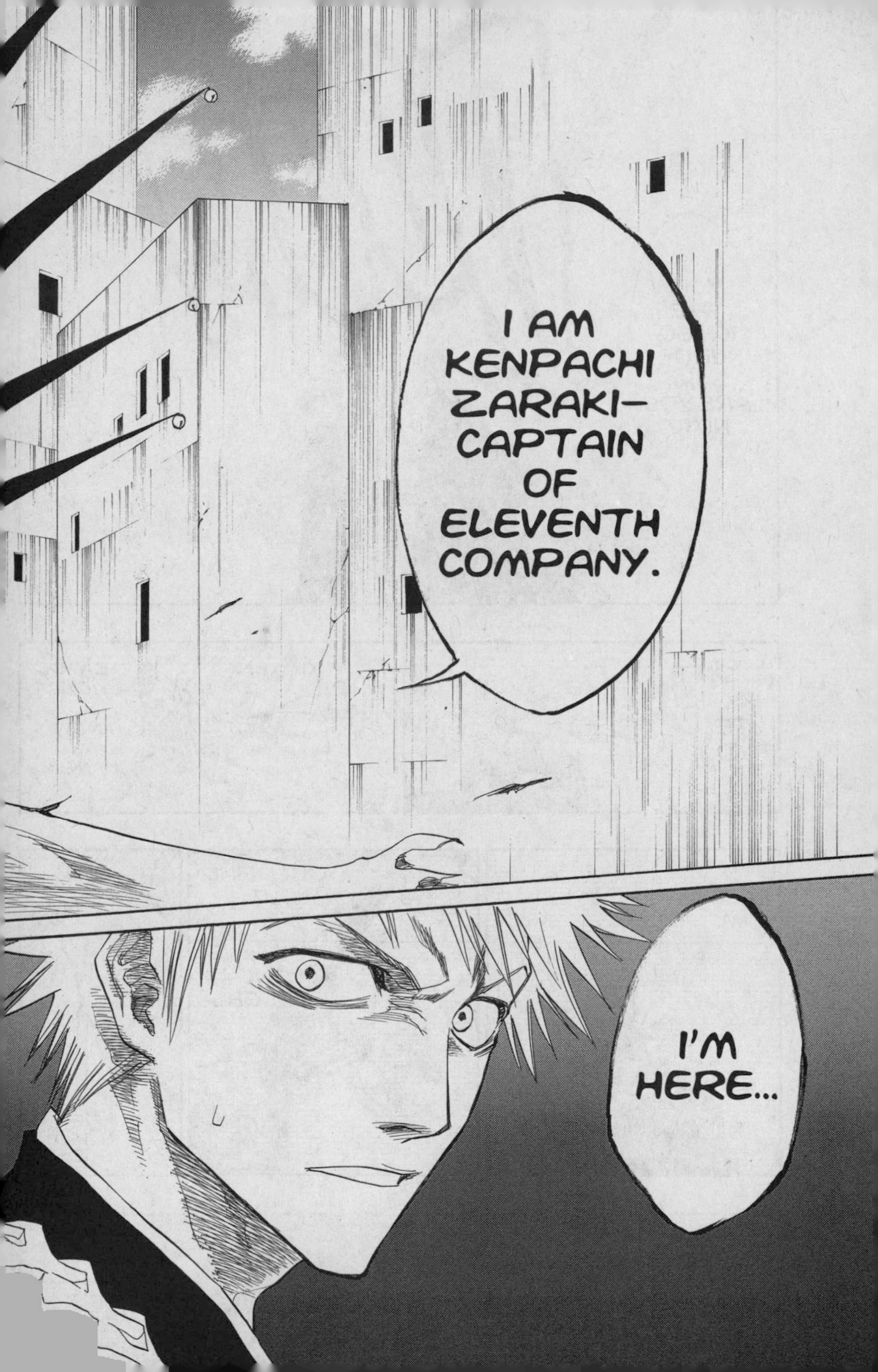
I AM KENPACHI ZARAKI–CAPTAIN OF ELEVENTH COMPANY.
I'M HERE...

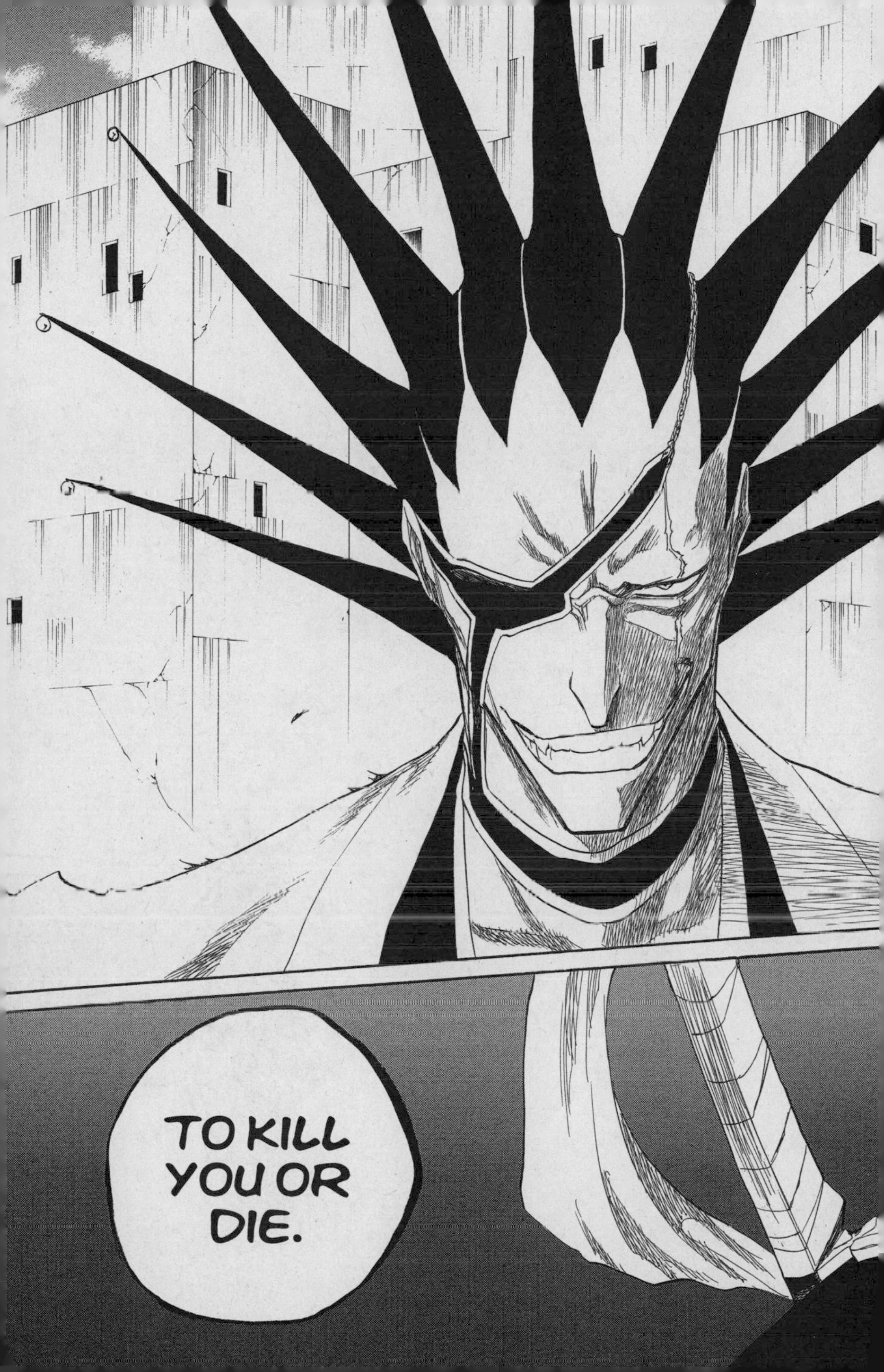
TO KILL YOU OR DIE.

SPECIAL
BOX SEAT

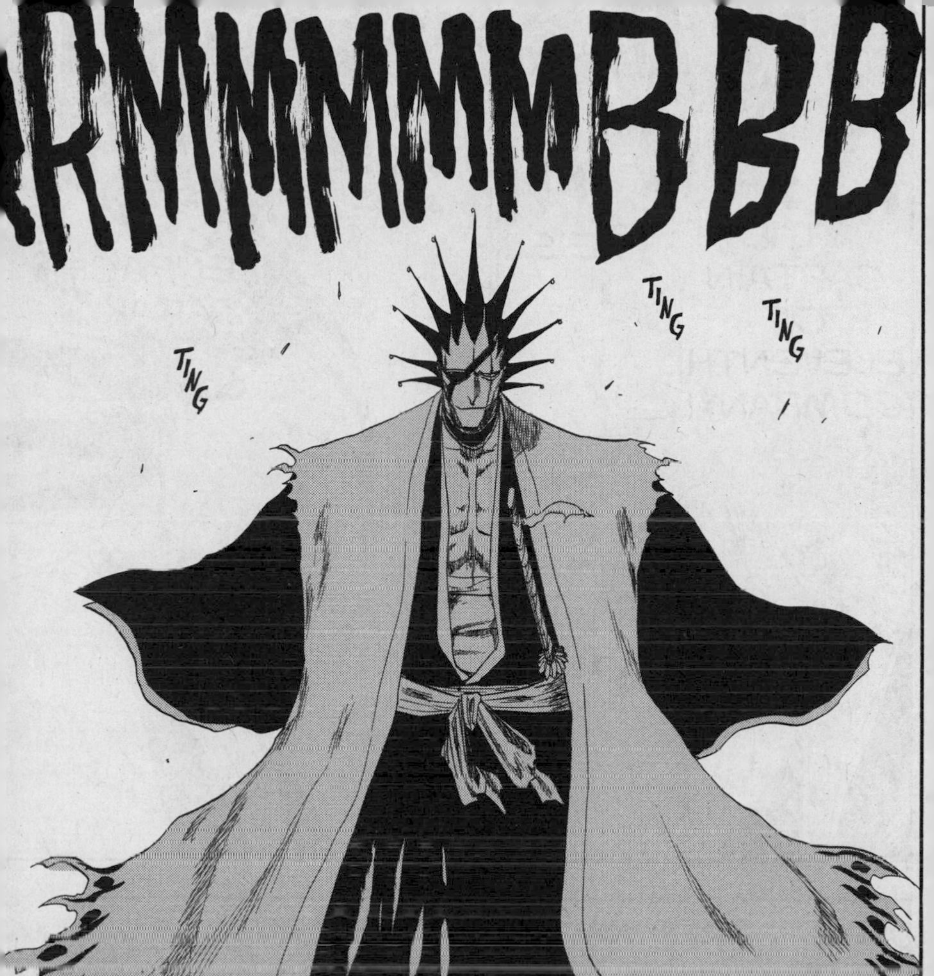
RMMMMMBBB
TING
TING
TING

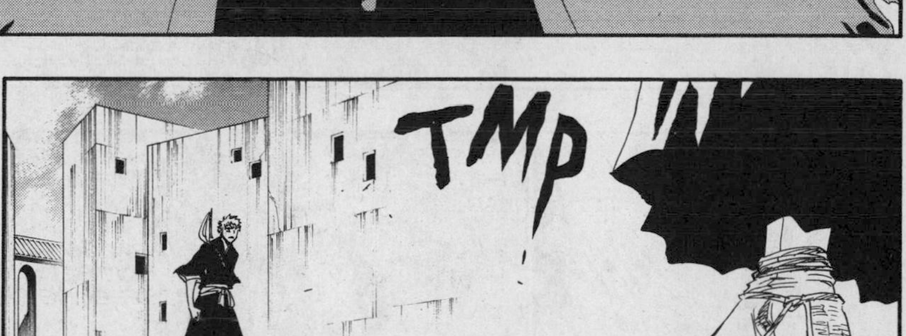
TMP

104. The Undead

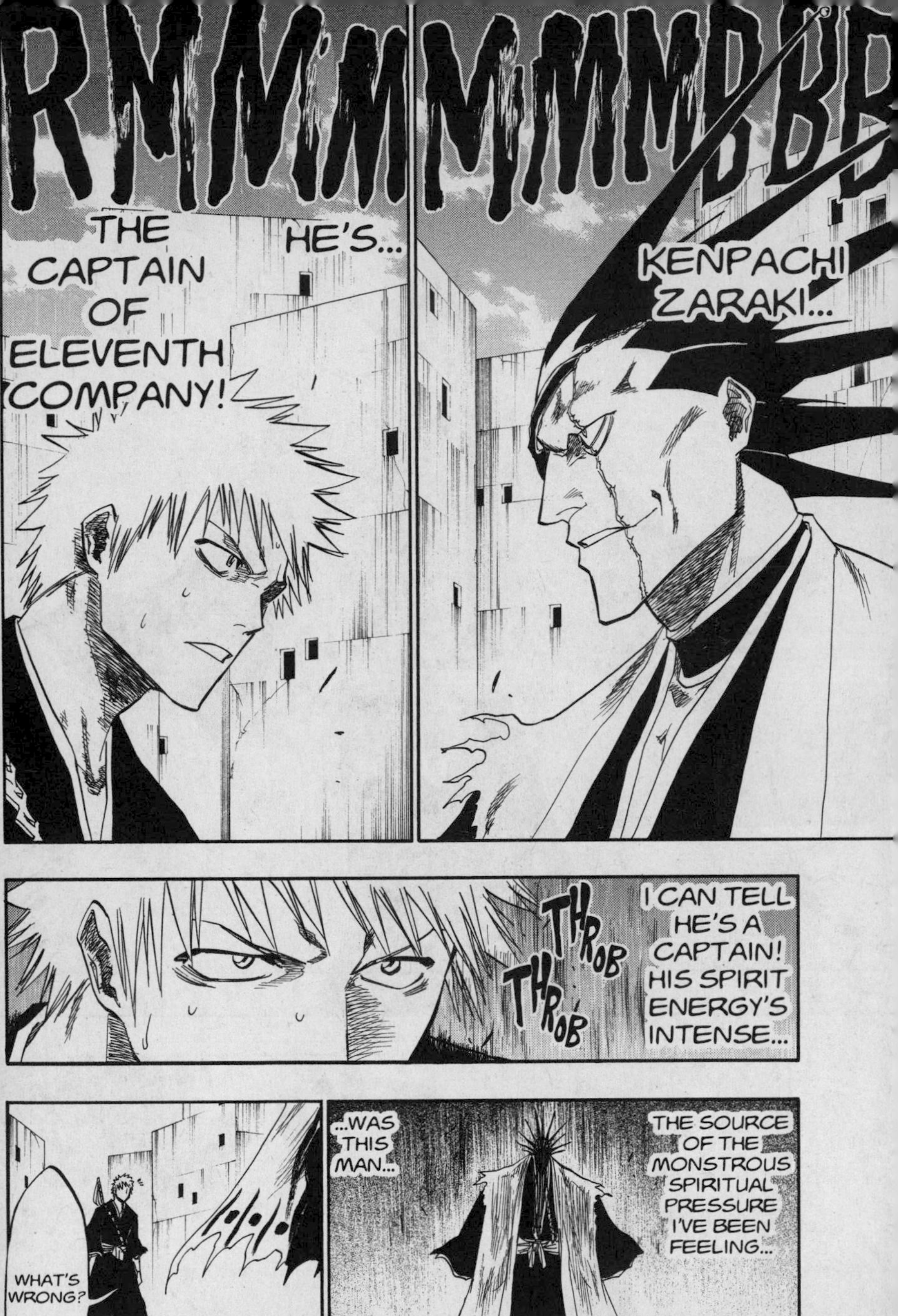
RMMMMMMBB
KENPACHI ZARAKI...
HE'S...
THE CAPTAIN OF ELEVENTH COMPANY!
I CAN TELL HE'S A CAPTAIN! HIS SPIRIT ENERGY'S INTENSE...
THROB
THROB
THE SOURCE OF THE MONSTROUS SPIRITUAL PRESSURE I'VE BEEN FEELING...
...WAS THIS MAN...
WHAT'S WRONG?

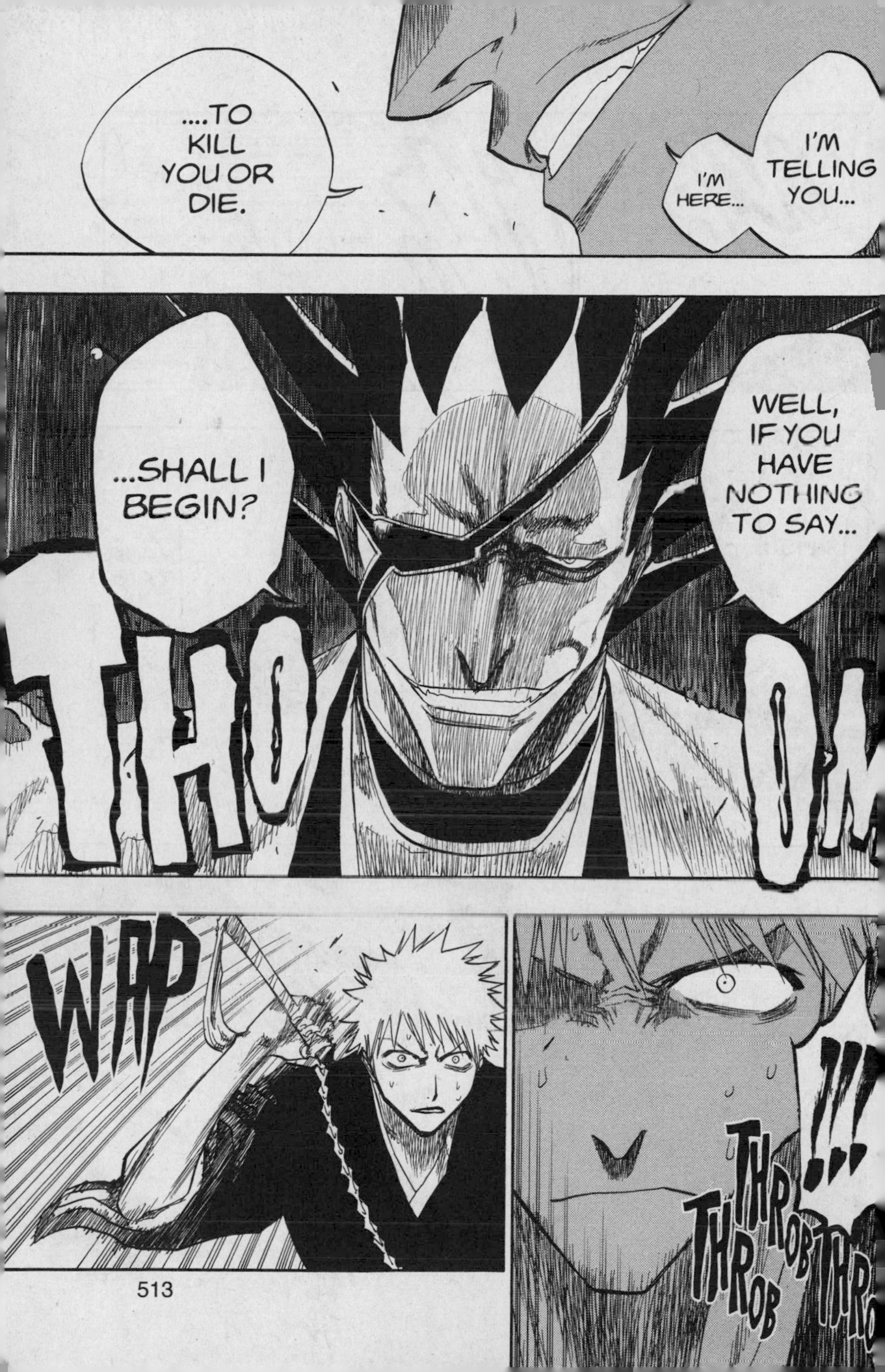
I'M TELLING YOU...
I'M HERE...
....TO KILL YOU OR DIE.
WELL, IF YOU HAVE NOTHING TO SAY...
...SHALL I BEGIN?
THOOM
!!
THROB THROB THRO
WAP

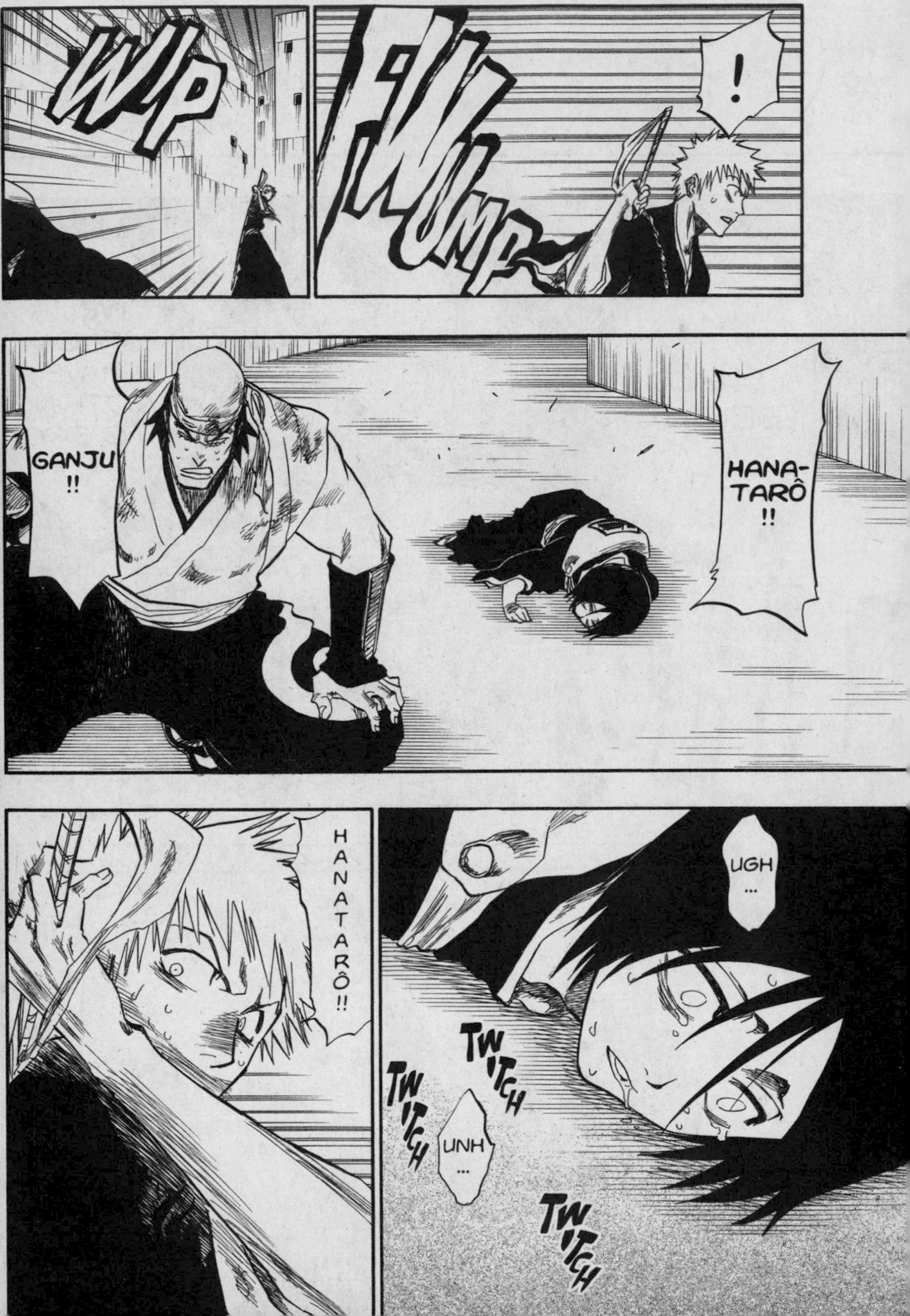
FWUMP
!
WIP
HANA-TARÔ!!
GANJU!!
UGH...
TWITCH
TWITCH
UNH...
TWITCH
HANATARÔ!!

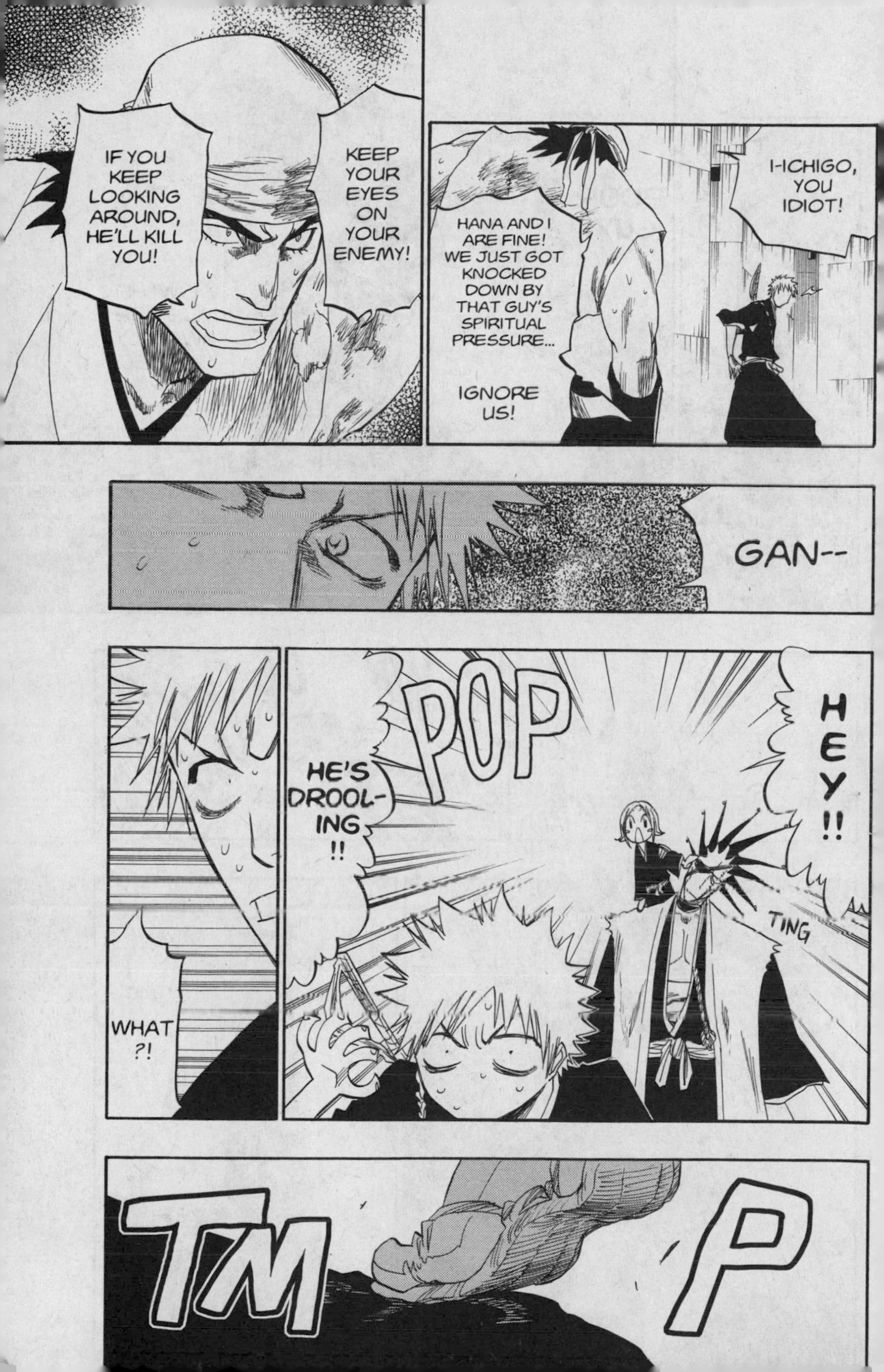
I-ICHIGO, YOU IDIOT!
HANA AND I ARE FINE! WE JUST GOT KNOCKED DOWN BY THAT GUY'S SPIRITUAL PRESSURE...
IGNORE US!
KEEP YOUR EYES ON YOUR ENEMY!
IF YOU KEEP LOOKING AROUND, HE'LL KILL YOU!
GAN--
HEY!!
TING
POP
HE'S DROOL-ING!!
WHAT?!
TM
P

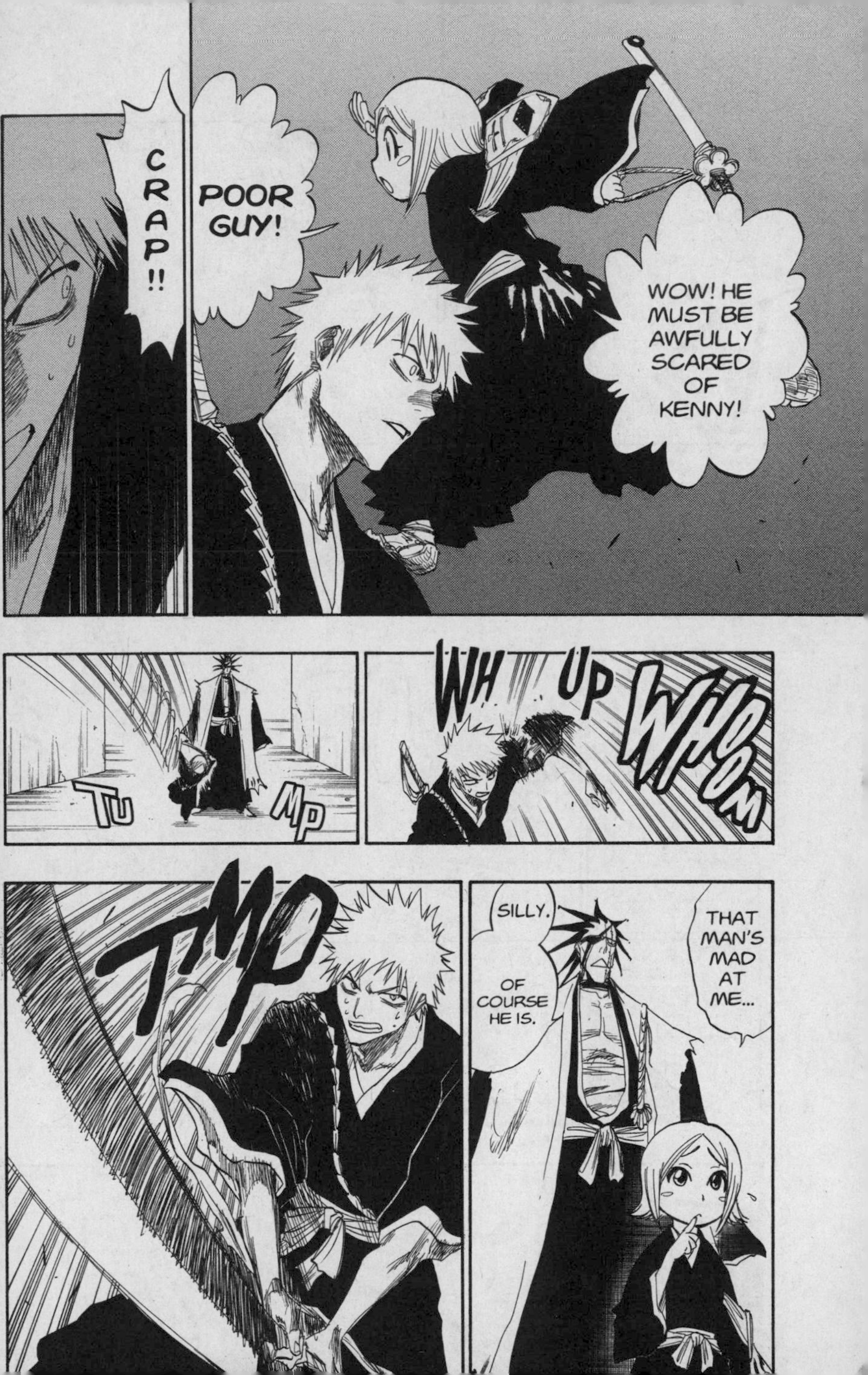
WOW! HE MUST BE AWFULLY SCARED OF KENNY!
POOR GUY!
CRAP!!
WH UP
WHOOM
TU MP
THAT MAN'S MAD AT ME...
SILLY.
OF COURSE HE IS.
TMP

READ THIS WAY

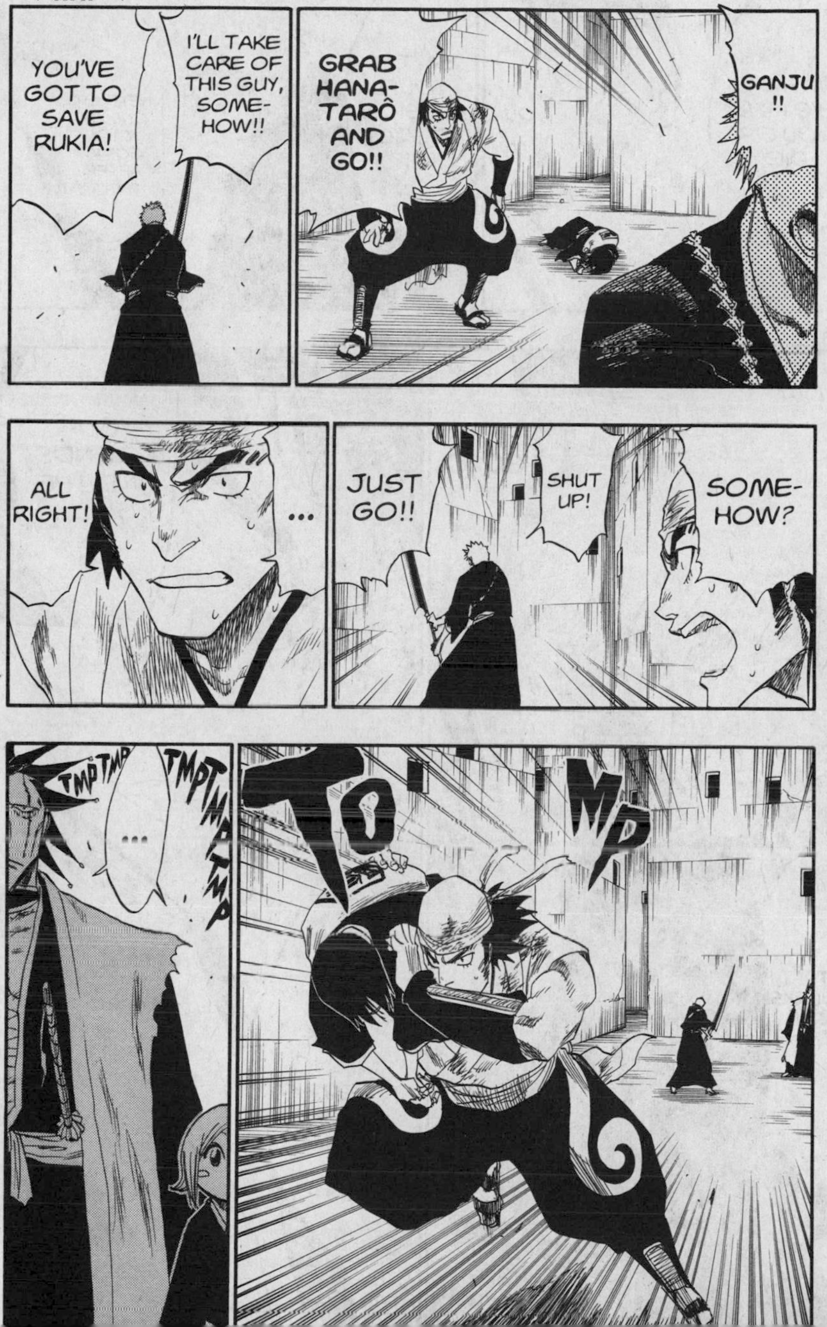
GANJU!!
GRAB HANA-TARÔ AND GO!!
I'LL TAKE CARE OF THIS GUY, SOME-HOW!!
YOU'VE GOT TO SAVE RUKIA!
SOME-HOW?
SHUT UP!
JUST GO!!
...
ALL RIGHT!
TOMP
TMPTMPTMPTMP
...
TMPTMP

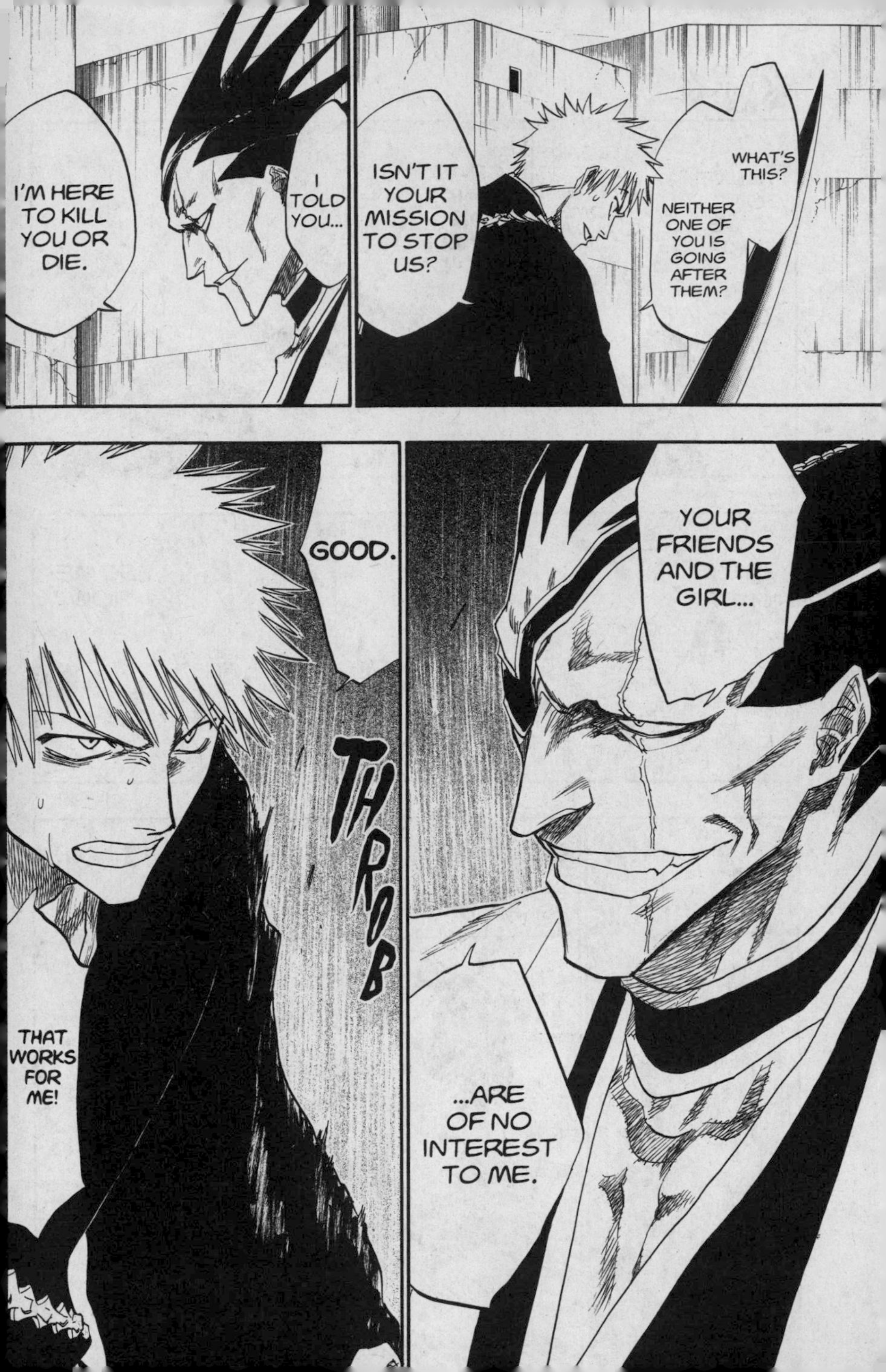
WHAT'S THIS?
NEITHER ONE OF YOU IS GOING AFTER THEM?
ISN'T IT YOUR MISSION TO STOP US?
I TOLD YOU...
I'M HERE TO KILL YOU OR DIE.
YOUR FRIENDS AND THE GIRL...
...ARE OF NO INTEREST TO ME.
GOOD.
THROB
THAT WORKS FOR ME!

104. The Undead

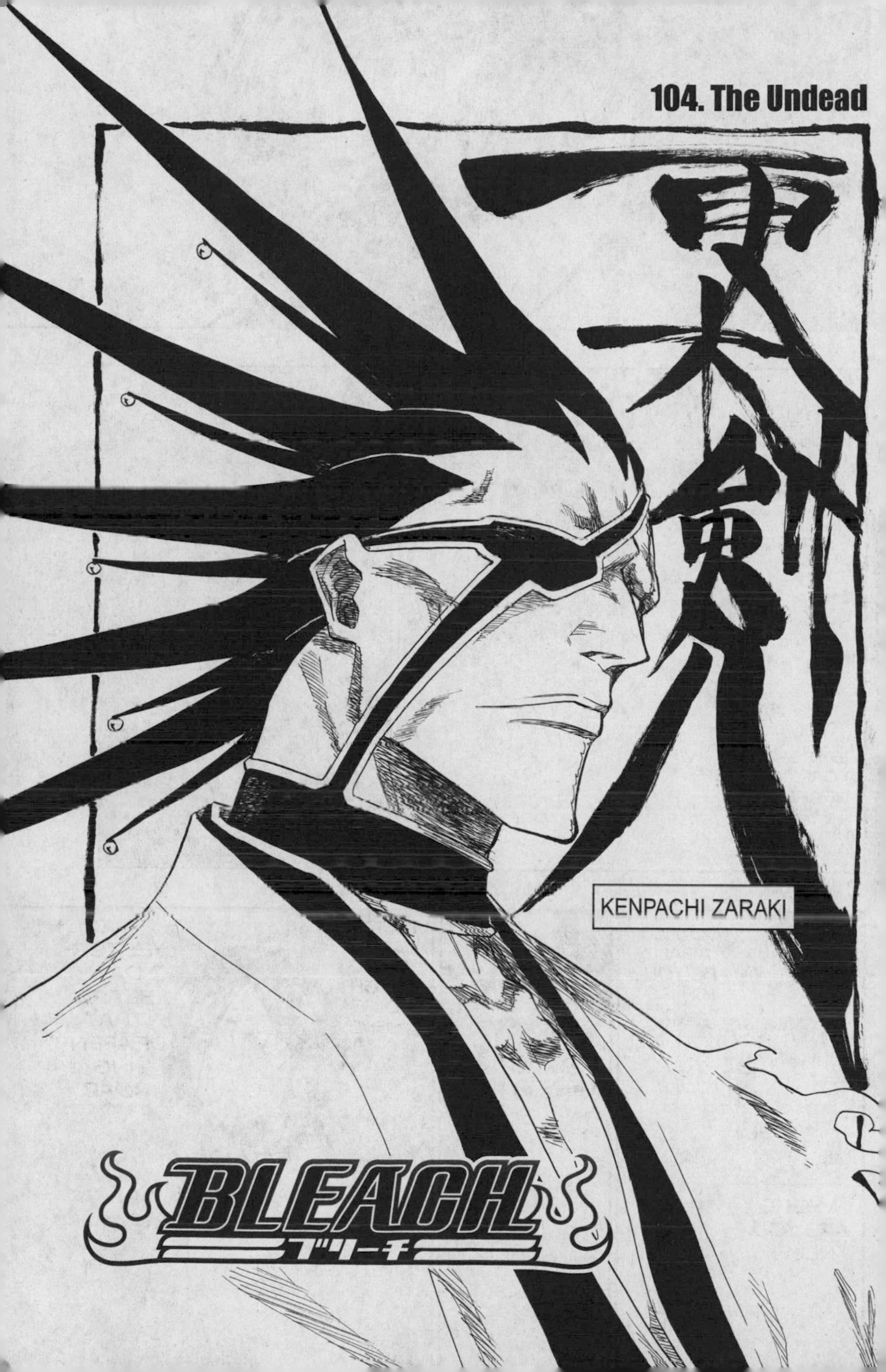
更木剣八
KENPACHI ZARAKI
BLEACH
ブリーチ

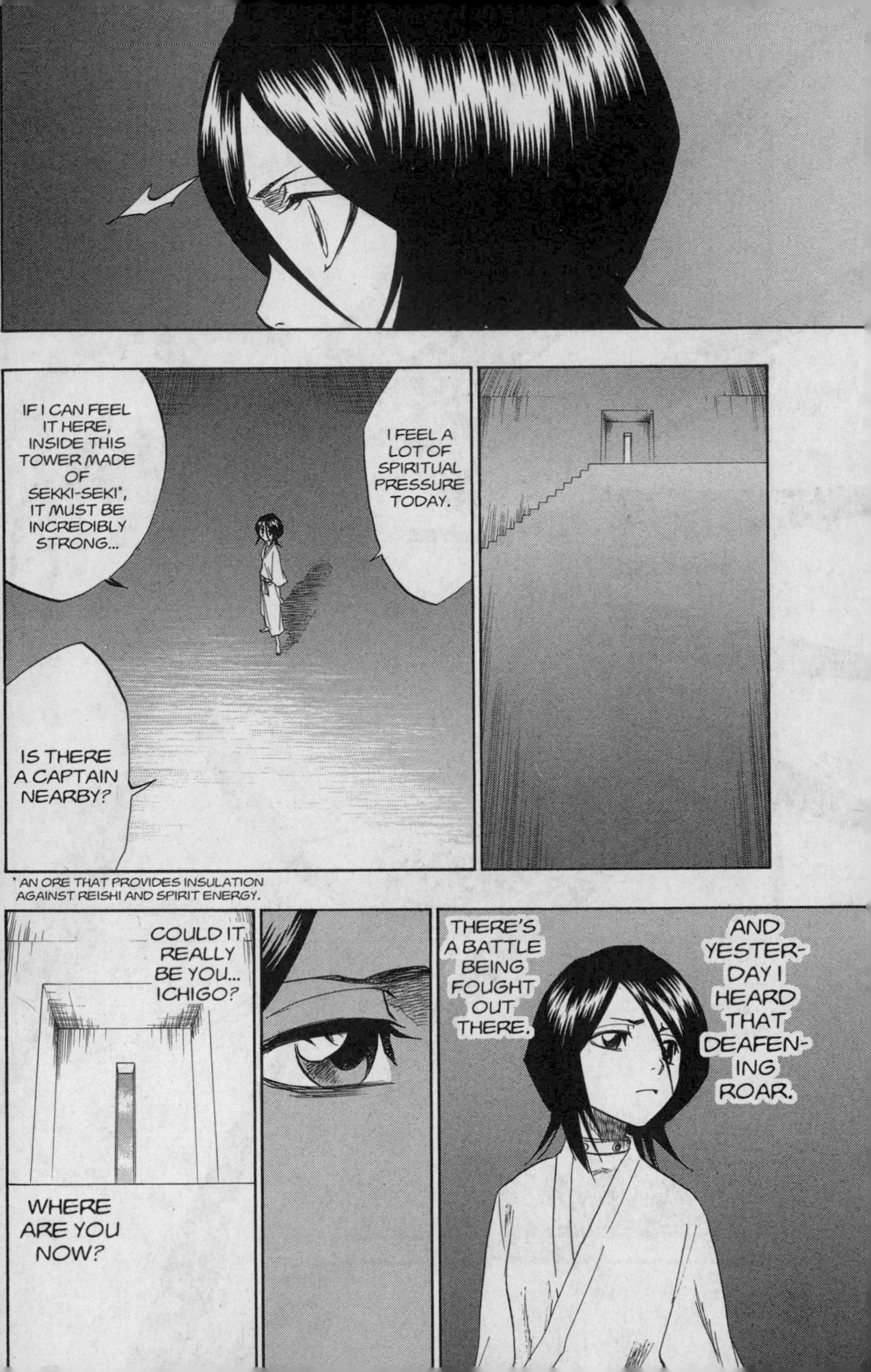
I FEEL A LOT OF SPIRITUAL PRESSURE TODAY.
IF I CAN FEEL IT HERE, INSIDE THIS TOWER MADE OF SEKKI-SEKI*, IT MUST BE INCREDIBLY STRONG...
IS THERE A CAPTAIN NEARBY?
AND YESTER-DAY I HEARD THAT DEAFEN-ING ROAR.
THERE'S A BATTLE BEING FOUGHT OUT THERE.
COULD IT REALLY BE YOU... ICHIGO?
WHERE ARE YOU NOW?

* AN ORE THAT PROVIDES INSULATION AGAINST REISHI AND SPIRIT ENERGY.

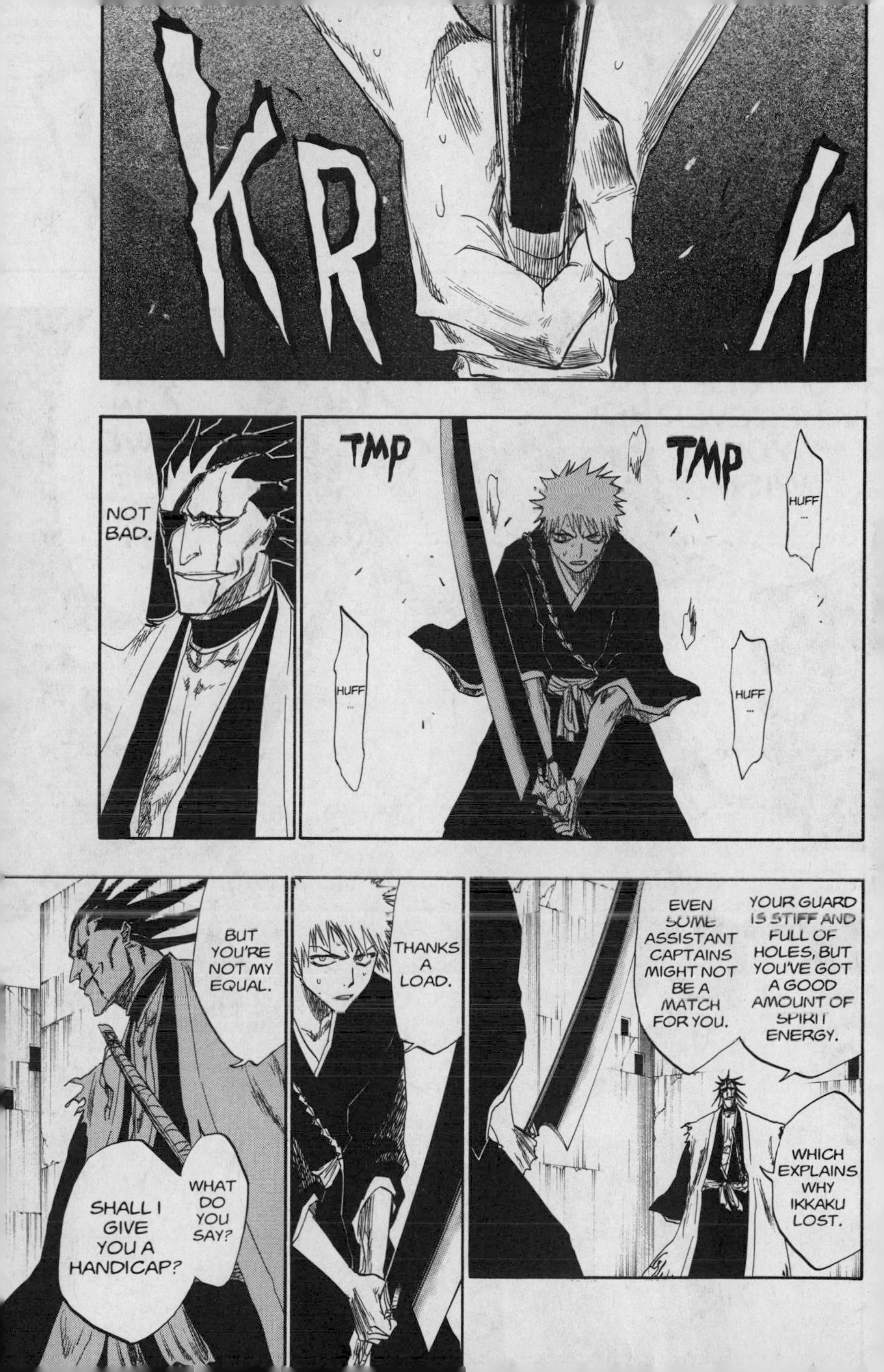
KRK
TMP TMP
HUFF...
HUFF...
HUFF...
NOT BAD.
YOUR GUARD IS STIFF AND FULL OF HOLES, BUT YOU'VE GOT A GOOD AMOUNT OF SPIRIT ENERGY.
EVEN SOME ASSISTANT CAPTAINS MIGHT NOT BE A MATCH FOR YOU.
WHICH EXPLAINS WHY IKKAKU LOST.
THANKS A LOAD.
BUT YOU'RE NOT MY EQUAL.
SHALL I GIVE YOU A HANDICAP?
WHAT DO YOU SAY?

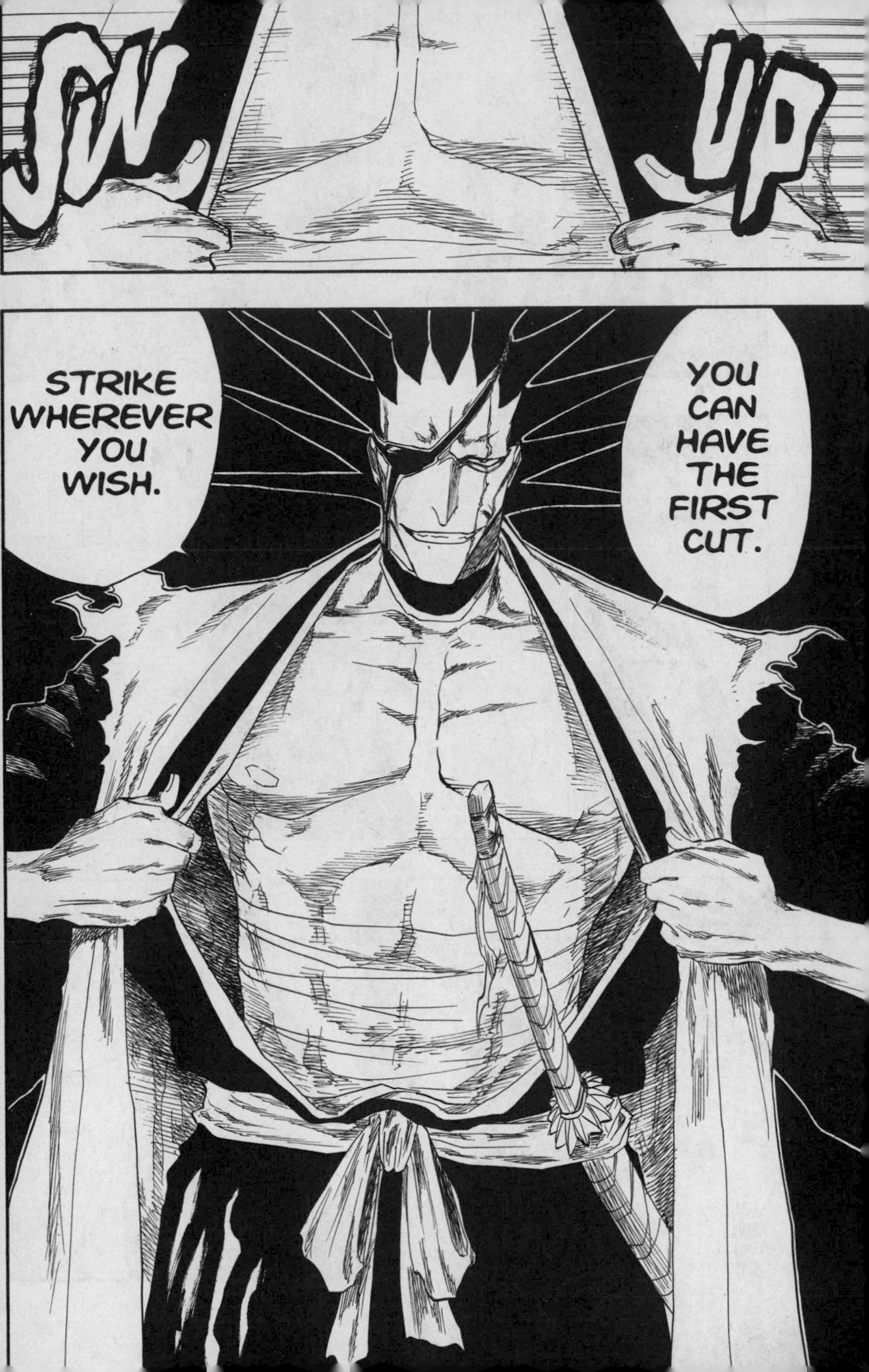
UP
YOU CAN HAVE THE FIRST CUT.
STRIKE WHEREVER YOU WISH.

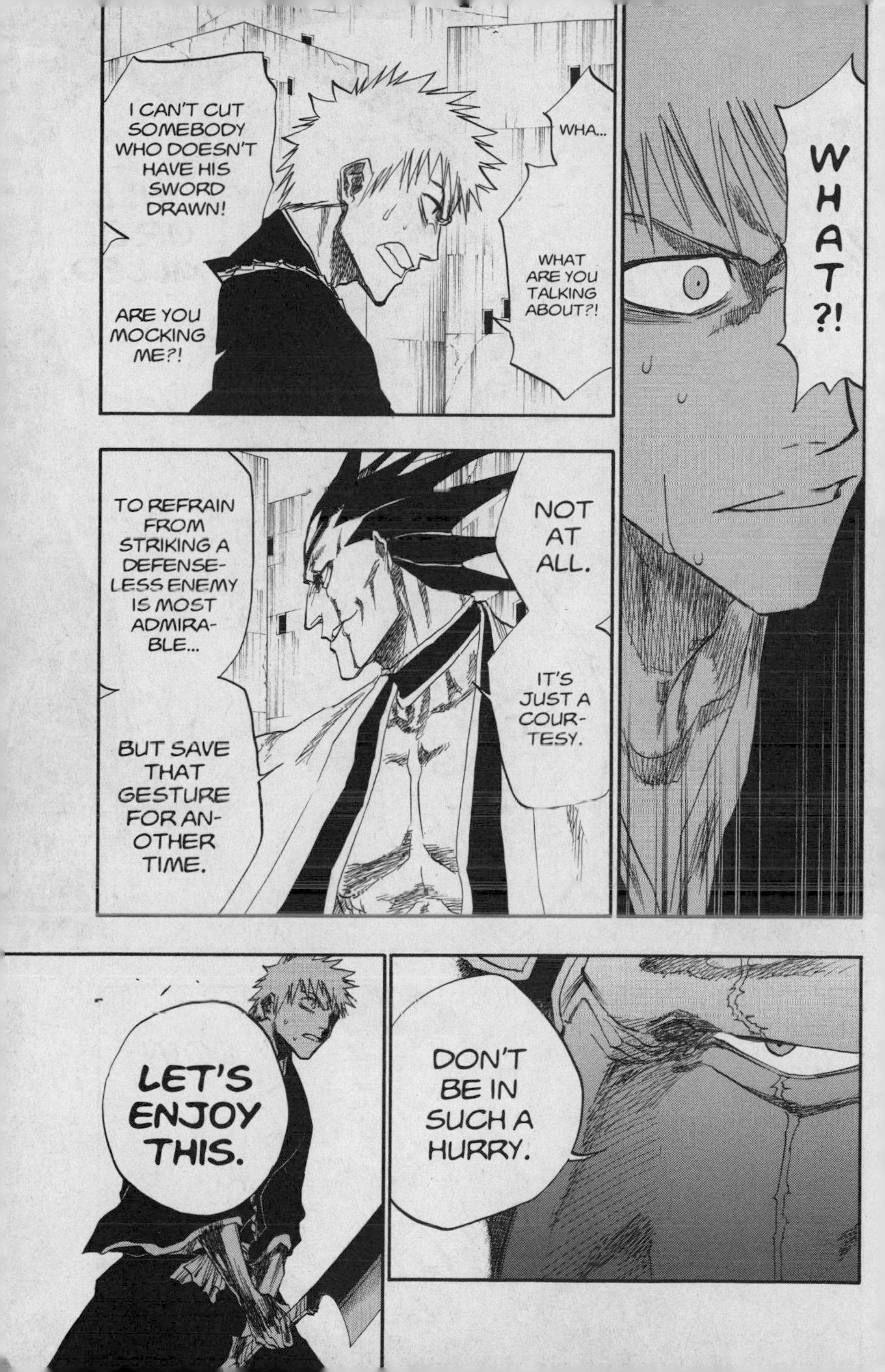
WHAT?!
WHA...
WHAT ARE YOU TALKING ABOUT?!
I CAN'T CUT SOMEBODY WHO DOESN'T HAVE HIS SWORD DRAWN!
ARE YOU MOCKING ME?!
NOT AT ALL.
IT'S JUST A COURTESY.
TO REFRAIN FROM STRIKING A DEFENSE-LESS ENEMY IS MOST ADMIRA-BLE...
BUT SAVE THAT GESTURE FOR AN-OTHER TIME.
DON'T BE IN SUCH A HURRY.
LET'S ENJOY THIS.

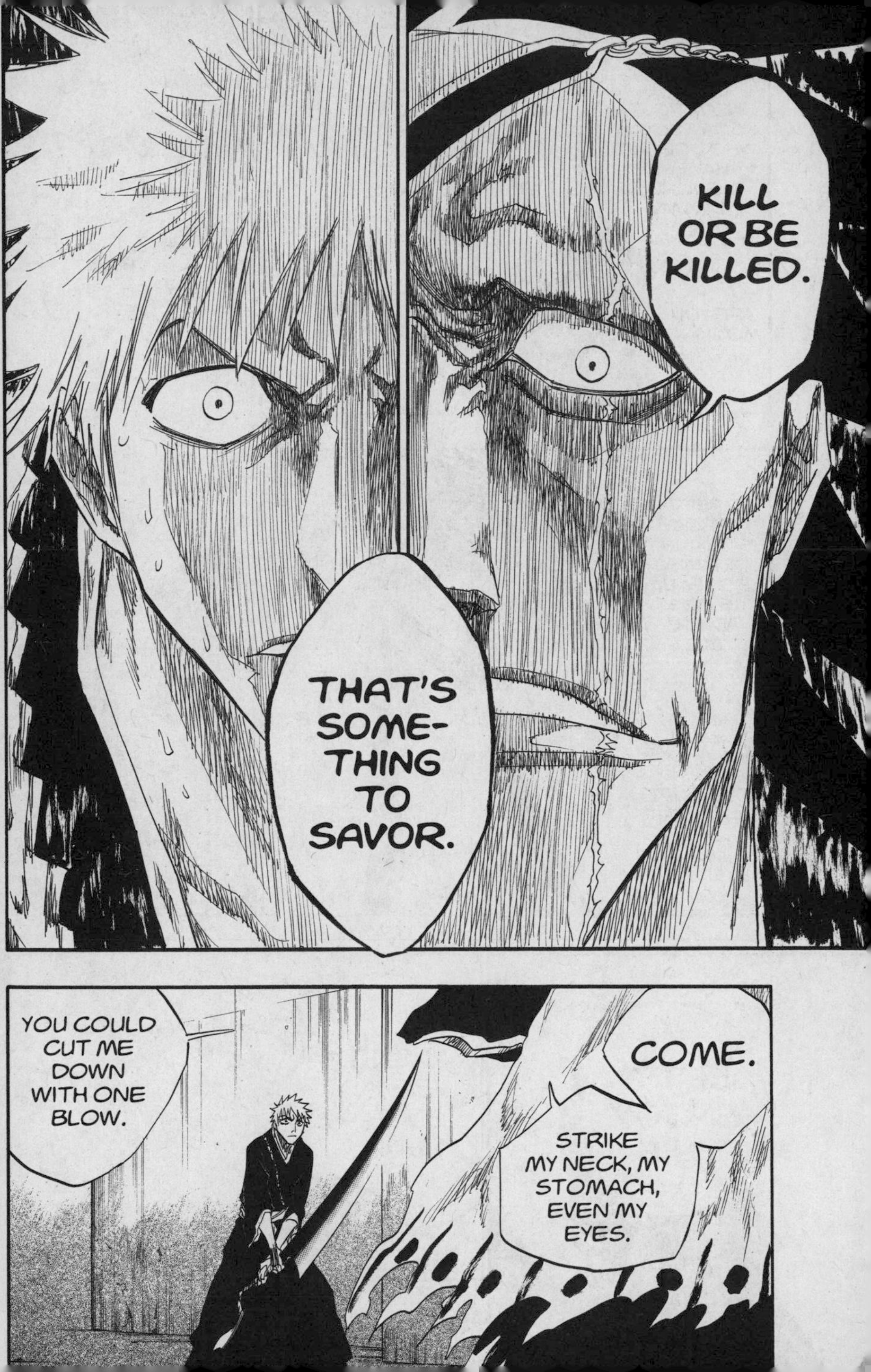
KILL OR BE KILLED.
THAT'S SOME-THING TO SAVOR.
COME.
STRIKE MY NECK, MY STOMACH, EVEN MY EYES.
YOU COULD CUT ME DOWN WITH ONE BLOW.

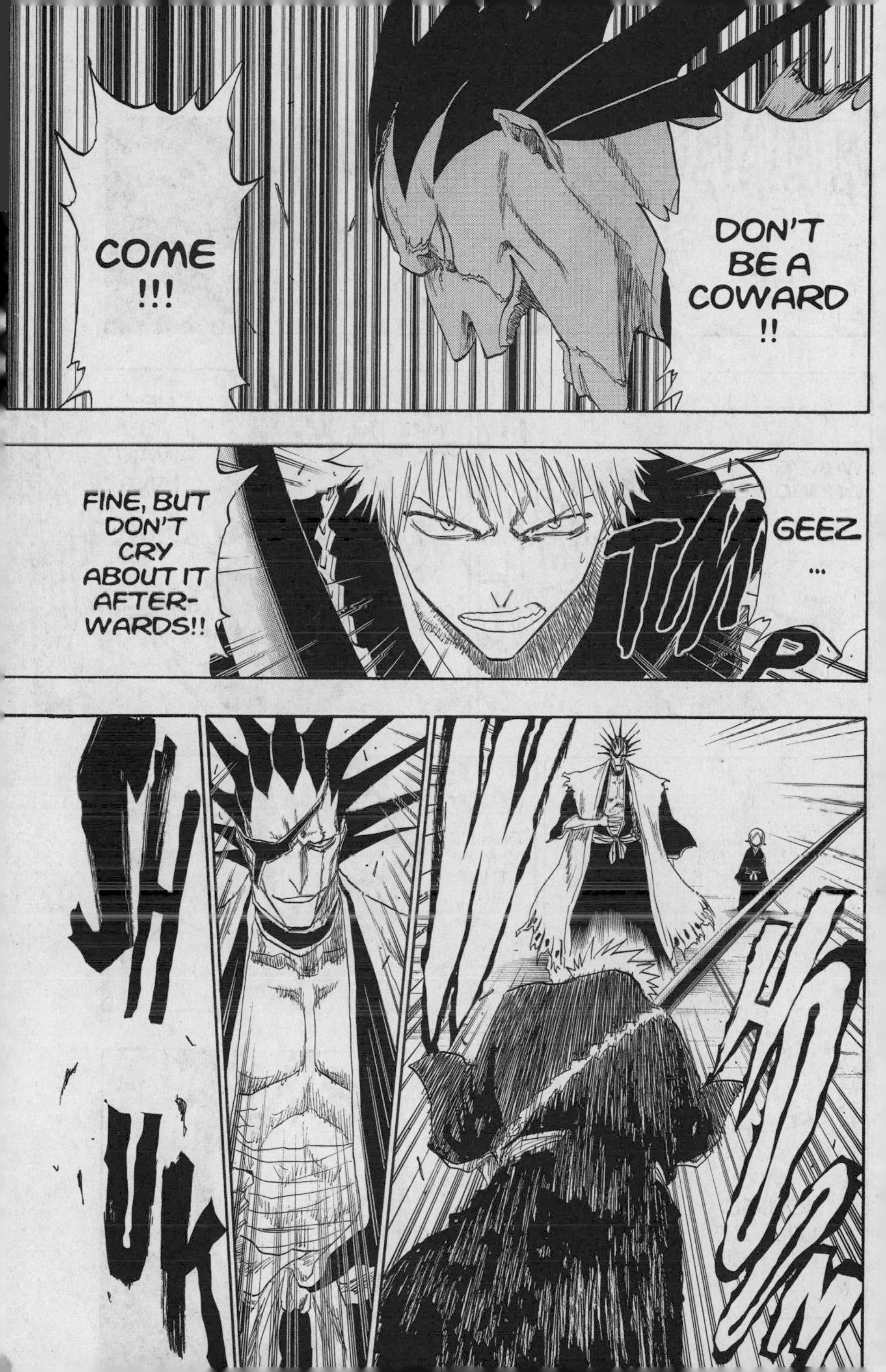
DON'T BE A COWARD !!
COME !!!
GEEZ ...
TMP
FINE, BUT DON'T CRY ABOUT IT AFTER-WARDS!!

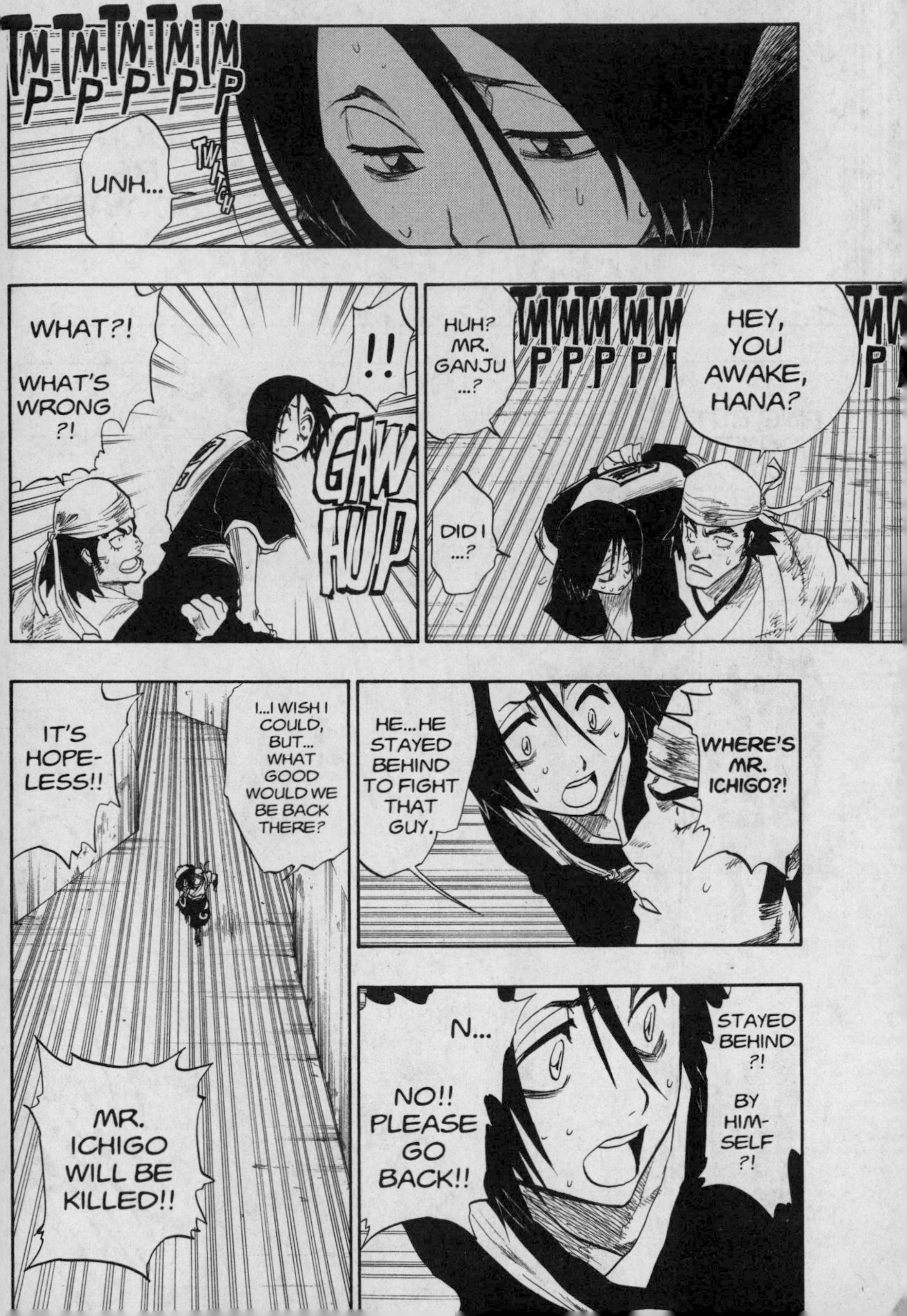
TMP TMP TMP TMP TMP
UNH...
TWITCH
HEY, YOU AWAKE, HANA?
TMP TMP TMP TMP TMP TMP
HUH? MR. GANJU ...?
DID I ...?
!!
GAWHUP
WHAT?!
WHAT'S WRONG ?!
WHERE'S MR. ICHIGO?!
HE...HE STAYED BEHIND TO FIGHT THAT GUY.
STAYED BEHIND ?!
BY HIM-SELF ?!
N...
NO!! PLEASE GO BACK!!
I...I WISH I COULD, BUT... WHAT GOOD WOULD WE BE BACK THERE?
IT'S HOPE-LESS!!
MR. ICHIGO WILL BE KILLED!!

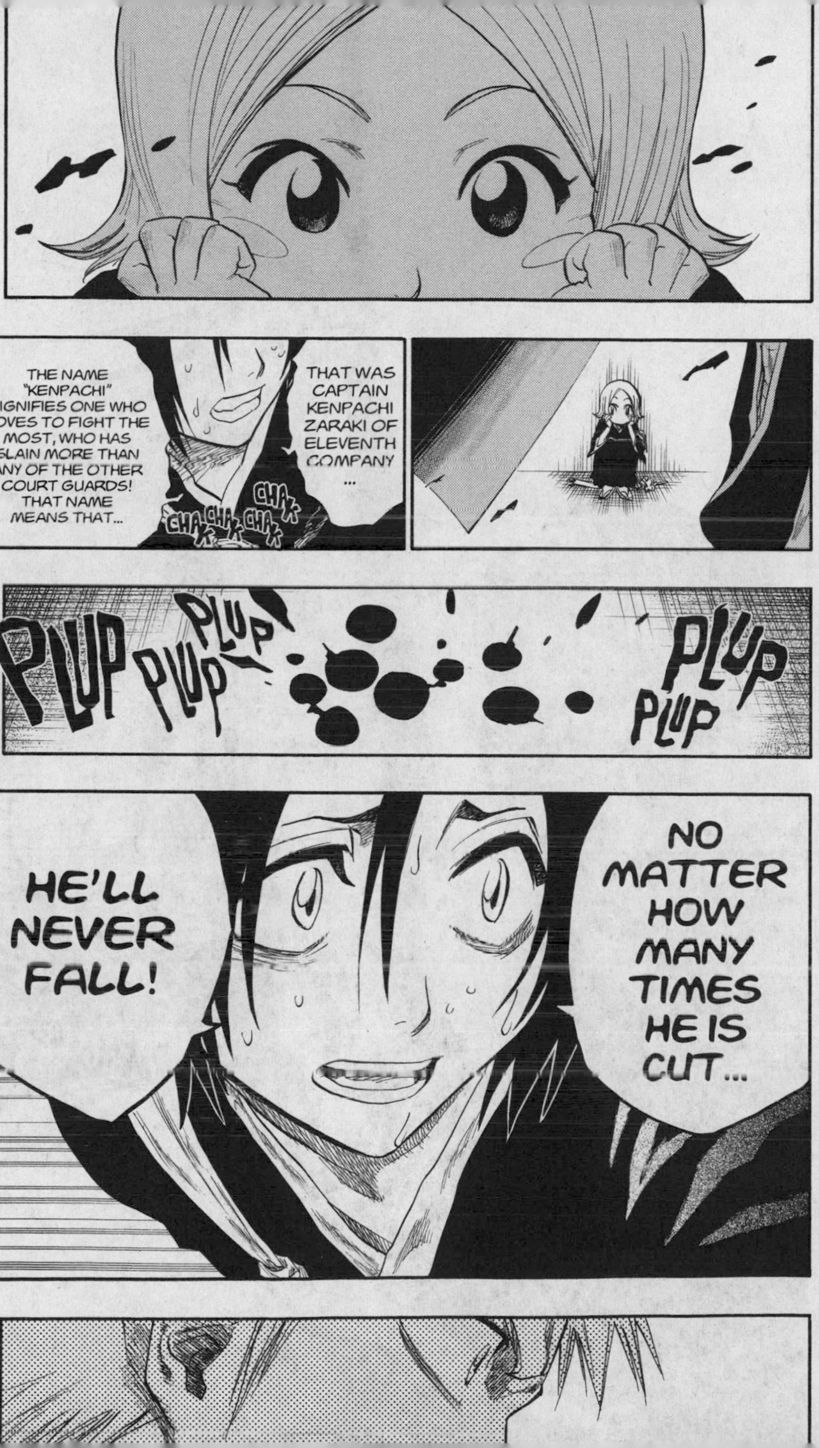
THAT WAS CAPTAIN KENPACHI ZARAKI OF ELEVENTH COMPANY ...
THE NAME "KENPACHI" SIGNIFIES ONE WHO LOVES TO FIGHT THE MOST, WHO HAS SLAIN MORE THAN ANY OF THE OTHER COURT GUARDS! THAT NAME MEANS THAT...
CHAK CHAK CHAK CHAK
PLUP PLUP
PLUP PLUP PLUP
NO MATTER HOW MANY TIMES HE IS CUT...
HE'LL NEVER FALL!

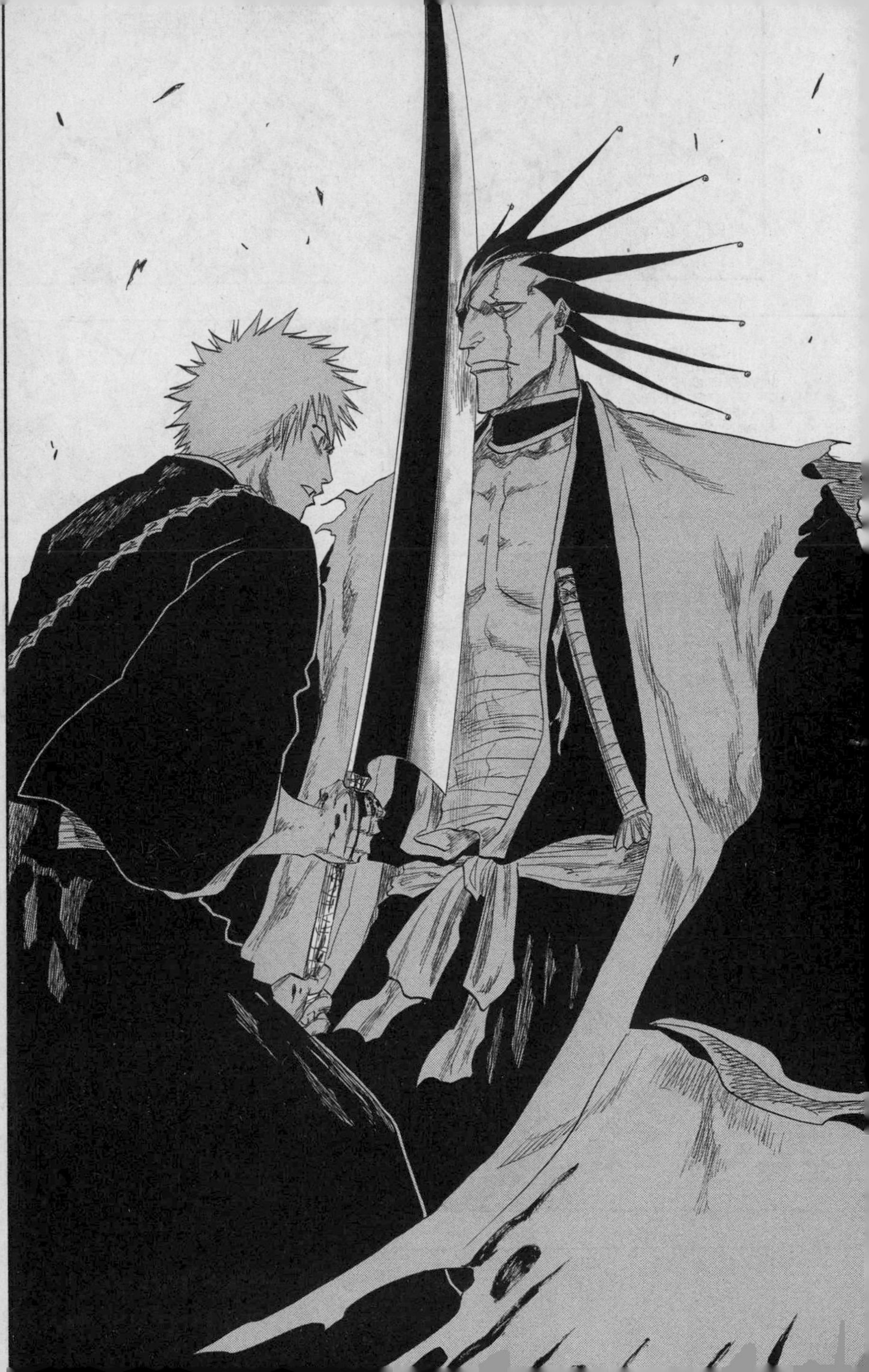

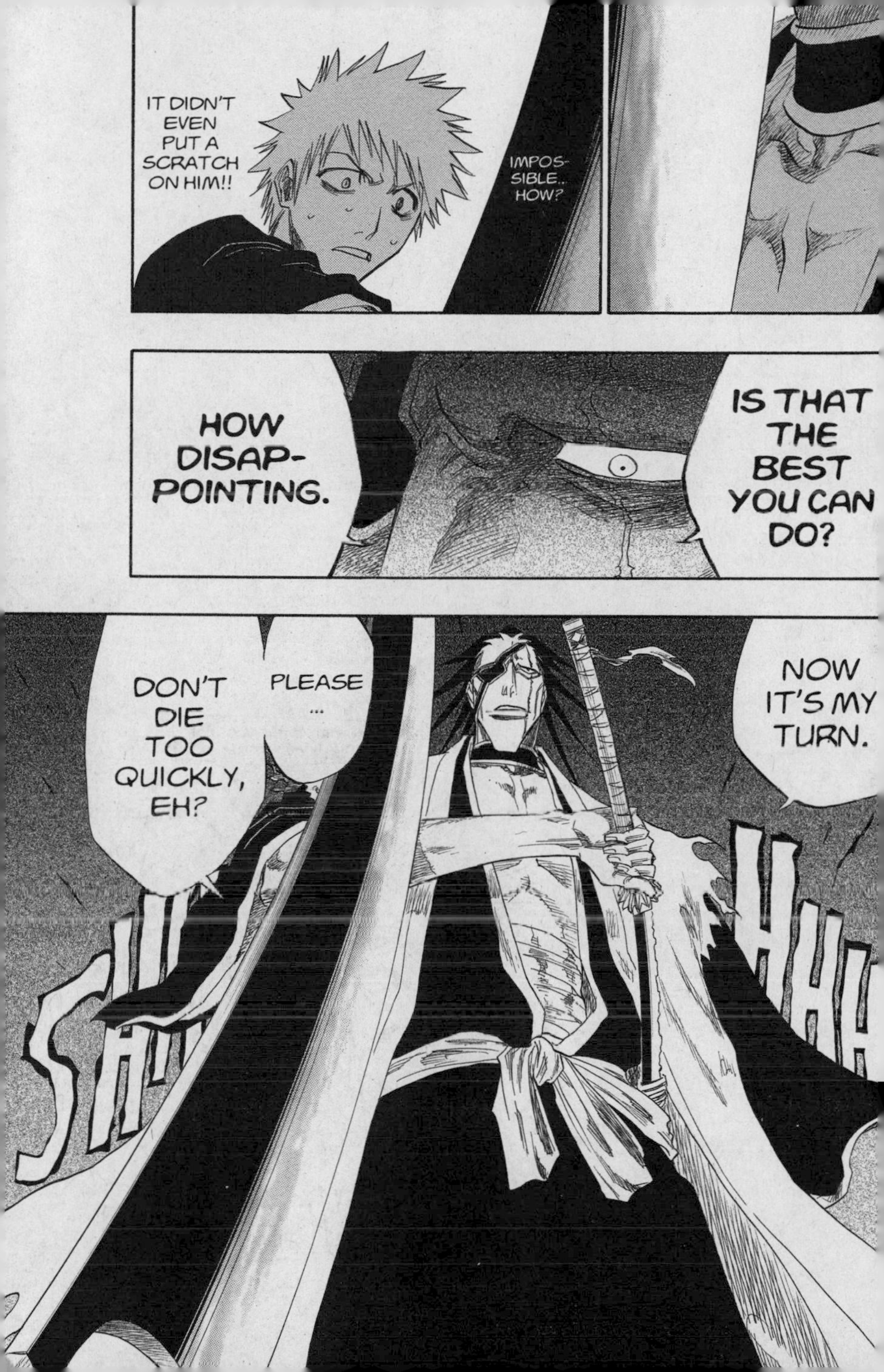
IMPOSSIBLE.. HOW?
IT DIDN'T EVEN PUT A SCRATCH ON HIM!!
IS THAT THE BEST YOU CAN DO?
HOW DISAPPOINTING.
NOW IT'S MY TURN.
PLEASE ...
DON'T DIE TOO QUICKLY, EH?

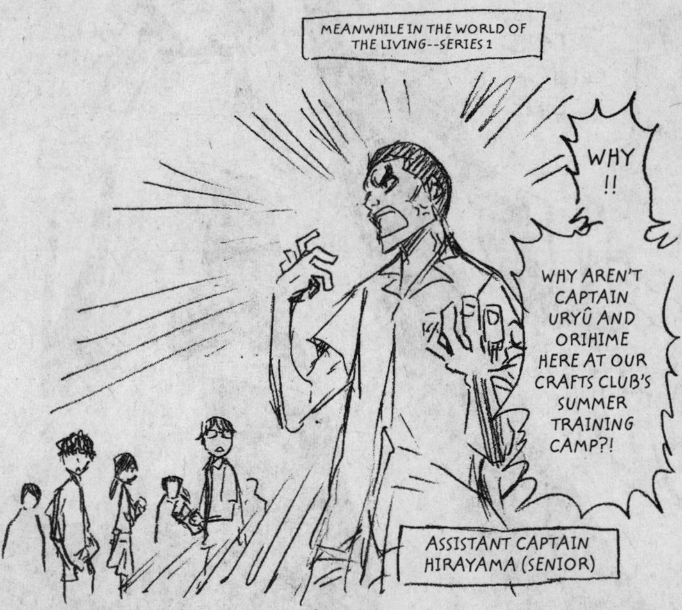
MEANWHILE IN THE WORLD OF THE LIVING--SERIES 1
WHY !!
WHY AREN'T CAPTAIN URYÛ AND ORIHIME HERE AT OUR CRAFTS CLUB'S SUMMER TRAINING CAMP?!
ASSISTANT CAPTAIN HIRAYAMA (SENIOR)

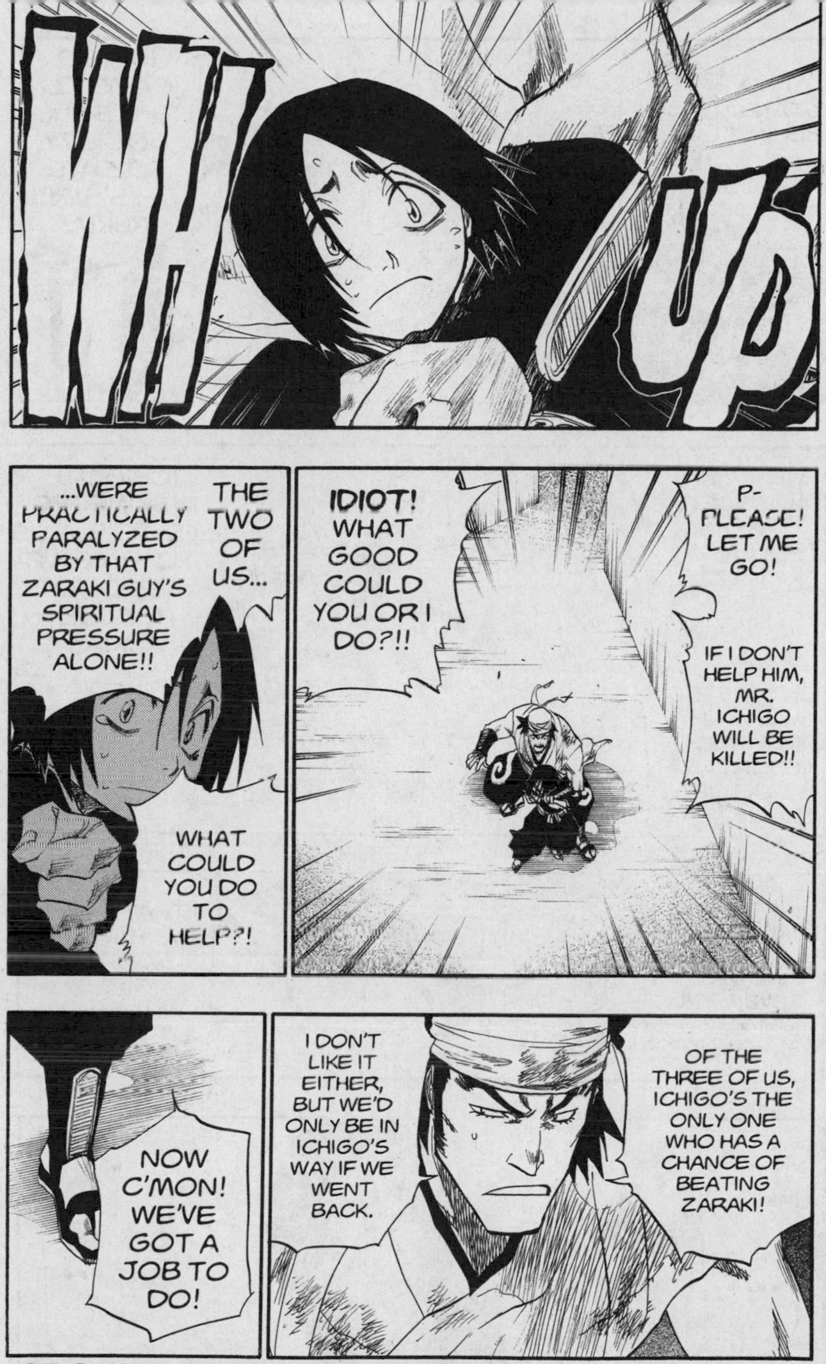
WHUD
P-PLEASE! LET ME GO!
IF I DON'T HELP HIM, MR. ICHIGO WILL BE KILLED!!
IDIOT! WHAT GOOD COULD YOU OR I DO?!!
THE TWO OF US...
...WERE PRACTICALLY PARALYZED BY THAT ZARAKI GUY'S SPIRITUAL PRESSURE ALONE!!
WHAT COULD YOU DO TO HELP?!
OF THE THREE OF US, ICHIGO'S THE ONLY ONE WHO HAS A CHANCE OF BEATING ZARAKI!
I DON'T LIKE IT EITHER, BUT WE'D ONLY BE IN ICHIGO'S WAY IF WE WENT BACK.
NOW C'MON! WE'VE GOT A JOB TO DO!

105. Spring, Spring, Meets the Tiger

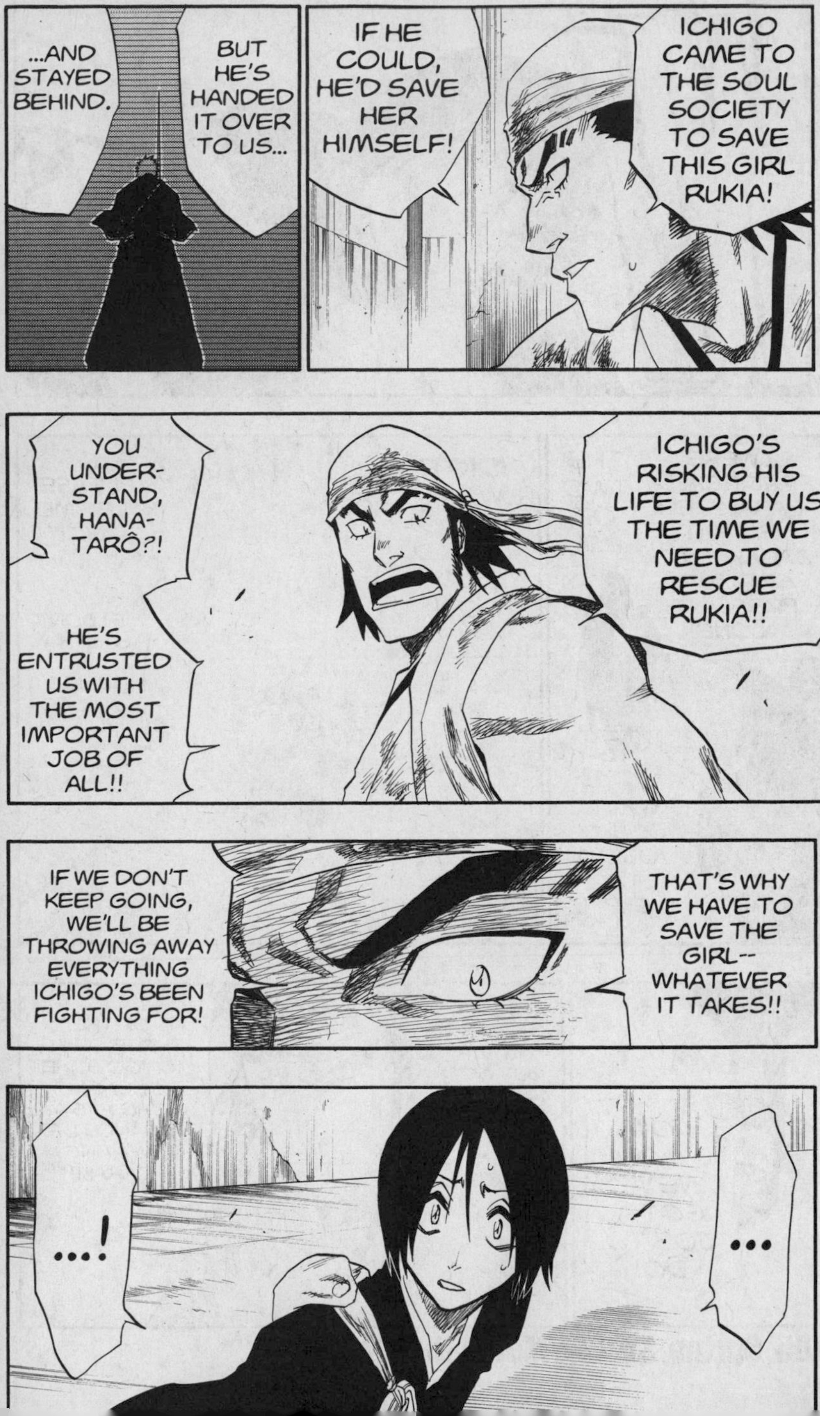
ICHIGO CAME TO THE SOUL SOCIETY TO SAVE THIS GIRL RUKIA!
IF HE COULD, HE'D SAVE HER HIMSELF!
BUT HE'S HANDED IT OVER TO US...
...AND STAYED BEHIND.
ICHIGO'S RISKING HIS LIFE TO BUY US THE TIME WE NEED TO RESCUE RUKIA!!
YOU UNDER-STAND, HANA-TARÔ?!
HE'S ENTRUSTED US WITH THE MOST IMPORTANT JOB OF ALL!!
THAT'S WHY WE HAVE TO SAVE THE GIRL-- WHATEVER IT TAKES!!
IF WE DON'T KEEP GOING, WE'LL BE THROWING AWAY EVERYTHING ICHIGO'S BEEN FIGHTING FOR!
...
...!

READ THIS WAY

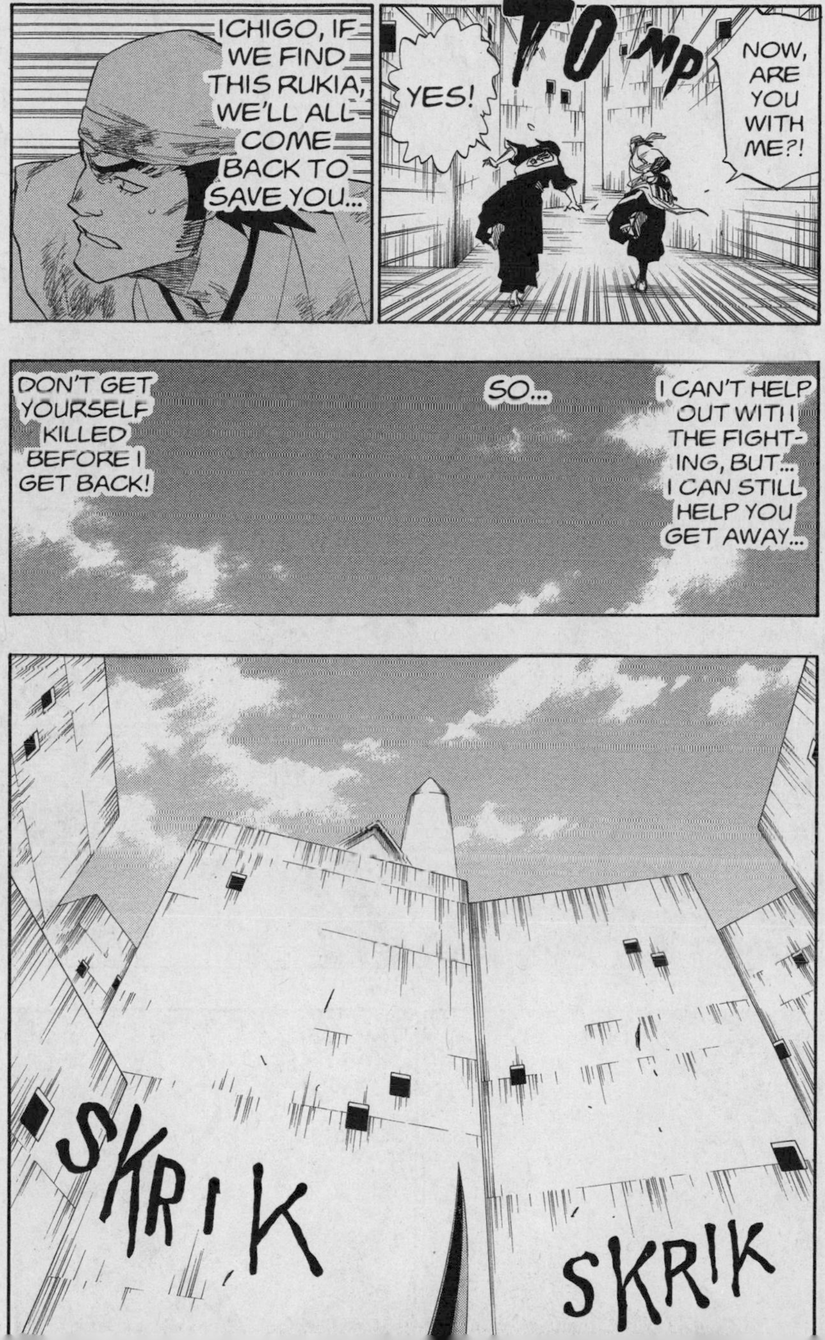
NOW, ARE YOU WITH ME?!
TOMP
YES!
ICHIGO, IF WE FIND THIS RUKIA, WE'LL ALL COME BACK TO SAVE YOU...
I CAN'T HELP OUT WITH THE FIGHTING, BUT... I CAN STILL HELP YOU GET AWAY...
SO...
DON'T GET YOURSELF KILLED BEFORE I GET BACK!
SKRIK
SKRIK

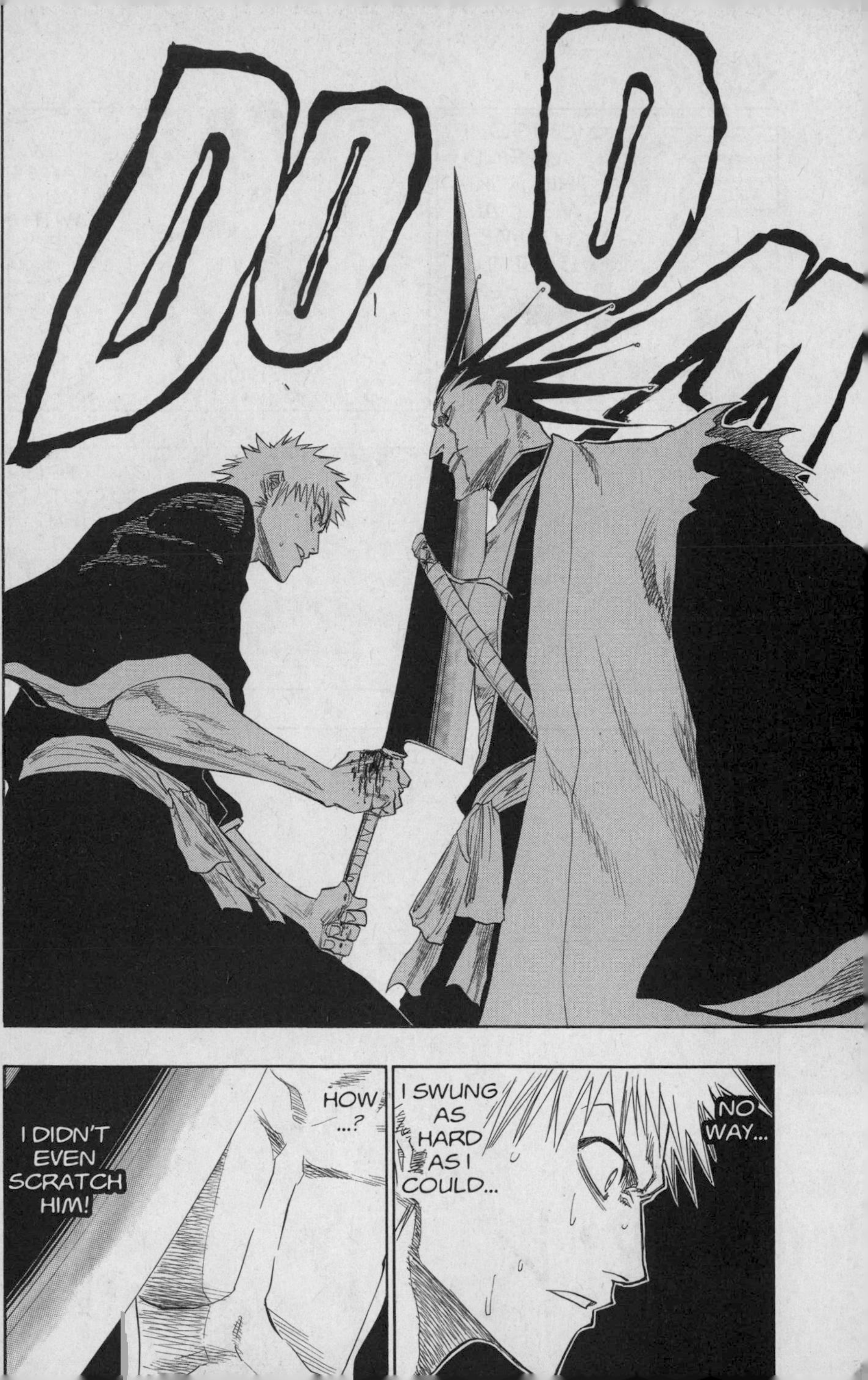
DOOM
NO WAY...
I SWUNG AS HARD AS I COULD...
HOW ...?
I DIDN'T EVEN SCRATCH HIM!

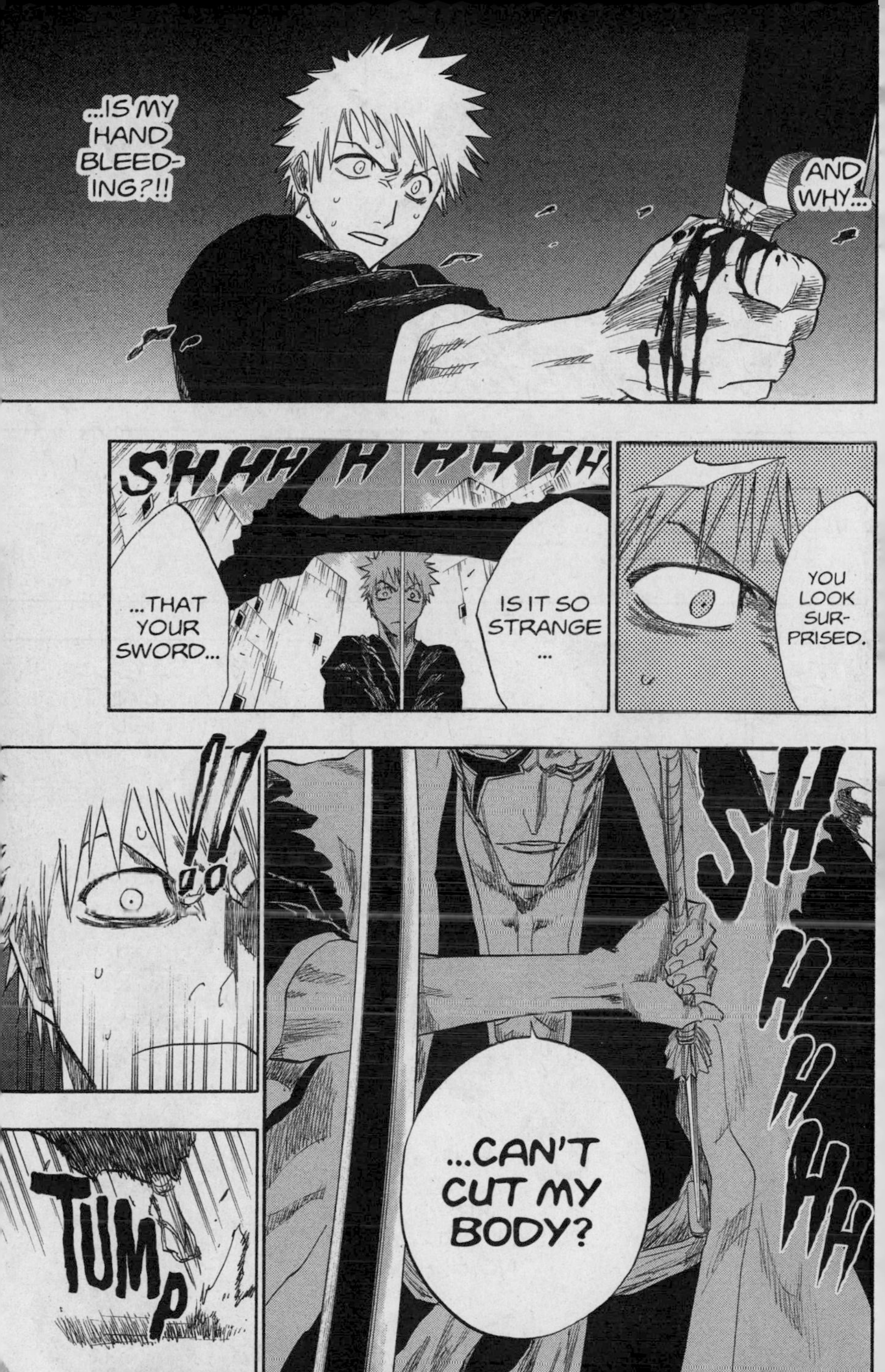
AND WHY...
...IS MY HAND BLEEDING?!!
YOU LOOK SURPRISED.
SHHHHHHHHH
IS IT SO STRANGE ...
...THAT YOUR SWORD...
SHHHHHHH
...CAN'T CUT MY BODY?
!!
TUMP

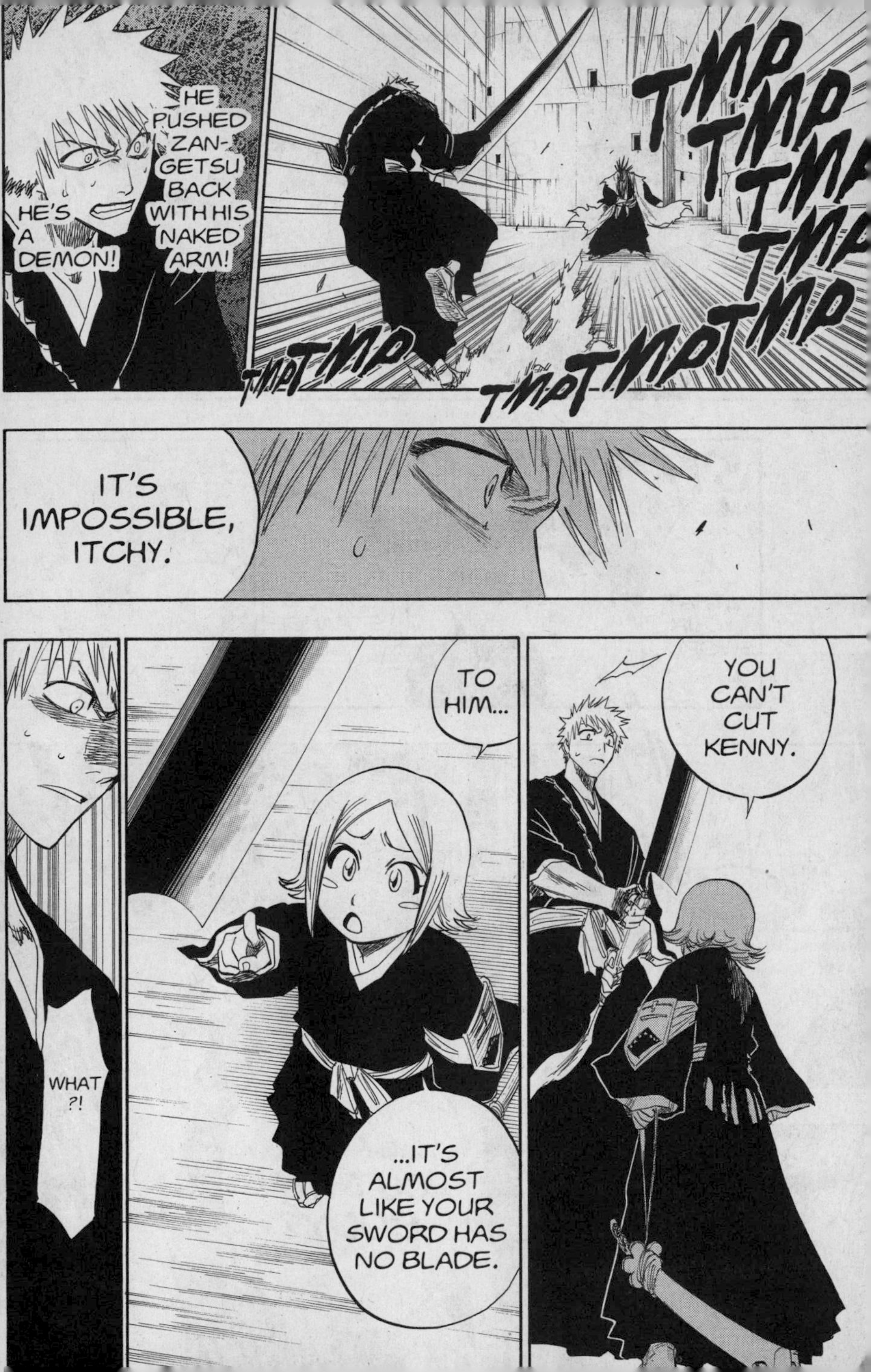
TMP TMP TMP TMP TMP TMP
TMP TMP TMP
TMP TMP
HE PUSHED ZAN-GETSU BACK WITH HIS NAKED ARM!
HE'S A DEMON!
IT'S IMPOSSIBLE, ITCHY.
YOU CAN'T CUT KENNY.
TO HIM...
...IT'S ALMOST LIKE YOUR SWORD HAS NO BLADE.
WHAT?!

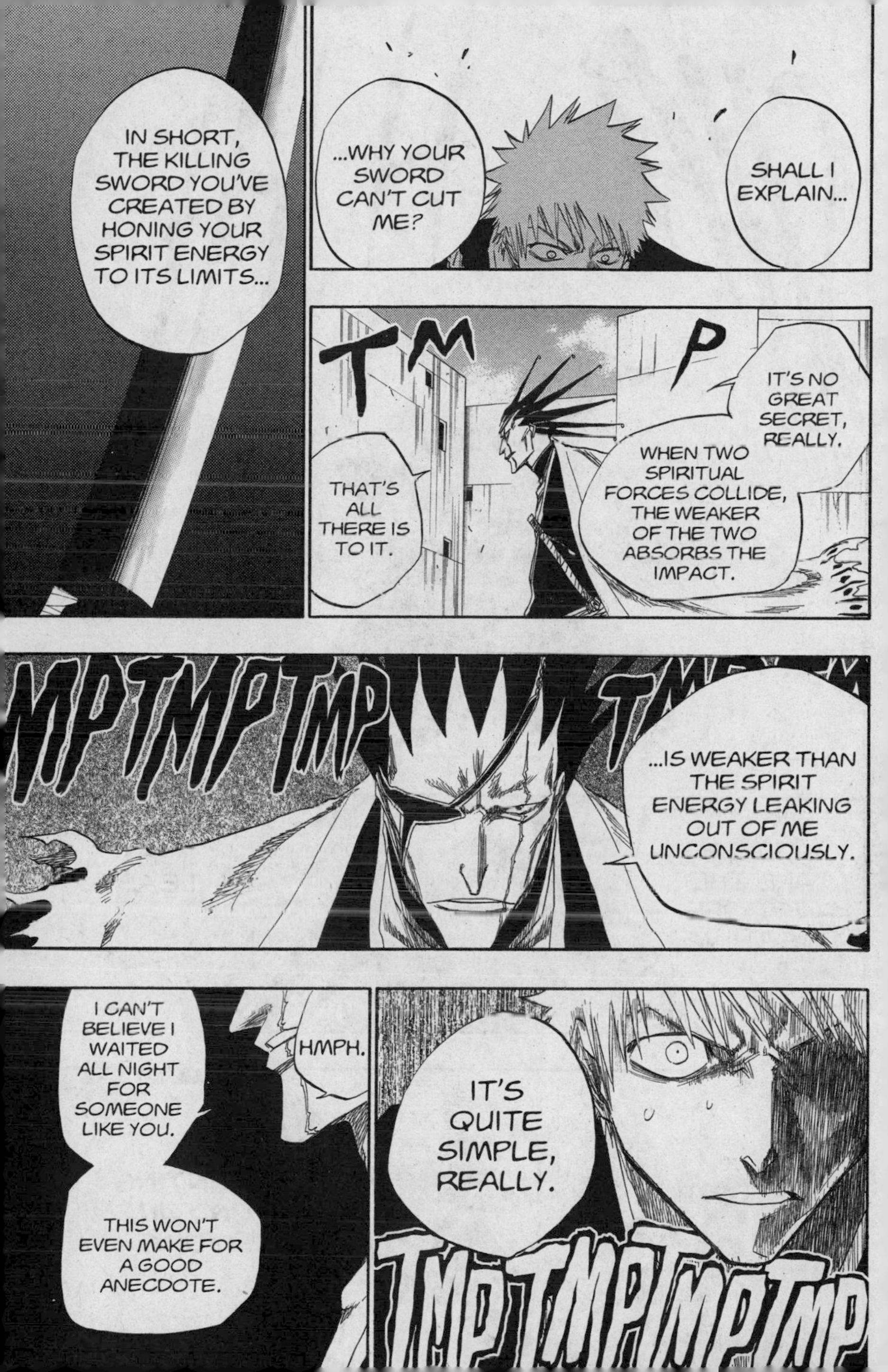
SHALL I EXPLAIN...
...WHY YOUR SWORD CAN'T CUT ME?
TMP
IT'S NO GREAT SECRET, REALLY.
WHEN TWO SPIRITUAL FORCES COLLIDE, THE WEAKER OF THE TWO ABSORBS THE IMPACT.
THAT'S ALL THERE IS TO IT.
IN SHORT, THE KILLING SWORD YOU'VE CREATED BY HONING YOUR SPIRIT ENERGY TO ITS LIMITS...
...IS WEAKER THAN THE SPIRIT ENERGY LEAKING OUT OF ME UNCONSCIOUSLY.
MPTMPTMP
IT'S QUITE SIMPLE, REALLY.
TMPTMPTMPTMP
HMPH.
I CAN'T BELIEVE I WAITED ALL NIGHT FOR SOMEONE LIKE YOU.
THIS WON'T EVEN MAKE FOR A GOOD ANECDOTE.

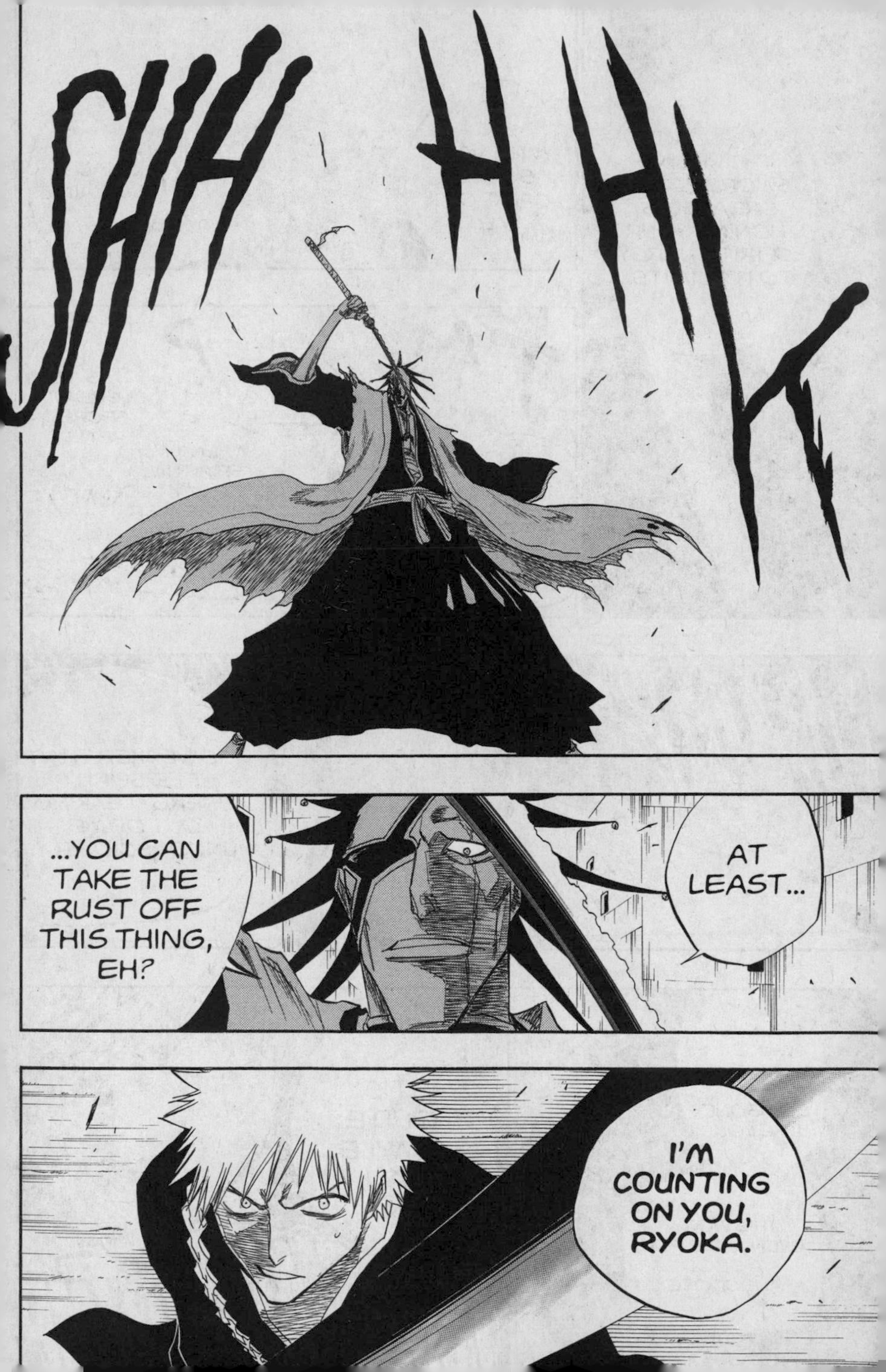
SHIIIIIK
AT LEAST...
...YOU CAN TAKE THE RUST OFF THIS THING, EH?
I'M COUNTING ON YOU, RYOKA.

105. Spring, Spring, Meets the Tiger

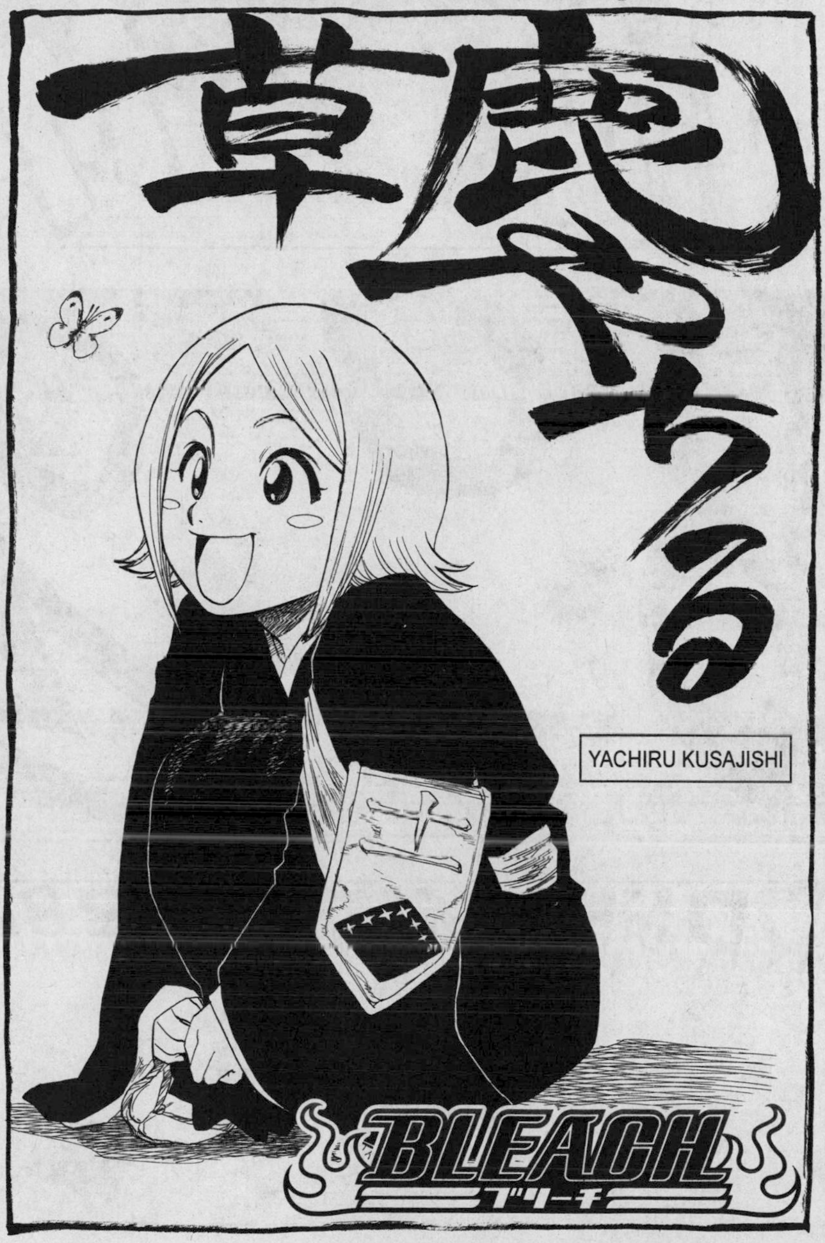
草鹿やちる
YACHIRU KUSAJISHI
BLEACH
ブリーチ

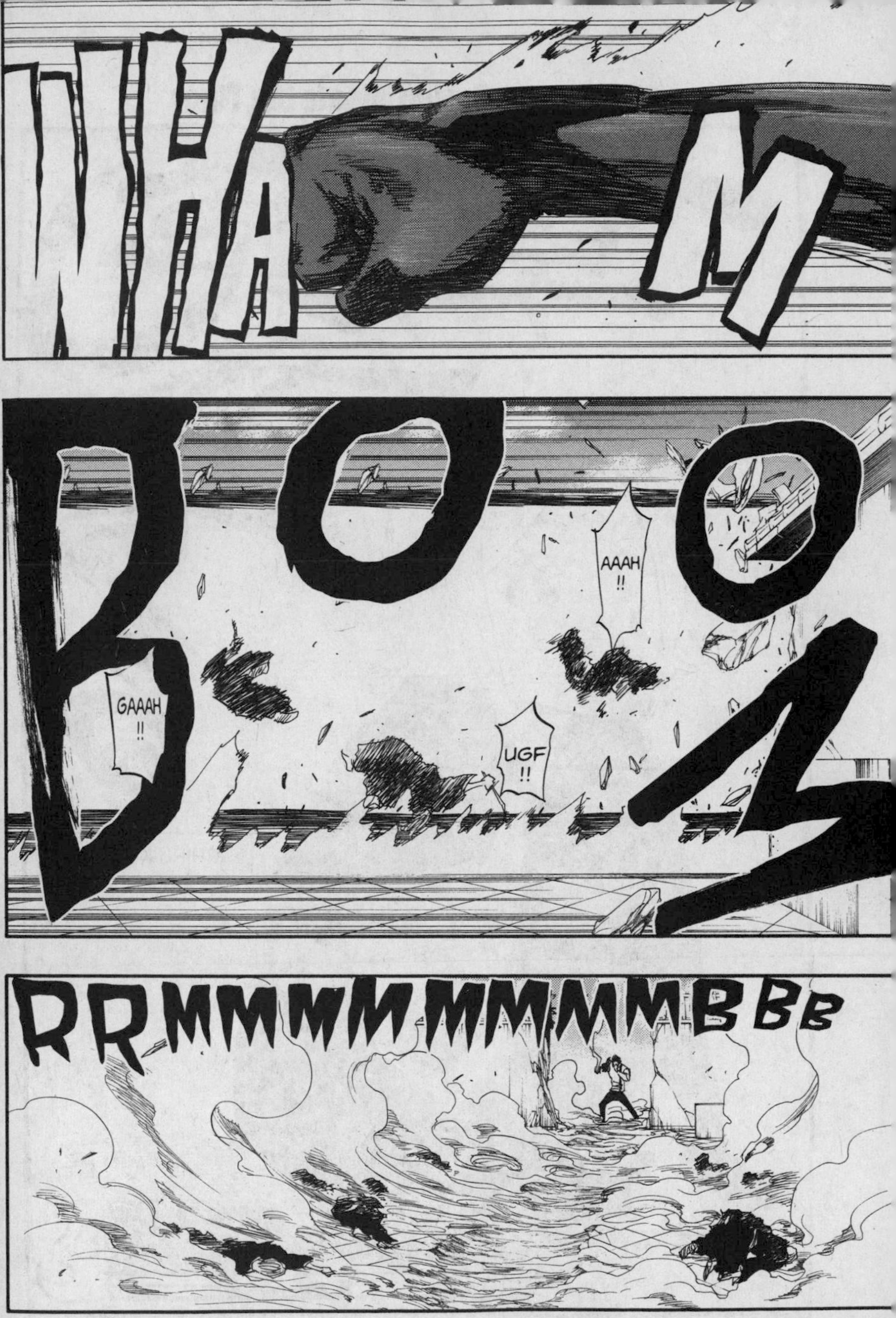
WHAM
BOOM
AAAH!!
UGF!!
GAAAH!!
RRMMMMMMMMBBB

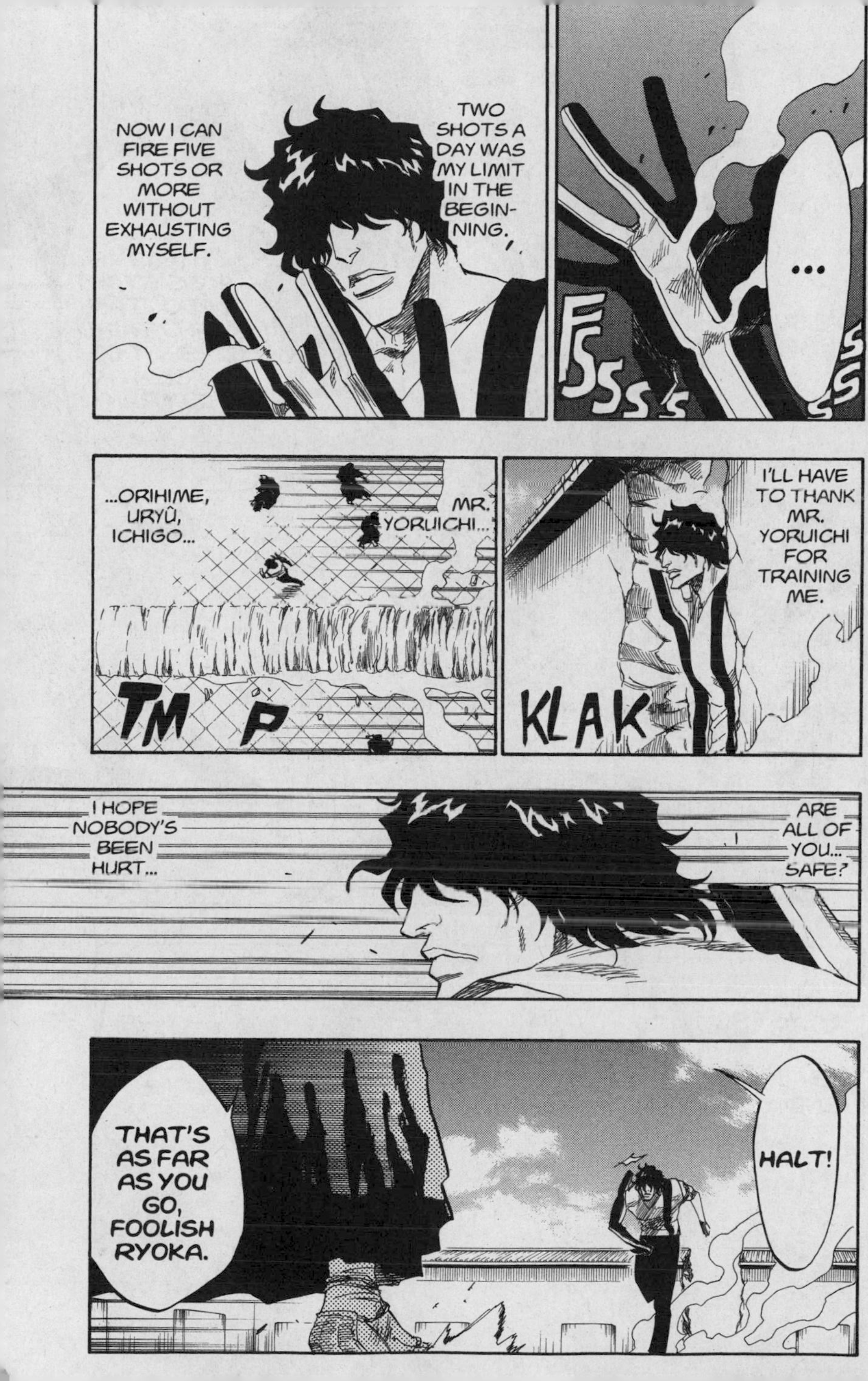
...
FSSSS
SSSS
TWO SHOTS A DAY WAS MY LIMIT IN THE BEGIN-NING.
NOW I CAN FIRE FIVE SHOTS OR MORE WITHOUT EXHAUSTING MYSELF.
I'LL HAVE TO THANK MR. YORUICHI FOR TRAINING ME.
KLAK
MR. YORUICHI...
...ORIHIME, URYŪ, ICHIGO...
TMP
ARE ALL OF YOU... SAFE?
I HOPE NOBODY'S BEEN HURT...
HALT!
THAT'S AS FAR AS YOU GO, FOOLISH RYOKA.

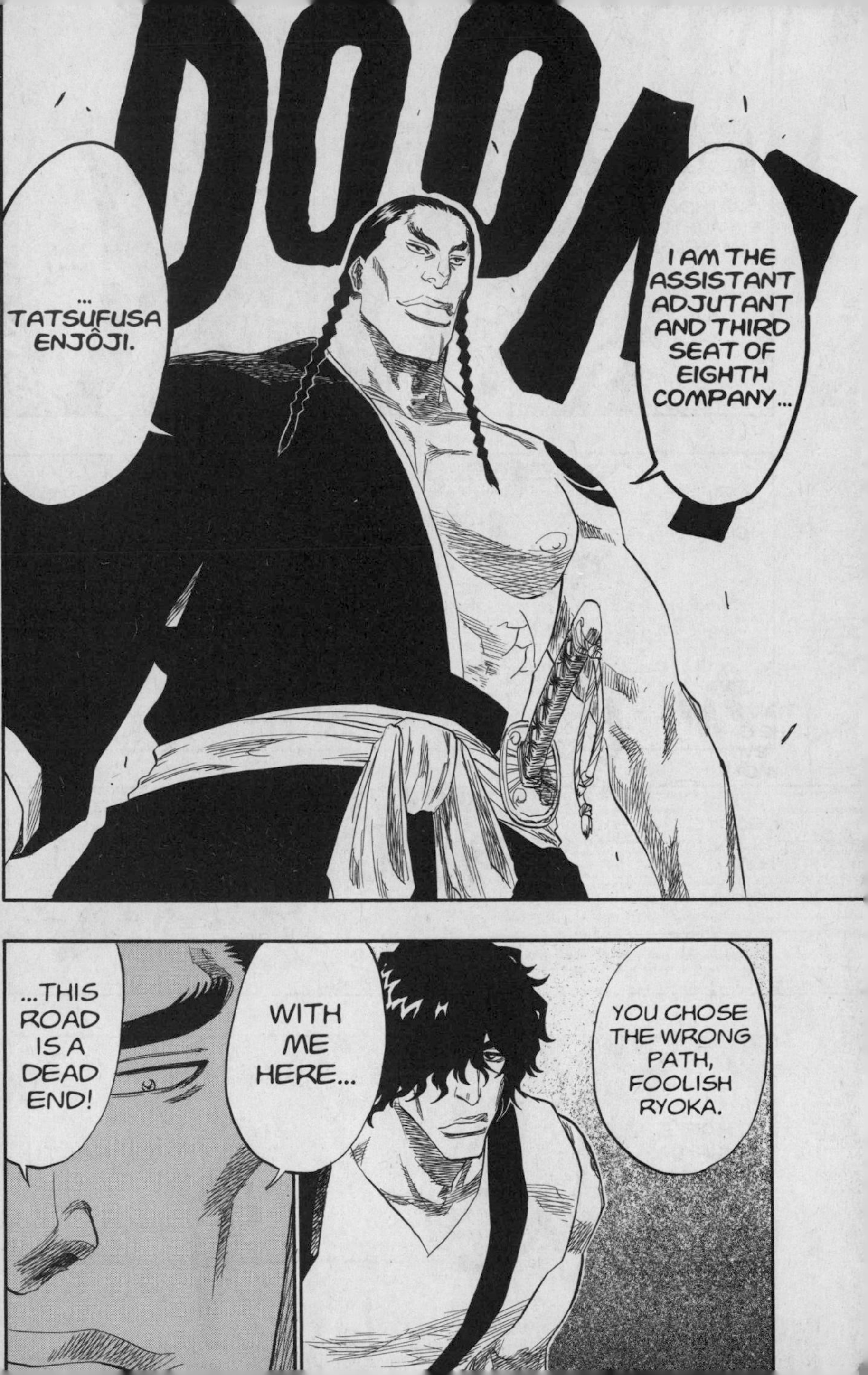
DOON
I AM THE ASSISTANT ADJUTANT AND THIRD SEAT OF EIGHTH COMPANY...
...TATSUFUSA ENJÔJI.
YOU CHOSE THE WRONG PATH, FOOLISH RYOKA.
WITH ME HERE...
...THIS ROAD IS A DEAD END!

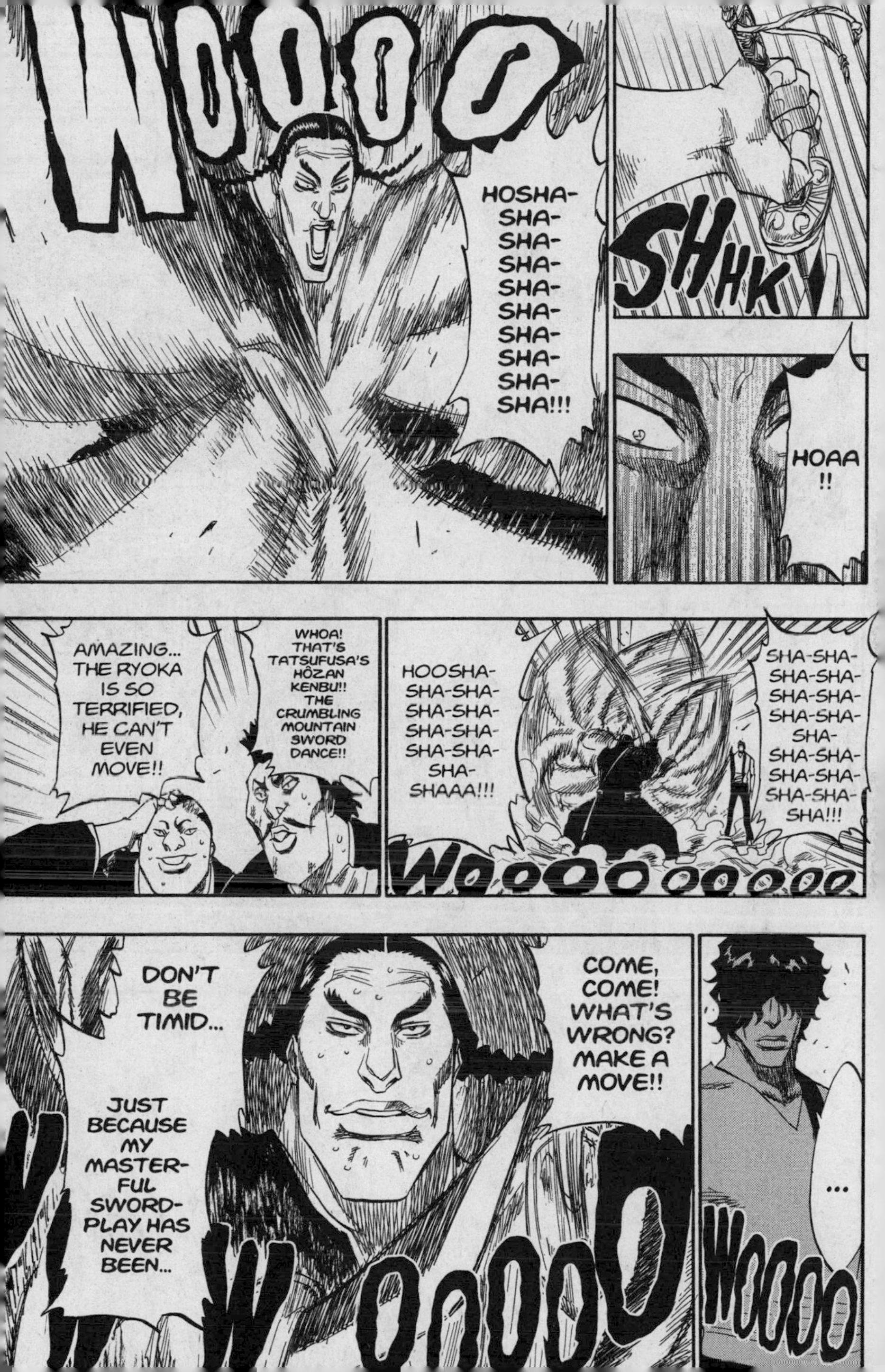
SHHK
HOAA!!
WOOOOO
HOSHA-SHA-SHA-SHA-SHA-SHA-SHA-SHA-SHA-SHA!!!
SHA-SHA-SHA-SHA-SHA-SHA-SHA-SHA-SHA-SHA-SHA-SHA-SHA-SHA-SHA-SHA!!!
HOOSHA-SHA-SHA-SHA-SHA-SHA-SHA-SHA-SHA-SHA-SHAAA!!!
WOOOOOOOOOO
WHOA! THAT'S TATSUFUSA'S HÔZAN KENBU!! THE CRUMBLING MOUNTAIN SWORD DANCE!!
AMAZING... THE RYOKA IS SO TERRIFIED, HE CAN'T EVEN MOVE!!
...
WOOOO
COME, COME! WHAT'S WRONG? MAKE A MOVE!!
DON'T BE TIMID...
JUST BECAUSE MY MASTERFUL SWORDPLAY HAS NEVER BEEN...
WOOOOO

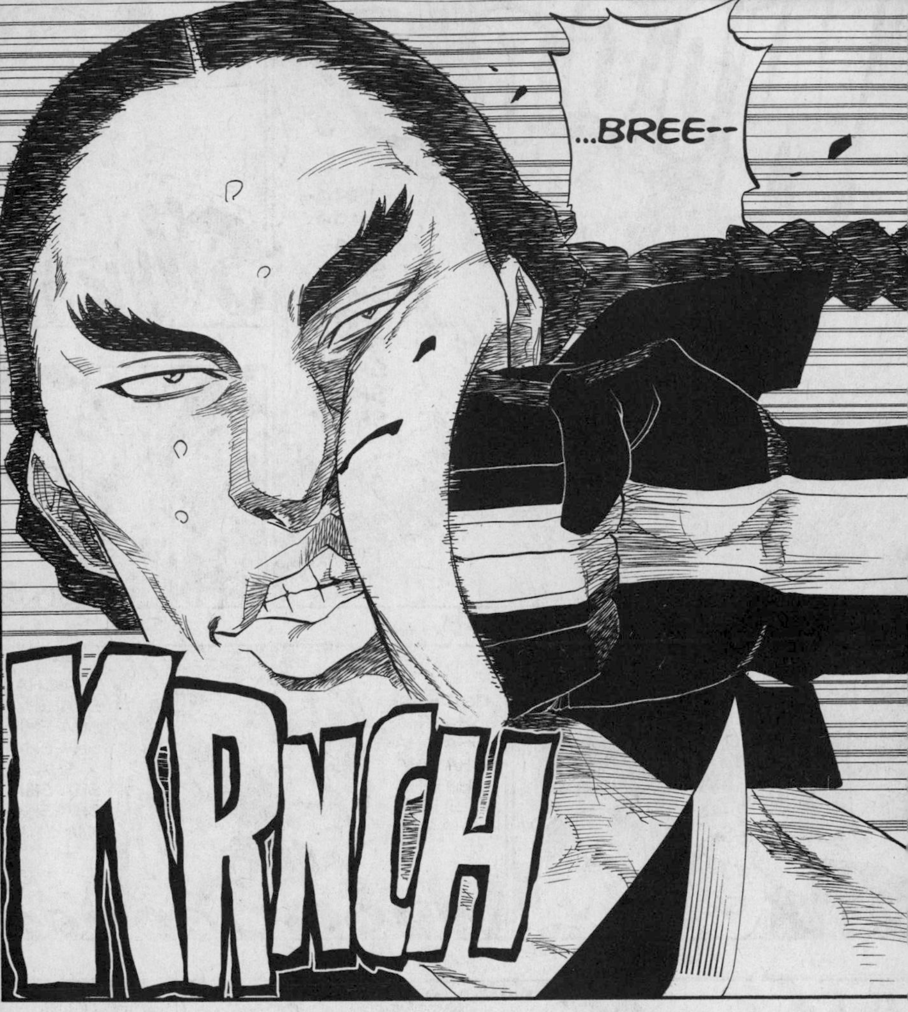
...BREE--
KRNCH
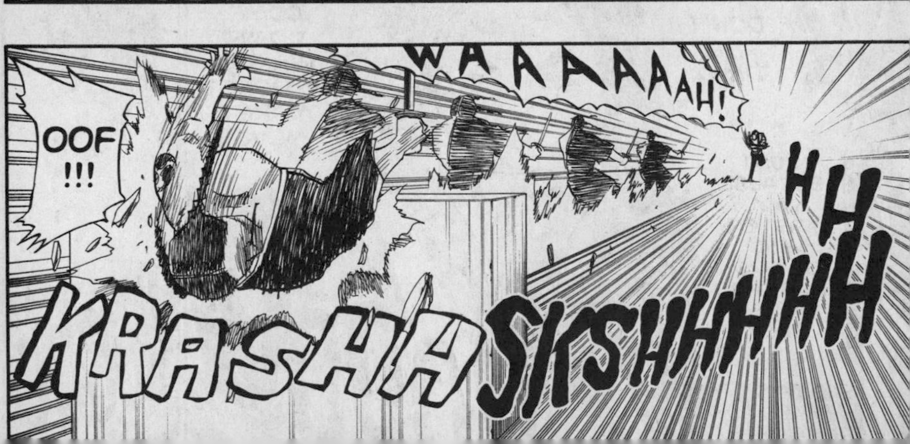
WAAAAAAAH!
OOF !!!
KRASHA
SKSHHHHHH

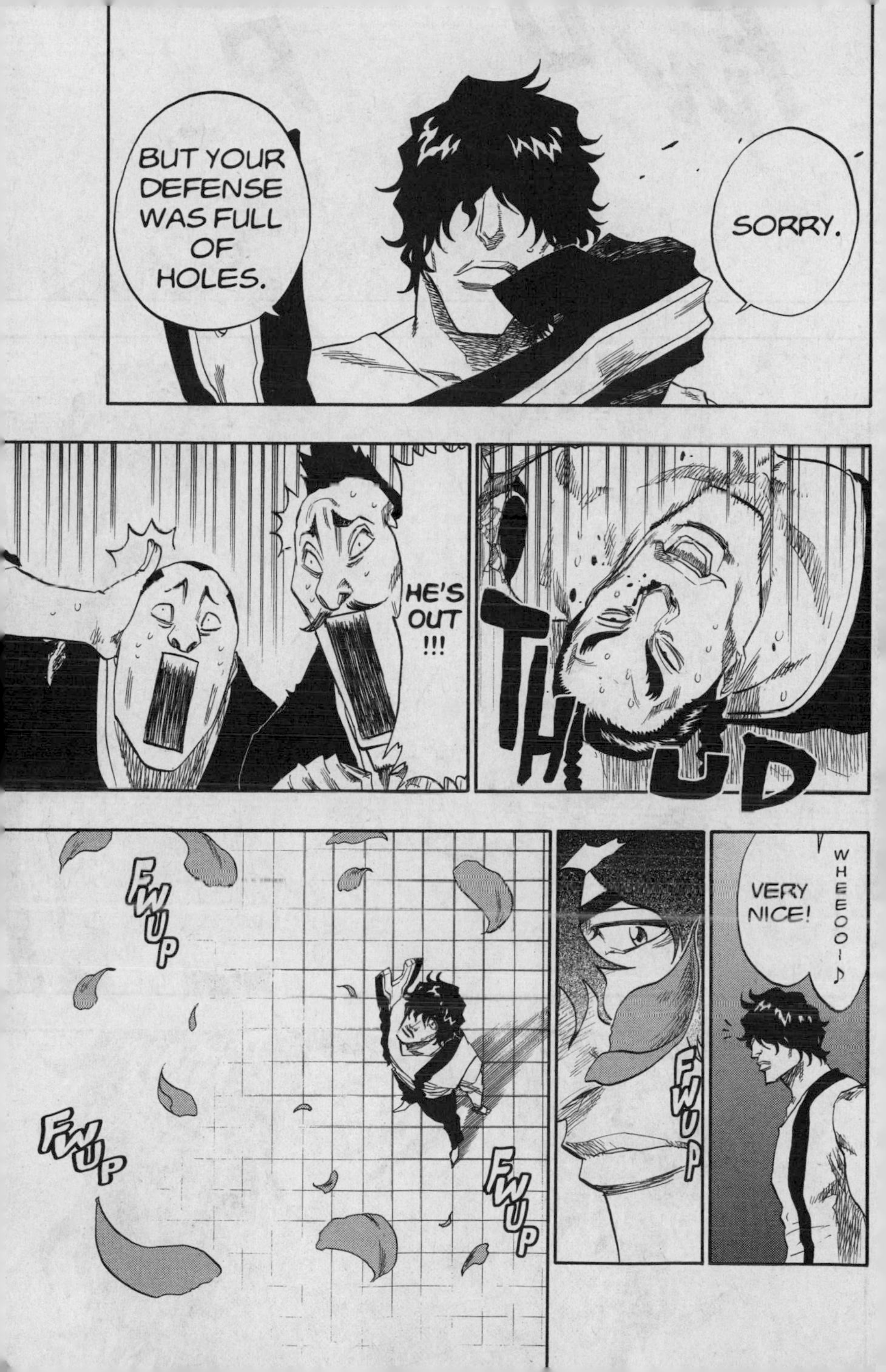
SORRY.
BUT YOUR DEFENSE WAS FULL OF HOLES.
THUD
HE'S OUT!!!
WHEEOO~♪
VERY NICE!
FWUP
FWUP
FWUP
FWUP

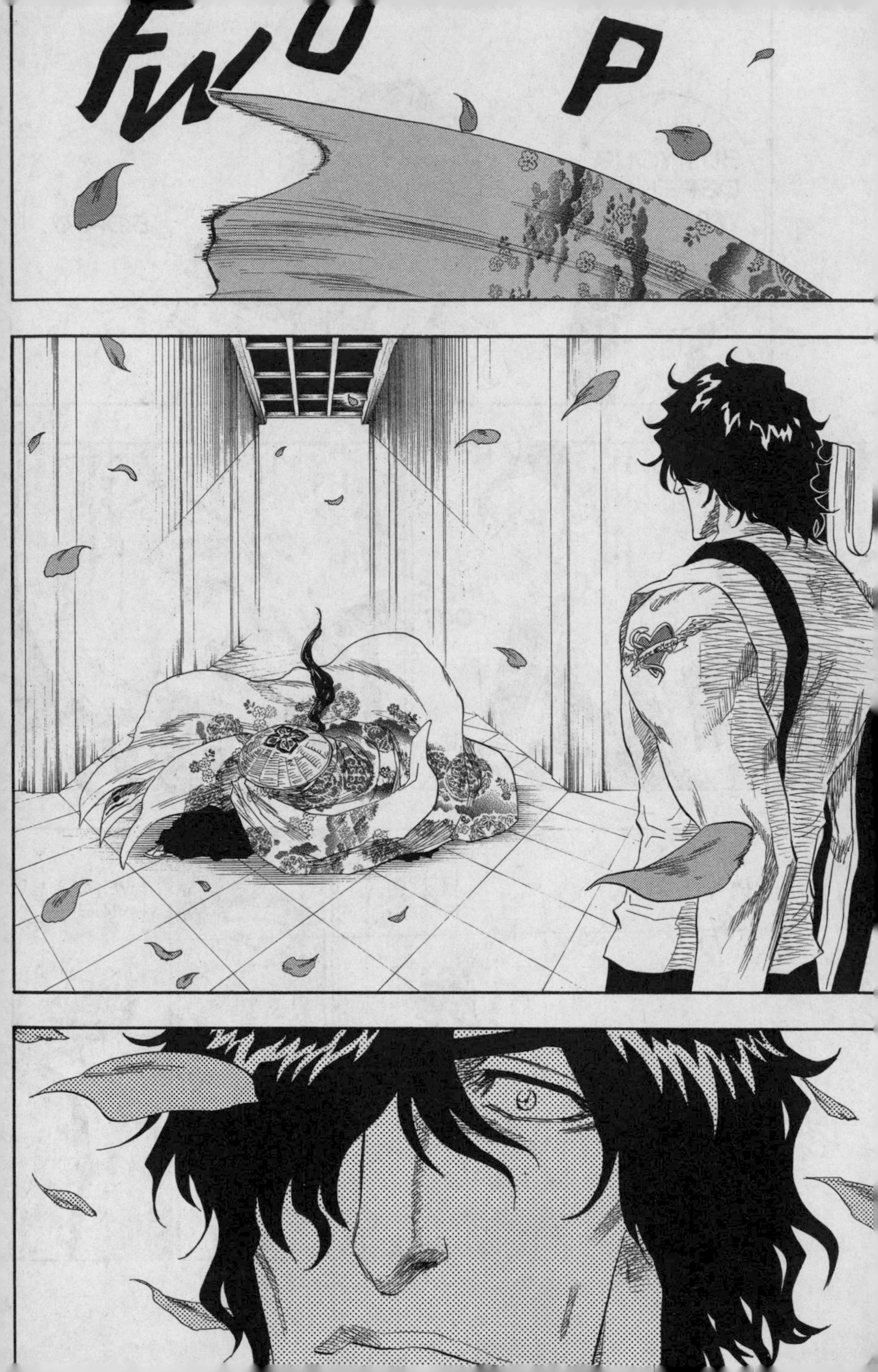
FWUP

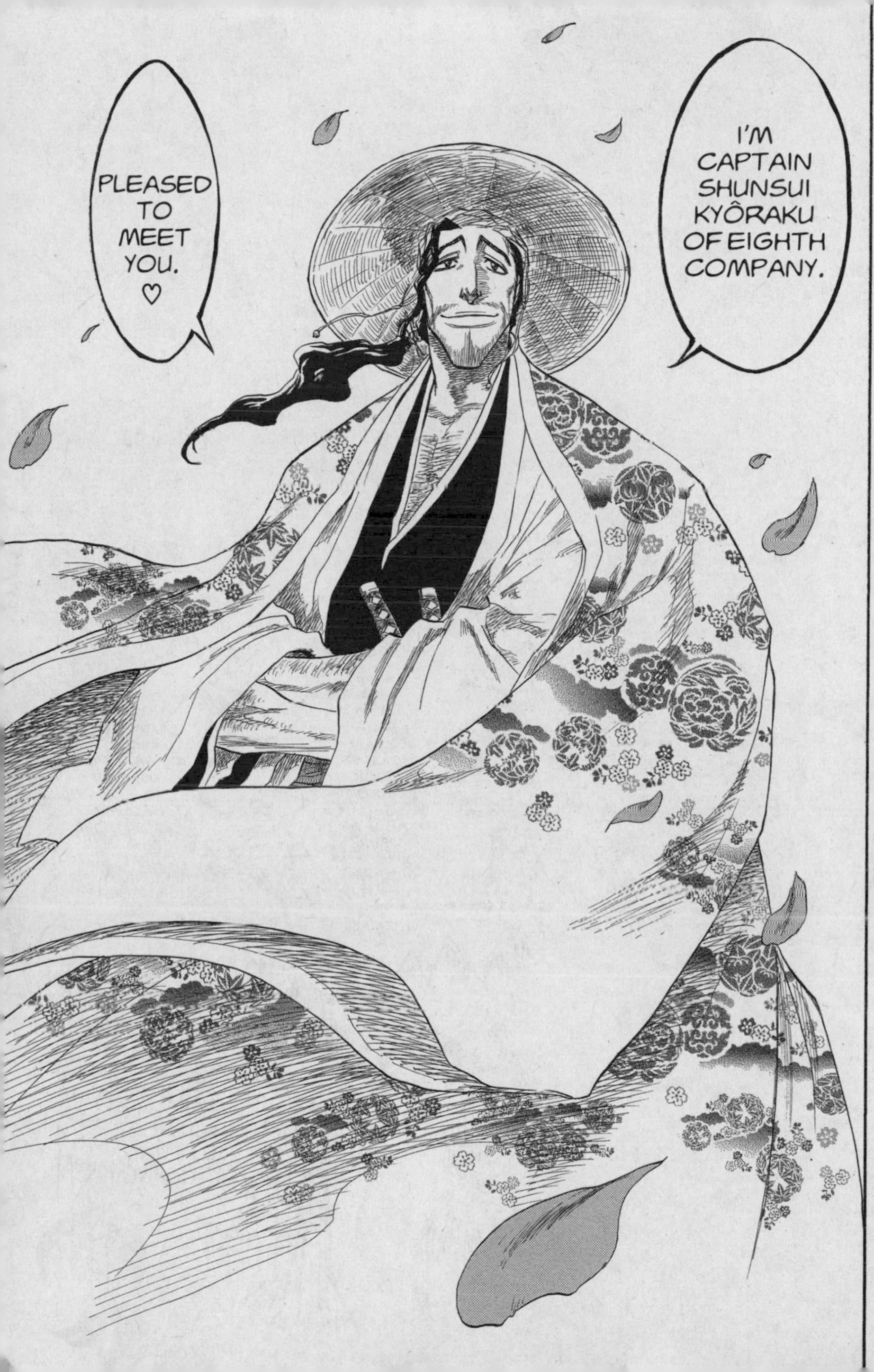
I'M CAPTAIN SHUNSUI KYÔRAKU OF EIGHTH COMPANY.
PLEASED TO MEET YOU. ♡

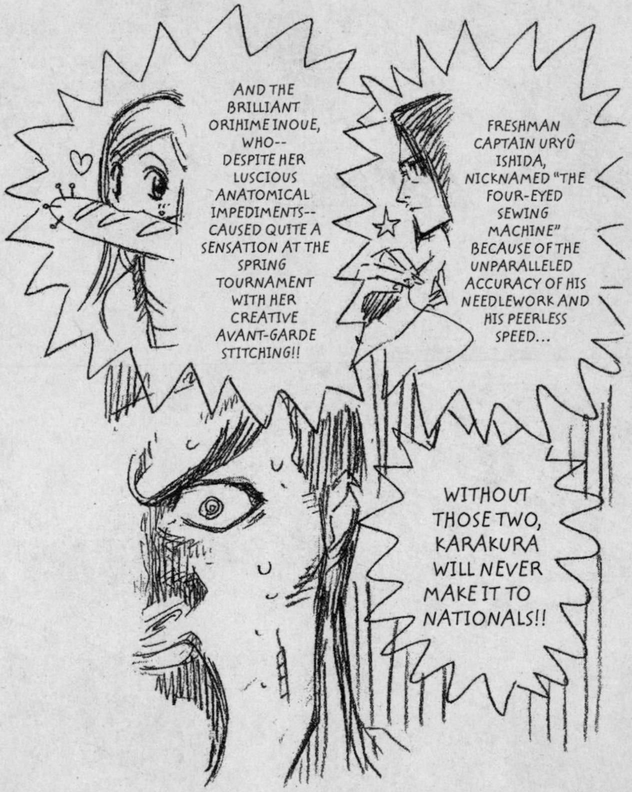
FRESHMAN CAPTAIN URYÛ ISHIDA, NICKNAMED "THE FOUR-EYED SEWING MACHINE" BECAUSE OF THE UNPARALLELED ACCURACY OF HIS NEEDLEWORK AND HIS PEERLESS SPEED...
AND THE BRILLIANT ORIHIME INOUE, WHO--DESPITE HER LUSCIOUS ANATOMICAL IMPEDIMENTS--CAUSED QUITE A SENSATION AT THE SPRING TOURNAMENT WITH HER CREATIVE AVANT-GARDE STITCHING!!
WITHOUT THOSE TWO, KARAKURA WILL NEVER MAKE IT TO NATIONALS!!

106. Cause to Confront

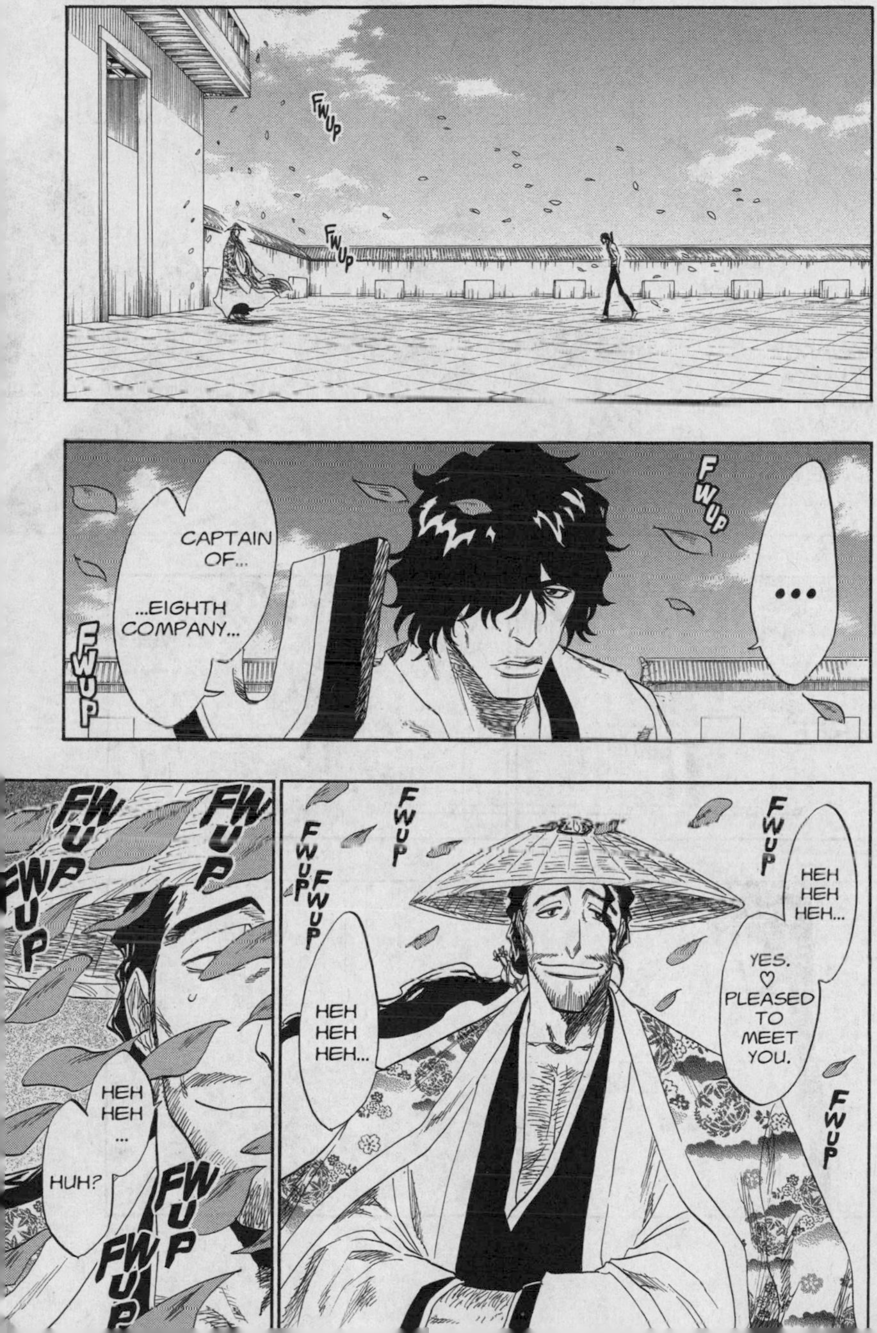
FWUP
FWUP
FWUP
...
CAPTAIN OF... ...EIGHTH COMPANY...
FWUP
FWUP
FWUP
HEH HEH HEH...
YES. ♡ PLEASED TO MEET YOU.
FWUP
FWUP
FWUP
HEH HEH HEH...
FWUP
FWUP
FWUP
HEH HEH ...
HUH?
FWUP
FWUP

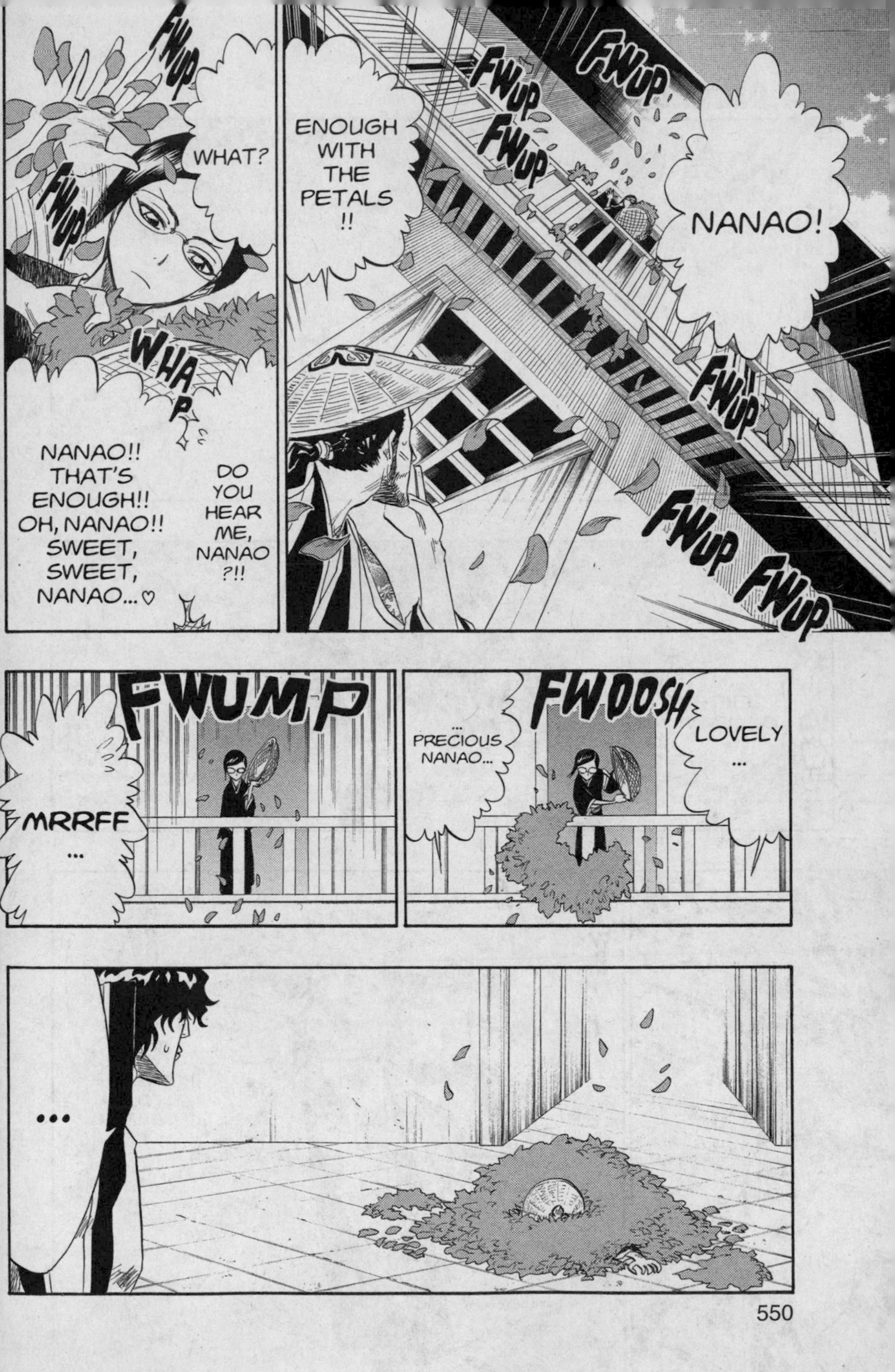

FWUP
NANAO!
FWUP
FWUP
ENOUGH WITH THE PETALS !!
FWUP
FWUP
FWUP
FWUP
WHAT?
FWUP
WHAP
DO YOU HEAR ME, NANAO ?!!
NANAO!! THAT'S ENOUGH!! OH, NANAO!! SWEET, SWEET, NANAO...♡
FWOOSH
LOVELY ...
... PRECIOUS NANAO...
FWUMP
MRRFF ...
...

READ THIS WAY

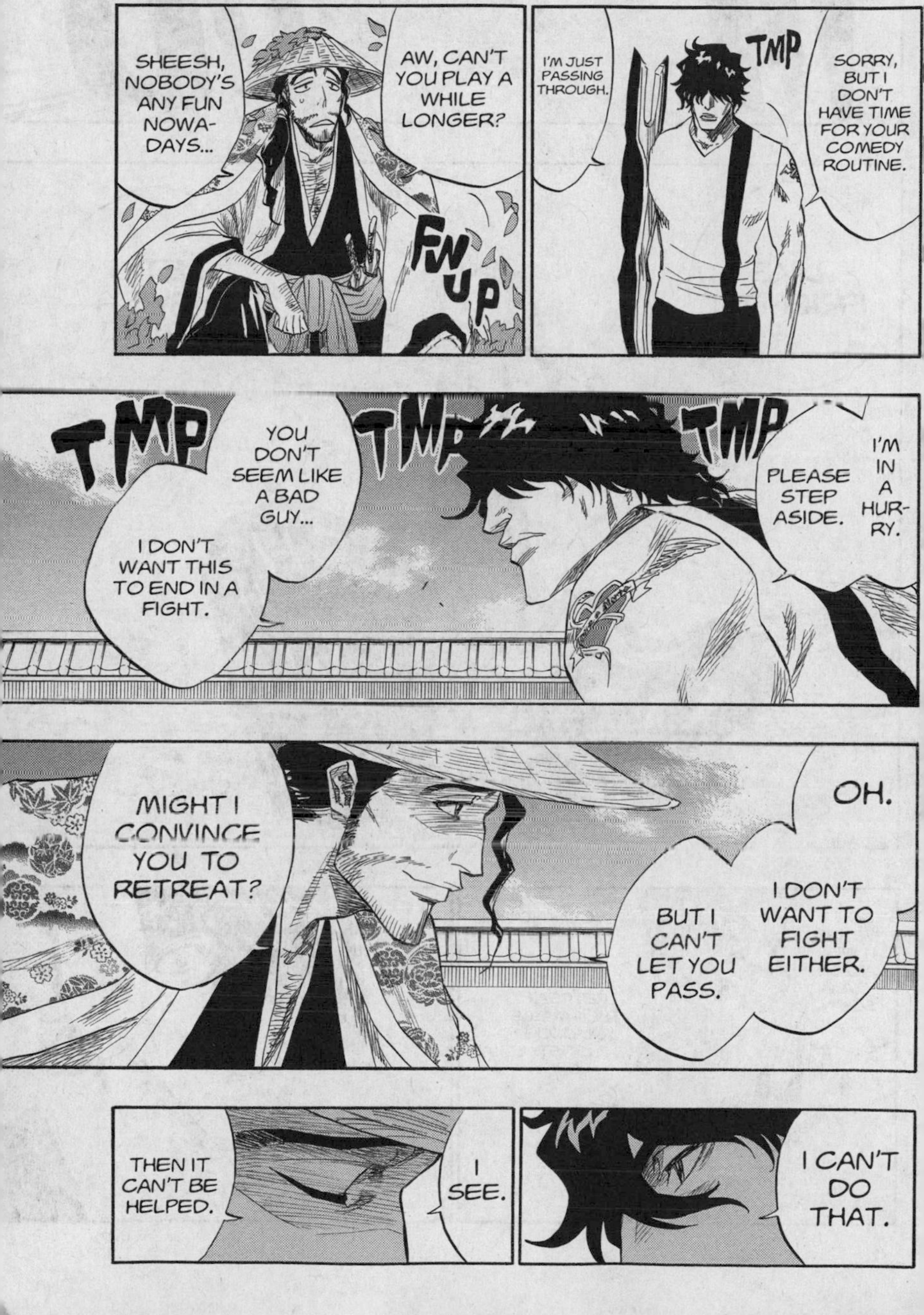
TMP
SORRY, BUT I DON'T HAVE TIME FOR YOUR COMEDY ROUTINE.
I'M JUST PASSING THROUGH.
AW, CAN'T YOU PLAY A WHILE LONGER?
SHEESH, NOBODY'S ANY FUN NOWA-DAYS...
FWUP
I'M IN A HURRY.
PLEASE STEP ASIDE.
TMP
TMP
TMP
YOU DON'T SEEM LIKE A BAD GUY...
I DON'T WANT THIS TO END IN A FIGHT.
OH.
I DON'T WANT TO FIGHT EITHER.
BUT I CAN'T LET YOU PASS.
MIGHT I CONVINCE YOU TO RETREAT?
I CAN'T DO THAT.
I SEE.
THEN IT CAN'T BE HELPED.

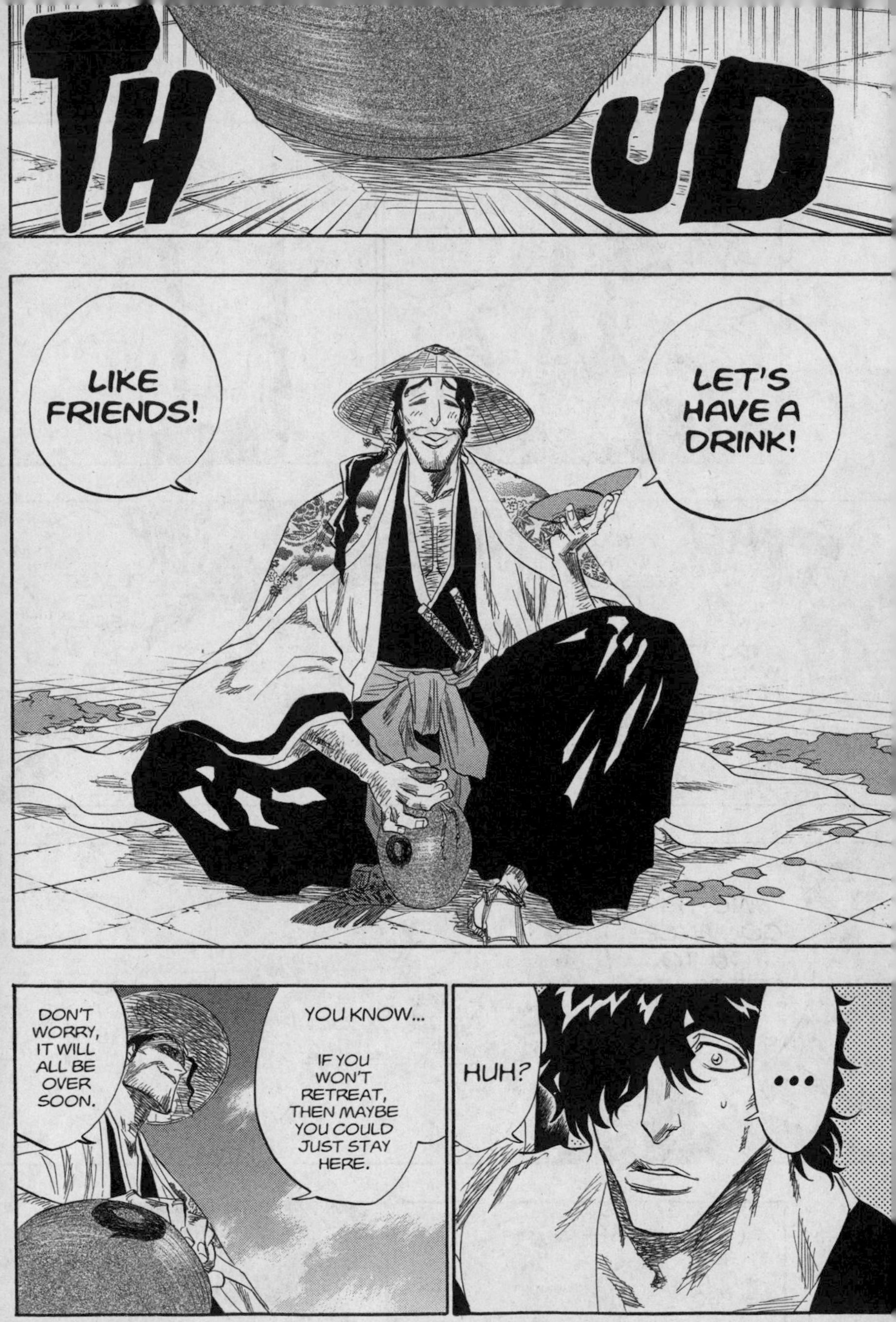
THUD
LET'S HAVE A DRINK!
LIKE FRIENDS!
...
HUH?
YOU KNOW...
IF YOU WON'T RETREAT, THEN MAYBE YOU COULD JUST STAY HERE.
DON'T WORRY, IT WILL ALL BE OVER SOON.

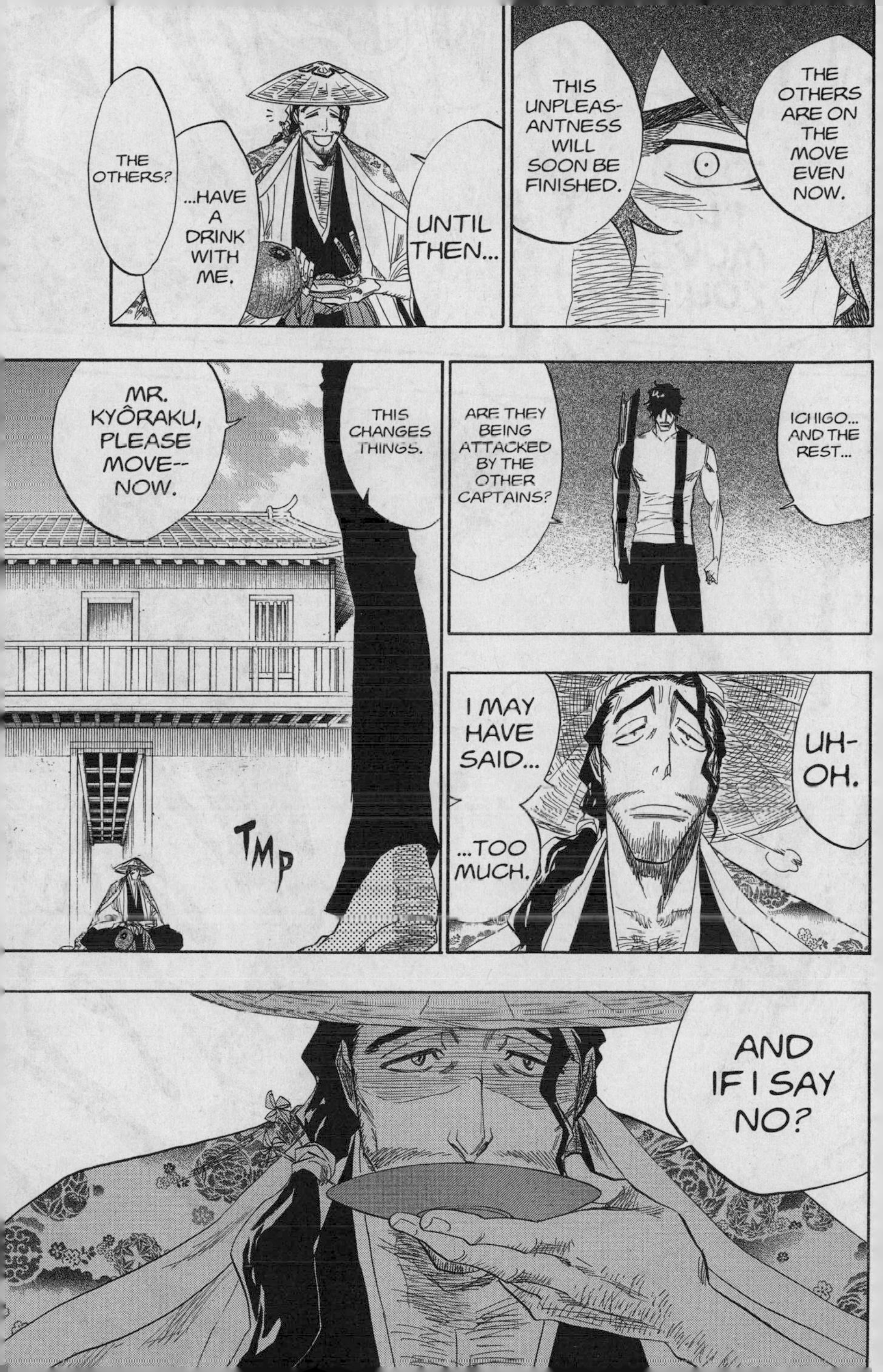
THE OTHERS ARE ON THE MOVE EVEN NOW.
THIS UNPLEAS-ANTNESS WILL SOON BE FINISHED.
UNTIL THEN...
...HAVE A DRINK WITH ME.
THE OTHERS?
ICHIGO... AND THE REST...
ARE THEY BEING ATTACKED BY THE OTHER CAPTAINS?
UH-OH.
I MAY HAVE SAID...
...TOO MUCH.
THIS CHANGES THINGS.
MR. KYÔRAKU, PLEASE MOVE--NOW.
TMP
AND IF I SAY NO?

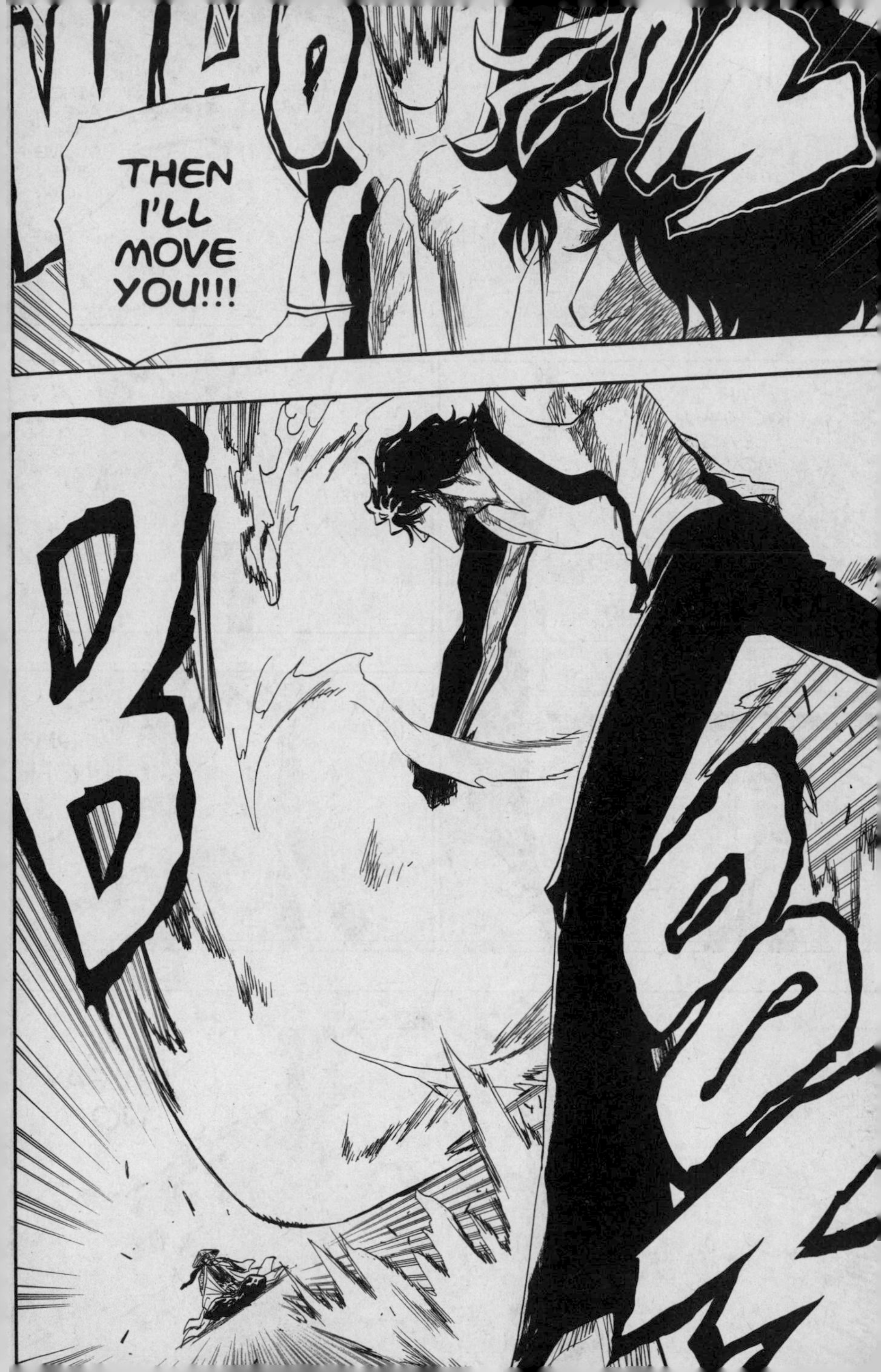
THEN I'LL MOVE YOU!!!

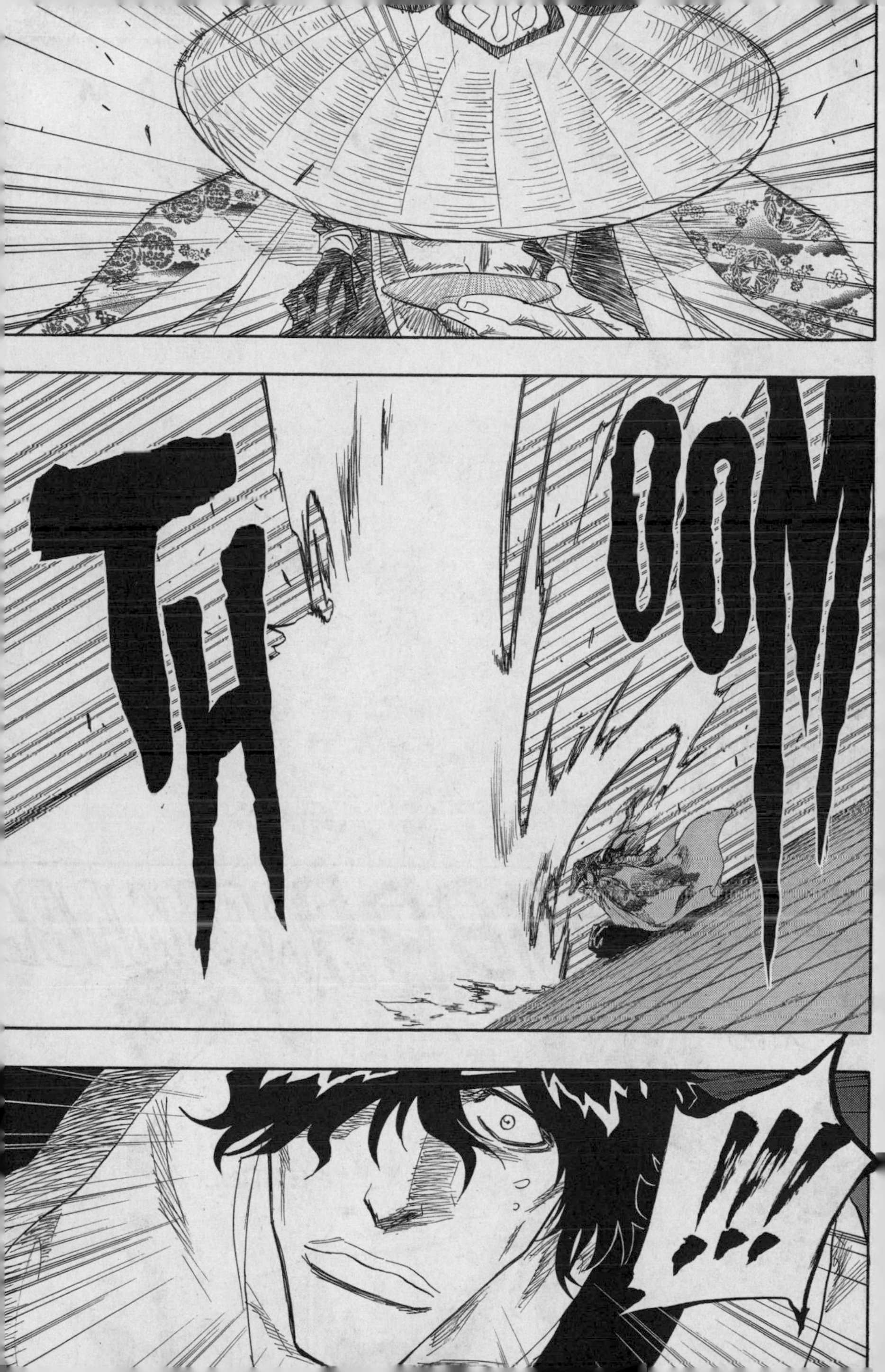
THOOM
!!!

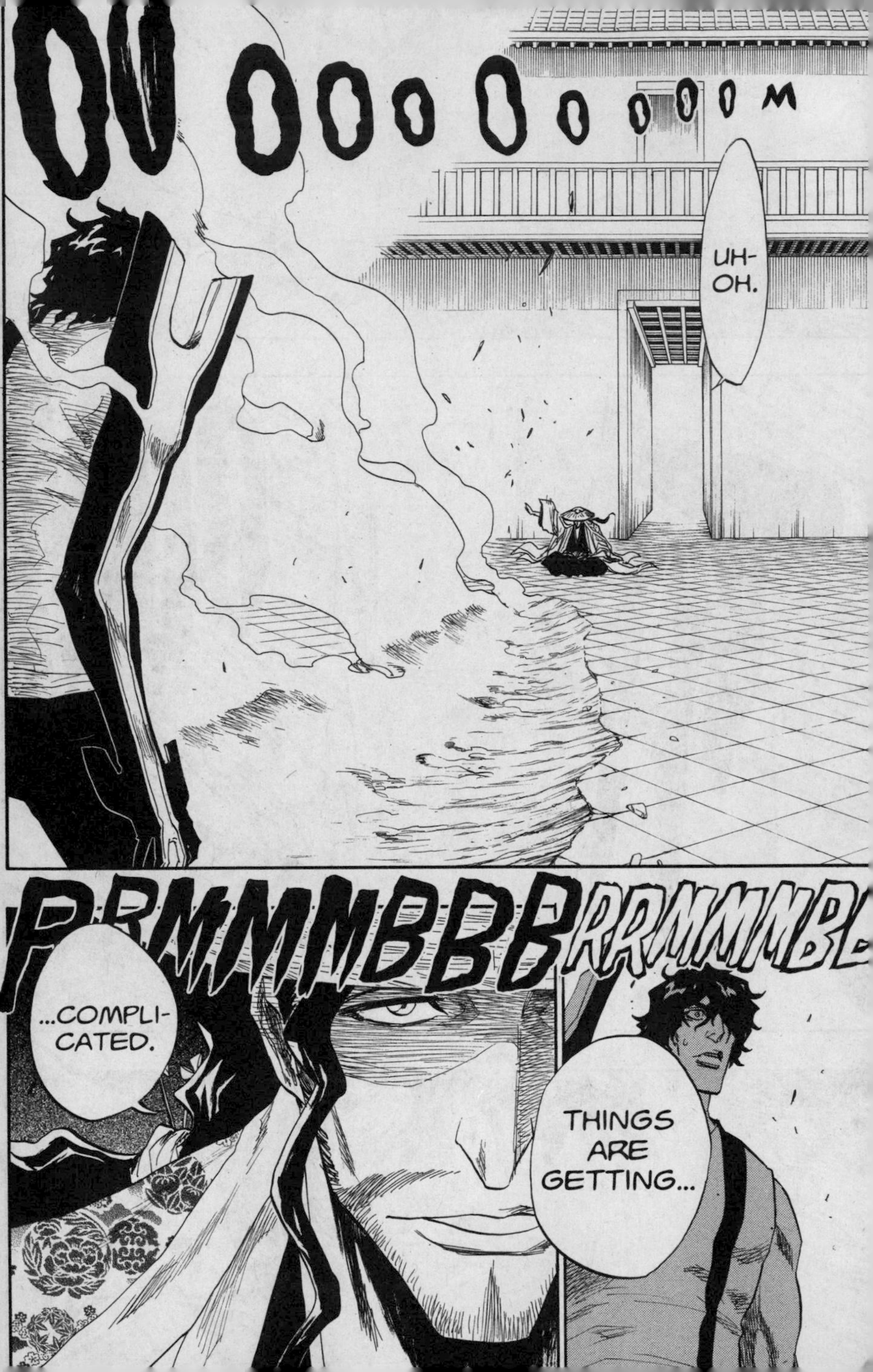
OOOOOOOOOOM
UH-OH.
BRMMMBBBRRMMMBL
THINGS ARE GETTING...
...COMPLICATED.

106. A Cause for Confront

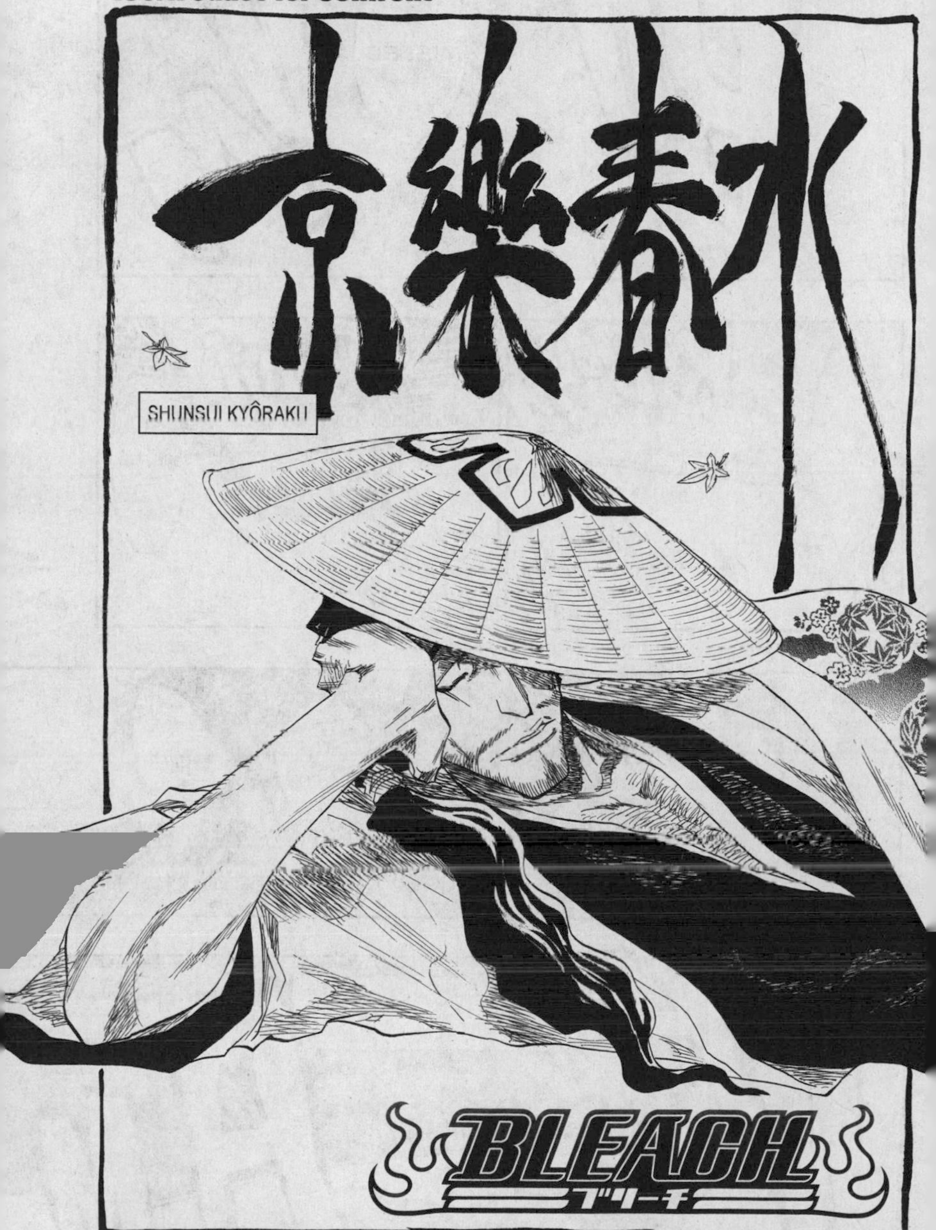
京樂春水
SHUNSUI KYÔRAKU
BLEACH
ブリーチ

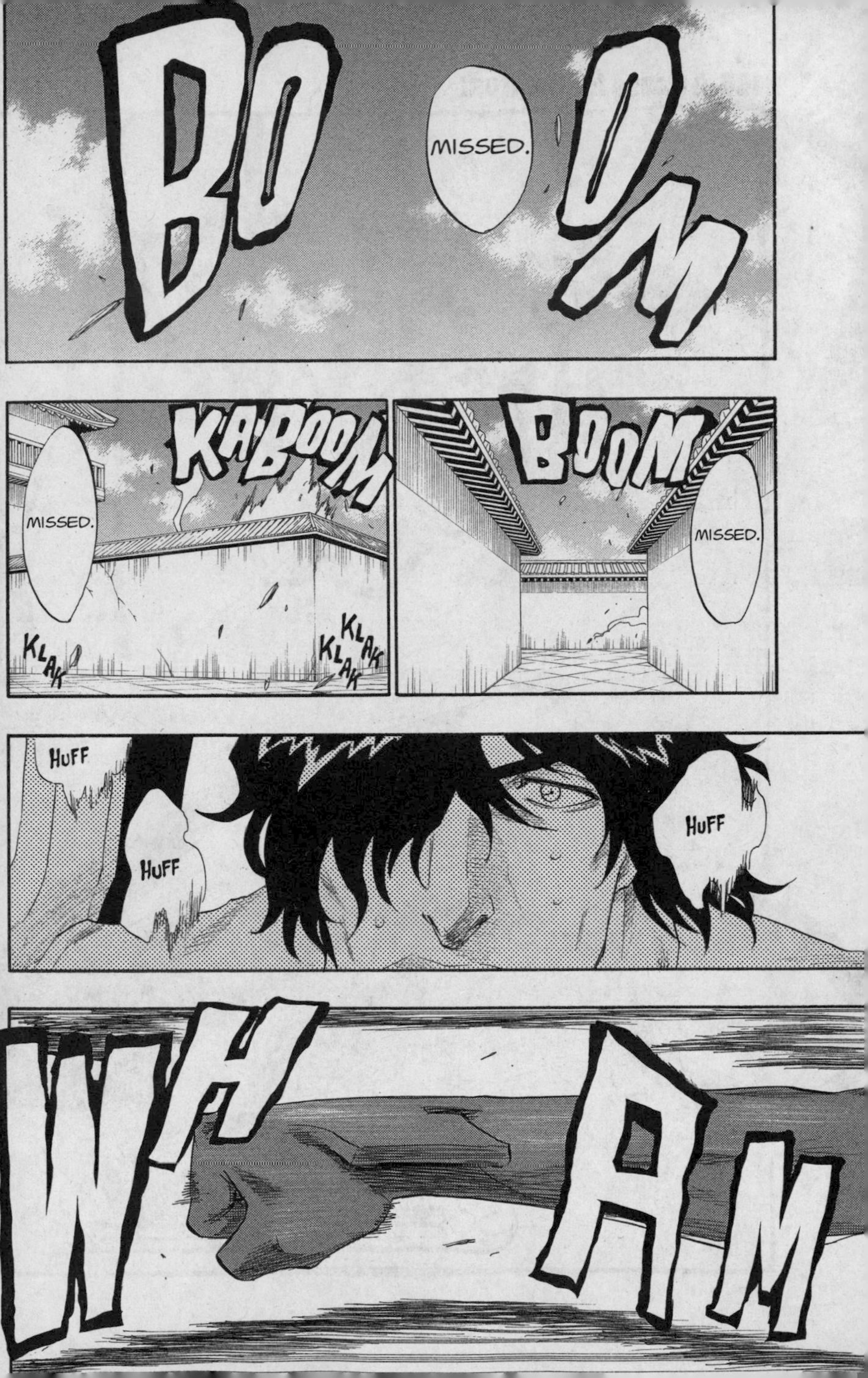
BOOM
MISSED.
BOOM
MISSED.
KA-BOOM
MISSED.
KLAK KLAK
KLAK
HUFF
HUFF
HUFF
WHAM

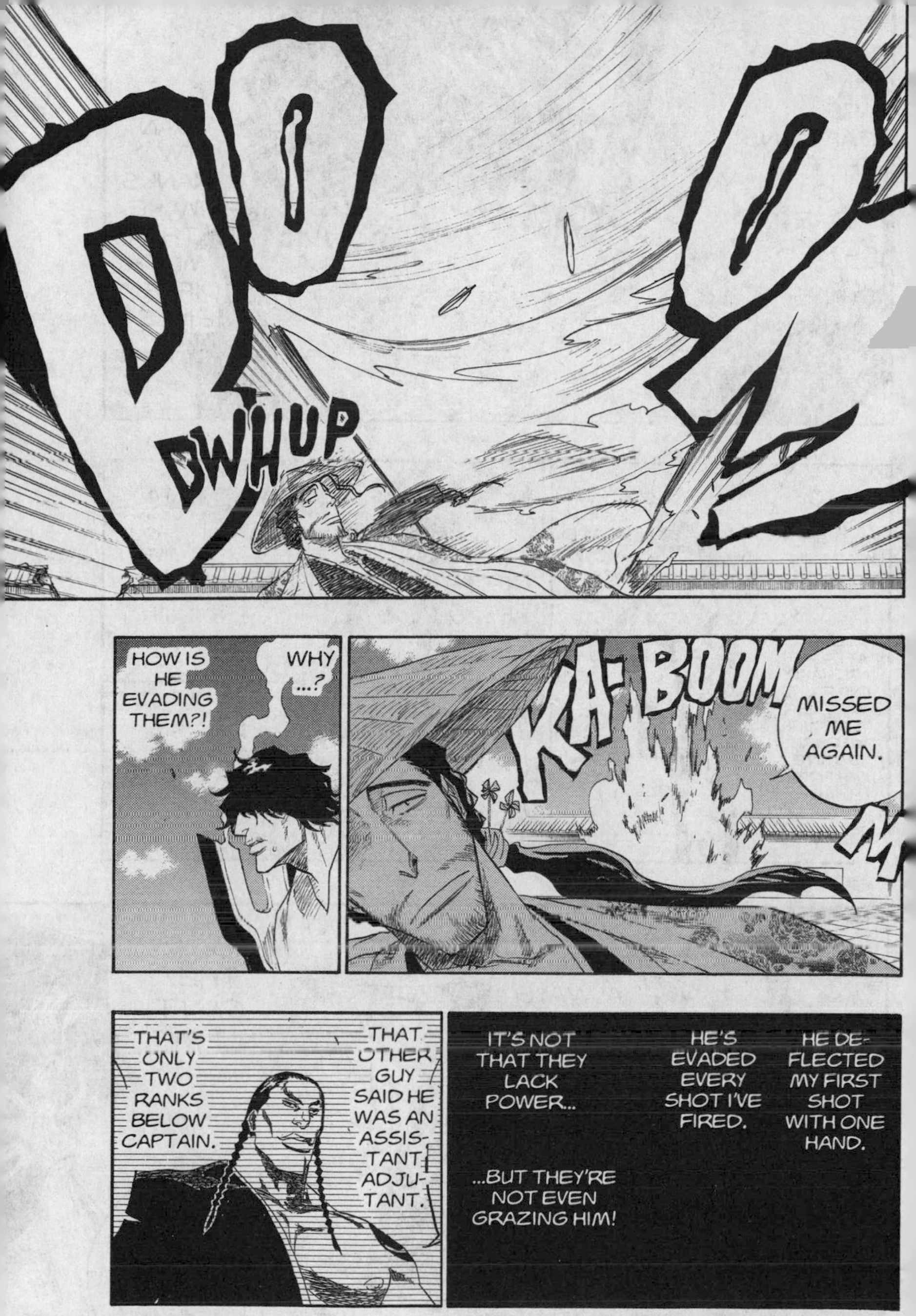
DOOOM
DWHUP
KA-BOOM
MISSED ME AGAIN.
WHY ...?
HOW IS HE EVADING THEM?!
HE DEFLECTED MY FIRST SHOT WITH ONE HAND.
HE'S EVADED EVERY SHOT I'VE FIRED.
IT'S NOT THAT THEY LACK POWER...
...BUT THEY'RE NOT EVEN GRAZING HIM!
THAT OTHER GUY SAID HE WAS AN ASSISTANT ADJUTANT.
THAT'S ONLY TWO RANKS BELOW CAPTAIN.

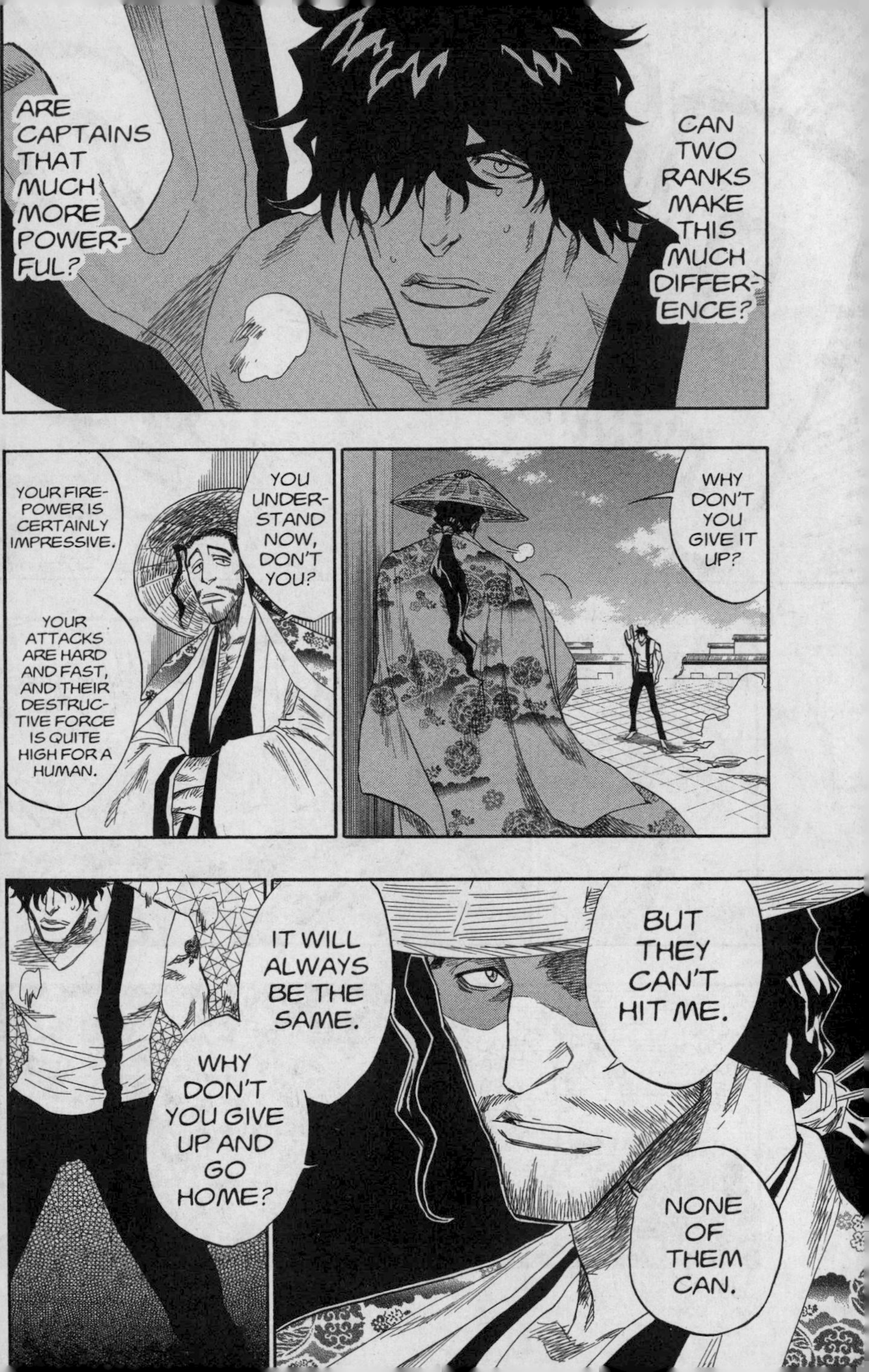
CAN TWO RANKS MAKE THIS MUCH DIFFERENCE?
ARE CAPTAINS THAT MUCH MORE POWERFUL?
WHY DON'T YOU GIVE IT UP?
YOU UNDERSTAND NOW, DON'T YOU?
YOUR FIREPOWER IS CERTAINLY IMPRESSIVE.
YOUR ATTACKS ARE HARD AND FAST, AND THEIR DESTRUCTIVE FORCE IS QUITE HIGH FOR A HUMAN.
BUT THEY CAN'T HIT ME.
NONE OF THEM CAN.
IT WILL ALWAYS BE THE SAME.
WHY DON'T YOU GIVE UP AND GO HOME?

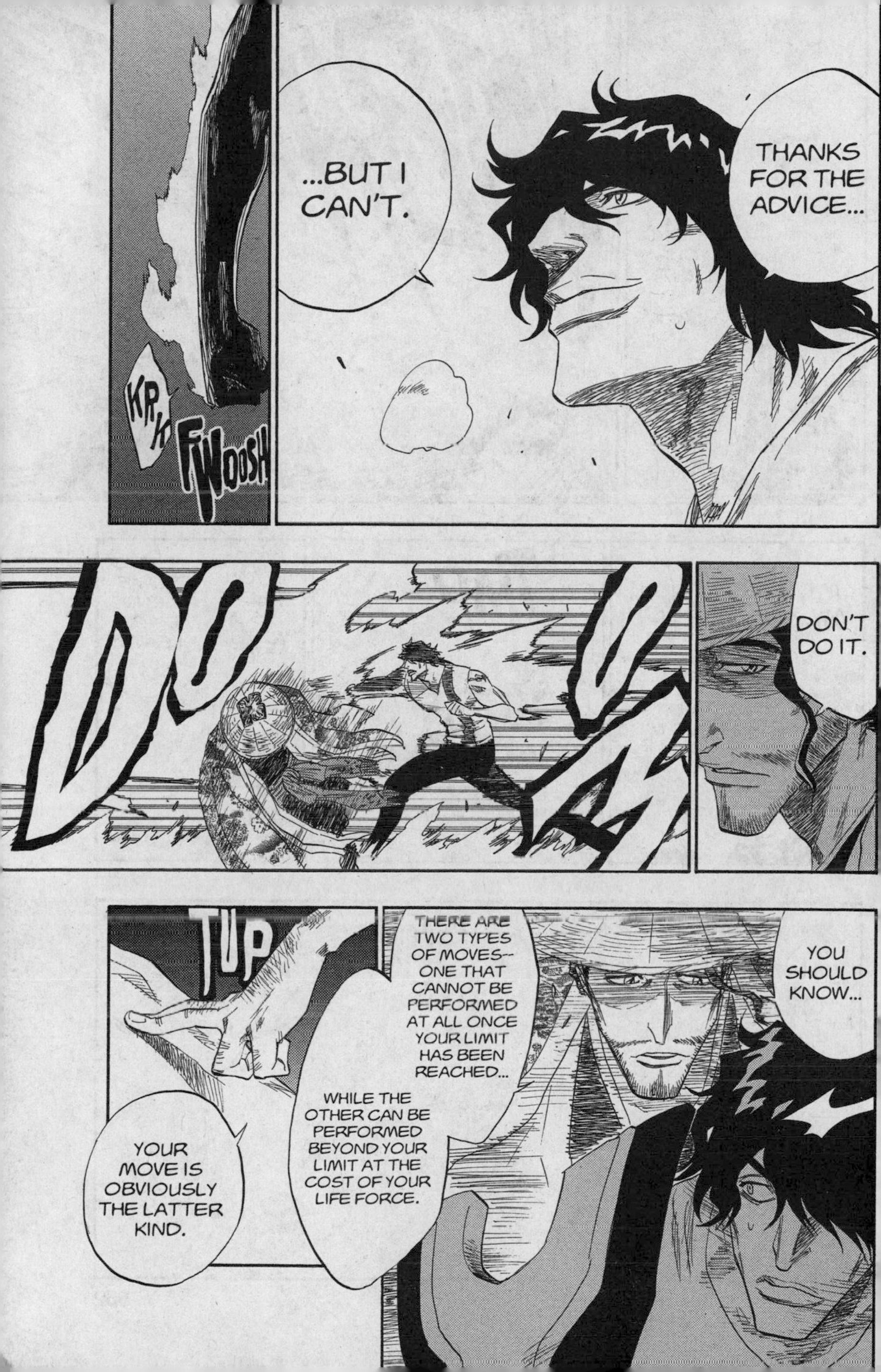
THANKS FOR THE ADVICE...
...BUT I CAN'T.
KRK
FWOOSH
DON'T DO IT.
DOOM
YOU SHOULD KNOW...
THERE ARE TWO TYPES OF MOVES-- ONE THAT CANNOT BE PERFORMED AT ALL ONCE YOUR LIMIT HAS BEEN REACHED...
WHILE THE OTHER CAN BE PERFORMED BEYOND YOUR LIMIT AT THE COST OF YOUR LIFE FORCE.
TUP
YOUR MOVE IS OBVIOUSLY THE LATTER KIND.

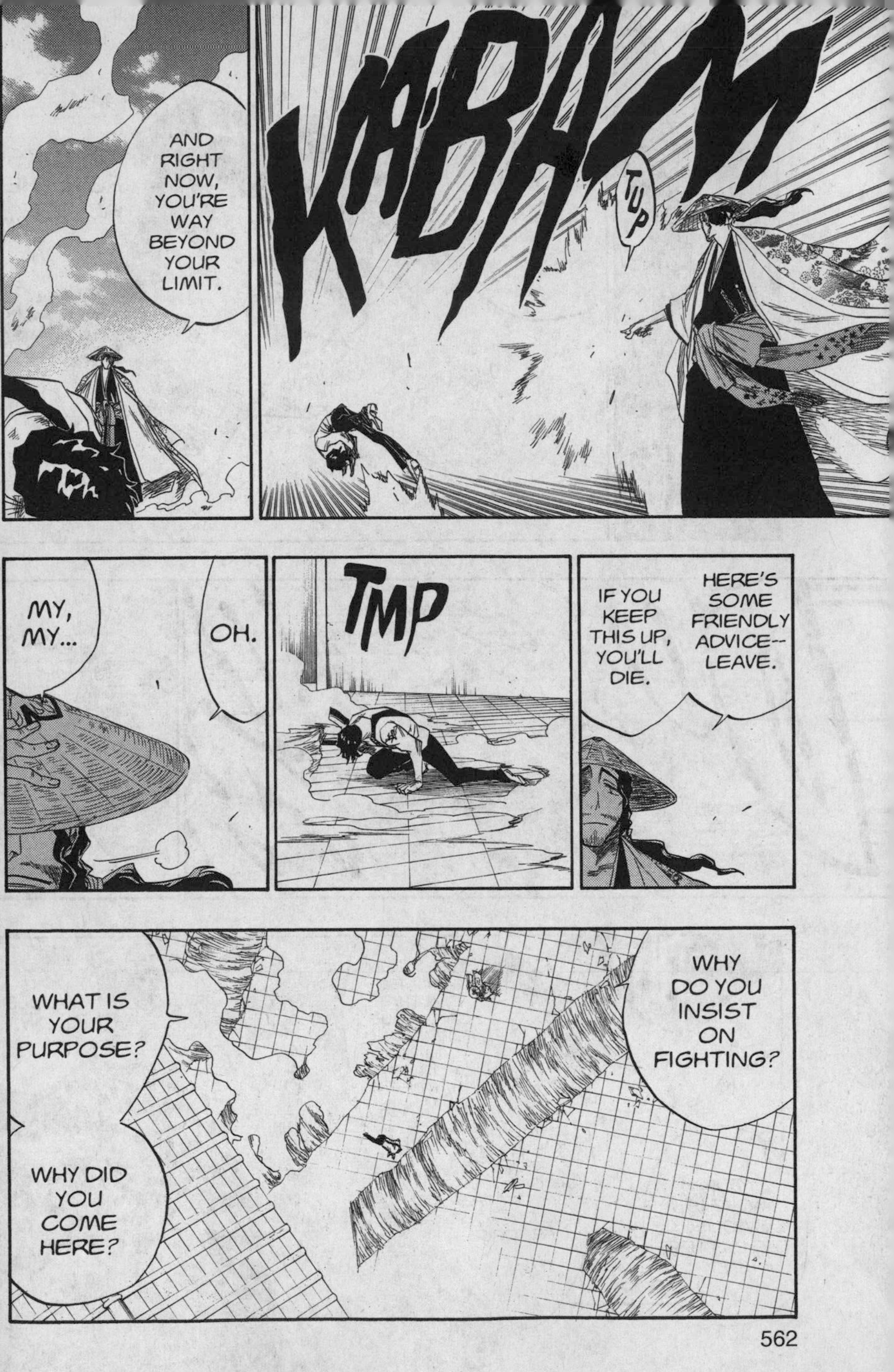
KABAM
TUP
AND RIGHT NOW, YOU'RE WAY BEYOND YOUR LIMIT.
HERE'S SOME FRIENDLY ADVICE--LEAVE.
IF YOU KEEP THIS UP, YOU'LL DIE.
TMP
OH.
MY, MY...
WHY DO YOU INSIST ON FIGHTING?
WHAT IS YOUR PURPOSE?
WHY DID YOU COME HERE?

READ THIS WAY

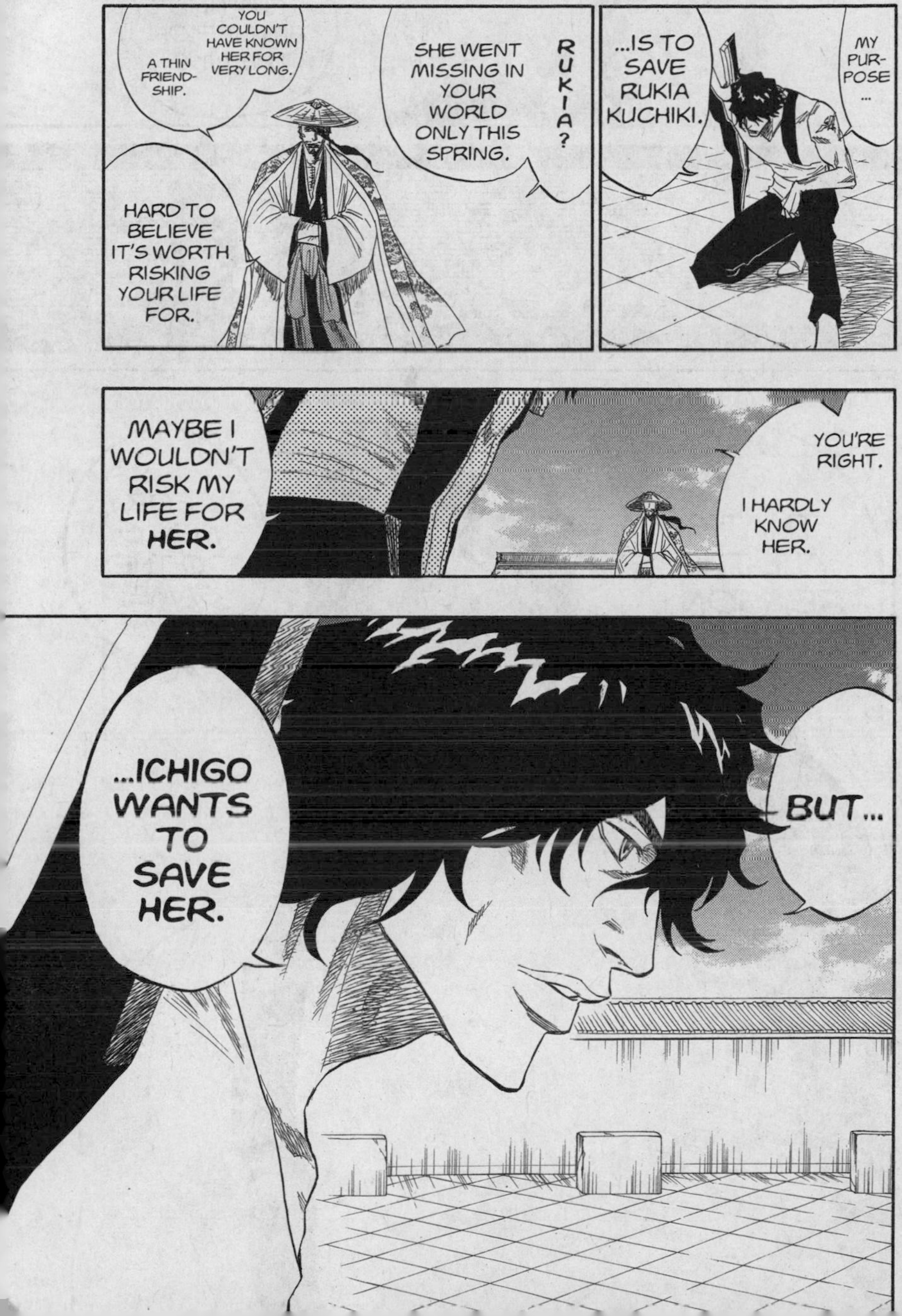
MY PURPOSE...
...IS TO SAVE RUKIA KUCHIKI.
RUKIA?
SHE WENT MISSING IN YOUR WORLD ONLY THIS SPRING.
YOU COULDN'T HAVE KNOWN HER FOR VERY LONG.
A THIN FRIENDSHIP.
HARD TO BELIEVE IT'S WORTH RISKING YOUR LIFE FOR.
YOU'RE RIGHT.
I HARDLY KNOW HER.
MAYBE I WOULDN'T RISK MY LIFE FOR HER.
BUT...
...ICHIGO WANTS TO SAVE HER.

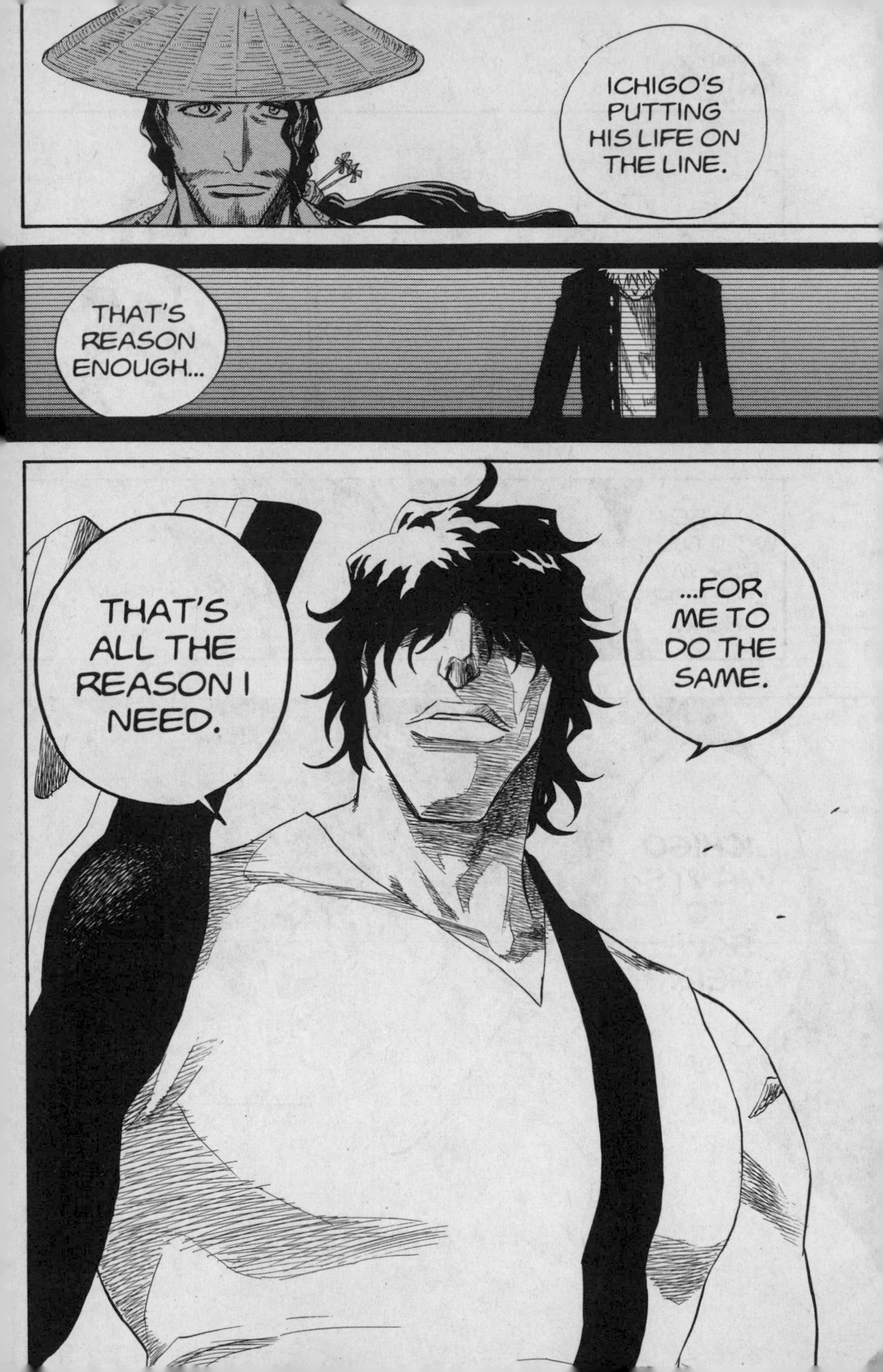
ICHIGO'S PUTTING HIS LIFE ON THE LINE.
THAT'S REASON ENOUGH...
...FOR ME TO DO THE SAME.
THAT'S ALL THE REASON I NEED.

OH. WELL...

YOUR RESOLVE SEEMS VERY STRONG.

IT WOULD BE DISRE-SPECTFUL FOR ME TO TRY TO TALK YOU OUT OF IT.

ALL RIGHT, THEN...

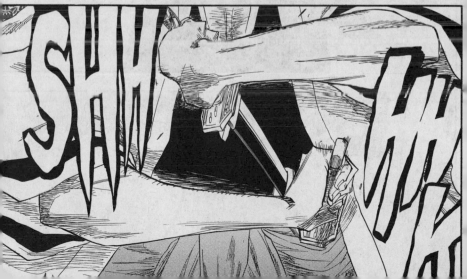

SHHH

HHHH

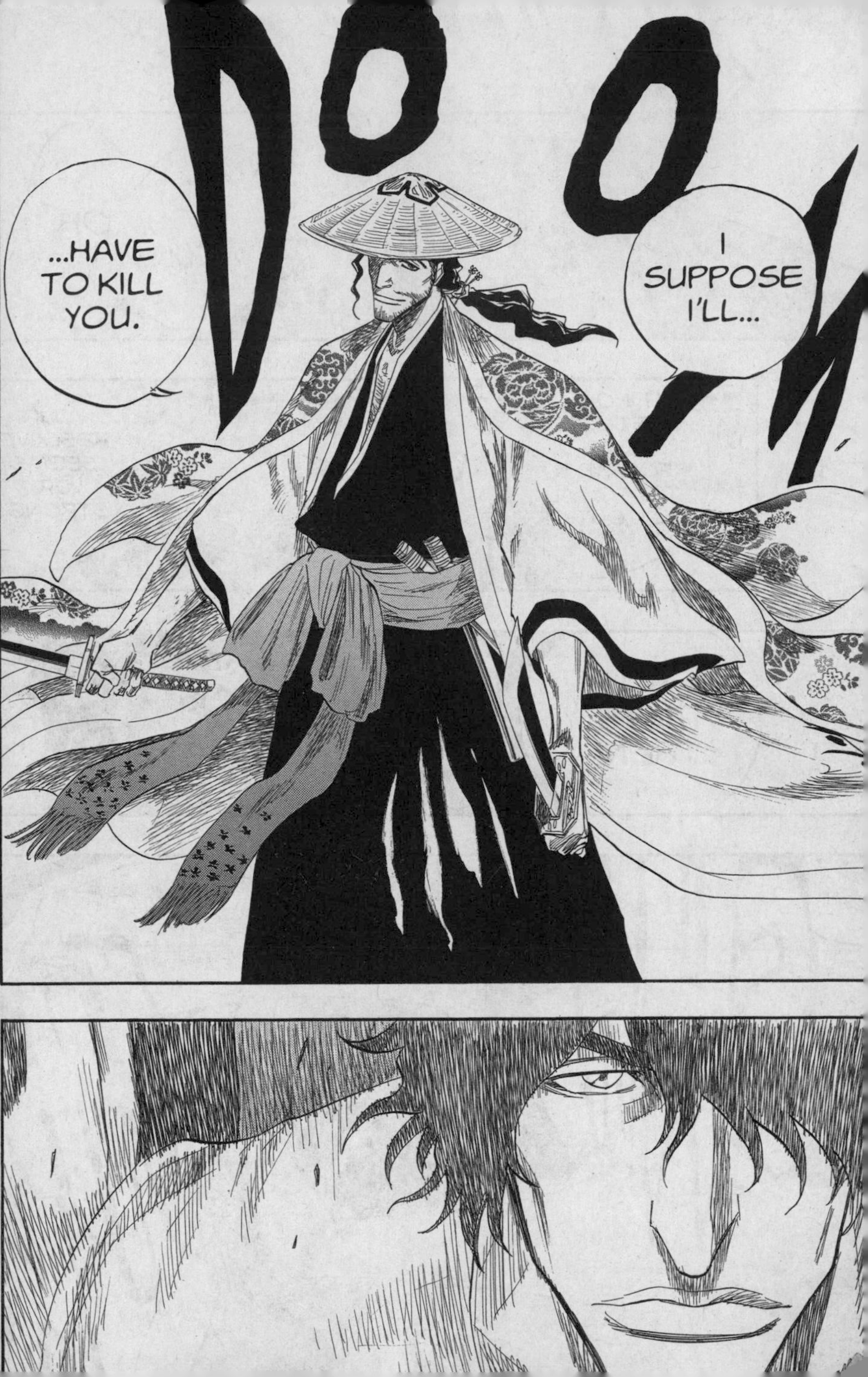
DOOM
I SUPPOSE I'LL...
...HAVE TO KILL YOU.

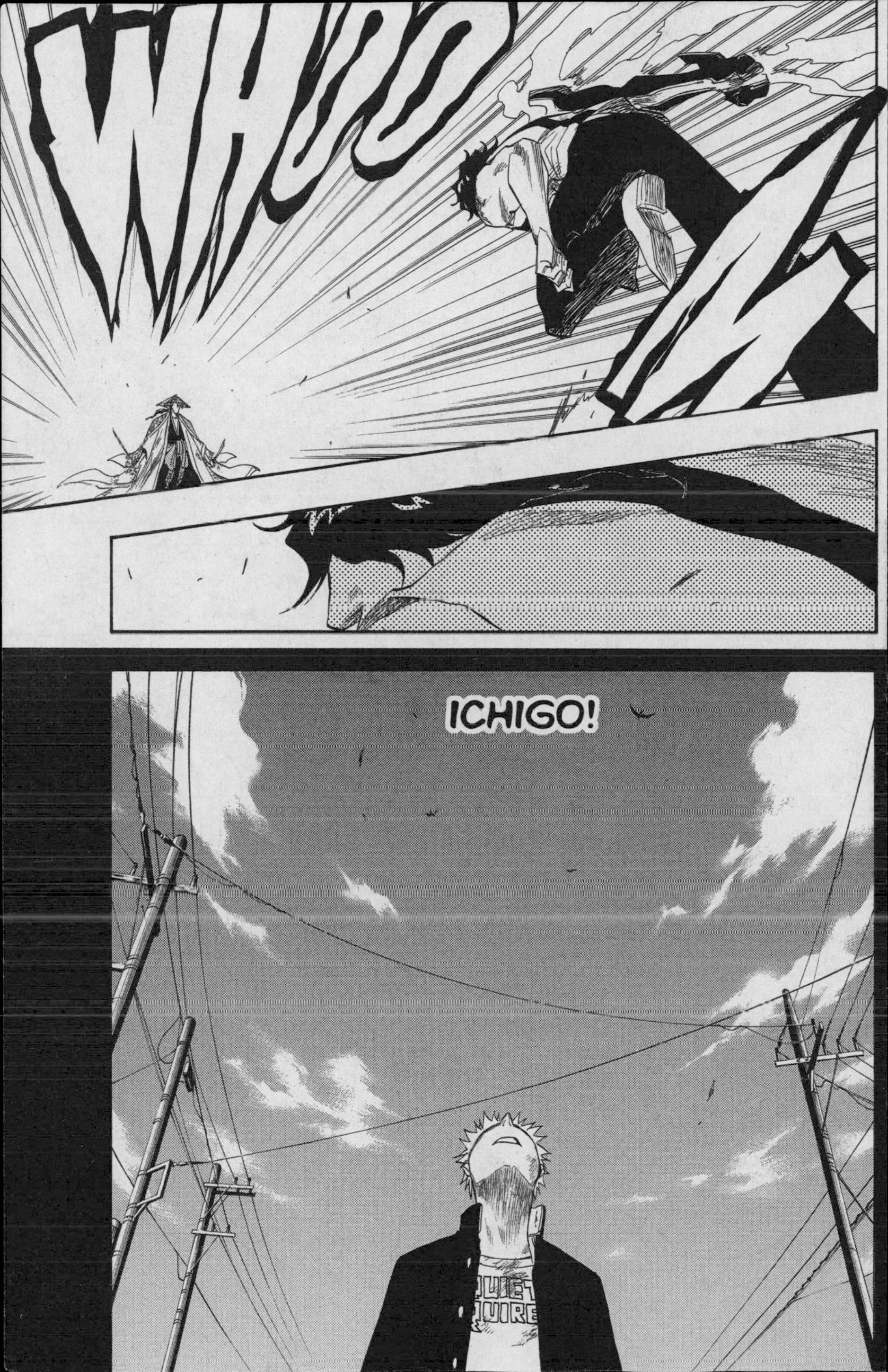
ICHIGO!

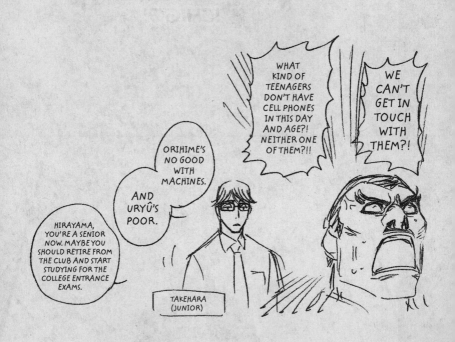

WE CAN'T GET IN TOUCH WITH THEM?!
WHAT KIND OF TEENAGERS DON'T HAVE CELL PHONES IN THIS DAY AND AGE?! NEITHER ONE OF THEM?!!
ORIHIME'S NO GOOD WITH MACHINES.
AND URYÛ'S POOR.
TAKEHARA (JUNIOR)
HIRAYAMA, YOU'RE A SENIOR NOW. MAYBE YOU SHOULD RETIRE FROM THE CLUB AND START STUDYING FOR THE COLLEGE ENTRANCE EXAMS.

107. Heat in Trust

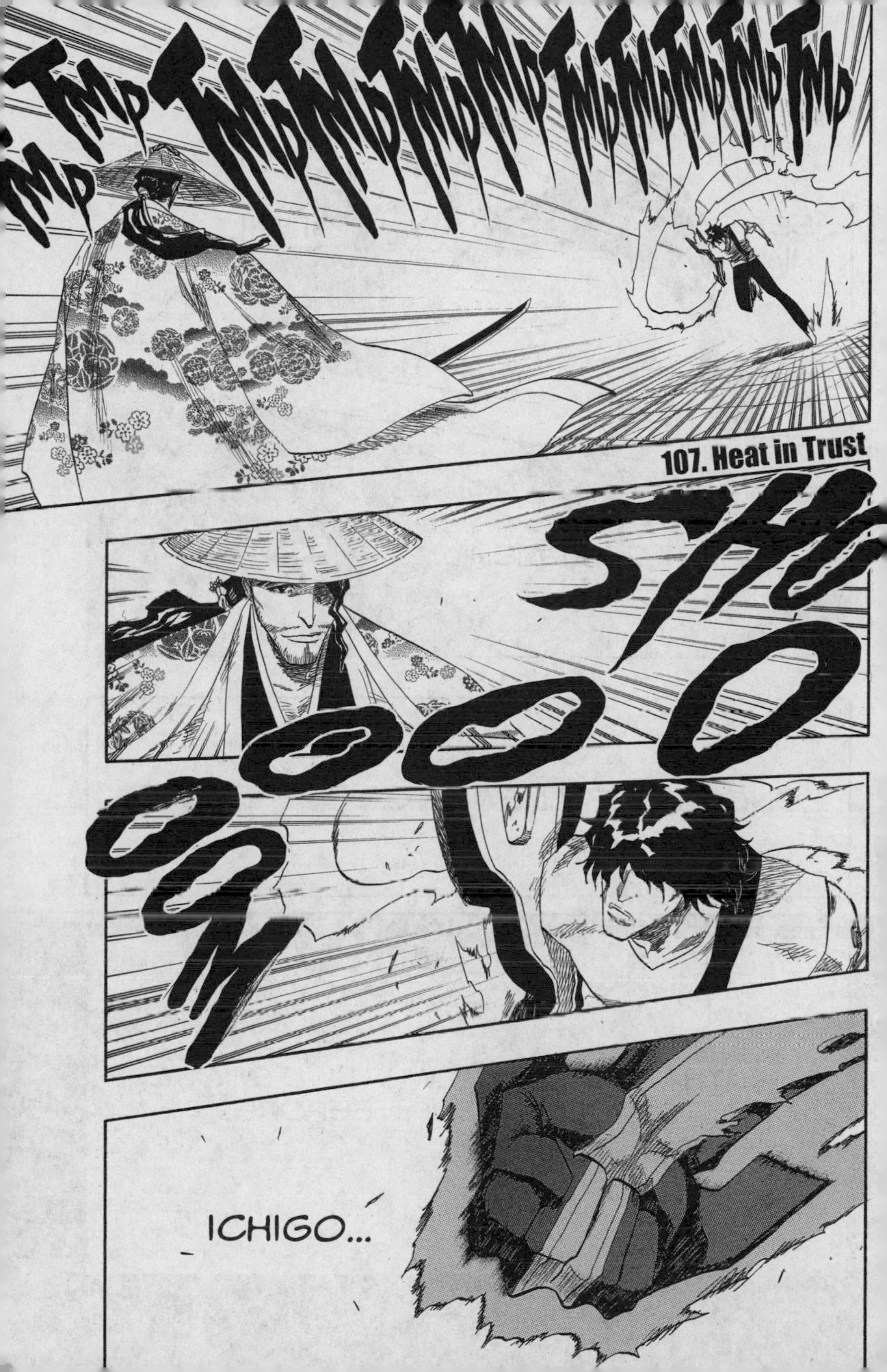
TMP TMP TMP TMP TMP TMP TMP TMP TMP TMP TMP TMP TMP
SHOOOOOOM
ICHIGO...

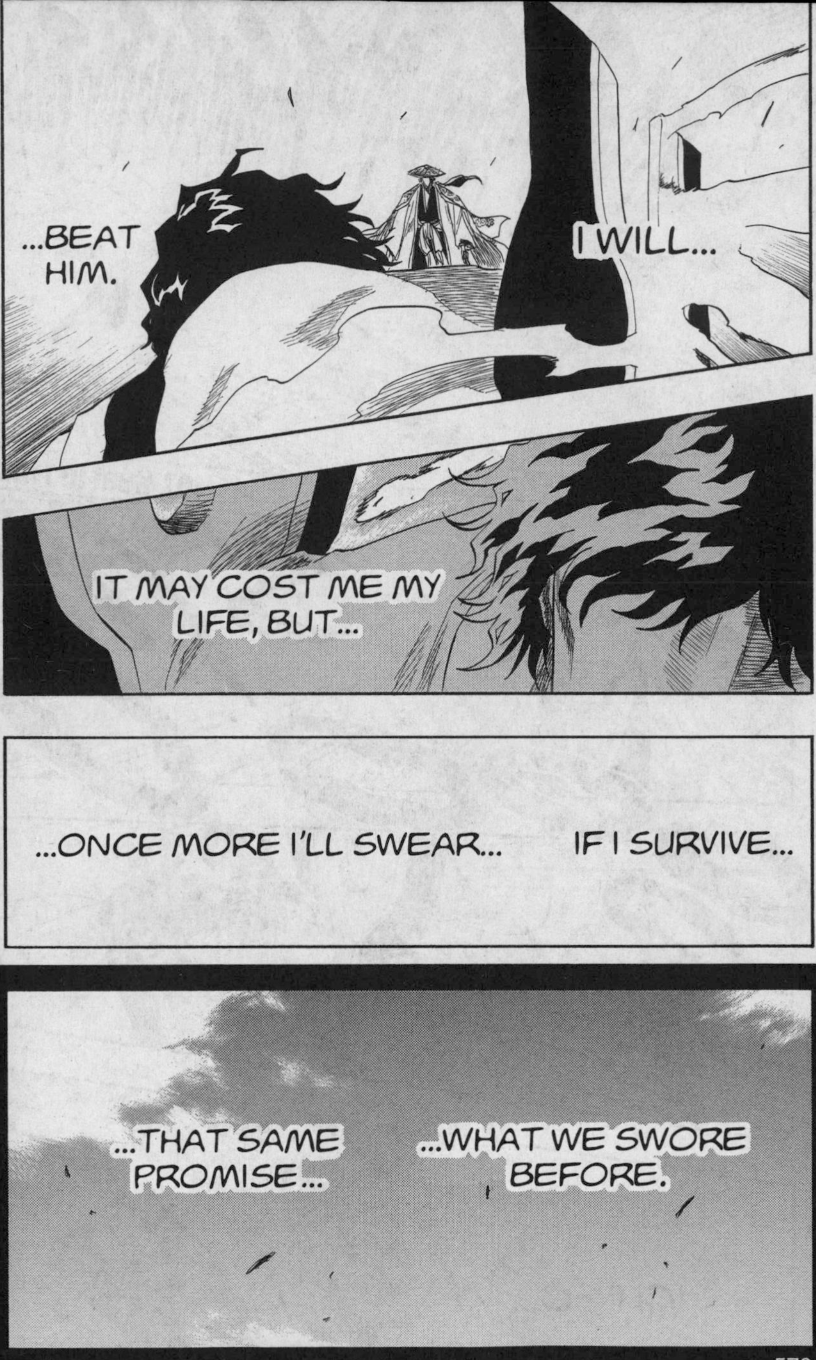
I WILL...
...BEAT HIM.
IT MAY COST ME MY LIFE, BUT...
IF I SURVIVE...
...ONCE MORE I'LL SWEAR...
...WHAT WE SWORE BEFORE.
...THAT SAME PROMISE...

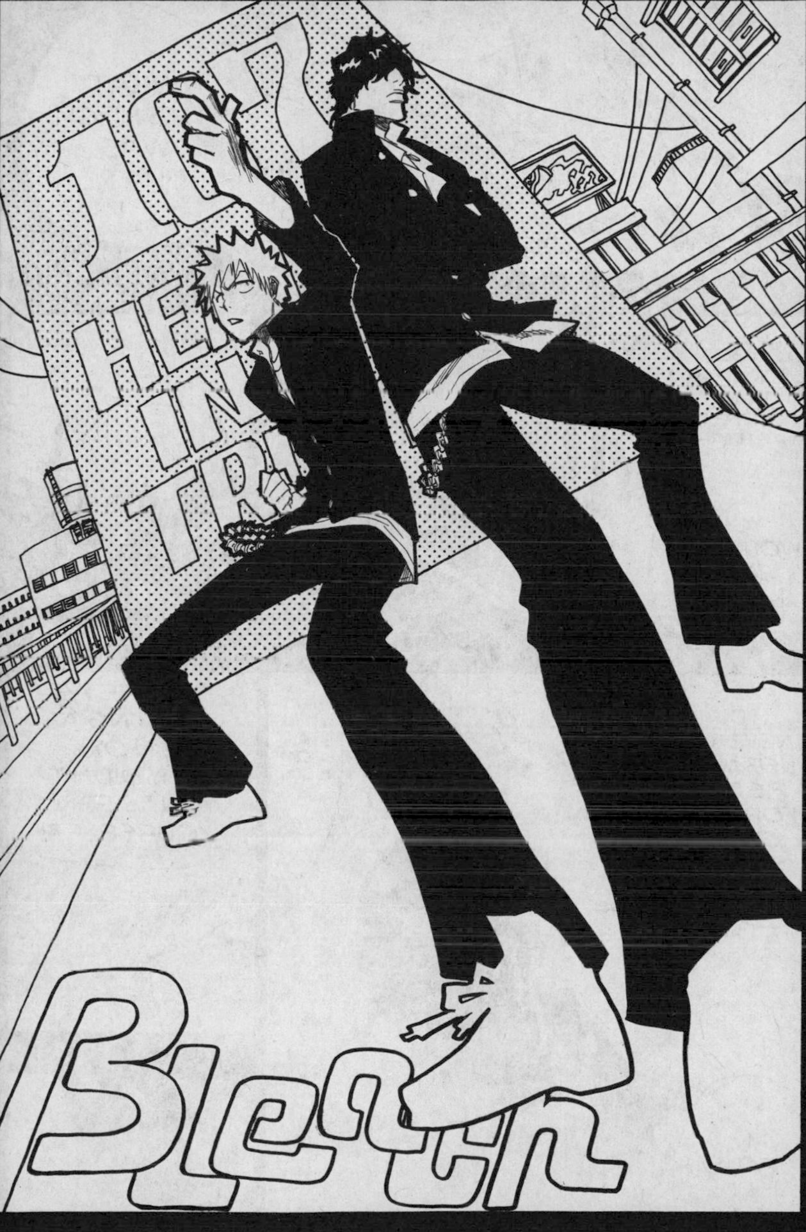
107
Bleach

107. Heat in Trust

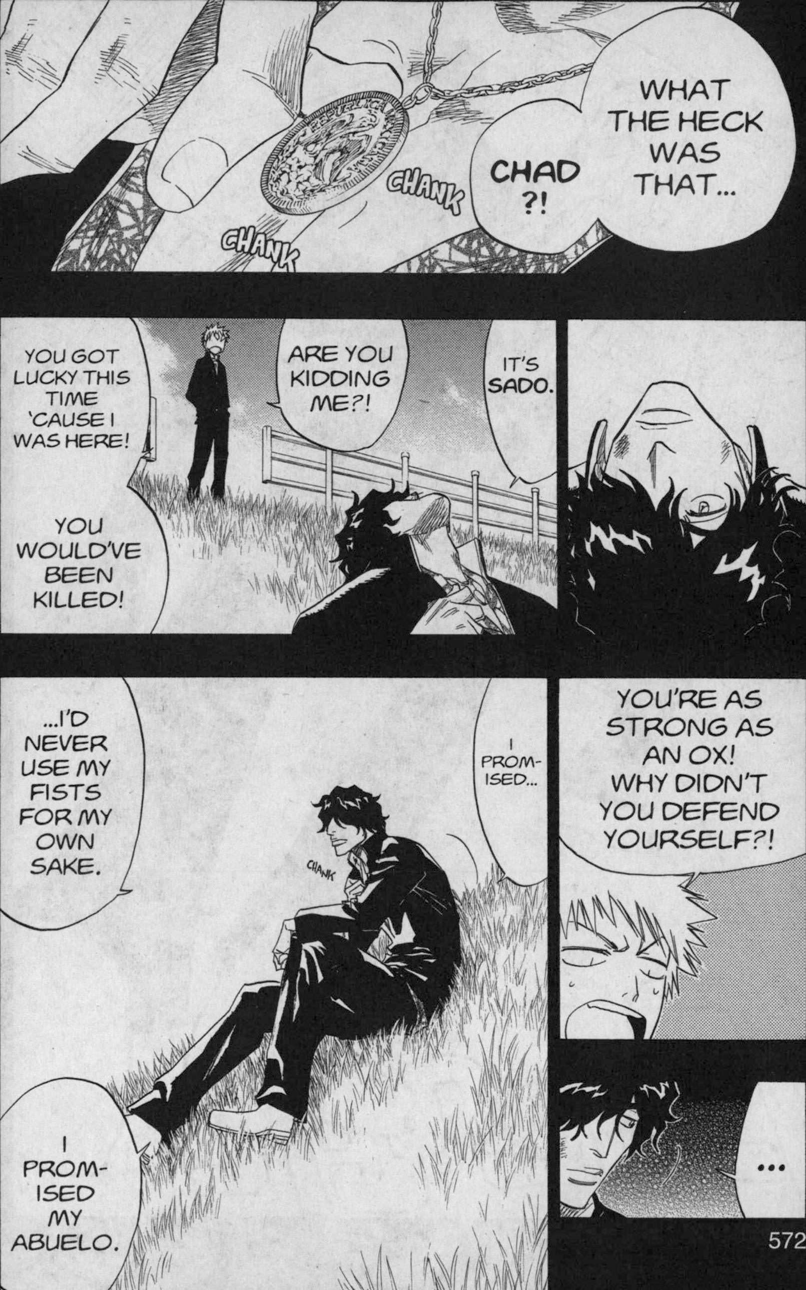
WHAT THE HECK WAS THAT...
CHAD ?!
CHANK
CHANK
IT'S SADO.
ARE YOU KIDDING ME?!
YOU GOT LUCKY THIS TIME 'CAUSE I WAS HERE!
YOU WOULD'VE BEEN KILLED!
YOU'RE AS STRONG AS AN OX! WHY DIDN'T YOU DEFEND YOURSELF?!
...
I PROM-ISED...
...I'D NEVER USE MY FISTS FOR MY OWN SAKE.
CHANK
I PROM-ISED MY ABUELO.

READ THIS WAY

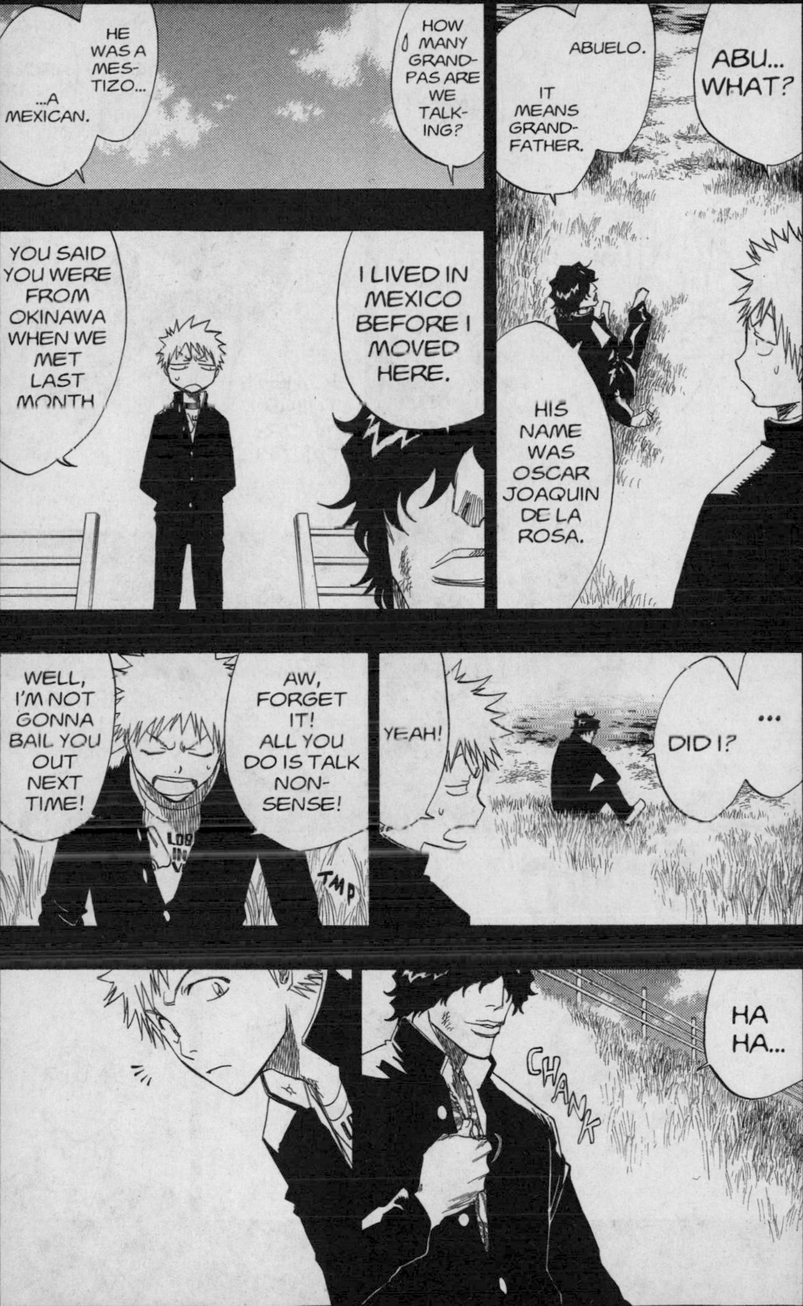

ABU... WHAT?
ABUELO.
IT MEANS GRANDFATHER.
HIS NAME WAS OSCAR JOAQUIN DE LA ROSA.
HOW MANY GRANDPAS ARE WE TALKING?
HE WAS A MESTIZO...
...A MEXICAN.
I LIVED IN MEXICO BEFORE I MOVED HERE.
YOU SAID YOU WERE FROM OKINAWA WHEN WE MET LAST MONTH
... DID I?
YEAH!
AW, FORGET IT! ALL YOU DO IS TALK NONSENSE!
WELL, I'M NOT GONNA BAIL YOU OUT NEXT TIME!
TMP
HA HA...
CHANK

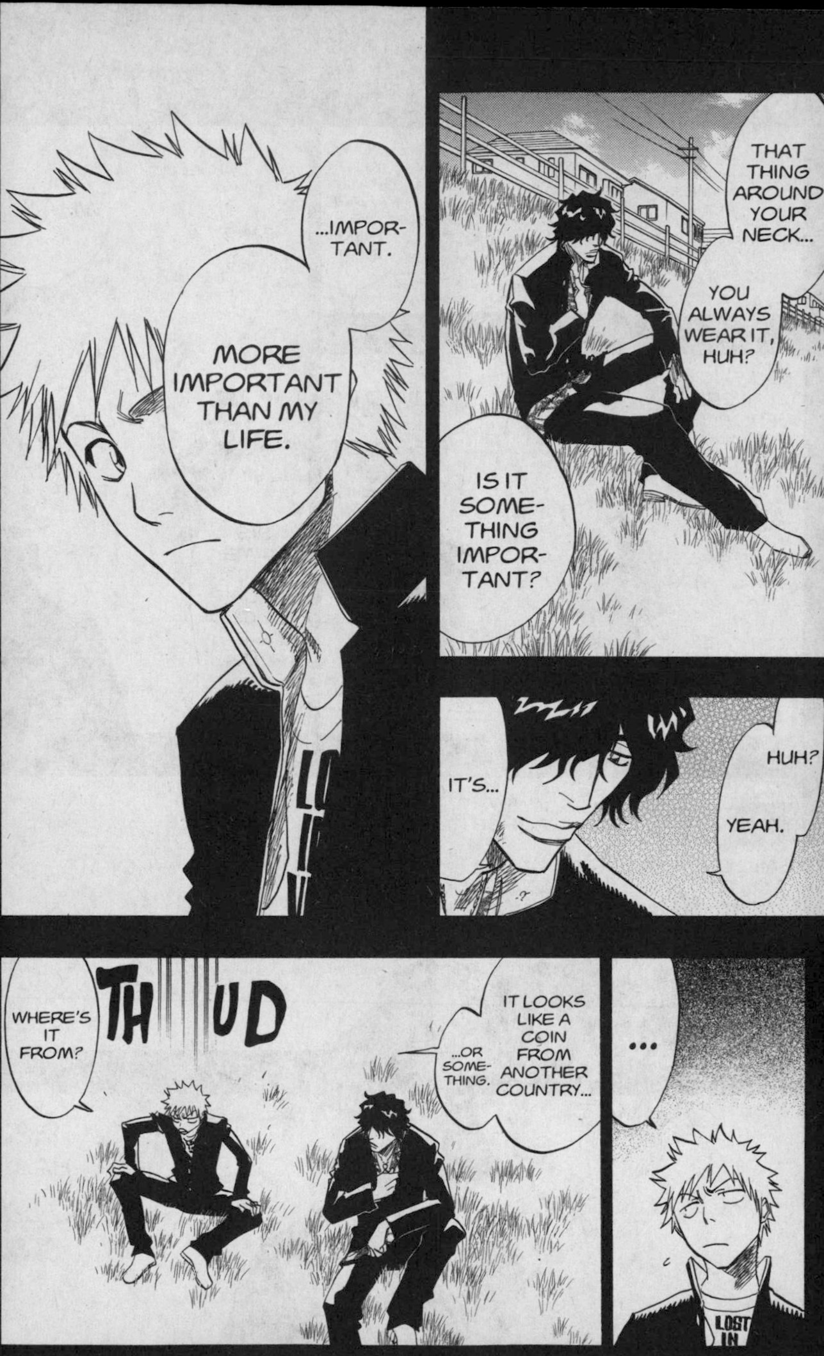
THAT THING AROUND YOUR NECK...
YOU ALWAYS WEAR IT, HUH?
IS IT SOME-THING IMPOR-TANT?
HUH?
YEAH.
IT'S...
...IMPOR-TANT.
MORE IMPORTANT THAN MY LIFE.
...
IT LOOKS LIKE A COIN FROM ANOTHER COUNTRY...
...OR SOME-THING.
THUD
WHERE'S IT FROM?

READ THIS WAY

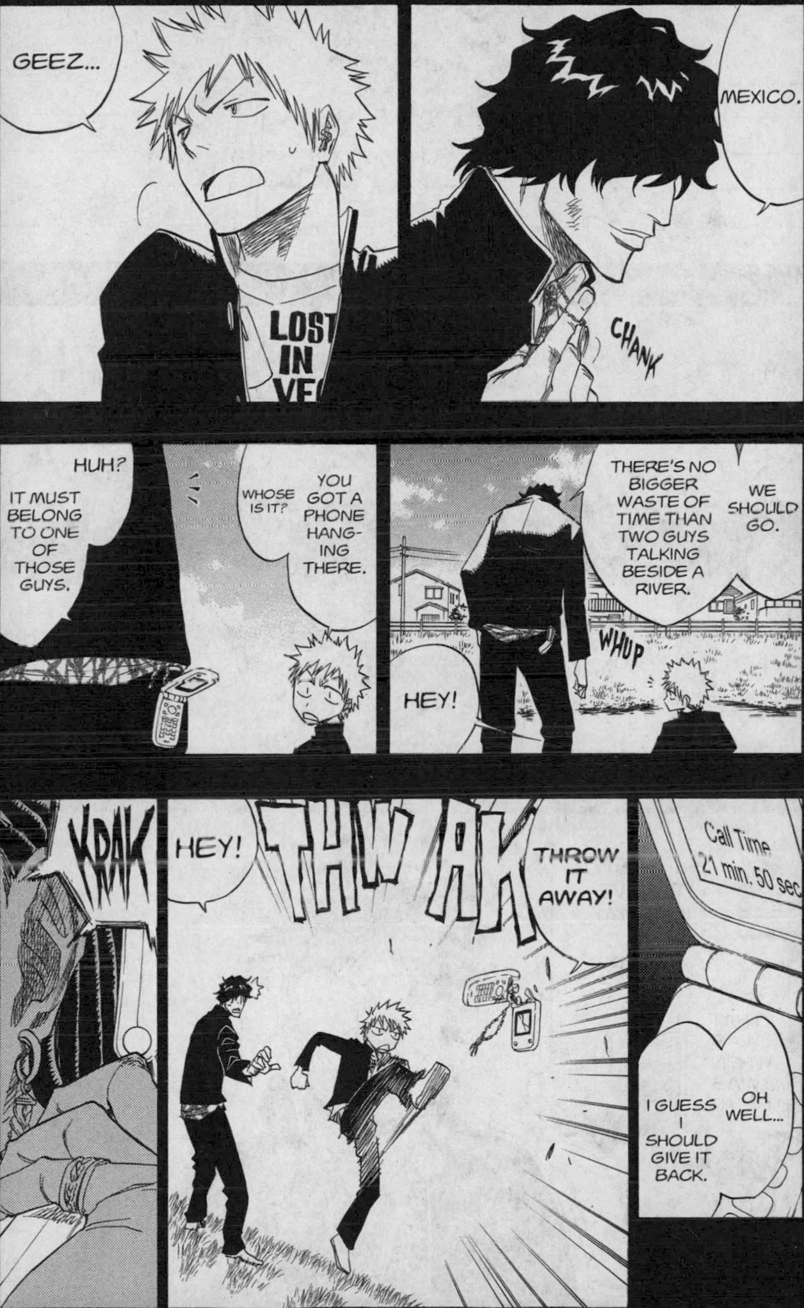
MEXICO.
CHANK
GEEZ...
WE SHOULD GO.
THERE'S NO BIGGER WASTE OF TIME THAN TWO GUYS TALKING BESIDE A RIVER.
WHUP
HEY!
YOU GOT A PHONE HANGING THERE.
WHOSE IS IT?
HUH?
IT MUST BELONG TO ONE OF THOSE GUYS.
Call Time
21 min. 50 sec
OH WELL...
I GUESS I SHOULD GIVE IT BACK.
THROW IT AWAY!
THWAK
HEY!
KRAK

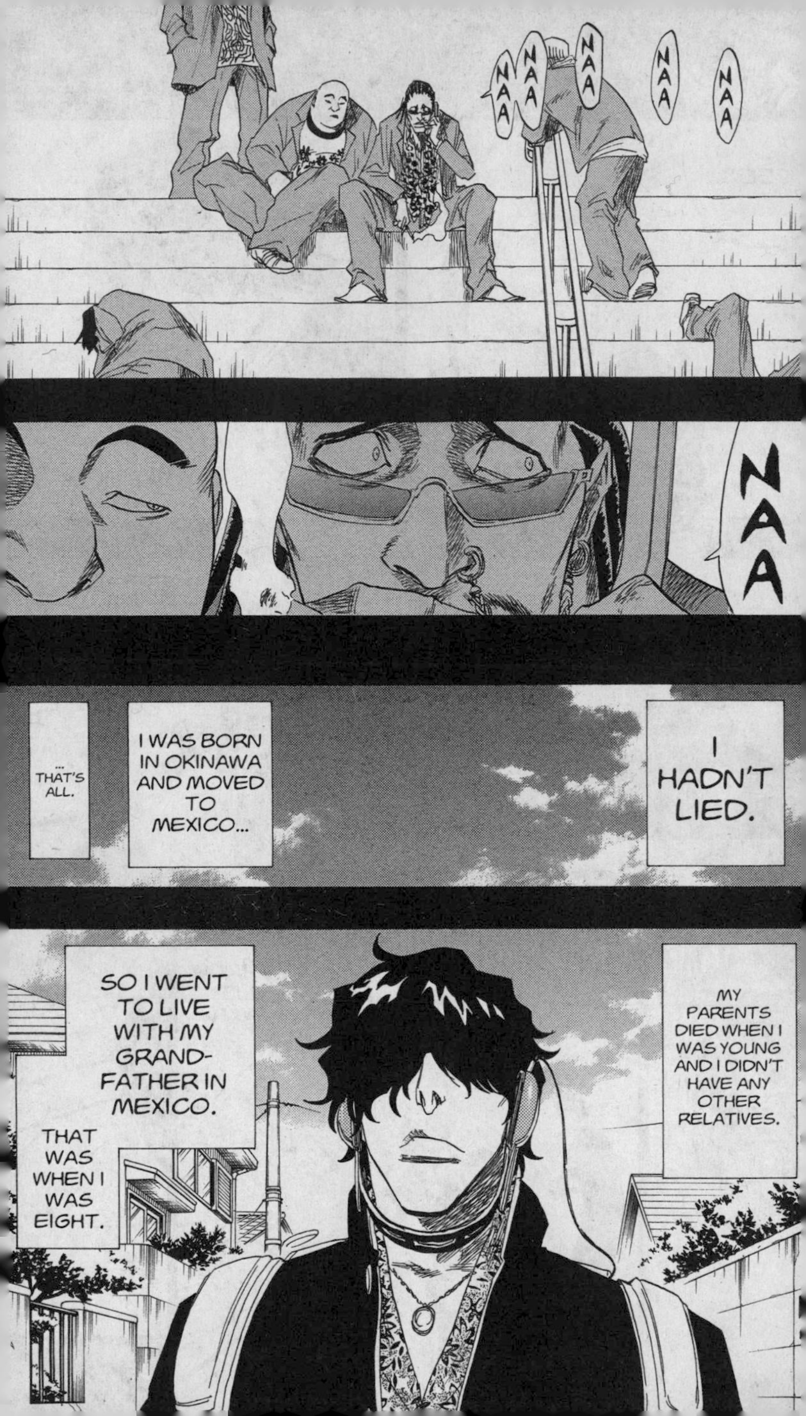
NAA
NAA
NAA
NAA
NAA
NAA
I HADN'T LIED.
I WAS BORN IN OKINAWA AND MOVED TO MEXICO...
... THAT'S ALL.
MY PARENTS DIED WHEN I WAS YOUNG AND I DIDN'T HAVE ANY OTHER RELATIVES.
SO I WENT TO LIVE WITH MY GRAND-FATHER IN MEXICO.
THAT WAS WHEN I WAS EIGHT.

READ THIS WAY

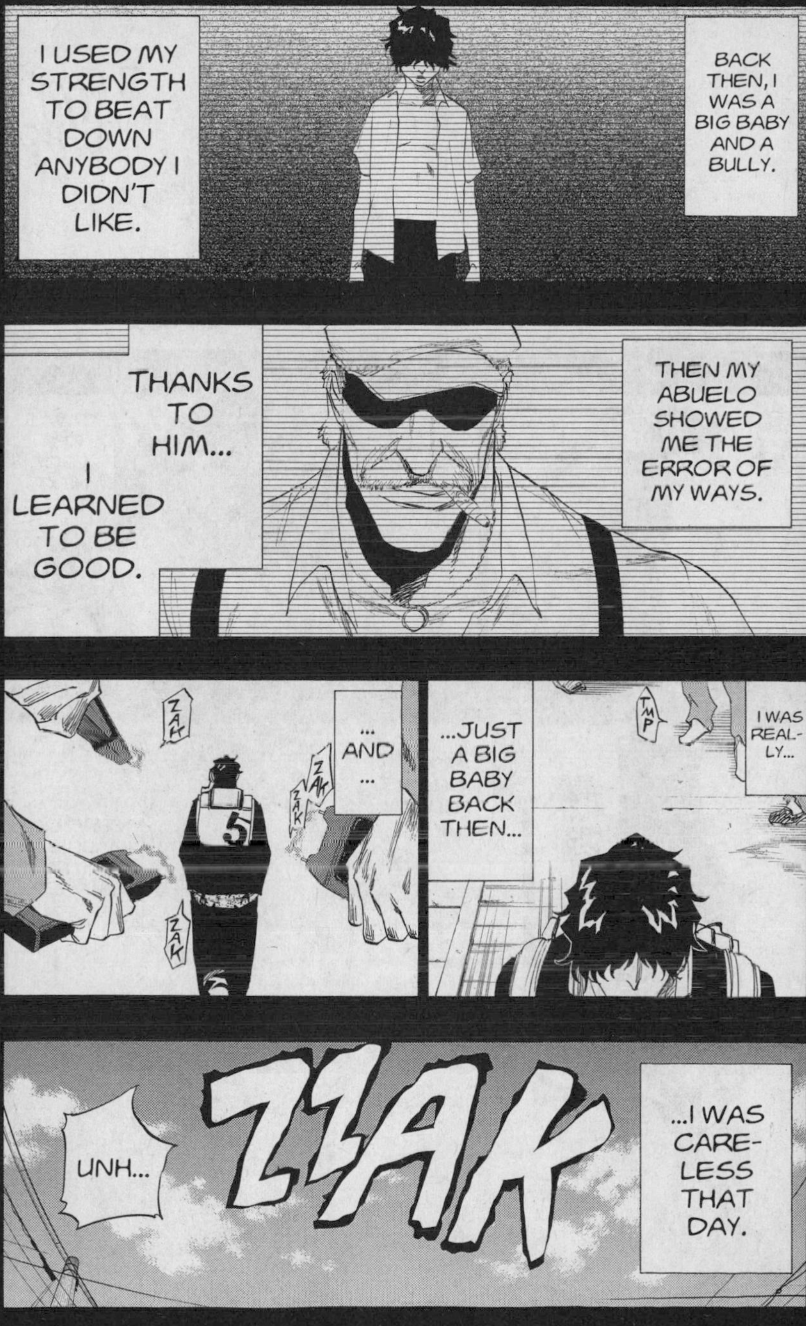

BACK THEN, I WAS A BIG BABY AND A BULLY.
I USED MY STRENGTH TO BEAT DOWN ANYBODY I DIDN'T LIKE.
THEN MY ABUELO SHOWED ME THE ERROR OF MY WAYS.
THANKS TO HIM...
I LEARNED TO BE GOOD.
I WAS REAL-LY...
TMP
...JUST A BIG BABY BACK THEN...
... AND ...
ZAK
ZAK
ZAK
ZAK
...I WAS CARE-LESS THAT DAY.
ZZAK
UNH...

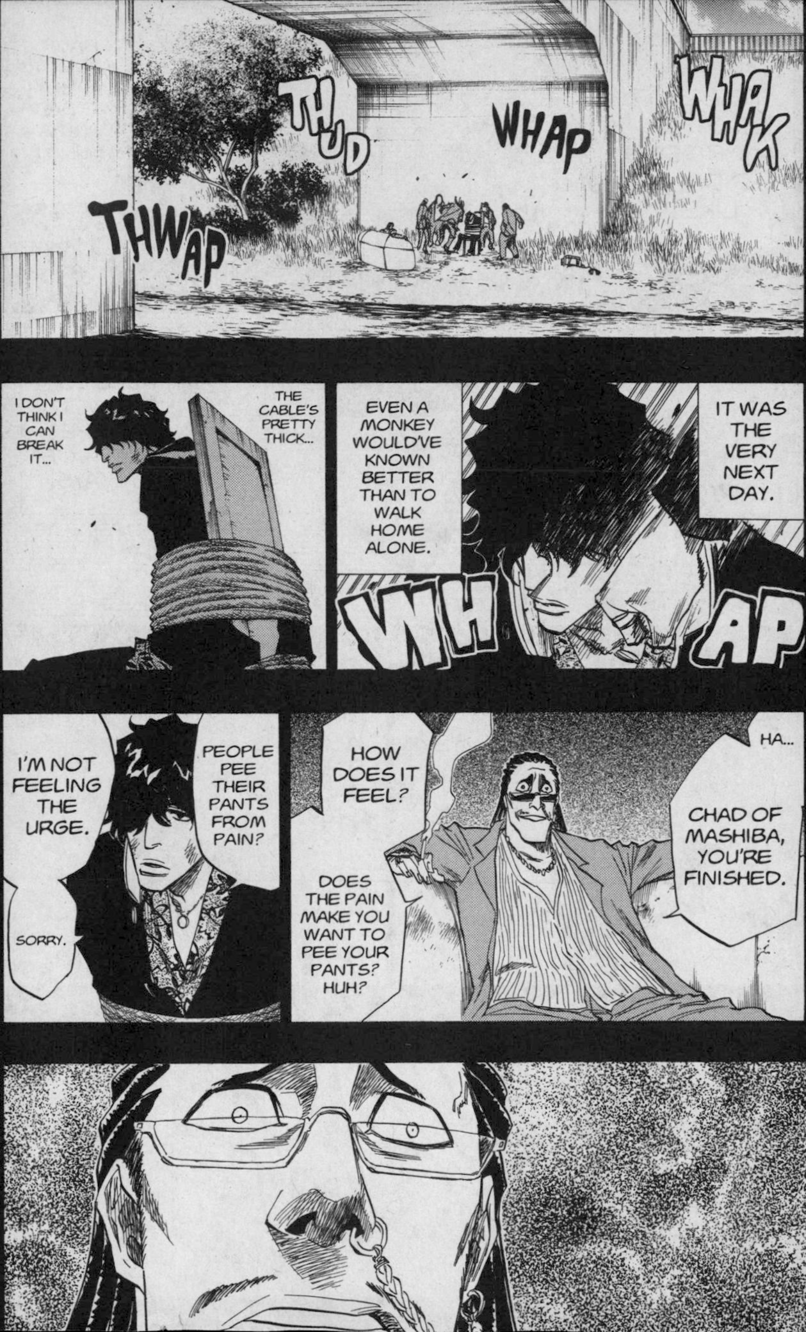
WHAK
WHAP
THUD
THWAP
IT WAS THE VERY NEXT DAY.
EVEN A MONKEY WOULD'VE KNOWN BETTER THAN TO WALK HOME ALONE.
WH AP
THE CABLE'S PRETTY THICK...
I DON'T THINK I CAN BREAK IT...
HA...
CHAD OF MASHIBA, YOU'RE FINISHED.
HOW DOES IT FEEL?
DOES THE PAIN MAKE YOU WANT TO PEE YOUR PANTS? HUH?
PEOPLE PEE THEIR PANTS FROM PAIN?
I'M NOT FEELING THE URGE.
SORRY.

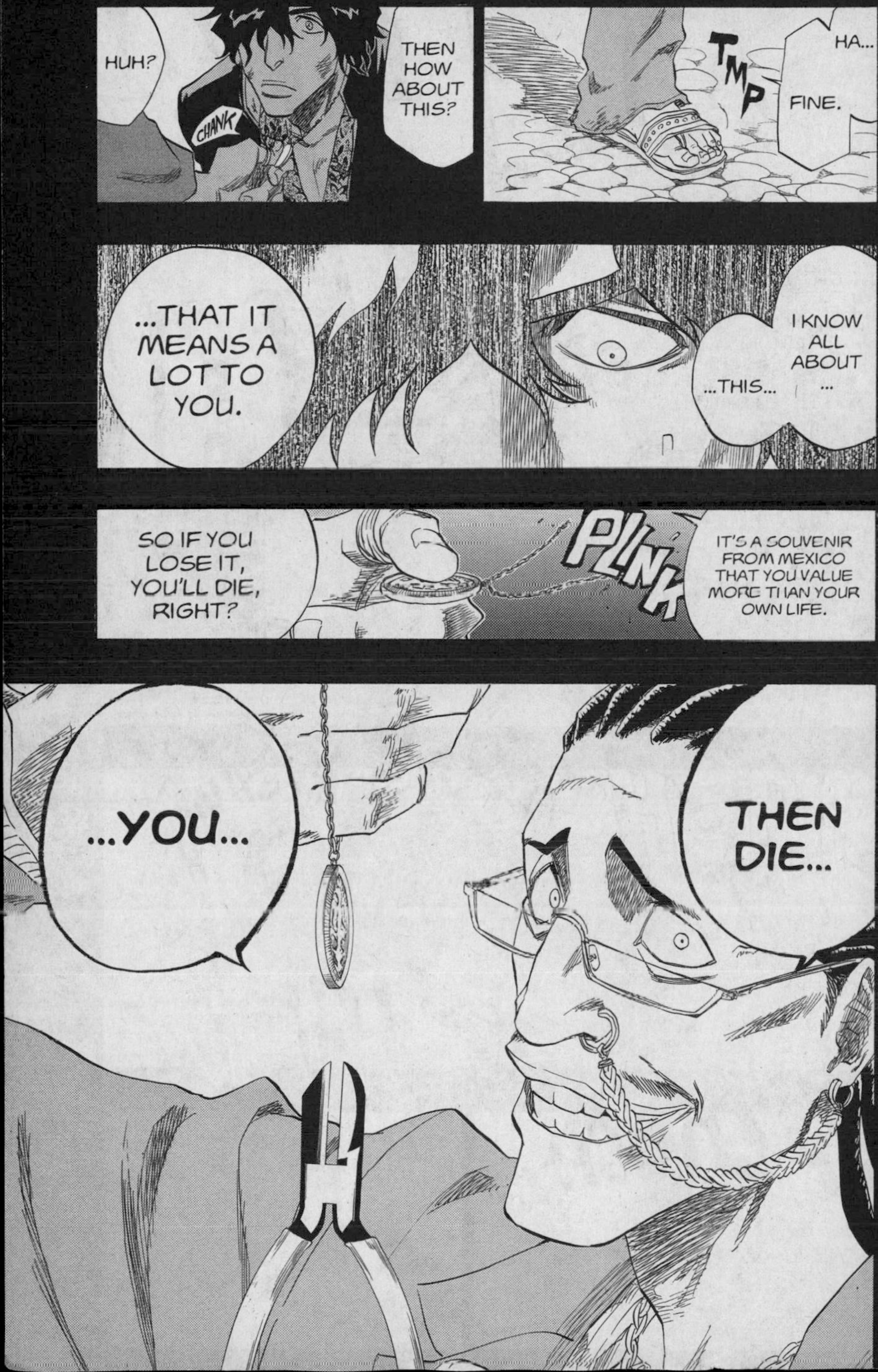
HA...
FINE.
TMP
THEN HOW ABOUT THIS?
HUH?
CHANK
I KNOW ALL ABOUT ...
...THIS...
...THAT IT MEANS A LOT TO YOU.
IT'S A SOUVENIR FROM MEXICO THAT YOU VALUE MORE THAN YOUR OWN LIFE.
PLINK
SO IF YOU LOSE IT, YOU'LL DIE, RIGHT?
THEN DIE...
...YOU...

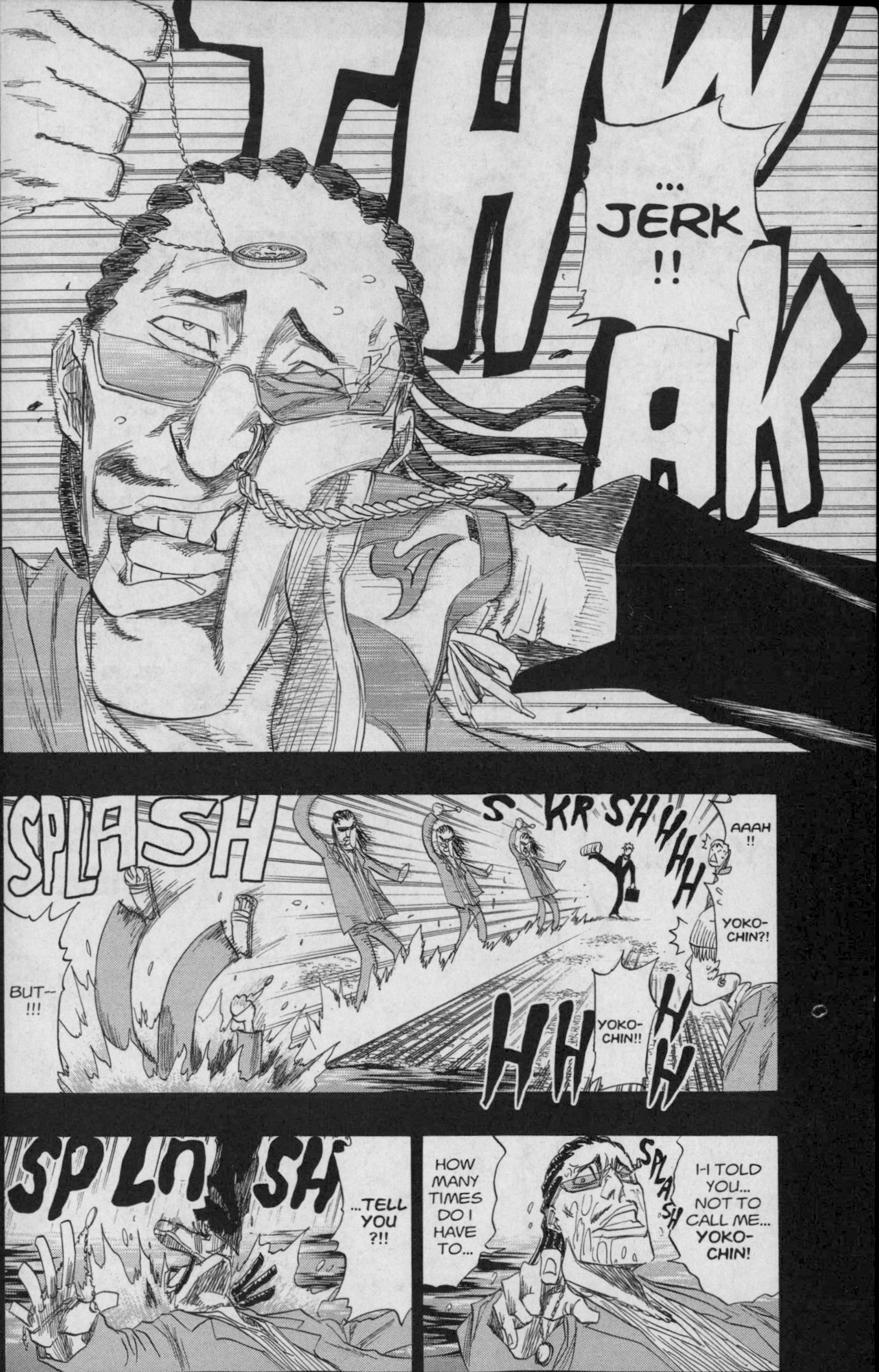
...JERK !!
AAAH !!
YOKO-CHIN?!
S KR SHHHHH
YOKO-CHIN!!
BUT-- !!!
SPLASH
I-I TOLD YOU... NOT TO CALL ME... YOKO-CHIN!
SPLASH
HOW MANY TIMES DO I HAVE TO...
...TELL YOU ?!!

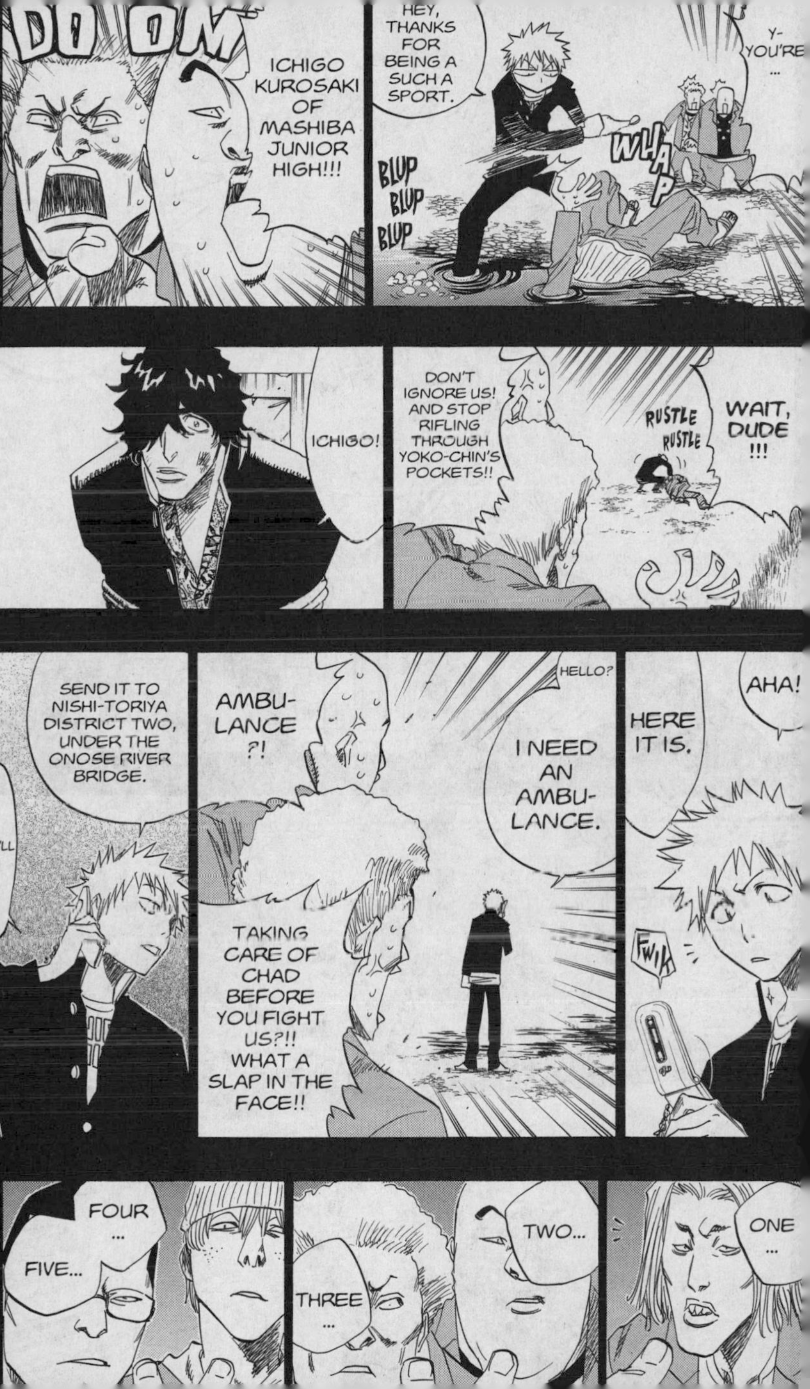
Y- YOU'RE ...
HEY, THANKS FOR BEING A SUCH A SPORT.
WHAP
BLUP BLUP BLUP
DOOM
ICHIGO KUROSAKI OF MASHIBA JUNIOR HIGH!!!
WAIT, DUDE !!!
RUSTLE RUSTLE
DON'T IGNORE US! AND STOP RIFLING THROUGH YOKO-CHIN'S POCKETS!!
ICHIGO!
AHA!
HERE IT IS.
FWIK
HELLO?
I NEED AN AMBULANCE.
AMBULANCE?!
TAKING CARE OF CHAD BEFORE YOU FIGHT US?!! WHAT A SLAP IN THE FACE!!
SEND IT TO NISHI-TORIYA DISTRICT TWO, UNDER THE ONOSE RIVER BRIDGE.
THERE'LL BE--
ONE ...
TWO...
THREE ...
FOUR ...
FIVE...

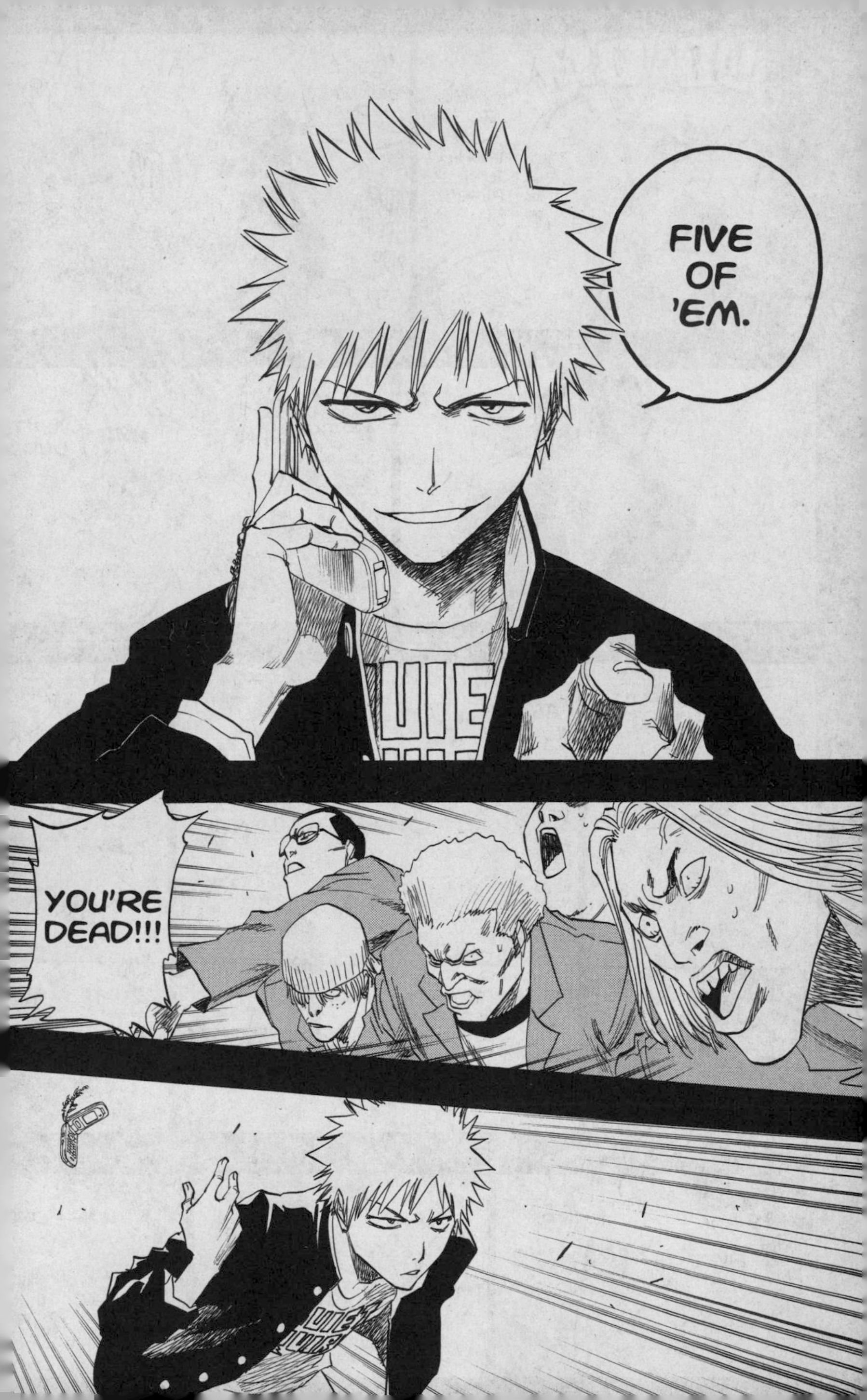
FIVE OF 'EM.
YOU'RE DEAD!!!

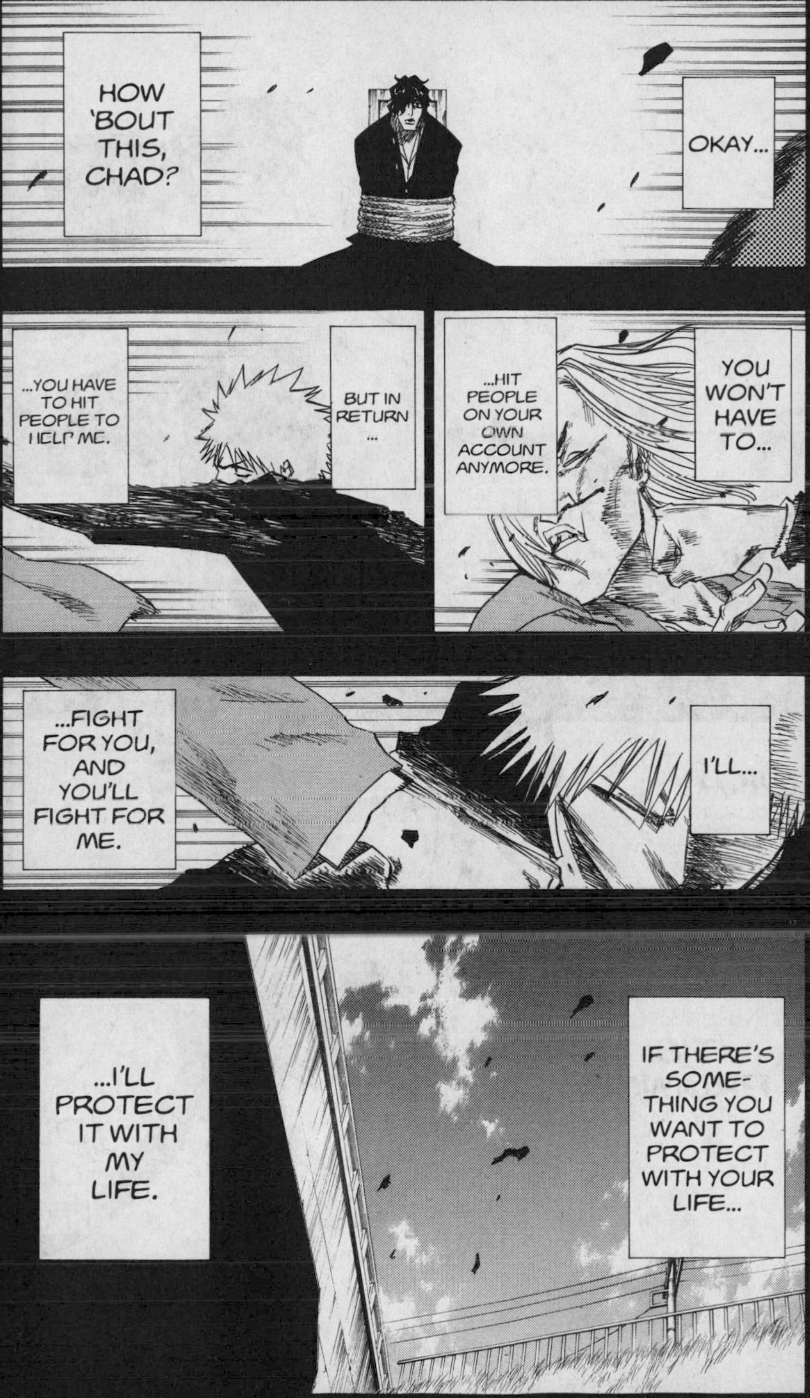
OKAY...
HOW 'BOUT THIS, CHAD?
YOU WON'T HAVE TO...
...HIT PEOPLE ON YOUR OWN ACCOUNT ANYMORE.
BUT IN RETURN...
...YOU HAVE TO HIT PEOPLE TO HELP ME.
I'LL...
...FIGHT FOR YOU, AND YOU'LL FIGHT FOR ME.
IF THERE'S SOME-THING YOU WANT TO PROTECT WITH YOUR LIFE...
...I'LL PROTECT IT WITH MY LIFE.

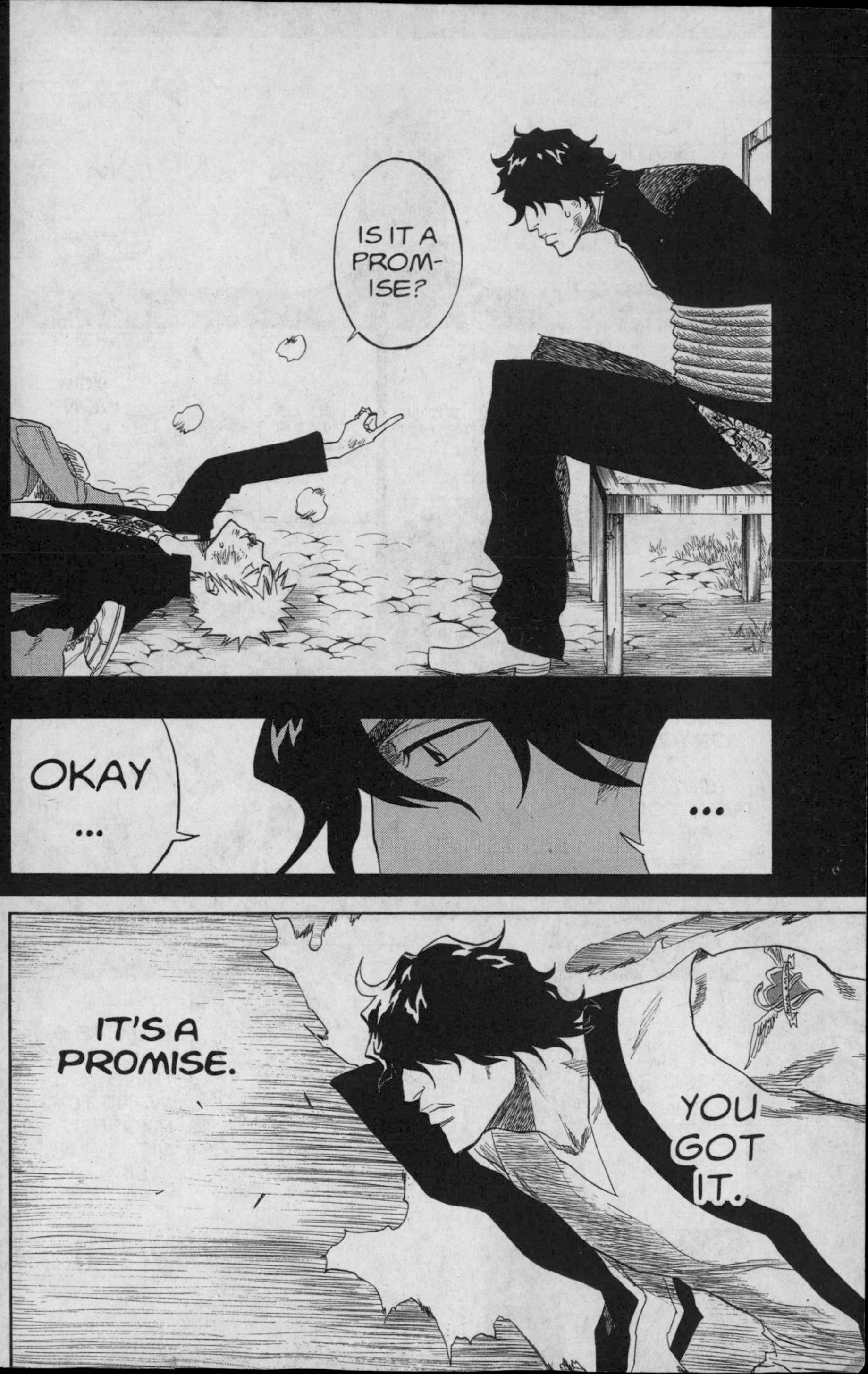
IS IT A PROM-ISE?
...
OKAY ...
IT'S A PROMISE.
YOU GOT IT.

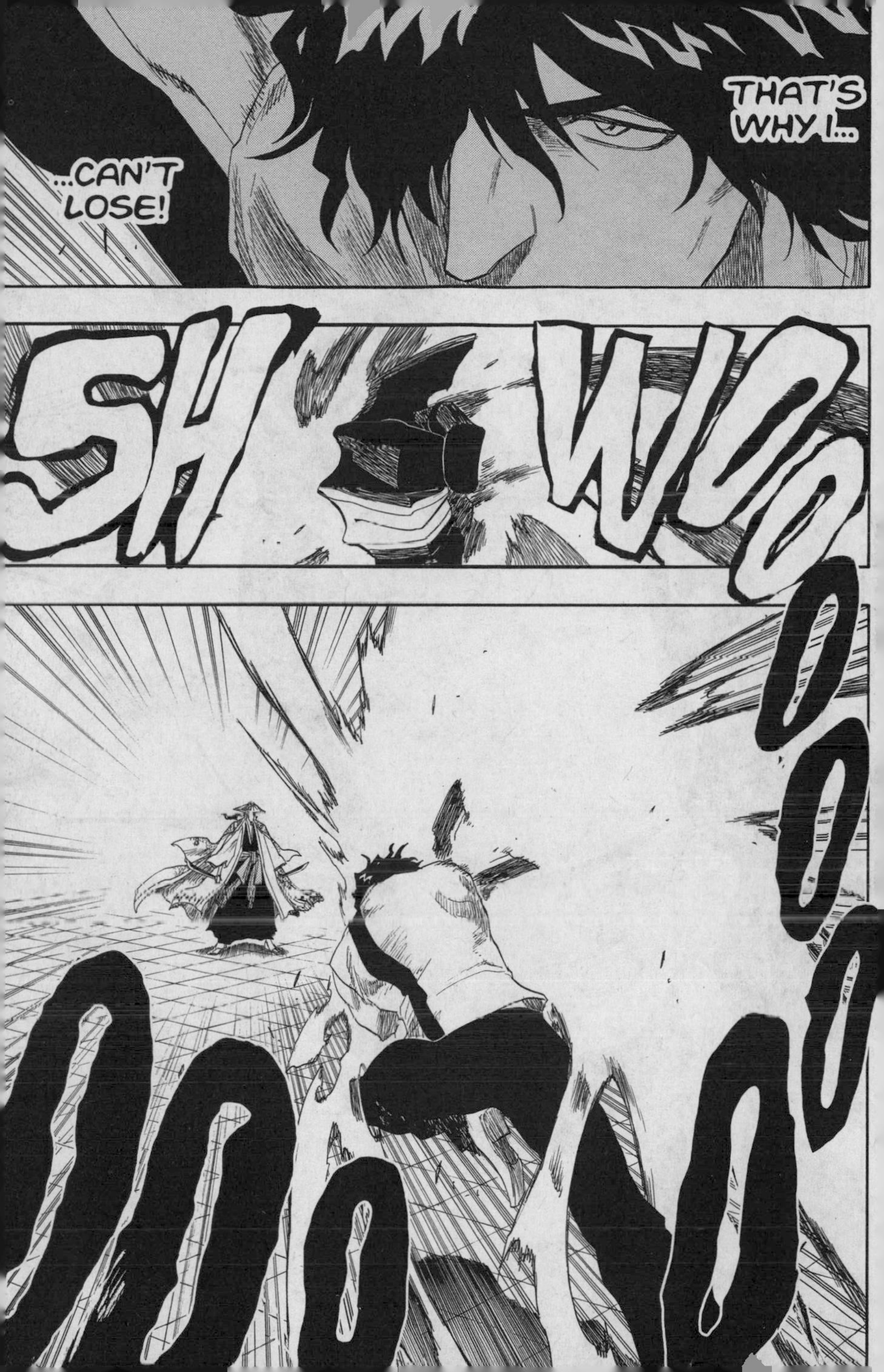
THAT'S WHY I...
...CAN'T LOSE!
SHWOOOOOOOOOOO

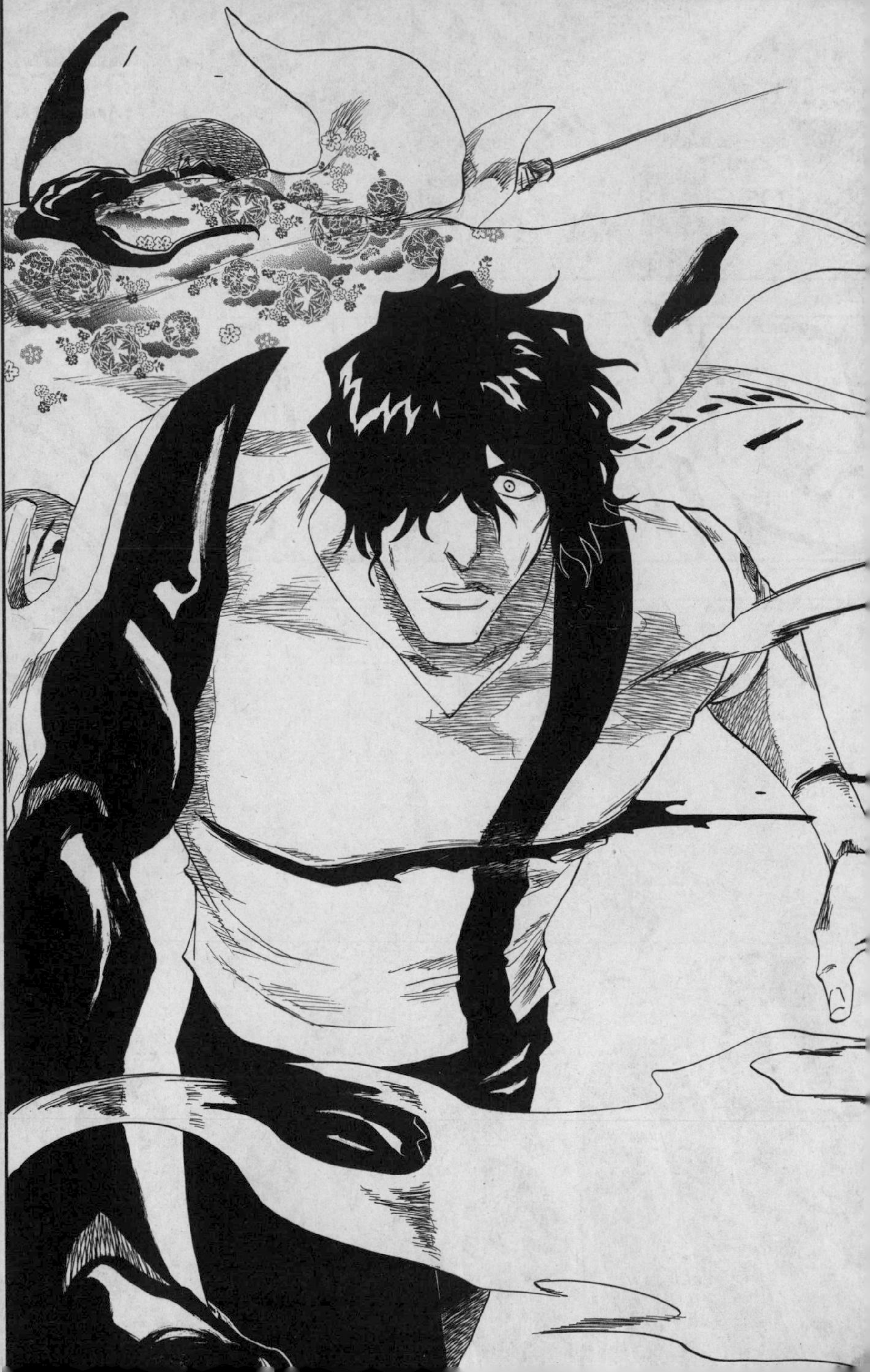

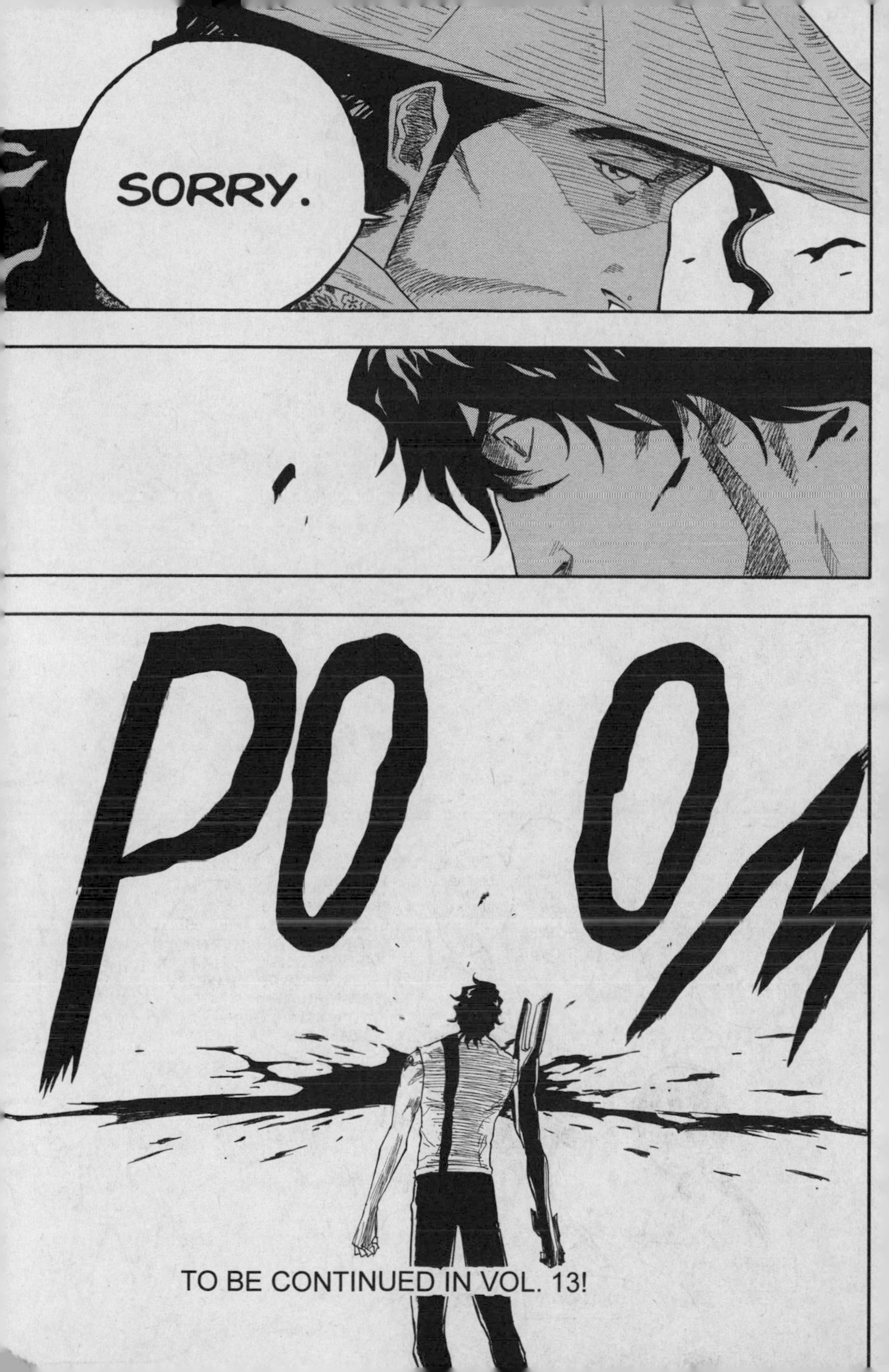
SORRY.
POOM
TO BE CONTINUED IN VOL. 13!

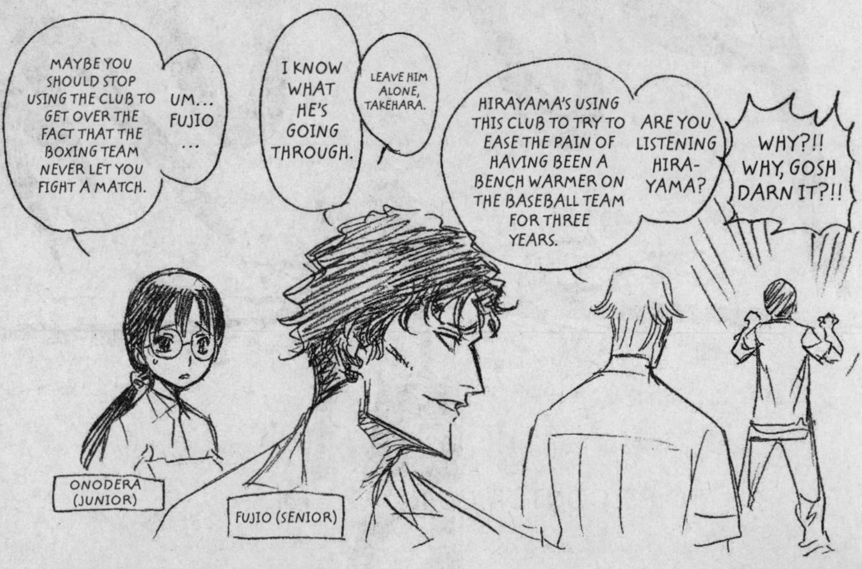
WHY?!! WHY, GOSH DARN IT?!!
ARE YOU LISTENING HIRA-YAMA?
HIRAYAMA'S USING THIS CLUB TO TRY TO EASE THE PAIN OF HAVING BEEN A BENCH WARMER ON THE BASEBALL TEAM FOR THREE YEARS.
LEAVE HIM ALONE, TAKEHARA.
I KNOW WHAT HE'S GOING THROUGH.
UM... FUJIO ...
MAYBE YOU SHOULD STOP USING THE CLUB TO GET OVER THE FACT THAT THE BOXING TEAM NEVER LET YOU FIGHT A MATCH.
FUJIO (SENIOR)
ONODERA (JUNIOR)

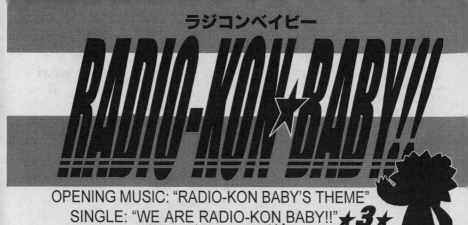

ラジコンベイビー

RADIO-KON★BABY!!

OPENING MUSIC: "RADIO-KON BABY'S THEME"
SINGLE: "WE ARE RADIO-KON BABY!!" ★3★

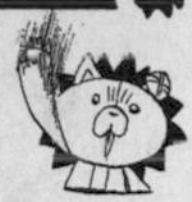

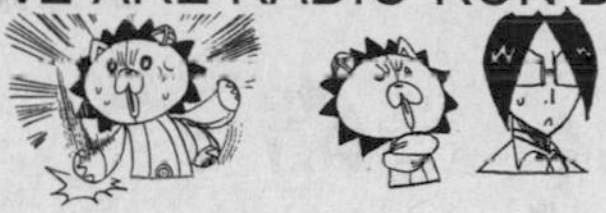

YO! HOW YOU GUY'S DOING?! IT'S BEEN A WHILE, HUH?!! TO TELL YOU THE TRUTH, I WAS SWEATING--I THOUGHT WE WERE FINISHED AFTER THE SECOND EPISODE!! BUT THE SUPER-POPULAR "RADIO-KON BABY"--THE FIRST THING TO GET CUT WHEN THERE ARE PAGE NUMBER CONSIDERATIONS--IS BACK FOR ITS THIRD INSTALLMENT!! OUR GUEST TODAY IS URYÛ ISHIDA!! THANK YOU VERY MUCH!!

...HELLO.

HEY!! WHAT'S THE MATTER, FOUR-EYES?!!

HURRY UP AND SIT DOWN!! OKAY, THE FIRST QUESTION IS... BUT BEFORE THAT, I GOTTA TELL YOU!! BECAUSE URYÛ'S IN THE CRAFTS CLUB, THERE WERE A BUNCH OF QUESTIONS ABOUT FIXING MY EARS AND RIPPING ME APART AND STUFF!! LISTEN UP!! I WOULDN'T LET THIS GUY LAY A FINGER ON MY BEAUTIFUL BODY!! GOT THAT, FOUR-EYES?! AND I DIDN'T SAY THAT TO SET UP A JOKE!!!

Q

I THOUGHT ARCHERS ALWAYS HOLD A BOW WITH THEIR LEFT HANDS REGARDLESS OF WHETHER THEY'RE LEFT- OR RIGHT-HANDED, BUT YOU HOLD IT WITH YOUR RIGHT. IS THAT SOME KIND OF QUINCY THING?

CHIMO--TOKYO

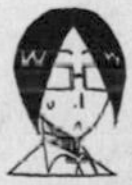

I DO?

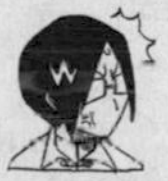

!!

Q

CAN URYÛ'S CAPE FLY?

ERI FUKADA--OITA

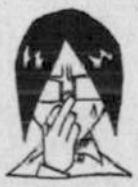

WHAT A QUESTION. DID I EVER SAY IT COULD FLY?

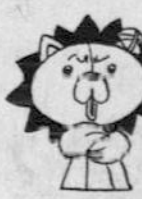

MAYBE SHE'S SEEN TOO MANY FLYING CAPES IN MOVIES AND STUFF. OR MAYBE SHE'S JUST MAKING FUN OF YOU.

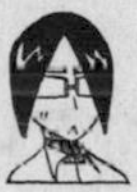

O-OKAY. I DON'T REALLY WANT TO ANYWAY.

Q

IN VOLUME 5 YOU SAID YOUR FAVORITE FOOD WAS MACKEREL STEWED IN MISO THAT YOU COOK YOURSELF. DOES THAT MEAN YOU LIVE ALONE? AND WHAT OTHER FOODS DO YOU LIKE?

KITE WATANABE--HOKKAIDO

GEEZ. WHAT A JERK.

NO.

Q

I HAVE A QUESTION FOR URYÛ. WHAT WAS YOUR NICKNAME AS A CHILD? ACTUALLY, CAN I CALL YOU "U-CHAN"?

AIKO ISHIMURA--NIIGATA

WHY? IT'S BEEN WORKING FINE SO FAR...

THEN YOU'VE BEEN SHOOTING YOUR BOW WITHOUT REALLY KNOWING THE PROPER WAY? DUDE, THAT'S DANGEROUS...

WELL...I WAS NEVER IN AN ARCHERY CLUB OR ANYTHING SO I DON'T REALLY KNOW WHAT'S RIGHT. ARE YOU SUPPOSED TO HOLD A BOW WITH YOUR LEFT HAND?

WHAT ?!

WAIT, IT'S NOT "QRACY," IT'S "QUINCY." THE LENGTH OF THE CAPE IS A MATTER OF INDIVIDUAL TASTE. MY MASTER ALWAYS SAID THAT A LONGER CAPE WAS COOLER.

Q

YOUR CAPE IS SHORT AND YOUR MASTER'S WAS LONG. DOES THE LENGTH OF THE CAPE INDICATE THE STRENGTH OF A QRACY?

YÛMA--HIROSHIMA

SO YOU'RE BASICALLY JUST A HOUSEWIFE.

IT'S NOT REALLY MY FAVORITE, BUT I'M GOOD AT MAKING CHIKUZEN-NI. THAT'S CHICKEN STEWED WITH TARO, BURDOCK, AND KONJAK*.

YOU REALLY ARE A JERK. OH WELL, THEN WHAT OTHER FOODS DO YOU LIKE?

WHAT DO YOU CARE? IT'S A PRIVATE MATTER. I DON'T WANT TO DISCUSS IT.

SERIOUSLY? WHY? YOUR PARENTS LIVE FAR AWAY OR SOMETHING?

YES, I LIVE ALONE.

*KONJAK IS KONNYAKU, A GELATINOUS SUBSTANCE MADE FROM INDONESIAN POTATOES.

HERE IT IS! THE BIGGEST QUESTION OF ALL!! THE SUSPICION THAT URYÛ ISHIDA IS UNCOOL!!!

Q

WHY IS YOUR FASHION SENSE SO BAD?

YAKINIKU YASSAN--OSAKA

Q

DO YOU FEEL COMFORTABLE WITH YOUR SENSE OF FASHION?

SEIKÔ MATSUOKA--YAMAGUCHI

...

I DUNNO? MAYBE YOU JUST DIDN'T MAKE A STRONG IMPRESSION ON THE READERS.

LIKE I SAID, IT'S NOT "QRACY," IT'S "QUINCY"! WHY DO SO MANY OF YOU REMEMBER IT INCORRECTLY?! WERE THESE QUESTIONS CHOSEN INTENTIONALLY?!

Q

DESPITE EVERYTHING YOU'VE SAID, ARE YOU INTO QRACY COSTUMES?

NANAE KUDO--HOKKAIDO

Q

WHEN YOU WERE LITTLE, YOU SAID, "WILL THIS TRADITIONAL QUINCY COSTUME EVER BE UPDATED? IT'S REALLY UNCOOL." WHAT KIND OF COSTUME WOULD YOU HAVE LIKED?

SEIYA IIDA--NIIGATA

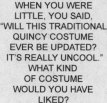

SEE?! SEE?! WELL?! HUH?! EVEN **YOU** THOUGHT THE CAPE WAS UNCOOL! THEN WHAT COSTUME WOULD YOU HAVE LIKED TO WEAR? HUH? SAY SOMETHING, MR. URYÛ "I'M NOT UNCOOL" ISHIDA!!

HMPH!!!

WELL, THERE SURE SEEMS TO BE A CONSENSUS REGARDING YOUR COOLNESS FACTOR HERE.

THAT'S INSULTING! THE ONLY REASON PEOPLE THINK THAT IS BECAUSE ICHIGO KEEPS SAYING MY CLOTHES ARE FUNNY! I DON'T THINK I'M SO UNCOOL...

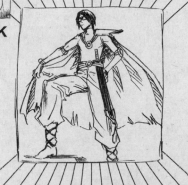

FINE. IF YOU MUST KNOW, I'LL SHOW YOU. I HAVE WITH ME A COSTUME THAT I DESIGNED BACK THEN. DON'T BE SURPRISED WHEN YOU SEE IT. IT'S SO COOL, I STILL GET GOOSE BUMPS WHEN I LOOK AT IT! I WAS OOZING WITH SUPER FASHION SENSE EVEN AS A YOUNG BOY!!!

YUCK...

WAITING FOR LETTERS!

ANY KIND OF QUESTION WILL DO!! BUT IF YOU SEND US A NAUGHTY QUESTION, PLEASE INCLUDE A RADIO NAME AS WELL AS YOUR REAL NAME, OTHERWISE THE KIDS AT SCHOOL WILL KNOW YOU'RE A PERV!! OUR NEXT GUEST WILL BE KISUKE URAHARA!! (UNCONFIRMED)

SEND YOUR QUESTION, NAME, ADDRESS, AGE, AND TELEPHONE NUMBER TO THE ADDRESS BELOW!!
SHONEN JUMP C/O VIZ MEDIA, LLC
★P.O. BOX 77010, SAN FRANCISCO, CA 94107★

SINGLE: "GOOD NIGHT, RADIO-KON BABY!" ENDING THEME MUSIC: WILLIE THE LION SMITH, "THE PANIC IS ON"

● ATTN: "BLEACH" RADIO-KON BABY!! ●

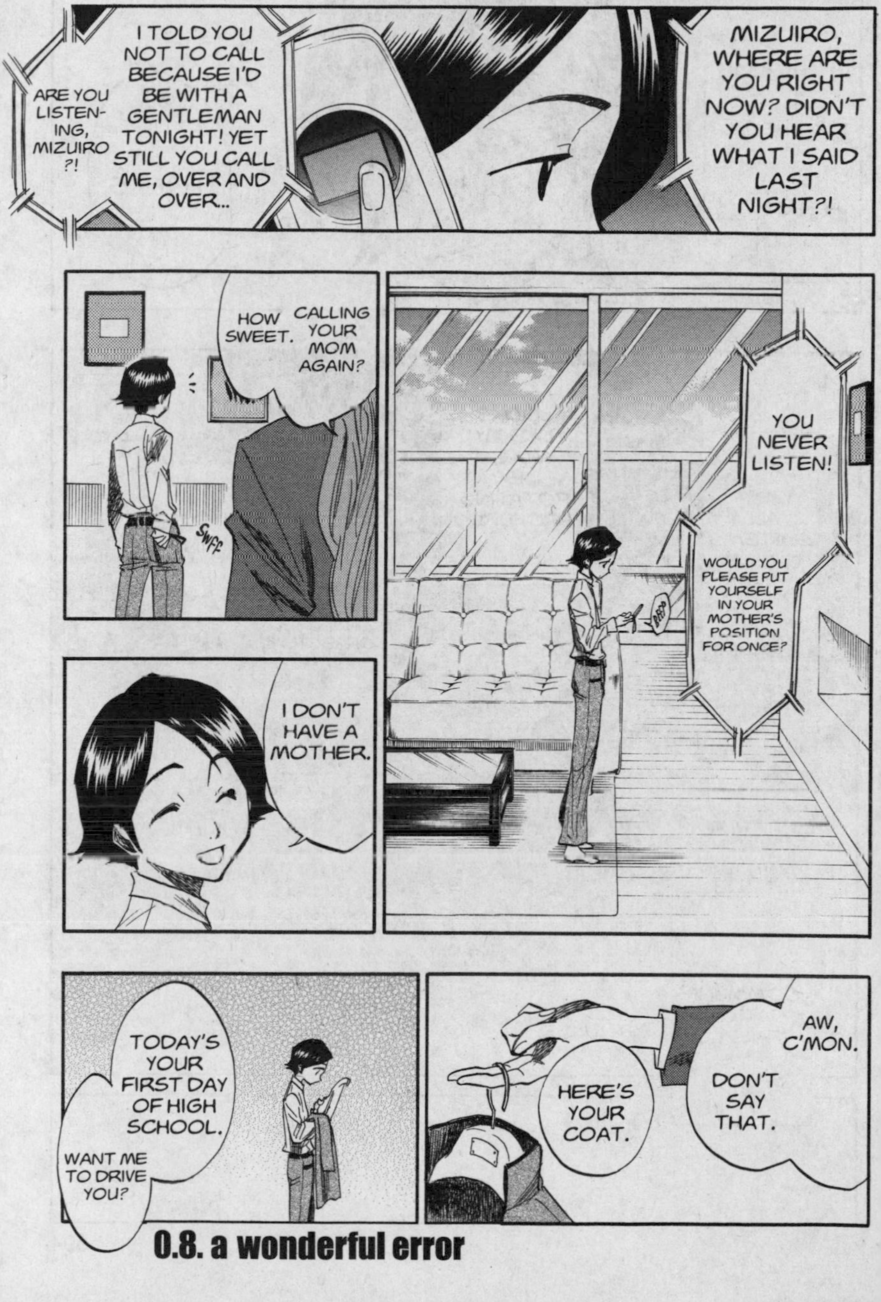
MIZUIRO, WHERE ARE YOU RIGHT NOW? DIDN'T YOU HEAR WHAT I SAID LAST NIGHT?!
I TOLD YOU NOT TO CALL BECAUSE I'D BE WITH A GENTLEMAN TONIGHT! YET STILL YOU CALL ME, OVER AND OVER...
ARE YOU LISTENING, MIZUIRO?!
YOU NEVER LISTEN!
WOULD YOU PLEASE PUT YOURSELF IN YOUR MOTHER'S POSITION FOR ONCE?
BEEP
CALLING YOUR MOM AGAIN?
HOW SWEET.
SWFF
I DON'T HAVE A MOTHER.
AW, C'MON.
DON'T SAY THAT.
HERE'S YOUR COAT.
TODAY'S YOUR FIRST DAY OF HIGH SCHOOL.
WANT ME TO DRIVE YOU?

0.8. a wonderful error

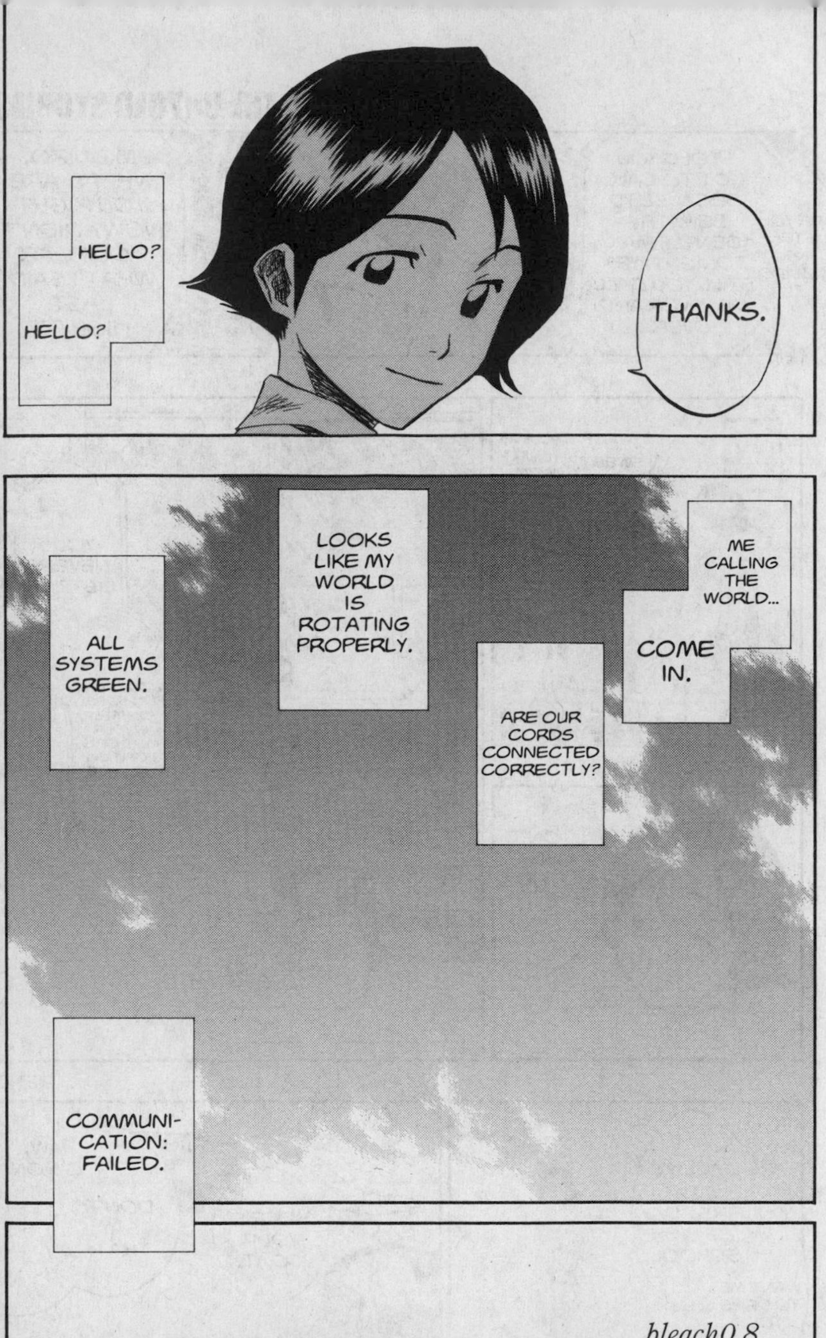
THANKS.
HELLO?
HELLO?
ME CALLING THE WORLD...
COME IN.
ARE OUR CORDS CONNECTED CORRECTLY?
LOOKS LIKE MY WORLD IS ROTATING PROPERLY.
ALL SYSTEMS GREEN.
COMMUNI-CATION: FAILED.
bleach0.8

READ THIS WAY

a wonderful error

TITE KUBO

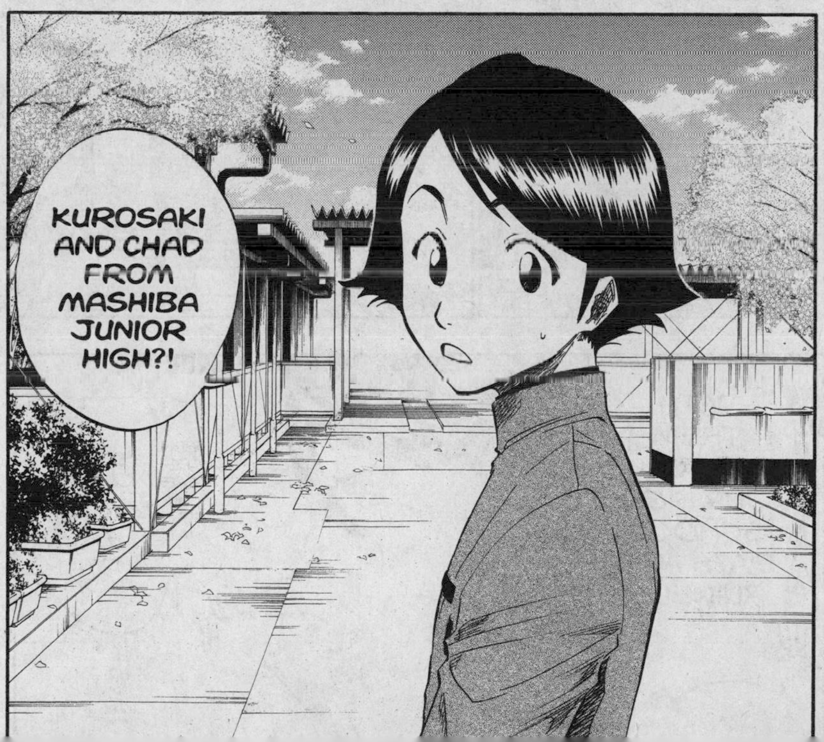
KUROSAKI AND CHAD FROM MASHIBA JUNIOR HIGH?!

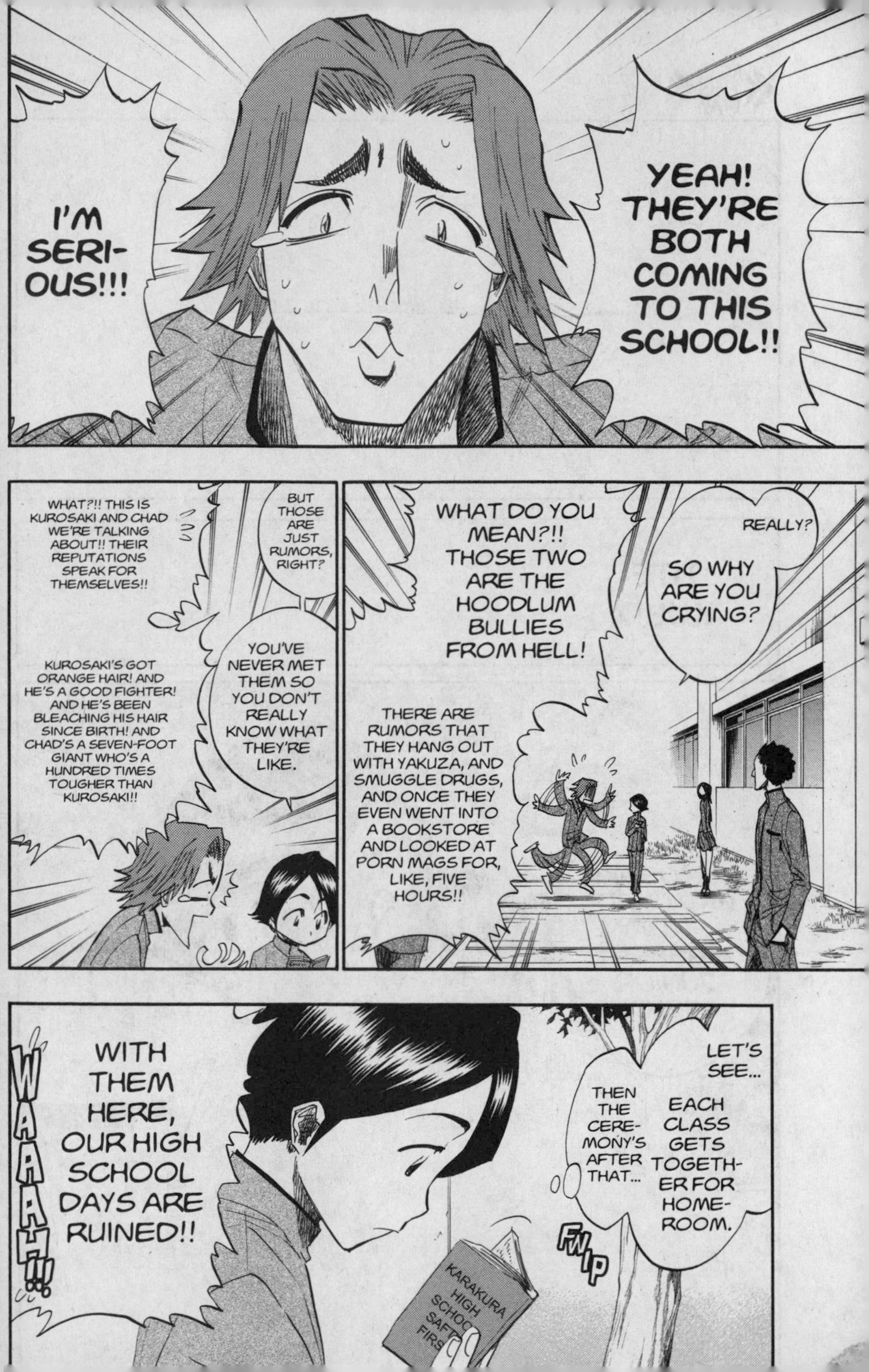
YEAH! THEY'RE BOTH COMING TO THIS SCHOOL!!
I'M SERI-OUS!!!
REALLY?
SO WHY ARE YOU CRYING?
WHAT DO YOU MEAN?!! THOSE TWO ARE THE HOODLUM BULLIES FROM HELL!
THERE ARE RUMORS THAT THEY HANG OUT WITH YAKUZA, AND SMUGGLE DRUGS, AND ONCE THEY EVEN WENT INTO A BOOKSTORE AND LOOKED AT PORN MAGS FOR, LIKE, FIVE HOURS!!
BUT THOSE ARE JUST RUMORS, RIGHT?
WHAT?!! THIS IS KUROSAKI AND CHAD WE'RE TALKING ABOUT!! THEIR REPUTATIONS SPEAK FOR THEMSELVES!!
YOU'VE NEVER MET THEM SO YOU DON'T REALLY KNOW WHAT THEY'RE LIKE.
KUROSAKI'S GOT ORANGE HAIR! AND HE'S A GOOD FIGHTER! AND HE'S BEEN BLEACHING HIS HAIR SINCE BIRTH! AND CHAD'S A SEVEN-FOOT GIANT WHO'S A HUNDRED TIMES TOUGHER THAN KUROSAKI!!
LET'S SEE...
EACH CLASS GETS TOGETH-ER FOR HOME-ROOM.
THEN THE CERE-MONY'S AFTER THAT...
FWIP
KARAKURA HIGH
WITH THEM HERE, OUR HIGH SCHOOL DAYS ARE RUINED!!
WAAAAH!!!

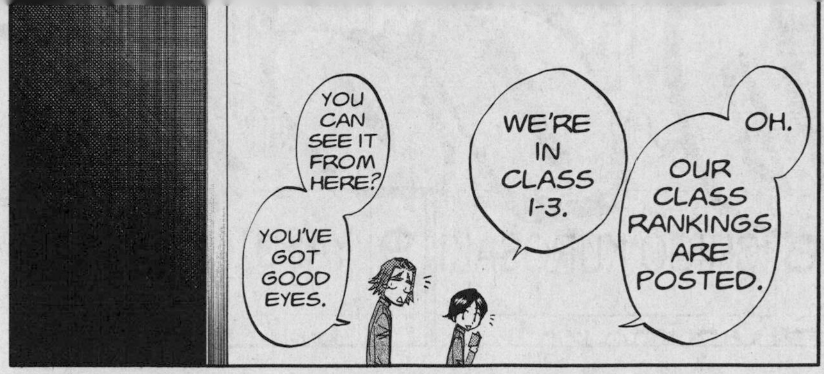
OH.
OUR CLASS RANKINGS ARE POSTED.
WE'RE IN CLASS 1-3.
YOU CAN SEE IT FROM HERE?
YOU'VE GOT GOOD EYES.

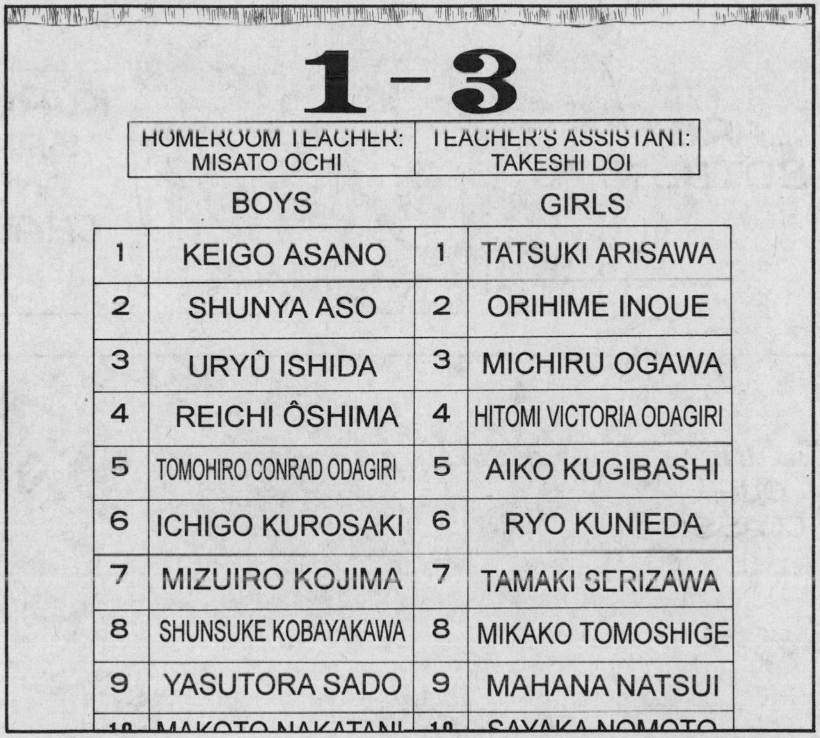
1-3

HOMEROOM TEACHER: MISATO OCHI	TEACHER'S ASSISTANT: TAKESHI DOI

BOYS		GIRLS	
1	KEIGO ASANO	1	TATSUKI ARISAWA
2	SHUNYA ASO	2	ORIHIME INOUE
3	URYÛ ISHIDA	3	MICHIRU OGAWA
4	REICHI ÔSHIMA	4	HITOMI VICTORIA ODAGIRI
5	TOMOHIRO CONRAD ODAGIRI	5	AIKO KUGIBASHI
6	ICHIGO KUROSAKI	6	RYO KUNIEDA
7	MIZUIRO KOJIMA	7	TAMAKI SERIZAWA
8	SHUNSUKE KOBAYAKAWA	8	MIKAKO TOMOSHIGE
9	YASUTORA SADO	9	MAHANA NATSUI
10	MAKOTO NAKATANI	10	SAYAKA NOMOTO

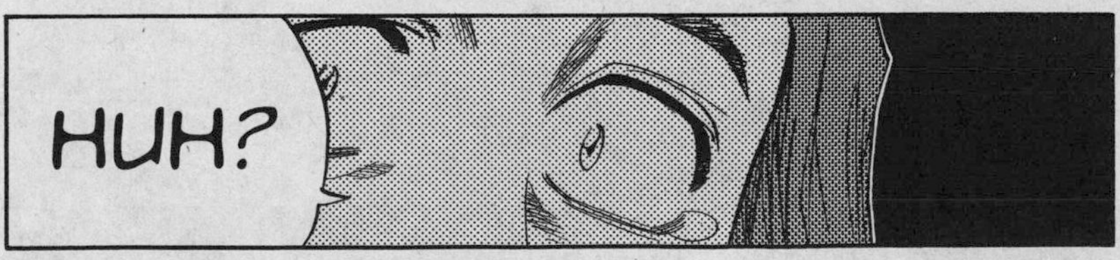
HUH?

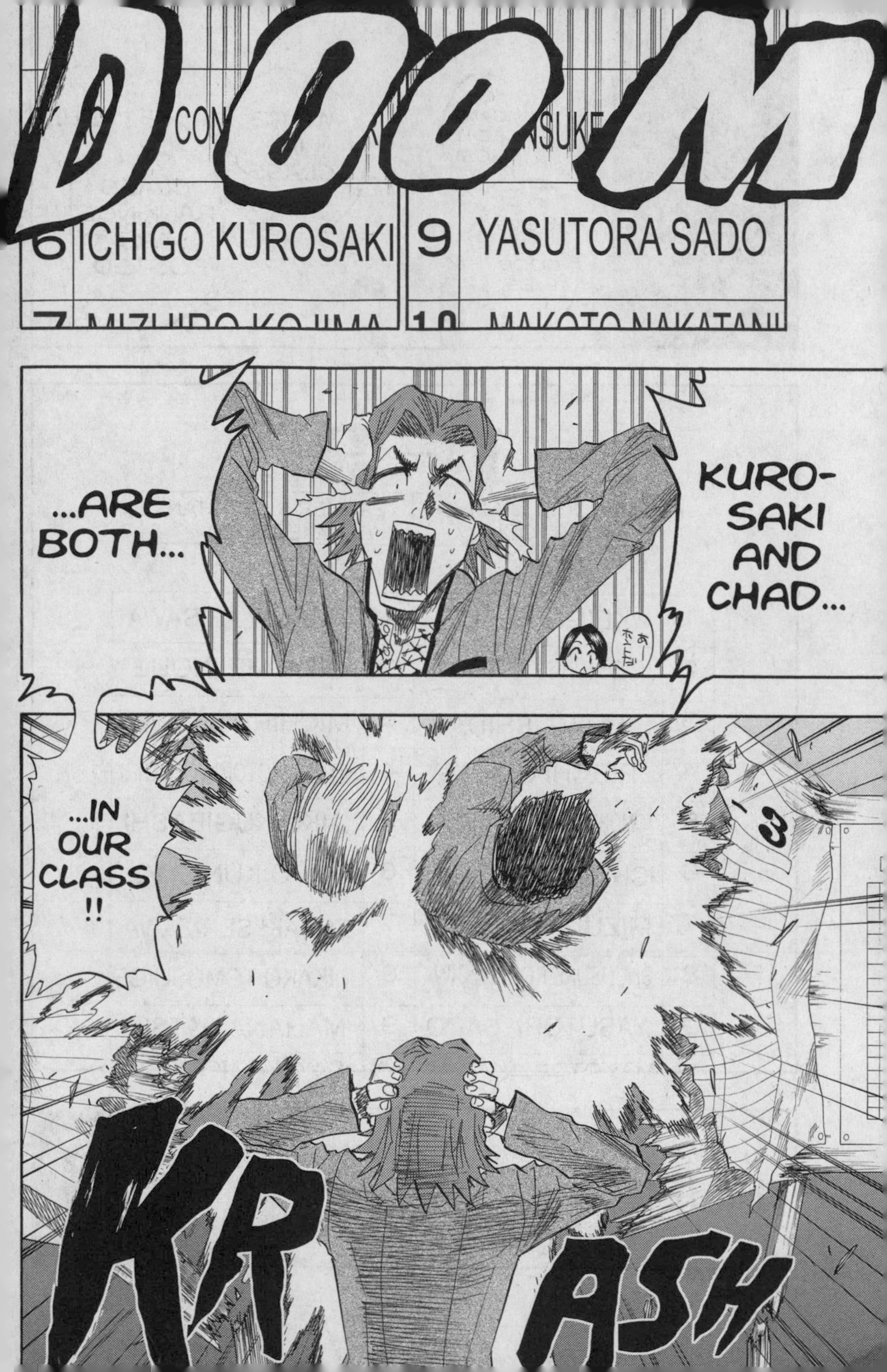
DOOM
6 ICHIGO KUROSAKI
9 YASUTORA SADO
KURO-SAKI AND CHAD...
...ARE BOTH...
...IN OUR CLASS !!
KRASH

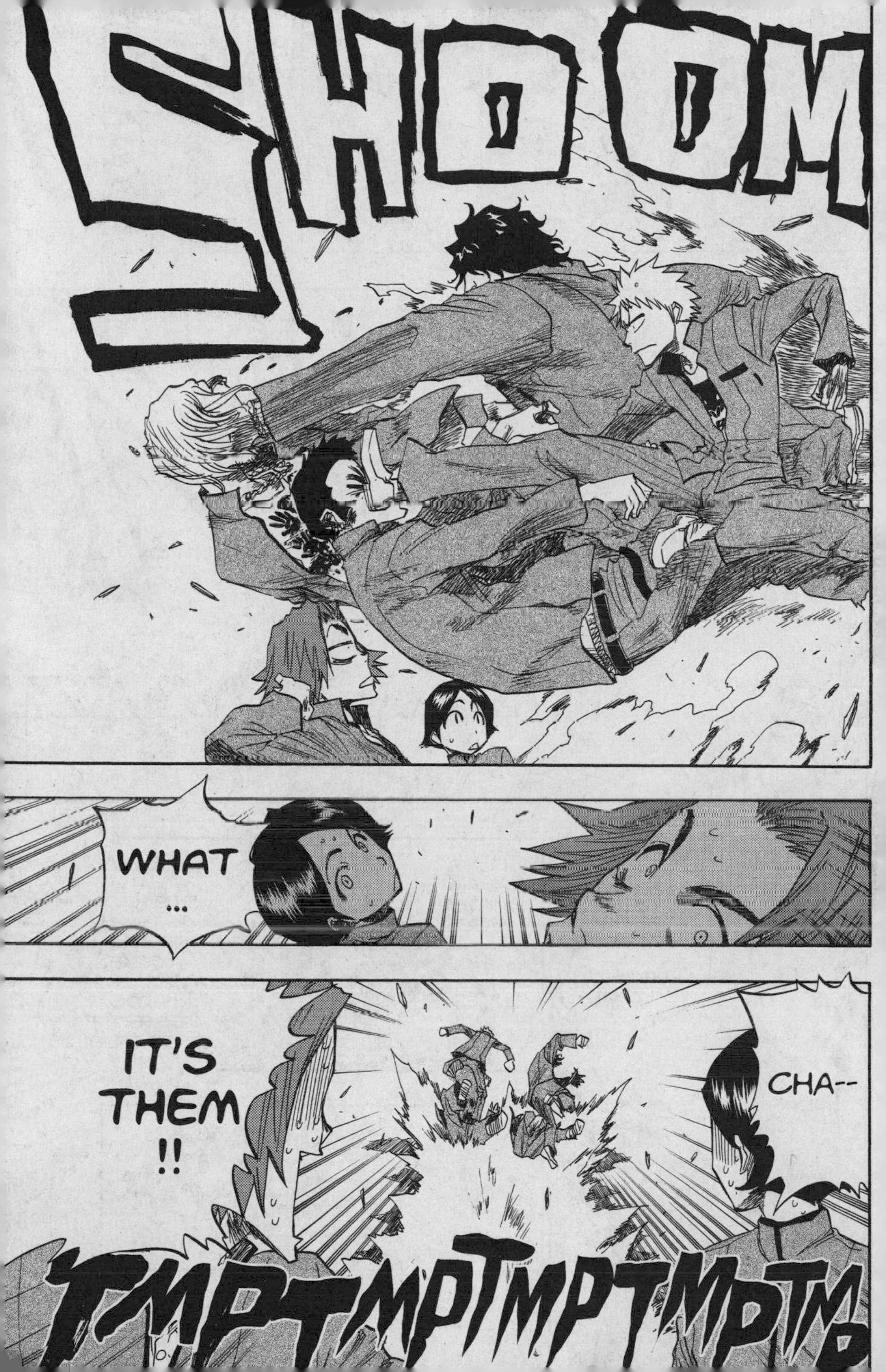
WHOOM
WHAT ...
CHA--
IT'S THEM !!
TMPTMPTMPTMPTMP

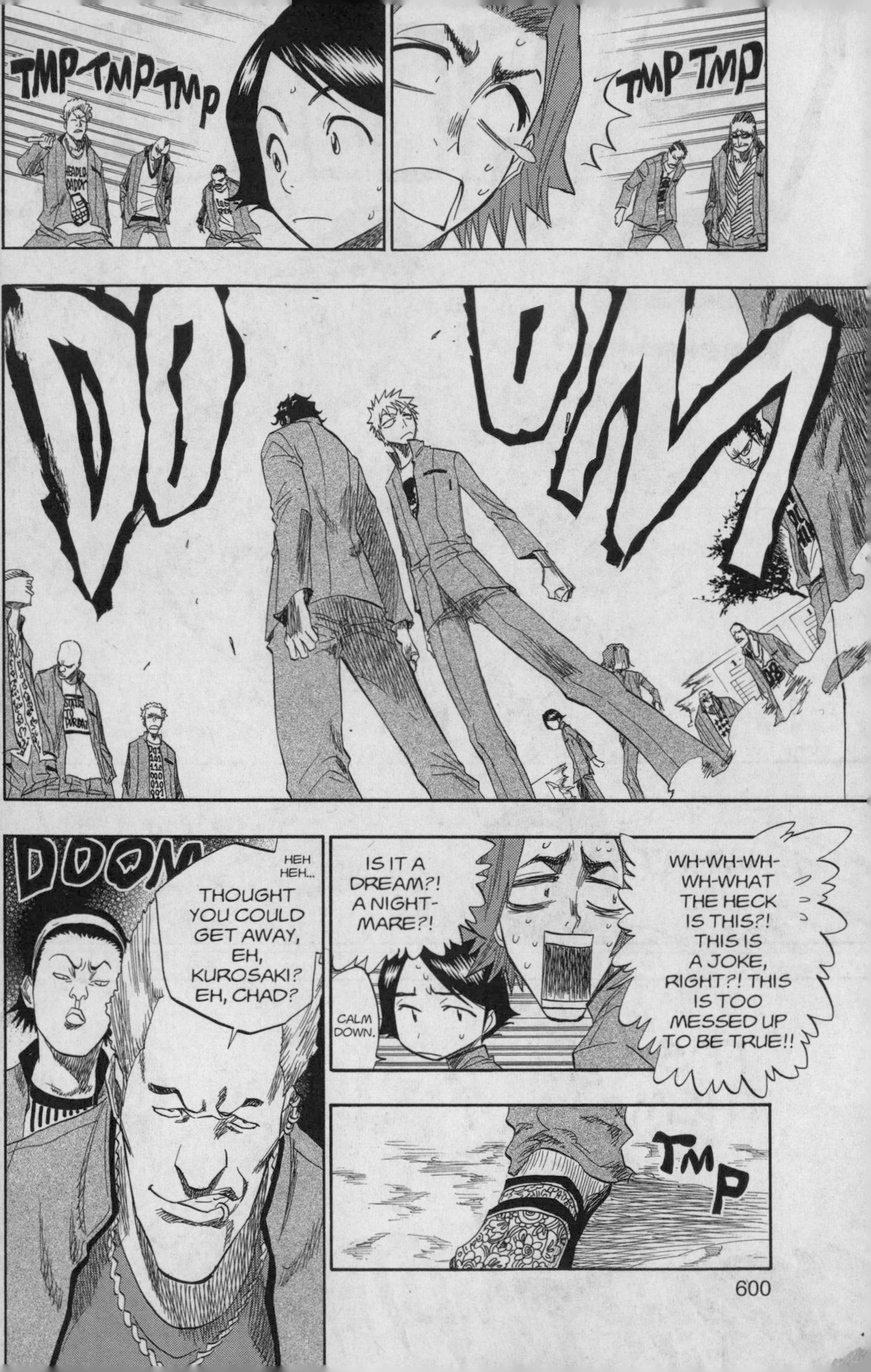

TMP TMP
TMP-TMP TMP
DOOM
WH-WH-WH-WH-WHAT THE HECK IS THIS?! THIS IS A JOKE, RIGHT?! THIS IS TOO MESSED UP TO BE TRUE!!
IS IT A DREAM?! A NIGHT-MARE?!
CALM DOWN.
TMP
DOOM
HEH HEH...
THOUGHT YOU COULD GET AWAY, EH, KUROSAKI? EH, CHAD?

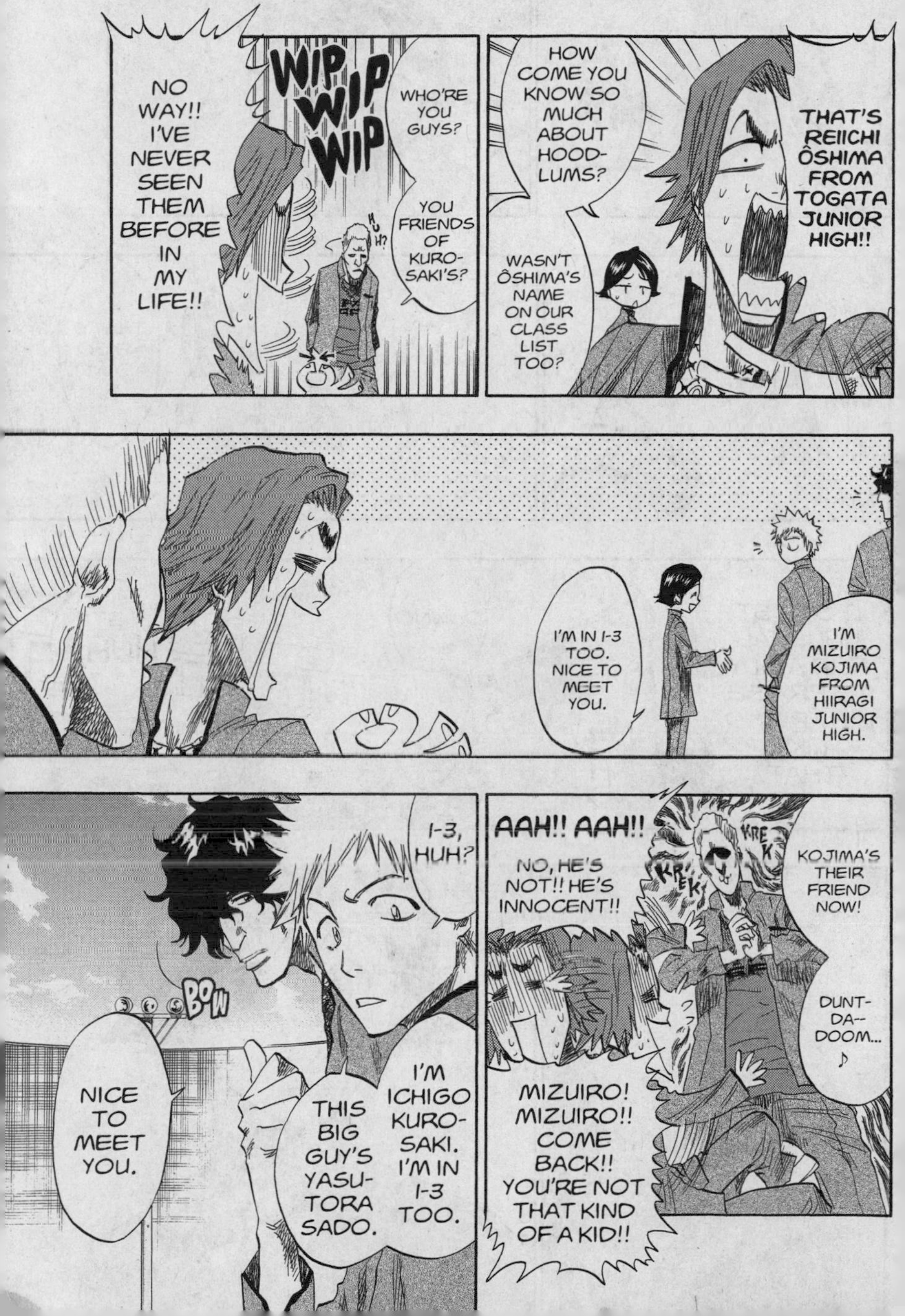
THAT'S REIICHI ÔSHIMA FROM TOGATA JUNIOR HIGH!!
HOW COME YOU KNOW SO MUCH ABOUT HOODLUMS?
WASN'T ÔSHIMA'S NAME ON OUR CLASS LIST TOO?
WHO'RE YOU GUYS?
YOU FRIENDS OF KUROSAKI'S?
WIP WIP WIP
HUH?
NO WAY!! I'VE NEVER SEEN THEM BEFORE IN MY LIFE!!
I'M MIZUIRO KOJIMA FROM HIIRAGI JUNIOR HIGH.
I'M IN 1-3 TOO. NICE TO MEET YOU.
KOJIMA'S THEIR FRIEND NOW!
KREK
KREK
AAH!! AAH!!
NO, HE'S NOT!! HE'S INNOCENT!!
DUNT-DA--DOOM... ♪
MIZUIRO! MIZUIRO!! COME BACK!! YOU'RE NOT THAT KIND OF A KID!!
1-3, HUH?
I'M ICHIGO KUROSAKI. I'M IN 1-3 TOO.
THIS BIG GUY'S YASUTORA SADO.
BOW
NICE TO MEET YOU.

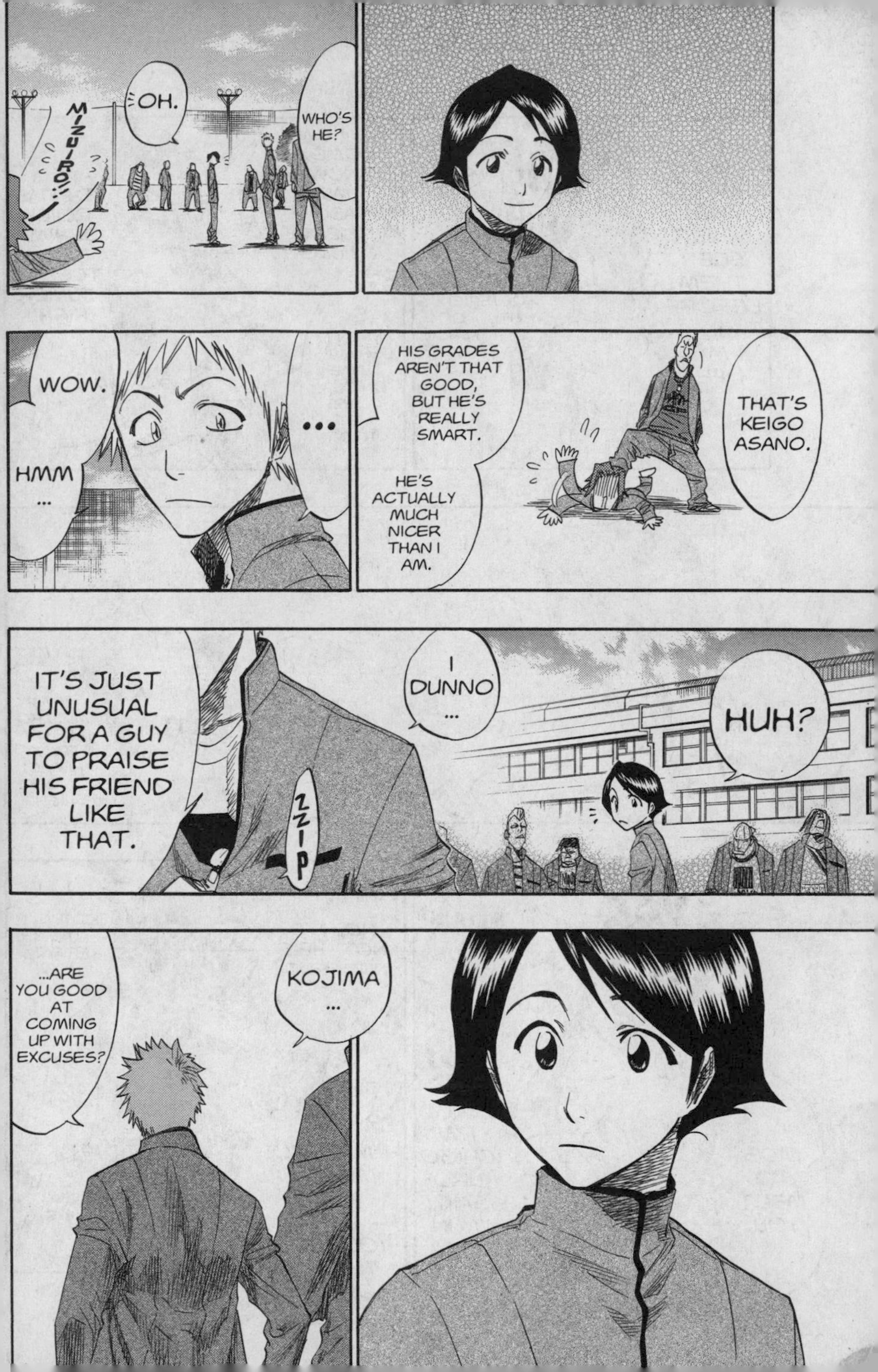
WHO'S HE?
OH.
MIZUIRO...!!
THAT'S KEIGO ASANO.
HIS GRADES AREN'T THAT GOOD, BUT HE'S REALLY SMART.
HE'S ACTUALLY MUCH NICER THAN I AM.
...
WOW.
HMM ...
HUH?
I DUNNO ...
IT'S JUST UNUSUAL FOR A GUY TO PRAISE HIS FRIEND LIKE THAT.
ZZIP
KOJIMA ...
...ARE YOU GOOD AT COMING UP WITH EXCUSES?

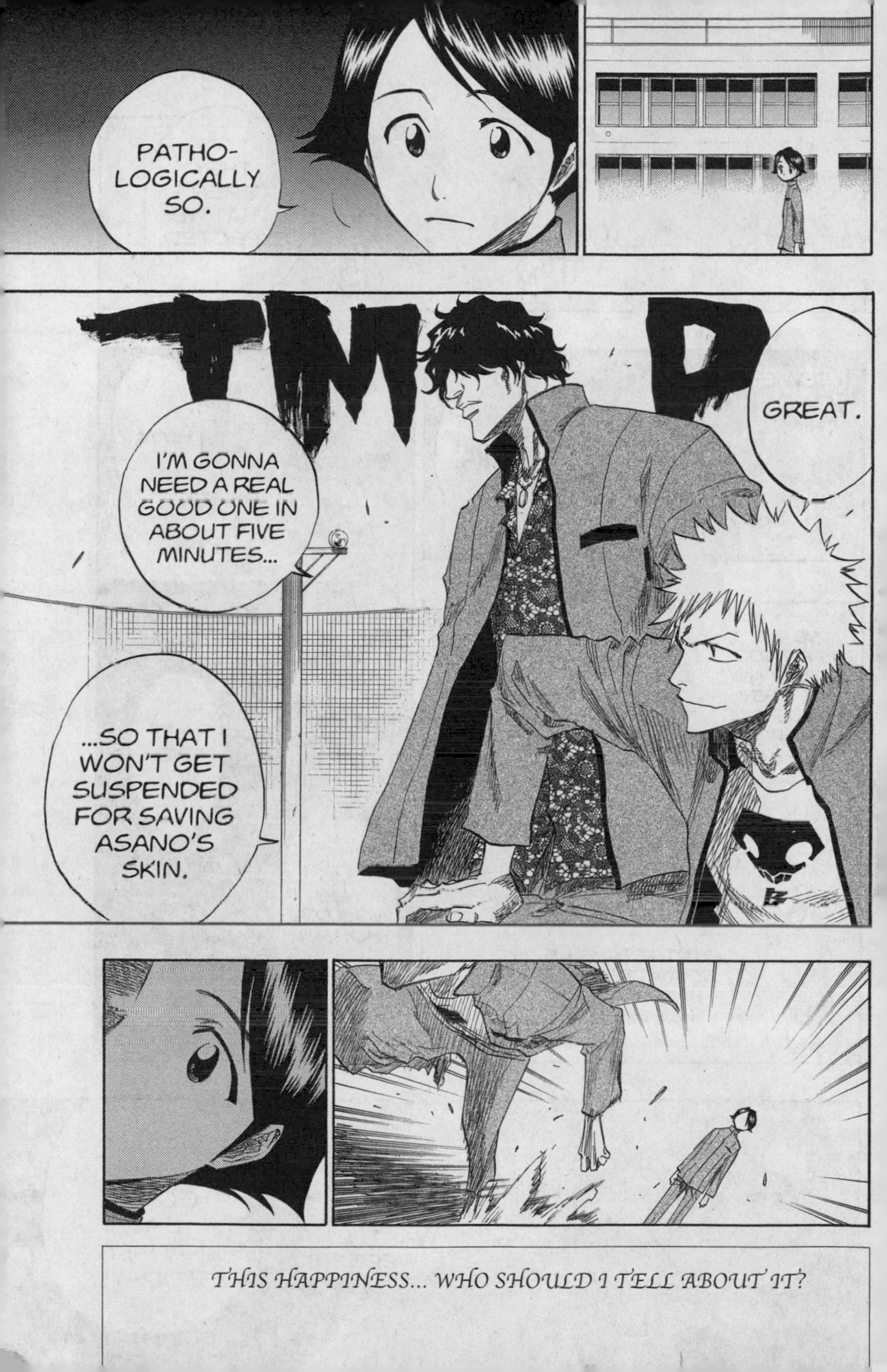
PATHO-LOGICALLY SO.
GREAT.
I'M GONNA NEED A REAL GOOD ONE IN ABOUT FIVE MINUTES...
...SO THAT I WON'T GET SUSPENDED FOR SAVING ASANO'S SKIN.
THIS HAPPINESS... WHO SHOULD I TELL ABOUT IT?

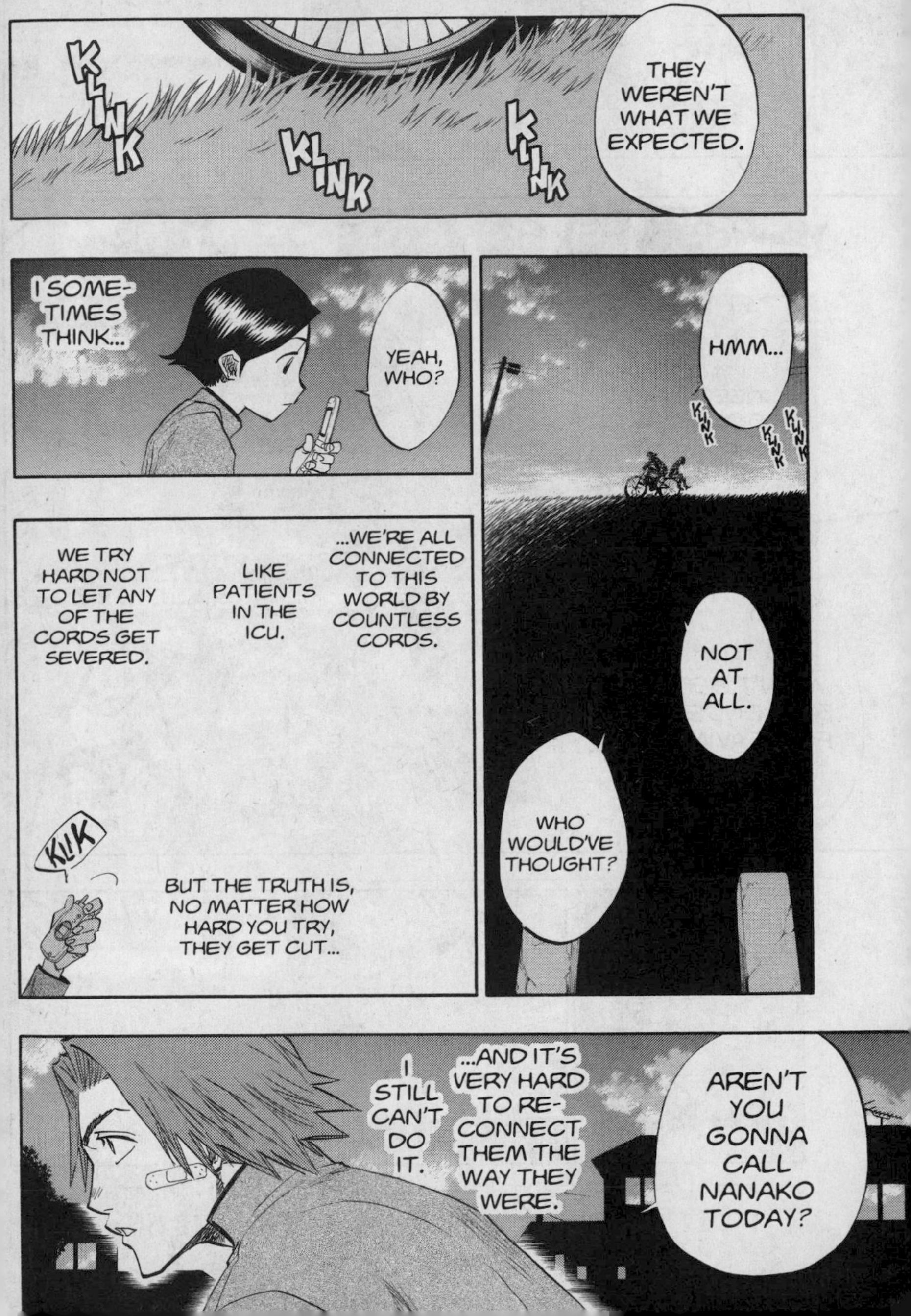

THEY WEREN'T WHAT WE EXPECTED.
KLINK
KLINK
KLINK
HMM...
KLINK
KLINK
KLINK
NOT AT ALL.
WHO WOULD'VE THOUGHT?
YEAH, WHO?
I SOMETIMES THINK...
...WE'RE ALL CONNECTED TO THIS WORLD BY COUNTLESS CORDS.
LIKE PATIENTS IN THE ICU.
WE TRY HARD NOT TO LET ANY OF THE CORDS GET SEVERED.
KLIK
BUT THE TRUTH IS, NO MATTER HOW HARD YOU TRY, THEY GET CUT...
AREN'T YOU GONNA CALL NANAKO TODAY?
...AND IT'S VERY HARD TO RE-CONNECT THEM THE WAY THEY WERE.
I STILL CAN'T DO IT.

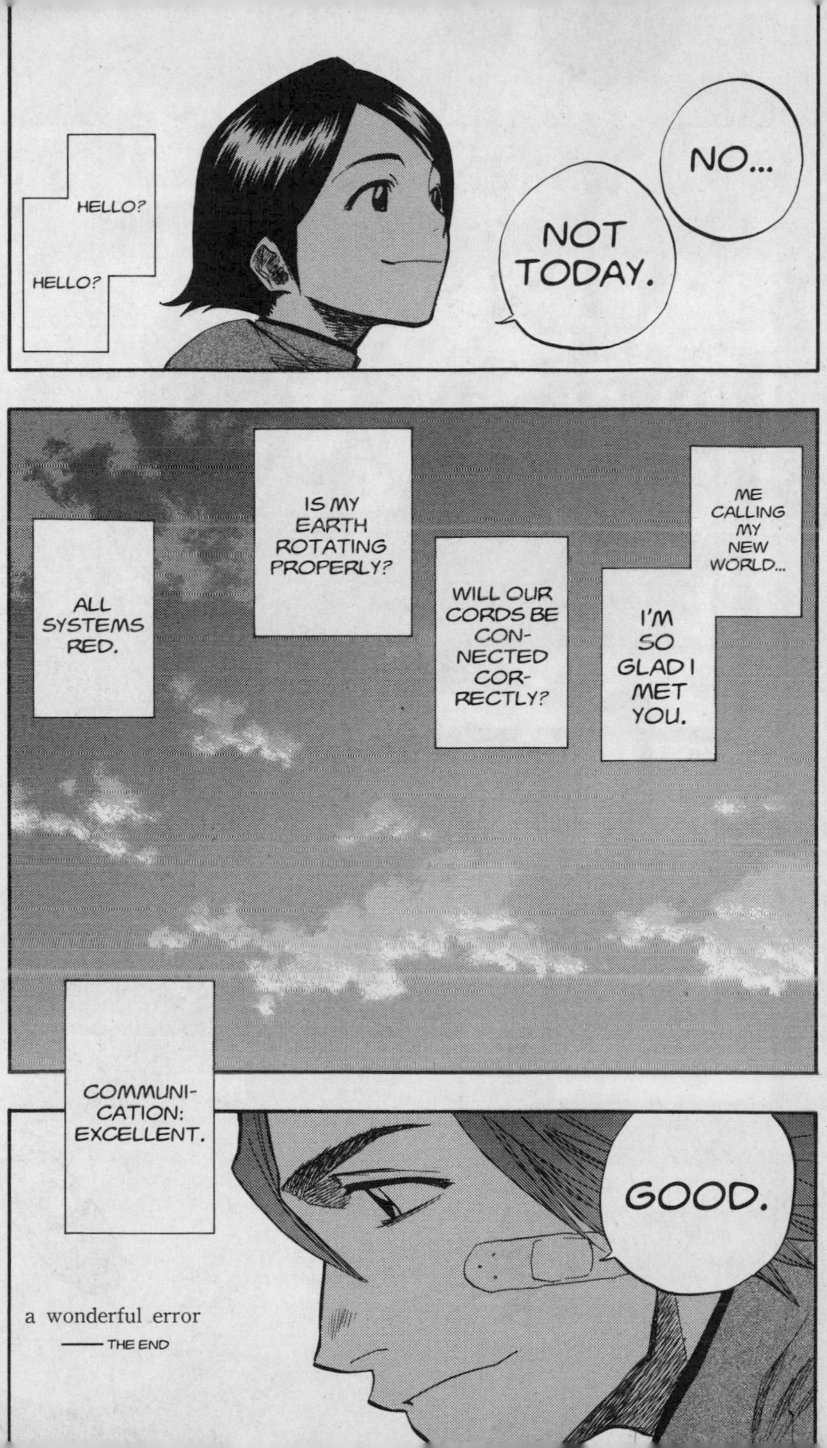
NO...
NOT TODAY.
HELLO?
HELLO?
ME CALLING MY NEW WORLD...
I'M SO GLAD I MET YOU.
WILL OUR CORDS BE CON-NECTED COR-RECTLY?
IS MY EARTH ROTATING PROPERLY?
ALL SYSTEMS RED.
COMMUNI-CATION: EXCELLENT.
GOOD.
a wonderful error
—— THE END

Next Volume Preview

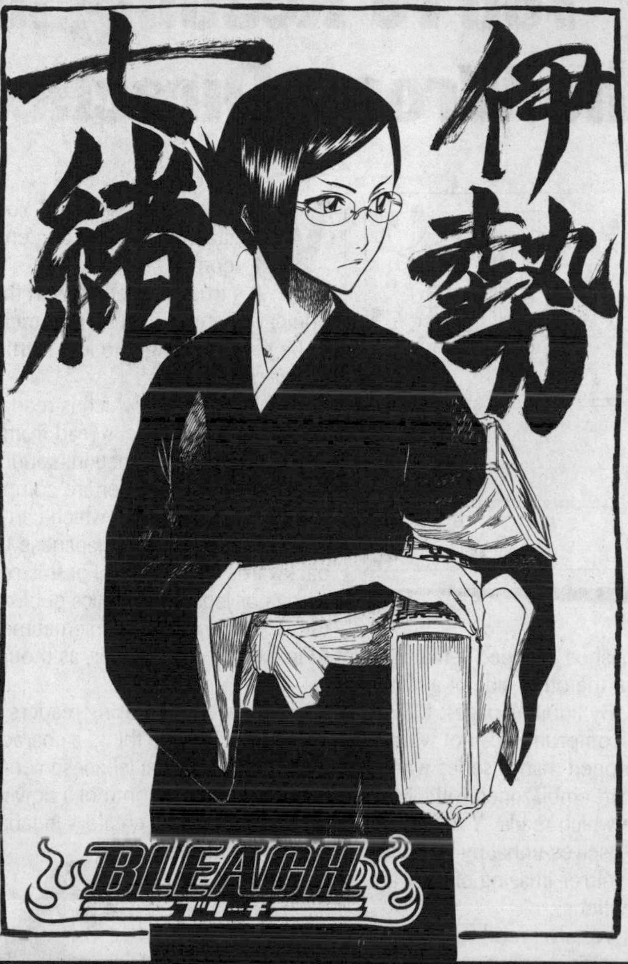
伊勢
七緒
BLEACH
ブリーチ

Ichigo and his friends have made it into the Soul Society, but they've been split up and are forced to face the enraged Soul Reapers without each other. Ichigo discovers where Rukia is being kept, but he has to go through her powerful and heartless brother to get to her!

BLEACH 3-in-1 Edition Volume 5 on sale May 2013!

You're Reading in the Wrong Direction!!

Whoops! Guess what? You're starting at the wrong end of the comic!

...It's true! In keeping with the original Japanese format, **Bleach** is meant to be read from right to left, starting in the upper-right corner.

Unlike English, which is read from left to right, Japanese is read from right to left, meaning that action, sound effects and word-balloon order are completely reversed... something which can make readers unfamiliar with Japanese feel pretty backwards themselves. For this reason, manga or Japanese comics published in the U.S. in English have sometimes been published "flopped"—that is, printed in exact reverse order, as though seen from the other side of a mirror.

By flopping pages, U.S. publishers can avoid confusing readers, but the compromise is not without its downside. For one thing, a character in a flopped manga series who once wore in the original Japanese version a T-shirt emblazoned with "M A Y" (as in "the merry month of") now wears one which reads "Y A M"! Additionally, many manga creators in Japan are themselves unhappy with the process, as some feel the mirror-imaging of their art skews their original intentions.

We are proud to bring you Tite Kubo's **Bleach** in the original unflopped format. For now, though, turn to the other side of the book and let the adventure begin...!

—Editor